INTERMEDIATE ACCOUNTING

The Dryden Accounting List

❦	Lee, Gilbart, Hipwell, and Hales	*Accounting*
❦	Gaber, Walgenbach, Hanson, and Hamre	*Introduction to Accounting*
	Brigham and Knechel	*Financial Accounting Using Lotus 1-2-3*
❦	Dauderis	*Financial Accounting: An Introduction to Decision Making*
❦	Gaber, Davidson, Stickney, and Weil	*Financial Accounting*
	Hoskin and Hughs	*Financial Accounting Cases*
❦	Williams, Deutsch, Stanga, and Holder	*Intermediate Accounting*
	Ketz, Campbell, and Baxendale	*Management Accounting*
	Maher, Stickney, Weil, and Davidson	*Managerial Accounting: An Introduction to Concepts, Methods, and Uses*
❦	Beechy	*Canadian Advanced Financial Accounting*
	Stickney	*Financial Statement Analysis*
❦	Clowes	*EDP Auditing*
	Douglas	*Governmental and Nonprofit Accounting: Theory and Practice*
	Ziebell and DeCoster	*Management Control Systems in Nonprofit Organizations*
	Bloom and Elgers	*Accounting Theory and Policy: A Reader*
❦	Most	*Accounting Theory*
	Belkaoui	*Accounting Theory*
❦	Skinner	*Accounting Standards in Evolution*
	Everett, Boley, Duncan, and Jamison	*HBJ Federal Tax Course*
	Williams and Miller	*GAAP Guide, College Edition*
	Bailey and Miller	*GAAS Guide, College Edition*

VOLUME 1 CHAPTERS 1–14

INTERMEDIATE ACCOUNTING

FIRST CANADIAN EDITION

JAN R. WILLIAMS, Ph.D., C.P.A.
University of Tennessee

ESTHER DEUTSCH, M.B.A., C.M.A.
Ryerson Polytechnic University

KEITH G. STANGA, Ph.D., C.P.A.
University of Tennessee

WILLIAM W. HOLDER, D.B.A., C.P.A.
University of South California

DRYDEN

A Division of Holt, Rinehart and Winston of Canada, Limited

Toronto   Montreal   Orlando   Fort Worth   San Diego   Philadelphia   London   Sydney   Tokyo

Canadian Cataloguing in Publication Data
Main entry under title:

Intermediate accounting

1st Canadian ed.
Includes index.
ISBN 0-03-922913-0

1. Accounting.   I. Williams, Jan R.

HF5635.W566 1994   657'.044   C93-093736-8

Publisher: Scott Duncan
Senior Editor and Marketing Manager: Ron Fitzgerald
Developmental Editor: Cheryl Teelucksingh
Marketing Co-ordinator: Lisa Whyatt
Director of Publishing Services: Jean Davies
Editorial Manager: Marcel Chiera
Supervising Editor: Carol Tong
Production Editor: Kathleen Vanderlinden
Production Manager: Sue-Ann Becker
Manufacturing Co-ordinator: Denise Wake
Copy Editor: Claudia Kutchukian
Cover and Interior Design: boyes and connolly
Typesetting and Assembly: Edwards Brothers Incorporated
Printing and Binding: Edwards Brothers Incorporated
Cover credit: Spencer Jones/Masterfile

This book was printed in the United States of America.
1 2 3 4 5   98 97 96 95 94

Preface

The primary subject of *Intermediate Accounting* is financial reporting for corporate business enterprises. Financial reporting practices of Canadian corporations involve a complicated but interesting combination of principles and procedures that have emerged over several decades. Many procedures can be explained by several broad accounting principles; others can be justified only by their having gained widespread acceptance in practice over many years.

The first Canadian edition of *Intermediate Accounting* provides the authors with an opportunity to balance a procedural explanation of currently applied accounting practices with a discussion of the theoretical framework on which those practices are based. Accounting students who seek professional success must understand both practice and theory to meet the challenges of the future.

We have also attempted to strike an appropriate balance between current practices and alternatives to current practice. To understand accounting as it exists in the present and as it may evolve in the future, students must understand alternatives to current practice.

Organization of the Text

The text is organized into five major sections:

Volume 1
Part 1   Theoretical Foundation for Financial Reporting and Revenue Recognition (Chapters 1–5)
Part 2   Tools of Accounting (Chapters 6–7)
Part 3   Asset Accounting (Chapters 8–14)
Volume 2
Part 4   Liability and Shareholders' Equity Accounting (Chapters 15–18)
Part 5   Additional Financial Reporting Issues (Chapters 19–25)

Part 1, Theoretical Foundation for Financial Reporting and Revenue Recognition, prepares students for the remainder of the text by providing the conceptual background necessary to understand generally accepted accounting principles and alternatives to those principles. Chapter 1 describes the important environmental factors and professional organizations that influence the development of corporate financial reporting. Chapter 2 presents the current conceptual framework of corporate financial reporting. This chapter explains the broad accounting principles that underlie many specific procedures currently used in the preparation of financial statements, which are then highlighted throughout the text as we illustrate their application to specific reporting practices. Chapter 3 introduces the nature and measurement of the elements of financial statements, stressing alternatives to current practice in an understandable way. Chapter 4 reviews the four basic financial statements that students should understand when beginning an intermediate accounting course. By discussing all of the financial statements in a single chapter, we can stress an important feature of financial statements: *articulation*. Chapter 5 covers revenue measurement and income presentation. This chapter was placed early in the text to explain concepts of revenue recognition that will be discussed from the balance sheet perspective throughout the remainder of the text.

Part 2, Tools of Accounting, covers two major topics. Chapter 6 reviews the accounting cycle and related practices used by business enterprises to keep adequate records efficiently and to prepare effective reports. Chapter 7 explains compound interest concepts in depth. These accounting tools are used frequently throughout the text.

Part 3, Asset Accounting, includes seven chapters (Chapters 8–14) that deal with the major asset categories typically found on corporate balance sheets: cash, receivables, inventories, investments, and capital tangible and intangible assets. Throughout these chapters, material that students have studied in introductory accounting courses is reviewed, and new, more advanced aspects of each asset category are discussed. Care has been taken to explain new material thoroughly and to make extensive use of examples and illustrations to enhance student understanding.

Part 4, Liability and Shareholders' Equity Accounting, includes four chapters. Chapter 15 addresses current and contingent liabilities, Chapter 16 discusses long-term debt, and Chapters 17 and 18 cover a variety of topics related to shareholders' equity. The purpose of this section is to make students aware of the alternative methods of corporate financing and the many accounting principles that are reflected in the liability and shareholders' equity sections of corporate balance sheets.

Part 5, Additional Financial Reporting Issues, covers several advanced topics that may be new to accounting students or that are mentioned only briefly in other accounting courses. Included are chapters on financial reporting of income taxes (Chapter 19), accounting for changes and correcting errors (Chapter 20), earnings per share (Chapter 21), reporting cash flow information in the Statement of Changes in Financial Position (Chapter 22), accounting for leases and pension costs (Chapters 23 and 24), and additional disclosure issues and financial analysis (Chapter 25).

All of the authors of this text teach intermediate accounting courses at their respective universities. We have listened carefully to students, colleagues, and faculty members at other colleges and universities and have incorporated many of their suggestions into this first Canadian edition. Most of the financial statement excerpts are current reporting examples. In general, the boxed articles found throughout the text are from the most current relevant readings. As this text goes to press, all authoritative accounting pronouncements that have been issued and that affect the content of intermediate accounting have been incorporated.

Some of the most difficult topics for intermediate accounting students are nonmonetary exchange of assets (Chapter 12), deferred income taxes (Chapter 19), accounting for leases (Chapter 23), and accounting for pension costs (Chapter 24). Extra attention was given to the presentation of these topics in an effort to reduce their complexity. Finally, Chapter 25 makes an attempt to strengthen, as well as streamline, the coverage of the dual subjects of financial statement disclosure and financial analysis.

End-of-Chapter Material

Questions, exercises, problems, cases, and judgement cases appear at the end of chapters. They offer opportunities for students to continue the learning process by applying concepts presented in the text. Appropriate questions, exercises, problems, and cases have been adapted from CMA and CPA examinations. Exercises, problems, cases, and judgement cases are preceded by a short phrase identifying the major subject of each item.

Questions typically involve a short discussion and emphasize the major points of the chapter. Some questions are multiple choice.

Exercises typically involve computations and usually focus on one major point.

Problems require computations and, often, discussion. They usually require the student to apply several major points discussed in the text.

Cases generally are extended discussion questions, often involving in-depth consideration of issues related to chapter topics. Cases provide students with opportunities to develop written communication skills in a context that is similar to what they will encounter in the accounting profession.

Judgement cases expose students to the uncertainties involved in the financial reporting process and the judgements professional accountants are required to make. Many of these cases require students to make and support decisions based on logical reasoning as well as knowledge of current accounting standards.

Features

The first Canadian edition of *Intermediate Accounting* has many features designed to help students. Each chapter begins with a list of objectives that preview the chapter and ends with a list of key points that highlight the most important subjects in the chapter.

The basic accounting principles discussed in Chapter 2 are highlighted in the margins throughout the text. This feature is designed to demonstrate how important accounting principles—such as revenue realization, matching, and consistency—are applied in practice.

Throughout the text, short readings are provided to expand students' understanding of accounting principles and the issues and controversies surrounding these principles. Most readings are taken from business periodicals, and they provide insight into the importance of corporate financial reporting to investors and creditors.

At appropriate points in the text, diagrams summarize complex procedures such as accounting for current and noncurrent marketable equity securities, recording of non-monetary assets, accounting for leases, and preparing earnings-per-share figures for companies with complex capital structures.

End-of-chapter Appendices present specialized subjects, complex topics, and less frequently used accounting methods. The Appendix to Chapter 1 includes the instructions for assembling the CICA *Handbook*.

Throughout the text, excerpts from published financial statements of major Canadian corporations illustrate how various accounting principles are applied. These excerpts are usually preceded by a brief description of the company to familiarize students with the nature of the reporting enterprise.

The 1992 annual report and basic financial statements of Canadian Pacific Limited are reproduced in their entirety and are cited throughout the text. The company's annual report is presented in Appendix A at the end of each text.

Supplements

For the Student
Study Guide Including Lotus® 1-2-3® Applications Manual by Barbara Trenholm, University of New Brunswick, and James M. Reeve, University of Tennessee. Part I of this manual contains a Study Guide consisting of the following sections for each chapter: Chapter Review, Learning Enrichment, Suggested Readings, Multiple-Choice Questions,

Exercises, and Solutions to Questions and Exercises. Part II contains the documentation necessary to build and run Lotus templates. These templates can be used to solve end-of-chapter material designated by the following logo:

A master disk is available free to instructors.

For the Instructor

Instructor's Manual by Esther Deutsch, Ryerson Polytechnic University, and Jane Campbell, University of Dayton. Most chapters in the Instructor's Manual contain the following sections: Text Objectives, Teaching Objectives, Major Topics, Chapter/Lecture Outline, Teaching Suggestions, Description of Selected Text Enrichment Material, Overview of End-of-Chapter Material by Topic, Overview of End-of-Chapter Material by Item, and a list of articles. In addition, the Instructor's Manual also includes a discussion guide for the judgement cases.

Instructor's Package to Lotus® 1-2-3® Applications by Barbara Trenholm, University of New Brunswick, and James M. Reeve, University of Tennessee. This package contains the Instructor's Manual, a Master Student Disk, and a Master Instructor's Disk for the electronic spreadsheet templates. The disks are 3½″ double-sided, double-density diskettes.

Solutions Manual, written by the textbook authors. This manual contains answers to all questions, exercises, problems, and cases in the text.

Test Resource Manual by Esther Deutsch, Ryerson Polytechnic University, and Michael Kennelley, Florida State University. Over 1200 questions are included in this manual, and each chapter consists of the following: ten to fifteen true/false questions, five to fifteen conceptual multiple-choice questions, five to ten application multiple-choice questions, six to nine problems, and one to three miscellaneous questions. Suggested examinations and solutions are also provided.

Computerized Test Bank. The Test Bank is available in a computerized format that allows instructors to edit and add questions and generate multiple versions of examinations, with answer keys.

Checklist of Key Figures. This list of principle figures for the textbook problems is provided free in class quantity.

Acknowledgements

Many people have contributed to the writing, review, revision, and publication of the first Canadian edition of *Intermediate Accounting*. The authors recognize the important contributions of these people and deeply appreciate their involvement in the revision.

One of the most useful forms of input when developing a text is the expert evaluation of accounting educators who invest time and effort in reviewing the manuscript. We received many thoughtful reviews of the material for the first Canadian edition and gave careful consideration to all suggestions made. We gratefully acknowledge the contributions of the following individuals who were willing to assist us:

Patricia Morrison	Ryerson Polytechnic University
Barbara Trenholm	University of New Brunswick
Norman Bell	Seneca College
Robert Bell	British Columbia Institute of Technology
John Heaphy	McGill University
Ronald Davidson	Simon Fraser University
Don Lockwood	University of British Columbia
Brian Duggan	University of Manitoba
Wendy Roscoe	Concordia University
Sylvia Sarkus	Ryerson Polytechnic University

The editorial staff at Holt, Rinehart and Winston of Canada, Limited has provided guidance, motivation, and inspiration for this revision. Ron Fitzgerald, acquisitions editor, provided overall guidance, and his personal interest in the project and in the authors has been a source of particular encouragement as we have attempted to meet the challenging deadlines required for this text. Developmental editor Cheryl Teelucksingh guided the project through its various stages. She, too, has shown great personal interest in the project and has impressed the authors with her understanding of the various components of the textbook and its supplements, as well as the desire of accounting professors for certain content changes. She has carefully chosen individuals to review the text, yet given the authors relative freedom to interpret those reviews. The copy editor, Claudia Kutchukian, has been a great help on this revision with her careful reading and editing of the manuscript. While the authors are responsible for the technical content of the text, much of its readability is due to Claudia's attention to clarity in structure and wording.

Our gratitude also goes to the other members of Harcourt Brace associated with our project, including Jean Lancee, Marcel Chiera, Sue-Ann Becker, Denise Wake, and Lisa Whyatt.

We want to thank our students and colleagues for their advice and counsel. Many useful suggestions from these individuals have been incorporated in this text. Particular mention is due to Barbara Trenholm, who is also the author of the student guide and the computer resource supplement. However, her contribution has extended far beyond these tangible components of this text. She has been and remains a valued consultant who is always willing to share judgements that draw from her outstanding teaching of intermediate accounting.

Throughout the text, we cite authoritative accounting literature published by the Canadian Institute of Chartered Accountants (CICA), American Institute of Certified Public Accountants (AICPA), and the Financial Accounting Standards Board (FASB). We are grateful for the work done by these organizations. We also acknowledge and thank the AICPA and the Institute of Management Accounting for allowing us to adapt material from past CPA and CMA examinations.

Our text includes many financial reporting examples taken from the published financial statements of Canadian corporations. We have also included several articles from Canadian and American business publications. We appreciate the willingness of these organizations to allow us to use this material, which greatly enriches the learning experience of students.

Finally, we wish to acknowledge the contributions of our families and friends during the period required to write this text. Perhaps their greatest contribution has been their patience and understanding during the many hours we were unable to be with them because we were working on the book. We recognize and appreciate their support and feel that much of the credit for this text rightfully belongs to them.

Jan R. Williams
Esther Deutsch
Keith G. Stanga
William W. Holder

Publisher's Note to Students and Instructors

This textbook is a key component of your course. If you are the instructor of this course, you undoubtedly considered a number of texts carefully before choosing this as the one that would work best for your students and you. The authors and publisher spent considerable time and money to ensure its high quality, and we appreciate your recognition of this effort and accomplishment. Please note the copyright statement.

If you are a student, we are confident that this text will help you to meet the objectives of your course. It will also become a valuable addition to your personal library.

Since we want to hear what you think about this book, please be sure to send us the stamped reply card at the end of the text. Your input will help us to continue to publish high-quality books for your courses.

Brief Contents

Contents

PART 2

TOOLS OF ACCOUNTING

PART 3

ASSET ACCOUNTING

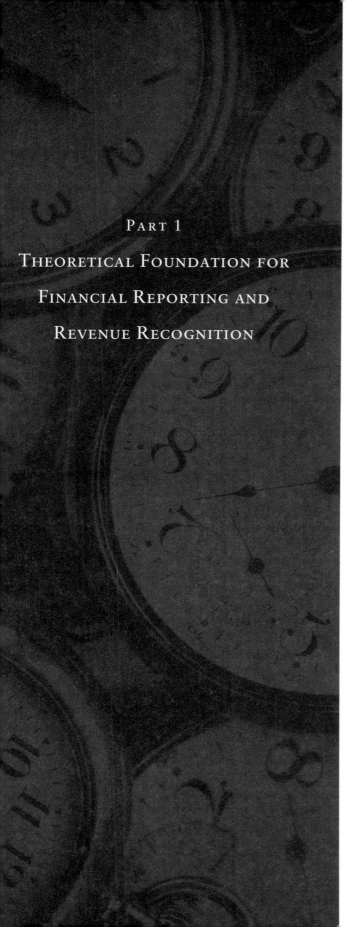

Chapter 1

The Financial

Accounting Environment

Objectives

1. To introduce and discuss financial accounting.

2. To distinguish clearly among preparers, auditors, and users of financial statements.

3. To introduce the concept of generally accepted accounting principles.

4. To explain how generally accepted accounting principles have been developed.

5. To indicate the major sources of generally accepted accounting principles.

6. To discuss major issues that are likely to affect the development of generally accepted accounting principles.

7. To introduce the subject of ethics in accounting.

Accounting as an Information System

Accounting **identifies, measures,** and **communicates** information about **economic entities** for use in making **economic decisions.** An accountant's primary task is therefore to supply information to help users, such as shareholders, bankers, and managers, make better decisions. These decisions determine how scarce resources are allocated within and among business enterprises. Accounting information helps society determine what goods and services to produce, as well as how and for whom to produce them. It should come as no surprise, then, that accounting is an exciting, often controversial discipline.

Accounting requires the use of theories of several fields of study, including economics, finance, psychology, sociology, communications theory, and political science. By applying psychological principles, for example, accountants learn how people process accounting information and how that information affects their decisions.

Internal and External Users

The two types of accounting information users are internal and external. The primary **internal users** are managers, who need accounting information to assist them in basic planning and control. Because of their authority within their companies, managers can usually obtain the internal information they need. When providing information to managers, accountants are not constrained by generally accepted accounting principles, which are principles that have substantial authoritative support. Instead, they prepare whatever information management finds most useful. The branch of accounting that is concerned with providing information for internal users is called **managerial,** or **management, accounting.** Managerial accounting is the subject of other textbooks and courses.

External users are those outside the business enterprise who have or contemplate having a direct or an indirect interest in the enterprise. They include present and potential owners (shareholders), lenders, suppliers, employees, and customers, as well as financial analysts, stock exchanges, regulatory authorities, and the general public. Compared with management, external users generally have much less authority to request information. When preparing information for external users, accountants follow generally accepted accounting principles established by the Accounting Standards Board in Canada and the Financial Accounting Standards Board in the United States. The use of such principles enhances the confidence and understanding of users and helps them to make more meaningful comparisons between companies.

Financial accounting, the subject of this textbook, is the branch of accounting that measures and reports the financial position of a business enterprise as well as changes in its financial position. The main output of the financial accounting process is a set of basic, general-purpose financial statements. As illustrated in Chapter 4, the basic financial statements are the balance sheet, income statement, statement of changes in financial position, and statement of retained earnings or statement of shareholders' equity. Financial accounting information is designed primarily to meet the needs of external users.

Basic Needs of External Users

Although there are many types of external users, financial accounting has traditionally focussed on meeting the needs of present and potential owners, such as preferred and common shareholders (investors), and creditors, such as bankers and bondholders. Investors and creditors are the most obvious external users of financial statements. Moreover, information that is useful to these two groups is likely to be useful to other external users as well.

Basically, investors and creditors want to know how much cash they will receive in return for their investment of cash or resources, and when they will receive it. Shareholders, for example, typically make decisions **to buy, sell, or hold equity investments.** Before they exchange cash for capital shares, they seek information that will help them to assess the amounts, timing, and uncertainties of expected cash flows in the form of dividends and appreciated market prices. Similarly, bank loan officers make decisions **to extend or not extend loans.** When making these decisions, bankers want information that will help them to assess their chances of receiving cash via interest and repayment of principal.[1]

Investment and credit decisions involve a comparison of expected cash outflows with expected cash inflows. In most cases, the outflows are known, based on, for example, the market price of the shares on the date of purchase or the amount of the loan requested. But the investor or creditor usually must **predict the amount of cash inflows and assess the risk that those inflows will be less than expected.** What an investor or creditor would really like is a knowledge of the future. However, no one can supply such knowledge directly.

The expected cash flows to investors and creditors are related to the expected cash flows to the enterprise to which they have committed their funds. More precisely: "Investors and creditors of profit oriented enterprises are interested, for the purpose of making resource allocation decisions, in predicting the ability of the entity to earn income and generate cash flows in the future to meet its obligations and to generate a return on investment."[2]

For an enterprise to generate favourable cash flows over the long run, it must operate profitably and remain solvent. Thus, **profitability** and **solvency** are two basic factors that investors and creditors evaluate based on the information in financial statements. Profitability refers to the ability of an enterprise to generate earnings. Solvency refers to its ability to pay its debts when they come due. A company may be highly profitable yet on the verge of bankruptcy due to a shortage of liquid assets such as cash and accounts receivable. Investors and creditors must therefore evaluate both aspects of a business enterprise.[3] Furthermore, if a business is to operate profitably and remain solvent, it must be **managed effectively.** Thus, financial statements can also be used to evaluate management's performance.

To summarize, investors and creditors provide cash or resources, and they want to know how much cash they will receive in return and when they will receive it. To help resolve these questions, they use financial statements to

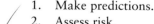

1. Make predictions.
2. Assess risk.
3. Evaluate profitability.
4. Evaluate solvency.
5. Evaluate management's performance.

These uses are interrelated.

---

[1]"Financial Statement Concepts," CICA *Handbook,* Paragraph 1000.15, March 1991.

[2]"Financial Statement Concepts," CICA *Handbook,* Paragraph 1000.12, March 1991.

[3]Lloyd C. Heath and Paul Rosenfield, "Solvency: The Forgotten Half of Financial Reporting," *Journal of Accountancy* (January 1979), pp. 48–54.

General-Purpose Financial Statements

Even when we narrow the list of external users to investors and creditors, we find that these users make different kinds of decisions under a variety of circumstances. Bankers, for example, make short-term, intermediate-term, and long-term loans to many different types of customers, so their needs for certain items of accounting information vary. Moreover, users differ in their ability to read, analyze, and understand accounting information. A shareholder with virtually no understanding of accounting information contrasts sharply with a Chartered Financial Analyst, who has met rigorous education, experience, and examination requirements. Clearly, the diversity of users poses a problem. Should accountants prepare tailor-made financial statements to meet the needs of a particular user? Or should they prepare a single, general-purpose set of financial statements to reasonably satisfy the needs of most users? Presently, financial accounting emphasizes general-purpose statements because (1) accountants believe that many users need similar information; (2) general-purpose statements are more favourable from a benefit/cost standpoint; and (3) tailor-made statements lack credibility. As a general rule, **the benefits of information (including financial accounting information) should exceed the costs of providing and using it.** In general-purpose financial statements, accountants strive to present information that is "capable of being understood by users. Users are assumed to have a reasonable understanding of business and economic activities and accounting, together with a willingness to study the information with reasonable diligence."[4]

Financial Statements and Financial Reporting

The main output of the financial accounting process today is a set of basic, general-purpose **financial statements**. These statements are as follows:

1. A **balance sheet**, which summarizes an enterprise's financial position at a particular point in time.
2. An **income statement**, which summarizes an enterprise's income and the components of income over a period of time.
3. A **statement of changes in financial position**, which summarizes an enterprise's cash receipts and cash payments during a period of time.
4. A **statement of retained earnings**, which describes the changes in an enterprise's retained earnings during a period, or a **statement of shareholders' equity**, which describes the changes in retained earnings as well as in other accounts that compose shareholders' equity.

Actual examples of these financial statements appear in annual reports to shareholders. Companies also present them in other disclosure media such as registration statements and annual reports filed with one of the provincial securities commissions. This textbook focusses on general-purpose financial statements, including their related notes (footnotes), which are an integral part of the statements. To familiarize you with financial statements, we have reproduced an actual set from Canadian Pacific Limited (a diverse management company that operates various businesses) in Appendix A at the end of Volume I. Take a few minutes to review these statements now; we will refer to them at various times

---

[4]"Financial Statement Concepts," CICA *Handbook*, Paragraph 1000.19, March 1991.

throughout the book. Additionally, Appendix A at the end of this volume contains most of the material presented in the 1992 annual report of Canadian Pacific Limited.

The output of the financial accounting process is not confined to financial statements. **Financial reporting** encompasses not only financial statements but also other means of communicating information that relates directly or indirectly to the financial accounting process. Corporate managers may communicate financial accounting information outside of the financial statements because they are required to do so by rule or custom or because they simply want to do so voluntarily.[5] Annual reports to shareholders, for example, include not only financial statements but also other information, such as financial highlights and a multi-year summary of important financial figures. They also include **nonfinancial information,** such as a description of major products and a listing of corporate officers and directors.[6]

Financial reporting provides a *major portion, but not all*, of the information needed by external users for making investment, credit, and similar decisions. Professional financial analysts, for example, usually gather and evaluate economic information (such as gross national product and government interest rate figures) and industry information (such as weekly and monthly production figures provided for many industries) before they analyze information about individual companies. Also, many analysts obtain information by talking with representatives of corporate management.

Characteristics and Limitations of Financial Statements

Some of the more important characteristics and limitations that apply to present-day financial statements are briefly described below.

1. **Financial nature.** The information in financial statements is primarily financial in nature. It is generally expressed in **units of money** regardless of changes in purchasing power.
2. **Business entities.** The information pertains to individual business entities (which may be a group of related companies) rather than to industries or to the entire economy.
3. **Estimates and judgement.** The information reflects estimates and judgement and is therefore inexact. Financial statements look more precise than they really are.
4. **Historical report.** The information reflects the financial effects of transactions and events that have already occurred. Financial statements do not contain future projections. Financial statements are the Balance Sheet, Income Statement, Statement of Retained Earnings, and the Statement of Changes in Financial Position. All these contain historical data. The annual report contains the financial statement and the forecasts and projections.
5. **General purpose.** The information is designed to reasonably meet the needs of many diverse users, particularly present and potential investors and creditors.

---

[5]"Financial Statement Concepts," CICA *Handbook,* Paragraph 1000.06, March 1991.

[6]To summarize certain key terms, **financial accounting** is the branch of accounting concerned with measuring and reporting the financial position of a business enterprise and the changes that occur in financial position. **Financial statements** (i.e., income statement, balance sheet, statement of changes in financial position, statement of retained earnings, statement of shareholders' equity) represent the main output of the financial accounting process. **Financial reporting** is a broad term that encompasses financial statements as well as other means of communicating information that relates directly or indirectly to the financial accounting process.

6. **Interrelatedness.** Financial statements are interrelated because measuring financial position is related to measuring changes in financial position. Thus we say that financial statements **articulate** with one another.
7. **Summarization and classification.** The information is summarized and classified in a manner designed to help meet users' needs.
8. **Several measurement bases.** Financial statements reflect several measurement or valuation bases (e.g., accounts receivable are reported at net realizable value, capital assets are usually reported at their original cost less accumulated depreciation).
9. **A single source.** Financial statements are only one source of the information needed by investors and creditors.
10. **Cost.** Financial statements involve a cost to provide and use. They can be justified only if the benefits they provide exceed the costs.

Objective of Financial Statements

The objective of financial statements is to communicate information that is useful to investors, members, contributors, creditors and other users ("users") in making their resource allocation decisions and/or assessing management stewardship. Consequently, financial statements provide information about:

    a.   an entity's economic resources, obligations and equity/net assets;
    b.   changes in an entity's economic resources, obligations and equity/net assets; and
    c.   the economic performance of the entity.[7]

Notice that the first part of the objective is the most general, while the next two are progressively more specific. Moreover, the third objective flows logically from the second, which in turn flows logically from the first. We explain these objectives more fully in the next chapter.

Preparers and Auditors of Financial Statements

Financial statements pertain to an economic entity such as a corporation. The **management** of that entity has the primary responsibility for preparing and disseminating its financial statements. Financial statements therefore contain **assertions**, or **representations made by management**, such as sales, net income, and total assets.

    Management's role in the financial reporting process has evolved over many years and is related to the fact that the corporation is the dominant medium for pooling productive resources in our economy. As corporations have grown in size, the separation between those who own the company (shareholders) and those who control it (managers) has widened. As a result, owners have demanded a periodic accounting from those to whom they have entrusted economic resources. This demand is met by the inclusion of a management report to shareholders in the annual report. A sample management report is part of the Appendix at the end of this book.

    Many critics have charged that management has too much responsibility in the financial reporting process. The critics claim that since financial statements are reports on management's performance, management should have less responsibility for determining the content of financial statements. Despite the critics' views, the traditional position of

---

[7]"Financial Statement Concepts," CICA *Handbook,* Paragraph 1000.15, March 1991.

the accounting profession has been that managers, because they are so familiar with company objectives and operations, are the people best suited to present pertinent company information to external parties.

To summarize, management has certain important **accountability** responsibilities to external parties. In discharging these responsibilities, management typically obtains the services of internal and external accountants.

Internal Accountants

Management hires **internal accountants** to work as employees within the company. Internal accountants perform many tasks, depending on the size and complexity of the enterprise. Perhaps their most important tasks are producing and analyzing many kinds of information designed to help management make better planning and control decisions. Should a company buy some new material-handling equipment? What is the optimal quantity of inventory for a company to order? When should a company order inventory? These are only a few of the questions that internal accountants can help to answer.

Internal accountants also design and implement accounting systems. In larger companies, they may serve on an **internal audit staff** that ensures that the company safeguards its assets, produces reliable accounting information, operates efficiently, and adheres to management policies.

The internal accountant's most important tasks that relate to financial accounting are **collecting data** and **preparing the financial statements**. Internal accountants must therefore understand and apply the accounting principles we discuss throughout this text.

Some internal accountants have achieved the **Chartered Accountant (CA)**, **Certified Management Accountant (CMA)** or **Certified General Accountant (CGA)** designation. As you might expect, not all internal accountants have earned a CA, CMA, or CGA. Moreover, not all persons who have one of these designations are internal accountants. Many people with accounting designations work in public accounting, colleges and universities, government, and elsewhere. In addition to meeting certain other requirements, a person wishing to earn a designation must pass rigorous examinations.

External Accountants

Although most managers and internal accountants are both competent and honest, an independent outside party is needed to attest to the fairness of management's financial statements so that users will have more confidence in them. This is the major role of **external** or **public accountants**.

Chartered Accountant (CA) is the major professional designation of those who practise public accounting in Canada. The U.S. counterpart is a Certified Public Accountant (CPA). Not all public accountants in Canada are CAs, and not all CAs practise public accounting. To become a CA, a person must satisfy certain education and experience requirements and pass a rigorous, uniform examination prepared and graded by the Canadian Institute of Chartered Accountants (CICA).

While CA firms provide such services as tax and management advisory services, their primary service is **auditing**, often called the **attest function**. External accountants are hired by shareholders as independent contractors, with the primary responsibility of examining the records of a company for the external users of financial statements. Basically, an **audit** consists of an examination of a company's financial statements, followed by the issuance of a report that expresses the auditor's opinion about whether the financial statements have been presented fairly in accordance with generally accepted accounting principles. The **auditor's report** lends credibility to management's financial statements so that users can be more confident that the statements accurately represent what they purport to represent.

The most common type of auditor's report is one in which the auditor issues an **unqualified opinion**, which means that among other things the auditor believes that the financial statements have been presented fairly in accordance with generally accepted accounting principles. Exhibit 1.1 illustrates a standard auditor's report in which an unqualified opinion is given. The wording was adopted by the accounting profession in 1988. In the **opening paragraph**, the auditor identifies the financial statements that were audited. The second paragraph, called the **scope paragraph**, describes the nature of the audit. The third paragraph, called the **opinion paragraph,** presents the auditor's opinion on the financial statements. An example of the auditor's report is shown in the Appendix at the end of this book, along with the notes to the financial statements of Canadian Pacific Limited.

Auditors may also render qualified opinions, adverse opinions, and disclaimers. A **qualified opinion** is given when the overall financial statements are fairly presented except for certain items that the auditor discloses. An **adverse opinion** means that the financial statements have not been presented fairly in accordance with generally accepted accounting principles. Finally, a **denial of opinion** means that the auditor could not evaluate the fairness of the financial statements and, as a result, expresses no opinion on them.[8]

Publicly owned companies and thousands of privately owned companies issue audited financial statements once each year. The provincial securities commissions and the stock exchanges require that the annual financial statements of companies subject to their jurisdiction be audited by independent CAs. Bankers often require a company's audited statements before making loans. When audited statements are not required, managers often have the statements prepared by an accountant from a review of the records.

Auditors must be **competent** and **independent** of any company whose financial statements they audit. To be competent, auditors must have a working knowledge of the generally accepted auditing standards[9] that govern how an audit should be conducted, as well as generally accepted accounting principles, many of which we cover in this textbook. To be independent, auditors must be honest and must not have any financial or family interest in the company they are auditing. Auditors must be independent *in fact* and *in appearance.* Users of financial statements simply will not attribute much importance to the auditor's opinion unless they believe that the auditor is independent of the company being audited.

Exhibit 1.2 provides an overview of the major parties directly involved in the financial reporting process. They include preparers, auditors, and users of financial statements.

Generally Accepted Accounting Principles (GAAP)

Basically, accounting principles are guidelines for gathering and communicating accounting information.[10] Imagine what would happen if companies were free to choose whatever accounting principles they preferred. One company might report its inventory at historical

---

[8]"Reservations in the Auditor's Report," CICA *Handbook*, Paragraphs 5510.13–26, October 1988.

[9]"Generally Accepted Auditing Standards," CICA *Handbook,* Paragraph 5100.02, March 1992.

[10]Accounting principles have also been called standards, concepts, procedures, rules, practices, and conventions.

Exhibit 1.1 Unqualified Auditor's Report

AUDITOR'S REPORT

To the Shareholders of

....

I have audited the balance sheet of

....

as at ...., 19...... and the statements of income, retained earnings and changes in financial position for the year then ended. These financial statements are the responsibility of the company's management. My responsibility is to express an opinion on these financial statements based on my audit.

I conducted my audit in accordance with generally accepted auditing standards. Those standards require that I plan and perform an audit to obtain reasonable assurance whether the financial statements are free of material misstatement. An audit includes examining, on a test basis, evidence supporting the amounts and disclosures in the financial statements. An audit also includes assessing the accounting principles used and significant estimates made by management, as well as evaluating the overall financial statement presentation.

In my opinion, these financial statements present fairly, in all material respects, the financial position of the company as at ...., 19...... and the results of its operations and the changes in its financial position for the year then ended in accordance with generally accepted accounting principles.

City   (signed) ....
Date   CHARTERED ACCOUNTANT

Source: Reprinted from "The Auditor's Standard Report," *CICA Handbook*, Paragraph 5400.26 (Toronto: CICA, 1989), p. 5584.

Exhibit 1.2 Preparers, Auditors, and Users of Financial Statements

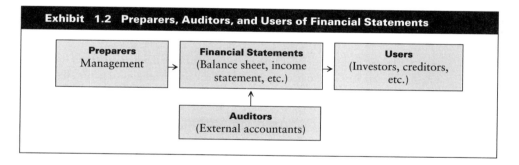

cost (the actual cost to purchase or produce the inventory), while others might use replacement cost, current selling price, or other measurements. Or one company might publish only an income statement while another might publish only a balance sheet. Such a situation could seriously reduce the ability of users to make valid comparisons between companies.

To help overcome this problem, the accounting profession has given some accounting principles the special status of **generally accepted accounting principles** (commonly called **GAAP**). Generally accepted accounting principles are those that have **substantial authoritative support**. Specifically, they represent

the consensus at any time as to which economic resources and obligations should be recorded as assets and liabilities, which changes in them should be recorded, when these changes should be recorded, how the recorded assets and liabilities and changes in them should be measured, what information should be disclosed and how it should be disclosed, and which financial statements should be prepared.[11]

Internal and external accountants must have a thorough knowledge of generally accepted accounting principles in order to prepare and attest to financial statements. Moreover, users should be familiar with these principles so that they can understand the nature and limitations of the information presented in financial statements.

In some ways, generally accepted accounting principles are similar to laws within our legal system in that the principles are formulated *by people*, often in an atmosphere in which considerable *political pressures* exist. Thus, instead of having been discovered in nature, Section 1000 of the CICA *Handbook* states that generally accepted accounting principles encompass "not only specific practices and procedures relating to particular circumstances but also broad principles and conventions of general application, including the underlying concepts described in this Section."[12] These principles should and do change as conditions warrant change. Furthermore, they are often *controversial*, as are laws that govern drinking, gambling, and many other areas. Just as laws should be judged based on how much they contribute to the achievement of society's goals, generally accepted accounting principles should be evaluated on the basis of how much they contribute to the **objectives of financial accounting**. Unlike laws, however, generally accepted accounting principles in Canada and the United States have largely been determined within the **private sector** rather than the public (government) sector of our economy. Financial statements prepared under GAAP have government assent that is supported by Section 44 of the Canada Business Corporations Act (CBCA).

Development of Generally Accepted Accounting Principles

Most of the progress made in the development of generally accepted accounting principles in Canada and the United States occurred during and after the 1930s. This progress was spurred by such factors as the growth of the corporate form of business organization in the early 1900s, with its separation of ownership from management; the introduction of income taxation in 1913 in the United States and in 1917 in Canada, which made accounting records necessary for tax purposes; the intense criticism of corporate reporting practices in the financial press during the early part of this century; and the stock market crash of 1929 and the depression that followed it.

Understanding generally accepted accounting principles requires a knowledge of the various organizations that have influenced their development. Primary among these are the Accounting Standards Board (AcSB) of the Canadian Institute of Chartered Accountants, the Society of Management Accountants of Canada (SMAC), the Certified General Accountants' Association (CGA), the Canadian Academic Accounting Association (CAAA), and the various provincial corporation departments and securities commissions. Publications by these and other organizations assist students of intermediate accounting and more advanced courses in financial accounting.

---

[11]"Financial Statement Concepts," CICA *Handbook,* Paragraph 1000.59, October 1991.
    [12]"Financial Statement Concepts," CICA *Handbook,* Paragraph 1000.60(a), October 1991.

Canadian Institute of Chartered Accountants (CICA)

The **Canadian Institute of Chartered Accountants (CICA)** is the national professional organization of CAs. This organization was incorporated as the Dominion Association of Chartered Accountants in 1902 and changed its name to the Canadian Institute of Chartered Accountants in 1949.

In 1934, the Canadian Companies Act and securities commissions were established by the Canadian government. The need for financial reporting standards and controls became evident after the stock market crash of 1929. The CICA's involvement in developing accounting principles began in 1946, when it issued its first recommendations in the form of a bulletin. *Bulletin No. 1* dealt with standards of financial statement disclosure. Several bulletins followed until 1968, when the CICA *Handbook* was introduced. The CICA *Handbook* converted the bulletins into loose-leaf format and included revisions of recommendations on unusual and nonrecurring items. Revisions to the CICA *Handbook* are introduced periodically, and 76 revisions were issued between 1968 and 1993. In 1974, the Accounting Research Committee was given the authority to publish *Accounting Guidelines.*

It wasn't until 1972 that the Canadian Securities Commission made the CICA *Handbook* the bible of financial reporting for its members. The government gave its support of the *Handbook* in 1975 when the Canada Business Corporations Act and the Ontario Securities Act were introduced. This support has remained strong except for the treatment of the Petroleum Incentives Program (PIP) grants. The institute's position was that the matching principle be followed and the grant be included in income when the exploration generated revenues and incurred expenses. The government and oil companies wanted to recognize the grants as income immediately as revenue. The government backed down and the institute's recommendations were implemented.

In addition to the CICA, there are provincial and territorial institutes whose members are also members of the CICA. The CICA issues many useful publications for accountants and accounting students, as well as a monthly journal, *CA Magazine*, that deals primarily with issues that are of concern to practising accountants.

Accounting Standards Board (AcSB)

In 1973, the Accounting Research and Auditing Standards Committee was divided into the Accounting Research Committee and the Auditing Standards Committee. The Accounting Research Committee was responsible for setting up the accounting recommendations. Its name was changed to the Accounting Standards Committee (AcSB) in 1982. In October 1991, the Accounting Standards Board (ASB), a fifteen-member committee, replaced the twenty-member AcSC. The AcSB is involved in developing and distributing literature on emerging issues, conducting studies, presenting exposure drafts, and publishing recommendations. The project development process is illustrated in Exhibit 1.3.

Research on various issues is done by staff who report their findings to the ASB. The research is developed into a project proposal and presented to the board. The statement of principles is developed as a basis on which the board discusses and debates its position on the issues. The exposure draft is prepared and circulated to interested parties. When the exposure period expires, the staff reviews the responses and presents this material to the board. If significant changes are required, a re-exposure draft is issued. When the

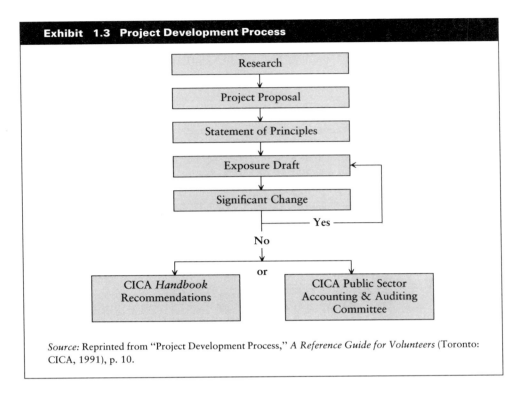

Exhibit 1.3 Project Development Process

Source: Reprinted from "Project Development Process," *A Reference Guide for Volunteers* (Toronto: CICA, 1991), p. 10.

exposure draft is accepted, it is published in *CA Magazine* along with the board's comments, and comments are invited from readers.

The CICA and the AcSB are influenced by the standards and practices of the American Institute of Certified Public Accountants and the International Accounting Standards Committee. For this reason, it is important for Canadian accounting students to have an overview of the structure of the standard-setting bodies in the United States.

International Accounting Standards Committee (IASC)

With the increase in international trade, there is a need for accountants all over the world to be able to interpret financial statements from other countries. As a result of a change in the trading environment, Section 1501 was added to the CICA *Handbook* in 1975. The purpose of this section is to provide the disclosure that is desirable by companies that report in an international environment. The disclosure for international purposes, however, should not override the Canadian regulations and recommendations.

American Institute of Certified Public Accountants (AICPA)

The **American Institute of Certified Public Accountants (AICPA)** is the U.S. professional organization of CPAs. In addition to many other useful publications, the AICPA publishes a monthly journal, *The Journal of Accountancy*, that deals primarily with current issues that are of concern to practising accountants.

Committee on Accounting Procedure (CAP)

The AICPA's first major involvement in developing accounting principles occurred in 1938 when it established the **Committee on Accounting Procedure (CAP)**. The CAP's

Annual Reports Often Don't Report Fully, Study Reports

TORONTO: Many of Canada's corporations are still not producing useful and relevant annual reports, says Jerry Trites, a partner in KPMG Peat Marwick Thorne's Halifax office.

Trites, a former chairman of the CICA's Auditing Standards Committee (now the Auditing Standards Board), was the chairman of a recent study group that has produced *Information to be Included in Annual Reports*. That study group surveyed the annual reports of 200 Canadian companies in 12 industry sectors, identifying 10 important areas requiring better information disclosures to meet users' needs.

"Annual reports are financial documents—not corporate storybooks," Trites says. "Their role is to communicate timely, relevant financial information to support economic decisions. And they must do so in a way that is understandable to key users—the company's shareholders, creditors and analysts/advisors."

But most aren't doing that. "Only 29% of the surveyed reports identified the company's fiscal and operating objectives for the coming year," Trites says. "Only 41% included a statement of environmental responsibilities—which is a serious omission, given the level of concern for the environment in Canada today. And a minuscule 3% disclosed information about the wealth created by the company's activities, and how this wealth was shared."

The study group also expressed concerns about the growing tendency for companies to issue two or more separate documents containing their financial information.

"An annual report should paint a complete financial picture," Trites explains. "Even though a company may release information using other vehicles, preparers must not assume that this information has actually reached users. Many users are unaware that these supplementary information vehicles exist. Others simply don't have the time to monitor a constant flow of releases."

In the end, Trites points out, most users still rely heavily on the annual report to make their decisions. For this reason, annual reports must integrate and interpret information that may be available from other sources, enabling users to fill their information gaps.

Trites advises financial executives to re-examine the openness with which information is disclosed in their company's annual reports. "In future, management will be expected to disclose information that may have been closely guarded in the past. It'll also have to be prepared to give the bad news with the good. A commitment to open, balanced disclosure is essential if annual reports are to remain relevant to users' needs."

Source: Reprinted from "Annual Reports Often Don't Report Fully, Study Reports," *The Bottom Line* (May 1992), p. 2.

purpose was to further the development of accounting principles, primarily by reducing the number of alternatives available for a given type of transaction or item. Although the CAP was dissolved in 1959, its 51 *Accounting Research Bulletins* (ARB) that have not been superseded by professional pronouncements are still important sources of generally accepted accounting principles.

Accounting Principles Board (APB)

In 1959, the AICPA replaced the CAP with the **Accounting Principles Board** (**APB**). From 1959 to 1973 the board issued 31 *Opinions* and four *Statements*. In 1970, the APB issued *Statement No. 4*, entitled "Basic Concepts and Accounting Principles Underlying Financial Statements of Business Enterprises."

Although the APB made significant progress in the development of generally accepted accounting principles, it was criticized for the broad principles within which to resolve problems. This is the same reason that the CAP had been criticized earlier. In response to these criticisms, the AICPA appointed a seven-person committee, chaired by Francis M. Wheat, to study the process of establishing accounting principles and to make recommendations for improvement. The Wheat Committee issued its report in March 1972, and this report led to the establishment of the Financial Accounting Standards Board.

Financial Accounting Standards Board (FASB)

Since July 1973, the **Financial Accounting Standards Board (FASB)** has been the official private-sector body charged with establishing and improving generally accepted accounting principles in the United States.[13]

The FASB issues three major types of pronouncements:

1. **Statements of Financial Accounting Standards (SFAS).** These establish new or amend existing generally accepted accounting principles.
2. **Interpretations.** These clarify, explain, or elaborate on SFAS, APB *Opinions*, or ARB. Interpretations are themselves a part of GAAP.
3. **Statements of Financial Accounting Concepts (SFAC).** These set forth objectives and concepts that the FASB uses as the basis for establishing and improving generally accepted accounting principles. SFAC do not establish generally accepted accounting principles within the scope of Rule 203, the *Code of Professional Conduct.*

Currently, the AICPA has an **Accounting Standards Executive Committee (AcSEC).** This committee issues *Statements of Position (SOP)*, which are intended to influence the development of accounting principles in specialized areas not covered by FASB pronouncements and *Issues Papers*, which are designed to identify financial accounting and reporting issues that AcSEC believes should be addressed or clarified by the FASB.

In addition to publishing *SOP* and *Issues Papers*, the AICPA also publishes *Industry Audit Guides* and *Industry Accounting Guides* and has an **Auditing Standards Board (ASB).** The ASB develops auditing standards and enforces professional ethics. Clearly, the ability of the FASB to survive as a private-sector, standard-setting body will depend to a large extent on how effectively it handles the many conflicting political pressures that it faces.

Provincial Securities Commissions

The level of share prices in Canada declined dramatically between 1929 and 1933. This occurrence made investors aware of the deficiency in the control of the information by public companies and the need for better disclosure of corporate information. The securities commissions do not protect investors from sustaining losses. Instead, their basic purpose is to ensure that companies provide investors with adequate information on which to base their investment decisions. Accordingly, companies under each provincial jurisdiction must report to their respective commission a substantial quantity of information.

---

[13]The Wheat Committee recommended use of the term "standards" instead of "principles" because of confusion over the meaning of "accounting principles." In this textbook we use the terms "principles" and "standards" interchangeably.

Each province controls and monitors the activities of the companies registered on its exchange (public trading in Canada is conducted through the Toronto, Montreal, Alberta, and Vancouver stock exchanges). The corporate reporting requirements vary slightly from annual reporting requirements to detailed annual reporting as well as summary quarterly reporting with varied supplemental information. The commissions are concerned with companies disclosing relevant financial and nonfinancial information on a timely basis.

The provincial securities commissions have some involvement in the standard-setting process, but they do not have the level of control of their U.S. counterpart, the Securities and Exchange Commission (SEC). The SEC has detailed reporting requirements for corporations trading shares under their control. The primary sources of the SEC's financial information requirements are **Regulation S-X, Accounting Series Releases (ASR), Staff Accounting Bulletins (SAB),** and **Financial Reporting Releases (FRR).**

Generally, securities commissions and private-sector standard-setting organizations co-operate with one another. The main ways in which the securities commissions have exerted their influence are by responding to planned and existing pronouncements of the AcSB and of its predecessors and by strongly encouraging these organizations to resolve emerging accounting problems.

Other Influences on Accounting Principles

The CICA and the provincial securities commissions are the organizations that have had the most influence in shaping generally accepted accounting principles as they exist today. However, other organizations, as well as income tax law, have also had an important impact.

Influencing Organizations

Canadian Academic Accounting Association (CAAA). This organization is dominated by accounting educators, although many practising accountants are active members. In addition to fostering improvements in accounting education and research, the CAAA has helped to develop accounting principles, especially in the area of financial accounting theory. This is the Canadian counterpart of the American Accounting Association.

Financial Executives Institute Canada (FEIC). The FEIC primarily comprises financial executives, such as controllers and treasurers, from large corporations. Members of this organization are an important subset of *preparers* of financial statements. Views expressed by FEIC members have played a significant role in the development of generally accepted accounting principles.

Accounting Standards Authority of Canada (ASAC). ASAC's membership includes accountants and representative user groups. The ASAC prepared the *Conceptual Framework for Financial Reporting* in 1987, the purpose of which was to provide an authoritative, coherent structure for objectives and broad fundamentals of financial accounting.

Income Tax Law

Income tax law has also influenced the development and implementation of accounting principles. For example, many smaller businesses maintain accounting records primarily for income tax purposes. Moreover, to avoid having to maintain one set of books for financial accounting purposes and another set for tax purposes, many companies use financial accounting principles that will reduce and postpone their income tax payments.

Although tax law has played a role in shaping generally accepted accounting principles, it is important to remember that **the principles that a company should use for tax purposes are not necessarily the same as those it should use for financial accounting purposes.** Tax accounting focusses on measuring taxable income using principles established by tax law. In contrast, a primary focus of financial accounting is measuring accounting income using generally accepted accounting principles. The objectives of tax law are to *raise money* for the operation of the government and to achieve certain *social goals.* The primary objective of generally accepted accounting principles is to *provide useful information* to investors, creditors, and other users. Since the objectives of tax accounting and financial accounting differ, the principles of tax accounting frequently differ from those of financial accounting. In Chapter 19, we examine financial accounting issues that relate directly to corporate income taxes.

Interestingly, many accountants feel that income tax law has often played a major role in the "nondevelopment" of GAAP. For example, the use of current value accounting in a company's primary financial statements is not a generally accepted accounting principle. One reason for this is accountants' fear that such accounting will create new kinds of income that the government will want to tax.

Sources of Generally Accepted Accounting Principles

As stated earlier, generally accepted accounting principles are those that have substantial authoritative support. The accounting profession has never published a complete, official list of such principles. Furthermore, because the profession has not defined precisely what is meant by the phrase "substantial authoritative support," the boundary separating generally accepted accounting principles from other principles is sometimes hazy. In practice, therefore, determining whether an accounting principle is generally accepted sometimes requires judgement. Accountants and auditors must be familiar with the sources of generally accepted accounting principles in order to answer difficult measurement and disclosure questions.

Generally accepted accounting principles can be classified into the four categories that follow. These categories are ranked from the most authoritative sources (Category A) to the least authoritative (Category D).

1. **Category A** contains the most authoritative sources of GAAP, which are issued by the AcSB, an authoritative body designated by the CICA Board of Governors, or were issued by its predecessor, the AcSC. These recommendations are presented in the *Handbook* in italics.
2. **Category B** contains desirable practices to be used when the AcSB recommendations do not fit a particular situation. This material appears in regular type in the *Handbook.*
3. **Category C** contains accounting guidelines and emerging issue abstracts included in the *Handbook.*
4. **Category D** contains other accounting literature, including CICA *Projects*, professional pronouncements from the FASB and IASC, and textbooks and journal articles. The isolated appearance of an accounting principle in a textbook or journal article should not be regarded as substantial authoritative support, but a consensus among several authors may be adequate support for an accounting principle not covered elsewhere in the literature.

Accountants should always record transactions in accordance with the *substance* (true nature) of the transactions. If the accounting treatment of a transaction is specified in a Category A recommendation, then the accountant should adhere to the Category A recommendation unless unusual circumstances exist. If the accounting treatment is *not* specified in a Category A recommendation, then the accountant should look for guidance in a source classified as Category B or C. Finally, the accountant should consider using a source in Category D only if an accounting treatment is not specified in Categories A, B, or C. Most of the CICA references in this text were issued by the AcSC.

Future Development of Generally Accepted Accounting Principles

Although considerable progress has been made in developing generally accepted accounting principles, much more work remains to be done. Some of the major issues that are likely to affect progress in this area are briefly discussed in the sections that follow.

Conceptual Framework Issue

A document that may ultimately have the greatest overall impact on the accounting standard-setting process is the *Conceptual Framework for Financial Reporting* issued by the Accounting Standards Authority of Canada. As stated earlier, this project sought to provide an authoritative, coherent structure for objectives and broad fundamentals of financial accounting. This structure is the basis for developing new financial accounting standards and eliminating inconsistencies that exist in current standards, and it provides a strong foundation to help the CICA resolve difficult accounting questions. The ASAC also intends that the structure will help everyone who has an interest in financial accounting to better understand the nature and limitations of financial accounting information.

To give you a more concrete idea of what the ASAC means by a conceptual framework, here are the major topics that the *Conceptual Framework in Financial Reporting* comprises:

1. Objective of financial reporting is to provide information for user decisions in a form that is understandable to the users.
2. Objective of financial reporting is to provide information for assessing cash flow prospects and changes in the resources of the entity.
3. Realization of the objectives through satisfaction of the users.[14]

The development of an authoritative conceptual framework has taken a lot of time, and there have been no easy, clear-cut answers to the questions that have arisen. The conceptual framework will continue to evolve, but changes to it will not likely occur as quickly as changes to accounting standards. In the long run, the CICA's success as a policy-making organization will probably depend heavily on the success of the Conceptual Framework document. Yet, a conceptual framework is unlikely to be a panacea. Certain factors will limit its usefulness: (1) the accounting policy-making process entails complex social choices; (2) the conceptual framework may not be interpreted uniformly by

---

[14]*Conceptual Framework for Financial Reporting, The Accounting Standards Authority of Canada,* Paragraph 122, 1987.

all CICA members at a given time; and (3) the CICA membership will continue to change over time, thereby possibly altering the ASAC's interpretation of the conceptual framework.

Economic Impact Issue

Accounting principles affect the allocation of scarce resources in our society because they determine the content of financial statements that investors, creditors, and others use to make many important decisions. Simply put, they help to determine who gets how much wealth.

In recent years, accounting principles have been directly linked to such issues as extended health care for retirees, bank lending policies, the merger movement, gross national product, national energy policy, and tax policy designed to encourage business investment. This fact has raised questions about whether and to what extent the CICA should be concerned with the economic impact of the standards that it sets. When the CICA established guidelines for oil- and gas-producing companies, for example, should it have been concerned only with trying to do what it considered correct according to accounting theory, or should it also have been concerned with doing what some energy producers claimed was best for the nation's energy program?

Perhaps less obvious but no less important is the fact that a *manager's behaviour*, as reflected in various operating and financial decisions, is often influenced by his or her knowledge of the information that accounting principles require. Indeed, some of a manager's compensation is often determined by the amount of net income reported in the company's financial statements. Recently, for example, Disney Corporation's CEO was awarded a contract that included "an annual cash bonus equal to 2% of Disney's net income in excess of a 9% return on equity. That clause alone resulted in a $6.8 million bonus last year when Disney's ROE hit 25%."[15]

Because of the actions of preparers and users of financial statements, accounting principles have an important *economic impact* on our society. Under current generally accepted accounting principles, for example, a company is not required to include all types of leases among its liabilities. Many people believe that if the CICA required companies to include all leases among their liabilities, companies would engage in fewer leasing transactions.

During the 1970s and 1980s, the economic impact issue began to play an increasingly important role in the standard-setting process of the AcSB. An awareness of this role helps to explain some of the generally accepted accounting principles that exist today.

In the future, the CICA is likely to be guided in its decisions primarily by the accounting theory that the AcSB has adopted from the Conceptual Framework document. However, the board will also consider the economic impact of its decisions by assessing the economic benefits and costs that its decisions are likely to produce, a process that will not be easy.

Private Versus Public Sector Issue

As noted earlier, private sector organizations have played the dominant role in shaping the development of generally accepted accounting principles in Canada. In the past, gov-

---

[15]John A. Byrne, Ronald Grover, and Todd Vogel, "Is the Boss Getting Paid Too Much?" *Business Week* (May 1, 1989), p. 52.

ernment has exerted relatively little direct influence on the standard-setting process. The most notable exceptions have been in the areas of accounting for the investment tax credit and accounting for oil- and gas-producing companies. Nevertheless, the provincial securities commissions have the legal authority to prescribe accounting principles, and government can effectively tell the commissions what to do. Will government ever decide that accounting principles should be formulated in the public sector?

Most accountants and other business people feel strongly that standard setting should remain in the private sector. A U.S. survey of the preferences of 1329 preparers, auditors, and users of financial reports "showed a clear preference for financial accounting reporting standards to be set within the private sector, by a body similar in composition to the current FASB."[16] The reasons for favouring the private sector determination of GAAP appear to be based on such important factors as objectivity, prestige and acceptability, expertise, competence, and image. Expertise is probably the most important of these factors.

In the final analysis, whether or not standard setting remains in the private sector will likely depend on how successful the CICA is in satisfying the various groups who are interested in its decisions, including the federal and provincial governments.

Uniformity Versus Flexibility Issue

People can usually think of several ways to account for a given type of transaction. Take depreciation for example. Generally accepted accounting principles support the concept that depreciation is a cost allocation process. But even though most accountants may agree with this concept, several depreciation methods are currently used, such as straight-line, double-declining balance, and productive output. The depreciation method that a company uses will influence the amount of its net income and other financial statement variables. This fact and the fact that people use financial statements to make *comparisons* between companies are the basis for one of the accounting profession's oldest debates: uniformity versus flexibility of accounting principles.

 Proponents of uniformity argue that company managers have too many accounting options available to them, and that these options create confusion and reduce the ability of financial statement users to make meaningful comparisons. Proponents of flexibility believe that some alternatives should be allowed, because each company is complex and unique.

Extreme uniformity or flexibility is disliked by most accountants. Strict uniformity would probably result in a "cookbook" prescribing in detail everything from procedures for gathering data to the precise format for financial statements. At the opposite extreme, unlimited flexibility would make it difficult for users to make comparisons among companies, and would undermine the integrity of the financial reporting process. The critical issue, therefore, is where on the uniformity/flexibility continuum the accounting profession should be.

One of the major tasks of accounting standards boards and committees has been to eliminate undesirable accounting alternatives. In doing this, accountants tend to emphasize the goal of **achieving comparability** rather than uniformity or flexibility. In order for financial statements to be comparable, any differences among the financial statements of different companies should reflect basic differences among the companies themselves and

[16]Joshua Ronen and Michael Schiff, "The Setting of Financial Accounting Standards—Private or Public?" *Journal of Accountancy* (March 1978), p. 69.

not merely among the accounting principles that they use. Achieving comparability requires: (1) identifying and describing the circumstances that justify or require the use of a particular accounting practice or method, [and] (2) eliminating the use of alternative practices under these circumstances.[17] Accomplishing this goal has not been and will not be easy. History reveals that when the accounting profession's critics feel that it has fallen short of achieving comparability, the cries for uniformity tend to become louder. A recent International Accounting Standards Committee exposure draft entitled *Comparability of Financial Information* recommends the elimination of alternative accounting choices. An important determinant of IASC's success will be the extent to which it contributes to comparability through an acceptable resolution of the uniformity/flexibility debate.

Market Efficiency Issue

Market efficiency is an issue with important implications for the uniformity/flexibility debate and for other accounting matters. Basically, in an **efficient market**, share prices behave as if they fully reflect publicly available information, including that reported in general-purpose financial statements. Although the evidence is not yet conclusive, a large body of empirical literature in accounting and finance suggests that the stock market is highly efficient.

An efficient market reacts to financial statements in a sophisticated manner. It is not fooled when two companies use different accounting methods. Instead, it recognizes that the numbers were generated by different methods. A high degree of market efficiency implies that the market is strongly influenced by the decisions of people who have considerable knowledge of accounting and business. In other words, an efficient market tends to be dominated by *sophisticated* rather than naive users of financial statements. A large portion of the market's efficiency is based on the reported financial results matching the expectations of the major traders.

An efficient market for accounting implies that many financial reporting issues can be resolved by a relatively simple strategy of **adequate disclosure**.[18] Consider the various depreciation methods. Those who believe that the market is highly efficient would argue that the reporting of several depreciation figures, each computed according to one of the widely used methods, involves only a small cost. Therefore, a company should use one method in its financial statements but disclose in the notes what depreciation would be under the other methods. Users, who are presumed to be sophisticated, can then adjust the statements to reflect the other methods if they so wish.

Efficient-market research has not been fully accepted by all accounting authorities. This is because the research pertains to the market as a whole and not to the behaviour of individual investors. Moreover, it says nothing about the information needs of financial statement users, such as bankers, whose decisions do not directly involve publicly traded shares. Nevertheless, the efficient market issue is one that may have an important effect on standard setting in Canada and the United States.

Big GAAP/Little GAAP Issue

General-purpose financial statements must conform with generally accepted accounting principles. These principles apply to any business regardless of its size or ownership char-

---

[17]"Financial Statement Concepts," CICA *Handbook*, Paragraph 1000.22, March 1991.

[18]See William H. Beaver, "What Should Be the FASB's Objectives?" *Journal of Accountancy* (August 1973), pp. 49–56.

acteristics. But consider a small, closely held business, such as a family-owned jewellery store or construction company. Do users of the financial statements of these kinds of businesses (primarily owners and bankers) really need the same types of information as users of the financial statements of such companies as Imperial Oil, BCE, and Canadian Pacific? Many people would say no. As a result, some people argue that one set of generally accepted accounting principles (which they would call "big GAAP") should apply to larger or publicly held companies, while a somewhat different set ("little GAAP") should apply to smaller or closely held companies.

The accounting profession has never defined precisely what constitutes a large or a small company. Accountants use the catchy term "big GAAP/little GAAP" to refer to the broad question of whether differential accounting principles should exist for different types of companies, whether based on size or ownership characteristics, or both.

Proponents of the big GAAP/little GAAP view believe that general-purpose financial statements of smaller companies are often unnecessarily costly because they include information that users do not really want. Proponents also feel that the cost of presenting all this information effectively precludes smaller companies from presenting information that is not required by GAAP but that users would find more useful. As a result, the proponents feel that present accounting standards tend to discriminate against smaller businesses.

The number and complexity of recommendations by the CICA have increased the importance of the big GAAP/little GAAP issue. The CICA is very concerned about this issue and has taken steps to reduce the financial reporting burden of smaller companies. As there are many more private companies than public companies, the big GAAP/little GAAP controversy will likely continue to influence the standard-setting process in the future.

Ethics in Accounting

Ethics has been a major news topic during the past several years. The media have bombarded us with stories about government officials using their political power for personal gain, corporate officers making money in the stock market by using insider information, and companies profiting from the sale of products that cause health hazards.

Everyone should behave in a way that is both legally and morally defensible. To behave legally, of course, means to obey laws. Morality provides fundamental guidelines to help people resolve conflicts and live together as a society. Thus, to behave in an ethical manner, a person must do what is right according to the current values of his or her society.

When applying accounting principles and in other aspects of their professional lives, accountants have a special obligation to observe high standards of ethical behaviour because of the trust given them by users of financial statements. Investors and creditors must believe in the integrity of financial statements if the statements are to have any value. Therefore, for accounting to continue as a useful institution in our society, accountants must have credibility. When an accountant engages in an illegal or unethical act, such as an independent auditor taking a bribe in exchange for allowing a company to falsify its financial statements, he or she undermines the integrity of the entire financial reporting process and of the accounting profession.

An accountant who encounters an ethical dilemma, such as being asked by management to misstate a company's revenues or expenses, should try to resolve the problem in a calm, reasoned manner. He or she should begin by evaluating all the facts and defining the ethical issues, and then identifying the parties who would be directly or indirectly affected by the decision made. Alternative courses of action should then be determined and their consequences compared. Next, the final decision should comply with high legal and moral standards of conduct. Finally, the accountant must have the courage and willpower to follow through with the ethical decision.

Fortunately, the accounting profession currently enjoys a high degree of moral credibility in the eyes of the general public. A recent nationwide survey of business people in the United States, indicated that accountants are regarded as having the highest business ethics of sixteen professions, ranking ahead of dentists and doctors.[19]

Concluding Remarks

Accounting seeks to identify, measure, and communicate information about economic entities that is useful in making economic decisions. Financial accounting is the branch of accounting that provides information about the financial position of a business enterprise and the changes that occur therein. Its primary focus is meeting the needs of external users such as shareholders and bankers.

General-purpose financial statements constitute the main output of financial accounting. Accountants prepare these statements in accordance with generally accepted accounting principles, which are largely determined by the private sector. Because these principles constantly change, the study of accounting is a lifelong process. As you study the remaining chapters of this book, continually question whether the accounting principles presented really aid the decision-making processes of external users. Do not assume that an accounting principle is desirable for society just because it is now generally accepted.

The following chapters will examine the hows, whys, and whats of intermediate accounting. Chapter 2 focusses on why, and deals with the basic theory of general-purpose financial statements.

Key Points

1. Accounting seeks to identify, measure, and communicate information about economic entities that is intended to be useful in making economic decisions. (Objective 1)
2. Financial accounting is the branch of accounting that is concerned with measuring and reporting the financial position of a business enterprise and the changes that occur in financial position. Financial accounting information is designed primarily to meet the needs of external users. (Objective 1)
3. External users of financial statements include present and potential owners, lenders, suppliers, employees, customers, financial analysts, stock exchanges, regulatory agencies, and the general public. (Objective 2)
4. Investors and creditors use financial statements to make predictions, assess risk, and evaluate profitability, solvency, and management's performance. (Objective 2)
5. The basic financial statements are the balance sheet, income statement, statement of changes in financial position, and statement of retained earnings or statement of shareholders' equity. (Objective 2)
6. The management of an economic entity has the primary responsibility for preparing its financial statements. (Objective 2)

---

[19]"Ethics Survey Ranks Accountants First," *Journal of Accountancy* (October 1989), p. 110.

7. Public (external) accountants examine financial statements and express an opinion about whether the statements have been prepared in accordance with generally accepted accounting principles. (Objective 2)
8. Auditors must be competent and independent from the companies they audit. (Objective 2)
9. Generally accepted accounting principles are those principles that have substantial authoritative support. (Objective 3)
10. The organizations that have had the most influence in developing generally accepted accounting principles are the Accounting Standards Board of the Canadian Institute of Chartered Accountants, Society of Management Accountants of Canada, Certified General Accountants' Association, Canadian Academic Accounting Association, and the various government departments and securities commissions in Canada, and the Committee on Accounting Procedure, Accounting Principles Board, Financial Accounting Standards Board, and Securities and Exchange Commission in the United States. (Objective 4)
11. Other organizations and income tax law have also affected the development of generally accepted accounting principles. (Objective 4)
12. CICA recommendations, desirable practices, and accounting guidelines are the most authoritative sources of generally accepted accounting principles. (Objective 5)
13. Several important issues are likely to affect the development of generally accepted accounting principles. These include the conceptual framework issue, the economic impact issue, the public versus private sector issue, the uniformity versus flexibility issue, the market efficiency issue, and the big GAAP/little GAAP issue. (Objective 6)
14. Accountants have a special obligation to observe high standards of ethical conduct because of the considerable trust given them by the users of financial statements. (Objective 7)

Appendix A: CICA *Handbook* Assembly Instructions

The CICA *Handbook* is usually received with two binders, a large blister pack of the filed contents, a package of dividers, the binder labels, and some packages of the revisions issued after the large blister pack was assembled.

1. Place one of the binder labels on each binder. Binders I and II will be used for accounting recommendations and auditing recommendations, respectively.
2. Start assembling the material with binder I and the large blister pack. Insert the ACCOUNTING RECOMMENDATIONS divider, followed by the pages up to the General Accounting, Section 1000 cover page.
3. Insert the 1000 GENERAL ACCOUNTING divider, followed by the pages up to the Specific Items, Section 3000 cover page.
4. Insert the 3000 SPECIFIC ITEMS divider, followed by the pages up to the Specialized Areas, Section 4000 cover page.
5. Insert the 4000 SPECIALIZED AREAS divider, followed by the pages up to the Accounting Guidelines table of contents page.
6. Insert the 4500 SUPPLEMENTARY FINANCIAL INFORMATION and ACCOUNTING GUIDELINES dividers, followed by the pages up to the EMERGING ISSUES COMMITTEE—ABSTRACTS OF ISSUES DISCUSSED table of contents page. The 4500 SUPPLEMENTARY FINANCIAL INFORMATION divider

may be excluded from your package. When this text went into production there were no recommendation pages for this section.

7. Insert the EIC ABSTRACTS divider, followed by the pages that go up to the CICA *Handbook* Volume II cover page.

8. Switch to binder II and insert the AUDITING RECOMMENDATIONS divider, followed by the pages up to the General Auditing, Section 5000 cover page.

9. Insert the 5000 GENERAL AUDITING divider, followed by the pages up to the Specific Items, Section 6000 cover page.

10. Insert the 6000 SPECIFIC ITEMS divider, followed by the pages up to the Specialized Areas, Section 7000 cover page.

11. Insert the 7000 SPECIALIZED AREAS divider, followed by the pages up to the Related Services, Section 8000 page.

12. Insert the 8000 RELATED SERVICES divider, followed by the pages up to the Auditing Guidelines table of contents page.

13. Insert the AUDITING GUIDELINES divider, followed by the pages up to the EDP Auditing Guidelines table of contents page.

14. Insert the EDP AUDITING GUIDELINES divider, followed by the pages up to the Topical Index Supplement (if one exists) or the Topical Index page 1.

15. Insert the TOPICAL INDEX divider, followed by the pages up to the Handbook Revisions cover page.

16. Insert the HANDBOOK REVISIONS divider, followed by the pages up to the Filing Instruction pages.

17. Insert the FILING INSTRUCTIONS divider and the Filing Instruction pages.

18. Place the additional revision packages in numerical order, starting with the revision following the revision instruction number filed in step 16. It is important to file the revisions individually in numerical order, because there may be pages inserted in one revision that are removed in a subsequent revision.

19. Follow the filing instructions as shown on the instruction sheet. Each instruction sheet has three columns. The first column shows the *Handbook* section name and/or number; the second column shows the page numbers of the pages to be withdrawn; and the last column shows the pages to be inserted and the date shown on the bottom of these pages. Withdraw the pages as indicated by the *Handbook* section and page number.

    The *Handbook* section number is printed in bold type at the bottom of each page and the page numbers appear in regular type at the spine margin of the binder. File the revisions in order. Do not group two revisions.

    There are gaps in the page numbers in the *Handbook*. At various points, a page may show the next page number to account for the gaps and allow for inclusion of future material within the existing structure.

20. When your *Handbook* is assembled, discard all the pages that were withdrawn. Remember to make sure that you are registered for future *Handbook* revisions; otherwise your book will become outdated.

Questions

Q1.1   Distinguish between internal and external users of accounting information.

Q1.2   What is financial accounting?

Q1.3 What is meant by "general-purpose financial statements"? Why does the accounting profession emphasize general-purpose statements instead of single-purpose statements?

Q1.4 Give three examples of accounting applications that illustrate the following point: "Financial statements are not usually as precise as they appear to be."

Q1.5 Identify five sources that investors and creditors commonly use to obtain information about specific companies.

Q1.6 Distinguish between financial statements and financial reporting.

Q1.7 Briefly explain the role of corporate management in the financial reporting process.

Q1.8 Briefly explain the professional designations of CGA, CMA, and CA.

Q1.9 What is an audit?

Q1.10 The following terms relate to auditor's reports. Define each one.

(a) Unqualified opinion.   (c) Adverse opinion.
(b) Qualified opinion.   (d) Denial of opinion.

Q1.11 What is meant by the term "generally accepted accounting principles"?

Q1.12 Distinguish among the following types of pronouncements:

(a) Accounting guidelines.   (d) Accounting recommendations.
(b) Emerging issues.   (e) Auditing recommendations.
(c) Exposure drafts.   (f) Auditing guidelines.

Q1.13 Briefly explain the professional responsibilities of an auditor as outlined in Section 5020 of the CICA *Handbook*. What is the significance of these responsibilities?

Q1.14 What are the major differences between the management report and the auditor's report?

Q1.15 What major steps does the CICA usually follow when formulating an accounting or auditing release?

Q1.16 What is the purpose of a securities commission?

Q1.17 What is the role of a provincial securities commission in establishing accounting standards?

Q1.18 Why do the principles of income tax law often differ from the principles of financial accounting?

Q1.19 Of what significance are financial analysts and commercial bank loan officers to the accounting profession?

Q1.20 Explain the various sources of generally accepted accounting principles, from the most authoritative to the least authoritative.

Q1.21 Briefly explain how accounting principles affect the manner in which our society allocates its scarce resources.

Q1.22 What is the uniformity versus flexibility issue?

Q1.23 Do generally accepted accounting principles apply only to larger companies? Explain.

Q1.24 What does "morality" mean, and why is it particularly important for accountants to observe high standards of moral behaviour?

Cases

C1.1 Sources of Information. Assume that you have recently graduated from university and your new boss asks you to speak to a local organization of business people. The topic of your speech is "Sources of Information That May Be Useful in Investment, Credit, and Similar Decisions."

Instructions

Identify the major sources that you should describe in your speech.

C1.2 The Accounting Profession. A friend of yours who is majoring in another business field has asked you what, if anything, besides the technical content of accounting courses distinguishes accounting from other business disciplines. Your friend does not understand why accountants can be designated as chartered accountants and what role CAs play in the business process.

Instructions

Develop a response to your friend's question. Consider the characteristics that distinguish a profession from other business or commercial endeavours. Also be sure to address the role of accounting in the functioning of our capital markets as well as its contribution to the management of business enterprises.

C1.3 Accounting Principles. At the completion of the Hardy Department Store audit, the company president asks about the meaning of the phrase "in conformity with generally accepted accounting principles" that appears in your audit report. The president observes that the meaning of the phrase must include more than what one normally considers to be "principles."

Instructions
(a) Explain the meaning of "accounting principles" as used in the auditor's report. (Do *not* discuss the significance of the words "generally accepted.")
(b) The president wants to know how you determine whether or not an accounting principle is generally accepted. Discuss the sources of evidence for determining whether an accounting principle has substantial authoritative support.
(c) The president believes that diversity in accounting practice will always exist among independent entities despite continual improvements in comparability. Develop arguments to support this belief.
(Adapted from AICPA.)

C1.4 Departures from GAAP. You are preparing the financial statements for your company, a chain of retail clothing stores, when the president calls you in to discuss an accounting problem. The issue involves a transaction that the company has just completed and that has a substantial effect on reported earnings. There is a CICA recommendation that deals generally with the issue; however, this particular transaction has a few characteristics that are not considered in the CICA recommendation. The president wishes to account for the transaction in a way that departs from the CICA provisions, and you see some validity in her position. First, the transaction is somewhat different from that contemplated by the CICA recommendation. While you do not consider the differences to be significant, you do believe that the accounting proposed by the president would better portray the economic substance of the transaction. Nevertheless, you believe that accounting for the transaction in the fashion prescribed by the CICA would also be reasonable. The president concludes the meeting with the following statement: "Study this issue for a while and write a position paper to let me know what you think. I know I can count on you to support any effort to put our best foot forward in the marketplace."

Instructions

Use the information provided in the case and the material in Chapter 1 to prepare a response that you believe is consistent with the responsibilities of a professional accountant.

C1.5 Standard-Setting Process. Your friend is a recent MBA graduate working as an investment loan officer at a bank. She took an introductory accounting course as part of the MBA program. In spite of achieving top marks in the course, she does not understand why it is difficult to compare the financial statements of different clients. She wants you to tell her why the CICA recommendations allow for all of these different rules to be considered generally accepted.

Instructions

Write a 250-word response to your friend. Include information from the CICA *Handbook* and Chapter 1 to support your explanation.

C1.6 Standard-Setting Process. The CICA was criticized for its auditing practices when several companies went bankrupt shortly after their audited financial statements were issued. The public questioned why the auditors did not discover and report the deficiencies in the operation.

Instructions

(a) Explain the auditors' role and responsibilities. Who are the auditors working for? Who is the auditors' superior?

(b) Do you think the auditors will be rehired if the auditor's report is qualified? Does this factor influence the scope of the audit and the contents of the report?

C1.7 Politicization in Standard Setting. Some accountants believe that the development and acceptance of generally accepted accounting principles (i.e., standard setting) is being politicized. Some use the term "politicization" in a narrow sense to mean influence by governmental agencies, particularly the securities commissions. Others use the term more broadly to mean the compromising that is done by bodies responsible for developing generally accepted accounting principles due to the influence and pressure of interested groups (e.g., CGA, CAAA, CMA, businesses through their various organizations, financial analysts, bankers, and lawyers).

Instructions

(a) Explain why the CICA *Handbook* recommendations are supported by government. What is your opinion of the intervention of government in the creation of generally accepted accounting principles?

(b) What arguments support the politicization view of standard setting?

(c) What arguments can be raised against the politicization view of standard setting?

(Adapted from CMA.)

C1.8 Income Tax Laws. One of your friends is a law school student who recently decided to take an introductory course in financial accounting. After his first day of class, she tells you: "I'm having some trouble understanding what financial accounting is all about. In law school, I learned how to calculate income according to tax laws. Why aren't the tax laws used to calculate income in financial accounting?"

Instructions
(a) Answer your friend's question.
(b) Discuss the significance of income tax law in the development of generally accepted accounting principles.

C1.9 Standard Setting for Leases. For many years, the accounting profession has debated the merits of two primary methods of accounting for leases by lessees (companies that lease assets from other enterprises): (1) capitalization of leases, which means that lessees record the present value of expected future lease payments as a liability and an asset, treating lease payments as reductions in the liability, and depreciating the recorded asset; and (2) expensing lease payments as they are made, with no initial recording of a lease asset or liability by the lessee.

When the CICA was discussing the issue of accounting for leases, it received several queries from the public that read in part as follows:

> A number of my friends and I are concerned with the possible effect of lease capitalization upon the financing costs of Canadian industry—which costs enter into the eventual prices to the public of goods and services. In an inflationary period, such suggested accounting practice may have a marked affect upon the prices to the public, of transportation, energy, food, and housing. It would be most unfortunate if a theoretical approach to financial disclosure assumed greater importance than the public good, especially when effective and more acceptable accounting methods are available for the protection of the investor.

Instructions
(a) Identify the broad issue in accounting standard setting that underlies the public concern.
(b) What effect, if any, do you think the points raised in the query should have on the CICA's deliberations in the matter of accounting for leases?

C1.10 Development Stage Companies. In April 1991, the CICA issued *Emerging Issues Committee, Abstract of Issue Discussed, Revenue and Expenditures During the Pre-operation Period*, EIC–27. This *Abstract* outlines the items to be deferred and expensed during the pre-operation period of a new business. This topic has received consideration by the business community, which feels that new businesses need some reporting incentives during their start-up period.

Instructions
(a) Do you believe that accounting recommendations should provide special rules for newly formed businesses? Why or why not?
(b) How long should the special treatment last? When should a business be considered operational?

C1.11 General Versus Detailed Standards. The public sometimes criticizes the CICA for some of its recommendations. One complaint is that the recommendations use a "cookbook" approach and are so narrow and detailed as to make implementation prohibitively expensive. Critics have cited the rules on pension costs and intangible capital assets as examples.

Instructions

When the CICA publishes an accounting standard, should the standard be written in a manner that is relatively general or relatively detailed in nature? Explain the rationale for your preference.

C1.12 Effects of Accounting Principles. An article that appeared in *Forbes* (November 28, 1988, p. 170) stated that "foreign companies have a walloping advantage over U.S. companies in playing the takeover game in this country. The advantage is intangible, but it's a big advantage all the same." The article explains that when a U.S. company acquires another company, generally accepted accounting principles require the U.S. company to amortize any payment that is made for goodwill. The goodwill is amortized over a maximum period of 40 years and causes the acquiring company's net income to be lower by the amount of the amortization. In contrast, under British accounting rules, when a British company acquires another enterprise, even one located in the United States, any amount paid for goodwill is immediately written off against shareholders' equity and is therefore never charged against the British company's net income.

Instructions

The Canadian accounting rules for intangibles mirror the U.S. rules. Do you believe that the British rules for goodwill give British companies an advantage over Canadian or U.S. companies when acquiring other companies? Present arguments to support your answer.

C1.13 Market Efficiency Issue. At an open meeting in July 1981, it was stated that the SEC "intends to apply the efficient market theory . . . to public offerings by widely-followed companies to take advantage of periodic reports filed under the Securities Exchange Act prior to a new registration statement." (Deloitte Haskins & Sells, *The Week in Review,* July 31, 1981, p. 1.)

Instructions
(a) What is an efficient market?
(b) Briefly indicate how you think the SEC could apply the efficient market theory "to take advantage of periodic reports filed under the Securities Exchange Act prior to a new registration statement."

C1.14 Big GAAP/Little GAAP Issue. In an open letter to the FASB, Alexander Grant & Company, a large, international CPA firm, stated

We are genuinely concerned that you are not reacting to a serious problem. A recent exchange of correspondence between the AICPA and the FASB makes it clear to us that the present FASB does not intend to consider relief from onerous accounting and disclosure requirements for the thousands of smaller and/or closely-held businesses across this country. (*Wall Street Journal*, October 25, 1977, p. 24.)

Instructions

(a) Take the position that the accounting profession should have one set of generally accepted accounting principles that apply to all companies, regardless of size or ownership characteristics. Develop arguments to support your position.

(b) Take the position that the accounting profession should have one set of generally accepted accounting principles for larger or publicly held companies and a different set for smaller or closely held companies. Develop arguments to support your position.

C1.15 Expense Reimbursement. As an accountant for a medium-sized company, you have recently returned from a five-day out-of-town assignment and are now completing your expense reimbursement form. Your employer has a written policy allowing you to claim reimbursement for your actual daily cost of meals up to a maximum of $35 per day. You are not required to provide receipts for the meals that you claim.

While you were on assignment, you ate meals for free at your aunt's home, but no one from your company knows because you worked on the assignment alone. You have learned through informal conversation that some of your fellow employees routinely request reimbursement for the maximum meal allowance of $35, even when the actual cost of their meals is much less.

Instructions

Would you claim reimbursement for the cost of your meals at the maximum daily rate allowed by your company ($35 × 5 days = $175)? Explain your answer.

Chapter 2

Financial Accounting Theory

Objectives

1. To describe financial accounting theory as it is currently applied. The theory consists of the following elements:

   a. Objectives

   b. Qualitative characteristics

   c. Assumptions

   d. Concepts and elements

   e. Broad principles

   f. Detailed principles

   g. Modifying conventions

One author defines accounting theory as "logical reasoning in the form of a set of broad principles that (1) provide a general frame of reference by which accounting practice can be evaluated and (2) guide the development of new practices and procedures."[1] This chapter provides an overview of descriptive financial accounting theory as it pertains to general-purpose external reporting by business enterprises. Note carefully the following terms from the preceding sentence:

1. **Overview.** In this chapter, we introduce the most important components of financial accounting theory. Entire textbooks have been devoted to explaining these and other components in more depth.
2. **Descriptive.** Descriptive theory refers to the ways in which accounting theory is currently applied. In contrast, normative theory attempts to prescribe how theory ought to be. This chapter is primarily descriptive.
3. **Financial accounting theory.** We present a logical framework that helps to explain why financial accounting is applied the way it is today.
4. **General-purpose external reporting.** The chapter focusses on a theoretical structure for general-purpose (rather than single- or limited-purpose), external (rather than internal) reporting.

A knowledge of accounting theory should help you to understand and apply generally accepted accounting principles as well as changes in those principles. Because accounting problems often appear to be routine, accountants sometimes get bogged down in the mechanics of problem solving and lose sight of the theory they seek to apply. For this reason, you should study this chapter carefully. Later, as you study other chapters, reread the appropriate sections of this chapter.

The accounting profession today does not have a single, comprehensive, generally accepted framework of accounting theory. As we pointed out in Chapter 1, however, the Accounting Standards Authority of Canada (ASAC) has developed a conceptual framework that it hopes will be accepted in the financial community. Recognize, therefore, that accounting is a relatively young and dynamic discipline for which a theoretical structure is still evolving. The theoretical framework presented in this chapter is based on several sources and represents descriptive financial accounting theory today.[2] Always strive for sound conceptual understanding that can help you to solve most accounting problems, whether you encounter them in a textbook, on an examination, or in the business world.

A Model of Financial Accounting Theory

Exhibit 2.1 presents the theoretical components discussed in this chapter. These components are **objectives, qualitative characteristics, assumptions, concepts and elements, broad principles, detailed principles,** and **modifying conventions.**[3] A move from the top to the bottom of the exhibit represents a move from general objectives to detailed principles, which are quite specific. Accountants traditionally have had less difficulty agreeing on the general components of the model than on the specific ones. Most accountants

---

[1]Eldon S. Hendricksen, *Accounting Theory*, 4th ed. (Homewood, IL: Irwin, 1982), p. 1.

[2]The framework that we present draws heavily from the works published by the ASAC in Canada and the FASB in the United States.

[3]The labels attached to certain components of the model vary somewhat in practice. Principles, for example, are sometimes called standards, concepts, procedures, rules, practices, and conventions.

Exhibit 2.1 Financial Accounting Theory: A Model

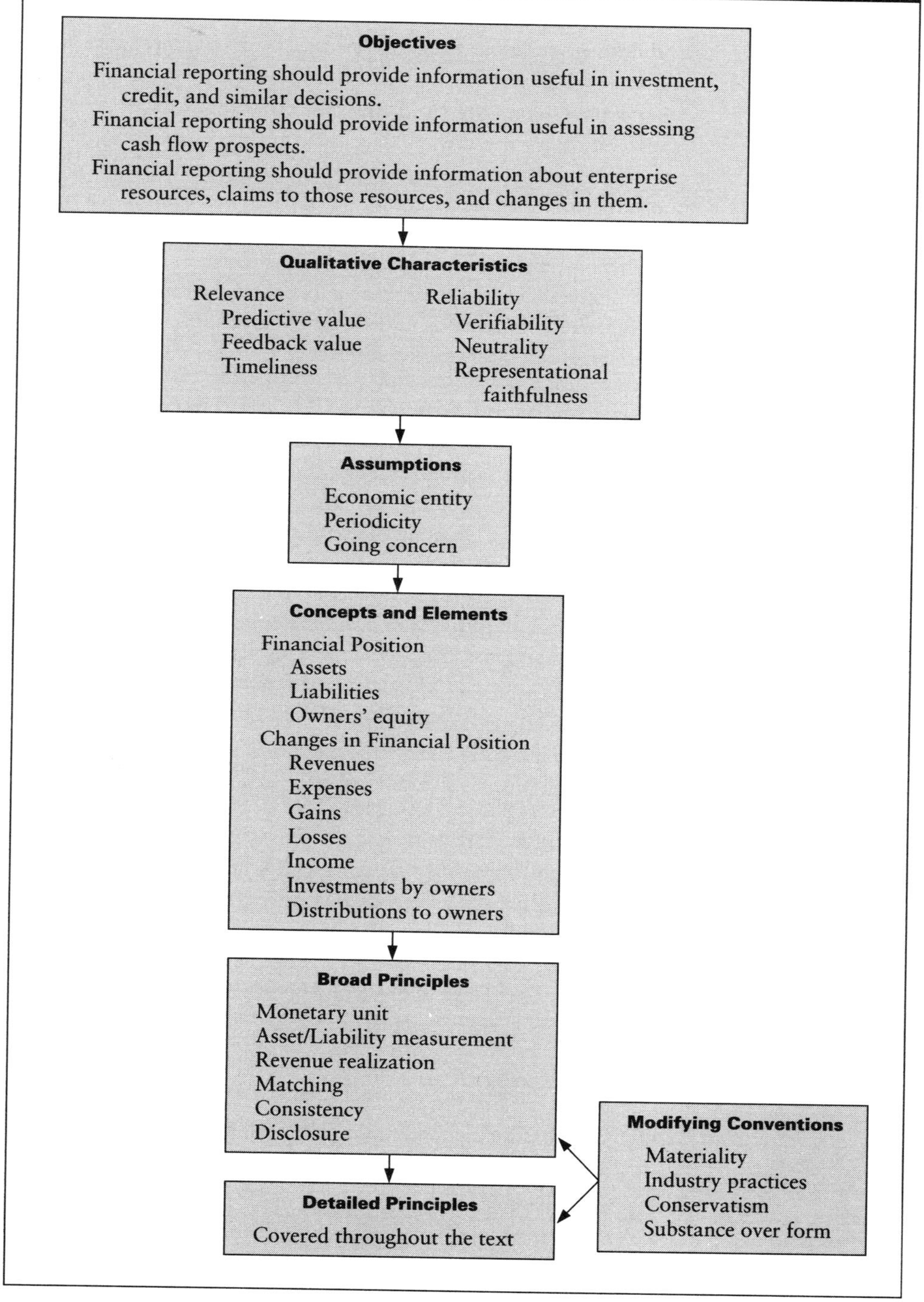

Objectives

Financial reporting should provide information useful in investment, credit, and similar decisions.

Financial reporting should provide information useful in assessing cash flow prospects.

Financial reporting should provide information about enterprise resources, claims to those resources, and changes in them.

Qualitative Characteristics

Relevance	Reliability
Predictive value	Verifiability
Feedback value	Neutrality
Timeliness	Representational faithfulness

Assumptions

Economic entity
Periodicity
Going concern

Concepts and Elements

Financial Position
   Assets
   Liabilities
   Owners' equity
Changes in Financial Position
   Revenues
   Expenses
   Gains
   Losses
   Income
   Investments by owners
   Distributions to owners

Broad Principles

Monetary unit
Asset/Liability measurement
Revenue realization
Matching
Consistency
Disclosure

Modifying Conventions

Materiality
Industry practices
Conservatism
Substance over form

Detailed Principles

Covered throughout the text

agree, for example, that an important accounting objective should be to provide useful information. On the other hand, less agreement exists about which principles the accounting profession should adopt to achieve the objective of providing useful information.

When studying the model of financial accounting theory, remember that the components are *not all independent of one another*. Many important **interrelationships** exist that are too complex to identify meaningfully in one model. Furthermore, accounting principles have not always developed on the basis of explicit objectives. As we pointed out in Chapter 1, "the term generally accepted accounting principles encompasses not only specific rules, practices and procedures relating to particular circumstances but also broad principles and conventions of general application."[4] For this reason, some accountants think that certain principles are inconsistent with certain objectives. These components may therefore change as a result of further development of accounting theory. Despite these limitations of the model, we believe that it provides a useful framework in which to study financial accounting.

Objectives of Financial Reporting

During the 1970s and 1980s, the Canadian Institute of Chartered Accountants spent time developing its objective for financial reporting in Canada. While the CICA was establishing guidelines for Canadian reporting, the American Institute of Certified Public Accountants (AICPA) published a major study called *Objectives of Financial Statements*. This study, commonly called the Trueblood Report, set forth several objectives but concluded that "the basic objective of financial testimony is to provide information useful for making economic decisions."[5] In 1978, the FASB issued *Statement of Financial Accounting Concepts No. 1*, entitled "Objectives of Financial Reporting by Business Enterprises,"[6] and in 1988 the CICA issued Section 1000, "Financial Statement Concepts." The FASB pronouncement was greatly influenced by the Trueblood Report.

The objective outlined in Section 1000 stems largely from the important needs of external users, who lack the authority to require the information that they want about a given enterprise. Furthermore, the objective is affected by the economic, legal, political, and social environment in Canada and, as a result, may change over time. Finally, the objective is affected by the characteristics and limitations of the information that financial reporting traditionally has provided.

Paragraph 1000.15 of the CICA *Handbook* has identified the objective of financial reporting. This broad objective includes the objectives outlined in Exhibit 2.1. The first part is the most general, while the next two parts are progressively more specific.

Useful Information

The objective of financial statements is "to communicate information that is useful to investors, members, contributors, creditors and other users ('users') in making their resource allocation decisions and/or assessing management stewardship."[7] This objective underscores the fact that financial reporting is not an end in itself. Instead, the *output* of

[4]"Financial Statement Concepts," CICA *Handbook,* Paragraph 1000.60, March 1991.

[5]"Basic Concepts and Accounting Principles Underlying Financial Statements of Business Enterprises," *APB Statement No. 4,* Paragraph 139, 1970.

[6]"Objectives of Financial Statements," *Report of the Study Group on the Objectives of Financial Statements* (New York: AICPA, 1973), p. 61.

[7]"Financial Statement Concepts," CICA *Handbook,* Paragraph 1000.15, March 1991.

the financial accounting process should serve as useful *input* for the making of rational investment, credit, and similar decisions in our society.

Traditionally, anyone proposing usefulness as an accounting objective has had to respond to the important questions: Useful to whom? And for what purpose? In stating its objective, the CICA's response to these questions is quite broad. As a result, the scope of financial reporting is not confined to one, or even a few, user groups. Instead, financial reporting attempts to serve many diverse users. These users, however, are expected to understand business affairs and be willing to spend reasonable amounts of time and effort analyzing accounting information. Accountants should always try to produce reports that are understandable to these kinds of users. Naive users of accounting information should consider taking steps to improve their understanding of business matters, or they should rely on professional advisors. **Understandability** to *reasonably informed users* is therefore a desirable quality of useful accounting information.[8]

Although providing useful information is the primary objective of financial reporting, accounting principles do not require companies to report all potentially useful information. Instead, a pervasive constraint stipulates that **accounting information should be provided only when the benefits of the information exceed the costs of providing and using it.** As you may imagine, trying to determine the benefits and costs of accounting information is highly subjective and can lead to honest differences of opinion between competent people. Benefits of accounting information are enjoyed by preparers (e.g., improved access to capital markets and favourable impact on a company's public relations), users (e.g., better investment and credit decisions), and consumers (e.g., steady supply of goods and services, more efficient functioning of the marketplace, and so forth). Most of the costs are initially paid by preparers but are then passed on to users of financial statements and consumers of the company's goods and services.[9]

Cash Flow Prospects

Rational investment, credit, and similar decisions are made after careful consideration of such factors as expected cost, risk, and return. As noted in Chapter 1, investors and creditors invest and lend cash, and they want to know how much cash they will receive in return and when they will receive it. Information that helps to resolve these uncertainties is regarded as useful.

Accordingly, the objective of financial reporting is to provide investors and creditors with information to be used in making resource allocation decisions and to predict the ability of an enterprise to earn income and generate cash.[10] Note that there is a difference between cash flows to investors and creditors and cash flows to a given enterprise to which they have committed funds. Chances of investors and creditors receiving cash via dividends, interest, and otherwise depend on the expected cash flows to the enterprise. If the enterprise succeeds in generating favourable cash flows, the probability of investors and creditors receiving favourable cash flow increases.

Enterprise Resources, Claims, and Changes

What information is helpful to investors, creditors, and other users in assessing prospective cash receipts from a business enterprise? Paragraph 1000.14 of the CICA *Handbook*

---

[8]"Financial Statement Concepts," CICA *Handbook,* Paragraph 1000.19, March 1991.

[9]"Financial Statement Concepts," CICA *Handbook,* Paragraph 1000.16, March 1991.

[10]"Financial Statement Concepts," CICA *Handbook,* Paragraph 1000.12, March 1991.

responds to this question: "Investors, members and contributors also require information about how the management of an entity has discharged its stewardship responsibility to those that have provided resources to the entity."[11] The elements of the financial statements that achieve the objective are "those that describe the economic resources, obligations and equity/net assets of an entity at a point in time, and those that describe changes in economic resources, obligations and equity/net assets over a period of time."[12]

Some of the most significant transactions and events that change a firm's resources and the claims to those resources are used to measure financial performance. The CICA states that "It is possible that an item will meet the definition of an element but still not be recognized in the financial statements because it is not probable that future economic benefits will be obtained or given up or because a reasonable estimate cannot be made of the amount involved."[13] Thus, investors and creditors may use past measures of earnings to help predict future earnings and, indirectly, to help predict their chances of receiving cash from a given enterprise.

The CICA believes that **accrual accounting** results in better performance measures than does cash basis accounting. However, the board has emphasized that "accrual accounting recognizes the effect of transactions and events in the period in which the transactions and events occur, regardless of whether there has been a receipt or payment of cash or its equivalent."[14] Thus, accountants provide useful historical measurements, but they cannot accurately predict the future and they surely do not make decisions for external information users.

While financial reporting focusses primarily on earnings, information about financial position as well as significant changes in financial position (besides earnings) is important when assessing an enterprise's cash flow prospects. Because management knows more about a firm than do outsiders, the usefulness of information can often be enhanced by management's explanation of the financial impact of certain transactions, events, and circumstances.

Qualitative Characteristics of Accounting Information

Given that the basic objective of external financial reporting is to provide information that is useful to people making rational economic decisions, a logical question is: What qualitative characteristics determine the usefulness of accounting information? Many studies have addressed this issue and have generally produced similar results.

The CICA believes that **relevance** and **reliability** are the two most fundamental qualitative characteristics of useful accounting information. Relevance means the capacity of information to make a difference in a decision by helping users to form predictions about the outcome of past, present, and future events or to confirm or correct prior expectations. For example, when shareholders decide to buy, sell, or hold equity investments, earnings-per-share information is generally regarded as highly relevant. In contrast, the serial numbers of capital assets, although highly reliable, are irrelevant information.

The major characteristics of relevant information are as follows:[15]

---

[11]"Financial Statement Concepts," CICA *Handbook*, Paragraph 1000.14, March 1991.
[12]"Financial Statement Concepts," CICA *Handbook*, Paragraph 1000.25, March 1991.
[13]"Financial Statement Concepts," CICA *Handbook*, Paragraph 1000.45, March 1991.
[14]"Financial Statement Concepts," CICA *Handbook,* Paragraph 1000.46, March 1991.
[15]"Financial Statement Concepts," CICA *Handbook*, Paragraph 1000.20, March 1991.

1. **Predictive value.** Information has predictive value when it can help users to increase the likelihood of correctly forecasting the outcome of events. For example, if "cash provided by operations" proves valuable in predicting loan default, it is said to have predictive value.
2. **Feedback value.** Information with feedback value enables users to confirm or correct expectations. A net income measure, for example, has feedback value if it can help shareholders to confirm or revise their expectations about a company's ability to generate earnings.
3. **Timeliness.** Information is timely when it is available to a decision maker before decisions are made. For example, one of the most important attributes of quarterly financial information is its timeliness.

To be relevant, information must have predictive value or feedback value or both, and it must be timely.

Information is reliable when it is in agreement with the actual underlying transactions and events, the agreement is capable of being independently verified, and the information is reasonably free of error and bias.[16] In other words, users can trust that reliable measurements will accurately represent the reality that the measurements claim to represent. For example, most people consider the amount of cash that a company has in its bank account to be highly reliable information. However, information about a company's projected earnings per share 50 years from now is usually not reliable.

Reliable information has three major characteristics:[17]

1. **Verifiability.** Information is considered verifiable when it is based on reasonable underlying evidence. Such evidence would permit all competent accountants to generate similar measurements under the same circumstances. The amount of a company's cash on hand, for example, is usually highly verifiable because accountants can simply count it.

    Because of the need for verifiability, financial accounting is based primarily on the results of **arm's-length exchange transactions**, in which unrelated parties act in their own best economic interests. Some accountants refer to the verifiability characteristic as "objectivity."
2. **Neutrality.** Information is neutral when it is free of bias toward a desired result or behaviour. Accounting information would not be neutral if it systematically produced results that favoured one group of users, such as bankers, over another, such as labour organizations.
3. **Representational faithfulness.** Information is representationally faithful when a measure or description agrees with the phenomenon that it claims to represent. A measure of a company's accounts receivable, for example, would have low representational faithfulness if it included a material amount of uncollectable accounts.

To be reliable, information must have all three of these characteristics.

Many accountants have argued that relevance and reliability may require important trade-offs. That is, to increase the relevance of accounting information, accountants may have to sacrifice some reliability, and vice versa. For example, generally accepted accounting principles call for reporting capital assets in the balance sheet at their historical cost.

---

[16]"Financial Statement Concepts," CICA *Handbook,* Paragraph 1000.21, March 1991.
    [17]"Financial Statement Concepts," CICA *Handbook,* Paragraph 1000.21(a)–(c), March 1991.

It is possible, however, that the current cost of capital assets is a more relevant, yet less reliable, measure than the historical cost of these assets. If so, the question then becomes: Which measure of capital assets, historical cost or current cost, results in information that is most useful? One of the great challenges of the accounting profession is to achieve an optimal balance between relevance and reliability to ensure that accounting information is as useful as possible. Arriving at this balance requires considerable research and generates many interesting debates in the financial community.

Assumptions

To provide information that is both relevant and reliable, and therefore useful, accountants begin by making certain assumptions. These assumptions, often called **postulates**, generally relate to things that are taken for granted. By starting with basic assumptions, other components in the theoretical framework may be logically derived.

Economic Entity Assumption

Applying the principles of accounting requires the identification of specific units of economic activity. Each unit serves as a focal point to guide the accountant's recording and reporting functions. Accordingly, accountants make the **economic entity assumption,** which says that **economic activities can be meaningfully associated with specific entities or units of accountability.** Typical examples of an economic entity are a person (such as a candidate for public office), a sole proprietorship, a partnership, and a corporation. The entity assumed may be somewhat narrow in scope, such as a division of a diversified company, or quite broad, as when consolidated financial statements are prepared for a group of corporations having common ownership. In any case, the name of the entity should appear at the top of the financial statements.

The economic entity assumption requires a careful separation of the financial affairs of a business (the entity) from the affairs of its owners and other businesses. For example, when a building contractor purchases lumber for an addition to his personal residence, this cost should not be included in the financial affairs of his building company.

Accountants sometimes ignore certain legal considerations when complying with the economic entity assumption. For example, the accounting records of a partnership must be kept separate and distinct from the records of the individual partners, even though the partners may be personally liable for partnership debts if liquidation occurs. Similarly, although a parent corporation and one or more subsidiaries constitute separate *legal* entities, accountants often prepare consolidated financial reports depicting the companies as a single *economic* entity. In addition to consolidated statements, accountants must prepare individual company statements for those companies combined into a consolidated form.

Periodicity Assumption

The most reliable method of calculating a new firm's income is to wait until the firm is finally liquidated. At that time, lifetime income can be measured as the amount of resources paid by the firm to the owners over the amount paid into the firm by the owners. Of course, measuring income only when a firm is terminated is not a practical way of satisfying the needs of financial statement users. Indeed, for information to be relevant and thereby have an impact on important decisions, it must be timely.

The need for timely dissemination of information has led accountants to make the **periodicity assumption: the economic activities of a firm can be meaningfully related to arbitrary time periods that are shorter than the firm's life.** In practice, annual, quarterly, and monthly time periods are commonly used. An annual period may be a calendar year, ending December 31, or a fiscal year, the end of which often coincides with the lowest point in a firm's business activities.

The economic activities of a typical business are complex and continuous. When a manufacturing firm buys a new machine, for example, the machine will likely last for several accounting periods. During these periods the machine will be used—with other machines, raw materials, and labour—to produce a product that may be sold at some future date for a price that is now uncertain. Given this interaction and uncertainty, no one can precisely determine the benefits of the machine to the firm. Therefore, depreciation expense under accrual accounting cannot be precisely determined for a period shorter than the life of the machine. As this example shows, financial reporting for any brief period requires estimates and professional judgement, and the accountant's measurements are therefore often tentative. In general, as the time period becomes shorter, it becomes increasingly difficult to make meaningful estimates, and the reliability of accounting information is reduced.

Going-Concern (Continuity) Assumption

The **going-concern assumption** holds that **in the absence of evidence to the contrary, accountants assume that entity operations will continue for a reasonable period of time; that is, the entity will not be liquidated in the near future.** There is no assumption that the entity will exist permanently but simply that it will last at least long enough to fulfill its plans and commitments. This assumption is supported by the fact that most businesses expect to operate for extended periods of time. This expectation is fostered by our relatively stable economic, political, and social environment, in which laws and customs afford certain rights and protections.

The going-concern assumption helps to provide a rationale for several important aspects of accounting. It permits assets to be defined as probable future economic benefits to a firm. Moreover, it supports the historical cost system of measurement, which is based on the premise that historical accounting information can be used to help predict interesting events. If, for example, a firm were expected to liquidate in the immediate future, its assets would be better stated at their net realizable value. The going-concern assumption also supports such interperiod allocation procedures as depreciation, amortization, and interperiod tax allocation. It would not make sense, for example, to depreciate a new machine over ten years if the company that owned it was expected to fold next year. Finally, the going-concern assumption serves as a basis for conventional balance sheet classification. Why list certain liabilities as long-term, for example, if the firm is expected to go out of business within six months?

The accountant should periodically reevaluate the logic of assuming a going concern for any given enterprise. Perhaps management would like to liquidate in the near future, or perhaps a long period of substantial losses will soon result in a forced liquidation. When evidence indicates that liquidation is imminent, the going-concern assumption should be abandoned in favour of the quitting-concern (i.e., liquidation) assumption, under which assets should be measured at their net realizable values and the priority rights of creditors should be reported. Accounting for companies under the quitting-concern assumption is covered in advanced accounting courses.

Concepts and Elements

The economic entity, periodicity, and going-concern assumptions support certain basic *concepts* and *elements*. The concepts are financial position and changes in financial position. The elements that compose financial position are assets, liabilities, and owners' equity; these elements appear on an entity's balance sheet. The major elements that explain the changes in an entity's financial position are revenues, expenses, gains, losses, income, investments by owners, and distributions to owners. Revenues, expenses, gains, losses, and income appear on an entity's income statement, while investments by and distributions to owners are summarized on its statement of shareholders' equity. The relationship between concepts and elements is illustrated in Exhibit 2.2.

Financial Position

The **financial position** of an entity is determined by its economic resources and the claims against those resources **at a particular point in time.**[18]

Financial position primarily consists of the following:

1. **Assets,** which are the probable future economic benefits obtained or controlled by an entity as a result of past transactions or events. Examples are cash, merchandise inventory, and land.
2. **Liabilities,** which are the probable future sacrifices of economic benefits arising from present obligations of an entity to transfer assets or provide services to other entities in the future as a result of past transactions or events. Examples are accounts payable, bonds payable, and unearned revenues.
3. **Owners' equity,** which is the residual interest in the assets of an entity that remains after deducting its liabilities. Examples of owners' equity in a corporation are preferred shares, common shares, and retained earnings. Owners' equity is used to describe the equity in a proprietorship or partnership. The equity of a proprietorship or partnership includes the capital and withdrawal accounts.

Changes in Financial Position

Changes in financial position are the result of certain events that occur **during a period of time.** These key elements account for changes in financial position:[19]

1. **Revenues,** that is, inflows or other enhancements of assets of an entity or settlements of its liabilities or both during a period, based on production and delivery of goods, provision of services, and other activities that constitute the entity's major operations. Examples are sales revenue, interest revenue, and rent revenue.
2. **Expenses,** which include outflows or other uses of assets or incurrences of liabilities or both during a period as a result of delivering or producing goods, rendering services, or carrying out other activities that constitute the entity's major operations. Examples are cost of goods sold, salaries expense, and advertising expense.

---

[18]"Financial Statement Concepts," CICA *Handbook,* Paragraph 1000.26, March 1991.

  [19]"Statement of Changes in Financial Position," CICA *Handbook,* Section 1540, March 1991.

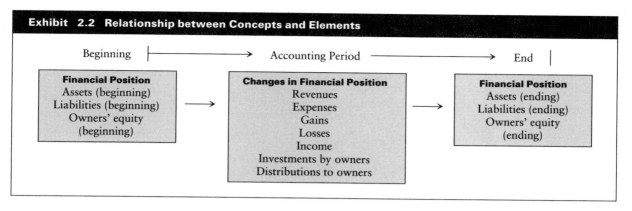

Exhibit 2.2 Relationship between Concepts and Elements

3. **Gains,** or increases in owners' equity (net assets) from peripheral or incidental transactions of an entity and from all other transactions and events affecting the entity during a period, except those that result from revenues or investments by owners. Examples are a gain on the sale of capital assets and a gain on the early retirement of long-term debt.

4. **Losses,** or decreases in owners' equity (net assets) from peripheral or incidental transactions of an entity and from all other transactions and events affecting the entity during a period, except those that result from expenses or distributions to owners. Examples are losses on the sale of investments and on litigation.

5. **Income,** which results from adding all revenues and gains for a period and subtracting all expenses and losses for the period.

6. **Investments by owners** are increases in owners' equity resulting from transfers from other entities of something valuable in exchange for ownership interests. Although assets (typically cash) are usually received as investments by owners, the consideration may also include services or satisfaction of liabilities of the enterprise.

7. **Distributions to owners** are decreases in owners' equity resulting from transferring assets, rendering services, or incurring liabilities to owners. One example is dividends declared.

The preceding definitions are broad. Although we have defined the term "assets," for example, we have not yet stated what attribute of assets (e.g., historical cost or current value) should be reported on the balance sheet. In order to give the elements a more concrete and practical focus, we must consider broad and detailed principles as well as modifying conventions. Most of the broad and detailed principles enable the accountant to recognize various items in financial statements.

Recognition in Financial Statements

Recognition is the process of including an item in financial statements as an asset, a liability, a revenue, an expense, or the like. A recognized item is represented by both words and numbers (e.g., Accounts receivable $40 000), and the amount is included in the financial statement totals.

For an item to be recognized, the following criteria must be met:

1. **Definition.** The item must meet the definition of an element of financial statements.
2. **Measurability.** The item must have a relevant attribute measurable with sufficient reliability.

3. **Relevance.** The information about the item must be capable of making a difference in user decisions.
4. **Reliability.** The information must be representationally faithful, verifiable, and neutral.

The above criteria should be applied in the context of a cost–benefit constraint (the benefits of information should exceed the costs of producing it) and a materiality threshold (the threshold varies depending on the size of the company and the monetary value of the statements). Note that the recognition criteria are derived from the qualitative characteristics of relevance and reliability and that the criteria help to make the definitions of the elements operational in resolving financial reporting issues.[20]

Broad Principles

To implement the concepts and elements, accountants apply certain generally accepted principles. Broad principles are those that have a pervasive impact on the form and content of financial statements. These principles relate to the basic accounting functions of *measurement* and *disclosure*.

Monetary Unit Principle

Quantification generally makes information more useful. Although it may be helpful to know that a firm generated net income during a particular period, it would be more helpful to know *how much*. Quantification decreases uncertainty about the firm's performance.

A measuring unit serves as a common denominator that permits variables (inventories, cost of goods sold, and so on) to be related to one another. A measuring unit also permits the aggregation of diverse items using basic arithmetic operations (addition, subtraction, and so on). In a barter economy, any valuable resource (for example, cows) could be used as a measuring unit. In a more advanced economy, such as that of Canada, money is a widely accepted medium of exchange. It is a convenient, customary, and understandable way of expressing wealth as well as changes in wealth. The **monetary**

Monetary Unit

unit principle maintains that **accountants should measure in units of money**, that is, **number of dollars**, or **nominal dollars**.

Money measures command over goods and services, just as the kilometre measures distance and the gram measures weight. Unfortunately, as a measuring unit, money has a major drawback. Most measuring units remain stable over time, but the ability of money to command goods and services—its **general purchasing power**, or **GPP**—usually changes. During a period of inflation (a rise in the overall level of prices), the GPP of money declines. Conversely, during a period of deflation (a decline in the overall level of prices), the GPP of money rises. Clearly, the economic problem of inflation has persisted in Canada for many years. This phenomenon has resulted in financial statements that reflect dollars of *mixed*, rather than uniform, purchasing power. A dollar invested in capital assets 30 years ago, for example, may be combined in financial statements with a dollar that resulted from sales made yesterday. Many observers feel that this tends to distort interperiod and intercompany comparisons and thereby reduces the usefulness of financial statements.

---

[20]"Financial Statement Concepts," CICA *Handbook,* Paragraph 1000.16, March 1991.

To help make financial statements more useful, some people have proposed that accountants stop measuring in nominal dollars and begin measuring in **constant dollars,** that is, dollars that have *uniform,* rather than mixed, purchasing power. These proposals usually call for companies to issue **constant-dollar financial statements,** a topic that we explain in Chapter 3. Current generally accepted accounting principles do not require companies to publish constant-dollar financial statements. The prevailing thought in the financial community is that, given the imprecise nature as well as the costs of preparing and interpreting constant-dollar financial statements, the distortive effects of inflation are not now sufficiently material to require a modification of the monetary unit principle. For this reason, we emphasize the monetary unit principle throughout the text.

Asset/Liability Measurement Principle

Asset/Liability Measurement

The **asset/liability measurement principle** (which we will sometimes refer to as the **measurement principle**) says that **assets and liabilities currently reported in financial statements are measured by different attributes, depending on the nature of the asset or liability and the relevance and reliability of the attribute measured.**[21] GAAP currently uses five different asset measurement attributes and specifies the circumstances under which each is required:

1. **Historical cost** (often simply called "cost") is the cash or cash-equivalent payment made to acquire an asset and put the asset to its intended use. The historical cost of a new machine, for example, includes the net invoice price as well as transportation, set-up, and break-in charges. Nonmonetary assets, such as inventories, property, plant, and equipment, and intangible assets are ordinarily measured at historical cost.[22]

2. **Current cost** is the cash-equivalent payment that a company would have to make today to acquire the same asset. Accountants measure some inventories at current cost.

3. **Current exit value in orderly liquidation** is the amount of cash an asset could be sold for in an orderly liquidation. Some investments in marketable securities are measured using this attribute.

4. **Expected exit value in due course of business,** often called **net realizable value,** is the amount of cash or cash-equivalent value that a company expects to receive for an asset in the ordinary course of business, less the costs of completing and selling the asset. Accountants use expected exit values to measure accounts receivable and some inventories.

5. **Present value of expected cash flows** is the discounted amount of the net cash inflows that an asset is expected to produce. Accountants use this attribute to measure long-term receivables.

Five similar attributes are used in present practice to measure liabilities. In the next chapter, we further explain and illustrate the various asset and liability measurement attributes.

---

[21]"Financial Statement Concepts," CICA *Handbook,* Paragraphs 1000.53–58, March 1991.

[22]Nonmonetary assets are those assets that cannot be expressed in terms of a fixed or predetermined number of dollars to be received by the reporting entity.

Each measurement attribute differs conceptually from the others, although different attributes often have the same dollar amounts. For example, the historical cost and current cost of a parcel of land are the same amount on the date that a company acquires the land. After the acquisition date, the two amounts usually differ.

Although current practice uses five different asset attributes, the historical cost attribute tends to dominate because of its wide use in measuring inventories, tangible, intangible, and capital assets. That is why current GAAP is commonly called **historical cost accounting**.

Historical cost is dominant for several reasons. First, people generally perceive it as the most reliable asset measurement attribute. Based on completed, arms'-length transactions, historical costs can be verified. Second, historical costs reliably measure an asset's current value on the date the asset was acquired. Third, if current values were more widely used, a company would need to revalue its assets and liabilities each time it prepared financial statements (annually, or perhaps even quarterly or monthly). Many people question whether the benefits of the resulting information would exceed the costs of providing it. Finally, government agencies, such as Revenue Canada, require that historical cost measurements be used in reports, such as tax returns, filed with them. These legal requirements have caused the historical cost system of measurement to be widely understood and established in the business community.

Many accountants and financial analysts question the relevance of historical cost measurements. For example, land acquired twenty years ago for $50 000 would be reported on today's balance sheet at its historical cost even though it may now be worth $200 000. Historical cost critics would argue that the $50 000 amount is irrelevant to user decisions. Another limitation of historical cost is that its proper determination is sometimes difficult and often requires estimates, allocations, and judgement. For example, what is the historical cost of a new machine acquired in exchange for an old machine plus a two-year, noninterest-bearing promissory note? We answer this question, and many similar ones, in later chapters.

Recent Accounting Standards Board work in such areas as pension accounting, accounting for income taxes, and financial instruments indicates that the board is becoming increasingly concerned about the proper recognition and measurement of assets and liabilities in corporate balance sheets.

Revenue Realization Principle

Companies engage in many different kinds of earning activities. Generally, these activities include planning, investing cash in productive assets, selling products or services to customers, collecting cash from customers, and providing warranty services. Collectively, a firm's earning activities constitute its earning process, and companies engage in this process with the goal of ultimately receiving more cash (hopefully much more) than they invested in productive assets. Because the goal of the earning process is to receive cash, it is logical for accountants to construct their measure of revenue based on past cash receipts or claims to future cash receipts that result from earning activities during an accounting period.

From a conceptual point of view, a firm generates revenue *continuously* during all phases of its earning process. In theory, therefore, accountants should initially measure revenue when a new product is planned, then measure additional revenue when the product is produced, when it is sold, and when cash is finally collected. As might be expected, measuring revenue during the early stages of an earning process is difficult because of the uncertainty about the amount of cash that the firm will ultimately receive.

Consequently, despite the theory that revenue is earned continuously, the accounting profession has had to resolve the following practical question: When can revenue be measured in a sufficiently reliable manner to enter it into the accounting records? The profession's answer to this question is found in the **revenue realization principle**. This principle states that **revenue should be recognized (recorded in the accounting records) when (1) the earning process is complete or virtually complete, and (2) the amount and timing of revenue are reasonably determinable**. When these two conditions are met, most of the uncertainty about the existence and amount of revenue has been resolved and revenue can be measured with sufficient reliability.

Revenue Realization

The two conditions for revenue realization (also called revenue recognition) are normally satisfied when a product is sold (when title passes from the seller to the buyer). Thus, an asset such as inventory should generally be carried at historical cost until an increase in its value is verified by a sale transaction. At the time of sale, most of the significant earning activities have been completed, and objective evidence provided by an exchange transaction supports the existence and amount of revenue to be recorded. Furthermore, expenses incurred to produce the revenue are either known or can be estimated with reasonable accuracy. Therefore, the accountant can apply the matching principle to measure periodic income.

The revenue realization principle also governs the recognition of revenue from sources other than product sales. For instance, revenue generated by providing services is recorded when the services have been rendered and are billable. Furthermore, revenue, such as rent revenue and interest revenue, that is generated by allowing others to use enterprise resources is usually recorded as time passes or as the resources are used.[23]

Because the revenue realization principle usually requires a sale, accountants measure revenue at the fair market value of the consideration given up in exchange for the value received. If this value is not available or clearly determinable, then the fair market value of the consideration received is used. Moreover, the requirement that the earning process be complete or virtually complete implies that any amount received in advance of providing goods or services must be recorded as a liability, such as unearned subscriptions revenue, until it is earned.

Although the revenue realization principle *normally* requires accountants to record revenue only when a sale occurs, a sale is not the only time when the two revenue realization conditions can be met. Contractors, for example, often engage in construction projects, such as office buildings and dams, that span several accounting periods. Rather than waiting until a contract is completed to measure revenue, contractors may choose to recognize revenue *during production* using the percentage-of-completion method. This method may be used when there is a definite contract price and when reasonable estimates can be made of progress toward project completion. As another example, revenue is sometimes recorded *at the completion of production*, before a sale has occurred. This procedure is appropriate for products, such as certain metals and agricultural commodities, for which a guaranteed market exists in which the firm can sell all that it has produced at a definite price. Finally, the recognition of revenue is sometimes delayed beyond the time of sale to the time *when cash is collected*. This occurs when significant uncertainty exists about the value of the assets received in the sale or the amount of additional expenses that will be incurred in connection with the sale. Under these circumstances,

---

[23]"Revenue," CICA *Handbook*, Paragraph 3400.09, September 1991.

which occasionally pertain to certain kinds of installment sales, either the installment sales method or the cost recovery method may be appropriate for recognizing revenue. The above discussion provides an introductory overview of the revenue realization principle; additional discussion appears in Chapter 5.

Matching Principle

Today, the income statement is generally regarded as the most important financial statement, and net income is one of the most significant numbers that accountants compute. In measuring periodic income, accountants usually apply the revenue realization principle first to determine when revenue should be recognized. Then they turn to the matching principle to determine when expenses should be recognized. The **matching principle** says that **costs should be recognized as expenses when the goods or services represented by the costs contribute to revenue.** In other words, accountants should attempt to associate (match) the revenues of an accounting period with the expenses incurred to generate those revenues.

Matching

From a conceptual point of view, the matching principle implies that the accountant should determine the extent to which the goods and services represented by historical costs have contributed to revenues during the accounting period. Costs that have contributed to revenues should be reported as expenses, and costs that are expected to contribute to revenues in the future should be reported as assets. This approach is called **direct matching,** but from a practical standpoint, it can be applied only to certain kinds of costs. For instance, a manufacturing company's costs for direct materials and direct labour can be reasonably identified with the firm's product (inventory). When the product is sold, sales revenue is recognized. Accordingly, because the direct materials and direct labour costs contributed directly to the sales revenue, those costs constitute expenses and should be reflected in the cost of goods sold. As another example, the costs of sales commissions can be directly related to the sales transactions. When sales revenue is recognized, the costs of related commissions should be expensed. Direct matching therefore involves associating expenses with revenues on the basis of a presumed **cause-and-effect relationship.**

Unfortunately, it is virtually impossible to accurately determine the extent to which the goods or services represented by most costs contribute to revenues. For example, when Dofasco Inc. purchases a new computer for use in its accounting department, who can precisely determine the pattern of the computer's contribution to revenues? When Mac-Millan Bloedel Limited incurs advertising costs, who can accurately assess the pattern of future benefits to the company? The lack of answers to these and similar questions often makes direct matching impractical, so accountants must use **indirect matching.** This approach involves estimates, and the accountant may try to match revenues with expenses based on a **systematic and rational allocation** of historical costs, such as depreciation expense or amortization expense. At times, however, the accountant cannot make a systematic and rational allocation, either because of the uncertainty of future revenues or the difficulty of reliably associating certain costs with future revenues. Under these circumstances, costs are reported as expenses in the period in which they are incurred. This is called **immediate recognition** of costs as expenses. Examples of such costs are advertising, and research and development. Note that accounting for these kinds of costs reflects the modifying convention of conservatism (discussed later in the chapter), the accountant's general guide for dealing with uncertain situations.

The revenue realization principle and the matching principle are the essence of the **accrual basis of accounting**. Under cash basis accounting, revenue is recorded only when received in cash, and expenses are recorded only when paid in cash. In contrast, accrual basis accounting requires recognition of revenues when earned (according to the revenue realization principle) and recognition of expenses when incurred (according to the matching principle). Differences between accrual basis and cash basis accounting are explained more fully in Chapter 3. To fully implement the accrual basis, the accountant must make certain adjusting entries at the end of every accounting period (as we explain in Chapter 6) in order to observe the principles of revenue realization and matching.

A final important point is that, in conventional accounting, income measurement is closely related to asset and liability measurement. Thus, the balance sheet and the income statement are said to be "fundamentally related." Notice, for example, that measuring depreciation expense, in compliance with the matching principle, directly affects the reported measurement of the asset that is being depreciated. The term **articulation** refers to the fundamental relationship among all financial statements prepared according to GAAP. Because of articulation, an accounting principle designed primarily to match revenues with expenses on the income statement may sometimes have an undesirable effect on asset or liability measurements on the balance sheet. Likewise, an accounting principle designed to better measure assets and liabilities may sometimes have an undesirable effect on matching revenues with expenses. Many accounting principles developed long ago (e.g., inventory accounting, depreciation accounting) appear to have a matching orientation, while many principles developed more recently (e.g., pension accounting, leases accounting) appear to have an asset and liability measurement orientation.

Consistency Principle

To formulate rational investment, credit, and similar decisions, users of accounting information typically make comparisons. Specifically, they compare circumstances of different companies (**intercompany comparisons**) and circumstances of a single company over time (**interperiod comparisons**). **Comparability** is therefore a desirable quality of useful accounting information that allows users to detect similarities in and differences between two underlying sets of objects or events.

Alternative generally accepted accounting principles exist in many areas of accounting. For example, in accounting for depreciation, a company may choose among the double-declining balance method, the units of production method, the straight-line method, and others. Because a company may choose among these alternatives, intercompany comparisons based on financial statements may sometimes be distorted. Nevertheless, these alternatives exist because different companies face substantially different circumstances. The accounting profession recognizes that the validity of intercompany comparisons is enhanced when differences between the financial statements of different companies result from basic differences between the companies themselves or from the nature of their transactions, and not merely from differences in accounting principles.[24] In the past, for example, some companies capitalized research and development (R & D) costs, while others expensed R & D costs when incurred. The CICA stated that capitalizing most kinds of R & D costs could not be justified, and in 1978 the Accounting Standards Committee issued Section 3450, which recommends expensing R & D costs

---

[24]"Financial Statement Concepts," CICA *Handbook,* Paragraph 1000.22, March 1991.

when incurred, but allows for the capitalization of development costs if the costs meet all of the criteria of Paragraph 3450.21.

The accounting profession sees a need for accurate interperiod comparisons, which help users of accounting information discern important trends. Knowing past trends, users can presumably make more accurate predictions about their prospects of receiving cash from an enterprise. To improve the interperiod comparability of accounting information, accountants observe the **consistency principle,** which holds that **accountants must measure and disclose information about an entity in the same manner from one accounting period to the next.** In other words, once a company adopts a certain set of accounting principles, it must observe those principles consistently over time. A company cannot use the first-in, first-out (FIFO) method of inventory cost determination in 1993; the specific identification method in 1994; the average cost method in 1995; and so forth. It should be noted, however, that the consistency principle does not require a company to measure and disclose all information in the same manner in a single accounting period. For example, it does not prohibit a company from using the FIFO method for one part of its inventories and the average cost method for another part.

Consistency

The consistency principle also does not prohibit a firm from changing from one accounting principle to another if it has a good reason for doing so. The CICA *Handbook* permits a change when there is evidence "that the change would result in a more appropriate presentation of events or transactions in the financial statements of the enterprise."[25] The accounting profession has not yet defined precisely what it means by the term "more appropriate." When a company changes from one accounting principle to another, it must clearly disclose the nature of, reason for, and dollar effects of the change. We cover accounting changes in Chapter 20.

The consistency principle is very important to independent auditors as part of their general review of the accounting records. The standard auditor's report that was adopted by the accounting profession in 1988 (see Exhibit 1.1 in Chapter 1) implies that the auditor is satisfied that the financial statements present fairly the financial position of the company. If a company makes a change in an accounting principle that has a material effect on the financial statements, then the auditor must be satisfied with the disclosure of the change. If the auditor believes that the change in accounting principles has been appropriately accounted for and justified by management, the auditor may issue an unqualified opinion on the financial statements. If the auditor disagrees, however, then she or he renders a qualified or an adverse opinion.

Disclosure Principle

The disclosure principle (often called adequate, fair, or full disclosure) is a significant and far-reaching component of accounting theory. In fact, the disclosure principle formed the basis for the securities legislation enacted in the United States in 1933 and 1934. In recognition of the prime importance of adequate disclosure, one of the generally accepted auditing standards of the CICA holds that informative disclosures in the financial statements are to be regarded as reasonably adequate unless otherwise stated in the [auditor's] report.[26]

Disclosure

Consistent with the accountant's aim of providing useful information, the **disclosure principle** calls for **revealing information that will be useful in the decision-making proc-**

---

[25]"Accounting Changes," CICA *Handbook,* Paragraph 1506.02, March 1991.
   [26]"Reservations in the Auditor's Report," CICA *Handbook,* Section 5510, October 1991.

esses of reasonably informed users. To determine an appropriate level of disclosure for a given company, an accountant must apply generally accepted accounting principles to the circumstances involved. This requires considerable professional judgement.

When disclosing information, the accountant must be an effective communicator. A delicate balance must be achieved between completeness and understandability. Although accountants want to issue complete financial reports, the understandability of the reports is impaired by excessive details. The disclosure principle requires that appropriate terminology be used in financial reports. Further, it implies that important information of an unfavourable nature should not be hidden by the use of crafty language, small type, and other unfair means.

Several methods of disclosure are commonly used. The most important information is in the **body of the financial statements**. For example, publicly held companies are required to disclose earnings-per-share information on the face of their income statements. **Notes** (footnotes) are an integral part of the financial statements and may effectively be used to disclose such facts as accounting policies, contractual restrictions, and certain details about leases. In addition, accountants use **schedules** to disclose such items as inventory (i.e., raw materials, work-in-process, and finished goods), operating expenses, and changes in the components of working capital. At times, **supplementary statements**, such as financial statements adjusted for inflation, constitute an effective method of disclosure.

Attempting to comply with the disclosure principle raises many interesting questions. For example, suppose that you are the independent auditor for a paper company. While examining the evidence for the financial statements, you discover that the company has violated an environmental protection statute. If the violation is discovered, the company could be sued for millions of dollars. How would you apply the disclosure principle under these circumstances? Clearly, adequate disclosure will continue to be a challenge in the years ahead.

Detailed Principles

Accountants use detailed principles to apply broad principles. Detailed principles are highly specific, and more than one level of detailed principles may exist in a given area of accounting. Accountants often use the terms "procedures" and "methods" when referring to detailed principles. With tangible capital assets, for example, accountants implement matching (a broad principle) by using depreciation (a detailed principle), which is computed by one of several methods (an even more detailed principle). Like broad principles, detailed principles relate to the basic accounting functions of measurement and disclosure.

Detailed principles are far too numerous to list and explain in this chapter. For this reason, they are covered in other chapters of this text and in other financial accounting courses. "Specific Items" and "Specialized Areas" of the CICA *Handbook* contain many detailed accounting principles.

Modifying Conventions

To be useful, accounting theory must be applied in the business world by individual accountants, who must use informed judgement to resolve many difficult questions. To help accountants resolve these questions practically and consistently, the accounting profession has adopted conventions (or customs) that modify basic accounting theory.

Reflecting the Truth

By systematically broadening the going concern concept, auditors can accurately assess audit risk.

In recent years, auditors have found themselves severely criticized after large public companies—such as the Northland Bank and the Canadian Commercial Bank—unexpectedly failed. What investors find hard to accept is that companies can fail only a few months after financial statements were issued with an unqualified audit report and no mention whatsoever of the company being in financial difficulty. A 1988 report by the Macdonald Commission—entitled *A Report of the Commission to Study the Public's Expectations of Audits*—showed that investors rely primarily on the auditor's report to obtain reliable information on a company's ability to continue in business.

A company's ability to carry on as usual is known as the going concern concept, an assumption that is described in the CICA *Handbook* as one of the basic principles governing financial statements. Any departure from that assumption, or any doubt as to its validity, may have serious consequences for several financial statement items. If the business is not (or may not be) a going concern, an evaluation method based on historical costs is no longer appropriate, and an alternative must be used.

However, there is no accounting standard that mandates what financial information is to be reported if the company is on the brink of serious financial problems. At present, the auditor's duty is to ensure that the financial statements are based on GAAP. The assumption is that the financial statements will contain sufficient information to explicitly inform the reader of any possibility of the company being unable to continue in business. In Canada, provided the financial statements are complete, the auditor is not obligated to report any doubts or misgivings about the company's going concern status.

In the United States, on the other hand, AICPA issued their Statement on Auditing Standards No. 59, *The Auditor's Consideration of an Entity's Ability to Continue as a Going Concern*. This standard requires the auditor to assess whether the entity will be able to continue operating for a given future period—generally the year following the date of the financial statements. According to both the U.S. standard and International Auditing Guideline No. 23, *Going Concern* (published in 1984 by the International Auditing Practices Committee of the International Federation of Accountants), if the auditor has doubts as to the company's ability to remain a going concern, an explanatory paragraph is to be included in the auditor's report.

Even though the Canadian standards do not yet impose this obligation, several firms have found themselves subject to the requirement—for example, firms that are subsidiaries of U.S. companies or whose securities are traded on U.S. stock exchanges. Therefore, in evaluating inherent risk, auditors should consider the possibility that the going concern assumption may be doubted, particularly since the economic costs could be significant should this assumption not hold.

The purpose of this article is to point out which aspects of financial statements will require the auditor's special attention, and outline systematic models to analyse inherent risk. Hopefully, this will help solve the problem of assessing the possibility that a business may cease to be a going concern.

Ceasing to Be a Going Concern

According to most auditing studies, a company ceases to be a going concern when it files for bankruptcy (or in Canada, when a receiver is appointed). However, from the auditor's viewpoint, bankruptcy is not the only sign that a company may be experiencing financial problems. Financially troubled companies have several other legal options before resorting to bankruptcy—such as agreeing to a takeover, merger, reorganization or liquidation. Each option may entail significant economic cost for all parties involved which, in a sense, signals an end to the original company. But the investors' real economic losses will have been incurred much earlier. And it is these losses that will indicate the number of possible lawsuits brought against the auditor.

If a firm is likely to face serious financial problems,[1] additional audit procedures may be required in order to ensure an accurate valuation of assets and liabilities. The auditor could then take steps to reduce the economic cost of problems before bankruptcy (or another legal option) becomes inevitable. Figure 1 illustrates the different economic or legal options according to our model of corporate failure.

CICA's *Handbook* section 5130 outlines a model that auditors must use in assessing audit risk. Composed of three risk components—inherent, non-control and non-detection—audit risk is the probability that the auditor will issue a clean opinion on financial statements containing a material error. Inherent risk is defined as the probability that an account balance or class of transactions contains major inaccuracies. Therefore, it is in the audi-

Continued

tor's best interest to clearly identify the inherent risk, since not doing so can entail major costs, including lawsuits and loss of credibility. In some circumstances, failure to identify a going concern problem can distort the financial statements, which directly affects the inherent risk. Auditors will have fulfilled their obligations if they inform the reader that, in their opinion, the company's continuation as a going concern is threatened.

FIGURE 1
Stages in Corporate Failure

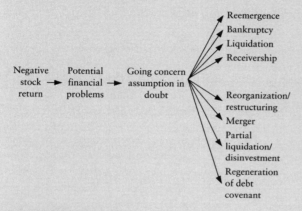

Inherent Risk

Our assessment of inherent risk has two parts: dynamic analysis of financial statements and analysis of qualitative factors. Information contained in financial statements is either static or dynamic. Static information, which includes the level of an item in the financial statements or a financial ratio at a given time, does not necessarily reflect a company's situation. Financial ratios may be even more deceptive because they vary greatly from one industry to another. Moreover, a ratio will not indicate future financial problems if the information is presented out of context. (For example, a working capital ratio of less than 1.5 may be a reflection of strength in the food sector and of weakness in the steel sector.) Dynamic information, on the other hand, better reflects the company's situation, and so is a more valuable tool for the auditor.

Deterioration of a company's operating framework is a dynamic phenomenon that indicates serious financial difficulties. In this case, the auditor should assess the trends shown by the financial statements in order to identify the indicators of future financial problems. An example of an item that signifies change is the company's stock returns.

It is up to the auditor to decide which item(s) on the financial statements is to be analysed, and then to deter-

mine the consistency of the information supplied. Dynamic accounting information, when incorporated into a systematic model of trend analysis in financial reporting, is highly useful here, since it serves to identify the items most at risk.

Above all, the auditor must ensure the accuracy of the company's net income figure.[2] It is not by chance that the materiality threshold in auditing engagements is usually based on operating income. Financial analysts also attach great importance to income, but they mainly try to determine its "quality," which they see as an indicator of the company's future cash flow.

According to the Financial Accounting Standards Board's (FASB) Statement of Financial Accounting Concepts No. 1, *The Objectives of Accounting for Business Enterprises*, income is a measure of the company's long-term cash flow: any unusual transaction affecting income should not affect long-term cash flows and, therefore, should not be part of the assessment of the company's future liquidity.

To arrive at a "real" income measure that can be used to predict future cash flows, it is necessary to eliminate the effect of gains or losses resulting from unusual transactions, as well as the effect of certain accounting practices adopted under the accrual method. The resulting trend should also provide information on the company's future financial situation. However, to obtain a complete analysis, the auditor must determine how consistent the income statement is with the balance sheet.

The balance sheet and the statement of changes in financial position can alert the auditor to possible financial problems down the road. There are two types of signals emitted by financial statements: those that reflect operating activities and those that reflect management decisions regarding the choice of accounting practices. To read the signals, eight financial management indicators are used:
- **Change in** adjusted net income in relation to assets;
- **Change in** accounts receivable that exceeds the change in sales;
- **Change in** inventory greater than the change in sales;
- **Change in** operating expenses greater than the change in sales;
- **Change in** interest expenses greater than the change in sales;
- **Change in** capital expenditures greater than the change in sales;
- **Change in** the maturity for interest-bearing debts; and
- **Decrease in** dividends (and redemption of shares).[3]

Continued

Qualitative Indicators

An analysis of a company's inherent risk would not be complete without an examination of the constraints that may affect the work and decisions of management. In our study, we used eight indicators of qualitative risk found in the literature (see, for example, *Auditing—An Integrated Approach* by A.M Lemon, A.A. Arens, and J.K. Loebbecke (Prentice Hall: Toronto, 1987)). These are:

- **Investment in** a different industrial sector (if the assets of this new sector represent 10% or more of the total assets);
- **Implementation of** a bonus plan;
- **Implementation of** a stock purchase plan;
- **Change in** control of the company;
- **Appreciable change in** the volume of transactions between related parties (based on sales and costs as a percentage of total sales and costs);
- **Change in** the number of locations;
- **Change in** stock ownership (change in percentage of shares held by the president); and
- **Change in** method of depreciation used.

These qualitative variables combined with the eight financial management indicators listed earlier can help the auditor distinguish between a healthy company and one that may experience financial difficulties. The use of discriminant models can yield valuable results for an auditor who knows how to use available financial data and qualitative data on inherent risk. Since the auditor is already making an estimate of inherent risk, it will be relatively easy to obtain the relevant data and fine-tune the models.

Putting It to Work

As an example of systematizing the assessment of inherent risk, we examined financial statements from 250 public companies listed on the Montreal Stock Exchange. The first group consisted of 112 healthy companies whose continuation as a going concern seemed assured; the second group was 138 companies in financial difficulty, with uncertain going concern status.

For our study, we defined the risk of a company not continuing as a going concern in terms of its market performance. Both financial and qualitative data, taken from the company's annual reports over a three-year period, were used. This three-year period preceded the first signal of failure—namely, a negative stock return.

For each company we examined eight financial variables and eight qualitative variables indicative of inherent risk. These risk indicators served as explanatory variables in the model for forecasting the entities' financial health. The results could also be used by the auditor to revise his or her estimates as to the acceptable overall risk for each audit engagement.

We used four distinct multivariate techniques: weighted least squares regression using the least squares criterion, linear discriminant analysis, logistic analysis, and classification via a decision tree (recursive partitioning).

Overall, the first three methods yielded non-validated classification rates ranging from 72% to 75%. What this inferred was that by using the statistical models, 75% of the firms in the sample could be correctly classified. The linear discriminant analysis model, with a validated rate of 69%, yielded much better results than the auditor obtains in practice. (In a separate study, H.C. Koh found that auditors had issued a reservation regarding the going concern assumption in only 54% of cases where companies later declared bankruptcy; see "Model Prediction and Auditor Assessments of Going Concern Status," *Accounting and Business Research*, Vol. 1, No. 84, 1991, pp. 331–338.)

Of the eight financial variables relating to the firm's operating activities, seven emerged as useful. These results indicate that healthy companies tend to increase their accounts receivable in relation to sales, but reduce their inventories. These two results are consistent, since a healthy company generally posts an increase in its sales, which in turn has a positive effect on both its accounts receivable and its inventory turnover rate.

An increase in operating expenses in relation to sales or an extension of the maturity date for debts tends to indicate financial problems ahead. For changes in debt maturities, it can be argued that managers who anticipate financial problems will try to refinance their debts in order to postpone the maturity date. Similarly, an increase in the amounts paid to shareholders through dividends and stock redemptions would indicate a decrease in investment opportunities, hence financial problems ahead. To a lesser extent, a decrease in adjusted net income and capital expenditures could also indicate future financial troubles.

Of the eight qualitative variables studied, two were validated by our models as signalling future problems. These were investments in a new industrial sector and a change in the depreciation method used. Therefore, it is important that the auditor conduct a thorough analysis of the reasons for any discretionary accounting changes made by managers.

Of special interest is the decision-tree classification technique, in which two variables alone generated a

Continued

classification rate of 74.8%. This technique produces a decision tree based on individual variables. Our analysis yielded a tree with two major branches that indicated possible financial difficulty: a change in operating expenses greater than .0412 in relation to the change in sales and, among companies registering a change in operating expenses of less than .0412, an increase of more than .69 per year in relative debt maturities.

Conclusion

While investors will often sustain significant losses without having to declare bankruptcy, the concept of a non-going concern business needs to be broadened if auditors are to accurately assess the overall audit risk. Accurate assessment of inherent risk through the integration of individual signals into a single diagnostic tool will benefit both the auditor and the investor.

We believe that audit judgment can be systematized by using statistical models. Accordingly, professional practitioners should consider maintaining internal data bases of clients' quantitative and qualitative data in order to facilitate fulfillment of the auditing mandate.

Endnotes

[1]For the purposes of this article, it is assumed that a company is experiencing serious financial problems and has a high risk of not

continuing in business if its annual stock return (adjusted for market) is less than −50%. A company's market value depends on discounted future cash flows. A reduction in a company's market value reflects either a downward revision of anticipated cash flows or an increase in the discount rate, which would be caused by an increase in the company's financial and operating risks. These two factors are indicative of financial problems that could threaten the company's continuation as a going concern.

[2]In terms of assessing inherent risk, CICA *Handbook* section 5130 calls on auditors to consider factors that might affect the accuracy of the financial statements. If company management foresees hard times and financial problems in the mid-term, it may be tempted to reduce the quality of its income by carrying out various transactions to inflate income in the short term, but have no effect on long-term trends.

[3]The relative changes are defined as follows (the example used changes in accounts receivable):

(Change in % of accounts receivable) − (Change in % of sales), where changes are defined as follows:

$[\text{Accounts receivable}_t - \text{E}_{t-1}(\text{Accounts receivable}_t)/\text{Accounts receivable}_{t-1}] \, \text{E}_{t-1}(\text{Accounts receivable}_t) = \text{Accounts receivable}_{t-1}$

Source: Reprinted from Denis Cormier, Michel Magnan, and Bernard Morard, "Reflecting the Truth," *CGA Magazine* (November 1992), pp. 45–49; 72.

To a large extent, accountants apply these modifying conventions by using generally accepted rules of broad and detailed accounting principles. Modifying conventions are therefore technically a part of generally accepted accounting principles. They are usually called modifying conventions, rather than accounting principles, because they cause the accountant to modify the "theoretically ideal" treatment of certain economic things and events. In other words, they enable the accountant to depart from a rigid interpretation of broad and detailed accounting principles in some cases. Modifying conventions may therefore be viewed as exceptions to accounting principles. These exceptions are justified on the grounds that accounting theory

1. Must yield information for which the benefits exceed the costs.
2. Must be applied in complex business enterprises among which facts and circumstances may differ substantially.
3. Must be applied under conditions of uncertainty.
4. Should focus on the economic substance of business transactions.

Materiality

All CICA recommendations assume that users of financial statements are interested in information that is significant to their decision-making process. While *all* transactions must be recorded and their effects ultimately reflected in the financial statements, the requirements of sound theory may be modified somewhat when dealing with immaterial items. For example, current generally accepted accounting principles require that extraordinary items (if they are material and meet the criteria of Section 3480.02) be presented in a separate section of the income statement. This disclosure principle presumably results in useful information, because a knowledge of extraordinary items should assist financial statement users to evaluate enterprise performance and to make important predictions. The question becomes: How large must an extraordinary item be to become material and thereby require separate disclosure? Clearly, a $100 tornado loss sustained by a multi-million-dollar company would not require separate disclosure, but would likely be combined with other items in the body of the income statement. Cluttering the financial statements with trivial details would be a disservice to statement users and may in some

Materiality
cases make the financial statements misleading. **Materiality**, therefore, is defined as follows: **"An item of information, or an aggregate of items, is material if it is probable that its omission or misstatement would influence or change a decision. Materiality is a matter of professional judgment in the particular circumstances."**[27] When making materiality decisions, accountants must decide whether knowledge of a particular item of information would likely affect a decision made by an informed user of financial statements. The materiality evaluation is complicated by a lack of knowledge about the specific ways in which accounting information influences investment, credit, and similar decisions.

Materiality decisions may involve quantitative as well as qualitative considerations. Quantitative considerations refer to such factors as the effect of the item on the company's earnings trend, or its relationship to key financial variables such as assets, liabilities, owners' equity, revenues, expenses, and net income. Qualitative considerations centre around the basic nature of the item. Does the item result in a contractual violation? Does the item represent an illegal transaction such as a bribe paid to a foreign official? Does the item represent an insider transaction, such as an interest-free loan made to the company president? Affirmative answers to these and similar questions may indicate that the item in question should be disclosed regardless of the dollar amounts immediately involved.

Materiality is one of the most complex, pervasive, and elusive components of accounting theory. Making materiality decisions requires considerable *judgement.* Because of differences in circumstances, an item that is judged material for one company may not necessarily be judged material for another company. To the dismay of some accountants, the accounting profession has not developed a comprehensive set of criteria to evaluate materiality dilemmas. A relatively small number of materiality guidelines are contained in authoritative accounting pronouncements about certain areas (e.g., earnings per share and segment reporting). The CICA's current position, however, is that no general standards of materiality can be formulated to take into account all of the considerations that enter into an experienced human judgement.

Industry Practices

Generally accepted accounting principles are intended for use in general-purpose external financial reporting by business enterprises. Accountants must therefore apply broad and detailed accounting principles to different kinds of companies. In applying these principles, accountants have found that certain industries (groups of similar companies) have peculiar characteristics that sometimes warrant a modification of accounting principles.

---

[27]"Financial Statement Concepts," CICA *Handbook,* Paragraph 1000.17, March 1991.

Industry Practices

The term **industry practices** refers to **modifications of accounting principles necessitated by the unusual characteristics of some industries**. Because these modifications presumably enhance the usefulness of accounting information, they have become generally accepted within the accounting profession and are therefore a part of GAAP.

For example, the investment company industry consists of firms that sell their own capital shares to the public and invest most of the proceeds in the securities of other entities. Thus, investment securities comprise most of the assets of a typical investment company. Given the importance of these securities and the fact that accountants can usually determine their market value in a sufficiently reliable manner, generally accepted accounting principles call for reporting the investment securities of investment companies at market value. Notice that this industry practice departs from historical cost measurement. Additionally, it constitutes an exception to the revenue realization principle, because the statement of operations (income statement) for an investment company includes unrealized increases and decreases (i.e., not verified by actual sales) in the value of investment securities held.

Industry practices cause many accounting principles to be modified. In fact, these practices have a significant impact on the published financial statements of such companies as banks, trust companies, credit unions, finance companies, life insurance companies, and public utilities. Knowledgeable preparers and users of external accounting information should be aware of industry practices and their role in the framework of GAAP. CICA's *Financial Reporting in Canada*, issued every two years, provides a comprehensive survey and analysis of industry practices.

Conservatism

Accountants try to produce reliable measurements, but often these measurements must be made in the presence of significant uncertainties. For example, over what period will a company benefit from research and development costs or from advertising costs? Given the difficult nature of such questions, accountants cannot always prepare precise financial statements.

When accountants attempt to resolve measurement uncertainties, they recognize that corporate managers tend to be confident and optimistic (sometimes too optimistic) about their companies. Moreover, many managers desire to maximize their reported earnings each period. From the pragmatic standpoint of avoiding unfavourable legal exposure, it is less risky for the accountant to understate than to overstate net income and net assets. Therefore, most accountants adopt a cautious attitude toward the inherent risks and uncertainties of the measurement process. This attitude is reflected in the modifying convention of conservatism.

Conservatism

The **conservatism** convention holds that **when faced with significant uncertainties about the solution to an accounting problem, an accountant should favour the solution that least favourably affects net income and net assets of the current period**.[28] Thus, conservatism is a practical and prudent, yet an imprecise, response to the problem of measurement risk. Implicit in the conservatism convention is the belief that, *when faced with significant uncertainties*, the accountant should observe the following moderating tendencies:

---

[28]"Financial Statement Concepts," CICA *Handbook,* Paragraph 1000.21(d), March 1991.

1. Measure revenues and gains lower rather than higher and later rather than earlier.
2. Measure expenses and losses higher rather than lower and earlier rather than later.
3. Measure net income lower rather than higher.
4. Measure assets lower rather than higher.
5. Measure liabilities higher rather than lower.
6. Measure owners' equity lower rather than higher.

Ideally, the accountant's measurements should be neither overstated nor understated. Conservatism is not a licence to deliberately understate net income and net assets. If a firm having cash of $100 000 reports only $25 000, this is not conservatism but inaccurate reporting.

Companies are not required to select the most conservative accounting treatment available in every situation. Thus, conservatism is not a basic accounting principle. Instead, it is more appropriately viewed as a modifying convention. For example, the common practice of immediately expensing the costs of major advertising programs is a modification of the matching principle, owing to the uncertainty associated with the existence and timing of future benefits.

Many examples of conservatism are found in accounting practice. These include the lower of cost or market rule for valuing inventories and marketable securities; accelerated depreciation; recording goodwill only when purchased in an arm's-length transaction; amortizing organization costs over a relatively brief period even though the firm benefits for its entire life; and immediately expensing most R & D and advertising costs even though future periods will likely benefit.

Many users of financial statements support the conservatism convention. Bankers, for example, recognize that the cost of lending to an applicant who defaults is usually higher than the cost of not lending to a loan applicant who would not have defaulted. Accordingly, bankers tend to support conservatism, including the lower of cost or market rule for inventory valuation. Moreover, most financial analysts evaluate enterprise performance on the basis not only of the quantity but also the quality of reported earnings. An important factor when assessing quality of earnings is the extent to which a firm uses conservative accounting policies. All other things being equal, many analysts look more favourably on a company that adopts conservative accounting policies. Such companies are sometimes said to have "conservative accounting personalities."

Substance Over Form

**Substance
Over Form**

Financial accounting is concerned with the legal as well as the economic effects of accountable events. But **when an apparent conflict exists between the economic substance and the legal form of a business transaction, accountants tend to emphasize economic substance.** To illustrate, computing earnings per common share appears to involve little more than dividing net income for a period by the average number of common shares outstanding. Certain securities, however, such as bonds that are convertible into common shares, may in substance be equivalent to common shares even though they are not common shares in legal form. Section 3500 of the CICA *Handbook* therefore requires accountants to include these types of securities in fully diluted earnings-per-share calculations under certain circumstances. By modifying the way in which accountants compute earnings-per-share numbers, the AcSB attempted to put economic substance over legal form.

As another example, accountants sometimes encounter long-term notes that have no stated interest rates. Legally, then, these notes do not bear interest. Nevertheless, the accounting profession recognizes that money has a time value, and as a result, the notes that companies typically issue contain interest even though the interest may not be explicitly stated. Accordingly, even though a long-term note may have no stated interest rate, Paragraph 1000.54(c) requires accountants to impute (estimate and record) interest under certain circumstances.

As a final example of putting substance over form, current accounting principles require a lessee to report certain kinds of leases as assets and liabilities even though the lessee does not actually own the leased property. In substance, these leases convey to lessees certain rights that are almost identical to the rights held by companies that purchase rather than lease their property.

Concluding Remarks

We cannot overemphasize the importance of developing a sound conceptual understanding of financial accounting. You should apply this understanding when solving the problems in this book, and avoid a procedural approach to solving problems that emphasizes mechanics and memorization. Accounting problems that appear in textbooks, on examinations, and in the business world are often complex and may vary in an endless number of ways. To solve these problems, accountants must have a solid base of theoretical knowledge. In the following chapters, we explain in more detail how the theory applies to specific accounting issues, and we highlight in the margins the key elements of accounting theory explained in Chapter 2.

The model presented in this chapter explains most, but not all, of financial accounting as accountants apply it today. In Chapter 1, we explained that because accounting principles help to determine how scarce resources are allocated in our economy, the Accounting Standards Board and its predecessor committees often have had to deal with political pressures in addition to deciding what is theoretically sound accounting. We believe that some accounting principles exist primarily because of political pressures, not because they are consistent with the model. The existence of these principles, however, does not mean that the model is worthless. Instead, it simply reflects the reality that accounting is a pragmatic discipline concerned with producing information that ultimately affects the welfare of people. At appropriate places throughout the text, we point out accounting principles that do not appear to exist primarily because of the model.

In the next chapter, we explore certain aspects of descriptive accounting theory in greater depth. We also introduce some proposals that, if adopted, would change the basic information that accountants currently report.

Key Points

1. Financial reporting should (1) provide information that is useful in investment, credit, and similar decisions; (2) provide information that is useful in assessing cash flow prospects; and (3) provide information about enterprise resources, claims to those resources, and changes in those resources. (Objective 1a)
2. Relevance and reliability are the two primary qualities of useful accounting information. (Objective 1b)
3. Financial accounting theory is based on three major assumptions, or postulates: (1) economic entity; (2) periodicity; and (3) going concern. (Objective 1c)

4. The assumptions listed above support basic concepts and elements. The first basic concept is financial position, and its elements are assets, liabilities, and owners' equity. The second basic concept is changes in financial position, and its major elements are revenues, expenses, gains, losses, income, investments by owners, and distributions to owners. (Objective 1d)

5. Accountants apply certain generally accepted accounting principles in order to implement the concepts and elements. Broad principles have a pervasive impact on the form and content of financial statements. The broad principles of financial accounting are: (1) monetary unit; (2) asset/liability measurement; (3) revenue realization; (4) matching; (5) consistency; and (6) disclosure. (Objective 1e)

6. Detailed principles are the highly specific ones that accountants use to apply the broad principles in practice. Detailed principles are numerous and are covered in later chapters of this text and in other courses. (Objective 1f)

7. Modifying conventions may be viewed as exceptions to accounting principles. These conventions are: (1) materiality; (2) industry practices; (3) conservatism; and (4) substance over form. (Objective 1g)

Questions

Q2.1 What is accounting theory?

Q2.2 What are the detailed objectives of financial reporting? How are these objectives interrelated?

Q2.3 Why are explicitly stated objectives considered important in the development of a structure of accounting theory?

Q2.4 In general, how much accounting knowledge does the accounting profession expect the users of financial statements to have? Why is it important for the accounting profession to state, at least in general terms, how much knowledge it expects users to have?

Q2.5 Briefly explain the qualities of relevance and reliability. How do these qualities relate to the basic accounting objective of providing useful information?

Q2.6 Explain the significance of the contention that relevance and reliability require important trade-offs.

Q2.7 Should the CICA require companies to report all information that users of financial statements regard as useful? Justify your answer.

Q2.8 Briefly explain each of the following accounting assumptions: economic entity, periodicity, and going concern.

Q2.9 Define the concept of financial position and each of the elements that compose it.

Q2.10 Explain the concept of changes in financial position and each of the elements that comprise these changes.

Q2.11 Briefly explain the monetary unit principle. Why is this principle criticized during periods of rapid inflation?

Q2.12 Briefly explain the asset/liability measurement principle. Why has the accounting profession traditionally preferred historical costs over current costs for measuring nonmonetary assets?

Q2.13 Briefly explain the revenue realization principle. When are the two conditions for revenue realization normally satisfied? At what times, other than at the time of sale, might it be appropriate under GAAP for a company to recognize revenue?

Q2.14 Briefly explain the matching principle.

Q2.15 Distinguish between cash basis and accrual basis accounting.

Q2.16 Briefly explain the consistency principle. Why is this principle important to the users of financial statements?

Q2.17 Does the existence of the consistency principle mean that:

(a) A company must use the same depreciation method in a given year to account for all of its depreciable assets?

(b) All companies in the steel industry must use the same inventory cost determination method, such as FIFO or weighted average?

(c) A company can never change from one generally accepted accounting principle to another?

Explain your reasoning for each answer.

Q2.18 Briefly explain the disclosure principle. In general, how does an accountant determine an appropriate amount of disclosure for a given company?

Q2.19 Briefly explain the modifying convention of materiality. Why is materiality regarded as one of the most pervasive aspects of accounting theory?

Q2.20 Briefly explain the term "industry practices." Cite three industries in which practices affect the information reported in corporate financial statements.

Q2.21 Briefly explain the modifying convention of conservatism. What do financial analysts mean when they say that certain companies have "conservative accounting personalities"?

Q2.22 Briefly explain the modifying convention of substance over form.

Exercises

E2.1 Assumptions, Principles, and Conventions. The following are the assumptions, broad principles, and modifying conventions discussed in Chapter 2:

(1) Economic entity assumption.

(2) Periodicity assumption.

(3) Going-concern assumption.

(4) Monetary unit principle.

(5) Conservatism.

(6) Revenue realization principle.

(7) Matching principle.

(8) Asset/liability measurement principle.

(9) Consistency principle.

(10) Disclosure principle.

(11) Materiality.

(12) Industry practices.

(13) Historical cost.

(14) Substance over form.

Instructions

Select the number corresponding to the assumption, broad principle, or modifying convention that best supports each of the following statements. Do not use any number more than once.

(a) A company allocates the cost of its intangible assets to the accounting periods in which the assets help to produce revenue.

(b) A company reports its financial statements in dollars that have mixed, rather than uniform, amounts of purchasing power.

(c) A company records a new computer at the cash-equivalent price paid to purchase it.

(d) A company estimates and records interest expense on a seven-year note payable that has no stated interest rate.

(e) A company reports major details about its leases in the notes to the financial statements.

(f) After adopting the first-in, first-out (FIFO) method of determining inventory costs, a company continues to use this method over time.

(g) A company that is uncertain about what depreciation method to use elects an accelerated method.

(h) The financial statements of an insurance company reflect some noticeable differences from those of most other types of companies.

(i) A small company separates its transactions from those of the owners.

(j) A company decides that whenever an asset costs less than $50, the cost will be charged to an expense account, even though the asset may benefit several accounting periods.

E2.2 Assumptions, Principles, and Conventions. Refer to the list presented in E2.1.

Instructions

Select the number corresponding to the assumption, broad principle, or modifying convention that best supports each of the following statements. Do not use any number more than once.

(a) The balance sheet of a small appraisal firm excludes the owner's personal automobile.
(b) Large companies ordinarily publish a complete set of financial statements at least once a year, regardless of whether the financial results are good or bad.
(c) A company should always report the important details about its long-term liabilities.
(d) When a company prepares financial statements according to GAAP, it ignores changes in the purchasing power of the dollar.
(e) Accounts receivable are reported at their net realizable value.
(f) The cost of a building is charged to expense in the accounting periods in which the building helps to produce revenue.
(g) A company ordinarily does not separately list each account receivable on its balance sheet.
(h) Leases on certain properties are reported as assets by companies that do not own the properties.
(i) Subscriptions received in advance by a magazine publisher are liabilities until the magazines are published.
(j) The amounts reported in financial statements should not ordinarily reflect a liquidation of the business.

E2.3 Assumptions, Principles, and Conventions. Refer to the list presented in E2.1.

Instructions

Select the number corresponding to the assumption, broad principle, or modifying convention that best supports each of the following statements. Do not use any number more than once.

(a) Most users of financial statements would not like companies to record sales before title to the inventory passes from the seller to the buyer.
(b) Most users would not want a company to charge the cost of a new building to expense in the year of acquisition.
(c) Users expect to know certain details about a company's pension plan.
(d) Many users trust the reliability of historical cost valuations of capital assets.
(e) User decisions would not likely be affected if a company listed petty cash separately on the balance sheet.
(f) Many users of financial statements prefer accounting principles, such as accelerated depreciation, that tend to state a company's income on the low side.
(g) Investors and creditors generally do not want financial statements to reflect a liquidation assumption unless it is likely that the firm will be liquidated in the near future.
(h) Users have trouble making interperiod comparisons when a company changes accounting principles from one year to the next.
(i) Many users believe that when convertible bonds are similar to common shares, the bonds should be treated as common shares for the purpose of computing earnings per share.

(j) Investors and creditors expect companies to issue financial reports at predetermined time intervals, and not only when the financial results are favourable to the reporting company.

E2.4 Assumptions, Principles, and Conventions. Refer to the list presented in E2.1.

Instructions

Select the number corresponding to the assumption, broad principle, or modifying convention that is most clearly *violated* by the accounting practice described in each statement below. Do not use any number more than once.

(a) A company charges the cost of new office equipment to expense in the year of purchase, although the equipment is expected to help produce revenue for many years.
(b) A company changes from weighted average to FIFO when accounting for inventories.
(c) A company that has been in business for 40 years prepares every financial statement in dollars that have the same amount of purchasing power.
(d) A company records sales after inventory has been produced but before it is sold.
(e) A company decides to publish financial statements only in years when it has good news to report.
(f) A company reports inventories, tangible assets, and intangible assets at current cost amounts on the balance sheet date.
(g) An electronics company owned by Mike Hardy reports the cost of Hardy's swimming pool as an asset on the balance sheet.
(h) A company having 150 accounts payable lists each account on the balance sheet.
(i) A company does not report the major details about its shareholders' equity.
(j) A company follows a policy of recording an item as an asset whenever the company is in doubt about whether the item is an asset or an expense of the current period.

E2.5 Asset Measurement. Mann Limited purchased a used delivery truck from Wall Ltd. on June 30, 1995. Wall had acquired the truck new on June 30, 1994, for $25 000 and had taken $5000 of depreciation for the fiscal year ending June 30, 1995. To acquire the truck, Mann issued to Wall 1000 of Mann's no-par value common shares. The shares were traded on the Montreal Stock Exchange, and on June 30, 1995, they had a fair market value of $24 per share. A reputable local mechanic estimated that the truck was worth $21 500 cash on June 30, 1995. Mann had offered Wall this amount, but Wall had refused. Immediately after Mann purchased the truck, Jones Corporation offered to buy it from Mann for $24 700 cash.

Instructions

(a) Record the appropriate journal entry on the books of Mann Limited on June 30, 1995.
(b) Explain the rationale for your answer to (a).

E2.6 Various Principles. Chase Ltd. recorded the following events as indicated during the current accounting period:

(1) The company purchased equipment on sale for $8000 cash. The equipment would have cost Chase $10 000 if it had not been on sale.

Equipment	10 000	
Cash		8 000
Revenue		2 000

(2) The company recorded depreciation on its capital assets. The dollar amount was correctly computed according to the straight-line method.

Retained Earnings	25 000	
Accumulated Depreciation		25 000

(3) An appraisal indicated that land acquired for $35 000 at the end of the previous accounting period was worth $40 000 at the end of the current period.

Land	5 000	
Gain from Holding Land		5 000

(4) Because the inflation rate during the current accounting period was 10 percent, the company reasoned that $40 000 of liabilities owed throughout the period could now be paid using "cheaper" dollars.

Liabilities	4 000	
Purchasing Power Gain		4 000

(5) The company purchased a pencil sharpener that was expected to last five years.

Miscellaneous Expense	12	
Cash		12

(6) The company gave its president a new swimming pool for her personal use at home.

Capital Assets	18 000	
Cash		18 000

(7) The company president accepted a three-month loan on the last day of the accounting period.

Accounts Receivable	20 000	
Cash		20 000

Instructions

(a) Using the theoretical model presented in the chapter, comment on the appropriateness of the manner in which Chase Ltd. has recorded each of the above events.
(b) Record the correct journal entries, if any, that Chase should have made for each of these events.

Cases

C2.1 Application of Accounting Theory. Rex Limited has just acquired 100 outstanding common shares of Luke, Inc., a large company whose shares trade on a major stock exchange. Over the years, the accounting profession has discussed three major methods that Rex might use to account for its investment in Luke:

(1) *The cost method.* Rex would record the investment at historical cost on the date acquired and continue to report it at cost until sold.

(2) *The lower of cost or market method.* Rex would record the investment at historical cost on the date acquired. If, on the balance sheet date, the fair market value of the shares is less than historical cost, Rex would report the investment at the lower market value.

(3) *The market value method.* Rex would record the investment at historical cost on the date acquired. On the balance sheet date, Rex would report the investment at the market value, regardless of whether the market value was above or below Rex's historical cost.

Instructions

Discuss the major pros and cons of each of these methods within the context of accounting theory. Which method do you feel the CICA *Handbook* should require? Explain the reasoning that supports your answer.

C2.2 Change in Accounting Policy Disclosure. A company may occasionally change from one accounting principle to another. For example, it may change from the weighted average method of inventory pricing to the FIFO method, and from the double-declining balance method of depreciation to the straight-line method. Paragraph 1506.16 of the CICA *Handbook* states that "for each change in an accounting policy in the current period, the following information should be disclosed: (a) description of the change; and (b) the effect of the change on the financial statements of the current period."

Instructions

Explain the accounting entries and disclosure method required for these types of transactions.

C2.3 Accrual Versus Cash Basis. According to Section 1000.15 of the CICA *Handbook*, a major objective of financial reporting is to provide information that helps shareholders, bankers, and others to assess their chances of receiving cash from a given enterprise. Nevertheless, the accounting profession believes that income statements prepared under the accrual basis of accounting are more useful than either cash basis income statements or statements of cash receipts and disbursements.

Instructions

(a) Distinguish clearly between the cash basis and the accrual basis of accounting.

(b) Distinguish clearly between (1) an accrual basis income statement, (2) a cash basis income statement, and (3) a statement of cash receipts and disbursements.

(c) Explain why an accrual basis income statement should be useful to shareholders, bankers, and other users when assessing their chances of receiving cash from a given enterprise.

C2.4 Income and Value. The general manager of the Michael Manufacturing Corporation received an income statement from his controller that covered the 1993 calendar year. "Joe," he said to the controller, "this statement indicates that a net income of

$2 million dollars was earned last year. You know the value of the company is not that much more than it was this time last year."

"You're probably right," replied the controller. "You see, there are factors in accounting that sometimes keep reported operating results from reflecting the change in the value of the company."

Instructions
Prepare a detailed explanation of the accounting conventions to which the controller referred. Include justification, to the extent possible, for the accounting methods generally used.
(Adapted from AICPA.)

C2.5 Asset Measurement. In 1965, Hashe Ltd. bought some land in British Columbia for $250 000. Today the land could be sold for $5 million.

Instructions
(a) In your opinion, would Hashe Ltd.'s financial statements be more useful to investors and creditors if the land were reported at $250 000 or at $5 million? Explain your answer.
(b) At what amount would generally accepted accounting principles require the land to be reported? Explain your answer.

C2.6 Revenue Realization. After the presentation of your report on the examination of the financial statements to the board of directors of Whitman Publishing Limited, one of the new directors says he is surprised the income statement assumes that an equal proportion of the revenue is earned with the publication of every issue of the company's magazine. He feels that the "crucial event" in the process of earning revenue in the magazine business is the cash sale of the subscription. He does not understand why—other than for the smoothing of income—most of the revenue cannot be "realized" in the period of the sale.

Instructions
Discuss the propriety of timing the recognition of revenue in Whitman Publishing Limited's accounts with

(a) The cash sale of the magazine subscription.
(b) The publication of the magazine every month.
(c) Both events, by recognizing a portion of the revenue with the cash sale of the magazine subscription and a portion of the revenue with the publication of the magazine every month.
(Adapted from AICPA.)

C2.7 Economic Versus Accounting Income. On May 5, 1994, Acker Corporation signed a contract with Hyde Associates under which Hyde agreed (1) to construct an office building on land owned by Acker, (2) to accept responsibility for procuring financing for the project and finding tenants, and (3) to manage the property for 50 years. The annual profit from the project, after debt service, was to be divided equally between Acker

Corporation and Hyde Associates. Hyde was to accept its share of future profits as full payment for its services in construction, obtaining finances and tenants, and management of the project.

By April 30, 1995, the project was nearly completed and tenants had signed leases to occupy 90 percent of the available space at annual rentals totalling $2 600 000. It was estimated that, after operating expenses and debt service, the annual profit would amount to $850 000. Hyde Associates believes that the economic benefit derived from the contract should be reflected on its financial statements for the fiscal year ended April 30, 1995. Management has directed that revenue be accrued in an amount equal to the commercial value of the services Hyde rendered during the year, that this amount be carried in contracts receivable, and that all related expenditures be charged against the revenue.

Instructions
(a) Explain the main difference between the economic concept of business income as reflected by Hyde's management and the measurement of income under GAAP.
(b) Discuss the factors to be considered in determining when revenue has been realized for the measurement of periodic income.
(c) Does Hyde's measurement of revenue and expense for the year agree with generally accepted accounting principles? Support your opinion by citing the factors to be considered for asset measurement and revenue and expense recognition.
(Adapted from AICPA.)

C2.8   Revenue Realization.   Tinsley Trading Stamps, Inc., was formed early this year to sell trading stamps throughout Western Canada to retailers who distribute the stamps free to their customers. Books for collecting the stamps and catalogues illustrating the merchandise for which the stamps may be exchanged are given free to retailers for distribution to stamp recipients. Centres with inventories of merchandise premiums have been established to redeem stamps. Retailers may not return unused stamps to Tinsley.

The following schedule expresses Tinsley's expectations of a "normal month's activity," defined as the level of operations expected when expansion of activities ceases or tapers off to a stable rate. The company expects this level to be attained in the third year, when stamp sales will average $2 million a month.

Month	Actual Stamp Sales	Merchandise Premium Purchases	Stamp Redemptions
6th	30%	40%	10%
12th	60	60	45
18th	80	80	70
24th	90	90	80
30th	100	100	95

Tinsley plans to adopt an annual closing date at the end of each twelve-month period.

Instructions
(a) Discuss the factors to be considered in determining when revenue should be recognized in measuring the income of a business enterprise.
(b) Discuss the accounting alternatives that should be considered by Tinsley for the recognition of its revenues and related expenses.

(c) For each accounting alternative discussed in (b), provide a balance sheet account and indicate how each should be classified.

(Adapted from AICPA.)

C2.9 Cost, Expense, and Loss. You have been asked to deliver your auditor's report to the board of directors of Brewington Manufacturing Corporation and to answer questions about the financial statements. After reading the statements, one director asks: "What are the precise meanings of the terms 'cost,' 'expense,' and 'loss'? These terms sometimes seem to identify similar items and at other times seem to identify dissimilar items."

Instructions
(a) Explain the meanings of "cost," "expense," and "loss" and their use in financial reporting under generally accepted accounting principles. Also discuss the distinguishing characteristics of the terms and their similarities and interrelationships.
(b) Classify each of the following items as cost, expense, loss, or other category, and explain how the classification of each item may change.
  (1) Cost of goods sold.
  (2) Bad debts expense.
  (3) Depreciation expense for machinery.
  (4) Organization costs
  (5) Spoiled goods.
(c) The terms "period cost" and "product cost" describe certain items in financial statements. Define these terms and distinguish between them. To what types of items does each apply?

C2.10 Matching. You are an accountant employed by a large CA firm. Crestwood Enterprises, one of your clients, is a manufacturer of paper and wood products. The company's president, Martha Dolby, is having trouble understanding her company's most recent income statement, which you audited. "The matching principle of accounting doesn't seem to make sense," Ms. Dolby tells you. "I know the principle says that costs should be recognized as expenses when the goods or services they represent contribute to revenue. The question I have is, how is my company supposed to know *when* the goods and services represented by our costs contribute to revenue? When we purchase a new machine for use in manufacturing, for example, the machine is used along with many other input factors to manufacture our products, which we then sell. Determining exactly how much the new machine contributes to revenues in a particular period is impossible. And I always thought that accountants tried to produce reliable information."

Instructions
(a) Answer Ms. Dolby's question.
(b) Explain how accountants try to make the matching principle operational.
(c) Describe how the matching principle is applied to account for each of the following types of costs and explain the rationale for each treatment.
  (1) Advertising costs.
  (2) Raw material costs.
  (3) Cost of equipment expected to last five years.
  (4) Cost of sales commissions.
  (5) Cost of a patent expected to benefit the company for seven years.

C2.11 Matching. The general ledger of Good Times, Inc., a corporation engaged in the development and production of television programs for commercial sponsorship, contains the following accounts before amortization at the end of the current year:

Account	Balance (Debit)
Sealing Wax & Kings	$51 000
The Messenger	36 000
The Desperado	17 000
Shin Bone	8 000
Studio Rearrangement	5 000

An examination of contracts and records reveals the following:

(1) The first two accounts listed above represent the total cost of completed programs that were televised during the accounting period just ended. Under the terms of an existing contract, "Sealing Wax & Kings" will be rerun during the next accounting period at a fee equal to 50 percent of the fee for the first program televised. The contract for the first run produced $300 000 of revenue. The contract with the sponsor of "The Messenger" provides that he may, at his option, rerun the program during the next season at a fee of 75 percent of the fee for the first program televised.

(2) The balance in The Desperado account is the cost of a new program that has just been completed and is being considered by several companies for commercial sponsorship.

(3) The balance in the Shin Bone account represents the cost of a partially completed program for a projected series that has been abandoned.

(4) The balance of the Studio Rearrangement account consists of payments made to a firm of engineers that prepared a report on using studio space and equipment more efficiently.

Instructions

(a) State the general principles of accounting that apply to the first four accounts.

(b) Describe how you would report each of the first four accounts in the financial statements of Good Times, Inc.

(c) In what way, if at all, does the Studio Rearrangement account differ from the first four?

(Adapted from AICPA.)

C2.12 Consistency. Everlast Tool Inc. is a large manufacturing concern that uses the FIFO method of inventory cost determination. The other major companies in Everlast's industry use the weighted average method. At a recent shareholders' meeting, one of Everlast's shareholders made the following statement:

> I'm having a lot of trouble comparing the performance of our company with that of others in the industry because we are the only company that uses FIFO. It seems to me that because of the consistency principle of accounting, we should be using weighted average so that our financial results will be consistent with those of our major competitors.

Instructions

Explain the consistency principle and evaluate the shareholder's statement.

C2.13 Consistency and Matching. Wyatt Ltd. had used the first-in, first-out (FIFO) method of inventory cost determination from the year the company was organized (1983) until 1988. In 1988, the company changed to the last-in, first-out method (LIFO) method. Management explained that the change was "to achieve a better matching of revenues and expenses." Assume that the current year is 1994 and that Wyatt's management wants to change back to FIFO. The reason management now gives for the change is "to achieve a better matching of revenues and expenses."

Instructions
In your opinion, should generally accepted accounting principles allow Wyatt to change back to FIFO in 1994? (For the purpose of answering this question, ignore the income tax restrictions on LIFO.) Explain the rationale for your opinion.

C2.14 Materiality. As a recent university graduate, you have been hired as an accountant with Broadfield Limited. Broadfield recently sustained an extraordinary loss due to a flood. In accounting, an extraordinary gain or loss is one that is unusual in nature, not expected to recur in the foreseeable future, and not the result of a decision or determination of management. Generally accepted accounting principles require companies to disclose extraordinary gains and losses in a specially labelled section of the income statement *if* they are judged to be material. The reason for special disclosure is to highlight extraordinary items in an effort to permit investors and creditors to make more meaningful evaluations of management's performance and more accurate predictions of future cash flows. If an extraordinary gain or loss is not considered material, it may be combined with other items in the income statement and not reported in a special extraordinary items category.

Broadfield's chief executive officer (CEO) has just entered your office and wants you to explain how the accounting profession would determine whether the extraordinary flood loss is material, and how it should be recorded in the financial statements.

Instructions
Explain to Broadfield's CEO the general factors that you believe should be considered in determining whether the flood loss is material. You need not attempt to develop precise, numerical materiality guidelines.

C2.15 Materiality. Assume that you are the independent auditor of a successful brewing company that has spent approximately 5 percent of each sales dollar on advertising during each of the past ten years. The company charges all advertising costs to expense in the period in which the costs are incurred, and in past years, it has separately disclosed the amount of advertising expense in its income statement.

This year, management has decided to save money by curtailing its advertising, and advertising expense for the year amounts to only 0.5 percent of sales. When examining the annual financial statements and notes, you find no mention of advertising expense for the period. Upon asking management about the omission, you are told:

> We have not disclosed advertising expense separately in our income statement because the amount clearly is immaterial. We don't want to clutter our financial statements, and thereby confuse our shareholders, by disclosing every minor detail concerning our oper-

ations. We have therefore included advertising in the "other expenses" category of our income statement.

Instructions

(a) Evaluate management's contention that this year's advertising expense is immaterial.

(b) What disclosure relating to the company's advertising do you recommend for this year? Defend your answer from the standpoint of accounting theory.

C2.16 Conservatism. Brian Langley has recently organized Langley Inc. to produce and sell consumer electronic products. As company president, Brian is currently trying to determine the accounting principles that his company should use. He says that "we will need to use accelerated depreciation for our depreciable assets because this method will produce conservative results and is therefore required by GAAP."

Instructions

Explain to Brian what accountants mean by "conservatism." In addition, explain whether conservatism will require Langley Inc. to use accelerated depreciation or whether Brian should use some other criteria in deciding what method to use.

Chapter 3

Nature and Measurement of the Elements of Financial Statements

Objectives

1. To introduce the measuring units that may be used in financial statements.

2. To discuss the nature and measurement of assets, liabilities, and owners' equity.

3. To discuss the nature, measurement, and components of net income.

4. To discuss the usefulness of accounting net income.

5. To present the arguments favouring and opposing the publication of financial forecasts.

In this chapter, we discuss assets, liabilities, owners' equity, revenues, expenses, gains, losses, and income. Financial forecasts are also discussed so that they can be contrasted with the information traditionally reported in financial statements.

Most concepts discussed in this chapter are applied within generally accepted accounting principles (GAAP).[1] Other concepts may be viewed as proposals for changing GAAP. If adopted by the accounting profession, these proposals would alter the present scope of accounting information.

This chapter provides a conceptual foundation that will help explain the strengths and limitations of conventional financial statements (i.e., statements prepared today in accordance with GAAP). The content of these statements is covered in Chapter 4. The conceptual foundation will also help you to understand some of the more serious proposals that have been made for changing conventional financial statements. We explain and illustrate these proposals more extensively in other chapters.

Measurement in Accounting

Accounting is a measurement and disclosure discipline. That is, accountants measure the various elements of a company's financial statements, such as assets, liabilities, equities, revenues, and expenses, and disclose their results to users in order to help them make better decisions. To be useful, the information that accountants choose to measure and disclose should be both relevant and reliable.

The term **measurement**[2] refers to the assignment of numbers to objects, such as inventories and capital assets, and events, such as purchases and sales. Measurement allows us to use numbers to conveniently relate certain objects and events to others. If, for example, we are told that one box weighs 100 kg and another weighs 200 kg, we know how heavy the second box is relative to the first without ever having seen or lifted either box. In accounting, the term **valuation** conveys the same meaning as "measurement." Accountants often say, for example, that a company's inventories are valued (measured) at a certain amount on the balance sheet.

The elements of financial statements are the subject matter of financial accounting and are the items accountants seek to measure. Users need measurements of assets, liabilities, and other elements to make rational investment, credit, and similar decisions. In order to measure the elements, we must first select a measuring unit and a financial attribute to measure.

Monetary Unit

To illustrate, assume that a company owns some land that we want to measure for financial reporting purposes. The measuring unit could be constant dollars that measure purchasing power as of the balance sheet date, or it could be nominal dollars that reflect the dollar's purchasing power at the time the land was acquired. The monetary unit principle requires the use of nominal dollars in conventional financial statements. The land has several financial attributes, such as how much it actually cost, how much it would cost to replace, and how much it could be sold for. Which one of these financial attributes should we measure? Although historical cost is the financial attribute required in conventional financial statements, other attributes could result in more useful information. Determining which measuring unit and which financial attribute would provide the most useful information are two major challenges that the accounting profession has faced for many years. We explore these issues more fully in later sections of this chapter.

---

[1]"Financial Statement Concepts," CICA *Handbook*, Paragraphs 1000.59–60, March 1991.

[2]"Financial Statement Concepts," CICA *Handbook*, Paragraph 1000.53, March 1991.

The Measuring Unit

Financial statements are expressed in money, which measures command over goods and services in the economy. If the general level of prices of goods and services remained constant over time, money would not be a controversial measuring unit to use in financial statements. Under these circumstances, money received or paid ten years ago could be compared meaningfully with money received or paid today, because both sums would represent the same amount of purchasing power or command over goods and services.

In reality, the general level of prices in the economy changes over time. An increase in the general price level means that money's command over goods and services has decreased; this is called **inflation**. Similarly, a decrease in the general price level, known as **deflation**, means that money's command over goods and services has increased. In Canada and in most other countries, inflation has existed for many years and is regarded by many people as simply a way of life. Between 1980 and 1990, for example, inflation in Canada rose by 19.5 percent. Persistent inflation has caused accountants to actively debate the pros and cons of the two measuring units that have been suggested for financial statements: **nominal dollars** (historical) and **constant dollars** (adjusted). The situation changed at the beginning of the nineties: the rate of inflation decreased and so the pressure for constant-dollar financial statements no longer prevails.

A nominal dollar is one that has not been adjusted for inflation (or deflation); a constant dollar is one that has been adjusted. Dollars are adjusted for inflation or deflation by using a **general price-level index**, which is a measure that reveals how much the average price of a given group of goods and services has changed over time. General price-level indices show the changes that have occurred over time in the overall level of prices in the economy. A general price-level index should be distinguished from a **specific price index**, which is a measure that reveals changes over time in the price of relatively specific goods or services, such as televisions or hospital care. The price of a specific good or service does not necessarily change at the same rate or even in the same direction as do prices in general. In a given year, for example, the inflation rate, which refers to prices in general, might be 10 percent, while the price of pocket calculators, a specific good, actually falls by 15 percent.

The most important general price-level indexes are the **Consumer Price Index** (CPI) and the **Gross Domestic Product Implicit Price Index**. The federal government derives each index by monitoring the changes over time that occur in the prices of the "market basket." Each index has its own market basket, or predetermined group of goods and services. The components of the market baskets are updated periodically to reflect changes in consumer requirements. When constructing an index, a base period is selected and assigned an index number of 100. All other periods are then assigned index numbers that relate to the base. If prices in general rose by 10 percent in the period immediately following the base period, for example, the new period would be assigned an index number of 110.

To illustrate the nominal-dollar and constant-dollar measuring units, suppose that a company acquired land for $10 000 at the beginning of the current year, when the general price-level index was 100. At the end of the year, the general price-level index was 110, which means that the inflation rate during the year was 10 percent. In an ending balance sheet prepared according to GAAP, we would report the land at $10 000. This amount is simply the historical cost of the land measured in nominal dollars. However, if we wanted to measure the historical cost of the same land using year-end constant dollars, the land would be measured at $11 000 ($10 000 × $^{110}/_{100}$). Observe that we measured the *historical cost* of the land in two ways; we did *not* measure the current market value of the land. Using the nominal-dollar measuring unit, we measured the historical cost at $10 000. Measured in constant dollars, the historical cost is $11 000. We derived different amounts simply because we used different measuring units. Because of inflation, we would need $11 000 at the end of the year to have the same purchasing power as $10 000 at the beginning of the year.

As another example of nominal- versus constant-dollar measurement, suppose that a company buys a product costing $200 at the beginning of the year, when the general price-level index is 110, and sells it for $220 at the end of the year, when the general price-level index is 121. How much income did the company earn as a result of these events?

Measured in nominal dollars, as required under GAAP, the income is $20, as shown below:

Sales (measured when the general price-level index was 121)	$220
Less: Cost of product sold (measured when the general price-level index was 110)	200
Nominal-dollar income	$ 20

Observe that the conventional nominal-dollar income of $20 is the result of matching a revenue ($220) and an expense ($200) that are measured in dollars having *different amounts of purchasing power*. In contrast, the income measured in year-end constant dollars is zero, as shown below:

Sales (measured when the general price-level index was 121)	$220
Less: Cost of product sold (measured when the general price-level index was 121: $200 × $^{121}/_{110}$ = $220)	220
Constant-dollar income	$0

Under the nominal-dollar approach, the company's income is $20 because the sale allowed the company to recover a larger *number of dollars* than was originally spent to buy the product. In contrast, under the constant-dollar approach, income is zero because the sale merely allowed the company to recover the same *amount of purchasing power* that was originally invested in the product.

As a final example contrasting the nominal-dollar and constant-dollar measuring units, suppose that at the beginning of the current year you invested $1000 in a savings account that will pay 6 percent interest on the last day of the year. Ignoring income taxes and assuming that the current annual inflation rate is 12 percent, how much income will you earn from your savings account during the year? The nominal-dollar income, which ignores inflation, would simply equal the interest of $60 ($1000 × 0.06) to be paid at year-end. This amount suggests that you will be $60 richer at the end of the year. Due to inflation, you were actually better off with $1000 at the beginning of the year than you will be with $1060 at year-end. The constant-dollar income for the period would reflect this reality by recognizing a loss of purchasing power as a result of holding cash during a period of inflation. On a constant-dollar basis, you would actually have become poorer by $60 during the year, computed as follows:

Interest revenue ($1000 × 0.06)	$ 60
Less: Purchasing power loss from holding cash [($1000 × 1.12) − $1000]	120
Constant-dollar loss	$ (60)

Conventional accounting ignores the purchasing power of the unit of measurement.

Purchasing power gains and losses exist when the measuring unit is constant dollars, but not when the measuring unit is nominal dollars. These gains and losses occur as a result of holding **monetary assets** (cash or claims to a fixed number of dollars of cash) or **monetary liabilities** (obligations to pay a fixed number of dollars of cash) during periods of inflation or deflation. During a period of inflation, a company gains purchasing power by being in debt because the debt can be paid with dollars having less purchasing power. On the other hand, a company loses purchasing power by holding monetary assets, such as cash, accounts receivable, and notes receivable, during a period of inflation, because the assets lose some of their potential for buying goods and services. The opposite results occur in periods of deflation. Purchasing power gains and losses are not presently reported in conventional financial statements because the measuring unit is the nominal dollar.

The desirability of using constant dollars as the measuring unit in financial statements has been one of the most widely discussed topics in financial accounting for several decades. Proponents claim that constant-dollar measurements would be useful to users of financial statements by revealing the impact of inflation on business enterprises. Opponents argue that constant-dollar measurements are imprecise and costly to prepare, inflation rates in Canada have not been high enough to warrant a departure from nominal-dollar accounting, and inflation is expected to remain low for several years. Conventional financial statements are now prepared using nominal dollars, and we emphasize the use of nominal dollars in this textbook. As you read the remaining chapters, however, remember the distinction between nominal dollars and constant dollars and that the use of nominal dollars creates certain distortions in financial statements. You will understand financial statements much better if you are aware of their strengths and limitations. Section 4510 of the CICA *Handbook*, entitled "Reporting the Effects of Changing Prices," required large corporations to report selected constant-dollar measurements as supplementary information to their basic financial statements. Section 4510 was introduced in 1982 when the annual inflation rate increased by 10.9 percent; it was removed in 1992 after a drop in the rate.

Now that we have examined the measuring units available for financial statements, we will discuss the nature and measurement of the major elements of financial statements.

Assets

Nature of Assets

In Chapter 2, we defined **assets** as probable future economic benefits obtained or controlled by an entity as a result of past transactions or events.[3] Assets have three essential characteristics:

1. They embody probable future economic benefits.
2. The economic benefits of assets must accrue to a particular entity.
3. They are the result of transactions or events that have already occurred.

These characteristics pertain to *all* assets, such as cash, accounts receivable, merchandise inventory, land, machinery, and patents. Historical cost is *not* an essential characteristic.

---

[3]"Financial Statement Concepts," CICA *Handbook*, Paragraphs 1000.29–31, March 1991.

Some assets, such as the land a city donates to attract a company to the area, may be acquired without cost.

The most important characteristic of an asset is the probable future economic benefits that usually result in net cash inflows to a company. A company may obtain the future economic benefits by exchanging the asset for something else of value or by using the asset. Two of a tire manufacturer's assets, for example, are the inventory of tires and the machinery used to make tires. The manufacturer usually derives benefits by exchanging the tire inventory for cash or claims to cash, and by using the machinery to manufacture tires that can later be sold.

Because the economic benefits of an asset are received in the future, accountants are sometimes uncertain about whether a particular item constitutes an asset. Cash is obviously an asset because it can buy goods and services. Uncollectable accounts receivable are not assets because of the absence of future benefits. But what about a new advertising program that merchants in Canadian border towns have initiated in an effort to convince consumers that they should buy in Canada? When a company spends money for the advertising, it hopes to derive future benefits. But the user of the company's financial statements may find it difficult to objectively evaluate the future benefits of this asset.

To qualify as an asset, the economic benefits of an item must be controlled by a particular entity. Public highways and public parks are therefore not considered assets of a particular company. Although the company may regularly use the highways to transport goods and use the parks for employee picnics, the company does not have the right to regulate the use of the highways and parks by others. However, private roads and parks that a company has built on its own land are considered assets because the company can regulate access by others.

In accounting, we define assets as probable future economic benefits rather than as physical objects. A subtle but important point is that the "bundle" of benefits, and not the physical object itself, is the essence of an asset. A building, for example, is a physical structure that may provide many benefits, such as office space and residual value, after it has been used. These *benefits* constitute the asset. At times, two or more entities may share the benefits that a building or other asset provides. In a building that is leased, for example, one party may have the right to use the property while another has the right to receive periodic rents and to realize the residual value of the property when the lease expires. In this case, the building provides economic benefits to both parties.

Assets result from past transactions or events of a particular entity. A ten-year-old machine becomes an asset to a particular company on the date the company acquires it, not when the machine was manufactured. Similarly, a machine that a company plans to acquire next year will not be an asset to the company until the acquisition occurs.

Measurement of Assets

Asset/Liability Measurement

Assets have several measurable financial attributes. As discussed in Chapter 2, conventional accounting emphasizes the historical cost attribute. That is why financial statements today are frequently referred to as historical-cost financial statements. But, as we saw in the previous section, historical cost is not an essential characteristic of an asset. Furthermore, historical cost is not the only attribute that accountants measure. Indeed, the asset measurements reported in financial statements today reflect a *mixture of financial attributes*.

A company operates in both an input market and an output market, and exchange prices exist in both markets. The financial attributes that may be used for asset measurement fall into two general categories that correspond to these markets, which are as follows:[4]

Market	Asset Measurement Category	Financial Attribute
Input	Input values	Historical cost
		Current cost
Output	Output values	Current exit value in orderly liquidation
		Expected exit value in due course of business
		Present value of expected cash flows

An **input market** is one in which a company acquires goods and services from suppliers, employees, and others. An **input value** refers to a measure of the amount a company has to give up to acquire the goods and services. In contrast, an **output market** is one in which a company sells its products to customers. An **output value** refers to a measure of the amount a company will receive in exchange for its product.

As we discuss these financial attributes, remember the following points:

1. Each attribute pertains to an existing asset.
2. Each attribute pertains to an actual transaction (one that has actually occurred), an expected transaction (one that is expected to occur), or a hypothetical transaction (one that would occur if certain circumstances existed).
3. Each attribute pertains to the past, the present, or the future.
4. Each attribute is used in practice for measuring certain kinds of assets under current GAAP.
5. Asset valuations (and income measurements) may differ significantly depending on which financial attribute is used. Under certain circumstances, the measurement of two or more financial attributes of a given asset may result in the same dollar amounts. Nevertheless, each attribute differs conceptually from the others.

Historical Cost

As we discussed in Chapter 2, the **historical,** or **acquisition, cost** of an asset is the amount of the cash or cash-equivalent payment made to render the asset operational. Historical cost is therefore an input value based on an actual past transaction. In conventional financial statements, historical cost is generally used to measure inventory; property, plant, and equipment; and intangible assets.

Historical costs are based on arm's-length exchange transactions that have occurred and can be verified by invoices, cancelled cheques, and other source documents. The historical cost of an asset equals the market value of the asset at the time the company acquired it. Changes in an asset's market value that occur after acquisition are generally ignored until the company sells the asset. The gain or loss is recognized after disposition of the asset.

Proponents of historical-cost measurement emphasize that historical costs are objective and reliable. Opponents argue that historical costs lack relevance because they fail to reflect current market values after a company acquires an asset.

---

[4]"Conceptual Framework for Financial Reporting," *The Accounting Standards Authority of Canada,* Paragraph 122 (Vancouver 1987), p. 321.

Current Cost

The **current cost** of an asset is the amount of the cash or cash-equivalent payment that a company would have to make today to acquire the same asset. Like historical cost, current cost is an input value, but unlike historical cost, current cost is based on a hypothetical present transaction. Suppose, for example, that a company owns land that it acquired a year ago for $20 000 (a historical cost). If the company would have to pay $25 000 for the land today, the land has a current cost of $25 000 to the company. Assuming that no inflation occurred during the year, the company has earned a $5000 **holding gain** simply by holding the land during a time when its market value increased. Holding gains are *not* separately recognized under generally accepted accounting principles, which, as we have stated, are based primarily on historical costs. However, applying the lower of cost or market rule when measuring inventories sometimes results in current-cost measurements that appear in conventional financial statements. We explain this rule in detail in Chapter 9.

Various methods can be used to determine the current costs of a company's assets. The current cost of a raw material may be determined by examining the prices listed in the supplier's current catalogue. It is often possible to determine the current cost of certain equipment used in operations by applying specific price indexes that measure changes in the price of the equipment over time. Appraisals may be effectively used to determine the current cost of such assets as land and specialized machinery.

Proponents argue that the use of current-cost measurements in financial statements would help users to make more accurate predictions of future cash flows and more meaningful evaluations of a company's financial position and performance. Critics contend that current-cost measurements are generally too subjective and unreliable to be useful in making investment and credit decisions.

Current Exit Value in Orderly Liquidation

The **current exit value** of an asset is the amount of cash the asset could be sold for in an orderly liquidation. In other words, the current exit value of a machine tells us how much cash a company could receive if it were to sell the machine in the normal course of business as opposed to a forced sale. Current exit value is an output value based on a hypothetical present transaction and is used today to measure the securities held by investment companies and certain other entities.

Recall that when an asset is measured at historical cost, changes in the asset's market value are generally ignored until the time of sale. In contrast, when an asset is measured at current exit value, changes in this value are recognized in both the asset valuation and income. Assume, for example, that a company buys an inventory item on December 31, 1994, for $100. Assume further that the current exit value of the item on that date is $140, and the company actually sells the item for $150 on March 3, 1995. Under the historical cost approach, the company would report the asset at $100 at the end of 1994 and would report income of $50 ($150 − $100) in 1995, when the asset is sold. The current exit value approach, in contrast, would require the company to report the asset at $140 at the end of 1994 and to report income of $40 ($140 − $100) during 1994 and $10 ($150 − $140) during 1995.

Proponents argue that current exit values are relevant because they reveal the cash receipts a company can command at the present time. On the other hand, critics maintain that companies acquire many assets for use rather than sale, and that current exit value measurements of most assets are unreliable. Critics further argue that some intangible assets, work-in-process inventory, and specialized capital assets, such as an oil refinery in a foreign country that has an unstable government, have no current exit values.

Expected Exit Value in Due Course of Business

The **expected exit value** of an asset, often called **net realizable value (NRV)**, is the amount of cash or cash-equivalent value that a company expects to receive for the asset in the ordinary course of business, minus the costs of completing and selling the asset. Suppose, for example, that a company owns some partially completed inventory that could be sold as is for $6000. Completing and selling the goods, which the company plans to do, will cost approximately $500, and the company estimates that the completed goods can be sold for $8000. Under these circumstances, the goods have a current exit value of $6000. The expected exit value of the goods in due course of business, however, is $7500 ($8000 − $500). Expected exit value is therefore an output value based on an expected future transaction. Changes that occur over time in an asset's expected exit value are recognized in both the asset valuation and income. In practice, expected exit values are used to measure accounts receivable and, under certain circumstances, inventories.

An asset's expected exit value is relevant to users because it indicates the net amount of cash the company expects to receive for the asset in the future. Expected exit values, however, are generally subject to the same criticisms as current exit values.

Present Value of Expected Cash Flows

An economic fact universally accepted by rational business people is that money has a time value, commonly called **interest**. Suppose that a neighbour you trust offers to give you, in exchange for cash, a written and signed IOU for $112 payable to you one year from now. How much cash would you be willing to pay for the IOU today assuming you want to earn 12 percent interest on your investment? Clearly you should not pay $112 because you would not earn any interest. The answer of course is $100 ($112 ÷ 1.12). We would say, then, that your neighbour's IOU has a **present value** as an asset to you of $100. To determine the present value we **discounted** the amount you would receive at the end of the year ($112) using a 12 percent discount rate.

Here's the point of the preceding exercise. Ultimately, the value of an asset to a company depends on the asset's ability to generate net cash inflows (cash inflows − cash outflows = net cash inflows) for the company in the future. Inventory, for example, has value because of the net cash inflows that generally result from the future sale. Equipment used in the manufacturing process has value because it is used to produce products that can later be sold to generate cash. The present value of an asset is the discounted amount of the net cash inflows that the asset is expected to generate. Present value, then, is an output value based on expected future transactions.

To determine the present value of an asset, we must discount all the expected net cash inflows. This process requires an estimate of (1) the **amount** of net cash inflows that an asset will generate, (2) the **timing** of those cash flows, and (3) the **discount rate**. Changes in an asset's present value are recognized in valuing the asset and in determining income. At this point, you should concentrate on *why* present value is an important financial attribute of assets. Computing present values is not difficult and is explained in Chapter 7.

Present value is widely regarded as the most relevant of the various asset valuation concepts. Assets are essentially expected future economic benefits, and present values tell us how much those benefits are currently worth to the company. The benefits are expressed as the net cash inflows that the company expects the asset to generate in the future. Little doubt exists that investors, creditors, and other users of financial statements would like to know the present value of a company's assets. The problem is that accountants cannot measure present value reliably for most types of assets. For example, a machine used in the manufacturing process is likely to be used with other machines, materials, and labour to produce a product that the company hopes to sell in the future for some amount of cash. But who knows whether the product will actually sell, how much it will sell for, and when the company will receive the cash from the sale? Who knows how much cash is attributable to the machine we are trying to measure, exclusive of the other factors (e.g., materials, labour, advertising) that are important in producing and selling the product? And what discount rate should we use to compute the present value? The difficulty of answering these kinds of questions is what makes the present-value approach impractical for most types of assets. However, the present-value approach is used in GAAP today for measuring certain long-term receivables under *Accounting Principles Board Opinion No. 21.*[5] In Canada, there is no equivalent recommendation; however, the practice is regarded as generally acceptable. The amount and timing of cash receipts for long-term receivables can usually be estimated with reasonable accuracy, and the discount rate used in practice is one that is reasonable at the time the receivable was created. The FASB is working on a major project that examines accounting measurements based on present value.

Summary

Historical Cost

Exhibit 3.1 summarizes the financial attributes we have discussed. Although each attribute is used under GAAP for measuring certain types of assets, the historical cost attribute is presently emphasized. Proponents of historical cost tend to emphasize the reliability of the measurement, while proponents of the alternatives to historical cost tend to emphasize the relevance of these measurements to users of a company's financial statements. Recall that relevance and reliability are the most important determinants of the usefulness of information. Assuming that relevance and reliability require important trade-offs, an important question facing the accounting profession is which financial attribute is in fact the most *useful* for decision making. Is it really the historical cost attribute, or is it some other one?

Liabilities

Nature of Liabilities

In Chapter 2, we defined **liabilities** as probable future sacrifices of economic benefits arising from present obligations of an entity to transfer assets or provide services to other entities in the future as a result of past transactions or events.[6] A liability has three essential characteristics:

1. It embodies a probable future sacrifice of economic benefits.
2. It obligates a particular entity to transfer assets or provide services in the future.
3. It is the result of a transaction or event that has already occurred.

The essential characteristics of a liability are similar to those of an asset, except that an asset entitles an entity to *receive* economic benefits, whereas a liability obligates the

---

[5]"Interest on Receivables and Payables," *APB Opinion No. 21*, 1971.
   [6]"Financial Statement Concepts," CICA *Handbook*, Paragraph 1000.32, March 1991.

Exhibit 3.1 Financial Attributes of Assets

Financial Attribute	Description	Transaction	Time
Input Values			
Historical cost	Amount of cash or cash-equivalent payment actually made to acquire the asset.	Actual	Past
Current cost	Amount of cash or cash-equivalent payment that a company would have to make today to acquire the same asset.	Hypothetical	Present
Output Values			
Current exit value in orderly liquidation	Amount of cash the asset could be sold for in an orderly liquidation.	Hypothetical	Present
Expected exit value in due course of business	Amount of cash or cash-equivalent value that a company expects to receive for the asset in the ordinary course of business, minus the costs of completing and selling the asset.	Expected	Future
Present value of expected cash flows	Amount of discounted net cash inflows that the asset is expected to generate.	Expected	Future

entity to *pay* economic benefits. Most liabilities, such as accounts payable, are settled by paying cash, but some, such as the liability for magazine subscriptions paid in advance, require settlement in the form of services or assets other than cash. For a liability to exist, it is not necessary to know either the exact amount of the liability or the identity of the parties to whom the entity is obligated. For example, companies report liabilities under product warranties in their financial statements without knowing the identity of the customers whose products will become defective and require servicing. The dollar estimates are based on past experience.

The most significant characteristic of a liability is the duty or requirement to sacrifice economic benefits in the future, either by expending assets or providing services. Liabilities may be payable on demand, on certain maturity dates, or when certain specific events occur. Because a liability entails a probable future sacrifice, uncertainty often exists about whether a particular item qualifies as a liability. For example, accounts payable, interest payable, and wages payable are clearly liabilities because they represent probable future sacrifices. On the other hand, determining that an entity will probably lose a lawsuit and therefore have to pay damages is much more difficult and requires considerable judgement and advice from lawyers.

Most liabilities, such as bonds payable, are evidenced by contracts or other agreements and by the fact that the entity incurring the liability usually receives proceeds (cash, other assets, or services). However, contracts and the receipt of proceeds are not essential characteristics of a liability. Some liabilities, such as income taxes and lawsuit settlements, result from governmental or legal actions and do not involve proceeds to the entity. Other liabilities, such as donations to charity, result from discretionary actions by an entity's management, and the entity does not receive proceeds.

A liability does not have to be legally enforceable, although most liabilities, such as notes payable, are.[7] A liability may exist simply because an entity is bound by custom or tradition to provide money, goods, or services in the future. A liability for year-end bonuses, for example, may exist because a company has always paid such amounts even without a contractual requirement to do so. When an obligation is not legally enforceable, determining whether a liability really exists can be extremely difficult. Under such circumstances, an accountant must apply careful professional judgement.

Probable future sacrifices alone do not constitute a liability. For a liability to exist, a particular entity must be obligated to transfer assets or provide services to other entities in the future as a result of past transactions or events. A company that has sold all of its inventory has no liability to pay for new inventory until it is acquired from another entity. Similarly, the amount shown in next year's budget for labour services is not a liability until the company has received the services.

Measurement of Liabilities

The five financial attributes discussed earlier for assets also pertain to liabilities.[8] But relative to asset measurement, liability measurement has received much less attention in the accounting literature. The measurement of a liability in practice is often the result of measuring the other side of the transaction that created the liability. When a company acquires an inventory item for $100 on credit, for example, the asset is measured at its historical cost of $100; the liability is also measured at $100, which is the amount the company expects to spend to liquidate the liability. In practice, a variety of financial attributes are used to measure liabilities.

Liabilities enable companies to delay payment. The cost of delaying payment is interest, or the time value of money. *Whether interest is explicitly stated or not, it is always inherent in liabilities.* Two issues in liability measurement therefore are (1) whether the interest should be separately recognized, and (2) what rate should be used to recognize the interest.

Each of the following financial attributes pertains to a liability that presently exists. Although each attribute is conceptually unique, the measurement of two or more financial attributes of a given liability may result in the same dollar amount under certain circumstances. Measurements of liabilities and income may differ considerably depending on the financial attribute used.

Present Value of Expected Cash Flows
Conceptually, a liability should be measured on a present-value basis, and many liabilities are currently measured this way. The present value of a liability is the discounted amount of the net cash outflows that are expected to be necessary to liquidate the liability. Suppose, for example, that a company has a debt of $1000 that is payable one year from today. Assuming an interest rate of 12 percent, the present value of the liability today is

---

[7]"Financial Statement Concepts," CICA *Handbook*, Paragraph 1000.34, March 1991.

[8]"Conceptual Framework for Financial Reporting," *The Accounting Standards Authority of Canada*, Paragraph 122 (Vancouver 1987), p. 322.

$892.86 ($1000 ÷ 1.12).[9] The $107.14 difference between $1000 and $892.86 is the interest expense that the company will incur by being indebted during the coming year. Under the present-value approach, the interest would be separately recognized and accounted for.

Present-value measurements reflect the time value of money and are required in current practice when measuring certain long-term payables under Section 3210 of the CICA *Handbook*. In practice, accountants apply the present-value approach throughout the time a liability exists by using a discount rate equal to the market rate of interest at the time the liability was initially incurred. This discount rate is called the historical market rate. Often the *historical market rate* is simply the interest rate stated in the loan agreement.

Expected Exit Value in Due Course of Business

The expected exit value of a liability is the amount of cash or cash-equivalent value that the company expects to pay to eliminate the liability in the ordinary course of business. The amount of the cash or cash-equivalent payment is not discounted to a present value. Assume that a company acquires some merchandise on credit. The goods cost $5000, which the company agrees to pay in 60 days. The expected exit value of the liability is $5000.

Expected exit values show how much cash the company expects to spend to liquidate a liability, but they ignore the time value of money completely. In the example above, the interest on the $5000 liability for 60 days is not separately considered. To illustrate this point more dramatically, assume that a company currently sells at par value $100 000, 12 percent, twenty-year bonds that the company expects to retire at maturity. The expected exit value of the bonds today would be $340 000 [$100 000 maturity value + $240 000 ($100 000 × 0.12 × 20) interest]. Recording the bond liability at $340 000 fails to reflect the economic reality that interest of $240 000 will be incurred during the twenty-year life of the bonds. Under current GAAP, the company would measure the bond liability at $100 000, an amount equal to the present value of the interest and principal payments required to liquidate the bonds.

Expected exit values are used under GAAP for measuring many liabilities. For example, accounts payable to suppliers are usually measured at expected exit values. The interest is ignored because the credit period is usually relatively brief and therefore the interest is immaterial. As another example, liabilities for product warranties are usually measured at their expected exit value. In this case, the interest is ignored because the amount and timing of payment are too uncertain to permit a meaningful estimate of the interest.

Historical Proceeds

The **historical proceeds** of a liability are the amount of the cash or cash-equivalent proceeds actually received when the liability was incurred. To illustrate, assume that a company receives $18 000 from magazine subscriptions paid in advance for three years. The company is obligated to provide the magazines, and it would measure the liability for unearned subscriptions revenue at $18 000, the amount of the cash proceeds received.

Historical proceeds are generally used under GAAP to measure liabilities for products or services that a company has agreed to provide in the future. The time value of money

---

[9]Computing present values is discussed more fully in Chapter 7.

is generally ignored for these types of liabilities because it is considered too impractical to measure.

Current Proceeds

The **current proceeds** of a liability are the amount of cash or cash-equivalent value that a company would receive today by incurring the same liability. The amount changes in response to changes in market interest rates and to changes in the perceived risk of the company that has the liability. As market interest rates rise, the current proceeds of a given liability tend to decrease; similarly, as market interest rates fall, the current proceeds tend to increase.

To illustrate, suppose that on January 1, 1994, a company issues a $10 000, 10 percent, two-year note payable with interest of $1000 ($10 000 × 0.10) payable at the end of each year. On that date, the market rate of interest is 10 percent, and the company receives proceeds of $10 000, because the present value of the note (including the interest) at the market rate of interest is $10 000. On December 31, 1994, the company pays $1000 of interest for the year 1994, the current market rate of interest is 12 percent, and the company's risk level is unchanged from the beginning of the year. Under these circumstances, the current proceeds of the note will be $9821.43 on December 31, 1994. This amount equals the $10 000 face amount plus $1000 of interest due at the end of 1995, divided by 1.12 ($11 000 ÷ 1.12 = $9821.43). We are saying, then, that *if* the company were to issue on December 31, 1994, a $10 000, 10 percent note with one year remaining to maturity, the company would obtain proceeds of $9821.43. The reason that the current proceeds are less than $10 000 is because the current market rate of interest (12 percent) exceeds the interest rate stated in the note (10 percent). A lender who invested $9821.43 in the note at the end of 1994 would earn 12 percent interest (the current market rate) during 1995 [$9821.43 + ($9821.43 × 0.12) = $11 000]. Notice that $9821.43 is simply the present value of the note computed using the current market rate of interest (12 percent) at the end of 1994.

We emphasize that the note payable in the previous example would be reported at $10 000 (not $9821.43) in conventional financial statements prepared at the end of 1994. This is so because $10 000 is the present value of the note at the end of 1994 computed using the market rate of interest that prevailed when the note was issued ($11 000 ÷ 1.10 = $10 000).

Under the current-proceeds approach to liability measurement, the time value of money is measured using a current rather than historical interest rate. Some people believe that the use of current proceeds would enhance the usefulness of financial statements for making predictions of cash flows and evaluations of management. But current proceeds depart from historical cost accounting and are not used for measuring liabilities under GAAP.

Current Exit Value in Orderly Liquidation

The current exit value of a liability is the amount a company would have to pay currently to eliminate the liability in a systematic manner. Assume, for example, that a company has $100 000 of bonds payable outstanding and that each of the 100 bonds was originally sold at par value of $1000. Assume further that market interest rates have fallen since the bonds were issued and that each bond now has a market price of $1050. In this example, the current exit value of the bonds is $105 000 ($1050 × 100), because this is the amount the company would have to pay currently to retire the bonds by purchasing them in the market.

When a liability requires specified cash payments, such as the bond liability in the example above, the current exit value and current proceeds will usually be the same amount. Nevertheless, current exit value and current proceeds differ conceptually. Current exit value refers to how much a company would have to *pay* to eliminate the liability; current proceeds refer to how much a company would *receive* by incurring the liability. Some people argue that current exit values would be relevant to users when assessing the ability of an entity to adapt to a changing environment. The counter-argument is that most companies do not intend to eliminate all of their liabilities currently. Like current proceeds, current exit value measurements represent a departure from historical cost accounting and are not used when measuring liabilities in financial statements prepared in accordance with GAAP.

Summary

The various financial attributes of liabilities are summarized in Exhibit 3.2.

Owners' Equity

Nature of Owners' Equity

Owners' equity is "the ownership interest in the assets of a profit oriented enterprise after deducting its liabilities."[10] In other words, owners' equity equals net assets, which are assets minus liabilities. Like liabilities, owners' equity represents an interest in the assets of an entity. But liabilities and owners' equity differ in several important aspects:

1. Liabilities represent the interest of creditors in the assets of an entity; owners' equity represents the interest of owners.
2. Liabilities rank ahead of owners' equity when an entity's assets are distributed. A company may not pay dividends to owners until it has made the required interest and principal payments to creditors. Moreover, when a company is liquidated, liabilities must be paid before distributions can be made to owners.
3. The amount of liability payments is usually more certain than is the amount of payments to owners. Oral or written agreements, such as bond contracts, usually specify how much cash a company must pay to liquidate its liabilities. The amount of dividend payments to owners, however, is usually determined at the discretion of a company's board of directors. There are specific equity securities that resemble liability payment obligations; examples are redeemable preferred shares[11] and term preferred shares.[12]
4. The timing of liability payments is usually more certain than the timing of payments to owners. Many liabilities have specific maturity dates; owners' equity does not mature.

Owners' equity represents the interest of parties who stand to lose the largest amount if an entity is unsuccessful and gain the largest amount if it is successful. Owners are the

---

[10]"Financial Statement Concepts," CICA *Handbook*, Paragraph 1000.35, March 1991.

[11]"Preferred Shares Whose Redemption is Outside of the Control of the Issuer, Emerging Issues Committee," CICA *Handbook*, EIC-13, February 1992.

[12]"Term Preferred Shares, Accounting Guidelines," CICA *Handbook*, December 1977.

Exhibit 3.2 Financial Attributes of Liabilities

Financial Attribute	Description	Transaction	Time
Present value of expected cash flows	Amount of discounted net cash outflows that are expected to be necessary to liquidate the liability.	Expected	Future
Expected exit value in due course of business	Amount of cash or cash-equivalent value that a company expects to pay to eliminate the liability in the ordinary course of business.	Expected	Future
Historical proceeds	Amount of cash or cash-equivalent proceeds actually received when the liability was incurred.	Actual	Past
Current proceeds	Amount of cash or cash-equivalent proceeds that a company would receive today by incurring the same liability.	Hypothetical	Present
Current exit value in orderly liquidation	Amount of cash that a company would have to pay currently to eliminate the liability in an orderly manner.	Hypothetical	Present

primary beneficiaries of an entity's net income, but they must also bear its losses. Owners' equity is originally created when owners invest cash or other assets in an entity. Subsequently, the interest of owners may be increased by additional investments and net income, and it may be decreased by distributions to owners (dividends) and net losses.

Owners' equity provides an important frame of reference when measuring a company's net income. In the absence of additional investments by owners or distributions to them during a period, net income for the period will equal the increase in owners' equity that occurred during the period.

Measurement of Owners' Equity

Asset/Liability Measurement

As indicated earlier, owners' equity is a **residual figure** derived by deducting liabilities from assets. The measurement of owners' equity is therefore not an independent process. Instead, it depends on the valuations assigned to the individual assets and liabilities. Suppose that a company had only one asset, an account receivable with an expected exit value of $10 000, and no liabilities. Under these circumstances, owners' equity would simply reflect the expected exit value measurement of $10 000 ($10 000 − $0). As we have seen, however, companies actually use a mixture of financial attributes (historical costs, expected exit values, present values, etc.) when measuring their individual assets and liabilities. Owners' equity therefore reflects a mixture of financial attributes. For this reason and because many assets and liabilities are simply too difficult to measure and report at all, owners' equity does not reveal the current market value of the company to its owners.

Net Income

In this section we discuss the nature, measurement, components, and usefulness of net income. Many people feel that net income is the most important single number that appears in the financial statements. Unlike cash on hand, the net income for a typical business cannot be seen or counted. The net income referred to in this section is the difference between revenue and expenses. Income concepts have been a highly controversial topic in accounting and economics.

Nature of Net Income

The economist J.R. Hicks defined an individual's income as the maximum amount the person could consume in a period and still be as well off at the end of the period as he or she was at the beginning.[13] This definition can be adapted to a business enterprise: the **net income** of a business is the increase in the net assets (owners' equity) of the firm, assuming no new capital contributions by the owners or dividend distributions by the business.[14] More precisely, the net income for a period equals the ending owners' equity, minus the beginning owners' equity, plus dividends declared during the period, minus additional capital contributions made during the period. To illustrate, assume that during a period a company had ending owners' equity of $25 000, beginning owners' equity of $20 000, dividends declared of $10 000, and additional capital contributions of $3000. Net income for the period would be $12 000 ($25 000 − $20 000 + $10 000 − $3000).

Important to an understanding of net income is the distinction between a return *of* capital and a return *on* capital. Shareholders invest in companies to earn a return *on* capital, or an amount in excess of their original investment. A return *of* capital is simply an erosion of the capital invested in the firm. Net income occurs only after the capital used from the beginning of the period is maintained. This concept is known as **capital maintenance**. In the Hicksian sense, the same level of "well-offness" must be maintained before net income can be said to exist. Revenues must be applied to the recovery of the resources used in the business before any net income can result. The capital used in the business does not have to be physically replaced with the exact same type of resources consumed: capital maintenance is a measurement concept, not a statement of how managers should reinvest resources.

To illustrate the concept of capital maintenance, consider a retail music store with all its capital invested in an inventory of 800 cassettes costing $5 each. If the retailer sells 600 cassettes at $7 each, the total return is $4200 (600 × $7). Therefore, at the end of the period, the retailer has 200 CDs and $4200. To determine net income, we must deduct from $4200 the amount of capital invested in the 600 CDs that were sold. One way of doing this is to deduct $3000 (600 × $5) from the $4200 as a return *of* capital and then consider the remaining $1200 (600 × $2) as a return *on* capital (i.e., net income). The retailer need not actually replace the 600 CDs that were sold. Our objective in deducting $3000 is merely to measure the capital consumed by the sale of 600 CDs so that we can determine net income.[15]

---

[13]J.R. Hicks, *Value and Capital* (Oxford: Clarendon Press, 1946), p. 172.

[14]"Financial Statement Concepts," CICA *Handbook*, Paragraph 1000.27, March 1991.

[15]Central to the concept of capital maintenance is the accountant's assessment of "well-offness." The accountant's definition of capital has a direct bearing on what is considered as net income. It is beyond the scope of this text to discuss the various concepts of capital. A lucid discussion can be found in Keith Shwayder, "The Capital Maintenance Rule and the Net Asset Valuation Rule," *Accounting Review* (April 1969), pp. 304–16.

Lifetime Net Income

The most definitive measure of net income can be made when a company is liquidated. At that time, the **lifetime net income** of the firm can be determined with certainty. Assuming no additional investments or withdrawals by owners, lifetime net income (or loss) would equal the cash initially invested by owners at the beginning of business, subtracted from the cash remaining for the owners at the end of business, after assets are liquidated and liabilities are satisfied. Over the life of the company, total revenues equal all cash receipts from earning activities (such as sales), and total expenses equal all cash disbursements for earning activities (such as payments to suppliers and employees). Lifetime net income therefore equals lifetime cash receipts from earning activities minus lifetime cash disbursements for earning activities, or net cash inflows from earning activities during the life of the company.

Periodic Net Income

Although the lifetime net income of an enterprise corresponds to its net cash flows from earning activities, this situation does not help the investor or creditor to make *timely* decisions. Investors and creditors are not interested in knowing the net income of a firm after final disposition of assets. Instead, they need periodic disclosures of operating performance in order to assess current investments and loans or to evaluate future capital commitments.

One function of the accountant is to provide statements of **periodic net income**. This presents a challenge because, in contrast to lifetime net income, periodic net income does not necessarily reflect cash flows for the period. At *some time* during the life of a company, a dollar should be received for every dollar of revenue reported by the company, but the cash receipts do not have to occur in the same period that the revenue is recognized. Likewise, at *some time* during the life of a company, a dollar should be spent for every dollar of expense reported by the company, but the cash payments do not have to occur in the same period that the expense is recognized. The accountant attempts to reconcile the recognition of revenues and expenses with the actual cash flows of past, present, and future periods. This reconciliation requires the recognition of certain assets and liabilities, as shown in Exhibit 3.3.

The upper left cell of Exhibit 3.3 represents the case of cash inflow preceding the recognition of revenue. Consider, for example, a business that rents space in return for a fee received in advance. When the fee is collected, there is no revenue, only the liability to provide rental space. Revenue is recognized only as rental space is provided. Likewise, the lower left cell of Exhibit 3.3 represents the case of cash outflow preceding the recognition of an expense. This occurs when a business pays cash in exchange for future services, such as prepaid insurance. The prepaid insurance represents the right to future protection that is amortized as an expense only as the protection is received.

The upper right cell of the exhibit illustrates transactions in which cash inflow follows revenue recognition. An example is interest on an investment in the bonds of another company. If the interest has been earned as of the end of an accounting period, then the interest must be recognized as a receivable and as revenue, even though the cash associated with the interest will not be received until the next accounting period. The lower right cell illustrates transactions in which cash outflow follows expense recognition. Frequently, at the end of a reporting period, an enterprise has received employee services for which it has not yet paid. The labour represents a liability that will later be compensated by actual cash payment.

Exhibit 3.3 Reconciliation Between Cash Flow and Revenue/Expense Recognition

	Cash Precedes Recognition	Cash Follows Recognition
Revenues	Liability Example: Unearned Rent Revenue	Asset Example: Accrued Interest Receivable
Expenses	Asset Example: Prepaid Insurance	Liability Example: Accrued Wages Payable

In each case, revenue and expense recognition for the period does not exactly correspond to cash flows. Although cash flows are reconciled with revenues and expenses over the lifetime of a company, it is unreasonable to postpone income measurement until business is terminated. Instead, methods must be used to measure periodic net income.

The Measurement of Periodic Net Income

The measurement of periodic net income depends on the valuation of assets and liabilities, since periodic net income is the change in net assets for the period, assuming no new capital contributions or dividends. At a very simple level, a cash basis system could be used to determine periodic income. In the following section, we compare cash basis accounting with traditional accrual basis accounting.

Cash Basis Accounting Versus Accrual Basis Accounting

Cash basis accounting defines revenues as cash inflows from earning activities, and expenses as cash outflows in earning activities. Frequently, cash inflows and outflows occur in different periods than the related events. For example, the purchase of machinery results in an immediate cash outflow but provides useful service over a period of years. **Accrual basis accounting** allows for such cases by recording the results of significant operating events when they occur rather than when cash is received or paid. Under accrual basis accounting, revenues are recognized when earned, regardless of when cash is received, and expenses are recognized when incurred, regardless of when cash is paid.

Because investors and creditors are interested in cash flows (see Chapter 2), wouldn't a simple cash basis income statement be preferable to an accrual basis statement? Most accountants think not. A cash basis system usually fails to provide valuable information about the earning capability of a firm. In addition, cash receipts and disbursements for successive periods are generally unrelated and can produce misleading trends.

Consider a college student who started a business, the Nimble Fingers Word Processing Service. The following events occurred during the first three months of the academic year.

September

Rented a computer for $25 on account.
Purchased paper for $30 on account.
Placed an advertisement in the campus newspaper for $40 on account.
Keyed several projects and charged customers a total fee of $200 on account.

October

Collected $200 in fees from customers.

November

Remitted payments to office equipment lessor, paper supplier, and campus newspaper.

Exhibit 3.4 shows the income statement and balance sheet under cash accounting. A close examination of these financial statements reveals some difficulties of cash basis accounting. If we evaluated the performance of Nimble Fingers based on the monthly cash flow figures, our conclusions would change from month to month. For September, we might conclude that the business accomplished nothing, because the financial statements contain all zeros. We know, however, that Nimble Fingers provided word processing services throughout September.

October appears more promising, with a large increase in net income, and we might conclude that the business is proving successful. This, however, is misleading, because we know, as early as the end of September, that of the $200 cash inflow reported in October, only $105 represents a return *on* invested capital, while the remaining $95 is a return *of* capital. This information is known, but the reporting is delayed under cash basis accounting.

The November income statement reports a net loss of $95. This turn of events leaves the outside observer unable to determine what might happen in December. The total net income for all three months is $105 ($0 + $200 − $95), which is accurate. What is not meaningful is the time period in which the $105 was disclosed. Under cash basis accounting, we must wait for the final cash payment in November before we have an accurate picture of the events for the first three months. This information was known with reasonable certainty as early as the end of September, but recognition was delayed until cash changed hands.

Accrual accounting alleviates these problems by recording net income when it was *earned* rather than when cash was collected or paid. Exhibit 3.5 presents the Nimble Fingers financial statements under accrual accounting. The information disclosed in September under accrual accounting differs markedly from that under cash accounting. Net income is disclosed in the period in which effort is applied to the word processing business, and accomplishments accrue as the jobs are completed. All net income is disclosed in September, when the main activities of the business were completed. After September, all that remains are the incidental activities of collecting customer accounts and satisfying creditor obligations. The income statement reflects this by attributing zero earnings to October and November. The balance sheet includes accounts receivable and accounts payable among the assets and liabilities in order to reconcile cash flow with revenue and expense recognition (Exhibit 3.3).

In both cash basis and accrual basis accounting, the net income for the period equals the change in the net assets, and the lifetime net income is $105. The two methods differ in the assignment of income to periods. Under accrual accounting, revenues and expenses are recorded at the earliest appearance of objective evidence, which frequently precedes cash flow. As a result, accrual accounting assigns income to the period in which it is earned, which is often a more timely measurement than that of cash basis accounting.

Measuring Income Under Accrual Accounting

Asset/Liability Measurement

The methods of measuring income under accrual accounting relate to the financial attributes used in measuring assets and liabilities, as discussed earlier in the chapter. Accrual basis income may be measured under historical cost, current cost, current exit value, expected exit value, and present value methods.

Exhibit 3.4   Financial Statements for Nimble Fingers Under Cash Basis Accounting

INCOME STATEMENT
(month ending)

	September	October	November
Revenues	$ —	$200	—
Expenses	—	—	$ 95
Net income (loss)	$ —	$200	$(95)

BALANCE SHEET
(last day of the month)

	September	October	November
Total assets (cash)	$ —	$200	$105
Owner's capital	$ —	$200	$105

To illustrate the various methods of measuring income under accrual accounting, consider the wholesaler Horizon Sales Inc. Horizon Sales has only one asset, an inventory of fur coats purchased on January 1, 1994. Information about the fur coats is as follows:

January 1, 1994

Fur coats are purchased at a cost of $100 000.

December 31, 1994

Current cost to replace the fur coats is $125 000.

Amount of cash that could be received in orderly liquidation (current exit value) of the fur coats is $133 000.

Amount of cash expected to be received for the fur coats after selling costs (expected exit value) is $135 000.

December 31, 1995

Fur coat inventory is sold for $144 000 on account.

January 1, 1996

$144 000 is collected from customers.

Historical Cost.   If the inventory of fur coats is measured under historical cost, recognition of income is delayed until the sale. This is consistent with the revenue realization principle, which requires that revenue be recorded only when the earning process is complete or virtually complete, and when the amount and timing of revenue are reasonably determinable. The objective evidence provided by the sale is usually necessary to satisfy the criteria for recognizing revenue. Therefore, net income of $44 000 ($144 000 − $100 000) would be recorded for Horizon Sales in 1995. Although historical cost is consistent with GAAP, it is helpful to understand the alternatives to conventional accounting methods.

Current Cost.   Under the current cost method, on December 31, 1994, Horizon Sales would write up the inventory to current cost ($125 000). The $25 000 difference between the beginning and ending balance of the inventory is called a holding gain (or holding

Exhibit 3.5 Financial Statements for Nimble Fingers Under Accrual Basis Accounting

INCOME STATEMENT
(month ending)

	September	October	November
Revenues	$200	$ —	—
Expenses	95	—	$ —
Net income (loss)	$105	$ —	$ —

BALANCE SHEET
(last day of the month)

	September	October	November
Cash	—	$200	$105
Accounts receivable	$200	—	—
Total assets	$200	$200	$105
Accounts payable	$ 95	$ 95	$ —
Owner's capital	105	105	105
Total liabilities and owner's capital	$200	$200	$105

loss if the ending balance is less than the beginning balance). The holding gain would be reported on the 1994 income statement. In 1995, the $19 000 difference between the selling price ($144 000) and the current cost valuation of the inventory on December 31, 1994 ($125 000) would be included in income.[16]

Current Exit Value. If we assume that the fur coats are reported at their current exit value, the holding gain for 1994 would be $33 000. This is the increase in the current exit value of the inventory from the beginning to the end of the period ($133 000 − $100 000 = $33 000). Horizon's 1995 current exit value income on the sale of the fur coats would be $11 000 ($144 000 − $133 000).

Expected Exit Value. As discussed previously, current exit value and expected exit value are likely to result in two different valuations of the same item because of the different assumptions used in each method. In the example of Horizon Sales, the holding gain for 1994 would be $35 000 ($135 000 − $100 000), while the expected exit value income recognized in 1995 would be $9000 ($144 000 − $135 000).

Present Value of Expected Cash Flows. To illustrate the measurement of earnings under present value, we must first assume that it was *known* when the fur coats were purchased on January 1, 1994, that $144 000 cash would be received for their sale two years later. This is, of course, an unrealistic assumption in the case of an inventory of fur coats.[17] As a result, we illustrate present value income measurement for Horizon Sales,

---

[16]If the current cost valuation of the inventory remained unchanged from December 31, 1994, to December 31, 1995, all of the $19 000 would be considered "current operating profit." If, however, the current cost valuation of the inventory changed during 1995, the $19 000 would be separated into two parts, current operating profit and holding gain. As an example, if the current cost valuation of the inventory was $134 000 on December 31, 1995, then $10 000 ($144 000 − $134 000) would be current operating profit, and $9000 ($134 000 − $125-000) would be a holding gain.

[17]The assumption of perfect foreknowledge is not so unreasonable in the case of assets and liabilities resulting in fixed cash flows. Examples include notes receivable and payable, which are contracts for certain cash flows in the future. In these cases, a present value approach is generally accepted.

bearing in mind the limitations of this approach to assets and liabilities with uncertain future cash flows.

Horizon Sales invested $100 000 in an asset (fur coats) that will be worth $144 000 in two years. The *annual* rate of growth necessary to increase the inventory from its present value of $100 000 to the future value of $144 000 is 20 percent.[18] For 1994, the investment is assumed to grow by 20 percent, or $20 000 ($100 000 × 0.20). Therefore, the inventory has a value of $120 000 on December 31, 1994. The $20 000, or the difference between the beginning and ending inventory valuation, is the income earned and reported in 1994. For 1995, the investment has a beginning value of $120 000. A 20 percent annual return on this amount yields $24 000 ($120 000 × 0.20) and increases the value of the inventory to $144 000. This is not a coincidence. The annual rate of return is determined so that the inventory balance increases to the selling amount of $144 000. The income earned in 1995 would be $24 000, and the increase in the inventory balance would reflect the 20 percent rate of return.

Summary

The net income of Horizon Sales under all five methods is summarized in Exhibit 3.6. Clearly, the *total income* on the sale of the fur coats is $44 000. The question is how to assign the $44 000 return on investment to the two periods. Under GAAP (historical cost), the $44 000 is reported in 1995, the year of the sale. Under the four alternatives to historical cost, at least part of the $44 000 is reported in 1994. This points to a frequent criticism of historical cost, namely, the delay in recognizing income. Critics of the historical cost method suggest that alternatives are generally more timely in the recognition of income and are therefore more relevant to users of financial statements in their attempts to predict future cash flows.

Historical cost proponents counter that the alternatives are too unreliable and also generate income numbers that are less likely to result in cash flows. For example, if the fur coats were sold for only $100 000 on December 31, 1995, the current cost and exit value (current and expected) methods would recognize income in 1994 and a loss in 1995. Supporters of historical cost argue that the reporting of income in 1994 under these methods could have harmed users, because that income failed to materialize. The uncertainty of eventual cash realization was too great and resulted in the reversal in 1995 of income recognized in 1994.

Components of Net Income

Net income is composed of revenues, expenses, gains, and losses. Each component can be defined according to the asset/liability view or the revenue/expense view. According to the **asset/liability view**, the components of net income are defined by reference to definitions of assets and liabilities. Under the **revenue/expense view**, the components of net income are defined without reference to definitions of assets and liabilities. Both views are used in practice, but the FASB and CICA currently favour the asset/liability view implied in the following definitions, which we presented in Chapter 2:[19]

---

[18]The annual rate of return can be determined with the aid of present value interest tables. Use of these tables is discussed in Chapter 7.

[19]"Financial Statement Concepts," CICA *Handbook*, Paragraphs 1000.37–40, March 1991.

Exhibit 3.6 Net Income of Horizon Sales Inc. for 1994 and 1995 Under Five Asset Valuation Methods			
Net Income Method	**1994**	**1995**	**Total**
Historical cost	—	$44 000	$44 000
Current cost	$25 000	19 000	44 000
Current exit value	33 000	11 000	44 000
Expected exit value	35 000	9 000	44 000
Present value of expected cash flows	20 000	24 000	44 000

1. **Revenues.** Inflows or other enhancements of assets of an entity or settlements of its liabilities or both during a period, based on production and delivery of goods, provision of services, and other activities that constitute the entity's major operations. Examples are sales revenue, interest revenue, and rent revenue. The major source of revenue is dependent on the type of operation. For example, a revenue source to one corporation may be considered miscellaneous income to another corporation.
2. **Expenses.** Outflows or other use of assets or incurrences of liabilities or both during a period as a result of delivering or producing goods, rendering services, or carrying out other activities that constitute the entity's ongoing major or central operations. Examples are cost of goods sold, salaries expense, and advertising expense.
3. **Gains.** Increases in owners' equity (net assets) from peripheral or incidental transactions of an entity and from all other transactions and events affecting the entity during a period, except those that result from revenues or investments by owners. Examples are a gain on the sale of capital assets and a gain on the early retirement of long-term debt.
4. **Losses.** Decreases in owners' equity (net assets) from peripheral or incidental transactions of an entity and from all other transactions and events affecting the entity during a period, except those that result from expenses or distributions to owners. Examples are losses on the sale of investments and on litigation.

Notice the references to assets, liabilities, and owners' equity (net assets). The components of net income are *not* defined independently of definitions of assets and liabilities. In a sense, the definitions of assets and liabilities are the reference point for the definitions of revenues, expenses, gains, and losses. This is called the asset/liability view.

According to the alternative conceptual approach—the revenue/expense view—revenues, expenses, gains, and losses are defined without direct reference to definitions of assets and liabilities. Proponents of this view disagree about the correct definition of the components of income, but they generally view revenues as a measure of the operating accomplishments of the enterprise in a particular period and expenses as the efforts necessary to generate the revenues for the period. Fundamental to this position is the principle

Matching

of matching expenses with revenues. Under the revenue/expense view, how we define assets and liabilities is secondary to how we define revenues and expenses. Assets and liabilities are essentially the debits and credits that remain after revenues and expenses are properly matched on the income statement.

Both the asset/liability view and the revenue/expense view are compatible with financial statements that *articulate* with one another. **Articulated financial statements**, which are the kind produced under GAAP, are fundamentally related or tied to one another.

The major issue in the asset/liability and revenue/expense controversy is which definition should take precedence. This is far from a trivial concern. Critics of the revenue/
expense view believe that the matching principle lacks objectivity. Furthermore, they
believe the income statement may be open to recognition of revenues and expenses that
are not changes in assets or liabilities. It is suggested that such revenues and expenses are
meaningless in understanding the change in wealth of a business. Under the revenue/
expense view, the balance sheet can become a "dumping ground" for nonresources and
nonobligations because of vague definitions of revenues and expenses. Supporters of the
asset/liability view impose an objective limit on what will be considered as admissible
revenues, expenses, gains, and losses. Only transactions that increase or decrease the
assets or liabilities of an enterprise can be considered revenues or expenses.

As indicated earlier, current practice reflects a *combination of both views*, which
makes the distinction between them difficult to observe. The CICA and the FASB have
decided to emphasize one view in order to guide future accounting policy decisions.
Because the accounting standard setters have supported the asset/liability view, we have
embraced this view throughout the conceptual discussion in this chapter.[20]

Usefulness of Accounting Net Income

In the mid-1960s, many critics of financial reporting argued that the net income number
was meaningless. They based their opposition on continued adherence to historical cost,
which they thought misrepresented reality. In addition, sceptics denounced the diversity
of acceptable accounting methods (e.g., weighted average versus FIFO in inventory costing) for determining net income. They suggested that managers could disclose net income
in various ways according to GAAP because of the lack of uniform measurement principles. Indeed, one author showed how identical firms could produce an earnings per
share of either $0.80 or $1.79, depending on the choice of accounting principles.[21] Critics
asserted that such ambiguity reduced the credibility of accounting income numbers as a
source of information to statement users. One financial analyst described the situation
this way:

> The accountant defines it [earnings] as what he gets when he matches costs against rev-
> enues, making any necessary allocations of costs to prior periods; or as the change in the
> equity account over the period. These costs are not economic definitions of earnings but
> merely descriptions of the motions the accountant goes through to arrive at the earnings
> number.[22]

Fortunately, subsequent research on the usefulness of net income disclosures has
lessened many of these concerns. One classic study investigated whether knowledge of
the next year's net income would be sufficient to earn superior returns in the price of a
company's shares.[23] Obviously, if such advance knowledge could not be used in profitable
investment strategy, it would be of little value. Results of this study indicated that if just

---

[20]"Financial Statement Concepts," CICA *Handbook*, Paragraphs 1000.44–52, March 1991.

[21]The illustration was provided by Leonard Spacek, "Business Success Requires an Understanding of Unsolved
Problems of Accounting and Financial Reporting," in J. Lories and R. Brealey, eds., *Modern Developments in
Investment Management* (New York: Praeger, 1972), pp. 630–44.

[22]Jack Treynor, "The Trouble with Earnings," *Financial Analysts Journal* (September 1972), p. 41.

[23]Ray Ball and Phillip Brown, "An Empirical Investigation of Accounting Income Numbers," *Journal of
Accounting Research* (Autumn 1968), pp. 159–78.

the direction of change in the next year's net income was known for a number of companies, investment decisions would consistently produce better-than-average returns. This suggests that disclosure of net income has value for investors.

Although strong evidence indicates that the net income number is useful for investor decision making, it says nothing about the timeliness of net income disclosures. Such information could have already reached investors in other forms. Investors could use alternative sources of information, such as investment advisory services and government reports, to estimate the current earnings of a company.

A study was conducted to test the timeliness of net income disclosures.[24] This study investigated whether present and potential investors reacted to the initial disclosure of the accounting net income number. Initial disclosure of a corporation's quarterly or annual earnings precedes the dissemination of quarterly or annual reports to shareholders. Major stock exchanges require listed companies to release earnings announcements to the press and wire services as soon as the information becomes available. Most Canadian corporations release earnings data via the provincial securities commission where they are registered and also provide this information directly to the news services. The earnings release is then printed in the business section of most major newspapers. Exhibit 3.7 shows typical annual and quarterly earnings data. If information in the release had already reached investors, we would not expect them to react to the net income disclosure. The study found that the volume of trading increases dramatically in the week the net income disclosure is released publicly, compared to the rest of the year. This finding supports the timeliness of net income disclosure.

Evidence strongly suggests that accounting net income is both useful and timely to investors in their buying and selling decisions. However, the question remains: Why do investors perceive the net income number as relevant information? The significance of net income can be viewed in two interrelated ways. In one sense, net income is a measure of *past* performance; in another sense, it is an indicator of *future* cash flows. These uses are discussed in the following sections.

Net Income as a Measure of Past Performance

A business enterprise begins operations by obtaining financing from its owners, and possibly from creditors. The cash received is then converted into labour, raw materials, plant, equipment, and other inputs of production. The goal of the organization is to convert these inputs to an output (product) whose value is greater than the sum of the inputs. This is accomplished by adding time, form, and place utility to the inputs. For example, grapes from the Rhine Valley can be pressed into wine; the bottled wine is then aged for several years, after which it may be shipped to a liquor store in Toronto. The inputs, including vineyard, wine press, storage area, and shipping, combine to produce a fine table wine that can be sold for an amount greater than the sum of the input costs. This is accomplished by adding time (the aging process), form (grapes to wine), and place (Germany to Toronto) to the product. This can be characterized as the **earning process** of the firm.

The earning process and financing activities of a firm become interrelated through time. Because firms must compete for investment dollars, the amount and cost of funds that a firm can obtain is a function of its earnings performance relative to other companies. Earnings tell owners and creditors how efficiently management converts inputs to

---

[24]William Beaver, "The Information Content of Annual Earnings Announcements," *Journal of Accounting Research* (Supplement 1968), pp. 67–92.

Exhibit 3.7 Earnings Announcement		

BCE Inc.

Year Dec. 31:	1991	1990
($ millions, except per share amounts)		
Revenues	$19 884	$18 373
Net income	1 329	1 062
Share earnings: net income	4.01	3.91
Quarter:		
Revenues	5 272	4 875
Net income	368	345
Share earnings: net income	1.11	1.05

Source: BCE Inc., *1991 Annual Report*.

outputs. Successful firms, as demonstrated by past earnings activities, enjoy a competitive advantage in the financing markets. In contrast, less successful firms may find their sources of capital diminished or unavailable. The result can be the final liquidation of an inefficient firm.

The earnings of an enterprise can be viewed as a "report card" of management's performance. Did management responsibly utilize the resources entrusted to them? If not, the shareholders have two choices: they can replace existing management, or they can sell their interest in the firm. However, the evaluation of management performance can be very difficult, especially if based solely on net income. Assume, for example, that the latest year-to-year net income results of a company show a 10 percent decrease. From this information alone, we might conclude that past performance is poor. However, if we know that during the same period the net income of all firms in the economy decreased by an average of 30 percent, we might conclude that our company performed well. An informed user of financial statements should also recognize that many events affecting a company's performance, such as floods and earthquakes, are beyond management's control.

Net Income as a Predictor of Cash Flows

Net income not only helps investors and creditors to evaluate the past performance of a firm, it also helps them to predict the cash returns they will receive. For shareholders, the value of shares relates to future dividends. For example, the price of a share is generally higher when shareholders expect to receive larger dividends, other things being equal. As a result, shareholders want information that helps them predict future dividends. Net income disclosures may be useful in this regard, because future dividends depend on future earnings.[25]

As a first step in predicting cash flow, present earnings should be separated into a transitory component and a permanent component.[26] The **transitory component** of net income is that part that investors do not expect again in the near future. Transitory income can result from unusual or incidental activities of limited duration or in uncon-

---

[25]"Future-Oriented Financial Information," CICA *Handbook*, Section 4250, 1989.

[26]A more detailed discussion of these two components of earnings and reporting considerations can be found in "Reporting Earnings," *FASB Discussion Memorandum*, 1979.

ventional markets. For example, a publishing company purchases a downtown parking lot as the site for a future office building. Until construction begins, the company operates the parking lot and collects parking fees. The parking fees are income of limited duration (until construction begins), are incidental to the main function of the company (publishing), and are therefore not expected to continue. Transitory income (or loss) can also result from unusual events, such as a casualty loss from an earthquake or an expropriation of capital assets by a foreign country.

The **permanent component** of net income is the part that investors expect to continue. Permanent income results from the primary functions of the enterprise. In the publishing company example, permanent income is generated from producing and marketing books. Permanent income is affected by changes in the demand for books, the price of the books, and the cost of producing the books.

Predictably, investors focus on permanent earnings because only they are useful in predicting income. Transitory earnings are not expected to affect future income. Because accounting policy makers, such as the FASB in the United States and the CICA in Canada, understand the importance of distinguishing between the two components of net income, various types of transitory earnings must presently be identified. In Chapter 4, we explore the reporting requirements for several of these nonrecurring events. Unfortunately, the financial reporting requirements for net income do not permit these two types of earnings to be clearly distinguished from each other.[27]

Creditors and investors have similar needs, but whereas investors are concerned with the ability of a firm to pay dividends, creditors are interested in the ability of a firm to make interest and principal payments on loans. Both investors and creditors are forward-looking in this regard. As a result, creditors also focus on the permanent component of net income in assessing the future earnings capability of the firm. Future earnings protect interest payments, because interest is paid to creditors before dividends are distributed to shareholders.

As the needs of investors and creditors are satisfied, so too are the needs of other users. Customers, for example, are interested in the longevity of an enterprise, especially if warranty contracts exist or if support is necessary for the product line (as in the case of computer equipment). Employees are concerned with job security and compensation; in both cases, the permanent net income can help predict employee income.

In summary, a firm's earnings are useful in making investment decisions. Net income reflects past performance and suggests future performance. Net income can tell financial statement users where the firm has been and, to a more limited degree, where it is going.

In present accounting practice, terms such as *net income* and *net earnings* are used interchangeably, and we make no distinction between them in this textbook. The FASB has indicated that in the future, however, it will attempt to enhance the usefulness of the income measurement by distinguishing between an enterprise's **earnings** and **comprehensive income**. Earnings will be considered a measure of an enterprise's performance during a period and will measure the extent to which revenues and gains associated with cash-to-cash cycles substantially completed during a period exceed expenses and losses associated with the same cycles. Comprehensive income will be considered a broad measure comprising all recognized changes in owners' equity except those resulting from investments by owners and distributions to owners. Certain transactions and events (e.g., changes in the market value of investments in marketable equity securities classified as noncurrent assets) will be included in the determination of comprehensive income but

---

[27]"Financial Statement Concepts," CICA *Handbook,* Paragraph 1000.37, March 1991.

will be excluded from earnings. The concepts of earnings and comprehensive income will likely evolve gradually over time. We explain the distinction between these concepts more fully in Chapter 5.

Financial Forecasts

Thus far in this chapter we have presented information about *past* and *current measurements*. However, financial statement users want information about the ability of a business to generate income *in the future*. Some observers have suggested that enterprises could provide this information directly to financial statement users in the form of published financial forecasts.

A **financial forecast** is a presentation that shows an enterprise's *expected* future financial position, results of operations, and cash flows based on conditions that management expects to exist and actions it expects to take. A financial forecast contrasts with a **financial projection**, which shows future financial position, results of operations, and cash flows that would exist if one or more *hypothetical* (but not expected) conditions or actions occurred. In other words, forecasts present what management *expects* to happen, while projections present what *would* happen if certain unexpected events (e.g., a labour strike) occurred. At the present time, neither of these two types of **prospective financial statements** is required by GAAP. However, some companies have in the past voluntarily disclosed financial forecasts, and there has been considerable discussion about the desirability of requiring the publication of forecasts by all companies as a part of GAAP.

Constructing a financial forecast requires making assumptions about the future state of the overall economy and the interaction of the firm with the economy. The accuracy of forecasts is directly related to the accuracy of these assumptions. As a result, some people have advocated publishing a range of forecasts during a given period. In this way, financial statement users would be aware of management's range of expectations, from pessimistic to optimistic, and could then select a scenario consistent with their own expectations.

In 1973, the Securities and Exchange Commission (SEC) reversed its long-standing opposition to public disclosure of financial forecasts by issuing guidelines for voluntary disclosures to be filed with the commission. Since that time, there has been a great deal of controversy about mandated public disclosure of financial forecasts. Various surveys have found widespread dissatisfaction with the concept of published financial forecasts.[28] In 1983 the Ontario and Quebec securities commissions adopted policies designed to improve future-oriented financial information. These policies arose from a survey conducted by the Ontario Securities Commission, which found major deviations between budgets and actual data.[29] Few companies publish financial forecasts. The Ontario and Quebec Securities Commissions followed the lead of the Securities and Exchange Commission (SEC) in the United States. For the rest of this chapter, we briefly discuss the arguments favouring and opposing public disclosure of financial forecasts.

Benefits of Public Disclosure

The major argument in favour of requiring disclosure of financial forecasts is that this disclosure would provide useful information to users of financial statements. Proponents

---

[28]See, for example, *Public Accounting in Transition: A Survey by Opinion Research Corporation* (Chicago: Arthur Andersen & Co., 1974), pp. 106, 107.

[29]"OSC Investigates Budget/Actual Shortfalls," *The Bottom Line* (April 1990), p. 17.

Steep Grade to FOFI

A new frontier is conquered as accounting standard setters approve *Handbook* Recommendations for FOFI

It's been a long and winding road to "Accounting Standards for Future-oriented Financial Information" (FOFI). So accounting standard setters have approached this relatively new frontier of financial information, which is well outside the boundaries of historical financial statements, with more than a little trepidation.

From its inception, delays have marked this section's passage. The uphill climb began in October 1982, when the AcSC approved a research proposal on financial forecasts aimed at developing standards covering the presentation and disclosure of financial forecasts in prospectuses, takeover bids, issuer bids, information circulars and interim and annual reporting. The first step, taken mainly to satisfy the Ontario Securities Commission, was to issue a guideline on financial forecasts in June 1983. It took another six years and the proposed standards' re-exposure to bring us to where we are today.

The re-exposure draft elicited 68 responses that the committee considered carefully in the course of drafting the final material. Many respondents expressed support for the re-exposure, while others limited their comments to specific issues. The few who expressed disagreement, or major concerns, focused on the lack of guidance on preparing FOFI, particularly for an entity in its startup phase.

Though the final material does reflect some changes, much has stayed the same. The distinction between limited use and general use (albeit under the terms "general purpose" and "special purpose") has been retained, as has the distinction between a forecast and a projection. The measurement standards focus on the quality of the assumptions underlying FOFI, the time period covered (not to extend beyond the time such information can be reasonably estimated) and the accounting policies to be used—which, incidentally, are the same as for historical financial statements.

Other areas remaining the same are special-purpose and general-purpose FOFI. The latter is presented in the format of historical financial statements and is to include, at the very least, an income statement, while the former is presented in the degree of detail and the format agreed to by the parties concerned.

Again, what hasn't changed is that both projections and forecasts must disclose a cautionary note indicating that results will vary, and must be labelled as either a forecast or a projection. Thus, it is essential to clearly state the effective date of the assumptions and the extent to which actual financial results are incorporated, as well as all aspects of significant assumptions, their nature and character, including hypotheses.

What's more, if the FOFI incorporates a change in accounting policy, that change and its effect must be duly noted. When special-purpose FOFI is presented, the identity of the intended users and the purpose of the information is to be disclosed, along with a caution that it may not be useful for other purposes—the same caution in effect when a projection is presented.

A good number of respondents made some useful suggestions regarding terminology which the committee adopted, among them the suggestion that "general use" and "limited use" should be defined by the terms of each engagement, and that a more useful distinction would be "general purpose" and "special purpose."

Certain other phrases were deemed problematic. For instance, one respondent thought the term "hypothetical assumptions" implied a "groundless assumption," while another pointed out that the phrase was internally redundant, since all assumptions are by nature hypothetical. In response to this, the word "hypothesis" was substituted for hypothetical assumptions.

In fact, the majority of comments concerned assumptions. Many respondents wanted to know how many types there were, how to define them and what standards they had to meet. Most wanted to know, for example, if it was true that there were only two types of assumptions (most probable and hypothetical), since neither was characterized specifically but was defined solely within the context of a forecast and a projection.

(Forecasts are based entirely on assumptions reflecting the entity's planned courses of action for the period covered, given management's judgment concerning the most-probable set of economic conditions. Projections are also based on these most-probable assumptions, in addition to a single hypothesis (or more)—which is an assumption consistent with the information's purpose but not necessarily the most probable in management's judgment.)

Everyone knows assumptions should be complete and internally consistent. Many respondents felt, however, that there should be more of an explanation provided about what constitutes "reasonable" and "suitably supported" ones.

Continued

The committee tackled the issue by requiring that all assumptions be "appropriate"—complete, internally consistent and reasonable. "Reasonable," in the context of "most probable," requires that the assumptions be consistent with planned courses of action for the period covered and, in the context of a hypothesis, that the hypothesis represent plausible circumstances and be consistent with the projection's purpose.

The final material also provides more guidance on what constitutes sufficient support. To be supportable, assumptions need to be based on an entity's past performance (or on that of similar entities, feasibility and marketing studies or other sources of objective corroboration). A hypothesis, however, does not have to be supportable.

Some respondents would have preferred more detailed preparation guidance, similar to that issued by the American Institute of Certified Public Accountants. But the committee decided such guidance was beyond the *Handbook*'s mandate, since it establishes general principles rather than detailed rules.

Respondents supported the requirement that the time period covered by FOFI not extend beyond the point where assumptions can be reasonably estimated. Though most agreed that forecasts normally encompass a relatively short period, some urged that an actual limit be set. The committee, however, was reluctant to table a limit for two reasons: (1) it wanted to avoid setting an arbitrary limit unless it was absolutely necessary; and (2) it believes situations will arise where assumptions can be supported for a longer period.

Many respondents also noted that disclosing all primary financial statements provides the user with better information than the statement of operations alone. The statement of cash flows provides a better picture of what cash flows can be expected and helps minimize the problem of arbitrary allocations in the income statements. The balance sheet provides information on economic resources, obligations and equity. The danger in not presenting all primary financial statements is that it might appear that the information omitted has been left out for a reason.

The committee resisted the temptation to require the presentation of all primary financial statements for general-purpose FOFI because FOFI's objective is to dictate which statements are the most relevant. Preparing a full set may place an unnecessary burden on the preparer in certain situations. And, since earnings per share is of particular interest to many users, the committee believes the income statement remains the statement to be mandated.

Both the committee and the respondents agreed that the presentation format for special-purpose FOFI should be in the form of a Recommendation, as opposed to being part of explanatory paragraphs—a decision that has now been acted on.

What concerned several respondents more than format was that the issues pertaining to startup entities weren't fully addressed in the re-exposure draft. The committee also wanted to redress this weakness, since entities in their startup phase are important users of FOFI, and the section would lose much of its usefulness if it couldn't be applied to them.

For that reason, it added an example with the proviso that such entities would often find it necessary to prepare projections rather than forecasts, particularly when certain key assumptions aren't supportable (due to a lack of historical data) and, as a result, don't meet the most-probable assumptions criteria.

Another concern of respondents was that the material stated that management was responsible for assumptions, but not for FOFI as a whole. Deciding this was a point well-taken, the committee amended the document to clarify management's responsibility in this regard.

The committee further agreed with respondents who thought the section should not be silent on the preparer's obligation to compare FOFI to actual information, to withdraw it when warranted by unusual circumstances, and to disclose subsequent changes, recognizing the user should be aware that it is prepared as of the effective date and its useful life is limited.

The committee did not think it possible or appropriate, however, to set rules that would apply in all situations. As a result, it decided the appropriate course of action was to inform users of the obligation the preparer was willing to assume. Should the preparer not assume responsibility for updating the FOFI, this fact should be disclosed.

With this last decision, the steep incline toward FOFI accounting standards has leveled out. *Handbook* Section 4250 will be published concurrently with the related auditing guideline, "Examination of a Financial Forecast or Projection Included in a Prospectus or Other Public Offering Document."

Source: Reprinted, with permission, from "Steep Grade to FOFI," *CA Magazine* (August 1989), pp. 49–50. Published by the Canadian Institute of Chartered Accountants, Toronto, Canada.

of requiring financial forecasts have argued that forecasts are essential for making more accurate predictions, which lead to informed investment and credit decisions. Investors and creditors could benefit from learning about management's plans and expectations. Relative to the outside investor, management generally knows more about the firm and at least as much about the impact of the external environment.

Managers could also benefit from the publication of financial forecasts. Financial forecasts put managers' reputations at stake and so provide a strong incentive to achieve the forecasted figures. Moreover, preparing forecasts for publication forces managers to plan for the future. Such planning may enable managers to take advantage of opportunities and avoid mistakes in judgement.

Some people argue that reporting forecasts is in the public interest because it reduces the opportunities for privileged insiders to profit from information that is not publicly available. Further, some argue that although certain forecasted information regularly appears in the business section of newspapers, the forecasts do not contain management's assumptions and are not subjected to the rigorous standards that would be applied if forecasts were a required part of GAAP.

Costs of Public Disclosure

The publication of financial forecasts has some serious limitations. A major concern is the possible misinterpretation of the forecasts by financial statement users. Because many investors are untrained in interpreting financial forecasts, they are likely to be unaware of the uncertainty of forecasts. Statement users may also have difficulty interpreting the variety of assumptions underlying a forecast. Moreover, across various firms, different forecast assumptions would lead to difficulty in comparing forecasts.

Another possible source of misinterpretation is management's tendency to bias forecasts. Managers may present overly optimistic forecasts to place the firm in the most favourable light. Such forecasts may help a firm obtain bank loans or may raise the share price, but the forecasts may also harm unwary investors as the actual operating results emerge. Likewise, managers may decide to play it safe by issuing overly conservative forecasts that are almost certain to be attained. If the forecast is exceeded, all the better. Unfortunately, outside investors may be misled into selling the shares or avoiding their initial purchase, only to find that the company was more prosperous than anticipated.

This tendency to bias forecasts can be mitigated by having an independent auditor examine the reasonableness of the assumptions. The auditor's report would state that an examination of the underlying assumptions was made and that they were found to be reasonable. However, because assumptions can prove faulty, the report would not guarantee future performance.

Management has long opposed the publication of financial forecasts because of the possibility of disclosing sensitive information, such as major marketing, product, or investment strategies. Competitors could develop counter-strategies to block a firm from realizing its goals, which, of course, would not benefit the forecasting company or its shareholders.

Another serious limitation of financial forecasts is the potential legal liability. What happens if actual results deviate sharply from forecasts? Blaming management for inaccurate forecasts is questionable when there has been an honest attempt to plan properly, make full disclosure, and manage as efficiently as possible. For example, airlines could not have predicted the effect of the 1973 OPEC oil embargo on their operating costs or the reduction in travel during the Persian Gulf War. To hold the airlines responsible for inaccurate forecasts under these circumstances would be unfair.

Some observers argue further that managers should not engage in the investment function by making financial forecasts. These critics suggest that financial forecasting is largely the domain of investors, who either reap the rewards of accurate forecasting or incur the penalties of inaccurate forecasting. Harvey Kapnick of Arthur Andersen & Co. has stated that "predictions of the future must be the responsibility of the investor. This is the essence of risk taking, and predicting and interpreting the future is the primary function in investment evaluation. No one can take action to insure [through lawsuits] the results of future events."[30]

Concluding Remarks

The issue of mandated disclosure of financial forecasts will be controversial for some time. In Canada, various securities and exchange commissions and the CICA have echoed the statements of the SEC and the FASB, which have been emphasizing disclosures that are future oriented. In contrast, most managers have opposed the concept for most of the reasons listed previously. In terms of the qualitative characteristics we presented in Chapter 2, proponents of financial forecasts argue that forecasts are relevant, while opponents argue that the information lacks sufficient reliability. At this time, it is difficult to predict the outcome of this controversy.

Financial accounting is constantly changing to achieve greater relevance and reliability. It is a discipline that has many interesting conceptual controversies. An understanding of only the present system of GAAP will not likely be adequate for a person whose future career will be spent preparing or using financial statements. Indeed, the education of the professional accountant (and other professional people) is continuous. You should think of a university degree program as a foundation on which to build knowledge and skills that will adapt to changing circumstances in an exciting world.

In this chapter, we have presented a conceptual discussion of the nature and measurement of the elements of financial statements. Throughout this discussion, we have presented alternatives to the present accounting model to acquaint you with not only what is presently accepted but also what may be accepted in the future. An understanding of this chapter should broaden your understanding of accounting and should help you to accommodate more contemporary accounting ideas. Moreover, this conceptual material should enhance your understanding of present generally accepted accounting principles. Current practice employs, to varying degrees, many of the ideas and valuation methods discussed in this chapter. In Chapter 4, we extend our presentation of GAAP for external reporting with an overview of the major financial statements.

Key Points

1. "Measurement" refers to the assignment of numbers to objects and events. To measure the elements of financial statements, we must select a measuring unit and a financial attribute to measure. (Objective 1)

2. The measuring units that have been suggested for use in financial statements are nominal dollars and constant dollars. A nominal dollar has not been adjusted for

---

[30]"Forecasting Earnings," *Forbes* (December 1, 1972), p. 37.

inflation or deflation; a constant dollar has been adjusted. Conventional financial statements use nominal dollars. (Objective 1)

3. A general price-level index indicates changes over time in the overall level of prices in the economy. A specific price index indicates changes over time in the price of a specific good or service. (Objective 1)

4. Purchasing power gains and losses are reported when financial statements are presented in constant dollars. These gains and losses result from holding monetary assets or liabilities during periods of inflation or deflation. (Objective 1)

5. Assets are probable future economic benefits that accrue to an entity as a result of past transactions or events. (Objective 2)

6. Financial attributes of assets include historical cost, current cost, current exit value in orderly liquidation, expected exit value in due course of business, and present value of expected cash flows. Conventional financial statements reflect a mixture of these attributes, although historical cost is emphasized. (Objective 2)

7. Liabilities are probable future sacrifices of economic benefits that obligate an entity to transfer assets or perform services in the future as a result of past transactions or events. (Objective 2)

8. Important issues in liability measurement are (1) whether the interest inherent in a liability should be recognized separately, and (2) what interest rate should be used to recognize the interest. (Objective 2)

9. Financial attributes of liabilities include present value of expected cash flows, expected exit value in due course of business, historical proceeds, current proceeds, and current exit value in orderly liquidation. Conceptually, a liability should be measured on a present value basis; many liabilities are measured this way under GAAP. (Objective 2)

10. Owners' equity equals net assets, which are assets minus liabilities. Owners' equity is not measured as an independent element of financial statements. Instead, its valuation depends on the valuations assigned to the individual assets and liabilities. (Objective 2)

11. Net income measures the change in net assets for a period of time, assuming no new capital contributions by the owners or dividend distributions by the business. (Objective 3)

12. Net income should be recognized only after the capital used from the beginning of the period is maintained. (Objective 3)

13. Lifetime net income is the total income of an enterprise from inception to termination. Lifetime revenues of an enterprise equal the total cash received from earning activities, and lifetime expenses equal the total cash disbursed for earning activities.

14. Periodic net income is the change in the wealth of a business over a short period of time, generally one year. (Objective 3)

15. Accrual basis accounting is generally preferred over cash basis accounting, because earnings disclosures under the accrual basis are more timely and less subject to unimportant fluctuations. (Objective 3)

16. Net income measurement under accrual accounting depends on the valuation concepts used to measure assets and liabilities. Unlike lifetime net income, periodic net income is affected by the valuation concepts employed. (Objective 3)

17. Net income is composed of revenues, expenses, gains, and losses. Each component can be defined by the asset/liability or revenue/expense view. According to the asset/liability view, the components of net income are defined by direct reference to definitions of assets and liabilities. Under the revenue/expense view, the components of net income are defined without reference to definitions of assets and liabilities. Both concepts are used in practice, but the CICA supports the asset/liability view. (Objective 3)

18. Strong evidence supports both the usefulness and timeliness of accounting net income. (Objective 4)

19. Accounting net income can be used to evaluate past performance and predict future earnings. (Objective 4)

20. Financial forecasts represent certain financial expectations of management. Considerable controversy presently exists about the possibility of requiring the publication of financial forecasts. The majority opinion today appears to be that the benefits of providing useful information, providing managerial incentives, reducing insider profits, and improving the forecast information that is currently published are outweighed by the costs of misinterpretation, biased forecasts, competitive disadvantages, potential legal liability, and the philosophy that future predictions are the responsibility of investors and creditors, not accountants. (Objective 5)

Questions

Q3.1 What does "measurement" mean? Why is measurement important in accounting?

Q3.2 What is the difference between nominal dollars and constant dollars? Which one of these measuring units does GAAP require? Why?

Q3.3 What is the difference between a general price-level index and a specific price index?

Q3.4 What are purchasing-power gains and losses? Are they reported in conventional financial statements? Explain why or why not.

Q3.5 Identify three essential characteristics of assets, and give ten examples of assets under GAAP.

Q3.6 Identify and define the financial attributes that may be used to measure assets.

Q3.7 Identify three essential characteristics of liabilities and give ten examples of liabilities under GAAP.

Q3.8 Identify and define the financial attributes that may be used to measure liabilities.

Q3.9 What does the term "owners' equity" mean? How does owners' equity differ from liabilities? Give five examples of items classified as owners' equity under GAAP.

Q3.10 How is owners' equity measured in conventional financial statements?

Q3.11 Provide a conceptual definition of "net income."

Q3.12 Explain the term "capital maintenance." Why is this concept important in determining income for a period?

Q3.13 What is lifetime net income? What are some distinguishing characteristics of lifetime net income? How does lifetime net income differ from periodic net income?

Q3.14 Define cash basis accounting. What are some disadvantages of this system?

Q3.15 Define accrual basis accounting. How can this system produce periodic net income numbers that are different under cash basis accounting for the same periods?

Q3.16 What are the advantages and disadvantages of using historical cost to determine income?

Q3.17 What are the components of net income? How are they similar?

Q3.18 How does the revenue/expense view of net income differ from the asset/liability view?

Q3.19 Is accounting net income a useful number? What are the uses of the accounting net income disclosure?

Q3.20 What is a financial forecast? What are the major advantages and disadvantages of future-oriented financial information?

Problems

P3.1 Nominal-Dollar Versus Constant-Dollar Measurement. Jim Arnold invested $300 000 in a parcel of land on January 1, 1995. He sold the land for $320 000 on December 31, 1995. The Consumer Price Index was 100 on January 1, 1995, and 105 on December 31, 1995.

Instructions

(a) Compute the gain or loss on the sale in accordance with GAAP. Disregard income taxes.
(b) Compute the gain or loss on the sale in constant end-of-1995 dollars. Disregard income taxes.
(c) Based only on the information presented above, was Arnold better or worse off at the end of 1995 than at the beginning? Explain your answer.
(d) In your opinion, should financial statements continue to emphasize the nominal-dollar measuring unit, or should they emphasize the constant-dollar measuring unit? Present arguments to support your position.

P3.2   Nominal-Dollar Versus Constant-Dollar Measurement.   At the beginning of 1995, Anne Reed purchased 2000 of Lambert Limited's common shares for $50 per share. During 1995, the general price level declined by 5 percent. At the end of 1995, Reed sold the 2000 shares for $48 per share.

Instructions

(a) Compute the gain or loss on the sale in accordance with GAAP. Disregard income taxes.
(b) Compute the gain or loss on the sale in constant end-of-1995 dollars. Disregard income taxes.
(c) Based only on the information presented above, was Reed better or worse off at the end of 1995 than at the beginning? Explain your answer.
(d) Did Reed have a purchasing power gain during 1995? Did she have a purchasing power loss during 1995? Explain your answers.

P3.3   Purchasing-Power Gains and Losses.   On January 1, 1995, Rice, Inc., sold merchandise to Tully, Inc. for $180 000 on account. Assume inflation was 10 percent during 1995, and as of December 31, 1995, Rice had not received the $180 000 payment due from Tully.

Instructions

(a) Calculate the amount of purchasing power gain or loss for Rice and for Tully.
(b) Explain why each company had a purchasing power gain or loss.
(c) Are purchasing power gains and losses reported in conventional financial statements? Why or why not?

P3.4   Nature of Assets.   You have been asked to determine whether each of the following items is an asset of Purdy Limited:

(1) One hundred of Seagram's common shares that Purdy has purchased.
(2) A provincially owned road constructed on land owned by Purdy.
(3) An order placed by Purdy for merchandise that the supplier has in a warehouse and will ship in ten days.
(4) A patent, owned by Purdy, to produce a drug that has been linked to cancer and banned by the Department of Health and Welfare. The drug will not be sold anywhere in the world.

(5) Ten $1000, 12 percent, twenty-year bonds of BCE that Purdy has purchased.
(6) The excellent credit reputation that Purdy has earned in the business community.
(7) A note receivable from a debtor who has been declared bankrupt and will not pay the amount owed to Purdy.
(8) A franchise that Purdy has acquired to market a successful product in three provinces.
(9) An order received from a customer for merchandise that Purdy will ship in five days.
(10) A machine that Purdy has purchased and received from a manufacturer.
(11) Merchandise owned by Jasper Limited that Purdy is holding on consignment. (Purdy is the consignee or selling agent and will try to sell the goods for Jasper.)
(12) A noncancellable lease that gives Purdy the right to use a machine owned by York Limited for five years, which is the estimated economic life of the machine.
(13) Cash received from a customer who has placed a prepaid order for merchandise to be shipped by Purdy in 30 days.
(14) A privately owned park that Purdy has built on its own land and that is often used by the city for sporting events.
(15) A parcel of land that has been given to Purdy by the province.

Instructions

Indicate whether each of the preceding items is an asset of Purdy Limited, according to GAAP. Briefly explain the reason for each of your decisions.

P3.5 Nature of Liabilities. You have been asked to determine whether each of the following items is a liability of Vinci Limited on December 31, 1995:

(1) The cash outlay expected to be made on January 7, 1996, to purchase equipment on that date.
(2) The amount expected to be needed to provide warranty services to customers for products sold before the end of 1995.
(3) The expected cash outlay for employee wages that will be earned during 1996.
(4) The obligation to provide future issues of a monthly newsletter for which subscriptions were prepaid during 1995.
(5) The obligation to provide merchandise to a customer who submitted a prepaid order on December 10, 1995.
(6) The obligation to fill orders expected to be made by regular customers during 1996.
(7) The obligation to distribute Vinci's own common shares to Vinci's shareholders as a result of a 10 percent stock dividend declared on December 15, 1995, and distributable on January 10, 1996.
(8) The obligation that may be required to settle a lawsuit against Vinci Limited that is pending on December 31, 1995. Vinci's attorneys expect to win the case.
(9) The obligation to retire at maturity $100 000, 12 percent, ten-year bonds issued at par value on December 31, 1995. (Interest on the bonds is to be paid annually, beginning on December 31, 1996.)
(10) The obligation to pay $120 000 interest ($100 000 $\times$ 0.12 $\times$ 10 years) on the bonds in (9) above.
(11) The burden associated with having earned a poor credit reputation during 1995.
(12) The obligation to provide office space to a tenant who paid six months' rent in advance on December 31, 1995.

Instructions

Indicate whether each of the preceding items is a liability, according to GAAP, of Vinci Limited on December 31, 1995. Briefly explain the reason for each of your decisions.

P3.6 Cash Versus Accrual Measurements. Violet Limited employs ten people. Salaries are paid biweekly, and certain employees occasionally receive salary advances. The company also owns several warehouses that it leases to various tenants. Some tenants are required to pay rent before using the warehouses, while others are allowed to use the warehouses before paying rent.

Violet Limited uses the conventional accrual basis of accounting, as required under GAAP. The amount of salaries expense was $91 000 and the amount of cash received from warehouse tenants was $137 000 for 1995. Selected information obtained from the company's comparative balance sheets is shown below:

	Dec. 31, 1994	Dec. 31, 1995
Prepaid salaries	$ 1 000	$ 3 000
Accrued salaries payable	5 000	2 500
Rent receivable	10 000	7 000
Unearned rent revenue	18 000	25 000

Instructions
(a) Compute the amount of cash paid for salaries during 1995.
(b) Compute the amount of rent revenue for 1995.

P3.7 Cash Versus Accrual Measurements. Victoria Limited employs several consulting companies. Some require payments in advance of performing services while others bill Victoria Limited after the services are rendered. Victoria Limited also leases office space to several law firms. Some law firms are required to pay rent in advance of using their offices, while others are allowed to use their offices before paying rent.

Victoria Limited uses the conventional accrual basis of accounting, as required under GAAP. The amount of cash paid to consulting companies was $48 000 and the amount of rent revenue earned from leasing office space was $66 000 during 1995. Selected information obtained from the company's comparative balance sheets is shown below:

	Dec. 31, 1994	Dec. 31, 1995
Prepaid consulting fees	$ 2 000	$5 000
Accrued consulting fees payable	7 000	2 000
Rent receivable	6 000	8 000
Unearned rent revenue	10 000	4 000

Instructions
(a) Compute the amount of consulting expense for 1995.
(b) Compute the amount of cash received from leasing office space during 1995.

P3.8 Cash Versus Accrual Statements. During the last four months of the academic year, the yearbook committee of Western Canada University produced and distributed the university's yearbook. The yearbook was published in April at a cost of $15 a copy.

The selling price was $22 each. If ordered in advance, the price was $18. The committee estimated that 9000 yearbooks would be sold for the 1994–95 academic year.

Previously, in February, the yearbook committee authorized the payment of $1500, which was the amount left from last year's yearbook sales, to the local newspaper, the campus newspaper, and a local radio station for advertising to be provided in March. In March, advance payments for 5000 yearbooks were received. The printing of 9000 year-books was completed in April and paid for on April 30. The difference between cash on hand and printing costs was made up by a short-term loan. In May, all advance orders were filled and 3500 more yearbooks were sold on a cash basis. The short-term loan of April was paid off in May, including an interest charge of $450. The unsold yearbooks were considered worthless and were therefore destroyed.

Instructions

(a) Prepare both cash basis and accrual basis monthly income statements and balance sheets for February, March, April, and May. (Identify the difference between assets and liabilities as "fund balance" rather than owners' equity, because the yearbook operation has no owners.) Disregard all taxes.

(b) What is the total income from yearbook sales for the 1994–95 academic year under each accounting method?

(c) From this problem, what is an obvious limitation of a cash-based system?

P3.9 Measurement of Income. Beau Hanna Sales Limited, an automobile dealership, started business on January 1, 1994, with $42 900 in cash. Hanna decided to "wait out" the current model year and start purchasing inventory when the 1995 models became available. As a result, the Hanna dealership purchased four new 1995 model automobiles on September 1, 1994. The costs of the new models were as follows:

Model	Cost
Astra	$ 8 800
Blaze	9 900
Cortez Deluxe	11 000
Dynasty Wagon	13 200

On November 1, the dealership sold the Astra for $10 340. On December 30, the manufacturer increased the wholesale price on the 1995 models by 10 percent. Hanna believed he could sell the Blaze, Cortez, and Dynasty for $12 210, $14 080, and $17 270, respectively. The sales agents' commissions were equal to 5 percent of the sales price.

During the calendar year 1995, the Blaze was sold for $12 430 and the Cortez for $14 410. Hanna still held the 1995 Dynasty on the lot as of October 1, 1995. He discounted the vehicle and finally sold it for $14 630 on October 15. On December 31, 1995, Beau Hanna Sales Limited ceased operations. Disregard all taxes.

Instructions

(a) Determine the net income for Beau Hanna Sales Limited for calendar years 1994 and 1995, assuming the automobile inventory is valued under (1) historical cost, (2) current cost, and (3) current exit value. Disregard all taxes.

(b) What is the lifetime net income of the Hanna dealership under each valuation method?

(c) Which pattern of income flows do you believe is most fair and reasonable?

P3.10 Measurement of Income. On January 1, 1994, Scotia Beer Limited began business with an $880 000 cash investment. The company did not intend to brew beer from raw materials but to use a newly developed aging process on beer purchased wholesale from other producers. After two years of aging by this special process, a top-quality premium beer was to result. One beer distributor was so impressed with the aging process that a contract was made for 20 000 barrels at a price of $60 a barrel, to be delivered and paid for on December 31, 1995.

On January 1, 1994, Scotia purchased 20 000 barrels of freshly brewed beer at $20 a barrel in order to start the aging process, which cost $1 per barrel per month. On December 31, 1994, the wholesale price of beer aged one year was $38 a barrel. The company estimated it could sell the beer for $45 a barrel after only one year of aging. On December 31, 1995, the aging process was completed and the beer was delivered to the distributor.

Instructions

(a) Prepare balance sheets for December 31, 1994, for Scotia Beer Limited under the following four valuation methods: (1) historical cost, (2) current cost, (3) current exit value, and (4) expected exit value. Disregard all taxes.

(b) What is the reported net income for 1994 and 1995 under each valuation method?

(c) Which pattern of income flows do you believe is most fair and reasonable?

P3.11 Cash Versus Accrual Statements. Cornwall University's 1994–95 hockey season began on December 1, 1994, and will end on March 31, 1995. The CU hockey arena (fully depreciated) holds 15 000 fans. The number of home dates per month are as follows: December, 7; January, 5; February, 5; and March, 5.

Five thousand seats per game are reserved for CU students at an admission price of $5 per student per game. The remaining seats are sold to alumni and other fans at a season-ticket cost of $308. Season-ticket orders are mailed on November 30. Season-ticket holders have the choice of paying the $308 as a lump sum by December 6 (the first home date) or using a payment plan of $77 per month with the first payment due by December 7. Forty percent of the season-ticket holders choose the payment plan.

The university also operates the concession stands, which cost $3000 per game and generate $8000 in cash revenues per game. All concession items are purchased COD seven days before a home date. There is no ending inventory of concession-stand items on December 31.

The major cost to the university in managing the arena is the utility bill for heating and lighting. The university receives the utility bill on the fifth of each month for the previous month's usage. The arena uses no heat or light in the off-season. Monthly usage during the hockey season is $240 000. Arena workers receive wages on a per-game basis and are paid on the day following a home date. The payroll cost for a home date is $12 000. In addition, the university insures the arena at a cost of $24 000 per year, which is paid in advance each December 1. The arena has $3000 cash left from the preceding hockey season.

On December 31, 1994, after a particularly exciting game in which CU upset their conference rival, the president of the university asks you to prepare financial statements for December. The president noticed that the arena was sold out for each of the home dates in December and, as a result, wants to know how much cash the arena operation is generating.

Instructions

(a) Prepare an income statement for December and a balance sheet on December 31, 1994, under a cash basis assumption. Develop an alternative set of statements under an accrual basis. (Identify the difference between assets and liabilities as "fund balance" rather than owners' equity, because a university does not have shareholders.) Disregard all taxes.

(b) Assuming the arena is used only for hockey, what will the arena operation earn for the period from December 1, 1994, to November 30, 1995?

(c) Show the president the shortcomings of cash-basis financial statements in evaluating the arena's operating performance for December.

Cases

C3.1 Income and Inflation. Whitfield Limited was formed on January 1, 1994. On that date, shareholders contributed $100 000 to the company in exchange for 10 000 of Whitfield's common shares. The company placed the $100 000 in a noninterest-bearing chequing account. For various unforeseen reasons, the company engaged in no further transactions during 1994. On December 31, 1994, the company still had $100 000 in its chequing account. Assume the inflation rate during 1994 was 5 percent.

Instructions

(a) According to GAAP, what is the amount of Whitfield's net income or loss for 1994? Explain your answer.

(b) In an economic sense, would Whitfield Limited generally be considered better off or worse off at the end of 1994 than at the beginning? Explain your answer.

(c) If you were in charge of setting GAAP, how much net income or loss would you require Whitfield to report for 1994? Explain your answer.

C3.2 Nature of Liabilities. Many companies promise to pay the cost of their employees' supplemental health care after they retire. In the past, generally accepted accounting principles have not required companies to include among their liabilities the obligations for postretirement supplemental health-care benefits. Instead, companies have simply accounted for these costs as expenses when the costs were paid, which of course was after the employees retired. This is sometimes referred to as the "pay as you go" basis of accounting for these costs.

The FASB has recently studied this accounting issue and has argued that companies should be required to account for the cost of postretirement supplemental health-care benefits during the periods in which the employees work for the company (i.e., before the employees retire). Such accounting would force many companies to report very large expenses and liabilities in their financial statements.

Many corporate managers have objected to the FASB's position, stating that such accounting is too imprecise and would cause many companies to drop or reduce postretirement supplemental health-care benefits. The managers also claim that the FASB's approach would substantially reduce corporate net income and shareholders' equity, and that some companies may even be forced to cut expenses in other vital areas, such as research and development.

In response to the managers' arguments, the FASB has argued that companies should be required to account for all of their obligations. Companies should not be excused from accounting for obligations just because they can only be estimated or because they adversely affect the company's financial statements. The CICA *Handbook* does not contain a recommendation on this issue.

Instructions

(a) Explain the theoretical rationale that supports the FASB's position on this accounting issue.
(b) Explain why you agree or disagree with the FASB's position.
(c) What is your opinion of the validity of the arguments that the corporate managers have raised?

C3.3 Measurement of Liabilities. On January 1, 1995, Hay Limited borrowed $50 000 cash from Crown Limited by signing a $50 000, 8 percent, two-year promissory note calling for interest of $4000 ($50 000 × 0.08 = $4000) to be paid at the end of 1995 and 1996. On the borrowing date, the market rate of interest for similar notes was 8 percent.

On December 31, 1995, Hay paid the $4000 interest for 1995. At that time, the market rate of interest for similar notes was 10 percent.

As the controller for Hay, you are trying to determine the amount the company should report for the note payable on December 31, 1995, in a balance sheet prepared in accordance with GAAP. You are considering the following alternatives:

(1) Report the note payable at $54 000. This amount equals the face amount of the note plus the interest that must be paid at the end of 1996 ($50 000 + $4000 = $54 000).
(2) Report the note payable at $49 090.91. This amount equals the amount in (1) above, discounted for one year at the current market interest rate of 10 percent ($54 000 ÷ 1.10 = $49 090.91).
(3) Report the note payable at $50 000. This amount equals the amount in (1) above, discounted for one year at the market interest rate of 8 percent that was in effect when the note was issued ($54 000 ÷ 1.08 = $50 000).

Instructions
Which of the above alternatives should you select? Explain your answer.

C3.4 Liabilities Versus Owners' Equity Jane Curren, an accountant employed by Ness Limited, has asked for your help in deciding whether each of the following items should be reported in Ness Limited's balance sheet as a liability or as shareholders' equity:

(1) An issue of subordinated income bonds that mature in ten years. The bonds provide for interest at an annual rate of 8 percent, to be paid only in those years during which the company's income is sufficient to cover the interest.
(2) An issue of preferred shares that Ness is required to redeem on specified future dates. The shares confer no voting rights and have a stated cumulative dividend rate of $8.
(3) An issue of preferred shares that Ness has an option to redeem at any time. The shares confer no voting rights and have a stated cumulative dividend rate of $9.

Instructions

(a) Explain how the substance over form modifying convention relates to the reporting problem indicated above.
(b) Indicate whether each listed item should be classified as a liability or as shareholders' equity. Explain your answers.

C3.5   Measurement of Shareholders' Equity.   On December 31, 1995, Raines Corporation reported total assets of $10 million, total liabilities of $4 million, and total shareholders' equity of $6 million. The shareholders' equity consisted of common shares of $1 million and retained earnings of $5 million. Raines had 100 000 no-par value common shares outstanding on December 31, 1995, and the market price per share on that date was $70.

Instructions

(a) Explain how shareholders' equity is measured in conventional accounting.
(b) Explain why the reported shareholders' equity of $6 million does not equal the ending market price per share multiplied by the shares outstanding ($70 × 100 000 = $7 000 000).

C3.6   Cash Versus Accrual Discussion.   Fishback Foundation is a not-for-profit organization dedicated to the support of the arts in the surrounding communities. The foundation has investments in real estate, shares, bonds, and mortgages, as well as unpaid pledges from supporters. The real-estate investments have outstanding mortgages. The foundation has been operating its accounting system on a cash basis since its inception in 1956. The trustees have embarked on a program to increase foundation activities, including an aggressive annual fund-raising campaign.

The trustees have decided that the foundation's accounting records should be audited annually, and they have engaged a CA firm to conduct the first audit. One of the auditors recommends that the foundation convert its accounting system from the cash basis to the accrual basis. The auditor has stated that accrual accounting is used in profit-making companies but has not been used extensively in governmental or not-for-profit organizations. The auditor believes that accrual accounting has many advantages and would be very useful to Fishback Foundation.

Instructions

(a) Describe how the foundation's statement of financial position and statement of receipts and disbursements prepared on an accrual basis would differ from those prepared on a cash basis.
(b) Identify and briefly explain the advantages accrual accounting provides to profit-making companies that would also be advantages to Fishback Foundation.
(c) Explain how the trustees' ability to evaluate the performance of the foundation's executive director would be improved if the foundation used financial statements prepared on the accrual basis rather than the cash basis.

(Adapted from CMA.)

C3.7   Measurement of Income.   Larry Jones bought a four-bedroom home on January 1, 1994, for $285 000 cash. After this purchase, Jones had only $45 000 cash left in his noninterest-bearing chequing account. On December 31, 1994, Jones could sell his house for $360 000 cash. At that time, he could engage in one of the following independent transactions:

(1) Sell the house and buy a similar four-bedroom home in the same town for $360 000.
(2) Sell the house and buy a similar four-bedroom home in another region of the country for $285 000.
(3) Sell the house and buy a similar four-bedroom home in another region of the country for $405 000.
(4) Sell the house and buy a six-bedroom home in the same town for $405 000.
(5) Not sell the house.

Instructions
(a) Determine the 1994 income (gain) Jones would record for each of the independent situations above, according to GAAP. Assume no transaction costs or taxes. Also assume that Jones is indifferent about regional location, and that all houses are of similar construction quality.
(b) How well does GAAP capture the economic substance of each transaction above?

C3.8 Asset/Liability Versus Revenue/Expense View. The following definitions of assets and liabilities are given in "Financial Statement Concepts," CICA *Handbook*, Paragraphs 1000.29–34, March 1991:

> **Assets**—are economic resources controlled by an entity as a result of past transactions or events and from which future economic benefits may be obtained.
> **Liabilities**—are obligations of an entity arising from past transactions or events, the settlement of which may result in the transfer or use of assets, provision of services or other yielding of economic benefits in the future.

Instructions
Are the preceding definitions consistent with the asset/liability or the revenue/expense view? What deficiencies can you identify in the above definitions?

C3.9 Usefulness of Forecasts. You and a friend are discussing whether corporate managers should be required to report financial forecasts in their companies' published annual reports. Your friend argues, "Forecasts are useful information because investors and creditors want to know as much as possible about the future when they make their decisions. Usefulness is the primary objective of corporate financial reporting. Therefore, if information is useful, then GAAP should require companies to report it."

Instructions
(a) If a certain type of information really is useful, should GAAP require companies to report it?
(b) Summarize the arguments for and against the required disclosure of financial forecasts.
(c) In your opinion, should companies be required to disclose financial forecasts? Defend your answer.

C3.10 Forecast Considerations and Assumptions. Eagle Electronics is a new company in the high-growth electronics field. It produces a unique electronic test package for the defence industry. Eagle Electronics, which has been run very successfully as a private company for two years, will be making its first public offering of common shares within the next month. Naturally, the company wants to obtain the highest price possible for the new offering. The treasurer of the company, Sam Easton, has suggested that the publication of a three-year earnings forecast may enhance the offering price of the new shares.

Instructions

What factors must Easton consider in the preparation of the earnings forecast? What shortcomings in the public disclosure of financial forecasts should Easton be aware of?

C3.11 Forecast Considerations and Assumptions. Hotel management must make many assumptions in preparing financial forecasts. The following are some variables management may have to consider:

(1) Gasoline prices.
(2) Aging population.
(3) Financing costs.
(4) Characteristics of automobiles.
(5) Land values.
(6) General economic conditions.
     The following background information comes from the annual report of Dreamy Inns of Canada, a fast-growing national motel chain.

The market that Dreamy Inns serves is broad and rapidly growing. Responding to today's more demanding traveller, we offer quality lodgings at better prices than our competitors. We cut out such expensive frills as elaborate lobbies, convention space, and meeting halls, and we pass the savings on to our guests. We offer all of the conveniences that travellers appreciate. Each of our strategically located properties provides a cluster of services in one convenient location: lodging, food, gasoline, gifts, and souvenirs.

Instructions

Explain how each of the above variables may be interpreted by the managers of Dreamy Inns in preparing a financial forecast.

Chapter 4

Basic Financial Statements

Objectives

1. To describe the major characteristics of basic financial statements.

2. To discuss and illustrate most major components of the income statement.

3. To discuss and illustrate the statement of retained earnings and the statement of shareholders' equity.

4. To discuss and illustrate the balance sheet, including the major classifications commonly used.

5. To provide a general introduction to the statement of changes in financial position.

6. To provide a general introduction to other topics related to basic financial statements.

Characteristics of Basic Financial Statements

What was the net income of George Weston Ltd. last year? Was this figure large or small in relation to the company's sales and to its shareholders' equity? What was the relationship last year between BCE's dividends and earnings? What proportion of Air Canada's assets at the end of last year did the company finance through debt? How did Cadillac Fairview use its cash resources last year? These are a few of the many questions that investors, creditors, and other users seek to answer based on information presented in companies' financial statements.

The basic financial statements are the **balance sheet, income statement, statement of changes in financial position, and statement of retained earnings** or **statement of shareholders' equity.** Companies usually present basic financial statements in their annual reports and in other disclosure media. The balance sheet summarizes the financial position of an enterprise **at a particular point in time.** The other basic statements summarize various changes in financial position that have occurred **during a period of time.**

Basic financial statements, which include the notes, have several important characteristics:

1. They are only a **subset,** although an important subset, of the information needed by users for making rational investment, lending, and similar decisions.
2. They are primarily **historical** in nature.
3. They **summarize** information.
4. They reflect many **estimates.**
5. They are **general-purpose** reports designed to serve the needs of many different users.
6. They **articulate** with one another (i.e., they are **interrelated**).

In this chapter, we review the form and content of the basic financial statements. In subsequent chapters, we discuss aspects of these statements in greater detail and thereby develop the statements more fully.

This chapter presents the statements in the order in which accountants typically prepare them (i.e., income statement; statement of retained earnings or statement of shareholders' equity; balance sheet; and statement of changes in financial position). To emphasize the interrelatedness of basic financial statements, the chapter presents a set of statements prepared for the Sunrise Corporation.[1]

Income Statement

The income statement, generally regarded as the most important financial statement, is used in two major ways:

1. **To predict cash flows.** Users of financial statements typically invest or lend cash, and they want to know *how much* cash they will receive in return and *when* they will receive it. Knowledge of a company's past income and its components helps

---

[1]A complete set of financial statements of Canadian Pacific Limited (a diversified corporation) is presented in Appendix A at the end of this book.

    We recommend *Financial Reporting in Canada*, 19th ed. (Toronto: CICA, 1992), a publication of the CICA from a survey of 300 Canadian corporations.

users to predict more accurately the company's future income and their own chances of receiving cash from the company.

2. **To evaluate management's performance.** Users regard the income statement as an important indication of management's success. Shareholders typically want to reward good managers and replace poor ones.

From a societal standpoint, measurements reported on the income statement help to ensure that we put our scarce resources to the best use and that the goods and services we want are available. If a company produces and distributes its products successfully, it should earn income. Moreover, a record of profitable operations should help the company to raise capital and other resources. Generally, resources should flow into companies that have unusually high incomes and out of those that sustain losses.

Elements of the Income Statement

Revenue Realization

Matching Asset/Liability Measurement

Accountants traditionally have measured a company's income by focussing on transactions that caused changes in the company's assets and liabilities during a period of time. These transactions include revenues, expenses, gains, and losses. As you might expect, accountants disagree about the best way to measure these components of a company's income. For example, we could measure expenses using current costs, opportunity costs, or historical costs. Traditionally, accountants have relied primarily on historical costs. Income measurement in conventional accounting primarily involves the **revenue realization, matching,** and **asset/liability measurement** principles, as discussed in Chapter 2.

The fundamental elements of the income statement and their relationships to net income are demonstrated in the following equation: Revenues − Expenses + Gains − Losses = Net Income or Loss.

A review of several definitions presented in Chapter 2 is appropriate at this point:[2]

1. **Revenues.** Inflows or other enhancements of assets of an entity or settlements of its liabilities or both during a period, based on production and delivery of goods, provision of services, and other activities that constitute the entity's major operations.
2. **Expenses.** Outflows or other use of assets or incurrences of liabilities or both during a period as a result of delivering or producing goods, rendering services, or carrying out other activities that constitute the entity's major operations.
3. **Costs.** Sacrifices incurred in acquiring resources. We include the term "cost" here so that you can differentiate it from the term "expense." Costs do not enter into the calculation of net income until they expire. An **expense** in conventional accounting is an **expired cost** (more precisely, an **expired historical cost**). In contrast, a cost that has not yet expired is reported as an **asset.**
4. **Gains and losses. Gains** are increases in owners' equity (net assets) from peripheral or incidental transactions of an entity and from all other transactions and events affecting the entity during a period, except those resulting from revenues or investments by owners. **Losses** are decreases in owners' equity (net assets) from peripheral or incidental transactions of an entity and from all other events affecting the entity during a period, except those that result from expenses or distributions to owners. Unlike revenues and expenses, which are measured and reported at **gross amounts,**

---

[2]These definitions are based largely on "Financial Statement Concepts," CICA *Handbook*, Paragraphs 1000.37–40, March 1991.

gains and losses are measured and reported at **net amounts**. For example, if a company paid $70 000 for land and later sold the land for $100 000, the company would report a $30 000 gain. This gain equals the gross selling price of $100 000, net of the land's cost of $70 000. In practice, gains are sometimes classified broadly as revenues; losses are sometimes classified broadly as expenses. An exception to this net presentation is interest. Interest income and interest expense are often shown separately under other income.

5. **Net income.** The net result of adding revenues and gains for a period and deducting expenses and losses for the period. Terms such as **earnings** and **profit** are often used as synonyms for **income**.

Several items that may appear on an income statement are somewhat peculiar and should be explained further at this time. These items include extraordinary gains and losses, unusual or infrequently occurring gains and losses that are not the result of determinations by management, and gains and losses resulting from the disposal of business segments.

Extraordinary Gains and Losses

Suppose that a company sustains a loss from an earthquake. Because this kind of loss is rare, users of financial statements could make more accurate predictions and more meaningful evaluations of management's performance if they knew about unusual and nonrecurring gains and losses. As a result, generally accepted accounting principles (GAAP) require companies to report **material** extraordinary gains and losses in a special section of their income statements.

Materiality

To be considered an extraordinary gain or loss, an event or transaction must meet *all* of the following characteristics:[3]

1. They are not expected to occur frequently over several years.
2. They do not typify the normal business activities of the entity.
3. They do not depend primarily on decisions or determinations by management or owners.

Note that to be considered extraordinary, an item must be unusual, nonrecurring, and not determinations of management. The term **extraordinary item** therefore has a technical meaning in accounting that differs from the everyday connotation of items that are simply unusual or peculiar. Furthermore, the criteria require the accountant to consider the specific **characteristics of the company** as well as the **environment in which it operates**. For example, an accountant would be more likely to judge a loss from a hurricane as extraordinary if it were sustained by a company located in Ottawa rather than by one located on the Atlantic Coast.[4]

Accountants must use *judgement* when applying the above criteria, which are inherently very restrictive and are rarely satisfied in practice.[5] In many cases, an event or transaction will meet the criteria only as the direct result of a **major casualty** (such as an earthquake), an **expropriation** (a takeover of property by a government), or a **prohibition** under a newly enacted law.

---

[3]"Extraordinary Items," CICA *Handbook*, Paragraph 3480.02, December 1989.
    [4]We are referring to a loss in excess of insurance proceeds or a loss not covered at all by insurance.
    [5]*Financial Reporting in Canada 1991*, 19th ed. (Toronto: CICA, 1992), pp. 184–92.

Following are some examples of events or transactions that meet all the criteria and should therefore be judged extraordinary:

1. A large portion of a vineyard's crops in the Okanagan Valley are destroyed by a hailstorm. Severe damage from hailstorms in this area are rare.
2. A cannery in Nova Scotia destroys a large quantity of inventory because of a government ban on canned goods containing cyclamates. Government prohibitions of this kind rarely occur.
3. An earthquake destroys an oil refinery in Alberta owned by a large multinational oil company. Earthquakes rarely occur in the area where the oil refinery is located.
4. A large fishery loses fishing vessels at sea. The insurance proceeds received result in a gain. This case meets the criteria of unusual and nonrecurring.

The CICA *Handbook* covers these exceptions and cites examples in Section 3480.

In contrast, here are some examples of events or transactions that should not be judged extraordinary because they do not meet all the criteria for extraordinary items:

1. An Ontario tomato grower's crop is damaged by frost in late May. Frost damage is normally experienced at this time of year every three or four years. In this case, the criterion of infrequent occurrence is not met.
2. A company that operates a chain of warehouses sells the excess land surrounding one of its warehouses. When the company buys property to establish a new warehouse, it usually buys more land than it will use because it expects the land to appreciate in value. In the past five years, there have been two instances in which the company sold such excess land. Here the criterion of infrequent occurrence has not been met, nor has the criterion of the transaction not being subject to management influence or decision been met.
3. A large, diversified company sells a block of shares from the portfolio of securities it has for investment purposes. This is the first sale from its portfolio. The criterion of unusual nature has not been met in this case because the company owns several securities. Management was involved in the decision to sell the investment.
4. A textile manufacturer with only one plant moves to another location. It has not relocated a plant in twenty years and has no plans to do so in the foreseeable future. Here, the criterion of unusual nature has not been met because, in general, moving from one location to another is a common business occurrence and is a decision of management.

Unusual or Infrequently Occurring Gains and Losses

 An accountant sometimes encounters a gain or loss that is unusual in nature, occurs infrequently, and is not based on decisions by management, *but not all three*. Such a gain or loss is therefore *not* extraordinary. Examples are gains or losses from the sale of plant assets, losses from inventory write-offs, and losses due to a strike. According to Paragraph 1520.3(l) of the CICA *Handbook*, these gains and losses should be reported as separate items in the income statement if they are material. They should *not* be reported in any way that implies they are extraordinary in nature.

Materiality

In practice, the distinction between extraordinary items and unusual or infrequently occurring items is sometimes hazy, but the third characteristic, not dependent on a decision or determination by management, limits the number of extraordinary items. Accountants should be aware that, because the income statement reports management's performance, many managers want to report gains as nonextraordinary and losses as extraordinary.

Disposal of a Business Segment

The term **segment of a business** refers to

> a component of an entity whose activities represent a separate major line of business or class of customer. A segment may be in the form of a subsidiary, a division, or a department provided that its assets, results of operations, and activities can be clearly distinguished, physically and operationally for financial reporting purposes, from the other assets, results of operations, and activities of the entity.[6]

A company may **dispose** of a segment of its business. For example, a company that has a furniture division and a clothing division may sell its clothing division.

Gains and losses from disposal of a business segment are *not* extraordinary items. Instead, they must be reported in a special income statement category called **discontinued operations.**[7] In Chapter 5, we discuss in detail the complex requirements for discontinued operations and illustrate how to report them in a comprehensive income statement.

Changes in Accounting Policies

A company may occasionally change from one accounting policy to another. For example, it may change from the first-in, first-out (FIFO) to the weighted average method of inventory cost determination, or from the declining balance method to the straight-line method of computing depreciation. Such changes are called **changes in accounting policies.** Changes are permitted under generally accepted accounting principles if the company can establish that the new policy is preferable to the old and will present more meaningful information to users of the financial statements.

Changes in accounting policies are *not* extraordinary items. Instead, changes in accounting policies are reported as adjustments to the opening retained earnings.[8] Financial reporting requirements for changes in accounting policies are complex. In Chapter 5, we discuss how to report accounting changes. Then, in Chapter 20, we explain the subject of accounting changes. Therefore, this chapter introduces you to the income statement, while Chapter 5 explains additional income statement reporting details at a time when you will be better able to understand their meaning and significance.

Income Statement Format

The form and content of the income statement have been greatly affected by recent professional pronouncements relating to such issues as intraperiod income tax allocation, accounting changes, discontinued operations, extraordinary items, and earnings per share. These issues are often complex and require careful study before the implications of income statement reporting can be fully understood. For this reason, we review in this section the fundamental aspects of the income statement format. In Chapter 5, we consider some additional reporting complexities of the income statement.

---

[6]"Discontinued Operations," CICA *Handbook*, Paragraph 3475.03, December 1989.

[7]"Income Statement," CICA *Handbook*, Paragraph 1520.02(b), August 1991.

[8]"Accounting Changes," CICA *Handbook*, Paragraphs 1506.02–21, March 1991.

The accounting profession has not adopted a uniform format for the entire income statement. Instead, it permits some flexibility, and this enables the practising accountant to structure an income statement that best fits the circumstances of the reporting entity. Nevertheless, many income statement disclosures (such as depreciation expense) are required by GAAP, and we discuss these required disclosures at appropriate places in this book. Accountants traditionally have presented the income statement in either a multiple-step or a single-step form.

Multiple-Step Form

A **multiple-step** income statement presents subtotals for gross margin and operating income before showing net income. Net income is therefore derived in intermediate steps. Exhibit 4.1 illustrates a multiple-step income statement for the Sunrise Corporation. In practice, many details shown in this example may be condensed or may be reported in notes or parenthetically. For example, the income statement may begin with net sales if the accountant thinks that the revenue contra account balances are immaterial. Moreover, the accountant may report only the totals for cost of goods sold, selling expenses, and general and administrative expenses. The details may be presented separately in the notes.

As Exhibit 4.1 suggests, a multiple-step format calls for deducting cost of goods sold from net sales to measure **gross margin on sales** (often called **gross profit on sales**). Gross margin is an intermediate measure of profitability that indicates the difference between the selling prices and the costs of products sold during the accounting period. For example, the gross margin earned by companies that produce cereal products is currently about 50 percent.

To the extent possible, **operating expenses** are usually divided into two categories: **selling expenses** relate to the sale of the company's products; **general and administrative expenses** relate to the general operations of the business.

Income from operations (also called **operating income**) is a measurement of the company's profitability as a result of its primary business activities. **Other revenues** and **other expenses** are related to the secondary activities of the company; these two sections are often combined. Note that Sunrise Corporation correctly reported an unusual item (loss on sale of long-term investments) as other expenses. As stated earlier, items that do not meet the criteria of Section 3480 must not be reported as extraordinary items.

Income before taxes and extraordinary item is an intermediate measure of income that would simply be called "income before taxes" if Sunrise Corporation did not have an extraordinary item. **Income tax** is the final expense deducted. The amount is determined by multiplying income before taxes and extraordinary item by the income tax rate, which we assume is 40 percent.[9] The amount therefore includes the income tax effect of all income statement items that appear before it. Income tax expense should always be shown separately, not combined with any other expenses.

Income before extraordinary item indicates how profitable the company was without considering the effects of the extraordinary item. Because extraordinary items are unusual and nonrecurring, many financial statement users rely heavily on the income before extraordinary item figure when they make predictions and evaluate management's performance.

The **extraordinary item** is presented next, as required by GAAP. In the exhibit, Sunrise Corporation reported an extraordinary *gain* because the proceeds received from a

Materiality

---

[9]So that we can concentrate on the basic form and content of financial statements without being diverted by income tax calculations, we assume a tax rate of 40 percent for the financial statements presented in this chapter.

Exhibit 4.1   Multiple-Step Income Statement

Sunrise Corporation
INCOME STATEMENT
For the Year Ended December 31, 1995

Sales Revenue			
Sales			$579 500
Less: Sales returns and allowances		$ 18 200	
Sales discounts		11 300	29 500
Net sales			550 000
Cost of goods sold			
Merchandise inventory, Jan. 1, 1995		40 000	
Purchases	$340 000		
Less: Purchase returns and allowances	(20 000)		
Purchase discounts	(6 800)		
Add: Transportation-in	11 800		
Net purchases		325 000	
Cost of goods available for sale		365 000	
Less: Merchandise inventory, Dec. 31, 1995		(35 000)	
Cost of goods sold			330 000
Gross margin on sales			220 000
Operating expenses			
Selling expenses			
Sales salaries	48 000		
Advertising	15 000		
Transportation-out	7 300		
Other selling expenses	2 700	73 000	
General and administrative expenses			
Office salaries	32 300		
Utilities	9 900		
Supplies	7 700		
Insurance	5 800		
Depreciation of building	2 500		
Bad debts	4 500		
Miscellaneous expenses	1 800	64 500	
Total operating expenses			137 500
Income from operations			82 500
Other revenues			
Interest		9 300	
Dividends		5 200	
Gain on sale of equipment		6 500	21 000
			103 500
Other expenses			
Interest		14 400	
Unusual item—loss on sale of long-term investments		5 100	19 500
Income before taxes and extraordinary item			84 000
Income tax expense			33 600
Income before extraordinary item			50 400
Extraordinary item—gain from expropriation of land, net of applicable income tax expense of $16 000			24 000
Net income			$ 74 400
Per common share			
Income before extraordinary item			$2.32
Extraordinary gain (net of tax)			1.20
Net income			$3.52

government expropriation of land exceeded the land's historical cost. An extraordinary gain or loss is always reported separately in a special section of the income statement. Further, the generally accepted accounting principle of **intraperiod tax allocation,** which is discussed in detail in Chapter 19, requires that the gross amount of an extraordinary gain be reduced by the amount of **income tax expense** associated with the gain. Similarly, it requires that the gross amount of an extraordinary loss be reduced by the amount of the **income tax reduction** associated with the loss. Extraordinary gains and losses are therefore always reported **net** of their income tax effects, or on a **net-of-tax basis.** Note in the exhibit that if the extraordinary gain had not been reported on a net-of-tax basis, the reported income tax expense (associated with income before taxes and extraordinary item) would have been $49 600 ($33 600 + $16 000). Income before extraordinary item would then have been reported as only $34 400 ($84 000 − $49 600). This error could cause some users to evaluate the company in a misleading (and in this case, less favourable) light. In 1990, the CICA introduced a special income statement category for discontinued operations. In Chapter 5, we present a comprehensive income statement that includes this category.

Net income includes the effects of all revenues, expenses, gains, and losses. The beneficiaries of net income are the shareholders, both preferred and common.

Earnings per common share is a widely used financial measurement that appears below net income.[10] Its beneficiaries are *common* shareholders. In the simplest case, an accountant calculates earnings per share by dividing net income by the weighted average number of common shares outstanding during the period. Sunrise Corporation had preferred shares outstanding and the preferred dividends were declared (see Exhibit 4.3). We therefore subtracted preferred dividends from net income when calculating earnings per common share. Note that because Sunrise Corporation had an extraordinary item, it reported *three* per-share numbers: (1) income before extraordinary item, (2) extraordinary gain (net of tax), and (3) net income after extraordinary item. Companies report these numbers separately to help users of financial statements make better predictions and more meaningful evaluations of management's performance. Calculating and reporting earnings per share can be extremely complex; we discuss and illustrate these complexities in Chapter 21.

Single-Step Form

In the **single-step** income statement, the accountant deducts total expenses from total revenues in a single step to measure net income. No separate disclosure is made of gross margin or operating income. Most companies that prepare single-step income statements deduct income tax as a separate, last item.[11] In Exhibit 4.2, we present a somewhat condensed single-step income statement. Such condensation is not essential. Indeed, **condensed income statements** may be presented in either a multiple-step or a single-step format. A typical annual report contains a condensed income statement. As you can see by comparing Exhibits 4.1 and 4.2, extraordinary items are reported in a special income statement category, regardless of the format used. Moreover, the multiple-step and single-step formats always contain the same information after income before taxes and extraordinary item.

---

[10]Enterprises with few shareholders are not required under generally accepted accounting principles to report earnings per share. Unless stated otherwise, you should assume in all end-of-chapter assignments that earnings per share is required.

   [11]*Financial Reporting in Canada 1990,* 19th ed. (Toronto: CICA, 1991), p. 147.

Exhibit 4.2 Single-Step Income Statement

Sunrise Corporation
INCOME STATEMENT
For the Year Ended December 31, 1995

Revenues		
Net sales		$550 000
Other revenues		21 000
Total revenues		571 000
Expenses		
Cost of goods sold	$330 000	
Selling expenses	73 000	
General and administrative expenses	64 500	
Interest	14 400	
Unusual item—loss on sale of long-term investments	5 100	
Total expenses		487 000
Income before taxes and extraordinary item		84 000
Income tax expense		33 600
Income before extraordinary item		50 400
Extraordinary item—gain from expropriation of land, less applicable income tax expense of $16 000		24 000
Net income		$ 74 400
Per common share		
Income before extraordinary item		$2.32
Extraordinary gain (net of tax)		1.20
Net income		$3.52

Note to Students: With either the multiple-step or the single-step form, generally accepted accounting principles require a special income statement category for discontinued operations. In Chapter 5, we discuss this category and present a comprehensive income statement that includes this category.

Multiple-Step Versus Single-Step Form

Many preparers and users of financial statements prefer the multiple-step form because it highlights gross margin and operating income. Others prefer the single-step form because it is often easier to understand and does not suggest a priority of expenses. In other words, the format does not imply that a company must recover its cost of goods sold expense before it can recover any other expenses. In reality, of course, a company must cover all of its expenses if it is to have net income. Proponents of the single-step form also point out that several terms often used in a multiple-step statement (especially "income from operations") have not been clearly defined by the accounting profession. A survey of the annual reports of 600 U.S. companies indicated that, in 1989, 232 companies used the single-step form while 368 companies used the multiple-step form.

Statement of Retained Earnings

The statement of retained earnings describes the changes in a company's retained earnings during a period and relates the income statement to the balance sheet. The retained earnings statement is usually fairly simple and may consist of three sections: (1) **prior period adjustments, correction of an error, and the cumulative effect of changes in accounting policies**; (2) **net income**; and (3) **dividends declared**. Users of financial statements can analyze the statement to determine whether any prior period adjustments exist and what relationship exists between a company's net income and its dividends. A statement of retained earnings for the Sunrise Corporation is shown in Exhibit 4.3.

Prior Period Adjustments and Accounting Changes

 Prior period adjustments are charged or credited directly to retained earnings. These items do not appear on the income statement of the period in which they occur. Paragraph 3600.03 of the CICA *Handbook* states

 Prior period adjustments should include only adjustments having all four of the following characteristics:

(a) are specifically identified with and directly related to the business activities of particular prior periods;

(b) are not attributable to economic events occurring subsequent to the date of the financial statements for such prior periods;

(c) depend primarily on decisions or determinations by persons other than management or owners; and

(d) could not be reasonably estimated prior to such decisions or determinations.[12]

A correction of an error that was made in the financial statements of a **prior period** is accounted for in the **current period** in a manner similar to a prior period adjustment.[13] The error may have resulted from mathematical mistakes, errors in selecting or applying accounting principles, or oversight or misuse of facts when the company prepared its erroneous financial statements.[14] Examples of errors include an overstatement of merchandise inventory at the end of the preceding period because of an inaccurate physical count, and an understatement of previously reported depreciation because of an error in computation. A change from an accounting policy that is not generally accepted to one that is generally accepted is considered to be a correction of an error.

In practice, correction adjustments due to errors are rare, yet they can sometimes have a significant effect on a company's financial statements. In a 1990 CICA survey of 300 Canadian companies, correction of errors was reported by two companies in 1990 and four in 1989.

An accountant must carefully distinguish a *correction of an error* from a **change in an accounting estimate**. A change in an accounting estimate results from the need for accountants to make many estimates. Changes in these estimates occur when new information or subsequent developments improve an accountant's judgement. Examples include changes in estimates of uncollectable accounts receivable and changes in the estimated service lives or salvage values of capital assets. Changes in accounting estimates are *not* prior period adjustments. These changes should be accounted for in the period of change if the change affects that period only, or in the period of change and future

---

[12]"Prior Period Adjustments," CICA *Handbook*, Paragraph 3600.03, March 1980.

[13]"Accounting Changes," CICA *Handbook*, Paragraph 1506.28, March 1991.

[14]"Accounting Changes," CICA *Handbook*, Paragraph 1506.26, March 1991.

Exhibit 4.3

Sunrise Corporation
STATEMENT OF RETAINED EARNINGS
For the Year Ended December 31, 1995

Retained earnings, Jan. 1, 1995, as previously reported		$ 45 600
Less: Correction of an error in a prior period—depreciation understated in		
1994 due to an error, less applicable income tax effect of $2000		3 000
Retained earnings, Jan. 1, 1995, as restated		42 600
Add: Net income		74 400
Subtotal		117 000
Less: Dividends declared on preferred shares ($0.80 per share)	$ 4 000	
Dividends declared on common shares ($0.60 per share)	12 000	16 000
Retained earnings, Dec. 31, 1995		$101 000

---

periods if the change affects both.[15] We explain corrections of errors and changes in accounting estimates in Chapter 20.

Prior period adjustments that result from realization of income tax benefits of preacquisition operating loss carryforwards of purchased subsidiaries are not covered extensively in this text. This topic is usually part of advanced accounting courses.

As shown in Exhibit 4.3, a correction of an error in a prior period adjustment is added to or deducted from the previously reported opening balance of retained earnings to derive a **restated (revised) opening balance.** Furthermore, a correction of an error in a prior period is reported **net of its related income tax effect,** as for extraordinary items. As we discuss in Chapter 19, the principle of intraperiod tax allocation requires that prior period adjustments and corrections be reported on a net-of-tax basis.

Net Income and Dividends

The net income figure on the statement of retained earnings is taken directly from the income statement. When a company sustains a **net loss** during a period, the loss is deducted on the retained earnings statement.

Dividends declared during the period are deducted on the retained earnings statement and dividends per share are ordinarily disclosed. Dividends declared may be in the form of cash, other assets, or the company's own shares. Further, they may relate to both preferred and common shares. Note that dividends declared are deducted on the statement since the declaration represents a reduction in retained earnings. Sometimes a company declares a dividend in one period but does not pay or distribute it until the next. As a result, dividends declared during a period may include an amount paid or distributed during the period and an amount that will be paid or distributed in the next period.

Combined Statement of Income and Retained Earnings

Exhibit 4.4 illustrates a **combined statement of income and retained earnings.** Some accountants favour this type of statement because it integrates important and related

---

[15]"Accounting Changes," CICA *Handbook*, Paragraphs 1506.22–.25, March 1991.

Exhibit 4.4

Sunrise Corporation
COMBINED STATEMENT OF INCOME AND RETAINED EARNINGS
For the Year Ended December 31, 1995

Net income*		$74 400
Add: Retained earnings, Jan. 1, 1995, as previously reported	$45 600	
Less: Correction of an error in a prior period—depreciation understated in 1994 due to an error, less applicable income tax effect of $2000	3 000	
Retained earnings, Jan. 1, 1995, as restated		42 600
Subtotal		117 000
Less: Dividends declared on preferred shares ($0.80 per share)	4 000	
Dividends declared on common shares** ($0.60 per share)	12 000	16 000
Retained earnings, Dec. 31, 1995		$101 000
Per common share**		
Income before extraordinary item		$2.32
Extraordinary gain (net of income taxes)		1.20
Net income		$3.52

*The items shown in Exhibits 4.1 or 4.2 would appear above net income.

**Alternatively, earnings per share may be presented parenthetically in the body of the combined statement of income and retained earnings.

information. Opponents claim that it is too complicated for many users and de-emphasizes net income by not placing this item at the bottom of the combined statement.

Statement of Shareholders' Equity

Sometimes a company also has changes in other accounts that comprise shareholders' equity. These changes occur as the company sells additional shares, retires its own shares, or engages in other kinds of capital share transactions. Such changes must be disclosed in a separate statement, in the basic statements, and in the notes to the financial statements. Changes in the number of shares outstanding should also be disclosed.[16]

Many companies report all of these changes in a separate statement of shareholders' equity. This statement combines the retained earnings statement with one that shows changes in all the other components of shareholders' equity. As a result, a company that reports a statement of shareholders' equity need not report a separate retained earnings statement. A statement of shareholders' equity for the Sunrise Corporation appears in Exhibit 4.5.

Balance Sheet

The balance sheet (sometimes called the **statement of financial position**) shows the financial position of an enterprise at a particular point in time. Investors, creditors, and other users of financial statements analyze an enterprise's balance sheet to evaluate such factors

[16]"Share Capital," CICA *Handbook*, Paragraph 3240.04, March 1975.

Exhibit 4.5

Sunrise Corporation
STATEMENT OF SHAREHOLDERS' EQUITY
For the Year Ended December 31, 1995

	Preferred Shares	Common Shares	Contributed Surplus	Retained Earnings	Total
Balance, Jan. 1, 1995, as previously reported	$50 000	$60 000	$25 000	$45 600	$180 600
Less: Prior period adjustment—correction of depreciation understatement in 1994 due to error, less applicable income tax effect of $2000				(3 000)	(3 000)
Balance, Jan. 1, 1995, as restated	50 000	60 000	25 000	42 600	177 600
Add: Net income				74 400	74 400
Less: Dividends declared on preferred shares ($0.80 per share)				(4 000)	(4 000)
Dividends declared on common shares ($0.60 per share)				(12 000)	(12 000)
Add: Common shares issued on Jan. 2, 1995 (8000 shares)		40 000	15 000		55 000
Balance, Dec. 31, 1995	$50 000	$100 000	$40 000	$101 000	$291 000

as **liquidity** (how close the assets are to cash realization), **capital structure** (what amount of assets has been financed by creditors and what amount by owners), and **financial flexibility** (the ability of a company to use its financial resources to adapt to change). Generally, companies that lack sufficient liquidity and financial flexibility, perhaps because virtually all of their assets are far removed from cash and a large proportion of their capital structure consists of debt, are less able than other companies to take advantage of attractive investment opportunities or to absorb adverse changes in operating conditions. Companies without sufficient liquidity and financial flexibility are therefore more likely to fail than other companies. The 1985 annual report of Texaco, Inc., contains an interesting disclosure that shows how a company's financial flexibility can sometimes be changed drastically. The disclosure says, "There was a significant change in Texaco's financial flexibility at December 31, 1985 attributable to the December 10, 1985 judgment of the Texas State District Court against Texaco and for Pennzoil in the amount of $10.5 billion (excluding interest)."

The balance sheet was once regarded as the most important financial statement, but, as stated earlier, most users now regard the income statement as paramount. Nevertheless, the balance sheet may be regaining some attention. The accounting standard setters are clearly giving renewed attention to the balance sheet, as indicated by the asset/liability view of earnings in recent standards in such areas as pensions and capital leases.

Elements of the Balance Sheet

The following equation presents the three major elements of the balance sheet:

$$Assets = Liabilities + Owners' Equity$$

In Chapter 2, we defined these elements as follows:

1. **Assets.**   Probable future economic benefits obtained or controlled by an entity as a result of past transactions or events.
2. **Liabilities.**   Probable future sacrifices of economic benefits arising from present obligations of an entity to transfer assets or provide services to other entities in the future as a result of past transactions or events.
3. **Owners' Equity/Net Assets.**   The residual interest in the assets of an entity that remains after deducting its liabilities.

Balance Sheet Classifications

Generally accepted accounting principles require a company to report its assets, liabilities, and owners' equity in several classifications or categories. Although some flexibility is permitted in selecting and naming balance sheet categories and in grouping specific items into them, the following categories (in the order shown) are representative of those usually found in practice:

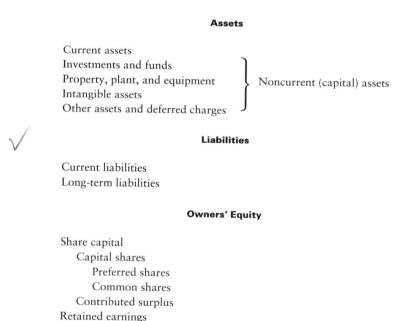

Assets

Current assets
Investments and funds
Property, plant, and equipment   } Noncurrent (capital) assets
Intangible assets
Other assets and deferred charges

Liabilities

Current liabilities
Long-term liabilities

Owners' Equity

Share capital
　　Capital shares
　　　Preferred shares
　　　Common shares
　　Contributed surplus
Retained earnings

Exhibit 4.6 shows the **account form** of balance sheet for Sunrise Corporation. In this form, the liabilities and owners' equity are listed to the right of the assets. The **report form** and the **financial position form** are also acceptable. The report form shows the liabilities and owners' equity directly below the assets. The financial position form shows current liabilities deducted from current assets to determine working capital; noncurrent assets are then added to working capital and noncurrent liabilities are deducted to arrive at owners' equity. Out of 300 companies surveyed by the CICA, 219 companies used the report form in their 1990 annual reports.[17]

---

[17]*Financial Reporting in Canada 1990*, 19th ed. (Toronto: CICA, 1991), p. 71.

Exhibit 4.6

Sunrise Corporation
BALANCE SHEET
December 31, 1995

Assets

Current Assets

Cash			$22 500
Marketable securities (at cost; market value $40 700)			40 000
Accounts receivable	$ 55 000		
Less: Allowance for doubtful accounts	4 500		50 500
Notes receivable			26 000
Merchandise inventory (at lower of average cost or market)			35 000
Prepaid expenses			
Supplies		5 350	
Insurance		4 650	10 000
Total current assets			$184 000

Investments and Funds

Investment in Case Limited common shares (at cost; market value $46 400)		41 800	
Land held for future plant site		55 000	
Plant expansion fund		48 700	
Total investments and funds			145 500

Property, Plant, and Equipment

Land			22 000
Building	100 000		
Less: Accumulated depreciation	30 000	70 000	
Equipment	80 000		
Less: Accumulated depreciation	20 000	60 000	
Total property, plant, and equipment			152 000

Intangible Assets

Goodwill			38 500

Other Assets

Unamortized discount		6 000	
Bond issue costs		8 000	14 000
Total assets			$534 000

Liabilities and Shareholders' Equity

Current Liabilities

Accounts payable	$ 47 400	
Notes payable	12 000	
Interest payable	4 200	
Salaries payable	6 400	
Commissions payable	1 000	
Income tax payable	10 000	
Advances from customers	7 200	
Unearned rent revenue	4 800	
Total current liabilities		$ 93 000

Long-Term Liabilities

Bonds payable (10%, due Dec. 31, 2005)		150 000
Total liabilities		243 000

Shareholders' Equity

Share capital

Capital shares

Preferred shares (no-par value, $8, cumulative and nonparticipating, 10 000 shares authorized, 5000 shares issued and outstanding)	65 000	
Common shares (no-par value, 25 000 shares authorized, 20 000 shares issued and outstanding)	125 000	
Total share capital		190 000
Retained earnings		101 000
Total shareholders' equity		291 000
Total liabilities and shareholders' equity		$534 000

Asset/Liability Measurement

The following discussion of each classification includes a brief indication of how some of the major items reported in it are valued on the balance sheet. You will see that although balance sheets are based largely on historical costs, they actually reflect several measurement attributes. Many of the remaining chapters in this book are organized within a balance sheet framework, and we explain in detail the nature and valuation of individual assets, liabilities, and owners' equity.

Assets

Current Assets. Current assets are cash and other assets that are reasonably expected to be realized in cash, sold, or consumed during the normal operating cycle of the business or within one year from the balance sheet date, whichever is *longer*.[18] An **operating cycle** for a given enterprise is the *average time* that it takes for the enterprise to spend cash for inventory, sell the inventory in exchange for a receivable, and collect the receivable in cash. The cycle thus progresses from cash, through inventories and receivables, back to cash.

Most companies have operating cycles that are shorter than one year. Some companies, however, such as those involved in distilling, tobacco, and lumber operations, have longer operating cycles. A balance sheet of one of these companies may therefore contain current assets, such as inventory, for which cash realization is not expected within the next year.

Current assets are usually listed in the order of their liquidity. The most common current assets are cash, short-term investments, receivables, inventories, and prepaid expenses.

Cash (on hand and on deposit) is included among current assets only if it is available for current operations. Any cash that has been restricted for other purposes should be reported in the investments and funds section of the balance sheet. Cash is reported at its face amount.

Short-term investments are those that are readily marketable and that management *intends* to convert into cash within the next year or operating cycle, whichever is longer. Often they consist entirely of marketable securities such as shares or bonds. These securities are normally reported at the lower of their cost or market value. Market value can be defined as the amount at which the securities are trading on a local stock exchange.

Receivables represent claims to cash. Accounts receivable typically compose the largest dollar value of receivables. An estimated allowance for doubtful accounts should be deducted from the gross amount of accounts receivable so that the accounts are properly reported at their **net realizable value** (estimated amount collectable).

Inventory in a merchandising company normally consists only of merchandise that is ready for sale to customers. On the other hand, the inventories of a manufacturing concern may consist of factory supplies, raw materials, work (goods) in process, and finished goods. Inventories are usually reported at the lower of cost or market value.

Prepaid expenses consist of such items as insurance, rent, advertising, taxes, and operating supplies. These items are not current assets in the sense that they will be converted into cash, but rather in the sense that if they had not been paid for in advance, they would require the use of current assets during the next year or operating cycle. A prepaid expense is reported at the amount of its unexpired or unconsumed cost.

In practice, the distinction between current and noncurrent assets is sometimes hazy and is based in part on judgement, custom, and materiality. For example, a company that

---

[18]"Current Assets and Current Liabilities," CICA *Handbook*, Paragraph 1510.01, August 1991.

Materiality

has a three-month operating cycle may report a two-year prepaid insurance policy as a current asset because the amount involved is immaterial. As another example, companies do not customarily report the following year's depreciation as a current asset, although a portion of capital assets will be consumed in the next year's operations.

Investments and Funds.   This category is used to report various types of investments and fund balances that management *intends* to hold for a period longer than the normal operating cycle or one year, whichever is longer, and that are *not* used in the business operations. Assets reported here need not be readily marketable. This category is often called **long-term investments,** or simply **investments.** Assets commonly included in this category are as follows:

1.   Long-term investments in securities of other companies, such as shares, bonds, and notes.
2.   Investments in capital assets that are not currently used in operations, such as land held for a future plant site or for speculation.
3.   Special fund balances accumulated for a particular purpose, such as future plant expansion.
4.   Cash surrender values of life insurance policies.

The valuation basis used for assets in this category depends on the type of asset. For example, a special fund balance is normally reported at the amount accumulated in the fund, while an investment in bonds is usually reported at face value plus unamortized premium (or face value minus unamortized discount). Long-term equity investments may be valued using the cost, lower of cost or market, or equity method, depending on whether the investment is readily marketable and on the extent of ownership interest held. We discuss the valuation of investments and funds more fully in Chapter 11.

Noncurrent (Capital) Assets

Property, Plant, and Equipment.   This section of the balance sheet reports assets that are tangible (have physical substance) and long-lived, and that are used in the business operations. **Plant (fixed) assets** is a shorter title that refers to property, plant, and equipment. Examples of plant assets are business sites (the land on which the business is located), buildings, equipment, machinery, furniture, fixtures, tools, containers, and natural resources. Accountants usually record depreciation or depletion on all plant assets except land. Plant assets are reported on the balance sheet at their historical cost less any accumulated depreciation or depletion. The term **book value** (or **net book value**) refers to the difference between cost and accumulated depreciation or depletion. The net book value of Sunrise Corporation's building is $70 000 ($100 000 − $30 000) (see Exhibit 4.6).

Intangible Assets.   Intangible assets are long-lived resources that lack physical substance but convey valuable rights and privileges to the business. Examples include patents, copyrights, goodwill, trademarks, franchises, and licences. An accountant usually cannot measure the value of intangible assets with sufficient objectivity to report it in the balance sheet. Therefore, the accountant initially records an intangible asset at cost, based on a completed, arm's-length exchange transaction. The cost is then allocated in a systematic manner over the periods benefited through a process called **amortization.**[19] The balance

---

[19]"Capital Assets," CICA *Handbook*, Paragraph 3060.31, October 1990.

sheet valuation assigned to an intangible asset is therefore its cost less amortization taken to date. Companies rarely report accumulated amortization in a separate contra account.

Other Assets and Deferred Charges.   This category includes assets that do not fit conveniently into one of the other four categories. Ideally, accountants should seldom use the other assets category since it is very general and since most assets can be classified into one of the other, more specific categories. Nevertheless, in practice, a wide variety of assets are reported as other assets.

Examples of other assets are machinery rearrangement costs, bond issue costs, organization costs, long-term rental prepayments, and prepaid income taxes resulting from the application of intraperiod tax allocation (a concept we explain in Chapter 19). The valuation reported is usually the unallocated cost. Accountants sometimes use the term **deferred charges** (meaning simply **delayed debits**) to describe certain assets in this category. A deferred charge is essentially a long-term prepayment of an expense. Many accountants avoid this term since, technically speaking, buildings, patents, and similar assets classified elsewhere are also deferred charges.

Liabilities

Current Liabilities.   Current liabilities are obligations whose liquidation is reasonably expected to require the use of existing resources properly classifiable as current assets or the creation of other current liabilities.[20] Notice that the definition of current liabilities is closely related to that of current assets. That is, if the satisfaction of a liability requires the use of existing current assets or the creation of other current liabilities, then the liability is considered current for accounting purposes. Current liabilities include the following:[21]

1.   Payables for items that have entered or relate directly to the operating cycle, such as accounts payable, wages payable, commissions payable, and income taxes payable.
2.   Collections received in advance of delivering goods or performing services, such as advances from customers for merchandise ordered or cash received for advance ticket sales.
3.   Other obligations that will be liquidated through the use of current assets or the creation of other current liabilities within the next year or operating cycle, whichever is longer. Examples include short-term notes payable resulting from the purchase of equipment and the currently maturing portion of long-term debt.

Not all short-term obligations require the use of current assets or the creation of other current liabilities during the next year or operating cycle. For example, a bond issue that matures during the next year may be paid using cash accumulated in a sinking fund (classified in the investments and funds category), or a short-term note payable may be refinanced on a long-term basis. These obligations should be reported as long-term rather than current liabilities. Current liabilities are normally listed in the order of their liquidation dates and reported at the amount to be paid.

Working capital (sometimes called **net working capital**) is the difference between total current assets and total current liabilities. Working capital is an approximate measure of the net amount of a company's relatively liquid resources, and many creditors

---

[20]"Current Assets and Current Liabilities," CICA *Handbook*, Paragraph 1510.03, August 1991.
[21]"Current Assets and Current Liabilities," CICA *Handbook*, Paragraphs 1510.03–09, March 1991.

believe that it constitutes a margin of safety for paying short-term debts.[22] Companies without adequate working capital may be more likely than others to have liquidity problems.

Because of the emphasis placed by many users of financial statements on working capital and on the size of a company's **current ratio** (current assets divided by current liabilities), corporate managers have at times wanted to incorrectly report certain non-current assets as current and certain current liabilities as long-term. Accountants and auditors must detect and request that management correct these errors before the financial statements are issued.

Long-Term Liabilities. Long-term liabilities are obligations that will not require the use of current assets or the creation of other current liabilities within the next year or operating cycle, whichever is longer. In other words, this category comprises all liabilities other than those properly classified as current. Examples of long-term liabilities are bonds payable, long-term notes payable, long-term obligations under warranty contracts, obligations under capital leases, and pension obligations. Conceptually, a long-term liability should be measured on the date incurred at an amount equal to the present value of the expected future payments.

When bonds payable are reported, any premium associated with the bonds should be added to the face or maturity value, while any discount should be reported under deferred charges. An obligation classified as long-term sometimes requires the use of current assets or the creation of other current liabilities within the next year or operating cycle, whichever is longer. Such an obligation, along with any related premium or discount, should be reclassified as a current liability. An example is a five-year note payable that matures within the next year and will be paid using cash that is classified as a current asset.

Some companies use a **deferred credits** category to report certain long-term obligations, such as deferred income taxes and collections received in advance of performing services on a long-term basis. Deferred credits are simply delayed credits that will increase reported income in future periods.

Owners' Equity

Owners' equity is a measure of the owners' interests in the assets of a business. Traditionally, the accountant measures individual assets and liabilities directly. Owners' equity is simply a residual, indirect measurement whose value depends on the values assigned to assets and liabilities.

The three primary forms of business organization are sole proprietorships, partnerships, and corporations. In proprietorships and partnerships, owners' equity is usually summarized in a single capital account for each owner. The balance in a capital account summarizes the owner's investments and withdrawals as well as his or her share of past net incomes and losses. The balance sheet of a proprietorship or partnership generally does not distinguish between amounts paid into the firm by owners and reinvested earnings, because government regulations usually do not restrict the amount of withdrawals that a proprietor or partner can make. Creditors of proprietorships and partnerships are usually more interested in the personal financial conditions of the owners, since, in the event of liquidation, owners may be held personally liable for business debts.

---

[22]For an interesting discussion of the limitations of the working capital concept, see Philip Fess, "The Working Capital Concept," *Accounting Review* (April 1966), pp. 266–70.

Corporations report owners' equity (usually called **shareholders'** or **stockholders' equity**) in two major categories: **share capital** (often called **contributed** or **invested capital**) and **retained earnings.** The use of these categories results in a shareholders' equity that is classified approximately according to **sources** of capital.

Historically, legal considerations have influenced the reporting of shareholders' equity. Because corporate shareholders cannot be held personally liable for company debts, most corporation acts state that corporations cannot distribute assets to shareholders if doing so would reduce owners' equity below a minimum amount, known as **legal** or **stated capital.** The legal capital of a given company depends on the laws of the jurisdiction in which the company is organized.

Share Capital.   This category is used to report amounts that shareholders have paid into the company in exchange for capital shares. This section of the balance sheet may be divided further by the type of capital shares.

Capital shares include various classes often referred to as preferred and common shares. Here, companies report the total amount received when the shares have no par or stated value. When the shares have a par or stated value per share, this value is multiplied by the number of shares issued. If a company has both preferred and common shares outstanding, it should report each type separately. Companies registered under the Canada Business Corporation Act and many provincial corporation acts must issue no-par value shares.

Materiality   **Contributed surplus** represents amounts received from **donated capital,** or **paid-in excess of the par or stated value** for par-value shares sold. Paid-in capital in excess of par may be presented as a single amount, but if several material sources of paid-in capital in excess of par exist, a breakdown by source may be helpful to financial-statement users.

Retained Earnings.   Retained earnings, which represent a company's accumulated earnings less its dividends, are added to total share capital and contributed surplus when determining total shareholders' equity. A negative (debit) balance in retained earnings, called a **deficit,** occurs when a company's losses and dividends exceed its earnings. An accountant should simply deduct a deficit from total share capital to arrive at total shareholders' equity.

The retained earnings category is sometimes divided into **appropriated** and **unappropriated** components. Companies may appropriate (or restrict) retained earnings for legal, contractual, or discretionary reasons. The amount appropriated is not available as a basis for declaring dividends during the time of appropriation. Companies usually disclose appropriations of retained earnings in the notes to their financial statements. Occasionally, however, a company may make a formal journal entry for the amount appropriated. This entry involves a debit to retained earnings and a credit to retained earnings appropriated for the designated purpose, such as future plant expansion. These kinds of entries ultimately produce balances in appropriated retained earnings accounts, such as Retained Earnings Appropriated for Future Plant Expansion or Retained Earnings Restricted by the Purchase of the Corporation's Own Shares. These accounts and their balances are reported as appropriated retained earnings.

When a company has created accounts for retained earnings appropriations, it reports the amount of its unappropriated retained earnings separate from the amounts appropriated. Unappropriated retained earnings are simply those available for declaring dividends.[23]

[23]A decision to declare dividends is, of course, influenced by many factors other than retained earnings.

Corporations that are under the Canada Business Corporations Act or many provincial acts can hold their own capital shares only under very limited circumstances. However, some provinces allow companies to purchase and hold their own shares that they previously sold to investors. A company may acquire its own shares for several reasons. For example, it may want to use the shares to satisfy employee stock-option contracts or to effect a merger. These shares are not assets but rather reductions in shareholders' equity. The vast majority of companies account for these shares at cost by debiting a treasury shares account for the cost of the shares purchased. The company later deducts the amount in the treasury shares account as the final account in the shareholders' equity section. This topic will not be covered in detail in this text because of its limited use in Canada.

Statement of Changes in Financial Position

A complete set of financial statements includes a statement of changes in financial position.[24] The primary purpose of this statement is to report information about a company's cash receipts and payments during a period. If used with the other basic financial statements, the statement of changes in financial position can help users to assess a company's ability to generate future net cash inflows, the company's ability to pay debts and dividends (outflows), the company's needs for external financing, the reasons for differences between income and related cash flows, and both the cash and non-cash aspects of the company's investing and financing transactions during the period.

Although the statement of changes in financial position provides considerable information about a company's current cash receipts and payments, the statement by itself does not provide a sound basis for making predictions about the company's future cash flows. Many current cash receipts result from decisions made in *past* periods (e.g., a decision made in an earlier period to invest in capital assets), and many current decisions involving cash payments are made with the aim of increasing *future* cash receipts (e.g., a decision made in the current period to invest in capital assets). Thus, the statement of changes in financial position should be used with the other basic financial statements to help investors and creditors assess such important factors as an entity's liquidity, financial flexibility, and profitability.

A statement of changes in financial position explains the change in a company's cash during the period. If a company invests in highly liquid short-term investments, such as treasury bills, then the statement should explain the change during the period in **cash and cash equivalents.**

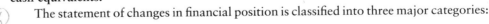

The statement of changes in financial position is classified into three major categories:

1. **Operating activities** include all transactions that are not properly classified as investing or financing activities. These activities include producing and selling goods and providing services. Generally, the cash flows from operating activities represent the cash effects of transactions that are reflected in the determination of income.
   a. Operating activities that produce cash *inflows* include:
      i.   Cash receipts from the sale of goods or services to customers.
      ii. Cash receipts from interest, dividends, and other sources that do not represent investing or financing activities.
      iii. Adjustment for non-cash items: depreciation and amortization.

---

[24]"Statement of Changes in Financial Position," CICA *Handbook*, Section 1540, August 1991.

    b.   Operating activities that produce cash *outflows* include:
       i.   Cash payments for the acquisition of inventory.
       ii.   Cash payments to employees and other suppliers of goods and services.
       iii.   Cash payments for taxes.
       iv.   Cash payments for interest.
       v.   Cash payments for other purposes that do not represent investing or financing activities.

2. **Financing activities** include obtaining resources from owners and paying dividends, and obtaining resources from creditors and repaying the amounts borrowed.
    a.   Financing activities that produce cash *inflows* include:
       i.   Cash receipts from the issuance of debt securities (short-term or long-term).
       ii.   Cash receipts from the issuance of equity securities.
    b.   Financing activities that produce cash *outflows* include:
       i.   Repayments of amounts borrowed.
       ii.   Cash payments of dividends.
       iii.   Cash payments to repurchase the company's own shares.

3. **Investing activities** include lending money and collecting loans, acquiring and disposing of securities that are not cash equivalents, and acquiring and selling long-term productive assets.
    a.   Investing activities that produce cash *inflows* include:
       i.   Cash receipts from the collection (or sale) of loans made to other enterprises.
       ii.   Cash receipts from the sale of assets such as investments in securities (other than cash equivalents) of other companies and property, plant, and equipment.
    b.   Investing activities that produce cash *outflows* include:
       i.   Cash outflows to make loans to other enterprises.
       ii.   Cash payments to acquire assets such as investments in securities (other than cash equivalents) of other companies and property, plant, and equipment.

Classification according to the three categories described above allows investors and creditors to assess significant relationships within and among a company's major activities: its operating, investing, and financing activities. The classification system provides useful information by linking cash flows that are often considered to be related, such as cash inflows from borrowing money and cash outflows to repay loans.

Exhibit 4.7 shows the statement of changes in financial position for the Sunrise Corporation. Preparation of such a statement requires comparative balance sheets as well as information that explains changes in the account balances during the period. We have *not* included all this information here, because at this point, you should concentrate on the basic form of the statement and the general types of information it conveys. You cannot verify all the numbers in Exhibit 4.7, but that is not our purpose at this time. After studying this chapter, you should have a basic understanding of the nature and purpose of the statement of changes in financial position. In Chapter 22, we discuss this statement in detail and explain how to prepare it.

As Exhibit 4.7 shows, the statement begins with cash flows from operating activities. Remember that operating activities encompass all transactions that are not properly classified as investing or financing activities. Net cash flow from operating activities does *not* include cash flows from certain transactions that are reflected in income but are investing or financing activities. For example, Sunrise had an unusual loss on the sale of long-term investments during 1995 (as shown in Exhibit 4.1). The sale of long-term investments is

Exhibit 4.7

Sunrise Corporation
STATEMENT OF CHANGES IN FINANCIAL POSITION
For the Year Ended December 31, 1995

Cash Flows from Operating Activities		
Cash received from customers	$538 700	
Interest received	2 100	
Dividends received	5 200	
Rent received	8 400	
Cash provided by operating activities		$554 400
Cash paid to suppliers and employees	455 900	
Interest paid	14 200	
Taxes paid	47 300	
Cash disbursed for operating activities		517 400
Net cash flow from operating activities		37 000
Cash Flows from Investing Activities		
Short-term loans made	(18 000)	
Collections on short-term loans	8 000	
Purchase of long-term investments	(14 000)	
Proceeds from sale of long-term investments	10 900	
Purchases of property, plant, and equipment	(38 800)	
Proceeds from disposals of property, plant, and equipment	76 400	
Net cash provided by investing activities		24 500
Cash Flows from Financing Activities		
Proceeds of short-term debt	23 000	
Payments to settle short-term debt	(25 000)	
Proceeds of long-term debt	50 000	
Payments to settle long-term note	(110 000)	
Proceeds from issuing common shares	55 000	
Dividends paid	(16 000)	
Net cash used by financing activities		(23 000)
Net increase in cash and cash equivalents		38 500
Cash and cash equivalents, Jan. 1, 1995		24 000
Cash and cash equivalents, Dec. 31, 1995		$ 62 500

really an investing activity, and accordingly, the loss is reflected in the calculation of the proceeds from the sale of long-term investments ($10 900).

Net cash flow from operating activities should be prominently disclosed, because users of financial statements generally are interested in evaluating the ability of a company to generate cash through its operations. Some companies can generate net income but not much cash. Over the long run, a business ordinarily must generate cash through its own operations if it is to survive. A company cannot simply depend on raising cash through such means as borrowing or selling capital assets. In Exhibit 4.7, we see that Sunrise generated a positive net cash flow of $37 000 as a result of its operating activities during 1995.

Cash flows from investing activities are reported in the next category shown in Exhibit 4.7. Observe how the cash outflows associated with each of the investing activities are deducted from related cash inflows. The statement shows that Sunrise generated

$24 500 from its investing activities during 1995, primarily by disposing of certain plant assets.

Cash flows from financing activities are also reported by subtracting cash outflows from related cash inflows. The statement shows that Sunrise's major financing activities during 1995 were the settlement of a long-term note payable and the issuance of common shares, thereby increasing the extent to which the firm relies on owner financing. Unlike the operating and investing activities, which *provided* cash during 1995, Sunrise's financing activities *used* cash of $23 000.

Taken together, Sunrise's operating, investing, and financing activities resulted in a net increase in cash and cash equivalents of $38 500. The term "cash and cash equivalents" (as opposed to "cash") is used near the bottom of the statement because Sunrise has marketable securities. These short-term, highly liquid investments are considered to be part of the company's cash-management program rather than a part of its operating, investing, or financing activities. If we add $24 000 of cash and cash equivalents at the beginning of 1995 to the $38 500 net increase in cash and cash equivalents, we find that Sunrise has cash and cash equivalents of $62 500 at the end of 1995.

Many other issues affect the form and content of the statement of changes in financial position. For example, when a company reports net cash flow from operating activities in the manner shown in Exhibit 4.7, a reconciliation of net income and net cash flow from operating activities must be provided in a separate schedule. This schedule is explained in Chapter 22.

Relationship Between Basic Financial Statements

As we stated earlier, the basic financial statements articulate with one another. Their relationship is summarized in simplified terms in Exhibit 4.8.

A company's financial position at a particular moment in time is shown on the balance sheet. The other basic financial statements summarize various types of changes in financial position that have occurred during a period of time. The income statement explains the changes in financial position that are the result of earnings activities. The statement of retained earnings or statement of shareholders' equity explains certain changes in the equity component of financial position. The statement of changes in financial position summarizes all important cash receipts and payments during a period.

The income statement reports the revenues, expenses, gains, losses, and net income for a period. The net income explains a part of the change in retained earnings that is shown on the statement of retained earnings or statement of shareholders' equity. The statement of changes in financial position summarizes the major cash-related activities that have occurred during the period. These statements are tied together by the beginning and ending balance sheets. All of the basic financial statements articulate with one another because of the double-entry system of accounting and because revenues, expenses, gains, losses, investments by owners, and distributions to owners represent cash flows associated with the economic resources and obligations presented on the balance sheet.

Articulation is an important concept to understand about financial statements. When a company computes depreciation on its capital assets, for example, this affects not only the income statement (depreciation expense) but also the balance sheet (accumulated depreciation). Most people believe that articulation is desirable because it accurately reflects the nature of a company's economic activities. Benefits usually require sacrifices, and sacrifices usually produce benefits. Double-entry accrual accounting, which we review

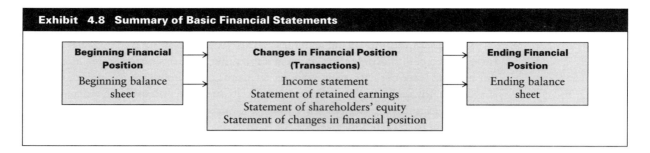

Exhibit 4.8 Summary of Basic Financial Statements

Beginning Financial Position	Changes in Financial Position (Transactions)	Ending Financial Position
Beginning balance sheet	Income statement Statement of retained earnings Statement of shareholders' equity Statement of changes in financial position	Ending balance sheet

in Chapter 6, ensures that financial statements prepared according to GAAP will articulate.

A minority view holds that financial statements could be improved if articulation were not required. Proponents of this view believe that articulation is an unnecessary constraint that limits the usefulness of financial statements. To illustrate this view, most people believe that LIFO inventory costing is generally desirable for the income statement (because cost of goods sold is measured at recent cost prices) but undesirable for the balance sheet (because inventory is measured at outdated historical costs). In contrast, FIFO is generally viewed as desirable for the balance sheet but undesirable for the income statement. A proponent of nonarticulated financial statements might argue that a company should be allowed to use LIFO on its income statement and FIFO on its balance sheet. Moreover, there is no need for the two statements to articulate. We emphasize that nonarticulated financial statements, although interesting, are *not* generally accepted today.

Other Financial Statement Topics

Disclosure

The **disclosure principle** requires an accountant to report information that might affect the decisions made by reasonably informed users of financial statements. To comply with this principle, an accountant usually must report in financial statements considerably more information than we have illustrated thus far in this chapter. Moreover, all of this information must be effectively communicated. In the remaining sections of this chapter, we will discuss several other topics pertaining to basic financial statements.

To help you understand the kinds of information that companies actually report, we have included a set of financial statements of Canadian Pacific Limited on the endpapers of this book. Look over these statements now, and refer to them frequently as you study the remaining chapters. Although the statements contain material that you have not yet encountered, you will understand them much better after you have studied this book.

Notes to Financial Statements

Financial statements are summaries that consist of dollar amounts and few words. **Notes to financial statements** are used to report information that does not fit in the body of the statements without reducing the understandability of the statements or that expands on information contained within the statements. **Notes are an integral part of the financial statements and therefore must be prepared and read carefully.** The notes often require several pages and are referenced in the financial statements.

Five major types of information are commonly disclosed in notes:

1. Information on **accounting policies.** Companies must disclose the major accounting policies that they use to prepare their financial statements.
2. Information on **subsequent events.** Companies are required to disclose certain types of events that occur between the date shown on the balance sheet and the date on which the financial statements are issued.
3. Information on **contingencies.** Companies often disclose certain contingencies, which are events, such as pending lawsuits, that involve uncertainty about possible gains or losses that will be resolved in the future. We discuss accounting for contingencies in Chapter 15.
4. Information on major **contracts, commitments, and restrictions.** Important details about leases and pension plans, for example, are usually reported in the notes.
5. Information that **amplifies data** presented in the body of the statements. For example, a company may provide a schedule that separates its inventories into raw materials, work-in-process, and finished goods.

Notes to financial statements should be concise, complete, and easily understood by a reader who has a reasonable understanding of business affairs and is willing to study the financial statements. The precise nature of disclosures required in notes is very detailed. We discuss these disclosures more fully at appropriate places in the remaining chapters.

Summary of Accounting Policies

Knowledgeable users recognize that the numbers reported in a company's financial statements depend on the accounting policies used to generate them. As a result, when analyzing financial statements, users typically want answers to questions such as: What inventory cost determination method (such as FIFO or average cost) does the company use? What depreciation method (such as double-declining balance or straight-line) does the company use?

To ensure that users have the information needed to answer these kinds of questions, Section 1505 of the CICA *Handbook* requires a company to disclose the accounting policies that it uses. The term "accounting policies" refers to the specific principles and methods that a company has adopted for preparing its financial statements. The accounting policies that a company discloses should be those that: (1) involve a selection from existing acceptable alternatives, (2) are peculiar to the reporting company's industry, or (3) are unusual or innovative applications of generally accepted accounting principles.

A company should preferably disclose its accounting policies in a separate **summary of significant accounting policies.** This summary should precede the notes to the financial statements or appear as the first note.[25]

Subsequent Events

Financial statements are seldom issued on the date shown on the balance sheet. Instead, a period of time usually elapses, during which the accountants and auditors complete their work on the statements. During this period, called the **subsequent period,** many important events can occur that have a material effect on the financial statements being prepared.

---

[25]"Disclosure of Accounting Policies," CICA *Handbook*, Paragraph 1505, March 1991.

Digging Into Firms' Footnotes

A well-known investment maxim says you should read financial statements from back to front.

That means you begin with the footnotes, which professionals say often contain more information than the financial statements themselves. Here you can find references to problems—such as outstanding lawsuits or investigations—which may affect the future of your investment.

Companies like to put their best foot forward in the letter to shareholders, just like a real estate agent emphasizes the good features of a building, warns Bob Tattersall of Howson Tattersall Investment Counsel Ltd. in Toronto.

But the notes to the financial statement are like the builder's blueprint, providing you with "the nuts and bolts of how the structure was created," he says.

One indication of a shaky foundation, particularly in this recessionary climate, is the appearance of a note entitled 'Going Concern Uncertainties.'

In the **Recsyn International Inc.** report for 1991, a note on the company's accounting policies disclosed its going concern assumptions: "While the financial statements have been prepared on the basis of accounting principles applicable to a going concern, several conditions and events cast substantial doubt on the validity of this assumption." Recsyn then provided details.

Read a going-concern note carefully, says John Carchrae, assistant director of accounting standards at the Canadian Institute of Chartered Accountants. And consider the implications. The company's ability to continue operating may depend, for example, on the continuing forbearance of its bankers, he says.

The CICA views a company's financial statements and accompanying notes as a package, all of which must be prepared according to generally accepted accounting principles (GAAP).

Before investing in a company, [you] should read the notes as part of the process of doing due diligence," says Jay Kellerman, a mergers and acquisitions lawyer with Smith Lyons Torrance Stevenson & Mayer in Toronto. "Look long and hard at the notes . . . I think they're invaluable."

Notes describe the company's transactions, expanding on line items in the balance sheet, income statement and statement of changes in financial position. They also outline the accounting policies underlying these statements.

"It's important to look at what's behind each number," says Carchrae, who cautions to resist being seduced by any single number, such as earnings per share.

He recommends you start with the footnote which sets out accounting policies, usually at the beginning of the section.

Here management discloses its revenue recognition, inventory pricing, consolidation and depreciation policies, among others. Once you know which accounting methods have been used, it's easier to compare the performance of this company with others in the same industry, Carchrae says.

Merchant bank **Hees International Bancorp Inc.**, for example, disclosed in its 1991 report that its merchant banking income was recorded on an accrual basis less a provision for uncollectible amounts.

The choice of accounting policies should also give you a clue about the conservatism of the company. After you analyse several companies in the same industry you begin to recognize some of the more common accounting practices, so that a different method should raise a red flag.

Also watch for a change in accounting policies, such as the method of depreciation.

For many years the disclosure of accounting changes was usually incomplete and led, in some cases, to charges that management used changes to manipulate earnings.

Management is now required to disclose changes in policies and estimates, and to correct previous errors. The notes detail the effect of such changes on current and previous statements.

Tattersall says the note which breaks down the company's business into segments is extremely useful. If you can see that a smaller division of the company is causing a disproportionate share of its problems, then you can bet the stock will go up sharply if the company announces it is selling that division, he says.

Notes can also provide important information about the company's significant assets and liabilities, including interest rates and due dates for long term debt.

These notes usually take a one-line item from the statements and break it into several component parts, sometimes providing another form of measurement, Carchrae says. Investment portfolios, for example, are carried at cost on the balance sheet but the market value is detailed in a note.

Indeed, notes are a way for management to provide you with concise explanations about other complicated matters, such as stock options, pension plans, leases and business combinations.

How does the company account for employee retire-

Continued

ment obligations? Although companies accrue liabilities for pension obligations, many don't accrue a liability for other post-employment benefits such as health care and life insurance, says Carchrae.

Imperial Oil Ltd.'s 1991 report estimates the company's share of the cost of certain health-care and life insurance benefits for almost all retired employees and surviving spouses. Note 12 gives an estimate of the year's expense as well as the long-term liability for these benefits.

Carchrae says you should also check how management reflects its potential environmental obligations. Is it accruing the costs the company will have to incur at the end of the useful life of the asset when the property has to be restored?

Imperial Oil, for example, says it has adopted new CICA recommendations that provisions be made for site-restoration costs. It then details the effect of the change on 1991 and prior years' statements.

Notes can alert you to other commitments or contingencies. They can tell you if there is a liability the firm may have to bear which has not been recorded in the financial statements because it cannot be reasonably estimated.

Kellerman says these notes sometimes include a throw-away line like "the company is vigorously defending the action."

Archer Communications Inc., for example, revealed to its shareholders in a note to its 1989 statements that it was the subject of an "informal investigation" by the U.S. Securities and Exchange Commission to determine whether Archer stock was being offered and sold in the U.S. in violation of securities laws. At that time management said it could not assess the potential liabilities of the investigation.

A year later, Archer conceded in a note that the SEC was conducting a "formal investigation," but again management claimed it was not able to assess the potential liabilities. The SEC continues to investigate. Last February, investors filed four lawsuits in a Los Angeles federal court against Archer, certain directors and officers, alleging violations of U.S. securities laws.

Finally, don't forget to read the note on subsequent events. It discloses anything material which has occurred after the date of the balance sheet.

Source: Reprinted from Susan Gittins, "Digging Into Firms' Footnotes," *The Financial Post* (April 6, 1992), p. 22.

Subsequent events are events that occur during the subsequent period, that is, between the date shown on the balance sheet and the date on which the financial statements are issued. Exhibit 4.9 illustrates the subsequent period, in relation to a set of 1995 financial statements. The subsequent period is from January 1, 1996, to February 28, 1996.

There are two types of subsequent events. The first consists of events that provide additional evidence about **conditions that existed on the balance sheet date** and that affect the estimates used in preparing the financial statements. The appropriate accounting for this type of subsequent event is to adjust the account balances reported in the financial statements to reflect the new information. For example, the bankruptcy of a major customer ten days after the balance sheet date usually reflects a condition (namely, the poor financial health of the customer) that existed on the balance sheet date, and the estimate of bad debts may therefore need to be revised upward to reflect the new information.

The second type of subsequent event is one that provides evidence about **conditions that arose after the balance sheet date.** Events of this type do not result in adjustments of the account balances of the previous period. They may, however, require disclosure in order to prevent the financial statements from being misleading. Examples of subsequent events that require disclosure are the purchase of a business, the loss of inventories or capital assets due to a casualty, and the sale of a bond or capital shares issue.[26]

Obviously, a subsequent event also affects the financial statements of the period in which the event occurs. For example, in the context of Exhibit 4.9, if a material sale of

---

[26]"Subsequent Events," CICA *Handbook,* Section 6550, May 1992.

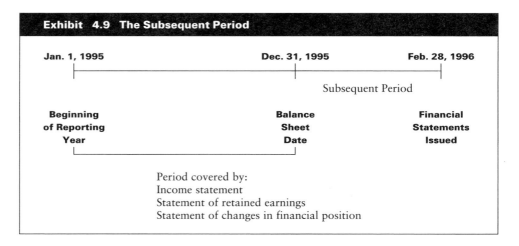

Exhibit 4.9 The Subsequent Period

Jan. 1, 1995   Dec. 31, 1995   Feb. 28, 1996

Subsequent Period

Beginning of Reporting Year   Balance Sheet Date   Financial Statements Issued

Period covered by:
Income statement
Statement of retained earnings
Statement of changes in financial position

common shares occurred on January 10, 1996, this event should be disclosed in the notes to the 1995 financial statements and recorded as a transaction in 1996. A more thorough treatment of subsequent events usually appears in auditing textbooks.[27]

Comparative Financial Statements

The financial statements illustrated in this chapter were prepared for one period only. In practice, **comparative financial statements** are ordinarily presented for two or more periods, as shown in the financial statements on the endpapers of this book. Such statements are more useful than single-period statements because they reveal important trends. When comparative financial statements are presented, all elements reported in the current period's statements should be comparable to those reported for the prior period(s). Any exceptions must be clearly explained.

Rounding of Amounts

The dollar amounts in financial statements are usually rounded. A recent survey of the annual reports of 300 companies found that 55 rounded to the nearest dollar, 204 rounded to the nearest thousand dollars, and 39 rounded to the nearest million dollars.[28] Rounding is justified because of materiality and the many estimates in financial statements. Failure to round may imply a degree of precision that simply does not exist in financial statements.

Disclosure Methods

Accountants use several methods of disclosure. Generally, the most important information is reported in the **body of the financial statements.** In addition to the account titles and amounts, **parenthetical disclosures** may be made in the body of the statements. For example, the market value of marketable securities may be shown in parentheses if it is greater than cost. Or a related asset and liability, such as inventory pledged as collateral

---

[27]"Subsequent Events", CICA *Handbook*, Section 3820, July 1979.

[28]*Financial Reporting in Canada 1990*, 19th ed. (Toronto: CICA, 1991), p. 16.

Checklist of Key Figures for Problems in

Intermediate Accounting, First Canadian Edition

Williams, Deutsch, Stanga, and Holder

Chapter 3
P3.1 (a) Gain, $20 000; (b) Gain, $5000
P3.2 (a) Loss, $4000; (b) Gain, $1000
P3.3 (a) Rice: Loss, $18 000; Tully: Gain, $18 000
P3.6 (a) Cash paid, $95 500; (b) Rent revenue, $127 000
P3.7 (a) Consulting expense, $40 000; (b) Cash received, $58 000
P3.8 (a) Cash basis income for May, $76 550; Accrual basis income for May, $31 550
(b) $30 050
P3.9 (a) For 1995: (1) $5296.50; (2) $1886.50; (3) ($1985.50); (b) $6319.50
P3.10 (a) Total assets: (1) $880 000; (2) $1 000 000; (3) $1 140 000; (4) $1 200 000
(b) For 1995: (1) $320 000; (2) $200 000; (3) $60 000; (4) -0-
P3.11 (a) Cash basis income, $2 273 000; Accrual basis income, $864 000; (b) $2 492 000

Chapter 4
P4.1 (a) & (b) Net income, $167 400
P4.2 (a) & (b) Net income, $54 000
(c) Retained earnings, $824 000
P4.3 (a) Retained earnings, $714 010
P4.4 (a) Net income, $49 200; Retained earnings, $192 200
P4.5 Total shareholders' equity, $1 039 580
P4.6 Total shareholders' equity, $1 800 400
P4.7 Total assets, $1 256 000
Total shareholders' equity, $678 500
P4.8 Total assets, $1 635 000
Total shareholders' equity, $1 042 000
P4.9 Total assets, $1 439 630
Total shareholders' equity, $718 500
P4.10 Total assets, $1 489 000
Total shareholders' equity, $815 000
P4.11 (a) Net income, $258 000
(b) Retained earnings, $315 000
(c) Total assets, $1 254 000
Total shareholders' equity, $651 000
P4.12 (a) Net income, $180 000
(b) Retained earnings, $197 000
(c) Total assets, $1 347 600
Total shareholders' equity, $658 600
P4.13 Net increase in cash, $46 000

Chapter 5
P5.1 (b) Gross profit to be recognized under percentage-of-completion method, $200 000

P5.2 Income before income taxes, $163 363
P5.3 (c) 1995 income to be recognized, $500 000
P5.4 (a) Income before income taxes, $1 506 500
P5.5 (a) 2. Income to be reported, $208 500
P5.6 (a) Income from continuing operations, $78 000
P5.7 (a) 2. Net income, $393 000
P5.8 (a) Net income, $1 751 425
P5.9 1995 net income, $1 248 000
P5.10 Net income, $280 480
P5.11 Earnings per share on net income, $7.36

Chapter 6
P6.1 (c) Unadjusted trial balance totals, $111 020
P6.2 (c) Unadjusted trial balance totals, $252 760
P6.3 (f) Net income and retained earnings, $1412; Total assets, $61 370; Total shareholders' equity, $51 412
P6.4 (g) Net income, $30 270; Retained earnings, $64 370; Total assets, $162 550; Total shareholders' equity, $104 370
P6.12 Trial balance totals, $92 500
P6.13 (d) Net income, $31 200; Retained earnings, $130 700; Total assets, $290 500; Total shareholders' equity, $230 700
P6.14 (d) Net income, $26 700; Retained earnings, $30 700; Total assets, $132 000; Total shareholders' equity, $80 700

Chapter 7
P7.1 $166.20 additional income
P7.2 Company A, $49 519.20; Company B, $36 174.60; Company C, $29 549.20; Company D, $23 433.20
P7.3 (a) $20 117.75; (b) $20 277.50
P7.5 (a) $5259.17; (b) $5781.41
P7.6 (a) $243 268.64; (b) $240 860.08
P7.7 (a) $157 908.84; (b) $107 908.84; (c) $2533.11
P7.8 (a) 28; (b) $15 528.77; (c) $17 931.84; (d) $26 347.77
P7.9 (a) $2591.67; (b) $448 166.60
P7.10 (a) $67 617.90; (b) $72 094.23
P7.11 (a) $2300; (b) $102 000; (c) $34 263.61; (d) $7576.00
P7.12 (b) $67 961.39
P7.13 (b) $37 127.56
P7.14 (a) 4%; (b) 10%; (c) 6%; (d) 10%; (e) 8%; (f) 10%
P7.15 (a) (1) $95 834.28; (2) $80 000.36; (3) $67 962.80
P7.16 (a) $439 995; (b) 4 years; (c) 5%
P7.17 (a) 16; (b) 10; (c) 7; (d) 17; (e) 5; (f) 12

P7.18 (a) $166.07; (b) (1) $520.73
P7.19 (a) $12 273.56; (b) $50 905.76
P7.20 (a) $9610.29; (b) $31 169.13

Chapter 8
P8.2 (a) Correct cash balance, $8036
P8.3 (a) Correct cash balance $5771
P8.4 (a) Correct amount of cash on May 31, $5771
P8.5 (a) Correct cash balance, $10 566
P8.6 (a) Correct amount of cash on November 30, $10 566
P8.7 (b) (1) Accounts receivable, $19 400
    (2) Accounts receivable, $20 000
P8.8 (b) Amount of adjusting entry:
    (1) $10 050; (2) $9900; (3) $10 100
    (4) $10 475
    (c) (2) & (3): Reduction of $10 050
P8.9 (a) $48 500; (c) Required charge to expense $33 500
P8.10 (c) Amount of adjusting entry, $60 300
P8.11 (b) Amount of adjusting entry, $11 360
P8.12 Credit to Allowance for Doubtful Accounts, $7700
P8.13 (b) Equity in assigned accounts receivable, $8860
P8.14 (a) (1) & (2): Proceeds from discounting note, $10 113
P8.15 (a) Proceeds from discounting Lyons note, $91 327.50
P8.16 Total of debits required to "Other Accounts," $34 511; Total of credits required to "Other Accounts," $40 720

Chapter 9
P9.1 (b) $23 500
P9.2 (b) $29 100
P9.3 (b) (1) Cost of goods sold, $72 100
    Ending inventory, $30 900
    (2) Cost of goods sold, $71 900
    Ending inventory, $31 500
P9.4 (a) Cost of goods sold: (1) $427 000; (2) $418 500; (3) $406 000
    (b) Cost of goods sold: (1) $427 000; (2) $420 900; (3) $411 000
P9.5 (a) Cost of good sold: (1) $122 500; (2) $126 389; (3) $132 500
    (b) Cost of goods sold: (1) $122 500; (2) $123 900; (3) $127 500
P9.6 (a) 1993 Net income, $48 000
P9.7 Decrease of $45 000
P9.8 Cost of goods sold: FIFO, $115 750; LIFO, $118 550; weighted average, $116 900
P9.9 (1) (a) LCM A, $23; B, $27; C, $45; D, $80
    (2) (a) LCM B, $24; B, $28; C, $45; B, $80
P9.10 Market: (1) 50; (2) 30; (3) 16; (4) 18; (5) 7; (6) 34; (7) 69; (8) 40
P9.11 (a) (1) $45 200; (2) $46 600; (3) $47 000
P9.12 (a) Corrected net income: 1990, $19 200; 1992, $21 600; 1995, $18 600

P9.13 Correct profits (losses): 1993, ($7850); 1994, $5550; 1995, $24 500
P9.14 (a) Total adjustment, $22 870
P9.15 Adjusted balances, $374 300
P9.16 (a) $59 110; (b) $47 100

Chapter 10
P10.1 $6000
P10.2 $6316
P10.3 $5930 or $5925
P10.4 $5330
P10.5 (a) $25 760
P10.6 1994, $97 500; 1995, $103 880
P10.7 (a) $29 814
P10.8 (a) $10 750; (b) $11 040
P10.9 (a) $74 428; (b) $71 748
P10.10 (a) $29 500 (b) $30 000; (c) 1994, $31 162; 1995, $25 760
P10.11 $23 000
P10.12 (a) $69 000
P10.13 Fire loss, $28 193.75
P10.14 $41 650
P10.15 (a) 20%; (b) $88 000; (c) $114 000
P10.16 Unit cost, small lots $12 000
P10.17 Insurance premium total $184

Chapter 11
P11.1 (a) Dec. 31, 1995 debit to Allowance to Reduce Current Marketable Securities to the Lower of Cost or Market, $7283
P11.2 August 1 allocation to stock rights, $5305
P11.3 December 31, 1995 debit to Allowance to Reduce CMES to LCM, $3800
P11.4 (b) June 30, 1995 interest revenue, $2407
P11.5 (b) 1995 gain on sale of bonds, $15 441
P11.6 (a) December 31, 1995 interest revenue, $257
P11.7 December 31 debit to cash, $47 515
P11.8 (b) 1995 investment balance, $1 343 400
P11.9 (b) Total operating income, $8 800 000
P11.10 (b) Equity in earnings, Fox Corp. $107 875
P11.11 (c) December 31, 1995 total assets, $308 482
P11.12 Total assets, $387 876.71

Chapter 12
P12.1 (b) Building cost, $318 182
P12.2 (e) Patent cost, $77 273
P12.3 December 31 interest expense, $2927
P12.4 Building costs, $360 174
P12.5 (b) Cost of land, $18 000
P12.6 (c) Cost of new equipment, $120 000
P12.7 (b) Annual repair and maintenance amount, $14 360
P12.8 Interest capitalized, $15 250
P12.9 August 1 capitalization of interest, $1250
P12.10 (b) Depreciation expense on building, $7875
P12.11 Asset E cost, $55 000
P12.12 (b) December 31, 1995 interest expense, $617

Chapter 13
P13.1 (a) 3. Year 5 double-declining balance, $4643
P13.2 (b) Net gain on asset disposals in 1995, $3750
P13.3 (b) Depreciation expense, building, $4361
P13.4 (b) Capitalized cost of office building, $3 302 250
P13.5 (a) December 5 loss of sale of machinery, $2575
P13.6 Asset Y, loss on sale, $5000
P13.7 Building cost, $523 875
P13.8 (c) Display fixtures 1993 depreciation, $26 400
P13.9 (b) Depreciation expense, $158 100
P13.10 1995 net income, $4 224 225
P13.11 (d) Depreciation expense, $80 700
P13.12 (b) Balance in Asset X, inventory system, $297 800
P13.13 (b) Total amount reimbursable, $666 667
P13.14 (a) Depreciation expense, Year 2, $11 083
P13.15 (a) Total assets, $9 626 900

Chapter 14
P14.1 (b) Amortization of intangibles, $645
P14.2 (a) Debit to Copyrights, $51 000
P14.3 (c) Research and development expense, $176 375
P14.4 (a) 1995 amortization of Patent B, $3809
P14.5 (b) Maximum price, $1 729 743
P14.6 (a) 3. Goodwill, $72 267
P14.7 (c) Goodwill, $440 615
P14.8 (a) Total intangibles, $118 886
P14.9 (b) Amortization of trademark, $962
P14.10 1. Land cost, $300 000
P14.11 December 31, 1995 amortization of Patent B, $15 467
P14.12 (b) Debit to Retained Earnings, $170 375

Chapter 15
P15.1 (a) Total current liabilities, $51 800
P15.2 (a) Value of machinery to be recorded, $31 000
Cash received from discounted note, $6750
(b) Total current liabilities, $84 815
P15.3 (a) Charge retained earnings for $54 250 for declaration of dividend
P15.4 (1) Credit to revenue account, $500 000
P15.5 (a) Total current liabilities, $2 776 000
(b) Total interest expense, $386 000
P15.6 (a) Adjustment required, $20 000
(b) Liability at end of year, $73 000
P15.7 (a) Estimated liability, $397 500
(b) Adjustment necessary, $347 500
P15.8 Part 2
(a) Promotion expense to be recognized, $4500
P15.9 (b) Premium liability for 1995, $2875
P15.10 (a) Token revenue, $254 300
P15.11 (a) Total current liabilities, $2 951 200
P15.12 (a) Total current liabilities 1994, $16 800 000

Chapter 16
P16.1 (a) Proceeds, $914 404
P16.2 (a) Bond issue price, $10 247 418

P16.3 (a) Present value of bonds, $768 855
(b) Net debit to cash, $743 855
P16.4 (a) Discount on bonds, $39 930
(b) April 30, 1995 discount amortized, $7986
P16.5 (a) Cash received, $3 310 000
P16.6 (a) Discount on bonds debit, $497 537
(b) Debit stock purchase warrants, $997 537
P16.7 (a) On May 1, 1994 credit interest expense $20 000
(b) Carrying amount of bonds on December 31, 1994, $2 055 932
P16.8 (a) Stated or nominal rate of interest, 9%
(b) Effective rate of interest, 8%
P16.9 (c) Noncurrent liability for bonds, $1 020 000
P16.10 (b) 1. Interest expense, $5760
P16.11 (a) Price at which bonds will be sold, $2 192 764
P16.12 (a) Loss on extinguishment, $1 115 000
(c) Net cash benefit per year, $115 200
P16.15 (a) Proceeds from issuance, $875 427

Chapter 17
P17.1 August 17 debit land account, $194 118
P17.2 June 1, Contributed Surplus from Retired Shares debit, $9500
P17.3 (b) Total shareholders' equity, December 31, 1994, $35 090 000
P17.4 Cash to defaulted subscriber, $6400
P17.5 (a) Retained Earnings debit from donated capital, $45 000
P17.6 (c) 1995, 14 900 preferred shares issued and outstanding
P17.7 December 31, 1994 total liabilities and shareholders' equity, $92 000
P17.8 (b) 2. Cost of treasury shares $2250
P17.9 (c) 24 000 shares of common to be issued
P17.10 September 30, 1995 total shareholders' equity $1 883 200
P17.11 December 31, 1995 balance in retained earnings, $5 551 887

Chapter 18
P18.1 (5) Eliminate appropriated retained earnings, $200 000
P18.2 (b) Total shareholders' equity, $287 000
P18.3 (b) Dividends to Class B Preferred, $58 000
(c) Dividends to Class B Preferred, $75 000
P18.4 December 31, 1995 total shareholders' equity, $3 925 000
P18.5 December 31, 1995 compensation expense recognized, $3000
P18.6 (b) December 31, 1995 retained earnings balance $12 625
P18.7 Total shareholders' equity, $3 076 500
P18.8 (b) Total dividends paid, 1995, $126 256
P18.9 December 31, 1994 common shares, $9 990 000
P18.10 December 31, 1995 retained earnings, $53 495
P18.11 (a) Retained earnings, $5 690 000

Chapter 19
P19.1 (b) December 31, 1994, credit to Deferred Income Tax, $22 000
P19.2 (c) December 31, 1995, credit to Deferred Income Tax, $34 000
P19.3 (c) December 31, 1995, credit to Deferred Income Tax, $22 575
P19.4 (a) Retained Earnings, Oct. 31, 1995, $676 554
P19.5 (c) December 31, 1994, credit to Deferred Income Tax, $5780
P19.6 (b) December 31, 1994, credit to Deferred Income Tax, $2720 (net)
P19.7 (b) December 31, 1995, credit to Deferred Income Tax, $15 000
P19.8 (a) 1994, net loss $377 840
P19.9 (b) Refund of past income taxes, $9800
P19.10 (c) 1995 cost reduction method net income, $575 800
P19.11 (a) 1994 Income tax expense, $272 108

Chapter 20
P20.3 Part 1, depreciation expense, 1995, $18 403
P20.4 (c) Debit to retained earnings, $3720
P20.5 (a) 1995 corrected net income, $23 600
P20.6 (b) 1995 corrected net income, $212 400
P20.7 (c) 1995 ending Retained Earnings, $252 000
P20.8 (b) 1995 cumulative effect of the change in accounting policy, $39 600 gain
P20.9 (a) 1995 cumulative effect of the change in accounting policy, $900 loss
P20.10 (a) correct net income, $23 100
P20.11 2. adjustment of the allowance for doubtful accounts, $14 500
4. adjustment of depreciation, $1450

Chapter 21
P21.1 (a) EPS on net income, $3.66
P21.2 (b) EPS, $1.25
P21.3 Step 6, fully diluted EPS, $0.76
P21.4 (a) 4. Fully diluted EPS, $2.17
P21.5 (b) 1995 EPS on net income, $0.10
P21.6 (b) Fully diluted EPS, $1.10
P21.7 (d) Fully diluted EPS, $2.06
P21.8 (c) Fully diluted EPS on income before extraordinary gain, $2.18
P21.9 Fully diluted EPS, $2.19

Chapter 22
P22.1 (a) Net cash provided by operating activities, $7000
P22.2 Net cash used by financing activities, $3000
P22.3 (b) 1. Net cash provided by operating activities, $212 250
P22.4 Net cash provided by operating activities, $46 236
P22.5 (b) Net cash used in financing activities, $252 250
P22.6 (b) Net cash used in investing activities, $120 000
P22.7 Company 6, cash received for the damage, $203 000
P22.8 Net cash provided by operating activities, $67 237
P22.9 Net cash provided by operating activities, $1 380 000
P22.10 (b) Net cash used in investing activities, $37 900
P22.11 Net cash provided by operating activities, $116 000
P22.12 Net cash provided by operating activities, $510 000

Chapter 23
P23.1 (b) Debit to amortization of leasehold improvements, $17 241
P23.2 (b) May 1, 1998 interest, $2292
P23.3 (b) Annual lease payment, $26 471
P23.4 (b) Interest revenue, $73 026
P23.5 (b) December 31, 1997 interest, $38
P23.6 (a) December 31, 1995 interest revenue, $95
P23.7 (b) Present value of lease, $1 500 000
P23.8 (b) December 31 amortization expense, $2300
P23.9 (b) 2. September 30, current liability balance, $9139
P23.10 (c) 1995 interest expense, $27 295
P23.11 (c) January 1, 1998 interest, $1107
P23.12 Loss before income taxes, $142 425

Chapter 24
P24.1 (b) Pension expense, $29 836
P24.2 (a) Net periodic pension cost, $67 100
P24.3 1996 Net periodic pension cost, $5116
P24.4 (b) Year 2000, amortization, $8000
P24.5 (b) 1996 unrecognized gain carried forward to 1997, $64 501
P24.6 (b) Pension expense, $129 280
P24.7 (b) 1995 pension liability, $26 092
P24.8 (b) Credit to prepaid/accrued pension cost, $4500
P24.9 (b) 1995, balance prepaid pension cost $73 200
P24.10 (a) 1996 recognition of gain, $223
P24.11 (b) Debit to pension expense, $20 500
P24.12 (c) Pension expense, $62 875

Chapter 25
P25.1 1995 fourth-quarter income before income tax, $148 000
P25.2 1995 fourth-quarter income tax expense, $64 820
P25.3 1995 net income, $642 020
P25.4 1995 third-quarter net income, $145 160
P25.5 (a) 1995 operating profit for manufacturing segment, $80 000
P25.6 (a) 1995 paper products segment operating loss, $2.86 million
P25.8 (a) 1995 agriculture segment operating profit, $32 million
P25.10 (a) 3.33; (k) 60.83 days; (v) 12%
P25.11 (a) 1. 4%; 3. 73 days; 5. 4.5 times
P25.12 (a) Total assets, $600 000; Net sales, $1 200 000; Cost of goods sold, $720 000

on a note payable, may be cross-referenced with a parenthetical remark beside the relevant title.

Notes to financial statements are used to report details that simply do not fit conveniently in the body of the statements. In addition, accountants often use **schedules** (presented alone or as part of the notes) to report such information as major inventory categories and operating expense details. The use of such schedules is particularly appropriate when a company prepares condensed financial statements.

Amount of Disclosure

An elusive problem that accountants face when preparing financial statements is deciding on an appropriate **amount (extent) of disclosure.** Accountants want to prepare financial statements that are reasonably complete, yet understandable. Clearly, to achieve understandability, an accountant must summarize many details. The question is: To what extent can the accountant summarize and still present statements that are sufficiently complete and therefore in compliance with the disclosure principle?

Deciding on an appropriate amount of disclosure in a given case depends on such related factors as the objectives of the statements, GAAP, the circumstances involved, the modifying convention of materiality, and professional judgement. Statements prepared for bankers, for example, are often fairly detailed in order to satisfy the bankers' needs. Those prepared for publication in annual reports to shareholders are often highly condensed.

As a general principle, the **offsetting** of assets and liabilities in the balance sheet is improper except when a specific legal right of offset exists. For example, cash in a bond sinking fund should not be offset against the bond liability, even though the company intends to use the cash to pay the bonds.

As another general principle, material **related-party transactions** should be disclosed. Examples are loans made by the company to its management or to a subsidiary.

Terminology

The language of accounting is technical, consisting of some words whose meanings differ from their everyday connotations. To communicate effectively, accountants must select words and phrases that the average user of financial statements can understand.

There is no requirement that the financial statements contain the same account titles that appear in the general ledger. For example, "accounts receivable" in the general ledger is sometimes reported on the balance sheet as "amounts due from customers."

The accounting profession has been very concerned with improving the terminology used in financial statements. The CICA *Handbook*, Section 3260, for example, noted that accountants have used the term "reserve" to describe asset contra accounts, liability accounts, retained earnings appropriations, and loss accounts. To avoid confusion, this section recommended that the use of "reserve" be limited to retained earnings appropriations.[29] The section further recommended that accountants stop using the term "surplus," because it may mislead users by implying an amount in excess of that needed. Accountants should use "paid-in capital" or "contributed capital" instead of "paid-in surplus" or "capital surplus." Likewise, the use of "retained earnings" is preferable to "earned surplus."

---

[29]"Reserves," CICA *Handbook*, Section 3260, October 1990.

One reason why we have mentioned these terminology recommendations is that the terms *not* recommended are still sometimes encountered in practice. We emphasize the use of modern, preferred terminology throughout this textbook. Remember that financial statements will not be useful if they do not communicate effectively.

Auditor's Report

As explained in Chapter 1, financial statements are often accompanied by an independent auditor's report. Financial statements contain the representations of the company's management. The functions of an independent auditor are to **examine the statements and express an opinion** that lends credibility to management's representations. This enables users to have greater confidence in the statements. Exhibit 1.1 (Chapter 1) presents a standard auditor's report, in which an unqualified opinion was given on the financial statements.

Conceptual Considerations

The financial statements discussed in this chapter are directly related to the model of financial accounting theory that we explained in Chapter 2 (see Exhibit 2.1). You may wish to review Exhibit 2.1 now and consider the following important points:

1. Financial statements help to accomplish the *objectives* of financial reporting, which are to provide useful information, information helpful in assessing cash flow prospects, and information about enterprise resources, claims to those resources, and changes in them.
2. Financial statements seek to provide information that is both relevant and reliable. Recall that relevance and reliability are the primary *qualitative characteristics* of useful accounting information.
3. Financial statements reflect the *assumptions* of economic entity (the entity identified at the top of the financial statements), periodicity (annual periods, quarterly periods, etc.), and going concern.
4. The *concepts* of financial position and changes in financial position are reflected in financial statements. Assets, liabilities, and owners' equity are the *elements* that compose financial position, while revenues, expenses, gains, losses, income, investments by owners, and distributions to owners are the major *elements* that compose changes in financial position.
5. The *broad principles* of monetary unit, asset/liability measurement, revenue realization, matching, consistency, and disclosure are all reflected in financial statements.
6. Financial statements also reflect numerous *detailed principles* that we will cover throughout this text.
7. The *modifying conventions* of materiality, industry practices, conservatism, and substance over form also affect financial statements.

Concluding Remarks

Financial statements are the culmination of an accountant's work. They constitute the *output* of the accounting information system and serve as *input* for investment, credit, and similar decisions that help to determine how resources are allocated in our society.

Financial statements are summaries that are primarily historical. They are interrelated and general-purpose, and they reflect many estimates. Underlying the information reported in financial statements are many important measurement and disclosure principles that we discuss throughout the text.

All financial statements bear the name of the reporting entity, the title of the statement, and the date or period of time covered. The balance sheet presents financial position at a particular point in time; the other basic statements present various changes in financial position during a period of time.

The financial statements discussed in this chapter are currently reported under generally accepted accounting principles. To help ensure that companies provide financial statements regularly, accountants follow certain steps during an accounting period. These steps, collectively called the **accounting cycle,** are presented in Chapter 6.

Key Points

1. The basic financial statements are the balance sheet, income statement, statement of changes in financial position, and statement of retained earnings or statement of shareholders' equity. (Objective 1)

2. Basic financial statements have several important characteristics:
   a. They are only a subset of the information needed by users for making rational investment, lending, and similar decisions.
   b. They are primarily historical in nature.
   c. They summarize information.
   d. They reflect many estimates.
   e. They are general-purpose reports designed to serve the needs of many different users.
   f. They articulate with one another. (Objective 1)

3. Extraordinary gains and losses result from events or transactions that are unusual in nature, not expected to recur in the foreseeable future, and not based on the decisions of management. (Objective 2)

4. A multiple-step income statement presents subtotals for gross margin and operating income; a single-step income statement does not. (Objective 2)

5. Prior period adjustments and the correction of an error made in the financial statements of a prior period should be charged or credited directly to the opening balance of the retained earnings. (Objective 3)

6. The major balance sheet categories are:
   a. Assets
      Current assets
      Noncurrent (capital) assets
         Investments and funds
         Property, plant, and equipment
         Intangible assets
         Other assets and deferred charges
   b. Liabilities
      Current liabilities
      Long-term liabilities
   c. Owners' equity
      Share capital
         Capital shares
            Preferred shares
            Common shares

Contributed surplus

Retained earnings (Objective 4)

7. The statement of changes in financial position provides information about the cash receipts and cash payments of an entity during a period. (Objective 5)

8. Notes (footnotes) are an integral part of the basic financial statements. (Objective 6)

9. The role of an independent auditor is to examine financial statements and express an opinion on them. (Objective 6)

Questions

Q4.1 What are the basic financial statements?

Q4.2 What are some important characteristics of the basic financial statements?

Q4.3 What are the criteria used to determine whether a gain or loss is extraordinary?

Q4.4 Why does the accounting profession require that extraordinary gains and losses be presented in a special section of the income statement?

Q4.5 Think of three examples of extraordinary items. (Do not use the examples presented in the chapter.)

Q4.6 Can gains and losses from disposal of a business segment and from changes in accounting policies be included in the extraordinary items category? Explain your answer.

Q4.7 Distinguish clearly between a multiple-step and a single-step income statement.

Q4.8 What are the advantages of using a multiple-step format for the income statement? What are the advantages of using a single-step format?

Q4.9 What does the term "prior period adjustments" mean? How should prior period adjustments be reported in the financial statements?

Q4.10 Suppose that in 1995 a company changes its estimate of the total useful life of its twelve-year-old building from 30 years to 40 years. For accounting purposes, what kind of an event is this, and how should the event be accounted for?

Q4.11 Define the term "current assets," and cite five examples of current assets.

Q4.12 Why are special fund balances and the cash surrender value of life insurance not usually reported among the current assets?

Q4.13 Define the term "current liabilities," and cite five examples of current liabilities.

Q4.14 Define the terms "working capital" and "current ratio."

Q4.15 Explain the various categories that may be used in the shareholders' equity section of the balance sheet.

Q4.16 Identify and briefly describe the major categories of a statement of changes in financial position.

Q4.17 Distinguish between a cash-basis income statement, a statement of cash receipts and disbursements, and a statement of changes in financial position. Which one is required by GAAP?

Q4.18 Why are the notes to the financial statements important to users?

Q4.19 Define the term "subsequent events." Indicate the two categories of subsequent events and the appropriate accounting treatment for each category in the financial statements of the period preceding the subsequent event.

Q4.20 What factors should affect an accountant's decision on how detailed a given set of financial statements should be?

Q4.21 Why is terminology an important aspect of accounting?

Q4.22 What are the roles of management and the independent auditor in relation to a set of financial statements?

Exercises

E4.1 Cost of Goods Sold. The following information pertains to Noe Inc., for the 1995 accounting period:

Transportation-out	$ 9 500	Transportation-in	$ 7 100
Purchases	150 000	Sales discounts	5 200
Sales returns	11 200	Purchase returns	6 000
Inventory, Dec. 31	25 800	Purchase discounts	3 000
Purchase allowances	2 300	Advertising expense	28 000
Sales	290 000	Sales allowances	3 600
Inventory, Jan. 1	40 000	Sales commission	70 000

Instructions

(a) Prepare the cost of goods sold section of Noe Inc.'s 1995 income statement.
(b) Compute the gross margin for 1995.
(c) Indicate how the accounts not used in (a) and (b) should be classified in the 1995 income statement.

E4.2 Income Statement Formats. The following information pertains to the 1995 accounting period of Reams Limited:

Cost of goods sold	$160 000
Dividend revenue	6 000
General and administrative expenses	21 000
Interest expense	5 000
Interest revenue	9 000
Net sales	290 000
Selling expenses	29 000
Income tax rate	40%
Number of common shares outstanding	10 000

Instructions

(a) Prepare a multiple-step income statement for 1995.
(b) Prepare a single-step income statement for 1995.

E4.3 Income Statement Sections. Rao Limited has been manufacturing and selling computers, household appliances, and medical supplies since 1981. The following events occurred during the company's 1995 accounting period:

(1) The company sold its computer division.
(2) The company lost one of its manufacturing plants because of the explosion of the gas furnace.
(3) The company lost its inventory held in a Middle Eastern country because of a government expropriation.
(4) The company sold its household appliance division.
(5) The company adopted the FIFO method of inventory cost determination. Prior to 1995, the company used the average cost method.
(6) The company adopted the straight-line method of accounting for all depreciable assets. Prior to 1995, the company used the double-declining balance method.

Instructions

Assume that each of the events listed is material and qualifies for reporting in the statement of retained earnings or one of the following income statement sections: (1) discontinued operations, (2) extraordinary items, and (3) other revenues or expenses. Where should each event be reported?

E4.4 Retained Earnings Statement. At the beginning of its 1995 calendar-year accounting period, Reaves, Inc., had retained earnings of $97 000. During 1995 the company earned a net income of $51 000 and declared cash dividends of $25 000 on its common shares. None of these dividends had been paid as of year-end. In addition, the company discovered that because of a mathematical error, depreciation expense had been overstated by $10 000 in 1994.

The company's income tax rate was 40 percent in 1994 and 1995. The company had 5000 common shares outstanding throughout 1995.

Instructions

Prepare a statement of retained earnings for Reaves for 1995.

E4.5 Combined Statement of Income and Retained Earnings. The following information pertains to the 1995 calendar-year accounting period of Laurentian Corporation:

Number of common shares outstanding throughout the year	20 000
Cost of goods sold	$161 200
Dividends declared	50 000
Loss from expropriation (extraordinary item)	20 000
General and administrative expenses	41 000
Loss due to write-off of worthless equipment (unusual item)	17 000
Net sales	418 000
Selling expenses	48 800

Laurentian Corporation reported retained earnings of $167 000 on December 31, 1994. During 1995, the company discovered that because of a material counting error, ending inventory for 1994 had been overstated by $16 000. The company's income tax rate was 40 percent in 1994 and 1995.

Instructions

Prepare a combined statement of income and retained earnings for Laurentian Corporation for 1995. Use the single-step format.

E4.6 Working Capital. The following information pertains to Calgary Limited on December 31 of the current year:

Equipment	$240 000
Accumulated depreciation—equipment	40 000
Accounts receivable	27 000
Prepaid insurance	3 000
Short-term notes payable	12 000
Cash	40 000
Bonds payable maturing in 20 years	110 000
Land	50 000
Accounts payable	30 000
Allowance for doubtful accounts	2 000
Merchandise inventory	34 000
Selling expense	29 000
Short-term investments	16 000
Wages payable	4 000
Premium on bonds payable	15 000
Interest Expense	8 000

Instructions

Compute Calgary Limited's working capital on December 31. Show all of your work clearly.

E4.7 Property, Plant, and Equipment and Long-Term Liabilities. The following are some of the account balances of Jasper Oil Limited on December 31, 1995, the end of the company's annual accounting period:

Land held for future building site	$ 92 000
Oil deposit	800 000
Term bonds payable (10%, due June 30, 2006)	400 000
Accumulated depreciation—equipment	180 000
Building	250 000
Land on which building is located	55 000
Notes payable (12%, due Apr. 30, 2000)	80 000
Equipment	360 000
Accumulated depletion of oil deposit	150 000
Notes payable (10%, due Aug. 31, 1996)	30 000
Accumulated depreciation—building	75 000
Serial bonds payable (11%, due July 31, 2001, to July 31, 2006, inclusive)	300 000
Unamortized discount on term bonds payable	8 000
Accumulated depreciation—furniture and fixtures	20 000
Bond issue costs	5 000
Furniture and fixtures	50 000

Instructions

(a) Prepare the property, plant, and equipment and long-term liabilities sections of Jasper Oil Limited's balance sheet on December 31, 1995.
(b) Indicate how Jasper Oil should classify any accounts that you did not use in (a).

E4.8 Shareholders' Equity. The following information pertains to Kelona Limited on December 31 of the current year:

(1) The company has preferred and common shares outstanding. The $2 preferred shares are cumulative and nonparticipating. A total of 20 000 shares were authorized, of

which 10 000 shares are issued and outstanding on December 31. Kelona sold its preferred shares for $20 per share.

(2) There were 50 000 common shares authorized, of which 40 000 shares are issued and outstanding on December 31. Kelona sold its common shares for $10 per share.

(3) The company has retained earnings of $1 800 000, of which $320 000 has been appropriated for plant expansion.

Instructions

Prepare the shareholders' equity section of Kelona's balance sheet on December 31.

E4.9 Balance Sheet. The following list of accounts and balances pertains to Costal Limited on December 31, 1995, the end of the company's annual accounting period:

Accounts payable	$ 28 000
Accounts receivable	37 000
Accumulated depreciation—furniture and fixtures	10 000
Advances from customers (pertaining to goods that Costal Limited will supply in 1996)	6 000
Allowance for doubtful accounts	1 800
Bond sinking fund	90 000
Bonds payable (14%, due Jan. 1, 2008)	150 000
Cash	26 000
Common shares (no-par value, 50 000 shares authorized, 30 000 shares issued and outstanding)	30 000
Franchise	86 000
Furniture and fixtures	70 000
Merchandise inventory	48 400
Contributed capital—donated land	60 000
Premium on bonds payable	4 000
Prepaid rent (pertains to the first quarter of 1996)	8 400
Retained earnings	?

Instructions

Prepare a balance sheet for Costal Limited on December 31, 1995.

E4.10 Missing Amounts in Financial Statements. The following independent cases pertain to a 1995 calendar-year accounting period:

	Case A	Case B	Case C	Case D
Revenues	$100 000	$200 000	?	?
Expenses	?	?	$ 50 000	$ 70 000
Net income	40 000	?	60 000	?
Retained earnings, Jan. 1	?	300 000	180 000	120 000
Dividends declared	50 000	70 000	?	30 000
Retained earnings, Dec. 31	120 000	310 000	?	?
Current assets, Dec. 31	?	60 000	100 000	?
Noncurrent assets, Dec. 31	420 000	?	580 000	300 000
Total assets, Dec. 31	500 000	?	?	410 000
Current liabilities, Dec. 31	?	30 000	?	20 000
Noncurrent liabilities, Dec. 31	270 000	?	170 000	?
Total liabilities, Dec. 31	?	140 000	?	?
Share capital, Dec. 31	?	520 000	210 000	100 000
Total shareholders' equity, Dec. 31	200 000	?	410 000	210 000

Instructions
Determine the missing amounts.

E4.11   Income Statement and Balance Sheet Classification.   Listed below are several categories that may be used in a multiple-step income statement and a balance sheet:

(1) Net sales.
(2) Cost of goods sold.
(3) Operating expenses.
(4) Other revenues.
(5) Other expenses.
(6) Extraordinary items.
(7) Current assets.
(8) Investments and funds.

(9)   Property, plant, and equipment.
(10) Intangible assets.
(11) Other assets—deferred charges.
(12) Current liabilities.
(13) Long-term liabilities.
(14) Capital shares.
(15) Contributed surplus.
(16) Retained earnings.

Instructions
Use the numbers above to show where each of the following items should usually be classified.

(a) Goodwill.
(b) Depreciation expense.
(c) Timberland.
(d) Buildings.
(e) Advertising.
(f) Transportation-out.
(g) Interest expense.
(h) Accounts payable.
(i) Copyrights.
(j) Patents.
(k) Bonds payable (due in twenty years).

(l)   Loss of property in Yarmouth due to a hurricane.
(m) Investment in subsidiary company.
(n) Write-off of inventories due to obsolescence.
(o) Bond sinking fund.
(p) Sales discounts.
(q) Preferred shares.
(r) Accumulated depreciation.
(s) Purchases discounts.
(t) Accounts receivable.

E4.12 Income Statement and Balance Sheet Classification.   Refer to the list of categories ((1)–(16)) in E4.11.

Instructions
Use the appropriate numbers to show where each of the following items should usually be classified.

(a) Cash.
(b) Allowance for doubtful accounts.
(c) Common stock dividend distributable.
(d) Merchandise inventory (ending).
(e) Note receivable (due in three months).
(f) Appropriation for plant expansion.
(g) Oil deposit.
(h) Premium on bonds that are payable in ten years.
(i) Transportation-in.
(j) Bond issue costs.

(k) Dividend revenue.
(l) Payment from common share subscriptions.
(m) Organization costs.
(n) Interest payable.
(o) Sales returns and allowances.
(p) Purchase returns.
(q) Note payable (due in five years).
(r) Wages payable.
(s) Common shares.
(t) Accumulated depletion.

E4.13 Income Statement and Balance Sheet Classification. Refer to the list of categories ((1)–(16)) in E4.11.

Instructions

Use the appropriate numbers to show where each of the following items should usually be classified.

(a) Salaries.
(b) Merchandise inventory (beginning).
(c) Gain from foreign exchange transactions.
(d) Building site.
(e) Note payable in five years.
(f) Investment in 100 shares of Petro-Canada's common shares that will likely be sold in three months.
(g) Prepaid insurance.
(h) Bad debts expense.
(i) Sinking fund bonds payable.
(j) Equipment used in the business.
(k) Purchase allowances.
(l) Building.
(m) Flood loss in an area that floods every two to three years.
(n) Appropriation for plant expansion.
(o) Land held for future plant sites.
(p) Reserve for bond sinking fund.
(q) Cash surrender value of life insurance.
(r) Raw materials.
(s) Donated capital—land.
(t) Discount on bonds payable (bonds are payable in thirteen years).

E4.14 Income Statement and Balance Sheet Classification. Refer to the list of categories ((1)–(16)) in E4.11.

Instructions

Use the appropriate numbers to show where each of the following items should usually be classified. If an item should not be reported on either an income statement or a balance sheet, indicate where it should be reported.

(a) Trademarks.
(b) Dividends declared.
(c) Purchases.
(d) Correction of an error made last year when computing depreciation expense.
(e) Franchise.
(f) Building that is being constructed for the company's own use.
(g) Small tools used in the business.
(h) Unearned rent revenue (will be earned in the first quarter of the next accounting period).
(i) Returnable containers used in the business.
(j) Machinery rearrangement costs.
(k) Bonds payable (due in six months; payment will be made from current assets).
(l) Equipment held for sale (was previously used in the business).
(m) Dividends payable.
(n) Appropriation for contingencies.
(o) Land held for future plant site.
(p) Deficit.
(q) Loss on sale of land.
(r) Taxes payable.
(s) Work-in-process.
(t) Unusual and nonrecurring loss of inventories due to expropriation by a foreign government.

E4.15 Statement of Changes in Financial Position. The following information pertains to Cormack Limited during 1995:

Dividends paid	$ 10 000
Cash received from customers	120 000
Proceeds from issuing common shares	25 000
Interest received	10 000
Proceeds from sale of long-term investments	6 000
Cash paid to suppliers and employees	95 000
Purchases of long-term investments	18 000
Income taxes paid	15 000

Cormack Limited had cash of $51 275 on January 1, 1995.

Instructions
Prepare a statement of changes in financial position for 1995.

E4.16 Subsequent Events. Lauer Limited's accounting period ends on December 31, and the company issues its financial statements on the following February 1. Below are some events that occurred during *1996*:

Jan. 4   Sale of common shares.

   7   Write-off of an account receivable because customer was formally declared
         bankrupt on January 7. The bankruptcy litigation was in process on
         December 31, 1995.

  12   Loss of a material portion of inventories because of a sudden flood.

  18   Purchase of a competing business.

  21   Purchase of additional inventory.

  27   Write-off of an account receivable because the customer's business was
         destroyed by an earthquake on January 27.

Instructions

Indicate the appropriate treatment for each of the above events in Lauer Limited's financial statements for 1995. Assume that each event is material.

Problems

P4.1 Income Statement Formats The following list of items pertains to the 1995 calendar-year accounting period of Matthews Inc.:

Advertising expense	$ 19 000
Gain on sale of investments	15 200
Interest expense	7 500
Interest revenue	8 900
Loss of inventory due to flood (considered unusual and nonrecurring)	21 000
Loss on write-off of plant assets due to obsolescence	21 800
Merchandise inventory, Dec. 31	80 000
Merchandise inventory, Jan. 1	62 000
Miscellaneous general and administrative expenses	7 800
Miscellaneous selling expenses	12 000
Office salaries expense	47 500
Office supplies expense	8 100
Purchases	455 000
Purchase discounts	8 700
Purchase returns and allowances	31 000
Sales	911 000
Sales discounts	15 200
Sales returns and allowances	22 800
Sales salaries expense	52 000
Transportation-in	13 700
Utilities expense	10 400

Matthews Inc., had 10 000 common shares outstanding throughout 1995. The company's income tax rate is 40 percent.

Instructions

(a) Prepare a detailed, multiple-step income statement for 1995.
(b) Prepare a condensed, single-step income statement for 1995.
(c) Which of the two forms of income statements do you prefer? Explain your answer.

P4.2 Corrected Income Statement and Statement of Retained Earnings. The accountant for Crown Limited has just handed you the income statement and retained earnings statement that follow:

Crown Limited
INCOME STATEMENT
As of December 31, 1995

Revenues		
Net sales		$638 000
Extraordinary gain from expropriation of property by a foreign government		50 000
Correction of understatement of 1994 ending inventory due to error		30 000
Rent revenue		11 800
Dividend revenue		7 200
Total revenues		737 000
Expenses		
Cost of goods sold	$328 000	
Selling expenses	109 600	
General and administrative expenses	84 200	
Interest expense	12 200	
Total expenses		534 000
Net income		$203 000

Crown Limited
STATEMENT OF RETAINED EARNINGS
As of December 31, 1995

Retained earnings, Jan. 1		$789 000
Add: Net income		203 000
		992 000
Less: Extraordinary loss of plant assets due to earthquake	$60 000	
Unusual loss on sale of long-term investments	23 000	
Dividends declared	37 000	120 000
Retained earnings, Dec. 31		$872 000

Additional Information

(1) You have determined that the account balances in the above statements are correct. The statements, however, are not presented according to GAAP.

(2) The company had 10 000 common shares outstanding throughout 1995.

(3) The company's income tax rate was 40 percent in 1994 and 1995. No income tax was included in the above statements.

(4) The company uses a calendar-year accounting period.

Instructions

(a) Prepare a condensed, multiple-step income statement for 1995 that complies with GAAP.

(b) Prepare a condensed, single-step income statement for 1995 that complies with GAAP.

(c) Prepare a statement of retained earnings for 1995 that complies with GAAP.

(d) From the standpoint of user decision making, why should extraordinary gains and losses be presented in a special section of the income statement?

P4.3 Corrected Statement of Retained Earnings. The bookkeeper for Dawson Limited recently prepared the following statement of retained earnings:

Dawson Limited
STATEMENT OF RETAINED EARNINGS
December 31, 1995

Retained earnings, Jan. 1, 1995		$619 572
Add: Net income for 1995	$93 477	
Gain on sale of land	85 420	
Gain from settlement of litigation that began in 1994	25 000	
Gain from foreign currency transaction	6 134	210 031
		829 603
Less: Dividends declared during 1995	20 000	
Loss of inventory caused by a government prohibition		
judged to be unusual and nonrecurring	50 000	
Recognition of salaries expense incurred in 1994 but		
erroneously not recognized in the 1994 income		
statement	19 500	
Loss from write-off of equipment leased to others	12 119	101 619
Retained earnings, Dec. 31, 1995		$727 984

Instructions

(a) Prepare a corrected statement of retained earnings for 1995. Assume an income tax rate of 40 percent and 10 000 common shares outstanding throughout 1995. The additions and deductions in the statement shown above are *before* income taxes, except for net income.

(b) Indicate specifically where Dawson Limited should report any items that do not belong on the statement of retained earnings.

P4.4 Combined Statement of Income and Retained Earnings. The following information pertains to the 1995 calendar-year accounting period of Chun Corporation:

Cost of goods sold	$222 600
Dividend revenue	7 590
Dividends declared	80 000
Gain on sale of investments (considered unusual or nonrecurring for this company)	89 340
General and administrative expenses	69 587
Interest expense	12 650
Loss from expropriation of property by a foreign government (considered unusual and nonrecurring)	48 000
Loss from settlement of litigation that began in 1994 (not considered unusual or nonrecurring for this company)	35 000
Loss of warehouse due to hurricane (considered unusual but recurring for this company)	42 150
Net sales	495 554
Selling expenses	63 473
Write-off of inventory due to obsolescence (considered unusual but recurring for this company)	17 024

Chun Corporation reported retained earnings of $187 000 on its balance sheet dated December 31, 1994. During 1995, it was discovered that $60 000 of revenue earned in 1994 had not been reported on the 1994 income statement that was prepared by the bookkeeper. The company had 5000 common shares outstanding throughout 1995.

Instructions
(a) Prepare a combined statement of income and retained earnings for 1995. Use the multiple-step format and assume an income tax rate of 40 percent.
(b) Do you favour a combined statement of income and retained earnings over separate statements of income and retained earnings? Explain your answer.

P4.5 Statement of Shareholders' Equity. Haven Limited reported the following amounts in the shareholders' equity section of its balance sheet dated December 31, 1994:

Preferred shares ($12 no-par value, 1000 shares issued)	$165 000
Common shares (10 000 no-par value shares issued)	385 000
Retained earnings	341 580

On January 3, 1995, the company sold 2000 additional common shares for $60 per share. During 1995, it was discovered that due to a new government regulation, $25 000 of revenue earned in 1994 had not been reported on the 1994 income statement.

Haven Limited reported a net income for 1995 of $55 000. The company declared cash dividends on the preferred shares and $7500 on the common shares at the end of *each* of the four quarters of 1995. Dividends are paid in cash 30 days after being declared to shareholders of record 20 days after the declaration date.

Instructions
Prepare a statement of shareholders' equity for the year ended December 31, 1995. Assume an income tax rate of 40 percent.

P4.6 Statement of Shareholders' Equity. Luther Limited reported the following amounts in the shareholders' equity section of its balance sheet dated December 31, 1994:

Preferred shares ($5 no-par value, 3000 shares)	$350 000
Common shares (no-par value, 10 000 shares)	775 000
Retained earnings	450 400

Additional Information
(1) On January 2, 1995, Luther sold 2000 additional common shares for $90 per share.
(2) Late in 1995, it was learned that, because of a mathematical error, an overstatement of depreciation expense by $37 500 had occurred in 1994.
(3) Luther reported a net income for 1995 of $82 500.
(4) Luther declared cash dividends of $15 000 on the preferred shares and $45 000 on the common shares during 1995.

Instructions
Prepare a statement of shareholders' equity for the year ended December 31, 1995. Assume an income tax rate of 40 percent.

P4.7 Balance Sheet. The following accounts and balances pertain to Zirkle Corporation on December 31, 1995:

Accounts payable	$ 38 300
Accounts receivable	43 900
Accumulated depletion	165 300
Accumulated depreciation	70 000
Advances from customers (advances pertain to goods that Zirkle Corporation will supply in 1996)	4 500
Advances to suppliers (advances pertain to goods that suppliers will provide in 1996)	7 100
Allowance for doubtful accounts	2 600
Appropriation for plant expansion	58 500
Bond issue costs	21 300
Bond sinking fund	190 700
Bonds payable (10%, due July 1, 2006)	500 000
Building	210 000
Cash	30 100
Cash surrender value of life insurance	12 300
Common shares (no-par value, 50 000 shares authorized, 40 000 shares issued and outstanding)	409 000
Franchise	21 840
Interest payable	3 000
Investment in bonds—long-term (at cost; market value $72 000)	65 000
Land	99 500
Land held for future plant site	138 000
Marketable securities—short-term (at cost that approximates market value)	18 570
Merchandise inventory (at lower of FIFO cost or market)	41 430
Note payable (12%, due Apr. 1, 1999)	25 000
Oil deposit	568 300
Organization costs	10 560
Prepaid insurance	4 300
Salaries payable	6 700
Unamortized discount on bonds payable	11 000
Unappropriated retained earnings	211 000

Instructions

Prepare a balance sheet in good form for Zirkle Corporation.

P4.8   Balance Sheet.   The following information pertains to Quinn Enterprises on December 31, 1995:

Patents	$160 000
Supplies	20 990
Common shares (no-par value, 20 000 shares authorized, 10 000 shares issued and outstanding)	500 000
Cash	50 000
Land	160 200
Machinery rearrangement costs	48 300
Unappropriated retained earnings	?
Serial 12% debenture bonds, $50 000 installments due annually from June 1, 1996, through June 1, 2005	500 000
Cash surrender value of life insurance	11 400
Trademarks	48 000
Appropriation for contingencies	80 000
Advances from customers (advances pertain to goods that Quinn Enterprises will provide in 1996)	15 875
Allowance for doubtful accounts	3 300
Plant expansion fund	203 100

Accounts payable	31 000
Accumulated depreciation—building	45 000
Investment in land (held for long-term speculative purposes)	196 500
Machinery and equipment	290 800
Unearned rent revenue (Quinn Enterprises will earn this revenue during the first quarter of 1996)	6 125
Accumulated depreciation of machinery and equipment	30 000
Building	250 000
Accounts receivable	73 410
Long-term investment in common shares (at cost; market value $98 700)	84 000
Note receivable (due on May 15, 1996)	21 000
Marketable securities (at cost; market value $44 430)	37 000
Notes payable (due in 1996)	40 000
Merchandise inventory (at lower of FIFO cost or market)	58 600

Instructions

(a) Prepare a balance sheet in good form for Quinn Enterprises. Compute the missing amount of unappropriated retained earnings.

(b) What are serial 12 percent debenture bonds? Explain the rationale for the financial reporting treatment of these bonds.

P4.9   Corrected Balance Sheet.   The bookkeeper for Totino Corporation has prepared the following balance sheet:

Totino Corporation
BALANCE SHEET
For 1995

Debits

Current Debits		
Cash	$ 36 000	
Cash surrender value of life insurance	18 000	
Building fund	112 000	
Accounts receivable	58 760	
Merchandise inventory	49 010	
Unamortized discount on bonds payable	12 000	
Total current debits		$ 285 770
Noncurrent Debits		
Marketable securities	25 300	
Advances to suppliers	7 500	
Prepaid rent	8 400	
Land held for future plant site	80 000	
Land	125 000	
Building	215 000	
Machinery and equipment	396 000	
Mineral deposit	327 000	
Goodwill	75 700	
Patents	41 300	
Machinery rearrangement costs	51 000	
Total noncurrent debits		1 352 200
Total debits		$1 637 970

Credits

Current Credits

Allowance for doubtful accounts	$ 4 340	
Accounts payable	42 630	
Interest payable	6 000	
Income tax payable	22 500	
Accrued pension costs	119 000	
Total current credits		$ 194 470

Noncurrent Credits

Accumulated depreciation of building	58 000	
Accumulated depreciation of machinery and equipment	66 000	
Accumulated depletion of mineral deposit	70 000	
Note payable	20 000	
Advances from customers	11 000	
Bonds payable	500 000	
Preferred shares	364 700	
Common shares	164 440	
Retained earnings	189 360	
Total noncurrent credits		1 443 500
Total credits		$1 637 970

Additional Information

 (1) You have determined that although the dollar amounts reported are correct, the balance sheet is not in accordance with GAAP.
 (2) Merchandise inventory is reported at the lower of average cost or market value.
 (3) The marketable securities, which had a market value of $32 600 on December 31, 1995, are reported at cost. Management plans to sell the securities in 1996.
 (4) The advances to suppliers pertain to goods that will be provided during 1996.
 (5) The prepaid rent applies to the first quarter of 1996.
 (6) The accrued pension costs will be paid after 2003.
 (7) The note payable is due on May 1, 1996.
 (8) The advances from customers pertain to goods that Totino Corporation will provide in 1996.
 (9) The bonds payable pay interest of 10 percent and are due on June 30, 2007.
(10) Relevant details about the preferred and common shares are as follows:
      Preferred shares: no-par value, $8, cumulative and nonparticipating, 20 000 shares authorized, 10 000 shares issued and outstanding.
      Common shares: no-par value, 50 000 shares authorized, 45 000 shares issued and outstanding.

Instructions

Prepare a balance sheet in good form for Totino Corporation.

P4.10 Corrected Balance Sheet. The bookkeeper for Lenhardt Limited prepared the following balance sheet on December 31, 1995:

Lenhardt Limited
BALANCE SHEET
December 31, 1995

Assets

Current assets	$ 558 525
Investments and funds	28 520
Property, plant, and equipment	723 600
Intangible assets	80 355
Other assets	98 000
Total assets	$1 489 000

Liabilities and Shareholders' Equity

Current liabilities	$162 000	
Long-term liabilities	562 000	
Total liabilities		$ 724 000
Shareholders' equity		765 000
Total liabilities and shareholders' equity		$1 489 000

Additional Information

(1) Current assets include cash, $83 000; merchandise inventory (at lower of FIFO cost or market), $75 125; note receivable (13 percent, due June 1, 1998), $100 000; investment in subsidiary (held for control), $215 000; and plant expansion fund, $85 400.

(2) Investments and funds include prepaid insurance (applicable to the first six months of 1996), $12 000; and bond issue costs, $16 520.

(3) Property, plant, and equipment includes land, $167 000; land held for future plant site, $146 600; building, $375 000 less accumulated depreciation, $45 000; and furniture and fixtures, $114 600 less accumulated depreciation, $34 600.

(4) Intangible assets include accounts receivable of $63 000 less an allowance for doubtful accounts of $4125; and organization costs, $21 480.

(5) Other assets consist of goodwill, $98 000.

(6) Current liabilities include accounts payable, $23 595; interest payable, $8405; and a note payable (12 percent, due May 1, 1998), $130 000.

(7) Long-term liabilities include serial 10 percent debenture bonds, $500 000 ($50 000 installments are payable annually from April 1, 1996, through April 1, 2005); advances from customers (advances pertain to goods that Lenhardt Limited will ship in 1996), $12 000; and retained earnings appropriated for bond retirement, $50 000.

(8) Shareholders' equity consists of common shares (no-par value, 50 000 shares authorized, 40 000 shares issued and outstanding), $470 000; and unappropriated retained earnings, $295 000.

Instructions

Prepare a balance sheet in good form for Lenhardt Limited.

P4.11 Income Statement, Retained Earnings Statement, and Balance Sheet. The information that follows was obtained from the accounting records of Marshall Limited on December 31, 1995, the end of the company's annual accounting period. The account balances shown have been updated through December 31.

Accounts payable	$ 52 500
Accounts receivable	78 000
Accumulated depletion	65 000
Accumulated depreciation	70 000
Advances from customers (advances pertain to goods that Marshall Limited will ship in 1996)	18 300
Allowance for doubtful accounts	3 000
Bond issue costs	31 000
Bond sinking fund	115 000
Bonds payable (10%, due June 1, 2008)	400 000
Building	275 000
Cash	41 110
Cash surrender value of life insurance	31 600
Common shares (no-par value, 20 000 shares authorized, 10 000 shares issued and outstanding throughout 1995)	336 000

Cost of goods sold	503 140
Dividend revenue	8 390
Dividends declared	100 000
Gain from expropriation of property by a foreign government (considered unusual and nonrecurring)	100 000
General and administrative expenses	253 430
Goodwill	53 100
Interest expense	50 000
Interest payable	12 500
Investment in common shares—long-term (at cost; market value $72 000)	67 000
Land	196 000
Land held for future plant site	140 000
Loss of plant assets due to flood (considered unusual and nonrecurring)	70 000
Loss on sale of long-term investments (considered unusual but not nonrecurring)	10 000
Marketable securities—short-term (at cost that approximates market value)	21 890
Merchandise inventory (at lower of FIFO cost or market)	73 500
Mineral deposit	236 400
Net sales	1 482 850
Note payable (12%, due May 1, 1999)	100 000
Patents	12 900
Prepaid insurance	8 500
Rent revenue	12 500
Salaries payable	19 700
Selling expenses	287 170
Unamortized discount on bonds payable	11 000

Marshall Limited had retained earnings of $157 000 on January 1, 1995. The company's income tax rate is 40 percent. Income taxes have already been paid.

Instructions

(a) Prepare an income statement (multiple-step format) for the year ended December 31, 1995.
(b) Prepare a statement of retained earnings for the year ended December 31, 1995.
(c) Prepare a balance sheet as of December 31, 1995.
(d) Provide evidence showing that the financial statements you prepared articulate with one another.

P4.12 Income Statement, Retained Earnings Statement, and Balance Sheet. The following are account balances of Atino Limited on December 31, 1995, the end of the company's annual accounting period. The account balances shown have been updated through December 31.

Net sales	$1 604 750
Dividends declared	200 000
Cash	118 000
Land	114 000
Franchise	89 900
Note receivable (14%, due July 30, 2000)	50 000
Accounts payable	53 700
Bond issue costs	13 000
Common shares (no-par value, 25 000 shares authorized, 10 000 shares issued and outstanding throughout 1995)	461 600
Note payable (12%, due June 1, 2001)	200 000

Other revenue	45 250
Supplies	12 300
Plant expansion fund	115 000
Accumulated depreciation—furniture and fixtures	37 000
Organization costs	21 700
Serial 10% debenture bonds ($50 000 installments are due annually from June 1, 1996, through June 1, 2003)	400 000
Loss of inventory due to earthquake (considered unusual and nonrecurring)	100 000
Land held for future plant site	90 000
Merchandise inventory (at lower of average cost or market)	87 400
Furniture and fixtures	123 000
Advances from customers (advances pertain to goods that Atino Limited will ship in 1996)	25 300
Cost of goods sold	657 500
Loss from write-off of plant assets due to obsolescence (considered unusual but not nonrecurring)	22 000
Investment in subsidiary (held for control)	179 000
Building	375 000
Interest expense	60 000
General and administrative expenses	296 400
Accounts receivable	75 000
Selling expenses	214 100
Allowance for doubtful accounts	3 700
Interest payable	10 000
Accumulated depreciation—building	75 000

Atino Limited reported retained earnings of $193 000 on its balance sheet dated December 31, 1994. On July 14, 1995, it was discovered that $40 000 of revenue earned during 1994 had been incorrectly omitted from the 1994 income statement. The omission was due to a new government regulation. The company's income tax rate was 40 percent in 1994 and 1995. Income taxes have already been paid.

Instructions

(a) Prepare an income statement (single-step format) for the year ended December 31, 1995.
(b) Prepare a statement of retained earnings for the year ended December 31, 1995.
(c) Prepare a balance sheet as of December 31, 1995.
(d) Provide evidence showing that the financial statements you prepared articulate with one another.

P4.13 Statement of Changes in Financial Position. The following events pertain to the 1995 calendar-year accounting period of Ramsey Limited:

(1) Received cash from the following sources:

(a)	From issuing short-term debt	$11 000
(b)	From issuing long-term debt	25 000
(c)	From selling land	21 000
(d)	From selling equipment	30 000
(e)	From issuing preferred shares	15 000
(f)	From collecting short-term loans	15 000
(g)	From dividends received	4 000
(h)	From customers	300 000
(i)	From interest received	16 000

(2) Paid cash for the following purposes:

(a)	To make short-term loans	$10 000
(b)	To purchase land	25 000
(c)	To liquidate long-term note	32 000
(d)	To pay dividends	26 000
(e)	To purchase equipment	44 000
(f)	To liquidate short-term debt	14 000
(g)	To pay suppliers and employees	210 000
(h)	To pay interest	5 000
(i)	To pay income taxes	25 000

Ramsey Limited had cash of $93 000 on January 1, 1995.

Instructions

Prepare a statement of changes in financial position for 1995.

Cases

C4.1 Extraordinary Items. As an audit partner of Lucke & Lucke, CAs, you are responsible for many clients. These events occurred during 1995:

(1) Patten Limited sustained a loss when it sold its computer division. Patten had been manufacturing computers and household appliances in separate divisions since 1981.

(2) Luce Limited lost some uninsured equipment because of an earthquake. This is the first earthquake to occur in the area where the equipment was located, and geologists believe that the area will not experience earthquakes in the future.

(3) Sutch Limited changed from the average cost method to the FIFO method of inventory cost determination.

(4) It was discovered that Cloninger Limited's bookkeeper forgot to deduct salvage value when computing straight-line depreciation for each of the two preceding years.

(5) Dobbs Corporation wrote off some capital assets because of obsolescence.

(6) Because of an expropriation, Nicley Limited lost all of its inventory held in a Middle Eastern country.

(7) Raines Enterprises determined that certain depreciable assets would probably have useful lives ten years longer than projected when the assets were purchased.

(8) Taft's Children's Wear destroyed a large portion of its inventory because of a government ban on the sale of clothing made of a flameproof fabric that causes skin irritations.

(9) White Inc., discovered that the ending inventory for the previous year had been misstated because of a counting error.

(10) Keene Limited lost some inventory because of a flood. Floods occur every three to five years in the area where the inventory was lost.

(11) Kilby Inc. lost all of its perishable inventory because its employees went on strike.

(12) International Business Enterprises had a gain from foreign currency transactions.

(13) Maull Corporation realized a gain from an insurance settlement. The settlement pertained to the company's South American plant, which was expropriated in 1995.

(14) Based on recent collection experience, Wertz Inc. changed the percentage used to estimate bad debts expense. The percentage was changed from 1 percent to 1.5 percent of net sales.

(15) Redmon Limited sustained a loss from selling some of the common shares in the company's investment portfolio.

Instructions

Indicate which of the above events should be reported as extraordinary items. If an event should not be reported as an extraordinary item, indicate the appropriate financial-statement category in which the event should be reported. Assume a multiple-step income statement format and that all events are material.

C4.2   Income and Cash Flows.   As an accountant for Eastpack Inc., you recently prepared the financial statements for the past year. The statements show that Eastpack had a substantial net income for the year; however, net cash flow from operating activities was a large *negative* amount. After studying the statements carefully, Eastpack's president questions whether the statements are correct. He says, "I thought that net income and net cash flow from operating activities were related concepts. I simply don't understand how we could have a large negative operating cash flow in the same period that we generated such high earnings."

Instructions

Assuming that Eastpack's financial statements are not erroneous, present major reasons that could explain why the company's net income substantially exceeds its net cash flow from operating activities.

C4.3   Estimates in Financial Statements.   Many companies promise to pay for their active employees' extended health care after they retire. Two alternative methods of accounting for the cost of medical benefits of retirees have been widely discussed in recent years. Method 1 treats the costs as expenses when the benefits are ultimately paid to retirees (i.e., after the employees retire). Method 2 attempts to better comply with the matching principle by estimating the future costs of retirees' health-care benefits and treating the costs as expenses during the period over which the retirees worked for the company. As the company recognizes the expense, a liability for future medical benefits would also be recognized.

In a *Business Week* article (September 16, 1989, p. 106), a financial analyst arguing in favour of Method 1 was quoted as saying, "It is better to be correctly wrong, and have no number in the financial statements, than to be approximately correct and mislead investors."

Instructions

Do you agree or disagree with the financial analyst? Explain the rationale that supports your answer.

C4.4   Estimates in Financial Statements.   Assume that you are a CA employed by an independent auditing firm. You and an accountant who works for one of your clients (a retail clothing company) are discussing the need to make estimates in the financial statements for the period just ended. The accountant states, "Financial statements presented in conformity with generally accepted accounting principles are described in the authoritative literature of the accounting profession as historical in nature. To me, that means that historical financial statements report transactions and events that have already happened and do not attempt to empound forecasts of future events into the measurements made in the statements. This simplifies the accountant's role and reduces the responsibilities assumed by a preparer of financial statements. I have approached the preparation of our company's financial statements in that manner. In a nutshell, our historical financial statements are just that: a treatise of what has already happened, unaffected by estimates of things that might happen in the future."

Instructions

Do the accountant's assertions accurately describe financial statements as they are presently prepared under GAAP? Explain the rationale that supports your answer.

C4.5   Financial Statement Deficiencies.   The following is the complete set of financial statements prepared by Harton Corporation:

Harton Corporation
STATEMENT OF INCOME
AND RETAINED EARNINGS
For the Fiscal Year Ended August 31, 1995

Sales		$3 500 000
Less returns and allowances		35 000
Net sales		3 465 000
Less cost of goods sold		1 039 000
Gross margin		2 426 000
Less:		
Selling expenses	$1 000 000	
General administrative expenses	1 079 000	2 079 000
Operating earnings		347 000
Add other revenue:		
Purchase discounts	10 000	
Gain on increased value of investments in real estate	300 000	
Correction of error in last year's statement	90 000	400 000
Ordinary earnings		747 000
Add extraordinary item—gain on sale of fixed asset		53 000
Earnings before income tax		800 000
Less income tax expense		380 000
Net earnings		420 000
Add beginning retained earnings		3 258 000
		3 678 000
Less:		
Dividends (12% stock dividend declared but not yet issued)	120 000	
Contingent liability (Note 2)	808 000	928 000
Ending unappropriated retained earnings		$2 750 000

Harton Corporation
BALANCE SHEET
August 31, 1995

Assets

Current Assets

Cash	$ 80 000	
Accounts receivable, net	110 000	
Inventory	130 000	
Total current assets		$ 320 000

Other Assets

Land and building, net	4 160 000	
Investments in real estate (current value)	1 508 000	
Goodwill (Note 1)	250 000	
Discount on bonds payable	42 000	
Total other assets		5 960 000
Total assets		$6 280 000

Liabilities and Shareholders' Equity

Current Liabilities

Accounts payable	$ 140 000	
Income taxes payable	320 000	
Stock dividend payable	120 000	
Total current liabilities		$ 580 000

Other Liabilities

Due to Willow Inc. (Note 2)	808 000	
Bonds payable (including portion due within one year)	1 000 000	
Total other liabilities		1 808 000
Total liabilities		2 388 000

Shareholders' Equity

Common shares	1 142 000	
Unappropriated retained earnings	2 750 000	
Total shareholders' equity		3 892 000
Total liabilities and shareholders' equity		$6 280 000

Notes to the Financial Statements

(1) As required by the federal income tax act, goodwill is written off at 10 percent of 50 percent of the cost of the goodwill. The goodwill was "acquired" in 1990.

(2) The amount due to Willow Inc. depends on the outcome of a lawsuit that is currently pending. The amount of loss, if any, is not expected to exceed $808 000, but the likelihood of this amount is difficult to predict.

Instructions

Identify and explain the deficiencies in the presentation of Harton's financial statements. There are no arithmetical errors in the statements. Organize your answer as follows:

(a) Deficiencies in the statement of income and retained earnings.
(b) The reporting deficiencies in the balance sheet should be presented in the solution.
(c) General comments.

If an item appears on both statements, identify the deficiencies for each statement separately.

(Adapted from AICPA.)

Chapter 5

Revenue Measurement and Income Presentation

Objectives

1. To discuss the theory and concepts underlying contemporary revenue-recognition practices.

2. To identify and describe acceptable methods of revenue recognition for long-term contracts and to describe the circumstances under which each method is appropriate.

3. To describe circumstances in which the installment sales and cost recovery methods of revenue recognition are acceptable.

4. To identify and describe acceptable methods of revenue recognition for franchises.

5. To describe the circumstances in which revenue should be recognized when the right of return exists.

6. To discuss the purposes and objectives of income determination.

7. To review the proper method of presenting a variety of irregular income statement items.

173

Complexities in Income Determination

**Revenue
Realization**

Matching

The determination and reporting of income is one of the most important topics in contemporary financial accounting. Crucial in determining net income is the timing of the recognition of revenue and related expenses. Applying the revenue realization principle, accountants must make many decisions about the timing and extent to which revenue is recognized. In applying the matching principle, we must also identify the expenses to be included in the determination of income. Finally, we must establish the appropriate form, organization, and content of the income statement.

The appropriate practices governing the recognition of revenue can be complicated. Consider, for example, accounting and reporting problems of aerospace companies (such as Boeing, Lockheed, and McDonnell Douglas) that agree—under a variety of long-term contracts—to provide research and development services and to produce aircraft, missiles, space vehicles, and support systems. Determining when and in what amount to recognize revenue and identifying the related expenses to be matched against the revenue are difficult problems.

After accountants decide how to recognize revenue and identify expense, they must prepare income statements to reflect the earning performance of enterprises. In earlier chapters, you learned several alternative methods of income presentation and how some transactions complicate the presentation of income. Accountants must often exercise judgement to choose the most appropriate format and extent of detail in presenting income.

This chapter begins by discussing concepts of accounting theory that underlie the recognition of revenue, and by illustrating the application of these concepts in several practical situations. Then the chapter looks more closely at theoretical questions that underlie the determination and presentation of income, and introduces some considerations that complicate presentation. Finally, a comprehensive model income statement summarizes our knowledge of income presentation.

Revenue Recognition: A Conceptual Analysis

**Revenue
Realization**

Before beginning this discussion, you need to have a good understanding of the term **revenue**. Historically, the word is derived from the French word *revenir*, which means "to return" or "to come again." Thus, "revenue" has its roots in a return-on-investment concept; that is, a business invests resources in a particular project or endeavour in the hope of earning a return on that effort.

Many attempts have been made to define the conceptual meaning of revenue. The CICA *Handbook* gives a particularly useful definition in "Revenue," Section 3400: "Revenue is the inflow of cash, receivables or other consideration arising in the course of the ordinary activities of an enterprise, normally from the sale of goods, the rendering of services, and the use by others of enterprise resources yielding interest, royalties and dividends."[1] Careful study of this definition reveals several important characteristics that an event must possess to qualify for recognition as an element of revenue.

**Revenue
Realization**

Accountants generally believe that revenue results from productive activity and is therefore earned or realized in a continuous fashion. For revenue to qualify for accounting recognition, however, at least three essential criteria must be met. The revenue must be

---

[1] "Revenue," CICA *Handbook*, Paragraph 3400.03, September 1986.

(1) earned, (2) measurable, and (3) collectable. Revenue should be recognized for accounting purposes at the earliest point at which all three of these criteria are met. Often the earliest point is the time of sale. Thus, in many situations, the recognition of revenue at the point of sale most closely follows the principles underlying the accrual basis of accounting.

Chapter 2 stated that revenue is typically recognized at the point of sale, because the sale signifies the completion of the earning process and the sale transaction establishes the amount of revenue to be recognized. Only collectability remains in question, and most sales are not made unless collectability is reasonably certain. At a minimum, companies can make reasonably accurate estimates of the extent to which credit sales will not be collected, and they establish credit and collection policies that tend to minimize the collectability problem. Thus, revenue recognition at the point of sale is an established practice that works well in most situations.

Revenue Realization

To illustrate, consider a company that manufactures and sells televisions to retail customers. From an economic perspective, the manufacturer combines raw materials and component parts with labour and overhead to construct a functioning television, thereby enhancing value. Stated simply, the productive process creates wealth and enhances value. The end product—a functioning television—is worth more than the sum of the value of its parts. This process alone, however, does not provide sufficient evidence of the realization of revenue to support accounting recognition. Specifically, until an external event (sale) takes place, there is inadequate evidence as to how much (measurable) revenue was earned in the manufacturing process and whether the enhancement in value will ever be realized (collected).

This description of revenue realization is similar to that presented in Paragraph 1000.47 of the CICA *Handbook*. The *Handbook* indicates that "revenues are generally recognized when performance is achieved and reasonable assurance regarding measurement and collectibility of the consideration exists."[2]

Consider the evidence supporting revenue recognition provided by a sale to an external party:

1. Few or no continuing obligations are retained by the seller (earned).
2. The relative value of the product sold is established by a market transaction between independent parties (measurability).
3. The buying party, who is deemed capable of paying the agreed-upon price, either pays or promises to pay the contract price (collectability).[3]

For sales situations in which one or more of these criteria are not met, the recognition of revenue should be deferred.

Substance Over Form

Sometimes sales are made to relatively poor credit risks with the condition that the seller regain control of the property if the buyer defaults. Such practices are common, for example, in the real estate industry. Repossession of the property pursuant to a loan default is not difficult, because real estate cannot be transported or hidden. Thus, certain types of real estate are frequently sold to relatively poor credit risks. In these cases, the real estate sale completes the earning process and provides a measure of the profit to be recognized, but the collectability of that revenue is not deemed adequately predictable. Recognition of revenue is therefore deferred until collectability is more assured.

---

[2]"Financial Statement Concepts," CICA *Handbook*, Paragraph 1000.47, March 1991.

[3]"Revenue," CICA *Handbook*, Paragraph 3400.07, September 1986.

As another example, magazine, book, and encyclopedia companies frequently sell annual or longer subscriptions, collecting the full fee in advance. The amount of revenue to be recognized ultimately is both collected and measurable; however, it remains unearned until the materials have been provided to the customers. Therefore, recognition is deferred until the revenue has been earned. In this situation, the earning process follows the point of sale.

Accountants must carefully analyze specific transactions to avoid recognizing revenue prematurely. They should accumulate and analyze objective evidence in light of the three criteria to assure compliance with GAAP. While many businesses conduct operations in a fashion compatible with recording revenue at the point of sale, many others require unique or unusual revenue-recognition practices.

Special Revenue-Recognition Problems

Industries and businesses with special revenue-recognition requirements frequently depend on complex, lengthy, or unusual earnings processes or contractual relationships between buyers and sellers. In this section, we explain several circumstances in which revenue is not recognized at the point of sale. Specifically, we consider the revenue-recognition problems inherent in long-term construction contracts, installment sales, franchises, and sales transactions involving the right of return. The Appendix to this chapter discusses revenue recognition in specialized situations involving real estate sales and retail land sales.

Long-Term Construction Contracts

In many industries, such as shipbuilding, aircraft design and production, and building construction, the earning activities of an enterprise are related to a number of large projects that extend through several accounting periods. The accounting and reporting problems of such activities relate primarily to the timing and extent of revenue to be recognized and the treatment of costs incurred in the productive process. Because of the variety of circumstances and contractual relationships in construction projects, alternative financial accounting methods have been developed. We now turn to these methods and the circumstances in which each is appropriate.

Accounting and Reporting Issues

The various methods developed to account for long-term contracting activity should not be viewed as equally acceptable in the same circumstances. Rather, each method is appropriate only when certain conditions are present.

When a large construction project is contemplated, the buyer and the builder usually draw up a contract prior to beginning construction. When such contracts are signed, a portion of the criteria necessary to recognize revenue is usually met. The construction company usually will not sign the contract if it has significant doubt about the buyer's ability to pay. For example, when an airplane manufacturer signs a contract with the Department of National Defence to develop and produce a new type of aircraft, the collectability of the contract amount is virtually assured. Although not all long-term contracts involve government buyers, construction companies usually accept only customers with an assured ability to pay the contract amount. The earning process is obviously not complete, however, and the amount of earnings to be ultimately realized in excess of costs incurred may still not be determinable. Therefore, the recognition of revenue must wait until both the earnings and measurability criteria are met. As previously stated, the principle that revenue is realized through the productive process is widely accepted in practice. Therefore, as development and production of the contract item proceed, revenue is said to be "earned." The final criterion of measurability, however, may still remain uncertain, and revenue should not be recognized in the accounting records until all three criteria are met.

Revenue Realization

Measuring the amount of revenue earned is particularly difficult in the area of long-term construction contracts. Even if the revenue is collectable and earned through production, the amount that has been earned and the related costs associated with the earning process may still not be determinable. The amount of revenue and expenses recognized during the production process relate to the **degree of completion** of the project and to the remaining costs and effort to be incurred in finishing the project.

Routine projects lend themselves to reliable predictions of costs and productive efforts. Other developmental projects may involve many uncertainties. Furthermore, some contracts specify how final sales prices will be determined. For example, a contract may guarantee the contractor reimbursement of all costs incurred plus some amount of profit. The profit portion may be stated as a certain number of dollars, a percentage above costs incurred, or an amount based on some other variable, such as days or hours of direct labour expended on the project. On the other hand, a contract may specify a total fixed amount to be received regardless of costs incurred. All these factors are considered in determining the appropriate accounting treatment for any specific situation.

Two basic methods are used in accounting for long-term construction contracts: the percentage-of-completion method and the completed-contract method. The **percentage-of-completion method** provides for the recognition of gross profit as production takes place. The **completed-contract method** defers recognition of gross profit until all production is complete and the customer's acceptance of the project is finalized.

Under the percentage-of-completion method, revenue and expenses are recognized to the extent that production has progressed. Therefore, estimates of costs and effort to complete the project are necessary to determine the amount of profit that should be recognized at interim points during construction. Specifically, the CICA *Handbook* states

> The percentage of completion is used when performances consist of the execution of more than one act, and revenue would be recognized proportionately by reference to the performance of each act.[4]

According to this statement, the selection of the method requires analysis of the *quality* of available evidence, primarily regarding the measurability of revenue earned. When effort has been expended on a long-term construction contract, it is generally agreed that both the earning and collectability criteria have been satisfactorily met. Therefore, the measurability of the revenue earned is the last critical prerequisite for the recognition of revenue. If the construction company can satisfactorily estimate the amount of revenue earned and the contract meets the following conditions, it should employ the percentage-of-completion method:

1. The contract specifies the enforceable rights of each party, the amount of consideration to be exchanged, and the manner and terms of settlement.

---

[4]"Revenue," CICA *Handbook*, Paragraph 3400.14, September 1986.

2. The buyer can be expected to honour the obligations of the contract.
3. The contractor can be expected to perform according to the terms of the contract.

The CICA *Handbook* confirms this position. Paragraph 3400.15 states, "The completed contract method would only be appropriate when performance consists of the execution of a single act or when the enterprise cannot reasonably estimate the extent of progress toward completion."[5]

Contractors are usually able to make the necessary reliable estimates and consequently should report most contracting activities by the percentage-of-completion method. This presumption is based on the notion that contractors would refuse contracts if reasonable estimates were impossible. However, if a construction company cannot meet the criteria for the percentage-of-completion method, then the completed-contract method is appropriate. In either case, disclosure of the method may be required.[6]

Percentage-of-Completion Method

In practice, contractors use two basic methods to measure the progress of the construction:

1. **Input measures** (e.g., ratio of costs incurred to total estimated costs).
2. **Output measures** (e.g., units of delivery).

A common input measure bases the progress on the ratio of the costs *already* incurred to the total *estimated* costs. In using costs incurred as a measure of degree of completion, the accountant must be cautious, because the costs may not be spread evenly over the contract period. For example, if a disproportionate amount of the costs were required in the early part of the contract period, costs incurred might not be a suitable measure of the degree of completion.

Output measures base the progress on the results achieved. One common output measure, the units-of-delivery approach, recognizes revenue when specific, discrete components of the project are completed and accepted by the buyer. The units-of-delivery approach to applying the percentage-of-completion method is most useful in contracts that require several large, but individual, components of production. For example, the construction of several condominium units or a group of similar ships or aircraft may be accounted for on a units-of-delivery basis. Revenue is recognized when a particular discrete component of the entire project is completed and delivered to or accepted by the customer. For example, if a construction company signs a contract to provide ten condominium units and completes four of the units—which are accepted by the buyer—at the end of the first year, then 40 percent of the total revenue provided under the contract should be recognized. The treatment of costs incurred under the contract, however, is not as obvious. In many contracts, certain costs incurred at the beginning of a contract relate to all of the units to be constructed. In the preceding example, the contractor should prorate such costs among the ten units rather than charge them immediately to expense. Costs of planning and design are especially significant in state-of-the-art production, such as the design and construction of defence or scientific projects that have never before been attempted. In the early stages, such projects frequently incur many **learning-curve costs** (i.e., expenditures necessary to learn how to do a particular construction project). Once

---

[5]"Revenue," CICA *Handbook*, Paragraph 3400.15, September 1986.
[6]"Revenue," CICA *Handbook*, Paragraph 3400.21, September 1986.

Matching

learned, the productive process may be replicated more easily and efficiently. Careful analysis and allocation of learning-curve costs to appropriate accounting periods are necessary to ensure a proper matching of revenues and expenses.

Completed-Contract Method

When reasonable estimates of the degree of completion are not possible, the completed-contract method of accounting for long-term contracts is applied. Under completed-contract accounting, no gross profit is recognized until the contract is completed and the products or services have been accepted by the buyer. At that time, all gross profit earned on the contract is recorded. Prior to the recognition of profit, contract costs are presented on the balance sheet as Construction in Progress, an inventory account.

When costs are incurred under a contract and charged to an inventory account, such as Construction in Progress, the accountant must ascertain that the amount reported as an asset does not exceed the **net realizable value** of the contract. Chapter 9 explains that the net realizable value of an item of inventory is defined as the sales (contract) value of the item less any costs still to be incurred to complete and sell the item. Thus, even under completed-contract accounting, estimates of the remaining costs are necessary to ensure that the Construction in Progress account is not overvalued. If we determine that the costs included as an asset under a particular contract exceed the net realizable value of the contract, we should write down the asset to its net realizable value and recognize a loss at that time.

A Long-Term Contract Example

The following example illustrates the appropriate accounting procedures for the percentage-of-completion and completed-contract methods. Dryden Construction Company agrees to build a large apartment building for Cozy Homes, Inc., for a total contract price of $5 million. Cozy Homes will make annual payments to Dryden, but the amounts of these payments cannot exceed the direct costs incurred by Dryden. The contract is signed on October 1, 1993, and Dryden's year-end is December 31. The contract provides Cozy Homes with a final inspection right to ensure compliance with the contract terms prior to accepting the completed project. Exhibit 5.1 provides further information about the contract.

Dryden bases its percentage-of-completion method on costs incurred rather than units delivered, because the contract calls for one large project rather than several separate projects. Dryden assumes that costs incurred will accurately measure the progress. Exhibit 5.2 presents the current year's gross profit calculations for the percentage-of-completion method. To illustrate the difference in the methods, Exhibit 5.3 shows the accounting entries for each contract year for both the percentage-of-completion and completed-contract methods. The resulting financial statement presentations for both methods are summarized in Exhibit 5.4.

These exhibits reveal that the only difference between the two methods is the timing of the recognition of gross profit on the contract. Both methods ultimately result in the recognition of the same total amount of gross profit ($600 000). The only balance sheet differences between the two methods relate to the carrying value of the Construction in Progress (inventory) account and Retained Earnings. Under the percentage-of-completion method, the amount of gross profit recognized is reflected as an increase in Construction in Progress and as an increase in Retained Earnings after being reported as an increase in net income in the income statement.

Exhibit 5.1 Long-Term Contracts—Illustrative Information

	Total contract price	$5 000 000		
	Total anticipated costs (at 10/1/93)	4 000 000		

Item	1993	1994	1995	Total
Costs incurred each year	$ 500 000	$2 500 000	$1 400 000	$4 400 000
Estimated costs to complete (at year-end)	3 500 000	1 250 000	—	—
Progress billings each year	400 000	2 000 000	2 600 000	5 000 000
Progress payments received each year	275 000	2 100 000	2 625 000*	5 000 000

*Since the contract was completed and accepted during 1995, the buyer paid the remaining balance of the total contract amount, computed as follows:

Contract amount		$5 000 000
Prior progress payments		
1993	$ 275 000	
1994	2 100 000	2 375 000
Remaining amount		$2 625 000

Exhibit 5.2 Revenue Recognized by Percentage-of-Completion Method

	1993	1994	1995
Total contract price	$5 000 000	$5 000 000	$5 000 000
Costs incurred to date	500 000	3 000 000	4 400 000
Anticipated costs to complete	3 500 000	1 250 000	—
Total estimated costs	4 000 000	4 250 000	4 400 000
Expected gross profit	$1 000 000	$ 750 000	$ 600 000
Percentage of completion			
$500 000/$4 000 000	12.5%		
$3 000 000/$4 250 000		70.6%	
$4 400 000/$4 400 000			100%
Gross profit earned to date			
$1 000 000 × 12.5%	$ 125 000		
$750 000 × 70.6%		$ 529 500	
$600 000 × 100%			$ 600 000
Less: Gross profit previously recognized	—	(125 000)	(529 500)
Current year gross profit	$ 125 000	$ 404 500	$ 70 500

Under the percentage-of-completion method, the amount of revenue to be recognized is calculated by determining the gross profit to be recognized during the current year and adding that figure to the actual costs incurred during the year. As Exhibit 5.2 shows, a revised estimate of the cumulative percentage of completion is computed each year. This percentage is applied to the expected gross profit (which will also vary as estimates of expected costs to be incurred are revised). The difference between the cumulative gross profit and the gross profit recognized in the previous year(s) is the current year's gross profit. The final entry in Exhibit 5.3 for each year under the percentage-of-completion method records revenues, costs, and the increase in Construction in Progress for the gross profit recognized.

Exhibit 5.3   Comparison of Completed-Contract and Percentage-of-Completion Journal Entries

| | | | Journal Entries | | | |
| | | | Completed-Contract | | Percentage-of-Completion | |
Date	Event	Accounts	Dr.	Cr.	Dr.	Cr.
1993	Contract signed	(No entry necessary to record contract commitment.)				
	Costs incurred	Construction in Progress	500 000		500 000	
		Cash		500 000		500 000
	Progress billings	Accounts Receivable	400 000		400 000	
		Contract Billings		400 000		400 000
	Billing collections	Cash	275 000		275 000	
		Accounts Receivable		275 000		275 000
	Revenue recognition	Construction in Progress	—		125 000	
		Cost of Earned Revenue	—		500 000	
		Construction Revenue		—		625 000
1994	Cost incurred	Construction in Progress	2 500 000		2 500 000	
		Cash		2 500 000		2 500 000
	Progress billings	Accounts Receivable	2 000 000		2 000 000	
		Contract Billings		2 000 000		2 000 000
	Billing collections	Cash	2 100 000		2 100 000	
		Accounts Receivable		2 100 000		2 100 000
	Revenue recognition	Construction in Progress	—		404 500	
		Cost of Earned Revenue	—		2 500 000	
		Construction Revenue		—		2 904 500
1995	Costs incurred	Construction in Progress	1 400 000		1 400 000	
		Cash		1 400 000		1 400 000
	Progress billings	Accounts Receivable	2 600 000		2 600 000	
		Contract Billings		2 600 000		2 600 000
	Billing collections	Cash	2 625 000		2 625 000	
		Accounts Receivable		2 625 000		2 625 000
	Revenue recognition	Construction in Progress	—		70 500	
		Cost of Earned Revenue	—		1 400 000	
		Construction Revenue		—		1 470 500
	Elimination of inventory	Contract Billings	—		5 000 000	
		Construction in Progress		—		5 000 000
	Recognition of costs and revenues on entire contract	Contract Billings	5 000 000		—	
		Cost of Earned Revenue	4 400 000		—	
		Construction Revenue		5 000 000		—
		Construction in Progress		4 400 000		—

Under the completed-contract method, the $5 000 000 of revenue and the $4 400 000 of costs are recognized in 1995, when the contract is complete and the uncertainties that preclude the use of the percentage-of-completion method are resolved. Actual companies may employ different account titles and certain other minor variations, but the procedures illustrated here are representative of the two methods.

Exhibit 5.4 shows the difference between the inventory account (Construction in Progress) and the Contract Billings as a *current* asset. The "current" classification of this

Exhibit 5.4 Comparison of Completed-Contract and Percentage-of-Completion Financial Statement Presentations

	Dec. 31, 1993		Dec. 31, 1994		Dec. 31, 1995	
Balance Sheet	Completed-Contract	Percentage-of-Completion	Completed-Contract	Percentage-of-Completion	Completed-Contract	Percentage-of-Completion
Current assets						
Accounts receivable	$ 125 000	$ 125 000	$ 25 000	$ 25 000	—	—
Inventory						
Construction in progress	500 000	625 000	3 000 000	3 529 500	—	—
Less: Contract billings	(400 000)	(400 000)	(2 400 000)	(2 400 000)	—	—
Construction in progress in excess of billings	100 000	225 000	600 000	1 129 500	—	—
Income Statement						
Construction revenue	—	$ 625 000	—	$ 2 904 500	$ 5 000 000	$ 1 470 500
Cost of earned revenue	—	(500 000)	—	(2 500 000)	(4 400 000)	(1 400 000)
Gross margin	—	$ 125 000	—	$ 404 500	$ 600 000	$ 70 500

item is based on the operating cycle definition. An asset is current if it is expected to be sold, consumed, or converted to cash within the next year (or operating cycle if the cycle exceeds one year). The period of the accounting cycle for long-term contracts, which frequently exceeds one year, is typically used to identify current assets.

If the contract provided for billings in excess of costs incurred, the Construction in Progress account could be less than the Contract Billings account. In this case, the difference is presented as a *current liability* labelled "Excess of Contract Billings over Construction in Progress" or another appropriate title.

Substance Over Form

Although the comparison of the percentage-of-completion and completed-contract methods in the Dryden example demonstrates the similarities and differences, *the methods are not equally acceptable in the same circumstances.* We must consider the circumstances and available evidence and select the *appropriate* method. The percentage-of-completion method is used when performance consists of more than one act and reasonably dependable estimates of the degree of completion can be made, because it presents the economic substance of the company's transactions and events more clearly and in a more timely fashion than does the completed-contract method. We use the completed-contract method only when reliable estimates of effort and resources to complete the project are not available. The percentage- of-completion method informs financial statement users of the volume of economic activity of the company.[7] While the completed-contract method is based on results as finally determined rather than on estimates, it does not reflect current performance when contract periods extend beyond one accounting period, and this method may result in irregular recognition of income.[8]

---

[7]"Revenue," CICA *Handbook,* Paragraph 3400.14, September 1986.

[8]"Accounting for Performance of Construction-Type and Certain Production-Type Contracts," *AICPA Statement of Position 81.1,* Paragraph 30, 1981.

A Hybrid Method

In certain types of contracts (e.g., cost-plus contracts in which the revenue will be the costs incurred plus a specified percentage), the contractor is assured of no loss. If the contractor is protected in this manner but is unable to make reasonable estimates of the percentage of completion, the AICPA's *Statement of Position 81–1* recommends a **hybrid method** described as the percentage-of-completion method based on a **zero profit margin**.[9] Under this method, revenue is recognized as an amount exactly equal to costs incurred until reasonably objective estimates of the percentage of completion can be made. In the earlier example, if Dryden Construction Company had used this method, revenue and costs would be recognized in 1993 and 1994 for $500 000 and $2 500 000 (the amount of costs incurred) respectively:

1993 Cost of Earned Revenue	500 000	
Construction Revenue		500 000
1994 Cost of Earned Revenue	2 500 000	
Construction Revenue		2 500 000

In 1995, the year in which the contract is completed, the entire gross profit is recognized, much as in the completed-contract method:

1995 Construction in Progress	600 000	
Cost of Earned Revenue	1 400 000	
Construction Revenue		2 000 000
Contract Billings	5 000 000	
Construction in Progress		5000,000

The first three entries in Exhibit 5.3 for each year would also apply to the hybrid method. The significant difference between the hybrid method and the completed-contract method is that the hybrid method requires the inclusion of both revenues and costs in the income statement for 1993 and 1994. Performance during the period would be included in the income statement, although the method would not have an impact on net income, since revenue and costs recognized would be equal. The zero profit margin approach gives financial statement users an indication of the volume of the company's business while deferring the recognition of gross profit until more reliable estimates of the degree of completion can be made.

Anticipated Losses on Contracts

Conservatism

During the contract period, the fact that a loss will be incurred on the contract may become apparent. Under all the methods presented above, a projected loss on a contract must be recognized immediately in conformity with the modifying convention of conservatism.

To illustrate, assume that Johnson Construction Company is using the completed-contract method on a project. At the end of 1995, the balance in the Construction in Progress account is $2 500 000, representing the costs incurred to date. If the company now projects a $350 000 loss on the contract because of unexpected cost increases in materials, labour, and overhead, the following entry is appropriate:

---

[9]"Accounting for Performance of Construction-Type and Certain Production-Type Contracts," *AICPA Statement of Position 81–1*, Paragraph 33, 1981.

| 1995 Loss on Construction Contract | 350 000 | |
| Construction in Progress | | 350 000 |

From this point forward, construction costs will be charged to the Construction in Progress account, and the balance in that account at the end of the contract will equal the contract revenue if the loss estimate is accurate. If the loss estimate is not accurate, an adjustment is made when the appropriate amounts are determinable.

Assume that on another contract Johnson is using the percentage-of-completion method. The Construction in Progress account at the end of 1995 has a balance of $6 500 000:

Construction costs incurred through 1995	$5 700 000
Gross profit recognized in previous years	800 000
Construction in Progress balance	$6 500 000

At the end of 1995, the company expects a $300 000 loss on the contract. The following entry should be made:

| 1995 Loss on Construction Contract | 1 100 000 | |
| Construction in Progress | | 1 100 000 |

The $1 100 000 loss represents a reversal of the $800 000 gross profit recognized in previous years, plus the $300 000 loss now expected on the contract. From this point forward, construction costs will be charged to the Construction in Progress account, and the balance in that account at the end of the contract will equal the contract revenue if the loss estimate is accurate. As in the completed-contract method, if the loss estimate is inaccurate, further adjustment must be made in the future as the appropriate amounts become determinable.

Installment Sales

The collectability of credit sales is usually predictable and reasonably assured as a result of credit approval, collection procedures, and historical evidence. In these cases, revenue is appropriately recognized at the point of sale. However, if a company makes credit sales to customers of relatively poor credit risk, recognition of revenue at the point of sale may be inappropriate. While such revenue may be deemed to have been earned and measurable, collectability remains uncertain. Therefore, the creditor should ordinarily defer the recognition of revenue until collecting the amount due. This practice is supported by the professional literature:

> There are exceptional cases where receivables are collectible over an extended period of time, and because of the terms of the transactions or other conditions, there is no reasonable basis for estimating the degree of collectibility. When such circumstances exist, and as long as they exist, either the installment method or the cost recovery method of accounting may be used. (Under the cost recovery method, equal amounts of revenue and expense are recognized as collections are made until all costs have been recovered, postponing a recognition of profit until that time.)[10]

[10]"Omnibus Opinion—1966," *APB Opinion No. 10,* Paragraph 12, 1966.

Conservatism

The **installment sales method** recognizes a portion of each cash collection as revenue and the remaining amount of cash collected as a recovery of cost. The **cost recovery method** treats all cash collected as a recovery of cost of the item sold until the full cost of the item sold is collected. Subsequent collections are treated entirely as revenue. The cost recovery method is even more conservative than the installment sales method, and application of the cost recovery technique is most desirable when the collectability of receivables is extremely uncertain.

Under the installment sales method, revenue is recognized on a pro rata basis as each installment is received. To illustrate, assume that Dryden Credit Company sells a $6000 automobile to a customer on November 1, 1995, under the following terms: The customer will pay $600 down and $150 per month for 36 months plus interest at 15 percent. Since Dryden Credit paid $4200 for the automobile, it will make a gross profit of $1800 on the sale. For simplicity, we will ignore the interest revenue, because it is not related to the recognition of profit on the sale.

Because of the significant uncertainty of collection resulting from granting credit to relatively poor credit risks, Dryden Credit uses the installment sales method of revenue recognition. Exhibit 5.5 presents the entries necessary to record the sale, collection of cash, and recognition of revenue. The gross profit percentage, which indicates the gross profit included in each payment received, is 30 percent, computed by dividing the gross profit by the sale price [($6000 − $4200)/$6000 = 0.30].

The Deferred Gross Profit account established at the point of sale is treated either as a contra account to Notes Receivable or as a deferred revenue (liability) account. The entry on December 31, 1995, which reflects the portion of cash collected that is recognized as revenue, may be made as each cash receipt occurs. If this practice is selected, each cash receipt of $150 (ignoring interest) is recorded in the following manner:

Cash	150	
Deferred Gross Profit	45	
Notes Receivable		150
Realized Gross Profit ($150 × 0.30 = $45)		45

The CICA *Handbook* does not provide detailed recommendations on accounting for installment sales, but it does outline the disclosure requirements as follows: "The amounts and, where practicable, maturity dates of instalment accounts maturing beyond one year should be disclosed. In some circumstances, it may be desirable to give information about the terms of instalment accounts."[11]

If different sales transactions result in different gross profit percentages, separate gross profit records must be kept for each sale. For example, if installment sales in 1994 result in a gross profit percentage of 32 percent and installment sales in 1995 result in a gross profit percentage of 34 percent, the receivables and deferred gross profit amounts related to 1994 sales must be kept separate from the 1995 sales so that a proper accounting may be made of the gross profit recognized as receivables collected.

Considering the uncertainty of collection for installment sales, it is not surprising that sellers typically retain a right of repossession (the right to take the property and resell it) if the buyer defaults. When inventory is thus acquired, the installment receivable and any deferred gross profit on the original sale must be eliminated. If the resale value of the

---

[11]"Accounts and Notes Receivable," CICA *Handbook,* Paragraph 3020.02, August 1991.

Exhibit 5.5 Installment Sales Accounting—Illustrative Entries			
Date	**Accounts**	**Dr.**	**Cr.**
Nov. 1, 1995	Cash	600	
	Notes Receivable	5400	
	Inventory		4200
	Realized Gross Profit* ($600 × 0.3)		180
	Deferred Gross Profit ($5400 × 0.3)		1620
	(*To record sale of automobile under installment sales method.*)		
Nov. 30, 1995	Cash	150	
	Notes Receivable		150
	(*To record receipt of payment.*)		
Dec. 31, 1995	Cash	150	
	Notes Receivable		150
	(*To record receipt of payment.*)		
Dec. 31, 1995	Deferred Gross Profit ($300 × 0.3)	90	
	Realized Gross Profit*		90
	(*To record revenue for the year based on cash received.*)		

*For income statement presentation purposes, the components of realized gross profit may be presented rather than the net amount of $270 ($180 + $90). In this situation, sales of $900 ($600 + $150 + $150) would be included in sales revenue and $630 ($900 × 0.7) would be included in cost of goods sold.

repossessed property is greater or less than the carrying amount of the receivable (face amount, less the deferred gross profit), a gain or loss is recognized.

To illustrate, assume that Dryden Appliance Company sells a refrigerator for $500 on an installment contract calling for 25 monthly payments of $20, plus interest. The refrigerator cost Dryden $420, resulting in a gross profit percentage of 16 percent [($500 − $420)/$500]. After ten payments, the customer discontinues paying and Dryden repossesses the refrigerator. The carrying amount of the receivable is as follows:

Receivable balance [$500 − 10 ($20)]	$300
Deferred gross profit balance [$80 − (10[$20] × 0.16)]	48
Carrying amount of installment receivable	$252

If the estimated resale value of the refrigerator is $200, the entry to record the repossession is as follows:

Repossessed Inventory	200	
Deferred Gross Profit	48	
Loss on Repossession	52	
Installment Receivables		300

If the estimated resale value of the refrigerator had been greater than $252, a Gain on Repossession would have been recorded.

Accounting for Franchise Activities

The growth of franchising as a commercial activity began to accelerate intensely during the 1960s and continues today. Many contentious accounting and reporting issues are posed by such activities, and these problems are resolved in the "Franchise Fee Revenue Accounting Guidelines" section of the CICA *Handbook*.[12] **Franchises** generally involve the creation or extension of a business in which two parties join together in a continuing contract with a joint public identity. Each party normally contributes resources. The **franchisor** generally contributes products, processes, equipment, company reputation, and trademarks. The **franchisee** generally provides operating capital and managerial and operational resources. Franchise activities are extremely broad; they cut across industry lines and are radically different in terms of organization, concept, and philosophy. For example, some franchise agreements provide for a relatively passive franchisor role after establishment, while others require extensive participation or the supply of products and skill on a continuing basis. Therefore, precise accounting and reporting standards are not possible. Certain broad guidelines, however, are provided by the "Franchise Fee Revenue, Accounting Guidelines."

The general bases for accounting and reporting practices are contained in the franchise agreement. Most such agreements require the franchisee to make a substantial initial payment, called a franchise fee, to the franchisor in consideration for the reputation, skill, products, and processes contributed by the franchisor. Financial accounting for the franchise fee in terms of revenue recognition is most controversial, and careful study of the franchise agreement is necessary.

The "Franchise Fee Revenue" guidelines section notes that the problem of recognizing revenue in regard to franchise fees generally results from two issues: (1) the point at which the fee is to be considered earned, and (2) the assessment of collectability of any unpaid portion of the fee. Initial fees are generally quite specific and, therefore, the amount of the initial fee is usually known. Most franchise agreements also call for continuing payments related to the level of franchisee business. For example, continuing payments to franchisors are usually based on the sales of products to franchisees or on a percentage of the franchisee's sales or profits.

The three revenue-recognition practices that are used with franchisees are summarized as follows:

1. **Cash basis.** This method calls for recording revenue when cash is received. Proponents cite the simplicity of application, the complexity of franchise agreements, and collection problems as support for this practice.
2. **Spread over life of agreement.** This method treats the initial fee as a prepayment for the privilege of using franchise rights. Accordingly, the prepayment should be recognized proportionately over the life of the franchise agreement. Franchisors agree that the franchise fee is payment for a confirmation of initial and continuing services and transfers of rights.
3. **Inception of the franchise agreement.** This method treats the sale of a franchise in a manner similar to the sale of any other commercial property, tangible or intangible. The sale represents the transfer of specified rights in exchange for specified consideration, and thus supports the recognition of revenue at the point of sale.

---

[12]"Franchise Fee Revenue, Accounting Guidelines," CICA *Handbook,* July 1984.

The "Franchise Fee Revenue" guidelines section finds merit in each argument under certain separate circumstances, and indirectly supports each in specific individual situations. In essence, revenue should be recognized when a franchise sale occurs *and* when all material obligations of the franchisor have been *substantially performed*. Substantial performance may take place at different points in time under different franchise agreements. Even if the franchise agreement requires no further franchisor services, revenue is not recognized if business conditions or informal policy indicates that substantial voluntary services are likely to be rendered by the franchisor.

Any unpaid franchise fees must also be assessed as to collectability prior to the recognition of revenue. If collection of the franchise fee is uncertain, the installment method or cost recovery method may be necessary to avoid a premature recognition of revenue.

Assume that in 1994 Sweets Corp. decided to sell bakery franchises in several large cities. Each franchise was sold for $40 000, $16 000 payable at signing, and $12 000 a year for two years starting one year after opening. No other payments were required from franchisees.

Sweets Corp. was obligated to provide considerable services to franchisees in opening and operating their operations for the first three years, including preparing promotional materials, setting up accounting systems, and training employees. Twenty percent of these franchising services were to be complete by the opening of the operation, and the remainder of the revenue was expected to be earned evenly over the three-year agreement.

The fair rate of interest during 1994 was 12 percent a year; thus, the present value of the two promissory notes of $12 000 each received from a franchisee was approximately $20 381 ($12 000 × 1.69005) on the date a franchise was sold. The notes were considered fully collectable.

One franchise was sold on June 30, 1994, and began operation on October 1, 1994. Sweets Corp. has a December 31 year-end. The franchise transactions were recorded by Sweets Corp. as follows:

June 30, 1994	Cash	16 000	
	Notes Receivable	24 000	
	Discount on Notes Receivable		3 719
	Unearned Franchise Fee Revenue		36 281
	(To record the receipt of the cash and the two notes from the franchisee.)		
Oct. 1, 1994	Unearned Franchise Fee Revenue	7 256	
	Franchise Revenue Earned		7 256
	(To recognize the franchise fee revenue to October 1, 1994.)		
Dec. 31, 1994	Unearned Franchise Fee Revenue	2 419	
	Franchise Revenue Earned		2 419
	(To recognize the franchise fee revenue to December 31, 1994:		
	[$36 281 − $7256] = ($29 025/36) = $806.25/month × 3 = $2418.75)		
Dec. 31, 1994	Discount on Notes Receivable	1 217	
	Interest Revenue		1 217
	(To recognize the interest earned to December 31, 1994:		
	[$20 281 × 0.12 × ½ = $1216.86])		
June 30, 1995	Cash	12 000	
	Notes Receivable		12 000
	(To record the receipt of the payment of the first note.)		

Dec. 31, 1995	Unearned Franchise Fee Revenue	9 675	
	Franchise Revenue Earned		9 675

(To recognize the franchise fee revenue to December 31, 1995: [$806.25/month × 12 = $9675])

Dec. 31, 1995	Discount on Notes Receivable	1 860	
	Interest Revenue		1 860

(To recognize the interest earned to December 31, 1995: [$20 281 × 0.12 × ½] + ($12 000 − [$3719 − $1217 − $1217] × 0.12 × ½) = $1216.86 + $642.90 = $1859.76]

June 30, 1996	Cash	12 000	
	Notes Receivable		12 000

(To record the receipt of the payment of the second note.)

Dec. 31, 1996	Unearned Franchise Fee Revenue	9 675	
	Franchise Revenue Earned		9 675

(To recognize the franchise fee revenue to December 31, 1996: [$806.25/month × 12 = $9675]

Dec. 31, 1996	Discount on Notes Receivable	642	
	Interest Revenue		642

(To recognize the interest earned to June 30, 1996: [$3719 − $1217 − $1860 = $642])

Many franchise agreements include clauses outlining royalties on purchases made by the franchisees and renewal terms and costs. The terms of an agreement are contingent on the type of operation and the potential of the franchise.

Revenue Recognition Where the Right of Return Exists

A company may sell an item with a provision allowing the customer to return it under certain circumstances. For example, a manufacturer may sell its products to a retailer with the **right to return** products that are unsatisfactory to the consumer. In such circumstances, the manufacturer should not recognize revenue until the following conditions are met:

(a) the seller of the goods has transferred to the buyer the significant risks and rewards of ownership, in that all significant acts have been completed and the seller retains no continuing managerial involvement in, or effective control of, the goods transferred to a degree usually associated with ownership; and

(b) reasonable assurance exists regarding the measurement of the consideration that will be derived from the sale of goods, and the extent to which goods may be returned.[13]

Disclosure Sales revenue and related expenses should be deferred because the revenue is not measurable and ultimate collection reasonably assured. Disclosure of the uncertainties of the circumstances and the enterprise's accounting policies are necessary to adequately inform users of the financial statements.[14]

To illustrate the recognition of revenue where the right of return exists, we will assume the following information about the Dryden Corporation for 1995:

---

[13]"Revenue," CICA *Handbook,* Paragraph 3400.07, September 1986.

[14]"Revenue," CICA *Handbook,* Paragraph 3400.18, September 1986.

Sales	$500 000
Cost of goods	$325 000
Expected returns	2% of sales
Actual returns during year (at selling price)	$6 000
Cash collected on receivables	$285 000

Since Dryden is able to make a reasonable estimate of returns, we will assume that all of the conditions for revenue recognition are met in the entries required to record sales and related transactions for 1995.

Accounts Receivable	500 000	
Cost of Goods Sold	325 000	
Sales		500 000
Inventory		325 000
(To record sales and cost of goods sold.)		
Sales Returns ($500 000 × 0.02)	10 000	
Inventory—Estimated Returns ($10 000 × 0.65)	6 500	
Allowance for Sales Returns		10 000
Cost of Goods Sold		6 500
(To record estimated sales returns.		
The 65% represents the cost-to-sales percentage in the sales: $325 000/$500 000 = 0.65.)		
Cash	285 000	
Accounts Receivable		285 000
(To record collection of receivables.)		
Allowance for Sales Returns	6 000	
Inventory ($6000 × 0.65)	3 900	
Accounts Receivable		6 000
Inventory—Estimated Returns		3 900
(To record sales returns and reclassification of inventory.)		

As a result of the recording of these transactions, net sales and cost of goods sold will be presented at $490 000 and $318 500, respectively, maintaining the 65 percent cost-to-sales ratio, as shown in the following computations:

Sales	$500 000	
Sales returns	10 000	$490 000
Cost of goods sold ($325 000 − $6500)		318 500
Gross margin		$171 500

Matching   This treatment is consistent with the matching principle. Accounts Receivable are presented at a net amount of $205 000, after considering $6000 of returns received, $285 000 of collections, and $4000 of estimated future returns:

Accounts receivable ($500 000 − $285 000 − $6000)	$209 000	
Allowance for estimated returns ($10 000 − $6000)	4 000	$205 000

The cost of inventory expected to be returned is presented in a special inventory classification, Inventory—Estimated Returns, at $2600 ($4000 × 0.65).

In this example, we assumed that the conditions for revenue recognition were met, and the question then became one of estimating returns and appropriately adjusting cost of goods sold so that the 65 percent cost-to-sales relationship is maintained in the income statement. Had the conditions for revenue recognition not been met, the sales and cost of goods sold amounts recognized in the first entry would have been deferred and recorded only when the conditions for revenue recognition were met.

Other Unusual Revenue-Recognition Circumstances

The timing and magnitude of revenue recognition remain complex and controversial areas for the accounting profession. Judgements are frequently required in determining when revenue should be recognized and in what amount. These circumstances raise the possibility of manipulation and the "managing" of earnings. Because of the central importance of revenue in the financial statements and the susceptibility to *abuse*, accountants must remain alert to the possibility of misstatement.

In our discussion of revenue recognition, we have emphasized situations involving physical products. Service industries, such as insurance, legal services, accounting services, management consulting, moving and storage, and banking, also encounter revenue-recognition problems. The questions of income determination for service industries are similar to those for product-related industries: When is revenue earned, measurable, and collectable? How should costs related to the generation of service revenue be treated? Few authoritative accounting pronouncements presently exist to help accountants answer these important questions. Theoretically, service revenue should be recognized when services are performed (earned), amounts can be objectively determined (measurable), and collection is reasonably assured (collectable). Expenses should be recognized as the rev-
Matching enues they helped to create are recognized, in accordance with the matching principle. Accountants must apply judgement in this important area of business activity. Undoubtedly, as the AcSB continues to refine accounting practices, particularly in specialized industries, more guidance concerning the recognition of revenue and the determination of income in service industries will be forthcoming.

As previously mentioned, many industries engage in transactions and business relationships that require unusual accounting and reporting practices. The Appendix to this chapter discusses financial accounting and reporting for additional situations that involve unique revenue-recognition problems.

The first part of this chapter has dealt with the criteria and circumstances that influence the recognition of revenue. Accounting and reporting standards have also been established in regard to the presentation of various items of revenue and expense in the income statement. The following sections consider theories, standards, and practices relevant to the format, organization, and content of the income statement.

Income Presentation

A major objective of financial reporting is to provide information to investors and creditors about **financial performance** during the reporting period. Although "performance" may refer to numerous aspects of an enterprise's operations, the AcSB has clearly designated **earnings** as a focal point for financial reporting: "The objective of financial statements is to communicate information that is useful to investors, members, contributors, creditors and other users ('users') in making their resource allocation decisions and/or assisting management stewardship."[15]

---

[15]"Financial Statement Concepts," CICA *Handbook*, Paragraph 1000.15, March 1991).

Revenue

Realization

Matching

Current accounting practice uses a transactions approach to income measurement. Under this approach, positive and negative asset and liability changes are measured and recognized in conformity with accounting principles, such as revenue realization and matching. The combined results of these changes is the determination of net income, one of the most prominent figures in financial reporting.

Objectives of Reporting Earnings

We could cite many objectives of reporting earnings. In Chapter 3, we examined the usefulness of accounting income figures and discussed net income as a measure of operating efficiency and a predictor of future cash flows.

The ability of management is a major factor in the success of a business enterprise, and income is the primary measure of business performance. Therefore, one objective of earnings is to *evaluate management efficiency* by comparing the results of management effort with some standard or goal. The objectives of business activity vary from enterprise to enterprise. A profit-oriented enterprise attempts to achieve some desired level of earnings as the basis for providing a desired level of cash flow to investors and creditors. Net income is a valuable measure of progress toward that goal. Periodic measures of earnings are useful in evaluating how well management has employed the resources at its disposal to achieve the desired level of earnings. The desired level of earnings may be determined in several ways, including management-established goals, industry averages, or individual investor expectations.

The primary focus of financial reporting is information about the enterprise's earnings and its components. *Information about earnings is generally more useful in predicting and evaluating future cash-flow potentials than is information about the enterprise's past cash flows.* Therefore, support for the presentation of earnings and its components is based primarily on the need for this information in assessing the enterprise's future activities, particularly those that have cash-flow prospects.

Inherent in the presentation of net income is the distinction between investment and income. **Investment** refers to the accumulated resources that the enterprise has as a result of contributions by investors. **Income** is the net result of the inflow of resources resulting from the employment of that investment. Another objective of reporting earnings is *to distinguish between the accumulation of investments and the accumulation of additional resources that result from the employment of investments.* These additional resources are either retained by the enterprise or distributed as dividends to the owners of the enterprise.

Alternative Income Concepts

We will now consider several alternative definitions of income that have been suggested by accounting theorists. The primary differences among these definitions are found in the treatment of wages, income taxes, interest, and preferred dividends.

Net Income to Shareholders

The current concept of income is founded on the notion that the amount identified as net income accrues to *all* shareholders. **Determinants** of income are those revenues, gains, expenses, and losses that are included in the computation of net income, such as sales revenue, cost of goods sold, operating expenses, interest expense, and income tax expense. Distributions of income are transfers of assets to owners of the enterprise, including both common and preferred shareholders. This concept of income, which is strongly emphasized in traditional accounting theory, is often identified as **net income to shareholders**. All expenses incurred in the generation of revenue are deducted in determining income, but no distributions to owners are deducted. Several alternative approaches to this concept are explained in the following sections.

Value Added Income

Under the value-added concept of income, a variety of interested parties are identified as the **recipients** of the income of the enterprise. The **value added** is the sales price of the enterprise's products or services minus the cost of the goods and services paid to other enterprises that produced those goods and services. Other groups who receive the advantages of enterprise operations—employees, creditors, government, and owners—are recipients of the income of the enterprise. Whereas the cost of goods sold is a determinant of income, expenditures such as income taxes, interest, and dividends are considered distributions of that income to the various recipients.

Enterprise Net Income

Under the concept of **enterprise net income**, income taxes and interest expense, as well as dividends, are considered distributions of income. Thus, the recipients of the income of the enterprise are creditors, government, and owners. The resulting income is much like the operating income figure that commonly appears in income statements today, because taxes and interest are frequently presented after that amount.

Net Income to Investors

Another variation of net income is **net income to investors**. Under this concept, all interest payments to creditors and dividend payments to shareholders are considered distributions of the enterprise's income, and all other distributions are considered determinants of income. This interpretation of income varies from current reporting practice only in that interest paid to creditors is treated as a distribution, rather than a determinant, of income.

Net Income to Residual Shareholders

The **residual** (or **common**) **shareholders** are typically thought of as the ultimate owners of the enterprise. Although the claim represented by preferred shares is legally that of an owner, there is some support for income to be regarded as the amount that accrues to the residual shareholders. This concept is reflected in the computation of earnings per share in which the net income (to all shareholders), as reported in the income statement, is reduced by the preferred dividend to derive an income figure accruing to the common shareholders. The resulting amount then becomes the basis for computing earnings per share. This view of income is consistent with the theory that common shareholders are the ultimate riskbearers and the group to whom the long-run profitability of the enterprise ultimately accrues.

Exhibit 5.6 summarizes the concepts of income and shows whether wages (return to employees), income taxes (return to government), interest (return to creditors), and preferred dividends (return to preferred shareholders) are treated as determinants or distributions of income under each concept. The concept of income reflected in current income presentation, net income to shareholders, is included in the fourth column.

Exhibit 5.6 Comparative Income Presentations (in thousands of dollars)

	(1) Value Added Income	(2) Enterprise Net Income	(3) Net Income to Investors	(4) Net Income to Shareholders	(5) Net Income to Residual Shareholders
Sales	$2000	$2000	$2000	$2000	$2000
Determinants of income					
Cost of goods sold	1000	1000	1000	1000	1000
Wages	—	400	400	400	400
Income taxes	—	—	150	150	150
Interest	—	—	—	200	200
Preferred dividends	—	—	—	—	50
	1000	1400	1550	1750	1800
Income	$1000	$ 600	$ 450	$ 250	$ 200
Distributions of income					
Wages	$ 400	—	—	—	—
Income taxes	150	$ 150	—	—	—
Interest	200	200	$ 200	—	—
Preferred dividends	50	50	50	$ 50	—
Common dividends	100	100	100	100	$ 100
Total distributions of income	$ 900	$ 500	$ 350	$ 150	$ 100
Groups to Whom Income Accrues					
Employees	X				
Government	X	X			
Creditors	X	X	X		
Preferred shareholders	X	X	X	X	
Common shareholders	X	X	X	X	X

Current Operating Performance Versus All-Inclusive Income

A continuing question about the presentation of income concerns which specific transactions, if any, should be *excluded* from income determination because of their unique
nature. Accountants agree that sales, cost of goods sold, and other similar revenue and
expense items should be included in the determination of net income. They also agree
that the results of capital transactions, such as dividends and share transactions, should
be excluded in determining net income. Opinions differ, however, on the proper treatment
of items that differ in nature from normal revenues and expenses, that do not recur in
any established pattern, or that represent adjustments of the income of some past accounting period.

Suppose, for example, that a company sustains a loss from an earthquake. Such a
loss is unusual and will not recur in any predictable pattern. If an objective of reporting
earnings is to provide information for predicting future events, should the company
include this loss in the measurement of income? Assume that in 1995 the company finds
an error in the determination of 1993 net income. Should it include the gain or loss
necessary to correct this error in the determination of 1995 net income? Special or irregular events like these are clearly part of the history of the enterprise's earnings, but their
unique characteristics have led to disagreement on the most appropriate way to present
them in the financial statements. The presentation of items such as those described above

has produced two opposing schools of thought: the **current operating performance view** and the **all-inclusive view**.

Proponents of the current operating performance view believe that a company's income should be based on its normal, recurring operations. That is, unusual items, non-recurring items, and items relating to other accounting periods should be *excluded* from the current year's measurement of income and reported as direct increases or decreases in retained earnings. These types of items would appear in the statement of retained earnings rather than the income statement. Proponents of this view believe that financial statement users rely heavily on reported measurements of *net income* but that they lack the knowledge necessary to understand the detailed components of an income statement. Proponents of this view also believe that financial statement users can make more accurate predictions and more meaningful evaluations of management performance if net income reflects only the normal, recurring activities of the business.

The opposite perspective is the all-inclusive view. Proponents of this view believe that net income for a period should equal the change in owners' equity during the period, except for dividends and capital share transactions. They contend that unusual items, events not recurring frequently, and items related to other accounting periods should be reported in the current income statement. Advocates of this view assume that financial statement users will not focus excessively on the bottom-line net income figure and that they will appropriately consider the components of net income when they interpret the enterprise's performance. All-inclusive advocates claim that irregular items tend to go unnoticed when not reported in the income statement. Considerable judgement is required to determine which items should be included under the current operating performance approach, which—according to all-inclusive proponents— allows management to manipulate reported income by including or excluding items as desired.

The CICA *Handbook* recommends that discontinued operations and extraordinary items be reported in the income statement net of tax after income from operations and that prior period adjustments be reported as an adjustment to the beginning balance of the retained earnings.[16]

Comprehensive Income

In 1984, the FASB issued "Recognition and Measurement in Financial Statements of Business Enterprises," *Statement of Financial Accounting Concepts No. 5*. In this statement, the concept of "comprehensive income" is introduced, and a distinction is drawn between comprehensive income and earnings.

Comprehensive income is defined as follows:

A broad measure of the effects of transactions and other events of an entity, comprising all recognized changes in equity (net assets) of the entity during a period from transactions and other events and circumstances except those resulting from investments by owners and distributions to owners.[17]

The concept of "earnings," on the other hand, is similar to net income in current practice. Earnings is a measure of performance for a period and to the extent feasible *excludes*

---

[16]"Prior Period Adjustments," CICA *Handbook,* Paragraph 3600.06, December 1980, and "Income Statement," CICA *Handbook,* Paragaraph 1520.02, August 1991.

[17]"Recognition and Measurement in Financial Statements of Business Enterprises," *FASB Statement of Financial Accounting Concepts No. 5*, Paragraph 39, 1984.

items that are extraneous to that period. In Canada, one example of an item that is excluded in present net income is the cumulative effect of a change in accounting policy. While the CICA expects that net income, profit, net loss, and other equivalent terms will continue to be used in financial statements as names for "earnings," we can reasonably expect some future changes in income statement content and display as the CICA puts into practice the concepts of comprehensive income and earnings. One possible outcome of this distinction is a movement back toward a current operating performance approach as extraneous transactions are identified as part of comprehensive income but not part of earnings from current operations.

Contemporary Income Presentation

Contemporary income presentation practices are based on the concept of income to shareholders (see Column 4, Exhibit 5.6). Emphasis is placed on the all-inclusive concept of income with limited exceptions. Concern for the presentation of the results of current operations, however, is apparent in the many separate classifications and subtotals required in the statement if certain types of events have taken place.

Throughout this text, various aspects of income statement presentation will be discussed and illustrated. In the following paragraphs, several important features of the income statement that will be considered in more detail in other chapters are briefly introduced. This discussion is followed by a discussion of the disposal of a segment of an enterprise and an explanation of how discontinued operations are reported in the income statement.

Single- and Multiple-Step Income Statements

Recall from Chapter 4 that a **single-step income statement** is a relatively simple presentation in which all revenues and gains included in pretax income are grouped together at the top of the statement. Next, all expenses and losses included in pretax income are grouped together and subtracted from the total of revenues and gains. This subtotal, reduced by income tax expense, is net income. In a **multiple-step income statement**, revenues from sales are presented first. From this amount, cost of goods sold is deducted to determine gross margin. Operating expenses, which may be classified into specific categories such as selling and administrative expenses, are deducted from the gross margin to obtain income from operations. Other income and expense items are added to or deducted from the income from operations to obtain net income. The resulting net income figure is the same for both statements, and the difference lies in the format and extent of detail. You may wish to refresh your memory about these two forms of income statement presentation by reviewing Exhibits 4.1 and 4.2.

Individually Identified Gains and Losses

Gains and losses that are unusual in nature or infrequent in occurrence are individually identified in the income statement. Under the multiple-step format, these items are usually displayed among other gains and losses, following income from operations. Examples of this type of item are gains and losses from the sale of capital assets or investment securities. Care should be taken not to present these items in a way that implies that they are extraordinary items. They are *not* presented on a net-of-tax basis, and earnings-per-share figures are not presented on these items.

Intraperiod Income Tax Allocation

Gains and losses presented in the financial statements in separate categories, such as extraordinary items, are presented on a net-of-tax basis. **Intraperiod income tax allocation** procedures require the determination of the income tax effect of these items and the direct association of the tax with the related gain or loss. A gain is reduced by the additional income tax resulting from that gain. A loss is reduced by the income tax benefit resulting from the reduction in income due to the inclusion of that loss. The income tax expense that relates to all revenues and expenses not separately classified is computed as if any separately classified item(s) did not exist.

Extraordinary Gains and Losses

Gains and losses that are judged to be unusual in nature and infrequent in occurrence and that do not depend primarily on decisions by management or owners are defined as **extraordinary** and are presented in a separate income statement category on a net-of-tax basis. This presentation is required in both single- and multiple-step income statements. An income subtotal immediately preceding extraordinary items entitled "income before extraordinary items" must be included in the income statement. This caption is followed by the extraordinary gain or loss, presented net of its tax effect, and then by the net income amount.

To illustrate the presentation of an extraordinary item, Exhibit 5.7 includes the partial consolidated income statement and a related note to the financial statements from the 1991 annual report of Torstar Corporation. Torstar is a broadly based information and entertainment communications company operating on a worldwide basis with about 45 percent of its revenues generated outside Canada. Note 12 of the 1991 financial statements, which appears at the bottom of Exhibit 5.7, explains the nature of the extraordinary item, specifically the settlement of expropriation of land in 1988.

Cumulative Effect of a Change in Accounting Policy

When an enterprise changes from one generally accepted accounting principle (or method of applying a principle) to another, the cumulative effect of that change is reported as an adjustment to the opening balance of retained earnings at the beginning of the period of change or with restatement of prior period statements, for comparative purposes. The cumulative effect may increase or decrease retained earnings depending on the nature of the specific change.

Corrections of Errors in Prior Period

Corrections of errors in previously issued financial statements and certain other adjustments are *not* included in the determination of net income. Primarily because they do not relate to the period in which they are recorded, these items (presented on a net-of-tax basis) belong in the retained earnings statement as adjustments to the beginning balance of the period, even though they are part of the enterprise's total earnings history.

Several types of events and transactions that are presented as prior period adjustments are discussed in Chapter 20. These include certain retroactive adjustments resulting from the application of authoritative accounting pronouncements.

Earnings Per Share

Earnings-per-share figures are included in the income statements of all publicly held companies. Other companies may choose to present earnings-per-share data, and several

---

Exhibit 5.7 Torstar Corporation, Example of Extraordinary Item

PARTIAL CONSOLIDATED INCOME STATEMENT
Years ended December 31, 1991 and 1990

	1991	1990
	(thousands of dollars)	
Income from continuing operations	19 422	55 184
Discontinued operations (note 10)	(22 847)	(12 972)
Income (loss) before extraordinary item	(3 425)	42 212
Extraordinary item (note 12)		4 209
Net income (loss)	($3 425)	$46 421
Average number of shares outstanding (thousands) (note 13)	38 743	38 590
Fully diluted earnings (loss) per Class A and Class B share (note 13)		
From continuing operations	$0.50	$1.43
Before extraordinary item	(0.09)	1.09
Net income (loss)	(0.09)	1.20

12. Extraordinary Item
In 1990, the company received additional proceeds of $4 209 000 (net of tax of $2 168 000) from a 1988 expropriation of land.

Source: Torstar Corporation, *1991 Annual Report.*

---

authoritative pronouncements require the presentation of earnings-per-share figures for certain income statement items.

When presented, earnings-per-share figures appear on the face of the income statement and may also be explained in related notes. A common practice is to present an earnings-per-share schedule (which parallels the income statement presentation) at the bottom of the income statement.

Exhibit 5.7 illustrates this method of presentation with Torstar Corporation's 1991 and 1990 comparative consolidated income statement, which includes a typical earnings-per-share presentation at the bottom.

The computation of earnings per share is complicated by the presence of convertible securities, stock options, warrants and rights, and other arrangements that include the possibility of changing the number of common shares outstanding. An in-depth discussion of this subject is found in Chapter 21.

Discontinued Operations

When an enterprise has disposed of a major portion of its operations, the results of *continuing operations* should be separated from the operating results of the *discontinued segment.* Any gain or loss on the disposal of the discontinued part of the business is also shown separately. Prior to the development of this income statement presentation technique and the change in the characteristics of extraordinary items, the most frequently reported extraordinary items in financial reports were gains and losses from the disposal of portions of business enterprises. The frequency of these items, combined with their

OSC Reviews Financial Statement Disclosure

The Ontario Securities Commission recently released its report on the 1990 annual Financial Statement Review Program, based on a random sample of 100 annual reports from about 2,000 active issuers. The objectives of the program are to challenge questionable accounting practices, ensure adequate disclosure, identify emerging issues and innovative transactions and promote improved financial reporting.

"There are really three main areas—income statements, standards and financial instruments—where we have reporting problems," says Brenda Eprile, the OSC's chief accountant, adding that the problems range from "not terribly misleading to investors, to somewhat misleading or confusing, to, in a few cases, very misleading." Some of the accounting could overstate earnings, and some financial statements disclose insufficient information.

Companies are also inconsistent in the calculation of operating income. "We have instances of what I would call 'interesting accounting.' Some companies are 'bending' the rules so that they boost or smooth reported net income and that makes it very difficult to compare companies' performances." The report notes that various techniques are used to modify reported net income, including capitalizing costs that should be expensed, recognizing revenue prematurely, avoiding asset writedowns and deferring gains on completed transactions.

Adds Eprile, "Income statement presentation is all over the map. Companies use different terminology to mean the same thing, or may use the same term but define it differently. There is considerable inconsistency across companies as to what items are included in long-term 'operating income.' For example, for some, the sale of operating assets investments is considered operating revenue, but for others it is not. On the flipside, consistency in the categorization of operating costs is also a problem because of the significant variation among companies. Commission staff is concerned because information is often picked off a financial statement and reported out of context in a magazine or newspaper article, which can then be misleading to shareholders or prospective investors in comparing investment alternatives."

According to the report, the accounting measurement and disclosure practices with respect to financial instrument transactions are increasingly divergent, and as Eprile notes, the effect of these differences in practice can be enormous as the use of financial instrument products grows. "In most cases, insufficient information is disclosed to enable an investor to understand the nature and extent of the transactions. As a result, investors and other financial statement users are unable to assess an issuer's exposure to financial instruments and the degree of counterpart risk."

She says it's difficult to bring any real discipline to financial statement reporting for many financial instruments because there are no set standards in place in Canada. "There is a lot of guidance from the United States but some of it is conflicting. This lack of authority makes things harder for us and we hope the standard setters will move along quickly on this matter." Other areas of OSC concern are the valuation of financial instrument investment portfolios held by financial institutions and the reporting of earnings per share, where the report notes that deviations from the *CICA Handbook* requirements "impair comparability and can be confusing and misleading."

What happens when the commission finds a discrepancy in a report? Explains Eprile, "We send comment letters to the company involved with a copy to their auditors, and give them four weeks to respond. They generally do so in writing, agreeing to make the necessary changes if required, or they come to see us with their advisers and we discuss the problem face to face. In many cases, the issues are resolved once the issuer provides additional information. No one likes to have a discrepancy pointed out,

Continued

but generally, people are very professional about it. They respect that we have a program in place and a job to do."

Like the 1989 report, the 1990 version is difficult to summarize because it avoids any indication of the extent of the accounting problems uncovered. Eprile says the commission staff omitted an overview because, "Although we have no problem saying we sent out 'X' number of comment letters, that really doesn't present a clear picture, because each case is different and the degree of discrepancy also varies. In some, a major change is required; in others, we simply warn the company to be on guard against the problem arising again in the future. Some companies have one item at issue while others have a few. So it's misleading to simply state, 'This many statements had problems,' because the range of problems is so broad."

She concludes, "It's difficult for me to come to a general conclusion about the state of public company accounting—I'm not a statistician and these 100 may not be a representative sample. We don't see a lot of offensive reporting, but we want issuers to realize we will review their financial statements and there are certain things we won't tolerate. We see this as 'preventive policing'—it's not a report card on how 'good' or 'bad' issuers are. We act as a check and balance in the system and we want to let companies know we are also there to offer advice and for consultation."

Source: Reprinted, with permission, from "OSC Reviews Financial Statement Disclosure," *CA Magazine,* May 1991, p. 10. Published by the Canadian Institute of Chartered Accountants, Toronto, Canada.

tendency to represent large dollar amounts, prompted the AcSC to establish the reporting standards for discontinued operations as part of Section 3475.[18]

Income or loss from the operations of a segment prior to its disposal and any gain or loss on the disposal are *not* extraordinary items under current accounting standards. These items are combined in a section of the income statement identified as **discontinued operations**. This section is *preceded* by an income subtotal, **income from continuing operations**. The income or loss from the operations of the disposed segment and the gain or loss from the actual disposal are presented separately on a net-of-tax basis. This section is followed by "net income" or "income before extraordinary item."

Earnings-per-share figures for income from continuing operations and net income are presented on the face of the income statement for publicly held companies. In practice, earnings-per-share figures are also frequently presented for the two components of discontinued operations or for the discontinued operations section as a single figure.

What constitutes a *segment* disposal (which, in turn, requires the company to present discontinued operations as described above)? A **segment** is a component of an enterprise whose activities represent a separate major line of business or a separate class of customer. A segment may be a subsidiary or other investee, a division, or a department, and the disposal may be accomplished by sale or abandonment. A major criterion distinguishing the disposal of a segment from other transactions requires that the assets and results of operations of the discontinued part of the business can be clearly distinguished physically, operationally, and for financial accounting purposes from other assets, results of operations, and activities of the enterprise. The inability to identify separately the results of operations of the discontinued unit suggests that the transaction is not a disposal of a *segment* of the business.

---

[18]"Discontinued Operations," CICA *Handbook,* Paragraph 3475.07, December 1989.

To illustrate the accounting and reporting for the disposal of a segment, assume that Ball Company has determined its preliminary aggregate operating figures for 1995 as follows:

Revenue from sales	$8 000 000
Cost of goods sold	3 500 000
Operating expenses	2 000 000
	5 500 000
Income before income tax	$2 500 000

At the end of the year, the company disposed of its nuts and bolts division, which was operationally separate from the rest of the business. Operating results of this division, which are included in the above aggregate figures, are as follows:

Revenue from sales	$1 500 000
Cost of goods sold	1 400 000
Operating expenses	800 000
	2 200 000
Loss before income tax	$ (700 000)

In addition, the actual disposal of the nuts and bolts division resulted in a $450 000 nonoperating loss before income tax, which is *not* included in the above figures:

Proceeds from the sale of nuts and bolts division	$ 6 500 000
Net book value of assets of nuts and bolts division	(6 950 000)
Loss on sale before income tax	$(450 000)

The appropriate income tax rate for all items is 40 percent.

The presentation of discontinued operations for Ball Company is illustrated in Exhibit 5.8. The revenue and expense amounts for continuing operations are determined by removing the figures for the discontinued division. The earnings-per-share figures are computed on the basis of 1 million common shares outstanding, with no preferred shares.

The disposal of a major segment of a business enterprise frequently takes place over an extended period of time. It is not unusual for such a disposal to begin in one accounting period and extend into one or more future accounting periods. In this situation, two dates are particularly important:

The **measurement date** is the date on which management adopts a formal plan of disposal. In the absence of a formal plan of disposal, the measurement date is the disposal date.

The **disposal date** is the effective date of sale if the disposal is by sale, or the date that operations cease if the disposal is by other means.[19]

If the measurement date is in one accounting period and the disposal date is in a subsequent accounting period, accounting for the disposal of the segment is more complex.

In presenting discontinued operations, any operating results after the measurement date are included in the gain or loss from disposal of the discontinued segment, rather than as the results of operations. At the measurement date, if a loss is expected from the

---

[19]"Discontinued Operations," CICA *Handbook,* Paragraph 3475.02(d),(e), December 1989.

Exhibit 5.8

Ball Company
INCOME STATEMENT
For the Year Ended December 31, 1995

Revenue from sales		$6 500 000
Cost of goods sold	$2 100 000	
Operating expenses	1 200 000	3 300 000
Income from continuing operations before income tax		3 200 000
Income tax expense (at 40%)		1 280 000
Income from continuing operations		1 920 000
Discontinued operations		
Loss from operations of discontinued nuts and bolts division, less applicable income taxes of $280 000	(420 000)	
Loss on disposal of nuts and bolts division, less applicable income taxes of $180 000	(270 000)	(690 000)
Net income		$1 230 000
Earnings per share		
Income from continuing operations		$1.92
Discontinued operations		
Loss from operations of nuts and bolts division	$(0.42)	
Loss on disposal of nuts and bolts division	(0.27)	(0.69)
Net income		$1.23

Conservatism

planned disposal, the estimated loss is recognized immediately. On the other hand, an anticipated gain from the disposal is not recognized until the gain is realized, which is usually at the disposal date. This procedure results in a *conservative* presentation of income, since an estimated loss is recognized immediately and an estimated gain is deferred until the later disposal date when it is fully realized.

In estimating whether a gain or loss will result from the disposal of the segment, the net amount expected to be received from the disposal includes any estimated costs and expenses directly associated with the disposal. Additionally, if the disposal will take time and continued operations of the segment are planned during the period of disposal, any estimated income or loss from operations is included in the estimated gain or loss on the disposal. Amounts of income or loss from operations included in the gain or loss on disposal are limited to amounts that can be reasonably projected. Normally such projections should not exceed a one-year period.

In addition to the information presented in the discontinued operations section of the income statement, the notes to the financial statements must disclose the following

Disclosure

information:

1. The identity and nature of the business segment that has been discontinued or is the subject of a formal plan of disposal.
2. The measurement date and either the disposal date or the period expected to be required for disposal.
3. The actual or expected manner of disposal.

Exhibit 5.9 Torstar Corporation, Note 10 Discontinued Operations

10. DISCONTINUED OPERATIONS

Heatset Printing

Effective December 1, 1990, the company sold the major assets (primarily three printing presses and related equipment) of its Heatset commercial printing operation. In exchange for the assets, the company received $11 912 000 of preferred shares in a subsidiary of Quebecor Inc. $6 552 000 of the shares were redeemed for cash in 1991. The remaining shares, which will be redeemed for cash (plus dividends of 5.5%) in December 1992, have been recorded on the balance sheet in receivables (included in Goodwill and other assets in 1990).

Third Party Distribution

Effective in 1991, the company discontinued the Third Party distribution operation of Harlequin's Australian book publishing company. This operation involved the distribution of products for other publishers in Australia.

Nelson Marketing

In February 1990, the company disposed of Nelson Marketing, a segment of the Miles Kimball marketing division which served specialty advertising buyers.

The results of these operations and the net loss on their sale or closure have been reported as discontinued operations in 1990. The net realizable value of the remaining assets and liabilities of the discontinued operations has been recorded on the balance sheet in Accounts payable.

Southam Inc.

During the fourth quarter of 1991 Southam announced its decision to sell its Graphics division. The results of operations of this business segment have been reported as a discontinued operation and previously reported financial statements have been restated.

Additional information related to these discontinued operations is as follows:

	1991	1990
	(thousands of dollars)	
Operating revenue		$36 948
Operating income		$5
Loss on sale or closure		(12 623)
Income tax recovery		5 100
		(7 523)
Equity in discontinued operations of Southam Inc. (note 4)	($22 847)	(5 454)
Total	($22 847)	($12 972)
Net provision included in accounts payable	($3 068)	($4 163)

Source: Torstar Corporation, *1991 Annual Report.*

4. A description and the carrying value by major class of the remaining assets and liabilities of the discontinued business segment at the balance sheet date.

5. Revenue applicable to the discontinued operation for the reporting period.[20]

Many of the items that must be disclosed are also necessary to establish the measurement date. Such information is frequently made available only through management action

---

[20]"Discontinued Operations," CICA *Handbook,* Paragraph 3475.13, December 1990.

Exhibit 5.10

Dryden Company
INCOME STATEMENT
For the Years Ended December 31, 1994 and 1995
(in thousands of dollars except earnings-per-share figures)

	1995	1994
Sales	$5525	$5108
Cost of goods sold	2100	1950
Gross margin	3425	3158
Selling and administrative expenses	1250	1200
Income from operations	2175	1958
Other income		
Gain on sale of plant assets	—	100
Dividend income	75	80
Other expenses		
Interest on long-term debt	(255)	(307)
Unrealized loss on valuations of current marketable equity securities	(92)	—
Income before income tax	1903	1831
Provision for income tax	761	732
Income from continuing operations	1142	1099
Discontinued operations		
Loss from operations of business segment, net of applicable income tax savings of $44 in 1995 and $48 in 1994	(66)	(72)
Loss on disposal of business segment, net of applicable income tax savings of $80	(120)	—
Income before extraordinary item	956	1027
Extraordinary item— gain on forced sale of assets to local municipality, net of applicable income taxes of $210	—	525
Net income	$ 956	$ 1552
Earnings per common share		
Income from continuing operations	$11.42	$10.99
Discontinued operations	(1.86)	(0.72)
Income before extraordinary item	9.56	10.27
Extraordinary gain	—	5.25
Net income	$ 9.56	$15.52

and estimates. Accountants, therefore, should attempt to gather additional objective evidence to support the assertions and disclosures contained in the financial statements.

When discontinued operations are presented in comparative financial statements, the operating results of the discontinued part of the business must be reclassified for the comparative year(s) for purposes of comparability and an amount of income from continuing operations must be presented for all years that are included in the statement.

Exhibit 5.9 presents Note 10, which is the disclosure of discontinued operations from the income statement of Torstar Corporation that appears in Exhibit 5.7.

Comprehensive Model Income Statement

The income statement in Exhibit 5.10 incorporates many of the revenue, expense, gain, and loss items that have been discussed in this chapter and will be discussed in several other chapters. The influence of the all-inclusive view can be seen in the inclusion of discontinued operations, extraordinary gain, and other revenues and expenses not directly related to operations. On the other hand, the influence of the current operating performance view can be seen in the separation of these items from normal, recurring transactions and the resulting subtotals, such as income from operations, income from continuing operations, and income before extraordinary item.

The following aspects of this statement are particularly worthy of attention and provide a review of several concepts covered earlier:

1. The provision for income tax incorporates the income tax effects of all transactions presented above that item in the income statement. All items below this item are presented on a net-of-tax basis.
2. The major types of irregular items are presented in the following order: discontinued operations, extraordinary item. Appropriate titles are assigned to the income figures that *precede* each of these items.
3. The discontinued operations segment is presented immediately before the extraordinary item and is divided into the results of *operations* of the discontinued segment and the loss on the *disposal* of the discontinued segment. This section is preceded by the caption, "income from continuing operations." All items in this section are presented on a net-of-tax basis.
4. The extraordinary gain is separately disclosed after the discontinued operations section and is presented on a net-of-tax basis.

While it is unlikely that a single income statement would contain all of the irregular items in Exhibit 5.10, it is important to understand the relation of each item to the others and to the income statement as a whole. The fictitious Dryden Company statement is presented to facilitate this understanding.

Concluding Remarks

Revenue
Realization
Matching

A great deal of the first part of this chapter centred on the accounting principles of *revenue realization* and *matching*. We determined that revenue is recognized when it is earned, measurable, and collectable. The *matching principle* is the basis for the income statement and requires a careful association of expenses with revenues. Frequently, this means that expenses are recognized in a different accounting period from the one in which they are actually incurred or paid.

Conservatism
Substance
Over Form

We have also seen that the modifying conventions of *conservatism* and *substance over form* are influential in the recognition of revenue and in the application of the matching principle.

Income statement presentation is an application of the *disclosure principle*. Many authoritative accounting pronouncements have been issued that deal with the content of the income statement and the placement of items within the statement. At the present time, the income statement is prepared on a modified all-inclusive basis, with only prior period adjustments and selected other items excluded. As the CICA implements its concept of comprehensive income, however, we can expect further refinement in income presentation.

Income presentation is one of the central themes of corporate financial reporting. In meeting the objectives of financial reporting, the income statement and information derived from that statement are particularly important. In this chapter, we have discussed revenue realization at the point of sale as the norm, and we have also discussed and illustrated several situations where revenue is logically recognized at other times and in somewhat unusual ways. We have also seen that careful preparation of the income statement and the proper ordering and wording of items within that statement are important in meeting the objectives of financial reporting. While there is some evidence in recent years that the AcSB is placing increased emphasis on the balance sheet in developing financial reporting standards, the income statement remains a vital part of financial reporting. Careful recognition of revenue and preparation of the income statement will undoubtedly continue to be a major responsibility of accountants in the future.

Key Points

1. Revenue is not recognized until it is earned, measurable, and collectable. In many situations, these conditions are met at the point of sale, although departures from revenue recognition at the point of sale are found in certain circumstances. (Objective 1)

2. The percentage-of-completion and completed-contract methods of accounting for long-term contracts are acceptable in different circumstances. Under the percentage-of-completion method, revenue is recognized throughout the construction period as objective evidence indicates the proper amount to be recognized. Under the completed-contract method, all revenue is deferred and recognized at the completion of the contract. (Objective 2)

3. The installment sales method defers the recognition of revenue until cash is collected, and this method is acceptable in financial reporting only when collectability is highly uncertain. (Objective 3)

4. Accounting for franchise fee revenue involves the deferral of recognition of revenue until the service has been performed or the obligation period has expired. (Objective 4)

5. When customers have the right to return products, certain conditions must be met before the revenue can be recognized. These conditions relate to the transfer of the risks and rewards of ownership from the seller to the buyer and the ability of the seller to make a reasonably objective estimate of the amount of returns. (Objective 5)

6. A major objective of financial reporting is to present information to investors and creditors concerning an enterprise's financial performance. The primary focus is information concerning earnings and its components. (Objective 6)

7. The presentation of income is carefully defined and structured in the authoritative literature. At the present time, income is presented in a manner consistent with a modified all-inclusive concept in that all items of profit and loss, except prior period adjustments and changes, are included in the income statement. (Objective 7)

8. "Discontinued operations," which follows the caption "income from continuing operations," is a separate section of the income statement and includes both the gain or loss from the disposal of a discontinued segment of the business and the operating income or loss of that segment. These items are separated from the income or loss from ongoing business activities. (Objective 7)

9. Discontinued operations and extraordinary items are presented in separate income statement categories on a net-of-tax basis. The cumulative effect of accounting changes and corrections is recorded as an adjustment to the opening balance of the retained earnings. (Objective 7)

Appendix A: Special Revenue-Recognition Practices

This appendix deals with the unique circumstances and business practices in industries that require unusual or complex revenue-recognition practices. The general criteria for revenue recognition developed in the body of this chapter apply equally to special industries and routine situations. Therefore, when studying this appendix, consider carefully how each of the practices specified by the accounting profession is consistent with general or fundamental concepts of revenue recognition. Although specific practices are discussed, the purpose of this appendix is to develop a conceptual understanding of these special circumstances rather than a detailed knowledge of the accounting procedures that are applied. The CICA *Handbook* does not address these topics, so many Canadian accountants prescribe to the guidelines issued in the United States or the CICA *Handbook* interpretations published by the Canadian Institute of Public Real Estate Companies (CIPREC).

Real Estate Transactions

A unique aspect of real estate transactions is that risk of uncollectable receivables is reduced by the nature of the asset sold. Land and other real property is relatively easy to repossess if the purchasing party fails to comply with the terms of the sales agreement. Real property is not readily transportable, does not generally depreciate in value, and is frequently not susceptible to damage and destruction. While the foregoing characteristics are usually associated with land, many buildings and structural improvements possess similar characteristics.

Since sellers of real estate recognize these characteristics of real estate, a greater credit risk may be assumed without creating an unacceptable risk of loss to the selling enterprise. Although the recovery of the investment in real estate may be assured to a greater degree than in other types of sales, the recognition of additional sales revenue should be carefully considered when the buyer is a poor credit risk.

Substance Over Form

Many real estate transactions are exceptionally complex, and the legal form of the transaction may often obscure the real economic substance of an event. The FASB's *Statement of Financial Accounting Standards No. 66* establishes general criteria for the timing of recognition of revenue and provides modifying conventions for use when the conceptual criteria for revenue recognition are not met at the time of the sale:

> [Revenue should be recognized] in full when real estate is sold, provided (a) the profit is measurable, that is, the collectability of the sales price is reasonably assured or the amount that will not be collectible can be estimated, and (b) the earning process is virtually complete, that is, the seller is not obliged to perform significant activities after the sale to earn the profit. Unless both conditions exist, recognition of all or part of the profit shall be postponed.[21]

If the collectability of the sales price is uncertain, as is the case in many real estate transactions, then the installment sales method of revenue recognition or the more conservative cost recovery method should be used. Furthermore, if the earning process is

---

[21]"Accounting for Sales of Real Estate," *FASB Statement of Financial Accounting Standards No. 66*, Paragraph 3, 1982.

incomplete, recognition of revenue moves from the time of sale to the time of the seller's performance of the earning process. Finally, no profit is recognized until a sale is actually consummated.

Certain requirements must be met in order to recognize revenue when the receivables are material after the sale and completion of the earning process. These criteria relate to: (1) the amount of the down payment, (2) the composition of the down payment, and (3) the terms regarding the receivable portion of the consideration.

In regard to the amount of the initial payment, a range from 5 percent to 25 percent of the purchase price, depending on the nature of the property sold, has been established for purposes of profit recognition.[22]

Even if a down payment is large enough to qualify for the recognition of profit, the composition of the payment and terms of collection must also be considered. Generally, the down payment must consist of cash or notes supported by irrevocable letters of credit from established lending institutions to support the immediate recognition of revenue. Buyers must also maintain a continuing financial commitment in that the payments being made must be sufficient to pay the total indebtedness, including interest.

If a buyer's down payment amount or quality or continuing investment is not adequate, then the installment sales method should normally be used to recognize revenue on the sale. However, if there is uncertainty as to whether the cost will be recovered if a buyer defaults or if the cost has already been recovered through down payment but future collections are uncertain, then the cost recovery method of revenue recognition is employed.

Accounting for Retail Land Sales

Land developers frequently acquire a large parcel of land, develop a master plan for subdivision and improvement, obtain construction approval, perform necessary improvements, and sell lots. Furthermore, certain characteristics inherent in retail land sales create special problems concerning the recognition of revenue and related expenses. Examples are small down payments, unenforceable sales contracts, and cancellation periods during which buyers can obtain refunds.

Consideration of the foregoing problems encouraged the AICPA to develop another *Industry Accounting Guide*; this one pertains to the timing and magnitude of revenue recognition.[23] This guide also became part of the *Statement of Financial Accounting Standards No. 66*. In essence, *SFAS No. 66* contains the following requirements for recording a sale:[24]

1. The buyer must make a down payment and regular subsequent payments throughout the period covered by any cancellation with refund right.
2. The aggregate payments, including interest, must at least equal 10 percent of the contract sales price.
3. Collection experience on similar sales must indicate that collection of the receivable is reasonably assured.

[22]"Accounting for Sales of Real Estate," *FASB Statement of Financial Accounting Standards No. 66*, Paragraph 54, 1982.

[23]"Accounting for Retail Land Sales," *AICPA Industry Accounting Guide*, 1973.

[24]"Accounting for Sales of Real Estate," *FASB Statement of Financial Accounting Standards No. 66*, Paragraph 45, 1982.

4. Generally, the receivable from the sale must not be subject to subordination to new loans on the property.
5. The seller must not be obligated to complete improvements of lots sold nor to construct facilities applicable to lots sold.

For transactions in which the first four criteria are met and substantial progress has been made toward the completion of requirement 5, the percentage-of-completion method is applicable.

Questions

Q5.1 What three conditions must be met for revenue to be recognized?

Q5.2 Why is the point of sale frequently used as the point of revenue recognition?

Q5.3 Why do long-term contracts pose a difficult revenue-recognition problem?

Q5.4 Under what circumstances should the percentage-of-completion method of recognizing revenue on long-term contracts be used?

Q5.5 Under what circumstances should the completed-contract method of recognizing revenue on long-term contracts be used?

Q5.6 What is the difference in accounting treatment of contract revenues and costs under the percentage-of-completion and completed-contract methods?

Q5.7 Assuming a contract is started in 1993 and completed in 1995, explain the procedure for estimating the amount of gross profit in each year if the percentage of completion is determined based on costs incurred to date as a percentage of total expected costs.

Q5.8 Under what circumstances is the installment sales method appropriate for financial reporting purposes? How does this method differ from recognizing revenue at the point of sale?

Q5.9 State briefly the criteria that must be met for revenue to be recognized if the customer has the right to return the purchased products. If one or more of these conditions are not met, what accounting procedures are appropriate?

Q5.10 Explain how the presentation of income contributes to meeting the primary objectives of financial reporting.

Q5.11 How does the presentation of income assist in judging management efficiency?

Q5.12 Explain the concept of "value added income." How does it differ from the concept of income underlying the income statement as currently prepared?

Q5.13 What is the difference between "income to shareholders" and "income to residual shareholders"?

Q5.14 Distinguish between the all-inclusive and current operating performance definitions of income in terms of the meaning of the final income figure resulting from each.

Q5.15 Distinguish between the collection of the franchise fees and the recognition of the franchise fee revenue.

Q5.16 What determines a "segment" in deciding whether the disposal of a portion of a business qualifies for separate disclosure in a discontinued operations section of the income statement?

Q5.17 Explain the meaning of the income subtotal "income from continuing operations."

Q5.18 Distinguish between the "measurement date" and the "disposal date." Explain their significance in reporting discontinued operations in the income statement.

Q5.19 State a rule for identifying those revenues, expenses, gains, and losses that must be presented on a net-of-tax basis in the income statement.

Q5.20 Which of the following is an example of an extraordinary item in reporting results of operations?
(a) A loss incurred because of a strike by employees.
(b) The write-off of deferred development costs believed to have no future benefit.
(c) A gain resulting from the devaluation of the Canadian dollar.
(d) A gain resulting from the province exercising its right of eminent domain on a piece of land used as a parking lot.
(Adapted from AICPA.)

Q5.21 Which of the following is *not* a generally practised method of presenting the income statement?
(a) Including prior period adjustments in determining net income.
(b) The single-step income statement.
(c) The consolidated statement of income.
(d) Including gains and losses from discontinued operations of a segment of a business in determining net income.
(Adapted from AICPA.)

Q5.22 Which of the following shows how the gain or loss from an event or transaction that meets the criteria for infrequent occurrence but not unusual nature should be disclosed?
(a) Separately in the income statement immediately after income from continuing operations.
(b) On a net-of-tax basis in the income statement immediately after income from continuing operations.
(c) As an extraordinary item treated accordingly in the income statement.
(d) Separately in the income statement as a component of income from continuing operations.
(Adapted from AICPA.)

Q5.23 When a company discontinues an operation and disposes of the discontinued segment, the transaction should be included in the income statement as a gain or loss on disposal reported as which of the following?
(a) A prior period adjustment.
(b) An extraordinary item.
(c) An amount after continuing operations and before extraordinary items.
(d) A bulk sale of fixed assets included in income from continuing operations.
(Adapted from AICPA.)

Exercises

E5.1 Long-Term Contract. Matthews Construction Company began work on a contract in 1994 and completed the contract in 1995. The total contract price was $4 200 000.

Information concerning the contract for 1994 and 1995 is as follows:

	1994	1995
Costs incurred during year	$ 600 000	$3 150 000
Estimated costs to complete at end of year	2 400 000	0
Billings during year	720 000	3 280 000
Collections during year	400 000	3 000 000

Instructions
(a) Determine the amount of the $4 200 000 contract price to be recognized each year under the completed- contract method.
(b) Determine the amount of the $4 200 000 contract price to be recognized each year under the percentage- of-completion method.

E5.2 Long-Term Contract. Quick-Build Construction Company contracted to construct a building for $450 000. Quick-Build began construction in 1994 and completed the project in 1995. Cost information for the project is as follows:

	1994	**1995**
Costs incurred	$200 000	$120 000
Estimated costs to complete	100 000	—

Quick-Build uses the percentage-of-completion method for recognizing income on the contract.

Instructions
(a) Determine the amount of income that the company should recognize in 1994 and 1995.
(b) Prove the amounts of income you have computed in (a) by computing the total income on the contract and comparing it with the incomes you have computed for 1994 and 1995.
(c) Prepare the journal entry required at the end of each year to recognize that year's income.

E5.3 Installment Sales. Mall Company, which began business on January 1, 1994, appropriately uses the installment sales method of recognizing revenue because of the uncertainty of the collection of its receivables. The following data pertain to 1994 and 1995:

	1994	**1995**
Installment sales	$350 000	$420 000
Cost of installment sales	280 000	315 000
General and administrative expenses	35 000	42 000
Cash collections on installment sales of:		
1994	150 000	135 000
1995	—	220 000

Instructions
(a) Determine the balance in the Deferred Gross Profit account at December 31, 1995.
(b) A 1994 sale resulted in a default in 1995. At the date of default, the balance of the installment receivable was $6400, and the repossessed merchandise had a fair value of $4750. Assuming the repossessed merchandise is recorded at fair value, determine the amount of gain or loss on the repossession.
(Adapted from AICPA.)

E5.4 Installment Sales. Ratner Company sells appliances through installment contracts. Because of the uncertainty of collection and the relatively high potential for repossession, the company appropriately recognizes revenue on an installment basis, deferring revenue recognition until cash is collected.

During 1994, Ratner determined that its gross profit percentage was 40 percent; during 1995 this percentage increased to 42 percent. Of $150 000 sales in 1994, Ratner collected $70 000 in 1994 and $50 000 in 1995. Of $170 000 sales in 1995, Ratner had collected $97 000 by year-end.

Instructions

For 1994 and 1995, compute the amounts of gross profit to be recognized and the amounts to be deferred at the end of the year.

E5.5   Rent Collected in Advance.   On August 1, 1995, Wilcox Company received $90 000 for one year's advance rent on space that it leases to another company. Wilcox Company's fiscal year ends on October 31.

Instructions

(a) Determine the portion of the $90 000 that should be recognized as revenue for the fiscal year ending October 31, 1995.
(b) Prepare the adjusting journal entry Wilcox should make on October 31, 1995, if the $90 000 was credited to Unearned Rent Revenue when it was received.
(c) Prepare the adjusting journal entry the company should make on October 31, 1995, if the $90 000 was credited to Rent Revenue when it was received.

E5.6   Right of Return.   Clark Company sold $225 000 of merchandise on credit to its customers during 1995. The cost of this merchandise was $153 000, and Clark uses a perpetual inventory system. Based on past trends, Clark expects returns of 2.5 percent of sales within 90 days of the sales transaction. During 1995, cash collections of receivables were $174 200, and the selling price of merchandise returned totalled $4050.

Instructions

(a) Prepare journal entries for all transactions and events mentioned above for Clark Company for 1995, the company's first year of operations.
(b) Indicate the items and dollar amounts that will appear in the 1995 income statement as a result of these events.

E5.7   Extraordinary Item.   Massey Production Company determines its pretax financial income for 1995 to be $1 420 000. The appropriate income tax rate for all income items is 35 percent. The company's reporting period ends on December 31. Included in pretax financial income are the following items:

(1) A loss of $335 000 on the destruction of a plant facility from a natural disaster. This item is considered both unusual in nature and infrequent in occurrence.
(2) A gain of $16 700 on the sale of shares owned in another company. Although Massey does not buy and sell share investments often, this type of transaction is common for companies of this type.

Instructions

Prepare the income statement to the extent possible from the information given, beginning with the caption "income before income tax."

E5.8 Special Income Items. Fairfield Fashions, Inc., has correctly determined the following information related to operations for 1995:

Revenue from sales	$650 000
Expenses	415 000
Income before income tax	$235 000

In reviewing the company's records, you discover the following items:

(1) During 1995, the company discovered an error in the amount of depreciation recognized in 1993 and 1994. The correction of this error, which has not been recorded, will result in an increase in depreciation for 1993 of $42 000 and for 1994 of $37 000.
(2) During 1995, an inventory loss of $37 800 was due to a government ban on certain flammable fabrics. This loss was considered both unusual and infrequent and has not been recorded.

During 1995, dividends of $62 500 were paid on 62 500 common shares, which were outstanding throughout 1995. Income taxes are to be recognized at 30 percent on all income items.

Instructions
Assuming that retained earnings at January 1, 1995, were previously reported as $590 000, prepare a partial income statement and a retained earnings statement for Fairfield Fashions, Inc., for calendar year 1995.

E5.9 Discontinued Operations. Wilbur Company, a holding company, has two operating subsidiaries: one manufacturing wheelbarrows and the other manufacturing toothbrushes. The wheelbarrow subsidiary has been unprofitable, and in late December 1994, Wilbur's management contracted to sell that subsidiary to another company for $60 000. The sale will be effective on April 1, 1995. Wilbur will operate the wheelbarrow subsidiary during the first three months of 1995, even though these operations are expected to result in a $10 000 loss (before income taxes).

At December 31, 1994, the carrying amount of Wilbur's investment in the wheelbarrow subsidiary is $100 000. Both the $40 000 loss on the sale of the investment and the $10 000 operating loss will be deductible on Wilbur's 1995 income tax return, resulting in an anticipated tax savings at an assumed 30 percent tax rate.

Instructions
Determine the amount of the "loss on disposal of wheelbarrow subsidiary, net of applicable income tax benefit" that should be presented in Wilbur's income statement for the year ended December 31, 1994.
(Adapted from AICPA.)

E5.10 Franchise. In 1994, Goody Inc. decided to sell bakery franchises in several locations in the Maritime provinces. Each franchise was sold for $60 000, payable $18 000 down and $14 000 a year for three years starting one year after the sale. Royalties of

2 percent of sales are to be paid by the franchisees to the franchisor for the term of the franchise operation.

Goody Inc. was obligated to provide considerable services to franchisees in opening and operating their operations for the first four years, including preparing promotional materials, setting up accounting systems, and training employees. The down payment of $18 000 was designed to cover the initial direct costs of the franchise contract and for the right to use the name Goody.

The fair rate of interest during 1994 was 8 percent a year; thus, the present value of the three promissory notes of $14 000 each received from a franchisee was approximately $36 079 on the date a franchise was sold. The notes were considered fully collectable, and the accountant for Goody recorded the sale of the franchise contract on April 30, 1994 as follows:

Cash	18 000	
Notes Receivable	42 000	
Franchise Revenue		60 000

Instructions
(a) Why is this entry incorrect? Explain your answer.
(b) Prepare the proper entry for April 30, 1994, and the entry on December 31, 1994, to recognize the revenue on the franchise contract.

E5.11 Extraordinary Items. The December 31, 1995, financial statements of Waller Corporation reported a total of $325 000 under the caption "extraordinary losses." An analysis further revealed that this amount was comprised of the following items:

(1) Waller recorded a loss of $75 000 in the abandonment of equipment formerly used in the business.
(2) In an unusual and infrequent occurrence, a loss of $90 000 was sustained as a result of hurricane damage to a warehouse.
(3) During 1995, several factories were shut down during a major strike by employees. Shutdown expenses totalled $140 000.
(4) Accounts receivable of $20 000 were written off as uncollectable.

Instructions
(a) Disregarding income taxes, compute the amount of loss that Waller should report as extraordinary on its 1995 statement of income.
(b) Explain the proper disclosure, if any, for any of the four items that should not be reported as extraordinary items.
(Adapted from AICPA.)

E5.12 Discontinued Operations. The following condensed statement of income of Banner Corporation, a diversified company, is presented for the two years ended December 31, 1995 and 1994.

	1995	**1994**
Net sales	$5 000 000	$4 800 000
Cost of sales	3 100 000	3 000 000
Gross profit	1 900 000	1 800 000
Operating expenses	1 100 000	1 200 000
Operating income	800 000	600 000
Gain on sale of division	450 000	0
Income before income taxes	1 250 000	600 000
Provision for income taxes	437 500	210 000
Net income	$ 812 500	$ 390 000

On January 1, 1995, Banner entered into an agreement to sell for $1 600 000 the assets and product line of one of its separate operating divisions. The sale was consummated on December 31, 1995, and resulted in a pretax gain on disposition of $450 000. This division's contribution to reported operating income before income taxes for each year was as follows:

1995	$(320 000) loss
1994	(250 000) loss

Assume an income tax rate of 35 percent.

Instructions

(a) In the preparation of a revised comparative statement of income, what amounts should Banner present for "income from continuing operations" for 1994 and 1995?
(b) In the preparation of a revised comparative statement of income, what amounts should Banner present for "discontinued operations" for 1994 and 1995?
(Adapted from AICPA.)

E5.13   Special Income Items.   Winter Company reports income before income tax of $952 000 for 1995. This figure includes the following items, which may require adjustment or reclassification before the formal income statement can be prepared:

(1) A change in depreciation method from the straight-line to the accelerated method resulted in a $40 000 loss that was due to the cumulative effect on previous years. Depreciation for 1995 was computed on the accelerated method.
(2) A gain of $127 500 on the excess of insurance recovery over the book value of a plant destroyed by a hurricane. This was the first hurricane in the province in over a century.
(3) A gain of $18 700 on the sale of noncurrent marketable equity securities.

All items are subject to 38 percent income tax. The end of the fiscal year is November 30, 1995. There were 20 000 common shares outstanding throughout the fiscal year.

Instructions

Prepare the income statement, beginning with "income before income tax," and provide computations.

E5.14 Income Statement Presentation. Pinson Company has accumulated information to be used in the preparation of its income statement for the year ended December 31, 1995. All items are on a pretax basis.

Sales	$7 750 000
Cost of goods sold	4 200 000
Operating expenses	1 600 000
Interest revenue	125 000
Extraordinary loss from major casualty	55 000
Cumulative effect (gain) of change in accounting policy	138 000
Gain from sale of discontinued business segment	123 000
Number of outstanding common shares throughout 1995	120 000
Income tax rate applicable to all items	35%

Instructions

Prepare a multiple-step income statement for 1995 to conform with GAAP.

E5.15 Correction of Income Statement. Friends, Inc., has prepared a preliminary income statement for 1995 as follows:

Friends, Inc.
INCOME STATEMENT
For the Year Ended December 31, 1995

Sales		$520 000
Cost of goods sold		221 000
Gross profit		299 000
Operating expenses		105 000
Income before special items		194 000
Special items		
Gain on the sale of land	$ 60 000	
Interest expense	(12 500)	
Loss on the sale of discontinued business segment	(14 000)	
Cumulative effect of change in method of overhead recognition	(35 800)	(2 300)
Income before income tax		191 700
Income tax expense		76 680
Net income		$115 020

You have been engaged to review this statement and revise it as appropriate. You determine that the gain on the sale of land should be presented as an extraordinary item because it resulted from the forced sale caused by newly enacted legislation. All items are subject to a 40 percent income tax. There were 50 000 common shares outstanding throughout the fiscal year.

Instructions

Prepare a revised income statement based on generally accepted accounting principles.

E5.16   Financial Statement Classification.   The following classification codes are to be used in completing this exercise:

Income Statement Categories/Items
 (1) Revenue.
 (2) Cost of goods sold.
 (3) Operating expenses.
 (4) Other revenues, expenses, gains, losses.
 (5) Discontinued operations.
 (6) Extraordinary items.

Items Omitted from the Income Statement
 (7) Cumulative effect of change in accounting policy.
 (8) Included in balance sheet.
 (9) Included in retained earnings statement.
 (10) Included in notes to the financial statements.
 (11) Omitted from the financial statements.

Instructions

Indicate the preferred code number for each of the following items. If an explanation is necessary, state it briefly. If more than one classification is needed, list all appropriate code numbers.

 (a) Accumulated depreciation—buildings.
 (b) Interest revenue.
 (c) Loss of plant from hurricane.
 (d) Revenues and expenses from segment disposed of during current year.
 (e) Dividends declared.
 (f) Gain on sale of capital assets.
 (g) Loss on expropriation of assets by foreign government.
 (h) Annual bonus paid to store manager.
 (i) Impact on previous years' earnings of changing depreciation method.
 (j) Correction of error in inventory that was carried forward from previous year.
 (k) Depreciation expense on manufacturing equipment.
 (l) Loss on disposal of a segment of the business.
 (m) Interest paid on outstanding debt.
 (n) Loss on sale of temporary marketable securities.
 (o) Changes in accounting policies.
 (p) Adjustment for change from unacceptable to acceptable accounting method.
 (q) Details of outstanding debt issues.
 (r) Revenue received in advance (to be earned in next accounting period).

Problems

P5.1   Long-Term Contracts.   Buildco Construction Company began operations January 1, 1995. During the year, Buildco entered into a contract with Pepperdine Company to construct a manufacturing facility. At that time, Buildco estimated that it would take five years to complete the facility at a total cost of $4 800 000. The total contract price for construction of the facility is $5 800 000.

During 1995, Buildco incurred $1 250 000 in construction costs related to the project. Because of rising material and labour costs, the estimated cost to complete the contract at the end of 1995 is $3 750 000. Pepperdine was billed for and paid 30 percent of the contract price in accordance with the contract agreement.

Instructions

Prepare schedules to compute the amount of gross profit to be recognized for the year ended December 31, 1995, and the amount to be shown as "cost of uncompleted contract in excess of related billings" or "billings on uncompleted contracts in excess of related costs" at December 31, 1995, under each of the following methods:

(a) Completed-contract method.
(b) Percentage-of-completion method.

Provide supporting computations in good form.
(Adapted from AICPA.)

P5.2 Installment Sales. Warren Corporation sells farm machinery on the installment plan. On June 1, 1995, Warren entered into an installment sale contract with Agriculture, Inc., for an eight-year period. Equal annual payments under the installment sale are $90 000 and are due on June 1. The first payment was made on June 1, 1995.

Additional Information
(1) The amount to be realized on an outright sale of similar farm machinery is $558 500.
(2) The cost of the farm machinery sold to Agriculture is $417 000.
(3) The finance charges relating to the installment period are $161 000 based on a stated interest rate of 8 percent, which is appropriate.
(4) The collection of installments due under the contract is reasonably assured.

Instructions

What income or loss before income taxes should Warren record for the year ended December 31, 1995, as a result of the above transaction? Show supporting computations in good form.
(Adapted from AICPA.)

P5.3 Long-Term Contracts. Fara Construction Company recognizes income under the percentage-of-completion method on its long-term contracts. During 1993, the company entered into a fixed-price contract to construct a bridge for $15 000 000. Contract costs incurred and estimated costs to complete the bridge were:

	Cumulative Contract Costs Incurred	Estimated Costs to Complete
At Dec. 31, 1993	$ 1 000 000	$8 000 000
At Dec. 31, 1994	5 500 000	5 500 000
At Dec. 31, 1995	10 000 000	2 000 000

Instructions
(a) Prepare a schedule and determine the estimated percentage of completion at the end of each year. (Round the percentage to the nearest two decimal points.)
(b) Prepare a schedule and determine the amount of revenue to be recognized each year. (Round dollars to the nearest thousand.)
(c) Prepare a schedule and determine the amount of income to be recognized each year.

(d) Prepare journal entries to record transactions for 1993 using the percentage-of-completion method, assuming that Fara billed its client $1 325 000 in 1993, of which $1 200 000 has been collected by the end of the year.

(Adapted from AICPA.)

P5.4 Installment Sales. Mann Company sells computers. On January 1, 1995, Mann entered into an installment sale contract with the Banner Company for a seven-year period expiring December 31, 2001. Equal annual payments under the installment sale are $1 000 000 and are due on January 1. The first payment was made on January 1, 1995.

Additional Information

(1) The cash selling price of the computer (i.e., the amount that would be realized on an outright sale) is $5 355 000.
(2) The cost of sales relating to the computer is $4 284 000.
(3) The finance charges relating to the installment period are $1 645 000, based on a stated interest rate of 10 percent, which is appropriate.
(4) Assume that the income tax rate is 30 percent.

Instructions

(a) What income (loss) before income taxes should Mann record as a result of this transaction for the year ended December 31, 1995? Show supporting computations in good form.
(b) Compute the amounts of gross profit to be recognized and the amounts to be deferred at the end of the year. Circumstances indicate that the collection of the installment sale is risky.

(Adapted from AICPA.)

P5.5 Long-Term Contracts. The directors of Myer Construction Company are meeting to determine which method of accounting for long-term construction contracts should be used in the company's financial statements: completed-contract or percentage-of-completion. You have been engaged to assist Myer's controller in preparing a presentation for the meeting.

Additional Information

(1) Myer commenced business on January 1, 1994.
(2) Construction activities for the year ended December 31, 1994 are summarized as follows:

Project	Total Contract Price	Billings Through Dec. 31, 1994	Cash Collections Through Dec. 31, 1994	Contract Costs Incurred Through Dec. 31, 1994	Estimated Additional Costs to Complete Contracts
A	$ 520 000	$ 350 000	$ 310 000	$ 424 000	$106 000
B	670 000	210 000	210 000	126 000	504 000
C	475 000	475 000	395 000	315 000	—
D	200 000	70 000	50 000	112 750	92 250
E	460 000	400 000	400 000	370 000	30 000
	$2 325 000	$1 505 000	$1 365 000	$1 347 750	$732 250

(3) All contracts are with different customers.
(4) Any work remaining to be done on the contracts is expected to be completed in 1995.

Instructions

(a) Prepare a schedule by project to compute the amount of revenue and income (or loss) before selling and general and administrative expenses for the year ended December 31, 1994, that would be reported under
(1) The completed-contract method.
(2) The percentage-of-completion method (based on estimated costs).
(b) Following is a balance sheet that compares balances resulting from the use of the two methods of accounting for long-term contracts. For each numbered blank space on the statement, supply the correct balance, indicating Dr. (Cr.) as appropriate. Disregard income taxes.

Myer Construction Company
BALANCE SHEET
December 31, 1994

Assets	Completed-Contract Method	Percentage-of-Completion Method
Cash	$XXXX	$XXXX
Accounts receivable		
Due on contracts	(1)	(5)
Cost of uncompleted contracts in excess of billings	(2)	—
Costs and estimated earnings in excess of billings on uncompleted contracts	—	(6)
Property, plant, and equipment, net	XXXX	XXXX
Other assets	XXXX	XXXX
	$XXXX	$XXXX

Liabilities and Shareholders' Equity		
Accounts payable and accrued liabilities	$XXXX	$XXXX
Billings on uncompleted contracts in excess of costs	(3)	—
Billings in excess of costs and estimated earnings	—	(7)
Estimated losses on uncompleted contracts	(4)	—
Notes payable	XXXX	XXXX
Common shares	XXXX	XXXX
Retained earnings	XXXX	XXXX
	$XXXX	$XXXX

(Adapted from AICPA.)

P5.6 Income Statement. Waddell, Inc., has prepared an income statement for the year ended June 30, 1995. This statement is presented for your evaluation as follows:

Waddell, Inc.
INCOME STATEMENT
For the Fiscal Year Ended June 30, 1995

Sales		$765 000
Cost of goods sold	$400 000	
Operating expenses	250 000	
Income tax expense	46 000	696 000
Income before extraordinary item		69 000
Extraordinary loss		24 000
Net income		$ 45 000

Additional Information

In reviewing the statement, you determine the following:

(1) The extraordinary loss resulted from the sale of a division of the company at $24 000 less than its book value. The division had been operating at a loss for several years, including a $15 000 operating loss included in the sales and expense figures in the company's income statement. The income tax benefit of the operating loss has been considered in computing the $46 000 income tax expense. The accountant who prepared the statement was not aware, however, that the loss on disposal would result in a 40 percent income tax benefit, and has included the entire $24 000 loss as an extraordinary item.

(2) The company sold 40 000 common shares on December 31, 1994, resulting in a total of 120 000 shares outstanding. The company has no preferred shares. The accountant was unaware of the need to present earnings-per-share figures.

(3) All income items are subject to a 40 percent income tax rate.

Instructions

(a) Prepare a revised income statement beginning with "income before income tax" for the year ended June 30, 1995. Provide computations to support your figures.

(b) Comment on why the operating results of a discontinued segment is presented as part of "discontinued operations."

P5.7 Income and Retained Earnings Statements. Mills Corporation is accumulating the last portions of financial data needed to prepare the financial statements for the year ended December 31, 1994. The retained earnings totalled $1 700 000 at January 1, 1994. Cash dividends of $39 000 were declared during 1994, but only $30 000 of these were paid in 1994. The 1994 estimated income before income taxes without considering the five activities described below is $920 000.

Additional Information

The information regarding the following activities has been taken from the company's records:

(1) A lawsuit arising from a 1992 claim was settled by the company during 1994 for $70 000. The loss has not been accrued and is due for payment in March 1995.

(2) The company sold one of several buildings in its Finishing Division at a gain of $20 000.

(3) Mills experienced a $200 000 loss of timber in 1994 due to the eruption of a volcano that had been inactive for over 50 years. The loss was not covered by insurance.

(4) The company changed its method for depreciating its buildings in 1994 from an accelerated method to straight-line. Total depreciation on the buildings through the end of 1993 would have been $260 000 lower by using the straight-line method.

(5) Office equipment purchased in January 1993 for $45 000 was incorrectly debited to office supplies expense. The straight-line method is used to depreciate office equipment for book purposes. The office equipment was estimated to have a three-year life with no expected scrap value. This error has not been corrected.

Assume Mills Corporation is subject to a 40 percent income tax rate on all transactions.

Instructions

(a) (1) Calculate the 1994 income from operations before income taxes for Mills Corporation, identifying adjustments, if any, that need to be made to the estimated income of $920 000.

(2) Prepare a partial statement of income for Mills Corporation for the year ended December 31, 1994, beginning with the amount for adjusted income from operations before income taxes, as calculated above.

(b) Prepare a statement of retained earnings for Mills Corporation for the year ended December 31, 1994.

(Adapted from CMA.)

P5.8 Income Statement. Information concerning the results of operations of Lewis Corporation for the calendar year 1995 is as follows:

Cost of goods sold	$2 985 000
Administrative expenses	1 300 000
Gain on the sale of marketable securities	15 000
Loss on sale of discontinued segment of business	95 000
Interest expense	65 000
Selling expenses	1 500 000
Sales	8 650 000
Loss on sale of capital assets	25 500
Cumulative effect (gain) resulting from change in depreciation method from double-declining balance to straight-line method	157 000
Correction of error (loss) in previous year's income, due to capitalization of research costs	76 000
Retained earnings, January 1, 1995	1 700 000
Dividends declared during 1995	240 000

Additional Information

(1) All income items are subject to a 35% income tax rate.
(2) The company had 1 million common shares outstanding during 1995.
(3) The following amounts related to the disposed segment are included in the appropriate revenue and cost figures:

Sales	$750 000
Cost of goods sold	600 000
Selling expenses	100 000
Administrative expenses	350 000
Interest expense	10 000

Instructions

(a) Prepare the income statement and the statement of retained earnings for Lewis Corporation for the year ended December 31, 1995.
(b) Explain your treatment of the cumulative effect of an accounting change and components of discontinued operations.

P5.9 Discontinued Operations. Barth Company, a diversified manufacturing company, had four separate operating divisions engaged in the manufacture of products in each of the following areas: food products, health aids, textiles, and office equipment.

Financial data for the two years ended December 31, 1994 and 1995, are as follows:

	Net Sales		Cost of Sales		Operating Expenses	
	1995	1994	1995	1994	1995	1994
Food products	$3 500 000	$3 000 000	$2 400 000	$1 800 000	$550 000	$275 000
Health aids	2 000 000	1 270 000	1 100 000	700 000	300 000	125 000
Textiles	1 580 000	1 400 000	500 000	900 000	200 000	150 000
Office equipment	920 000	1 330 000	800 000	1 000 000	650 000	750 000
	$8 000 000	$7 000 000	$4 800 000	$4 400 000	$1 700 000	$1 300 000

Additional Information

On January 1, 1995, Barth adopted a plan to sell the assets and product line of the office equipment division, and the company expected to realize a gain on this disposal. On September 1, 1995, the division's assets and product line were sold for $2 100 000 cash, resulting in a gain of $640 000 (exclusive of operations during the phase-out period).

The company's textiles division had six manufacturing plants, which produced a variety of textile products. In April 1995, the company sold one of these plants and realized a gain of $130 000. After the sale, the operations at the plant that was sold were transferred to the remaining five textile plants, which the company continued to operate.

In August 1995, the main warehouse of the food products division, located on the banks of the St. Lawrence River, was flooded when the river overflowed. The resulting damage of $420 000 is not included in the financial data given above. Historical records indicate that the St. Lawrence River normally overflows every four to five years, causing flood damage to adjacent property.

For the two years ended December 31, 1995 and 1994, the company had interest revenue of $70 000 and $40 000, respectively, which was earned on investments.

The provision for income tax expense for each of the two years should be computed at a rate of 35 percent.

Instructions

Prepare in proper form a comparative statement of income for Barth Company for the two years ended December 31, 1995 and 1994.
(Adapted from AICPA.)

P5.10 Income Statement. Perry Company has always prepared its income statement on the current operating performance basis. Because the statements have been used strictly for internal purposes, adherence to GAAP has not been a major consideration.

In early 1995, the company's accountant contacts you for advice in preparing income and retained earnings statements for 1994 in accordance with generally accepted accounting principles for use with a bank loan application. The accountant presents you with the following statements, which had been prepared for internal use:

Perry Company
INCOME STATEMENT
For the Year Ended December 31, 1994

Sales revenue	$851 000
Cost of goods sold	415 000
Gross profit	436 000
Operating expenses	305 000
Income before income tax	131 000
Income tax expense	55 020
Net income	$ 75 980

Perry Company
RETAINED EARNINGS STATEMENT
For the Year Ended December 31, 1994

Retained earnings, January 1, 1994		$1 405 000
Additions		
Gain on the sale of investments*	$275 500	
Net income for 1994	75 980	351 480
		1 756 480
Deductions		
Extraordinary loss—major casualty*	72 500	
Cumulative effect of change in accounting policy in 1994*	69 600	
Cash dividends, 1994	75 000	
Stock dividends, 1994	50 000	(267 100)
Retained earnings, December 31, 1994		$1 489 380

*Presented on net-of-tax basis.

You determine that all items are appropriately described, that all items subject to income tax appropriately reflect a 42 percent income tax rate, and that the company had 75 000 common shares outstanding throughout 1994.

Instructions

Prepare income and retained earnings statements for 1994 in accordance with generally accepted accounting principles, including all relevant disclosures that can be determined from the data given. Provide computations to support your financial statement items.

P5.11 Income Statement. The following trial balance of Garr Corporation at December 31, 1994, has been adjusted except for income tax expense:

Garr Corporation
TRIAL BALANCE
December 31, 1994

Account	Dr.	Cr.
Cash	$ 675 000	
Accounts receivable (net)	1 695 000	
Inventory	2 185 000	
Property, plant, and equipment (net)	8 660 000	
Accounts payable and accrued liabilities		$ 1 895 000
Income tax payable		360 000
Common shares		5 975 000
Retained earnings, 1/1/94		3 350 000
Net sales—Regular		10 750 000
—Plastics Division		2 485 000
Cost of sales—Regular	5 920 000	
—Plastics Division	1 650 000	
Selling and administrative expenses		
—Regular	2 600 000	
—Plastics Division	660 000	
Interest income—Regular		65 000
Gain on litigation settlement—Regular		200 000

Depreciation adjustment from accounting change—		
Regular	350 000	
Gain on disposal of Plastics Division		150 000
Income tax expense	835 000	
	$25 230 000	$25 230 000

Additional Information

Other financial data for the year ended December 31, 1994:

Income tax expense

Estimated tax payments	$475 000
Accrued	360 000
Total charged to income tax expense (estimated)	$835 000
Tax rate on all types of income	40%

Gain from litigation settlement is not considered infrequent.

Discontinued operations

On October 31, 1994, Garr sold its Plastics Division for $2 950 000 when the carrying amount was $2 800 000. For financial statement reporting, this sale was considered a disposal of a segment of a business. Since there was no phase-out period, the measurement date was October 31, 1994.

Change in depreciation method

On January 1, 1994, Garr changed to the 150 percent declining balance method from the straight-line method of depreciation for certain of its capital assets. The pretax cumulative effect of this accounting change was determined to be a charge of $350 000.

Capital structure

Common shares, no-par, traded on a national exchange:

	Number of Shares
Outstanding at 1/1/94	200 000
Issued on 7/1/94 as a 15% stock dividend	30 000
	230 000

Instructions

Using the multiple-step format, prepare a formal income statement for Garr for the year ended December 31, 1994. All components of income tax expense should be appropriately shown. (*Hint:* The 15 percent stock dividend should be treated as outstanding for the entire year in computing earnings-per-share figures.)
(Adapted from AICPA.)

Cases

C5.1 Methods of Revenue Recognition. AMB Industries has three operating divisions: Queenswood Construction Division, Paperback Publishing Division, and Protection Securities Division. Each division maintains its own accounting system and method of revenue recognition.

Queenswood Construction Division. During the fiscal year ended November 30, 1995, Queenswood Construction Division had one construction project in process. A $24 000 000 contract for construction of a civic centre was granted on June 19, 1995, and construction began on August 1, 1995. Estimated costs of completion at the contract date were $20 million over a two-year period from the date of the contract. On November 30, 1995, construction costs of $6 000 000 had been incurred, and progress billings of $6 600 000 had been made. The construction costs to complete the remainder of the project were reviewed on November 30, 1995, and were estimated to amount to only $12 million due to an expected decline in raw materials costs. Revenue recognition is based on the percentage-of-completion method.

Paperback Publishing Division. The Paperback Publishing Division sells large volumes of novels to a few book distributors that in turn sell to several national bookstore chains. Paperback Publishing allows distributors to return up to 30 percent of sales, and distributors give the same terms to bookstores. While returns from individual titles fluctuate greatly, the returns from distributors have averaged 20 percent in each of the past five years. A total of $8 million of paperback sales were made to distributors during fiscal year 1995. On November 30, 1995, $3 million of fiscal 1995 sales were still subject to return privileges over the next six months. The remaining $5 million of fiscal 1995 sales had actual returns of 21 percent. Sales from fiscal 1994, totalling $2 million, were collected in fiscal 1995 less 18 percent returns. This division records revenue according to the method referred to as "revenue recognition when the right of return exists."

Protection Securities Division. Protection Securities Division works through manufacturers' agents in various cities. Orders for alarm systems and down payments are forwarded from agents, and the division ships the goods FOB factory directly to customers (usually police departments and security companies). Customers are billed directly for the balance due plus actual shipping costs. The firm received orders for $6 million of goods during the fiscal year ended November 30, 1995. Down payments of $600 000 were received, and $5 million of goods were billed and shipped. Actual freight costs of $100 000 were also billed. Commissions of 10 percent on product price are paid to manufacturing agents after goods are shipped to customers. Such goods are warranted for 90 days after shipment, and warranty returns have been about 1 percent of sales. Revenue is recognized at the point of sale by this division.

Instructions

(a) There are a variety of methods for revenue recognition. Define and describe each of the following methods, and indicate which ones are in accordance with GAAP.
    (1) Point of sale.   (3) Percentage of completion.
    (2) Completed contracts.   (4) Installment contract.
(b) Compute the revenue to be recognized in fiscal year 1995 for each of the three operating divisions of AMB Industries in accordance with generally accepted accounting principles.

(Adapted from CMA.)

C5.2 Income Statement Presentation. Phillips Company is a major manufacturer of foodstuffs whose products are sold in grocery and convenience stores throughout Canada. The company's name is well known and respected, because its products have been marketed nationally for over 50 years.

In April 1995, the company was forced to recall one of its major products. A total of 35 people in Vancouver were treated for severe intestinal pain, and eventually three of these people died from complications. All of them had consumed Phillips' product.

The product causing the problem was traced to one specific lot. Phillips keeps samples from all lots of foodstuffs. After thorough testing, company management and the legal authorities confirmed that the product had been tampered with after it had left the company's plant and was no longer under the company's control.

All of the product was recalled from the market—the only time a Phillips product has been recalled nationally and the only time it has been tampered with. People who still had the product in their homes, even though it was not from the affected lot, were encouraged to return the product for credit or refund. A media campaign was designed and implemented by the company to explain what had happened and what the company was doing to minimize any chance of a recurrence. Phillips decided to continue the product with the same trade name and wholesale price. However, the packaging was redesigned completely to be tamper-resistant and safety-sealed. This required the purchase and installation of new equipment.

The corporate accounting staff recommended that the costs associated with the tampered product be treated as an extraordinary charge on the 1995 financial statements. Corporate accounting was asked to identify the various costs that could be associated with the tampered product and related recall. These costs (in thousands) are as follows:

(1)	Credits and refunds to stores and consumers	$20 000
(2)	Insurance to cover lost sales and idle plant costs for possible future recalls	4 000
(3)	Transportation costs and off-site warehousing of returned product	4 000
(4)	Future security measures for other Phillips products	6 000
(5)	Testing of returned product and inventory	800
(6)	Destroying of returned product and inventory	2 400
(7)	Public relations program to reestablish brand credibility	1 800
(8)	Communication program to inform customers, answer inquiries, prepare press releases, etc.	1 600
(9)	Higher cost arising from new packaging	700
(10)	Investigation of possible involvement of employees, former employees, competitors, etc.	500
(11)	Packaging redesign and testing	2 000
(12)	Purchase and installation of new packaging equipment	5 000
(13)	Legal costs for defence against liability suits	600
(14)	Lost sales revenue due to recall	22 000

Phillips' estimated earnings before income taxes and before consideration of any of the above items for the year ending December 31, 1995, are $200 million.

Instructions
(a) Phillips Company plans to recognize the costs associated with the product tampering and recall as an extraordinary charge.
   (1) Do you agree that these costs qualify as an extraordinary charge?
   (2) Describe the placement and terminology used to present these costs in the 1995 income statement.
(b) Refer to the fourteen cost items identified by Phillips' corporate accounting staff.
   (1) Identify by number the cost items that should be included in the costs of the recall for 1995.
   (2) For any item that is not included in the cost of the recall, explain why it would not be included in the extraordinary charge.
(Adapted from CMA.)

C5.3 Income Statement Classification. Willis Company, a publicly held regional manufacturer of western-style clothing, uses a calendar year for financial reporting. During 1993, Willis purchased a small chain of retail specialty clothing stores that was privately owned and had been a good customer of Willis for a number of years.

Susan Helms was hired as controller of Willis Company in May 1994. In preparation for the 1995 budget, she completed a detailed comparison of the 1994 performance with the 1993 figures as reported. This analysis revealed the following items that affected the reported figures for 1993:

(1) The accounts receivable at December 31, 1993, were understated by $63 000. A subsidiary ledger had a balance with a transposed number. The Accounts Receivable control account was reduced by this amount in the adjusting entries of 1993.

(2) In May 1994, $60 000 was received in settlement for a $130 000 claim against a vendor for defective merchandise. The claim was filed in March 1993, but no receivable was recorded by Willis because the vendor's financial condition was very weak.

(3) In 1994, Willis paid $48 000 for additional federal income tax that was determined to be due for 1990 by a Revenue Canada audit.

(4) Willis paid $75 000 in August 1994 to settle an employee discrimination suit filed in September 1993 by a labour union that charged bias in promotion practices. No liability had been recorded in 1993, but the suit had been disclosed in the notes to the 1993 financial statements.

(5) The retail chain Willis acquired in 1993 recorded its bad debts on the direct write-off basis even though the chain had significant credit sales and bad debt losses. The chain was included in the consolidated earnings of Willis for 1993. Susan Helms estimated that the chain would have had an allowance for doubtful accounts of $50 000 if an allowance system had been used.

Instructions

Discuss how Susan Helms should handle each of the five situations in preparing the 1994 financial statements, paying particular attention to whether the items should be treated as prior period adjustments or as part of 1994 income.
(Adapted from CMA.)

Judgement Cases

J5.1   Bad Debt Accounting and Revenue Recognition.   Foreign Ideas, Inc., is a wholesaler of electronic products such as television sets, stereo equipment, and microwave ovens. The company, located in Alberta, wishes to discuss an accounting and financial reporting issue with you because your firm is the company's auditor. The company sells many of its products to retail outlets located in Mexico. The receivables that arise from these sales are denominated in Canadian dollars. That is, although the Mexican retailers will sell the products to Mexican nationals for pesos, those retailers will have to convert the pesos into Canadian dollars in order to pay Foreign Ideas the amounts owed.

Near the end of the past year, the exchange rate between the two currencies changed abruptly and significantly. From a relatively stable ratio of about 2 pesos to 1 dollar, the exchange rate is now about 4 pesos to 1 dollar. This change adversely affects the ability of the Mexican retailers to pay Foreign Ideas the amounts due. To illustrate, suppose Foreign Ideas sold a Mexican retailer a television for $400. If the Mexican retailer sold the product to one of its customers for 1600 pesos, those pesos could be converted to $800 dollars, and the obligation to Foreign Ideas could easily be settled. Now, however, 1600 pesos will bring only $400 dollars when converted by the Mexican retailer. The loss in the conversion rate limits the ability of the Mexican retailers to sell Canadian products, convert their proceeds, and pay for the products.

Foreign Ideas' financial officer describes the above conditions and acknowledges that estimating the amount of bad debts expected from the Mexican receivables has proved difficult. He then states the company's intentions as follows:

What we propose to do is to follow CICA *Handbook*, Section 3290, "Contingencies," very carefully. We are also mindful of the wording "reasonably estimated" and "likely," which provide that the amount of a loss that should be reported is the best estimate of the expected loss within the range when only a range of loss can be estimated. If no amount of loss within the range appears to be a better estimate than any other, however, then the low end of the range should be accrued. That is what we propose to do.

The range of loss that we face this year extends from the total amount of our Mexican receivables to the amount that proved uncollectable in past years. Because the change in the exchange rate was so recent, abrupt, and significant, we are unable to identify any amount within the range that appears to be more likely than any other amount. We just don't have enough experience with a situation like this. By the way, we have stopped anything other than COD shipments to most of our international customers. So, it is only the receivables that existed at the end of the year that are in question. Therefore, in accordance with Section 3290, we are going to accrue the same amount we did last year. That is the low end of the range that seems to us to meet the requirements of the CICA *Handbook.*

We need to know if you agree with our analysis, because we are going to inform our banker of our preliminary operating results later this week and don't want to struggle with this issue when the audit begins.

Instructions

Do you agree with the chief financial officer's analysis and resolution? (Address this issue without regard to the fact that accounting for loss contingencies is discussed primarily in Chapter 15 of this textbook.)

J5.2   Income Statement Presentation.   Paper Tiger, a manufacturer of a wide variety of paper products, owns and operates forest lands in several locations in western Canada and the United States. Recently, a volcano erupted and destroyed a large forest owned by the company in Oregon. That forest is the only timber that the company owned near the volcano. The loss of the forest is very large relative to the company's financial statements, and the company is concerned about the preparation of its income statement for the year and the manner in which the loss should be reported.

The president of Paper Tiger maintains that the loss has never happened before and is clearly unusual. Furthermore, the president believes that the mere size of the item suggests that it should be presented as an extraordinary loss.

You are the engagement partner of the company's auditor and have been consulted as to whether the loss can be considered an extraordinary item. As you are reviewing the relevant authoritative accounting literature, you happen to hear a newscast that states that eruptions of the volcano are expected to continue into the foreseeable future. You have directed your assistant to consult the U.S. Geological Survey, and that research confirms that eruptions are, in fact, expected to continue indefinitely.

Instructions

Determine whether you believe the loss can be reported as an extraordinary item in Paper Tiger's income statement, and justify your position. Be sure to cite the appropriate authoritative accounting literature in your answer, and provide your reasoning as to how that literature should be applied in this particular situation.

Chapter 6

The Accounting Cycle

Objectives

To discuss and illustrate the steps in the accounting cycle. These steps are as follows:

1. Identify transactions.

2. Analyze transactions.

3. Record transactions in journals.

4. Post to ledger accounts.

5. Prepare an unadjusted trial balance.

6. Prepare adjusting entries.

7. Prepare an adjusted trial balance.

8. Prepare financial statements.

9. Prepare closing entries.

10. Prepare a post-closing trial balance (optional).

11. Prepare reversing entries (optional).

231

The primary objective of financial reporting is to provide information that is useful in making investment, lending, and similar decisions. To provide this information, accountants follow a sequence of steps during an enterprise's accounting period, which is usually one year. This sequence is called the **accounting cycle** or the **accounting process**.

In this chapter, we review the steps in the accounting cycle. Most students have been introduced to these steps in previous courses; however, a thorough review of the accounting cycle will reinforce the knowledge required to understand the remainder of this text.

The widespread use of computers has had a profound impact on business data processing in recent years. In this chapter, however, we emphasize manual processing methods often used by smaller businesses. Emphasizing a manual system enables us to illustrate the accounting cycle in the simplest, most understandable manner. The chapter covers the basic accounting functions of recording and summarizing business data that accountants carry out regardless of whether a company processes information manually, mechanically, or electronically. The computer removes the repetitive and balancing functions and produces the journals and reports from the initial data entered. In addition, computerized accounting packages have features for producing cheques when payments are due or blocking shipments to customers who have exceeded their credit limit or are in arrears.

Steps in the Accounting Cycle

Step 1. Identify Transactions

The initial step in the accounting cycle is identifying transactions so that they can be properly recorded. Broadly defined, a **transaction** is an event that (1) changes a firm's financial position *and* (2) can be measured with sufficient objectivity. For example, a cash purchase of supplies is a transaction that changes a firm's financial position by increasing one asset (supplies) and decreasing another (cash). In contrast, hiring a new office manager is not presently considered a transaction under generally accepted accounting principles. A major reason why hiring activities are not considered accountable events is that their impact on the firm's financial position is too uncertain to measure in a sufficiently reliable manner.

Transactions may be external or internal in nature. **External transactions** are those that involve outside parties; examples include sales, purchases, and loans. **Internal transactions** are those confined to the accounting entity itself; examples are depreciation, amortization, and conversion of production costs into inventory.

A firm's accounting system should identify pertinent information about every transaction. When a transaction occurs, a **source document,** often called a **business paper**, is prepared as evidence of the transaction. For external transactions, for example, a sales invoice is a source document that supports a sale transaction, a cheque supports a payment transaction, and a promissory note supports a loan. Depreciation schedules, amortization schedules, and inventory schedules are common examples of source documents for internal transactions. To verify the accuracy of financial statement information, an accountant should be able to trace financial statement numbers to the source documents. This tracing process is important to the auditing function. The term **audit trail** refers to the evidence that links the balances shown in the financial statements with the thousands of transactions that are summarized in those balances.

Step 2. Analyze Transactions

After identifying transactions, the accountant determines their impact on financial position as represented by the basic equation Assets = Liabilities + Owners' Equity. This analysis occurs within the **double-entry system** of accounting. These entries are made in records called **accounts,** and every transaction affects at least two accounts.

There are several forms of accounts. The simplest form is the **T account.**

Account Title	
Debits (left side)	Credits (right side)

The T account is a convenient and widely used instructional device.

Proper analysis of a transaction requires an understanding of the major types of accounts and the manner in which debit and credit entries affect each, as summarized in Exhibit 6.1.[1]

Note that the **normal balance** in an account coincides with what is done to increase the balance in the account. For example, we increase the balance in an asset account with a debit; the normal balance in an asset account is therefore debit.

Remember that any transaction affects financial position as represented by the basic equation Assets = Liabilities + Owners' Equity. Revenue and expense accounts are also reflected in this equation because they are **temporary extensions of owners' equity,** as shown in Exhibit 6.1. Companies use these temporary accounts to determine net income. With these accounts, they measure revenue and expense activities in many individual accounts and thereby avoid excessive detail in the Owners' Equity account. At the end of the accounting period, the balances in the revenue and expense accounts are transferred to the Owners' Equity account via the closing process (explained in Step 9).[2]

Step 3. Record Transactions in Journals

After the information shown on source documents has been gathered and analyzed, it is entered in chronological order in a journal. Thus, a **journal** is a chronological record of transactions. The process of recording transactions in a journal is called **journalizing.** Because this marks the first time that transactions are recorded in the debit-and-credit framework, a journal is often called a **book of original entry.**

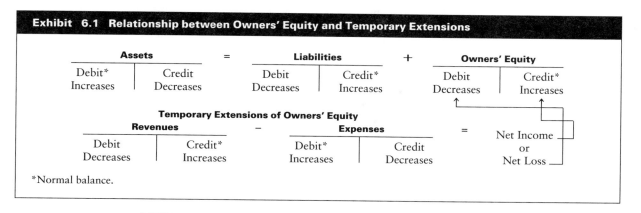

Exhibit 6.1   Relationship between Owners' Equity and Temporary Extensions

---

[1]Other types of accounts will be discussed at appropriate places in the text.

[2]Gain accounts (e.g., gain on sale of land) function in the same way as revenue accounts; loss accounts (e.g., loss of building caused by fire) function in the same way as expense accounts.

General Journal

The most fundamental journal is the **general journal**, often called simply the journal. A **simple journal entry** consists of one debit and one credit. **A compound journal entry** consists of two or more debits or two or more credits. To illustrate, consider the following two transactions of Brookshire Corporation during October:

Oct. 1 Sold merchandise to Johnson Company for $1200 on account.
Purchased machinery from Roberts Tool Company for $10 000. Paid $2000 cash and signed a 90-day, 12 percent promissory note for the remainder of the purchase price.

These transactions would be entered in Brookshire's general journal as follows:

General Journal					Page J7
Date		Description	Post. Ref.	Dr.	Cr.
Oct.	1	Accounts Receivable—Johnson Co.	111	1 200	
		Sales	401		1 200
		Sold merchandise to Johnson Company on account.			
	4	Machinery	161	10 000	
		Cash	101		2 000
		Notes Payable	211		8 000
		Purchased machinery from Roberts Tool Company. Paid $2000 cash and signed a 90-day, 12% promissory note for balance.			

As shown above, the account to be debited is customarily listed before the account to be credited. The account credited is also indented to distinguish it clearly from the account debited.

Special Journals

Although all transactions could be recorded in a general journal, a business usually has several **special journals** in addition to a general journal in order to facilitate the efficient recording of large numbers of similar transactions. Common types of special journals and the nature of the transactions recorded in each are listed below:

Type of Special Journal	Nature of Transactions Recorded
Sales journal	Sales of merchandise on credit
Cash receipts journal	Receipts of cash from any source
Purchases journal	Purchases of merchandise on credit[3]
Cash payments journal	Payments of cash for any purpose
General journal	Transactions that don't fit any of the special journals

The number, purpose, and format of special journals vary considerably. Each business must decide on its special journals based on its needs. The topic of special journals is covered in more depth in Appendix B at the end of this chapter.

---

[3]Sometimes a purchases journal is expanded to record *all* credit purchases, including merchandise, equipment, and supplies.

When a company uses special journals, it uses the general journal to record all transactions that do not fit the special journals. The general journal, then, is an integral part of an accounting system whether or not special journals are used. For this reason, and because the general journal offers a convenient instructional format, we use it throughout the text to illustrate the application of various accounting concepts and principles.

Step 4. Post to Ledger Accounts

General Ledger

After transactions have been journalized, the next step is to transfer the information to accounts in the general ledger. This transfer process is called **posting**. Posting may occur at various times during an accounting period, and it involves reorganizing information from a chronological system to a system of individual accounts that brings all like items (e.g., all cash items) together in one place. To illustrate, the journal entries shown earlier for Brookshire Corporation are posted to these general ledger T accounts:

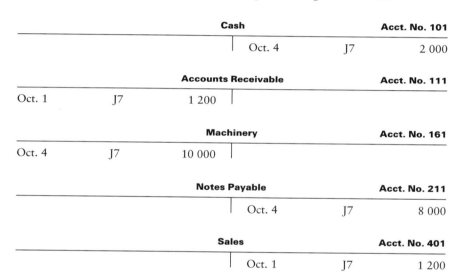

As shown, the accountant must post each part of every general journal entry.

The **general ledger**, often called simply the **ledger**, consists of many accounts. Each account is a record of information about a particular asset, such as Cash and Accounts Receivable; liability, such as Accounts Payable and Notes Payable; owners' equity, such as Common Shares and Retained Earnings; revenue, such as Sales and Service Fees Earned; and expense, such as Salaries and Advertising. Based on the scope of its operations and the extent of detail desired for reporting purposes, a business determines the exact nature of its accounts.

Certain ledger accounts are called real accounts, whereas others are known as nominal accounts. **Real, or permanent, accounts** remain open. These include asset, liability, and owners' equity accounts. Real accounts measure stocks of things, such as resources or debts, that exist at a certain point in time. **Nominal, or temporary, accounts** are closed at the end of every accounting period. These include revenue and expense accounts. Nominal accounts measure flows, such as sales or cost of goods sold, that occur over time. During an accounting period, **mixed accounts** contain both real and nominal components. At the end of the period, adjusting entries separate mixed accounts into their real and nominal components. For example, before adjusting entries, the Supplies account usually has both consumed (nominal) and unconsumed (real) portions. An adjusting entry places the consumed portion in a nominal account (Supplies Expense) and allows the unconsumed portion to remain in a real account (Supplies). After the accountant makes adjusting entries, all accounts in the ledger are either real or nominal.

The general ledger ordinarily includes certain adjunct and contra accounts. An **adjunct account** is one whose balance is added to the balance in the account to which it relates. For example, Freight-In is an adjunct account to Purchases, and Premium on Bonds Payable is an adjunct account to Bonds Payable. A **contra,** or **offset, account** is one whose balance is subtracted from the balance in the account to which it relates for financial statement presentation. For instance, Sales Discounts is a contra account to Sales, and Allowance for Doubtful Accounts is a contra account to Accounts Receivable. Adjunct and contra accounts are closed at the end of an accounting period only if the accounts they relate to are also closed.

Subsidiary Ledgers

In addition to a general ledger, most businesses have one or more **subsidiary ledgers**. The purpose of a subsidiary ledger is to store the details of certain general ledger accounts. For example, a company may have thousands of credit customers. While it is certainly necessary to know the total amount that these customers owe the company, it is also essential to know the name and address of each customer and how much each one owes. This information facilitates the billing process and is useful when the company makes credit-granting decisions. Rather than have a separate Accounts Receivable account for each customer in the general ledger, firms usually create an Accounts Receivable subsidiary ledger. This ledger is often in the form of a tray of alphabetized cards, with each card representing a customer's account. The Accounts Receivable account in the general ledger then becomes a **control,** or **main, account** that is supported by many detailed accounts in the subsidiary ledger.

When a subsidiary ledger exists, posting must appear in both the control account and the appropriate subsidiary ledger accounts. The control account is debited for the total debits and credited for the total credits made to the subsidiary ledger accounts. After all accounts have been posted, the balance in the control account should equal the total of the individual account balances in the subsidiary ledger. To assure this equality, the accountant periodically reconciles each control account with its subsidiary ledger accounts.

Why use subsidiary ledgers? One important reason is to reduce the number of accounts in the general ledger. With fewer accounts, it is easier to avoid errors and to find them when they occur. Subsidiary ledgers also facilitate the division of labour in an accounting department. Individuals with limited accounting experience can often be assigned responsibility for one or more subsidiary ledgers, and work on the various ledgers can thereby proceed simultaneously. A subsidiary ledger can support any general ledger account. Subsidiary ledgers are often set up for Cash (when a company has several bank accounts), Accounts Receivable, Merchandise Inventory (when a company uses a perpetual inventory system), Capital Assets, Accounts Payable, Capital Shares, Selling Expenses, and Administrative Expenses.

Step 5. Prepare an Unadjusted Trial Balance

A **trial balance** is a list of general ledger accounts and their debit or credit balances. It summarizes, usually on one sheet of paper, information that appears in a company's general ledger. The accountant prepares a trial balance at the end of every accounting period before making the adjusting entries. Because the account balances do not yet reflect adjustments, the trial balance prepared at this time is often called an **unadjusted trial balance**.

A trial balance serves two main purposes:

1. It provides evidence that total debits in a company's general ledger equal total credits.
2. It provides information that helps the accountant to formulate adjusting entries.

The unadjusted trial balance for Maple Limited at December 31, 1995, follows. Information pertaining to this company, which uses a calendar-year accounting period, will be used to help explain the subsequent steps in the accounting cycle.

Maple Limited
UNADJUSTED TRIAL BALANCE
December 31, 1995

Account	Dr.	Cr.
Cash	$ 21 079	
Accounts receivable	60 000	
Allowance for doubtful accounts		$ 500
Note receivable	10 000	
Merchandise inventory	57 606	
Prepaid insurance	1 200	
Land	40 000	
Building	100 000	
Accumulated depreciation—building		10 000
Office equipment	120 000	
Accumulated depreciation—office equipment		24 000
Accounts payable		38 405
Unearned rent revenue		4 800
Long-term note payable		72 000
Common shares, no-par value		115 000
Retained earnings		34 215
Sales		523 000
Purchases	187 000	
Purchase returns		2 000
Purchase allowances		2 500
Purchase discounts		3 600
Freight-in	7 250	
Sales salaries expense	78 000	
Advertising expense	24 000	
Freight-out	6 000	
Miscellaneous selling expenses	5 141	
Officers' salaries expense	76 000	
Professional services	23 000	
Utilities expense	8 244	
Miscellaneous administrative expenses	5 500	
Totals	$830 020	$830 020

Step 6. Prepare Adjusting Entries

Revenue
Realization

Under the **cash basis of accounting**, revenue is recorded only when it is received, and expenses are recorded only when they are paid. In contrast, the **accrual basis of accounting** requires recognition of revenue when it is earned, according to the revenue realization

Matching

principle, and recognition of expenses when they are incurred, according to the matching principle. Under accrual basis accounting, the cash inflows typically associated with a given period's revenues may occur in past, present, or future periods. Similarly, the cash outflows typically associated with a given period's expenses may occur in past, present, or future periods. Thus, the primary difference between cash basis and accrual basis accounting is the timing of the recognition of revenues and expenses.

Current generally accepted accounting principles require accrual basis accounting, because this system generates measures of performance and financial position that are superior to those of cash basis accounting. To help implement accrual basis accounting, the accountant makes certain **adjusting entries** (often called **adjustments**) at the end of every accounting period. Adjusting entries are initially recorded in the general journal, then posted to the appropriate general ledger accounts. If an entry requires an account that is not in the general ledger, the accountant simply creates a new account.[4]

Purpose of Adjusting Entries

Revenue
Realization

Matching

Adjusting entries permit an accurate measurement of earnings and financial position on the accrual basis. Adjusting entries are based on the principles of **revenue realization** and **matching** (see Chapter 2). Every adjusting entry allocates revenues or expenses between current and future periods. Moreover, every adjusting entry affects both a balance sheet account (asset or liability) and an income statement account (revenue or expense).[5]

Accumulating Adjusting Data

An external event such as a purchase or sale signals the accountant to record the transaction. At the end of the accounting period, however, no external events signal the accountant to record adjusting entries. How then does the accountant determine the nature and amounts of adjusting entries to record? Basically, the accountant carefully considers each account in the trial balance and examines certain source documents. Accounts that have mixed balances (i.e., mixed accounts) must be separated into real and nominal components. In addition, certain information not reflected on the trial balance must be entered in the accounting records. For example, the presence of Prepaid Insurance on the trial balance causes the accountant to inquire whether any insurance has expired and therefore should be charged to expense. This inquiry normally involves a review of the company's insurance policies. A Notes Receivable account usually leads the accountant to review the notes to determine whether any interest has been earned. Interest earned should be entered in a revenue account. Because many adjusting entries repeat from one accounting period to the next, accountants can often gain insight into the nature and amounts of the current period's adjusting entries by examining the ones that were made at the end of the preceding period or at the same period in the previous year.

Classification of Adjusting Entries

We will classify adjusting entries using the following three categories:

---

[4]"Financial Statement Concepts, Recognition Criteria," CICA *Handbook,* Paragraphs 1000.41–52, March 1991.

[5]Certain **correcting entries** and **reclassification entries** are sometimes made during the adjustment process. For example, a correcting entry might be made to charge to Advertising Expense an amount that was mistakenly charged to Research and Development Expense during the year. A reclassification entry might be made to reclassify to current liability status the portion of long-term debt that will mature within the next year. As these examples suggest, a correcting or reclassification entry often affects only nominal accounts or only real accounts.

1. Accruals.
2. Deferrals.
3. Special items.

Accruals. Accruals are adjusting entries that normally fulfill *one* of the following conditions:

1. A revenue is recognized before the related cash receipt.

   or

2. An expense is recognized before the related cash payment.

Accruals are appropriate for revenues and related assets, and for expenses and related liabilities that increase or accumulate gradually during the accounting period. Rather than recording these items weekly, daily, or even more frequently, the accountant records them by making adjusting entries at the end of the accounting period.[6]

As an example of **accrued revenues** (accrued assets), Maple Limited acquired a $10 000, one-year, 12 percent note receivable dated July 1, 1995, with interest payable at maturity. This note represents money loaned by the company and is reflected on its trial balance. The revenue realization principle holds, in part, that revenue generated by allowing others to use enterprise assets, such as money, should be recorded as time passes. Accordingly, the company should make the following adjusting entry on December 31, 1995, the end of the company's annual accounting period:

Dec. 31 Interest Receivable	600	
Interest Revenue		600

(To accrue interest for 6 months on note receivable, computed as follows: $10 000 × 0.12 × 6/12 = $600.)

Revenue Realization

The adjusting entry assigns the $600 of interest revenue to 1995, the period in which the revenue was earned according to the revenue realization principle. The cash receipt associated with the interest will occur in the next accounting period, specifically on June 30, 1996 (the maturity date of the note).

As an example of **accrued expenses** (accrued liabilities), on October 1, 1995, Maple Limited issued a $72 000, ten-year, 10 percent note payable, with interest payable annually on September 30. September 30, 1996, is therefore the first date on which interest will be paid. Nevertheless, the money borrowed was used during the last three months of 1995. Accordingly, the cost of that money (interest) must be reported as an expense in 1995 to comply with the matching principle. The accountant should make the following adjusting entry:

Matching

Dec. 31 Interest Expense	1800	
Interest Payable		1800

(To accrue interest for 3 months on note payable, computed as follows: $72 000 × 0.10 × 3/12 = $1800.)

The adjusting entry assigns the $1800 of interest expense to the current accounting period (1995), the period in which the expense was incurred. The cash payment associated with the accrued interest will occur on September 30, 1996.

---

[6]"Financial Statement Concepts, Recognition Criteria," CICA *Handbook*, Paragraph 1000.46, March 1991.

Maple Limited must make one other major accrual, that of income tax expense. This is usually the final adjusting entry, because the amount depends on the size of a company's pretax income. We will therefore make this entry later in the chapter, after we have calculated Maple's 1995 income before taxes.

Deferrals. Deferrals are adjusting entries required to separate mixed accounts into their real and nominal components. A deferral-type adjusting entry typically fulfills *one* of the following conditions:

1. A revenue is recognized after the related cash receipt.
    or
2. An expense is recognized after the related cash payment (or incurrence of a liability).

In Exhibit 6.2, we compare accruals with deferrals.

Adjusting entries to reflect **deferred (unearned) revenues** are necessary for mixed accounts in which a portion of the balance represents revenue that has been earned currently and a portion represents revenue that will be earned in one or more future accounting periods. For example, Maple Limited's trial balance shows unearned rent revenue of $4800. The lease shows that the $4800 represents one year's rent received in advance on an office in the company's building. When the amount was received on September 1, 1995, the following entry was made:

Sep. 1 Cash	4800	
Unearned Rent Revenue		4800
(To record cash received for payment of rent revenue in		
advance.)		

Revenue Realization

The revenue realization principle holds, in part, that revenue generated by allowing others to use an enterprise asset, such as an office, is earned as time passes. Accordingly, on December 31, 1995, the following adjusting entry is required to reflect the fact that one-third of the $4800 has been earned:

Dec. 31 Unearned Rent Revenue	1600	
Rent Revenue		1600
(To record revenue earned on office rented, computed		
as follows: $4800 \times {}^{4}\!/_{12} = \$1600$.)		

As usual, the adjusting entry affects a balance sheet account (Unearned Rent Revenue) and an income statement account (Rent Revenue). After the entry has been posted, the Unearned Rent Revenue account has a $3200 credit balance ($4800 − $1600 = $3200). This balance is a liability, because it represents the company's obligation to provide the rented asset (i.e., the office) during the first eight months of the next accounting period.

Some companies follow the practice of **crediting a revenue account** whenever revenues are collected in advance of being earned. If Maple had observed this practice, it would have debited Cash and credited Rent Revenue for $4800 on September 1, 1995. Then, on December 31, 1995, the adjusting entry would have been as follows:

Dec. 31 Rent Revenue	3200	
Unearned Rent Revenue		3200
(To record the unearned revenue from office rent paid		
in advance, computed as follows: $4800 \times {}^{8}\!/_{12} = \$3200$)		

Exhibit 6.2 Comparison of Accruals and Deferrals

Accrued Revenue	Revenue recognition Cash receipt
Deferred (Unearned) Revenue	Cash receipt Revenue recognition
Accrued Expense	Expense recognition Cash payment
Deferred (Prepaid) Expense	Cash payment (or incurrence of liability) Expense recognition

(each timeline labeled "Time")

The amounts reported on the 1995 financial statements would be the same as before, because the economic circumstances have not changed. At December 31, 1995, therefore, rent revenue would still be $1600 and unearned rent revenue would still be $3200.

Adjusting entries to reflect **deferred (prepaid) expenses** are necessary for mixed accounts in which a portion of the balance represents an expense that has been incurred currently and a portion represents an expense that will be incurred in one or more future accounting periods. For example, Maple Limited's trial balance shows prepaid insurance of $1200. The insurance policy shows that this amount represents the cost of fire protection for one year, paid in advance on April 1, 1995. When the original amount was paid, the company debited Prepaid Insurance and credited Cash.

Matching

The matching principle recognizes costs as expenses when the goods or services represented by the costs contribute to revenue. During 1995, three-fourths of the insurance protection has presumably contributed to revenue. The expired portion of the insurance cost must therefore be entered in an expense account. The following adjusting entry is required:

Dec. 31 Insurance Expense   900
        Prepaid Insurance   900
        (*To record expired portion of insurance, computed as follows:* $1200 × 9/12 = $900.)

Notice once again that the adjusting entry affects a balance sheet account (Prepaid Insurance) and an income statement account (Insurance Expense). After posting, the Prepaid Insurance account has a $300 debit balance. This balance represents an asset: specifically, the right to receive fire insurance protection during the first three months of the next accounting period.

Some companies follow the practice of **debiting an expense account** for short-term prepayments. If Maple had observed this practice, it would have debited Insurance Expense and credited Cash for $1200 on April 1, 1995. On December 31, 1995, the adjusting entry would require a debit to Prepaid Insurance and a credit to Insurance Expense for $300. The amounts reported on the 1995 financial statements would be the same as before: insurance expense for 1995 would still be $900, and prepaid insurance at December 31, 1995, would still be $300.

Matching

The matching principle further requires that Maple Limited record depreciation on its building and office equipment. These assets have contributed to revenues throughout

1995; accordingly, a portion of their cost must be allocated to 1995 expense. Maple uses the straight-line method to depreciate the building and office equipment over 50 and 10 years, respectively. Furthermore, the company expects each asset to have no salvage value.[7] The adjusting entry is:

Dec. 31 Depreciation Expense—Building	2 000	
Depreciation Expense—Office Equipment	12 000	
Accumulated Depreciation—Building		2 000
Accumulated Depreciation—Office Equipment		12 000

(*To record depreciation, computed as follows:*

$$\text{Building} \frac{\$100\ 000 - 0}{50 \text{ years}} = \$2000$$

$$\text{Office Equipment} \frac{\$120\ 000 - 0}{10 \text{ years}} = \$12\ 000)$$

Note that a compound entry was made to record depreciation. Two simple entries would also have been appropriate. Once again, the adjusting entry affects a balance sheet account (Accumulated Depreciation) and an income statement account (Depreciation Expense). Accumulated Depreciation is a contra account that permits the balance sheet to show both the cost and the accumulated depreciation of the major types of capital assets. Both pieces of information are generally considered relevant and are required disclosures.[8] The cost of an asset minus its accumulated depreciation is often called the asset's **book value**, or **net book value**.

When a company incurs costs that will likely benefit several accounting periods, such as the cost of buildings and equipment, the normal procedure is to debit an asset account instead of an expense account. Therefore, adjusting entries to record long-term cost allocations, such as depreciation, are usually similar to the one illustrated above.

Special Items.   These are adjusting entries that do not fit neatly into the accrual and deferral categories and are therefore classified separately. Common examples include the adjusting entries for bad debts expense and for cost of goods sold in a company that uses the periodic inventory system.

Companies that sell on credit do not usually expect to collect all of their accounts receivable. Therefore, some portion of credit sales made during a period and some portion of accounts receivable at the end of the period will likely never be collected in cash. To reflect these expectations, companies make an adjusting entry to record **estimated bad debts**.[9]

Procedures for estimating bad debts expense are covered in Chapter 8. For now, assume that all of Maple Limited's sales are on credit and that the company expects that 0.5 percent of its sales will never be collected. The company makes the following adjusting entry:

---

[7]Under the straight-line method, depreciation is computed using the following formula:

$$\text{Annual depreciation} = \frac{\text{Cost} - \text{Salvage value}}{\text{Years of service life}}$$

[8]"Capital Assets," CICA *Handbook*, Paragraphs 3060.58–59, October 1990.
[9]"Accounts and Notes Receivable," CICA *Handbook*, Paragraphs 3020.12–14, July 1978.

Dec. 31 Bad Debts Expense   2615
      Allowance for Doubtful Accounts   2615
    (To record estimated bad debts, computed as follows:
    $523 000 × 0.005 = $2615.)

Matching

The adjusting entry assigns bad debts expense of $2615 to the current accounting period, where it is matched on the income statement with the revenue from credit sales. Credit sales give rise to the uncollectables. Bad debts expense is regarded as a cost of making credit sales, and recording it helps implement the matching principle. The credit in the above entry is not made to Accounts Receivable because we do not yet know which specific accounts will become uncollectable. The Allowance for Doubtful Accounts is a contra account to Accounts Receivable; we therefore subtract it from Accounts Receivable on the balance sheet. Accounts receivable minus allowance for doubtful accounts is often called the **net realizable value** of accounts receivable. The net realizable value of Maple's accounts receivable at December 31, 1995, is $56 885 [$60 000 − ($500 + $2615)]. The $500 amount is the balance in the Allowance for Doubtful Accounts before adjustments are made.

An outflow of resources is associated with most expenses. This outflow may occur in past, present, or future periods. In regard to bad debts, however, no such outflow occurs. Instead, there is simply a reduction in the inflow of cash expected. Thus, bad debts expense is somewhat peculiar, and some accountants think it should be treated as a revenue contra account (perhaps called Sales Uncollectable) rather than an expense. We have treated the adjusting entry for bad debts as a special item because of its peculiar nature.

Another special item is the **adjustment for cost of goods sold**. A company using the periodic inventory system debits Purchases whenever it makes a merchandise purchase. Furthermore, the recording of a sale does not involve entries in either the Cost of Goods Sold or Merchandise Inventory accounts. As a result, the Merchandise Inventory balance shown on the ending trial balance is the balance that was on hand at the *beginning* of the accounting period.[10] The objectives of the cost of goods sold adjustment are therefore threefold:

1. To enter the ending inventory balance in the Merchandise Inventory account and remove the beginning inventory balance. The ending balance can then be presented on the ending balance sheet.
2. To close all of the accounts included in the calculation of net purchases. These accounts include Purchases, Purchase Returns, Purchase Allowances, Purchase Discounts, and Freight-In.
3. To enter the Cost of Goods Sold expense in the accounting records. Cost of goods sold is computed using the following formula:

Cost of Goods Sold = Beginning Inventory + Purchases
                  − Purchase Returns − Purchase Allowances
                  − Purchase Discounts + Freight-In
                  − Ending Inventory

---

[10]Throughout this chapter, we assume that a periodic inventory system is used. In Chapter 9, we review in detail the differences between periodic and perpetual systems.

To illustrate, Maple Limited's physical inventory count at the end of 1995 shows merchandise costing $43 756. The adjusting entry for cost of goods sold is:

Dec. 31	Merchandise Inventory (Dec. 31)	43 756	
	Purchase Returns	2 000	
	Purchase Allowances	2 500	
	Purchase Discounts	3 600	
	Cost of Goods Sold	200 000	
	Merchandise Inventory (Jan. 1)		57 606
	Purchases		187 000
	Freight-In		7 250
	(To record cost of goods sold and ending inventory.)		

The adjusting entry accomplishes the three objectives described above. Actually, the entry is nothing more than the implementation of the basic cost of goods sold formula in general journal form. After the entry is posted, the Cost of Goods Sold account will have a $200 000 debit balance. Because Cost of Goods Sold is a nominal account, it must be closed during the closing process.

The adjusting entry for cost of goods sold is part adjusting and part closing. Some accountants prefer to treat it as a closing entry. Because it is peculiar, we have classified it as a special item.

Step 7. Prepare an Adjusted Trial Balance

After journalizing and posting the adjusting entries, the accountant prepares an **adjusted trial balance** that reflects the company's adjusting entries. An adjusted trial balance serves three major purposes:

1. It provides evidence that, after the adjusting entries have been made, total debits in a company's general ledger equal total credits. The trial balance thus helps to control errors made during the adjustment process.
2. It enables the accountant to calculate income before taxes so that the adjusting entry for income tax expense can be made.
3. It provides a convenient listing of account balances for use in the financial statements.

The adjusted trial balance of Maple Limited appears on page 245. Note that the columns are subtotalled and income before taxes is informally calculated. This calculation does not have to be shown in detail on the adjusted trial balance. Income before taxes is the difference between the income statement accounts with credit balances and the income statement accounts with debit balances. For Maple Limited, this difference is $80 000.

Income tax expense is typically a major expense. Unlike most other expenses, it can be computed only after calculating income before taxes. Maple Limited's income tax rate is 44 percent.[11] The figure entered in the income statement is an estimate for matching purposes. The company therefore records the accrual of its income tax expense as follows:

---

[11]In this chapter, we review the accounting cycle without being diverted by the mechanics of calculating income taxes. We therefore assume that a tax rate of 44 percent applies to all income and that no differences exist between the company's pretax accounting income and its taxable income. In Chapter 19, we discuss and illustrate how to account for income taxes under more complex circumstances.

Dec. 31 Income Tax Expense   35 200
      Income Tax Payable   35 200
    (*To accrue income tax expense at a rate of 44%.*)

As usual, this adjusting entry is journalized and posted to the affected general ledger accounts listed near the bottom of the adjusted trial balance. The columns are then totalled.

Maple Limited
ADJUSTED TRIAL BALANCE
December 31, 1995

Account	Dr.	Cr.
Cash	$ 21 079	
Accounts receivable	60 000	
Allowance for doubtful accounts		$ 3 115
Note receivable	10 000	
Interest receivable	600	
Merchandise inventory	43 756	
Prepaid insurance	300	
Land	40 000	
Building	100 000	
Accumulated depreciation—building		12 000
Office equipment	120 000	
Accumulated depreciation—office equipment		36 000
Accounts payable		38 405
Interest payable		1 800
Unearned rent revenue		3 200
Long-term note payable		72 000
Common shares, no-par-value		115 000
Retained earnings		34 215
Sales		523 000
Interest revenue		600
Rent revenue		1 600
Cost of goods sold	200 000	
Sales salaries expense	78 000	
Advertising expense	24 000	
Freight-out	6 000	
Miscellaneous selling expenses	5 141	
Officers' salaries expense	76 000	
Professional services	23 000	
Utilities expense	8 244	
Interest expense	1 800	
Insurance expense	900	
Depreciation expense—building	2 000	
Depreciation expense—office equipment	12 000	
Bad debts expense	2 615	
Miscellaneous administrative expenses	5 500	
Subtotal	840 935	840 935
Income tax expense	35 200	
Income tax payable		35 200
Total	$876 135	$876 135

Income before taxes $= \$523\ 000 + 600 + 1600 - 200\ 000$
$- 78\ 000 - 24\ 000 - 6000 - 5141$
$- 76\ 000 - 23\ 000 - 8244 - 1800$
$- 900 - 2000 - 12\ 000 - 2615$
$- 5500 = \$80\ 000$

Income tax expense $= \$80\ 000 \times 0.44 = \$35\ 200$

Step 8. Prepare Financial Statements

Using the information on the adjusted trial balance, the accountant prepares the formal **financial statements**.[12] The accountant ordinarily prepares financial statements in the following order: (1) income statement, (2) statement of retained earnings, (3) balance sheet, and (4) statement of changes in financial position. Many small corporations, proprietorships, and partnerships exclude the statement of changes in financial position from their financial statements. These basic financial statements are explained in Chapter 4. Preparing the statement of changes in financial position requires more information than appears on the adjusted trial balance. In Chapter 22, we discuss and illustrate how to prepare this statement. The income statement, statement of retained earnings, and balance sheet for Maple Limited appear in Exhibit 6.3. We present these statements for illustrative **Materiality**   purposes; most accountants would probably combine several of the items shown, based on materiality considerations.

Step 9. Prepare Closing Entries

After preparing the financial statements, the accountant prepares **closing entries**. These entries are made at the end of the accounting period. They are first recorded in the general journal, then posted to the appropriate ledger accounts.

The accountant closes *only* the nominal accounts. Furthermore, *all* nominal accounts are closed. To **close an account** means to reduce its balance to zero. Closing nominal accounts is logical, because they measure activities or flows that have occurred *during a given period of time*. At the end of the period, nominal accounts have served their purpose. Their balances must therefore be reduced to zero so that the accounts can be used to measure activities in the *next* accounting period.

Because nominal accounts are temporary extensions of owners' equity (see Exhibit 6.1), their balances may be transferred directly to an owners' equity account (Retained Earnings in the case of a corporation) during closing. However, most accountants transfer revenue and expense balances to a clearing account called **Income Summary** (or **Revenue and Expense Summary**). This account merely summarizes the net income or loss for the period, and its balance is closed (i.e., reduced to zero and transferred) to owners' equity.[13] The income summary account is only used in the closing entries and never appears on any of the financial statements. Closing entries are formulated based on the nominal account balances shown on the adjusted trial balance. The closing entries for Maple Limited follow.

---

[12]Financial statements may also be prepared using a worksheet, as discussed in Appendix A. A **worksheet** is used to accumulate and organize the information required to prepare financial statements.

[13]Some corporations (especially those that declare dividends quarterly) record the declaration of a dividend by debiting a **Dividends Declared** account, while others charge Retained Earnings directly. Dividends Declared is a nominal account and is presented on the statement of retained earnings. It normally has a debit balance and is closed directly to Retained Earnings at the end of the accounting period:

Dec. 31 Retained Earnings	XXX	
Dividends Declared		XXX
(To close the Dividends Declared account.)		

In sole proprietorships and partnerships, Drawing accounts are used instead of Dividends Declared. Drawing accounts are closed directly to Owners' Capital at the end of the accounting period.

Dec. 31 Sales	523 000	
Interest Revenue	600	
Rent Revenue	1 600	
Income Summary		525 200
(*To close revenue accounts.*)		

Dec. 31 Income Summary	480 400	
Cost of Goods Sold		200 000
Sales Salaries Expense		78 000
Advertising Expense		24 000
Freight-out		6 000
Miscellaneous Selling Expenses		5 141
Officers' Salaries Expense		76 000
Professional Services		23 000
Utilities Expense		8 244
Interest Expense		1 800
Insurance Expense		900
Depreciation Expense—Building		2 000
Depreciation Expense—Office Equipment		12 000
Bad Debts Expense		2 615
Miscellaneous Administrative Expenses		5 500
Income Tax Expense		35 200
(*To close expense accounts.*)		

Dec. 31 Income Summary	44 800	
Retained Earnings		44 800
(*To close the Income Summary account.*)		

Although compound entries were used to illustrate the closing process, it would also have been appropriate to use a series of simple entries. Note that after closing entries are posted, zero balances will exist in each revenue account, each expense account, and the Income Summary clearing account. Furthermore, the ending balance in the Retained Earnings account is $79 015 ($34 215 + $44 800). Through no coincidence, this is the same figure reported for Retained Earnings on Maple's balance sheet dated December 31, 1995.

Step 10. Prepare a Post-Closing Trial Balance (Optional)

After journalizing and posting the closing entries, the accountant usually prepares a **post-closing trial balance**. This is simply a listing of general ledger accounts and their balances after the closing entries have been made. The post-closing trial balance therefore consists entirely of real accounts. Its purpose is to provide evidence that equal debits and credits exist in the general ledger after closing. The post-closing trial balance is not a required step in the accounting cycle, because its purpose is solely error detection.

Step 11. Prepare Reversing Entries (Optional)

The final step in the accounting cycle is to journalize and post **reversing entries**. These entries bear the first date of the new accounting period. They are called reversing entries because they are the reverse or opposite of certain adjusting entries made at the end of

Exhibit 6.3 Preparation of Financial Statements

Maple Limited
INCOME STATEMENT
For the Year Ended December 31, 1995

Sales revenue			
Sales			$523 000
Cost of goods sold			
Merchandise inventory, Jan. 1, 1995		$ 57 606	
Purchases	$187 000		
Less: Purchase returns	2 000		
Purchase allowances	2 500		
Purchase discounts	3 600		
Add: Freight-in	7 250		
Net purchases		186 150	
Cost of goods available for sale		243 756	
Merchandise inventory, Dec. 31, 1995		43 756	
Cost of goods sold			200 000
Gross margin on sales			323 000
Operating expenses			
Selling expenses			
Sales salaries	78 000		
Advertising	24 000		
Freight-out	6 000		
Miscellaneous	5 141	113 141	
Administrative expenses			
Officers' salaries	76 000		
Professional services	23 000		
Utilities	8 244		
Insurance	900		
Depreciation of building	2 000		
Depreciation of office equipment	12 000		
Bad debts	2 615		
Miscellaneous	5 500	130 259	
Total operating expenses			243 400
Income from operations			79 600
Other revenues			
Interest		600	
Rent		1 600	2 200
			81 800
Other expense			
Interest			1 800
Income before taxes			80 000
Income tax expense ($80 000 × 0.44)			35 200
Net income			$44 800
Earnings per share ($44 800 ÷ 10 000 shares outstanding)			$4.48

Maple Limited
STATEMENT OF RETAINED EARNINGS*
For the Year Ended December 31, 1995

Retained earnings, Jan. 1, 1995	$ 34 215
Add: Net income	44 800**
Retained earnings, Dec. 31, 1995	$79 015

Maple Limited
BALANCE SHEET
December 31, 1995

Assets

Current Assets

Cash		$ 21 079	
Accounts receivable	$ 60 000		
Less: Allowance for doubtful accounts	3 115	56 885	
Note receivable		10 000	
Interest receivable		600	
Merchandise inventory		43 756	
Prepaid insurance		300	
Total current assets			$132 620

Plant assets

Land		40 000	
Building	100 000		
Less: Accumulated depreciation	12 000	88 000	
Office equipment	120 000		
Less: Accumulated depreciation	36 000	84 000	
Total plant assets			212 000
Total assets			$344 620

Liabilities and Shareholders' Equity

Current Liabilities

Accounts payable	$ 38 405	
Interest payable	1 800	
Income tax payable	35 200	
Unearned rent revenue	3 200	
Total current liabilities		$78 605

Long-Term Liabilities

Notes payable		72 000
Total liabilities		150 605

Shareholders' Equity

Share capital		
Common shares, no-par value, 10 000 shares issued and outstanding	115 000	
Retained earnings	79 015†	
Total shareholders' equity		194 015
Total liabilities and shareholders' equity		$344 620

*Maple Limited declared no dividends during 1995. If dividends had been declared, they would be subtracted on the retained earnings statement, as discussed and illustrated in Chapter 4.

**This number was obtained from the income statement.

†This number was obtained from the statement of retained earnings.

the preceding period. Reversing entries do not mean that the adjusting entries reversed were unnecessary or inaccurate.

The sole purpose of reversing entries is to *simplify* the subsequent recording of certain kinds of recurring transactions. Because their only purpose is simplification, reversing entries are optional. To illustrate, recall that on December 31, 1995, Maple Limited had outstanding a $72 000, ten-year, 10 percent note payable, with interest payable annually on September 30. In Exhibit 6.4, we summarize selected accounting entries pertaining to the note under alternative assumptions about reversing entries.

Under either assumption, the interest expense recorded for the first nine months of 1996 is $5400 ($1800 × 3). Therefore, either assumption results in the same amounts on the 1996 financial statements. Making the reversing entry on January 1, however, eliminates the need to allocate the September 30 interest payment between the amount currently expensed and the amount previously accrued. This may seem like a trivial simplification for Maple Limited, with its single note payable. However, some companies have many notes payable. Moreover, the recording of interest payments is often assigned to an employee who has little accounting experience. Under these circumstances, a qualified accountant may well decide to make reversing entries to simplify the recording of interest payments by the employee. At the end of the period, the accountant can then analyze each note payable and formulate the appropriate adjusting entry for accrued interest.

The following categories of adjusting entries may be reversed: (1) adjusting entries to record accruals (either revenues or expenses), and (2) adjusting entries to record deferrals when the original amount to which the adjusting entry pertains was recorded in a nominal account. For example, an adjusting entry debiting Prepaid Insurance and crediting Insurance Expense may be reversed, because it is a deferral in which the original amount was recorded in a nominal account (i.e., Insurance Expense). In contrast, an adjusting entry debiting Insurance Expense and crediting Prepaid Insurance should not be reversed, because although the adjusting entry is a deferral, the original amount was recorded in a real account (i.e., Prepaid Insurance). Reversing entries should not record the cost of an asset that has expired, nor should they reinstate liabilities that no longer exist.

A company may choose to reverse any number of adjusting entries as long as the entries fall into one of the two categories discussed above. Because reversing entries are optional, companies should not make them unless the benefits of doing so exceed the costs.

Conceptual Considerations/Concluding Remarks

Of all the steps in the accounting cycle, the preparation of adjusting entries typically gives intermediate accounting students the most trouble. The following broad principles from the theoretical model in Chapter 2 are important to remember when preparing adjusting entries:

1. **Revenue realization.** Under the accrual basis of accounting, certain adjusting entries are necessary to ensure that revenues will be recognized in the period in which they are earned, regardless of when the cash inflows associated with the revenues occur.
2. **Matching.** Under the accrual basis of accounting, certain adjusting entries are necessary to ensure that expenses will be recognized in the period in which they are incurred, regardless of when the cash outflows associated with the expenses occur.

Exhibit 6.4   Effect of Reversing Entries

	Assumptions				
Event	**Accrued Interest Expense Is Reversed**			**Accrued Interest Expense Is Not Reversed**	
Dec. 31, 1995					
Adjusting entry to accrue interest expense	Interest Expense 1800			Interest Expense 1800	
	Interest Payable	1800		Interest Payable	1800
Dec. 31, 1995					
Closing entry applicable to accrued interest expense	Income Summary 1800			Income Summary 1800	
	Interest Expense	1800		Interest Expense	1800
Jan. 1, 1996					
Reversing entry	Interest Payable 1800			No entry	
	Interest Expense	1800			
Sept. 30, 1996					
Payment of interest	Interest Expense 7200			Interest Expense 5400	
	Cash	7200		Interest Payable 1800	
				Cash	7200

Together, the revenue realization and matching principles are the essence of the accrual basis of accounting. The need to implement these principles explains why adjusting entries are necessary at the end of every accounting period.

Key Points

1. A transaction is an event that changes a company's financial position and can be measured with objectivity. (Objective 1)
2. Source documents serve as evidence that transactions have occurred. (Objective 1)
3. A journal is a chronological record of transactions. A company should always have a general journal and may have one or more special journals. (Objective 3)
4. Posting involves transferring information from journals to accounts in a ledger. A company should always maintain a general ledger and may have one or more subsidiary ledgers. (Objective 4)
5. The unadjusted trial balance provides evidence that total debits in a company's general ledger equal total credits. It also provides information that helps to formulate adjusting entries. (Objective 5)
6. Adjusting entries permit accurate measurement of earnings and financial position on the accrual basis. (Objective 6)
7. Adjusting entries are based on the revenue realization and matching principles. (Objective 6)
8. An adjusted trial balance provides a convenient listing of account balances that may be used to prepare the financial statements. (Objective 7)
9. The accountant usually prepares financial statements in the following order: income statement, statement of retained earnings, balance sheet, statement of changes in financial position. (Objective 8)
10. Closing entries transfer nominal account balances to owners' equity. After closing, all nominal accounts should have zero balances. (Objective 9)
11. A post-closing trial balance consists entirely of real accounts. (Objective 10)
12. Accountants use reversing entries to simplify the subsequent recording of certain kinds of recurring transactions, such as interest payments. (Objective 11)

The Other Costs of Capital

Beyond the financial aspects, raising capital involves changes to relations among owners, management, bankers, and other investors. In turn, these changes can result in strategic and operational shifts for small and medium-sized enterprises.

Every company owner, corporate treasurer and chief financial officer is concerned about the cost of capital. The cost-of-capital calculations contained in theoretical models focus primarily on the financial costs in determining the "optimal" (i.e., lowest cost) combination of debt and equity for a company's capital structure. For small and medium-sized enterprises, however, the range of options assumed in theoretical models is often not available as these organizations have limited access to public equity, bond, debt, and money markets. These companies usually have two basic choices when raising capital; bank debt and equity.

Each of these choices has associated costs of both a financial (in terms of interest or dividend requirements) and a non-financial nature. Companies usually focus on the financial costs of any given capital-raising option, but it is often the non-financial costs which can more profoundly impact on an organization and its on-going activities and operations. The nature of these non-financial costs must therefore be understood and factored into the decision-making process of any capital-raising initiative.

The requirements of banks and other financial institutions, for both operating and term loans, are relatively basic: security and serviceability. The costs involved, in addition to the interest rate, can include legal fees, commitment fees, monitoring fees, administration fees, work fees, prepayment fees, and other similar charges levied by financial institutions to compensate for the costs of reviewing and administering loan facilities. The range and magnitude of these charges have increased dramatically in recent years. Borrowers should anticipate fees of between one and three per cent of the amount borrowed when budgeting for the cost of new debt facilities.

The Other Costs

The more significant costs, and those which are much more difficult to quantify, relate to the raising of equity. For companies that can't access the public markets, equity must be raised from private sources. Although there can be financial costs associated with the process, the more significant costs are the potential implications which the selling of equity to an outside investor can have for the company and its owners and management.

The first challenge which must be addressed when the need for equity has been identified is that of sourcing. Depending on the amount required, the options can include friends and relatives; corporate investors who may have some strategic desire to obtain a window on the firm's industry or market; or large institutional pools of capital such as venture capital funds or pension funds and insurance companies that may desire to diversify their investment portfolios with positions in smaller, private companies with above-average growth potential. There are many potential benefits to a company in having such investors. But there are also aspects of the relationships which must be clearly understood from the outset in order to minimize possible misunderstandings and the resulting aggravation and inherent costs. Friends and relatives often invest for personal reasons. As a result, they are usually flexible with regard to the manner in which the relationship is structured and documented.

The relationship with a corporate investor will be influenced by the strategic purpose of the investment. But it will likely require some aspect of a company's operations, be it research, production, marketing or distribution, to become more closely aligned with the corporate investor. The nature of the relationship with an institutional investor is not as easily defined. As a result, the costs to a company can be significant if an investor's interests and desires are not clearly understood at the outset of any relationship.

An investor's objective is to maximize the return from any investment. In order to accomplish this, a number of steps must be taken, and issues resolved, before an investor will be prepared to go forward. Most investors will undertake a detailed investigation of any company under consideration for investment. In addition to meeting with management, touring facilities, examining and evaluating historic operating and financial information, and undertaking market research and competitive analysis studies, investors will require a detailed business plan. This plan should, in simple terms, outline where the company has come from, where it is going and how it is planning to get there.

Continued

A business plan should outline an organization's history, the products or services it provides, the markets it operates in, the major competitors in those markets, and what the company's competitive advantage is vis-à-vis those competitors. It should also outline the opportunities that are perceived to exist in the market and management's strategy to address those opportunities.

The plan should also detail the experience and abilities of the senior management team and illustrate that all of the functional skills required to execute the plan are in place. Historic financial information (five years if available), prepared by the company's accountant should be included. Included too should be an outline of the amount of capital required and its intended use, and detailed financial forecasts outlining the anticipated performance of the company subsequent to the investment.

Preparing the business plan, and responding to an investor's other questions and requirements, will involve a considerable investment of time and resources by a company and its management, but are essential if capital is to be attracted.

Valuation of the Company

In most new investment situations, the issue that usually causes most disagreements, and the one which represents the most obvious "cost," is the valuation of the company. In many cases, the owners of a company have a different perception about the company's value than do outside investors. In addition to an investor's basic objective of maximizing financial return, there are a number of other considerations involved in any valuation process.

Investors must be comfortable that the potential return on an investment is sufficient to justify the associated level of risk. The higher the perceived risk, the higher the required return. This risk/return analysis takes into consideration the growth prospects for the company, its competitive environment, the size of the available market, and the opportunity cost of the funds to the investor with respect to other investment options that may be available. If, for example, analysis indicates that the best a company can achieve, assuming all goes according to plan, is a doubling of its revenues and earnings over the next five years, the amount of equity required to achieve a desired rate of return would be much larger than for a company that could, again in the best case scenario, achieve revenue and earnings growth of ten times over the same time frame.

Another consideration that enters the valuation process is the existing level of investment in the business. Most investors will attempt to give full value to a company as it exists immediately prior to an investment. This will reflect the company's worth today which may, or may not, reflect the amount of previous investment in the company. Investors are not prepared to pay for forecasted earnings, as they believe that, without their investment, these future earnings would not be achievable. Nor are they prepared to pay for past sins or mistakes. If money was misspent in the past a new investor will not ascribe any value to such a use of funds. Conversely if a company's earnings, market position, or assets indicate a valuation in excess of what a company's balance sheet would suggest is warranted, most investors are prepared to give the existing shareholders value for these achievements. Investors are, for the most part, prepared to value a company at what it is worth today and then go together into the future with the existing owners and management.

Structuring ROI

An investor's return analysis will also take into consideration the method by which, and the time frame within which, they will be able to realize on the investment and generate the return. There are a limited number of ways investor liquidity can be achieved. Each way has potential implications and costs to a company and its shareholders. Some investors will include as part of an investment agreement a put option. A put option gives the investor the ability to compel the company to repurchase its equity after a certain period of time at a predetermined price (e.g., a certain price/earnings multiple, net book value or some multiple thereof, a certain percentage increase in the original amount invested, etc.). If an investor exercises a put, it is incumbent on the company to raise the capital required to repurchase the shares. This could necessitate raising additional debt or reselling the equity to another investor. However the repurchase is accomplished, the company will likely need to reconfigure its financial and capital structure. Such a process could, of course, involve significant financial and non-financial costs.

Other liquidity options include taking the company public, thus providing investors an exit through the public markets, or selling the company to a third party. Going public involves significant initial and on-going costs. In Canada, it is not a realistic option for most small and medium-sized companies, given the structure of the public market investors. These parties are more inclined to invest

Continued

in larger companies for reasons of volatility, control, and market float.

The process of going public also has significant associated costs. The president of one medium-sized Canadian company that recently completed an initial public offering (IPO) on the Toronto and Montreal Stock Exchanges estimated the out-of-pocket expenses directly related to the process to be approximately 10% of the amount raised ($2.5 million on a $25 million issue). These costs included the underwriting fees, the accounting and legal fees, printing expenses, "road show" presentation costs, and listing fees. In addition, the process is very time-consuming and diverts attention from the day-to-day operation of the business. This particular executive noted in retrospect that the decision was not entirely rational.

If a company does go public, there are numerous on-going costs associated with listing, reporting and shareholder relations. (Another medium-sized TSE-listed company estimates the on-going costs of being public are approximately $250,000 per year.) In addition, the reporting and disclosure requirements of a public company put increases pressure on management, force a focus on quarterly results, and require attention to be paid to the price of the stock and the public's perception of the company. All of these can have significant associated costs.

Controlling the Company and a New Relationship

The option of selling the company, or part of it, to a third party could require control of the company to change hands. This could have significant negative implications for management. If control doesn't change, there will still likely be a difference in the nature of the relationship, as the new investor will likely have taken the position for strategic reasons. As a result, the new investor will want to exploit some aspects of the company's technology, production process, products, markets, or distribution and service systems. Moreover, modified reporting streams and formats, or physical relocation of facilities or employees may be required. Once again, all of these possibilities have associated financial as well as non-financial costs.

Both going public and sale to a third party can have significant benefits to an organization, but they can also have significant explicit and implicit costs. Before any investment, therefore, there should be a clear understanding of both parties' objectives and intentions. If the investor requires liquidity within a certain period of time, this should be known in advance as it could influence the strategic direction taken and decisions made.

If the original shareholders desire to take the company public, or cash out within a certain time frame, this should also be discussed as it will influence the manner in which the relationship is structured. The owners may want to pass the company on to their children or management. This may limit an investor's options and, if the issue isn't discussed and resolved prior to the investment, difficulties could arise for both parties in the future.

A number of other issues in the on-going relationship between an investor and a company could cause problems. It is important that these issues also be resolved prior to any investment. The method by which this is accomplished is through a shareholders' agreement. A shareholders' agreement reflects the negotiations between the parties, and documents the nature of the relationship and the obligations and expectations of each party. The areas addressed can include the level of shareholder compensation, capital expenditures, the timing and formating of financial budgeting and reporting, dividend policy, restrictions on the raising of future debt and equity and other, similar issues relating to the financing and operating of the company. In addition, most shareholders' agreements will also provide the investor the right to appoint one or more representatives to the company's board of directors. This will allow the investor to monitor performance and contribute to the strategic decision-making process.

Each of the issues addressed in the shareholders' agreement will have some impact on the company's operations, as any new initiatives, or change in strategic direction, will have to be undertaken in consultation with the outside shareholders. Investors are usually willing to consider deviations from the agreement but a clear explanation must be provided as to the reason that the change is felt to be of benefit to the company.

Investors have made their initial investment based on a certain set of expectations and beliefs. The shareholders' agreement provides the only mechanism by which these expectations can be quantified, qualified and controlled. Investors invest in management and, for the most part, believe in the management team's ability to run the company. Investors do, however, want to maintain some control over the financial resources of an organization and have some ability to monitor performance relative to plan.

Although the costs of this type of capital can be significant, in terms of both actual financial requirements and other, more difficult-to-quantify costs, the benefits can be

Continued

substantial. To minimize the potential "costs" of raising equity capital, it is important that a company investigate potential investors with as much "due diligence" as investors use in evaluating the company and its management. An investor's objectives must be compatible with the company's. The company and its management must feel comfortable that they can work with the investor to achieve those objectives. Money is a commodity. To minimize the costs and maximize the returns when raising capital, a company should identify a partner it will be able to work with over the long term, and one that can bring more to the company than just a chequebook. In this way, the "costs" will be minimized and the returns on the capital will be maximized.

Source: Reprinted from an article in *CMA Magazine*, by Edward G. Anderson, "The Other Costs of Capital" (December/January 1993), pp. 19–22.

Appendix A: The Worksheet

Using a Worksheet to Prepare Annual Statements

A **worksheet** is a multicolumn sheet of paper that accountants often use to accumulate and organize the information required to prepare financial statements. Worksheets facilitate the preparation of financial statements by (1) providing a place where adjusting entries can be made informally before they are journalized and posted, (2) providing an orderly means whereby each account can be classified according to the financial statement in which it will appear, and (3) providing a balancing mechanism that helps to uncover accounting errors. Worksheets are never published, because they are not formal financial statements.

In practice, many different worksheet formats exist. The format used in any given case depends on individual or company preferences. A twelve-column worksheet for Maple Limited is shown in Exhibit 6.5. This worksheet includes the same basic data presented earlier in the chapter. Maple Limited's worksheet consists of six pairs of amount columns. Sometimes accountants reduce the worksheet's size by eliminating the adjusted trial balance columns or by combining the retained earnings and balance sheet columns. The financial statement balances, of course, are not affected by worksheet size. Maple Limited's worksheet has no columns for the statement of changes in financial position. Preparing this statement may require a separate worksheet, which we explain in Chapter 22. The following steps are required to prepare the worksheet:

1. Enter the unadjusted trial balance in the first pair of amount columns and determine that the columns balance.
2. Enter all adjusting entries, except income taxes, in the adjustments columns. Then subtotal these columns to determine that they balance. In Exhibit 6.5, the adjusting entries are identified by small letters (a–g) and are presented in the order in which they are discussed in the chapter. Note that when an adjustment requires an account that is not listed in the unadjusted trial balance, the new account is listed below the unadjusted trial balance totals. When a worksheet is used, the adjusting entries are usually made informally in the adjustments columns before they are journalized and posted. Errors can then be found and corrected before entering them into the formal accounting records.

Exhibit 6.5

Maple Limited
WORKSHEET
For the Year Ended December 31, 1995

Accounts	Unadjusted Trial Balance Dr.	Unadjusted Trial Balance Cr.	Adjustments Dr.	Adjustments Cr.	Adjusted Trial Balance Dr.	Adjusted Trial Balance Cr.	Income Statement Dr.	Income Statement Cr.	Retained Earnings Dr.	Retained Earnings Cr.	Balance Sheet Dr.	Balance Sheet Cr.
Cash	21 079				21 079						21 079	
Accounts receivable	60 000				60 000						60 000	
Allowance for doubtful accounts		500		(f) 2 615		3 115						3 115
Notes Receivable	10 000				10 000						10 000	
Merchandise inventory, Jan. 1, 1995	57 606			(g) 57 606								
Prepaid insurance	1 200			(d) 900	300						300	
Land	40 000				40 000						40 000	
Building	100 000				100 000						100 000	
Accumulated depreciation—building		10 000		(e) 2 000		12 000						12 000
Office equipment	120 000				120 000						120 000	
Accumulated depreciation—office equipment		24 000		(e) 12 000		36 000						36 000
Accounts payable		38 405				38 405						38 405
Unearned rent revenue		4 800 (c)	1 600			3 200						3 200
Long-term note payable		72 000				72 000						72 000
Common shares		115 000				115 000						115 000
Retained earnings, Jan. 1, 1995		34 215				34 215				34 215		
Sales		523 000				523 000		523 000				
Purchases	187 000			(g) 187 000								
Purchase returns		2 000	(g) 2 000									
Purchase allowances		2 500	(g) 2 500									
Purchase discounts		3 600	(g) 3 600									
Freight-in	7 250			(g) 7 250								
Sales salaries expense	78 000				78 000		78 000					
Advertising expense	24 000				24 000		24 000					
Freight-out	6 000				6 000		6 000					

Continued

Exhibit 6.5 Continued

Account	Trial Balance Dr	Trial Balance Cr	Adjustments Dr	Adjustments Cr	Adjusted Trial Balance Dr	Adjusted Trial Balance Cr	Income Statement Dr	Income Statement Cr	Balance Sheet Dr	Balance Sheet Cr
Miscellaneous selling expenses	5 141				5 141		5 141			
Officers' salaries expense	76 000				76 000		76 000			
Professional services	23 000				23 000		23 000			
Utilities expense	8 244				8 244		8 244			
Miscellaneous administrative expenses	5 500				5 500		5 500			
	830 020	830 020								
Interest receivable			(a) 600		600				600	
Interest revenue				(a) 600		600		600		
Interest expense			(b) 1 800		1 800		1 800			
Interest payable				(b) 1 800		1 800				1 800
Rent revenue				(c) 1 600		1 600		1 600		
Insurance expense			(d) 900		900		900			
Depreciation expense—building			(e) 12 000		12 000		12 000			
Depreciation expense—office equipment			2 000		2 000		2 000			
Bad debts expense			(f) 2 615		2 615		2 615			
Merchandise inventory, Dec. 31, 1995			(g) 43 756		43 756				43 756	
Cost of goods sold			(g) 200 000		200 000		200 000			
			273 371	273 371	840 935	840 935	445 200	525 200		
Income tax expense			(h) 35 200		35 200		35 200			
Income tax payable				(h) 35 200		35 200				35 200
			308 571	308 571	876 135	876 135				
Net income							44 800			44 800
							525 200	525 200		
							79 015	79 015		
Retained earnings, Dec. 31, 1995							79 015	79 015	395 735	395 735

3. Determine the adjusted account balances by combining the unadjusted trial balance amounts with the adjustments amounts. Extend the adjusted balances in the adjusted trial balance columns. Subtotal these columns to determine that they balance.
4. Extend each debit account balance in the adjusted trial balance to the debit column of the financial statement in which the balance will appear. Similarly, extend each credit account balance to the credit column of the financial statement in which the balance will appear.
5. Subtotal the income statement columns. The difference between the columns is the *pretax* income or loss for the period. For Maple Limited, the difference is $80 000 ($525 200 − $445 200), and it represents pretax income.
6. Compute the income tax expense by applying the appropriate income tax rate to the pretax income. The income tax expense for Maple Limited is $80 000 × 0.44 = $35 200.
7. Enter the income tax accrual in the adjustments columns. Then extend the income tax expense balance to the debit column of the adjusted trial balance and the income statement. Extend the income tax payable balance to the credit column of the adjusted trial balance and the balance sheet. Total the adjustments columns and the adjusted trial balance columns.
8. Enter net income in the income statement debit column to balance the two income statement columns. The balancing figure is also entered in the retained earnings credit column.
9. Subtotal the retained earnings columns and enter the balance, which is ending retained earnings, in the retained earnings debit column and the balance sheet credit column.
10. Total the balance sheet columns and determine that they balance.

Maple Limited's financial statements may now be prepared directly from the worksheet. These statements would match those illustrated in the chapter. After the statements are prepared, the adjusting entries are journalized and posted on the basis of information shown in the adjustments columns of the worksheet. To complete the accounting cycle, the accountant would close the nominal accounts as illustrated in the chapter. Finally, the accountant may prepare a post-closing trial balance and reversing entries.

Using a Worksheet to Prepare Interim Statements

Most companies formally prepare adjusting and closing entries only at the end of each fiscal year. Nevertheless, companies typically desire interim (e.g., monthly or quarterly) financial statements in addition to annual statements. At the end of each interim period, the accountant enters the necessary adjustments on a worksheet similar to the one for Maple Limited and does not formally record them in journals or ledgers. Adjustments shown on the year-end worksheet then pertain to the entire year; these amounts are journalized and posted to the accounts in the general ledger.

Because the balance sheet represents financial position at a point in time, the accountant obtains information about assets and equities directly from the balance sheet columns of an interim worksheet. Conversely, revenue and expense amounts on an interim worksheet are cumulative from the beginning of the fiscal year. Therefore, to determine revenues and expenses associated with a particular interim period, the accountant must subtract revenues and expenses attributable to previous interim periods from the corresponding amounts shown on the worksheet. To illustrate, assume that a company closes its books each December 31. To prepare an income statement for March, the accountant must subtract the revenues and expenses for January and February from the corresponding amounts shown on the March 31 worksheet. To prepare an income statement for the second quarter, the accountant must subtract the revenues and expenses for the first quarter from the corresponding amounts shown on the June 30 worksheet. Like the income statement, the retained earnings statement pertains to a certain period of time. It is therefore prepared like the income statement.

Appendix B: Special Journals

The general journal format we use throughout this book de-emphasizes certain procedural details and enables us to better illustrate how to apply basic accounting concepts and principles. In practice, most businesses have several special journals in addition to a general journal. Special journals typically process most of a company's transactions. This Appendix will review some of the more common types of special journals.

A special journal is used to initially record a single type of transaction that often recurs. A company may create a special journal to handle virtually any kind of routine transaction. However, it still needs a general journal to record transactions that do not fit the intended purpose of one of its special journals. Typically, adjusting entries, correcting entries, closing entries, reversing entries (if used), and entries for transactions that occur infrequently, such as the sale of common shares in exchange for land, are recorded in the general journal.

What are the advantages of special journals? First, special journals save time in journalizing and posting transactions. When journalizing, there is no need to rewrite account titles; when posting, transaction totals rather than individual amounts may be transferred to general ledger accounts. By simplifying the journalizing and posting requirements for routine transactions, special journals tend to reduce the number of errors made. Moreover, errors are easier to pinpoint once they have occurred.

Another use for special journals is to permit a division of labour within the accounting department. Instead of several people attempting to use the general journal simultaneously, certain individuals can assume responsibility for one or more special journals. This often enables the company to better utilize employees with limited accounting experience. Such separation of duties also strengthens the company's internal control system.

Each business must determine which types and formats of special journals it needs based on the nature of its transactions. The types and formats presented below are for illustrative purposes only.

Sales Journal

The sales journal is a chronological listing of all *credit* sales of merchandise. For a company that makes 5000 credit sales a month, a sales journal relieves the company of (1) recording 5000 general journal entries debiting Accounts Receivable and crediting Sales, and (2) posting these entries individually to the general ledger. A sales invoice or ticket typically initiates an entry in a sales journal.

An abbreviated sales journal of Star-Bright, Inc., is presented in Exhibit 6.6. Special journals are normally arranged in columns. Star-Bright's sales journal contains five

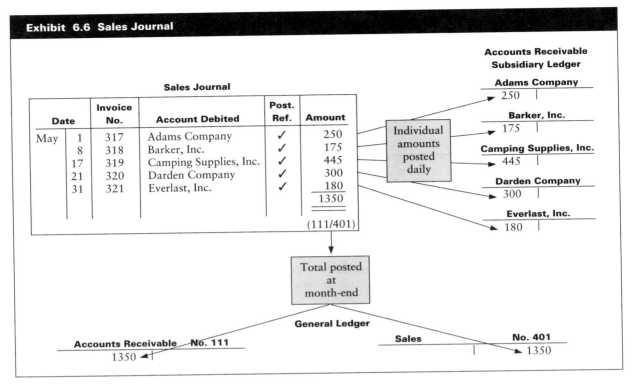

Exhibit 6.6 Sales Journal

columns. We assume in this example that the company's credit terms are 2/10, n/30.[14] If credit terms varied by customer, a journal column could easily be added to record the terms of each sale.

The process of posting from a sales journal is depicted by the arrows. Individual amounts in the sales journal are posted daily as debits to the appropriate accounts in the accounts receivable subsidiary ledger. Daily posting provides up-to-date credit records and facilitates the billing process. The check marks in the posting reference column indicate that individual accounts have been posted. At the end of each month, the amount column *total* is posted to the general ledger as a debit to the Accounts Receivable control account and a credit to Sales. The notation (111/401) at the bottom of the amount column indicates that general ledger accounts bearing these numbers have been posted. Note that if each sale were recorded in the general journal instead of the sales journal, each debit and credit would have to be separately posted to the general ledger. This would be time-consuming and expensive. As the sales journal illustrates, posting any journal involves making equal debits and credits in the general ledger. Moreover, the sum of the debits (or credits) posted to subsidiary ledger accounts should equal the amount posted as a debit (or credit) to the related control account.

Cash Receipts Journal

The cash receipts journal records all cash receipts, including those resulting from cash sales. Star-Bright's cash receipts journal in Exhibit 6.7 consists of nine columns, five of

---

[14]In other words, a customer who pays within 10 days after the invoice date may deduct 2 percent from the invoice price; a customer who does not pay within the 10-day discount period must pay the gross invoice amount within 30 days after the invoice date.

Exhibit 6.7 Cash Receipts Journal

Cash Receipts Journal

Date		Account Credited	Explanation	Post. Ref.	Cash Debit	Sales Discount Debit	Accounts Receivable Credit	Sales Credit	Sundry Accounts Credit
May	3	Sales	Cash sales		500			500	
	11	Adams							
		Company	Payment in full	✓	245	5	250		
	14	Notes Payable	90-day, 10% loan from						
			City National Bank	211	2000				2000
	27	Barker, Inc.	Payment in full	✓	175		175		
	31	Darden							
		Company	Payment in full	✓	294	6	300		
					3214	11	725	500	2000
					(101)	(402)	(111)	(401)	(X)

Total debits = $3225   Total credits = $3225

which are used to record amounts. The following posting features of the cash receipts journal are noteworthy:

1. Column *totals* for cash, sales discounts, and sales are posted at the end of each month. Individual amounts are not posted. The account numbers posted are inserted parenthetically at the bottom of these columns to indicate that posting has occurred.
2. The term "sundry accounts" means various individual accounts. Therefore, sundry accounts are posted *individually*. The account number 211 in the posting reference column indicates that the Notes Payable account has been posted. The (X) notation at the bottom of the Sundry Accounts column signifies that the column total is not posted.
3. Amounts in the accounts receivable column are posted *individually and in total*. Individual amounts, referenced by the check marks, are posted daily as credits to the customer accounts in the accounts receivable subsidiary ledger. The column total is posted at the end of the month as a credit to the Accounts Receivable control account in the general ledger. The notation (111) at the bottom of the column indicates that the column total has been posted.

Purchases Journal

Some companies use a purchases journal to record *all* credit purchases; others use it to record only credit purchases of *merchandise*. A purchase invoice normally initiates each entry in a purchases journal. Star-Bright's purchases journal in Exhibit 6.8 consists of six columns; its purpose is confined to recording credit acquisitions of merchandise. To record all credit acquisitions in its purchases journal, the company would have to add columns to record items such as supplies and equipment.

Individual amounts in the purchases journal are posted daily as credits to the appropriate accounts in the accounts payable subsidiary ledger. The check marks in the posting reference column indicate that individual accounts have been posted. The column *total*

Exhibit 6.8 Purchases Journal

Purchases Journal

Date		Account Credited	Invoice Date	Terms	Post. Ref.	Amount
May	1	Modern Supply Company	Apr. 29	2/10, n/30	✔	200
	16	Dresser, Inc.	May 15	2/10, n/60	✔	550
	18	Office Products Distributors	May 16	n/30	✔	450
	24	Ebenezer, Inc.	May 23	1/10, n/30	✔	196
	31	Wilson Manufacturing Company	May 29	2/10, n/30	✔	254
						1650
						(501/201)

is posted to the general ledger at the end of each month as a debit to the Purchases account and a credit to the Accounts Payable control account. The notation (501/201) at the bottom of the amount column signifies a monthly posting.

Cash Payments Journal

The cash payments journal records all cash payments, including those resulting from cash purchases. Star-Bright's cash payments journal in Exhibit 6.9 consists of ten columns, five of which are amount columns. Significant posting features in the cash payments journal are described below.

1. Column *totals* for cash, purchase discounts, and purchases are posted at the end of each month. The account numbers posted are inserted parenthetically at the bottom of these columns to indicate that posting has occurred.
2. Amounts in the sundry accounts column are posted *individually*. The account numbers 131 and 517 in the posting reference column indicate postings made to the Prepaid Insurance and Advertising Expense accounts, respectively. The (X) notation at the bottom of the sundry accounts column signifies that the column total is not posted.
3. Amounts in the accounts payable column are posted *individually and in total*. Individual amounts, referenced by the check marks, are posted daily as debits to the supplier accounts in the accounts payable subsidiary ledger. The column total is posted at the end of the month as a debit to the Accounts Payable control account in the general ledger. The (201) notation at the bottom of the column indicates that the column total has been posted.

Other Special Journals

We have illustrated only the four most common special journals. Remember, however, that companies may use other types.

For example, many companies use a voucher system, in which a voucher is prepared for each transaction that requires a cash payment. A **voucher** is a source document containing detailed information about a liability and its payment. Each voucher is recorded in a journal called a **voucher register**. This journal is similar to an expanded purchases journal and thus replaces the purchases journal. Cheques are drawn only in payment of

Exhibit 6.9 Cash Payments Journal

Cash Payments Journal

Date		Cheque No.	Account Debited	Explanation	Post. Ref.	Cash Credit	Purchase Discount Credit	Accounts Payable Debit	Purchases Debit	Sundry Accounts Debit
May	2	477	Purchases	Cash purchases		300			300	
	8	478	Modern Supply Company	Payment in full	✓	196	4	200		
	12	479	Prepaid Insurance	Fire insurance policy	131	450				450
	25	480	Dresser, Inc.	Payment in full	✓	539	11	550		
	31	481	Advertising	WACK Radio Station	517	250				250
						1735	15	750	300	700
						(101)	(502)	(201)	(501)	(X)

Total credits = $1750   Total debits = 1750

approved vouchers. A **cheque register**, which is merely a modified cash payments journal, replaces the cash payments journal in a voucher system.

A **payroll register** is a widely used journal for recording payroll information. A **sales returns and allowances journal** and a **purchases returns and allowances journal** are often used by companies that have many such transactions.

___

Questions

Q6.1 Describe the purpose of the accounting cycle and list in sequence the steps involved. *Page 231*

Q6.2 Describe the nature of source documents and list five examples.

Q6.3 State whether the normal balance in each of the following accounts is debit or credit:

(a) Prepaid Insurance. −
(b) Wages Expense. −
(c) Sales. +
(d) Accounts Payable. +
(e) Gain on Sale of Land. +
(f) Accumulated Depreciation. +
(g) Discount on Bonds Payable. −
(h) Common Shares. +
(i) Dividends. −
(j) Loss on Sale of Investments. −
(k) Sales Returns. −

Q6.4 Does a debit increase or decrease the balance in each of the following types of accounts?

(a) Revenue. −
(b) Liability. −
(c) Expense. +
(d) Asset +
(e) Owners' equity. −

Q6.5 What is a journal? Why might a company want to use several special journals?

Q6.6 Give an example of a general journal entry to record each of the following:

(a) An increase in an asset and an increase in a liability.
(b) A decrease in a liability and a decrease in an asset.
(c) An increase in an expense and a decrease in an asset.

(d) An increase in an asset and an increase in a revenue.

(e) An increase in an asset and an increase in owners' equity.

Q6.7 What is a general ledger? Why is posting to general ledger accounts necessary?

Q6.8 Distinguish between real, nominal, and mixed accounts.

Q6.9 What is a subsidiary ledger and a control account? Why might a company want to use several subsidiary ledgers?

Q6.10 What are the major purposes of an unadjusted trial balance? Does an unadjusted trial balance prove that no errors have been made during an accounting period?

Q6.11 Distinguish between the cash basis and the accrual basis of accounting.

Q6.12 What are adjusting entries? Why are they needed?

Q6.13 A company recently made an adjusting entry to record depreciation and another to record accrued interest on notes receivable. How does each entry relate to an accounting principle?

Q6.14 Describe how an accountant accumulates the information needed to prepare adjusting entries.

Q6.15 Distinguish between accruals and deferrals.

Q6.16 Give two examples of adjusting entries that are based on the revenue realization principle. Give two examples that are based on the matching principle.

Q6.17 Give an example that illustrates two ways in which an adjusting entry applicable to prepaid rent might be recorded.

Q6.18 Give an example that illustrates two ways in which an adjusting entry applicable to unearned subscriptions revenue might be recorded.

Q6.19 What are the purposes of the cost of goods sold adjustment assuming the use of a periodic inventory system?

Q6.20 What are the major purposes of an adjusted trial balance?

Q6.21 Why is the income tax adjustment usually the final adjusting entry prepared?

Q6.22 Why are the following statements usually prepared in the sequence indicated?

(a) Income statement.

(b) Statement of retained earnings.

(c) Balance sheet.

Q6.23 What are closing entries? Why are they needed?

Q6.24 What types of accounts appear on a post-closing trial balance?

Q6.25 What are reversing entries? Why are these entries often desirable?

Q6.26 (Appendix A) What is a worksheet? How does a worksheet facilitate the preparation of financial statements?

Exercises

E6.1 Debit/Credit Rules. A list of accounts follows:

(1) Sales.

(2) Common Shares.

(3) Accounts Payable.

(4) Salaries Expense.

(5) Accounts Receivable.

(6) Dividends.

(7) Interest Earned.

(8) Retained Earnings.

(9) Goodwill.

(10) Bonds Payable.

(11) Accumulated Depreciation.

(12) Unearned Subscriptions Revenue.

(13) Dividends Payable.

(14) Premium on Bonds Payable.

(15) Preferred Shares.

(16) Allowance for Doubtful Accounts.

(17) Investment in Bonds.

(18) Advertising Expense.

(19) Sales Returns.

(20) Retained Earnings Appropriated for Plant Expansion.

Instructions

State whether the balance in each account is increased by a debit or a credit.

E6.2 Journal Entries. During July, Rogoski Company engaged in the transactions listed below. The company uses a periodic inventory system.

July 2 Purchased on account merchandise costing $25 000.
   2 Paid $600 of freight charges in connection with merchandise referred to above.
   6 Purchased land for $10 000.
   10 Sold merchandise for cash of $9000.
   14 Borrowed $8000 by signing a 90-day, 10 percent note.
   16 Sold 1000 no-par value common shares for $15 000.
   19 Sold merchandise on account for $6000.
   23 Sold land that was purchased on July 6. The cash selling price was $11 000.
   27 Received a $1000, 90-day, 8 percent note from a customer on account.
   31 Paid July salaries of $5000.

Instructions
Record the above transactions in general journal form.

E6.3 Posting. Ness Inc. recorded the following journal entries during its first month of operations:

Aug. 1 Cash	20 000	
Common Shares		20 000
3 Prepaid Rent	1 200	
Cash		1 200
7 Equipment	5 000	
Cash		5 000
11 Purchases	4 000	
Accounts Payable		4 000
13 Accounts Receivable	7 000	
Sales		7 000
24 Cash	2 000	
Accounts Receivable		2 000
27 Accounts Payable	3 000	
Cash		3 000
31 Salaries Expense	1 400	
Advertising Expense	200	
Utilities Expense	100	
Cash		1 700

Instructions
(a) Set up a general ledger and post each journal entry to appropriate T accounts.
(b) Prepare an unadjusted trial balance on August 31.

E6.4 Correcting Entries. A trial balance for Will Hurt, DDS, at the end of his first month in practice is presented below:

Will Hurt, DDS
TRIAL BALANCE
May 31

Account	Dr.	Cr.
Cash	$ 9 560	
Supplies	11 730	
Prepaid rent	6 800	
Equipment	58 000	
Accounts payable		$ 9 640
Will Hurt, capital		75 000
Revenues from patients		5 450
Salaries expense	1 300	
Utilities expense	400	
Miscellaneous office expenses	300	
Will Hurt, drawing	2 000	
	$90 090	$90 090

Additional Information

Upon examining Hurt's books, you discover the following:

(1) Cash of $300 received from a patient had been recorded as $500. (Hurt renders services on a cash basis only.)
(2) A $964 purchase of supplies on account had been recorded as $469.
(3) A $2000 purchase of equipment had been charged to prepaid rent.
(4) A $677 payment on account had been recorded as $776.

Instructions

(a) Journalize the necessary correcting entries on May 31. (Do not record adjusting entries.)
(b) Prepare a corrected trial balance.

E6.5   Adjusting and Reversing Entries.   The following information pertains to Dano Company for the current year:

(1) On November 1, the company received a $5000, 90-day, 10 percent note from a customer.
(2) Accrued wages as of December 31 amount to $2175.
(3) On September 1, the company received $2400 for rent paid in advance for eight months on a warehouse that Dano Company leases to Moore Company. Dano Company credited a nominal account.
(4) On October 1, the company paid $1800 for a two-year fire insurance policy and debited a nominal account.
(5) The company computes $10 000 of depreciation for the year.
(6) The company estimates $2635 of bad debts for the year.

Instructions

(a) Prepare the necessary adjusting journal entries on December 31, the end of the company's annual accounting period.
(b) Assuming that Dano Company wants to make reversals, prepare the reversing entries that are appropriate on January 1 of the next accounting period.

E6.6 Adjusting Entries.   Amy Wong owns the Wong Hair Styling Centre. A trial balance for the business at the end of its first year of operations follows:

Wong Hair Styling Centre
TRIAL BALANCE
December 31

Account	Dr.	Cr.
Cash	$13 000	
Supplies	14 000	
Prepaid rent	12 000	
Equipment	25 000	
Accounts payable		$ 3 000
Note payable		20 000
Wong, capital		7 000
Styling revenues		56 500
Advertising expense	7 000	
Salaries expense	13 000	
Utilities expense	2 500	
	$86 500	$86 500

Additional Information
(1) A physical count reveals that supplies costing $1000 are on hand at year-end.
(2) Rent on the shop was paid in advance for two years on January 1.
(3) The equipment was acquired on January 1. It has an estimated useful life of ten years and no expected salvage value. Wong elects to use the straight-line depreciation method.
(4) The note payable relates to a one-year, 8 percent loan obtained from First National Bank on April 1.
(5) Salaries earned by employees but unpaid to them at year-end amount to $1680.

Instructions
Using the trial balance and the additional information presented above, prepare the necessary adjusting entries in general journal form at December 31.

E6.7 Cost of Goods Sold and Gross Margin.   Selected account balances for Janzen Company on December 31 are shown below. Each account has a normal balance.

Account	Balance
Freight-out	$ 12 000
Merchandise inventory, Dec. 31	43 000
Purchase discounts	3 000
Sales returns	11 000
Freight-in	8 000
Sales discounts	7 000
Merchandise inventory, Jan. 1	30 000
Purchase returns	6 000
Sales allowances	9 000
Purchase allowances	4 000
Purchases	200 000
Sales	370 000

Instructions
(a) Prepare a schedule showing the computation of cost of goods sold.
(b) Calculate the amount of gross margin.

E6.8 Financial Statements. The adjusted trial balance of Gibney Company on December 31 appears below:

Account	Dr.	Cr.
Cash	$ 27 000	
Accounts receivable	50 000	
Allowance for doubtful accounts		$ 3 000
Note receivable (short-term)	10 000	
Merchandise inventory	20 000	
Prepaid rent (for one year)	6 000	
Equipment	100 000	
Accumulated depreciation		15 000
Accounts payable		23 000
Salaries payable		2 000
Income tax payable		22 000
Common shares (no-par value; 3000 outstanding)		100 000
Retained earnings		50 000
Sales		215 000
Interest revenue		6 000
Cost of goods sold	100 000	
Salaries expense	20 000	
Rent expense	6 000	
Advertising expense	17 000	
Depreciation expense	10 000	
Bad debts expense	3 000	
Miscellaneous expense	5 000	
Income tax expense	22 000	
Dividends	40 000	
	$436 000	$436 000

Instructions
Prepare an income statement, a statement of retained earnings, and a balance sheet.

E6.9 Closing Entries. Refer to the information presented for Gibney Company in E6.8.

Instructions
(a) Journalize the closing entries on December 31.
(b) Prepare a post-closing trial balance.

E6.10 Closing Entries. Listed below are the adjusted account balances of Beli Company on December 31. Each account has a normal balance.

Account	Balance
Accounts payable	$ 40 000
Accounts receivable	37 000
Accumulated depreciation—equipment	20 000
Advertising expense	8 000
Allowance for doubtful accounts	1 000
Bad debts expense	1 000
Cash	30 000
Common shares	30 000
Cost of goods sold	101 000
Depreciation expense—equipment	10 000
Equipment	100 000
Income tax expense	16 000
Interest expense	6 000
Interest payable	3 000
Merchandise inventory	50 000
Note payable	30 000
Prepaid rent	4 000
Rent expense	12 000
Retained earnings	53 000
Salaries expense	20 000
Sales	236 000
Sales returns	11 000
Freight-out	5 000
Utilities expense	2 000

Instructions

Prepare closing entries in general journal form at December 31.

E6.11 Reversing Entries. Berger Publishing Company made the following adjusting entries on December 31, 1995:

(1)	Rent Receivable	2000	
	Rent Revenue		2000
(2)	Insurance Expense	700	
	Prepaid Insurance		700
(3)	Property Tax Expense	1200	
	Property Tax Payable		1200
(4)	Subscriptions Revenue	2400	
	Unearned Subscriptions Revenue		2400
(5)	Supplies Expense	850	
	Supplies		850
(6)	Amortization Expense	1700	
	Copyrights		1700
(7)	Bad Debts Expense	650	
	Allowance for Doubtful Accounts		650
(8)	Advertising Revenue	3300	
	Unearned Advertising Revenue		3300

Instructions

Assuming that the company wants to make reversals, prepare all reversing journal entries that are appropriate on January 1, 1996.

E6.12 Reversing Entries. On November 1, 1995, Moncy Company issued at par $200 000 of twenty-year, 8 percent bonds with interest payable semi-annually on April 30 and October 31. The company uses a calendar-year accounting period.

Instructions

Record all appropriate journal entries using a table similar to the one shown below.

	Assumption	
Event	**Moncy Company makes reversing entries for accrued interest.**	**Moncy Company does not make reversing entries for accrued interest.**
12/31/95 adjusting entry to record accrued interest		
12/31/95 entry to close accrued interest		
1/1/96 reversing entry applicable to accrued interest		
4/30/96 entry to record payment of interest		
10/31/96 entry to record payment of interest		

E6.13 Accrual Accounting. A recent comparative balance sheet of Gonzales Inc. showed the following information:

		Balance	
Explanation		**12/31/94**	**12/31/95**
Interest receivable		$100	$400
Consulting fees receivable		700	300
Prepaid insurance		500	700
Supplies		400	200
Salaries payable		500	800
Utilities payable		300	200
Unearned subscriptions revenue		600	800
Unearned advertising revenue		600	200

Selected information about the company's 1995 revenues and expenses (accrual basis) appears below:

Revenues		**Expenses**	
Interest	$1400	Insurance	$2200
Consulting fees	5000	Supplies	1200
Subscriptions	7500	Salaries	4300
Advertising	3000	Utilities	2000

Instructions
(a) Compute the amount of 1995 cash receipts from each of the following sources: (1) interest, (2) consulting fees, (3) subscriptions, and (4) advertising.
(b) Compute the amount of 1995 cash payments for each of the following purposes: (1) insurance, (2) supplies, (3) salaries, and (4) utilities.

E6.14 Accrual Accounting. A recent comparative balance sheet of Sims Company revealed the following information:

Explanation	Balance 12/31/94	12/31/95
	Balance	
	12/31/94	**12/31/95**
Interest receivable	$200	$300
Consulting fees receivable	800	200
Prepaid insurance	600	800
Supplies	500	100
Salaries payable	600	900
Utilities payable	400	100
Unearned subscriptions revenue	700	900
Unearned advertising revenue	700	400

Selected information about the company's 1995 cash receipts and disbursements appears below:

Explanation	Cash Receipts	Cash Disbursements
Interest	$3500	
Consulting fees	3000	
Insurance		$2900
Supplies		1200
Salaries		4400
Utilities		1000
Subscriptions	7000	
Advertising	4200	

Instructions

Compute each of the following income statement amounts for 1995 under the accrual basis of accounting: (1) interest revenue, (2) consulting fees earned, (3) insurance expense, (4) supplies expense, (5) salaries expense, (6) utilities expense, (7) subscriptions revenue, and (8) advertising revenue.

E6.15 (Appendix B) Special Journals. Maher Company uses the following journals: sales, sales returns and allowances, purchases, purchases returns and allowances, cash receipts, cash payments, and general. The following events occurred during December:

(1) Borrowed money from bank.
(2) Purchased merchandise for cash.
(3) Received defective merchandise from customers and granted credit.
(4) Discovered that a cash purchase of equipment in October had inadvertently been charged to the Land account at that time.
(5) Received payments made by customers on account.
(6) Computed annual depreciation.
(7) Made cash sales.
(8) Purchased merchandise on account.
(9) Paid accounts payable.
(10) Collected cash from customers on account.
(11) Made credit sales.
(12) Issued common shares for legal services received.
(13) Paid December rent.
(14) Returned defective merchandise to suppliers and received credit.

Instructions

Indicate the journal in which the company should record each of the above events.

E6.16 (Appendix B) Special Journals. Presented below are several transactions of Mankel Company that occurred during December 1995. The company uses a periodic inventory system and a calendar-year accounting period.

Dec. 1 Purchased merchandise on account from Marek Company for $420.
  4 Sold merchandise to Larry Gordon for $205 cash.
  5 Paid Rip Company $440 on account.
  8 Borrowed $10 000 from City & Provincial Bank and signed a one-year, 8 percent note.
  12 Sold merchandise on account for $1400 to Hoffmann, Inc.
  13 Signed a two-year, 9 percent note for $20 000 in exchange for land purchased from Windsor Corporation.
  17 Received $275 on account from Mancini Company.
  20 The company discovered that a $5000 purchase of equipment on November 14, 1995, had inadvertently been entered in the Land account.
  22 Purchased merchandise from Moore Company for $170 cash.
  30 Paid a utility bill of $235 for services received in December.
  31 Estimated depreciation for the year at $4000.
  31 Determined that $400 of prepaid insurance had expired during 1995.

Instructions
(a) Record the above transactions in general journal form.
(b) Assume that Mankel Company uses the following journals: sales, cash receipts, purchases, cash payments, and general. Indicate where the company should record each transaction.

E6.17 (Appendix B) Sales Journal. Hudgens Company began operations on May 1 and had the following credit sales during May:

Date	Customer	Invoice No.	Amount
May 1	Macy Company	101	$550
8	Gresham, Inc.	102	280
16	Epling Enterprises	103	675
21	Davis Company	104	460
31	Cathey, Inc.	105	600

Instructions
(a) Set up a sales journal and record each of the above transactions.
(b) Post the journal entries to appropriate general and subsidiary ledger accounts.

E6.18 (Appendix A) The Worksheet. Presented below is the unadjusted trial balance of Meisenheimer Inc., on December 31, the end of the company's annual accounting period.

Account	Dr.	Cr.
Cash	$ 26 000	
Note receivable	5 000	
Prepaid rent	12 000	
Equipment	100 000	
Accumulated depreciation		$ 20 000
Accounts payable		17 000
Common shares		30 000
Retained earnings		15 000
Consulting revenues		175 000
Salaries expense	90 000	
Travel expense	10 000	
Utilities expense	6 000	
Dividends	8 000	
	$257 000	$257 000

Additional Information

This information is available on December 31:

(1) Accrued interest on note receivable is $250.
(2) Seventy-five percent of the prepaid rent shown above has expired.
(3) Depreciation expense for the year is $12 000.
(4) The December utility bill of $550 has not been paid or recorded.
(5) The income tax rate is 40 percent.

Instructions

Prepare a twelve-column worksheet (as shown in Appendix A).

Problems

P6.1   Journal Entries and Posting. Sanchez Company started business on June 1. The company uses a periodic inventory system and records purchases of merchandise at gross amounts. The following transactions occurred during June:

June 1 Issued 1000 no-par value common shares for $60 000.
    2 Borrowed $10 000 by signing a one-year, 10 percent note.
    3 Purchased the following for cash:

	Cost
Land	$10 000
Building	30 000
Equipment	5 000
Total	$45 000

    4 Purchased a three-year fire insurance policy for $4800. (Debit an asset account.)
    5 Purchased office supplies for $4000. (Debit an asset account.)
    6 Received merchandise and an invoice dated June 5 from Reath, Inc. for $6000. Credit terms are 2/10, n/30.
    6 Paid freight of $300 on merchandise received from Reath, Inc.
    8 Sold merchandise on credit to Kerley Company, for $20 000. Terms are n/30.
  10 Purchased merchandise from Kim, Inc. for cash of $6000.
  12 Returned $600 of defective merchandise to Kim, Inc. and received a cash refund.
  14 Sold merchandise for cash of $5000.
  15 Paid Reath, Inc. the amount of the June 5 invoice, less the discount.
  17 Received merchandise returned by Kerley Company. Granted credit of $1000.

20 Received one-year's rent of $4800 in advance on a small office. (Credit a liability account.)

23 Received merchandise and an invoice dated June 21 from Fogle, Inc., for $7500. Credit terms are 1/10, n/60.

25 Sold merchandise on credit to Corey Company for $3000. Terms are n/30.

29 Received payment in full from Kerley Company. (See June 8 and June 17 transactions.)

30 Paid the following June expenses:

Salaries	$1900
Advertising	600
Utilities	500
Total	$3000

Instructions

(a) Record each of the June transactions in a general journal.

(b) Post each journal entry to appropriate general ledger accounts.

(c) Prepare an unadjusted trial balance on June 30.

P6.2   Journal Entries and Posting.   Presented below is an unadjusted trial balance for Gilhula Company on November 30:

Gilhula Company
UNADJUSTED TRIAL BALANCE
November 30

Account	Dr.	Cr.
Cash	$ 14 000	
Accounts receivable	21 000	
Allowance for doubtful accounts		$ 1 000
Notes receivable	7 000	
Merchandise inventory, Jan. 1	15 000	
Prepaid insurance	3 000	
Prepaid rent	8 000	
Investment in Lee Company shares	20 000	
Equipment	60 000	
Accumulated depreciation		10 000
Accounts payable		11 000
Note payable		5 000
Common shares		40 000
Retained earnings		61 000
Sales		110 000
Sales returns	4 000	
Purchases	55 000	
Purchase returns		2 000
Purchase discounts		1 000
Freight-in	5 000	
Salaries expense	20 000	
Advertising expense	6 000	
Utilities expense	3 000	
Interest expense	-0-	
	$241 000	$241 000

Additional Information

The following transactions occurred during December:

Dec. 1 Sold the investment in Lee Company shares for $14 000.
   3 Received a $4000, 90-day, 9 percent note from a customer on account.
   4 Purchased merchandise for cash of $3600.
   6 Paid the $5000 note listed in the unadjusted trial balance. The note, which matured on Dec. 6, was for 120 days at 8 percent interest.
   7 Paid $8000 of accounts payable. Cash discounts of 2 percent were taken.
   8 Returned $400 of defective merchandise purchased on Dec. 4 and received a cash refund.
   9 Collected $10 000 from customers on account.
   11 Wrote off uncollectable accounts receivable of $800.
   13 Purchased merchandise on account for $3000. Terms are n/30.
   13 Paid freight of $200 on merchandise purchased.
   16 Received merchandise returned by a customer. Granted credit of $800.
   18 Sold merchandise on account for $9000.
   22 Made cash sales of $5000.
   23 Purchased a one-year insurance policy for $1900.
   28 Purchased $10 000 of equipment for use in the business. Paid $2000 cash and signed an $8000, one-year, 8 percent note.
   31 Paid the following expenses:

Salaries	$1800
Advertising	600
Utilities	300
Total	$2700

Instructions

(a) Record each of the December transactions in a general journal. (Do not record adjusting entries.)
(b) Set up general ledger accounts and enter the opening balances for December. Post each journal entry to appropriate accounts.
(c) Prepare an unadjusted trial balance on December 31.

P6.3 Accounting Cycle. Coomer Consulting Company began operations on December 1. The following transactions occurred during the first month:

Dec. 1 Sold 500 no-par value common shares for $50 000 cash.
   1 Purchased equipment for $30 000 cash. (The equipment has an estimated useful life of ten years and no expected salvage value. The company plans to use straight-line depreciation.)
   1 Purchased a one-year insurance policy for $4800. (The company records all prepaid amounts in *real,* i.e., balance sheet, accounts.)
   1 Paid $9600 office rent in advance for one year.
   2 Purchased on account supplies costing $8000.
   10 Received $2000 from a client for services rendered.
   16 Borrowed $5000 from City Bank and signed a 90-day, 8 percent note.
   30 Paid half of the amount owed for the purchase of supplies on December 2.
   31 Billed clients $6000 for services rendered during December.
   31 Paid $500 for advertisements run in the local newspaper during December.
   31 Paid the utility bill for $180 for December.
   31 Paid December salaries of $2500.

Instructions

(a) Record the December transactions in general journal form.
(b) Post the journal entries to general ledger T accounts.
(c) Prepare an unadjusted trial balance at December 31.
(d) Journalize and post all necessary adjusting entries. (A count reveals that supplies costing $7000 are on hand December 31. The income tax rate is 40 percent.)
(e) Prepare an adjusted trial balance.
(f) Prepare an income statement, a statement of retained earnings, and a balance sheet for December.
(g) Journalize and post closing entries.
(h) Prepare a post-closing trial balance.

P6.4 Accounting Cycle. Presented below is the post-closing trial balance of Beal Corporation on December 31, 1994:

Beal Corporation
POST-CLOSING TRIAL BALANCE
December 31, 1994

Account	Dr.	Cr.
Cash	$ 12 000	
Accounts receivable	18 000	
Allowance for doubtful accounts		$ 900
Merchandise inventory	23 000	
Prepaid rent	24 000	
Equipment	50 000	
Accumulated depreciation		10 000
Accounts payable		21 000
Income tax payable		11 000
Common shares		40 000
Retained earnings		44 100
	$127 000	$127 000

Following is a summary of transactions that occurred during 1995:

(1) Purchased merchandise on account for $85 000. (The company uses a periodic inventory system.)
(2) Paid freight charges of $4600 on merchandise purchased.
(3) Sold merchandise as follows:

On account	$145 000
For cash	62 900
Total	$207 900

(4) Collected $136 000 of accounts receivable.
(5) Wrote off uncollectable accounts of $850.
(6) Paid the income tax liability that was reported on December 31, 1994.
(7) Paid $78 000 on accounts payable.
(8) Paid the following expenses:

Salaries	$21 000
Advertising	12 000
Utilities	8 000
Telephone and telegraph	4 400
Total	$45 400

(9) Declared dividends of $10 000. The company will pay the dividends early in 1996.

Additional Information

This information is available on December 31, 1995:

(1) The company estimates that 1 percent of credit sales made during 1995 will never be collected.
(2) A physical count reveals that merchandise costing $19 000 is on hand at year-end.
(3) One-half of the prepaid rent as of December 31, 1994, expired during 1995.
(4) The equipment has an estimated useful life of ten years and no expected salvage value. The company uses straight-line depreciation.
(5) The income tax rate for 1995 is 40 percent.

Instructions

(a) Set up general ledger T accounts for the post-closing trial balance accounts and for the following accounts: Dividends Payable, Sales, Cost of Goods Sold, Purchases, Freight-In, Salaries Expense, Advertising Expense, Utilities Expense, Telephone and Telegraph, Bad Debts Expense, Rent Expense, Depreciation Expense, Income Tax Expense, Dividends, and Income Summary. Enter the opening balances for 1995 in the general ledger T accounts.
(b) Journalize the 1995 transactions in the order in which they are presented above. Use the number to the left of each transaction to indicate the date.
(c) Post the journal entries to the general ledger T accounts.
(d) Prepare an unadjusted trial balance.
(e) Journalize and post adjusting entries.
(f) Prepare an adjusted trial balance.
(g) Prepare an income statement, a statement of retained earnings, and a balance sheet.
(h) Journalize and post closing entries.
(i) Prepare a post-closing trial balance.

P6.5 Adjusting Entries. The following transactions occurred during the 1995 calendar-year accounting period of Pavaroni Company.

April 1 Paid $4000 to a local television station for commercial time that will be broadcast evenly over twelve months, beginning in April.
June 1 Received $6000 from a tenant paying rent in advance for one year.
Sept. 1 Paid $1200 for a one-year fire insurance policy.
Nov. 1 Received $24 000 from customers for subscriptions paid in advance for one year.

Instructions

(a) Assuming the company has entered the above receipts and payments in *real* (balance sheet) accounts, journalize the adjustments required on December 31, 1995.
(b) Assuming the company has entered the above receipts and payments in *nominal* (income statement) accounts, journalize the adjustments required on December 31, 1995.

(c) Under the assumption in (a), compute the adjusted account balances for the 1995 financial statements for all accounts in your adjusting entries.

(d) Under the assumption in (b), compute the adjusted account balances for the 1995 financial statements for all accounts in your adjusting entries.

P6.6 Adjusting and Reversing Entries. Bower Publishing Company recorded the following transactions during its 1995 calendar-year accounting period:

Mar. 1 Received $18 000 from customers for subscriptions paid in advance for one year.

Apr. 1 Paid $2400 for a one-year fire insurance policy.

Aug. 1 Received $9000 from a tenant paying rent in advance for six months.

Oct. 1 Paid $6000 to a local radio station for advertising time. The station agreed to broadcast two ads each month for twelve months, beginning in October.

Instructions

(a) Journalize the above transactions assuming that the company enters in *real* (balance sheet) accounts the amounts that are received or paid in advance.

(b) Based on (a), journalize the necessary adjustments on December 31, 1995.

(c) Assuming that the company uses reversing entries, journalize the reversals that are appropriate for the adjusting entries in (b).

(d) Journalize the above transactions assuming that the company enters in *nominal* (income statement) accounts the amounts that are received or paid in advance.

(e) Based on (d), journalize the necessary adjustments on December 31, 1995.

(f) Assuming that the company uses reversing entries, journalize the reversals that are appropriate for the adjusting entries in (e).

P6.7 Adjusting and Reversing Entries. The following information pertains to Fred's Laundry Service on June 30, 1995, the end of the company's fiscal year:

(1) On March 1, 1995, the company purchased a three-year fire insurance policy for $3600. A *real* (balance sheet) account was debited.

(2) The company's estimate of bad debts for the fiscal year is $2000.

(3) On October 1, 1994, the company received $12 000 for rent received in advance for one year for storage space that it leases to Hall Company. A nominal account was credited.

(4) The company's estimate of depreciation for the year is $12 000.

(5) On April 1, 1995, the company paid $1800 to the local newspaper for advertising space and debited a nominal account. The newspaper agreed to publish four ads each month for one year, beginning in April.

(6) On May 31, 1995, the company borrowed $10 000 from Citizens' Bank and signed a 120-day, 8 percent note.

(7) Employees have earned wages of $640 that the company has not paid or recorded as of June 30, 1995.

(8) On December 1, 1994, the company purchased at par value ten $1000, 8 percent, twenty-year bonds of Hope, Inc. The bonds pay interest semi-annually on May 31 and November 30.

(9) On March 1, 1995, the company received $12 000 for laundry service that it will provide for one year, beginning on that date. A *real* (balance sheet) account was credited.

(10) Property taxes owed and unrecorded as of June 30 total $1300.

Instructions

(a) Prepare adjusting entries in general journal form at June 30, 1995.

(b) Assuming that the company wants to make reversing entries, identify the adjusting entries that it may appropriately reverse.

P6.8 Adjusting and Reversing Entries. Presented below is the trial balance of Skinner Company at December 31, 1995, the end of the company's annual accounting period.

Account	Dr.	Cr.
Cash	$ 26 000	
Accounts receivable	25 000	
Allowance for doubtful accounts	150	
Merchandise inventory, Jan. 1	53 000	
Investment in Slaton, Inc. bonds	30 000	
Land	47 000	
Building	200 000	
Accumulated depreciation—building		$ 22 500
Equipment	80 000	
Accumulated depreciation—equipment		24 000
Accounts payable		19 000
Note payable		50 000
Common shares		100 000
Retained earnings, Jan. 1		176 028
Sales		452 000
Interest revenue		2 700
Rent revenue		9 000
Purchases	280 380	
Purchase returns and allowances		11 180
Freight-in	10 000	
Salaries expense	86 200	
Rent expense	21 000	
Utilities expense	7 678	
	$866 408	$866 408

Additional Information

(1) Eighty percent of 1995 sales were made on credit. The company estimates that 2 percent of credit sales will never be collected.

(2) A physical count reveals that merchandise costing $50 000 is on hand at year-end.

(3) On March 17, 1994, the company purchased 30 $1000, 8 percent, twenty-year bonds of Slaton, Inc. The bonds pay interest semi-annually on March 31 and September 30.

(4) The company computes annual depreciation as follows: Building, 2.5 percent of cost; Equipment, 5 percent of cost.

(5) The note payable relates to a 90-day, 8 percent loan obtained from Northwest Bank on October 20, 1995.

(6) The company has rented a portion of its building to Purdy's Retail Store since July 1, 1993. The rent is $6000 per year, payable by Purdy's in advance each July 1.

(7) As of December 31, employees had earned salaries of $5200 that the company had not paid or recorded.

(8) The company has rented a warehouse from the Suda Storage Company since October 1, 1994. The rent is $12 000 per year, payable by Skinner Company in advance each October 1.

(9) The utility bill for December 1995 is $621. As of December 31, this amount had not been paid or recorded.

(10) The company's income taxes for the year are $27 180, to be paid in 1996.

Instructions

(a) Prepare the adjusting entries in general journal form on December 31, 1995.

(b) Identify the broad accounting principle that underlies each adjusting entry. (*Hint:* Review the principles discussed in Chapter 2.)

(c) Refer to the part of your answer in (b) that pertains to the cost of goods sold adjustment. Explain why the broad accounting principle you identified applies to this adjustment.

(d) Assuming that Skinner Company wants to make reversing entries, identify the adjusting entries that the company may appropriately reverse.

P6.9 Adjusting and Reversing Entries. Presented below is the trial balance of Renfro Corporation at December 31, 1995, the end of the company's annual accounting period:

Renfro Corporation
TRIAL BALANCE
December 31, 1995

Account	Dr.	Cr.
Cash	$ 14 925	
Accounts receivable	24 000	
Allowance for doubtful accounts		$ 300
Note receivable	4 000	
Merchandise inventory, Jan. 1	10 000	
Supplies	1 300	
Prepaid insurance	3 000	
Land	70 000	
Building	60 000	
Accumulated depreciation—building		6 000
Equipment	20 000	
Accumulated depreciation—equipment		4 000
Goodwill	9 375	
Accounts payable		8 600
Unearned rent revenue		7 200
Bonds payable (20-year, 10 percent)		100 000
Common shares		60 000
Retained earnings, Jan. 1		17 000
Sales		200 000
Purchases	95 000	
Purchase returns		3 000
Freight-in	8 000	
Salaries expense	30 000	
Travel expense	7 000	
Advertising expense	16 000	
Freight-out	10 000	
Telephone expense	5 000	
Utilities expense	11 000	
Interest expense	7 500	
	$406 100	$406 100

Additional Information

(1) The company makes all its sales on credit. It estimates that 1.5 percent of sales made during 1995 will never be collected.

(2) The note receivable is a 90-day, 8 percent note taken from a customer on December 1, 1995.

(3) A physical inventory indicates that merchandise costing $20 000 is on hand December 31, 1995.

(4) A count reveals that supplies costing $400 are on hand December 31, 1995.

(5) The prepaid insurance account pertains to a three-year fire policy purchased on July 1, 1994, for $3600.

(6) The following information concerns the building and equipment:

	Estimated Useful Life in Years	Estimated Salvage Value	Depreciation Method
Building	40	None	Straight-line
Equipment	20	None	Straight-line

(7) The company recorded $10 000 of goodwill when it acquired a competing firm on October 1, 1993. Renfro Corporation uses the straight-line method of amortizing goodwill.

(8) On July 1, 1995, the company leased a portion of its building to Kinzer Company and received a cheque for $7200 for one year's rent paid in advance.

(9) The company issued the bonds payable at par value on October 1, 1992. The bonds pay interest semi-annually on March 31 and September 30.

(10) Salaries earned but unpaid to employees as of year-end totalled $2700.

(11) On December 17, 1995, the company paid $1800 for advertising time on a local television show that will be broadcast on January 12, 1996.

(12) A utility bill of $1340 for December 1995 has been received but not yet recorded or paid.

(13) Property taxes that accrued during 1995 amounted to $3100.

(14) The company determines that income tax expense for 1995 is $8900. This amount will be paid in 1996.

Instructions

(a) Prepare adjusting entries in general journal form at December 31, 1995.

(b) Identify the broad accounting principle that underlies each adjusting entry. (*Hint:* Review the principles discussed in Chapter 2.)

(c) Refer to the part of your answer in (b) that pertains to the adjusting entry for the building and equipment (i.e., depreciation). Explain why the broad accounting principle you identified applies to this adjusting entry.

(d) Identify adjusting entries that Renfro Corporation may appropriately reverse, assuming that the company wants to make reversing entries.

P6.10 Reconstructing Adjusting Entries. Presented below are trial balances of Grayson Company at December 31, 1995:

Trial Balance

Account	Unadjusted Dr.	Unadjusted Cr.	Adjusted Dr.	Adjusted Cr.
Cash	$ 14 000		$ 14 000	
Accounts receivable	22 000		22 000	
Allowance for doubtful accounts	56			$ 2 000
Note receivable	10 000		10 000	
Interest receivable			1 000	
Supplies	6 000		3 209	
Merchandise inventory, Jan. 1	20 000			
Merchandise inventory, Dec. 31			25 000	
Prepaid rent	18 000		6 000	
Equipment	120 000		120 000	
Accumulated depreciation— equipment		$ 30 000		40 000
Accounts payable		12 000		12 000
Salaries payable				2 000
Income tax payable				16 000
Common shares		40 000		40 000
Retained earnings		67 265		67 265
Sales		205 631		205 631
Interest revenue				1 000
Cost of goods sold			102 840	
Purchases	107 840			
Salaries expense	29 000		31 000	
Miscellaneous expenses	8 000		8 000	
Supplies expense			2 791	
Rent expense			12 000	
Depreciation expense			10 000	
Bad debts expense			2 056	
Income tax expense			16 000	
	$354 896	$354 896	$385 896	$385 896

Instructions

Based on the above information, reconstruct the adjusting journal entries that Grayson Company made on December 31, 1995.

P6.11 Effects of Adjusting Entries. At the end of 1995, Coe Company failed to record the adjusting entries indicated below:

(1) Accrued wages owed to employees.
(2) Depreciation of plant assets.
(3) Earned portion on one year's rent that had been received by Coe in advance on July 1, 1995, and recorded in a liability account.
(4) Estimate of bad debts.
(5) Unexpired portion of a one-year fire insurance policy that Coe paid for on September 1, 1995, and charged to a nominal account.
(6) Accrued interest on an investment in bonds.

Instructions

Prepare a table similar to the one below, and indicate the effect of each error on the 1995 financial statement elements shown. Use the following code in marking your answers: 0 = overstated, U = understated, and NE = no effect. Assume that each error is independent of the others.

Error	Total Revenues	Total Expenses	Net Income	Total Assets	Total Liabilities	Share-holders' Equity
Example: Failed to record accrued interest on note payable.	NE	U	O	NE	U	O
(1)						
(2)						
(3)						
(4)						
(5)						
(6)						

P6.12 (Appendix B) General and Special Journals. Corkland Company began operations on May 1. The company uses a periodic inventory system. All credit sales are subject to terms of 2/10, n/30. The following transactions occurred during May:

May 1 Issued 10 000 no-par value common shares for $60 000.
   2 Issued 1000 no-par value common shares for land valued at $7000.
   3 Purchased a building for $30 000. Cheque no. 101 was issued.
   5 Received merchandise and an invoice dated May 2 from Brown Company for $2000. Terms are 1/15, n/30.
   7 Sold merchandise on credit to Albert Company for $3000. Invoice no. 1001 was issued.
   9 Purchased merchandise from Dantley Company for cash of $1500. Cheque no. 102 was issued.
  11 Sold merchandise on credit to Hadler Company for $2500. Invoice no. 1002 was issued.
  12 Received merchandise and an invoice dated May 10 from Gatlin Company for $4000. Terms are 2/10, n/60.
  13 Sold merchandise to Roundtree Company for cash of $6300.
  15 Issued cheque no. 103 for $1980 to Brown Company in payment of May 2 invoice, less the discount.
  16 Received a cheque for $2940 from Albert Company in payment of May 7 invoice, less the discount.
  18 Received a cheque for $2450 from Hadler Company in payment of May 11 invoice, less the discount.
  19 Issued cheque no. 104 for $3920 to Gatlin Company in payment of May 10 invoice, less the discount.
  24 Received merchandise and an invoice dated May 23 from Early Company for $1000. Terms are 2/10, n/30.
  25 Sold merchandise on credit to Canton Company for $8000. Invoice no. 1003 was issued.
  28 Received merchandise and an invoice dated May 26 from Ison Company for $1800. Terms are 3/15, n/30.
  31 Sold merchandise on credit to Jasper Company for $2800. Invoice no. 1004 was issued.

Instructions
(a) Record the transactions for May using the following journals: sales, purchases, cash receipts, cash payments, and general.

(b) Post the appropriate amounts in a general ledger and in accounts receivable and accounts payable subsidiary ledgers. Systematically number all accounts and use posting references.

(c) Prepare a trial balance on May 31.

(d) Reconcile the subsidiary ledgers with the appropriate control accounts.

P6.13 (Appendix A) The Worksheet, Financial Statements, Adjusting and Closing Entries. Defiore Company has adopted a calendar-year accounting period. The company's unadjusted trial balance on December 31 appears below:

Account	Dr.	Cr.
Cash	$ 36 775	
Accounts receivable	30 000	
Allowance for doubtful accounts	225	
Merchandise inventory, Jan. 1	42 000	
Investment in bonds (long-term)	20 000	
Land	52 000	
Building	100 000	
Accumulated depreciation—building		$ 25 000
Equipment	50 000	
Accumulated depreciation—equipment		25 000
Accounts payable		32 000
Common shares (no-par value, 10 000 shares)		100 000
Retained earnings, Jan. 1		109 500
Sales		475 000
Interest revenue		1 500
Rent revenue		12 000
Purchases	305 000	
Purchase returns		12 000
Salaries expense	88 000	
Advertising expense	22 000	
Utilities expense	6 000	
Supplies expense	30 000	
Dividends	10 000	
	$792 000	$792 000

Additional Information

This information is available on December 31:

(1) The company estimates that bad debts expense for the year is $3500.
(2) The December 31 merchandise inventory is $50 000.
(3) Unrecorded interest of $500 has accrued on the investment in bonds.
(4) The company estimates depreciation for the year as follows: Building, $2500; Equipment, $5000.
(5) One-fourth of the rent revenue shown in the trial balance has *not* been earned as of December 31.
(6) Employees have earned salaries of $4000 that the company has not paid or recorded.
(7) The cost of supplies on hand December 31 is $12 000.
(8) The income tax rate is 40 percent.

Instructions

(a) Enter the unadjusted trial balance on a twelve-column worksheet (as in Appendix A).
(b) Enter the adjusting entries on the worksheet.

(c) Complete the worksheet.

(d) Prepare an income statement, a statement of retained earnings, and a balance sheet.

(e) Record the adjusting and closing entries in the general journal.

P6.14 (Appendix A) The Worksheet, Financial Statements, Adjusting and Closing Entries. Presented below is the unadjusted trial balance of Gaudet, Inc. on December 31, the end of the company's annual accounting period:

Account	Dr.	Cr.
Cash	$ 4 500	
Accounts receivable	18 000	
Allowance for doubtful accounts		$ 300
Notes receivable (due in 6 months)	10 000	
Merchandise inventory, Jan. 1	23 000	
Prepaid insurance	4 800	
Land	40 000	
Building	50 000	
Accumulated depreciation—building		20 000
Equipment	20 000	
Accumulated depreciation—equipment		12 000
Accounts payable		21 000
Dividends payable		8 000
Unearned rent revenue		6 000
Common shares (no-par value, 10 000 outstanding)		50 000
Retained earnings, Jan. 1		22 000
Sales		225 000
Purchases	123 000	
Freight-in	7 000	
Salaries expense	34 000	
Advertising expense	8 000	
Utilities expense	4 000	
Dividends	18 000	
	$364 300	$364 300

Additional Information

This information is available on December 31:

(1) Accrued interest on notes receivable totals $500.

(2) Employees have earned salaries of $1500 that the company has not yet paid or recorded.

(3) One-half of the unearned rent revenue was earned during the year.

(4) Three-fourths of the prepaid insurance shown above expired during the year.

(5) Depreciation for the year is as follows: Building, $2000; Equipment, $4000.

(6) Bad debts expense for the year is $900.

(7) The inventory on hand December 31 has a cost of $27 000.

(8) The income tax rate is 40 percent.

Instructions

(a) Enter the unadjusted trial balance on a twelve-column worksheet (as in Appendix A).

(b) Enter the adjusting entries on the worksheet.

(c) Complete the worksheet.

(d) Prepare an income statement, a statement of retained earnings, and a balance sheet.

(e) Record the adjusting and closing entries in the general journal.

Cases

C6.1 Accrual Accounting. Assume that you are working in the office of a small business client of your CA firm. The client has always maintained accounting records but has never prepared a set of financial statements completely in accordance with GAAP. Now, however, the client needs a bank loan, and the banker has required a set of financial statements prepared according to GAAP. Your client has asked for your help in understanding the meaning of accrual accounting.

Instructions

(a) How does accrual accounting affect the determination of income? Include in your discussion what constitutes an accrual and a deferral, and give appropriate examples of each.

(b) Compare accrual accounting and cash accounting.

(Adapted from AICPA.)

C6.2 Periodic Financial Reporting. Firms prepare annual financial statements for internal management and for distribution to outside parties. In addition, many firms prepare summary reports or statements quarterly, monthly, and weekly for both internal use and external distribution. The frequency of reporting may affect the preparation cost and objectivity of the reports or statements.

Instructions

(a) Explain why the accounting period that is appropriate for internal and external reporting for most firms is one year.

(b) Explain in general terms why summary reports or statements are prepared for reporting periods of less than one year. Give an example why (1) internal management and (2) an outside party may want reports or statements that cover a shorter period.

(c) Adjustments to the accounting records are made when summary reports or statements are prepared annually, quarterly, or monthly.

(1) Explain why these adjustments are needed.

(2) Cite examples of adjustments that would have to be made to the accounting records.

(d) How is the objectivity of financial information in summary reports or statements affected when more frequent reports are prepared?

(Adapted from CMA.)

Chapter 7

Compound Interest Concepts

Objectives

1. To distinguish clearly between simple and compound interest.

2. To discuss and illustrate the fundamentals of compound interest.

3. To discuss and illustrate how to solve each of the following types of compound interest problems in accounting contexts:
   Amount and present value of a single sum.
   Amount and present value of an ordinary annuity.
   Amount and present value of an annuity due.
   Amount and present value of a deferred annuity.

A dollar received today is worth more than a dollar received one year from today. This is true even if we ignore inflation, because the dollar received today can be invested to earn a return. Thus, we could place $1.00 in a 6 percent savings account today and have $1.06 at the end of one year.

Money has been regarded as a valuable resource ever since scientists discovered that it doesn't grow on trees. It comes as no surprise, then, that money cannot be used free of charge. Money has a time value, commonly called **interest,** that people must consider when making rational investment and credit decisions.

Interest is the cost of using money over time. From the standpoint of a borrower, interest is the excess money that is paid over the amount that was borrowed. From the standpoint of the lender, interest is the excess money that is received over the amount that was loaned. The value of money changes over time, and therefore cash inflows and outflows that occur at different points in time are not directly comparable. Accordingly, they should not be lumped together but should be compared as of a common point in time. We may choose to compare cash flows as of some future time. Usually, however, we compare them as of the present time, because the present is the time within which we live and think.

To illustrate, assume that you have just decided to sell your wristwatch. Allen offers you $100, payable immediately, while Baker offers $103, to be paid in one year. Assuming that you can earn a 6 percent return on your money, which offer should you accept? Clearly, if we compare the alternatives as of one year hence, we find that Allen's offer is worth $106 ($100 × 1.06), whereas Baker's offer is worth only $103. Making the comparison as of the present time, we find that Allen's offer is worth $100 while Baker's offer is worth less ($103 ÷ 1.06 = $97.17). In either case, Allen's offer should be accepted. Note that, because money has a time value, we could not meaningfully compare the two offers until we determined the value of each offer as of a common point in time.

In this chapter, we explain and illustrate the fundamentals of compound interest. The time value of money has so many applications in business that it is often covered in several university courses, such as accounting, finance, economics, and mathematics. You must acquire a working knowledge of compound interest concepts to understand many topics covered in subsequent chapters. Examples are accounting for certain notes receivable and notes payable under "Financial Statement Concepts" in Paragraph 1000.54(c) of the CICA *Handbook,* accounting for bonds as investments and liabilities, accounting for leases under "Leases" in Section 3065, accounting for pension plans under "Pension Costs and Obligations," accounting for sinking funds, and accounting for installment contracts. That money has a time value is clearly recognized in J.A. Milburn's *Incorporating the Time Value of Money Within Financial Accounting,* a 1988 CICA Research Study, which frequently requires accountants to estimate and record interest even though a long-term note may contain no stated interest rate.

In this chapter, we are not concerned with changes in the general purchasing power of money over time (inflation or deflation). We will compare various sums of money without regard to the ability of those sums to buy goods and services. Assuming a 6 percent interest rate, for example, the question of whether $1.00 today can buy more or fewer goods and services than $1.06 can one year hence is beyond the scope of this chapter. More on this issue appears in Chapter 3.

Simple Versus Compound Interest

Interest is earned over a period of time. Therefore, a stated interest rate relates to a particular time period. Interest is normally stated as an **annual percentage rate,** such as

8 percent or 10 percent, and therefore we assume throughout the text that a stated interest rate is a rate **per year** unless indicated otherwise.

There are two types of interest: simple and compound. **Simple interest** is earned only on the principal sum of money invested. The formula for simple interest is

$$i = prt$$

where i = simple interest
p = principal sum of money
r = interest rate per unit of time
t = time expressed in units that correspond to the interest rate

For example, if $1500 is borrowed at 8 percent for one year, the simple interest is $1500 $\times$ 0.08 $\times$ 1 = $120. If the same amount is borrowed for only six months, simple interest is $1500 $\times$ 0.08 $\times$ $^{6}/_{12}$ = $60. **Note that r and t must correspond with each other.** If r is an annual rate, t must be expressed in years; if r is a monthly rate, t must be expressed in months; and so forth.

Simple interest is used in many short-term (less than one year) business transactions. Recall that we assumed simple interest in Chapter 6 when we illustrated adjusting entries for the accrual of interest on notes receivable and notes payable.

Compound interest is earned on the principal sum of money invested *and* on the interest accumulated. In other words, the principal earns interest and the accumulated interest earns interest. To illustrate, assume that $1500 is invested for three years at 8 percent. A comparison of simple versus compound interest on this investment appears in Exhibit 7.1.

Notice that with compound interest, the accumulated amount at the end of each year becomes the new principal sum on which interest is earned during the next year. Notice further that $29.57 ($389.57 − $360.00 or $1889.57 − $1860.00) of additional interest resulted from compound interest.[1] This is the interest on prior interest accumulations, which can be verified as shown in Exhibit 7.2.

Compound interest is used in most long-term (beyond one year) business transactions. Although interest is typically stated as an annual percentage rate, when compound interest is assumed, interest may be compounded (calculated and added to principal) for periods of less than one year. For example, interest may be compounded semi-annually, quarterly, monthly, daily, or even continuously.[2] To avoid repetition, we make the customary assumption throughout the text that a stated annual interest rate is compounded annually, unless indicated otherwise.

The rate of return with the simple interest calculation is 8 percent ($120 ÷ $1500 = 0.08). The same principal with interest compounded quarterly will provide a rate of return of 8.243 percent ($123.65 ÷ $1500.00 = 0.08243). The benefits of compounding become self-evident when it is viewed over a longer period of time. The compound interest calculation is shown in Exhibit 7.3.

Called the "eighth wonder of the world" by some people, compound interest has impressive power to make a sum of money grow. Francis Baily, a nineteenth-century British astronomer, determined that a British penny invested at 5 percent compound interest at the birth of Christ would have yielded enough gold by the year 1810 to fill 357 million earths. As another example, when Benjamin Franklin died in 1790, he left

---

[1]The rate of return under the simple interest method is 8 percent ($360/$1500/3 years = 0.08) versus a rate of return of 8.67 percent ($389.57/$1500/3 years = 0.0867%) under the compound interest method.

[2]Continuous compounding is accomplished using logarithms.

Exhibit 7.1 Simple Interest

$$i = prt \quad \$1500 \times 0.08 \times 3 = \$360$$
Accumulated amount at the end of three years is:
$$\$1500 + \$360 = \$1860$$

Compound Interest

(A) Year	(B) Principal		(C) Rate		(D) Time		(E) Compound Interest	(F) Accumulated Amount (B + E)
1	$1500.00	×	0.08	×	1	=	$120.00	$1620.00
2	1620.00	×	0.08	×	1	=	129.60	1749.60
3	1749.60	×	0.08	×	1	=	139.97	1889.57
						Total	$389.57	

Exhibit 7.2

Year	Prior Interest Accumulation		Rate		Time		Interest on Prior Interest Accumulation
1	—*	×	0.08	×	1	=	—
2	$120.00**	×	0.08	×	1	=	$ 9.60
3	249.60†	×	0.08	×	1	=	19.97
						Total	$29.57

*   No interest was accumulated prior to Year 1.
** This is the $120.00 interest for Year 1.
†   This is the $120.00 interest for Year 1 plus the $129.60 interest for Year 2.

Exhibit 7.3

No. of Months	Principal at the Beginning		Rate 8% ÷ 4 = 2%		Time		Interest on Prior Interest Accumulation
3	$1500.00*	×	0.02	×	1	=	$ 30.00
3	1530.00**	×	0.02	×	1	=	30.60
3	1560.60†	×	0.02	×	1	=	31.21
3	1591.81††	×	0.02	×	1	=	31.84
						Total	$123.65

*   No interest was accumulated prior to the first quarter.
** This is the principal + $30 interest at the end of the first quarter.
†   This is the principal $1530.00 + $31.21 interest at the end of the second quarter.
†† This is the principal $1560.60 + $31.84 interest at the end of the third quarter.

about $4600 to the cities of Boston and Philadelphia under the condition that the money not be used for 100 years. By 1890, the $4600 had grown to $332 000.[3]

Basic Concepts

The fundamental concepts underlying all compound interest problems are as follows:

1. **Present value (*PV*).** Present value usually refers to a value at the present time (today) of cash flows to be received in the future. More generally, it refers to a value at the beginning of any time span that is of concern.

2. **Future value (*FV*).** This usually refers to a value at some time in the future of cash received today. More generally, future value can refer to a value at the end of any time period that is of concern.

3. **Interest rate (*i*).** This refers to a rate that corresponds to the length of each compounding period. The rate is computed by dividing the annual interest rate by the number of times a year interest is compounded.[4] For example, if interest is stated at 8 percent, compounded annually (once per year), the interest rate is 8 percent per annual period (0.08 ÷ 1). If interest is stated at 8 percent, compounded semi-annually (twice per year), the interest rate is 4 percent per semi-annual period (0.08 ÷ 2). And if interest is stated at 8 percent, compounded quarterly (four times per year), the interest rate is 2 percent per quarterly period (0.08 ÷ 4).

4. **Time periods (*n*).** This refers to the number of compounding periods. It may be computed by multiplying the number of years involved by the number of compounding periods in each year. For example, interest for three years, compounded semi-annually, involves 6 (3 × 2) compounding periods. Likewise, interest for three years, compounded quarterly, involves 12 (3 × 4) compounding periods.

Using these four fundamental concepts, we can solve compound interest problems.

Quite often, sketching the known components in the form of a **time diagram** aids in understanding and resolving the compound interest problem. The four concepts discussed above are depicted in the following time diagram:

---

[3]Robert L. Rose, "Compounding: It's Boring but a Wonder," *Wall Street Journal* (June 17, 1985), p. 23.

[4]The interest rate (i) is called a **stated,** or **nominal, rate.** Furthermore, the term **frequency of compounding** (usually denoted by the letter n) refers to the number of times a year interest is compounded.

It is worthwhile to note that whenever m is greater than 1, the effective or true rate of interest (r) on an investment is greater than the stated annual rate. The **effective rate** is the rate that, when compounded annually, generates the same annual interest as the stated annual rate does when compounded m times per year. The effective rate may be calculated using the following formula:

$$r = (1 + i)^n - 1$$

For example, if the stated annual rate is 8 percent compounded quarterly, the effective annual rate is:

$$
\begin{aligned}
r &= (1 + i)^n - 1 \\
&= (1 + 0.02)^4 - 1 \\
&= (1.02)^4 - 1 \\
&= 1.08243 - 1 \\
&= 0.08243 \\
&= 8.243\%
\end{aligned}
$$

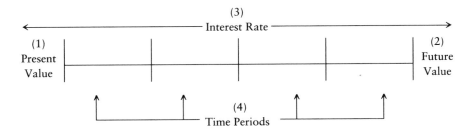

Single Sum Problems

Single sum problems (sometimes called lump sum problems) involve a single sum of money and generally fall into one of the following categories:

1. Problems that focus on the future value of a single sum of money that is left on deposit for a certain number of periods at a certain interest rate per period.
2. Problems that focus on the present value of a single sum of money that is discounted for a certain number of periods at a certain interest rate per period.

Amount (Future Value) of a Single Sum

In everyday conversation, "amount" refers to any amount, past, present, or future. In discussions of compound interest, amount refers only to a *future value*. The amount of a single sum is therefore the future value to which the sum will accumulate if left on deposit for a certain number of periods at a certain interest rate per period. For example, in the earlier discussion of simple and compound interest, $1889.57 (a future value) is the amount to which $1500 (a single sum of money) will accumulate if left on deposit for three years at 8 percent compounded annually. The solution is illustrated in the time diagram in Exhibit 7.4. Note that the arrow points to the right, the direction of the future value.

The period-by-period approach used earlier to calculate future value is somewhat cumbersome, and it would be even more so in a problem involving more than three periods. To simplify the calculations, the basic compound interest formula is applied:

$$FV = PV(1 + i)^n$$

where FV = future value of a single sum
PV = present value (principal sum) of a single sum
i = interest rate per compounding period
n = number of compounding periods

Applying this formula, we find that $1889.57 is indeed the future value:

$$
\begin{aligned}
FV &= PV(1 + i)^n \\
&= \$1500\,(1 + 0.08)^3 \\
&= \$1500\,(1.08)^3 \\
&= \$1500\,(1.25971) \\
&= \$1889.57
\end{aligned}
$$

Note that the formula consists of four variables: FV, PV, i, and n. If we know the values of *any* three, we can solve for the fourth using algebra.

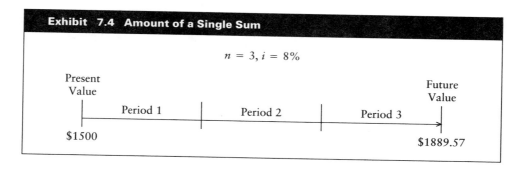

Exhibit 7.4 Amount of a Single Sum

$$n = 3, i = 8\%$$

Present Value

Future Value

| Period 1 | Period 2 | Period 3 |

$1500

$1889.57

Focus for a moment on the $(1 + i)^n$ part of the formula. Because of the frequent need to apply compound interest concepts in the business world, tables have been published that provide solutions for $(1 + i)^n$ for many combinations of i and n. We will refer to each of these solutions as a **future value factor** (*fvf*). Table 7.1 at the end of this chapter contains future value factors for most of the commonly encountered i and n values.[5] It can be used to save time in solving problems that involve the amount of a single sum.

Table 7.1 is entitled "Amount of 1" because it gives the amounts (future values) to which 1 (such as 1 dollar, 1 peso, or 1 mark) will accumulate if left on deposit for n periods at i compound interest. If we know the amount to which 1 will accumulate, we can find the amount to which any single sum will accumulate by simply multiplying the single sum by the amount to which 1 will accumulate. Note that the table consists of rows of compounding periods (n) and columns of interest rates (i). A future value factor is located at the intersection of each row and column.[6] For example, the future value factor of $n = 5$ and $i = 10\%$ is 1.61051. To illustrate finding a table factor, Exhibit 7.5 presents a portion of Table 7.1 with the factor boxed for $n = 5$ and $i = 10\%$ (1.61051).

To really understand the solutions to compound interest problems, you should remember how Table 7.1 was constructed—that is, by solving $(1 + i)^n$ for different combinations of i and n values. It is no surprise that future value factors increase with each increase in i or n.

Because we know that $FV = PV(1 + i)^n$ and $(1 + i)^n = fvf$, we can now state Equation 7.1:

$$FV = PV \times fvf_{n|i}$$

where FV = future value of a single sum
PV = present value (principal sum) of a single sum
$fvf_{n|i}$ = future value factor (from Table 7.1) for the relevant n and i

The expression $fvf_{n|i}$ is read as "*fvf* sub n at i" or "*fvf* angle n at i." When solving a compound interest equation, inserting the values for n and i ensures that you will locate and use the correct table factor.

Recall that we have determined, using both a period-by-period approach and a formula approach, that $1889.57 is the future value of $1500 deposited for 3 years at

---

[5]Table 7.1, as well as the other tables at the end of the chapter, are partial. In practice, more comprehensive tables are widely available. Of course, any compound interest table can be extended by using the formula on which the table is based.

[6]Notice that each table factor is rounded to five decimal places. In practice, tables rounded to ten places are often used when dealing with extremely large numbers in order to minimize the effects of rounding.

Exhibit 7.5 Finding the Future Value Factor of $n = 5$, $i = 10$ percent Using Table 7.1 (Amount of 1)

Periods (n)	8%	10%	12%
1	1.08000	1.10000	1.12000
2	1.16640	1.21000	1.25400
3	1.25971	1.33100	1.40493
4	1.36049	1.46410	1.57352
5	1.46933	1.61051	1.76234
6	1.58687	1.77156	1.97382

8 percent compounded annually. Now we can use Equation 7.1 and Table 7.1 to implement a third approach to solving the problem. This approach is the easiest of all, because some of the calculations have already been performed and the results appear in Table 7.1. First, note in Table 7.1 that the *fvf* for $n = 3$ and $i = 8\%$ is 1.25971. Now we can say

$$
\begin{aligned}
FV &= PV - fvf_{n|i} \\
&= \$1500 \times fvf_{3|8\%} \\
&= \$1500(1.25971) \\
&= \$1889.57
\end{aligned}
$$

Because of the computational ease and time savings offered by compound interest tables, we emphasize a table-based solution to the problems in this chapter.

Accounting Examples

Problem 1. At the beginning of Year 1, New Brunswick Electric Company deposited $50 000 in a special building fund that earns 8 percent interest compounded quarterly. How much cash will be in the fund at the end of Year 10? What is the future value of the $50 000 fund?

Solution 1. In this problem we know the present value ($50 000), the interest rate per period ($0.08 \div 4 = 0.02$), and the number of periods (4 periods per year $\times$ 10 years = 40 periods). We must solve for the future value, which we do with Equation 7.1 and Table 7.1:

$$
\begin{aligned}
FV &= PV \times fvf_{n|i} \\
&= \$50\ 000 \times fvf_{40|2\%} \\
&= \$50\ 000\ (2.20804) \\
&= \$110\ 402
\end{aligned}
$$

Problem 2. To keep things simple, let's modify Problem 1. Assume that New Brunswick Electric Company wants to accumulate $110 402 for the purchase of a new building. If at the beginning of Year 1 the company deposited $50 000 in a special building fund that earns 8 percent interest compounded quarterly, how many years will it take for the fund to accumulate to $110 402? When will the future value be reached?

Solution 2. We know the present value ($50 000), the future value ($110 402), and the interest rate per period ($0.08 \div 4 = 0.02$). We are asked to solve for the number of years, which we can easily do using Equation 7.1 and Table 7.1. Since $FV = PV \times fvf_{n|i}$, we can divide both sides of the equation by PV:

$$fvf_{n|i} = \frac{FV}{PV}$$

$$fvf_{n|2\%} = \frac{\$110\ 402}{\$\ 50\ 000}$$

$$= 2.20804$$

Now that we know the future value factor and the interest rate per period, we simply run our finger down the 2 percent column of Table 7.1 until we find 2.20804. Since 2.20804 is found at $n = 40$, we conclude that it will take 10 years (40 quarterly interest periods ÷ 4) to accumulate $110 402. If we had not found the number 2.20804 in the 2% column of Table 7.1, we could have approximated our answer using linear interpolation, a procedure explained later in the chapter.

Problem 3. Suppose that the problem were phrased this way. New Brunswick Electric Company wants to accumulate $110 402 for the purchase of a new building. If at the beginning of Year 1 the company deposited $50 000 in a special building fund in which interest is compounded quarterly, what annual rate of interest is required for the $50 000 deposit to accumulate to $110 402 at the end of year 10? In which column on the Year 10 line of Table 7.1 will you find the factor 2.20804?

Solution 3. We follow the same approach taken in Problem 2, except that we look for the future value factor of 2.20804 in Table 7.1 along the row in which $n = 40$ (10 years × 4 compounding periods per year). Because 2.20804 is in the 2% column, we conclude that the required annual rate of interest is 8 percent (0.02 × 4).

Present Value of a Single Sum

Determining the present value of a single sum is the inverse of determining the amount of a single sum. Instead of moving forward in time using accumulation to determine a future value, we move backward in time using **discounting** to determine a present value. For example, suppose that we want to know the present value of $1889.57 to be received or paid in three years discounted at 8 percent compounded annually. We could prepare a decumulation table similar to the compound interest accumulation table presented earlier. Instead of going forward in time, we would go backward, and instead of multiplying each year's principal by 1.08, we would multiply by 1 ÷ 1.08 (which is the same as dividing by 1.08), as shown in Exhibit 7.6. The time diagram in Exhibit 7.7 illustrates the solution to the problem. The arrow in the diagram points to the left, which is the direction of the present value.

That $1500 is the present value (the decumulated amount at the beginning of Year 1) is no surprise, because this problem was used earlier to explain the amount of a single sum. Preparing decumulation tables is tedious and time-consuming. Fortunately, there are easier ways to solve the problem.

Remember that the basic compound interest formula is

$$FV = PV(1 + i)^n$$

If we divide both sides of this equation by $(1 + i)^n$, we get

Exhibit 7.6 Compound Discount

(A) Year	(B) Principal		(C) Discount Rate		(D) Time		(E) Decumulated Interest	(F) Compound Discount (B + E)
1	$1889.57	×	$\frac{1}{1.08}$	×	1	=	$1749.60	$139.97
2	1749.60	×	$\frac{1}{1.08}$	×	1	=	1620.00	129.60
3	1620.00	×	$\frac{1}{1.08}$	×	1	=	1500.00	120.00
								$389.57

Exhibit 7.7 Present Value of a Single Sum

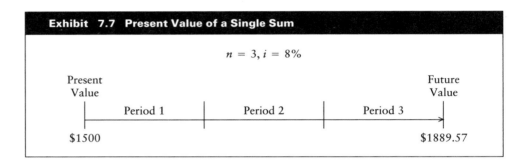

$$n = 3, i = 8\%$$

Present Value — Period 1 — Period 2 — Period 3 — Future Value

$1500 $1889.57

$$PV = \frac{FV}{(1 + i)^n}$$

We can now apply this formula to the problem and determine that $1500 is indeed the present value:

$$PV = \frac{FV}{(1 + i)^n}$$
$$= \frac{\$1889.57}{(1.08)^3}$$
$$= \frac{\$1889.57}{1.25971}$$
$$= \$1500$$

We can easily rewrite the above formula as follows:

$$PV = FV \times \frac{1}{(1 + i)^n}$$

The $\frac{1}{(1 + i)^n}$ part of the equation is simply the reciprocal (inverse) of the formula used to calculate the amount of 1. Tables that provide solutions for $\frac{1}{(1 + i)^n}$ for combinations of i and n are widely available. We will refer to each of these solutions as a **present value factor** (*pvf*). A present value factor is simply the reciprocal of the future value factor for a given i and n. Table 7.2 at the end of the chapter contains present value factors for many i and n combinations. Given the formula used to construct the table, you should not be surprised that present value factors decrease with an increase in n or i. Note that the table is entitled "Present Value of 1." If we know the present value of 1 for a certain i and n, we can easily compute the present value of any single sum by multiplying the single sum by the present value of 1.

Because we know that $PV = FV \times \dfrac{1}{(1 + i)^n}$ and $\dfrac{1}{(1 + i)^n} = pvf$, we can now state Equation 7.2:

$$PV = FV \times pvf_{n \rceil i}$$
$$\text{where } PV = \text{present value (principal sum) of a single sum}$$
$$FV = \text{future value of a single sum}$$
$$pvf_{n \rceil i} = \text{present value factor (from Table 7.2) for the relevant } n \text{ and } i$$

Equation 7.2 saves time in solving problems for the present value of a single sum. To illustrate its application to the example problem, we first find in Table 7.2 that the pvf for $n = 3$ and $i = 8\%$ is 0.79383. Now we can state the following:

$$PV = FV \times pvf_{n \rceil i}$$
$$= \$1889.57 \times pvf_{3 \rceil 8\%}$$
$$= \$1889.57 \, (0.79383)$$
$$= \$1500$$

Accounting Examples

Problem 4.   What is the value at the beginning of Year 1 of a noninterest-bearing note that has a maturity value of \$10 000 at the end of Year 4? Assume that the market rate of interest for similar notes is 8 percent compounded annually.

Solution 4.   We know the future value (the \$10 000 maturity value), the interest rate per period (8 percent), and the number of periods (four). We can solve for the present value by using Equation 7.2 and Table 7.2:

$$PV = FV \times pvf_{n \rceil i}$$
$$= \$10\,000 \times pvf_{4 \rceil 8\%}$$
$$= \$10\,000 \, (0.73503)$$
$$= \$7350.30$$

In other words, \$7350.30 is the sum that a person would pay today to receive \$10 000 at the end of four years, assuming 8 percent interest compounded annually. That the note could only be sold at a discount (\$10 000 − \$7350.30 = \$2649.70) appears reasonable, because the note has no stated interest and similar notes yield 8 percent.

As in the examples concerning the amount of a single sum, we could alter the information in Problem 4 to illustrate solutions for other variables. However, the point should now be clear: we are dealing with one basic equation of four variables. When three of the variables are known, solving for the one that is unknown is not difficult.

Problem 5.   One of your clients, I.M. Rich, wants to put aside some money to buy her son an \$8000 automobile when he graduates from university in four years. Assuming that Ms. Rich will earn 6 percent, compounded annually, on her savings during the first two years and 8 percent, compounded semi-annually, during the last two years, how much should she deposit at the beginning of the four-year period?

Solution 5. Once again, we are seeking the present value of a single sum ($20 000). However, in this case the interest rate and the frequency of compounding change after the second year. We therefore need to break down the problem into two components. First, compute the present value, as of the beginning of the third year, of $20 000 to be received at the end of four semi-annual periods discounted at 4 percent per period. (Remember that the 8 percent interest is compounded semi-annually during the last two years.) Second, compute the present value, as of the beginning of the first year, of the value calculated in the first step when discounted for two years at 6 percent. Thus, we have

$$
\begin{aligned}
\textbf{Step 1.} \quad PV &= FV \times pvf_{n|i} \\
&= \$20\ 000 \times pvf_{4|4\%} \\
&= \$20\ 000\ (0.85480) \\
&= \$17\ 096
\end{aligned}
$$

The value $17 096 is the present value as of the beginning of the third year. To determine the present value as of the beginning of the first year, we must perform Step 2.

$$
\begin{aligned}
\textbf{Step 2.} \quad PV &= FV \times pvf_{n|i} \\
&= \$17\ 096 \times pvf_{2|6\%} \\
&= \$17\ 096\ (0.089000) \\
&= \$15\ 215.44
\end{aligned}
$$

Ms. Rich should therefore deposit $15 215.44 so that she will have the $20 000 required to purchase the automobile at the end of the four-year period.

Remember from this example that **whenever a compound interest problem appears complex, try to solve the problem by dividing it into its components.**

Annuity Problems

An annuity is a series of equal receipts or payments, called **rents,** that occur at uniform intervals at a constant interest rate.[7] This book assumes a standard annuity, in which interest is compounded once at the end of each interval. Annuities commonly occur at annual, semi-annual, quarterly, or monthly intervals. Lease payments, sinking fund payments, mortgage payments, and retirement payments are only a few examples of annuities that accountants encounter every day.

Annuities may be classified as ordinary annuities or annuities due.[8] The difference lies solely in the timing of the rents. With an **ordinary annuity,** the rents occur at the *end* of each period. With an **annuity due,** the rents occur at the **beginning** of each period. In both kinds of annuities *one* rent occurs during each period, either at the beginning (annuity due) or at the end (ordinary annuity). For this reason, the symbol *n* in annuity problems refers to either the number of compounding periods or the number of rents.

As in the single sum problems discussed earlier, annuities involve present and future value concepts. Whereas earlier discussions dealt with the present and future values of a

---

[7]Note that the term *rents* refers to a series of equal receipts or payments of any kind. In compound interest discussions, use of this term is not confined to its everyday connotation of payments on a leased asset.

[8]Ordinary annuities are sometimes called *annuities in arrears,* while annuities due are sometimes called *annuities in advance.*

single sum, the following sections concern the present and future values of multiple sums, each of which is equal in size.

Amount (Future Value) of an Ordinary Annuity

As shown earlier, a single sum of $1500 left on deposit for three years at 8 percent will accumulate to 1889.57. What is the amount (future value) at the end of three years of *three periodic rents of $1500 each* that occur at the end of each year at 8 percent compounded annually? The question involves the amount of an ordinary annuity.

As the time diagram in Exhibit 7.8 suggests, computing the amount of an ordinary annuity involves nothing more than computing the total amount of a series of single sums.[9] Algebraically, we have

			Amount of the
3rd Rent	**2nd Rent**	**1st Rent**	**Ordinary Annuity**
$1500	+ $1500 (1.08)	+ $1500 (1.08)² =	$4869.60

Note that although the annuity encompasses three periods, only two rents earn interest. The first rent earns interest during periods two and three. The second rent earns interest during period three only. The third rent earns no interest, because it occurs at the end of the three-year span. In an amount of an ordinary annuity of n rents, only n − 1 rents will earn interest, because the last rent occurs at the end of the annuity term and no interest period exists for that rent. **An amount of an ordinary annuity focusses on a future value and the last rent occurs at the end of the annuity term.**

Of course, the $1500 rent in the preceding equation could be factored out:

$$\$1500 (1 + 1.08 + 1.08^2) = \$4869.60$$
$$\$1500 (1 + 1.08 + 1.1664) = \$4869.60$$
$$\$1500 (3.2464) = \$4869.60$$

Turn to Table 7.3 at the end of the chapter and locate the factor for $n = 3$, $i =$ 8%. You will see that it is 3.24640, the number by which we multiplied $1500 in the last equation. Note that Table 7.3, entitled "Amount of an Ordinary Annuity of 1," contains factors for many combinations of n and i. Each factor is an **amount of an ordinary annuity factor (*aoaf*)**. Each factor could have been determined by the approach used above for $n = 3$ and $i = 8\%$, but the following formula was applied to save time in generating each factor:

$$aoaf_{n\,|\,i} = \frac{(1 + i)^n - 1}{i}$$

Each table factor, then, is based on an equation that incorporates values for both n and i.

---

[9]You may find it helpful to verify this statement by applying Equation 7.1 and Table 7.1 to each of the $1500 rents. This would give the following results:

1st rent	$1500 (1.16640)	=	$1749.60
2nd rent	1500 (1.08000)	=	1620.00
3rd rent	1500 (1.00000)	=	1500.00
	Total		$4869.60

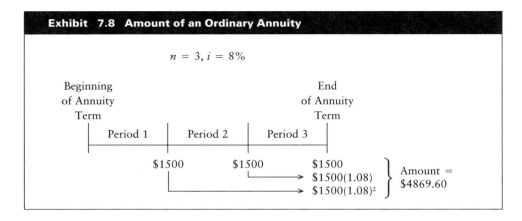

Exhibit 7.8 Amount of an Ordinary Annuity

$n = 3, i = 8\%$

Using Table 7.3, we can find the amount to which an ordinary annuity of any size rent will accumulate. We simply multiply the size of each rent by the amount to which an ordinary annuity of 1 will accumulate. Expressed algebraically, we have Equation 7.3:

$$AOA = R \times aoaf_{n|i}$$

where AOA = amount (future value) of an ordinary annuity of n rents at i interest rate

R = size of each periodic rent

$aoaf_{n|i}$ = amount of an ordinary annuity of 1 factor (from Table 7.3) for the relevant n and i

Notice that Equation 7.3 contains four variables (AOA, R, n, and i), and if we know the values of any three, we can solve for the fourth using algebra.

Accounting Examples

Problem 6. On January 1 of the current year, Control Systems Corporation creates a sinking fund to accumulate cash that will be needed to retire a $1 million issue of bonds payable that matures in ten years. Accordingly, the company decides to make twenty semi-annual payments of $30 000 each into a sinking fund. The first payment will be made on June 30 of the current year, and the fund is expected to earn interest at 10 percent compounded semi-annually. How much cash will be in the fund at the end of ten years?

Solution 6. The problem clearly involves an annuity, because periodic payments (rents) of $30 000 each will be placed in a sinking fund. Furthermore, it is an ordinary annuity, because the initial rent occurs at the end of the first semi-annual period. Because the payments are made semi-annually, we know that $n = 10 \times 2 = 20$ and $i = 10\% \div 2 = 5\%$. We must determine the amount of an ordinary annuity of twenty rents of $30 000 each at 5 percent interest. Using Equation 7.3 and Table 7.3, we have

$$
\begin{aligned}
AOA &= R \times aoaf_{n|i} \\
&= \$30\ 000 \times aoaf_{20|5\%} \\
&= \$30\ 000\ (33.06595) \\
&= \$991\ 978.50
\end{aligned}
$$

Unfortunately, the amount in the sinking fund at the end of ten years will be $8021.50 ($1 000 000 − $991 978.50) less than the company needs to retire the bonds.

Problem 7.   Referring to Problem 6, how much would Control Systems Corporation have to deposit at the end of each semi-annual period to accumulate $1 million in the sinking fund at the end of ten years?

Solution 7.   In Problem 6, semi-annual deposits of $30 000 left the company $8021.50 short of its goal of $1 million. Thus, logic dictates that the company will have to deposit somewhat more than $30 000 each period. To find the exact size of each deposit, we refer to Equation 7.3. Dividing both sides of the equation by $aoaf_{n|i}$ and substituting the values of the known variables, gives us the following:

$$R = \frac{AOA}{aoaf_{n|i}}$$
$$= \frac{\$1\ 000\ 000}{aoaf_{20|5\%}}$$
$$= \frac{\$1\ 000\ 000}{33.06595}$$
$$= \$30\ 242.59$$

Control Systems Corporation must therefore deposit $30 242.59 at the end of each semi-annual period to accumulate $1 million at the end of ten years.

Problem 8.   One of your clients, Tom Mack, tells you that he wants to accumulate a $10 000 cash gift for his new baby daughter by depositing $300 at yearly intervals beginning one year from now. The periodic deposits will be placed in a 6 percent savings account. When Tom accumulates the $10 000, how old will his daughter be?

Solution 8.   We know that this problem involves an ordinary annuity, because the periodic deposits of $300 begin one year from now. Furthermore, we know the desired future amount ($10 000), the size of the periodic rents ($300), and the interest rate per period (6 percent). The unknown that we seek is the number of periods, which we can determine by rewriting Equation 7.3 and using Table 7.3. Dividing both sides of the equation by R and substituting the known values, we have

$$aoaf_{n|i} = \frac{AOA}{R}$$
$$aoaf_{n|i} = \frac{\$10\ 000}{\$300}$$
$$= 33.33333$$

We now search the 6% column of Table 7.3 for the factor 33.33333. We won't find it, but we can determine that it would lie between 30.90565 (the factor for $n = 18$) and 33.75999 (the factor for $n = 19$). Because it is closer to the factor for $n = 19$, we conclude that it will take almost nineteen years for Tom Mack to accumulate $10 000. In other words, Tom's daughter will be almost nineteen years old when she receives the $10 000 gift from her father.

A closer approximation may be achieved by using linear interpolation. In general, when a factor is computed but does not appear in the pertinent compound interest table, interpolation may be used to find a reasonable approximation of the unknown number of periods (n) or interest rate (i).[10] The smaller the range of interpolation, the smaller the error will be. Interpolation is based on the principle of proportion, as the following format suggests:

---

[10]An exact answer may be determined using logarithms.

	When n is:	The corresponding $aoaf$ is:
	18	30.90565
	?	33.33333
	19	33.75999

$$ 1 \left\{ x \left\{ \begin{array}{cc} 18 & 30.90565 \\ ? & 33.33333 \\ 19 & 33.75999 \end{array} \right\} 2.42768 \right\} 2.85434 $$

We can set up the following proportion: $\dfrac{x}{1} = \dfrac{2.42768}{2.85434}$

Solving for x, we find that it equals 0.85. Since x is the distance between 18 and n, we conclude that $n = 18 + 0.85 = 18.85$ (18 years and 10.2 months). Tom's daughter, then, will be approximately 18.85 years old when she receives her gift. Any time you want to interpolate, set up a proportion similar to the one shown above.

Problem 9.   Referring to the information in Problem 8, what interest rate would Tom Mack have to earn on his investment so that he could give his daughter the $10 000 present on her eighteenth birthday?

Solution 9.   Logic dictates that since it would take approximately 18.85 years to accumulate $10 000 at 6 percent interest, Tom will have to earn more than 6 percent to accumulate the same amount in less time. Once again, dividing both sides of Equation 7.3 by R, we have

$$ aoaf_{n|i} = \frac{AOA}{R} $$

Therefore, $aoaf_{18|i} = \$10\ 000/\$300 = 33.33333$. Looking across the $n = 18$ row of Table 7.3, we determine that 33.33333 would lie between 30.90565 (the factor for $i = 6\%$) and 37.45024 (the factor for $i = 8\%$). Approximating the answer through interpolation we have

$$ 2\% \left\{ x \left\{ \begin{array}{cc} 6\% & 30.90565 \\ ? & 33.33333 \\ 8\% & 37.45024 \end{array} \right\} 2.42768 \right\} 6.54459 $$

Setting up a proportion, we have $\dfrac{x}{2\%} = \dfrac{2.42768}{6.54459}$

Solving for x, we find that it equals 0.74 percent. Since x is the distance between 6% and i, we conclude that $i = 6\% + 0.74\% = 6.74\%$. Tom Mack would thus have to earn roughly 6.74 percent interest if he wanted to give his daughter $10 000 on her eighteenth birthday.

Amount (Future Value) of an Annuity Due

Earlier, we stated that an annuity due is one in which the rents occur at the *beginning* of each period. Further, we saw that $4869.60 is the amount of an *ordinary* annuity of three annual rents of $1500 each at 8 percent. What is the amount at the end of three years of three annual rents of $1500 each that occur at the *beginning* of each year at 8 percent compounded annually?

As the time diagram in Exhibit 7.9 suggests, an annuity due begins with a rent and ends one period *after* the last rent. Thus, if we took the amount of an ordinary annuity of three $1500 rents at 8 percent and left all the money on deposit at 8 percent for one additional period, we would have the amount of an annuity due of three $1500 rents at 8 percent. For any given values of n and i, the amount of an annuity due is greater than the amount of an ordinary annuity by the interest on the latter amount for one period. Stated differently, the amount of an annuity due for given values of n and i is equal to the amount of an ordinary annuity of $n + 1$ rents at i interest rate, *minus* one rent (the final rent).

An amount of an annuity due focusses on a future value, and last rent occurs one period before the end of the annuity term. In an amount of an annuity due of n rents, all of the n rents earn interest. Note carefully in Exhibit 7.9 that the third rent earns interest for one period, the second rent earns interest for two periods, and the first rent earns interest for three periods. Algebraically,

$$\$1500\,(1.08) + \$1500\,(1.08)^2 + \$1500\,(1.08)^3 = \$5259.17$$

Factoring out the $1500 rent, we get

$$\$1500\,(1.08 + 1.08^2 + 1.08^3) = \$5259.17$$
$$\$1500\,(1.08 + 1.1664 + 1.25971) = \$5259.17$$
$$\$1500\,(3.50611) = \$5259.17$$

In the last equation, 3.50611 is simply a factor for computing the amount of an annuity due (***aadf***) where $n = 3$ and $i = 8\%$. We could construct a table of these factors and call it "Amount of an Annuity Due of 1." However, the relationship between the amount of an ordinary annuity and the amount of an annuity due is so straightforward that a separate table is unnecessary. We can use the "Amount of an Ordinary Annuity of 1" table (Table 7.3) to determine an *aadf* simply by finding the factor for $n + 1$ periods and i, and subtracting 1 from the factor we find. Stated algebraically,[11]

$$aadf_{\overline{n}|i} = aoaf_{\overline{n+1}|i} - 1$$

To illustrate, let's use Table 7.3 to calculate $aadf_{3|8\%}$. We simply look up the table factor for $n + 1 = 4$ periods and $i = 8\%$, and we find 4.50611. Subtracting 1 from this, we get 3.50611. Now that we know how to derive an *aadf* using Table 7.3, we can state Equation 7.3A:

$$AAD = R \times aadf_{\overline{n}|i}$$

where AAD = amount of an annuity due of n rents at i interest rate

R = size of each periodic rent

$aadf_{\overline{n}|i}$ = amount of an annuity due of 1 factor (from Table 7.3, as adjusted) for the relevant n and i

---

[11] A second way to derive $aadf_{\overline{n}|i}$ is as follows:

$$aadf_{\overline{n}|i} = aoaf_{\overline{n}|i}(1 + i).$$

Although this approach is correct, it is more difficult to use when i is the unknown variable.

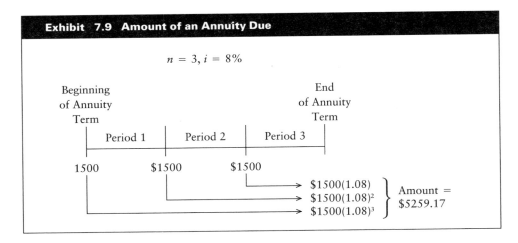

Exhibit 7.9 Amount of an Annuity Due

Because of the values of n and i determine the value of $aadf_{n|i}$, Equation 7.3A consists of four variables: AAD, R, n, and i. Remember that if we know the values of any three, we can solve for the fourth using algebra.

Accounting Example

Problem 10. Warren Wilson has created a fund for his retirement in 35 years. He deposits $3000 today in a special 8 percent account, and he plans to make periodic deposits of $3000 each at annual intervals over the next 34 years. How much cash will be in Wilson's retirement fund when he retires?

Solution 10. Because the initial rent occurs at the beginning of the first year, we are dealing with an annuity due. Specifically, we are asked to calculate the amount (a future value) of an annuity due of 35 rents of $3000 at 8 percent. Using Equation 7.3A and Table 7.3, as adjusted, we have

$$
\begin{aligned}
AAD &= R \times aadf_{n|i} \\
&= \$3000 \times aadf_{35|8\%} \\
&= \$3000\,(aadf_{35+1|8\%} - 1) \\
&= \$3000\,(187.10215 - 1) \\
&= \$3000\,(186.10215) \\
&= \$558\ 306.45
\end{aligned}
$$

Present Value of an Ordinary Annuity

We have seen that the amount of an ordinary annuity of three annual rents of $1500 each at 8 percent is $4869.60. Accountants must often solve problems that are the inverse of this one; for example: What is the present value of an ordinary annuity of three annual rents of $1500 each discounted at 8 percent? The time diagram in Exhibit 7.10 illustrates the solution.

A present value of an ordinary annuity focusses on a present value, and the first rent occurs one period after the beginning of the annuity term. Note carefully that the initial rent occurs at the end of the first time period, consistent with our definition of an ordinary annuity. When the present value of an ordinary annuity of n rents is computed, each rent is discounted.

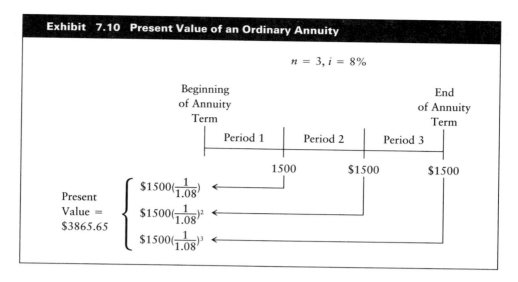

Exhibit 7.10   Present Value of an Ordinary Annuity

In Exhibit 7.10, we compute the present value of an ordinary annuity by computing the present value of each rent and summing the results. Algebraically, we have

	1st Rent		2nd Rent		3rd Rent		Present Value of the Ordinary Annuity

$$\$1500(\tfrac{1}{1.08}) \; + \; \$1500(\tfrac{1}{1.08})^2 \; + \; \$1500(\tfrac{1}{1.08})^3 \; = \quad \$3865.65$$

Factoring out the $1500 rent, we have

$$\$1500\,[(\tfrac{1}{1.08}) + (\tfrac{1}{1.08})^2 + (\tfrac{1}{1.08})^3] = \$3865.65$$
$$\$1500\,(0.92593 + 0.85734 + 0.79383) = \$3865.65$$
$$\$1500\,(2.57710) = \$3865.65$$

Locate the table factor for $n = 3$, $i = 8\%$ in Table 7.4. Through no coincidence, it is 2.57710, the number we multiplied by $1500 in the last equation. Table 7.4 is titled "Present Value of an Ordinary Annuity of 1." It contains many factors, each of which we will call a **present value of an ordinary annuity factor (*pvoaf*)**. Although each *pvoaf* could have been calculated by the approach illustrated above for $n = 3$ and $i = 8\%$, the following formula is used to save time:

$$pvoaf_{n\rceil i} = \frac{1 - \dfrac{1}{(1 + i)^n}}{i}$$

As the title indicates, Table 7.4 includes present value factors assuming an ordinary annuity of 1. For given n and i values, we can easily calculate the present value of an ordinary annuity of any size rent: we simply multiply the size of each rent by the present value of an ordinary annuity of 1.

We can state Equation 7.4 algebraically as follows:

$$PVOA = R \times pvoaf_{n|i}$$

where $PVOA$ = present value of an ordinary annuity of n rents at i interest rate

R = size of each periodic rent

$pvoaf_{n|i}$ = present value of an ordinary annuity of 1 factor (from Table 7.4) for the relevant n and i

Of the four variables ($PVOA$, R, n, and i), any three must be known to solve for the fourth.

Accounting Example

Problem 11. On January 1 of the current year, Allied Steel Company issues $5 million of 8 percent, twenty-year term bonds that pay interest semi-annually each June 30 and December 31. How much cash will the bonds sell for if, on January 1, the market rate of interest for bonds similar to those of Allied Steel Company is 10 percent?

Solution 11. Note that Allied's bonds have a **coupon interest rate** (often called **nominal rate** or **stated rate**) of 8 percent. This is simply the annual rate of interest stated in the bond contract. This rate is used to compute the amount of cash that will be paid as interest to bondholders each year. Note also that when the bonds are sold, the **market rate of interest** (often called the **yield rate** or the **effective rate**) for similar bonds is 10 percent. What would entice bond investors to purchase Allied's 8 percent bonds when these investors could purchase similar bonds that earn 10 percent?

Of course, the bonds must sell for a price that is less than their par or face value. In other words, the bonds will sell at a **discount,** the amount necessary to bring the yield rate on Allied's bonds up to the 10 percent market rate. Logic also dictates that when the coupon rate exceeds the market rate, the bonds will sell at a **premium.** When the two rates are equal, the bonds will sell at **par.**

Now that we have used intuition, let's formulate a more precise solution to the problem. First, recognize that since the bonds pay interest semi-annually, they include 20 $\times$ 2 = 40 periods (n = 40), and the stated interest rate per period is 8% $\div$ 2 = 4%. Second, recognize that in addition to paying the $5 million maturity value (a single sum) to bondholders in twenty years, Allied must also pay $200 000 (0.04 $\times$ $5 000 000) interest at the end of each semi-annual period for twenty years. The interest payments constitute an ordinary annuity. Finally, recognize that to compute the present value of the bonds (the price bondholders would be willing to pay on January 1), we must discount the maturity value and the interest annuity using the market rate of interest per period, so i = 10% $\div$ 2 = 5%. Now we can determine the present value of Allied's bonds using the following two steps:

Step 1. Compute the present value of the single sum maturity value of $5 000 000 for n = 40 and i = 5%. (Use Equation 7.2 and Table 7.2.)

$$PV = FV \times pvf_{n|i}$$
$$= 5\ 000\ 000 \times pvf_{40|5\%}$$
$$= \$5\ 000\ 000\ (0.14205)$$
$$= \$710\ 250$$

Step 2. Compute the present value of the ordinary interest annuity of $200 000 for n = 40 and i = 5%. (Use Equation 7.4 and Table 7.4.)

$$PVOA = R \times pvoaf_{n|i}$$
$$= \$200\ 000 \times pvoaf_{40|5\%}$$
$$= \$200\ 000\ (17.15909)$$
$$= \$3\ 431\ 818$$

Summing the results of Steps 1 and 2, we get $710 250 + $3 431 818 = $4 142 068, which is the present value of the bonds. Thus, if bondholders pay $4 142 068 for Allied's bonds, they will earn 10 percent, compounded semi-annually, on their investment. Note that our intuition was correct: the bonds sell at a discount of $857 932 ($5 000 000 − $4 142 068). This discount is simply extra interest that Allied must pay. To help implement the matching principle, this discount must be amortized over the life of the bond issue. We discuss discount (and premium) amortization more fully in Chapter 16.

Matching

The bond pricing problem illustrates that **it is often helpful to divide a seemingly complex problem into its components.** Sometimes this involves more than one equation and table. Nevertheless, the same basic compound interest concepts apply.

Present Value of an Annuity Due

Recall that an annuity due is one in which the rents occur at the beginning of each time period. In an earlier section, we saw that $3865.65 is the present value of an ordinary annuity of three rents of $1500 each discounted at 8 percent. Now we will simply change the timing of the $1500 rents and ask this question: What is the present value of three annual rents of $1500 each that occur at the *beginning* of each year (an annuity due) discounted at 8 percent? Once again, a time diagram (Exhibit 7.11) helps us to visualize the solution. Note that the initial rent is not discounted, because it occurs at the beginning of the three-year span. In general, when the present value of an annuity due of *n* rents is computed, only $n - 1$ rents will be discounted. **A present value of an annuity due focusses on a present value, and the first rent occurs at the beginning of the annuity term.**

As shown in Exhibit 7.11, an annuity due begins with a rent and ends one period *after* the last rent. Therefore, if we computed the present value of an annuity due of three $1500 rents at 8 percent and then *discounted* all the money at 8 percent for one more period, we would have the present value of an ordinary annuity of three $1500 rents at 8 percent. Similarly, if we computed the present value of an ordinary annuity of three $1500 rents at 8 percent and then *compounded* all the money at 8 percent for one period into the future, we would have the present value of an annuity due of three rents of $1500 at 8 percent. For any given values of *n* and *i*, the present value of an annuity due will be greater than the present value of an ordinary annuity by the interest on the latter amount for one period. Stated somewhat differently, the present value of an annuity due for any given values of *n* and *i* will be equal to the present value of an ordinary annuity of $n - 1$ rents at *i* interest rate, *plus* one rent (the initial rent).

As Exhibit 7.11 suggests, we could compute the present value of an annuity due by computing the present value of each rent and summing the results. Expressed algebraically, we get

$$\$1500 + \$1500(\frac{1}{1.08}) + \$1500(\frac{1}{1.08})^2] = \$4174.91$$

Factoring out the $1500 rent, we get

$$\$1500 [1 + (\frac{1}{1.08}) + (\frac{1}{1.08})^2] = \$4174.91$$
$$\$1500 (1 + 0.92593 + 0.85734) = \$4174.91$$
$$\$1500 (2.78327) = \$4174.91$$

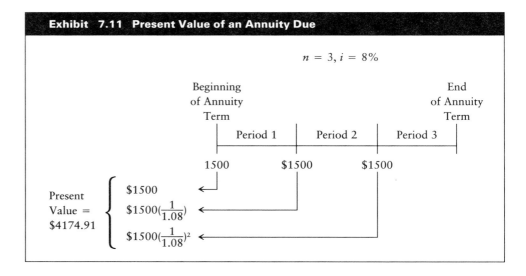

Exhibit 7.11 Present Value of an Annuity Due

$n = 3, i = 8\%$

The 2.78327 component in the last equation is simply a factor for computing the present value of an annuity due (*pvadf*) where $n = 3$ and $i = 8\%$. A complete table of these factors would be called a "Present Value of an Annuity Due of 1" table. We have not constructed such a table because we already have Table 7.4, and we know that a relatively simple relationship exists between the present value of an ordinary annuity and the present value of an annuity due. Thus, we can use Table 7.4 to determine a *pvadf* simply by finding the factor for $n - 1$ periods and i, and adding 1 to the factor. Stated algebraically,[12]

$$pvadf_{\overline{n}|i} = pvadf_{\overline{n-1}|i} + 1.$$

To illustrate, let's use Table 7.4 to calculate $pvadf_{\overline{3}|8\%}$. Looking at the table, we find that the factor for $n - 1 = 2$ periods and $i = 8\%$ is 1.78326. Adding 1 to this number, we get 2.78326. (*Note:* The 1 is included because the first rent is immediate; therefore, there is no change in the value of this rent.)

Now that we know how to use Table 7.4 to calculate a *pvadf*, we can state Equation 7.4A:

$$PVAD = R \times pvadf_{\overline{n}|i}$$

where $PVAD$ = present value of an annuity due of n rents at i interest rate

R = size of each periodic rent

$pvadf_{\overline{n}|i}$ = present value of an annuity due of 1 factor (from Table 7.4, as adjusted) for the relevant n and i

The four variables that make up Equation 7.4A are $PVAD$, R, n, and i. As usual, if we know the values of any three, we can solve for the fourth.

---

[12]A second way to compute $pvadf_{\overline{n}|i}$ is as follows:

$$pvadf_{\overline{n}|i} = pvadf_{\overline{n}|i}(1 + i).$$

Although this approach is correct, it is more difficult to use when i is the unknown variable.

Accounting Examples

Problem 12. On June 1 of the current year, Rockwell Drilling Company signed a twelve-year, noncancellable lease with Equipment Leasing Corporation. The lease gave Rockwell the right to use certain drilling equipment that had a twelve-year estimated useful life and no salvage value. In exchange, Rockwell agreed to make twelve annual lease payments of $15 000 each, beginning on June 1. Assuming a relevant interest rate of 10 percent, what is the present value of the lease on June 1?

Solution 12. Because the initial lease payment occurs at the beginning of the first interval, the lease payments represent an annuity due. To determine the present value of the lease, we compute the present value of an annuity due of twelve rents ($n = 12$) of $15 000 each at $i = 10\%$. Using Equation 7.4A and Table 7.4, we have

$$
\begin{aligned}
PVAD &= R \times pvadf_{n|i} \\
&= \$15\ 000 \times pvadf_{12|10\%} \\
&= \$15\ 000\ (pvadf_{12-1|10\%} + 1) \\
&= \$15\ 000\ (6.49506 + 1) \\
&= \$15\ 000\ (7.49506) \\
&= \$112\ 425.90
\end{aligned}
$$

Observe that the *timing* of the lease payments impacts the present value of the lease. **In general, the timing of cash inflows and outflows has an important impact on the valuation of assets and liabilities and on the measurement of revenues and expenses in accounting.**

Problem 13. Jane Tomas retired today after 40 years with the Stork Candy Company. She has accumulated $187 298.32 in her retirement account, and she wants to withdraw $20 000 annually, beginning today, for as long as her retirement money lasts. Assuming that all money in Jane's account earns 10 percent interest, how many $20 000 annual withdrawals can she make?

Solution 13. We know that $187 298.32 is the present value of an annuity due of n rents of $20 000 each at $i = 10$ percent. Dividing both sides of Equation 7.4A by R, we have

$$
\frac{PVAD}{R} = pvadf_{n|i}
$$

$$
\text{or } pvadf_{n|i} = \frac{PVAD}{R}
$$

Substituting the known values for $PVAD$, R, and i, we have

$$
pvadf_{n|10\%} = \frac{\$187\ 298.32}{\$20\ 000}
$$

$$
pvadf_{n|10\%} = 9.36492
$$

Of course, we should not look for 9.36492 in Table 7.4, because we have seen that this table assumes an ordinary annuity. However, remember that $pvadf_{n|i} = pvadf_{n-1|i} + 1$. Subtracting 1 from both sides of this equation, we get

$$
pvadf_{n|i} - 1 = pvadf_{n-1|i}
$$

Substituting the known values, we get

$$
9.36492 - 1 = pvadf_{n-1|10\%}
$$

$$
\text{or } pvadf_{n-1|10\%} = 8.36492
$$

Now we can search the 10% column in Table 7.4 until we find 8.36492. We find it in the $n = 19$ row. Since 19 is the *pvoaf* for $n - 1$ rents, we conclude that Jane Tomas can make 20 withdrawals ($19 + 1 = 20$) from her retirement account. If we had not found 8.36492, we could have interpolated to approximate n.

Deferred Annuities

In a deferred annuity, the initial rent occurs two or more periods in the future. That is, the initial rent does not occur at either the beginning or the end of the first time period but at some later date. For computational convenience, it is customary to treat all deferred annuities as deferred ordinary annuities instead of deferred annuities due. We will therefore omit the adjective "ordinary" when referring to deferred annuities.

The **deferral period** is the length of time between the present and the *beginning* of the first period in which a rent occurs. Remember, therefore, that the deferral period ends one period *before* the initial rent occurs. Thus, if an annuity begins to produce rents at the end of six periods, we say that it is deferred five periods. Similarly, an annuity that is deferred for nine periods will produce its first rent at the end of ten periods. The time diagram in Exhibit 7.12 illustrates an annuity of three annual rents of $1500 at 8 percent, deferred four years.

The deferral period does not affect the calculation of an amount (future value). Because there is nothing on deposit to accumulate interest during the deferral period, the amount of a deferred annuity is the same as the amount of an annuity that is not deferred, assuming that the two annuities have the same values for n, i, and R. In the example above, the amount would be $4869.60, the same figure computed in the discussion of the amount of an ordinary annuity.

On the other hand, assuming that the two annuities have the same values of n, i, and R, the present value of a deferred annuity is less than the present value of an annuity that is not deferred. The reason is that when we compute a present value, we must discount through the deferral period.

The easiest way to compute the present value of a deferred annuity is to find the *pvoaf* for the *total* number of periods involved; that is, the number of periods that the annuity is deferred (k) plus the number of periods in which rents occur (n). Then subtract the *pvoaf* associated with the ordinary annuity that is nonexistent during the deferral period. The resulting factor is then multiplied by the size of the periodic rent. Algebraically, we have Equation 7.5:

$$PVDA = R \times (pvoaf_{k+n|i} - pvoaf_{k|i})$$

where $PVDA$ = present value of an ordinary annuity of n rents at i interest rate, deferred k periods

R = size of each periodic rent

$pvoaf_{k+n|i}$ = present value of an ordinary annuity factor for the *total* number of periods involved

$pvoaf_{k|i}$ = present value of an ordinary annuity factor for the number of periods in which no rents occur

If we want to know the present value of an annuity of three annual rents of $1500 at 8 percent deferred four years, we would proceed as follows:

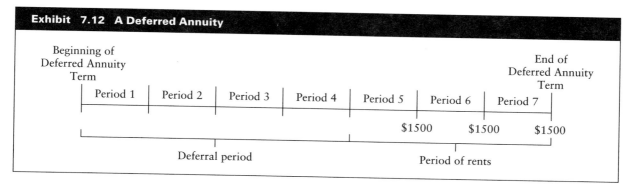

Exhibit 7.12   A Deferred Annuity

Beginning of
Deferred Annuity
Term

End of
Deferred Annuity
Term

| Period 1 | Period 2 | Period 3 | Period 4 | Period 5 | Period 6 | Period 7 |

$1500 $1500 $1500

Deferral period   Period of rents

$$PVDA = R \times (pvoaf_{7|8\%} - pvoaf_{4|8\%})$$
$$= \$1500 \, (5.20637 - 3.31213)$$
$$= \$1500 \, (1.89424)$$
$$= \$2841.36$$

Another way to compute the present value of a deferred annuity is to first compute the present value of the annuity at the beginning of the first period in which a rent occurs (using Equation 7.4 and Table 7.4) and then discount this single sum to the present (using Equation 7.2 and Table 7.2). Following this approach, we find that the present value of the annuity at the beginning of Period 5 is $3865.65 ($1500 × 2.57710). Discounting this single sum to the present, we find that it equals $2841.37 ($3865.65 × 0.73503). The $0.01 discrepancy ($2841.37 − $2841.36) between answers is the result of rounding.

Accounting Example

Problem 14. Sam Persaud purchases a $50 000 annuity contract that promises a return of 8 percent compounded annually. Sam will receive fifteen equal annual payments, the first of which is due ten years from now. How much will each annual payment be?

Solution 14. Because the annuity begins to produce rents at the end of ten years, we say that it is deferred nine years. Therefore, we know that $50 000 is the present value of an ordinary annuity of fifteen annual rents at 8 percent, deferred nine years. To solve for the size of the periodic rent, we divide both sides of Equation 7.5 by $(pvoaf_{k+n|i} - pvoaf_{k|i})$:

$$R = \frac{PVDA}{(pvoaf_{k+n|i} - pvoaf_{k|i})}$$
$$= \frac{\$50\,000}{(pvoaf_{24|8\%} - pvoaf_{9|8\%})}$$
$$= \frac{\$50\,000}{10.52876 - 6.24689}$$
$$= \frac{\$50\,000}{4.28187}$$
$$= \$11\,677.14$$

Concluding Remarks

When solving a compound interest problem, you should first determine what type of problem you are being asked to solve. Distinguishing between single sum problems and

Time Is Money

It is said that accounting, like law, is a profession that has a rule for every situation. If that's true, then why don't accountants have a consistent standard for when, and under what circumstances, to use one of the most fundamental measurements of finance itself—the time value of money?

As anyone who has bought a bank CD knows, the yield on an investment is basically a function of how much money is invested at what rate of return for how long. In theory, both assets and liabilities of corporations can be measured in the same way. For liabilities: How much money would be needed today to pay for an obligation that does not come due for 5 or 10 years—future health obligations of not-yet-retired workers, say, or the projected pension liabilities of a firm 10 or 20 years in the future? For assets: What is the "present value" of a financial asset—a mortgage, say, or a corporate bond—that is due to mature in the year 2013? In both cases, the solution comes from taking the future value or cost of the asset or liability in question, then using an assumed rate of interest over the period of time involved to "discount" it back to its present value.

Unfortunately, the accountants who actually prepare financial reports have few—and often highly inconsistent—rules for when and how to make those calculations in preparing balance sheets. "Financial statements are becoming irrelevant to business decision making," complains G. Michael Crooch, partner at Arthur Andersen. "We are not measuring items according to their economic value because we're ignoring the time value of money."

Now at last the Financial Accounting Standards Board seems willing to face the problem, by adding a discounting project to its agenda. New rules are years away, but they eventually could have a dramatic effect on corporate financials. Depending upon what FASB finally decides, present value accounting could be used for virtually any transaction that involves a long delay before final settlement. Potential targets for discounting include impaired assets, product and manufacturers' warranties, and loss reserves for property-casualty insurers.

Present value accounting could in some ways be quite a boon to corporations, by reducing the liability side of their balance sheets. How? By recognizing that $1 million payable in 1994 is not as effectively large a liability as $1 million payable in 1989. That's common sense. If you were to take $600,000 and invest it at a relatively modest 10%, it would equal $1 million by the time the liability would need to be paid. Thus the effective liability is not $1 million but $600,000.

For example, under current FASB income tax accounting rules, deferred taxes must be booked in full, rather than discounted forward to the time when they are due. Thus, General Electric had a $3.1 billion deferred tax reserve in 1987. "That $3.1 billion is more than we'll really have to pay, considering the interest effect," notes Bernard Doyle, GE's manager of corporate accounting services. We're not talking peanuts. The discounted value of that liability is hundreds of millions of dollars less than book value.

In a few cases, present value accounting is already required by FASB. Under a new FASB statement regarding pension accounting, General Electric in 1987 reported only a $15.5 billion liability based on an 8.5% rate of return; without discounting for present value, the liability would have been much greater.

Present value accounting obviously helps a company put its best foot forward, and of course could be abused. How? By making unrealistically high assumptions about interest rates. "Experience has shown that, in many cases, insurers have not been adequately funded in the past," notes Denis Callaghan, analyst at Alex. Brown. "If they were allowed to use discounting, the problem could get worse." Maybe, but any company that overdiscounts the future liability risks having to take major writeoffs as the liabilities come due. All in all, present value accounting has lots to recommend it.

Arthur Wyatt, Arthur Andersen & Co. accounting partner, sums up: "Any company routinely considers present values when doing deals. Why shouldn't investors have that information in the financial statements?"

Source: Reprinted from Penelope Wang, "Time Is Money," *Forbes,* January 9, 1989, p. 300. Reprinted with permission of *Forbes* magazine, January 9, 1989. © Forbes Inc., 1989.

annuity problems is fairly easy, because periodic rents of equal size clearly indicate an annuity problem.

On the other hand, distinguishing between the following types of annuity problems is often difficult:

1. Amount of an ordinary annuity.
2. Amount of an annuity due.

3. Present value of an ordinary annuity.
4. Present value of an annuity due.

To help you see the differences among these four types of annuity problems, Exhibit 7.13 compares them in one illustration. **When solving an annuity problem that seems difficult, draw a time diagram and remember the following points:**

1. An annuity problem involves a value that represents a single sum of money. This value may occur either before or after the rents. If the value (which may be the unknown variable) occurs *after* the rents, the value is an *amount* (future value). Consequently, we have an amount of an annuity problem. To determine whether the annuity is ordinary or due, note the timing of the *final rent*. If the final rent occurs *at the same time* as the value, we have an amount of an ordinary annuity problem. If the final rent occurs *one period* before the value, we have an amount of an annuity due problem.

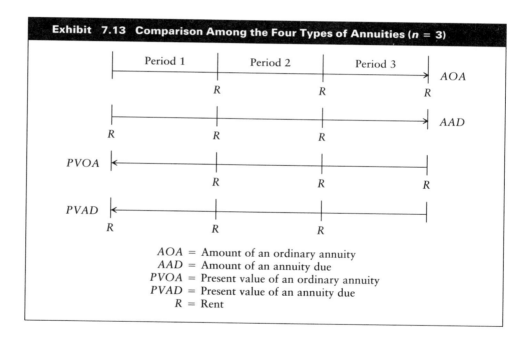

Exhibit 7.13 Comparison Among the Four Types of Annuities ($n = 3$)

AOA = Amount of an ordinary annuity
AAD = Amount of an annuity due
$PVOA$ = Present value of an ordinary annuity
$PVAD$ = Present value of an annuity due
R = Rent

Exhibit 7.14 Summary of Compound Interest Equations

Equation Number	Equation	Appropriate Table
7.1	$FV = = PV \times \mathrm{fvf}_{n|i}$	7.1
7.2	$PV = FV \times \mathrm{pvf}_{n|i}$	7.2
7.3	$AOA = R \times \mathrm{aoaf}_{n|i}$	7.3
7.3A	$AAD = R \times \mathrm{aadf}_{n|i}$	7.3 (adjusted)
7.4	$PVOA = R \times pvoaf_{n|i}$	7.4
7.4A	$PVAD = R \times \mathrm{pvadf}_{n|i}$	7.4 (adjusted)
7.5	$PVDA = R \times (pvoaf_{k+n|i} - poaf_{k|i})$	7.4

Exhibit 7.15 Characteristics of Annuity Problems

Type of Annuity Problem	Focus	Rents
Amount of an ordinary annuity	A future value	End of each period. Final rent occurs at same time as future value.
Amount of an annuity due	A future value	Beginning of each period. Final rent occurs one period before future value.
Present value of an ordinary annuity	A present value	End of each period. Initial rent occurs one period after the present value.
Present value of an annuity due	A present value	Beginning of each period. Initial rent occurs at same time as present value.

2. If the value (which may be the unknown variable) in the problem occurs before the rents, the value is a *present value*. Consequently, we have a present value of an annuity problem. To determine whether the annuity is ordinary or due, observe the timing of the *first rent*. If the first rent occurs *one period after* the value, we have a present value of an ordinary annuity problem. If the first rent occurs *at the same time* as the present value, we have a present value of an annuity due problem.

A deferred annuity is not difficult to recognize, because the first rent occurs two or more periods after the beginning of the annuity term (see Exhibit 7.12).

Once you have identified the problem, you can solve it using the appropriate equation(s) and table(s). The major equations presented in this chapter are summarized in Exhibit 7.14. After you gain experience working with the equations, you may find that you can simplify writing them by omitting the letters that precede the letter f (for factor). For example, Equation 7.3 can be concisely written as $AOA = R \times f_{n\mid i}$. If you simplify the writing of an equation, take care to use the correct type of factor when solving the equation.

Finally, try to form the habit of examining your answers to compound interest problems from a common-sense perspective. We know, for example, that the present value of $1000 discounted for two years at 8 percent could not possibly be $8573.40. The actual present value is only $857.34. Obviously, misplacing a decimal can greatly affect the solution to a compound interest problem.

In the remaining chapters of this textbook, you will be asked to apply many of the tools discussed in this chapter and the previous chapter on the accounting cycle. The next chapter, which covers cash and receivables, is the first of a series of seven chapters that explain the asset side of the balance sheet. As we move into our study of various types of assets, you will see how these tools are applied.

Key Points

1. Simple interest is earned only on the principal sum of money invested; compound interest is earned not only on the principal but also on the interest accumulated. (Objective 1)

2. Four fundamental concepts underlie all compound interest problems:
   a. Present value (*PV*).   c. Interest rate (*i*).
   b. Future value (*FV*).   d. Number of time periods (*n*). (Objective 2)
3. In a compound interest problem, the values of *i* and *n* should reflect the number of times a year that interest is compounded. (Objective 2)
4. An amount of a single sum problem focusses on the future value to which a single sum of money will accumulate if left on deposit for a certain number of periods at a certain interest rate per period. (Objective 3)
5. A present value of a single sum problem focusses on the present value of a single sum of money that is discounted for a certain number of periods at a certain interest rate per period. (Objective 3)
6. An annuity is a series of equal receipts or payments, called rents, that occur at uniform time intervals at a constant interest rate. In an ordinary annuity, the rents occur at the end of each time period; in an annuity due, the rents occur at the beginning of each time period. Present value and future value concepts apply to annuities, just as these concepts apply to single sum problems. (Objective 3)
7. Important characteristics of the major types of annuity problems are summarized in Exhibit 7.15. (Objective 3)
8. A deferred annuity is one in which the initial rent occurs two or more periods in the future. A deferral period does not affect the calculation of an amount, but it does affect the calculation of present value. (Objective 3)
9. When solving a compound interest problem, you should read the problem carefully to determine the type of problem you are dealing with, solve the problem using the appropriate equations and tables, and make sure your answer seems reasonable. (Objective 3)
10. A complex problem can usually be solved by dividing it into its components. (Objective 3)

Questions

Q7.1 Explain what is meant by the time value of money.
Q7.2 Distinguish between simple and compound interest.
Q7.3 Distinguish between the amount of a single sum and the present value of a single sum.
Q7.4 What is an annuity?
Q7.5 Distinguish between an ordinary annuity and an annuity due.
Q7.6 Distinguish between the amount of an ordinary annuity and the amount of an annuity due.
Q7.7 Distinguish between the present value of an ordinary annuity and the present value of an annuity due.
Q7.8 What is a deferred annuity?
Q7.9 Explain how the factors in each of the following future and present value tables (at the end of this chapter) were calculated:
(a) Table 7.1.   (c) Table 7.3.
(b) Table 7.2.   (d) Table 7.4.
Q7.10 Explain how an "Amount of 1" table could be converted to a "Present Value of 1" table.
Q7.11 Explain how an "Amount of an Ordinary Annuity of 1" table could be converted to an "Amount of an Annuity Due of 1" table.
Q7.12 Explain how a "Present Value of an Ordinary Annuity of 1" table could be converted to a "Present Value of an Annuity Due of 1" table.
Q7.13 Indicate the number of compounding periods (*n*) and the interest rate per period (*i*) for each of the following:
(a) Three years, 12 percent compounded annually.

(b) Three years, 12 percent compounded semi-annually.
(c) Three years, 12 percent compounded quarterly.
(d) Three years, 12 percent compounded monthly.

Q7.14 Assuming that $n = 15$ and $i = 10\%$, what is
(a) The amount of 1?
(b) The present value of 1?
(c) The amount of an ordinary annuity of 1?
(d) The amount of an annuity due of 1?
(e) The present value of an ordinary annuity of 1?
(f) The present value of an annuity due of 1?

Exercises*

E7.1 To what amount will $7500 accumulate if it is deposited for five years at 10 percent, assuming

(a) Simple interest?
(b) Interest compounded annually?
(c) Interest compounded semi-annually?
(d) Interest compounded quarterly?

E7.2 Assuming an interest rate of 8 percent, compounded quarterly, how many years will it take for a deposit of $1800 to accumulate to $2674.71?

E7.3 What annual interest rate, when compounded annually, would cause an initial deposit of $6600 to accumulate to $25 063.50 in fourteen years?

E7.4 Amy Rooks plans to send each of her two daughters to university. For the first daughter, Amy will need $25 000 in three years; Amy plans to accumulate this amount by depositing a certain sum today in a three-year GIC that pays 6 percent interest compounded annually. For the second daughter, Amy will need $50 000 in seven years; Amy plans to accumulate this amount by depositing a certain sum today in a seven-year certificate of deposit that pays 8 percent interest compounded annually. What is the total amount of cash that Amy needs to deposit today?

E7.5 Ray Robusto has deposited $2000 on the same day of each month for the last two years in an account that pays 12 percent interest, compounded monthly. He made the last deposit today. How much money does Ray now have in his account?

E7.6 Ben Rollo has $30 000 today as a result of having deposited equal amounts of cash in a savings account every six months for twelve years. The account pays interest of

---

*Brief descriptions of the exercises and problems in this chapter are not given so that students can practise learning how to recognize the different types of compound interest problems. As indicated in the chapter, learning to recognize the different types is very important.

6 percent, compounded semi-annually. Assuming that the last deposit was made today, how much was each deposit?

E7.7 As of today, Bill Morie has accumulated $114 550 in a retirement account that pays 10 percent interest, compounded annually. He accumulated this sum by depositing $2000 at annual intervals during each year that he worked in the clothing business. The last deposit was made today. How many deposits did Bill make?

E7.8 Jane Harts has $9433.42 today as a result of having deposited $750 at annual intervals for the last ten years. The last deposit was made today. Assuming annual compounding, what interest rate did Jane earn on her periodic deposits?

E7.9 Roger Frankenberg plans to deposit $2750 in his savings account today and at each of the next 35 monthly intervals, for a total period of three years. Assuming that Roger's money earns interest of 12 percent, compounded monthly, how much money will Roger have in his account at the end of three years?

E7.10 Helen Freeman wants to accumulate $50 000 at the end of eighteen years and will make eighteen equal annual deposits into a fund that pays 8 percent interest, compounded annually. Helen will make the final deposit one year before the $50 000 sum is accumulated. How much will each deposit be?

E7.11 When Tom Wilkerson's son was born, Tom deposited $250 in a special savings account that pays interest at 8 percent compounded annually. Later, Tom deposited $250 on each of his son's birthdays. How old is Tom's son if today is his son's birthday and, just *before* Tom makes his current deposit, the amount accumulated in the account is $7331.07?

E7.12 Paul Rechenbach deposited $1000 annually in an investment account for five years, ending one year ago. Assuming that interest is compounded annually and that Paul has accumulated $6715.61 in his account as of today, what stated interest rate did he earn?

E7.13 Brenda Schmierbach wants to earn an interest rate of 10 percent, compounded quarterly. How much money should she pay today to an insurance company for the right to receive $12 000 at quarterly intervals, starting three months from now, for the next eight years?

E7.14 Today, Harold Reed deposited $18 000 in a savings account that pays 6 percent interest compounded semi-annually. Harold wants to liquidate the balance in his account by making equal semi-annual withdrawals, starting six months from now, for four years. How large will each withdrawal be?

E7.15 Doris Boadt has $60 207.90 in a savings account that pays 6 percent interest compounded annually. How many annual withdrawals of $5000 each can she make from the account, assuming that she makes the first withdrawal one year from now?

E7.16 Paul Yamato buys an automobile having a cash price of $6473.70 with $1500 down and payments of $2000 annually for three years. Assuming annual compounding, what is the stated interest rate in this transaction?

E7.17 Assuming that she wants to earn interest of 12 percent compounded monthly, how much money should Maria Rucci pay today to an insurance company for the right to receive $5000 each month for 36 months, with the initial $5000 to be received today?

E7.18 Rita Rogow wants to use all the money in her $30 000 savings account to pay for her university education, which begins today. The account pays 10 percent interest, compounded annually. What constant amount of cash can she withdraw at the beginning of each of her four years in university?

E7.19 Fred Granger currently owes a debt of $3167.46. The debt accrues interest at 10 percent, compounded annually on the unpaid balance. How many annual payments of $500 each will Fred have to make to liquidate the debt and interest, assuming that he makes the first payment today?

E7.20 Angela Wishart purchased a new video recorder that had a cash price of $526.59. She made an $80 down payment and paid the balance in $80 installments at the end of each year for seven years. What is the stated annual interest rate?

E7.21 Assume that it is now the beginning of Year 1. Answer each of the following questions, assuming an interest rate of 6 percent compounded annually.

(a) What is the amount at the end of Year 10 of ten annual deposits of $7000 each, the first of which is made at the end of Year 1?

(b) What is the amount at the end of Year 20 of ten annual deposits of $7000 each, the first of which is made at the end of Year 11?

(c) As of the beginning of Year 11, what is the present value of ten annual receipts of $7000 each, the first of which is received at the end of Year 11?

(d) As of the beginning of Year 1, what is the present value of ten annual receipts of $7000 each, the first of which is received at the end of Year 11?

(e) Why are the correct answers to (a) and (b) the same?

(f) Why are the correct answers to (c) and (d) different?

Problems*

P7.1 Friendly Credit Union, whose slogan is "our interest is more interesting," currently pays interest at a rate of 8 percent, compounded quarterly. Better Credit Union, whose slogan is "our interest interests more," pays 8 percent, compounded annually. If you want to deposit $10 000 for five years, what would be the total additional interest that you could earn by depositing the money in Friendly Credit Union rather than Better Credit Union?

P7.2 McDonald Company deposited $20 000 with each of four investment companies at the following terms:

Investment Company	Annual Rate	Compounded	Investment Term in Years
A	12%	Annually	8
B	10%	Quarterly	6
C	10%	Semi-annually	4
D	8%	Quarterly	2

What will be the balance in each investment account at its maturity?

P7.3 Joan Ricca was informed by the attorney managing her deceased uncle's estate that the following deposits would be made in her new savings account at the end of each of the following years:

Year	Deposit
1994	$5000
1995	3000
1996	4000
1997	6000

The account pays 8 percent interest, compounded annually.

Instructions

(a) Assuming that Joan makes no additional deposits or withdrawals, what will be the balance in her savings account at the end of 1997, immediately after the last deposit?

(b) What would be the balance in the savings account at the end of 1997 if, instead of the deposits shown above, a deposit of $4500 were made at the end of each year?

---

*Brief descriptions of the exercises and problems in this chapter are not given so that students can practise learning how to recognize the different types of compound interest problems. As indicated in the chapter, learning to recognize the different types is very important.

(c) Explain the similarities and differences in the techniques you used to solve (a) and (b).

P7.4 Sean Christoff has admired for many years a refurbished Model T automobile owned by his neighbour. Thus, Sean quickly accepted his neighbour's recent offer to sell the car. Which of the following two payment options offered by the neighbour should Sean take?

(1) $4650 cash payable immediately.
(2) $5500 cash payable in one sum after two years.

Sean knows that he can earn 8 percent, compounded annually, on his money.

P7.5 Your neighbour has a $7000 noninterest-bearing note receivable that matures at the end of three years. You recently inherited $20 000, and you know that you could earn 10 percent, compounded annually, on investments that are similar in risk to your neighbour's note. Your goal is to maximize your income.

Instructions
(a) What is the maximum amount of cash that you would be willing to pay today for your neighbour's note?
(b) What is the maximum amount of cash that you would be willing to pay today if the $7000 note paid you interest of 3 percent at the end of each year? (*Hint:* you will receive $7000 × 0.03 = $210 at the end of Years 1, 2, and 3 and the $7000 maturity value at the end of year 3.)
(c) Explain why the amounts in (a) and (b) are *maximum* amounts.

P7.6 On February 1, 1995, Fraser Tool Company leased equipment from French Manufacturing Corporation. The lease term is three years, which equals the estimated economic life of the equipment. The lease requires Fraser to make 36 monthly rental payments of $8000 each, with the first payment due on February 1, 1995.

Instructions
(a) Assuming a relevant interest rate of 12 percent compounded monthly, what is the present value of the lease to Fraser Tool Company on February 1, 1995?
(b) Answer (a) again, assuming that the first of the 36 monthly rental payments is made on March 1, 1995.

P7.7 Henry Hudson, a local dentist, opens a tax-deferred retirement account that pays 8 percent interest, compounded annually. He plans to deposit $2000 at annual intervals for 25 years, with the initial deposit made today.

Instructions
(a) How much cash will Henry have in his account when he retires at the end of 25 years?

(b) How much of the sum that you calculated in (a) is interest?

(c) What equal-size deposits would Henry have to make at the beginning of each year to accumulate $200 000 at the end of 25 years?

P7.8   Laura Boley retired from Howden Company today with $165 766.20 in a retirement account that pays 8 percent interest compounded annually.

Instructions

(a) How many $15 000 annual withdrawals can Laura make from her account if she makes the first withdrawal one year from now?

(b) What equal amount should she withdraw at the end of each year if she wants to make the final withdrawal 25 years from today?

(c) What equal amount should she withdraw annually if she wants to make a total of fifteen withdrawals, with the initial withdrawal made today?

(d) What equal amount should she withdraw annually if she wants to make a total of fifteen withdrawals, with the initial withdrawal made five years from now?

P7.9   Pam Bearden plans to retire twenty years from today. She wants to build a registered retirement savings plan by making twenty annual deposits, with the first deposit made today. Pam wants to make twenty annual withdrawals of $25 000 each from her retirement account, with the initial withdrawal made twenty years from now. The retirement account will earn 12 percent interest, compounded annually.

Instructions

(a) What equal amounts should Pam deposit in her account?

(b) What is the total amount of interest that Pam will earn on the money in her account?

P7.10   Tuff Trucking Company purchased a new truck from Mann Motor Company in exchange for a three-year, noninterest-bearing promissory note with a maturity value of $90 000. The market rate of interest for similar notes is 10 percent, compounded annually.

Instructions

(a) What is the historical cost of the truck to Tuff Trucking Company?

(b) Answer (a) again, assuming that the $90 000 note paid interest of 2 percent at the end of each year for three years. (*Hint:* The note pays interest of $90 000 × 0.02 = $1800 to the holder at the end of each of the three years, and it pays the maturity value of $90 000 at the end of the third year.)

P7.11   Scott Kelso buys a new home today costing $67 736.39. He makes a $10 000 down payment and gets a ten-year mortgage loan for the balance. The mortgage bears interest at 10 percent, compounded quarterly, and calls for equal quarterly payments, starting three months from now.

Instructions
(a) How much will each quarterly payment be?
(b) What is the total sum of cash that Scott will spend on the down payment and the loan?
(c) What is the total amount of interest that Scott will pay on the loan?
(d) What is the total amount of interest that Scott could save if he could get the required loan at 8 percent compounded quarterly?

P7.12 Bryja Company will need $2 500 000 at the end of twenty years to retire a maturing issue of term bonds. To accumulate the desired sum, the company deposits $62 500 at the end of each year in a sinking fund that pays 6 percent interest compounded annually.

Instructions
(a) At the end of twenty years, will the fund be sufficient to retire the bonds?
(b) If your answer to (a) is no, what equal amount of cash would the company have to deposit at the end of each of the twenty years to accumulate the desired sum?

P7.13 Readett Company wants to purchase a new warehouse in three years. The company expects the warehouse to cost $525 000 at that time. To accumulate this amount, the company plans to make twelve quarterly deposits of $36 000 each in a special account that pays 10 percent interest compounded quarterly. The first deposit is made today.

Instructions
(a) At the end of three years, will the amount in the fund be sufficient to purchase the warehouse?
(b) If your answer to (a) is no, what equal amount of cash would the company have to deposit at the beginning of each quarter to accumulate $525 000 at the end of three years?

P7.14 Determine the stated annual interest rate in each of the following independent cases (assume annual compounding in each case):

(a) A deposit of $1300 accumulates to $1850.30 in nine years.
(b) A person lends $75 131 today in exchange for $100 000 to be received at the end of three years.
(c) Periodic deposits of $1200 made at the end of each year accumulate to $25 218.08 at the end of fourteen years.
(d) Periodic deposits of $2800 made at the beginning of each year accumulate to $57 075.97 at the end of eleven years.
(e) An annuity contract purchased for $53 373.90 promises to pay $5000 at the end of each year for the next 25 years.
(f) A person borrows $50 000 in exchange for a written promise to pay $4821.78 at the beginning of each year for 30 years, with the first payment due now.

P7.15   On April 1, 1995, Rechichar Corporation issues 10 percent, twenty-year bonds payable with a total par value of $80 000. Interest is payable semi-annually on September 30 and March 31.

Instructions

(a) How much will the bonds sell for if, on April 1, 1995, the market rate of interest for similar bonds is
  (1) 8 percent   (2) 10 percent?   (3) 12 percent?
(b) Make the journal entry for Rechichar Corporation to record the bond issuance under each of the three assumptions in (a).
(c) Explain the meaning and accounting treatment of "discount on bonds payable."

P7.16   Stinnette Company has projected substantial growth in sales over the next five years. To ensure that sufficient funds are available for capital expansion, Stinnette plans to deposit $75 000 in a building fund at the end of each year for the next five years.

Instructions

(a) What will be the balance in the fund at the end of the fifth year if interest is earned at 8 percent, compounded annually?
(b) How many years will it take for the fund to accumulate $348 075 if interest is earned at 10 percent, compounded annually?
(c) What interest rate, compounded annually, would be necessary to accumulate $414 422 by the end of the fifth year?

P7.17   How many *years* are involved in each of the following independent situations?

(a) A deposit of $3600 accumulates to $9145.26 at 6 percent, compounded annually.
(b) A person lends $22 819.50 today in exchange for $50 000 to be received in the future, which includes interest at 8 percent, compounded semi-annually.
(c) Deposits of $300 at the end of each quarter accumulate to $11 115.36 at the end of the final quarter. The interest rate is 8 percent, compounded quarterly.
(d) Deposits of $600 at the beginning of each year accumulate to $14 787.25 at the end of the final year. The interest rate is 4 percent, compounded annually.
(e) A person deposits $1635.14 today in a savings account that pays interest at 8 percent, compounded quarterly. The account is liquidated by withdrawals of $100 at the end of each quarter, with the initial withdrawals made at the end of the first quarter.
(f) A person deposits $1777.37 today in a savings account that pays interest at 6 percent, compounded annually. The account is liquidated by annual withdrawals of $200, with the initial withdrawal made today.

P7.18   On January 1, 1993, Vicki Wrightson buys new furniture costing $5000. To pay for it, she signs a promissory note calling for equal monthly payments for three years. The first payment is due in one month. The note bears interest at 12 percent, compounded monthly.

Instructions
(a) How much will each monthly payment be?
(b) How much interest will Vicki pay on the furniture loan in each of the following years:
     (1) 1993?   (2) 1994?   (3) 1995?

P7.19   Craig Wesson wants to establish a special retirement fund from which he can make five annual withdrawals of $20 000 each, with the first withdrawal to be made on January 1, 2002. Wesson wants to make four equal annual contributions to the retirement fund, beginning January 1, 1995, and ending January 1, 1998. Wesson wants the fund to be exhausted after the final withdrawal on January 1, 2006. The fund will earn 10 percent interest, compounded annually.

Instructions
(a) What equal amount should Wesson contribute to the fund?
(b) What is the total amount of interest that Wesson will earn on the money in his fund?

P7.20   Otto Farber wants to establish a university fund for his son, Eddie. Farber estimates that Eddie will require $15 000 per year for four years, beginning September 1, 2001, and ending September 1, 2004. Farber wants to make three equal annual contributions to the university fund, beginning September 1, 1995, and ending September 1, 1997. Farber wants the fund to be exhausted after the final withdrawal on September 1, 2004. The fund will earn 12 percent interest, compounded annually.

Instructions
(a) What equal annual amount should Farber contribute to the fund?
(b) What is the total amount of interest that Farber will earn on the money in his fund?

P7.21   John Lindon wants to buy a log cabin kit from Homely Homes, Inc., for $20 000 cash. The best alternative use of John's money is an investment account that pays 8 percent interest, compounded annually. John expects that it would take him two years working part-time to complete the exterior of the cabin and an additional year to finish the interior. If John decides to buy the kit, he will leave his present part-time job of making Christmas ornaments from pine-cones. As a result, he will lose $2000 cash income at the end of each of the three years that he worked on the cabin.

    The cabin would be constructed on a lake in a retirement community. John expects that the annual rent for the first five years after completion would be $2400 and for the second five years would be $3600. Rental payments would be due at the beginning of each year. John expects that he would sell the cabin for $26 000 after renting it for ten years.

Instructions
Using appropriate compound interest concepts, determine whether the log cabin is a sound economic investment for John Lindon. Disregard income taxes.

Cases

C7.1 Historical Cost.   In Chapter 2, we stated that the historical cost of an asset equals the cash equivalent price of acquiring the asset and putting it to its intended use. Suppose that on June 1, 1995, Edmonton Corporation buys 100 common shares of Calgary Company as an investment in exchange for a three-year note. The note has a face amount of $14 049.29 and no stated interest rate. Calgary Company is a small, closely held enterprise, and the market value of its common shares is not readily determinable. On June 1, 1995, the market rate of interest for notes similar to the one issued by Edmonton is 12 percent.

Instructions

(a) How should Edmonton determine the historical cost of its investment in Calgary Company?
(b) Justify your answer to (a) from the standpoint of accounting theory.

C7.2 Revenue Realization. On December 31, 1995, Western Galleries, Inc. sold a unique painting to Black Company in exchange for a five-year note receivable. The note had a face amount of $161 051 and no stated interest rate. The market rate of interest for similar notes on December 31, 1995, was 12 percent. The painting could not be appraised in a reliable manner.

Instructions

Explain how Western Galleries should determine the amount of revenue to recognize on the sale for the period ending December 31, 1995.

C7.3 Provincial Lottery. A Canadian province recently ran a full-page advertisement in major provincial newspapers announcing that it was sponsoring a lottery in which the winner would receive $1 million. The fine print near the bottom of the ad indicated, "The $1 million will be paid in $50 000 annual installments over twenty years."

Instructions

Do you feel that the province's ad is fair and reasonable, or is it misleading? Defend your position with appropriate arguments, disregarding income taxes.

Table 7.1 Amount of 1

$$fvf_{\overline{n}|i} = (1 + i)^n$$

Periods (n)	1%	2%	2.5%	3%	4%	5%
1	1.01000	1.02000	1.02500	1.03000	1.04000	1.05000
2	1.02010	1.04040	1.05063	1.06090	1.08160	1.10250
3	1.03030	1.06121	1.07689	1.09273	1.12486	1.15763
4	1.04060	1.08243	1.10381	1.12551	1.16986	1.21551
5	1.05101	1.10408	1.13141	1.15927	1.21665	1.27628
6	1.06152	1.12616	1.15969	1.19405	1.26532	1.34010
7	1.07214	1.14869	1.18869	1.22987	1.31593	1.40710
8	1.08286	1.17166	1.21840	1.26677	1.36857	1.47746
9	1.09369	1.19509	1.24886	1.30477	1.42331	1.55133
10	1.10462	1.21899	1.28008	1.34392	1.48024	1.62889
11	1.11567	1.24337	1.31209	1.38423	1.53945	1.71034
12	1.12683	1.26824	1.34489	1.42576	1.60103	1.79586
13	1.13809	1.29361	1.37851	1.46853	1.66507	1.88565
14	1.14947	1.31948	1.41297	1.51259	1.73168	1.97993
15	1.16097	1.34587	1.44830	1.55797	1.80094	2.07893
16	1.17258	1.37279	1.48451	1.60471	1.87298	2.18287
17	1.18430	1.40024	1.52162	1.65285	1.94790	2.29202
18	1.19615	1.42825	1.55966	1.70243	2.02582	2.40662
19	1.20811	1.45681	1.59865	1.75351	2.10685	2.52695
20	1.22019	1.48595	1.63862	1.80611	2.19112	2.65330
21	1.23239	1.51567	1.67958	1.86029	2.27877	2.78596
22	1.24472	1.54598	1.72157	1.91610	2.36992	2.92526
23	1.25716	1.57690	1.76461	1.97359	2.46472	3.07152
24	1.26973	1.60844	1.80873	2.03279	2.56330	3.22510
25	1.28243	1.64061	1.85394	2.09378	2.66584	3.38635
26	1.29526	1.67342	1.90029	2.15659	2.77247	3.55567
27	1.30821	1.70689	1.94780	2.22129	2.88337	3.73346
28	1.32129	1.74102	1.99650	2.28793	2.99870	3.92013
29	1.33450	1.77584	2.04641	2.35657	3.11865	4.11614
30	1.34785	1.81136	2.09757	2.42726	3.24340	4.32194
31	1.36133	1.84759	2.15001	2.50008	3.37313	4.53804
32	1.37494	1.88454	2.20376	2.57508	3.50806	4.76494
33	1.38869	1.92223	2.25885	2.65234	3.64838	5.00319
34	1.40258	1.96068	2.31532	2.73191	3.79432	5.25335
35	1.41660	1.99989	2.37321	2.81386	3.94609	5.51602
36	1.43077	2.03989	2.43254	2.89828	4.10393	5.79182
37	1.44508	2.08069	2.49335	2.98523	4.26809	6.08141
38	1.45953	2.12230	2.55568	3.07478	4.43881	6.38548
39	1.47412	2.16474	2.61957	3.16703	4.61637	6.70475
40	1.48886	2.20804	2.68506	3.26204	4.80102	7.03999

Table 7.1   Amount of 1

6%	8%	10%	12%	16%	20%	24%	Periods (n)
1.06000	1.08000	1.10000	1.12000	1.16000	1.20000	1.24000	1
1.12360	1.16640	1.21000	1.25440	1.34560	1.44000	1.53760	2
1.19102	1.25971	1.33100	1.40493	1.56090	1.72800	1.90662	3
1.26248	1.36049	1.46410	1.57352	1.81064	2.07360	2.36421	4
1.33823	1.46933	1.61051	1.76234	2.10034	2.48832	2.93163	5
1.41852	1.58687	1.77156	1.97382	2.43640	2.98598	3.63522	6
1.50363	1.71382	1.94872	2.21068	2.82622	3.58318	4.50767	7
1.59385	1.85093	2.14359	2.47596	3.27841	4.29982	5.58951	8
1.68948	1.99900	2.35795	2.77308	3.80296	5.15978	6.93099	9
1.79085	2.15892	2.59374	3.10585	4.41144	6.19174	8.59443	10
1.89830	2.33164	2.85312	3.47855	5.11726	7.43008	10.65709	11
2.01220	2.51817	3.13843	3.89598	5.93603	8.91610	13.21479	12
2.13293	2.71962	3.45227	4.36349	6.88579	10.69932	16.38634	13
2.26090	2.93719	3.79750	4.88711	7.98752	12.83918	20.31906	14
2.39656	3.17217	4.17725	5.47357	9.26552	15.40702	25.19563	15
2.54035	3.42594	4.59497	6.13039	10.74800	18.48843	31.24259	16
2.69277	3.70002	5.05447	6.86604	12.46768	22.18611	38.74081	17
2.85434	3.99602	5.55992	7.68997	14.46251	26.62333	48.03860	18
3.02560	4.31570	6.11591	8.61276	16.77652	31.94800	59.56786	19
3.20714	4.66096	6.72750	9.64629	19.46076	38.33760	73.86415	20
3.39956	5.03383	7.40025	10.80385	22.57448	46.00512	91.59155	21
3.60354	5.43654	8.14027	12.10031	26.18640	55.20614	113.57352	22
3.81975	5.87146	8.95430	13.55235	30.37622	66.24737	140.83116	23
4.04893	6.34118	9.84973	15.17863	35.23642	79.49685	174.63064	24
4.29187	6.84848	10.83471	17.00006	40.87424	95.39622	216.54199	25
4.54938	7.39635	11.91818	19.04007	47.41412	114.47546	268.51207	26
4.82235	7.98806	13.10999	21.32488	55.00038	137.37055	332.95497	27
5.11169	8.62711	14.42099	23.88387	63.80044	164.84466	412.86416	28
5.41839	9.31727	15.86309	26.74993	74.00851	197.81359	511.95156	29
5.74349	10.06266	17.44940	29.95992	85.84988	237.37631	634.81993	30
6.08810	10.86767	19.19434	33.55511	99.58586	284.85158	787.17672	31
6.45339	11.73708	21.11378	37.58173	115.51959	341.82189	976.09913	32
6.84059	12.67605	23.22515	42.09153	134.00273	410.18627	1210.36292	33
7.25103	13.69013	25.54767	47.14252	155.44317	492.22352	1500.85002	34
7.68609	14.78534	28.10244	52.79962	180.31407	590.66823	1861.05403	35
8.14725	15.96817	30.91268	59.13557	209.16432	708.80187	2307.70699	36
8.63609	17.24563	34.00395	66.23184	242.63062	850.56225	2861.55667	37
9.15425	18.62528	37.40434	74.17966	281.45151	1020.67470	3548.33027	38
9.70351	20.11530	41.14478	83.08122	326.48376	1224.80964	4399.92954	39
10.28572	21.72452	45.25926	93.05097	378.72116	1469.77157	5455.91262	40

Table 7.2 Present Value of 1

$$pvf_{\overline{n}|\,i} = \frac{1}{(1 + i)^n}$$

Periods (n)	1%	2%	2.5%	3%	4%	5%
1	0.99010	0.98039	0.97561	0.97087	0.96154	0.95238
2	0.98030	0.96117	0.95181	0.94260	0.92456	0.90703
3	0.97059	0.94232	0.92860	0.91514	0.88900	0.86384
4	0.96098	0.92385	0.90595	0.88849	0.85480	0.82270
5	0.95147	0.90573	0.88385	0.86261	0.82193	0.78353
6	0.94205	0.88797	0.86230	0.83748	0.79031	0.74622
7	0.93272	0.87056	0.84127	0.81309	0.75992	0.71068
8	0.92348	0.85349	0.82075	0.78941	0.73069	0.67684
9	0.91434	0.83676	0.80073	0.76642	0.70259	0.64461
10	0.90529	0.82035	0.78120	0.74409	0.67556	0.61391
11	0.89632	0.80426	0.76214	0.72242	0.64958	0.58468
12	0.88745	0.78849	0.74356	0.70138	0.62460	0.55684
13	0.87866	0.77303	0.72542	0.68095	0.60057	0.53032
14	0.86996	0.75788	0.70773	0.66112	0.57748	0.50507
15	0.86135	0.74301	0.69047	0.64186	0.55526	0.48102
16	0.85282	0.72845	0.67362	0.62317	0.53391	0.45811
17	0.84438	0.71416	0.65720	0.60502	0.51337	0.43630
18	0.83602	0.70016	0.64117	0.58739	0.49363	0.41552
19	0.82774	0.68643	0.62553	0.57029	0.47464	0.39573
20	0.81954	0.67297	0.61027	0.55368	0.45639	0.37689
21	0.81143	0.65978	0.59539	0.53755	0.43883	0.35894
22	0.80340	0.64684	0.58086	0.52189	0.42196	0.34185
23	0.79544	0.63416	0.56670	0.50669	0.40573	0.32557
24	0.78757	0.62172	0.55288	0.49193	0.39012	0.31007
25	0.77977	0.60953	0.53939	0.47761	0.37512	0.29530
26	0.77205	0.59758	0.52623	0.46369	0.36069	0.28124
27	0.76440	0.58586	0.51340	0.45019	0.34682	0.26785
28	0.75684	0.57437	0.50088	0.43708	0.33348	0.25509
29	0.74934	0.56311	0.48866	0.42435	0.32065	0.24295
30	0.74192	0.55207	0.47674	0.41199	0.30832	0.23138
31	0.73458	0.54125	0.46511	0.39999	0.29646	0.22036
32	0.72730	0.53063	0.45377	0.38834	0.28506	0.20987
33	0.72010	0.52023	0.44270	0.37703	0.27409	0.19987
34	0.71297	0.51003	0.43191	0.36604	0.26355	0.19035
35	0.70591	0.50003	0.42137	0.35538	0.25342	0.18129
36	0.69892	0.49022	0.41109	0.34503	0.24367	0.17266
37	0.69200	0.48061	0.40107	0.33498	0.23430	0.16444
38	0.68515	0.47119	0.39128	0.32523	0.22529	0.15661
39	0.67837	0.46195	0.38174	0.31575	0.21662	0.14915
40	0.67165	0.45289	0.37243	0.30656	0.20829	0.14205

Table 7.2 Present Value of 1

6%	8%	10%	12%	16%	20%	24%	Periods (n)
0.94340	0.92593	0.90909	0.89286	0.86207	0.83333	0.80645	1
0.89000	0.85734	0.82645	0.79719	0.74316	0.69444	0.65036	2
0.83962	0.79383	0.75131	0.71178	0.64066	0.57870	0.52449	3
0.79209	0.73503	0.68301	0.63552	0.55229	0.48225	0.42297	4
0.74726	0.68058	0.62092	0.56743	0.47611	0.40188	0.34111	5
0.70496	0.63017	0.56447	0.50663	0.41044	0.33490	0.27509	6
0.66506	0.58349	0.51316	0.45235	0.35383	0.27908	0.22184	7
0.62741	0.54027	0.46651	0.40388	0.30503	0.23257	0.17891	8
0.59190	0.50025	0.42410	0.36061	0.26295	0.19381	0.14428	9
0.55839	0.46319	0.38554	0.32197	0.22668	0.16151	0.11635	10
0.52679	0.42888	0.35049	0.28748	0.19542	0.13459	0.09383	11
0.49697	0.39711	0.31863	0.25668	0.16846	0.11216	0.07567	12
0.46884	0.36770	0.28966	0.22917	0.14523	0.09346	0.06103	13
0.44230	0.34046	0.26333	0.20462	0.12520	0.07789	0.04921	14
0.41727	0.31524	0.23939	0.18270	0.10793	0.06491	0.03969	15
0.39365	0.29189	0.21763	0.16312	0.09304	0.05409	0.03201	16
0.37136	0.27027	0.19784	0.14564	0.08021	0.04507	0.02581	17
0.35034	0.25025	0.17986	0.13004	0.06914	0.03756	0.02082	18
0.33051	0.23171	0.16351	0.11611	0.05961	0.03130	0.01679	19
0.31180	0.21455	0.14864	0.10367	0.05139	0.02608	0.01354	20
0.29416	0.19866	0.13513	0.09256	0.04430	0.02174	0.01092	21
0.27751	0.18394	0.12285	0.08264	0.03819	0.01811	0.00880	22
0.26180	0.17032	0.11168	0.07379	0.03292	0.01509	0.00710	23
0.24698	0.15770	0.10153	0.06588	0.02838	0.01258	0.00573	24
0.23300	0.14602	0.09230	0.05882	0.02447	0.01048	0.00462	25
0.21981	0.13520	0.08391	0.05252	0.02109	0.00874	0.00372	26
0.20737	0.12519	0.07628	0.04689	0.01818	0.00728	0.00300	27
0.19563	0.11591	0.06934	0.04187	0.01567	0.00607	0.00242	28
0.18456	0.10733	0.06304	0.03738	0.01351	0.00506	0.00195	29
0.17411	0.09938	0.05731	0.03338	0.01165	0.00421	0.00158	30
0.16425	0.09202	0.05210	0.02980	0.01004	0.00351	0.00127	31
0.15496	0.08520	0.04736	0.02661	0.00866	0.00293	0.00102	32
0.14619	0.07889	0.04306	0.02376	0.00746	0.00244	0.00083	33
0.13791	0.07305	0.03914	0.02121	0.00643	0.00203	0.00067	34
0.13011	0.06763	0.03558	0.01894	0.00555	0.00169	0.00054	35
0.12274	0.06262	0.03235	0.01691	0.00478	0.00141	0.00043	36
0.11579	0.05799	0.02941	0.01510	0.00412	0.00118	0.00035	37
0.10924	0.05369	0.02673	0.01348	0.00355	0.00098	0.00028	38
0.10306	0.04971	0.02430	0.01204	0.00306	0.00082	0.00023	39
0.09722	0.04603	0.02209	0.01075	0.00264	0.00068	0.00018	40

Table 7.3 Amount of an Ordinary Annuity of 1

$$aoaf_{\overline{n}|\,i} = \frac{(1 + i)^n - 1}{i}$$

Periods (n)	1%	2%	2.5%	3%	4%	5%
1	1.00000	1.00000	1.00000	1.00000	1.00000	1.00000
2	2.01000	2.02000	2.02500	2.03000	2.04000	2.05000
3	3.03010	3.06040	3.07562	3.09090	3.12160	3.15250
4	4.06040	4.12161	4.15252	4.18363	4.24646	4.31012
5	5.10101	5.20404	5.25633	5.30914	5.41632	5.52563
6	6.15202	6.30812	6.38774	6.46841	6.63298	6.80191
7	7.21354	7.43428	7.54743	7.66246	7.89829	8.14201
8	8.28567	8.58297	8.73612	8.89234	9.21423	9.54911
9	9.36853	9.75463	9.95452	10.15911	10.58280	11.02656
10	10.46221	10.94972	11.20338	11.46388	12.00611	12.57789
11	11.56683	12.16872	12.48347	12.80780	13.48635	14.20679
12	12.68250	13.41209	13.79555	14.19203	15.02581	15.91713
13	13.80933	14.68033	15.14044	15.61779	16.62684	17.71298
14	14.94742	15.97394	16.51895	17.08632	18.29191	19.59863
15	16.09690	17.29342	17.93193	18.59891	20.02359	21.57856
16	17.25786	18.63929	19.38022	20.15688	21.82453	23.65749
17	18.43044	20.01207	20.86473	21.76159	23.69751	25.84037
18	19.61475	21.41231	22.38635	23.41444	25.64541	28.13238
19	20.81090	22.84056	23.94601	25.11687	27.67123	30.53900
20	22.01900	24.29737	25.54466	26.87037	29.77808	33.06595
21	23.23919	25.78332	27.18327	28.67649	31.96920	35.71925
22	24.47159	27.29898	28.86286	30.53678	34.24797	38.50521
23	25.71630	28.84496	30.58443	32.45288	36.61789	41.43048
24	26.97346	30.42186	32.34904	34.42647	39.08260	44.50200
25	28.24320	32.03030	34.15776	36.45926	41.64591	47.72710
26	29.52563	33.67091	36.01171	38.55304	44.31174	51.11345
27	30.82089	35.34432	37.91200	40.70963	47.08421	54.66913
28	32.12910	37.05121	39.85980	42.93092	49.96758	58.40258
29	33.45039	38.79223	41.85630	45.21885	52.96629	62.32271
30	34.78489	40.56808	43.90270	47.57542	56.08494	66.43885
31	36.13274	42.37944	46.00027	50.00268	59.32834	70.76079
32	37.49407	44.22703	48.15028	52.50276	62.70147	75.29883
33	38.86901	46.11157	50.35403	55.07784	66.20953	80.06377
34	40.25770	48.03380	52.61289	57.73018	69.85791	85.06696
35	41.66028	49.99448	54.92821	60.46208	73.65222	90.32031
36	43.07688	51.99437	57.30141	63.27594	77.59831	95.83632
37	44.50765	54.03425	59.73395	66.17422	81.70225	101.62814
38	45.95272	56.11494	62.22730	69.15945	85.97034	107.70955
39	47.41225	58.23724	64.78298	72.23423	90.40915	114.09502
40	48.88637	60.40198	67.40255	75.40126	95.02552	120.79977

Table 7.3 Amount of an Ordinary Annuity of 1

6%	8%	10%	12%	16%	20%	24%	Periods (n)
1.00000	1.00000	1.00000	1.00000	1.00000	1.00000	1.00000	1
2.06000	2.08000	2.10000	2.12000	2.16000	2.20000	2.24000	2
3.18360	3.24640	3.31000	3.37440	3.50560	3.64000	3.77760	3
4.37462	4.50611	4.64100	4.77933	5.06650	5.36800	5.68422	4
5.63709	5.86660	6.10510	6.35285	6.87714	7.44160	8.04844	5
6.97532	7.33593	7.71561	8.11519	8.97748	9.92992	10.98006	6
8.39384	8.92280	9.48717	10.08901	11.41387	12.91590	14.61528	7
9.89747	10.63663	11.43589	12.29969	14.24009	16.49908	19.12294	8
11.49132	12.48756	13.57948	14.77566	17.51851	20.79890	24.71245	9
13.18079	14.48656	15.93742	17.54874	21.32147	25.95868	31.64344	10
14.97164	16.64549	18.53117	20.65458	25.73290	32.15042	40.23787	11
16.86994	18.97713	21.38428	24.13313	30.85017	39.58050	50.89495	12
18.88214	21.49530	24.52271	28.02911	36.78620	48.49660	64.10974	13
21.01507	24.21492	27.97498	32.39260	43.67199	59.19592	80.49608	14
23.27597	27.15211	31.77248	37.27971	51.65951	72.03511	100.81514	15
25.67253	30.32428	35.94973	42.75328	60.92503	87.44213	126.01077	16
28.21288	33.75023	40.54470	48.88367	71.67303	105.93056	157.25336	17
30.90565	37.45024	45.59917	55.74971	84.14072	128.11667	195.99416	18
33.75999	41.44626	51.15909	63.43968	98.60323	154.74000	244.03276	19
36.78559	45.76196	57.27500	72.05244	115.37975	186.68800	303.60062	20
39.99273	50.42292	64.00250	81.69874	134.84051	225.02560	377.46477	21
43.39229	55.45676	71.40275	92.50258	157.41499	271.03072	469.05632	22
46.99583	60.89330	79.54302	104.60289	183.60138	326.23686	582.62984	23
50.81558	66.76476	88.49733	118.15524	213.97761	392.48424	723.46100	24
54.86451	73.10594	98.34706	133.33387	249.21402	471.98108	898.09164	25
59.15638	79.95442	109.18177	150.33393	290.08827	567.37730	1114.63363	26
63.70577	87.35077	121.09994	169.37401	337.50239	681.85276	1383.14570	27
68.52811	95.33883	134.20994	190.69889	392.50277	819.22331	1716.10067	28
73.63980	103.96594	148.63093	214.58275	456.30322	984.06797	2128.96483	29
79.05819	113.28321	164.49402	241.33268	530.31173	1181.88157	2640.91639	30
84.80168	123.34587	181.94342	271.29261	616.16161	1419.25788	3275.73632	31
90.88978	134.21354	201.13777	304.84772	715.74746	1704.10946	4062.91304	32
97.34316	145.95062	222.25154	342.42945	831.26706	2045.93135	5039.01217	33
104.18375	158.62667	245.47670	384.52098	965.26979	2456.11762	6249.37509	34
111.43478	172.31680	271.02437	431.66350	1120.71295	2948.34115	7750.22511	35
119.12087	187.10215	299.12681	484.46312	1301.02703	3539.00937	9611.27913	36
127.26812	203.07032	330.03949	543.59869	1510.19135	4247.81125	11918.98612	37
135.90421	220.31595	364.04343	609.83053	1752.82197	5098.37350	14780.54279	38
145.05846	238.94122	401.44778	684.01020	2034.27348	6119.04820	18328.87306	39
154.76197	259.05652	442.59256	767.09142	2360.75724	7343.85784	22728.80260	40

Table 7.4   Present Value of an Ordinary Annuity of 1

$$pvoaf_{\overline{n}|\,i} = \dfrac{1 - \dfrac{1}{(1 + i)^n}}{i}$$

Periods (n)	1%	2%	2.5%	3%	4%	5%
1	0.99010	0.98039	0.97561	0.97087	0.96154	0.95238
2	1.97040	1.94156	1.92742	1.91347	1.88609	1.85941
3	2.94099	2.88388	2.85602	2.82861	2.77509	2.72325
4	3.90197	3.80773	3.76197	3.71710	3.62990	3.54595
5	4.85343	4.71346	4.64583	4.57971	4.45182	4.32948
6	5.79548	5.60143	5.50813	5.41719	5.24214	5.07569
7	6.72819	6.47199	6.34939	6.23028	6.00205	5.78637
8	7.65168	7.32548	7.17014	7.01969	6.73274	6.46321
9	8.56602	8.16224	7.97087	7.78611	7.43533	7.10782
10	9.47130	8.98259	8.75206	8.53020	8.11090	7.72173
11	10.36763	9.78685	9.51421	9.25262	8.76048	8.30641
12	11.25508	10.57534	10.25776	9.95400	9.38507	8.86325
13	12.13374	11.34837	10.98318	10.63496	9.98565	9.39357
14	13.00370	12.10625	11.69091	11.29607	10.56312	9.89864
15	13.86505	12.84926	12.38138	11.93794	11.11839	10.37966
16	14.71787	13.57771	13.05500	12.56110	11.65230	10.83777
17	15.56225	14.29187	13.71220	13.16612	12.16567	11.27407
18	16.39827	14.99203	14.35336	13.75351	12.65930	11.68959
19	17.22601	15.67846	14.97889	14.32380	13.13394	12.08532
20	18.04555	16.35143	15.58916	14.87747	13.59033	12.46221
21	18.85698	17.01121	16.18455	15.41502	14.02916	12.82115
22	19.66038	17.65805	16.76541	15.93692	14.45112	13.16300
23	20.45582	18.29220	17.33211	16.44361	14.85684	13.48857
24	21.24339	18.91393	17.88499	16.93554	15.24696	13.79864
25	22.02316	19.52346	18.42438	17.41315	15.62208	14.09394
26	22.79520	20.12104	18.95061	17.87684	15.98277	14.37519
27	23.55961	20.70690	19.46401	18.32703	16.32959	14.64303
28	24.31644	21.28127	19.96489	18.76411	16.66306	14.89813
29	25.06579	21.84438	20.45355	19.18845	16.98371	15.14107
30	25.80771	22.39646	20.93029	19.60044	17.29203	15.37245
31	26.54229	22.93770	21.39541	20.00043	17.58849	15.59281
32	27.26959	23.46833	21.84918	20.38877	17.87355	15.80268
33	27.98969	23.98856	22.29188	20.76579	18.14765	16.00255
34	28.70267	24.49859	22.72379	21.13184	18.41120	16.19290
35	29.40858	24.99862	23.14516	21.48722	18.66461	16.37419
36	30.10751	25.48884	23.55625	21.83225	18.90828	16.54685
37	30.79951	25.96945	23.95732	22.16724	19.14258	16.71129
38	31.48466	26.44064	24.34860	22.49246	19.36786	16.86789
39	32.16303	26.90259	24.73034	22.80822	19.58448	17.01704
40	32.83469	27.35548	25.10278	23.11477	19.79277	17.15909

Table 7.4 Present Value of an Ordinary Annuity of 1

6%	8%	10%	12%	16%	20%	24%	Periods (n)
0.94340	0.92593	0.90909	0.89286	0.86207	0.83333	0.80645	1
1.83339	1.78326	1.73554	1.69005	1.60523	1.52778	1.45682	2
2.67301	2.57710	2.48685	2.40183	2.24589	2.10648	1.98130	3
3.46511	3.31213	3.16987	3.03735	2.79818	2.58873	2.40428	4
4.21236	3.99271	3.79079	3.60478	3.27429	2.99061	2.74538	5
4.91732	4.62288	4.35526	4.11141	3.68474	3.32551	3.02047	6
5.58238	5.20637	4.86842	4.56376	4.03857	3.60459	3.24232	7
6.20979	5.74664	5.33493	4.96764	4.34359	3.83716	3.42122	8
6.80169	6.24689	5.75902	5.32825	4.60654	4.03097	3.56550	9
7.36009	6.71008	6.14457	5.65022	4.83323	4.19247	3.68186	10
7.88687	7.13896	6.49506	5.93770	5.02864	4.32706	3.77569	11
8.38384	7.53608	6.81369	6.19437	5.19711	4.43922	3.85136	12
8.85268	7.90378	7.10336	6.42355	5.34233	4.53268	3.91239	13
9.29498	8.24424	7.36669	6.62817	5.46753	4.61057	3.96160	14
9.71225	8.55948	7.60608	6.81086	5.57546	4.67547	4.00129	15
10.10590	8.85137	7.82371	6.97399	5.66850	4.72956	4.03330	16
10.47726	9.12164	8.02155	7.11963	5.74870	4.77463	4.05911	17
10.82760	9.37189	8.20141	7.24967	5.81785	4.81219	4.07993	18
11.15812	9.60360	8.36492	7.36578	5.87746	4.84350	4.09672	19
11.46992	9.81815	8.51356	7.46944	5.92884	4.86958	4.11026	20
11.76408	10.01680	8.64869	7.56200	5.97314	4.89132	4.12117	21
12.04158	10.20074	8.77154	7.64465	6.01133	4.90943	4.12998	22
12.30338	10.37106	8.88322	7.71843	6.04425	4.92453	4.13708	23
12.55036	10.52876	8.98474	7.78432	6.07263	4.93710	4.14281	24
12.78336	10.67478	9.07704	7.84314	6.09709	4.94759	4.14742	25
13.00317	10.80998	9.16095	7.89566	6.11818	4.95632	4.15115	26
13.21053	10.93516	9.23722	7.94255	6.13636	4.96360	4.15415	27
13.40616	11.05108	9.30657	7.98442	6.15204	4.96967	4.15657	28
13.59072	11.15841	9.36961	8.02181	6.16555	4.97472	4.15853	29
13.76483	11.25778	9.42691	8.05518	6.17720	4.97894	4.16010	30
13.92909	11.34980	9.47901	8.08499	6.18724	4.98245	4.16137	31
14.08404	11.43500	9.52638	8.11159	6.19590	4.98537	4.16240	32
14.23023	11.51389	9.56943	8.13535	6.20336	4.98781	4.16322	33
14.36814	11.58693	9.60857	8.15656	6.20979	4.98984	4.16389	34
14.49825	11.65457	9.64416	8.17550	6.21534	4.99154	4.16443	35
14.62099	11.71719	9.67651	8.19241	6.22012	4.99295	4.16486	36
14.73678	11.77518	9.70592	8.20751	6.22424	4.99412	4.16521	37
14.84602	11.82887	9.73265	8.22099	6.22779	4.99510	4.16549	38
14.94907	11.87858	9.75696	8.23303	6.23086	4.99592	4.16572	39
15.04630	11.92461	9.77905	8.24378	6.23350	4.99660	4.16590	40

Cash and Receivables

PART 3

ASSET ACCOUNTING

Objectives

1. To discuss and illustrate the financial accounting and reporting requirements for cash and receivables classified as current assets.

2. To explain the accounting for a petty cash fund.

3. To discuss and illustrate the preparation of a bank reconciliation and a proof of cash.

4. To explain the accounting for credit sales.

5. To discuss and illustrate the accounting for uncollectable accounts receivable.

6. To explain certain financing methods under which companies use their accounts receivable to generate cash.

7. To discuss and illustrate the accounting for notes receivable.

In Part 1 of this book, we discussed the theoretical basis for financial reporting, and in Part 2, we presented the tools of accounting. In Part 3, our focus shifts to asset accounting. Each of the seven chapters in Part 3 discusses important measurement and disclosure principles that relate to certain assets, and each is related to the theoretical framework presented in Chapter 2. Recall that, in Chapter 2, we defined assets as probable future economic benefits obtained or controlled by a particular entity as a result of past transactions or events. The Canadian Pacific Limited balance sheet printed in Appendix A at the end of this text, shows several of the assets discussed in Part 3.

This chapter focusses on cash and receivables classified as current assets. Cash and receivables classified as noncurrent assets are discussed in Chapter 11. Recall that, in Chapter 3, we discussed the nature of asset valuation. Generally, the valuation of cash and short-term receivables is less complex and controversial than the valuation of most other assets.

The assets described in this chapter are highly liquid (i.e., cash or close to cash realization) and are therefore important in assessing a company's overall liquidity. An empirical study provided evidence that users of financial statements are becoming more concerned about liquidity evaluations: "While security analysts used to be concerned primarily with earnings per share, they are now devoting increased attention to the balance sheet and cash flow. Liquidity analysis plays a significant part in security analysts' evaluation of companies."[1]

Cash

Composition of Cash

Cash is the standard medium of exchange in business transactions. It includes currency, coins, cheques, bank drafts, money orders, and demand deposits (chequing accounts). Savings accounts are also usually considered cash, because banks generally do not enforce their legal right to demand notice before the depositor makes a withdrawal. As a result, savings account balances are usually available for immediate expenditure.

Most companies maintain several general ledger accounts for cash in order to provide management with adequate details concerning cash balances. For example, a company might establish the following:

1. A **petty cash** account for currency and coins (called a petty cash fund) used to make small disbursements.
2. A **cash on hand** account for undeposited cash receipts.
3. A separate **cash in bank** account for each chequing account maintained.

External users of financial statements are generally interested in the total amount of cash that a company has and in the relationship between this amount and other financial statement amounts. That is why companies typically combine the amounts shown in the various cash accounts and report only a single total as "cash" on the balance sheet.

Asset/Liability Measurement

The valuation of cash is not highly controversial: cash is simply reported at its **face amount**. The classification of cash as current or noncurrent depends on management's intended use of the cash. To be classified as a current asset, cash must be available for

---

[1]Morton Backer and Martin L. Gosman, *Financial Reporting and Business Liquidity* (New York: National Association of Accountants, 1978), p. 251.

use in current operations. Because it is highly liquid, cash is usually listed first among the current assets. A material amount of cash that has been restricted or designated for some current purpose, such as the payment of current bond interest, should be reported separately among the current assets. On the other hand, cash that is not available for current purposes, such as cash accumulated in a sinking fund to retire the principal amount of long-term bonds, should be reported in the investments and funds category and not in current assets.[2]

Several noteworthy considerations in accounting for cash are described below.

1. **Certificates of deposit (CDs) or Guaranteed Investment Certificates (GICs)** should normally be included in short-term investments instead of cash, because banks usually impose substantial interest penalties that discourage holders from making withdrawals before the certificates mature.

2. **Postdated cheques, NSF cheques** (not sufficient funds cheques, those that cannot be covered by funds in the debtor's bank account), and **IOUs** should be reported as receivables rather than cash.

3. **Expense advances,** such as advances for employee travel, and **postage stamps** should be reported as prepaid expenses, not cash. These items will become expenses and are not normally converted into cash.

4. **A bank overdraft,** which occurs when a depositor has written cheques for a sum greater than that in the depositor's bank account, should be reported as a current liability, except when the depositor has sufficient funds in another account with the *same bank* to cover the account that is overdrawn. Under these circumstances, which may arise when a company maintains a regular operating account and a payroll account with the same bank, the bank will transfer funds to the overdrawn account if the depositor fails to do so. As a result, the depositor may appropriately offset the overdraft against the cash balance and report the net amount of cash among the current assets.

   Some companies maintain a line of credit at their bank. This line of credit is in the form of a demand loan. When a bank account goes into overdraft, a note is completed as collateral for the amount of the increase in the overdraft.

5. **Undelivered or outstanding cheques,** as of the balance sheet date, should be considered part of a debtor's cash. Technically, cheques drawn by a company should not be deducted from the company's cash balance until they have been mailed or otherwise delivered. As a result, liabilities that the cheques are intended to liquidate still exist and should be reported as current payables.

6. **Compensating balances** are minimum amounts that a company agrees to maintain in a bank chequing account as partial consideration for a loan or line of credit. Compensating balances limit the amount of cash that a company can spend in everyday operations. Moreover, compensating balances increase a company's effective interest cost if they are higher than the chequing account balances that the company would normally maintain. For these reasons, a company should disclose information about compensating balances in the notes to its financial statements. An example of such a note is as follows:

During 1993, informal arrangements were maintained with a number of banks, which generally required the Company to maintain compensating cash balances of 8 percent of

---

[2]"Cash," CICA *Handbook,* Section 3000, December 1968.

the loan commitments plus 8 percent of the average daily outstanding debt balances. At December 31, 1993, the cash balance includes $9.5 million of such compensating balances.

Management of Cash

Companies need cash to buy goods and services, to pay off debts, and to make distributions to owners. Because of its critical importance to any business, cash must be managed effectively. As the chief executive of Firestone Tire & Rubber Company has stated: "Cash becomes the final determinant in the way you run a company."[3] Effective cash management involves striking a delicate balance between *risk* and *profitability*. On the one hand, managers try to avoid having too little cash on hand in order to minimize the company's risk of insolvency. On the other hand, they try to avoid excessive cash balances because uninvested cash does not contribute to the company's profits.

Effective cash management requires careful planning and control. The major aspect of **cash planning** is the **cash budget**, which is an internal statement of projected cash inflows, outflows, and balances. Among other things, the cash budget enables managers to prepare in advance for such activities as the raising of additional cash through borrowing, and the investing of idle cash in productive assets. Cash planning is usually covered in managerial accounting and financial management courses.

Cash control is an important part of a firm's **internal control system**. Internal control has been defined as "Policies and procedures established and maintained by management to assist in achieving its objective of ensuring, as far as practical, the orderly and efficient conduct of the entity's business."[4] Internal control includes **accounting controls**, which relate to the safeguarding of assets and the reliability of financial records, and **administrative controls**, which relate to operational efficiency and adherence to managerial policies. Accountants should have a general awareness of administrative controls, including statistical analyses, time and motion studies, performance reports, employee training programs, and quality controls.[5] In addition, accountants should have a thorough understanding of accounting controls. External accountants review the internal controls as part of the audit, but the responsibility for implementing and monitoring these controls rests with internal accountants. Several important **principles of internal accounting control** are listed below.

1. Company personnel should be competent and honest, and they should be given specific responsibilities.
2. The responsibility for a series of related events, such as receiving merchandise and paying for it, should be divided between two or more persons.
3. The accounting function should be separated from the custodianship of company assets.
4. Adequate accounting records should be kept at all times.
5. Certain clerical personnel should be rotated among various jobs.
6. Assets should be protected by insurance and by physical safeguards.
7. An internal audit staff should be maintained if management believes the benefits of having such a staff exceed the costs.

---

[3]Thomas O'Hanlon, "Less Means More at Firestone," *Fortune* (October 20, 1980), p. 116.

[4]"Internal Control in the Context of an Audit," CICA *Handbook,* Paragraph 5200.03, March 1992.

[5]"Internal Control in the Context of an Audit," CICA *Handbook,* Sections 5200–220.C, March 1992.

Maintaining an adequate system of internal accounting control for all assets is important, but it is particularly important for cash. Cash appeals to virtually everyone and is relatively easy to steal if not properly safeguarded. If one person, for example, both receives and records a company's cash, that person can easily pocket some of the receipts and fail to record them. The specific features of internal accounting controls over cash vary from company to company. Generally, however, these controls are designed to ensure that

1. Responsibilities are divided between those employees who account for cash and those who have custody of it.
2. All cash receipts are recorded when received and deposited immediately and intact in the bank.
3. All disbursements are made for authorized purposes.
4. All disbursements, except for small ones made from petty cash, are made by cheque.

Specific accounting controls for cash are usually covered in more depth in auditing courses. Two important control measures designed to help safeguard a company's cash—the maintenance of a petty cash fund and the periodic reconciliation of the bank statement—are discussed in the sections that follow.

Petty Cash

A business should generally make all payments by cheque. But most businesses find it inconvenient or impossible to write cheques for such small items as taxi fares, newspaper delivery charges, postage, courier charges, and minor supplies. A company usually pays for these kinds of items from a **petty cash fund**, often called an **imprest cash fund**. A petty cash fund is established for a fixed amount and allows a company to effectively control small amounts of cash fairly easily. The following discussion explains how such a fund works.

1. A responsible employee is appointed **petty cashier**. A cheque drawn payable to petty cash is cashed, and the petty cashier places the money in the petty cash fund (which is often kept in a locked box). The cheque that establishes the fund is usually for an amount ($300, for example) that the company estimates will last from two to four weeks. The following journal entry is required:

Petty Cash	300	
Cash		300

2. As time passes, the petty cashier disburses money from the fund. To evidence each disbursement, the petty cashier places in the fund a prenumbered receipt that is signed by the person who received cash. The amount of petty cash on hand and the amounts shown on the signed receipts should always equal the original amount of the fund ($300 in our example). The company does *not* make journal entries when petty cash is disbursed.
3. When the amount of cash in the fund is low, the petty cashier submits the signed receipts and requests reimbursement from the general cashier for an amount that will increase the cash in the fund to the original amount. At this time, the receipts are

cancelled so that no one can use them again. In addition, the company records increases in those expenses (or other accounts) that are documented by the receipts.

Now assume that after three weeks only $25 remains in the petty cash fund. The signed receipts show the following petty cash disbursements:

Postage	$ 45
Office supplies	102
Transportation-in	125
Total	$272

Because the fund contains only $25, the general cashier must write a cheque for $275 ($300 − $25) to restore the fund to its original amount ($300). After the cheque is written, the company makes the following journal entry:

Postage Expense	45	
Office Supplies Expense	102	
Transportation-in	125	
Cash Short and Over	3	
Cash		275

The cheque is then cashed and the money is placed in the petty cash fund.

Cash Short and Over is a nominal account that is debited for cash shortages and credited for overages. Such shortages and overages usually result from errors in making change or failure to obtain receipts for very small amounts. A debit balance in the Cash Short and Over account at the end of a period should be reported as a miscellaneous expense and a credit balance as a miscellaneous revenue. However, a material cash shortage resulting from a cause such as theft should be charged to a receivable account if the company expects to recover the amount of the shortage. If recovery is not expected, the company should charge a loss account.

Materiality

Observe that the company debited the Petty Cash account when the fund was established and made no other entries in this account. At the end of an accounting period, therefore, the petty cash fund should ordinarily be replenished. This ensures that all expenses paid with petty cash are recorded and that the petty cash on hand corresponds with the amount shown in the Petty Cash account. If for some reason the fund is not replenished at the end of an accounting period, the company should still debit the appropriate expense accounts, but it should credit the Petty Cash account directly. Over time, the pattern of petty cash disbursements may suggest that the original amount of the petty cash fund is either too low or too high. If this occurs, the amount of petty cash and the balance shown in the Petty Cash account should be increased or decreased accordingly. For example, if the company in the above example increases the fixed amount of the petty cash fund from $300 to $400, the following journal entry would be made:

Petty Cash	100	
Cash		100

Cash in Bank

The cash that a business has on hand may include petty cash funds, change funds (funds used to make change with customers), and undeposited receipts. As stated earlier, a business normally keeps most of its cash in one or more chequing accounts. The chequing account gives a company a **double record** of its cash transactions: the company's own record plus that provided by the bank. The bank's record is summarized on a monthly **bank statement.**

An accountant verifies the cash on hand simply by counting it. In contrast, because the cash in a chequing account cannot be conveniently counted, accountants verify it by preparing a bank reconciliation.

Bank Reconciliation

When a company receives a bank statement, the company's accountant should immediately prepare a **bank reconciliation.** This schedule explains any differences between a company's book balance of cash and the bank statement balance. A bank reconciliation helps to identify errors made by the depositor or by the bank in recording cash transactions. It also helps in making journal entries to update the depositor's accounting records.

On a depositor's books (accounting records), the cash balance in a bank account is an asset. On the bank's books, the cash in the depositor's account is a liability. Because the depositor and the bank do not simultaneously record all transactions, and because either party can make mistakes, the asset balance on the depositor's books usually does not equal the liability balance on the bank statement. Many factors may explain why the two balances differ:

1. **Deposits in transit.** These are additions to cash in the bank that the depositor has recorded but that do not appear on the bank statement. For example, on the last day of the month, the depositor may place the day's cash receipts in the bank's night depository, to be recorded by the bank on the next business day. These receipts should appear on the next month's bank statement.

2. **Outstanding cheques.** These are cheques that the depositor has issued and recorded but that have not yet cleared the bank and will not be deducted on the bank statement until they are deposited in the bank of the payee and processed through the banking system.

3. **Bank collections.** Promissory notes are often made payable at the payee's bank. The bank may therefore collect a note for the depositor and credit the proceeds to the depositor's account. Such collections made near the end of a month may appear on the bank statement but not yet appear on the depositor's books because the depositor is not yet aware of the collection. These types of transactions are not common in the Canadian business environment.

4. **Bank charges.** The bank often makes various charges that are not yet recorded on the depositor's books, such as charges for bank services, chequebooks, NSF cheques, and repayment of depositor loans.

5. **Bank errors.** Occasionally, a bank error might affect the depositor's account. For example, the bank might erroneously charge one company's cheque to another company's account. The depositor should instruct the bank to correct such errors. The occurrence of these types of errors should be reduced by the use of encoded cheques.

6. **Depositor errors.** Sometimes an error is made in the depositor's accounting records (commonly called a **book error**). For example, the depositor may have written a cheque for one amount but recorded the cheque at a different amount. The depositor should promptly correct the accounting records.

An accountant may prepare a bank reconciliation by reconciling from the bank statement balance to the book balance, or vice versa. Accountants prefer, however, to reconcile from both of these balances to the **correct cash balance.** Such a reconciliation is relatively easy to understand, it shows in one place the information needed for making journal entries, and it indicates the correct cash balance that a company can spend from its chequing account (the balance after all errors are corrected and all outstanding items clear the bank). A convenient form for this type of bank reconciliation is shown in Exhibit 8.1.

Observe that the bank reconciliation is divided into two sections: "balance per bank statement" and "balance per books." The logic of the additions and deductions in each section is not difficult to understand. Both sections end with the same "correct cash balance." This is the amount of cash that the depositor can spend from the chequing account and the amount that should appear on the depositor's balance sheet.

Usually, the depositor must make journal entries after the reconciliation is completed to update the depositor's accounting records. These entries are based on the items added or deducted in the "balance per books" section. Additions and deductions in the other section either have already been recorded by the depositor or represent errors that the bank must correct.

To illustrate, assume that Todd, Inc. keeps all of its cash in a chequing account. An examination of the company's accounting records and its bank statement for the month ended May 31, 1995, revealed the following information:

1. The cash balance shown as of May 31 on the bank statement was $17 631.
2. The cash balance shown as of May 31 on the company's books was $15 214.
3. A deposit of $1500 mailed to the bank on May 31 did not appear on the bank statement.
4. On May 30, the bank collected a note receivable for Todd, Inc. and credited the proceeds of $2100 to the company's account. The proceeds included $100 of interest, all of which the company earned during 1995. Todd, Inc. has not yet recorded the collection.
5. Outstanding cheques as of May 31 were as follows:

No. 902	$ 132
No. 922	870
No. 923	1645

6. The company discovered that cheque no. 916, written in May for $527 in payment of an account payable, had been incorrectly recorded as $257.
7. The bank returned a cheque for $538 that the company deposited on May 29. The cheque was drawn by a customer who did not have sufficient funds in his bank account to cover the cheque. There was a $10 NSF cheque fee. Depending on company policy, this fee may be charged to an expense account or charged back to the issuer of the NSF cheque.
8. The bank statement showed a $12 service charge for May.

The bank reconciliation for Todd, Inc. is shown in Exhibit 8.2. As stated earlier, the journal entries to update the depositor's accounting records should be based on the items added or deducted in the "balance per books" section.

Exhibit 8.1 Bank Reconciliation Form

Balance per bank statement		$XXX
Add: Deposits in transit	$XX	
Bank errors that understate the balance per bank statement (e.g., the bank charges someone else's cheque to the depositor's account)	XX	XX
		XXX
Deduct: Outstanding cheques	XX	
Bank errors that overstate the balance per bank statement (e.g., the bank charges one of the depositor's cheques to someone else's account)	XX	XX
Correct cash balance		$XXX
Balance per books		$XXX
Add: Deposits credited by the bank but not yet recorded by the depositor (e.g., collection of a promissory note)	$XX	
Book errors that understate the balance per books (e.g., the depositor writes a cheque for $10 but deducts $100 on the books)	XX	XX
		XXX
Deduct: Bank charges not yet recorded by the depositor (e.g., bank service charges and NSF cheques)	XX	
Book errors that overstate the balance per books (e.g., the depositor writes a cheque for $100 but deducts $10 on the books)	XX	XX
Correct cash balance		$XXX

Exhibit 8.2

Todd, Inc.
BANK RECONCILIATION
May 31, 1995

Balance per bank statement		$17 631
Add: Deposits in transit		1 500
		19 131
Deduct: Outstanding cheques		
No. 902	$ 132	
No. 922	870	
No. 923	1 645	2 647
Correct cash balance		$16 484
Balance per books		$15 214
Add: Note and interest collected by bank		2 100
		17 314
Deduct: Bank service charge	$ 12	
NSF cheque received from customer, includes $10 fee	548	
Error made in recording cheque no. 916 ($527 − $257)	270	830
Correct cash balance		$16 484

Cash	2100	
Notes Receivable		2000
Interest Revenue		100
(*To record collection of note and interest by bank.*)		
Miscellaneous Expense	12	
Cash		12
(*To record bank service charge.*)		
Accounts Receivable	538	
Miscellaneous Expense	10	
Cash		548
(*To record NSF cheque.*)		
Accounts Payable	270	
Cash		270
(*To correct error made in recording cheque no. 916.*)		

These entries may be combined into a single compound entry. When the entries are posted, Todd, Inc.'s cash account will show a balance of $16 484, the correct amount as shown on the bank reconciliation.

An accountant should reconcile the monthly bank statement for each chequing account that a company maintains. If a company has more than one chequing account, the amount of cash to report on a balance sheet will be the sum of the correct cash balances shown on the bank reconciliations and any cash that the depositor has on hand.

Proof of Cash

Auditors frequently prepare an expanded version of the bank reconciliation known as a **four-column bank reconciliation,** or simply a **proof of cash.** A proof of cash includes four reconciliations:

1. A reconciliation of the bank statement and book balances of cash at the end of the *previous month*.
2. A reconciliation of the cash receipts (deposits) shown on the bank statement with those shown on the books for the *current month*.
3. A reconciliation of the cash payments shown on the bank statement with those shown on the books for the *current month*.
4. A reconciliation of the bank statement and book balances of cash at the end of the *current month*.

The proof of cash is a stronger control measure than the single-column bank reconciliation. Auditors frequently prepare a proof of cash when a company is found to have weak internal control over cash. Because it provides a reconciliation of cash transactions as well as cash balances, the proof of cash makes it easier to pinpoint errors made by the company or the bank. This feature is particularly important when a company has made cash transfers from one bank account to another during the month. If a transfer is shown as a payment from one account but is not shown as a receipt by the other, an accountant or auditor will want to know why. We illustrate how to prepare a proof of cash in the Appendix to this chapter.

Desktop Forgery

Paul Sjiem-Fat, a Netherlands Antilles national living in Boston's North Station neighborhood, claimed on a Bank of Boston credit card application to be an employee of the Dutch consulate. After he defrauded the bank of about $20,000, the bank discovered that his employment claim was a lie, and, since it involved impersonation of a diplomat, the Secret Service was called in, a search warrant was issued and Sjiem-Fat's apartment was raided.

Investigating this seemingly routine case, the Secret Service stumbled upon its first-ever case of computer forgery. It is certainly not going to be the last. While crooks are only just beginning to learn the game, the possibilities are nearly endless: letters of credit, job recommendations, property records, insurance claims, expense account receipts, college transcripts, business licenses. In short, many of the paper credentials on which society relies are henceforward suspect.

What made this Boston case especially alarming was that Sjiem-Fat used no sophisticated equipment. In his apartment police found a personal computer, a laser printer and nine bogus checks totaling $146,500. In a highly original—and perhaps pioneering—way, Sjiem-Fat was using ordinary desktop publishing tools as instruments of crime.

Here is what he apparently did. With the sort of desktop publishing equipment you can buy at any computer retailer, Sjiem-Fat convincingly forged Digital Equipment Corp. letterheads with a phony name, Paul Marques, and a phony vice president title. He also created phony cashier's checks from banks like First American and Chase Manhattan. Stewart Henry, an investigator with the U.S. Secret Service, explains: "He used the official emblems from three different banks and transferred them onto blank check paper with a laser printer. This was the first time we had ever seen anything like this."

According to investigators, Sjiem-Fat used bogus checks to buy computers from various Boston suppliers. After taking delivery of the computers, he sold them for cash to buyers in the Caribbean area.

An isolated case? Not necessarily. Just last month a rash of computer-generated fake checks hit the Phoenix area. "These look like they were done by putting corporate logos onto check paper with a desktop publishing system," says Gail Thackery, an assistant attorney general for Arizona.

Coupled to a good printer and the right software, the personal computer is a powerful publishing device. It can create and store logos as well as type in all sizes and styles. With a scanner, it can read in a document, then modify and reprint it. It is, above all, quite accessible to the amateur. Now you can produce professional-looking brochures and blank business forms without hiring a master printer. You can also, if your taste runs that way, run off a bogus check or two.

The existence of all these potential counterfeiting tools is scary enough, but an unrelated development threatens to turn the situation into a disaster for the banking industry. This other problem is a federal statute compelling banks to give their customers quick access to funds from deposited checks.

The quick-access rule was heralded as a victory for consumers. But it was an even bigger victory for con artists. Why? Today's forger can make crisp and convincing business checks, deposit them into an account opened previously under a fake name, demand cash after waiting as little as three days, and be out of town long before the forgeries are discovered. If the forger has chosen as target a corporation with a large balance and a lot of check volume, it's next to impossible for either the bank or the corporation to detect the scheme without doing a monthly statement reconciliation. And that reconciliation can't possibly take place within three days of when a bogus check is deposited.

In the past, a forger had to have access to professional printing equipment and presses. He either owned a print shop, bribed someone who worked at one, or made do with whatever materials he could copy by hand. The risk of detection was high. Not any longer. The boom in desktop publishing has brought a flood of typesetting products to market, at declining prices and increasing capabilities.

"The market for this equipment has gone wild in the last year," says James Cavuoto, a Torrance, Calif. desktop publishing expert. "It's only a matter of time before the crooks catch on to the opportunity." They clearly already have.

Source: Reprinted from David Churbuck, "Desktop Forgery," *Forbes,* November 27, 1989, pp. 246–53. Reprinted with permission of *Forbes* magazine, November 27, 1989. © Forbes Inc. 1989.

Receivables

Receivables are claims held against others for money, goods, or services. They generally result in an inflow of cash. An enterprise should classify a receivable as a *current asset* only if collection of the receivable is expected within the next year or operating cycle, whichever is longer. Other receivables should be reported in the investments and funds category or in other assets, as we discuss and illustrate in Chapter 11.

Because of the operating cycle concept, when current assets include installment receivables, but "where practicable, maturity dates of installment accounts maturing beyond one year should be disclosed."[6] These receivables are often collectable over periods that are longer than one year after the balance sheet date. Accounting for installment receivables is discussed in Chapter 5.

Asset/Liability Measurement

Proper accounting for a receivable requires an assessment of the **amount, timing,** and **uncertainty** associated with its collection. In theory, an accountant should initially value (measure) a receivable at an amount equal to the present value of the cash that the enterprise expects to collect. Such a valuation reflects the time value of money: an enterprise earns **interest** by waiting to collect money. The amount of interest is the difference between a receivable's maturity value and its present value. In practice, accountants often ignore interest for short-term receivables, because they regard the amount as immaterial.

Materiality

Receivables may be classified as **trade receivables** or **nontrade receivables,** which are generally reported separately on the balance sheet. Trade receivables result from sales of goods or services to customers. They usually compose most of the total dollar value of a company's receivables. All other receivables are nontrade. Examples of nontrade receivables include:

1. Receivables from officers or employees.
2. Advances to subsidiaries.
3. Various types of deposits made with other parties (e.g., power or telephone companies).
4. Claims against insurance companies.
5. Dividends receivable (from other companies).
6. Interest receivable.

A receivable may be represented by an open account (a nonwritten promise to pay) or by a note (a written promise to pay). Thus, **accounts receivable** and **notes receivable** are reported separately on the balance sheet. They are discussed in the sections that follow.

Accounts Receivable

In a broad sense, the term "accounts receivable" includes all receivables not evidenced by written promises to pay. But accountants usually restrict the term to open accounts that have resulted from selling goods or services on credit. Because accounts receivable are important assets to many companies, they must be managed effectively. Such management involves a trade-off between the revenues generated by credit sales and the costs associated with carrying the resulting accounts receivable.

---

[6]"Accounts and Notes Receivable," CICA *Handbook,* Paragraph 3020.02, August 1991.

Generally accepted accounting principles require companies to report accounts receivable at **net realizable value.** This is the amount that the company expects to collect, and it equals the face amount of the receivables less an estimated uncollectable amount. Because of materiality, accountants generally ignore the interest inherent in the face amount of accounts receivable.

Recording Credit Sales

Recording accounts receivable is closely related to the revenue realization principle (discussed in Chapter 2). That is, a seller should record a receivable that arises from a sale of goods on the date that the sale occurs. This is also when the seller recognizes revenue. Under most circumstances, the sales revenue and the related receivable should be recorded at the precise moment that title passes from the seller to the buyer. For practical reasons, however, accounts receivable and related sales revenue are usually recorded when the seller ships the goods.

Trade Discounts. A trade discount is an amount that a seller deducts from a list price to determine the invoice price of goods sold. List prices are quoted in the seller's catalogues or price lists, while trade discounts usually appear in a separate schedule. A trade discount, then, is merely a convenient device that manufacturers and wholesalers often use to price their goods. The use of trade discounts enables a company to revise its prices periodically without having to reprint its catalogues and to set different prices for different types of customers and for different quantities sold.

Neither sellers nor purchasers should record trade discounts in their accounts. To illustrate, assume that Smith Ltd. sells 100 footballs to Todd, Inc. for the list price of $30 each, less a trade discount of 40 percent. The invoice price is therefore $18 ($30 − $12) per football and the total invoice price is $1800 ($18 × 100). Here is how Smith Ltd. should record the transaction:

Accounts Receivable	1800	
Sales		1800

Many sellers express trade discounts in a series such as 40/20/10. The use of multiple trade discounts allows the seller to conveniently vary the selling price based on such factors as the type of customer or the quantity purchased. If the terms are 40/20/10, a customer may receive a trade discount of (1) 40 percent, (2) 40 percent and 20 percent, or (3) 40 percent, 20 percent, and 10 percent, depending on the circumstances. Suppose, for example, that Smith Ltd. sells Model 21 televisions for the list price of $100 each, less the following discounts:

40%	If 50 or fewer TVs are purchased.
40% and 20%	If more than 50 but fewer than 100 TVs are purchased.
40%, 20%, and 10%	If 100 or more TVs are purchased.

Assuming that customers Aim, Bar, and Cam purchase 30, 60, and 200 televisions, respectively, Exhibit 8.3 shows how Smith Ltd. would determine the invoice price for each customer.

Trade discounts can be used to differentiate between types of customers. An example would be an operation with the following: retail sales without discounts; wholesale sales with a 40 percent discount; distributor sales that qualify for discounts of 40 percent and

Exhibit 8.3 Trade Discount

Customer	Quantity Purchased	Applicable Trade Discount	Invoice Price Per Unit	Total Invoice Price
Aim	30	40%	$100 − ($100 × 40%) = $60	$60 × 30 units = $1800
Bar	60	40% and 20%	$100 − ($100 × 40%) = $60 $60 − ($60 × 20%) = $48	$48 × 60 units = $2880
Cam	200	40%, 20%, and 10%	$100 − ($100 × 40%) = $60 $60 − ($60 × 20%) = $48 $48 − ($48 × 10%) = $43.20	$43.20 × 200 units = $8640

20 percent; manufacturer sales that qualify for discounts of 40 percent, 20 percent, and 10 percent.

Cash Discounts. Companies frequently offer cash discounts to their credit customers. A **cash discount** is a reduction on an invoice price that is offered to buyers to encourage prompt payment. Companies use trade discounts to *establish* an invoice price and cash discounts to *reduce* the invoice price. From the seller's point of view, a cash discount is called a **sales discount;** from the purchaser's point of view, a cash discount is called a **purchase discount.** A cash discount is usually expressed in terms such as 2/10, n/30 or 2/10, EOM (end of month). Terms of 2/10, n/30 mean that the buyer may deduct 2 percent from the invoice price if payment is made within ten days of the invoice date. A buyer who does not pay within the ten-day discount period must pay the gross invoice amount within 30 days of the invoice date.

Purchasers generally take cash discounts offered to them because it is usually advantageous to do so. Suppose, for example, that Smith Ltd. sells goods to Todd, Inc. for an invoice price of $1000, terms 2/10, n/30. Todd, Inc. can liquidate its debt by paying $980 within ten days of the invoice date. In effect, $980 is the **cash price** of the goods. Instead of paying the $980 by the tenth day, Todd, Inc. may choose to pay a $20 premium in order to keep the $980 for an additional twenty days (30 days − 10 days). This choice will result in an interest rate of 2.04 percent ($20 ÷ $980) for twenty days. This is equivalent to an effective *annual* rate of 36.7% ($0.0204 \times {}^{360}\!/_{20}$). Most companies try to avoid such a high interest cost.

In theory, an account receivable and the related sales revenue should be measured net of any cash discounts allowable. This is consistent with the **net method** of recording credit sales. In Exhibit 8.4, we compare the net method with the **gross method** of recording credit sales. The net method correctly states the receivable at its realizable value on the date of sale, and correctly states the amount of revenue earned on that date. Under the net method, the receivable and the related revenue are recorded at an amount that equals the **cash equivalent price** on the date of sale. Remember that sellers offer cash discounts to encourage buyers to pay promptly. A buyer who fails to take a cash discount has in effect decided to engage in a deferred payment transaction. The buyer therefore incurs an interest cost, and the seller earns interest revenue. The interest that the seller earns is reflected in the Sales Discounts Not Taken account. The seller should report the balance in this account on the income statement as financial revenue.

Most companies record credit sales at gross amounts by using the gross method. When the seller later receives the buyer's payment, the seller records any cash discounts

Exhibit 8.4 Net and Gross Methods of Recording Credit Sales

Transaction	Net Method		Gross Method		
July 1					

Jam Company sells merchandise for $100, terms 2/10, n/30.	Accounts Receivable
	    Sales
		98
		    98
			Accounts Receivable
			    Sales
				100	100

Alternative Assumption No. 1					
July 10					

Jam Company receives payment that buyer made within the discount period	Cash
	    Accounts Receivable
		98
		    98
			Cash
			Sales Discounts
			    Accounts Receivable
				98
				2
					100

Alternative Assumption No. 2					
July 30					

Jam Company receives payment that buyer made after the discount period	Cash
	    Accounts Receivable
	    Sales Discounts Not
	      Taken
		100
		    98
		
		    2
			Cash
			    Accounts Receivable
				100	100

taken in a Sales Discounts account. The seller later deducts the balance in this account from sales to arrive at net sales. Although the gross method tends to result in an overstatement of accounts receivable and sales revenue, it is practical and convenient, and it enables a company to make a year-end adjusting entry to estimate sales discounts and thereby eliminate material errors from financial statements.

Accounting for Uncollectable Accounts

Companies sell on credit, rather than only for cash, to increase total sales and thereby increase profits. But a company that sells on credit assumes the risk that some customers will not pay their accounts. When an account becomes uncollectable, the company sustains a **bad debt loss.** These losses are simply one of the costs of doing business on credit. Accounting for bad debt losses would be fairly easy if the losses occurred in the same period as the sale. In reality, bad debt losses often occur in subsequent periods.

One method of accounting for uncollectable accounts, called the **direct write-off method,** involves debiting Bad Debts Expense and crediting Accounts Receivable in the period in which the company determines that the accounts are uncollectable.[7] This method is based on actual rather than estimated bad debt losses. However, the direct write-off method usually violates the matching principle. The reason is that the bad debts expense is often recognized in a later accounting period than the one in which the related sales revenue was recognized. The result is a mismatching of sales revenue and bad debts expense. In addition, the direct write-off method leads to the reporting of accounts receiv-

---

[7]An entry debiting Accounts Receivable and crediting Bad Debts Expense would be made if an account that had been written off was later recovered in the *same* accounting period. If a recovery occurred in a *subsequent* accounting period, Accounts Receivable would be debited and Bad Debts Recovered (a revenue account) would be credited. An entry debiting Cash and crediting Accounts Receivable would be made to record the collection.

able at an amount greater than their net realizable value (i.e., at an amount greater than the company expects to collect), which violates the asset/liability measurement principle.

Use of the direct write-off method may be appropriate if a company's bad debt losses are immaterial or if a company is unable to reasonably estimate its losses from uncollectable receivables. Generally, however, the inability to estimate bad debt losses suggests that collectability is so uncertain that the company should defer the recognition of revenue beyond the time of sale. As we explained in Chapter 5, if a company makes a credit sale to a customer who is a relatively poor credit risk, recognition of revenue should occur after the time of sale, and either the installment sales method or the cost recovery method of accounting may be used. Most companies, however, make credit sales only to customers who have a reasonable credit standing, and accordingly, the general rule in accounting is to recognize revenue at the time of sale. Because bad debt losses are usually material, and because most companies can reasonably estimate these losses based on their own collection experience or that of other similar companies, use of the direct write-off method is discouraged.

Companies that can estimate their uncollectables use the **allowance method** to account for them. Under this method, a company estimates the total amount of its uncollectable accounts at the end of every accounting period. As we discuss later in the chapter, this estimate may be based on credit sales or on accounts receivable. The company records the estimate in a year-end **adjusting entry** similar to the one shown below (the $5200 amount is assumed).

Bad Debts Expense	5200	
Allowance for Doubtful Accounts		5200

The balance in Bad Debts Expense usually appears as an operating expense on the income statement, where the expense is matched with sales revenue.[8] The Allowance for Doubtful Accounts (also called the Allowance for Uncollectable Accounts or the Allowance for Bad Debts) is a contra account to Accounts Receivable. The allowance is therefore deducted from accounts receivable on the balance sheet to estimate the net realizable value of the receivables. The use of an allowance account relieves a company of the necessity of crediting individual customer accounts each time it estimates bad debts. Obviously, when a company estimates bad debts and makes an adjusting entry, it does not yet know which accounts will become uncollectable. The allowance method tends to overcome the matching and asset valuation problems inherent in the direct write-off method. That is why accountants prefer the allowance method, even though it is based on estimated figures.

Accountants usually consult with a company's credit department personnel to estimate the amount of bad debts. As indicated earlier, the company's collection experience and that of similar companies are usually the most important factors in determining the estimate. These factors should be evaluated in the context of current and projected circumstances that may affect the company's future collection experience. Assessing the

---

[8]Because uncollectables are *expected* when a company makes credit sales, a strong argument can be made that uncollectables should not be included in revenue. Therefore, the estimated amount of a company's bad debts should be treated as a revenue offset (similar to sales returns) rather than an expense. Following this approach, a company should debit Sales—Uncollectables instead of Bad Debts Expense when it estimates bad debts. The balance in Sales—Uncollectables would later appear as a deduction from sales on the income statement.

In practice, companies usually debit Bad Debts Expense. The rationale is that even if a receivable proves uncollectable, it existed on the date of sale and revenue was generated for the full amount of the sale.

collectability of accounts receivable is a challenging task, particularly in the difficult economic climate that many companies have faced in recent years. When estimating bad debts under the allowance method, accountants may use either an income statement approach or a balance sheet approach.

Matching

Income Statement Approach. Under this approach to the allowance method, an accountant first determines the average percentage relationship between a company's *credit sales* and its actual bad debt losses. This percentage is then multiplied by credit sales for the current year to estimate bad debts expense.

The income statement approach is so called because it emphasizes the Bad Debts Expense account rather than the Allowance for Doubtful Accounts. With the income statement approach, credit sales (an income statement number) is multiplied by a percentage to estimate the amount of bad debts expense (another income statement number) as accurately as possible. This approach emphasizes the matching principle, because the bad debts estimate is based directly on the related sales revenue. Exhibit 8.5 presents facts to illustrate two approaches to the allowance method for Smith Ltd., an enterprise that uses a calendar-year accounting period.

To illustrate the income statement approach, let us further assume that in previous years actual bad debt losses have averaged 1 percent of credit sales each year, and the company expects this percentage to continue in the future. Here is the adjusting entry that the company should make on December 31, 1995:

Bad Debts Expense	2100	
Allowance for Doubtful Accounts		2100
($210 000 × 0.01 = $2100)		

Observe that we made the above entry without considering the previous balance ($400 credit) in the Allowance for Doubtful Accounts. The reason is that under the income statement approach, we focus on Bad Debts Expense, not on the Allowance account. After the above entry is posted, Bad Debts Expense will have a balance of $2100, and the balance in Allowance for Doubtful Accounts will be $2500 ($400 + $2100).

In another variation of the income statement approach, bad debts expense is based on a percentage of total sales (cash and credit) rather than only credit sales. The use of a percentage based on credit sales is logical, because bad debts arise only from credit sales. Nevertheless, the use of total sales is acceptable, since it would produce reasonable results if a company's mix of cash and credit sales is fairly stable over time.

The income statement approach requires the examination of the balance in the Allowance for Doubtful Accounts. This examination is to ensure that the existing balance is not overstated or understated. If there is a discrepancy in this account, it would be a change in an accounting estimate.

Balance Sheet Approach. The primary objective of this approach to the allowance method is to report accounts receivable on the balance sheet at net realizable value. To accomplish this objective, the balance sheet approach focusses on establishing a **desired balance** in the Allowance for Doubtful Accounts. The desired balance equals the estimated amount of uncollectable accounts receivable. This is the amount that, when subtracted from accounts receivable, will reduce the receivables to their net realizable value. Reporting accounts receivable at their net realizable value is consistent with the asset/liability measurement principle.[9]

---

[9]An allowance for doubtful accounts is acceptable for tax purposes when the allowance is based on specifically identified uncollectable accounts. This procedure is explained in Revenue Canada Taxation, "Bad Debts and Reserves for Doubtful Debts," *Interpretation Bulletin IT-442R,* September 6, 1991.

Exhibit 8.5

Smith Ltd.
Facts to Illustrate Allowance Method

Credit sales made during 1995	$210 000
Accounts receivable 12/31/95	50 000
Allowance for doubtful accounts, 12/31/95, before adjustment	400 (credit balance)

Percentage of Accounts Receivable. A simple way to implement the balance sheet approach is to multiply the year-end accounts receivable balance by a percentage that the company estimates from experience will be uncollectable. The product is the desired balance in the Allowance account. The adjusting entry to estimate bad debts is then recorded for the amount that is necessary to produce the desired balance.

To illustrate, return to Exhibit 8.5. Assume that instead of using the income statement approach, Smith Ltd. elects to use the balance sheet approach, and it estimates that approximately 4 percent of the accounts receivable balance on December 31, 1995, will be uncollectable. The company should make the following adjusting entry on December 31, 1995:

Bad Debts Expense	1600	
Allowance for Doubtful Accounts		1600

Notice that the above entry reflects the amount necessary to produce the desired balance in the Allowance account. The computation is shown below:

Desired balance in Allowance account ($50 000 × 0.04)	$2000
Less: Credit balance in Allowance account before adjustment	400
Amount of adjusting entry	$1600

After the above entry is posted, Bad Debts Expense will have a balance of $1600; the balance in the Allowance account will be $2000 ($400 + $1600).

The Allowance account sometimes has a *debit* balance before adjustment. As we illustrate later in the chapter, a company writes off uncollectable accounts by debiting the Allowance account and crediting Accounts Receivable. A debit balance in the Allowance account therefore occurs when a company has written off a greater amount of accounts receivable than it had previously estimated as uncollectable. This is an error in an estimate that is corrected with a charge in the income statement for the year when the error is detected. A debit balance in the Allowance account before adjustment would simply be *added* to the desired balance in order to determine the amount of the adjusting entry. For example, if Smith Ltd. had a $400 *debit* balance (instead of a $400 *credit* balance) in its Allowance account before adjustment, the company would make the adjusting entry on December 31, 1995, for $2400 ($2000 + $400). The computation is shown below.

Desired balance in Allowance account ($50 000 × 0.04)	$2000
Less: Debit balance in Allowance account before adjustment	400
Amount of adjusting entry	$2400

Aging of Accounts Receivable.   A more accurate way to implement the balance sheet approach is to determine the desired balance in the Allowance account by aging the accounts receivable. Here the accountant groups a company's individual accounts receivable into categories based on how long they have been outstanding. This schedule is called an **aging of accounts receivable** (see Exhibit 8.6). Next, the total in each category is multiplied by an estimated uncollectable percentage. The accountant then adds the products to derive a total amount that is estimated to be uncollectable. Because this is the desired total in the Allowance account, the adjusting entry to estimate bad debts should be recorded for the amount necessary to produce the desired balance.

The percentages shown in Exhibit 8.7 are based on a company's collection experience and on the advice of its credit department personnel. Higher percentages are usually associated with the higher-age categories because, generally, the longer that an account has been outstanding, the less likely it is to be collected.

To illustrate, refer again to Exhibit 8.5. Assume that Smith Ltd. now elects to estimate its bad debts using the aging form of the balance sheet approach and that it prepares the information shown in Exhibits 8.6 and 8.7. The company should make the following adjusting entry on December 31, 1995:

Bad Debts Expense	1969	
Allowance for Doubtful Accounts		1969

Note once again that the above entry is for the amount necessary to produce the desired balance in the allowance account. The computation is shown below.

Desired balance in Allowance account (total estimated amount uncollectable shown in Exhibit 8.7)	$2369
Less: Credit balance in Allowance account before adjustment	400
Amount of adjusting entry	$1969

After the above entry is posted, Bad Debts Expense will have a balance of $1969, and the Allowance account will have a balance of $2369 ($400 + $1969). If the Allowance account had a $400 *debit* balance (instead of a $400 *credit* balance) before adjustment, the adjusting entry would be for $2769 ($400 + $2369).

Summary and Evaluation of Approaches.   There are two basic approaches to the allowance method of accounting for uncollectable accounts. Each has two forms or variations:

1. Income statement approach.
    a. Percentage of credit sales.
    b. Percentage of total sales.
2. Balance sheet approach.
    a. Percentage of accounts receivable.
    b. Aging of accounts receivable.

A company may use any form of the allowance method to estimate its bad debts because all are acceptable under GAAP. The income statement approach emphasizes the matching principle, while the balance sheet approach emphasizes the reporting of accounts receivable at their net realizable value. Notice that both approaches demonstrate that financial statements **articulate** with one another. Under the income statement

Exhibit 8.6

Smith Ltd.
AGING OF ACCOUNTS RECEIVABLE
December 31, 1995

	Accounts Receivable Balance 12/31/95	Time Outstanding				
Customer		**Under 30 Days**	**30–60 Days**	**61–120 Days**	**121–180 Days**	**Over 180 Days**
Adams Company	$ 1 200	$ 900	$ 300			
Blunt & Company	600			$ 600		
Carver Enterprises	750	600	150			
Dandridge Inc.	350					$ 350
⋮	⋮	⋮	⋮	⋮	⋮	⋮
Zimmerman Company	500				500	
Total	$50 000	$39 300	$5 600	$3 400	$600	$1 100

Exhibit 8.7

Smith Ltd.
ESTIMATED AMOUNT UNCOLLECTABLE BASED ON AGING ANALYSIS
December 31, 1995

Time Outstanding	Amount	Estimated Percentage Uncollectable	Estimated Amount Uncollectable
Under 30 days	$39 300	1%	$ 393
30–60 days	5 600	6%	336
61–120 days	3 400	25%	850
121–180 days	600	40%	240
Over 180 days	1 100	50%	550
Total	$50 000		$2369

approach, what we do to benefit the income statement directly affects the balance sheet; under the balance sheet approach, what we do to benefit the balance sheet directly affects the income statement.

Remember that all variations of the allowance method are based on **estimates**. A company's actual bad debt losses will therefore equal its estimates only by chance. Under the income statement approach, the percentage of credit sales usually produces the most accurate results, because bad debt losses relate only to credit sales. Under the balance sheet approach, an aging of accounts receivable generally produces the most accurate results. In practice, many companies estimate their uncollectable accounts using one approach and then apply another approach to determine whether a reasonable result has been obtained. For example, a company might use the percentage of credit sales approach and determine that a bad debts adjusting entry for $12 000 is necessary. To check the reasonableness of the $12 000 amount, the company might age the accounts receivable and determine that an adjusting entry for only $10 000 is necessary. As a result of applying these two approaches concurrently, the company might finally decide to make an adjusting entry for $11 000.

Over time, a company may determine that its estimates of bad debts were too high or too low, and the company's allowance for doubtful accounts balance before year-end adjustment thus contains an excessive credit or debit balance. When this occurs, the company should change the percentage that it uses to estimate bad debts. Such a change is an example of a **change in an accounting estimate**, and as we discussed briefly in Chapter 4 and will discuss in more depth in Chapter 20, the change should be accounted for in current and future periods. In other words, the company should begin using a revised percentage to estimate its bad debts but should not make a prior period adjustment.

Writing Off Uncollectable Accounts.   When all reasonable attempts to collect an account have failed, a company's credit manager should authorize the accounting department to write off the account as uncollectable. Assume that the following balances were taken from the accounting records of Smith Ltd.:

Accounts receivable	$100 000 (Debit)
Allowance for doubtful accounts	1 700 (Credit)

If the company's credit manager decides that an account of $500 from W. Grant is uncollectable, the following entry should be made:

Allowance for Doubtful Accounts	500	
Accounts Receivable		500

The accountant would post the above entry to the appropriate general and subsidiary ledger accounts. After posting, the Accounts Receivable balance will be $99 500:

Accounts Receivable

100 000	
	500
99 500	

Allowance for Doubtful Accounts

	1700
500	
	1200

Notice that although the write-off reduces accounts receivable and the Allowance account, it has no effect on the net realizable value of the receivables:

	Before Write-off	**After Write-off**
Accounts receivable (Debit)	$100 000	$99 500
Allowance for doubtful accounts (Credit)	1 700	1 200
Net realizable value	$ 99 300	$99 300

Collection of Accounts Written Off.   Occasionally, a company collects all or part of an account that it wrote off as uncollectable. When this occurs, the company should first reverse, to the extent of the recovery, the entry that it made to write off the account. Then the company should record the collection in the usual manner. To illustrate, refer to the information presented earlier for Smith Ltd., and assume that Smith later collects the account of $500 from W. Grant. Smith should record the following entries:

Accounts Receivable	500	
Allowance for Doubtful Accounts		500
(*To reinstate W. Grant's account.*)		
Cash	500	
Accounts Receivable		500
(*To record the collection.*)		

Notice that there are two entries rather than a single entry debiting Cash and crediting the Allowance account. Making two entries is preferable, since this permits Smith Ltd. to accumulate in its accounts receivable subsidiary ledger a complete record of its credit experience with W. Grant.

Other Applications of the Allowance Method

Matching

Asset/Liability Measurement

Our discussion of the allowance method has thus far been confined to its use in accounting for uncollectable accounts. We have seen that through the use of estimates, the allowance method enables a company to better match expenses and revenues and to report receivables at their net realizable value. The same logic applies to the use of the allowance method in accounting for other items that affect the cash realization of accounts receivable. For example, a company may use the allowance method to account for

1. Sales discounts that customers will probably take (assuming that the company records accounts receivable at gross amounts).
2. Anticipated sales returns and allowances.
3. Anticipated collection costs (e.g., lawyer's fees) that the company will incur when trying to collect accounts receivable.
4. Anticipated freight costs that customers will be allowed to deduct from their remittances because of the company's shipping terms.

To illustrate, assume that Smith Ltd. determines from experience that the actual cost of collecting its accounts receivable averages 1 percent of the year-end accounts receivable balance. If the current year-end accounts receivable balance is $100 000, the company should make the following adjusting entry:

Collection Expense	1000	
Allowance for Collection Expense		1000
($100 000 $\times$ 0.01 = $1000)		

Collection expense would be reported as an operating expense on the income statement, and the allowance for collection expense would be deducted from accounts receivable on the balance sheet. In a subsequent period, the company would charge actual collection costs to the Allowance account, and would credit Cash or other appropriate accounts.

Adjusting entries similar to the one shown above are appropriate for recording estimated sales discounts, sales returns and allowances, and freight costs. In each case, a contra revenue account (e.g., Sales Discounts) or an expense account (e.g., Transportation-out or Delivery Expense) is debited and the appropriate Allowance account is credited. The effect of these entries is to reduce current net income and lower the net realizable value of accounts receivable reported on the balance sheet. For example, Torstar Corporation, a broadly based information and entertainment communications company, uses the allowance method to account for anticipated book returns. In its 1991 annual report, the company reported a provision of $64 million at December 31, 1991 and $60 million at December 31, 1990.

Despite the theoretical merits of applying the allowance method to items other than uncollectable accounts, most companies do not do so. Instead of estimating these items in advance, companies usually account for them when they actually occur. This approach, which is required for income tax purposes, is justified under GAAP because of immateriality and because the amounts involved often do not fluctuate significantly from year to year.

Use of an Allowance Account When a Right to Return Exists

Materiality

Many companies allow customers to return defective merchandise. Some companies, such as those in the newspaper, perishable food, and book publishing industries, permit customers to return merchandise under certain circumstances even when the merchandise is not defective. These circumstances may include customer dissatisfaction or an inability of the customer to resell the product.

The seller should recognize revenue at the time of sale only if *all* risks and rewards of ownership have been transferred. Paragraph 3400.18(b) of the CICA *Handbook* does not mention the right to return, but states that revenue should not be recognized when the amount of a return is significant or unpredictable. If the amounts of the sales returns are expected to be material in relation to total sales, the companies are offering their customers the right to return. In these cases, the allowance method of accounting for sales returns can be used to properly recognize revenue at the time of sale.

To illustrate, assume that Smith Ltd. gives customers the right to return products. Recent experience indicates that customers will return approximately 20 percent of the merchandise Smith Ltd. has sold and that the company can later resell this merchandise for approximately 60 percent of the original sales price. During the current year, Smith Ltd. made sales of $100 000. Here is the adjusting entry the company should make at year-end, assuming a perpetual inventory system:

Sales Returns	20 000	
Inventory—Estimated Returns	12 000	
Allowance for Sales Returns		20 000
Cost of Goods Sold		12 000

The Inventory—Estimated Returns account is a current asset and shows the net realizable value of inventory that is expected to be returned ($100 000 $\times$ 0.2 $\times$ 0.6 = $12 000). The allowance for sales returns is deducted from accounts receivable on the balance sheet. The effect of the above entry is to reduce gross margin and current assets by $8000.

Suppose now that during the first month of the next accounting period, a customer returns merchandise that had an original sales price of $1000. Assuming that the customer has not paid for the goods, Smith Ltd. should make the following entry:

Inventory—Returned Goods	600	
Allowance for Sales Returns	1000	
Inventory—Estimated Returns		600
Accounts Receivable		1000

The right to return is different from goods transferred on consignment. The title to consignment goods remains with the vendor, while the purchaser holds title to goods sold with the right to return.

Use of Accounts Receivable to Generate Cash

Instead of waiting until customers pay their accounts, companies often want the cash immediately. This is usually accomplished by **pledging, assigning,** or **factoring** the accounts.

The key conceptual issue under each of the three alternatives is whether a **borrowing transaction** or a **sale transaction** has occurred. In a borrowing transaction, the receivables are simply used as collateral to obtain a loan. The borrowing company continues to report the receivables as assets and also reports the interest expense and the liability for the loan. In a sale transaction, the selling company receives cash, removes the receivables from the accounting records, and typically recognizes a loss on the receivables sold. The selling company does not recognize a liability because the receivables have actually been sold.[10]

Pledging Accounts Receivable.

Companies sometimes obtain loans by pledging their accounts receivable as collateral. In a pledging arrangement, the borrower agrees to collect its accounts receivable and to use the proceeds to repay the lender. The borrower records the loan and related interest in the usual manner, and the loan balance is reduced as the borrower remits its collections. If the borrower defaults, the lender can recover the amount owed by selling the accounts pledged.

If a company has pledged some or all of its accounts receivable, the company should disclose the amount pledged, either parenthetically or in a note to its financial statements.

Assigning Accounts Receivable.   An assignment of accounts receivable is a more formal type of pledging arrangement. In an assignment, a borrower (called the **assignor**) transfers its rights in some or all of its accounts receivable to a lender (called the **assignee**) in exchange for a loan. The money received from collecting the accounts is later used to pay off the loan.

An assignment is evidenced by a **financing agreement** and a **promissory note,** both of which are signed by the assignor. The financing agreement may indicate that the assignment is on either a **non-notification** or a **notification** basis. When accounts are assigned on a non-notification basis, as is usually the case, customers are not informed that their accounts have been assigned. As a result, they continue to make payments to the assignor,

---

[10]"Transfer of Receivables," CICA *Handbook,* EIC–9, November 1989.

who in turn forwards them to the assignee. When accounts are assigned on a notification basis, customers are notified to make their payments directly to the assignee.

The assignor retains ownership of the accounts assigned. As a result, the assignor assumes the risk that accounts receivable will not be realized for their full face amount because of such factors as sales discounts, sales returns and allowances, and bad debt losses.

Before entering into an assignment, the assignee (usually a bank or a finance company) analyzes the borrower's accounts receivable. The assignee generally refuses to lend money secured by accounts believed to be too risky. Furthermore, the assignee usually lends only a certain percentage (often between 60 percent and 90 percent) of the face amount of the accounts that it is willing to lend against. This helps to insulate the assignee from collection losses that the assignor might sustain. As additional protection, the assignee frequently requires the assignor to substitute new accounts for ones that become past due or uncollectable. Naturally, the assignee charges interest for the loans that it makes. In addition, the assignee usually requires a **service charge** for processing the assignment.

To illustrate, assume that on December 31, 1994, Smith Ltd. assigns $100 000 of accounts receivable to National Trust under a non-notification arrangement. National Trust advances $80 000 less a service charge of $1600, and Smith Ltd. signs a promissory note that provides for interest of 1 percent per month on the unpaid loan balance. Smith Ltd. should make the following entries on December 31:

Assigned Accounts Receivable	100 000	
Accounts Receivable		100 000
Cash	78 400	
Service Charge Expense	1 600	
Notes Payable		80 000

The first entry transfers the assigned accounts to a separate account. The second entry records the receipt of cash on the loan.

To continue the illustration, a series of 1995 transactions and the corresponding journal entries appear below.

1. From January 1 to January 31, Smith Ltd. collected assigned accounts of $60 000, less sales discounts of $700 and sales returns and allowances of $1300.

Cash	58 000	
Sales Discounts	700	
Sales Returns and Allowances	1 300	
Assigned Accounts Receivable		60 000

2. On January 31, Smith Ltd. remitted the January collections to National Trust.

Notes Payable	57 200	
Interest Expense ($80 000 $\times$ 0.01)	800	
Cash		58 000

3. From February 1 to February 28, Smith Ltd. collected $29 000 of assigned accounts and wrote off as uncollectable $3000 of assigned accounts.

Cash	29 000	
Allowance for Doubtful Accounts	3 000	
Assigned Accounts Receivable		32 000

4. On February 28, Smith Ltd. paid off the remaining loan balance and transferred the remaining balance in Assigned Accounts Receivable to Accounts Receivable.

Notes Payable ($80 000 − $57 200)	22 800	
Interest Expense ($22 800 × 0.01)	228	
Cash		23 028
Accounts Receivable	8 000	
Assigned Accounts Receivable		8 000
($100 000 − $60 000 − $32 000)		

Disclosure

Materiality

Smith Ltd. should separately disclose the specifically assigned accounts receivable if they are material. Moreover, Smith should disclose its equity in the assigned accounts, either parenthetically or in a note. A note in the 1994 financial statements, for example, might say that "on December 31, 1994, Smith Ltd. had $20 000 ($100 000 − $80 000) equity in its assigned accounts receivable."

The example provides a general view of accounting for assigned accounts receivable. In practice, the accounting requirements depend in part on the financing agreement. A general description of this agreement should be disclosed in the note to the assignor's financial statements.

Factoring of Accounts Receivable. In a factoring arrangement, a company (the **seller**) sells its accounts receivable to a financial institution (the **factor**). In most cases, the factor is a bank or a finance company. Factoring differs from an assignment in that the seller actually transfers ownership of its accounts receivable to the factor. Although accounts may be factored **with recourse** (the factor may hold the seller liable if debtors do not pay), accounts are usually factored **without recourse** (the factor bears the risk that debtors will not pay). Moreover, accounts are usually factored on a notification basis.

The details of a factoring arrangement vary and should be spelled out in a factoring contract. A typical factoring arrangement is continuous. The factor maintains a credit department that performs all functions related to the seller's accounts receivable. In addition to deciding to whom the seller may extend credit, the factor assumes responsibility for billing, collecting, and bad debt losses. The seller ships merchandise to approved customers and immediately sells the receivables to the factor. Thus, the advantage of factoring to a seller are immediate cash and relief from the burden of carrying accounts receivable. Factoring arrangements are common in the textile, apparel, carpet, and furniture industries. Moreover, the use of credit cards such as American Express, VISA, and MasterCard is in essence a form of factoring.

When accounts are factored, the factor charges a **factoring fee** for its services of credit approval, billing, collecting, and assuming bad debt losses. This fee is usually 1 percent to 3 percent of the net amount of the receivables factored. The factor then credits the seller's account for the net amount of the receivables factored less the factoring fee. The factor may also withhold some predetermined amount (usually about 10 percent of the net amount of receivables factored) to protect itself against sales returns and allowances.

To illustrate, assume that on September 1, 1995, Riley Limited factors $20 000 of accounts receivable without recourse with First Finance Corporation on a notification basis. First Finance charges a factoring fee of 3 percent of the amount of receivables factored. In addition, First Finance withholds 10 percent of the amount of receivables factored to cover sales returns and allowances. Riley would make the following journal entry on September 1:

Cash	17 400	
Receivable from Factor (20 000 × 0.10)	2 000	
Loss on Factoring Accounts Receivable ($20 000 × 0.03)	600	
Accounts Receivable		20 000

Riley Limited would classify the Receivable from Factor as a current asset. This account would later be credited when sales returns and allowances occur and when the factor remits the ending balance in Riley's account.

Notice in the above example that Riley Limited factored accounts receivable *without recourse* and accounted for the factoring as a sale. Accordingly, the accounts receivable are removed from the accounting records, and no liability is recorded.

When receivables are factored *with recourse,* the transfer is not recognized as a sale unless the following conditions are met:

1. The company selling the account surrenders control of the future economic benefits embodied in the receivables.
2. The obligation of the company selling the accounts can be reasonably estimated.
3. The company buying the receivables cannot under normal conditions expect the company selling the receivables to repurchase these receivables.

If these conditions are not met, the amount of the proceeds from the transfer of the receivables should be reported as a liability, because the transaction is now regarded as a borrowing, not a sale. Assume that Riley Limited factored its receivables with recourse and did not satisfy all of the three conditions. Under these circumstances, Riley Limited would account for the transfer of receivables as a borrowing and would make the following journal entry on September 1:

Cash	17 400	
Receivable from Factor (20 000 × 0.1)	2 000	
Interest Expense ($20 000 × 0.03)	600	
Payable to Factor		20 000

Notice that the accounts receivable of $20 000 that were factored are not removed from Riley's accounting records. These accounts are still considered assets of Riley's, and now Riley has a collateralized loan for which it must account. If the transaction had incorrectly been accounted for as a sale, Riley Limited would have been permitted to engage in **off-balance-sheet financing.** That is, the company would have been permitted to borrow money without having to report the liability.

The appropriate accounting practices for a factoring arrangement depend on the specific agreement. If a company has entered into a factoring agreement, the company should briefly describe the agreement in the notes to its financial statements.

Notes Receivable

A promissory note, often called simply a **note,** is a written promise to pay a certain sum of money at a designated time. The note is signed by the **maker** and is usually made payable to the order of a specified **payee**, who in turn may endorse the note and thereby sell (discount) it to a subsequent holder. From a payee's viewpoint, a note represents a receivable and therefore an asset. Notes receivable are more desirable than accounts receivable for the following reasons:

1. Notes are often easier to collect, because they represent written claims. Thus, their use may reduce a company's bad debt losses.
2. Notes can usually be converted into cash by discounting them with a bank or another lender, and this process (which we explain in a subsequent section) is usually quicker and cheaper than assigning or factoring accounts receivable.
3. Notes receivable usually bear a specified rate of interest, while accounts receivable do not.

Companies may acquire notes receivable in exchange for merchandise when customers need credit for a period longer than usual for open accounts. Occasionally, companies acquire notes in exchange for accounts receivable claims against customers who simply need additional time to pay their accounts. Notes receivable may also result from the sale of other assets and from lending money. In Canada, accounts receivable claims are rarely converted to notes. The following sections are included to illustrate the theory used for discounting notes.

Valuation of Notes Receivable

Asset/Liability Measurement

As indicated earlier in the chapter, notes receivable should be valued initially at an amount equal to the present value of the cash that the company expects to collect. This approach is theoretically sound because it recognizes the time value of money.

If a company can reasonably estimate the amount of its uncollectable notes receivable, it should establish an allowance for such notes in a manner similar to that used for accounts receivable. Companies that acquire many notes as a result of selling merchandise can usually estimate their uncollectables with reasonable accuracy.

Because money has a time value, all commercial notes contain interest. Nevertheless, notes are commonly classified as either **interest-bearing** or **noninterest-bearing**. Interest-bearing notes specifically state a certain interest rate; noninterest-bearing notes do not. In a noninterest-bearing note, the interest is included in the face amount of the note and is not explicitly stated.

Interest-Bearing Notes Receivable.   Because interest-bearing notes receivable specifically state a certain interest rate, the present value of the note at the time of issuance equals its face amount, assuming that the interest rate is reasonable. Consequently, such notes are initially recorded at their face amount (which equals their present value). Interest revenue is then recognized on the accrual basis as time passes.

To illustrate, assume that on October 1, 1994, Smith Ltd., which uses a calendar-year accounting period, sells merchandise having a sales price of $1000 to Bin Company in exchange for a one-year, interest-bearing note. The note has a face amount of $1000 and a stated interest rate of 12 percent (equal to the going market rate for similar notes) payable at maturity. Smith Ltd. would account for the note as shown in Exhibit 8.8.

Noninterest-Bearing Notes Receivable.   The present value of a noninterest-bearing note receivable is less than its face amount. The reason is that the face amount includes interest even though no interest is specifically stated. Although it is theoretically correct to account for this interest, many companies fail to do so.

Exhibit 8.8   Accounting for Interest-Bearing Notes Receivable

Transaction	Entry		
Oct. 1, 1994 Smith Ltd. sells merchandise having a sales price of $1000 to Bin Company in exchange for a one-year, interest-bearing note. The note has a face amount of $1000 and a stated interest rate of 12 percent (equal to the going market rate for similar notes) payable at maturity	Notes Receivable Sales	1000	1000
Dec. 31, 1994 Smith Ltd. computes accrued interest for three months ($1000 × 0.12 × ³⁄₁₂ = $30).	Interest Receivable Interest Revenue	30	30

Sept. 30, 1995
Smith Ltd. collects principal and interest at maturity.*
	Cash
	  Note Receivable
	  Interest Receivable
	  Interest Revenue
		1120	1000
			30
			90

*The illustration assumes that Smith Ltd. does not make reversing entries.

To illustrate, let us assume that on October 1, 1994, Smith Ltd. sells merchandise having a sales price of $1000 to Bur Company in exchange for a one-year, noninterest-bearing note. The note has a face amount of $1120, and the going market rate for similar notes is 12 percent. The note therefore has a present value of $1000, an amount that equals the sales price of the merchandise as well as the face amount of the note ($1120) divided by 1.12. Smith Ltd. would account for the note using one of the alternative methods shown in Exhibit 8.9.

Under Method 1, the note is initially recorded at its present value of $1000. This is done by debiting Notes Receivable for the face amount ($1120) and crediting Discount on Notes Receivable for the total amount of interest that the note contains ($120). Notice that the interest equals 12 percent of the sales price of $1000 for one year. The balance in the Discount account is deducted from notes receivable on the balance sheet. Consequently, if Smith Ltd. prepared a balance sheet on October 1, the company would report a net amount of $1000, which equals the present value of the note on that date.

Observe that the present value of the Bur Company note ($1000) is the same as the present value of the Bin Company note recorded in the previous example. The reason is that these are similar one-year notes with maturity values of $1120. Under Method 1, as shown in Exhibit 8.9, $30 of interest revenue is recorded in 1994 and $90 in 1995. These are the same amounts recorded for the Bin Company note in Exhibit 8.8. Method 1 is theoretically correct because it reflects the economic reality that money has a time value. Method 1 puts substance (i.e., the economic fact that the note contains interest) over form (i.e., the fact that the note has no stated interest rate). Notes receivable, sales, and interest revenue are all correctly reported under Method 1.

In practice, many companies use Method 2 to record short-term, noninterest-bearing, trade notes receivable. These companies initially record such notes at their face amount,

Substance Over Form

Exhibit 8.9 Accounting for Noninterest-Bearing Notes Receivable

Transaction	Method 1: Record at Present Value (theoretically correct)			Method 2: Record at Face Amount (theoretically incorrect)		
Oct. 1, 1994 Smith Ltd. sells merchandise having a sales price of $1000 to Bur Company in exchange for a one-year, noninterest-bearing note. The note has a face amount of $1120 and the going market rate for similar notes is 12 percent.	Notes Receivable Sales Discount on Notes Receivable*	1120	1000 120	Notes Receivable Sales	1120	1120
Dec. 31, 1994 Smith Ltd. computes accrued interest for three months ($1000 × 0.12 × ³⁄₁₂ = $30)	Discount on Notes Receivable Interest Revenue	30	30	No entry		
Sept. 30, 1995 Smith Ltd. collects principal and interest at maturity.**	Cash Discount on Notes Receivable Notes Receivable Interest Revenue	1120 90	1120 90	Cash Notes Receivable	1120	1120

*Some firms prefer *not* to use a Discount account. These firms would debit Notes Receivable for $1000 on October 1 and for $30 on December 31. They would then credit Notes Receivable for $1030 on September 30, 1995. This approach is an acceptable variation of Method 1 because it produces essentially the same results.

**The illustration assumes that Smith Ltd. does not make reversing entries.

not at their present value. The use of Method 2 leads to several misstatements in the financial statements. In the example shown in Exhibit 8.9, sales, net income, assets, and shareholders' equity would each be overstated in 1994, while interest revenue would be understated. In 1995, interest revenue and net income would be understated.

FASB's *Accounting Principles Board Opinion No. 21,* which we explain in Chapter 11, requires companies, under certain circumstances, to impute (estimate and record) interest in transactions involving receivables and payables for which there is either no stated interest or an unreasonable amount of stated interest. Applying the principles set forth in this pronouncement would produce the results shown under Method 1. However, *APB Opinion No. 21* states that it is not intended to apply to "receivables and payables arising from transactions with customers or suppliers in the normal course of business which are due in customary trade terms not exceeding approximately one year."[11] Consequently, many companies use Method 2 to account for these types of notes receivable. Because the receivables are short-term, an argument can be made that the amount of

---

[11]"Interest on Receivables and Payables," *APB Opinion No. 21,* Paragraph 3, 1971.

Materiality

interest often is not material. In addition, net income may not be significantly distorted if the receivables occur fairly evenly over time.

Discounting Notes Receivable

Most notes are **negotiable,** which means that a payee may transfer its rights to collect a note to a subsequent holder. On the maturity date, the holder collects the amount of the note's maturity value from the maker.

When a note is negotiable, therefore, the payee may obtain cash before the maturity date by **discounting** (selling) the note at a bank or another entity. To discount the note, the payee endorses it. In rare cases, the endorsement is made without recourse, which means that the endorser avoids future liability on the note. Usually, however, banks require that endorsements be made with recourse, which means that the endorser agrees to pay the holder if the maker does not. Consequently, endorsers typically remain **contingently liable** on notes receivable that they have discounted.

Contingent liabilities, discussed more fully in Chapter 15, are obligations that must be paid if certain conditions occur. For example, if the maker of a note fails to pay the holder on the maturity date, an endorser (with recourse) must pay. Users of financial statements want to know about a company's contingent obligations. Consequently, Section 3290 of the CICA *Handbook* requires companies to disclose contingent liabilities that relate to notes receivable discounted, even if there is only a remote chance that the company will actually have to pay.[12]

When a company discounts a note at a bank, the company receives cash **proceeds.** These proceeds, which the bank calculates, are equal to the **maturity value** of the note less the bank's **discount.** To calculate the discount, the bank multiplies the maturity value of the note by the bank's **discount rate** (the interest rate that the bank charges for discounting the note) and by the **remaining time to maturity.** These calculations are illustrated in the following example.

Suppose that on March 1, 1995, Todd, Inc. receives a $10 000, 90-day, 10 percent note from a customer on account. Thirty days later, on March 31, 1995, Todd, Inc. discounts the note with recourse at Nation Trust. The bank's discount rate is 12 percent, and Todd, Inc. receives proceeds of $10 045, computed as follows:

Face amount of note	$10 000
Interest to maturity ($10\ 000 \times 0.10 \times \frac{90}{360}$) (1)	250
Maturity value of note[13]	10 250
Bank discount ($10\ 250 \times 0.12 \times \frac{60}{360}$) (2)	205
Proceeds	$10 045

How should Todd, Inc. account for the note receivable discounted? Similar to the use of accounts receivable to generate cash, the key conceptual issue in accounting for notes receivable discounted is whether a borrowing transaction or a sale transaction has occurred in substance. In practice, most notes receivable are accounted for as sales transactions, because most notes are discounted with recourse, and the three conditions for recognizing a transfer of receivables with recourse as a sale are usually satisfied (see

---

[12]"Contingencies," CICA *Handbook*, Section 3290, December 1989.

[13]Remember that the maturity value equals the face amount of a noninterest-bearing note.

(1) Interest at 10 percent that would be earned over the term of the note.

(2) Discounting of the note at an interest rate of 12 percent for the discounting period of 60 days.

page 361). Also, those notes receivable issued without recourse are recognized as sales transactions.

Assuming that the three conditions have been met and the transfer of receivables with recourse can be recognized as a sale, Todd, Inc. should account for the note receivable discounted (with recourse) using one of the two approaches shown in Exhibit 8.10. Because most makers pay their notes at maturity, the **footnote approach** is easier to apply. Under this approach, Notes Receivable is credited when a note is discounted, and the contingent liability is disclosed in a note such as: "The company is contingently liable for $10 250 on a note receivable discounted at the bank. It does not expect the maker of the note to default." The company, of course, stops making this disclosure when it is no longer contingently liable on the note. Instead of using a note, the company may disclose essentially the same information parenthetically on the balance sheet.

When a note has been discounted, the bank will try to collect the maturity value from the maker on the maturity date. If the maker defaults, the bank must promptly notify the endorser. Therefore, the endorser who has not heard from the bank within a few days after the maturity date can generally assume that the maker has paid the note and thereby ended the endorser's contingent liability. If, on the other hand, the maker does not pay the bank, we say that the note has been **dishonoured**. In this case, the bank promptly notifies the endorser and holds the endorser liable for the full maturity value plus any **protest fee** (any reasonable cost that the bank incurs in protesting the note). The endorser pays the bank and then has a claim against the maker for the full amount paid. Because the endorser pays the note, the endorser no longer has a contingent liability to the bank.

To illustrate the accounting entries involved, assume that on the maturity date, May 30, 1995, the customer pays National Trust the amount owed, thereby ending Todd, Inc.'s contingent liability. As shown in Exhibit 8.10, Todd, Inc. would not make an entry under the note approach but would under the **contra account approach.** In practice, the entry required under the contra account approach would likely be made a few days after the maturity date, because a company that is contingently liable on a note does not usually know on the maturity date that the maker has paid.

Assume now that instead of paying the note on May 30, 1995, the customer dishonoured it and the bank charged Todd, Inc. with the maturity value plus a protest fee of $25. Under these circumstances, Todd, Inc. should make the appropriate entry or entries shown in Exhibit 8.10.

Dishonoured Notes Receivable is a special note receivable account and should be reported separately from notes receivable on the balance sheet. This account should be used for all dishonoured notes receivable, whether or not they have been discounted. Todd, Inc. will earn interest on the amount in this account at the rate allowed by law. The Dishonoured Notes Receivable account should be credited if Todd, Inc. collects from the maker. If the company cannot collect the dishonoured note, it should write off the amount uncollectable to an Allowance for Uncollectable Notes account, assuming that it uses such an account for its notes receivable.

Remember that the above example assumes that Todd, Inc. discounted the note receivable on a *with recourse* basis and that the three conditions for recognizing a transfer of receivables with recourse as a sale had been satisfied. If the note had been discounted *without recourse*, Todd, Inc. would still account for the discounting as a sale, but *no contingent liability would exist.* On the other hand, if the note had been discounted on a *with recourse* basis and any of the three conditions had *not* been met, Todd, Inc. would account for the discounting transaction as a borrowing instead of a sale. Accordingly,

Exhibit 8.10 Accounting for Discounted Notes Receivable

Transaction	Note Approach		Contra Account Approach	
Mar. 1, 1995 Todd, Inc. receives a $10 000, 90-day, 10 percent note from a customer on account.	Notes Receivable Accounts Receivable	10 000 10 000	Notes Receivable Accounts Receivable	10 000 10 000
Mar. 31, 1995 Todd, Inc. discounts the note (with recourse) at National Trust at a discount rate of 12 percent.	Cash Notes Receivable Interest Revenue	10 045 10 000 45	Cash Notes Receivable Discounted Interest Revenue	10 045 10 000 45
Alternative Assumption No. 1 **May 30, 1995** The customer pays National Trust.	No entry		Notes Receivable Discounted Notes Receivable	10 000 10 000
Alternative Assumption No. 2 **May 30, 1995** The customer dishonours the note, and the bank charges Todd, Inc. with the maturity value plus a protest fee of $25.	Dishonoured Notes Receivable Cash	10 275 10 275	Dishonoured Notes Receivable Cash Notes Receivable Discounted Notes Receivable	10 275 10 275 10 000 10 000

Todd, Inc. would make the following journal entry on March 31, when the note was discounted:

Cash	10 045	
Liability for Notes Receivable Discounted		10 000
Interest Revenue		45

Liability for Notes Receivable Discounted is a current liability account. In this case an actual liability, not a contingent liability, would exist. The Notes Receivable account would remain on Todd, Inc.'s books on March 31. If the customer paid National Trust on May 30, Todd, Inc. would make the following entry:

Liability for Notes Receivable Discounted	10 000	
Notes Receivable		10 000

On the other hand, if the customer dishonoured the note on May 30, Todd, Inc. would make the following entries:

Dishounored Notes Receivable	10 275	
Cash		10 275

| Liability for Notes Receivable Discounted | 10 000 | |
| Notes Receivable | | 10 000 |

Balance Sheet Presentation of Receivables

Materiality

As stated earlier, an enterprise should classify a receivable as a current asset only if collection is expected within the next year or operating cycle, whichever is longer. Within the current assets category, trade receivables should be reported separately from nontrade receivables. Moreover, a company should report separately those receivables that reflect **related-party transactions,** such as loans made by the company to officers or to affiliated companies. Accounts and notes receivable should be segregated when the amount of each is material. Exhibit 8.11 shows a report produced by the CICA from a survey of receivables disclosure from 300 Canadian companies.

Cash and receivables are two examples of **financial instruments**. In 1991, the CICA issued an exposure draft on financial instruments with proposed recommendations that disclosure include information about financial instruments that have off-balance-sheet risk and concentrations of credit risk. These disclosures are explained in Chapters 16 and 25.

Conceptual Considerations

The following elements of the theoretical model discussed in Chapter 2 are particularly important to the topics in this chapter.

Asset/Liability Measurement

1. **Asset/liability measurement principle.** Cash is measured at its face amount, accounts receivable are measured at net realizable value, and notes receivable are measured at present value on the date received. Also, the balance sheet approach to the allowance method of accounting for uncollectable accounts is consistent with this principle.

Revenue Realization

2. **Revenue realization principle.** A company ordinarily should record revenue and the related receivable that arises from a sale of goods on the date that the sale occurs. Only in exceptional cases does GAAP permit the recognition of revenue either before or after the time of sale.

Matching

3. **Matching.** The income statement approach to the allowance method of accounting for uncollectable accounts helps a company to more accurately match the expense of uncollectable accounts with the sales revenue that is associated with those accounts.

Substance Over Form

4. **Substance over form.** When receivables are transferred with recourse from one company to another, such as by factoring accounts receivable or discounting a note receivable, the transferor should account for the transfer as a sale of the receivables only if three conditions are met. These conditions help to establish whether the transfer of receivables is in substance a sale of the receivables or whether it is really a borrowing transaction.

When accounting for noninterest-bearing notes receivable, recording the note initially at its present value is theoretically better than recording the note at its face amount because substance is considered more important than form in financial accounting.

Exhibit 8.11   Segregation of Receivables

| | Number of Companies | | | | Percentage | | | |
	1990	1989	1988	1987	1990	1989	1988	1987
One figure shown for receivables	210	202	202	207	71	68	68	71
More than one figure for receivables	78	86	85	76	26	29	29	26
Different types of receivables indicated by separate figures not disclosed	3	3	4	7	1	1	1	2
Receivables not disclosed separately	6	5	4	4	2	2	2	1
	297	296	295	294	100	100	100	100

Source: Reprinted from *Financial Accounting in Canada,* Nineteenth Edition (Toronto: CICA, 1991), p. 75.

Concluding Remarks

Cash is the standard medium of exchange in business transactions, and receivables are claims held against others that generally result in a future inflow of cash. To be classified as a current asset, cash must be available for use in current operations. Similarly, receivables are properly classified as current assets only when they are collectable within the next year or operating cycle, whichever is longer.

Cash and receivables are two examples of monetary assets because they are fixed or determinable in terms of the number of dollars on hand or to be received, regardless of how prices change. For this reason, the valuation of cash and receivables is less controversial than the valuation of nonmonetary assets. In the next two chapters, we focus on accounting for inventory. Inventory is a current asset that is nonmonetary in nature and is considerably more challenging to value than either cash or receivables.

Key Points

1. Cash may include currency, coins, cheques, bank drafts, money orders, chequing accounts, and savings accounts. (Objective 1)
2. On a balance sheet, cash is valued at face amount and classified as a current asset only if the cash is available for use in current operations. (Objective 1)
3. A petty cash fund is used to disburse small amounts of currency and coins for such items as taxi fares, postage, and minor supplies. (Objective 2)
4. A bank reconciliation is a schedule that explains any differences between a company's book balance of cash in a particular bank account and the bank statement balance. (Objective 3)
5. A proof of cash is an expanded, four-column reconciliation that is a stronger control measure than the single-column bank reconciliation. (Objective 3)
6. The preparation of either a bank reconciliation or a proof of cash usually indicates that a company has to make certain adjusting entries to update its accounting records. (Objective 3)
7. Receivables are claims held against others for money, goods, or services. (Objective 1)
8. A receivable should be valued initially at an amount equal to the present value of the cash that the company expects to collect. A receivable should be classified as a current asset only if collection is expected within the next year or operating cycle, whichever is longer. (Objective 1)

9. From the standpoint of accounting theory, the net method of recording credit sales is better than the gross method, but most companies use the gross method because of its convenience and materiality. (Objective 4)
10. The allowance method, rather than the direct write-off method, should be used when accounting for uncollectable accounts. (Objective 5)
11. The allowance method requires that bad debts be estimated by an income statement approach or a balance sheet approach. (Objective 5)
12. The income statement approach emphasizes the matching principle and requires that the adjusting entry for bad debts be made without considering the previous balance in the Allowance for Doubtful Accounts. (Objective 5)
13. The balance sheet approach emphasizes the reporting of accounts receivable at net realizable value and requires that the previous balance in the Allowance for Doubtful Accounts be considered in recording the adjusting entry for bad debts. (Objective 5)
14. In addition to its use in accounting for uncollectable accounts, the allowance method can be used in accounting for other items that affect the cash realization of accounts receivable (e.g., sales discounts). (Objective 5)
15. Many companies use accounts receivable to generate cash immediately by pledging, assigning, or factoring the accounts. Each method of accounts receivable financing has important financial statement implications. (Objective 6)
16. Although some notes have no stated interest rate, all commercial notes contain interest, because money has a time value. (Objective 7)
17. Theoretically, we should always account for the interest component of a note receivable, whether or not the interest is explicitly stated. In practice, many companies do not separately account for the interest component of short-term, noninterest-bearing trade notes receivable because of materiality. (Objective 7)
18. A company may use either a note approach or a contra account approach to accounting for certain notes receivable that are discounted. (Objective 7)

Appendix A: Preparing a Proof of Cash

As stated earlier in this chapter, auditors often prepare a four-column bank reconciliation, also called a proof of cash. To illustrate how to prepare a proof of cash, we will use the information presented earlier in the chapter for preparing a bank reconciliation for Todd, Inc. for the month ended May 31, 1995. In addition, assume that the following facts pertain to Todd, Inc. during June 1995:

1. The cash receipts (deposits) shown on the June bank statement are $78 839. These receipts include the deposits of $1500 that were in transit on May 31.
2. The cash receipts shown on the company's books during June are $79 864.
3. The cash payments shown on the June bank statement are $76 188. These payments include the cheques totalling $2647 that were outstanding on May 31.
4. The cash payments shown on the company's books during June are $77 261.
5. The cash balance shown as of June 30 on the bank statement is $20 282.
6. The cash balance shown as of June 30 on the company's books is $17 817.
7. A deposit of $3600 mailed to the bank on June 30 does not appear on the June bank statement.
8. On June 30, the bank collected a note receivable for Todd, Inc. and credited the proceeds of $3175 to the company's account. The proceeds included $185 of interest,

all of which the company earned during 1995, and a $10 collection fee. Todd, Inc. has not yet recorded the collection.

9. Outstanding cheques as of June 30 total $2910.
10. The bank statement shows a $20 service charge for June.

The proof of cash for Todd, Inc. appears in Exhibit 8.12. The form is divided into two sections, like the form in Exhibit 8.1. In the "per bank statement" section, we reconcile from four amounts shown on the bank statement to the correct (true) amounts. In the "per books" section, we reconcile from four amounts shown on the company's books to the same correct amounts that are determined in the "per bank statement" section. The first column of the proof of cash is simply the single-column bank reconciliation prepared at the end of May (see Exhibit 8.2); the fourth column is a single-column reconciliation for June. The second column reconciles the June receipts, and the third column reconciles the June payments.

To prepare a proof of cash, we may begin by completing the top line in each section. We do this simply by copying the necessary information from the bank statement and the company's books. Next, we copy in the first column the information shown in the fourth column of the proof of cash prepared for the previous month. We then prepare in the fourth column a single-column reconciliation for the current month. Finally, each reconciling item in one of the two outside columns is ordinarily added or deducted in one of the two inside columns.

Exhibit 8.12

Todd, Inc.
PROOF OF CASH
For June 1995

	May 31 Balance	June Receipts	June Payments	June 30 Balance
Per bank statement	$17 631	$78 839	$76 188	$20 282
Deposits in transit				
May 31	1 500	(1 500)		
June 30		3 600		3 600
Outstanding cheques				
May 31	(2 647)		(2 647)	
June 30			2 910	(2 910)
Correct amounts	$16 484	$80 939	$76 451	$20 972
Per books	$15 214	$79 864	$77 261	$17 817
Note and interest collected by bank less collection fee				
May	2 100	(2 100)		
June		3 175		3 175
Bank service charge				
May	(12)		(12)	
June			20	(20)
NSF cheque	(548)		(548)	
Error made in entering cheque no. 916	(270)		(270)	
Correct amounts	$16 484	$80 939	$76 451	$20 972

A logical analysis of each reconciling item should enable you to determine whether to add or deduct the item. For example:

1. The May 31 deposits in transit of $1500 are deducted from the June receipts shown on the bank statement. Because this amount is a May receipt that is shown as a receipt on the June bank statement, we must deduct it in order to derive the correct amount of June receipts.
2. The outstanding cheques of $2910 on June 30 are added to the June payments shown on the bank statement. Because these cheques are June payments that simply have not cleared the bank as of June 30, we must add them in order to derive the correct amount of June payments.
3. The note and interest collected by the bank in June ($3175) are added to the June receipts shown on the company's books. Because this amount is a June receipt not yet shown on the company's books, we must add it in order to derive the correct amount of June receipts.
4. The bank service charge of $12 for May is deducted from the June payments shown on the company's books. Because this amount is a May payment (i.e., the bank charged the company's chequing account in May) that the company recorded as a payment in June, we must deduct it in order to derive the correct amount of June payments.

Remember that a company must usually prepare journal entries based on the information shown on its bank reconciliations. Our illustration assumes that Todd, Inc. prepares such entries near the beginning of the month that follows each reconciliation. In practice, many companies do this because they do not receive their bank statements in the mail on the last day of each month. When a company wants to prepare accurate financial statements (e.g., at year-end), the company should record its journal entries as transactions of the month to which the bank reconciliation pertains.

As with the single-column bank reconciliation, preparation of a proof of cash usually requires a company to make journal entries to update its accounting records. The entries necessary for Todd, Inc. are suggested by the information shown in the "per books" section of the proof of cash:

Cash	3175	
Miscellaneous Expense	10	
Notes Receivable		3000
Interest Revenue		185
(*To record collection of note and interest by bank.*)		
Miscellaneous Expense	20	
Cash		20
(*To record bank service charge.*)		

Questions

Q8.1   What are the normal components of cash?

Q8.2   What are the guidelines for the valuation and classification of cash on the balance sheet?

Q8.3   How should a company report each of the following items?
  (a) Bank overdrafts.

(b) Certificates of deposit.

(c) NSF cheques received from customers.

(d) Expense advances made to employees.

(e) Postdated cheques received from customers.

(f) Postage stamps.

(g) IOUs received from employees.

Q8.4 What do accountants mean by the term "internal control"?

Q8.5 Why should a company divide the responsibility for a series of related transactions between two or more persons?

Q8.6 What is the purpose of a petty cash fund?

Q8.7 Explain the nature of a Cash Short and Over account.

Q8.8 What is a bank reconciliation? What purposes does it serve?

Q8.9 What is a proof of cash? What purposes does it serve?

Q8.10 What does the term "receivables" mean? How should receivables be classified on the balance sheet?

Q8.11 How should short-term receivables be valued on the balance sheet?

Q8.12 What is the difference between a trade discount and a cash discount?

Q8.13 Explain the distinction between the net method and the gross method of recording credit sales. Which method do companies generally use? Why?

Q8.14 Briefly compare the direct write-off method and the allowance method of accounting for uncollectable accounts.

Q8.15 Assume that a company uses the allowance method of accounting for uncollectable accounts. What is the major argument in favour of using the income statement approach? What is the major argument in favour of using the balance sheet approach?

Q8.16 Why does the Allowance for Doubtful Accounts sometimes have a debit balance?

Q8.17 What is the theoretical argument for using the allowance method to account for expected sales returns and allowances? (Assume that the expected amount is material.)

Q8.18 Why is it theoretically correct to account for interest when accounting for a non-interest-bearing note receivable?

Q8.19 What is the fundamental difference between the note approach and the contra account approach to accounting for notes receivable discounted?

Exercises

E8.1 Cash Components. The controller of Wiser Women's Wear is trying to determine the total amount to report as cash on a balance sheet dated December 31. The following items are being considered:

(1) Currency and coins in a change fund (used for making change with customers) on December 31.

(2) NSF cheques received during December from customers on account and returned by the bank with December bank statement.

(3) Certificates of deposit held on December 31.

(4) Cheques that the company has drawn payable to suppliers. Cheques have been recorded but not mailed as of December 31.

(5) Postage stamps on hand December 31.

(6) Correct cash balance on December 31 in special chequing account used for writing payroll cheques.

(7) Petty cash on hand December 31.

(8) A cheque received from a customer and dated January 5 of the following year.

(9) IOUs from company personnel.

(10) Correct cash balance on December 31 in Chemical Bank general chequing account.

Instructions

(a) Identify the items that the controller should report as cash on the December 31 balance sheet.
(b) Indicate the proper balance sheet reporting for items that the company should not include as cash.

E8.2 Cash Components. The following information pertains to Weber Limited on December 31:

Correct cash balance in general chequing account with First Provincial Bank	$3 261
Overdraft in special chequing account with Victoria Bank (Weber does not have another account with Victoria Bank)	290
Cash accumulated in a special fund that will be used for plant expansion in five years	15 187
Cash surrender value of life insurance	3 265
Cash travel advances in the hands of company salespersons	1 296
Currency and coins in a petty cash fund (the company has not replenished the fund to the imprest amount of $200)	58
Ninety-day treasury bill maturing February 27	20 000

Instructions

(a) Calculate the total amount that Weber company should report as cash in the current assets section of the balance sheet dated December 31.
(b) Indicate the proper balance sheet reporting of items that you omitted in (a).

E8.3 Petty Cash. On April 1, Dyer Insurance Agency established an imprest petty cash fund for $300 by writing a cheque on City Provincial Bank. On April 23, the fund contained the following:

Currency and coins	$ 26
Receipts for office supplies expense	84
Receipts for postage expense	167
Receipts for advertising expense	18

On April 26, Dyer wrote a cheque to increase the fund to the imprest amount.

Instructions

Prepare the necessary journal entries to record the petty cash transactions during April.

E8.4 Cash Balance before Adjustments. The following information pertains to Egerton Inc. as of November 30:

Bank statement balance	$2148
Bank service charge for November (not previously recorded on Egerton's books)	17
Cheques outstanding	215
Interest on bank balance credited by bank during November (not previously recorded on Egerton's books)	37
Deposit in transit	490
Cheque issued by Egentin Ltd. was deducted from Egerton Inc.'s account by the bank	560

Instructions

Based on the above information, compute the general ledger cash balance on November 30 before adjustments.

E8.5 Bank Reconciliation. The following information pertains to Ninja, Inc., as of September 30:

Cash balance per general ledger	$2585
Cash balance per bank statement	2705
Cheques outstanding	350
Bank service charge shown on September bank statement	10
Error made by Ninja, Inc., in recording a cheque that cleared the bank in September (cheque was drawn in September for $145 but recorded at $185)	40
Deposit in transit	260

Instructions

Prepare a September bank reconciliation for Ninja, Inc.

E8.6 Cash to Report. The bookkeeper for Bressler Limited recently prepared the following bank reconciliation:

Bressler Limited
BANK RECONCILIATION
September 30

Balance per bank statement			$12 642
Add: Deposit in transit		$870	
Cheque book printing charge		21	
Error made in recording cheque no. 1782 (issued in September to acquire equipment)		160	
NSF cheque from a customer returned with the bank statement, includes $10 fee		500	1 551
			14 193
Deduct: Outstanding cheques			
No. 1763	$235		
No. 1795	168		
No. 1796	45	448	
Note collected by bank (includes $60 interest and $10 collection)		950	1 398
Balance per books			$12 795

Instructions

(a) What amount should Bressler report as cash on the balance sheet dated September 30? Assume that the company has $910 cash on hand on September 30.
(b) Prepare the necessary compound journal entry.

E8.7 Bank Reconciliation. Archer Corporation keeps all of its cash in a chequing account. An examination of the company's accounting records and bank statement for the month ended June 30 revealed the following information:

(1) The cash balances as of June 30 are

Bank statement balance	$8469
Book balance	8524

(2) A deposit of $950 that was placed in the bank's night depository on June 30 does not appear on the bank statement.
(3) The bank statement shows that on June 30, the bank deposited $935 from principal and interest on a GIC held by Archer. The proceeds included $35 interest, all of which Archer earned during the current accounting period. Archer has not yet recorded the collection.
(4) Cheques outstanding on June 30 are

No. 151	$150
No. 157	48
No. 166	72

(5) Archer discovered that cheque no. 159, written in June for $183 in payment of an account payable, had been recorded in the company's records as $138.
(6) Included with the June bank statement was an NSF cheque for $240 that Archer had received from Engin Inc. (in account on June 26). Archer has not yet recorded the returned cheque. The bank charged a $10 fee for processing the NSF cheque.
(7) The bank statement shows a $15 service charge for June.

Instructions

(a) Prepare a June 30 bank reconciliation for Archer.
(b) Prepare the necessary journal entries.
(c) Post the journal entries to Archer's cash account and determine the adjusted cash balance.

E8.8 (Appendix) Proof of Cash. The following information pertains to the cash of Hines Limited:

(1)

	July 31	August 31
Balance shown on bank statement	$2738	$2696
Balance shown in general ledger before reconciling the bank account	2578	2500
Outstanding cheques	863	1015
Deposit in transit	685	1245

(2)

	For August
Deposits shown on bank statement	$5588
Charges shown on bank statement	5630
Cash receipts shown on company's books	5398
Cash payments shown on company's books	5476

(3) The bank service charge was $18 in July (recorded by the company during August) and $24 in August (not yet recorded by the company).

(4) Included with the August bank statement was a cheque for $480 that had been received on August 25 from a customer on account. The returned cheque, marked "NSF" by the bank, has not yet been recorded on the company's books. The bank charged $20 for processing the NSF cheque.

(5) During August, the bank collected $750 of bond interest for Hines Limited and credited the proceeds to the company's account. The company earned the interest during the current accounting period but has not yet recorded it.

(6) During August, the company issued a cheque for $696 for equipment. The cheque, which cleared the bank during August, was incorrectly recorded by the company for $896.

Instructions

Prepare a proof of cash for August.

E8.9 Recording Credit Sales. Penato, Inc., engaged in the following transactions during August:

Aug. 1 Sold merchandise to A Limited for $5000; terms 2/10, n/30.
    2 Sold merchandise to B Inc. for $20 000; terms 2/10, n/30.
   11 Received payment from B Inc. for the August 2 sale.
   30 Received payment from A Limited for the August 1 sale.

Instructions

Prepare general journal entries for these transactions on Penato's books, using
(a) The net method of recording credit sales.
(b) The gross method of recording credit sales.

E8.10 Bad Debts. The following data pertain to two companies that have calendar-year accounting periods:

	1995 Credit Sales	Accounts Receivable Dec. 31, 1995	Allowance for Doubtful Accounts Dec. 31, 1995 Before Adjustment
Song Limited	$200 000	$25 000	$150 credit balance
Wong Limited	500 000	60 000	250 debit balance

Instructions

Journalize the necessary adjusting entry on December 31, 1995, based on the following independent assumptions:

(a) For Song Limited, assuming the company estimates that 1 percent of credit sales are uncollectable.
(b) For Song Limited, assuming the company estimates that 6 percent of the accounts receivable balance on December 31, 1995, will be uncollectable.
(c) For Wong Limited, assuming the company estimates that 0.5 percent of credit sales are uncollectable.
(d) For Wong Limited, assuming the company estimates that 5 percent of the accounts receivable balance on December 31, 1995, will be uncollectable.

E8.11 Bad Debts.   The following information pertains to Truan Inc.:

(1) Sales made during 1995:

Cash	$100 000
Credit	320 000
Total	$420 000

(2) Accounts receivable classified by age on December 31, 1995:

Age of Accounts	Accounts Receivable Balance
Under 30 days	$40 000
30–60 days	20 000
61–120 days	10 000
Over 120 days	5 000
Total	$75 000

(3) The Allowance for Doubtful Accounts had a $400 credit balance before adjustment on December 31, 1995.

Instructions
Prepare the adjusting entry on December 31, 1995, to record estimated bad debts under each of the following:

(a) The income statement approach, assuming that the uncollectable rate is 1 percent of credit sales.
(b) The income statement approach, assuming that the uncollectable rate is 0.75 percent of total sales.
(c) The balance sheet approach, assuming that the uncollectable rate is 5 percent of gross accounts receivable.
(d) The balance sheet approach, assuming that the following uncollectable percentages are appropriate: under 30 days, 1 percent; 30–60 days, 3 percent; 61–120 days, 10 percent; over 120 days, 30 percent.
(e) Discuss the accounting principles that support the income statement approach to calculating bad debt expense.

E8.12 Aging Schedule.   An aging of Sidlowski Limited's accounts receivable on December 31, 1995, reveals the following information:

Time Outstanding	Amount of Accounts Receivable
Under 30 days	$ 80 000
30–60 days	16 000
61–120 days	12 000
121–180 days	8 000
Over 180 days	4 000
Total	$120 000

Based on past experience, the company believes that the following uncollectable percentages are appropriate: under 30 days, 1.5 percent; 30–60 days, 3 percent; 61–120 days, 15 percent; 121–180 days, 30 percent; over 180 days, 60 percent.

Instructions

Using the aging of accounts receivable variation of the balance sheet approach, prepare the adjusting entry on December 31, 1995, to record estimated bad debts, assuming that the balance in the Allowance for Doubtful Accounts before adjustment is:

(a) $440 credit.
(b) $560 debit.

Discuss the accounting principles that support the balance sheet approach to calculating bad debt expense.

E8.13   Accounts Receivable—Selected Events.   Sidnknecht, Inc., reported the following information on its balance sheet dated December 31, 1994:

Accounts receivable	$53 800
Less: Allowance for doubtful accounts	2 400
	$51 400

The following events occurred during 1995:

(1) Made credit sales of $210 000 and cash sales of $56 000.
(2) Collected $201 800 from customers on account.
(3) Wrote off $3300 of accounts considered to be uncollectable.
(4) Collected $400 from customers whose accounts had been written off as uncollectable.
(5) Estimated that 6 percent of the accounts receivable balance at year-end would prove to be uncollectable.

Instructions

Prepare journal entries to record the above events.

E8.14   Allowance Method for Sales Returns.   Levy Limited uses the allowance method to account for its sales returns. Based on past experience, Levy estimates that customers will return approximately 10 percent of the goods that the company sold. The company also estimates that it can resell goods returned by customers for approximately 70 percent of the original selling price. Levy's sales during the current accounting period were $400 000. The company uses a perpetual inventory system.

Instructions

(a) Prepare an adjusting journal entry to record estimated sales returns for the current accounting period.
(b) Prepare a journal entry to record the return in the next accounting period of goods that Levy sold for $4000. Assume that the customer had not paid for the goods.

E8.15   Assigning Accounts Receivable.   On July 2, Foggin Inc. assigned $50 000 of accounts receivable to its bank on a non-notification basis. On that date, the bank advanced $40 000, less a service charge of 1 percent of the total accounts assigned, and Foggin signed a $40 000 note bearing interest of 1 percent per month on the unpaid loan balance at the beginning of the month.

During July, Foggin collected $33 000 on assigned accounts. The company remitted this amount to the bank on July 31.

During August, the company collected the remaining balance of assigned accounts. On August 31, the company paid off the remaining loan balance.

Instructions

Record the above events in general journal form.

E8.16   Factoring Accounts Receivable.   On February 1, Fotis Inc. factored $80 000 of accounts receivable without recourse with Fast Finance Corporation on a notification basis. Fast Finance charged a factoring fee of 3 percent of the amount of receivables factored. To cover sales returns and allowances, Fast Finance withheld 5 percent of the amount of receivables factored.

Instructions

Prepare the necessary journal entry for Fotis on February 1.

E8.17   Pledging, Assigning, and Factoring.   On September 30, Hebert Inc. engaged in the following transactions:

(1) Obtained a $20 000, 30-day, 9 percent loan from First Provincial Bank. The company pledged $20 000 of accounts receivable as security for the loan.
(2) Assigned $25 000 of accounts receivable on a non-notification basis to Commercial Bank. The bank advanced $21 000, less a service charge of $420, and Hebert signed a $21 000 note calling for interest of 1 percent per month on the unpaid loan balance.
(3) Factored $60 000 of accounts receivable without recourse on a notification basis with Quick Finance Corporation. Quick Finance charged a factoring fee of 2 percent of the amount of receivables factored and withheld 10 percent of the amount factored.

Instructions

Journalize each of the above transactions on September 30.

E8.18 Interest-Bearing Notes Receivable. On November 1, 1994, Breece Manufacturing Limited sold land in exchange for a $60 000, 8 percent, 90-day promissory note. The 8 percent interest rate was the going market rate for similar notes. Breece had paid $22 000 to acquire the land in 1984. When the note matured, Breece collected principal and interest. Use 360 days per year in your calculations.

Instructions

Prepare all journal entries (including an adjusting entry) required to record the above events on Breece's books in 1994 and 1995. Assume that Breece uses a calendar-year accounting period and does not make reversing entries.

E8.19 Recording Notes Receivable. On October 1, 1994, Bridges, Inc., sold merchandise having a sales price of $5000 and received a one-year promissory note with a face amount of $5500. The note had no stated interest rate, although the market rate for similar notes was 10 percent. When the note matured, Bridges collected the face amount. Bridges, Inc., uses a calendar-year accounting period and does not make reversing entries. Use 360 days per year in your calculations.

Instructions

(a) Prepare all journal entries (including an adjusting entry) required to record the above events on Bridges' books, assuming that the company records the note at present value.

(b) Prepare all journal entries required to record the above events on Bridges' books, assuming that the company records the note at face amount.

(c) From a theoretical standpoint, is it better for Bridges to record the note at present value or at face amount? Explain your answer.

E8.20 Discounting Notes Receivable. Aoki Limited has the following three notes receivable:

Note	Date of Note	Face Amount	Interest Rate	Time of Note
A	April 1, 1995	$30 000	8%	90–day
B	May 1, 1995	40 000	9%	90–day
C	May 16, 1995	60 000	10%	60–day

Instructions

For each note, calculate the proceeds that Aoki would receive by discounting the note on May 31, 1995, at a rate of 8 percent. Use 360 days per year in your calculations.

Problems

P8.1 Petty Cash. The following events pertain to Arp's Supply House:

June 1 Established an imprest petty cash fund for $400 by writing a cheque on Candor County Bank.

     12 Wrote a cheque to replenish the fund. The fund contained:

Currency and coins	$ 16
Receipts for transportation-in	303
Receipts for postage expense	66

20 Wrote a cheque to replenish the fund and to increase the imprest amount to $500. The fund contained:

Currency and coins	$ 36
Receipts for transportation-in	277
Receipts for postage expense	70
Receipts for charitable contributions	25

Instructions

Prepare the necessary journal entries to record the petty cash transactions during June.

P8.2 Bank Reconciliation. Hinson Limited keeps all of its cash in a chequing account. Presented below are the company's bank reconciliation prepared at the end of May, the general ledger account for cash, and a summary of the company's bank statement for June.

Hinson Limited
BANK RECONCILIATION
May 31

Balance per bank statement	$6250
Add: Deposits in transit	225
	6475
Deduct: Outstanding cheques	418
Correct cash balance	$6057
Balance per books	$6072
Deduct: Bank service charge	15
Correct cash balance	$6057

Cash

Balance, June 1	6 057	June disbursements	25 679
June receipts	26 182		

Summary of Hinson Limited's
Bank Statement for June

Balance, June 1	$ 6 250
Deposits shown for June	25 692
Note and interest collected during June less the collection fee	1 565
Cheques that cleared during June	(25 707)
June service charge	(17)
Balance, June 30	7 783

Additional Information

(1) During June, Hinson incorrectly recorded two cheques. Cheque no. 507 was drawn for $233 but recorded as $323; cheque no. 521 was drawn for $180 but recorded as $18. Both cheques were issued in payment of accounts payable and cleared the bank in June.

(2) During June, the bank erroneously charged a $210 cheque of Minson Inc. to Hinson's account.

(3) A note for $1500 and interest was collected by the bank during June; $75 represents interest, all of which Hinson earned during the current year. The bank deducted the collection fee of $10. The company has not yet recorded the collection.

Instructions

(a) Prepare a June 30 bank reconciliation.

(b) Prepare journal entries to bring Hinson Limited's accounting records up to date.

(c) What amount should Hinson report as cash on the balance sheet dated June 30?

P8.3 Bank Reconciliation. Witt Limited uses a calendar-year accounting period. The following information is available about the company's cash:

Witt Limited
BANK RECONCILIATION
April 30

Balance per bank statement		$4942
Add: Deposit in transit		610
		5552
Deduct: Outstanding cheques		
No. 606	$177	
No. 607	248	425
Correct cash balance		$5127
Balance per books		$5139
Deduct: Bank service charge		12
Correct cash balance		$5127

First Provincial Bank
General Account: Witt Limited

Date	Debits		Credits	Balance
4–30				4 942
5–01			610	5 552
5–02	177			5 375
5–04	248	755	1 552	5 924
5–05	437			5 487
5–09	489		3 621	8 619
5–12	705		1 986	9 900
5–20	930			8 970
5–22	423			8 547
5–26			2 549	11 096
5–29	255 NSF			10 841
5–30	20 DM	5 798		5 023
5–31	14 SC		1 290 CM	6 299
	Total debits $10 251		Total credits $11 608	

Legend: DM: Debit memo NSF: Not sufficient funds cheque
CM: Credit memo SC: Service charge

Witt Limited's Cash Account
Taken From General Ledger

Cash

Balance, April 30	5 139	Cash Payments Journal, May 31	10 816
Cash Receipts Journal, May 31	10 583		

Information Taken from Witt Limited

Cash Receipts Journal			Cash Payments Journal		
Date	Cash Debit		Date	Cheque No.	Cash Credit
5–03	1 552		5–01	608	755
5–08	3 621		5–03	609	473
5–12	1 986		5–06	610	489
5–25	2 549		5–11	611	705
5–31	875		5–16	612	930
	10 583		5–21	613	243
			5–27	614	511
			5–29	615	5 798
			5–30	616	346
			5–31	617	566
					10 816

Additional Information

(1) During May, a collection charge of $20 that was applicable to Hitt Limited was erroneously deducted by the bank from Witt Limited's account.

(2) The credit memo shown on the bank statement relates to a note that the bank collected on Witt's behalf. The note had a face value of $1200, and Witt earned interest of $100 during the current accounting period. There was a $10 collection fee. The company has not yet recorded the collection.

(3) Witt failed to record the bank service charge for April (see April reconciliation).

(4) The NSF cheque shown on the bank statement had been received during May from a customer on account. The return of the cheque has not yet been recorded by Witt.

(5) Witt made two errors in recording cash payments during May:

Cheque No.	Actual Amount of Cheque	Amount Recorded
609	$437	$473
613	423	243

Cheque no. 609 was for delivery expense; cheque no. 613 was issued to purchase equipment.

Instructions

(a) Prepare a bank reconciliation dated May 31.

(b) Prepare the necessary journal entries.

(c) Why is it prudent for the company accountant to prepare the bank reconciliation on a timely basis?

P8.4 Appendix—Proof of Cash. Refer to the information given for Witt Limited in P8.3.

Instructions

(a) Prepare a proof of cash for May.

(b) Prepare the necessary journal entries.

P8.5 Bank Reconciliation. The accounting period of Riblett Inc. ends on December 31. The following information is available about the company's cash:

Riblett Inc.
BANK RECONCILIATION
October 31

Balance per bank statement			$18 005
Add: Deposit in transit			1 790
			19 795
Deduct: Outstanding cheques			
No. 773		$4 563	
No. 774		2 118	6 681
Correct cash balance			$13 114
Balance per books			$11 534
Add: Note collected by bank			
Principal		1 500	
Interest earned during current accounting period		100	1 600
			13 134
Deduct: Bank service charge			20
Correct cash balance			$13 114

Coronet Provincial Bank
General Account: Riblett Inc.

Date	Debits		Credits	Balance
10–31				18 005
11–01			1 790	19 795
11–02	4 563			15 232
11–04	2 118	4 567	5 967	14 514
11–05	963			13 551
11–06			3 410	16 961
11–07	2 515			14 446
11–11			1 037	15 483
11–13	2 264			13 219
11–18	3 325			9 894
11–24	964		4 255	13 185
11–28	619		750 CM	13 316
11–29	3 000	35 DM	500 CM	10 781
11–30	665 NSF	22 SC		10 094
Total debits $25 620			**Total credits $17 709**	

Legend: DM Debit memo NSF: Not sufficient funds cheque
CM: Credit memo SC Service charge

Riblett Inc.'s Cash Account
Taken from General Ledger

Cash

Balance, Oct 31	11 534	Cash Payments Journal, Nov. 31	21 575
Cash Receipts Journal, Nov. 30	18 269		

Information Taken From Riblett Inc.

Cash Receipts Journal		Cash Payments Journal		
Date	Cash Debit	Date	Cheque No.	Cash Credit
11–03	5 967	11–01	775	4 567
11–06	3 410	11–04	776	963
11–11	1 037	11–05	777	2 515
11–23	4 255	11–10	778	3 264
11–30	3 600	11–17	779	3 325
	18 269	11–22	780	694
		11–27	781	619
		11–28	782	760
		11–29	783	3 000
		11–30	784	1 868
				21 575

Additional Information

(1) After preparing the October 31 reconciliation, Riblett failed to record the necessary journal entries.

(2) The NSF cheque had been received during November from a customer on account. Riblett has not yet recorded the return of the cheque. The $665 charge back includes a $15 returned fee.

(3) The credit memos shown on the bank statement pertain to $750 of bond interest that Riblett earned during the current accounting period and that the bank collected on the company's behalf (collection not yet recorded on Riblett's books) and a $500 collection made for Niblett Inc. that the bank erroneously credited to Riblett's account.

(4) The $35 debit memo shown on the bank statement pertains to the rental of a safety deposit box during November.

(5) Riblett made two errors in recording cash payments during November:

Cheque No.	Actual Amount of Cheque	Amount Recorded
778	$2264	$3264
780	964	694

Cheque no. 778 was issued to purchase equipment; cheque no. 780 was for advertising expense.

Instructions

(a) Prepare a bank reconciliation dated November 30.
(b) Prepare the necessary journal entries. Assume all bank charges are expensed.

P8.6 (Appendix) Proof of Cash. Refer to the information given for Riblett Limited in P8.5.

Instructions

(a) Prepare a proof of cash for November.
(b) Prepare the necessary journal entries. Assume all bank charges are expensed.

P8.7   Recording Credit Sales.   Minor, Inc., began operations in 1995. During the year, the company sold merchandise with a gross invoice price of $100 000. All sales were subject to credit terms of 3/10, n/60. Of the total sales of $100 000, the company received payments for 50 percent within the discount period and 30 percent after the discount period had expired. The company had not collected the other 20 percent as of year-end.

Instructions
(a)   Prepare general journal entries to record the above transactions using: (1) the net method of recording credit sales, and (2) the gross method of recording credit sales.
(b)   What financial statement balances would Minor report on December 31, 1995, for sales, sales discounts not taken, sales discounts, and accounts receivable under (1) the net method, and (2) the gross method?
(c)   Which of the two methods of recording credit sales is theoretically superior? Why?

P8.8   Accounts Receivable—Selected Events.   Olson Department Store reported the following information on its balance sheet dated December 31, 1994:

Accounts receivable	$138 000
Less: Allowance for doubtful accounts	7 000
	$131 000

Additional Information
The company engaged in the following transactions during 1995:
(1)   Made cash sales of $320 000 and credit sales of $670 000.
(2)   Collected $650 800 from customers on account.
(3)   Wrote off $7200 of accounts considered to be uncollectable.
(4)   Collected $600 from customers whose accounts had been written off as uncollectable.

Instructions
(a)   Prepare journal entries to record the above transactions.
(b)   Journalize the adjusting entry to record estimated bad debts at the end of 1995 under each of the following independent assumptions:
  (1)   The company estimates that 1.5 percent of credit sales are uncollectable.
  (2)   The company estimates that 1.0 percent of total sales are uncollectable.
  (3)   The company estimates that 7 percent of the accounts receivable balance at the end of 1995 will be uncollectable.
  (4)   The company estimates that 75 percent of the year-end balance of accounts receivable has an uncollectable percentage of 3 percent; the remaining 25 percent has an uncollectable percentage of 20 percent.
(c)   Assume that the company estimates its bad debts on the basis of assumption (b-1).
  (1)   Show how accounts receivable would be presented on the balance sheet prepared at the end of 1995.
  (2)   What is the dollar effect of the year-end bad debt adjustment on the pretax income for 1995?
  (3)   What is the dollar effect of the year-end bad debt adjustment on the working capital (current assets minus current liabilities) reported at the end of 1995?

P8.9 Aging Schedule. Harding Corporation operates in an industry that has a high rate of bad debts. On December 31, 1995, before any year-end adjustments, Harding's Accounts Receivable balance was $600 000 and its Allowance for Doubtful Accounts balance was $25 000. The year-end balance reported in the statement of financial position for the allowance for doubtful accounts will be based on the aging schedule shown as follows:

Time Outstanding	Amount of Accounts Receivable	Probability of Collection
Under 15 days	$300 000	0.98
16–30 days	200 000	0.90
31–45 days	50 000	0.80
46–60 days	30 000	0.70
61–75 days	10 000	0.65
Over 75 days	10 000	0.00

Instructions

(a) What is the appropriate balance for the Allowance for Doubtful Accounts on December 31, 1995?

(b) Show how accounts receivable would be presented on the balance sheet on December 31, 1995.

(c) What is the dollar effect of the year-end bad debt adjustment on the pretax income for 1995?

(Adapted from CMA.)

P8.10 Aging Schedule. From inception of operations to December 31, 1994, Dunn Corporation provided for uncollectable accounts receivable under the allowance method: provisions were made monthly at 2 percent of credit sales; bad debts written off were charged to the Allowance account; recoveries of bad debts previously written off were credited to the Allowance account; and no year-end adjustments to the Allowance account were made. Dunn's usual credit terms are net 30 days.

The balance in the Allowance for Doubtful Accounts was $130 000 at January 1, 1995. During 1995, credit sales totalled $9 million, interim provisions for doubtful accounts were made at 2 percent of credit sales, $90 000 of bad debts were written off, and recoveries of accounts previously written off amounted to $15 000.

Instructions

(a) Prepare a schedule analyzing the changes in the Allowance for Doubtful Accounts for the year ended December 31, 1995. Use the income statement approach.

(b) Dunn installed a computer facility in November 1995, and an aging of accounts receivable was prepared for the first time as of December 31, 1995. A summary of the aging is as follows:

Classification by Month of Sale	Balance in Each Category	Estimated Percent Uncollectable
Nov–Dec. 1995	$1 140 000	2%
July–Oct.	600 000	10
Jan.–June	400 000	25
Prior to 1/1/95	130 000	75
	$2 270 000	

A review of collectability of the account balances in the "prior to 1/1/95" aging category, revealed that receivables totalling $60 000 related to 1993. Effective with the year ended December 31, 1995, Dunn adopted a new accounting method for estimating the allowance for doubtful accounts at the amount indicated by the year-end aging analysis of accounts receivable.

Instructions

(a) Prepare a schedule for the computation of the allowance based on the aged analysis of the accounts receivable as of December 31, 1995.

(b) Prepare the journal entry for the year-end adjustment to the Allowance for Doubtful Accounts balance as of December 31, 1995.

(c) Discuss the benefits and deficiencies of the two approaches to computing the allowance for doubtful accounts. Use the problem material as an example.

(Adapted from AICPA.)

P8.11   Aging Schedule.   Keene Limited sells office equipment and supplies to many organizations in the city and surrounding area on contract terms of 2/10, n/30. In the past, over 75 percent of the credit customers have taken advantage of the discount by paying within ten days of the invoice date.

The number of customers taking the full 30 days to pay has increased within the last year. Current indications are that less than 60 percent of the customers are now taking the discount. Bad debts as a percentage of gross credit sales have risen from the 1.5 percent provided in past years to about 4 percent in the current year.

The controller has responded to a request for more information on the deterioration in collections of accounts receivable with the report reproduced below.

Keene Limited
Finance Committee Report
Accounts Receivable Collections
May 31, 1995

The fact that some credit accounts will prove uncollectable is normal. Annual bad debt write-offs have been 1.5 percent of gross credit sales over the past five years. During the last fiscal year, this percentage increased to slightly less than 4 percent. The current Accounts Receivable balance is $1.2 million. The condition of this balance in terms of age and probability of collection is as follows:

Proportion of Total	Age Categories	Probability of Collection
68%	Not yet due	99%
15%	Less than 30 days past due	96.5%
8%	30 to 60 days past due	95%
5%	61 to 120 days past due	91%
2.5%	121 to 180 days past due	60%
1.5%	Over 180 days past due	10%

The Allowance for Doubtful Accounts had a credit balance of $30 250 on June 1, 1994. Keene has provided for a monthly bad debts expense accrual during the current fiscal year based on the assumption that 4 percent of gross credit sales will be uncollectable. Total gross credit sales for the 1994–95 fiscal year amounted to $3 million. Write-offs of bad accounts during the year totalled $108 750.

Instructions

(a) Prepare an accounts receivable aging schedule for Keene Limited using the age categories identified in the controller's report showing
    (1) The amount of accounts receivable outstanding for each age category and in total.
    (2) The estimated amount that is uncollectable for each category and in total.
(b) Compute the amount of the year-end adjustment necessary to bring Allowance for Doubtful Accounts to the balance indicated by the age analysis. Then prepare the necessary journal entry to adjust the accounting records.
(c) Assume a recessionary environment with tight credit and high interest rates.
    (1) Identify steps Keene Limited might consider to improve the accounts receivable situation.
    (2) Evaluate each step identified in terms of the risks and costs involved.
(Adapted from CMA.)

P8.12 Changing an Accounting Estimate of Bad Debts. Provo Limited has been in business for five years, but its financial statements have never been audited. Engaged to perform an audit for 1995, you find that the company's balance sheet has no allowance for doubtful accounts. Bad debts have simply been expensed as written off, and recoveries have been credited to income collected. The company's policy is to write off at December 31 of each year those accounts on which no collections have been received for three months. The installment contracts are for two years. Installment contracts are signed when installment sales are made; they outline the terms of the sale.

Upon your recommendation, the company agrees to revise its accounts for 1995 to reflect the allowance method of accounting for bad debts. The estimate of bad debts is to be based on a percentage of sales that is derived from the experience of prior years.

Statistics for the past five years are as follows:

Charge Year	Sales	Accounts Written Off and Year of Sale					Recoveries and Year of Sale
		1991	1992	1993	1994	1995	
1991	$100 000	$ 550					(1991) $100
1992	250 000	1 500	$1 000				(1992) 400
1993	300 000	500	4 000	$1 300			(1993) 500
1994	325 000		1 200	4 500	1 500		(1994) 600
1995	275 000			2 700	5 000	1 400	

Accounts receivable at December 31, 1995, were as follows:

1994 sales	$ 15 000
1995 sales	135 000
	$150 000

Instructions

Prepare the adjusting journal entry or entries with appropriate explanations to set up the Allowance for Doubtful Accounts. Support each item with computations. Disregard income tax implications.
(Adapted from AICPA.)

P8.13 Assigning and Factoring Accounts Receivable. The following information pertains to Carolina Textiles, Inc:

June 1 Assigned $75 000 of accounts receivable to City Bank on a non-notification basis. The bank advanced $64 000, less a service charge of $1600. Carolina signed a $64 000 promissory note bearing interest of 1 percent per month on the unpaid loan balance.
    28 Collected assigned accounts of $50 000, less sales returns and allowances of $1500.
    29 Sold goods on account for $80 000.
    30 Remitted the June 28 collection to City Bank.
    30 Factored $50 000 of accounts receivable without recourse with Eastward Chartered Bank on a notification basis. Eastward Chartered Bank charged a factoring fee of 3 percent of the amount of receivables factored and withheld 10 percent of the amount factored to cover sales returns and allowances.

Instructions
(a) Journalize the above events on Carolina's books.
(b) Assume that Carolina wants to prepare a balance sheet dated June 30. Discuss the financial reporting requirements for those receivables that pertain to the assignment and factoring arrangements.

P8.14 Notes Receivable Discounted. The following events pertain to Troyer Limited:

May 1 Troyer receives a $10 000, 90-day, 10 percent note in satisfaction of West Limited's account receivable of $10 000.
    31 Troyer discounts the note with recourse at First Bank. The discount rate is 8 percent. Relevant circumstances indicate that the discounting should be accounted for as a sale of the note.
July 30 West Limited pays First Bank the total amount owed on the note. Use 360 days per year in your calculations.

Instructions
(a) Prepare journal entries to record the above events on Troyer's books using each of the following approaches to accounting for notes receivable discounted:
    (1) Note approach.   (2) Contra account approach.
(b) Assume that instead of paying the note on July 30, West Limited dishonours it. First Bank charges Troyer with the maturity value and a $20 protest fee. Journalize the entry or entries required for Troyer on July 30 under the:
    (1) Note approach.   (2) Contra account approach.
(c) What is the fundamental difference between these two approaches to accounting for notes receivable discounted?

P8.15 Notes Receivable. The following events pertain to Rosa Inc.:

Dec. 1, 1994	Rosa Inc. sells merchandise to Luna Limited. The merchandise has a selling price of $10 000, and Rosa receives a one-year promissory note that has a face amount of $11 000 and no stated interest rate. The market rate for similar notes is 10 percent.
Dec. 16, 1994	Rosa sells land to Lyons Limited in exchange for a $90 000, 10 per-cent, 90-day promissory note. The 10 percent interest rate equals the going market rate for similar notes. The cost of the land to Rosa is $60 000.
Jan. 30, 1995	Rosa discounts the Lyons note with recourse at County Bank. The discount rate is 8 percent. Relevant circumstances indicate that Rosa Inc. should account for the discounting as a sale of the note.
Mar. 16, 1995	Lyons pays County Bank the full amount owed.
Nov. 30, 1995	Luna pays Rosa the full amount owed.

Rosa Inc. uses a calendar-year accounting period and does not make reversing entries. The company records notes receivable at present value on the date received, and it uses the note approach to accounting for notes receivable discounted. Use 360 days per year in your calculations.

Instructions
(a) Prepare journal entries (including adjusting entries) to record the above events on Rosa's books.
(b) Should Rosa recognize interest earned on the Luna note? Explain the rationale for your answer.
(c) Assume that the Luna and Lyons notes are dishonoured when they mature. County Bank charges Rosa with the maturity value of the Lyons note and a $60 protest fee. Journalize the entry or entries required for Rosa on March 16, 1995, and November 30, 1995.

P8.16 Notes Receivable. You are examining Nichols Corporation's financial statements for the year ended December 31, 1995. Your analysis of the 1995 entries in the Trade Notes Receivable account is as follows:

Nichols Corporation
ANALYSIS OF TRADE NOTES RECEIVABLE
For the Year Ended December 31, 1995

Trade Notes Receivable

Date		Folio	Debit	Credit
Jan. 1	Balance forward		$118 000	
Feb. 28	Received $25 000, 6% note due 10/29/95 from Daley, whose trade account was past due.	MEMO		
28	Discounted Daley Note at 6%.	CR		$ 24 960
Mar. 29	Received noninterest-bearing demand note from Edge, the corporation's treasurer, for a loan.	CD	6 200	
Aug. 30	Received principal and interest due from Allen and, in accordance with agreement, two principal payments in advance.	CR		34 200
Sept. 4	Paid protest fee on note dishonoured by Charnes.	CD	5	

Nov. 1	Received cheque dated 2/1/96 in settlement of Bailey note. The cheque was included in cash on hand 12/31/95.	CR		8 120
Nov. 4	Paid protest fee and maturity value of Daley note to bank. Note discounted 2/28/95 was dishonoured.	CD	26 031	
Dec. 27	Accepted furniture and fixtures with a fair market value of $24 000 in full settlement from Daley.	GJ		24 000
31	Received cheque dated 1/3/96 from Edge in payment of 3/29/95 note. (The cheque was included in petty cash until 1/2/96, when it was returned to Edge in exchange for a new demand note of the same amount.)	CR		6 200
31	Received principal and interest on Charnes note.	CR		42 437
31	Accrued interest on Allen note.	GJ	1 200	
	Totals		$151 436	$139 917

Additional Information

(1) Balances at January 1, 1995, were a debit of $1400 in the Accrued Interest Receivable account and a credit of $400 in the Unearned Interest Income account. The $118 000 debit balance in the Trade Notes Receivable account consisted of the following three notes:

Allen note dated 8/31/89, payable in annual installments of $10 000 principal plus accrued interest at 6% each Aug. 31	$70 000
Bailey note discounted to Nichols at 6 percent on 11/1/94, due 11/1/95	8 000
Charnes note for $40 000 plus 6% interest dated 12/31/94, due on 9/1/95	40 000

(2) No entries were made during 1995 to the Accrued Interest Receivable account or the Unearned Interest Income account, and only one entry for a credit of $1200 on December 31 appeared in the Interest Income account.

(3) All notes were from trade customers unless otherwise indicated.

(4) Debits and credits offsetting Trade Notes Receivable debit and credit entries were correctly recorded unless the facts indicate otherwise.

(5) Nichols Corporation uses the contra account approach when accounting for notes receivable discounted. Notes receivable are discounted with recourse and are properly accounted for as sales. The company also follows the practice of debiting Trade Accounts Receivable instead of Dishonoured Notes Receivable when a customer dishonours a note.

Instructions

(a) Prepare a worksheet to adjust each entry to correct or properly reclassify it, if necessary. Enter your adjustments in the proper columns to correspond with the date of each entry. Do not combine related entries for different dates. Your completed worksheet will provide the basis for one compound journal entry to correct all entries to Trade Notes Receivable and related accounts for 1995. Formal journal entries are not required. In addition to the information in the above analysis, the following headings are suggested:

ADJUSTMENT OR RECLASSIFICATION REQUIRED

Trade Notes Receivable	Trade Accounts Receivable	Interest Income	Other Accounts	Amount
Debit (Credit)	Debit (Credit)	Debit (Credit)	Account Title	Debit (Credit)

(b) Prepare a single journal entry to correct the recorded transactions.
(Adapted from AICPA.)

Cases

C8.1 Outstanding Cheques. You are the controller for Reider, Inc., a company that uses a calendar-year accounting period. Walter Brush, a new person on the accounting staff, has just prepared a bank reconciliation dated December 31, 1995, and has determined that outstanding cheques total $14 895. Brush believes that this amount should be classified as liabilities on Reider's year-end balance sheet, because the cheques have not cleared the bank as of December 31.

Instructions

Explain how Reider, Inc. should account for the outstanding cheques on its year-end balance sheet.

C8.2 Notes Receivable and Bad Debts. Gann Limited has significant amounts of trade accounts receivable. Gann uses the allowance method to estimate bad debts instead of the direct write-off method. During the year, some direct accounts were written off as uncollectable, and some that were previously written off as uncollectable were collected.

Gann also has some interest-bearing notes receivable for which the face amount plus interest at the prevailing rate of interest is due at maturity. The notes were received on July 1, 1994, and are due on June 30, 1996.

Instructions

(a) What are the deficiencies of the direct write-off method?
(b) What are the two basic allowance methods used to estimate bad debts, and what is the theoretical justification for each?
(c) How should Gann account for the collection of the specific accounts previously written off as uncollectable? Assume Gann has an Allowance for Doubtful Accounts account.
(d) How should Gann report the effects of the interest-bearing notes receivable on its December 31, 1995, balance sheet and its income statement for the year ended December 31, 1995? Why?
(Adapted from AICPA.)

C8.3 Notes Receivable and Bad Debts.

Part 1. On July 1, 1994, Mayes Limited, a calendar-year company, sold special-order merchandise on credit and received in return an interest-bearing note receivable from the customer. Mayes Limited will receive interest at the prevailing rate for a note of this type. Both the principal and interest are due in one lump sum on June 30, 1995.

Instructions

(a) When should Mayes Limited report interest income from the note receivable? Discuss the rationale for your answer.

(b) Assume that the note receivable was discounted without recourse at a bank on December 31, 1994. How would Mayes Limited determine the amount of the discount, and what is the appropriate accounting for the discounting transaction?

Part 2. On December 31, 1994, Mayes Limited had significant amounts of accounts receivable as a result of credit sales to its customers. Mayes Limited uses the allowance method based on credit sales to estimate bad debts. Based on past experience, 1 percent of credit sales normally will not be collected. This pattern is expected to continue.

Instructions

(a) Discuss the rationale for using the allowance method based on credit sales to estimate bad debts. Contrast this method with the allowance method based on the balance in the Trade Receivables accounts.

(b) How should Mayes Limited report the Allowance for Doubtful Accounts on its balance sheet at December 31, 1994? Also, describe the alternatives, if any, for presentation of bad debts expense in Mayes Limited's 1994 income statement.

(Adapted from AICPA.)

C8.4 Notes Receivable, Assigning, and Factoring. On July 1, 1994, Harris Limited sold special-order merchandise on credit and received in return an interest-bearing note receivable from the customer. Harris will receive the prevailing rate of interest for a note of this type. Both the principal and interest are due in one lump sum on June 30, 1995.

On September 1, 1994, Harris sold special-order merchandise on credit and received in return a noninterest-bearing note receivable from the customer. The prevailing rate of interest for a note of this type is determinable. The note receivable is due in one lump sum on August 31, 1996.

Harris also has significant amounts of trade accounts receivable as a result of credit sales to its customers. On October 1, 1994, some trade accounts receivable were assigned to Davidson Finance Corporation on a with-recourse, non-notification basis for an advance of 75 percent of their amount, at an interest charge of 20 percent on the balance outstanding.

On November 1, 1994, other trade accounts receivable were factored on a without-recourse basis. The factor withheld 5 percent of the trade accounts receivable factored as protection against sales returns and allowances and charged a finance charge of 3 percent.

Instructions

(a) How should Harris determine the interest revenue for 1994 on the
  (1) Interest-bearing note receivable? Why?
  (2) Noninterest-bearing note receivable? Why?

(b) How should Harris report the interest-bearing note receivable and the noninterest-bearing note receivable on its balance sheet at December 31, 1994?

(c) How should Harris account for subsequent collections on the trade accounts receivable assigned on October 1, 1994, and the payments to Davidson Finance? Why?

(d) How should Harris account for the trade accounts receivable factored on November 1, 1994? Why?

(Adapted from AICPA.)

C8.5   Credit Card Plan.   One of your corporate clients operates a full-line department store that dominates its market area, is easily accessible to public and private transportation, has adequate parking facilities, and is near a large, permanent military base. The president of the company seeks your advice on a proposal he received.

A local bank in which your client has an account recently affiliated with a popular national credit-card plan and has invited your client to participate. Under the plan, affiliated banks mail credit-card applications to people in the community who have good credit ratings, regardless of whether they are bank customers. If the recipient wishes to receive a credit card, he or she completes, signs, and returns the application and installment credit agreement. Card holders may charge merchandise or services at any participating establishment throughout the country.

The bank guarantees payment to all participating merchants on invoices that have been properly completed, signed, and validated with the impression of credit cards that have not expired or been reported stolen or otherwise cancelled. Local merchants, including your client, may turn in all card-validated sales tickets or invoices to their affiliated local bank at any time and receive immediate credits to their chequing accounts of 96.5 percent of the face value of the invoices. If card users pay the bank in full within 30 days for amounts billed, the bank levies no added charges against them. If they elect to make their payments under a deferred payment plan, the bank adds a service charge with an effective annual interest rate of 18 percent on unpaid balances. Only the local affiliated banks and the franchisor of the credit-card plan share in these revenues.

The 18 percent service charge approximates what your client has been billing customers who pay their accounts over an extended period on a schedule similar to that of the credit-card plan. Participation in the plan does not prevent your client from continuing its credit business.

Instructions

(a) What are (1) the positive and (2) the negative financial and accounting factors that your client should consider in deciding whether to participate in the credit-card plan? Explain.

(b) If your client participates in the plan, which income statement and balance sheet accounts may change materially as the plan becomes fully operative? (Such factors as market position, sales mix, prices, and markup are expected to remain about the same as in the past.) Explain.

(Adapted from AICPA.)

Judgement Cases

J8.1   Troubled Notes Receivable.   Sam Farmer is the chief financial officer for a small Canadian corporation operating in Alberta that manufactures farm implements and offers long-term credit to buyers. In fulfilling the financing function, the company makes a number of noninterest-bearing loans. Under the terms of these loans, the borrower signs a note for an amount greater than the funds actually lent, and the interest revenue to the company is implicit in the difference between the amount lent and the amount to be repaid (i.e., the discount on the note receivable). Farmer is aware that the CICA *Handbook* does not address this issue and that the provisions of *APB Opinion No. 21*, "Interest on Receivables and Payables," require the company to amortize the discount on the long-term receivables. The company has consistently recognized interest revenue in this manner.

Recently, Farmer read an article in the local newspaper that described the financial implications of a recent drought in the area in which many of the company's best customers operate. While there is no evidence that any financial difficulties are being experienced by the company's customers, the article states that many farming operations are expected to go bankrupt. Farmer believes that some of the company's notes receivable may eventually become uncollectable or only partially collectable. He wonders whether his company should continue to recognize interest revenue on those loans that have some uncertainty as to their ultimate collectability.

Instructions

Help Farmer decide what to do. If you believe that additional evidence is necessary before making any decisions, describe the evidence that Farmer should obtain in attempting to resolve the problem.

J8.2 Receivable Classification. You are the independent CA for Enos, Inc., an electronic products wholesaler. Enos has recently made an important sale to a retail company that is opening several new outlets. Due to the size of the sale, Enos has allowed the retailer to acquire the goods by signing a three-year, interest-bearing note rather than requiring the normal credit terms of 30 days. Enos uses a one-year time period for classifying current assets and liabilities on its balance sheet, and this practice is still appropriate in light of the recent sale to the retailer.

When you explain to Enos' management that the receivable should be classified as noncurrent because of its maturity date, management objects, stating that the company intends to discount the receivable without recourse at a local bank fairly soon after the balance sheet date. Management asserts that although the bank normally used by the company does not engage in such transactions, other banks would be quite willing to do so because they commonly do so for other businesses. Enos' management further objects to classifying the receivable as a noncurrent asset because such a classification would cause the company to violate one of its lending covenants that requires a minimum amount of working capital.

The retailer is a fairly small company that has been a customer of Enos for many years. You recall a recent, rather negative, newspaper article about the retailer's financial difficulties due to keen competition from other large chains of electronics retailers.

Your audit of Enos is now almost complete, and Enos will not accomplish the transfer of the receivable prior to the issuance of the financial statements.

Instructions

Would you accept classifying the receivable as a current asset? Explain your answer. If you believe that additional evidence is needed to resolve the case, be sure to identify the nature of that information as part of your solution.

Chapter 9

Inventories: Basic Valuation Methods

Objectives

1. To discuss and illustrate the financial accounting and reporting requirements for inventories.

2. To explain the methods used to determine inventory quantities on hand.

3. To explain the nature of costs that should be included in inventory.

4. To discuss and illustrate various inventory cost flow methods.

5. To discuss and illustrate the valuation of inventory at the lower of cost or market value.

6. To indicate exceptional cases under generally accepted accounting principles of inventory valuation above cost.

7. To indicate effects of inventory errors on financial statements.

8. To explain conceptual considerations in accounting for inventories.

Inventories

Inventories are goods that are held for sale in the ordinary course of business and goods that are in production or that will soon be used in production. A **service business**, such as a legal firm, normally has no inventories. In contrast, inventories are one of the most important assets of **merchandising businesses** and **manufacturing businesses**, which typically derive most of their revenues from sales of inventories. Moreover, cost of goods sold is usually the largest expense of such companies. It is not surprising, then, that the managers of merchandising and manufacturing companies often devote substantial resources to inventory planning and control. Furthermore, users of financial statements regard inventory information as extremely important when they make investment, lending, and similar decisions.

In this chapter and the next, we discuss the accounting valuation of inventories. Inventories are physical resources, and our primary concern is how accountants obtain a financial representation of such resources for external reporting purposes. Most of our discussion focusses on **inventory valuation methods**, often called **inventory pricing methods**, that companies use to prepare their external financial statements in accordance with GAAP. This chapter presents an overview of basic valuation methods; Chapter 10 introduces several additional methods.

Acquisition of Inventories

A merchandising company buys finished inventory and later resells it. In contrast, a manufacturing company produces its inventory. In doing so, a manufacturing company incurs the following **manufacturing,** or **production, costs:**[1]

1. **Direct materials.** Raw materials costs that can be traced directly and practically to units of the firm's product. In the case of a manufacturer of wooden desks, for example, the cost of the wood is a direct materials cost.
2. **Direct labour.** Labour costs that can be traced directly and practically to units of the firm's product. For the desk manufacturer, the costs of employing staff to assemble the desks are direct labour costs.
3. **Manufacturing, or factory, overhead.**   All manufacturing costs, other than direct materials and direct labour, that are necessary to construct the company's product. For the desk manufacturer, overhead includes, for example, the costs of factory maintenance, depreciation of factory equipment, and glue used on certain parts of each desk.

Direct materials and direct labour are referred to as *prime costs*. Direct labour and manufacturing overhead are considered *conversion costs*.

Classification of Inventories

A merchandising company has one class of inventory, commonly called **merchandise,** or **merchandise inventory.** A manufacturing company, however, may have the following four categories of inventory:

---

[1]"Inventories," CICA *Handbook*, Paragraph 3030.02, September 1973.

1. **Raw materials.** Goods that can be traced directly to units of the firm's product. An example is the desk manufacturer's inventory of wood.
2. **Factory supplies.** Goods that can be traced only indirectly to units of the firm's product. An example is the desk manufacturer's supply of glue. Generally, it is not practical to trace glue to specific desks. The cost of factory supplies used is an element of overhead that is commonly called **indirect materials.**
3. **Work (goods) in process.** Goods that are partially completed. Goods in process have been assigned appropriate manufacturing costs and will remain in production until completed. It is impossible for a manufacturing operation to complete by the end of the period all of the units started during the period. The value assigned to these goods is based on the percentage completed as at the balance sheet date.
4. **Finished goods.** Products that are completed and ready for sale. Finished goods have been assigned their full share of manufacturing costs.

Flow of Inventory Costs

Asset/Liability Measurement

Matching

Exhibit 9.1 compares the typical flow of inventory costs in a merchandising company with that in a manufacturing company. Note that inventory costs are initially accounted for as assets. In other words, a company's inventory is first measured at its historical cost. To implement the matching principle, the costs are expensed in the period in which the inventory is sold. In this way the revenue generated by the sale of inventory can be related to the costs incurred to purchase or produce it.

A merchandising company and a manufacturing company calculate cost of goods sold in somewhat different ways. In the comparison shown in Exhibit 9.2, we assume a periodic inventory system.

Note in Exhibit 9.2 that a merchandising company adds the cost of its net purchases to the cost of its beginning inventory to derive the cost of goods available for sale. Because a manufacturing company produces (rather than purchases) its finished goods inventory, it adds the cost of goods manufactured to its beginning inventory. We discussed the calculation of net purchases in Chapter 6. The computation of the cost of goods manufactured by Parker Company is shown in Exhibit 9.3 (dollar amounts assumed). The schedule of cost of goods manufactured is generally used for internal purposes and is seldom published.

Observe in Exhibit 9.3 that to calculate cost of goods manufactured, we add the total manufacturing costs incurred during the period to the beginning work-in-process inventory. The total ($257 000) tells us the amount of manufacturing costs that we must account for during the period. From this total, we subtract the cost of the ending work-in-process inventory (the partially completed goods on hand at the end of the period) to derive the cost of goods manufactured during the period ($242 000). As noted in Exhibit 9.2, the cost of goods manufactured is included in the calculation of a manufacturing company's cost of goods sold.

As our discussion suggests, a manufacturing company accounts for inventories somewhat differently from a merchandising company. For example, many manufacturing companies use **direct costing** (also called **variable costing**) for internal reporting purposes, because this method enables managers to better plan and control their company's operations. Under direct costing, the accountant classifies all manufacturing costs as either variable or fixed. Variable manufacturing costs are those that vary in total in direct proportion to changes in production volume. They include direct materials, direct labour, and variable overhead. Fixed manufacturing costs, in contrast, are those that remain

Exhibit 9.1 Flow of Inventory Costs

	Time	Asset	Time of Sale	Expense
Merchandising Company		Merchandise Inventory $\longrightarrow$	|	Cost of Goods Sold
			|	
Manufacturing Company	Direct Materials Used $\longrightarrow$ Direct Labour Manufacturing Overhead	Work-in-Process Inventory $\longrightarrow$ Finished Goods Inventory $\longrightarrow$	|	Cost of Goods Sold
			|	

Exhibit 9.2 Calculation of Cost of Goods Sold

Merchandising Company	Manufacturing Company
Beginning Merchandise Inventory	Beginning Finished Goods Inventory
+ Net Purchases	+ Cost of Goods Manufactured
= Cost of Goods Available for Sale	= Cost of Goods Available for Sale
− Ending Merchandise Inventory	− Ending Finished Goods Inventory
= Cost of Goods Sold	= Cost of Goods Sold

Exhibit 9.3

Parker Company
SCHEDULE OF COST OF GOODS MANUFACTURED
For the year Ended December 31

Direct materials used		
Raw materials inventory, Jan. 1	$ 23 000	
Add: Net purchases of raw materials	157 000	
Cost of raw materials available for use	180 000	
Less: Raw materials inventory, Dec. 31	25 000	$155 000
Direct labour		47 000
Manufacturing overhead		
Indirect labour	12 000	
Indirect materials	3 000	
Factory utilities	5 000	
Depreciation of factory building	3 500	
Depreciation of factory equipment	6 000	
Taxes on factory properties	7 000	
Miscellaneous factory expenses	1 500	38 000
Total manufacturing costs incurred during the year		240 000
Add: Work-in-process inventory, Jan. 1		17 000
Total manufacturing costs to account for		257 000
Less: Work-in-process inventory, Dec. 31		15 000
Cost of goods manufactured		$242 000

constant in total as production volume changes over a relevant range of production. Fixed manufacturing costs are confined to such overhead costs as property taxes and depreciation. Under the direct costing method, the accountant records as inventory costs only the variable manufacturing costs. Fixed overhead costs are expensed in the period in which they are incurred, because it is assumed that a company incurs these costs primarily to allow production to occur.

Direct costing contrasts with **absorption costing**, in which fixed overhead costs are treated as a part of the cost of inventory. Proponents of absorption costing point out that because both variable and fixed overhead costs are normally necessary to produce specific goods, both costs should be inventoried. Generally accepted accounting principles require the use of absorption costing for external reporting purposes, because most accountants view fixed overhead as an important component of the historical cost of inventory that is manufactured. Paragraph 3030.06 of the CICA *Handbook* recommends that the *applicable share of overhead expense be applied* to the cost of goods manufactured. The share of overhead includes the variable costs and a portion of the fixed costs.

Many manufacturing companies use standard costs to account for their inventories. Primarily a management tool, **standard costing** requires a company to accumulate inventory costs using amounts that *should be* incurred to manufacture the inventory, rather than actual costs. Standard costing allows a company to detect variances between what it should cost to produce a product and what it actually costs. Standard costs are acceptable for external reporting under GAAP, however, if they reasonably approximate actual costs determined using a recognized cost flow method. Peculiarities in accounting for inventories of manufacturing companies, such as direct costing and standard costing, are covered more extensively in managerial or cost accounting courses.

Nature of the Inventory Valuation Problem

Inventory accounting problems would be relatively simple if a company instantaneously sold all the inventory that it purchased or produced. In most cases, however, there is a lag between the time at which goods are purchased or produced and the time at which they are sold. As a result, most companies have an inventory of unsold goods on hand at the end of the accounting period, and accountants must then resolve the question of how to allocate the cost of goods available for sale between (1) the goods on hand (ending inventory) and (2) the goods sold.

The accountant may determine cost of goods sold **residually**, that is, by subtracting the cost of the ending inventory from the cost of goods available for sale. To do this, the accountant must value the ending inventory directly, which means resolving the following important questions:

1.   What is the physical quantity of goods on hand?
2.   What is the accounting valuation of those goods?

Determination of Inventory Quantities

The method for determining the physical quantity of goods on hand differs depending on whether a company uses a periodic or a perpetual inventory system. Regardless of the system used, the accountant must understand the general principles to determine which goods properly belong in inventory and which goods do not.

Periodic Versus Perpetual Inventory System

Under a **periodic inventory system**, inventory quantities are *not* maintained on a day-to-day basis in the accounting records. Instead, at the end of each accounting period, the quantity of unsold goods is determined by a physical count. The accountant then determines the inventory's cost by using one of the generally accepted inventory cost flow methods discussed later in this chapter. The inventory cost thus derived is subtracted from the cost of goods available for sale to determine the cost of goods sold. In a periodic system, therefore, cost of goods sold is a residual figure that includes the cost of goods actually sold as well as the cost of those lost by theft, spoilage, and similar causes. Although a periodic system is not ideal for inventory planning and control, it is relatively inexpensive and is often appropriate for products that turn over rapidly and have low unit costs, such as groceries and hardware.

In contrast, a **perpetual inventory system** requires the accountant to maintain continuous records of the quantity of inventory on hand. Under a perpetual system, an account may be established for each product; these accounts are kept in an **inventory subsidiary ledger**. The account for each product shows increases and decreases, as well as the balance on hand. In a complete perpetual system, the subsidiary ledger accounts are maintained in cost dollars as well as in units. Consequently, the balance in the merchandise inventory control account in the general ledger should agree with the total of the individual account balances in the subsidiary ledger.

In a perpetual system, it is still desirable to physically count the inventory at least once each year, but the count need not occur at year-end. This count tests the accuracy of the perpetual records. An actual count frequently reveals differences between the records and the physical units on hand. These differences may exist for several reasons, including theft, breakage, and inaccurate recording or counting. Whenever a careful count indicates differences, the accounting records should be verified and appropriately adjusted. If, for example, the accounting records show inventory on hand costing $10 000 but the physical count indicates only $9885, the following entry is necessary:

Inventory Shortage	115	
Merchandise Inventory		115
(*To record inventory shortage:* $10 000 − $9885 = $115.)		

Materiality

Inventory Shortage is a loss account that, if material in amount, should be reported separately in the income statement. Many companies simply report inventory shortages as part of cost of goods sold. This practice is justified on the grounds that some shortages may be considered a normal cost in the selling process. However, when inventory shortages are included in cost of goods sold, the gross margin ratio becomes distorted.

Although the perpetual system is more costly than the periodic system to implement, it facilitates better inventory planning and control. In the past, perpetual records were used primarily for low-volume, high-cost items, such as jewellery, fur coats, and automobiles. In recent years, however, the widespread use of computers has enabled companies to maintain perpetual records for a greater variety of inventory items. With computers, companies can conveniently store and retrieve large amounts of data in a cost-effective manner. Many companies account for part of their inventories on a periodic basis and the remainder on a perpetual basis.

In a periodic inventory system, merchandise purchases are debited to the Purchases account. Throughout the accounting period, therefore, the Merchandise Inventory account contains only the balance that was on hand at the beginning of the period. At the end of the period, the accountant makes an adjusting entry to record the ending inventory as well as the cost of goods sold for the entire period, as discussed in Chapter 6. In contrast, under a perpetual system, the Merchandise Inventory and Cost of Goods Sold accounts are continually maintained. Merchandise purchases are therefore charged directly to an Inventory account. Moreover, an entry to record a sale is accompanied by an entry that reduces the Inventory account and recognizes an increase in Cost of Goods Sold. At the end of the accounting period, an adjusting entry is not required, because the Inventory account reflects the balance on hand and the Cost of Goods Sold account reflects the expense incurred during the entire period. The proper accounting for selected merchandise transactions under periodic and perpetual inventory systems is shown in Exhibit 9.4.

Goods to Include in Inventory

The general rule for determining what items to include in inventory is that goods belong to the entity that has legal title, regardless of where the goods are located. Consequently, when title to goods passes from seller to buyer, the seller should record a sale and exclude the goods from inventory. The buyer in turn should record a purchase and include the goods in inventory.

Title to goods may pass at any time expressly agreed to by buyer and seller. When the time of title passage is not expressly agreed upon, the buyer takes title when goods exist and are identified to the contract, and the seller has completed performance in regard to delivering the goods. If goods are shipped **FOB (free on board) shipping point**, title passes to the buyer when the seller delivers the goods to the carrier. The seller transfers ownership for the goods to the buyer as soon as the goods leave the seller's premises. The seller's premises would be the truck if the goods are delivered by the seller, or a common carrier if the goods are shipped by a common carrier. Title to goods shipped **FOB destination** passes when the goods arrive at their ultimate destination. The seller retains ownership of the goods until the goods arrive at the agreed-upon destination. The buyer records the purchase when the goods arrive at the agreed-upon destination. If the buyer agrees to pick up the goods at the seller's place of business, title passes when the seller has completed the goods and identified them to the contract.

Application of the legal title rule may pose problems when a company owns goods that are located elsewhere or when it holds goods that belong to someone else. We discuss these problems in the following sections.

Goods in Transit

Materiality

During an accounting period, the accountant normally records purchases when goods are received and sales when goods are shipped, regardless of the precise moment at which title passes. This procedure is expedient, and because title usually passes in the same period, no material misstatements occur in the financial statements.

On the other hand, the accountant should carefully analyze the invoice terms of goods that are in transit at the end of an accounting period to determine who has legal title. The analysis should encompass goods purchased as well as goods sold. Goods shipped FOB shipping point belong to the buyer; those shipped FOB destination belong to the seller. When analyzing goods in transit, the accountant should examine invoices for several days before and after the end of the accounting period in order to ensure a

Exhibit 9.4   Accounting under Periodic and Perpetual Inventory Systems

Transaction	Periodic Inventory System		Perpetual Inventory System	

Purchase merchandise costing $4000 on account	Purchases 4000
	    Accounts Payable 4000
			Merchandise Inventory 4000
			    Accounts Payable 4000	

Pay freight of $45 on purchase	Transportation-in 45
	    Cash 45
			Merchandise Inventory 45
			    Cash 45	

Return defective merchandise costing $250	Accounts Payable 250
	    Purchase Returns 250
			Accounts Payable 250
			    Merchandise Inventory 250	

Sell goods costing $3000 on account for $6000	Accounts Receivable 6000
	    Sales 6000
			Accounts Receivable 6000
			    Sales 6000
			 Cost of Goods Sold 3000
			    Merchandise Inventory 3000	

proper cutoff at year-end. The journal entries for these situations are shown in Exhibit 9.5.

Consigned Goods

A **consignment** is a method of marketing goods in which the owner (the **consignor**) transfers physical possession of certain goods to an agent (the **consignee**) who sells the goods on the owner's behalf. Goods on consignment should be included in the consignor's inventory and excluded from the consignee's inventory. The consignor becomes liable for the cost of the goods when the goods are sold to a third party. Similarly, goods in the hands of others for sale, storage, processing, or other reasons should be included in the inventory of the party holding title. Accounting for consignments is covered in advanced accounting courses.

Determination of Inventory Valuation at Cost

Asset/Liability Measurement

In accordance with the asset/liability measurement principle, the quantity of inventory on hand should be valued initially at its historical cost. Two questions must be answered when determining an inventory cost valuation:

1. What costs should be included in inventory?
2. What method should be used to associate inventory costs with the physical units on hand?

Costs to Include in Inventory

An accountant must differentiate between product costs and period costs. **Product costs** "attach to" the inventory. These costs are initially capitalized and are regarded as assets (i.e., inventory). When the inventory is later sold, the product costs expire and are therefore charged to expense (cost of goods sold). In contrast, **period costs** are expensed in the period in which they are incurred. In other words, period costs are not inventoried, because their relationship to the product (inventory) is generally considered too difficult

Exhibit 9.5 Accounting Records of the Buyer (Goods in Transit)

Transaction	FOB Shipping Point		FOB Destination	
Dec. 28, 1994				
Goods costing $40 000 were shipped by the seller to the buyer	Purchases* Accounts Payable	40 000 40 000		
Dec. 31, 1994				
Year-end inventory	List as inventory in transit		Not shown in inventory	
Jan. 6, 1995				
Goods arrive at the destination			Purchases* Accounts Payable	40 000 40 000

*Assuming a periodic inventory system.

to trace. Selling expenses, general and administrative expenses, and income tax expense are examples of period costs.

Product costs are the "laid down" costs incurred, either directly or indirectly, to purchase or produce inventory as well as to bring the inventory to a condition and location for sale. These costs include direct materials, direct labour, and overhead. They also include the invoice cost of purchased merchandise as well as the costs of inbound transportation, insurance, inspection, handling, warehousing, and purchasing.[2]

The specific content of product costs varies somewhat between companies. Many companies use only the invoice cost plus the cost of inbound transportation to value inventories of purchased goods. Other costs that should in theory be inventoried (such as insurance, handling, and purchasing costs) are treated as period costs. This treatment is justified on the ground that it is often impossible to meaningfully allocate certain indirect costs to inventory. The treatment is considered acceptable if a company applies it *consistently* over time to either a certain portion or to all of its inventories. Inventory costs capitalized for financial reporting purposes may differ from those capitalized for income tax purposes.[3]

Consistency

Generally accepted accounting principles do not permit a company to capitalize the interest cost associated with inventories that are routinely manufactured or otherwise produced in large quantities on a repetitive basis. However, interest cost should be capitalized if it is a material part of the cost of acquiring inventory items that are constructed as discrete projects, such as ships.[4] For these items, interest cost represents an important component of historical cost. Companies should also capitalize interest as part of the historical cost of acquiring certain capital assets. We explain interest capitalization more fully in Chapter 12.

Materiality

Invoice Cost

The invoice cost itself is the largest component of product cost for purchased inventory. To determine the invoice cost, **trade discounts** and GST are subtracted from the list price and invoice total, respectively. The trade discounts are not entered in the accounting

---

[2]"Inventories," CICA *Handbook,* Paragraph 3030.02, September 1973.

[3]"Inventories," CICA *Handbook,* Paragraph 3030.01, September 1973.

[4]"Interest Capitalized—Disclosure Considerations," CICA *Handbook,* Section 3850, August 1987.

records, and GST paid on purchases is deducted from the GST collected on sales to reduce the GST payment.[5] Theory and practice usually differ on whether the invoice cost component of product cost should also exclude **cash discounts**.[6]

In theory, the cost of purchases (and of inventory) should be measured net of cash discounts allowable. This is known as the **net method** of recording purchases; it is compared with the **gross method** in Exhibit 9.6. The cost measured under the net method represents the cash-equivalent price on the date of purchase and therefore the correct historical cost. Cash discounts encourage early payment; any discount not taken represents the cost of engaging in a deferred payment transaction. Accordingly, this cost should be shown as a financing expense on the income statement.

In practice, most companies record purchases (and inventory) at gross invoice amounts. Cash discounts taken are recorded in a Purchase Discounts account at the time of payment, and this balance is deducted from purchases when measuring cost of goods sold.[7] This procedure is theoretically deficient in two major respects. First, it technically

Matching

violates the matching principle, because discounts are recorded only when cash is paid rather than when the purchases that give rise to the discounts are made. Second, the procedure does not allocate discounts taken between goods sold and those on hand. This tends to understate cost of goods sold and overstate net income and ending inventory.

Consistency

Despite its theoretical shortcomings, the gross method is supported on the practical grounds that (1) it is more convenient than the net method from a bookkeeping stand-

Materiality

point, and (2) if applied consistently over time, it usually produces no material errors in the financial statements.

Transportation Costs

If practical, the costs of inbound transportation should be allocated to specific units of inventory purchased. This procedure, which is facilitated by the use of a perpetual inventory system, permits transportation charges to be appropriately reflected in cost of goods sold as well as in ending inventory. Transportation costs are inventoried because they are an important part of the cost of acquiring goods. In the purchase of coal, for example, rail transportation costs constitute a substantial portion of inventory costs.

In a periodic inventory system, inbound transportation charges are usually accumulated in a nominal account entitled Transportation-in or Freight-in. Theoretically, the balance in this account at the end of an accounting period should be allocated in a reasonable manner between cost of goods sold and ending inventory. Instead of imple-

Conservatism

menting this approach, firms often use the more expedient alternative of including all transportation-in costs in the calculation of net purchases. Although the expedient

Materiality

approach tends to overstate cost of goods sold and understate net income and ending inventory, it is often supported on the grounds of conservatism, materiality, and consis-

Consistency

tency of application.

---

[5]A **trade discount** is a reduction from a catalogue list price granted by manufacturers and wholesalers of certain products. The use of trade discounts enables a company (1) to revise its prices periodically without having to reprint its catalogues, and (2) to set different prices for different types of customers. See Chapter 8 for a detailed explanation of the application of trade discounts.

[6]A **cash discount** is a reduction from the amount of an invoice that is offered for early payment of cash, usually expressed in terms such as "2/10, n/30." As we explained in Chapter 8, the effective annual interest cost associated with not paying within ten days is 36.7 percent. It is usually advantageous for a company to take all available cash discounts, even if the company must borrow money to do so.

[7]Some companies treat purchase discounts as financial revenue similar to interest. This treatment lacks theoretical support. A purchaser of goods who pays for them within the discount period has not thereby made a loan to the seller. Because no loan has been made, no financial revenue has been realized.

Exhibit 9.6 Net and Gross Methods of Recording Purchases

Transaction	Net Method		Gross Method	
July 1				
ABC Company purchases merchandise for $100, terms 2/10, n/30.	Purchases* Accounts Payable	98 98	Purchases* Accounts Payable	100 100
Alternative Assumption No. 1				
July 10				
ABC Company pays within the discount period.	Accounts Payable Cash	98 98	Accounts Payable Purchase Discounts Cash	100 2 98
Alternative Assumption No. 2				
July 30				
ABC Company pays after the discount period.	Accounts Payable Discounts Lost (or Interest Expense) Cash	98 2 100	Accounts Payable Cash	100 100

*Assuming a periodic inventory system.

Inventory Cost Flow Methods

Inventory costs flow into a business and are treated as assets when goods are purchased or manufactured; they flow out and are charged to expense when goods are sold. The difference between the cost inflows and the cost outflows represents the cost of the inventory on hand.

If inventory unit cost prices remained constant over time, the process of inventory cost determination would be relatively simple. That is, it would simply involve multiplying the quantity of each inventory item on hand by its constant unit cost and summing the results. In reality, of course, unit costs usually fluctuate. With inflation, they tend to rise over time. The reality of fluctuating unit costs underscores the critical importance of the various inventory cost flow methods. When reflecting on these methods, keep the following points in mind:

Asset/Liability Measurement

1. Each method leads to a determination of inventory and cost of goods sold based on historical cost.
2. A company can use one method to account for a certain portion of its inventories (such as raw materials) and other methods to account for different portions (such as finished goods).

Consistency Disclosure

3. The method(s) adopted should be used consistently over time and should be disclosed in the financial statements.

Specific Identification Method

The **specific identification method** requires a company to maintain detailed records that permit the accountant to identify individually the actual unit costs of (1) inventory items on hand and (2) inventory items sold. Each item of inventory is identified (e.g., a code on a sales tag) with its actual unit cost. When an item is sold, the difference between its selling price and its actual cost represents the gross margin.

At first glance, this method seems appealing. For one thing, the flow of inventory costs corresponds with the physical flow of goods. In addition, the method may be used with either a periodic or a perpetual inventory system.

Despite its appeal, the specific identification method has theoretical and practical shortcomings. On the theoretical side, the method is often criticized because it may permit management to manipulate income. Suppose, for example, that a company offers two identical gold watches for $500 each. Due to recent fluctuations in gold prices, one watch cost $250 and the other $350. Management can earn a gross profit of either $250 or $150 from the sale of one watch simply by choosing which watch to sell. The introduction of scanners and electronic point-of-sale devices has eliminated the detailed record-keeping requirements of the specific identification method to inventories that consist of relatively expensive, slow-moving items, such as automobiles, farm equipment, art objects, fur coats, jewellery, and long-term construction projects.

Cost Flow Methods Based on Assumptions

Because it is rarely feasible to specifically identify inventory unit costs, most companies make an **assumption** about the way inventory costs flow through the business. The major cost flow assumptions available under GAAP and the method of implementing each are as follows:

Cost Flow Assumption	**Cost Flow Method**
1. Cost flow is in the same order in which costs were incurred.	1. First-in, first-out (FIFO).
2. Cost flow is an average of the costs incurred.	2. Average cost.
3. Cost flow is in the reverse order in which costs were incurred.	3. Last-in, first-out (LIFO).

A survey of the 1990 annual reports of 300 companies found that 271 companies reported inventories. Some companies used more than one method of cost determination, and the use of FIFO, average cost, and LIFO was reported by 121, 95, and 6 companies, respectively. Only one of the companies using LIFO used it for all of its inventory.[8]

In reflecting on the FIFO, average cost, and LIFO methods, bear in mind that each method reflects an **assumed cost flow pattern**. Any method may be used **regardless of the way in which goods physically flow through the business**. For example, goods may (and usually do) physically flow in the FIFO manner, yet LIFO may be used as the cost flow method.

Masse Limited is a merchandising concern that, for accounting purposes, identifies its inventory items using a combination of numbers and letters. The following inventory data for the company's Product 19-C for the current year will be used to illustrate the application of the FIFO, average cost, and LIFO methods.

Date	Product 19-C	Number of Units	Unit Cost	Total Cost
Jan. 1	Inventory on hand	300	$5	$ 1 500
Mar. 21	Purchase	900	6	5 400
Aug. 19	Purchase	600	7	4 200
Nov. 3	Purchase	200	8	1 600
	Available for sale	2 000		$12 700

[8]"Inventories," *Financial Reporting in Canada*, 19th ed. (Toronto: CICA, 1991), pp. 77–78.

We will assume that 800 units of Product 19-C were sold on May 27 and another 800 units were sold on October 9. A physical count on December 31 indicates that 400 units of Product 19-C are on hand.

First-In, First-Out (FIFO) Method.   The FIFO method is based on the assumption that inventory costs should be matched with sales revenue in the same order in which the costs were incurred. The most recent costs incurred are therefore used in determining the cost of inventory on hand. Assuming a periodic system, the cost of the 400 units of Product 19-C on hand is determined as follows:

Most recent costs (Nov. 3 purchase)	200 units × $8	$1600
Next most recent costs (Aug. 19 purchase)	200 units × $7	$1400
Inventory, Dec. 31	400	$3000

Recall that cost of goods sold is a residual figure determined by subtracting the cost of the ending inventory from the cost of goods available for sale. For Product 19-C, cost of goods sold under FIFO is $9700 ($12 700 − $3000). Note that under the FIFO method, cost of goods sold consists of the earliest costs incurred [(300 units × $5) + (900 units × $6) + (400 units × $7) = $9700].

The FIFO method produces the same cost figures regardless of whether a company uses a periodic or a perpetual system. For example, if Masse Limited maintained perpetual records for Product 19-C, the company would use a form similar to the one shown in Exhibit 9.7. Observe in the exhibit that the cost of goods sold and the ending inventory are still $9700 and $3000, respectively.

The FIFO method has been supported on the grounds that its assumed cost flow pattern corresponds closely to the physical flow of goods in most businesses. Therefore, when goods physically move in the first-in, first-out manner, the FIFO method approximates specific identification. Unlike specific identification, however, FIFO gives management little opportunity to manipulate income.

In terms of financial statement impact, the use of FIFO produces an ending inventory cost based on the most recent acquisition prices. This cost frequently approximates current replacement cost, another fact often cited in support of FIFO. On the other hand, because the balance sheet and income statement articulate with one another, the use of FIFO produces a cost of goods sold figure that is based on the earliest costs incurred. These costs often depart considerably from current replacement costs. The value of the balance sheet inventory under FIFO is comprised of prices from the most recent purchases. The failure of FIFO to match current costs with current revenues on the income statement is perhaps the most frequently cited shortcoming of this method.

Average Cost Method.   The average cost method is based on the assumption that a weighted average of all inventory costs should be used to measure inventory cost flow. This average is computed by dividing the total cost of goods available for sale by the total number of units available for sale. Assuming a periodic system, the cost of the 400 units of Product 19-C on hand is determined as follows:

Weighted average unit cost	$12 700 ÷ 2000 = $6.35
Inventory, Dec. 31	400 units × $6.35 = $2540

Cost of goods sold is therefore $10 160 ($12 700 − $2540). We can verify this by multiplying the 1600 units sold by $6.35 (1600 × $6.35 = $10 160). Note that a *weighted average*, rather than a *simple average*, unit cost figure should be used. A weighted average

Exhibit 9.7 Perpetual Inventory: FIFO Method

| | Purchased | | | Sold | | | Balance | | |
Date	Number of Units	Unit Cost	Total Cost	Number of Units	Unit Cost	Total Cost	Number of Units	Unit Cost	Total Cost
Jan. 1							300	$5	$1500
Mar. 21	900	$6	$5400				300	5	1500
							900	6	5400
May 27				300	$5	$1500			
				500	6	3000	400	6	2400
Aug. 19	600	7	4200				400	6	2400
							600	7	4200
Oct. 9				400	6	2400			
				400	7	2800	200	7	1400
							200	7	1400 ⎫ Ending
Nov. 3	200	8	1600				200	8	1600 ⎬ inventory
				Cost of goods sold $9700					= $3000

reflects the number of units acquired at each price; a simple average [($5 + $6 + $7 + $8) ÷ 4 = $6.50] does not.

When used with a perpetual inventory system, the average cost method is called the **moving average method**. Under this method, a new weighted average unit cost must be **computed after every purchase**; the average is therefore said to "move." The moving average method for Product 19-C is illustrated in Exhibit 9.8.

Observe carefully that a new weighted average unit cost is computed after each purchase. This is done by dividing the total cost of goods available for sale (immediately after the purchase) by the total number of units available for sale (immediately after the purchase). For example, the weighted average unit cost after the first purchase (March 21) is computed as follows:

Jan. 1	Inventory	300 units × $5	$1500
Mar. 21	Purchase	900 units × $6	5400
	Available for sale immediately after Mar. 21 purchase	1200 units	$6900

Weighted average unit cost = $6900 ÷ 1200 = $5.75

The same procedure is used to determine the weighted average unit cost after the August 19 and November 3 purchases.

Under the average cost method, the cost of the ending inventory usually differs depending on whether a company uses a periodic or a perpetual inventory system. It follows that when ending inventories differ, cost of goods sold figures also differ. These differences are shown below for Product 19-C.

Exhibit 9.8   Perpetual Inventory: Moving Average Method

	Purchased			Sold			Balance			
Date	Number of Units	Unit Cost	Total Cost	Number of Units	Unit Cost	Total Cost	Number of Units	Unit Cost	Total Cost	
Jan. 1							300	$5.00	$1500	
Mar. 21	900	$6	$5400				1200	5.75*	6900	
May 27				800	$5.75	$4600	400	5.75	2300	
Aug. 19	600	7	4200				1000	6.50*	6500	
Oct. 9				800	6.50	5200	200	6.50	1300	
Nov. 3	200	8	1600				400	7.25*	2900	} Ending inventory = $2900
				Cost of goods sold $9800						

*Weighted average unit cost is computed after each purchase.

Average Cost Method	Ending Inventory	+	Cost of Goods Sold	=	Cost of Goods Available for Sale
Periodic system	$2 540		$10 160		$12 700
Perpetual system	2 900		9 800		12 700

The average cost method is supported on the basis that it generally produces figures for both ending inventory and cost of goods sold that lie between those produced under the FIFO and LIFO methods. The method is essentially a compromise solution to the complex question of how we should assume that inventory costs flow through a business. Furthermore, the method is relatively easy to apply, and it affords management little opportunity to manipulate income.

On the other hand, the weighted average method is not as accurate as FIFO in approximating the current cost of the ending inventory, nor is it as accurate as LIFO in approximating the current cost of goods sold. Furthermore, average cost corresponds with the physical flow of goods only when goods available for sale are sold in essentially a random pattern, which may occur with inventories of liquid products such as chemicals and petroleum.

Last-In, First-Out (LIFO) Method.[9]   The LIFO method assumes that inventory costs should be matched with sales revenue in the reverse order in which the costs were incurred (the opposite of FIFO).[10] Inventory is therefore valued at the earliest costs incurred. Referring to Masse Limited and assuming a periodic system, we determine the LIFO cost of the ending inventory of 400 units of Product 19-C as follows:

Earliest costs (Jan. 1 inventory)	300 units × $5	$1500
Next earliest costs (Mar. 21 purchase)	100 units × $6	$ 600
Inventory, Dec. 31	400	$2100

[9]The LIFO coverage in this text will be reduced because LIFO is used by few Canadian companies, and this method of inventory valuation cannot be used for income tax in Canada.

[10]LIFO is an outgrowth of the **base stock method,** which some companies in the United States used early in the twentieth century. Because the base stock method is not acceptable for income tax purposes and is not considered an important method for financial reporting purposes, it is not covered in this textbook.

Observe that the ending inventory of 400 units is divided into two layers (300 units × $5 and 100 units × $6). Cost of goods sold is $10 600 ($12 700 − $2100) and consists of the most recent costs incurred [(200 units × $8) + (600 units × $7) + (800 units × $6) = $10 600].

The application of LIFO using a perpetual system for Product 19-C is shown in Exhibit 9.9. Under the perpetual system, units sold are costed at the time of sale. Because LIFO is therefore applied currently throughout the period rather than only at the period's end, LIFO results usually differ between a periodic and a perpetual system. These differences are shown below for Product 19-C.

LIFO Method	Ending Inventory	+	Cost of Goods Sold	=	Cost of Goods Available for Sale
Periodic system	$2 100		$10 600		$12 700
Perpetual system	2 600		10 100		12 700

Observe that for Product 19-C, cost of goods sold is higher under the periodic than under the perpetual system. This is because of the timing of the purchases and sales and because the unit cost prices of Product 19-C rose steadily during the current year. In our example, the cost of goods sold differences relate to the sale on October 9. Under the perpetual system, the October 9 sale was costed using the most recent cost prices at that time [(600 units × $7) + (100 units × $6) + (100 units × $5) = $5300]. Under the periodic system, the October 9 sale was costed using the most recent cost prices as of the end of the year [(200 units × $8) + (600 units × $7) = $5800]. In the United States, many companies that experience rising inventory costs use LIFO for tax purposes, because it tends to produce a higher cost of goods sold and therefore less income taxes. American tax law states that companies using LIFO for tax purposes must also use it for financial reporting purposes. Consequently, a company that uses LIFO with a perpetual system often restates its cost of goods sold and inventory at year-end to conform with the results that would have occurred under a periodic system. This restatement is done for income tax and external financial reporting purposes. In Canada, the LIFO method of cost determination cannot be used for tax purposes.

Applying LIFO to each of a company's products, as we have done for Masse Limited's Product 19-C, is called the **specific goods method** of applying LIFO. This method requires that LIFO be applied to *each product* in a company's inventory.

Major Arguments for LIFO.   LIFO is perhaps the most controversial inventory cost flow method. Nevertheless, certain theoretical and economic arguments support its use. From a theoretical standpoint, the use of LIFO is often said to produce a better matching of cost of goods sold expense (measured using recent cost prices) with sales revenue (measured using recent selling prices). As a result, it is often claimed that LIFO produces a better measure of net income than either FIFO or average cost. When inventory costs are rising, net income normally includes a component called **inventory profits.** These profits equal the difference between the current replacement cost of sales and the cost of sales determined using a generally accepted cost flow method. Inventory profits are illusory, however, because they generally must be used to replace depleted inventories at higher costs. The LIFO method greatly reduces inventory profits, thereby causing net income to more accurately reflect an amount that can be distributed to shareholders and still enable the company to replace its inventories. Many financial analysts consider the use of LIFO as a favourable factor when they evaluate the **quality of a company's earn-**

Matching

Exhibit 9.9   Perpetual Inventory: LIFO Method

Date	Purchased Number of Units	Unit Cost	Total Cost	Sold Number of Units	Unit Cost	Total Cost	Balance Number of Units	Unit Cost	Total Cost	
Jan. 1							300	$5	$1500	
Mar. 21	900	$6	$5400				300	5	1500	
							900	6	5400	
May 27				800	$6	$4800	300	5	1500	
							100	6	600	
Aug. 19	600	7	4200				300	5	1500	
							100	6	600	
							600	7	4200	
Oct. 9				600	7	4200				
				100	6	600				
				100	5	500	200	5	1000	
Nov. 3	200	8	1600				200	5	1000	} Ending
							200	8	1600	} inventory
				Cost of goods sold $10 100						= $2600

ings. During periods of rising prices, LIFO tends to produce net income and inventory measurements that reflect conservatism.[11]

LIFO is often supported on the economic grounds that, during periods of rising prices, its use tends to lower taxable income and thereby postpone income tax payments until the time, if ever, that inventory unit costs or physical quantities decline. U.S. federal income tax law permits a company to compute taxable income using LIFO only if the company also uses LIFO for financial reporting. This is known as the **LIFO conformity requirement,** and as the name implies, this requirement pertains only to LIFO. With the major exception of LIFO, a company does not have to use the same methods for financial reporting purposes as it uses for income tax purposes, or vice versa.

The LIFO conformity requirement has deterred some companies from adopting LIFO. Nevertheless, occasionally high inflation rates have made LIFO one of the most popular accounting methods in past years. One author has estimated that the use of LIFO has permitted General Electric Company to save approximately $1 billion of income taxes during a 25-year period ending in 1979.[12] Such tax savings enhance a company's availability of cash. This increased cash flow is in effect an interest-free loan of indefinite and perhaps permanent duration. It reduces borrowing requirements and thereby tends to lower interest costs, which in turn contributes even further toward improving a company's cash flow.

Major Arguments Against LIFO.   Despite the theoretical and economic advantages of LIFO, the method has been attacked for several reasons. The major arguments against LIFO are summarized below.

---

[11]Not all companies have experienced a trend of rising inventory costs over time. Some companies in the electronics industry, for example, have experienced declining costs. For these companies, using FIFO is considered more conservative than using LIFO.

[12]S. Thomas Moser, "LIFO: Inflation Lifeline," *Management Focus* (March–April 1981), p. 24.

1. LIFO inventories are often valued using outdated cost prices. Some say that LIFO-valued inventories are unrealistic because they fail to reflect current costs. When inventory valuations are unrealistic, related measurements, such as working capital, the current ratio, and inventory turnover, are also distorted.

2. The LIFO cost flow assumption is usually opposite to the physical flow of goods. Only a few types of inventories, such as coal or gravel, physically flow in a LIFO manner.

3. When a liquidation of LIFO inventory layers occurs, outdated costs tend to be matched with sales revenue, thereby reducing the matching benefits that LIFO generally produces. Matching outdated costs with current revenues is said to produce an unrealistic measure of net income. Frequently, the liquidation of LIFO layers is involuntary, as when a strike disrupts production or a supplier fails to deliver goods on a timely basis at the end of an accounting period. A LIFO liquidation can sometimes have a material impact on a company's financial statements. For example, in 1980, Bethlehem Steel Corporation had a LIFO liquidation that increased the company's income by 77 percent. In the same year, a LIFO liquidation by the Firestone Tire and Rubber Company increased the company's income by 65 percent.[13]

4. The use of LIFO permits income manipulation, such as by making end-of-period purchases designed to preserve existing inventory layers. At times, these purchases may not even be in the best economic interests of the company.

5. The variations in methods of applying LIFO as well as the fact that most LIFO users have adopted it at different times tend to distort intercompany comparisons, even those made between two LIFO companies in the same industry.

6. During periods of rising inventory costs, the use of LIFO for tax purposes in the United States, coupled with the conformity requirement, creates a paradox. That is, it postpones taxes and thereby makes the firm better off economically, yet it lowers reported net income and thereby makes the firm appear *worse* than it would under FIFO or average cost. Many managers are reluctant to adopt LIFO out of fear that the reduced reported earnings will cause investors to penalize the market price of their company's shares. Although the empirical studies in this area have not produced consistent results, research suggests that this fear may be unjustified, because changes to LIFO do not appear to result in unfavourable market reactions.[14] A retired chairman of General Electric Company has speculated that some managers may not want to use LIFO because "most top executive contracts are tied to reported earnings."[15]

Materiality

Comparison of Results Between FIFO, Average Cost, and LIFO.   Exhibit 9.10 summarizes the financial statement impact of the FIFO, average cost, and LIFO methods of accounting for Product 19-C of Masse Limited for the current year. We do not show the results under the specific identification method, because they depend on which units were sold and which are on hand.

As Exhibit 9.10 suggests, certain key financial statement variables for Masse Limited differ depending on which cost flow method the company adopts. These variables include

---

[13]Allen I. Schiff, "The Other Side of LIFO," *Journal of Accountancy* (May 1983), pp. 120–21.

[14]See, for example, Shyam Sunder, "Stock Price and Risk Related to Accounting Changes in Inventory Valuation," *Accounting Review* (April 1975), pp. 305–15. It is also worth noting that the LIFO conformity requirement does not prohibit the disclosure of supplemental non-LIFO income information. This supplemental information, such as the amount of net income that would have been reported if the FIFO method had been used, cannot be presented on the face of the financial statements.

[15]Reginald H. Jones, quoted in *Journal of Accountancy* (July 1981), p. 28.

	FIFO		Average Cost		LIFO	
	Periodic System	**Perpetual System**	**Periodic System**	**Perpetual System**	**Periodic System**	**Perpetual System**
Exhibit 9.10 Comparison of Results Under FIFO, Average Cost, and LIFO						
Cost of goods available for sale	$12 700	$12 700	$12 700	$12 700	$12 700	$12 700
Cost of ending inventory (Dec. 31)	3 000	3 000	2 540	2 900	2 100	2 600
Cost of goods sold	$ 9 700	$ 9 700	$10 160	$ 9 800	$10 600	$10 100

Disclosure

inventory, total current assets, working capital, cost of goods sold, gross margin, and net income. The fact that the various cost flow methods produce different financial statement effects underscores the importance of each company disclosing the method(s) that it uses.

Because the unit cost of Product 19-C rose steadily during the current year, FIFO produces the lowest cost of goods sold figure, while LIFO used with a periodic system produces the highest. The nature of the differences produced under the various cost flow methods depends primarily on the direction and magnitude of unit cost movements as well as on the length of time that a company has used LIFO.

Selection of a Cost Flow Method

We have just seen that the various inventory cost flow methods can lead to substantially different financial statement results. We also know that accountants seek to produce information that enables users to make meaningful intercompany comparisons. To help ensure the propriety of these comparisons, differences between the financial statements of different companies should result from basic differences between the companies themselves or from the nature of their transactions, and not merely from differences in accounting principles.[16] Given these facts, why does GAAP permit companies to choose among several inventory cost flow methods?

The basic reason is that circumstances can differ substantially between companies. Accountants generally believe that a company should have some leeway in selecting a cost flow method that is most appropriate in light of the circumstances the company faces. The accounting profession has therefore tended to favour **some flexibility,** rather than **strict uniformity,** when formulating accounting principles. Nevertheless, two of the great challenges of the Accounting Standards Board and its predecessor committees have been (1) to identify the circumstances that warrant the use of a particular accounting principle and (2) to eliminate alternative principles that are not justified by differences in circumstances.

Given the alternatives currently available under GAAP, what basic criterion should a corporate manager use in selecting an inventory cost flow method? Section 3030.08 of the CICA *Handbook* states "The selection of the most suitable method for determining the cost will depend upon the particular circumstances of each enterprise and the industry in which it is engaged."[17] The phrase "upon the particular circumstances" has not been

---

[16]"Inventories," CICA *Handbook,* Paragraph 3030.08, September 1973.
[17]"Inventories," CICA *Handbook,* Paragraph 3030.08, September 1973.

well defined. As a result, this often conveys significantly different meanings to different people. The absence of more concrete criteria for selecting a cost flow assumption has increased the importance of judgement. Many companies appear to select a method based largely on factors such as tax minimization, steady growth in reported earnings, and so forth. Thus, it seems fair to say that financial statements today often reflect certain differences that are unrelated to basic differences between companies or their transactions.

When a company adopts a cost flow method for a portion or all of its inventories, it should use the method consistently over time. As stated earlier, the accountant should disclose the method(s) in the financial statements. When a company changes to another cost flow method, the accountant should disclose the nature of the change, the justification for the change, and the dollar effects of the change on income. We explain accounting changes in Chapter 20.

Inventory Valuation at the Lower of Cost or Market (LCM)

Acountants initially value inventory items by multiplying quantities on hand by unit costs derived under a cost flow method (specific identification, FIFO, etc.). The resulting valuation is at historical cost. In inventory accounting, GAAP requires a departure from historical cost measurement when the utility of inventory has declined below cost. This departure is known as the **lower of cost or market rule**, or simply the **LCM rule**.

The LCM rule is stated as a departure from the cost basis of pricing the inventory.The application of the LCM rule is required when the utility of the goods is no longer as great as its cost. Where there is evidence that the utility of goods, in their disposal in the ordinary course of business, will be less than cost, whether due to physical deterioration, obsolescence, changes in price levels, or other causes, the difference should be recognized as a loss in the current period. This is generally accomplished by stating such goods at a lower level commonly designated as market.

A company purchases or manufactures inventory for ultimate sale. The term **utility of goods** thus refers to the ability of the goods to generate revenue via sales. Utility is a subjective concept, and **market value** is used simply as a practical means of measuring it. Therefore, if the market measure of goods on hand at the end of the current period has declined below cost, the accountant should report the difference as a loss in the period in which the decline occurred.

Meaning of Market

What does "market" mean? Section 3030.11 of the CICA *Handbook* recommends that "a term, more descriptive of the method of determining market, such as 'replacement cost,' 'net realizable value' or 'net realizable value less normal profit margin,' would be preferable."[18] The choice of the market determination is left to the professional judgement of accountants. Net realizable value has become the accepted determination of market, as evidenced by Exhibit 9.11.

In the United States, the determination of the market price has specific limits, which are stated as follows in the AICPA's *Accounting Research Bulletin No. 43*:

---

[18]Gertrude Mulcahy, "The Use and Meaning of 'Market' in Inventory Valuation Research Study," in *Inventories* (Toronto: CICA, 1963), p. 1083.

Exhibit 9.11   Disclosure of Methods of Cost and Market Determination

	Number of Companies			
	1990	1989	1988	1987
Net realizable value	228	223	216	213
Replacement cost	68	72	71	76
Net realizable value less normal profit margin	12	12	13	12
Estimated net realizable value	9	10	10	13
Lower of replacement cost and net realizable value	5	5	6	7
Estimated realizable value	5	5	5	6
Various other bases	13	13	13	13

Source: Reprinted from *Financial Reporting in Canada,* Nineteenth Edition (Toronto: CICA, 1991), p. 79.

As used in the phrase lower of cost or market the term market means current replacement cost (by purchase or by reproduction, as the case may be) except that:

(1) Market should not exceed the net realizable value (i.e., estimated selling price in the ordinary course of business less reasonably predictable costs of completion and disposal); and

(2) Market should not be less than net realizable value reduced by an allowance for an approximately normal profit margin.[19]

Generally, therefore, market means **current replacement cost** on the balance sheet date. In the case of purchased inventories, this cost includes not only the purchase price that would have to be paid for the quantities usually purchased, but also incidental acquisition costs such as freight and handling. For manufactured inventories, replacement cost is based on current materials prices, prevailing labour rates, and current overhead costs. Note that replacement cost is an **input,** or **entry, value,** because it represents an amount that would have to be paid to acquire inventory.

The reason for using replacement cost to represent market (and therefore utility) is that declines in replacement cost are often associated with declines in selling prices. Selling prices, however, may be influenced by other factors. *ARB No. 43* therefore states that in applying the LCM rule, "judgment must always be exercised and no loss should be recognized unless the evidence indicates clearly that a loss has been sustained."[20] To help accountants determine whether or not a loss has been sustained, the bulletin specifies an upper and a lower limit within which market must fall. Each limit is an **output,** or **exit, value,** because each is based directly on expected selling prices that the firm will receive for the goods being valued.

The upper limit on market, commonly called the **ceiling,** is **net realizable value.** This is the amount used most frequently in Canada to determine the market price. The lower limit, commonly called the **floor,** is **net realizable value reduced by an allowance for an approximately normal profit margin.** This method is ranked third in the survey shown in Exhibit 9.11. These concepts are illustrated below for one unit of inventory Item Q.

---

[19]*Accounting Research Bulletin No. 43*, Ch. 4, Statement 6.
　[20]*Accounting Research Bulletin No. 43*, Ch. 4, Paragraph 9.

Estimated selling price in the ordinary course of business	$10
− Reasonably predictable costs of completion and disposal	1
= Net realizable value (ceiling)	9
− Allowance for an approximately normal profit margin (30% of selling price)	3
= Net realizable value less an allowance for an approximately normal profit margin (floor)	$ 6

When applying the LCM rule in the United States, *replacement cost is used as market only when it falls between the ceiling and the floor.* On the other hand, *if replacement cost is greater than the ceiling, the ceiling is used as market.* The use of a ceiling is defended on the grounds that if inventory were reported at more than its net realizable value, the amount reported would exceed the inventory's utility. This would result in a loss when the inventory is sold. If *replacement cost is less than the floor, the floor is used as market.* Limiting market to the floor is defended on the basis that writing down inventory items below the floor understates the inventory's utility and thereby permits the recognition of an abnormally high profit when the inventory is sold.

From a practical standpoint, the LCM rule requires (1) selecting as market the middle amount from among the ceiling, replacement cost, and floor, and (2) selecting the lower of cost or market to use for inventory valuation purposes. Exhibit 9.12 lists four inventory items. The assumed dollar amounts are on a per unit basis.

Observe in Exhibit 9.12 that for each item, U.S. market is the middle value selected from among the ceiling, replacement cost, and floor. *After* we have determined market, we compare it with cost. The lower of cost or market is then entered in the LCM column. Unit amounts in the U.S. LCM column are the correct ones to use for inventory valuation purposes. Note that these amounts represent the cost for Item A, the ceiling for Item B, the replacement cost for Item C, and the floor for Item D. The net realizable value was used as the Canadian market value, and the Canadian LCM column has the cost for Item A and the market (NRV) for items B, C, and D.

The LCM rule applies to goods that a company will sell in the ordinary course of business. At times, a company may own damaged, deteriorated, or obsolete goods that it cannot sell in the usual manner. Such goods should be carried in a separate account and, for accounting purposes, should be valued below cost, at their estimated selling prices less disposal costs. The accounting principles that should be used for inventory received in a trade-in are discussed in Chapter 12; accounting for repossessed inventory is presented in Chapter 5.

Methods of Applying the LCM Rule

Consistency

In the preceding example, we assumed that the LCM rule was applied to each item in inventory. Actually, a company may choose to apply the rule to (1) each inventory item, (2) major categories of items, or (3) the inventory as a whole. According to *ARB No. 43,* the application method selected should most clearly reflect periodic income. Moreover, the method should be applied consistently over time. Most companies use the individual item method.[21] Regardless of what method is used, the quantity of each item should initially be multiplied by (1) unit costs to derive aggregate cost, and (2) unit market values

---

[21]Lower of cost or market must be applied to each inventory item for federal income tax purposes.

Exhibit 9.12 The LCM Rule in the United States and Canada

Inventory Item	Net Realizable Value Ceiling[a]	Replacement Cost[b]	NRV less Normal Profit Floor[c]	U.S. Market[d]	Canadian Market[e]	Cost[f]	U.S. LCM[g]	Canadian LCM[h]
	Market Determinants							
A	$7	$6	$5	$6	$7	$3	$3	$3
B	7	8	5	7	7	9	7	7
C	7	6	5	6	7	8	6	7
D	7	4	5	5	7	8	5	7

[a]Net realizable value (the estimated selling price, assumed to be $10, less reasonably predictable costs of completion and disposal, assumed to be $3).

[b]The current replacement cost as of the balance sheet date.

[c]Net realizable value less a normal profit margin (normal profit is assumed to be 20% of the $10 selling price).

[d]The middle amount selected from among the ceiling, replacement cost, and floor.

[e]Net realizable value was used for the market determination.

[f]Determined using a cost flow method (specific identification, FIFO, etc.).

[g]Lower of cost or market (the lower amount selected from the cost and market). This amount is used for inventory valuation purposes on the balance sheet in the United States.

[h]Lower of cost or market (the lower amount selected from the cost and market). This amount is used for inventory valuation purposes on the balance sheet in Canada.

to derive aggregate market.[22] This is shown in Exhibit 9.13, in which we assume the same inventory items (A, B, C, and D) as in Exhibit 9.12. For simplicity, we assume that 1000 units of each item are on hand.

Observe in Exhibit 9.13 that the final inventory valuation is $24 000, $26 000, or $27 000, depending on how the LCM rule is applied. In certain cases, the results under the different methods may be equal. If the results are not equal, applying LCM to individual items produces the lowest inventory valuation; applying it to inventory as a whole produces the highest.

Once an inventory item has been written down to a value below cost, that value is regarded as its "new cost" for purposes of subsequent accounting. If the market value of an item that has been written down subsequently increases, the increase is not reflected in the accounts until a sale occurs.

Recording LCM in the Accounts

When application of the LCM rule indicates that inventory should be reported at market, how should this be recorded? Ideally, a loss account should be debited and a valuation allowance account (an inventory *contra* account) should be credited. To illustrate, let's assume the following facts for Bradley Limited:

Inventory, Jan. 1, at cost	$ 50 000
Purchases during the year	200 000
Inventory, Dec. 31	
At cost	40 000
At market	33 000

[22]Multiplying by unit costs overcomes the problem of having to compare more than one unit cost with a single unit market value. Under the FIFO method, for example, more than one unit cost may exist for certain inventory items.

Exhibit 9.13 Methods of Applying LCM Rule − Market = NRV

	Number of units	Unit Cost	Unit Market	Aggregate Cost	Aggregate Market	(1) Individual Items	(2) Major Categories	(3) Inventory as a Whole
Category I								
Item A	1000	$3	$6	$ 3 000	$ 6 000	$ 3 000		
Item B	1000	9	7	9 000	7 000	7 000		
Subtotal				12 000	13 000		$12 000	
Category II								
Item C	1000	8	7	8 000	7 000	7 000		
Item D	1000	8	7	8 000	7 000	7 000		
Subtotal				16 000	14 000		14 000	
Total				$28 000	$27 000			$27 000
Inventory valuation						$24 000	$26 000	$27 000

(Header spanning columns (1), (2), (3): **LCM Applied to**)

If the company uses the periodic inventory system, the cost of goods sold adjusting entry would appear as shown below.

Dec. 31 Inventory, Dec. 31	40 000	
Loss on Reduction of Inventory Cost to Market	7 000	
Cost of Goods Sold	210 000	
Inventory, Jan. 1		50 000
Allowance to Reduce Inventory Cost to Market		7 000
Purchases		200 000

On the other hand, the following adjusting entry would be made if the company uses a perpetual system:

Dec. 31 Loss on Reduction of Inventory Cost to Market	7000	
Allowance to Reduce Inventory Cost to Market		7000

Under either system, cost of goods sold would be reported at $210 000 and the loss of $7000 would be shown in the body of the income statement (*not* as an extraordinary item). A clear distinction is therefore made between an *expense* associated with *goods sold* and a *loss* associated with holding *goods on hand*. Separating the expense from the loss is conceptually correct, since the two amounts are caused by different factors. Moreover, a separate reporting of the two amounts may help financial statement users to make more accurate predictions of future cash flows.

The Allowance account is deducted from inventory on the balance sheet:

Inventory, at cost	$40 000	
Less: Allowance to reduce inventory cost to market	7 000	$33 000

Disclosure   Use of the Allowance account facilitates the disclosure of the ending inventory at both cost ($40 000) and market ($33 000).

At the end of the next accounting period, the Allowance account should be closed to the Beginning Inventory if a periodic system is used or to Cost of Goods Sold if a perpetual system is used. This avoids overstatement of the beginning inventory and cost of goods sold. If the market value of the ending inventory is below cost, the difference should again be entered in the Loss and Allowance accounts.

Materiality

In practice, a number of acceptable variations of the above procedure are encountered. Conceptually, these variations are less desirable than the procedure described above. They may be supported, however, on the grounds of materiality and practicality. For example, the LCM rule is sometimes applied in the accounts by

1. Debiting Cost of Goods Sold (instead of the Loss account) and crediting the Allowance account.
2. Debiting the Loss account and crediting the Inventory account (instead of the Allowance account).
3. Debiting Cost of Goods Sold (instead of the Loss account) and crediting the Inventory account (instead of the Allowance account).

When an Allowance account is used, some accountants leave it open and merely adjust it upward or downward at year-end so that it agrees with the difference between cost and market. An increase in the Allowance account requires the recognition of a loss. A decrease requires the recognition of a recovery of loss, sometimes called a gain. The balance in the Allowance account is never reduced below zero. In other words, a debit balance should never exist in the Allowance account, because it would cause the carrying value of the inventory to exceed cost.

Pros and Cons of LCM

The LCM rule is an example of the modifying convention of conservatism. It permits accountants to recognize a loss on inventory, even though evidence of the loss does not result from a sale. The rule has a long history in accounting. Its early use was supported as a means of achieving balance sheet conservatism at a time when creditors were the primary users of external financial statements and the balance sheet was regarded as the most important financial statement. Current financial reporting emphasizes the income statement, and the LCM rule is now supported on the basis that it produces a conservative income measure in the current period.

Many users of financial statements support the LCM rule because they think it reduces their risk of making poor decisions. In a study involving in-depth interviews of important financial statement users, Morton Backer found that "all but one of the 74 bankers interviewed favored the lower of cost or market rule. . . . The security analysts also overwhelmingly supported the rule. Only four of these 72 analysts interviewed opposed the rule."[23]

Despite the alleged benefits of the LCM rule, it has long been one of the most controversial elements of GAAP. Critics have levelled many arguments against it, some of which are listed below.

---

[23]Morton Bacher, *Financial Reporting for Security Investment and Credit Decisions* (New York: National Association of Accountants, 1970), p. 104.

1. The rule requires a write-down to market when cost exceeds market, but it does not permit a write-up to market when market exceeds cost. Some accountants consider this inconsistent and illogical.
2. The rule permits the use of several (four in United States) different inventory measures. Some inventory items may therefore be valued at cost, while others are valued using ceiling, replacement cost, and floor amounts. The existence of these different valuation bases may inhibit the ability of statement users to make valid intercompany and interperiod comparisons.
3. Different methods may be used to apply the LCM rule (i.e., to individual items, major categories, or inventory as a whole) and to record it in the accounts. As a result, intercompany comparisons may be distorted.
4. Determining a "normal profit" in order to establish a floor is difficult and subjective. These profits vary between inventory items and over time as selling prices and cost prices change.
5. Valuing an inventory item at the floor in order to prevent an abnormally high profit on its sale may be closer to income manipulation than to income measurement. While management's function is to earn a profit, the accountant's function is to measure and report it.
6. The LCM rule may produce conservative results in the first year of its use. However, when the lower inventory costs are charged to cost of goods sold in a subsequent period, net income tends to be greater and therefore unconservative.
7. The rule is often complicated to apply. Furthermore, there is reason to suspect that many preparers and users of financial statements may not adequately understand it.[24]

Inventory Valuation Above Cost

Thus far, we have discussed the valuation of inventory at cost and at the lower of cost or market. In Chapter 3, we discussed several alternatives to conventional historical cost measurement. These include current cost (replacement cost), current exit value in orderly liquidation, expected exit value in due course of business (net realizable value), and present value of expected cash flows. Many critics of historical cost accounting believe that accounting information would be more useful if inventories were consistently measured using any of the alternatives to conventional historical cost. Some accountants, for example, believe that inventories should be measured and reported at current cost, regardless of whether the current cost measurement is above or below historical cost. Although many theoretical arguments lend support to the valuation of inventory at amounts greater than historical cost, such valuation is permissible under GAAP only in certain exceptional cases.

For example, construction companies often engage in projects that take several years to complete, such as office buildings, ships, and dams. Instead of waiting until the end of a project to recognize income, these companies may, under GAAP, choose to recognize income *during production* using the percentage-of-completion method. Under this method, an inventory account called Construction in Progress consists of **historical costs incurred plus income recognized to date**. The reporting of inventory in this manner is considered appropriate for these companies, given the unusual nature of the construction

---

[24]Morton Bacher, *Financial Reporting for Security Investment and Credit Decisions* (New York: National Association of Accountants, 1970), p. 104.

business. We further explain and illustrate the percentage-of-completion method in Chapter 5.

The reporting of inventory at net realizable value, even though such value may be above cost, is permitted under GAAP in certain exceptional cases. Precious metals that have a fixed monetary value and no substantial marketing costs may be reported at net realizable value. Similarly, certain agricultural and mineral products, units of which are interchangeable, can be sold immediately at quoted market prices, and are difficult to cost appropriately, may be reported at net realizable value. In addition, it is customary for companies within certain industries to report inventories at net realizable value, because it is virtually impossible for them to determine costs with sufficient objectivity. A meat-packing company, for example, buys its raw material "on the hoof" and divides it into many cuts, such as ribs and chuck. Since any allocation of the cost of the animal to the resulting cuts would be purely arbitrary, these companies value their inventories of cuts at net realizable value.

When a company values its inventory above cost, the company is considered to have earned income before the time of sale. Clearly, this is an exceptional treatment, given the revenue realization principle. Financial statements of companies that value inventories above cost should disclose the valuation basis used.

Effects of Inventory Errors on Financial Statements

Inventory errors often occur when counting, pricing, or extending inventory amounts. Inventory errors may also arise because certain goods have been either incorrectly included or incorrectly excluded when the inventory was taken. We may better appreciate the importance of accurately accounting for inventories by focussing on the impact of certain inventory errors on financial statements. Several common types of errors made in accounting for merchandise and the effects of each are summarized below.

1. The company's accountant incorrectly includes in the ending inventory the cost of certain goods that do not belong to the company.
    a. If the credit purchase of the goods has *not* been recorded, the effects will be an overstatement of ending inventory, an understatement of cost of goods sold, and an overstatement of net income and ending retained earnings.
    b. If the credit purchase of the goods has been recorded, then *two* errors will have occurred (i.e., incorrectly including the goods in inventory *and* incorrectly recording the purchase). The effects will be an overstatement of ending inventory and of accounts payable. Cost of goods sold, net income, and ending retained earnings, however, will be correctly stated, because both purchases and ending inventory are overstated by the same amounts and therefore offset one another in the calculation of cost of goods sold and net income.
2. The company's accountant incorrectly excludes from ending inventory the cost of certain goods that belong to the company.
    a. If the credit purchase of the goods has been recorded, the effects will be an understatement of ending inventory, an overstatement of cost of goods sold, and an understatement of net income and ending retained earnings.
    b. If the credit purchase of the goods has *not* been recorded, then *two* errors will have occurred (i.e., incorrectly excluding the goods from inventory *and* incorrectly failing to record the purchase). The effects will be an understatement of ending inventory and of accounts payable. Cost of goods sold, net income, and

How to Prevent Inventory Fraud

Goods can disappear both on and off company premises

Next to cash, inventory is the most common target of employee embezzlement. There are many ways a devious employee can successfully embezzle corporate inventory. The simplest and most common method is to conceal inventory in personal belongings and walk out with it.

Another common practice is to add excess quantities to orders that are being shipped to customers. They then enter into "profit-sharing" arrangements with either customers' drivers or their own firm's drivers, depending on who delivers the goods.

A third, less obvious, method involves consumption of inventory—such as food or cigarettes—during the working day. Each incident might not represent a large dollar loss. But on a cumulative basis, it can add up.

Inventory fraud also can take place away from the company's premises. For example, an employee could process paperwork that records goods as being received by the company, while the shipment is diverted. This, again, can involve collusion with delivery drivers, or simply an employee who picks up merchandise and delivers only a portion of the goods—but reports the complete receipt.

In addition to the above methods of inventory misappropriation, companies that lease warehouse space or use contractors for intermediary processing could find themselves victims of fraud by means of having their inventory misused.

The misuse of customers' inventory is not uncommon by suppliers who hold inventory that a company has paid for until delivery.

There has been more than one occasion where a company's auditors have attempted to physically inspect such inventory on the supplier's premises only to find that it has been "borrowed" by the supplier for shipment to another customer. The supplier's intention would be to replace the inventory when needed. Since this inventory had been paid for by the company, the supplier is in fact misappropriating the company's inventory for its own benefit.

Another type of inventory misuse occurs when contractors "short-ship" a product when it is returned to the company for further processing. Typically, the control procedures after the merchandise has been purchased and enters the production cycle are not as tight as when it first arrives or when it eventually leaves the company's premises.

Thus, if the inventory is not properly tracked through the system—including shipping to and from contractors—then shrinkages and losses cannot be properly monitored.

So what can a company do to minimize and prevent inventory fraud?

There are various methods of prevention. The first issue to resolve is the level of risk associated with a particular inventory. This means that the individual company must determine how valuable its inventory is to the average employee. Is it readily usable or saleable?

For example, if a company's inventory consists of 45 gallon drums of chemicals, then it is extremely difficult for an employee to physically remove and transport them. It also would be difficult to convert the chemicals into cash.

However, if the inventory consists of end-user products such as garments or electronic components, the value of the item to the employee is far greater and therefore the temptation would increase. Thus, the risk of theft associated with the type of inventory increases as the employee's ability to exchange this inventory for cash increases.

Having established the level of risk, management can then assess the extent that controls should be implemented.

Such controls should be carefully selected so that they produce maximum results at minimum expense. But it must be remembered that it is extremely difficult to guard against fraud when there is collusion among several employees in responsible positions.

Thus it's imperative that all inventory controls be backed up by meticulous physical inventory counts on a regular basis to identify any shortages. If there are any, then investigation may be necessary to determine where the leak is occurring and to identify the culprits.

15 Ways a Business Can Curb Inventory Fraud

1. Maintain perpetual inventory records on a current basis and ensure adequate division of duties between accounting clerks and inventory personnel.
2. Maintain segregated inventory receiving and shipping areas.
3. Utilize signed requisitions or documents to authorize the release of inventories.
4. Have orders verified for quantities by a second employee prior to shipment.
5. Have inventories counted regularly and periodically.
6. Have physical inventory counts compared to perpetual inventory records with all discrepancies investigated and approved by management.

Continued

7. Have management prepare and supervise the procedures for physical inventory counts.
8. Utilize non-inventory employees for inventory counts in conjunction with inventory personnel in teams of two.
9. Utilize closed circuit television monitor systems for all entrances and exits to inventory warehouse.
10. Disallow any employee bags, packages or similar items which could conceal inventory from inventory storage areas.
11. Have all inventory receiving and shipping documents signed and dated in order to fix responsibility.
12. Ensure that inventory is maintained in a neat and orderly fashion.

13. Regularly perform physical inspection of all goods held by outsiders on behalf of the company.
14. Ensure proper and adequate controls over the sale of scrap or sales to employees or through a factory outlet store.
15. Perform regular gross profit tests to estimate inventories and compare these estimates to perpetual records and physical counts.

Source: Reprinted from Philip C. Levi, CFE, FCA, partner at Bessner Gallay Schapira Kreisman, "How to Prevent Inventory Fraud," *Montreal Gazette*, June 29, 1992.

ending retained earnings, however, will be correctly stated, because both purchases and ending inventory are understated by the same amounts and therefore offset one another in the calculation of cost of goods sold and net income.

When considering the effects that inventory errors have on net income, remembering the following relationships is often helpful. For simplicity, we ignore expenses other than cost of goods sold in the three equations below.

Equation 1:	$S - CGS = NI$
Equation 2:	$BI + P - EI = CGS$
Equation 3:	$S - BI - P + EI = NI$
where	$S = $ Sales (net)
	$CGS = $ Cost of goods sold
	$NI = $ Net income
	$BI = $ Beginning inventory
	$P = $ Purchases (net)
	$EI = $ Ending inventory

Equation 3 indicates that an overstatement (understatement) of either the beginning inventory or purchases tends to decrease (increase) net income, because the beginning inventory and purchases are subtracted when measuring net income. In contrast, an overstatement (understatement) of ending inventory tends to increase (decrease) net income because ending inventory is added when measuring net income.

The types of inventory errors discussed previously relate to purchase transactions. Similar errors may arise in relation to sales transactions. For example, the cost of certain goods that have actually been sold may erroneously be included in the ending inventory.

The various types of inventory errors just discussed affect the current accounting period. Recognize, however, that an error in the ending inventory of the current period has the opposite effect in the next period, because the ending inventory of one period is the beginning inventory of the next. If the error is not corrected in the second period, it will offset the error made in the first period.

Correcting an inventory error requires a logical analysis of the error's effects on the financial statements. The appropriate correction depends in part on when the error is detected. An error in the ending inventory of one period that is discovered near the end of the next, for example, requires a prior period adjustment. Chapter 20 discusses the topic of error correction in greater depth.

Conceptual Considerations/Concluding Remarks

Throughout this text, we stress the importance of understanding the relationship between the individual topics covered and the theoretical model presented in Chapter 2. The following elements of the model are especially pertinent in inventory accounting:

Asset/Liability Measurement

1. **Asset/liability measurement principle.** The primary basis of accounting for inventories is historical cost. Remember that determining historical cost is not as easy as it may appear. Resolving important issues such as what costs should be inventoried and what cost flow method should be used is a real challenge to the accountant.

Revenue Realization

2. **Revenue realization principle.** When an increase in the value of inventory is verified by a sale, revenue is usually recorded. Only in exceptional cases may accountants properly value inventory above cost and therefore recognize revenue before the time of sale.

Matching

3. **Matching principle.** The cost of the inventory sold must be charged to expense in the period in which the sale occurs. By doing so, the sales revenue is matched with the cost of the goods sold to produce the revenue.

Consistency

4. **Consistency principle.** A company should account for its inventories using the same methods over time. This principle is particularly important in inventory accounting, because several alternative accounting methods exist.

Disclosure

5. **Disclosure principle.** The following disclosure guidelines should be observed when reporting inventories on the balance sheet and in the related notes:

   a. Report inventories in the current assets section.
   b. Disclose separately each major class of inventory, such as raw materials, work-in-process, finished goods, factory supplies, and goods on consignment. Remember to include in inventory only those goods for which the company (i.e., the accounting entity) has legal title on the balance sheet date.
   c. List inventories in order of their liquidity. See Canadian Pacific Limited's balance sheet and note found in Appendix A of this text.
   d. Disclose parenthetically, in a footnote, or in a summary of significant accounting policies the inventory cost flow method used (FIFO, average cost, etc.) as well as the basis used in pricing the inventory (cost or LCM). Also disclose any methods used that are peculiar to the firm's industry.
   e. If the company has made a change in its inventory accounting policies, disclose the nature of and justification for the change. The effect of the change on income should also be disclosed. We explain accounting changes in Chapter 20.
   f. Subtract the amount in an inventory allowance account (such as the Allowance to Reduce Inventory Cost to Market) from the amount in the Inventory account to derive the net amount. Report all three amounts on the balance sheet or in the related notes.
   g. Do *not* offset the cost of inventories pledged as collateral against the loan liability. These inventories are properly reported as assets. However, the nature of the pledge agreement should be disclosed.
   h. Do *not* include in inventories advance payments made to suppliers for goods that the company has ordered but to which title has not been received as of the

balance sheet date. These advances should be reported after inventories in an account called Advances to Suppliers.

Exhibit 9.14 shows recent inventory disclosures of the Journey's End Corporation.
6. **Industry practices.** This modifying convention sometimes requires the reporting of inventories at amounts above cost. Companies in the meat-packing industry, for example, typically value their inventories of cuts at net realizable value.

Exhibit 9.14 Example of Inventory Disclosure

Journey's End Corporation
CONSOLIDATED BALANCE SHEET

	July 31	
	1991	**1990**
	(thousands of dollars)	
Assets		
Current Assets		
Cash	$ 3 296	$ 3 772
Accounts Receivable	15 775	14 201
Income Taxes Recoverable	1 926	—
Inventories (Notes 2, 10)	75 380	90 902
Deposits	143	2 167
	96 520	111 042

Notes to Consolidated Financial Statements
Years Ended July 31

1. Summary of Significant Accounting Policies

(d) Inventories
Inventories consist of raw land, completed buildings, buildings under development including the cost of land, land lease costs, land improvements, building construction costs, chattels, carrying costs including mortgage and syndication costs, bank interest capitalized, realty taxes, legal fees and other direct expenses. Provision is made for any costs which are not considered recoverable. Accordingly, the carrying value of these inventories is at the lower of cost and net realizable value.

2. Inventories
Inventories consist of completed properties which are available for sale or syndication, properties under development, and various parcels of land for sale or future development and are summarized as follows:

	1991	**1990**
	(in thousands)	
Properties completed	$53 017	$52 159
Properties under development	—	28 302
Land	22 363	10 441
	$75 380	$90 902

Source: Journey's End Corporation, *1991 Annual Report.*

7. **Conservatism.** This modifying convention is reflected in the LCM rule. Under this rule, a departure from historical cost measurement is required when the utility of inventory has declined below cost.

---

1. Inventories are goods that are held for sale in the ordinary course of business, and goods that are in production or that will soon be used in production. (Objective 1)
2. To value an inventory for financial reporting purposes, an accountant must determine (1) the physical quantity of goods on hand and (2) the accounting valuation that should be associated with those goods. (Objective 1)
3. Inventory quantities are maintained on a day-to-day basis in a perpetual inventory system, but not in a periodic system. (Objective 2)
4. Inventory items should be included in the inventory of the entity that has legal title. Goods in transit at the end of an accounting period that were shipped FOB shipping point belong to the buyer; those shipped FOB destination belong to the seller. Consigned goods belong to the consignor. (Objective 2)
5. To determine the cost of inventory, an accountant must determine (1) what costs to include in inventory and (2) what method to use in associating inventory costs with the physical units on hand. (Objectives 1 and 2)
6. Product costs are inventoried; period costs are charged to expense in the period in which they are incurred. (Objective 3)
7. Trade discounts and GST are deducted when determining product costs. In theory, cash discounts should also be deducted, but in practice, most companies account for inventory at gross invoice amounts (i.e., without deducting cash discounts). (Objective 3)
8. Inventory cost flow methods include specific identification, FIFO, average cost, and LIFO. Each method leads to a valuation of inventory and cost of goods sold based on historical cost. (Objective 4)
9. The specific identification method requires that the actual unit costs of goods on hand and goods sold be identified individually. In contrast, the FIFO, average cost, and LIFO methods reflect assumed cost flow patterns. (Objective 4)
10. LIFO cannot be used for income tax purposes in Canada. In the United States, if a company elects to use LIFO for income tax purposes, it must also use LIFO for financial reporting purposes. The LIFO method is an important exception to the general principle that a company does not have to use the same methods for financial reporting purposes that it uses for income tax purposes. (Objective 4)
11. A company should select the inventory cost flow method that most clearly reflects its periodic income. Once selected, the method should be used consistently over time and disclosed in the financial statements. (Objective 4)
12. Inventory should ordinarily be reported on a balance sheet at the lower of cost or market value. In essence, the term "market" refers to the middle value selected from among the ceiling, replacement cost, and floor amounts. (Objective 5)
13. The lower of cost or market rule may be applied to each inventory item, to major categories of items, or to inventory as a whole. (Objective 5)
14. The lower of cost or market rule is an exception to historical cost measurement of inventories that is justified on the basis of conservatism. (Objective 5)
15. The valuation of inventory at an amount greater than historical cost is permissible under GAAP only in certain exceptional cases. (Objective 6)
16. Inventory errors can cause several important misstatements to occur in the financial statements. (Objective 7)
17. The following elements of accounting theory are especially important in the area of inventory accounting: asset/liability measurement, revenue realization, matching, consistency, disclosure, industry practices, and conservatism. (Objective 8)

Q9.1 What are the major differences between merchandising and manufacturing companies regarding the classification of inventories and the calculation of cost of goods sold? Why do these differences exist?

Q9.2 The primary basis of accounting for inventories under GAAP is historical cost. Identify three inventory valuation methods that are alternatives to historical cost, and briefly explain why these methods are not generally accepted today.

Q9.3 What is a periodic inventory system? What is a perpetual system? What factors should a manager consider when deciding which system the company should use?

Q9.4 What general rule determines which goods properly belong in a company's inventory? How does the accountant apply this general rule to goods in transit on the balance sheet date and to consigned goods?

Q9.5 Distinguish between product costs and period costs.

Q9.6 Why is the net method of recording purchases theoretically superior to the gross method?

Q9.7 What are the major arguments for and against the specific identification method of inventory cost determination?

Q9.8 What are the major arguments for and against the FIFO method of inventory cost determination?

Q9.9 What are the major arguments for and against the average cost method of inventory cost determination?

Q9.10 What are the major arguments for and against the LIFO method of inventory cost determination?

Q9.11 What basic problem does the existence of several inventory cost flow methods within GAAP create for external users of financial statements? How does the accounting profession justify these alternative methods?

Q9.12 What basic criterion should a company manager use in selecting an inventory cost flow method? Why is this criterion difficult to apply?

Q9.13 What are the major arguments for and against the LCM rule in accounting for inventories?

Q9.14 What does the term "market" mean in the context of the LCM rule?

Q9.15 What is the rationale for ceiling and floor limits on market under the LCM rule?

Q9.16 Under what circumstances, if any, is it appropriate under GAAP to value inventories at amounts greater than historical cost?

Q9.17 Relate inventory accounting to the asset/liability measurement principle, revenue realization principle, and matching principle.

Q9.18 Why is the consistency principle especially important in inventory accounting?

Q9.19 Relate inventory accounting to the conservatism modifying convention.

E9.1 Cost of Goods Sold. Listed below are selected accounts and their balances that appeared on the unadjusted trial balance of Biswal, Inc., at April 30, 1995, the end of the company's annual fiscal period. Each account has a normal balance.

Sales returns	$12 000
Merchandise inventory	35 000
Transportation-out	14 000
Purchase returns	5 000
Sales	300 000
Advertising expense	15 000
Transportation-in	8 000
Purchases	135 000
Sales discounts	4 000
Sales commissions	12 000
Officers' salaries expense	40 000

A physical count on April 30 indicates that merchandise costing $28 000 is on hand.

Instructions

(a) Prepare the adjusting journal entry to record cost of goods sold on Biswal's books at April 30, 1995.
(b) What account(s) in (a) will Biswal have to close when it prepares closing entries on April 30, 1995?
(c) Indicate where the accounts you did not include in (a) should appear in Biswal's financial statements.
(d) Prepare a schedule of cost of goods sold for Biswal, Inc., for the year ending April 30, 1995.
(e) Calculate the gross margin.

E9.2   Cost of Goods Manufactured. Information pertaining to Mapp Manufacturing Corporation for the year ended December 31, 1995, is as follows:

Indirect labour	$45 000
Salesperson's salaries expense	42 000
Raw materials inventory, Dec. 31	53 000
Depreciation expense on factory properties	30 000
Work-in-process, Jan. 1	40 000
Direct labour	110 000
Factory utilities expense	20 000
Finished goods, Dec. 31	96 000
Work-in-process, Dec. 31	33 000
Advertising expense	25 000
Raw materials inventory, Jan. 1	60 000
Indirect materials used	7 000
Purchases of raw materials	400 000
Property taxes expense on factory	18 000
Finished goods, Jan. 1	68 000
Returned purchases of raw materials	10 000
Net sales	835 000
Miscellaneous factory expenses	4 000

Instructions

(a) Prepare a schedule of cost of goods manufactured for the year ended December 31, 1995.
(b) Calculate the cost of goods sold.
(c) Calculate the gross margin.

E9.3   Direct Versus Absorption Costing. The following information pertains to Newlin Manufacturing Limited during its first year of business:

Sales	10 000 units
Production	13 000 units
Cost per unit produced	
Direct materials	$1.00
Direct labour	3.00
Variable overhead	2.50
Fixed overhead	1.50

Instructions

Calculate the cost of the company's year-end inventory, assuming (1) absorption costing and (2) direct costing.

E9.4   Periodic and Perpetual Systems.   Infantcar, Inc., is a wholesaler of infant car seats. At the beginning of 1995, the company's inventory consisted of 900 car seats priced at $30 each. During 1995, the following events occurred:

(1)   Purchased 8000 car seats on account at $30 each, terms n/30.
(2)   Returned 500 defective car seats to supplier and received credit.
(3)   Paid for 6000 of the car seats purchased in (1).
(4)   Sold 7900 car seats on account for $56 each, terms n/30.
(5)   Received 200 car seats returned by a customer and gave credit. The goods were in excellent condition and were therefore returned to regular inventory.
(6)   Received cash for 6800 of the car seats sold in (4).
(7)   Physical count at year-end revealed 600 units on hand.

Instructions

(a)   Prepare journal entries (including adjusting entries) to record the above events on Infantcar's books, assuming that the company uses (1) a periodic system and (2) a perpetual system.

(b)   What is the company's cost of goods sold for 1995 under (1) the periodic system and (2) the perpetual system? Explain any difference you find between the two numbers.

E9.5   Goods in Transit.   Pulley Limited had the following purchase and sale transactions near the end of 1995:

No.	Transaction	Terms	Date Merchandise Shipped by Seller	Date Merchandise Received by Buyer
1	Purchase	FOB shipping point	12/26/95	1/5/96
2	Purchase	FOB destination	12/26/95	1/5/96
3	Sale	FOB shipping point	12/26/95	1/5/96
4	Sale	FOB destination	12/26/95	1/5/96

Instructions

For each transaction, indicate whether Pulley Limited should include the merchandise in its inventory at December 31, 1995. Assume that all dollar amounts are material. Explain your answer in each case.

E9.6   Goods to Include in Inventory.   As the independent CA for Raye Corporation, state whether the goods in each of the following 1995 events should be included in Raye's inventory for the fiscal year ending June 30, 1995. Explain your answer in each case.

(1)   Finished goods pledged as collateral for a 90-day loan from Winnipeg Bank were on hand June 30.

(2) An order, accompanied by cash payment for the total sales price, was received on June 29 for goods that Raye shipped on July 2.

(3) Raye made advance payments of $3000 to suppliers for goods ordered but not shipped as of June 30.

(4) On June 30, Raye shipped goods FOB destination to Shagle Corporation, which received the goods on July 5.

(5) On June 29, Senape Ltd. shipped goods FOB shipping point to Raye. Raye received the goods on July 2.

(6) Certain raw materials owned by Raye were at Ramer Limited for processing on June 30.

(7) Raye had certain goods on hand for which it was acting as a selling agent for Newbrough Ltd.

(8) On June 26, Mazzola, Inc., shipped goods FOB destination to Raye. Raye received the invoice on June 30 and the goods on July 2.

(9) On June 29, Harbison Corporation shipped goods FOB shipping point to Raye. Raye received the invoice and the goods on July 2.

(10) On June 30, Raye sent goods to a consignee and prepaid the freight charges. The consignee received the goods on July 5.

E9.7 Goods to Include in Inventory. During an annual audit at December 31, 1995, you find the following transactions:

(1) Merchandise costing $2116 was received on January 3, 1996, and the related purchase invoice was recorded January 5. The invoice showed the shipment was made on December 29, 1995, FOB destination.

(2) Merchandise costing $815 was received on December 28, 1995, and the invoice was not recorded. You located it in the hands of the purchasing agent; it was marked "on consignment."

(3) A packing case containing a product costing $965 was not included in the physical inventory because it was marked "hold for shipping instructions." Your investigation revealed that the customer's order was dated December 18, 1995, but that the case was shipped and the customer billed on January 10, 1996. The product was a stock item of your client.

(4) Merchandise received on January 6, 1996, costing $720 was entered in the purchase register on January 7, 1996. The invoice showed shipment was made FOB supplier's warehouse on December 31, 1995. Because it was not on hand December 31, it was not included in inventory.

(5) A special machine, made to order, was finished and in the shipping room on December 31, 1995. The customer was billed on that date, and the machine was excluded from inventory although it was shipped on January 4, 1996.

Instructions

Assume that the amount is material in each case. State whether the merchandise should be included in the client's inventory, and explain your decision.
(Adapted from AICPA.)

E9.8 Net Versus Gross Method. Rao Limited, which uses a periodic inventory system, had the following merchandise transactions during December 1995:

Dec. 1 Purchased merchandise from Hall Ltd. for $1000, terms 2/10, n/30.
   2 Purchased merchandise from Wall Corporation for $2000, terms 3/10, n/30.
   11 Paid Wall Corporation for Dec. 2 purchase.
   30 Paid Hall Ltd. for Dec. 1 purchase.

Instructions

(a) Prepare the general journal entries to record the above transactions on the books of Rao Limited using (1) the net method of recording purchases and (2) the gross method of recording purchases.
(b) Discuss the accounting logic of the net method and the gross method of recording purchases.

E9.9 FIFO and LIFO. Holcomb, Inc., is a wholesaler of footballs. The following information pertains to the company's inventory during July 1995:

Balance, July 1	2000 units @ $11
Purchase July 12	2000 units @ $12
Purchase, July 26	2000 units @ $15
Balance, July 31	2500 units

Instructions

Assuming that Holcomb uses a periodic inventory system, calculate each of the following amounts for July 1995:

(a) Ending inventory under FIFO.
(b) Cost of goods sold under LIFO.
(c) Ending inventory under LIFO.
(d) Cost of goods sold under FIFO.

E9.10 FIFO, Average Cost, and LIFO. Sweet Food Limited sells honey. The following information is available from the company's inventory records for 1995:

	Jars	Cost per Jar
Inventory, Jan. 1	200	$1.00
Purchases		
Jan. 16	300	1.50
Feb. 22	600	2.00
Mar. 3	500	2.50
Mar. 19	400	3.00

During the first quarter of 1995, the company sold 1400 jars at $5 each. The company uses a periodic system. A physical inventory on March 31 reveals 600 jars on hand.

Instructions

Prepare a schedule in the form shown below, and compute the missing values. Show all supporting computations.

| | Inventory Mar. 31, 1995 | 1st Quarter, 1985 | | |
		Sales	Cost of Goods Sold	Gross Margin
LIFO	$	$	$	$
FIFO				
Average				
Cost				

E9.11 FIFO, Average Cost, and LIFO.   Marcee, Inc., uses Raw Material Q in its production process. The following changes occurred in Marcee's inventory of Raw Material Q during October:

Oct.	1	Balance on hand	100 units @ $27
	6	Purchased	300 units @ $25
	14	Purchased	600 units @ $28
	25	Purchased	400 units @ $21
Oct.	9	Issued to production	200 units @ ?
	28	Issued to production	800 units @ ?

Instructions
(a) Assuming that Marcee maintains complete perpetual records for Raw Material Q, compute the cost of the inventory at October 31 and the cost of materials issued to production during October using the (1) FIFO, (2) moving average, and (3) LIFO methods. (Round unit cost calculations to three places.)
(b) Assuming that Marcee uses a periodic system to account for Raw Material Q, compute the cost of the inventory at October 31 and the cost of materials issued to production during October using the (1) FIFO, (2) average cost, and (3) LIFO methods. (Round unit cost calculations to three places.)

E9.12 Effects of LIFO and FIFO.   Neilson Ltd. began operations on January 1, 1992, and adopted the LIFO method of inventory pricing for its financial statements. The following additional facts pertain to the company:

Year	Reported Net Income	Ending Inventory Under LIFO	Ending Inventory That the Company Would Have Reported Under FIFO
1992	$ 60 000	$ 8 000	$15 000
1993	72 000	12 000	22 000
1994	90 000	18 000	12 000
1995	120 000	26 000	17 000

The company's income tax expense has consistently been 40 percent of income before taxes.

Instructions
Calculate the amount of net income the company would have reported for 1992, 1993, 1994, and 1995 under the FIFO method.

E9.13 Lower of Cost or Market. For each of the following independent cases, determine the correct unit value for inventory valuation under the LCM rule (1) most popular in Canada and (2) in the United States.

Case	Historical Cost	Cost to Replace	Net Realizable Value (NRV) Ceiling	(NRV) Less Normal Profit Margin Floor
A	$50	$48	$60	$53
B	78	76	86	72
C	38	37	48	40
D	80	82	79	71
E	23	20	27	22
F	18	17	20	16
G	60	61	59	50
H	89	84	97	88

E9.14 Lower of Cost or Market. Olinger, Inc., compiled the following inventory information on November 30, 1995, the end of the company's fiscal year:

	Quantity	Unit Cost	Unit Market
Category X			
Product 1	400	$20	$18
Product 2	500	28	32
Category Y			
Product 3	700	17	19
Product 4	600	18	14
Category Z			
Product 5	400	35	39
Product 6	300	31	28

Instructions

Compute Olinger's inventory valuation at November 30, 1995, assuming that the company applies the LCM rule to (1) each product, (2) major categories of products, and (3) inventory as a whole.

E9.15 Lower of Cost or Market. The following information pertains to Loveday, Inc., at December 31, 1995:

Inventory, Jan. 1	$ 75 000
Purchases during 1995	325 000
Inventory, Dec. 31	
Cost	60 000
Market	50 000

Before 1995, application of the LCM rule never produced a need to write down the company's inventory to an amount below cost.

Instructions

Prepare the necessary adjusting journal entries to record cost of goods sold and to reflect the application of the LCM rule under each of the following assumptions:

(a) The company uses a periodic inventory system and applies the LCM rule using a loss account and a valuation allowance account.
(b) The company uses a periodic inventory system and applies the LCM rule using neither a loss account nor a valuation allowance account.
(c) The company uses a perpetual inventory system and applies the LCM rule using a loss account and a valuation allowance account.
(d) The company uses a perpetual inventory system and applies the LCM rule using neither a loss account nor a valuation allowance account.

E9.16 Inventory Errors.   Greene, Inc., began operations on January 1, 1994. The following data pertain to the company's first two years in business:

	Reported Amount	Correct Amount
Inventory		
Dec. 31, 1994	$ 20 000	$ 40 000
Dec. 31, 1995	35 000	35 000
Net Income		
For 1994	60 000	?
For 1995	66 000	?
Retained earnings		
Dec. 31, 1994	60 000	?
Dec. 31, 1995	126 000	?

During 1994 and 1995, the company's income tax expense rate was 40 percent, and the company declared no dividends.

Instructions

Compute the correct amount for each of the following variables:
(a) Net income for 1994.
(b) Net income for 1995.
(c) Retained earnings, December 31, 1994.
(d) Retained earnings, December 31, 1995.

E9.17 Inventory Errors.   Gresham Limited uses a periodic inventory system and sells its merchandise for 100 percent above cost. The following events occurred near the end of the first year of operations (Year 1):

(1) The company recorded a credit sale of goods to which it had not surrendered legal title as of the end of Year 1. These goods were excluded from the company's ending inventory.
(2) The company failed to record the credit sales of goods to which it surrendered legal title during Year 1. The company included the goods in its ending inventory.
(3) The company included certain goods to which it had not yet received legal title in its ending inventory. The company did not record a purchase of these goods.

(4) The company recorded a credit purchase of goods to which it received legal title during Year 1. Although the goods had not been sold by year-end, the company did not include them in its ending inventory.

(5) The company recorded a credit purchase of goods to which it did not receive legal title during Year 1. These goods were included in the company's ending inventory.

(6) The company failed to record the credit purchase of goods to which it received legal title during Year 1. Although the goods had not been sold by year-end, the company did not include them in its ending inventory.

Instructions

Set up a matrix like the one below. At the intersection of each row and column, indicate the effect of the event on the financial statement variable at the end of Year 1, using the following codes: O = Overstated, U = Understated, NE = No Effect. Treat each event independently. (Note: You should have 36 answers in the completed matrix.)

Event No.	Total Revenues	Total Expenses	Net Income	Total Assets	Total Liabilities	Total Shareholders' Equity
1						
2						
3						
4						
5						
6						

E9.18 Accrual Basis and Cash Flows. The following data were taken from the financial statements of Fishburne, Inc., a calendar-year merchandising corporation:

(1) Balance sheet data:

	Dec. 31, 1994	Dec. 31, 1995
Trade accounts receivable, net	$ 84 000	$ 78 000
Inventory	150 000	140 000
Accounts payable, merchandise (credit)	(95 000)	(98 000)

(2) Total sales were $1 200 000 for 1995 and $1 100 000 for 1994. Cash sales were 20 percent of total sales each year.

(3) Cost of goods sold was $840 000 for 1995.

(4) Variable general and administrative (G&A) expenses for 1995 were $120 000. They have varied in proportion to sales; 50 percent have been paid in the year incurred and 50 percent the following year. Unpaid G&A expenses are not included in accounts payable above.

(5) Fixed G&A expenses, including $35 000 depreciation and $5000 bad debt expense, totalled $100 000 each year. Eighty percent of fixed G&A expenses involving cash were paid in the year incurred and 20 percent the following year. Each year, there was a $5000 bad debt estimate and a $5000 write-off. Unpaid G&A expenses are *not* included in accounts payable above.

Instructions

(a) Compute the amount of cash collected during 1995 resulting from total sales in 1994 and 1995.
(b) Compute the amount of cash disbursed during 1995 for purchases of merchandise.
(c) Compute the amount of cash disbursed during 1995 for variable and fixed general and administrative expenses.

(Adapted from AICPA.)

E9.19 Current Value Accounting. The controller of Connelly Corporation, Mr. Colson, is discussing a comment you made in the course of presenting your audit report:

> . . . And frankly, I agree that we, too, are responsible for finding ways to produce more relevant financial statements that are as reliable as the ones we now produce. For example, suppose the corporation acquired a finished item for inventory for $40 when the general price-level index was 110. And later, the item was sold for $75 when the general price-level index was 121 and the current replacement cost was $54. We could calculate a holding gain.

Instructions

(a) Explain to what extent and how current replacement costs are already used in generally accepted accounting principles to value inventories.
(b) Compute the amount of the holding gain in Mr. Colson's example.
(c) Why is the use of current replacement cost for both inventories and cost of goods sold preferred by some accounting authorities to the generally accepted use of FIFO or LIFO?
(d) Why do some authorities believe that the present market resale (exit or output) price is a conceptual improvement on current replacement (entry or input) cost for inventory measurement?

(Adapted from AICPA.)

Problems

P9.1 Goods to Include in Inventory. Butler, Inc., uses a periodic inventory system and a fiscal year ending September 30. On September 30, 1994, the company correctly reported inventory on hand costing $14 500. During the fiscal year ending September 30, 1995, the company recorded purchases of $45 000. A physical count on September 30, 1995, revealed that goods costing $21 000 were on hand. The following material events occurred between September 23 and October 7, 1995:

(1) Goods costing $3000 that Butler was holding as a consignee were included in the physical count.
(2) An invoice for goods costing $4600 was received and entered as a credit purchase on September 29. The goods arrived on October 2. The supplier shipped the goods FOB destination on September 27.
(3) An invoice for goods costing $4100 was received and entered as a credit purchase on October 3. The goods arrived on that date and were in satisfactory condition. The supplier shipped the goods FOB shipping point on September 29.
(4) Goods that Butler specially purchased from an overseas supplier for ultimate sale to Digital Enterprises, Inc., were included in the physical count. A contract between Butler and Digital pertaining to the goods states that "title passes when buyer approves the goods." A representative from Digital Enterprises inspected and approved the goods in Butler's warehouse on September 28. Butler shipped the goods

and recorded a sale on October 4. The goods cost $2500 and were sold on credit for $3600.

(5) Goods costing $800 and housed in a special storeroom were inadvertently overlooked when the physical count was taken.

(6) An invoice for goods costing $3100 was received and entered as a credit purchase on September 28. The supplier shipped the goods FOB shipping point on September 26. The receiving report indicates that Butler received the goods on October 1.

Instructions

(a) Make all necessary correcting entries in general journal form for the fiscal year ending September 30, 1995. Assume that the adjusting entry for cost of goods sold has not been made and that the books for the year have not been closed.

(b) Compute the correct inventory amount for Butler's balance sheet dated September 30, 1995.

(c) Make the adjusting journal entry to record the cost of goods sold for the fiscal year ending September 30, 1995.

P9.2 Goods to Include in Inventory. Tower Limited of North York uses a periodic inventory system and a fiscal year ending April 30. The company makes all its merchandise purchases and sales on credit. The following information is available from the company's inventory records:

Beginning inventory, May 1, 1994	$20 000
Purchases, May 1, 1994–April 30, 1995	90 000
Purchase returns, May 1, 1994–April 30, 1995	2 000
Ending inventory, April 30, 1995 (per physical count)	16 000

The following events occurred near the end of the fiscal year that ended on April 30, 1995:

(1) Goods costing $4000 received on April 27 were recorded as a purchase twice.

(2) Goods shipped by rail from North York to a Vancouver customer were recorded as a sale on April 30. The goods cost $3600; the selling price was $6000. The goods were shipped on April 30, FOB Vancouver. Tower Limited did not include these goods in its physical inventory.

(3) Goods costing $3500 received on April 29 were recorded as a purchase on May 2.

(4) Goods costing $4500 were recorded as a purchase on May 5. A Quebec supplier shipped the goods to North York by rail, FOB Quebec, on April 30.

(5) Goods costing $5000 held by Bailey Corporation on consignment were not counted. Tower Limited recorded a sale of $8000 when it shipped the goods to Bailey on April 23.

(6) Goods costing $3800 were received on April 18 and returned for credit on April 20 because they were not satisfactory. Tower Limited did not record these events.

Instructions

(a) Make all necessary correcting entries in general journal form for the fiscal year ending April 30, 1995. Assume that the adjusting entry for the cost of goods sold has not been made and that the books for the year have not been closed.

(b) Compute the correct inventory amount for Tower Limited's balance sheet dated April 30, 1995.

(c) Make the adjusting journal entry to record the cost of goods sold for the fiscal year ending April 30, 1995.

P9.3 Net Versus Gross Method. Theo, Inc., began operations in 1995. The company maintains complete perpetual records for its merchandise inventory. During 1995, Theo purchased merchandise having a gross invoice cost of $100 000. All purchases were made under the terms 2/10, n/30. Theo paid freight charges of $5000 for the merchandise.

During the year, Theo paid for 80 percent of the merchandise within the discount period; it paid for the other 20 percent after the discount period had expired. Theo sold 70 percent of the merchandise it acquired for cash of $120 000; the other 30 percent remains in inventory at year-end.

Instructions
(a) Prepare the general journal entries to record the above transactions on Theo's books using (1) the net method of recording purchases and (2) the gross method of recording purchases.
(b) What financial statement balances would Theo report at December 31, 1995, for sales, cost of goods sold, gross margin, discounts lost (or interest expense), and ending inventory under (1) the net method and (2) the gross method?
(c) Which method of recording purchases (net method or gross method) is generally regarded as theoretically superior? Why?

P9.4 FIFO, Average Cost, and LIFO. The following information pertains to Sonare calculators of Compu Corporation for the month of June, 1995:

Date	Calculators	Units	Unit Cost	Unit Selling Price
June 1	Beginning inventory	1000	$52	
7	Purchase	3000	50	
12	Sale	2000		$100
17	Purchase	6000	45	
22	Purchase	2000	43	
28	Sale	7000		100
30	Ending inventory	3000		

Instructions
(a) Assuming that the company uses a periodic inventory system, calculate the cost of the ending inventory and the cost of goods sold using (1) the FIFO method, (2) the average cost method, and (3) the LIFO method. (Round unit cost calculations to three places.)
(b) Assuming that the company uses a perpetual inventory system, calculate the cost of the ending inventory and the cost of goods sold using (1) the FIFO method, (2) the average cost method, and (3) the LIFO method. (Round unit cost calculations to three places.)
(c) Calculate the amount of gross margin in (a1, 2, 3) and (b1, 2, 3).
(d) Assume that the inflation rate (i.e., the increase in the overall level of prices in the economy) was 1 percent during June 1995. Use your answer to (c) to logically evaluate the claim that the use of LIFO produces lower earnings during inflationary periods.

P9.5 FIFO, Average Cost, and LIFO. The following inventory information pertains to Resting-Boy recliners of Fine Furniture Ltd. for the year ended December 31, 1995:

Date	Recliners	Units	Unit Cost	Total Cost
Jan. 1	Inventory on hand	200	$150	$ 30 000
Apr. 3	Purchase	300	175	52 500
Sept. 28	Purchase	400	200	80 000
	Available for sale	900		$162 500

The company sold 400 recliners on June 25 and 300 on December 10. A physical count on December 31 indicates that 200 recliners are on hand.

Instructions

(a) Assuming that the company uses a periodic inventory system, calculate the cost of the ending inventory and the cost of goods sold using (1) the FIFO method, (2) the average cost method, and (3) the LIFO method. (Round unit cost calculations to three places.)

(b) Assuming that the company uses a perpetual inventory system, calculate the cost of the ending inventory and the cost of goods sold using (1) the FIFO method, (2) the average cost method, and (3) the LIFO method. (Round unit cost calculations to three places.)

P9.6 Effects of LIFO and FIFO. Seminole, Inc., began operations on January 1, 1992, and adopted the LIFO method of inventory pricing in their financial statements. Condensed income statements for Seminole, Inc. for 1992–95 follow:

	1992	1993	1994	1995
Net sales	$250 000	$300 000	$400 000	$480 000
Cost of goods sold	125 000	150 000	200 000	240 000
Gross margin	125 000	150 000	200 000	240 000
Sales and administration expenses	75 000	75 000	75 000	75 000
Pretax income	50 000	75 000	125 000	165 000
Income taxes (40%)	20 000	30 000	50 000	66 000
Net income	$ 30 000	$ 45 000	$ 75 000	$ 99 000

Seminole's comparative balance sheets showed the following LIFO inventory amounts at December 31: 1992, $25 000; 1993, $27 000; 1994, $30 000; and 1995, $38 000.

Notes to Seminole's financial statements indicated that, if the company had used the FIFO inventory method, December 31 inventories would have been as follows: 1992, $35 000; 1993, $42 000; 1994, $50 000; and 1995, $65 000.

Instructions

(a) Using the condensed format shown above, prepare income statements for Seminole, Inc., for 1992–95, assuming that the company had used FIFO since its inception.

(b) Explain the underlying factors that cause Seminole's net income under FIFO to differ from its net income under LIFO.

P9.7 Effect of Change from FIFO to LIFO. Manford Manufacturing Ltd. manufactures two products: Hoop and Soop. On December 31, 1994, Manford used the FIFO inventory method. On January 1, 1995, Manford changed to the LIFO method. The cumulative effect of this change is not determinable, and as a result, the ending inventory of 1994 under FIFO is also the beginning inventory for 1995 under LIFO. Any layers added during 1995 should be costed by reference to the first acquisitions of 1995, and any layers liquidated during 1995 should be considered a permanent liquidation.

The following information was available from Manford's inventory records for the last two years:

	Hoop		Soop	
	Units	Unit Cost	Units	Unit Cost
1994 Purchases				
Jan. 7	5 000	$4.00	22 000	$2.00
Apr. 16	12 000	4.50		
Nov. 8	17 000	5.00	18 500	2.75
Dec. 13	10 000	6.00		
1995 Purchases				
Feb. 11	3 000	7.00	23 000	3.00
May 20	8 000	7.50		
Oct. 15	20 000	8.00		
Dec. 23			15 500	3.50
Units on Hand				
Dec. 31, 1994	15 000		14 500	
Dec. 31, 1995	16 000		12 000	

Instructions

Compute the effect of the change from the FIFO to the LIFO inventory method on income before income taxes for the year ended December 31, 1995.
(Adapted from AICPA.)

P9.8 Effects of FIFO, LIFO, and Average Cost. The controller of the Tegano Corporation, a retail company, prepared three different schedules of gross margin for the first quarter ended September 30, 1995:

	Sales ($10 per unit)	Cost of Goods Sold	Gross Margin
Schedule A	$280 000	$118 550	$161 450
Schedule B	280 000	116 900	163 100
Schedule C	280 000	115 750	164 250

The computation of cost of goods sold in each schedule is based on the following data:

	Units	Cost per Unit	Total Cost
Beginning inventory, July 1	10 000	$4.00	$40 000
Purchase, July 25	8 000	4.20	33 600
Purchase, Aug. 15	5 000	4.13	20 650
Purchase, Sept. 5	7 000	4.30	30 100
Purchase, Sept. 25	12 000	4.25	51 000

The president of the corporation cannot understand how three different gross margins can be computed from the same set of data. As controller, you have explained that the three schedules are based on three different assumptions concerning the flow of inventory costs: FIFO, weighted average, and LIFO. Schedules A, B, and C were not necessarily prepared in this sequence of cost flow assumptions.

Instructions

Prepare three separate schedules computing cost of goods sold and supporting schedules. Show the composition of the ending inventory under each of the three cost flow assumptions.
(Adapted from AICPA.)

P9.9 Lower of Cost or Market. Yarbro Limited manufactures four products and prices its inventory using the lower of average cost or market value. The company maintains a normal profit margin rate of 20 percent of selling price. Yarbro's accountant gathered the following information, all on a per unit basis, at December 31, 1995:

Product	Historical Cost	Current Replacement Cost	Estimated Selling Price	Estimated Cost to Dispose
A	$24	$23	$30	$ 3
B	28	24	40	5
C	45	48	70	10
D	81	82	90	10

Instructions

(a) Prepare a schedule to determine the correct unit values for the inventory valuation of each product under the LCM rule (1) using the United States reporting requirements and (2) using the Canadian interpretation of market as the net realizable value (NRV).

(b) Explain the rationale for the use of selling prices when applying the LCM rule.

P9.10 Lower of Cost or Market. Selected items of merchandise information for eight independent cases appear below. In each case, the normal profit margin rate is 30 percent of selling price.

Instructions

Set up a table similar to the one below, and compute the missing values.

Case	Estimated Selling Price	Estimated Cost to Dispose	NRV Ceiling	Allowance for Normal Profit Margin	NRV Less Normal Profit Floor	Replacement Cost	Market	Historical Cost	LCM
1	$60		$50			$52		$51	
2		$5		$15		28		33	
3			18	6			$16		$15
4	30	4						20	18
5	10		9			7		8	
6		6		12		35			32
7			69	24		72		70	
8	70	9				37		42	

P9.11 Lower of Cost or Market. The following inventory information pertains to Yokoyama, Inc., at December 31, 1995:

		Per Unit			
	Quantity	Original Cost	Cost to Replace	Net Realizable Value	NRV Less Normal Profit Floor
Appliances					
Product W	500	$25	$22	$27	$23
Product X	300	31	33	36	29
Sporting Goods					
Product Y	600	14	18	20	13
Product Z	800	21	21	20	15

Instructions
(a) Determine the inventory valuation at December 31, 1995, assuming that the company applies the LCM rule to (1) each product, (2) major categories of products, and (3) the inventory as a whole. Assume the rules of the United States for market.
(b) The accountant for Yokoyama is trying to determine which one of the three amounts in (a) she should use in the company's published financial statements. What major factors should she consider?

P9.12 Inventory Errors. Condensed income statements for Penner Limited for 1990–95 appear below.

	Year Ending December 31					
	1990	1991	1992	1993	1994	1995
Net sales	$125 000	$132 000	$141 000	$156 000	$163 000	$176 000
Cost of goods sold	75 000	80 000	85 000	94 000	98 000	106 000
Gross margin	50 000	52 000	56 000	62 000	65 000	70 000
Sales and administrative expenses	30 000	31 000	34 000	39 000	41 000	45 000
Pretax income	20 000	21 000	22 000	23 000	24 000	25 000
Income taxes (40%)	8 000	8 400	8 800	9 200	9 600	10 000
Net income	$ 12 000	$ 12 600	$ 13 200	$ 13 800	$ 14 400	$ 15 000

The previous statements were prepared without knowledge of the following inventory errors:

Date	Inventory
Dec. 31, 1989	Correctly stated
Dec. 31, 1990	Understated $12 000
Dec. 31, 1991	Overstated $8000
Dec. 31, 1992	Understated $6000
Dec. 31, 1993	Correctly stated
Dec. 31, 1994	Overstated $12 000
Dec. 31, 1995	Overstated $6000

Instructions

(a) Using the condensed format shown above, prepare corrected income statements for Penner Limited for 1990–95.

(b) Describe the overall impact that the correction of the inventory errors in (a) has on the company's earnings trend.

P9.13 Inventory Errors. You have been asked to review the records and prepare corrected financial statements for Lufkin Corporation. The books of account are in agreement with the following balance sheet:

Lufkin Corporation
BALANCE SHEET
December 31, 1995

Assets		Liabilities and Shareholders' Equity	
Cash	$ 5 000	Accounts payable	$ 2 000
Accounts receivable	10 000	Notes payable	4 000
Notes receivable	3 000	Capital shares	10 000
Inventory	25 000	Retained earnings	27 000
	$43 000		$43 000

A review of Lufkin's books indicates that the following errors and omissions had not been corrected during the applicable years:

Dec. 31	Inventory Overvalued	Inventory Undervalued	Prepaid Expense	Unearned Revenue	Accrued Expense	Accrued Revenue
1992	—	$6000	$900	—	$200	—
1993	$7000	—	700	$400	75	$125
1994	8000	—	500	—	100	—
1995	—	9000	600	300	50	150

According to the books, profits are $5500 in 1993, $6500 in 1994, and $7500 in 1995. No dividends were declared during these years and no adjustments were made to retained earnings.

Instructions

Prepare a worksheet to develop the correct profits for 1993, 1994, and 1995 and the adjusted balance sheet accounts as of December 31, 1995. (Disregard possible income tax effects.)

(Adapted from AICPA.)

P9.14 Sales and Purchases Cutoff. You have been engaged to audit M Limited for the year ended December 31, 1995. M Limited, a wholesale chemical business, makes all sales at 25 percent over cost.

Shown below are portions of M Limited's sales and purchases accounts for the calendar year 1995.

Sales

Date	Reference	Amount	Date	Reference	Amount
12/31	Closing entry	700 590	Balance forward		658 320
			12/27	SI#965	5 195
			12/28	SI#966	20 000
			12/28	SI#967	1 302
			12/31	SI#969	5 841
			12/31	SI#970	7 922
			12/31	SI#971	2 010
		700 590			700 590

Purchases

Date	Reference	Amount	Date	Reference	Amount
Balance forward		360 300	12/31	Closing entry	385 346
12/28	RR#1059	3 100			
12/30	RR#1061	8 965			
12/31	RR#1062	4 861			
12/31	RR#1063	8 120			
		385 346			385 346

RR = Receiving report.
SI = Sales invoice.

You observed the physical inventory of goods in the warehouse on December 31, 1995, and were satisfied that it was properly taken. When you conducted a sales and purchases cutoff test (to determine that these transactions are recorded in the proper period), you found that at December 31, 1995, the last receiving report that had been used was no. 1063 and that no shipments had been made on any sales invoices with numbers larger than no. 968. You also obtained the following additional information:

(1) Included in the physical inventory were chemicals that had been purchased and received on receiving report no. 1060 but for which an invoice was not received until 1996. The cost was $4366.

(2) In the warehouse at December 31, 1995, were goods that had been sold and paid for by the customer but that were not shipped until 1996. They were all sold on sales invoice no. 965 and were not inventoried. The sales agreement between M Limited and this customer provided that title to the goods passes as soon as the customer pays for the goods and the seller processes the customer's order.

(3) On the evening of December 31, 1995, there were two railway cars on M Limited's siding:

(a) Car #AR38162 was unloaded on January 2, 1996, and received on receiving report no. 1063. The freight was paid by the vendor.

(b) Car #BAE74123 was loaded and sealed on December 31, 1995, and was switched off the company's siding on January 2, 1996. The sales price was $12 700 and the freight was paid by the customer. This order was sold on sales invoice no. 968.

(4) Two cars of chemicals enroute to Z Pulp and Paper Ltd. were temporarily stranded on December 31, 1995, on a railroad siding. They were sold on sales invoice no. 966 and the terms were FOB destination.

(5) A truckload of material enroute to M Limited on December 31, 1995, was received on receiving report no. 1064. The material was shipped FOB destination and freight of $75 was paid by M Limited. However, the freight was deducted from the purchase price of $975.

(6) Chemicals exposed to rain in transit and deemed unsalable were included in the physical inventory. Their invoice cost was $1250 and freight charges of $350 had been paid on the chemicals.

Instructions

(a) Compute the adjustments that should be made to M Limited's physical inventory at December 31, 1995.
(b) Prepare the adjusting entries required as of December 31, 1995.
(Adapted from AICPA.)

P9.15 Inventory Reconciliation. Hillard Limited cans two food commodities, which it stores at various warehouses. The company uses a perpetual inventory system under which the finished goods inventory is charged with production and credited for sales at standard cost. The details of the finished goods inventory are maintained on computer diskettes by the tabulating department in units and dollars for the various warehouses.

The accounting department receives copies of daily production reports and sales invoices. Units are then extended at standard cost and a summary of the day's activity is posted to the Finished Goods Inventory general ledger control account. Next the sales invoices and production reports are sent to the tabulating department for processing. Every month the control account and detailed tabulation records are reconciled and adjustments are recorded. The last reconciliation and adjustments were made at November 30, 1995.

Your CA firm observed the taking of the physical inventory at all locations on December 31, 1995. The inventory count began at 4:00 P.M. and was completed at 8:00 P.M. The company's figure for the physical inventory is $342 400. The general ledger control account balance at December 31 was $384 900, and the final "tab run" of the inventory computer file showed a total of $403 300.

Unit cost data for the company's two products are as follows:

Product	Standard Cost
A	$2
B	3

A review of December transactions disclosed the following:

(1) Sales invoice no. 1301, Dec. 2, was priced at standard cost for $11 700 but was listed on the accounting department's daily summary at $11 200.
(2) A production report for $23 900, Dec. 15, was processed twice in error by the tabulating department.
(3) Sales invoice no. 1423, Dec. 9, for 1200 units of product A was priced at a standard cost of $1.50 per unit by the accounting department. The tabulating department corrected the error but did not notify the accounting department of the error.
(4) A shipment of 3400 units of Product A was invoiced by the billing department as 3000 units on sales invoice no. 1504, Dec. 27. The error was discovered by your review of transactions.
(5) On December 27, the Halifax warehouse notified the tabulating department to remove 2200 unsalable units of Product A from the finished goods inventory, which it did without receiving a special invoice from the accounting department. The accounting department received a copy of the Halifax warehouse notification on

December 29 and prepared a special invoice, which was processed in the normal manner. The units were not included in the physical inventory.

(6) A report for the production on January 3 of 2500 units of Product B was processed for the Saskatoon plant as of December 31.

(7) A shipment of 300 units of Product B was made from the Montreal warehouse to Ken's Markets, Inc., at 8:30 P.M. on December 31 as an emergency service. The sales invoice was processed as of December 31. Hillard Limited prefers to treat the transaction as a sale in 1995.

(8) The working papers of the auditor observing the physical count at the Windsor warehouse revealed that 700 units of Product B were omitted from Hillard's physical count. Hillard concurred that the units were omitted in error.

(9) A sales invoice for 600 units of Product A shipped from the Jasper warehouse was mislaid and was not processed until January 5. The units were shipped on December 30.

(10) The physical inventory of the Victoria warehouse excluded 350 units of Product A marked "reserved." Investigation revealed that this merchandise was being stored as a convenience for Steve's Markets, Inc., a customer. This merchandise, which has not been recorded as a sale, is billed as it is shipped.

(11) A shipment of 10 000 units of Product B was made on December 27 from the Jasper warehouse to the Windsor warehouse. The shipment arrived on January 6 but had been excluded from the physical inventories.

Instructions

Prepare a worksheet to reconcile the balances for the physical inventory, Finished Goods Inventory general ledger control account, and tabulating department's detail of finished goods inventory ("tab run"). Use the format shown below.

	Physical Inventory	General Ledger Control Account	Tabulating Department's Detail of Inventory
Balance per client	$342 400	$384 900	$403 300

(Adapted from AICPA.)

P9.16 Corrected Inventory. You are auditing Handy Manufacturing Corporation for the year ended December 31, 1995. To reduce the workload at year-end, the company took its annual physical inventory under your observation on November 30, 1995. The company's Inventory account, which includes raw material and work-in-process, is on a perpetual basis and the FIFO method of pricing is used. There is no finished goods inventory. The company's physical inventory revealed that the book inventory of $58 410 was understated by $3000. To avoid distorting the interim financial statements, the company decided not to adjust the book inventory, except for obsolete inventory items, until year-end.

Your audit revealed the following information about the November 30 inventory:

(1) Pricing tests showed that the physical inventory was overpriced by $2200.

(2) Footing and extension errors resulted in a $150 understatement of the physical inventory.

(3) Direct labour included in the physical inventory amounted to $10 000. Overhead was included at the rate of 200 percent of direct labour. You determined that the amount of direct labour was correct and the overhead rate was proper.

(4) The physical inventory included obsolete materials recorded at $250. During December, these obsolete materials were removed from the inventory account and charged to Cost of Sales.

Your audit also disclosed the following information about the December 31 inventory:

(1) Total debits to certain accounts during December are listed below.

Purchases	$24 700
Direct labour	12 100
Manufacturing overhead	25 200
Cost of sales	68 600

(2) The cost of sales of $68 600 included direct labour of $13 800.
(3) Normal scrap loss on established product lines is negligible. However, a special order started and completed during December had excessive scrap loss of $800, which was charged to Manufacturing Overhead.

Instructions

(a) Compute the correct amount of the physical inventory at November 30, 1995.
(b) Without prejudice to your solution to (a), assume that the correct amount of the physical inventory at November 30, 1995, was $55 250. Compute the amount of the inventory at December 31, 1995.
(Adapted from AICPA.)

Cases

C9.1 LIFO. Jack Schaad, president of Pickett, Inc., recently read an article that claimed that at least 100 of the country's largest 500 companies were considering lobbying the government to have the LIFO method for valuing inventories deductible for tax purposes. The article stated that the firms wanted to switch to LIFO to (1) neutralize the effect of inflation in their financial statements, (2) eliminate inventory profits, and (3) reduce the amount of income taxes on their current tax returns. Schaad wonders if he should join the lobbyists and asks you to evaluate whether the switch would benefit his company.

Pickett currently uses the FIFO method of inventory valuation in its periodic inventory system. The company has a high inventory turnover rate, and inventories represent a significant proportion of the assets.

In discussing this trend toward LIFO inventory with business friends, Schaad has been told that the LIFO system is more costly to operate and will provide little benefit to companies with high turnover. Schaad intends to use the inventory method that is best for the company in the long run and not to select a method just because it is the current fad.

Instructions

(a) Explain to Mr. Schaad what inventory profits are and how the LIFO method of inventory valuation could reduce them.
(b) Explain to Mr. Schaad the differences between LIFO, FIFO, and average cost methods of inventory valuation.
(Adapted from CMA.)

C9.2 FIFO and LIFO. Mize Ltd. is considering changing its inventory valuation method from FIFO to LIFO for financial statement purposes because of the matching principle. However, management wishes to consider all of the effects on the company, including its reported performance, before making the final decision.

The inventory account, currently valued on the FIFO basis, consists of 1 million units at $7 per unit on January 1, 1995. There are 1 million common shares outstanding as of January 1, 1995, and the cash balance is $400 000.

The company has made the following forecasts for the period 1995–97:

	1995	1996	1997
Unit sales (in millions of units)	1.1	1.0	1.3
Sales price per unit	$10	$10	$12
Unit purchases (in millions of units)	1.0	1.1	1.2
Purchase price per unit	$7	$8	$9
Annual depreciation (in thousands of dollars)	$300	$300	$300
Cash dividends per share	$0.15	$0.15	$0.15
Cash payments for additions to and replacement of plant and equipment (in thousands of dollars)	$350	$350	$350
Income tax rate	40%	40%	40%
Opening expense (exclusive of depreciation) as a percent of sales	15%	15%	15%
Common shares outstanding (in millions)	1	1	1

Instructions

(a) Prepare a schedule that illustrates and compares the following data for Mize Ltd. under the FIFO and LIFO inventory methods for 1995–97. Assume the company would begin LIFO at the beginning of 1995.

(1) Year-end inventory balances.   (3) Earnings per share.
(2) Annual net income.   (4) Cash balance.

Assume all sales are collected in the year of sale and all purchases, operating expenses, and taxes are paid during the year incurred.

(b) Using the data above, your answer to (a), and any additional issues you believe need to be considered, prepare a report that recommends whether or not Mize Ltd. should change to the LIFO inventory method. Support your conclusions with appropriate arguments.

(Adapted from CMA.)

C9.3 Insurance Costs, LCM, and LIFO. Bagchi Limited purchased a significant amount of raw materials inventory for a new product that it is manufacturing. Bagchi purchased insurance on these raw materials while they were in transit from the supplier.

Bagchi uses the lower of cost or market rule for these raw materials. The replacement cost of the raw materials is above the net realizable value and both are below the original cost.

Bagchi uses the average cost inventory method for these raw materials. In the last two years, each purchase has been at a lower price than the previous purchase, and the ending inventory quantity for each period has been higher than the beginning inventory quantity for that period.

Instructions

(a) What is the theoretically appropriate method that Bagchi should use to account for the insurance costs on the raw materials while they were in transit from the supplier? Why?

(b) (1) At which amount should Bagchi's raw materials inventory be reported on the balance sheet? Why?

(2) In general, why is the lower of cost or market rule used to report inventory?

(c) What would have been the effect on ending inventory and cost of goods sold had Bagchi used the LIFO inventory method instead of the average cost inventory method for the raw materials? Why?

(Adapted from AICPA.)

Judgement Cases

J9.1 Recognizing a Sale. You are the controller for Glenuck Corporation, a large, publicly held manufacturer of electronic products and component parts. The company recognizes sales revenue according to the accrual basis of accounting.

Today's date is January 20, 1995, and you have just completed your initial draft of the financial statements for Glenuck's accounting period that ended on December 31, 1994. The income statement shows that the company's earnings per share (EPS) for 1994 are considerably lower than had been previously expected. In fact, the 1994 EPS are lower than EPS for 1993, and this breaks a ten-year trend of rising EPS.

Glenuck's chief executive officer, Jon Weimer, enters your office and lets you know that he is extremely displeased with these earnings results. He is especially concerned about the potential negative effect of the EPS decline on the company's share price, and subsequent shareholder reaction.

Mr. Weimer then brings up the subject of a large order of compact disc players that Glenuck had recently manufactured under a special order placed by Sound Magic Corporation, a national retail electronics chain. The contract with Sound Magic had provided that the CD players would be manufactured according to Sound Magic's precise specifications and that title to the goods would pass "on the date Sound Magic approves the goods." Glenuck Corporation produced the goods during 1994, and a Sound Magic representative inspected and approved them on January 3, 1995. Glenuck then shipped the goods on January 3.

Mr. Weimer observes that the preliminary 1994 income statement does not reflect the large sale made to Sound Magic. He points out that if the income statement could be revised to include the sale, EPS for 1994 would be comfortably higher than for 1993. Glenuck could then continue its string of unbroken EPS increases, and Glenuck's shareholders would be happy. Mr. Weimer tells you that he has a way to convince the independent auditors to go along with his plan, but he does not explain exactly what he has in mind.

You inform Mr. Weimer that generally accepted accounting principles permit a sale to be recognized only when title to goods in inventory passes from a seller to a buyer, in this case, on January 3, 1995. Mr. Weimer then states that "the goods in question were completed in 1994, and it only seems fair and reasonable to recognize the sales revenue in 1994. The fact that Sound Magic did not inspect the goods until January 3, 1995 is trivial."

Mr. Weimer then suggests that you revise the 1994 income statement to reflect the sale of the special order merchandise to Sound Magic. As he leaves your office, he reminds you of the need for everyone at Glenuck to be a team player.

Instruction

Would you revise the 1994 income statement in accordance with Mr. Weimer's instructions? Explain in detail the rationale that supports your decision. As a part of your explanation, include a discussion of the major parties who would be affected by your decision.

J9.2 Lower of Cost or Market Decision. Joy Toys, Inc. typically manufactures most of its product in anticipation of the Christmas season. Sometimes the company will quickly design and manufacture a toy to take advantage of fads (such as Ninja Turtles or sports heroes) that sweep the nation.

During the accounting period that just ended, the company designed and produced a large quantity of a doll named for an Olympic skater, which the company anticipated rushing to market before the winter Olympics. The toy was endorsed by the skater. Shortly before Joy Toys was set to begin taking orders for the doll, another skater failed to pass a drug test at a pre-Olympic event. As a result, the Olympic committee has set up an inquiry into the practices of all the athletes it is planning to send to the Olympics.

The outcome of the inquiry could tarnish the image of the skater who endorsed the doll, and it may not be marketable at a price and volume necessary for Joy Toys to recover its cost of production.

Joy Toys must file its financial statements for the most recent accounting period with the Ontario Securities Commission later this week, and its president does not want to recognize any losses in the value of the inventory of dolls. He believes that if the skater is cleared by the inquiry, the toy will "sell like hotcakes," and that the chances of a favourable finding are "better than 75 percent."

Instructions

Do you believe that Joy Toys should recognize a loss on its inventory of dolls in the financial statements for the accounting period just ended? Support your answer with careful analysis and reasoning.

J9.3 Inventory Reporting Foliage Partners, Ltd. is a limited partnership formed to fund the cultivation and sale of a variety of tropical plants. The investors provide funding to the limited partnership, which in turn advances monies to a contract grower, Green Top Growers (GTG), Inc., which is then responsible for acquiring the plants and plant materials, planting and cultivating the plants until their maturity, and then selling them on behalf of the limited partnership. GTG, a closely held company whose financial statements are not audited, is involved in a number of such arrangements and also grows plants on its own behalf. GTG has existed for ten years, although it has expanded substantially only in the last two. The types of plants in question take between eighteen months and three years to grow.

You are the accountant for Foliage Partners and are currently preparing its financial statements for the year just ended. Because the limited partnership has only recently been formed, the project is not far along at this time. The monies advanced to GTG so far are intended to provide only for the acquisition of the plants and plant materials and their initial planting. GTG is authorized to acquire the plant materials in the form of seeds, seedlings, or cuttings, limited only in such a fashion as to meet the projected growing schedules in the partnership agreement.

As of the partnership's balance sheet date, GTG had acquired the required seeds and seedlings and planted them in accordance with the agreement. The cuttings will be made from stock plants owned by GTG and then planted by GTG on behalf of Foliage Partners. On a recent visit to the GTG's facilities, you noticed that none of the cuttings have been made, although GTG has a large number of stock plants from which, according to GTG's president, the cuttings will soon be taken.

The general partner of the Foliage Partners believes that the balance sheet description of the amounts advanced to GTG should be characterized as plant inventory. She readily agrees to disclosing the fact that the inventory is held and is being cultivated by a contract grower and that the inventory will continue to be cared for by GTG on behalf of the limited partnership. You nevertheless wonder whether calling all of the amounts advanced to GTG "plant inventory" is appropriate in light of the fact that the cuttings have not yet been completed. The president responds to your concerns in the following fashion:

> The cuttings exist. They simply have not yet been separated from the stock plants. Moreover, we have paid GTG and they are obligated to perform according to the contract. The plant material exists, is growing at this time, and was growing at the balance sheet date. I believe that those cuttings exist, belong to the limited partnership, and should be so reported. To do otherwise might unduly alarm the investors by causing them to believe that the project is behind schedule or otherwise troubled when, in fact, it is not. We only recently funded the partnership and things are going perfectly. Why plant any seeds of doubt if, in fact, none exist?

Instructions

What should the amounts advanced to GTG by the partnership be called on the partnership's balance sheet? Do you believe that it would be acceptable to refer to the items as "plant inventory"? Defend your answers with appropriate arguments. Regardless of your answers to these questions, what information do you believe should be disclosed about the state of the inventory and costs paid to the contract grower?

Chapter 10

Inventories: Additional Valuation Methods

Objectives

1. To discuss and illustrate the conventional retail method.

2. To discuss and illustrate the average cost retail method.

3. To discuss and illustrate the retail FIFO method at lower of average cost or market.

4. To discuss and illustrate the retail LIFO method at cost.

5. To discuss and illustrate the gross margin method.

6. To discuss and illustrate the relative sales value method.

7. To discuss and illustrate accounting for purchase commitments.

The previous chapter provided an overview of basic inventory valuation methods. The objective of this chapter is to explain and illustrate several additional methods: conventional retail, average cost retail, retail FIFO, retail LIFO, gross margin, relative sales value, and accounting for purchase commitments. Some of these methods may initially appear to be more complex than they really are. However, one reason that companies use them is to simplify the enormous clerical tasks that accounting for inventory can produce.

Retail Inventory Method

The **retail inventory method** is a reversed markup procedure of inventory pricing used by many retail businesses, such as department stores. The main advantage of the method is that it produces accounting information and facilitates inventory control at less cost than other methods that could be used in retail concerns. Ending inventory and cost of goods sold figures derived under the retail method are acceptable for financial reporting and income tax purposes. Some larger retail stores have computer-coded price tags and scanners to reduce the inventory as soon as the sale is registered. However, there are still many smaller retailers who do not have the technology to maintain a perpetual inventory.

When applying the retail method, the accountant records the beginning inventory, purchases, and sales in the accounts in the usual manner under a periodic inventory system. Moreover, supplementary records are kept of additional information, including the beginning inventory and net purchases, each stated at **retail** (i.e., **selling**) **prices**. The accumulation of supplementary records at retail prices is facilitated by the fact that retail companies usually price their merchandise for sale when ordered or soon after acquisition. The accountant divides the **cost of goods available for sale** during a period by the **retail value of the same goods** to produce a cost-to-retail percentage that is commonly called the **cost percentage**. This percentage reflects the relationship between cost and retail that prevails in the *current* period. Sales for the period are then deducted from the retail value of goods available for sale to derive an ending inventory valued at *retail prices*. The accountant multiplies the ending inventory at retail by the cost percentage to derive an *estimate* of the **historical cost** of the ending inventory to use for balance sheet reporting purposes. Cost of goods sold may then be computed in the usual manner for a periodic system. Alternatively, cost of goods sold may be computed by multiplying the sales for the period by the cost percentage. The following simplified example illustrates the essence of the retail method:

Asset/Liability Measurement

	At Cost	At Retail
Beginning inventory	$ 9 800	$ 14 000
Net purchases	65 200	86 000
Goods available for sale	$75 000	$100 000
Cost percentage ($75 000 ÷ $100 000 = 0.75)		
Deduct:		
Sales		80 000
Ending inventory		
At retail		$ 20 000
At cost ($20 000 × 75%)	$15 000	
Cost of goods sold		
($9800 + $65 200 − $15 000 = $60 000 *or*		
$80 000 × 0.75 = $60 000)	$60 000	

Observe that the retail method enables us to calculate the cost of the ending inventory without knowing how many physical units are actually on hand. Nevertheless, a company using the retail method **must count its physical inventory at least once each year** for good internal control. Goods counted are extended at retail prices and compared with the inventory at retail value derived under the retail method. Differences may occur for several reasons, including shoplifting, theft, breakage, inaccurate records, and an inaccurate physical count. If the physical count has been performed correctly, the accounting records should be adjusted to agree with it.

The retail method has three main uses:

1. The retail method enables a company to estimate its inventory at any time without a physical count, because both cost and retail figures are always available. These estimates are used for annual as well as interim reporting purposes.
2. Even when the inventory is counted, the retail method enables a company to take its physical inventory at marked selling prices. This expedites the work of personnel, since they do not have to refer to purchase invoices, and salespeople are usually familiar with the retail prices of the items they sell.
3. The retail method provides results that are useful when determining insurance coverage and settlements.

The major limitation of the retail method is that the cost percentage is merely an average of all goods reflected in its calculation. The average yields accurate results if the same relationship between cost and selling price exists for all goods or if the mix of goods in ending inventory is the same as that in the goods available for sale. Because some departure from these conditions usually occurs, the retail method produces accounting values of ending inventory and cost of goods sold that are only *approximations*. When the relationship between cost and selling price varies substantially between departments, the accountant should apply the retail method separately to each department, thus improving the accuracy of the method. Ending inventory costs computed in each department are summed to derive the cost for the entire inventory.

A company using the retail method does not have to apply the method to its entire inventory. For example, a large department store may use the retail method when accounting for certain types of merchandise, such as men's clothing, and the specific identification method when accounting for others, such as expensive jewellery.

When applying the retail method, the accountant adds transportation-in and subtracts purchase discounts when computing net purchases in the cost column. These two items are not added or subtracted in the retail column because the original retail price of the inventory is ordinarily set in a manner that reflects them. Purchase returns and purchase allowances are subtracted in the cost and retail columns because these items reduce the amount of goods purchased.

The sales amount that should be subtracted in the retail column should be net of any sales returns and allowances. Sales discounts, however, are not subtracted from sales because they are financial in nature and are not part of the initial markup that is applied to goods purchased. Employee discounts and normal shrinkage (due to damage, theft, etc.) should be subtracted (just as sales are) in the retail column because these items represent normal reductions of the original retail value of goods available for sale during the period. For example, the regular selling price of a product is $100 and the cost is $60. This means that the original markup is $40 ($100 − $60) or the cost percentage is 60 percent ($60 ÷ $100). If this item were purchased by an employee who qualifies for a 20 percent discount, then the net price would be $80. The employee discount of $20 must be included in the retail method of calculating inventory. If the employee discounts are ignored, the inventory at cost will be incorrect at 75 percent ($60 ÷ $80).

Retail Method Terminology

The previous example was simplified in order to introduce the rationale, uses, and limitations of the retail method. To properly handle the complexities encountered in practice, accountants must understand the meaning of each of the following important terms used by retailers:

1. **Original retail price.** The price at which merchandise is first marked for sale to customers. This price includes an initial markup equal to the difference between the original retail price and the cost.
2. **Additional markup.** The amount added to the original retail price. Markups are added to the retail price of the goods, which are expected to sell at above the original markup.
3. **Markup cancellation.** Cancellation, either in part or in total, of an additional markup. A markup cancellation should not reduce the selling price below the original retail price.
4. **Net markup.** The amount of additional markups less markup cancellations. The net markup for any item should not be negative.
5. **Markdown.** The amount subtracted from the original retail price. A markdown occurs when the retail price of an item with the original markup is reduced, or when an item with an additional markup is reduced below the original retail price.
6. **Markdown cancellation.** Cancellation, either in part or in total, of a markdown. A markdown cancellation does not increase the selling price above the original retail price. Markdown cancellations can occur when items that were marked down for a sale go back to their normal retail prices after the sale period.
7. **Net markdown.** The amount of markdowns less markdown cancellations.

Assume that a retail concern purchases a new line of summer dresses for $60 each and immediately prices each dress for sale at $100. The *original retail price* is therefore $100. This price, which actually includes an *initial markup* of $40, is now an important point of reference when labelling future changes in selling price. If, in response to great demand for the dresses, the company raises the selling price to $110, we have an *additional markup* of $10. If the price is later lowered from $110 to $106, we have a *markup cancellation* of $4. The net markup is now $6. Suppose that near the end of the summer the company lowers its selling price from $106 to $90. This action represents a *markup cancellation* of $6 ($106 − $100) and a *markdown* of $10 ($100 − $90). If the company later raises the price from $90 to $92, we have a *markdown cancellation* of $2. The *net markdown* is now $8 ($100 − $92).

The descriptions of the retail method in this chapter will use the following data:

	At Cost	At Retail
Inventory, Jan. 1	$10 000	$13 000
Net purchases	47 600	64 000
Additional markups		7 000
Markup cancellations		4 000
Markdowns		12 000
Markdown cancellations		8 000
Sales		56 000

The **conventional retail method at lower of cost or market** produces an ending inventory that approximates the **lower of average cost or market**, which we will refer to simply as lower of cost or market. Observe in our example on page 462 that the lower of average cost or market is $14 400 ($20 000 × 0.72). The lower of average cost or market method of computing the cost percentage includes the sales figures at their expected selling price.

Average cost retail method is $15 160 ($20 000 × 0.758) in our example on page 463 and includes the net markups as well as net markdowns when computing our cost percentage. If, on the other hand, we had ignored net markups as well as net markdowns when calculating our cost percentage, the cost percentage would have been 74.8 percent ($57 600 ÷ $77 000). Note that the $57 600 amount equals the cost value of the beginning inventory ($10 000) plus the cost value of the net purchases ($47 600), and the $77 000 amount equals the retail value of the beginning inventory ($13 000) plus the retail value of the net purchases ($64 000). Ending inventory at cost would then have been $14 960 ($20 000 × 0.748).

Retail FIFO lower of cost or market includes net markups *and* net markdowns when calculating our cost percentage. The cost percentage is 71 percent ($47 600 ÷ $67 000). Note that the $67 000 amount equals the retail value of the net purchases ($64 000) plus the net markups ($3000). Ending inventory at lower of average cost or market is $14 200 ($20 000 × .71).

Retail LIFO at cost includes net markups *and* net markdowns when calculating our cost percentage. The cost percentage is 75.6 percent ($47 600 ÷ $63 000). Note that the $47 600 amount equals the net purchases at cost. The retail value includes the net purchases ($64 000) plus the net markups ($3000) minus the net markdowns ($4000). Ending inventory at cost is $15 292 [$10 000 (beginning inventory at cost) + $7000 (increase in the inventory at retail) × 0.756].

Conventional Retail Method (Lower of Average Cost or Market)

The existence of additional markups, markup cancellations, markdowns, and markdown cancellations introduces new complexities to the retail method. First, a company's accounting system must permit an accurate accumulation of each of these items in supplementary records. Second, because these items represent adjustments to the original retail price, they must be included in a logical manner in the basic retail inventory procedures that we illustrated earlier.

The conventional retail method, the one most commonly used by retailers, requires (1) including net markups when calculating the cost percentage and (2) subtracting net markdowns along with sales when measuring the ending inventory at retail. In other words, the accountant computes the cost percentage *after* considering net markups but *before* considering net markdowns. These procedures are illustrated in the example that follows.

The conventional retail method produces an ending inventory that approximates the lower of average cost or market, which we will refer to simply as lower of cost or market. As these numbers illustrate, the conventional retail method produces the lowest ending inventory valuation when compared with alternative methods of handling net markups and net markdowns.

Conventional retail method (lower of cost or market)

	At Cost	At Retail
Beginning inventory	$10 000	$13 000
Net purchases	47 600	64 000

Additional markups		$ 7 000
Less: Markup cancellations		4 000
Net markups		3 000
Goods available for sale	$57 600	80 000
Cost percentage ($57 600 ÷ $80 000 = 0.72)		
Deduct: Sales		(56 000)
Markdowns	12 000	
Less: Markdown cancellations	8 000	
Net markdowns		(4 000)
Ending inventory at retail		$20 000
At lower of cost or market ($20 000 × 0.72)	14 400	
Cost of goods sold	$43 200	

Are the results under the conventional retail method simply the most conservative, or do they really approximate those achieved by applying the lower of cost or market rule? Suppose that a company began operations near the end of a year and bought only a single item of merchandise that it was unable to sell. The item cost $100 and was originally priced to sell for $200. The retail price was subsequently raised to $250 (an additional markup of $50). Later the price was lowered to $125 (a markup cancellation of $50 and a markdown of $75). The following illustration shows how to value the ending inventory item using the conventional retail method:

	At Cost		At Retail
Beginning inventory	—		—
Net purchases	$100.00		$200
Additional markup		$50	50
Retail price with additional markup			$250
Reducing the retail price to $125 as follows:			
Less: Markup cancellation		50	
Net markup			—
Goods available for sale	100.00		200
Cost percentage ($100 ÷ $200 = 0.50)			
Deduct:			
Sales			—
Markdown		75	
Less: Markdown cancellation		—	
Net markdown			(75)
Ending inventory			
At retail			$125
At lower of cost or market ($125 × 0.50)	$ 62.50		

The lower of cost or market valuation produced by the conventional retail method approximates the inventory's **net realizable value less an allowance for a normal profit margin**. In our example, the inventory item that cost $100 was originally priced at $200 to allow a 50 percent profit margin based on selling price. The sales price of the item was finally reduced to $125. This price indicates that the item's **utility** (its ability to produce future revenue) has declined. Observing the lower of cost or market rule requires that we recognize the decline in the current period, the one in which it occurred. This reflects the conservatism modifying convention. Accordingly, the conventional retail method produces an ending inventory valuation of $62.50, an amount clearly below the historical cost of $100. Note that the lower of cost or market valuation of $62.50 represents the estimated selling price ($125) less an allowance for a normal profit margin of 50 percent of selling price ($125 × 0.50 = $62.50).

We emphasize that the conventional retail method only *approximates* an ending inventory valuation at lower of cost or market. The method does not measure market by comparing net realizable value (NRV), replacement cost, and NRV less normal profit margin as required for reporting in the United States, but it does meet the requirements of Section 3030 of the CICA *Handbook*. Moreover, accountants apply the method to many inventory items, not simply to a single unit. An averaging effect therefore occurs. The conventional retail method is also limited because it assumes that markdowns apply only to goods sold during a period. This assumption is justified on the ground that goods marked down are more likely than not to have been sold during the period. In reality, however, some of the goods marked down may still be in ending inventory.

Average Cost Retail Method

The average cost retail method of estimating inventory requires (1) including net markups and (2) subtracting net markdowns when calculating the cost percentage.

The average cost retail method produces an ending inventory that approximates the cost. As these numbers illustrate, the average cost retail method produces a higher ending inventory valuation when compared with the conventional method of handling net markups and net markdowns. These procedures are illustrated in the following example:

Average cost retail method

	At Cost		At Retail
Beginning inventory	$10 000		$13 000
Net purchases	47 600		64 000
Subtotal	$57 600		$77 000
Additional markups		$ 7 000	
Less: Markup cancellations		4 000	
Add: Net markups			3 000
Markdowns		12 000	
Markdown cancellations		8 000	
Deduct net markdowns			(4 000)
Goods available for sale	$57 600		76 000
Cost percentage			
($57 600 ÷ $76 000 = 0.758)			
Deduct: Sales			(56 000)
Ending inventory at retail			$20 000
Ending inventory at average cost			
($20 000 × 0.758)	15 160		
Cost of goods sold	$42 440		

The average cost retail method can be compared to the conventional method by comparing the calculations. Suppose that a company began operations near the end of a year and bought only a single item of merchandise that it was unable to sell. The item cost $100 and was originally priced to sell for $200. The retail price was subsequently raised to $250 (an additional markup of $50). Later, the price was lowered to $125 (a markup cancellation of $50 and a markdown of $75). The following illustration shows how to value the ending inventory item using the average cost retail method:

	At Cost		At Retail
Beginning inventory	—		—
Net purchases	$100		$200
Additional markup		$50	
Less: Markup cancellation		50	
Net markup			—
Markdown		75	
Less: Markdown cancellation			—
Net markdown			(75)
Goods available for sale	100		125
Cost percentage ($100 ÷ $125 = 0.80)			
Deduct:			
Sales			—
Ending inventory			
At retail			$125
At cost ($125 × 0.80)	$100		

The inclusion of the net markups and net markdowns equals the cost in our example, but this method will only *approximate* an ending inventory valuation at cost when applied to inventory that includes a mixture of products. An averaging effect therefore occurs. The average cost retail method is also limited because it assumes that the ratio of marked up and marked down goods is constant in the goods sold and the goods in inventory.

Retail FIFO Method

Many companies adapt the retail method to reflect the FIFO cost flow assumption. This adaptation is called the retail FIFO method. Use of this method assumes retailers sell all of the beginning inventory before selling the goods purchased during the current period.

Compared with the conventional retail method, the retail FIFO method requires two important changes when calculating the periodic cost percentage:

1. The beginning inventory is separated from the calculation of the cost percentage. Thus, the beginning inventory is excluded to ensure that the resulting cost percentage reflects cost and retail prices of the current period only.
2. a. **Lower of cost or market.** Net markups are *included* with the net purchases in the calculation of the cost percentage. The rationale for excluding the markdowns in the calculation of the cost percentage is that markdowns apply only to goods sold during a period. This assumption is justified on the grounds that goods marked down are more likely than not to have been sold during the period.
    b. **Cost.** Net markups as well as net markdowns are *included* in the calculation. In other words, the accountant computes the cost percentage *after* considering both net markups and net markdowns. The rationale for including both in the cost

percentage is that FIFO is a method of arriving at *cost*, not lower of cost or market.

If we now make the simplified assumption that the level of specific retail prices remained *constant* during the year, here is how we would determine the cost percentage and the FIFO at lower of cost or market for the ending inventory:

Retail FIFO method (at lower of cost or market)

	At Cost		At Retail
Net purchases	$47 600		$64 000
Additional markups		$ 7 000	
Less: Markup cancellations		4 000	
Add: Net markups			3 000
	47 600		67 000
Cost percentage ($47 600 ÷ $67 000 = 0.71)			
Beginning inventory	10 000		13 000
Cost of goods available for sale	57 600		80 000
Deduct: Sales			(56 000)
Markdowns		12 000	
Markdown cancellations		8 000	
Deduct: Net markdowns			(4 000)
Ending inventory at retail			$20 000
Ending inventory FIFO at lower of cost or market ($20 000 × 0.71)	14 200		
Cost of goods sold	43 400		

Note that the beginning inventory was included in the calculation of the cost of goods sold. Net markups were included and net markdowns were excluded in the calculation of the cost percentage (71 percent). The beginning inventory was included in the cost of goods available for sale, then the cost percentage of 71 percent was used to convert the inventory at retail ($20 000) to the inventory at FIFO lower of cost or market of $14 200.

This example shows the cost percentage excluding the beginning inventory and the cost of goods sold including the beginning inventory. The ending inventory is calculated at the cost percentage based on the current period net purchases.

The FIFO retail method at cost would have a cost percentage of 75.6 percent ($47 600 ÷ $63 000). The net purchases at cost are $47 600 and at retail are $63 000 (net purchases + net markups − net markdowns). The ending inventory using FIFO at cost would be $15 120 ($20 000 × 0.756).

Retail LIFO Method at Cost

Matching

Many companies adapt the retail method to reflect the LIFO cost flow assumption. This adaptation is called the retail LIFO method. Use of this method enables retailers to secure the matching benefits that LIFO usually produces while at the same time reducing substantially the clerical burden of applying LIFO.

Compared with the conventional retail method, the retail LIFO method requires two important changes when calculating the periodic cost percentage.

1. The beginning inventory is *excluded* from the calculation. Under retail LIFO, the sole purpose of the cost percentage is to price any new LIFO layer that might be added in the current period. Thus, the beginning inventory is excluded to ensure that the resulting cost percentage reflects cost and retail prices of the current period only.

2. Net markups as well as net markdowns are *included* in the calculation. In other words, the accountant computes the cost percentage *after* considering both net markups and net markdowns. The rationale for including both in the cost percentage is that LIFO is a method of arriving at *cost*, not lower of cost or market.

If we now make the simplifying assumption that the level of specific retail prices remained *constant* during the year, here is how we would determine the cost percentage and the LIFO cost of the ending inventory:

Retail LIFO method at cost

	At Cost		At Retail
Net purchases	$47 600		$64 000
Additional markups		$ 7 000	
Less: Markup cancellations		4 000	
Add: Net markups			3 000
Markdowns		12 000	
Markdown cancellations		8 000	
Deduct: Net markdowns			(4 000)
Subtotal	47 600		63 000
Cost percentage ($47 600 ÷ $63 000 = 0.756)			
Beginning inventory at retail			13 000
Cost of goods available for sale			76 000
Deduct: Sales			(56 000)
Ending inventory at retail			$20 000
Ending inventory at retail			$20 000
Beginning inventory increase at retail			13 000
Inventory increase at retail			$ 7 000
Ending inventory at LIFO cost			
Beginning inventory at cost	$10 000		
Add: Inventory increase at cost			
($7000 × 0.756)	5 292		
Ending inventory	$15 292		

Note that the beginning inventory was excluded and the net markups and net markdowns were included in the calculation of the cost percentage (75.6 percent). The cost percentage was then used to convert the inventory *increase* that occurred during the year from a retail measure ($7000) to a cost measure ($5292). The cost of the inventory increase was then added to the cost of the beginning inventory to derive the cost of the ending LIFO inventory ($15 292).

The above example is very simplified; in reality, the retail dollar (like the cost dollar) is rarely a stable device for measuring inventory changes. Indeed, the level of specific retail prices usually fluctuates over time. Therefore, the retail LIFO method requires us to measure all inventory changes in **retail dollars of the base year**. The term "base year" refers to the *beginning* of the year in which a company adopts the retail LIFO method.

The retail LIFO method is similar to the dollar-value LIFO. In fact, the retail LIFO method is sometimes called the **dollar-value retail LIFO method**. The discussion of the retail LIFO method has been limited to an introduction to its basic operation because of its infrequent use in Canada.

Gross Margin Method

The **gross margin method** (often called the **gross profit method**) is widely used to obtain the **estimated cost** of an ending inventory for interim financial statements and insurance claims. The method requires adding the beginning inventory at cost to the net purchases at cost to produce the cost of goods available for sale during the period. Net sales for the period are then multiplied by a gross margin on sales percentage, and the result is subtracted from net sales to produce an estimated cost of goods sold figure. This figure is then subtracted from the cost of goods available for sale to produce an estimate of the cost of the ending inventory, as shown below:

Beginning inventory (measured at cost)		$ 30 000
Net purchases (measured at cost)		150 000
Cost of goods available for sale		180 000
Deduct:		
Net sales (measured at selling prices)	$200 000	
Less: Estimated gross margin		
($200 000 × 0.2)	40 000	
Estimated cost of goods sold		160 000
Estimated cost of ending inventory		$ 20 000

Dollar amounts for the beginning inventory, net purchases, and net sales are taken directly from the company's accounting records. The estimated gross margin on sales percentage (20 percent in this example) is a **historical rate** (not a current rate such as the one we use under the retail method) that reflects recent past experience. Typically, it is an average of the percentages applicable to the past few years.

Notice the similarity between the procedures used in applying the gross margin method and those used in calculating cost of goods sold in a periodic inventory system. In both calculations, we begin by deriving the cost of goods available for sale. Under the gross margin method, we then subtract the estimated cost of goods sold to obtain the estimated cost of the ending inventory. Under the periodic system, we subtract the cost of the ending inventory from the cost of goods available for sale to derive the cost of goods sold.

Gross Margin on Sales Percentage

Under the gross margin method, we use a **gross margin on sales percentage** when reducing net sales to an estimated cost basis. Gross margin percentages are usually derived and expressed in relation to selling prices. To illustrate, if a soccer ball costs $8 and sells for $10, the gross margin is $2. The gross margin percentage based on selling price is therefore 20 percent ($2 ÷ $10 = 0.2). The remaining 80 percent ($8 ÷ $10 = 0.8) is called the cost of goods sold percentage. The gross margin on sales percentage and the cost of goods sold percentage always sum to 100 percent.

At times, a gross margin percentage may be based on cost prices instead of selling prices. Using the same basic data shown above for the soccer ball, the gross margin percentage based on cost is 25 percent ($2 ÷ $8 = 0.25). When we are given a gross margin on cost percentage, we should first convert it to a gross margin on sales percentage in order to correctly apply the gross margin method. The following widely used formulas enable us to convert a gross margin on cost percentage to a gross margin on sales percentage, and vice versa:

$$\text{Gross margin on sales percentage} = \frac{\text{Gross margin on cost percentage}}{100\% + \text{Gross margin on cost percentage}}$$

$$\text{Gross margin on cost percentage} = \frac{\text{Gross margin on sales percentage}}{100\% - \text{Gross margin on sales percentage}}$$

Obviously, only the first formula is required to find an unknown gross margin on sales percentage. Accountants nevertheless should be familiar with both types of conversions.

The following examples illustrate how to apply the formulas:

Gross Margin on Sales Percentage		Gross Margin on Cost Percentage
20% (given)	⟶	$\frac{20\%}{100\% - 20\%} = 25\%$
25% (given)	⟶	$\frac{25\%}{100\% - 25\%} = 33\frac{1}{3}\%$
$\frac{50\%}{100\% + 50\%} = 33\frac{1}{3}\%$	⟵	50% (given)
$\frac{100\%}{100\% + 100\%} = 50\%$	⟵	100% (given)

Because cost prices are less than selling prices, each gross margin on cost percentage is greater than the related percentage based on sales. The gross margin on sales percentage is often called the **markup on sales**; similarly, the gross margin on cost percentage is frequently called the **markup on cost**.

Uses of the Gross Margin Method

Remember that we use an average *historical* (as opposed to a current) gross margin on sales percentage to implement the gross margin method. A major assumption of this method is that this percentage reasonably approximates the rate of gross margin in the current period. Because this rate usually differs to some extent from the average historical rate, the gross margin method yields only an *estimate* of the cost of the ending inventory. This estimate generally approximates the results under whatever inventory cost flow method the company uses (FIFO, average cost, and so forth). An exception may occur when a company uses some complex method of LIFO consisting of several layers of outdated costs. In this case, the ending inventory estimate under the gross margin method may depart considerably from the actual LIFO cost; we must therefore use caution when interpreting the results produced by the gross margin method.

The estimates produced by the gross margin method are generally considered too imprecise for use in annual financial statements prepared according to GAAP. Nevertheless, many companies use the method when preparing their internal and external interim reports (i.e., monthly or quarterly reports). Companies that use the gross margin method in their external interim reports and companies that use other methods than those used for annual reporting purposes "should disclose the method used at the interim date and any significant adjustments that result from reconciliations with the annual physical inventory."[1]

Accountants often use the gross margin method to estimate the cost of an inventory lost by theft, fire, or other casualty. The information needed to apply the method may be taken directly from the accounting records. If the records have been lost, an accountant can sometimes construct estimates of the needed information using prior years' financial statements, microfilm copies of bank records showing details of receipts and disbursements, and contact with suppliers and customers. When inventory has been lost, a company may apply the gross margin method to help determine an insurance settlement. We must remember, however, that the method produces an estimate of the *historical cost* of the inventory lost. Insurance coverage and settlements are often based on *replacement costs.* Thus, the results of the gross margin method may need adjusting to an estimated current replacement cost basis.

If the inventory loss is the result of a fire, there may be some inventory that is not damaged and some that is not entirely damaged. The partially damaged inventory may have a market value and the insurance claim should be for only the portion lost. Another factor to consider is inventory that declines in value when held for a period of time. The following illustration begins with the estimated cost of the ending inventory from page 467, and includes undamaged inventory with a sales value of $2500, merchandise with a cost of $1000 that had a market value of $600, and a write-down of 10 percent for the remainder for obsolescence.

Estimated cost of ending inventory	$20 000
Less: Undamaged inventory with a sales value of $2500, gross profit of ($2500 × 0.2 = $500), and a cost of $2000	2 000
Subtotal	$18 000
Less: Write-down of the inventory at 10%	1 800
Subtotal	$16 200
Deduct: Salvage value received from the sale of damaged merchandise	600
Amount to be recovered	$15 600

Auditors often use the gross margin method as a rough test of the validity of inventory cost determined under either a periodic or a perpetual system. If a material difference exists between the ending inventory cost determined using the gross margin method and that determined under the company's accounting system, the auditor should inquire about the reasons for the difference. This inquiry may simply reveal that the gross margin on sales percentage used in the gross margin method does not properly reflect current conditions. On the other hand, the inquiry may reveal errors made when determining cost within the company's accounting system.

Some companies with December 31 year-ends find it inconvenient to take inventory on that date. These companies may take their physical inventory on November 30 and estimate the inventory for December 31 from the accounting records using the gross margin method. The physical count on November 30 meets the annual physical requirements, and the estimated inventory on December 31 is used for the financial statements.

---

[1]"Interim Reporting to Shareholders," CICA *Handbook,* Section 1750.23, December 1989.

Gross Margin Method Applied to Classes of Goods

Gross margin percentages sometimes vary considerably among different classes of goods within a single company. When such variation occurs, the use of a single, company-wide gross margin percentage assumes that goods in the various classes are sold in the same mix each period. This assumption is, of course, seldom valid. As a result, we should apply the gross margin method separately to each class of goods, thereby enhancing the method's accuracy. We can then sum the ending inventory costs determined for each class to produce an overall cost for the company's inventory.

Relative Sales Value Method

A company purchases inventory items of different value in a lump sum or as a basket of goods. The total price is paid, and then the purchaser must allocate the cost among the individual units in the basket. Often the only method of allocating the cost to each unit is by using the relationship among the economic utility of the various components of the basket. Examples of these situations would be land subdivided for housing units, or plants or trees of varying size purchased as a unit or inventory clearance from a store.

Assume that 40 hectares of land are purchased for $600 000. This land is divided into housing lots with roads and facilities. The developer invests an additional $300 000 to have the land subdivided into individual lots.

The developer estimates that after subdividing the land it will yield the following:

- 20 corner units considered as prime locations with a selling price of $15 000 per unit.
- 50 units on a crescent considered as the second-best locations with a selling price of $9000.
- 150 units on the remaining available land with a selling price of $5000.

Exhibit 10.1 shows how the developer's costs are allocated among the lots.

Loss From Purchase Commitments

Companies often enter into irrevocable contracts that guarantee the price and delivery of products and materials sold or used in their operation. If the value of the contract is material, then the details of the contract should be disclosed in the notes to the financial statements.[2]

In a period of rising prices, most of these contracts prove to be advantageous for the company and shield it from price increases. However, on some occasions the contracted products may have price fluctuations, and the contract price may exceed the market price on the financial statement date. This situation leads to a liability that, for matching purposes, should be recorded in the period in which the loss was incurred. The entry that must be recorded is a loss in the income statement and a liability to be applied against future purchases.

Matching

---

[2]"Contractual Obligations," CICA *Handbook*, Section 3280, December 1978.

Exhibit 10.1   Relative Sales Value of Allocating Costs

Type	Quantity of Lots	Unit Sales Price	Total Sales Value	Allocation Formula	Cost Allocated
Corner	20	$15 000	$ 300 000	$300 000/$1 500 000 × $900 000	$180 000
Crescent	50	9 000	450 000	$450 000/$1 500 000 × $900 000	270 000
Regular	150	5 000	750 000	$750 000/$1 500 000 × $900 000	$450 000
			$1 500 000		

Total Cost: Purchase Price	$600 000
Development Costs	300 000
	$900 000

Entry to record the total purchase cost

Corner Lots Inventory, 20 units	180 000	
Crescent Lots Inventory, 50 units	270 000	
Regular Lots Inventory, 150 units	450 000	
Cash		900 000

Assume that a dishwasher manufacturer with a December year-end entered into a contract on October 15, 1994, to purchase 50 000 gear boxes for delivery at $25 each over the next year. By year-end, 8000 gear boxes were received at the contracted price.

After the company entered into the agreement with the local supplier, a new Japanese company introduced a similar gear box that sells for $23. Your entries under these circumstances would be as follows:

December 31, 1994: Year-end entry.

Loss from Purchase Commitment	84 000	
Liability for Purchase Commitment		84 000

(To record loss from commitment to purchase 42 000 gear boxes at $25. The market price on December 31, 1994, is $23.)

Commitment balance: 50 000 − 8 000 = 42 000 gears
Commitment loss per unit:
    Commitment price $25 − Market price $23 = $2

January 25, 1995: Received 5000 gear boxes.

Purchases	115 000	
Liability for Purchase Commitment	10 000	
Accounts Payable		125 000

(To record the purchase of 5000 gear boxes at the contract price of $25. $2 per unit was set up as a liability at December 31, 1994.)

Concluding Remarks

The inventory methods presented in this chapter may at first appear complex and imprecise. Remember, though, that accountants seek to provide **useful information** for which the **benefits exceed the costs.** Many large companies have tens of thousands, sometimes

Seven Keys to Better Inventory Management

The challenges for inventory management can be met logically and effectively by tackling these seven key areas.

The starting point for improved inventory management has to be an effective sales forecasting process. Sales forecasts are a key determinant of inventory turnover and service performance—including fill rates (or stock-outs) and order delivery cycle time.

Good sales forecasting means staying close to the customer to monitor sales trends and to anticipate both seasonal fluctuations and the "life cycle" of new, mature, and declining stock items. It also requires tracking leading indicators that foreshadow changes in underlying or structural demand. Finally, an effective sales forecasting process provides for measurement and feedback on forecasting accuracy.

Managing customer service is the second prerequisite to improved inventory management. Customer service standards must be established in consultation with customers so that their needs are reflected in fill rates and lead times. Most customers expect consistent, reliable service. Establishing and monitoring service standards—and alerting customers in advance to a failure to meet these standards—can go a long way toward good customer relations and effective inventory management. And a positive customer relationship can often facilitate product substitution rather than a lost sale when an unavoidable stock-out occurs.

The distributor provides the essential link between the product supplier and the ultimate customer. This means that relationships with suppliers are just as important as relationships with customers. Suppliers need the distributor to get their product to the end user. But the distributor needs consistent, reliable service performance by the supplier to meet its own customer service performance standards. Typically, suppliers want distributors who contract for significant volumes and have a solid financial base. In many industries, suppliers provide annual volume discounts to encourage large orders and cash discounts to encourage prompt payment. But from the distributor's viewpoint, good inventory management often means minimizing order quantities and maximizing order frequency—taking into account supplier lead times and fill rates and customer demand patterns.

Striking a balance between the sometimes conflicting objectives of suppliers and distributors requires a close working relationship between the two. Open communication through personal contacts at all levels frequently provides important inventory management benefits to the distributor including lower minimum order quantities, higher promotional discounts and improved payment

terms. Moreover, a close working relationship with major suppliers can pave the way for the return of excess and slow-moving stock to the supplier—an important element in improved distributor inventory management. But developing and maintaining a close working relationship with major suppliers must also be based on solid information—and this means keeping accurate supplier performance statistics that will support distributor negotiations.

The fourth key is to set tough but realistic inventory turnover objectives. Inventory budgets should be set from the bottom up, based on projected turnover of individual inventory items or product lines. Ideally, those responsible for controlling inventory levels and meeting customer service standards should be responsible for establishing the inventory budget. And the inventory budget should be broken down by month in order to properly reflect seasonality and other demand factors.

Effective distribution inventory management also requires an understanding and appreciation of inventory carrying costs. The distinction between financing and operating costs (including facilities and handling costs) and the distinction between fixed versus variable costs (at least over the short run) are important to informed inventory decision-making. Similarly, information on the cost of initiating and processing inventory orders can provide important insights into determining economic order quantities.

Good information systems are another prerequisite to effective inventory management. Timely and accurate information on demand, stock status, service performance (both from vendors and to customers) and suggested replenishment quantities can provide managers with the competitive edge in inventory management. Typically, successful distributors have relatively simple but effective computer-based information systems. But they also continually seek out opportunities to refine their systems so that they can respond quickly and effectively to changes.

Finally, effective inventory management requires discipline to follow relatively simply policies and procedures carefully and consistently. Training buyers in the basics of inventory management—and the organization's specific inventory systems and procedures—can positively impact on all aspects of inventory management.

Source: Reprinted from an article in *CMA Magazine,* by Kenneth G. Koehler, "Seven Keys to Better Inventory Management" (July/ August 1990), p. 18.

hundreds of thousands, of products. To account for such large and diverse inventories in a cost-effective manner, the methods described in this chapter are often helpful.

<table>
<tr><td>**Key Points**</td><td>

1. The retail inventory method is a reversed markup procedure of inventory pricing used by many retail businesses such as department stores. (Objectives 1 through 4)

2. The conventional retail method requires that we include net markups when calculating the cost percentage and subtract net markdowns along with sales when measuring the ending inventory at retail. The method produces an ending inventory valuation that approximates the lower of cost or market. (Objective 1)

3. The average cost retail method requires that we include net markups and net markdowns when calculating the cost percentage. The method produces an ending inventory valuation that approximates the average cost. (Objective 2)

4. The retail FIFO method at lower of cost or market requires that we include net markups when calculating the cost percentage and subtract net markdowns along with sales when measuring the ending inventory at retail. The method produces an ending inventory valuation that approximates the lower of cost or market. (Objective 3)

5. The retail LIFO method is an adaptation of the retail method used by many retailers to reflect the LIFO cost flow assumption. When calculating the periodic cost percentage under the retail LIFO method, the beginning inventory is excluded, while net markups and net markdowns are included. Under this method, we apply LIFO on the basis of changes in base-year retail dollars associated with a pool of similar goods. LIFO layers are expressed in retail dollars rather than in physical units; retail LIFO is therefore very similar to dollar-value LIFO. (Objective 4)

6. The gross margin method is used to estimate the cost of an inventory. The method relies on the use of a historical gross margin on sales percentage. Although the estimate produced by this method is generally considered too imprecise for use in annual financial statements, the method is frequently used for interim reporting purposes, for estimating the cost of an inventory lost by fire or other casualty, and for testing the reasonableness of an inventory cost derived in some other manner. (Objective 5)

7. The relative sales value method is used to allocate a lump-sum payment for inventory items among the individual items. (Objective 6)

8. Disclosure of a significant purchase commitment should be provided to the users of the financial statements. When the purchase commitment indicates a contingent loss, the loss should be reported in the financial statements when the amount can reasonably be estimated. (Objective 7)

</td></tr>
</table>

<table>
<tr><td>**Questions**</td><td>

Q10.1 Briefly describe the general operation of the retail inventory method.

Q10.2 What are the major uses of the retail method?

Q10.3 What major assumption about the composition of the ending inventory is inherent in the retail method?

Q10.4 What is the meaning of each of the following terms?
(a) Original retail price.   (e) Markdown.
(b) Additional markup.   (f) Markdown cancellation.
(c) Markup cancellation.   (g) Net markdown.
(d) Net markup.

Q10.5 Explain why the conventional retail method produces an ending inventory valuation that approximates the lower of cost or market.

</td></tr>
</table>

Q10.6 Explain the major differences between the conventional retail method and the retail FIFO method with regard to the manner in which the periodic cost percentage is calculated. Why do these differences exist?

Q10.7 Briefly describe the operation of the retail FIFO method.

Q10.8 Briefly describe the operation of the gross margin method.

Q10.9 Distinguish between a markup on cost and a markup on sales price.

Q10.10 Should we use a gross margin on cost percentage or a gross margin on sales percentage when applying the gross margin method? Why?

Q10.11 What are the major uses of the gross margin method?

Q10.12 Briefly describe the operation of the relative sales value method.

Q10.13 List situations in which the relative sales value method would be used for inventory valuation.

Q10.14 Why would a company enter into a purchase contract?

Q10.15 What situation would result in a loss from a purchase commitment?

Q10.16 How should a loss from a purchase commitment be recorded?

Exercises

E10.1 Conventional Retail Method. The following information was taken from the accounting records of Gibbs Department Store for the current year:

	Cost	Retail
Beginning inventory	$15 000	$20 000
Net purchases	60 000	75 000
Net markups		5 000
Net markdowns		6 000
Sales		79 000

Instructions

Calculate the ending inventory using the conventional retail method.

E10.2 Conventional Retail Method. The information shown below was taken from the financial records of Harvey's Hardware Store:

Inventory, Jan. 1, 1995	
At cost	$ 6 000
At retail	10 000
Purchases during 1995	
At cost	37 540
At retail	67 000
Purchase returns during 1995	
At cost	1 140
At retail	2 000
Additional markups during 1995, at retail	6 000
Markdowns during 1995, at retail	8 000
Markup cancellations during 1995, at retail	1 000
Markdown cancellations during 1995, at retail	3 000
Transportation-in during 1995, at cost	1 600
Sales during 1995, at retail	65 000

Instructions

Calculate the inventory valuation at December 31, 1995, using the conventional retail method.

E10.3 Conventional Retail Method. Gwinn Department Store uses the retail inventory method. Information relating to the computation of the inventory at December 31, 1995, is as follows:

	Cost	Retail
Inventory, Jan. 1, 1995	$ 41 000	$ 96 000
Purchases	394 810	607 400
Purchases returns	9 900	15 400
Freight-in	14 490	
Net markups		46 000
Net markdowns		30 000
Sales		560 000

Estimated normal shrinkage due to breakage and theft is 3 percent of sales.

Instructions

Calculate the estimated inventory on December 31, 1995, at the lower of cost or market using the conventional retail method.

E10.4 Conventional Retail Method. The following data pertain to Canning Limited for 1995:

	Cost	Retail
Inventory, Jan. 1	$15 000	$25 000
Net purchases	30 000	65 000
Net markups		10 000
Net markdowns		15 000
Sales		52 520

Instructions

Calculate the estimated ending inventory on the basis of lower of cost or market using the retail method.

E10.5 Average Cost Retail. Using the data presented in E10.4, calculate the cost of the ending inventory using the average cost retail method. (Round the cost percentage to three decimal places.)

E10.6 Retail FIFO at Lower of Cost or Market. Using the data presented in E10.4, calculate the cost of the ending inventory using the retail FIFO method.

E10.7 Retail FIFO Cost. Truax Limited uses the retail FIFO inventory method. The following information pertains to the company's 1995 accounting period:

	Cost	Retail
Inventory, Jan. 1, 1995	$30 000	$43 000
Purchases	140 000	180 000
Freight-in	10 000	
Net markups		35 000
Net markdowns		15 000
Sales		180 000

Instructions

Assuming that the inventory on January 1, 1995, is the base inventory and that there was no change in the price index during the year, compute the inventory at December 31, 1995, using the retail FIFO cost method. (Round the cost percentage to three decimal places.)

E10.8   Average Cost Retail.   Using the data presented in E10.7, calculate the cost of the ending inventory using the retail average cost method. (Round the cost percentage to three decimal places.)

E10.9   Retail LIFO.   The following data pertain to McCammon Supply Limited for the current year:

	Cost	Retail
Inventory, Jan. 1 (base LIFO layer)	$18 250	$25 000
Sales		88 700
Net markups		7 000
Net markdowns		10 000
Net purchases	75 000	103 000

Instructions

Calculate the cost of the ending inventory at December 31 using the retail LIFO method. Assume no change in the level of retail prices during the year.

E10.10   Gross Margin Percentages.   Prepare a table similar to the one shown below and fill in the missing amount for each case.

Case	Gross Margin on Sales Percentage	Gross Margin on Cost Percentage
1	20%	
2		200%
3	33⅓%	
4		20%
5	75%	
6		66⅔%

E10.11   Gross Margin Method.   On May 2, 1995, a fire destroyed the entire uninsured merchandise inventory of Walter Limited. You obtained the following data:

Inventory, Jan. 1, 1995	$10 000
Purchases, Jan. 1 through May 2	70 000
Sales, Jan. 1 through May 2	80 000
Gross margin on sales percentage	25%

Instructions

Calculate the estimated fire loss to report in Walter Limited's income statement for 1995.

E10.12 Gross Margin Method. Drexler Limited uses the gross margin method to estimate its inventories for interim reporting purposes. The following data pertain to the company:

Inventory, Jan. 1, 1995	$40 000
Purchases, Jan. 1 through Mar. 31, 1995	120 000
Sales, Jan. 1 through Mar. 31, 1995	180 000
Markup on cost	25%

Instructions

Calculate the estimated cost of the inventory at the end of the first quarter of 1995.

E10.13 Gross Margin Method. You are the independent auditor for Profit's Department Store. Tomorrow is the last day of the current fiscal year. The store will be closed and you will observe the taking of the physical inventory to accurately determine its cost.

Profit's accounting records as of the end of today provide the following data that pertain to the current fiscal year: sales, $446 000; sales returns, $20 000; beginning inventory, $80 000; purchases, $194 000; purchase returns, $4000; transportation-in, $10 000.

The average rate of gross margin on sales during the last three years is 40 percent.

Instructions

Estimate the cost of the ending inventory.

E10.14 Gross Margin Method. The following data were obtained from the accounting records of Tully, Inc.:

Inventory, July 1	$12 000
Purchases	
July	60 000
August	70 000
September	79 600
Sales	
July	70 000
August	82 000
September	90 000

The company's markup on cost has averaged 25 percent during the past few years.

Instructions

Estimate the ending inventory costs for July, August, and September for monthly reporting purposes.

E10.15   Relative Sales Value Method. Goreland Office Furniture Ltd. purchased the following inventory of a bankrupt competitor for $460 000.

Quantity	Description	Unit Sales Value
1000	Steno chairs	$ 30
600	Steno desks	500
800	Filing cabinets	300

Instructions

Allocate the total cost of the goods and give Mr. Goreland a unit cost for each item.

E10.16   Relative Sales Value Method. Burson Land Development purchased three farms outside Saskatoon city limits for a total cost of $2 200 000. The company plans to convert this land into custom-built industrial buildings. Mr. Carter, the president of Burson, has asked you to advise him on how the costs per unit can be established.

Instructions

Prepare a short, point-form report outlining your recommendations and the additional information required before you can do the calculations.

E10.17   Purchases Commitment. In June 1, 1994, Sutton Manufacturing Ltd. signed a three-year agreement to purchase steel sheet from its major supplier. The agreement states that the steel mill will be Sutton's only supplier of this major raw material at a price of $20 per sheet for the first two years of the agreement, and $22 per sheet for the last year. Sutton's annual usage is 150 000 sheets.

Sutton has a calendar year-end, and the controller has asked for your advice on the reporting requirements for the agreement. The market price for the steel sheets was $18 on December 31, 1994.

Instructions

Prepare the report.

E10.18   Purchases Commitment. Using the data presented in E10.17, prepare the report based on a market price of $22 for the steel sheets on December 31, 1994.

Problems

P10.1   Conventional Retail Method. The following information pertains to Hutchens Limited for the fiscal year ended June 30, 1995:

	Cost	Retail
Inventory, July 1, 1994	$12 600	$20 000
Purchases	46 160	80 500
Purchase returns	1 860	3 000
Purchase allowances	900	1 500
Transportation-in	4 000	
Additional markups		8 000
Markdowns		13 000
Markup cancellations		4 000
Markdown cancellations		8 000
Gross sales		84 000
Sales returns		2 000
Employee discounts granted		1 000
Normal breakage		2 000

Instructions

Calculate the June 30, 1995, inventory at lower of cost or market using the conventional retail method.

P10.2 Average Cost Retail. Using the data presented in P10.1, calculate the cost of the ending inventory using the average cost retail method. (Round the cost percentage to four decimal places.)

P10.3 Retail FIFO at Lower of Cost or Market. Using the data presented in P10.1, calculate the cost of the ending inventory using the retail FIFO method at lower of cost or market. (Round the cost percentage to three decimal places.)

P10.4 Conventional Retail Method. Brown Store applies the conventional retail method to each of its three departments in order to estimate its monthly inventories for internal reporting purposes. The following information for January 1995 is available from the company's accounting records:

	Department					
	Men's Clothing		Women's Clothing		Infants' Wear	
	Cost	Retail	Cost	Retail	Cost	Retail
Beginning inventory	$1 003	$1 700	$2 040	$4 000	$1 176	$2 800
Net purchases	3 797	6 000	5 960	11 500	3 624	8 800
Net markups		300		500		400
Net markdowns		700		900		500
Sales		5 000		10 000		8 000

Instructions

Calculate the estimated January 31 inventory for Brown Store by applying the conventional retail method to each department separately and summing the results.

P10.5   Conventional Retail Method. Doucette Department Store, Inc. uses the retail inventory method to estimate ending inventory for its monthly financial statements. The following data pertain to a single department for October 1995:

Inventory, Oct. 1	
At cost	$20 000
At retail	30 000
Purchases (exclusive of freight and returns)	
At cost	100 151
At retail	146 495
Freight-in	5 100
Purchase returns	
At cost	2 100
At retail	2 800
Additional markups	2 500
Markup cancellations	265
Markdowns (net)	800
Normal spoilage and breakage	3 600
Sales	134 730

Instructions
(a) Using the conventional retail method, prepare a schedule computing the estimated lower of cost or market inventory on October 31, 1995.
(b) A department store using the conventional retail inventory method estimates the cost of its ending inventory at $29 000. An accurate physical count reveals only $22 000 of inventory at lower of cost or market. List the factors that may have caused the difference between the computed inventory and the physical count.
(Adapted from AICPA.)

P10.6   Retail FIFO at Lower of Cost or Market. Hathaway Limited adopted the retail FIFO method on January 1, 1993. On that date, the company's inventory at retail prices was $111 111, its cost percentage was 45 percent, and a suitable retail price index was 100. Additional information for 1993, 1994, and 1995 appears below. (Round the cost percentages to three decimal places.)

	1993	1994	1995
Beginning inventory at retail	$111 111	$122 151	$124 551
Net purchases			
At cost	86 000	101 200	112 800
At retail	205 000	233 000	247 000
Net markups at retail	10 000	7 000	9 000
Net markdowns at retail	15 000	20 000	16 000
Sales at retail	188 960	217 600	225 140

Instructions
(a) Calculate the cost of ending inventory for each year using the retail FIFO method.
(b) Calculate the cost of goods sold for each year under the retail FIFO method.

P10.7   Retail FIFO at Lower of Cost or Market. Under your guidance, Sam's Sporting Goods Store installed the retail method of accounting for its merchandise inventory as of

January 1, 1995. (Round the cost percentages to three decimal places.) When you pre-pared the store's financial statements on June 30, 1995, the following data were available:

	Cost	Selling Price
Inventory, Jan. 1	$26 900	$40 000
Markdowns		10 500
Additional markups		19 500
Markdown cancellations		6 500
Markup cancellations		4 500
Purchases	86 200	111 800
Sales		123 000
Purchase returns and allowances	1 500	1 800
Sales returns and allowances		6 000

Instructions

(a) Prepare a schedule to compute the store's June 30, 1995, inventory under the retail FIFO at lower of cost or market method. Assume that the level of retail prices has remained constant.

(b) Without prejudice to your solution to (a), assume that you computed the June 30, 1995, inventory to be $45 150 at retail and the cost percentage to be 80 percent. The level of retail prices has increased from 100 at January 1 to 105 at June 30. Prepare a schedule to compute the June 30, 1995, inventory under the retail FIFO method.

(Adapted from AICPA.)

P10.8 Conventional Retail and Retail FIFO. Conner Corporation, which uses the conventional retail inventory method, wishes to change to the retail FIFO method beginning with the accounting year ending December 31, 1995. Amounts indicated by the firm's accounting records are as follows:

	Cost	Retail
Inventory, Jan. 1, 1995	$5 210	$ 15 000
Net purchases in 1995	47 250	100 000
Net markups in 1995		7 000
Net markdowns in 1995		2 000
Sales in 1995		95 000

Assume that all net markups and net markdowns apply to 1995 purchases and that it is appropriate to treat the entire inventory as a single department. Also assume that the level of specific retail prices remained constant in 1995.

Instructions

Compute the inventory valuation at December 31, 1995, using:

(a) The conventional retail method.

(b) The retail FIFO method at lower of cost or market. (Round the cost percentage to four decimal places.)

(Adapted from AICPA.)

P10.9   Conventional Retail and Retail FIFO.   On January 2, 1995, Barton Corporation installed the retail method of account for its merchandise inventory. When you undertook the preparation of Barton's interim report of earnings on June 30, 1995, the following data were available:

	Cost	Retail
Inventory, Jan. 1	$ 95 413	$141 700
Markdowns		44 700
Additional markups		51 100
Markdown cancellations		13 300
Markup cancellations		3 140
Purchases	285 221	444 600
Sales		471 600
Purchases returns	6 474	10 660
Sales returns		18 900
Employee discounts		6 400
Shrinkage—2% of net sales		

Instructions

Compute the inventory valuation at June 30, 1995, using:

(a)   The conventional retail method.
(b)   The retail FIFO method at lower of cost or market. (Round the cost percentages to four decimal places.)
(Adapted from AICPA.)

P10.10   Conventional Retail and Retail LIFO at Cost.   Tutterow Department Store converted from the conventional retail method to the retail LIFO method on January 1, 1994. In your examination of the financial statements for the year ended December 31, 1995, management asks that you give a summary of certain computations of inventory costs for the past three years.

The following information is available:

(1)   The inventory at January 1, 1993, had a retail value of $45 000 and a cost of $27 500, based on the conventional retail method.
(2)   Transactions during 1993 were as follows:

	Cost	Retail
Gross purchases	$282 000	$490 000
Purchase returns	6 500	10 000
Purchase discounts	5 000	
Gross sales		492 000
Sales returns		5 000
Employee discounts		3 000
Freight-in	26 500	
Net markups		25 000
Net markdowns		10 000

(3)   The retail value of the December 31, 1994, inventory was $56 100, the cost percentage for 1994 under the retail LIFO method was 62 percent, and the retail price index was 102 percent of the January 1, 1994, price level.

(4) The retail value of the December 31, 1995, inventory was $48 300, the cost percentage for 1995 under the retail LIFO method was 61 percent, and the retail price index was 105 percent of the January 1, 1994, price level.

Instructions

(a) Prepare a schedule showing the computation of the cost of inventory on hand at December 31, 1993, based on the conventional retail method.

(b) Prepare a schedule showing the computation of the cost of inventory on hand at December 31, 1993, based on the retail LIFO method. Tutterow Department Store does not consider beginning inventories in computing its retail LIFO cost percentage. Assume that the retail value of the December 31, 1993, inventory was $50 000.

(c) Without prejudice to your solution to (b), assume that you computed the December 31, 1993, inventory (retail value $50 000) under the retail LIFO method at a cost of $28 000. Prepare a schedule showing the computations of the cost of the store's 1994 and 1995 year-end inventories under the retail LIFO method.

(Adapted from AICPA.)

P10.11 Gross Margin Method. A major portion of Wadley Limited's inventory was stolen on the night of August 16, 1995. A physical count the next day revealed that goods costing $10 000 were still on hand. Your examination of the company's accounting records reveals the following:

Inventory, Jan. 1, 1995	$ 25 000
Transactions, Jan. 1 through Aug. 16, 1995	
Purchases	87 000
Purchase returns	2 500
Transportation-in	5 400
Sales	141 500
Sales returns	5 000

The company began operations early in 1994, and its income statement for that year appears below.

Wadley Limited
INCOME STATEMENT
For the Year Ended December 31, 1994

Net sales		$195 000
Cost of goods sold		117 000
Gross margin on sales		78 000
Operating expenses		
Selling expenses	$11 000	
Administrative expenses	17 000	
Total		28 000
Income before income taxes		50 000
Income tax expense		20 000
Net income		$ 30 000

Instructions

Estimate the cost of the inventory that was stolen.

P10.12 Gross Margin Method. On the night of September 30, 1995, a fire destroyed most of the merchandise inventory of Spradlin, Inc. All goods were completely destroyed except for (1) partially damaged goods that normally sell for $10 000 and that had an estimated net realizable value of $2500 after the fire, and (2) undamaged goods that normally sell for $6000.

Condensed income statement information for the past three years appears below.

	1994	1993	1992
Net sales	$500 000	$300 000	$100 000
Cost of goods sold	384 000	220 000	71 000
Gross margin	116 000	80 000	29 000
Operating expenses	25 000	20 000	9 000
Income before income taxes	91 000	60 000	20 000
Income tax expense	36 400	24 000	8 000
Net income	$ 54 600	$ 36 000	$ 12 000

The company estimates that the rate of gross margin on sales in 1995 is equal to the weighted average rate for the past three years.

The following data are available from the company's accounting records, which were locked in a fireproof safe:

Inventory, Jan. 1, 1995	$46 000
Net purchases, Jan. 1 through Sept. 30, 1995	423 750
Net sales, Jan. 1 through Sept. 30, 1995	525 000

Instructions

(a) Estimate the amount of the fire loss, assuming that Spradlin, Inc. does not carry insurance on its inventory.

(b) Assume that Spradlin does have insurance on the inventory and that you are the adjuster for the insurance company. How might you argue that Spradlin's loss is really smaller than the amount you computed in (a)?

P10.13 Gross Margin Method. Carter Supplies, Inc. lost most of its inventory in a fire in December just before the year-end physical inventory was taken. Corporate records disclose the following:

Inventory (beginning)	$80 500
Purchases	240 000
Purchase returns	15 000
Sales	350 000
Sales returns	8 000
Gross profit is 25% of sales	

Merchandise with a selling price of $20 000 remained undamaged after the fire, and the damaged merchandise has a salvage value of $3750. The company does not carry fire insurance on its inventory. It is estimated that the year-end inventory would have been subject to a normal 5 percent write-down for obsolescence.

Instructions

Prepare a formal schedule computing the fire loss incurred by Carter Supplies, Inc. (Do not use the retail inventory method.)

P10.14 Gross Margin Method. On April 15, 1995, fire damaged the office and warehouse of Yon Wholesale Corporation. The only accounting record saved was the general ledger, from which the following trial balance was prepared:

Yon Wholesale Corporation
TRIAL BALANCE
March 31, 1995

Cash	$ 7 000	
Accounts receivable	27 000	
Inventory, Dec. 31, 1994	50 000	
Land	24 000	
Building and equipment	120 000	
Accumulated depreciation		$ 27 200
Other assets	3 600	
Accounts payable		23 700
Accrued liabilities		7 200
Capital stock		100 000
Retained earnings		47 700
Sales		90 400
Purchases	42 000	
Other expenses	22 600	
	$296 200	$296 200

Additional Information

(1) The fiscal year of the corporation ends on December 31.

(2) An examination of the April bank statement and cancelled cheques revealed that cheques written April 1–15 totalled $11 600, including $5700 for accounts payable as of March 31, $2000 for April merchandise shipments, and $3900 for other expenses. Deposits during the same period amounted to $10 650, which consisted of receipts on account from customers, with the exception of a $450 refund from a vendor for merchandise returned in April.

(3) Correspondence with suppliers revealed unrecorded obligations at April 15 of $8500 for April merchandise shipments, including $1300 for shipments in transit on that date.

(4) Customers acknowledged indebtedness of $26 400 at April 15, 1995. It is estimated that customers owe another $5000 that will never be acknowledged or recovered. Of the acknowledged indebtedness, $600 will probably be uncollectable.

(5) The companies insuring the inventory agreed that the corporation's fire loss claim should be based on the assumption that the overall gross margin on sales percentage for the past two years was in effect during the current year. The corporation's audited financial statements disclosed the following:

	Year Ended December 31	
	1994	**1993**
Net sales	$400 000	$300 000
Net purchases	226 000	174 000
Beginning inventory	45 000	35 000
Ending inventory	50 000	45 000

(6) Inventory with a cost of $6500 was salvaged and sold for $1350. The balance of the inventory was a total loss.

Instructions

Prepare a schedule computing the amount of the inventory fire loss, including a proper supporting schedule of the computation of the gross margin on sales percentage. *(Adapted from AICPA.)*

P10.15 Gross Margin Method. Reese Corporation is an importer and wholesaler. Its merchandise is purchased from a number of suppliers and is warehoused by Reese until it is sold to customers.

In conducting the audit for the year ended June 30, 1995, the company's CA determined that the internal control system was good. Accordingly, the physical inventory was observed at an interim date, May 31, 1995, instead of at year-end.

The following information was obtained from the general ledger:

Inventory, July 1, 1994	$ 87 500
Physical inventory, May 31, 1995	95 000
Sales for 11 months ended May 31, 1995	840 000
Sales for year ended June 30, 1995	950 000
Purchases for 11 months ended May 31, 1995 (before audit adjustments)	675 000
Purchases for year ended June 30, 1995 (before audit adjustments)	790 000

The CA's audit disclosed the following information:

Shipments received in May and included in the physical inventory but recorded as June purchases	$7 500
Shipments received in unsalable condition and excluded from physical inventory (credit memos had not been received nor had chargebacks to vendors been recorded)	
Total at May 31, 1995	1 000
Total at June 30, 1995 (including the May unrecorded chargebacks)	1500
Deposit made with vendor and charged to purchases in April 1995 (product was shipped in July 1995)	2000
Deposit made with vendor and charged to purchases in May 1995 (product was shipped, FOB destination, on May 29, 1995, and was included in May 31, 1995, physical inventory as goods in transit)	5 500

Instructions

In audit engagements in which interim physical inventories are observed, a frequently used auditing procedure is to test the reasonableness of the year-end inventory by the gross margin method. Prepare in good form the following schedules:

(a) Computation of the gross margin on sales percentage for the 11 months ended May 31, 1995.
(b) Computation by the gross margin method of cost of goods sold during June 1995.
(c) Computation by the gross margin method of the June 30, 1995, inventory.
(Adapted from AICPA.)

P10.16 Relative Sales Value Method. Jacker Real Estate purchased land on the outskirts of Barrie, Ontario. Jacker's president felt that this region of the province was beginning to develop into an industrial centre. The land cost Jacker $1 800 000 and was developed for a cost of $300 000. Jacker has prepared the following plan for the types of lots and has estimated the sales value for each lot:

Quantity	Description	Unit Sales Value
10	Lots with frontage on two streets	$45 000
31	Medium-size lots	30 000
81	Small lots	20 000

All costs incurred in addition to the acquisition and development costs are allocated on a per-lot basis. To date, $183 000 in costs have been incurred for the foundation and $61 000 for the building permits.

Instructions
Compute the unit cost for each lot.

P10.17 Relative Sales Value Method. Haland Liquidators Ltd. is in the process of auctioning off the assets of an estate. You purchased three paintings in a lump sum transaction for $90 000. Your insurance company has asked you to provide them with a unit cost, and an accountant has told you that this can be accomplished by using the relative sales value method. The market values of the paintings are $28 800, $52 400 and $61 600, and the policy premium is $2 per $1000 cost.

Instructions
Compute the insurance premium for each painting.

P10.18 Purchases Commitment. On March 15, 1995, Keilly Ltd., a retail photo sales and developing shop, signed an agreement to sell Silcronic film under its own label, "Keil-cron." The contract price was $3.00 per roll with an expected retail price of $4.50. This was a two-year agreement, with Keilly guaranteeing to purchase a minimum of 2000 rolls of film per month.

A competitor of Silcronic film has approached Keilly Ltd. with a similar offer at a cost of $2.50 per roll and no minimum order quantity. It appears that the new offer is the common industry contract.

The purchases to June 30, 1995, were 1200 in March, 2200 in April, 2150 in May, and 2000 in June.

Instructions
Prepare the reporting requirements for the June 30, 1995 financial statements.

P10.19 Purchases Commitment. Using the data presented in P10.18, prepare the reporting requirements for the June 30, 1995, financial statements with the following changes to the contract: the market price of the film is $3.50 per roll on June 30, 1995, and there is no minimum purchase quantity requirement.

C10.1   Impact of Changing from FIFO to LIFO.   Chip Henry, president of Dowling Enterprises, is thinking about changing his company's method of inventory pricing from FIFO to LIFO. Dowling Enterprises is a large, publicly held manufacturer of a wide variety of products whose costs are expected to increase steadily in the near future. LIFO is not acceptable for tax purposes, and Henry wonders what impact that would have on his company. Henry is concerned, though, that using LIFO could lower his company's net income, stock market price, working capital, and current ratio (current assets divided by current liabilities). He fears that while using LIFO may match revenue and expenses, investors and creditors may not look favourably on the company reporting lower income in the future.

Instructions
Advise Henry as to whether or not Dowling Enterprises should adopt LIFO. Provide rationale for your advice, and be sure to address Henry's concerns about LIFO.

C10.2   Retail Method.   Mizysak Paint Limited, your client, manufactures paint. The company's president, Mr. Mizysak, has decided to open a retail store to sell Mizysak paint as well as wallpaper and other supplies that would be purchased from other suppliers. He has asked you for information about the retail method of pricing inventories at the store.

Instructions
Prepare a report for the president explaining the retail method of pricing inventories. Your report should include the following points:

(a)   Description and accounting features of the retail method.
(b)   Conditions that may distort the results under the method.
(c)   Advantages of using the method when compared to cost methods of inventory pricing.
(d)   Accounting theory underlying the treatment of net markdowns and net markups under the method.
(Adapted from AICPA.)

C10.3   Inventories and Cash Basis Accounting.   The owner of Lutz's Retail Hardware computes income on a cash basis. At the end of each year, he takes a physical inventory and computes the cost of all merchandise on hand. To this he adds the ending balance of accounts receivable, because he considers this a part of inventory on the cash basis. Using this logic, he deducts from this total the ending balance of accounts payable for merchandise and arrives at what he calls inventory (net).

The following information has been taken from Lutz's cash basis income statements:

	1995	1994	1993
Cash received	$173 000	$164 000	$150 000
Cost of goods sold			
Inventory (net), Jan. 1	8 000	11 000	3 000
Total purchases	109 000	102 000	95 000
Goods available for sale	117 000	113 000	98 000
Inventory (net), Dec. 31	1 000	8 000	11 000
Cost of goods sold	116 000	105 000	87 000
Gross margin	$ 57 000	$ 59 000	$ 63 000

The following additional information is available:

	1995	1994	1993
Cash sales	$151 000	$147 000	$141 000
Credit sales	24 000	18 000	14 000
Accounts receivable, Dec. 31	8 000	6 000	5 000
Accounts payable for			
merchandise, Dec. 31	33 000	20 000	13 000

Instructions

(a) Without reference to the above, discuss the various cash basis concepts of revenue and income and indicate the conceptual merits of each.

(b) Is the gross margin for Lutz's Retail Hardware being computed on a cash basis? Evaluate and explain the approach used, with illustrative computations of the cash basis gross margin for 1994.

(c) Explain why the gross margin for Lutz's Retail Hardware shows a decrease while sales and cash receipts are increasing.

(Adapted from AICPA.)

Judgement Cases

J10.1   Gross Profit Method.   Danton Distributors Inc. has a problem with taking its annual physical inventory, because the inventory should be counted on June 30. Danton's managers selected the June 30 year-end to avoid the problems of a physical count on New Year's Eve. It appears that they have not avoided the problem, because most of their staff plan festivities for June 30, as the commencement of the July 1 holiday.

Danton's managers have heard that the gross profit method is fairly accurate. They have instructed you, as their accountant. to use the gross profit method for the financial statements.

Instructions

Would you follow management's instructions? Explain in detail the rationale that supports your decision. As a part of your explanation, include a discussion on the merits and disadvantages of the gross profit method of estimating the inventory.

J10.2   Retail Method.   Katie's Kids Klothes uses the conventional retail method of valuing its inventories. In past years, the company has had a stable cost-to-retail relationship for its inventory due to buying from one manufacturer and marking up the goods by a fixed percentage. Because of excellent sales and a lack of competition, Katie's has not previously needed to mark down any of its goods.

In the current year, however, two national department store chains have opened stores in Katie's small town. Those department stores have provided intense competition, and Katie's has found itself buying products from a variety of manufacturers with lower costs, reducing markup on many of its goods, and marking down various items of inventory. Despite these adjustments, Katie's is unable to sell all of certain products.

As an independent CA, you are beginning the audit of Katie's for the current year and have also been asked to consult on Katie's problems related to the new competition. Of particular concern is determining the value of Katie's ending inventory. In past years, you have been able to determine the inventory value at retail by simply counting the items on the shelves and extending the quantities by the retail prices noted on each item. The retail value of the inventory was then reduced to a lower of cost or market valuation by multiplying the retail value by the appropriate cost percentage. You had little concern about obsolete or unsalable goods, because little inventory remained at year-end and what remained was always sold quickly after year-end.

At the end of the current year, there is a large amount of inventory on hand because Katie's had bought larger quantities to obtain lower prices, and disappointing sales levels had resulted from the increased competition. You are also aware that the stable cost percentage of past years is uncertain today, and that the value of some of the inventory may be impaired below its net realizable value less the normal gross margin amount. Katie Helder, the owner of the store, has stated, "Let's just get these financial statements out as quickly as possible and turn our attention to solving my business problems. By the way, I don't expect to spend any more money than last year on producing the financial statements. Times are getting real tough here."

Instructions
Describe the methods that you believe should be applied to value Katie's inventory at the end of the current year. Be specific in your answer, and identify procedures that you believe should be applied in light of the company's changed conditions. Also comment on the owner's statement about the cost of preparing the financial statements. What should you do in regard to preparing the financial statements and the concerns about your fee?

Chapter 11

Investments and Funds

491

Enterprises invest in income-producing securities issued by other companies for a variety of reasons, including (1) earning a return on otherwise temporarily idle cash, (2) accumulating resources to retire long-term bonds, and (3) acquiring the capital shares of another enterprise to gain influence, control, or some other business advantage. Pertinent accounting issues concern the classification (current or noncurrent), measurement (valuation basis and cost flow), and disclosure of relevant information, including the accounting methods followed.

This chapter discusses the financial accounting and reporting implications of a variety of investment activities and circumstances. We first consider accounting concepts and practices for short-term, or temporary, investments. Next, we discuss the issues associated with accounting for long-term, or noncurrent, investments. Both sections consider investments in both equity and debt securities. Finally, we discuss several special problems associated with investments.

Temporary Investments

This section deals with accounting measurement and disclosure problems of various investments considered to be current assets. You will recall that **current assets** are defined as cash and other assets that can reasonably be expected to be sold, used up, or converted to cash within one year or the normal operating cycle, whichever is *longer*.[1]

Cash or investments that may mature or be sold in the near future may be restricted or designated by management for some noncurrent purpose. Even though these assets are highly liquid, they should be classified as noncurrent on the basis of management intent. For example, if a company acquires a short-term treasury bill of the federal government to earn a return on otherwise temporarily idle cash, the investment is considered **current.** If the same treasury bill is acquired to provide a fund for the retirement of bonds payable that mature in several years, however, then the investment is considered **noncurrent.** Cash and investments should also be considered noncurrent when held (1) to acquire or construct a noncurrent asset, (2) to acquire influence or control over another business, or (3) to achieve some other continuing business advantage. Thus, the objective of the investment—as well as the marketability of the security held—must be considered in classifying the asset.

Conceptually, we may view the operating cycle of a business as the time and activity required for resources to be productively applied, a product manufactured and sold or service rendered, and cash finally collected (as illustrated in Exhibit 11.1). If there are several operating cycles each year, then a one-year period should be used as the basis for classifying current assets. If the period of time represented by an operating cycle is greater than one year, however, the longer operating cycle is used for purposes of classifying current assets. For example, operating cycles exceed one year in the lumber, tobacco, and distillery businesses. Enterprises that have no clear operating cycle should adopt a one-year period for purposes of distinguishing between current and noncurrent assets.

Therefore, investments classified as current assets should represent securities acquired with temporarily idle cash. The investments are also expected to be liquidated within a year or an operating cycle, whichever is longer. Excess cash may be invested in either equity or debt securities. The following section considers accounting and reporting practices for temporary investments in equity securities.

---

[1]"Current Assets and Current Liabilities," CICA *Handbook,* Paragraph 1510.01, August 1991.

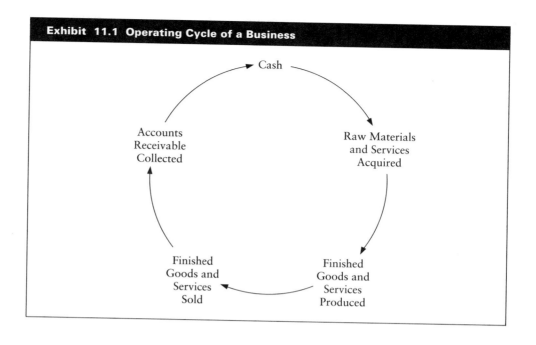

Exhibit 11.1 Operating Cycle of a Business

Temporary Investments in Equity Securities

The term "marketable" identifies securities for which sales prices or bid and ask prices are available from a securities exchange or in the over-the-counter market. When the sale of shares is restricted by a governmental or contractual requirement, the shares are considered nonmarketable unless the restriction can be removed within one year.

An **equity security** is any instrument representing an ownership interest or the right to acquire or dispose of ownership shares in an enterprise at a fixed or determinable price. Thus, the term includes warrants, common and preferred shares, and certain other ownership instruments. The term does *not* include preferred shares that must be redeemed or that are redeemable at the discretion of the investor. For example, if a capital share can be presented to the issuing corporation and redeemed for cash, an investor should not consider the share an equity security. Rather, such an item is considered a receivable of the investor. Furthermore, equity securities do *not* include treasury shares or convertible bonds. In short, "equity securities" are outstanding shares and other instruments that are not subject to a maturity or call date.

Valuation of Marketable Equity Securities

All marketable equity securities owned by an investing company should be recorded at their original cost (or fair market value if donated) and divided into two separate portfolios: current and noncurrent. Subsequent to acquisition, each portfolio is reported in the financial statements at the lower of cost or market. In Canada, investments may be reported at lower of individual cost or market, or lower of aggregate cost or market.[2] In the United States, the lower of cost or market rule requires that each portfolio should be valued at the lower of *aggregate* cost or market as of the balance sheet date.

---

[2]"Temporary Investments," CICA *Handbook,* Paragraph 3010.06, August 1991.

Conservatism

Remember that conservatism is one of the modifying conventions of financial accounting theory. The role of conservatism is to ensure that business risks and uncertainties are given adequate consideration in the financial statements, and it generally requires the recognition of apparent losses and the deferral of all gains until realized.

Accountants value all assets that are to be sold or otherwise converted directly into cash at amounts not exceeding the net realizable value of the assets. Marketable equity securities are valued at the lower of cost or market, as are items of inventory. Accounts receivable are also reported at net realizable value, which is the amount of cash expected to be collected after estimating uncollectable accounts. In the case of marketable equity securities, the CICA merely requires a conservative valuation basis consistent with other assets that are held for exchange or collection.

An Illustration of Accounting for Current Marketable Equity Securities

To illustrate, assume that Stable Limited acquires 500 common shares of Ace Enterprise at $25 per share as a temporary investment. The following entry would record the purchase:

Current Marketable Equity Securities (CMES)	12 500	
Cash		12 500
($25 × 500 shares = $12 500)		

The asset title Current Marketable Equity Securities is used in this entry. Other appropriate titles frequently used are Temporary Investments and Short-Term Investments. In addition to the Ace shares, we will assume that Stable also holds several other equity securities from Stress Limited as temporary investments, all of which were purchased during 1993. Exhibit 11.2 illustrates the determination of the aggregate cost, aggregate market value, and total lower of cost or market for the entire current portfolio of marketable equity securities held by Stable Limited at December 31, 1993.

Application of the lower of cost or market rule indicates that the carrying amount of this current portfolio should be $24 800 or $25 800, the individual or aggregate lower of cost or market value of the portfolio, because both of these amounts are lower than the $28 100 aggregate cost. The difference between the cost of the market is accounted for as a valuation allowance, and a loss is recognized in the income of the period.

Unrealized Losses. We recognize the decline in market value below cost of a current portfolio of securities even if we expect the decline to be short-term and **unrealized** in that the shares have not yet been sold.

We measure unrealized gains and losses as the difference between the market value and the cost of the marketable equity security portfolio at the balance sheet date. The following entry reflects this determination for Stable Limited using the total market value of the securities:

Dec. 31, 1993 Loss on Valuation of CMES	2300	
Allowance to Reduce CMES to Lower of Cost or		
Market (LCM)		2300
($28 100 − $25 800 = $2300)		

Allowance to Reduce CMES to Lower of Cost or Market is a contra asset, or valuation allowance, to the marketable equity securities account. The valuation allowance is subtracted from the cost of marketable equity securities to arrive at a lower of cost or

Exhibit 11.2 Lower of Aggregate Cost or Market Valuation: Current Portfolio, December 31, 1993

Security	(1) Number of Shares	(2) Cost per Share	(3) Market Price per Share	(4) Per Share Lower of Cost or Market	(5) (Col. 1 × Col. 2) Total Cost	(6) (Col. 1 × Col. 3) Total Market Value	(7) (Col. 1 × Col. 4) Total Lower of Cost or Market
Ace Enterprise, common shares	500	$25	$27	$25	$12 500	$13 500	$12 500
Stress Limited, preferred shares	1000	15	12	12	15 000	12 000	12 000
Stress Limited, warrants	300	2	1	1	600	300	300
Aggregate totals					$28 100	$25 800	$24 800

market valuation of the current equity portfolio for presentation in the balance sheet. Whenever the valuation allowance account has a positive (credit) balance, the current portfolio is valued at market. In contrast, if the valuation allowance account has a zero balance, the current equity portfolio is valued at cost. The valuation allowance cannot have a negative (debit) balance, because the securities cannot be carried in the accounts in excess of their cost.

In the 1993 balance sheet, Stable Limited will include current marketable equity securities, less the valuation allowance, among the current assets:

Marketable securities	$28 100
Less: Allowance to reduce marketable securities to market	2 300
	$25 800

The loss account debited in the previous entry, Loss on Valuation of CMES, is presented in the 1993 income statement of Stable Limited.

Unrealized Loss Recoveries. If the market value of the portfolio rises in subsequent years, losses already recognized may be partially or fully recovered. Losses that are recovered in future years because of increases in market value are reflected in the financial statements in the period of the recovery. Loss *recoveries* are recognized only to the extent of previously recognized losses. To illustrate, Exhibit 11.3 reflects the December 31, 1994, current marketable equity security portfolio of Stable Limited.

The entry to record the change in total market value of the current marketable equity security portfolio during 1994 is

Dec. 31, 1994 Allowance to Reduce CMES to LCM	2300	
Loss Recovery on Valuation of CMES		2300
(*To remove valuation allowance for market recoveries.*)		

Even though the market recovery is so large that it causes the total market value of the entire portfolio to exceed its aggregate cost, the portfolio is written up only to its original cost by bringing the valuation allowance to a zero balance. Therefore, the unrealized loss recovery (gain) to be recognized in the income statement is limited to the previously recognized losses. If the increase in the market value of the portfolio only partially

Exhibit   11.3   Lower of Aggregate Cost or Market Valuation: Current Portfolio, December 31, 1994

	(1)	(2)	(3)	(4)	(5)	(6)	(7) (Col. 1 × Col. 4)
			Market	Per Share		(Col. 1 × Col. 3)	
	Number of	Cost per	Price per	Lower of Cost or	(Col. 1 × Col. 2)	Total Market	Total Lower of Cost or
Security	Shares	Share	Share	Market	Total Cost	Value	Market
Ace Enterprise, common shares	500	$25	$32	$25	$12 500	$16 000	$12 500
Stress Limited, preferred shares	1000	15	13	13	15 000	13 000	13 000
Stress Limited, warrants	300	2	1	1	600	300	300
Aggregate totals					$28 100	$29 300	$25 800

recovers previously recognized losses, then the portfolio is valued at market, and a partial unrealized loss recovery is recognized in income.

As an example, if the total market value of Stable's current marketable equity security portfolio were $27 900 (instead of $29 300), the valuation allowance account must have a $200 balance ($28 100 − $27 900). Since the valuation allowance account has a balance of $2300 from the previous period, a journal entry to reduce the valuation allowance by $2100 would be necessary:

Dec. 31, 1994	Allowance to Reduce CMES to LCM	2100	
	Loss Recovery on Valuation of CMES		2100

This leaves a $200 credit balance in the valuation allowance, resulting in a portfolio carrying value of $27 900 ($28 100 − $200) in the 1994 balance sheet.

Notice that the credit to the loss recovery account is not the same as a credit to the loss account. The loss of 1993 is a nominal account that has been closed to Retained Earnings. Therefore, an increase in market prices that recovers previously recognized losses cannot be accounted for by credits to the loss account. To do so would result in the reporting of a "negative loss" in the income statement. Such an accounting is unattractive from an informational perspective. Creating a separate Loss Recovery account is more meaningful.

Realized Gains and Losses.   *FASB Statement No. 12* defines a **realized gain** or **loss** as the difference between the net proceeds from the sale of a marketable equity security and its cost.[3] Other circumstances giving rise to realized losses are discussed later in this chapter.

When a company disposes of a current marketable equity security by sale or otherwise, accountants generally recognize a realized gain or loss to the extent of the difference between the original cost of the security and the proceeds received from its disposition. The valuation allowance account attaches to the whole portfolio of current marketable equity securities, and not to individual equity securities within the portfolio. As a result, the valuation allowance is not adjusted in any way when various individual securities are sold. The purpose for this procedural approach is to ease the record-keeping burden. Current marketable equity securities are, by their nature, acquired and disposed of with

---

[3]*FASB Statement of Financial Accounting Standards No. 12*, Paragraph 7.

great regularity. Attaching the valuation allowance to each equity security would add a great burden to the accounting system. A corporation frequently invests in many different marketable equity securities and has a high trading volume. Thus, the method of adjusting the valuation allowance on the complete portfolio at the end of the reporting period is more economical than maintaining subsidiary valuation allowance records for each security.

To illustrate a sale, assume that Stable Limited sells all of its Ace common shares (Exhibit 11.3) for $20 a share early in 1995. The following entry is necessary to record the sale:

Jan. 15, 1995	Cash	10 000	
	Loss on Disposal of CMES	2 500	
	CMES		12 500
	($20 × 500 shares = $10 000)		

This entry does not affect the valuation allowance in any way, because that account is adjusted only at each balance sheet date. Therefore, if the sale of Ace common shares were the only activity during 1995, and if the market value of the remaining securities remained constant, then the situation at the end of 1995 would be as illustrated in Exhibit 11.4.

Because the aggregate cost of the portfolio exceeds the aggregate market value, a $2300 entry is necessary to adjust the valuation allowance ($15 600 − $13 300 = $2300). The difference between the aggregate cost and aggregate market value at the balance sheet date represents what the balance in the valuation allowance account should be. If the valuation allowance contains a balance from the previous year, then an entry is made for the amount of the difference between the current balance of the valuation allowance and the amount that the valuation allowance should contain. In the Stable illustration, the aggregate market value exceeded the aggregate cost of the current marketable equity securities portfolio at December 31, 1994 (Exhibit 11.3), and the valuation allowance account was completely eliminated at that date. Therefore, it is necessary to prepare the following entry for the full $2300 excess of aggregate cost over aggregate market value at December 31, 1995:

Dec. 31, 1995	Loss on Valuation of CMES	2300	
	Allowance to Reduce CMES to LCM		2300

This entry is necessary even though there has been no change in either the cost or market values of the securities remaining in the portfolio following the sale of the Ace common shares. An unrealized loss (due merely to the absence of the Ace shares at December 31, 1995) is reported in the 1995 income statement.

This treatment places a heavy emphasis on distinguishing between realized gains or losses and unrealized gains or losses. A company may recognize an *unrealized* loss in one period if the market value of a security declines below cost, and a *realized* loss in the following period if the security is sold for less than its cost. In these circumstances, an unrealized loss recovery may also be recognized in the period of disposal. To illustrate, assume that Stable Limited buys a single share of Remote, Inc. for $100 a share as a temporary investment on January 10, 1994. Assume further that the market value of the Remote share declines to $80 at December 31, 1994, and that this investment was the

Exhibit 11.4 Lower of Aggregate Cost or Market Valuation: Current Portfolio, December 31, 1995

Security	(1) Number of Shares	(2) Cost per Share	(3) Market Price per Share	(4) Per Share Lower of Cost or Market	(5) (Col. 1 × Col. 2) Total Cost	(6) (Col. 1 × Col. 3) Total Market Value	(7) (Col. 1 × Col. 4) Total Lower of Cost or Market
Stress Limited, preferred shares	1000	$15	$13	$13	$15 000	$13 000	13 000
Stress Limited, warrants	300	2	1	1	600	300	300
Aggregate totals					$15 600	$13 300	$13 300

only one made by Stable. The following entries would record the acquisition of the share and recognize the unrealized loss:

Jan. 10, 1994 CMES   100
      Cash   100
Dec. 31, 1994 Loss on Valuation of CMES   20
      Allowance to Reduce CMES to LCM   20

If we now assume that Stable Limited sells the Remote, Inc. share on February 4, 1995, for $80 and makes no further acquisitions of marketable equity securities during 1995, the following entries are necessary:

Feb. 4, 1995 Loss on Disposal of CMES   20
      Cash   80
         CMES   100
      (*To report sale of security at loss of $20.*)
Dec. 31, 1995 Allowance to Reduce CMES to LCM   20
         Loss Recovery on Valuation of CMES   20
      (*To remove valuation allowance account.*)

This unusual result of recognizing an unrealized loss in one year and an unrealized loss recovery in the next occurs because of the significance placed on distinguishing between realized and unrealized losses. If the December 31, 1995, adjusting entry had been omitted, then the $20 loss would have been recognized twice, once as unrealized at the end of 1994 and then again as realized in February 1995. Only the December 31, 1995, adjusting entry eliminates this undesirable effect. The combined income statement effect for 1994 and 1995 properly reflects a $20 loss. In practice, such results are generally not directly observed, because corporations hold many different securities in their portfolios. The impact on the valuation allowance of transactions such as those illustrated above is combined with the market value changes of all securities in the portfolio and not recognized separately. Nevertheless, reported results of operations are directly affected in the manner described.

Dividend Revenue. Dividends on capital share investments are ordinarily recorded as revenue when they are received by debiting Cash and crediting Dividend Revenue. Dividends that have been declared by the company issuing the shares but have not been received by the end of the investing company's financial reporting period should be recognized as a receivable and as revenue. Dividend revenue should *not* be anticipated and recognized prior to declaration, however.

Disclosure

Financial Statement Disclosures. The CICA requires disclosure of the basis of valuation and market value for marketable securities.

Furthermore, if a company engages in several transactions that involve the same class of security, assumptions concerning the cost flow of the securities may be necessary. In this regard, marketable securities may be viewed in a fashion similar to items of inventory. The method of cost valuation is weighted average for both financial reporting and income tax purposes.

Exhibit 11.5 contains a summary of the segregation and types of temporary investments reported by 300 Canadian companies. It is clear from this survey that almost 80 percent of the companies reporting temporary investments combined their temporary investments with cash.

Summary

Exhibit 11.6 presents the significant accounting practices involved in accounting for marketable securities. The flowchart provides a summary and review tool to ensure your complete understanding of accounting for current marketable equity securities.

Temporary Investments in Debt Securities

Debt securities differ from equity securities in several important ways. Debt securities represent amounts loaned to the company issuing the security in contrast to the ownership interest represented by equity securities. Return on debt securities, called **interest,** is fixed in amount and timing in comparison with dividends on equity securities, which are declared at the discretion of the issuing company. Finally, debt securities have a fixed maturity date while equity securities usually do not.

Companies may acquire debt securities for relatively short periods of time. If a debt security is *not marketable*, a current maturity date is generally necessary for classifying the investment as a current asset. The maturity date of a *marketable* debt instrument, however, does not necessarily indicate whether or not the item is considered current. As in the case of equity securities, management intent is an important consideration in the classification of investment securities. For example, a company may acquire a note or bond of another company with an immediate maturity date. If the acquiring company places the security in a noncurrent investment fund, the investment is classified as noncurrent. The noncurrent classification of such an investment possessing a short-term maturity date is based on management's intent to reinvest the funds at maturity for some noncurrent purpose. In contrast, if a company invests temporarily idle cash in marketable bonds that have a distant maturity date with the intention of disposing of the investment quickly, a current classification is appropriate. Management intent is therefore an important consideration in classifying investments in both debt and equity securities. Of course, the expressed intent of corporate management should be supported by logic and corroborative evidence, such as the purposes of the investment, the history of similar activities, a ready market for the security, and events subsequent to the balance sheet date.

Section 3010 of the CICA *Handbook,* "Temporary Investments," applies to both equity and debt securities with the following: "When the market value of temporary

Exhibit 11.5 Disclosure of Segregation and Types of Temporary Investments

	Number of Companies			
	1990	1989	1988	1987
Combined with cash	79	86	90	76
Shown separately	20	32	34	45
Combined with				
Term deposits	2	2	1	2
Cash and term deposits	—	—	—	1
One figure shown separately and one combined with				
cash	1	1	1	2

Source: Reprinted from *Financial Reporting in Canada,* Nineteenth Edition (Toronto: CICA, 1991), p. 73.

investments has declined below the carrying value, they should be carried at market value."[4]

Therefore, market valuation is required for current marketable debt securities whenever the investment has suffered a decline in market value that is not due to a temporary condition. In such a case, a loss should be reported in the income statement in the period of the investment write-down. Except for this condition, however, some of the latitude in accounting for and reporting marketable debt securities is not allowed for marketable equity securities.

While marketable equity securities must be written down to market for any material market declines, current generally accepted accounting principles require that individual debt securities be written down only for non-temporary declines. Should a company choose to apply the lower of cost or market policy to its entire portfolio of debt securities, no guidance is provided as to whether this should be done at the individual security level, to the portfolio in the aggregate, or in some other manner. Little guidance is available to help accountants distinguish between temporary and permanent declines. Although accountants may write down debt securities treated as current assets for *temporary* market declines, such a practice is not mandatory. Finally, *Accounting Research Bulletin No. 43* does not consider whether or not loss recoveries taking place in later periods may be recognized. Since the practice is not prohibited and, in fact, is required for current marketable equity securities, accountants may logically apply the same practices to debt securities as are applied to current marketable equity securities. Exhibit 11.7 compares current GAAP requirements for each type of current marketable security.

The exhibit shows that the accounting practices specified by the three documents permit differences rather than prescribe them. That is, no differences are explicitly established by any of the statements. Rather, Section 3010 and *ARB No. 43* are merely silent about some of the accounting issues addressed by *SFAS No. 12*. As a result, practice varies somewhat in this area; however, logic and consistency support treating current marketable equity and debt securities in a similar fashion. This means that all current marketable securities would be treated in accordance with the more precise requirements of *SFAS No. 12*. The authors support this position because it provides consistency in the recording of temporary investment transactions.

---

[4]"Temporary Investments," CICA *Handbook,* Paragraph 3010.06, August 1991.

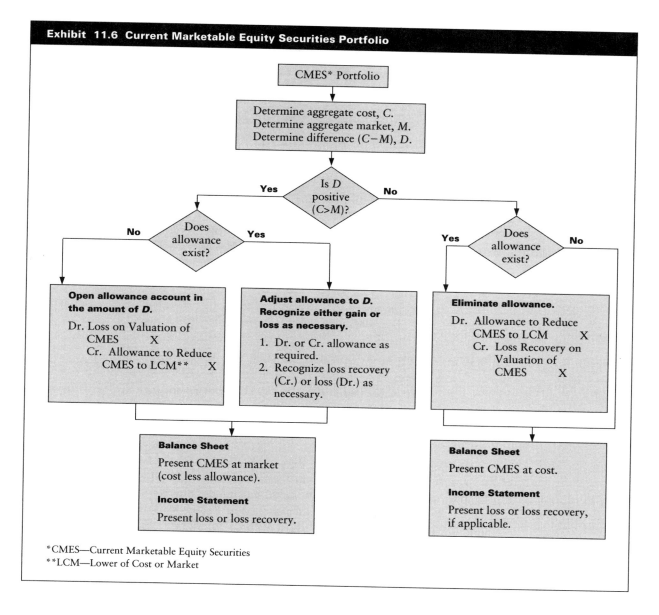

Exhibit 11.6 Current Marketable Equity Securities Portfolio

CMES* Portfolio

Determine aggregate cost, C.
Determine aggregate market, M.
Determine difference (C−M), D.

Is D positive (C>M)?

Yes ← → **No**

Does allowance exist? — **No** / **Yes**

Does allowance exist? — **Yes** / **No**

Open allowance account in the amount of D.

Dr. Loss on Valuation of
   CMES   X
  Cr. Allowance to Reduce
     CMES to LCM**   X

**Adjust allowance to D.
Recognize either gain or loss as necessary.**

1. Dr. or Cr. allowance as required.
2. Recognize loss recovery (Cr.) or loss (Dr.) as necessary.

Eliminate allowance.

Dr. Allowance to Reduce
   CMES to LCM   X
  Cr. Loss Recovery on
    Valuation of
    CMES   X

Balance Sheet

Present CMES at market (cost less allowance).

Income Statement

Present loss or loss recovery.

Balance Sheet

Present CMES at cost.

Income Statement

Present loss or loss recovery, if applicable.

*CMES—Current Marketable Equity Securities
**LCM—Lower of Cost or Market

The following example demonstrates acceptable accounting practices for temporary investments in debt securities. Assume that Stable Limited acquires bonds of Timeless Corporation on March 1, 1994. The bonds are dated January 1, 1994, pay interest semi-annually at a stated rate of 12 percent, mature in 2001, and were acquired by Stable for $10 200 (102 percent of par) plus accrued interest.

The acquisition or issue price of a bond is frequently stated as a percentage of par or face value. In this case, the bond was acquired at an amount 2 percent greater than the par amount of the bond, or at "102." Furthermore, certain transaction costs, such as broker fees, are frequently incurred in the acquisition of bonds and are considered part of the cost of the bonds. In this simplified example, no costs are considered except the direct cost of the bonds and related accrued interest. Stable Limited would make the following journal entry:

Exhibit 11.7 Accounting for Short-Term Investments

Issue	Temporary Investments (Section 3010)	Marketable Equity Securities (SFAS No. 12)	Marketable Debt Securities (ARB No. 43)
Valuation basis	Lower of cost or market.	Lower of aggregate cost or market.	Cost reduced to market for value declines of individual securities not due to temporary conditions.
Criterion for loss recognition	Declines to market recognized in income.	All market declines recognized in income.	Declines not due to temporary conditions recognized in income.
Loss recoveries	Silent. Many accountants follow the guidelines of *SFAS No. 12*.	All market recoveries to the extent of previously recognized unrealized losses.	No specification of market value recoveries.

Mar. 1, 1994 Short-Term Debt Investment	10 200	
Interest Receivable	200	
Cash		10 400

(*To record acquisition of Timeless Corporation bonds.*)

The total cash investment is computed as follows:

$$\$10\ 000 \times 102\% \quad = \$10\ 200 \text{ Bond price}$$
$$\$10\ 000 \times 12\% \times \tfrac{2}{12} = \underline{\quad 200} \text{ Accrued interest}$$
$$\text{Total cash investment} \quad \underline{\$10\ 400}$$

The debit of $200 to Interest Receivable could also have been charged to Interest Revenue. In that case, when the semi-annual interest is received, the entire cash received ($10 000 × 0.12 × 6/12 = $600) would be credited directly to the Interest Revenue account. Resuming the example in which Interest Receivable was charged, we find that the following entry would be necessary on June 30, 1994, to record the receipt of the interest payment:

June 30, 1994 Cash	600	
Interest Revenue		400
Interest Receivable		200

(*To record semi-annual interest payment,*
$10 000 × 0.12 × 6/12 = $600, ⅓ *of which had previously been recorded as receivable.*)

Note that the $200 amount paid in excess of par value ($10 200 − $10 000 = $200) is not amortized. Accountants usually do not amortize a difference between the purchase price and the par value of a temporary debt investment on the assumption that the investment is short-term and will not be held to maturity. This treatment is consistent with the overall objectives of short-term investments; that is, a temporary productive application of otherwise idle resources.

Finally, if Stable Limited sells the bond on November 1, 1994, at 97 plus accrued interest, the following entry is necessary:

Nov. 1, 1994	Cash	10 100	
	Loss on Sale of Debt Investment	500	
	Short-Term Debt Investment		10 200
	Interest Revenue		400

(*To record sale of bond at 97, plus accrued interest for four months:* $10 000 \times 0.12 \times \frac{4}{12} = \$400$.)

The cash received is the sum of $9700 ($10 000 \times 0.97$) plus $400 interest accrued from July 1 ($10 000 \times 0.12 \times \frac{4}{12}$). Since the bond cost $10 200 and was sold for $9700, a loss of $500 is recognized.

Noncurrent Investments

Companies frequently invest in the securities of different enterprises for purposes other than the temporary investment of idle cash. These investments are excluded from current assets and reported as noncurrent investments in the investing company's balance sheet.

In addition to the reasons mentioned earlier, such as accumulating funds for the retirement of debt or the ability to control another enterprise, a company may make long-term investments in another business for other reasons. For example, a company that desires to expand operations to a new product line or geographic area may presently lack adequate liquid resources. The company may discover, however, that it can capitalize on such opportunities immediately by investing in other enterprises that are already involved in those activities. Because the appropriate accounting treatment is affected by management's intent, accountants should understand completely the nature and purpose of the investment.

Noncurrent Investments in Equity Securities

If one company acquires the equity securities of another company as a noncurrent investment, the investment must be classified as one of the following types:

1. **Passive.** The investment is made in order to earn a return (dividends or long-term capital increment). Securities may be voting or nonvoting. Securities are reported at the *lower of cost or market,* when the market decline is other than temporary.
2. **Significant influence.** The investment is made in order to affect the operating or financial policies of the investee and to earn a return. Securities must convey voting rights to the investor to establish influence. Securities are reported by using the *equity method,* in which investee earnings (net income), net of dividends received, are recognized by the investor.
3. **Control.** The investment is made to obtain the ability to mandate operating or financial policies of a subsidiary and to earn a return. Securities must convey voting rights to permit control. The financial statements of the investee are *consolidated* with those of the investor, because in substance only a single economic entity exists.

Substance Over Form

Determination of whether an investment is passive or designed to obtain significant influence or control of the investee is based primarily on the magnitude of the investment. Accounting and reporting practices differ for each type of equity investment. Exhibit 11.8 presents the nature and objective of each type of investment and describes the general

Exhibit 11.8 Summary of Investments in Equity Securities

Issue	Level of Investment		
	Less than 20%	20%–50%	More than 50%
Ownership of voting shares			
Character of investment	Passive	Significant influence	Control
General reporting practice	Lower of cost or market*	Equity method	Consolidation
Primary relevant literature	CICA Paragraph 3050.02(c); SFAS No. 12; ARB No. 43, Ch. 3	CICA Paragraph 3050.02(a); APB Opinion No. 18	CICA Paragraph 1580.14; ARB No. 51; APB Opinions 16 and 17; SFAS No. 94

*When the decline is other than temporary.

reporting practice for each. The sections that follow consider the conceptual differences and accounting practices for each of the three types of equity investment.

Passive Equity Investments

Our previous discussion of marketable equity securities revealed that CICA *Handbook* Section 3010 specifies accounting and reporting practices for current portfolios of marketable equity securities. Now we will consider financial accounting and reporting standards in Section 3050 for *noncurrent* portfolios of marketable equity securities.

Conservatism

In Canada, unlike in the United States, the noncurrent portfolio is *not* valued at the lower of aggregate cost or market at each balance sheet date. The loss in value of the noncurrent investment is written down only if the loss is other than temporary. The write-down of the other than temporary loss on the noncurrent investment is included in the income of the period of the decline.[5]

Paragraph 3050.24 of the CICA *Handbook* outlines the conditions under which the impairment in the value of an investment may be indicated. When any of these conditions persist for three or four years, the value of the investment is presumed to be impaired whether the loss is realized or unrealized.[6] This practice differs from the practice specified by FASB for non-current marketable equity securities.

The FASB distinguishes between realized and unrealized losses for the noncurrent portfolio by stating that **only realized losses should be recognized in income**. Although the carrying amount of the noncurrent marketable equity securities portfolio is reduced from aggregate cost to a lower aggregate market, only *permanent* aggregate market declines are recognized in the income of the period. Aggregate market declines that are *temporary*, while requiring recognition in the asset valuation allowance, do not result in losses reported in the income statement.[7] Rather, companies in the United States report a temporary aggregate market decline below aggregate cost as a direct reduction of shareholders' equity, thereby avoiding the recognition of a loss in the income statement. The FASB gives three conditions under which losses on noncurrent investments must be treated as realized losses and recognized in income in the year of the loss: (1) a sale or disposal of the security, (2) a **permanent decline** in the market value of an individual security below its cost,[8] or (3) a transfer of the security to the current marketable equity security classification, or vice versa.

---

[5]"Long-Term Investments," CICA *Handbook,* Paragraph 3050.20, August 1991.

[6]"Long-Term Investments," CICA *Handbook,* Paragraph 3050.24, August 1991.

[7]*FASB Statement of Financial Accounting Standards No. 12,* Paragraph 11.

[8]*FASB Statement of Financial Accounting Standards No. 12,* Paragraphs 7, 10–11.

Conditions 1 and 2 provide convincing evidence that a permanent loss has been sustained by the investing company, which requires income statement recognition of the loss. Transfers of securities between the current and noncurrent portfolios (condition 3) may also give rise to a realized loss on the income statement. The purpose of this condition is to prevent managers from "dressing up" the income statement via classification changes between current and noncurrent investments in equity securities. In the absence of condition 3, a manager could transfer a security with a large unrealized loss position to the noncurrent portfolio. This would effectively remove the recognition of the unrealized loss from the income statement and, hence, arbitrarily improve net income. Condition 3 reduces the incentive for this type of behaviour by requiring a loss position to be recognized in income upon portfolio reclassification of the securities.

Changes in the value of marketable equity securities taking place after the balance sheet date should *not* be reflected in the financial statements, even if such a decline is considered permanent. However, in the United States, when changes in the market value of securities take place after the balance sheet date, the amount of gain or loss to be recognized is measured by the market value of the securities at the balance sheet date.

When cash dividends are received on passive investments in marketable equity securities, revenue is recognized in the amount of the dividend. For example, if Stable Limited receives a dividend of $3000 from Volunteer Corporation, the following entry is needed:

Cash	3000	
Dividend Revenue		3000
(To record receipt of cash dividend.)		

Occasionally, an investee company declares a dividend that exceeds its existing retained earnings or the income earned since the investor purchased the shares. In such cases the recipient company recognizes the receipt of a *liquidating dividend* and, instead of recognizing dividend revenue, records a recovery of a portion of the original investment. Liquidating dividends are fairly common in mining and petroleum operations.[9] To illustrate, assume that Stable Limited receives a $1000 liquidating dividend from Volunteer Corporation. The following entry should be made:

Cash	1000	
Net CMES		1000
(To record receipt of liquidating dividend.)		

To expand our illustration, assume that the investor owns 15 percent of its outstanding common shares of the investee. The investee's net income post-acquisition by the investor was $4000, and a $1000 dividend is received:

Cash	1000	
NCMES		400
Dividend Revenue		600
(To record receipt of cash and liquidating dividend.)		

The cash dividend is from the investor's pro rata share of the post-acquisition income ($4000 $\times$ 0.15 = $600). The liquidating dividend is the $1000 cash received, less the cash dividend of $600, to equal $400.

---

[9] "Long-Term Investments," CICA *Handbook,* Paragraph 3050.02(c), August 1991.

Passive investments in *nonmarketable* equity securities, such as shares of a closely held corporation, should be carried at cost unless there is clear evidence of an impairment in carrying value. Since no market value exists, such investments are not considered current except in unusual circumstances, such as an imminent sale.

Equity Investments Representing Significant Influence

Different accounting practices are required if the level of a long-term investment in voting marketable equity securities reaches a point at which significant influence is exercised by the investor over the operating and financial policies of the investee. The ability to significantly influence an investee company provides evidence that the earnings and losses of the investee have direct implications for the investor.

The range of business activities and purposes for which significant influence investments are made is broad. If an investor exercises significant influence over an investee, then the investor should accrue a portion of the income earned by the investee during that period. The amount of investee income to be reported as an increase in the investment account and as income to the investor is based on the level of the equity investment in the investee.

The **equity method** of accounting for significant influence investments is a sound accounting principle, because the carrying amount of the investment is directly affected by the results of the investee's operations.[10] Application of the equity method represents a type of "automatic valuation" accounting. An investment in the voting shares of a company represents, in substance, an investment in the net assets of that company. Changes in the investee's net assets that result from earnings or dividend payments result in changes in the investment account of the investor under the equity method.

Revenue Realization

The equity method is an example of accrual accounting. The investor company recognizes its share of the investee earnings on the income statement in the period earned. The income is later realized either via dividend distributions by the investee or disposition of the investment by the investor. The undistributed earnings (earnings retained after dividends are distributed) of the investee represent an increase in the net assets of the investee. A profitable investee company should experience a rise in the market value of its outstanding equity as the net assets increase from undistributed earnings. Therefore, the cash flow that an investor could realize from the disposition of the investment is simply the realization of previously recognized income.

The automatic valuation represented by the equity method is a surrogate for measuring the investment at current value. Indeed, if the current value of the investee equity shares were the accepted method of valuation, the equity method would be unnecessary. If the equity method of accounting were *not* required for investors having significant influence, income would be recognized when dividends were received or when the investment was sold. In the latter case, if the investment was sold for a price greater than original cost, the gain would be both recognized and realized in the period of disposition. This approach would have the undesirable effect of delaying the recognition of income until the investment was sold and then recognizing in a single period the lump sum gain (or loss). In contrast, the equity method provides for a more timely recognition of earned income from equity investments.

The ability to exercise significant influence may be evident in several ways. For example, representation on the investee's board of directors, material intercompany transactions, technological dependency of the investee, and other relationships may indicate an

---

[10]"Subsidiaries," CICA *Handbook*, Paragraph 1590.03(a), August 1991.

ability to exercise significant influence. Because of the difficulties in determining whether an investor exercises significant influence over the investee, Paragraph 3050.04 of the CICA *Handbook* establishes a threshold level of investment to guide practice. It states that a direct or indirect investment of 20 percent or more in the *voting* interest of an investee indicates, **in the absence of contrary evidence,** that an investor has the ability to exercise significant influence over an investee.[11] This paragraph thus establishes a presumption of significant influence arising at investment levels of 20 percent or more. The presumption may be rebutted, however, if evidence is available to support alternative practices. Recently, several companies have applied the equity method of accounting to holdings of investee voting shares as small as 5 percent to 10 percent, contending that even such small investments create significant influence if the rest of the investee's shares are widely distributed.

It is important to note that Paragraph 3050.04 does not absolutely require application of the equity method if 20 percent or more of the voting shares of an investee is held. The CICA *Handbook* provides guidance as to what types of evidence may overcome the presumption of significant influence arising at investment levels of 20 percent or more of the voting shares, but companies may look to the United States for additional examples. *FASB Interpretation No. 35* provides five examples of evidence that tend to rebut the presumption of significant influence, even if 20 percent or more of the voting shares are held:

Opposition by the investee, such as litigation or complaints to governmental regulatory authorities, challenges the investor's ability to exercise significant influence.

The investor and investee sign an agreement under which the investor surrenders significant rights as a shareholder.

Majority ownership of the investee is concentrated among a small group of shareholders who operate the investee without regard to the views of the investor.

The investor needs or wants more financial information to apply the equity method than is available to the investee's other shareholders (for example, the investor wants quarterly financial information from an investee that publicly reports only annually), tries to obtain that information, and fails.

The investor tries and fails to obtain representation on the investee's board of directors.[12]

Finally, although the test for significant influence is based on voting shares, the equity method is applied only to investments in common shares, whether or not they are voting shares. Thus, the investment level used to assess the existence of significant influence may differ from the investment level used in accounting for the investment.

A Basic Example of the Equity Method. An investor applying the equity method bases the recognition of income and the accompanying increase in the investment account on the percentage of shares represented by the investment. The receipt of dividends is treated as a reduction of the carrying amount of the investor's investment account. The

---

[11]"Long-Term Investments," CICA *Handbook,* Paragraph 3050.04, August 1991.
[12]"Criteria for Applying the Equity Method of Accounting for Investments in Common Stock: An Interpretation of APB Opinion No. 18," *FASB Interpretation No. 35,* 1981, Paragraph 4.

receipt of dividends represents a partial conversion of the investment to cash from equity in the investee's assets.

The following example illustrates accounting practices appropriate for the equity method. Assume that Stable Limited acquires a 25 percent interest in the voting shares of Thomas Limited on January 1, 1995. Also assume that Thomas Limited has only one class of common shares, all of which is voting, and that both companies report on a calendar-year basis. If Stable paid $500 000 for the investment, and Thomas reports a net income of $100 000 for 1995 and pays a $20 000 dividend on December 31, 1995, the following entries are necessary:

Jan. 1, 1995   Investment in Equity Securities   500 000
                     Cash   500 000
                (To record acquisition of 25% voting interest in Thomas Limited.)
Dec. 31, 1995 Investment in Equity Securities   25 000
                     Equity in Investee Income   25 000
                (To record equity in investee net income: $100 000 × 0.25 = $25 000.)
Dec. 31, 1995 Cash   5 000
                     Investment in Equity Securities   5 000
                (To record receipt of dividend: $20 000 × 0.25 = $5000.)

Excerpts from the 1995 balance sheet and income statement of Stable Limited would appear as follows:

Stable Limited
PARTIAL BALANCE SHEET
December 31, 1995

Noncurrent assets
  Investment in equity securities
  ($500 000 + $25 000 − $5000 = $520 000) $520 000

Stable Limited
PARTIAL INCOME STATEMENT
For the Year Ended December 31, 1995

Other revenue
Equity in investee income $25 000

The favourable impact of the investee's earnings are, thus, immediately reflected in the investor's financial statements. The dividends received by the investor are treated as a partial recovery or liquidation of the investment. Financial reporting for investments accounted for under the equity method contain many additional significant issues, and the following paragraphs discuss several of these.

The Existence of Positive and Negative Differential.   One issue arises in applying the equity method if the investor pays more or less for an investment than the book value of the underlying assets. For example, if the earning potential of the investee is abnormally high, the current value of the investee's net assets as represented by the market value of the investee's shares is frequently greater than the carrying amount on the investee's books.

If an excess amount is paid to acquire an equity interest in specifically identifiable undervalued assets, the difference is amortized over the individual lives of those assets.[13] For example, assume that the book value of the net assets (assets minus liabilities) of Thomas Limited in the previous example is $1 960 000, and that Stable Limited acquires a 25 percent ownership interest for a cost of $500 000. A 25 percent ownership in Thomas' net assets, however, equals only $490 000 ($1 960 000 × 0.25); therefore, Stable Limited paid $10 000 more for the investment than is represented by the book value. If the management of Stable Limited concludes that this differential represents an excess of the current value over the book value of Thomas Limited's plant assets, which have a ten-year life, the following entry to amortize this differential is necessary at the end of each year:

Equity in Investee Income	1000	
Investment in Equity Securities		1000
($10 000 ÷ 10 years = $1000)		

Combining this entry with the earlier ones results in $24 000 being included in the net income of the investor ($25 000 − $1000) and an investment in the balance sheet of $519 000 [$500 000 + ($25 000 − $1000) − $5000]. After $1000 has been amortized each year for ten years, the $10 000 excess of cost over book value will have been fully amortized, and this adjustment will no longer be necessary.

In practice, accountants frequently find it difficult to determine which specific assets are overvalued or undervalued and how much of the difference relates to general excess earning capacity. If the differential relates to excess earning capacity rather than to specific assets, the excess is considered **goodwill**. The CICA *Handbook* specifies that amounts recorded for goodwill must be amortized over a period not exceeding 40 years.[14] Accountants frequently attribute all of the difference between the cost of an equity method investment and the book value of the underlying net assets to goodwill, because information about the value of specific assets is difficult to obtain. Furthermore, differences caused by this simplifying assumption are normally not material. Therefore, in most situations, any excess of cost over the book value of the underlying assets is amortized as goodwill over a period of no greater than 40 years. For example, in Stable Limited's acquisition of Thomas Limited—resulting in a $10 000 difference between cost and book value—if the $10 000 is interpreted as goodwill with a twenty-year life, $500 would be amortized against the Equity in Investee Income account each year ($10 000/20 years = $500).

Any **negative differential** (excess of book value acquired over investment cost) is usually amortized in a similar fashion; however, the amortization results in *increases,* rather than decreases, in Equity in Investee Income and Investment in Equity Securities. For example, assume that the book value of the net assets (assets minus liabilities) of Thomas Limited in the previous example is $2 040 000 and that Stable Limited acquires a 25 percent ownership interest for a cost of $500 000. A 25 percent ownership in Thomas's net assets, however, equals only $510 000 ($2 040 000 × 0.25); therefore, Stable Limited paid $10 000 less for the investment than is represented by the book value. This differential should be assigned to the nonmonetary assets. If the nonmonetary assets have a fair value of $300 000, these assets would be recorded at $290 000.

---

[13]"Long-Term Investments," CICA *Handbook,* Paragraph 3050.12, August 1991.

[14]"Capital Assets," CICA *Handbook,* Paragraph 3060.32, October 1990.

Investee Operating Losses.   Another significant accounting issue arises if an investee company incurs operating losses to such an extent that application of the equity method reduces the investor's asset account to zero. To illustrate, assume that Thomas Limited incurs a $50 000 net loss. Stable Limited prepares the following entry:

Equity in Investee Loss	12 500	
Investment in Equity Securities		12 500
($50 000 × 0.25 = $12 500)		

This entry is appropriate unless it brings the investment account to a credit (negative) balance. Investors ordinarily discontinue applying the equity method if the investment account reaches zero, unless the investor (1) has guaranteed the indebtedness of the investee or (2) is otherwise committed to provide financial support. For example, if the shares of the investee were acquired from the investee at less than par, then the investor may be obligated (in the event of investee dissolution) to contribute amounts that would make the investment equal to the par value of the shares. In such cases, the Investment account may properly contain a credit balance and be reported as a liability to the extent of any contingent obligation.

The investor may suspend the use of the equity method because the recognition of investee net losses reduces the investment balance to zero, and therefore the conditions (described earlier) that would require the continued recognition of investee losses do not apply. The investor should resume applying the equity method if the investee becomes profitable again only after the investor's share of the net income equals the net losses that were not recognized during the period of suspension.

Change of Ownership Share.   If the investor reduces its share in the investee from 20 percent or more to less than 20 percent, its reporting requirements should be changed. The change in accounting for the investment from equity to cost would be conditional on the investor's eliminating significant influence in the investee. The cost of the investment is deemed to be the carrying value of the investment at the time of the change.[15]

Sale of an Investment.   When all or part of an equity-method investment is sold, the seller removes the appropriate percentage of the existing investment balance and determines a gain or loss by comparing the proceeds from the sale with that amount. For example, Stable Limited owned 10 000 shares of Alexander, Inc. common shares, which represented 40 percent of Alexander's voting shares. Stable has appropriately applied the equity method, and the investment balance at the time of sale was $125 000, including the original cost adjusted for Stable's share of Alexander's net incomes and net losses, dividends, and amortization of positive and negative differential. If Stable sells 2000 of the shares on June 1, 1995, for $35 000, the following entry is required:

June 1, 1995 Cash	35 000	
Investment in Equity		
Securities (²⁄₁₀ × $125 000)		25 000
Gain on Sale of Equity Securities		10 000

The $10 000 gain represents the excess of the $35 000 received over a pro rata share (²⁄₁₀ or 20 percent) of the carrying amount of the investment. Since 2000 of 10 000 shares are being sold, ²⁄₁₀ of the carrying value of the investment, or $25 000, is taken out of

---

[15]"Long-Term Investments," CICA *Handbook,* Paragraph 3050.16, August 1991.

the investment account. If the entire investment had been sold the entire investment account would have been eliminated at $125 000 and compared with the cash received to determine the amount of gain or loss.

The equity method is a complicated accounting procedure that involves application principles that are beyond the scope of this textbook. For example, the two companies involved may have intercompany transactions that require elimination. Also, the percentage of shares held by the investor may change, and as a result, the investor may be required to change to or from the equity method. These procedures are generally given greater attention in advanced accounting texts that provide in-depth coverage of business combinations and consolidated financial statements.

Disclosure

Equity Method Disclosures. Section 3050 of the *Handbook* requires the following disclosures for investments in common shares when such investments are significant to the financial position and results of operations of the investor:[16]

1. Name of each investee.
2. Percentage of ownership of common shares.
3. Accounting policies with respect to the investment. (In cases where 20 percent or more of the voting shares is held and the equity method is not used, or where less than 20 percent of the voting shares is held and the equity method is used, the following should be disclosed: name of the investee and the reason(s) for departure from the 20 percent guideline.)
4. Difference between investor's carrying value and the underlying equity in net assets, and the accounting treatment for this difference.
5. Aggregate value, based on quoted market price, of the investment in common shares of each identified investee that is not a subsidiary.
6. Summarized financial information of investees (either individually or combined).
7. Material effects of the possible exercise of options or warrants, possible conversions, etc.

Exhibit 11.9 shows the equity method disclosures from the 1991 annual report of TransAlta Utilities Corporation. "TransAlta is the largest investor-owned electric utility in Canada. TransAlta has developed, owned and operated major thermal power plants for more than 30 years. It currently produces about 70 per cent of the electric energy consumed by electric utility customers in the province."[17] The investments totals of $36.9 million in 1991 and $35.8 million in 1990 represent the balances resulting from applying the equity method for AEC Power Ltd. and the cost method for Sherritt Gordon Limited, as described in the financial statement note identifying accounting policies employed in the preparation of the statements. The disclosure in Exhibit 11.9 includes the note numbered 2, which describes the investments.

Equity Investments Representing Control of investee

If a company acquires an investment in the voting shares of an investee that exceeds 50 percent, the investor is presumed to be capable of controlling the investee's operating and financial policies. The investor is then called the **parent** and the investee is called the **subsidiary**. In such circumstances, accountants prepare **consolidated financial statements** for the two entities rather than separate financial statements for each. This practice is

Substance Over Form

---

[16]"Long-Term Investments," CICA *Handbook*, Paragraphs 3050.29–33, August 1991.
[17]TransAlta Utilities Corporation, *1991 Annual Report* (Calgary: 1992).

Exhibit 11.9 Equity Investment Disclosures

TransAlta Utilities Corporation

Consolidation and Investments

The consolidated financial statements include the accounts of the corporation and all subsidiaries, of which TransAlta Resources Corporation, TransAlta Fly Ash Ltd., Kanelk Transmission Company Limited and Farm Electric Services Ltd. are active.

TransAlta Resources Corporation holds investments and constructs and operates cogeneration facilities. TransAlta Fly Ash Ltd. processes and sells fly ash gathered at the corporation's coal-fired generating plants. Kanelk Transmission Company Limited owns facilities interconnecting the corporation's transmission system between the Crowsnest Pass region and the Kananaskis River valley and in doing so passes through a portion of British Columbia. Farm Electric Services Ltd. is a non-profit entity which organizes, constructs, operates and maintains, at cost, electric distribution systems owned by rural electrification co-operative associations.

TransAlta Resources' investment in AEC Power Ltd. is accounted for by the equity method and its investment in Sherritt Gordon Limited convertible notes is accounted for at cost.

2. Investments

	December 31	
	1991	**1990**
AEC Power Ltd.	**$15.8**	$15.8
Sherritt Gordon Limited	**21.1**	—
Canada Northwest Energy Limited	—	20.0
	$36.9	$35.8

AEC Power Ltd. owns and operates the utilities plant that supplies electric energy and steam on a cost-of-service basis to the Syncrude project for production of synthetic crude oil from the Alberta oil sands. The investment consists of 50 per cent of the voting common shares, which represents one third of the outstanding shares.

In October 1991, TransAlta received $29.0 million in convertible notes of Sherritt Gordon Limited in exchange for its interest in Canada Northwest Energy Limited. At December 31, 1990 the investment in Canada Northwest was classified as a discontinued operation and carried at a cost of $20.0 million. The difference between the value of the consideration received and the corporation's carrying cost of its previous investment in Canada Northwest will be included in earnings over five years.

During 1990, the corporation discontinued equity accounting for its investment in Canada Northwest and ceased operations in a wholly owned subsidiary, TransAlta Energy Systems Corporation, resulting in a loss of $110 million.

Source: TransAlta Utilities Corporation, *1991 Annual Report.*

based on the position that the two separate legal entities represent only one *economic* entity as a result of the majority investment. Therefore, financial reporting reflects the economic reality—not the legal form of organization—by consolidating the financial statements of the companies. Accounting and reporting practices underlying consolidated financial statements, while similar to the equity method, are discussed at length in advanced accounting texts and are discussed here only briefly.[18]

---

[18]For an excellent discussion of financial accounting and reporting for various business combinations, see Arnold J. Pahler and Joseph E. Mori, *Canadian Advanced Accounting: Concepts and Practice,* 4th ed. (San Diego: Harcourt Brace Jovanovich, 1991).

Consolidating the financial statements of two or more corporations involves aggregating the adjusted trial balances of each company after eliminating the residual effects of all intercompany transactions. Such transactions may involve buying and selling, lending and borrowing, and investing activities. Furthermore, *consolidated net income* generally remains the same whether the investor applies the equity method to the investee or fully consolidates the investee into a complete set of consolidated financial statements. The difference between the equity method and the **consolidation method** is one of degree of detail disclosed rather than of earnings measurement. Under the equity method, only a single asset account and revenue account are presented in the investor's financial statements, which represent the investment in the investee. Hence, the equity method is frequently called a **single-line consolidation.** The consolidation approach requires adding the specific individual asset, liability, revenue, and expense accounts of the subsidiary to those of the parent for financial reporting purposes. Any **minority interest**—outstanding shares held by individuals or entities other than the parent company—is usually shown outside the shareholders' equity of the consolidated entity.

The annual reports of many major companies include consolidated financial statements. The 1991 annual report to shareholders of BCE Inc. provides an excellent example. "BCE is a management holding corporation whose core businesses are the provision of telecommunications services and the manufacture of telecommunications equipment. BCE also has major interests in financial services and in a number of other businesses." All of its financial statements are titled with the word "consolidated," such as the consolidated statement of changes in financial position. The summary of significant accounting policies includes the following statement: "The investments in associated companies (20 percent to 50 percent owned) are accounted for by the equity method."

Noncurrent Investments in Debt Securities

A company may acquire the debt securities of other businesses as long-term investments for such reasons as (1) accumulating liquid resources for some noncurrent purpose, and (2) earning an acceptable rate of return on those liquid resources during the accumulation process. These objectives contrast with the purposes of making short-term investments in debt securities; that is, to invest temporarily excess cash for a short period of time. Because of these differing investment objectives, accounting practices for noncurrent debt investments differ from those appropriate for current debt investments.

Recording Bond Investments

When a company acquires the debt securities of another company as a noncurrent investment, the acquisition price frequently differs from the maturity value of the debt instrument. The rate of interest stated on a security, which was established when it was issued, may have become unrealistic as a result of changing economic conditions in money markets, changes in the risk class of the company issuing the bond, or other factors. In such cases, buyers are willing to pay more or less for the security than its stated or face value. If this occurs, the difference between the cash paid to acquire a security and the face value of the security is viewed as an adjustment of the security's stated rate of interest.

In general, investments in bonds and notes receivable are recorded at the fair market value of the consideration given for the security. When debt securities are acquired solely for cash, their value is presumed to be the amount of cash paid. If a security is exchanged for *noncash consideration,* the fair market value of this consideration is presumed to represent the present value of the security. If the fair market value of the noncash consideration is not determinable, however, we must then select an appropriate interest rate and compute the present value of the security by using the techniques described in Chapter 7. In such cases, the interest rate to be used in valuing the transaction can be affected by several considerations, such as the credit standing of the issuer, any restrictive covenants in the security, tax consequences, and collateral. Prevailing rates of interest for similar securities of issuers with similar credit ratings also help in the selection of an appropriate interest rate for determining the present value. The objective in selecting an interest rate is to approximate the rate that would have been incurred in an arm's-length transaction involving lending of cash.

Substance Over Form

In some circumstances, a stated rate of interest may not represent the rate that would exist in an arm's-length transaction. For example, the existence of related parties and related-party transactions may indicate that the stated rate of interest is not reasonable. In such situations, stated or unstated rights and privileges may alter the effective, or actual, rate of interest. If a right to abnormal purchase or sales discounts is granted as part of the consideration for a loan, the difference between the present value of the security and the cash loaned is properly regarded as an element of interest and the effective rate of interest implicit in such notes will differ from the stated rate.

Accounting for Premium and Discount

Any **premium** or **discount** recognized in conjunction with a debt investment is treated as a direct increase (premium) or reduction (discount) in the carrying amount of that investment. That is, a debt investment is originally presented in the balance sheet at its present value: its market value when it is acquired. The related premium or discount is then amortized as an adjustment to interest revenue over the life of the security by using the effective rate of interest.[19] The effective rate of interest is represented by the discount rate that equates the purchase price with the two future cash flows (interest payments and maturity amount) obtainable from the investment. We apply the effective rate of interest to the carrying value at the beginning of each period to determine annual interest. In this manner, a constant rate of interest is recognized over the life of the investment. The difference between the total interest revenue, determined by applying the effective rate of interest to the carrying amount and the cash received during the period, represents the amount of premium or discount to be amortized. This is consistent with amortization practices discussed in Chapters 4 and 7.

Materiality

In the United States, the straight-line method of amortizing premium or discount is not acceptable unless the results of applying that method are not materially different from the **effective interest method** (also called the **compound interest method** or the **interest method**) described above.

A Comprehensive Example

The following example illustrates the recording of noncurrent investments in debt securities. Assume that Stable Limited acquires ten $1000 bonds of Leverage Limited on January 1, 1993, as a long-term investment at 89.2 (i.e., at 89.2 percent of the face amount). The bonds mature in five years and bear a stated rate of interest of 9 percent, payable annually on December 31. The following entry would record the acquisition of the bonds:

---

[19]"Interest on Receivables and Payables," *APB Opinion No. 21*, Paragraph 15.

Jan. 1, 1993 Investment in Bonds   10 000
                    Discount on Bond Investment   1 080
                    Cash   8 920

The computations are as follows:

$1000 × 10   = $10 000 Face amount
$1000 × 10 × 89.2% =   (8 920) Cash paid
                         $ 1 080 Discount

   The determination of the interest rate (12 percent) implicit in this transaction requires trial and error, because it represents a present value problem involving both an annuity and a single amount. To illustrate, note that when Stable bought the Leverage bonds, rights to two cash flows were acquired:

1. Interest payments of $900 (0.09 × $1000 × 10) per year for five years.
2. The maturity value of $10 000 at the end of five years.

   Since Stable Limited is willing to pay only $8920 for both of these rights, there is some interest rate (*r*) that will equate both future cash flows (interest and principal) with the investment price or present value (*PV*) of $8920. The equation can be expressed as follows:

   PV of the interest payment annuity for five years at *r* rate + PV of the maturity value in five years at *r* rate = PV of total investment

   In the case of Stable Limited, the equation would become:

   $900 yearly for five years at *r* + $10 000 in five years at *r* = $8920

Both the present values of an annuity (series of interest payments) and an amount (single principal payment) are involved, so we must estimate the effective rate by using the present value tables in Chapter 7. Since the bonds were acquired below par value, the effective rate is logically greater than the stated rate of 9 percent.
   Trying 12 percent, we compute as follows:

($900 × 3.60478*) + ($10 000 × 0.56743**) ≈ $8920
$3244*** + $5674*** ≈ $8920
$8918 ≈ $8920

*3.60478 is the present value of five payments of $1 at 12 percent. See Table 7.4.
**0.56743 is the present value of $1 due five years from now at 12 percent. See Table 7.2.
***These numbers have been rounded to the nearest dollar.

   The effective interest rate of 12 percent approximately equates both of the future cash flows with the amount paid for the investment and is therefore the effective rate of interest. If a higher or lower rate had been selected originally, then the computation would have failed to equate the two numbers, thereby requiring the testing of different rates until the equation was satisfied.

At the end of the year, the 9 percent interest payment is received and a portion of the discount on the bonds is amortized:

Dec. 31, 1993	Cash	900	
	Interest Revenue		900
	(0.09 × $10 000 = $900)		
Dec. 31, 1993	Discount on Bond Investment	170	
	Interest Revenue		170
	(*To record amortization of discount:*		
	$8920 × 0.12 = $1070; $1070 − $900 = $170.)		

During the first year of the investment, 12 percent is earned on the carrying amount of the investment. Since the carrying amount of the investment during the year is $8920, then $1070 ($8920 × 0.12) total interest revenue is earned. Only $900 ($10 000 × 0.09) is received in cash, however, and the difference of $170 ($1070 − $900) represents the amount of discount to be amortized. Exhibit 11.10 presents an amortization table developed for Stable Limited as an aid to accounting for this investment.

At the end of the second year, the effective interest rate (12 percent) is applied to the investment's carrying amount at the beginning of the *second* period. Because $170 of discount was amortized at the end of the first year, the carrying amount of the investment increased by that amount, as demonstrated in the following computation:

Investment in bonds	$10 000
Discount at Jan. 1, 1994 ($1080 − $170)	910
Carrying amount at Jan. 1, 1994	$ 9 090

The carrying amount of the investment is $9090 at the beginning of the second year. By multiplying the carrying value of the note by the effective interest rate (12%), we compute the total interest revenue for the second year to be $1091. Again, since $900 of this amount is received in cash, the difference of $191 ($1091 − $900) represents the amount of discount to be amortized as additional interest revenue. This process continues each year until all of the discount has been amortized and the bonds mature with the discount fully amortized. No gain or loss is recognized at the maturity of the bonds, as reflected in Exhibit 11.10. The carrying value of the investment at the maturity date is $10 000.

If the straight-line method of amortization had been used in this example, the amount of amortization would be $216 ($1080/5) per year. As in the effective interest method, the carrying amount of the bond investment would increase to $10 000, except the increase would accumulate in equal increments of $216. Compared to the effective interest method, the straight-line method is conceptually inferior. The interest revenue is overstated in the earlier years and understated in the latter years for a bond purchased at a discount. The opposite pattern would hold for bonds purchased at a premium. As a result, the straight-line amortization method is not generally acceptable unless the periodic difference between it and the effective interest method is immaterial.

Materiality

How would these procedures differ if the bonds had been acquired at a **price greater than par value?** The effective interest rate would be less than the stated rate. This rate is applied to the carrying amount of the investment to determine interest revenue for the period, which would be an amount less than the cash received. The difference between the interest revenue and the cash received is amortized as a *reduction* in the carrying

Exhibit 11.10   Amortization Table for Investment in Bonds at Discount

		(1) (12% carrying value [Col. 6]) Total Interest Revenue	(2) (9% × $10 000) Cash Received	(3) (Col. 1 − Col. 2) Discount To Be Amortized	(4) Face Amount of Bonds	(5) (Reduced by Col. 3) Remaining Discount	(6) (Col. 4 − Col. 5) Carrying Amount
Date	Explanation						
Jan. 1, 1993	Acquisition of bonds	—	—	—	$10 000	$1080	$8 920
Dec. 31, 1993	Recognition of interest	$1070	$900	$170	10 000	910	9 090
Dec. 31, 1994	Recognition of interest	1091	900	191	10 000	719	9 281
Dec. 31, 1995	Recognition of interest	1114	900	214	10 000	505	9 495
Dec. 31, 1996	Recognition of interest	1139	900	239	10 000	266	9 734
Dec. 31, 1997	Recognition of interest	1166*	900	266	10 000	—	10 000

*Minor rounding adjustment in 1997 figures to eliminate remaining discount.

amount of the investment. As in the case of an investment acquired at a discount, the straight-line method of amortization is appropriate only if it renders amounts that do not vary from those materially obtained from the effective interest method.

Materiality

To illustrate, assume that Stable Limited acquired the $10 000 par value bonds at $10 400, which results in an approximate effective interest rate of 8 percent. The journal entries to record the acquisition of the bonds on January 1, 1993, and to recognize interest revenue at December 31, 1993, are as follows:

Jan. 1, 1993	Investment in Bonds	10 000	
	Premium on Bond Investment	400	
	Cash		10 400
Dec. 31, 1993	Cash	900	
	Interest Revenue ($10 400 × 0.08)		832
	Premium on Bond Investment		68

The December 31, 1993, entry reduces the premium on bond investment to $332 ($400 − $68), and interest revenue for 1994 is computed as $827 ($10 332 × 0.08, rounded). If straight-line amortization were applied, annual amortization of the premium would be $80 ($400/5 years).

In both the discount and premium examples illustrated above, we have debited the Investment in Bonds account for the par value of the bonds and used a separate Discount or Premium on Bond Investment account for the difference between the acquisition price of the investment and the par value of the bonds. The Investment in Bonds account and the Discount or Premium on Investment account are usually combined for presentation in the balance sheet and may be combined in the company's records as well. If the investment is carried in a single investment account rather than in separate accounts as illustrated here, amortization of any discount or premium is made directly to the Investment account. In the previous example, if a single investment account had been used, the following entries would have been appropriate:

Jan. 1, 1993	Investment in Bonds	10 400	
	Cash		10 400
Dec. 31, 1993	Cash	900	
	Interest Revenue		832
	Investment in Bonds		68

In this text and in the problem material at the end of this chapter, we assume that a separate Discount or Premium account is used **unless otherwise indicated.** The separate Discount or Premium account is then combined with the Investment account into a single amount for balance sheet presentation.

Sale of Debt Investments

If bonds are sold before their maturity date, a gain or loss may arise. Because any premium or discount recognized at the acquisition of a bond has been subject to amortization since acquisition, the amount of gain or loss depends in part on the remaining unamortized premium or discount. Returning to the previous example where Stable purchased bonds for $8920, including a $1080 discount, assume that Stable sells the Leverage bonds on June 30, 1995, for $10 200 plus accrued interest. The following entries would be necessary to update the accounts:

June 30, 1995	Interest Receivable	450	
	Interest Revenue		450
	(To accrue interest for January 1–June 30, 1995:		
	$10 000 × 0.09 × $\frac{6}{12}$ = $450.)		
June 30, 1995	Discount on Bond Investment	107	
	Interest Revenue		107
	(To amortize discount on bonds for the period Jan. 1, 1995 through		
	June 30, 1995.)		

Calculations for the discount are as follows:

$9281 × 12% × $\frac{6}{12}$	$557
Less: Amount to be received in cash	(450)
Discount to be amortized	$107

This amount can also be determined as half of the 1995 amortization in Exhibit 11.10 (½ × $214). A third entry would be required to record the sale:

June 30, 1995	Cash	10 650	
	Discount on Bond Investment	612	
	Gain on Sale of Bonds		812
	Investment in Bonds		10 000
	Interest Receivable		450
	(To record receipt of cash, $10 200 + $450 = $10 650; elimination of		
	remaining discount, $719 − $107 = $612; elimination of investment in		
	bonds; and recognition of gain.)		

The gain of $812 can be verified as follows:

Cash received, excluding interest		$10 200
Carrying amount of investment at June 30, 1995:		
Face value	$10 000	
Unamortized discount ($719 − $107)	(612)	(9 388)
Gain on sale of investment		$ 812

In this example, we have assumed that the entire investment in the bonds held by Stable Limited was sold. If only part of the bonds had been sold, the entries to record interest receivable, amortization of discount, and the sale would be made for only that part of the investment that was sold. For example, if four of the ten bonds had been sold, only $180 of interest revenue would be recognized ($450 × 0.4%); only $43 of bond discount amortization would be recognized ($107 × 0.4); and a gain of only $325 would be recognized ($812 × 0.4).

In the above illustration, the bond investment was sold at a gain because the cash received was *greater* than the carrying amount (face value, less the unamortized discount). Had the cash received been *less* than the carrying amount, a loss would have been recognized on the sale equal to the difference between the cash received and the carrying amount.

Additional Investment Considerations

Several additional investment instruments may be held by companies and classified as marketable equity securities. Specifically, stock purchase warrants and stock rights may be held by an investing company and included in the current or noncurrent marketable equity securities portfolio. Also, an investor may receive shares through the issuance of dividends and splits by the investee, adding to the number of shares held by the investor. In this section, we introduce these situations briefly and consider them from the perspective of the investor. In Chapters 16, 17, and 18, we cover these topics in greater depth when we consider them from the perspective of the issuing company. In this section, we also introduce accounting for the cash surrender value of life insurance and the accumulation of cash in a fund for a specified future purpose, such as retirement of long-term debt.

Stock Purchase Warrants

Stock purchase warrants convey to the holder the ability to buy a given number of shares at a stated price for a specified period of time. These warrants are often issued when a company sells bonds or shares to make the primary securities more attractive.

When an investor acquires a stock purchase warrant along with another security such as a bond or preferred shares, we must allocate the price paid between the two securities. This is accomplished by using the relative market values of the two securities as indicated in the following formula:

$$\text{Allocated cost of stock warrants} = \frac{\text{Fair market value of warrants}}{\text{Fair market value of warrants} + \text{Fair market value of other security}} \times \text{Total cost of investment}$$

For example, assume that Stable Limited purchases ten $1000 bonds for $1050 each and receives with every bond ten detachable stock purchase warrants, each of which may be used to acquire one additional common share. Immediately after the securities are acquired, separate markets arise for the warrants and the bonds because the warrants are detachable and the two securities can sell separately. The fair market value of each bond is $1025, while the fair market value of each warrant is $5. The following calculation is necessary to allocate the total cost:

$$\text{Cost of warrants} = \frac{\$5 \times 100 \text{ warrants}}{\left[\begin{array}{c} (\$5 \times 100 \text{ warrants}) \\ + \\ (\$1025 \times 10 \text{ bonds}) \end{array} \right]} \times (\$1050 \times 10 \text{ bonds})$$

$$= \$488.37$$

The following entry records the acquisition of the two securities:

Investment in Bonds	10 012	
Stock Purchase Warrants	488	
Cash		10 500
(*To record acquisition of bonds with stock purchase warrants.*)		

Each warrant has an allocated cost of $4.88 ($488 ÷ 100). Since the life of most warrants is limited, they must be exercised or sold, or else they become worthless.

To illustrate the accounting for stock warrants subsequent to purchase, assume that the bond investor exercises half of the warrants (50 warrants). Further assume that the investor can exercise each warrant by paying $50 for one common share. The journal entry would appear as follows:

Marketable Equity Securities	2744	
Stock Purchase Warrants (50 × $4.88)		244
Cash ($50 × 50)		2500
(*To exercise 50 stock purchase warrants.*)		

The market price of the shares when the warrants are exercised does not determine the cost of the stock acquired. Rather, the cost is determined by the $4.88 allocated cost of the warrant plus the $50 cash paid when the warrant is exercised. If the remaining 50 warrants are sold for $6 each, a gain is recognized as follows:

Cash (50 × $6)	300	
Stock Purchase Warrants (50 × $4.88)		244
Gain on Sale of Warrants		56
(*To record the sale of the remaining warrants.*)		

Warrants that expire unexercised or unsold are eliminated from the accounting records by recognizing a loss equal to the allocated cost of the expired warrants. To illustrate, assume that the investor allowed the 50 warrants that were not exercised in the previous example to expire rather than selling them. A loss is recognized as follows:

Loss on Expiration of Stock Purchase Warrants	244	
Stock Purchase Warrants		244
(*To record expiration of warrants.*)		

Stock Rights

Stock rights are distributed by a corporation to employees or shareholders on a pro rata basis to permit them to maintain their proportionate interest in the corporation pursuant to a new share issue. Although one right is usually issued for each share held, the number of rights required to purchase an additional share depends on the terms of the offering. Rather than exercise the right to purchase additional shares, the shareholder may choose instead to sell the rights on the open market.

When stock rights are received, the accountant for the investor allocates the cost of the original share investment between (1) the original investment and (2) the rights just received. This allocation should be based on the relative fair market values of the rights and the shares at the time the rights are received. When separate stock rights are issued, a market price will exist for them as well as for the related shares, because the two securities can be traded separately. The following formula should be used to determine the amount to be assigned to the rights:

$$\text{Allocated cost of stock rights} = \frac{\text{Fair market value of rights}}{\text{Fair market value of rights} + \text{Fair market value of shares}} \times \text{Total cost of investment}$$

For example, assume that Stable Limited acquires 100 of Cypress Limited's common shares for $75 per share and later receives a stock right for each share held. If the market value of the rights is $5 per right and the value of the shares is $88 ¾ per share at the time the rights are received, the following calculation is necessary:

$$\text{Allocated cost of rights} = \frac{(100 \times \$5)}{(100 \times \$5) + (100 \times \$88.75)} \times (100 \times \$75) = \$400$$

A journal entry is then made to reflect the allocation of cost to the new investment:

Investment in Stock Rights	400	
Investment in Common Shares		400
(*To record receipt of stock rights.*)		

If the rights are sold, a gain or loss is recognized if the proceeds from the sale differ from the allocated cost of $4 per right ($400/100 = $4). If the rights are exercised and new shares are acquired, the cost of the new shares is calculated as the $4 allocated cost of the rights plus the additional amount paid for the shares. If the rights expire and become worthless, then the Investment in Stock Rights account is eliminated with a recognized loss equal to the allocated cost. The loss represents the dilution of the ownership interest experienced by the investor because of nonexercise of the rights. The journal entries to account for the disposition of stock rights whether they are exercised, sold or allowed to expire are similar to those for stock purchase warrants presented in the previous section.

Stock Dividends and Stock Splits

Occasionally, a company may receive shares of the investee company by issuance of a *share dividend* or *share split*. In such cases, the recipient (investor) of the additional shares makes no accounting entry. Rather, a memorandum is written to indicate that the original investment cost must now be allocated over the greater number of shares, thereby *lowering the cost per share*. Under Canadian income tax law, stock dividends are taxable at the market value of the shares on the issue date.

To illustrate, assume that Stable Limited holds 200 of Hill Limited's common shares that were purchased for $11 000 ($55 a share) when Hill declares a 10 percent stock dividend. Stable will receive an additional 20 (200 × 0.1) of Hill shares. Subsequent to the dividend, Stable holds 220 shares at a cost of $11 000, or $50 per share ($11 000/220 = $50). If 50 shares are then sold for $60 per share, the following entry is appropriate:

Cash (50 × $60)	3000	
Investment in Common Shares (50 × $50)		2500
Gain on Sale of Shares		500
(*To record sale of 50 shares of Hill Limited's common shares.*)		

The remaining 170 (220 − 50) of Hill shares are carried on Stable's books at $8500 ($11 000 − $2500), or $50 per share ($8500/170 = $50).

If Hill Limited issued a share split rather than a share dividend, the same procedure would be followed. However, the increase in shares would be much greater than 10 percent; for example, it could be 100 percent or 200 percent.

Cash Surrender Value of Life Insurance

A company can insure the lives of its key executives and name the company as beneficiary. The purpose of this arrangement is to compensate the company for the loss of services arising from the untimely death of important members of management.

Two forms of insurance are commonly used: term and whole life insurance. With **term life insurance,** the company is simply buying protection for the loss of the insured individual. The insurance does not represent an investment, and the premiums are ordinarily expensed as paid. **Whole life insurance,** on the other hand, has the unique feature of accumulating cash surrender value in addition to providing insurance protection. The cash surrender value represents an investment to the company in that it can borrow the accumulated cash value from the insurance company or terminate the policy and receive the cash surrender value outright. When a company pays an annual premium on whole life insurance, part of the premium is recognized as insurance expense. The remaining portion represents an increase in cash surrender value and should, therefore, be recognized as an increase in an investment asset. The amount of the annual premium reflecting an increase in the cash surrender value is specified by the insurance contract. The insurance contract will frequently include a schedule of cash surrender values listed by the number of years the policy has been in effect. On the financial statements of the investing company, the cash surrender value should be disclosed as a noncurrent asset, because corporations do not usually intend to terminate insurance policies within the operating cycle.

To illustrate the accounting for cash surrender values, assume that Stable Limited takes out a whole life policy that names the company as beneficiary. The insurance contract calls for coverage of $200 000 on the life of Stable's chief executive officer (CEO) in return for premiums of $3500 per year. The cash surrender value schedule indicates the cash value increases for the first three years as follows:

End of Coverage Year	Cash Surrender Value
1	—
2	$ 500
3	1100

Because the first year's premium does not result in an increased cash surrender value, the entire $3500 premium is debited to Insurance Expense when paid. The following journal entries record the second and third years' premiums:

Insurance Expense	3000	
Cash Surrender Value of Life Insurance	500	
Cash		3500
Insurance Expense	2900	
Cash Surrender Value of Life Insurance ($1100 − $500)	600	
Cash		3500

Notice that the increase in the cash surrender value is debited to an investment account, Cash Surrender Value of Life Insurance, and the remainder of the $3500 premium is debited to Insurance Expense.

If Stable's CEO died at the end of the fifth year of coverage when the cash surrender value was $3700, the following journal entry would be necessary to record the receipt of the death benefit:

Cash	200 000	
Cash Surrender Value of Life Insurance		3 700
Gain from Life Insurance Settlement		196 300

A corporation may also establish life insurance coverage for the benefit of employees and their named beneficiaries. Since this type of insurance is for the benefit of each employee, not the company, all of the premium is considered a form of compensation expense. Any accumulation of cash surrender value belongs to the employee and should not be identified as a company asset.

Funds

Business enterprises establish special funds for a variety of purposes, including bond or other debt redemption, future plant expansion, and pension commitments. When such funds are established, several significant accounting and reporting issues arise.

Fund assets may be held and managed by corporate personnel, or fund resources may be transferred to a **fiscal agent** or **trustee,** such as a bank, for administration. Although many long-term special funds are created in compliance with such things as contractual provisions, bond indentures, or covenants in debt instruments or pension plans, others are the result of internal management decisions.

To illustrate, assume that Stable Limited management decides to create a bond-retirement fund in the amount of $10 000. The following entry would be necessary:

The Bankers' New Headache

How's this for bizarre accounting? Suppose you're carrying wide neckties in inventory at cost, $4 million. Suddenly skinny ties become fashionable and the value of your wide tie inventory drops to $1 million. You keep the old ties on the books at $4 million, arguing to your accountants that wide ties will be fashionable again someday, and you'll be able to realize their historical value then—all the time selling off wide ties for less than their carrying value.

Something similar to this has been common practice among banks, savings and loans and other financial institutions for years. The game isn't played with neckties, of course. It's played with their huge portfolios of fixed-income securities. Here's how:

When a financial institution buys debt securities, it generally allocates them to either a long-term "investment" account, or a short-term "trading" account. The accountants let the institution keep "investment" securities on the books at historical cost, on the theory that the company plans to hold them until maturity, when they can be redeemed at par.

By contrast, "trading" securities have to be carried at current market value. If interest rates fall and the values of the securities rise, earnings and capital surplus are credited. But if rates rise and the securities' values fall, the drop must be charged against earnings and surplus. Reported earnings can thus fluctuate violently, even if no securities are sold.

In the past, banks and thrifts have protected themselves against writing up and down their portfolios by putting most of their securities into "investment" accounts. But then they buy and sell the securities anyway. This stabilizes reported earnings—but at a cost of misstating the value of the bonds on the balance sheet. If interest rates rise and bond prices plunge, a bank's or a thrift's assets look as strong as ever—though they're not. It's akin to carrying those wide ties in inventory at pre-skinny-tie prices.

Worse, financial institutions can (and do) easily bury investment losses by "cherry picking"—selling the securities that have appreciated, while quietly sitting on those that are worth less than the balance sheet says.

Consider Columbia Savings & Loan, whose chairman, Thomas Spiegel, just resigned under attack for investing too much of its portfolio in risky junk bonds. At the end of 1988 Columbia had $8.7 billion of fixed-income securities. Of that, only $320 million, or 4%, was carried at market values. The rest, deemed investment securities, was carried at cost.

Was Columbia holding its investments until they matured? Hardly. In 1988 the thrift sold over $5 billion of fixed-income securities—more than half its portfolio.

Gains from selling the securities amounted to almost two-thirds of pretax earnings, $83 million. Recently, Columbia got a taste of how much market valuation can hurt. In August Congress required thrifts to divest themselves of their junk bonds within five years. Under generally accepted accounting principles, assets held for sale have to be valued at the lower of cost or market. On Sept. 30 Columbia marked its junk bond portfolio down to market value, taking a $351 million writeoff.

Columbia is not an isolated case. Virtually all of the thrift industry's profits over the last five years came from selling investment securities. Yet at the end of 1988 the top 30 thrifts had only 2% of their assets in trading or held-for-sale accounts.

What of the big commercial banks? They, too, allot most of their securities to "investment" accounts. For example, at the end of 1988, Citicorp had $15.2 billion of investment assets, and $3.9 billion of trading assets.

Finally, under pressure from the Securities & Exchange Commission, the accounting rulemakers appear ready to make financial institutions carry more of their securities at market values. In mid-January the American Institute of Certified Public Accountants' standard-setting committee is scheduled to vote on new rules. If they are passed, as seems likely, the new rules say that banks, savings and loan associations, finance companies, and credit unions may classify their debt securities as "investments," and value them at cost, under only two conditions. The financial institution must have (a) the financial ability to hold the securities to maturity, and (b) the intention—barring unforeseen events—to hold them long enough to recover their book value. Otherwise the securities must be put in a trading account—carried at market value—or in a "held for sale" account, carried at the lower of cost or market value.

What if a bank sells lots of "investment" securities, saying there were "unforeseen events"? The new rules will probably provide that any institution that sells, for virtually any reason, over 10% of its investment securities in a year must mark its entire portfolio to the lower of cost or market.

Under the new rules, earnings are likely to be much more volatile. The American Bankers Association (which is lobbying hard against the new rules) recently released a study of the effect of market value accounting on bank earnings at a time of volatile interest rates. In spring 1981, national banks with over $1 billion in assets would have earned $1 billion in aggregate. Six months later the group

Continued

would have lost $1.5 billion. Three months after, earnings would have rebounded to $4 billion, and then dropped back to $1.5 billion. Over the same period, using the historical cost method, earnings would have been constant at about $1 billion.

Does this volatility matter? After all, if banks really hold their securities until maturity, the ups and downs will average out. But this doesn't mollify Jerry Von Rohr, chairman of little Mega Bancshares, Inc., a three-bank holding company in St. Ann, Mo. "We're sitting here earning better than 1% on assets," he says. "Now suddenly [under the proposed rules], Mega pops up in the *St. Louis Post Dispatch* with a loss. What will public perception be? What will our customers think?"

As part of their lobbying effort, the bankers contend that forcing them to mark their "investment" securities to market will discourage purchases of long-term securities—which fluctuate more in price than short-term ones—mak-

ing it hard for business and the Treasury to issue long-term debt.

"That's a real red herring," says John Kreischer of the accounting firm Kreischer, Miller, and head of the accountants' committee developing the new proposal. "Banks don't invest in long-term securities to begin with. They buy two-year securities, maybe three. And if the investment made economic sense before, it will still."

In any case, says Timothy Lucas of the Financial Accounting Standards Board, "It is not appropriate for us to encourage people to buy long-term debt by setting up accounting standards that mislead them." It's hard to argue with that.

Source: Reprinted from Dana Wechsler, "The Bankers' New Headache," *Forbes,* January 8, 1990, pp. 76–80. Reprinted with permission of *Forbes* magazine, January 8, 1990. © Forbes Inc., 1990.

Bond-Retirement Fund Cash	10 000	
Cash		10 000
(To establish bond-retirement fund.)		

If Stable Limited's management decides to acquire treasury bills so that the fund will earn interest, the investment is recorded at cost:

Bond-Retirement Fund Investment	10 000	
Bond-Retirement Fund Cash		10 000
(To record acquisition of treasury bills by bond-retirement fund.)		

Subsequent accounting for investments made by such a fund follow the principles previously described and depend on the nature, extent, and investment objectives of the fund. Dividends and interest earned on fund investments are debited to the Bond-Retirement Fund Investment account.

When fund assets are transferred to a fiscal agent, the fund assets and related liabilities may be excluded from the financial statements. Liabilities are excluded only to the extent that the company's obligations have been discharged. Pension fund assets and liabilities are frequently accounted for in this manner. Bond sinking funds and related bonds payable are normally reported in corporate financial statements, however, even if sinking fund assets have been transferred to a fiscal agent. Although a fund may consist of a variety of assets, such as cash and investments in several types of securities, all these assets are normally aggregated into a single account for balance sheet presentation.

A fund is usually created by an original contribution and augmented by additional contributions and the earnings of the fund itself. If a company desires to accumulate a certain amount in the fund by some specific date, it will need estimates of the earning power of the assets in the fund in order to ascertain the specific amount of the contributions. The company may then use present value techniques to determine the future contribution necessary to accumulate the desired amount. The accountant should monitor the performance of the fund in terms of earnings and contributions to ascertain whether the fund is accumulating resources at the level anticipated in the original present value calculation. If fund assets earn at a level higher than anticipated, the remaining contributions may be reduced. Conversely, if the fund performs more poorly than planned, the company must increase its contributions to meet its goals for the fund. The techniques incident to evaluating the earnings performance of a fund involve the compound interest concepts discussed in Chapter 7.

Market Value: An Alternative to Practice

Many accounting theorists have advocated accounting for marketable securities at market value, without regard to the relationship of that value to historical cost. The primary virtue of accounting for marketable securities at market value is to provide decision makers with current and useful information that reports the economic consequences of holding investments during an accounting period. This method would require revaluation of investments at the end of each accounting period, based on market value at that time. It is not widely employed in financial reporting at the present time, except for certain specialized industry situations.

Revenue Realization

The market value method raises an interesting question of revenue recognition. Some argue that the periodic adjustment in value should be recognized in the determination of income, much like the current portfolio unrealized loss and loss recovery examples in this chapter, but with the use of market value not limited to historical cost. Others prefer that unrealized gains and losses be accumulated in shareholders' equity, much like the noncurrent portfolio adjustment presented earlier, but with use of market value not limited to historical cost. Accounting theorists have advocated the use of current value for asset accounting and balance sheet presentation for many years. These include Moonitz and Sprouse,[20] Edwards and Bell,[21] Chambers,[22] Sterling,[23] and Beaver.[24] Marketable securities have often been used by these authors to illustrate their particular approach to the valuation of assets at current or market value. After decades of research in this area, Sterling concludes: "In research different people from different schools of thought using different postulates and different research methods have drawn the same conclusion: Marketable securities ought to be valued at market. That conclusion has not been challenged in the research literature."[25] In practice, however, the predominant method of measuring and reporting marketable securities remains historical cost or some variation of cost, such as the lower of cost or market or the equity method.

More recently, Foran and Foran attempted to evaluate marketable equity security accounting in light of the FASB's conceptual framework. They correctly state that one purpose of the framework is to be a standard of comparison by which current practice can be evaluated. These authors carefully analyzed market value and lower of cost or

---

[20]Robert T. Sprouse and Maurice Moonitz, "A Tentative Set of Broad Accounting Principles for Business Enterprise," in *Accounting Research Study No. 3* (New York: AICPA, 1962).

[21]E.O. Edwards and P.W. Bell, *The Theory of Measurement of Business Income* (Berkeley: University of California Press, 1964).

[22]R.J. Chambers, *Accounting Evaluation and Economic Behavior* (Englewood Cliffs, NJ: Prentice-Hall, 1966).

[23]Robert R. Sterling, *The Theory of the Measurement of Enterprise Income* (Lawrence, KS: The University Press of Kansas, 1970).

[24]William H. Beaver, "Reporting Rules for Marketable Equity Securities," *Journal of Accountancy* (October 1971), pp. 57–61.

[25]Robert R. Sterling, "Accounting Research, Education and Practice," *Journal of Accountancy* (September 1973), pp. 43–50.

market procedures against the individual parts of the conceptual framework, concluding that it is unnecessary to delay recognition until a cash-to-cash cycle is complete. They recommend that the FASB implement its conceptual framework by revising accounting for marketable securities so that it will be consistent with the current objectives, qualitative characteristics, elements, and recognition and measurement standards of financial reporting.[26] Section 4210 of the CICA *Handbook* recommends the use of moving average market value for equity portfolio investments held by life insurance enterprises.[27]

Concluding Remarks

In this chapter, we have considered accounting practices and theory related to accounting for investments in equity and debt securities and introduce several other investment accounting issues. Accounting procedures currently employed in practice to measure investment assets are heavily based in historical cost, as the following summary indicates:

Investment Type	Current Accounting Practice
Equity—Current	Lower of cost or market (LCM), applied to individual securities*
Noncurrent	
Passive	Cost—unless market decline is other than temporary*
Significant influence	Equity method
Control	Consolidated financial statements
Debt—Current	Cost or LCM, applied on individual securities
Noncurrent	Historical cost, adjusted for portion of premium or discount already recognized as adjustment to interest revenue

*Unrealized losses and loss recoveries included in income.

The variations to historical cost found in these accounting procedures represent the unique attributes of the markets in which these securities exist and purposes for which they are held by the investing company.

You have also been introduced to the criticisms of market value accounting for marketable securities. Current value accounting, of which market value is one example, is sometimes criticized for its lack of objectivity in that the company holding the asset (i.e., investment) has not participated in the market that would be used to establish the accounting valuation. Others observe that we use market value in accounting for current and noncurrent marketable equity securities, as well as selected other assets, when the market declines by requiring a lower of cost or market approach. If market is sufficiently objective when it is below cost to permit its use, is it not equally objective when market is above cost? Some argue that the lower of cost or market method lacks internal consistency in that assets valued in this manner may be carried at either cost or market value.

Consistency

The use of current value, including market value, will undoubtedly continue to receive significant attention as it is evaluated in light of the conceptual framework. In our opinion, accounting research should play an increasingly important role in this evaluation.

---

[26]Nancy J. Foran and Michael E. Foran, "SFAS No. 12 and the Conceptual Framework," *Accounting Horizons* (December 1987), pp. 43–50.

[27]"Life Insurance Enterprises," CICA *Handbook*, Paragraph 4210.04, March 1991.

Key Points

1. Companies invest in a variety of securities for many business reasons. (Objective 1)
2. Investments in voting equity securities must be classified as either passive, significant influence, or control in nature. (Objective 2)
3. Classification of securities between current and noncurrent categories involves assessing management intent, marketability, maturity dates of the security, and other corroborative evidence. (Objective 2)
4. Marketable securities representing passive investments should be valued at cost unless the decline in the market is other than temporary. (Objective 3)
5. Unrealized losses and unrealized loss recoveries on the current marketable equity securities portfolio are recognized in the income statement of the period of the change. (Objective 4)
6. Unrealized losses on noncurrent marketable equity securities portfolios are recognized when the decline is other than temporary. The unrealized loss is not recovered unless the investment is sold. (Objective 4)
7. Investments in voting shares that provide the investor with significant influence over the investee are accounted for by using the equity method. (Objective 4)
8. A proportionate amount of the investee's net income is accrued by an investor using the equity method, whereas dividends are reported as reductions of the Investment account. (Objective 4)
9. Investment of more than 50 percent in the voting shares of an investee results in control of the investee by the investor, and consolidated financial statements are appropriate. (Objective 4)
10. Business enterprises frequently establish funds for a variety of reasons, such as meeting bond maturities or pension commitments and expanding plant operations. (Objective 4)
11. Extensive financial statement disclosures are required for material investments. (Objective 5)
12. Accounting for marketable securities at market value, while not widely used at the present time, has conceptual merit and has been suggested by accounting researchers as an alternative to current practice. (Objective 6)

Questions

Q11.1   What methods of cost identification are most commonly used for securities that have been sold?

Q11.2   In accounting for temporary investments in bonds, how should one treat discounts or premiums for financial reporting purposes?

Q11.3   Distinguish between temporary and noncurrent investments. Why is it possible for purchases of a specific company's shares to be a current investment for one company and a long-term investment for another?

Q11.4   Explain the difference in the cost and equity methods of accounting for a long-term investment in common shares.

Q11.5   How should the excess of investment cost over the proportionate share of the investee's book value at the date of acquisition be recognized in the investor's balance sheet? Discuss the implications of this excess for the income statement.

Q11.6   How is a stock dividend that is received by an investor company recognized for accounting purposes?

Q11.7   Give three circumstances under which an investment that is accounted for by the cost method will be written down.

Q11.8   What are "current assets" as the term is used to classify amounts on a balance sheet? How may marketable securities qualify as current assets?

Q11.9 With regard to marketable equity securities, when should realized gains be recognized?

Q11.10 With marketable equity securities, in what circumstances should realized losses be recognized?

Q11.11 The CICA *Handbook* specifies that a direct or indirect investment of 20 percent or more of the voting shares of an investee company leads to a *presumption* that, in the absence of evidence to the contrary, an investor has an ability to exercise significant influence over an investee. What are some examples of "contrary evidence" that might tend to refute this presumption?

Q11.12 What is a stock right? What three events can transpire after receiving a stock right? How are they accounted for?

Q11.13 In accounting for long-term investments in bonds, what causes premiums and discounts? How are these items accounted for while the investment is held?

Q11.14 How are investee operating losses accounted for under the equity method?

Q11.15 Distinguish between the accounting for temporary investments in marketable equity securities and noncurrent investments in marketable equity securities when the investor owns less than 20 percent of the investee's shares.

Q11.16 What is the cash surrender value of a life insurance policy? How should the cash surrender value be presented in the balance sheet?

Q11.17 What is a fund? What are the significant issues related to accounting for a fund?

Q11.18 Describe the market value method of accounting for marketable securities. Why is it advocated by some accounting theorists over those methods currently used?

Q11.19 A company may acquire a stock purchase warrant in conjunction with another investment. What procedure is required to place a value on the warrant?

Q11.20 A company that holds an investment in the common shares of another company may receive additional shares when the investee distributes a stock dividend or a stock split. Describe the appropriate accounting for the newly acquired shares in these circumstances.

Exercises

E11.1 Current Marketable Equity Securities. Murphy Manufacturing Limited had the following securities in its current marketable equity securities portfolio on December 31, 1994:

	Cost	Market
Clark Company Ltd.	$ 25 000	$ 28 000
MacDonald Limited	50 000	47 000
Huron Inc.	30 000	25 000
Lawton, Inc.	15 000	4 000
Total	$120 000	$104 000

All the securities were purchased during December 1994. The following events took place during 1995:

Mar. 15 Lawton, Inc., filed for protection under the federal bankruptcy laws. The market value of Murphy's holdings in Lawton shares fell to $500. Lawton's situation was apparently permanent.

June 5 One thousand shares of Orbit Electronics were purchased at $28 per share as a temporary investment. The brokerage commission on this purchase was $140.

July 17 Half of the MacDonald Limited holdings were sold for $31 000, net of commissions.

Nov. 10 Murphy's management decided to begin developing a controlling interest in Huron Inc., and the Huron shares were transferred to a noncurrent equity investment status. The Huron shares had a market value of $29 000 on the transfer date.

On December 31, 1995, the market value of Murphy's holdings in marketable equity securities appeared as follows:

Clark Company Ltd.	$19 000
MacDonald Limited	30 000
Orbit Electronics	24 000
Lawton, Inc.	400
Huron Inc.	30 000

Instructions

Provide the appropriate journal entries relating to the marketable securities. Beginning with the December 31, 1994, adjusting entry, list the entries in chronological order.

E11.2 Current Debt Investments. During 1995, Richfield Limited made several transactions in current marketable debt instruments. Richfield uses the lower of cost or market method, applied on an individual security basis, for valuation of these investments.

Jan. 31   Richfield purchased $10 000 face amount, 11 percent bonds at 103 plus accrued interest. Interest is payable on July 1 and January 1.
Feb. 28   Richfield purchased $20 000 face value, 10 percent bonds at 97 plus accrued interest. Interest is payable on July 1 and January 1.
July 1   Interest on both bond investments was received.
Aug. 31   Richfield sold half of the 11 percent bonds at 95 plus accrued interest.
Oct. 1   Richfield sold half of the 10 percent bonds at 101 plus accrued interest.
Dec. 31   Interest was accrued.
      31   The market prices of the bonds were as follows:

11% bonds	102
10% bonds	95

Instructions

Provide the appropriate journal entries for the above transactions. Round all amounts to the nearest dollar.

E11.3 Current and Noncurrent Marketable Equity Securities. Nifty Thrifty Supermarkets invests in marketable equity securities for long-term funding purposes. On February 15, 1994, Nifty Thrifty made the following purchases:

	Market Price per Share (including commissions)
900 shares Alberts	$99
500 shares Browns	42
300 shares Carsons	33

During 1994, the following transactions took place:

June 30   Nifty Thrifty received dividends of $3700 on the three investments.
Aug. 1   150 shares of Browns were sold for $45 per share. Commissions on the transaction were $120.
Sept. 15 200 shares of Alberts were sold for $98 per share. Commissions on the transaction were $180.
Nov. 11   The remaining Alberts shares were transferred to a temporary investment status when the Alberts shares was trading for $94 per share.

On December 31, 1994, the per-share market values of Nifty Thrifty's holdings were as follows:

Alberts	$90
Browns	41
Carsons	30

On December 31, 1995, the market values of Nitty Thrifty's holdings were as follows:

Alberts	$85
Browns	43
Carsons	29

Instructions

The market value declines are considered to be permanent.

(a) Provide the appropriate journal entries for Nifty Thrifty's transactions and adjustments.
(b) In the balance sheet and income statement, what reporting distinctions are made in accounting for *temporary* versus *noncurrent* investment portfolios? Outline your answer by utilizing the December 31, 1994, information on Nifty Thrifty Super-markets.

E11.4 Current Debt and Equity Investments. At the beginning of 1995, Dennis Limited held in its Current Investments account the following:

(1) $150 000 face amount, 8 percent bonds purchased at a cost of $137 000.
(2) 1200 no-par value, $3.50 preferred shares purchased at a cost of $66 000.

Interest on the bonds is payable on March 31 and September 30, and the preferred dividend is paid quarterly on a calendar-year basis. On October 31, 1995, half the bonds were sold for $77 000 (including accrued interest) and 500 shares were sold for $24 000.

Instructions

Prepare the necessary journal entries for 1995. Assume all dividends declared were received by December 31, 1995, and round all amounts to the nearest dollar.

E11.5 Noncurrent Debt Investments. Mouser Co. Inc. purchased $20 000 face value, ten-year, zero coupon bonds (bonds with a zero nominal interest rate) for $9264 on January 1, 1995, for long-term funding purposes. On the same date, Mouser purchased $30 000 face value, five-year, 8 percent bonds that were priced to yield 6 percent, with interest payable annually on December 31. Mouser utilizes the effective interest method of amortization and carries the investment and any related discount or premium in separate accounts.

Instructions

(a) List the journal entries needed to record the purchase of the bond investments. Round all amounts to the nearest dollar.

(b) List the journal entries related to the interest on the bond investments for December 31, 1995. Round all amounts to the nearest dollar.
(c) Why are bond investments sometimes purchased at prices that differ from their face value?

E11.6 Noncurrent Debt Investments. The following is a partial effective interest amortization table for a bond investment due in eight years:

Date	Interest Revenue	Cash Received	Amortization	Present (Carrying) Value
Jan. 1, 1994				$11 000
July 1, 1994	$440	$600	$160	?
Jan. 1, 1995				

Instructions
(a) Is the effective rate less than or greater than the nominal rate?
(b) Is the carrying value less than or greater than the face value?
(c) What is the nominal rate?
(d) What is the effective rate?
(e) What is the carrying value on July 1, 1995?
(f) What is the face amount of the bond investment?
(g) What will be the sum of the amortization column for the eight years?
(h) At the end of eight years, what will be the final carrying value?

E11.7 Noncurrent Debt Investments. On September 1, 1994, Adams Limited purchased $300 000 face value, 8 percent bonds, which would mature in eight years. The bonds were purchased as a long-term investment at a price to yield 12 percent compounded semi-annually. Interest is payable on August 31 and February 28.

Instructions
Round amounts to the nearest dollar.

(a) Using the appropriate present value table in Chapter 7, compute the purchase price of the bonds and prepare the journal entry to record their purchase, with any premium or discount in a separate account from the par value.
(b) Prepare the December 31, 1994, adjusting entry.
(c) Prepare the February 28, 1995, journal entry.

E11.8 Cost and Equity Methods. Phillips, Inc., owns exactly 20 percent of the voting common shares (10 000 shares) of Rand Limited. The investment cost $250 000 and was purchased on January 1, 1995, when Rand's common shares were selling at $25 per share and the total recorded amount of shareholders' equity was $900 000. During 1995, Rand Limited reported net income of $85 000 and paid $50 000 in cash dividends. At December 31, 1995, Rand Limited had recorded shareholders' equity of $935 000 and the common shares were selling at $22 per share. Rand has no preferred shares in its capital structure, and Phillips's investment in Rand is considered to be a noncurrent investment, with any excess of cost over book value attributable to goodwill with an expected twenty-year life.

Instructions

Consider each of the following cases independently.

(a) Assuming Phillips, Inc., has significant influence over Rand Limited, prepare the general journal entries to record the above, and indicate the balance sheet and income statement amounts that will be presented by Phillips for 1995 concerning this investment.

(b) Assuming Phillips, Inc., does *not* have significant influence over Rand Limited, prepare the general journal entries to record the above, and indicate the balance sheet and income statement amounts that will be presented by Phillips for 1995 concerning this investment.

E11.9 Equity Method. On January 1, 1995, Quails Limited purchased 20 percent of Green Limited's outstanding common shares for $1 000 000 when the underlying book value of the company was $4 500 000. Forty percent of the excess is attributable to assets with a remaining life of eight years, and the remainder to unrecorded goodwill to be amortized over 40 years. Green Limited reported net income of $280 000 in 1995 and declared dividends of $0.90 per share on all 200 000 outstanding shares.

Instructions

Prepare Quails's journal entries, relative to the Green investment, that are required on December 31, 1995.

E11.10 Equity Method With Losses. On January 1, 1991, Kids Stuff Toy Limited purchased a 40 percent influential interest in Clothes for Tots, Inc., for $110 000. The subsequent earnings and dividend distributions of Clothes for Tots were as follows:

Year	Net Income (Loss)	Dividends
1991	$ 50 000	$60 000
1992	(160 000)	40 000
1993	(150 000)	10 000
1994	20 000	—
1995	140 000	10 000

Instructions

(a) For each of the five years, determine Kids Stuff's reported income (loss) from the investment in Clothes for Tots. Determine the balance of the investment account at the end of 1995.

(b) Assume Clothes for Tots' investment is unchanged; but, they own only 15 percent and do not have significant influence. For each of the five years, determine Kids Stuff's reported dividend revenue from the investment in Clothes for Tots. Assume that the decline in the value of the investment is not considered permanent.

E11.11 Sinking Fund. Krippin Manufacturing Limited established a sinking fund on January 1, 1994, for the retirement to a bond issue. The following transactions occurred:

Jan. 1, 1994	Established a sinking fund with $270 000 cash.
Jan. 18	Purchased marketable equity securities for $250 000.
July 15	Paid fund expenses of $10 000.
Sept. 9	Sold marketable equity securities having an original cost of $60 000 for $53 000.
Dec. 20	Received dividends on marketable equity securities of $15 000.
Feb. 12, 1995	Purchased certificate of deposit for $50 000.
Dec. 31	Interest and dividends of $27 000 were received.
Dec. 31	Sold all securities in the fund for $275 000 and retired an outstanding bond issue of $300 000. The remaining fund balance was transferred back to the corporate Cash account.

Instructions
Provide the appropriate journal entries for these transactions.

E11.12 Cash Surrender Value. On January 2, 1993, Lambert Limited insured its president with a $100 000 face value life insurance policy, with Lambert as the beneficiary. Premiums are $1900 per year and are payable each January 2, beginning in 1993. The cash surrender value after each payment is made for the first three payments is as follows:

Cash Surrender Value	
Jan. 2, 1993	—
Jan. 2, 1994	$300
Jan. 2, 1995	$650

Lambert records each payment in a prepaid expense account, appropriately adjusting that account each December 31, the end of its financial reporting period.

Instructions
Prepare all general journal entries required for this insurance policy from January 2, 1993, through December 31, 1995.

E11.13 Stock Rights. Stout Limited owns 1200 shares purchased for $75 per share. One right is received for each outstanding share; the market values of the shares and rights at the issuance date of the rights are $90 and $4, respectively. Two rights are required to purchase one share at $80.

Stout exercises 500 rights one month later, sells 400 rights at $5.30 per right toward the end of the year, and allows the remaining rights to expire.

Instructions

Round all amounts to the nearest dollar.

(a) Provide the appropriate journal entry for:
   (1) The receipt of the rights.
   (2) The exercise of 500 rights.
   (3) The sale of 400 rights.
   (4) The expiration of the remaining rights.
(b) Is the account carrying the original investment in shares reduced when stock rights are received? Why or why not? Could the receipt of the stock rights be recorded as a memorandum entry similar to that for stock dividends? Explain your answer.

E11.14   Equity Method.   On January 1, 1995, Holland Shipbuilders, Inc. purchased a 35 percent interest in Vernon Iron Works at $20 per share. As a result, Holland was able to appoint two members of the board of directors. The balance sheet of Vernon Iron Works appeared as follows on January 1, 1995:

Vernon Iron Works
BALANCE SHEET
January 1, 1995

Assets

Current assets		$ 20 000
Land		40 000
Fixed assets	$160 000	
Accumulated	(50 000)	110 000
Total assets		$170 000

Liabilities and Shareholders' Equity

Current liabilities	$ 15 000
Long-term liabilities	75 000
Common shares (no-par value, 6000 shares authorized, issued, and outstanding)	50 000
Retained earnings	30 000
Total liabilities and shareholders' equity	$170 000

Vernon had a net income of $25 000 and declared dividends of $10 000 during 1995. The depreciable assets of Vernon are undervalued by $30 000. The average remaining life of the depreciable assets is six years. Holland Shipbuilders amortizes goodwill over a twenty-year period.

Instructions

Round all amounts to the nearest dollar.

(a) Provide Holland's journal entry to record the acquisition of 35 percent of Vernon Iron Works.
(b) Provide the journal entry to record Holland's share in the income and dividends of Vernon Iron Works.
(c) Provide the journal entry to amortize the excess of investment cost over equity. (*Hint*: Remember that Holland is purchasing only 35 percent of the $30 000 amount by which the depreciable assets are undervalued.)

E11.15 Cost and Equity Method. On January 1, 1993, Overland Railroad Limited established significant influence over K&K Railroad by acquiring 60 000 common shares, a 30 percent interest, for $570 000. The book value of K&K was $1 300 000 on January 1, 1993. Since this purchase, K&K earned income and paid dividends as follows:

Year	Net Income	Dividends
1993	$180 000	$100 000
1994	310 000	140 000

The market value per share on K&K common shares on December 31, 1993 and 1994, was $8 and $9, respectively. The decline was not expected to be permanent. Overland Railroad incorrectly accounted for this investment as if significant influence had not been established.

Instructions

(a) As a result of incorrectly applying accounting principles, the financial statements of Overland Railroad Limited are incorrect. At December 31, 1993 and 1994, were the following accounts overstated, understated, or correct? If incorrect, by what amount? Show supporting computations. Assume that any excess of cost over book value should be amortized over 30 years.

  (1) Net Investment in K&K Railroad.
  (2) Net Income.

(b) If the K&K investment were sold on January 1, 1995, would a greater gain be reported under the incorrect approach or the equity method? Which method better assigns income to periods? Discuss your reasoning.

E11.16 Current Marketable Equity Security Sale. The temporary marketable equity security portfolio of Fowler Limited is as follows on December 31, 1994:

	Cost	Market	Loss
Thayer Limited	$16 000	$14 000	$ 2 000
Webber, Inc.	21 000	20 000	1 000
Lincoln Limited	32 000	25 000	7 000
Totals	$69 000	$59 000	$10 000

On December 31, 1994, Fowler's accountant established a lower of cost or market (LCM) valuation for the current marketable equity securities (CMES) by the following adjusting journal entry:

Dec. 31, 1994 Loss on Valuation of CMES	10 000	
Allowance to Reduce CMES to LCM		10 000
(*To adjust CMES to LCM valuation.*)		

Prior to this journal entry no allowance account existed.

On January 2, 1995, Fowler sold all of its holdings in Lincoln for the market price of $25 000. Fowler's accountant has proposed the following entry to record this sale:

Jan. 2, 1995	Cash	25 000	
	Allowance to Reduce CMES to LCM	7 000	
	CMES		32 000

Instructions

(a) Do you agree with the accountant's entry? Why or why not?

(b) According to the GAAP, what entry would be required on Jan. 2, 1995, to record the sale of the Lincoln shares?

(c) Referring to your answer in (b), how would you respond to the criticism of the Fowler accountant when she says that the loss is being recognized in income twice—once in 1994 when the market declined below cost, and once in 1995 when the securities were actually sold?

(d) How would the entries be made if these investments were long-term investments and the declines were other than temporary?

E11.17 Stock Purchase Warrants. Esau Limited purchased ten units of a bond and three stock purchase warrants in Frank, Inc., at $1050 per unit. Immediately after, the bonds were selling for $1040 and the warrants were selling for $12 each.

Instructions

Determine the cost that should be associated with each individual security involved in the purchase.

Problems

P11.1 Current Marketable Equity Securities. Synthetic Fuels Limited has invested its idle cash in temporary marketable equity securities. Synthetic Fuels uses the average method of assigning cost to security investments. On January 31, 1993, the following investments were made:

	Market Price per Share (including commissions)
500 shares of West	$ 47
1000 shares of IBX	100
700 shares of Macs	70

On March 31, 1993, IBX issued a 20 percent stock dividend. Cash dividends of $12 000 were declared and paid by the three investments.

On September 7, 1993, Synthetic Fuels Limited invested additional idle cash in the following temporary investments:

	Market Price per Share (including commissions)
200 shares of West	$51
400 shares of IBX	86

On December 20, 1993, Synthetic Fuels sold 1100 shares of IBX for $90 per share.

The market values per share of Synthetic Fuels' temporary investment holdings on December 31, 1993, were:

West	$48
IBX	88
Macs	55

On February 28, 1994, Synthetic Fuels Limited sold 300 shares of West at $45 per share. Dividends of $7000 were earned by Synthetic Fuels on March 31, 1994. The company purchased 200 additional shares of IBX at $85 per share on August 31, 1994.

The market values of Synthetic Fuels' temporary investment holdings on December 31, 1994, were:

West	$49
IBX	83
Macs	65

There were no investment transactions in 1995, and on December 31, 1995, the market values for Synthetic Fuels' holdings were:

West	$48
IBX	87
Macs	78

Instructions

(a) Provide the appropriate journal entries for the transactions and adjustments from January 31, 1993, to December 31, 1995.
(b) Comment briefly on the impact that the periodic valuation of these securities at the lower of cost or market has on Synthetic Fuels' net income.

P11.2 Stock Rights. Elliott, Inc. engaged in the following transactions during 1995:

Jan. 6   Purchase of 500 common shares of Kann Ltd. at $87 per share. Brokerage commissions were $390. The Kann shares are to be held for long-term funding purposes.

May 24   Kann issued a 10 percent stock dividend, followed by a cash dividend of $2.70 per share.

Aug. 1   Elliott, Inc. received one stock right from Kann for every share of Kann common held. Four stock rights entitled the owner to purchase one share of Kann common at $50 per share. Each right had a market value of $11, while Kann common was trading ex-rights (without rights) at $80 per share. The stock rights expire on August 1, 1996.

Sept. 21 Elliott sold 200 Kann stock rights for $13.50 per right.

Sept. 30 300 stock rights were exercised for the acquisition of Kann common.

Dec. 31   The market value for Kann stock rights was $16.50 per right. Kann common closed at $68 per share.

Instructions

Provide the appropriate journal entries and year-end adjustments for the Elliott, Inc. transactions, rounding all amounts to the nearest dollar.

P11.3 Current Marketable Equity Securities. Wampler Ltd. used idle cash to invest in current marketable equity securities. The following table summarizes relevant information related to the CMES portfolio for the years 1993–95:

Marketable Equity Securities

	Date Purchased	Shares Purchased	Purchase Price	Market Price per Share		
				12/31/93	12/31/94	12/31/95
Sax	1/15/93	700	$45	$44	$46	$47
Xon	3/1/93	400	47	50	45	49
Citco	9/21/93	1000	56	50	51	53
STL	2/2/94	500	31	29	25	26

In 1994, Wampler sold 200 shares of Sax for $28 per share and 400 shares of Citco for $52 per share.

Instructions

Provide all the appropriate journal entries relating to the current marketable equity securities portfolio for 1993–95.

P11.4 Long-Term Bond Investment. Pillar, Inc. decided to invest in bonds to achieve long-term funding objectives. On January 2, 1993, Pillar purchased $100 000 face amount, 6 percent bonds due in three years. The bonds were priced to yield an effective interest rate of 10 percent. Interest is payable semi-annually on June 30 and December 31. Pillar utilizes the effective interest method of amortization and adjusts the carrying value of the bonds on interest payment dates. On June 30, 1994, Pillar sold half the bond investment at 99.

Instructions

Round all amounts to the nearest dollar.

(a) Compute the price paid for the investment, and provide the appropriate journal entry for the acquisition on January 2, 1993, assuming Pillar uses a separate discount or premium account on bond investments.
(b) Provide the appropriate journal entries related to the bond investment through December 31, 1995. Construct a table similar to the one in Exhibit 11.10 (page 517) to determine the proper amortization, adjusted for the June 30, 1994, sale.

P11.5 Long-Term Bond Investment. On June 1, 1994, Warner, Inc. purchased as a long-term investment 800 of the $1000 face value, 8 percent bonds of Universal Corporation for $738 300. The bonds were purchased to yield 10 percent interest. Interest is payable semi-annually on December 1 and June 1. The bonds mature on June 1, 1999. Warner uses the effective interest method of amortization. On November 1, 1995, Warner sold the bonds for $795 000. This amount includes the appropriate accrued interest.

Instructions

Round all amounts to the nearest dollar.

(a) Prepare a schedule of interest revenue and bond discount amortization for the original bond investment from June 1, 1994, to June 1, 1999.

(b) Prepare a schedule showing the income or loss before income taxes from the bond investment that Warner should record for the years ended December 31, 1994 and 1995. Show supporting computations in good form.

(Adapted from AICPA.)

P11.6   Long-Term Bond Investment.   On May 1, 1994, Pope Limited purchased for long-term funding purposes $20 000 face amount, 12 percent bonds, due in three years, at 105.076. The bonds pay interest on May 1 and November 1. Pope utilizes the effective interest method of amortization on interest dates and at calendar year-end. Pope sold $5000 face amount bonds for 101.5 plus accrued interest on August 1, 1995.

Instructions

Round all amounts to the nearest dollar.

(a) Provide the appropriate journal entries for the bond investment from the date of original purchase through December 31, 1995, assuming Pope Limited does *not* use a separate discount or premium account on bond investments. Construct an effective interest amortization table to support your journal entries based on the $20 000 investment without regard to the August 1, 1995, sale. (*Hint:* You must first determine the effective interest rate by trial and error.)

(b) Write a brief explanation of how your answer to (a) would differ had Pope Limited carried the investment account at par value, with any premium or discount in a separate account. Illustrate your explanation by preparing again the journal entries for the purchase of the investment on May 1, 1994, and the interest received on November 1, 1994.

(c) Might a rational business person ever purchase bonds with a $20 000 face value for an amount greater than this? Why or why not?

P11.7   Sinking Fund.   Whisper Ltd. has established a sinking fund for the purpose of redeeming a bond issue. The following transactions relate to this fund for 1995:

Jan. 1   Dividends of $6500 received on North Limited shares held in the fund.
Jan. 14   Expenses of $365 paid by the fund.
Feb. 23   Annual company contribution of $77 500 transferred to the fund.
Apr. 1   Purchased at par, $120 000 of 8 percent bonds plus accrued interest. Interest payable June 30 and December 31.
May 31   Sold bonds purchased on April 1 at 102 plus accrued interest.
Aug. 17   Sold $450 000 of sinking fund assets for $432 700.
Nov. 30   Received dividends of $8200 on Wood Ltd. shares.
Dec. 22   Sold remaining fund assets for 105 percent of carrying value for $680 400.
Dec. 23   Fund cash now totals $1 247 515, of which $1 200 000 is used to retire bond issue.
Dec. 31   Remaining fund cash returned to the general Cash account.

Instructions

Prepare journal entries for these transactions.

P11.8 Equity Method. On June 30, 1993, Miller Limited purchased 30 percent of the outstanding common voting shares of Rex Ltd. for $1 300 000. At that time, the net assets of Rex Ltd. amounted to $4 million. The level of investment is sufficient to give Miller significant influence over the activities of Rex. Any difference between the purchase price and the underlying book value of Rex Ltd.'s net assets is due to the following:

(1) Land is undervalued by $25 000.
(2) Depreciable assets with a ten-year life are worth $30 000 more than the book value.
(3) Goodwill is determined to exist for any remaining difference between cost and book value. Goodwill is estimated to have a useful life of 25 years from the date of the share purchase described above. The following relates to Rex Ltd.:

Year	Net Income	Dividends Declared and Paid on December 31
1993	$100 000	$25 000
1994	120 000	40 000
1995	75 000	—

Instructions

(a) Prepare all necessary journal entries for the transactions described above on the books of Miller Limited through 1995.
(b) Compute the investment account balance on December 31, 1993, 1994, and 1995. (*Hint:* By purchasing 30 percent of the outstanding common shares of Rex Ltd., Miller Limited has purchased only 30 percent of the undervalued amount of land [$25 000] and depreciable assets [$30 000]. Also, recall that land is not subject to amortization.)

P11.9 Equity Method. Porter Limited has made substantial dollar investments in several companies over the past several years in order to diversify and to reduce Porter's dependence on the high-quality steel market. Porter has manufactured high-quality steel for over 50 years. The company policy has been to acquire a substantial portion, but not a majority, of the equity issues of specialty product companies that have been identified as good performers in growth industries. Porter exercises significant influence over the management of these companies because it has at least a 25 percent representation on each of the boards of directors of these companies.

The following schedule presents the companies in which Porter has invested, the percentage of ownership in each company, and the carrying amount of the investment as of December 31, 1994.

Company	Percentage Ownership	Carrying Amount of Investment as of Dec. 31, 1994
Specialty Alloy	15%	$72 000 000
Aerospace, Inc.	40	10 000 000
Temper, Inc.	30	8 000 000
Air Flow, Inc.	30	100 000

Investment performance varied greatly among the companies during 1995. Presented below is a schedule of the income and dividend performance of each company and the market value of its outstanding shares. An interpretation of the information follows:

1995 Performance

Company	Income (Loss)	Dividends Paid	Market Value of Outstanding Shares as of Dec. 31, 1995
Specialty Alloy	$50 000 000	$8 000 000	$540 000 000
Aerospace, Inc.	8 000 000	2 000 000	35 000 000
Temper, Inc.	(6 000 000)	500 000	10 000 000
Air Flow, Inc.	(800 000)	none	1 400 000

Temper, Inc. lost a substantial portion of the market for one of its product lines because a competitor introduced a lower-priced model based on technology not available to Temper. This was the cause of the current year's loss. Management has restructured the company so that it will be profitable in the future, although the level of dollar profits will be reduced from those experienced in the past. Consequently, the market value of the Temper shares is not expected to return to the levels experienced when it was purchased. The $10 million market value reflects this restructuring.

Air Flow, Inc. expects to be profitable from now on. The current year's loss contains the final expenditures incurred in the redevelopment of its product lines. A substantial number of orders for future deliveries have been received.

Instructions

Porter Limited reports on a calendar-year basis and is preparing its 1995 financial statements in accordance with generally accepted accounting principles.

(a) Determine the amount that each of the investments Porter holds in the four companies contributes to the total investment that should be reported on the December 31, 1995, balance sheet. Use the equity or cost method as required in Section 3050 of the CICA *Handbook*.
(b) Calculate the amount of income each investment contributes to Porter's income for 1995.

(Adapted from CMA.)

P11.10   General Equity Investments. On December 31, 1994, ABM, Inc. reported as long-term investments the following marketable equity securities:

Danner Corp., 5000 of common shares (a 1% interest)	$125 000
Ewing Corp., 10 000 of common shares (a 2% interest)	160 000
Fox Corp., 25 000 of common shares (a 10% interest)	700 000
Marketable equity securities at cost	985 000

Additional Information

On May 1, 1995, Danner issued a 10 percent stock dividend, when the market price of its shares was $24.

On November 1, 1995, Danner paid a cash dividend of $0.75 per share.

On August 5, 1995, Ewing issued, to all shareholders, stock rights on the basis of one right per share. Market prices at date of issue were $13.50 per share (ex-rights) and $1.50 per right. ABM sold all its rights on December 16, 1995, for net proceeds of $18 800.

On June 30, 1995, ABM paid $1 520 000 for 50 000 additional common shares of Fox Corp.'s, which represented a 20 percent investment in Fox. The fair value of all of Fox's identifiable assets net of liabilities was equal to their carrying amount of $6 350 000. As a result of this transaction, ABM owns 30 percent of Fox and can exercise significant influence over Fox's operating and financial policies. ABM amortizes goodwill over a 40-year period.

ABM's initial 10 percent interest of 25 000 of Fox's common shares were acquired on January 2, 1994, for $700 000. At that date, the net assets of Fox totalled $5 800 000, and the fair value of Fox's identifiable assets net of liabilities was equal to their carrying amount.

Market prices per share of the marketable equity securities, all listed on a national securities exchange, were as follows:

	December 31	
	1994	**1995**
Danner Corp., common	$22	$23
Ewing Corp., common	15	14
Fox Corp., common	27	29

Fox reported net income and paid dividends as follows:

	Net Income	**Dividends per Share**
Year ended 12/31/94	$350 000	None
Six months ended 6/30/95	200 000	None
Six months ended 12/31/95	370 000	$1.30
(Dividend was paid 10/1/95)		

There were no other intercompany transactions between ABM and Fox.

Instructions

(a) Prepare a schedule setting forth for each investment the transactions and computations necessary to determine the ending balance in ABM's December 31, 1995, balance sheet.

(b) Prepare a schedule showing all revenue, gains, and losses relating to ABM's long-term investments for the year ended December 31, 1995.

(Adapted from AICPA)

P11.11 Correction of Errors. The following asset side of the balance sheet was provided by the Krause Corporation on December 31, 1995:

Krause Corporation
December 31, 1995

Assets

Cash	$ 20 000
Temporary marketable equity securities (market: $16 000)	22 000
Inventory	30 000
Current assets	72 000
Noncurrent investment in 8%, 11-year bonds (at face value; cost: $87 711)	100 000
Noncurrent marketable equity securities (at market; cost: $62 000)	75 000
Plant assets	100 000
Less: Accumulated depreciation	(25 000)
Total assets	$322 000

The long-term investment in bonds was purchased on January 1, 1995. The difference between cost and face value was recognized on the 1995 income statement as an unrealized gain on the acquisition date. The interest on the bonds is payable annually on December 31. The noncurrent marketable equity securities include a 30 percent interest in Alomar Ltd. This investment (with a $45 000 market value on December 31, 1995) was purchased on January 2, 1995, for $40 000 and represents a significant influence. Alomar had net income of $50 000 and dividends of $20 000 in 1995. Krause reported 1995 net income of $57 000. The books for Krause Corporation have not been closed for 1995. Assume that all items are material.

Instructions
(a) Provide correcting and adjusting journal entries for Krause Corporation in light of the information given. Any discount or premium on the bond investment is to be carried in a separate account from the face value.
(b) What is Krause's correct net income for 1995? Show your computations.
(c) Recast the asset side of the December 31, 1995, balance sheet for Krause Corporation according to generally accepted accounting principles.

P11.12 Comprehensive Investment Analysis. The following correct balance sheet was provided by Chakos, Inc. on December 31, 1994:

Chakos, Inc.
BALANCE SHEET
December 31, 1994

Assets

Current marketable equity securities	$ 12 000.00	
Less: Allowance to reduce CMES to LCM	(1 500.00)	$ 10 500.00
Other current assets		40 000.00
Total current assets		50 500.00
Investment in bonds		94 793.25
Noncurrent investment in marketable securities*		50 000.00
Investment in Baxter Ltd. (accounted for by the equity method)**		75 000.00
Land		74 500.00
Total assets		$344 793.25

Liabilities and Owners' Equity

Current liabilities	$ 35 000.00
Bonds payable (issued at face value)	100 000.00
Common shares (no-par value, 40 000 shares)	100 000.00
Retained earnings	109 793.25
Total liabilities and owners' equity	$344 793.25

*The noncurrent investment in marketable securities has been written down from the original investment of $75 000.

**The investment in Baxter Ltd. is a 25 percent interest and represents significant influence.

The market values of the investments held by Chakos, Inc. on December 31, 1995, were:

Current marketable equity securities	$ 11 000
Noncurrent marketable equity securities	45 000
Investment in bonds	100 000
Investment in Baxter Ltd.	70 000

All market value declines are considered permanent.

Chakos did not have any significant financing or investing transactions during 1995. The bond investment was an $80 000 face amount, ten-year, 12 percent bond purchased on December 31, 1990. Interest is received annually on December 31. Chakos uses the effective interest method of amortization. Baxter Ltd. reported income for 1995 of $100 000 and declared dividends of $80 000. The operating income of Chakos, Inc. for 1995 was $15 000. Current liabilities on December 31, 1995, were $35 000. Assume no taxes.

Instructions

Prepare the December 31, 1995, balance sheet for Chakos, Inc. Provide a supporting schedule to derive the balances for retained earnings and other current assets.

Cases

C11.1 Bond Investment. Wilson Limited purchased $1 million of face amount, 5 percent, six-year bonds at 71.22 on January 1, 1992. Calendar year 1995 was a poor year for Wilson because of declining revenues and tighter operating margins. The company had an operating income of only $100 000 on revenues of $2 million, or 5 percent. The treasurer decided to remedy the situation by selling the $1 million face amount, 5 percent bonds on December 31, 1995, at 90 and recognizing a gain for that period. The following calculation determined the gain on the sale:

Proceeds	$900 000
Carrying value	712 200
Gain	$187 800

As a result of this transaction, Wilson Limited's net income totalled $287 800, or 14.4 percent of sales. The treasurer was very pleased. The company was now above the industry-wide profitability average for 1995, the shareholders would be satisfied, and the treasurer's year-end bonus, which is based on net income, would be almost triple what it would have been before the transaction. As the treasurer's assistant, you are not comfortable with his remedy. You confront the treasurer and tell him, "I have some good news and some bad news."

Instructions
(a)   What is the "good news"?
(b)   What is the "bad news"?

C11.2   Equity Method.   On page 524 is a reprint from *Forbes'* "Numbers Game" column. The article is critical of the use of the equity method.

Instructions
Read the article carefully. Do you agree with its conclusions? Why or why not? How would you respond to the allegations presented in this article?

Judgement Cases

J11.1   Current and Noncurrent Classification Issues.   Your client, Come Clean, Inc., specializes in the removal and treatment of a hazardous waste that is created by other companies in their productive processes. This particular toxic waste was only identified five years ago. Because little was known about some of its toxic properties, liability insurance was not available prior to the most recent year. In prior years, the company was required by a provincial regulatory agency to perpetually maintain a large fund in lieu of liability insurance to compensate anyone injured by the activities of the company in disposing of the waste. To date, no claims have been made and none are known to exist. Further, the company was successful in acquiring liability insurance last year, and the province has agreed that the fund no longer needs to be maintained.

The assets in the fund are marketable equity securities of a wide range of large corporations. At the end of the preceding year, the aggregate market value of the fund had declined below the aggregate cost, due primarily to a broad and sudden decline in the stock market shortly before year-end. At that time, you believed that the decline in the market value was other than a temporary decline. In light of the economic conditions in the country and the dim prospects for the future, you wrote down these securities to their market value. The loss was included in the determination of income in that period.

Since that time, the value of the portfolio has gradually risen, and you believe that it will eventually equal or exceed their original cost. However, the fund is no longer required, and the company has been selling the securities to expand capacity or replace obsolete equipment. You note that the market value of the securities sold have all exceeded their original costs, and realized gains have been appropriately recorded. The president of Come Clean, Inc. has informed you that he intends to use the proceeds from the sale of the fund securities to replace outdated plant assets and to increase the disposal capacity of the company. He contends that the securities are presently trading at higher than their recorded cost and should be sold. You argue that the book cost is below the original cost, and you suggest holding the securities until they increase above their original cost. The stock market average is moving up, and the economy is improving.

Instructions
Prepare a report for the president of Come Clean, Inc. to explain the accounting treatment of long-term investments when a loss in value is other than temporary, and to explain the recording of the subsequent sale. Support your answer with consideration of the relevant factors and accounting principles.

J11.2   Equity Method.   Hi-Flyer Airline, Inc. acquired a 25 percent interest in the voting shares of a large regional travel agency, We-Book-Em, Inc. Originally, the airline planned to use the travel agency as a "feeder" for a charter business it intended to develop. The airline has since abandoned the charter business program, but it continues to hold stock in the travel agency. Hi-Flyer has appropriately applied the equity method of accounting to its interest in the travel agency, and that investment has been largely profitable.

Now, however, the travel agency has lost three accounts that collectively represented 40 percent of its revenue. Its cash flow and profitability forecasts reveal anticipated losses through each of the next five years. The value of We-Book-Em shares has also been adversely affected, and the amount of Hi-Flyer's related investment account substantially exceeds the market value of the shares and any price that might be realized in a unitary sale of the interest. You have just received the latest audited financial statements of the travel agency, which discuss the loss of the contracts but do not contain any write-down of assets or loss in the corresponding income statement.

Hi-Flyer does not intend to sell its interest and now plans to acquire an even larger share of the travel agency in order to gain control and finally implement its own charter and reservation service. The president tells you, "We know how to make lemonade out of lemons and that is exactly what we are going to do with We-Book-Em. While our program won't be launched for at least three years and we don't expect it to generate material amounts of revenue for five, we are quite confident that the more distant future is very, very rosy."

You are pondering the implications of the situation when you read that Section 3050 of the CICA *Handbook* recommends the realization of a loss when the decline in the value of the investment is other than temporary. You become concerned that some kind of a write-down in the carrying amount of the We-Book-Em investment might be necessary. You are also aware that the major lending institution assisting Hi-Flyer has expressed concern about the debt/equity ratio and net income level reported recently by the airline. Any write-down of the investment in We-Book-Em would certainly increase the concerns of Hi-Flyer's lenders and would be resisted strongly by the management of Hi-Flyer.

Instructions

Is a write-down of the investment in We-Book-Em necessary at this time? If you believe that a current write-down of the investment is or may be necessary, be sure to describe the amount of the write-off that will be required. Draw on your knowledge of equity method accounting as well as other accounting standards and principles.

Chapter 12

Property, Plant, and Equipment: Acquisition and Disposal

Objectives

1. To describe the roles of tangible and intangible assets in the revenue-producing process.

2. To discuss the basic accounting principles that underlie accounting for tangible and intangible assets.

3. To apply the asset/liability measurement principle to specific capital assets in a variety of circumstances.

4. To discuss the proper accounting treatment of tangible capital-asset expenditures that are incurred after the initial acquisition of the related assets.

5. To discuss transactions that result in the disposal of tangible capital assets, including their sale, abandonment, destruction, or exchange for other assets.

6. To identify and discuss those limited situations in which a departure from historical cost is warranted in accounting for tangible capital assets.

Classification of Tangible and Intangible Capital Assets

Although capital assets are used in the production or distribution of goods or services in virtually all businesses, they vary in nature because of the differences in the business activities of enterprises. These assets include both tangible properties, such as equipment and buildings, and intangible assets, such as patents and franchise rights. **Tangible assets are often called property, plant, and equipment** or simply **plant assets** or **fixed assets. Assets lacking physical substance** are typically referred to as **intangible assets.**

All tangible and intangible capital assets have two primary characteristics in common:

1. **They are acquired as operating assets.** Tangible and intangible assets are acquired for use in the production or distribution of goods or services. They are *not* acquired primarily for purposes of resale, even though they may later be sold.
2. **They are relatively long-lived.** Tangible and intangible assets are expected to have relatively long lives in terms of their contribution to the production and distribution of goods and services. In most cases, therefore, the cost of these assets is allocated as an expense over their productive lives.[1]

Despite these similarities, characteristics of specific tangible and intangible assets vary considerably. For example, although most are readily transferable between enterprises, others cannot be separated from the original enterprise. Furthermore, some are natural resources, while others are man-made properties. Numerous classifications of tangible and intangible capital assets are available. In this text, we use the classifications that follow:

Asset Classification	Example Assets	Allocation of Cost
Tangible Capital Assets		
Property, plant, and equipment subject to depreciation	Buildings Equipment Furniture Fixtures	Depreciation
Property not subject to depreciation	Land	
Natural resources	Oil and gas reserves Mineral deposits	Depletion
Intangible Capital Assets		
Separately identifiable	Patents Copyrights Trademarks Franchises Leaseholds	Amortization
Not separately identifiable	Goodwill	Amortization

[1]"Capital Assets," CICA *Handbook*, Paragraph 3060.04, December 1990.

Chapters 12, 13, and 14 deal with accounting for tangible and intangible capital assets. The balance sheet inside the front endpapers of this book lists "Properties" as an asset category in the balance sheet of Canadian Pacific Limited. These assets include significant investments in tangible assets that are used in the day-to-day operations of the company. We discuss tangible capital assets in Chapters 12 and 13.

The first part of this chapter presents general principles of accounting for all capital assets. We then focus on specific issues concerning the acquisition and disposal of various types of tangible assets. Chapter 13 covers the depreciation and depletion of tangible assets and includes several special accounting problems. In Chapter 14 the accounting principles discussed in Chapters 12 and 13 are applied to intangible assets, and several problems associated with accounting for these assets are identified and discussed. Because a detailed discussion of depreciation is included in Chapter 13, this chapter uses only straight-line depreciation.

Definitions and Basic Accounting Principles

Capital assets are acquired primarily for use in the production and distribution of goods and services, are expected to be used over a relatively long period, and have tangible physical properties. Although tangible assets are apparent through their physical qualities, their value lies in their **service potential:** the positive contribution that the asset is capable of making to the revenue-producing process of the enterprise. Service potential can also exist in an intangible asset, in the form of rights and privileges that accrue to the holder of the asset. Exchange of assets is discussed later in this chapter.

Several principles that underlie accounting for all tangible and intangible assets are discussed in the following sections. Application of the principles to specific assets, problems encountered in applying the principles, and specified exceptions to the general principles are discussed throughout this and subsequent chapters.

**Asset/Liability
Measurement**

 Principle 1. Tangible and intangible capital assets are initially recorded at historical cost.

Tangible and intangible assets are *initially* measured and recorded at **historical cost,** which is the cash price or the cash-equivalent value of other consideration. The cash or cash-equivalent price represents the bargained value of the asset at the time of acquisition. From the viewpoint of the acquirer, the cash or cash-equivalent price represents the future value of the service potential expected from the asset.

The method of accounting for historical cost for tangible and intangible assets is broader than simply the cash or cash-equivalent price. All costs related to the acquisition and preparation of an asset for its intended use are considered part of the asset's cost. In addition, subsequent costs to extend the useful life of the asset (beyond that originally expected) or to increase either the quantity or quality of service rendered by the asset are considered part of its cost. In a survey of 297 companies reporting capital assets, 97 percent used cost as their basis of valuation.[2]

 Historical cost, as applied to tangible and intangible assets, is best described as a **full-cost concept,** because it includes expenditures related to the acquisition of an asset and the continuing enhancement of the service potential of the asset.

---

[2]"Property, Plant and Equipment," in *Financial Reporting in Canada*, 19th ed. (Toronto: CICA, 1991), p. 96.

Matching

Principle 2. The cost of tangible and intangible assets is allocated as depreciation, depletion, or amortization in a systematic and rational manner to achieve a matching of expenses and revenues during the useful life of the asset.

As tangible and intangible assets are used in the production of revenue, their *future* service potential declines. Since these assets are established at historical cost, this decline in service potential is measured by treating a portion of historical cost as an expense in the periods that benefit from the use of the asset. From the accountant's perspective, **depreciation** is the process of allocating the cost of property, plant, and equipment as an expense to those periods during which the asset contributes to the revenue-producing process. The terms **depletion** and **amortization** are used to describe this allocation process for **natural resources** and intangible assets, respectively.

Although expenditures for a tangible or an intangible asset are typically made when the asset is initially acquired, the cost is allocated as an expense over the useful life of the asset; only *part* of the cost is charged as an expense in the period of acquisition. This

Matching

procedure is important to the process of matching revenues and expenses in determining net income.

Methods to determine depreciation expense must be **systematic** and **rational.** A systematic method calculates the periodic depreciation charge in advance or on the basis of the activity level during a particular period. A rational method identifies the association between the amount of depreciation expense recognized and the decline in the service potential of the asset during the period. Chapter 13 covers in detail a number of systematic methods that are widely practiced. Specific circumstances must be considered in evaluating the rational feature of a particular method.

(3)   **Principle 3.** The establishment of cost and the subsequent allocation of that cost is necessarily based on many estimates and assumptions about the use of the capital asset.

Estimates and assumptions are an important part of accounting for capital assets. If cash transactions are not used in acquiring the assets and if costs related to acquisition are incurred, judgements must be made in determining the historical cost. Cost allocation methods (i.e., depreciation, depletion, and amortization) require an estimate of useful life in terms of calendar time, service time, or productive output. Finally, an estimate of residual (or salvage) value is required in applying the various cost allocation methods that are used in practice.

An additional judgement must estimate the pattern of the decline in the service potential of a tangible or an intangible asset. Since the allocation method must be rational, it should reflect—to the extent possible—the estimated decline in the service potential of the asset on a periodic basis over its estimated useful life.

    Principle 4. The unallocated cost of a capital asset, called "book value," is *not* intended to approximate the current market value of the asset.

Matching

As indicated in Principle 2, the process for allocating the cost of capital assets to those periods that benefit from their use is important in matching revenues and expenses to determine net income. The historical cost of the asset, less accumulated depreciation, depletion, or amortization, is called **book value.** We can define book value best in terms of the process followed in its calculation: the historical cost reduced by the accumulated depreciation, depletion, or amortization recognized to date. Alternatively, book value can be defined as the *unallocated* portion of the historical cost of the asset.

Given how book value is determined, we cannot expect it to equal the current market value of the asset. After an asset is acquired, its market value may remain constant, may decline, or may increase. If the market value declines, it may or may not equal the book value. The term "book value" may be a misnomer, because it seems to imply that the number measures the current worth of the asset. Although "unallocated cost" is more descriptive of the number, "book value" is widely used in practice. While book value does not equal the current value of the asset, depreciation policy should generally be applied so that the book value does not exceed the current value of the asset.

Determining Costs of Specific Items of Property, Plant, and Equipment

Property, plant, and equipment—or simply fixed assets—should be established in appropriate accounts at cost. The full cost includes expenditures necessary to acquire the assets and to prepare them for their intended use. The following sections develop and apply the full-cost concept to specific types of capital assets.

Land

The cost of land includes a variety of expenditures related to the acquisition of the land and its preparation for use as intended by the acquiring enterprise. Several major expenditures should be capitalized as the cost of land:

1. The original bargained acquisition price.
2. Commissions related to acquisition.
3. Legal fees related to acquisition.
4. Cost of surveys.
5. Cost of an option to buy the acquired land.
6. Cost of removing unwanted buildings from the land, less any proceeds from salvage.
7. Unpaid taxes (to date of acquisition) assumed by the purchaser.
8. Cost of permanent improvements (e.g., landscaping) and improvements maintained and replaced by the government (e.g., streetlights and sewers).

What happens when some of these costs are incurred but the land is *not* acquired? For example, in deciding whether or not to acquire a parcel of land, a company may pay for surveys, purchase options, and other items related to several parcels of land, but eventually buy only one. While a case can be made that costs associated with land not acquired are necessary expenditures for the land acquired, in our opinion, such costs should be expensed as incurred. The relationship between such costs and the acquired land is indirect, and care must be taken not to capitalize costs in an amount that exceeds the fair value of the acquired land.

Expenditures for land improvements that have limited lives should be capitalized in accounts other than the Land account and depreciated over their estimated useful lives. Examples are private driveways, sidewalks, fences, parking lots, and easements or rights of way of limited duration.

Land and other capital assets that are held for speculative or other investment purposes should be classified as investments rather than as property, plant, and equipment. Taxes and other expenditures required to maintain these assets should be capitalized as part of the cost of the assets if they are not producing revenue while they are considered an investment. If the assets produce revenue (e.g., through rental), these expenditures should be treated as expenses and matched against the revenue that the investments generate.

Land is generally considered to have an unlimited life and is not expected to decline in service potential as it is used. Thus, land is usually carried at the original cost figure and not depreciated over the periods during which it is used in the operations of the enterprise.

Buildings

The cost of a building includes all necessary expenditures to acquire or construct and prepare the building for its intended use. The following major expenditures should be capitalized as part of the cost of a building.

If acquired by purchase:

1. The original bargained purchase price of the building.
2. Cost of renovation necessary to prepare the building for its intended use.
3. Cost of building permits related to renovation.
4. Unpaid taxes (to date of acquisition) assumed by the purchaser.

If acquired by construction:

1. Cost of constructing new building, including materials, labour, and overhead.
2. Cost of excavating land in preparation for construction.
3. Cost of plans, blueprints, specifications, and estimates related to construction.
4. Cost of building permits.
5. Architectural and engineering fees.
6. Interest cost when an extended period of time is required for construction.[3]

The cost of a building that is acquired but immediately removed to prepare the land for construction of a new building should be treated as part of the cost of the *land* rather than as part of the cost of the new building. As we indicated earlier, the cost of removal is treated as part of the land cost. Also, the cost of removing an existing building that the new purchaser actually used for a time should be treated as an adjustment to the gain or loss on the disposal of the old building rather than as part of the cost of the land or the newly constructed building.

Care must be taken to distinguish between building costs and the cost of other assets, such as removable fixtures. The latter represent separate assets that should be recorded in appropriate asset accounts and depreciated over their expected useful lives. This holds even if they were acquired with the building and used in a manner closely related to it.

Machinery, Equipment, Furniture, and Fixtures

Machinery, equipment, furniture, and fixtures are various types of property, plant, and equipment that are used by enterprises in the production and distribution of goods and

---

[3]The subjects of overhead as part of the cost of internally constructed capital assets and capitalization of interest are covered later in this chapter.

services. The following list includes some of the costs that should be capitalized in the appropriate asset accounts:

1. The original bargained acquisition price.
2. Freight, insurance, handling, storage, and other costs related to acquiring the asset.
3. Cost of installation, including site preparation, assembling, and installing.
4. Cost of trial runs and other tests required before the asset can be put into full operation.
5. Cost of reconditioning equipment acquired in a used state. Cost of removing the old equipment to make room for the new equipment is a cost of the old equipment. However, accidental damage to a machine being removed or installed is an expense of the period.

Making the proper distinction in the accounting records among the types of property, plant, and equipment is important because the estimated lives of assets and the methods of depreciating them vary among the various asset categories.

Natural Resources

Natural resources (e.g., timber, coal, and oil) represent tangible assets that are recorded at cost when they are acquired. These costs are then allocated, usually on a production basis, as depletion to the periods benefiting from the use of the natural resources, as we explain in Chapter 13.

The cost of natural resources includes the original purchase price plus exploration and development costs related to the location and extraction of the resources.[4] Other capital assets, separate from the natural resource, are frequently acquired for use in the development and production of natural resources. Buildings and equipment, for example, are typically used in the successful exploitation of natural resources. These assets are established in separate accounts and depreciated over the shorter of (1) their expected useful lives or (2) the expected useful life of the related natural resource.

Other Capital Assets

Types of property, plant, and equipment are as numerous as types of enterprises. Each enterprise must acquire those capital assets required to succeed in its line of business. In addition to the more common tangible assets—land, buildings, machinery, equipment, furniture, fixtures, and natural resources—a wide variety of assets is used by some enterprises. Several of these are discussed in the following paragraphs.

Returnable containers are used in certain types of businesses to transfer products between the enterprise and its customers. Such containers may represent a significant asset, especially when a large number are in circulation at any particular time. In some cases, the customer makes no deposit; the container is simply returned by the customer or picked up by the enterprise after it has been used. In these cases, the enterprise typically uses an inventory method whereby the asset cost is increased as units are acquired and reduced as a periodic count or estimate reveals the number of units that are no longer in use. The reduction may be due to normal wear and tear, breakage, or other causes. The

---

[4]Unique problems associated with accounting for exploration costs in the oil and gas industry are covered in Chapter 14.

amounts of deposits that are intended to be returned later represent a liability of the enterprise. This liability is often called **deposits from customers.** Returnable containers that are not returned within a reasonable period should be treated as sales at the deposit amount. To complete the matching process, the cost of unreturned containers should then be charged to an appropriate expense.

Matching

Miscellaneous tools and other small items of equipment are another type of capital asset, despite their relatively low unit cost. The practical limitations of capitalizing and depreciating a large number of inexpensive assets result in the cost of such items being treated as expenses when incurred, or later on an inventory basis similar to that for returnable containers. Materiality is an important consideration in these situations, and a departure from the strict application of the matching principle may be justified if expensing small assets or using an inventory approach does not have a significant impact on the financial statements.

Materiality

Matching

In a manufacturing process, various tools and other devices are used to mould, stamp, cut, and shape materials. Such devices, commonly called *patterns and dies,* should be capitalized in appropriate asset accounts and depreciated over their estimated useful lives. If such devices are useful only in a particular job rather than in a continuous manufacturing process, they should be charged to cost for that particular job.

Problems of Establishing Historical Cost

The concept of full cost, whereby capital assets are established at the cost of acquisition and preparation for intended use, is more easily stated than applied. Numerous problems are encountered in attempting to apply this general principle to specific situations. Judgement is required in assessing which expenditures should be classified as part of the cost of assets and which costs should be treated in other ways.

This section discusses several frequently encountered problems: cash discounts; deferred-payment plans; internally constructed assets; capitalization of interest; acquisition by issuing securities; basket purchases; and installation, preparation, and start-up costs. Although these problems and their resolutions can apply to a wide range of capital assets, they are illustrated here in the context of specific tangible assets.

Cash Discounts

The bargained purchase price of an asset is the cash paid or the cash-equivalent price. If cash discounts are available for early payment, should cost include or exclude the cash discount? A related question is whether the amount of the recorded cost should depend on whether or not the cash discount is taken.

Theoretically, the cash-equivalent price should equal the original price *minus* any cash discount available, **whether or not the discount is taken,** because the net amount is the price at which the asset could be acquired in a cash transaction. If the discount is not taken, a **discount lost** should be recorded and treated as an expense in the current period.

As an example, assume that Elmwood Limited acquired equipment with a list price of $88 000 with terms 2/10, n/30. The asset should be recorded at the net amount of $86 240 [$88 000 − (0.02 × $88 000)]:

Equipment	86 240	
Accounts Payable		86 240

If payment is made within the ten-day period, the $86 240 payment of accounts payable is recorded. If payment is made after the ten-day period, however, the following entry is appropriate:

Accounts Payable	86 240	
Discount Lost	1 760	
Cash		88 000

Materiality

Recording the asset at the **net amount** is preferable, because this represents the cash-equivalent price. However, some accountants record the asset at the total price paid ($88 000 in the above example) if the discount is not taken. The basis for this treatment is that the total price was the actual amount paid; in some particular circumstances, it may not be appropriate or possible for management to take the discount. Materiality may be an important consideration in these decisions, because relatively small discounts may not have a significant impact on the financial statements.

Deferred-Payment Plans

Assets may be acquired on a long-term financing plan whereby periodic payments are made or a single payment is made at some future date. An asset acquired in this manner should be recorded at the current cash-equivalent price and any interest included in the financing plan recognized as expense in the appropriate period(s). The objective of this practice is to distinguish properly between the portion of payments that represents the historical cost of the asset acquired and the portion representing interest charges for the credit received. Failure to make this distinction results in a misstatement of the cost of the asset, depreciation expense, and interest expense.

If interest is not stated in a deferred-payment contract, if the stated interest is not reasonable in view of current market conditions, or if the face amount of the obligation differs from the current selling price for the same or equivalent asset, interest may need to be *imputed*. The amount of the obligation is assumed to include the **acquisition price** of the asset and **interest charges**. The obligation is recorded at the asset's estimated fair value, and the difference between the face amount of the obligation and the estimated fair value of the asset at the date of acquisition is recognized as interest over the life of the obligation. The asset and related obligation should be recorded at an amount equal to (1) the fair value of the asset being acquired, (2) the market value of the obligation, or (3) the present value of the obligation determined by present value techniques that use an estimated interest rate. The most objectively determinable of the first two measures should generally be used. Many accountants prefer using the market value of the obligation because of the reliability of the amount. In some cases, however, the amounts for (1) and (2) are not available and the value of the asset and related obligation must be estimated by the third method. If either of the first two methods is used to record the transaction, the difference between the **face value of the note** and the **recorded amount of the asset** must be used to compute a rate upon which the recognition of interest will be based. If the third method is used, the borrower's (i.e., purchaser's) incremental borrowing rate should be used as a basis for computing the recorded amount of the asset, the obligation, and the subsequent recognition of interest. This process is a specific application of the general process of imputing interest required by *Accounting Principles Board Opinion No. 21* that we discussed in Chapter 11. Exhibit 12.1 summarizes the processes used in accounting for deferred-payment acquisitions.

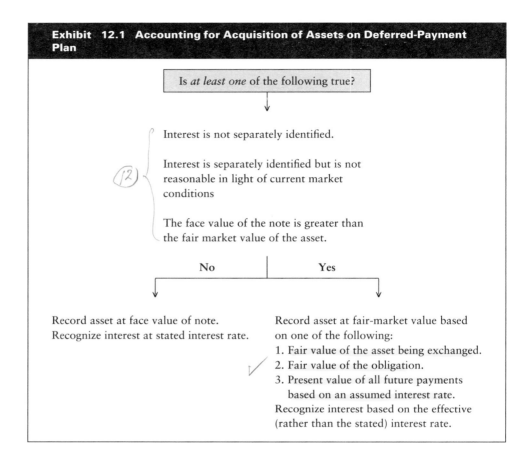

Exhibit 12.1   Accounting for Acquisition of Assets on Deferred-Payment Plan

Is *at least one* of the following true?

Interest is not separately identified.

Interest is separately identified but is not reasonable in light of current market conditions

The face value of the note is greater than the fair market value of the asset.

No   Yes

Record asset at face value of note. Recognize interest at stated interest rate.

Record asset at fair-market value based on one of the following:
1. Fair value of the asset being exchanged.
2. Fair value of the obligation.
3. Present value of all future payments based on an assumed interest rate.
Recognize interest based on the effective (rather than the stated) interest rate.

Two independent examples illustrate the process of imputing interest on such acquisitions. In the first example, we will assume that Elmwood Production Limited acquired a used machine by issuing a $150 000 noninterest-bearing note. The transaction took place on December 31, 1992, and payment is due on December 31, 1995. Neither the market value of the note nor the fair value of the property are determinable. Recently, however, Elmwood paid 12 percent interest on similar transactions.

Since no stated interest rate exists and market values of the note and the asset are unknown, the portion of the note representing interest must be separated by using the 12 percent interest rate. Using the present value of 1 factor from Table 7.2, we can determine the present value as follows:

$$\text{Present value of note} = \text{Face value} \times pvf_{\overline{n}|i}$$
$$= \$150\ 000 \times pvf_{\overline{3}|12\%}$$
$$= \$150\ 000 \times 0.71178)$$
$$= \$106\ 767$$

The cost of the machinery is recorded at $106 767 and the note payable, net of a discount to reduce the face value of $150 000 to its present value, is recorded at the same amount. This may be done by using a separate Discount account as follows:

Machinery	106 767	
Discount on Notes Payable	43 233	
Notes Payable		150 000

The discount of $43 233 is then recognized as interest over the life of the note according to the following schedule (amounts rounded to the nearest dollar):

Date	Interest Computation	Carrying Value of Obligation
		$ 106 767
Dec. 31, 1993		
Interest recognition	$(0.12 \times \$106\ 767 = \$12\ 812)$	12 812
		119 579
Dec. 31, 1994		
Interest recognition	$(0.12 \times \$119\ 579 = \$14\ 349)$	14 349
		133 928
Dec. 31, 1995		
Interest recognition	$(\$150\ 000 - \$133\ 928 = \$16\ 072)$	16 072
	OR 133,928 × 12% = 16,071	150 000
Payment of note		(150 000)
		—

Interest at December 31, 1995, can also be determined by applying the 12 percent rate to the carrying value of the obligation, as was done in 1993 and 1994. The following computation would result: $12\% \times \$133\ 928 = \$16\ 071$. The $1 difference from the amount in the preceding schedule is due to a rounding difference caused by stating the amounts in whole dollars. One way to get around this rounding problem is to adjust for the difference between the face value and carrying value of the note in the last year, as we did in the schedule.

The following entry recognizes the interest at December 31 of each intervening year:

	1993	1994	1995
Interest Expense	12 812	14 349	16 072
Discount on Notes Payable	12 812	14 349	16 072

As each entry recognizing interest is made, the carrying value of the note is increased, as indicated in the schedule above. The final payment at December 31, 1995, is made by a debit to the Notes Payable account and a credit to the Cash account for $150 000. The cost of the asset for purposes of depreciation and financial statement presentation is $106 767.

Capital acquisitions resulting in *multiple* payments may also require interest imputations. To illustrate, Elmwood Production Limited acquired a used machine by issuing three $50 000 noninterest-bearing notes, payable one, two, and three years from the transaction date of December 31, 1992. Neither the market value of the notes nor the fair value of the asset is determinable. In recent similar transactions, however, Elmwood paid 12 percent interest.

As in the previous case, no interest rate is stated and the market values of the notes and asset are not determinable. The portion of the notes representing interest must be separated by using the appropriate present value factor for an ordinary annuity from Table 7.4, as follows:

Face value of notes (representing both principal and interest)	$150 000
Present value of notes	
($50 000 × $pvoaf_{\overline{3}|\ 12\%}$)	
($50 000 × 2.40183)	(120 092)
Amount of imputed interest	$ 29 908

The purchase of the asset and the related obligation are then recorded as follows:

Machinery	120 092	
Discount on Notes Payable	29 908	
Notes Payable		150 000

The portion of each $50 000 payment representing interest is separated and recognized periodically over the life of the notes according to the following schedule:

Date	Interest Computation	Carrying Value of Obligation
		$120 092
Dec. 31, 1993		
Interest recognition	(0.12 × $120 092)	14 411
Payment		(50 000)
		84 503
Dec. 31, 1994		
Interest recognition	(0.12 × $84 503)	10 140
Payment		(50 000)
		44 643
Dec. 31, 1995		
Interest recognition	(0.12 × $44 643)	5 357
Payment		(50 000)
		-0-

An entry is made to record the periodic payment and to recognize interest at December 31 of each intervening year, as follows:

	1993	1994	1995
Notes Payable	50 000	50 000	50 000
Cash	50 000	50 000	50 000
Interest Expense	14 411	10 140	5 357
Discount on Notes Payable	14 411	10 140	5 357

This series of entries results in the complete elimination of the obligation of $120 092 recognized at the date of acquisition and the proper recognition of interest expense for the intervening accounting periods. The cost of the asset for purposes of depreciation and financial statement presentation is $120 092.

Imputing interest for an asset acquisition is required in order to distinguish between the historical cost of the capital asset and interest expense. This, in turn, results in a proper measurement of the asset in the balance sheet, and interest expense and depreci-

Asset/Liability Measurement

**Substance
Over Form**

ation expense in the income statement. It is also an interesting example of the principle of substance over form in that we recognize interest expense on debt obligations that are in form noninterest-bearing. Failure to impute interest in those situations described in Exhibit 12.1 results in improper figures for these important financial statement items.

Internally Constructed Assets

In certain circumstances, companies construct their own capital assets rather than acquire them from other enterprises. For some companies, this is done routinely and is an expected part of business operations; for others, this is done only occasionally. Several frequently cited reasons for constructing assets internally are:

1. To acquire needed productive services at prices lower than those from external sources.
2. To make use of facilities and personnel that would otherwise be idle in slack periods.
3. To produce specialized assets that might not otherwise be available.
4. To ensure the privacy of information concerning future production plans.

Historical cost applies to capital assets that are developed internally as well as acquired from external sources. However, measuring the cost of internally constructed assets poses some unusual problems. Costs of producing inventory are generally identified in terms of material, labour, and overhead costs.[5] This classification also provides the basis for determining the cost of capital assets that are constructed internally.

Accountants generally agree that materials and direct labour should be included in the cost of an internally constructed asset, since they represent both tangible materials and payment to employees involved in the production of the asset. Overhead costs are more controversial, however, because they are indirect costs of production that are not closely associated with any specific product or constructed asset.

Several positions exist concerning inclusion of manufacturing overhead in the cost of internally constructed assets. One position holds that the costs of such assets should *not* include any overhead charge because of the indirect nature of overhead and the inability to associate overhead charges with the particular asset being constructed. The basis of this assumption is that overhead costs are the same whether or not assets (other than inventory produced for resale) are being constructed. However, the exclusion of overhead does not appear viable if overhead costs increase as a result of constructing capital assets internally. A second position thus requires only *incremental* overhead to be included in the cost of the internally constructed asset. While intuitively logical, isolating the increase in overhead costs that can be specifically identified with constructing an asset internally is often difficult.

The concept of full cost supports a third position concerning the amount of overhead, if any, to be capitalized as part of the cost of an asset that is constructed internally. This position holds that the asset should be charged overhead on the same basis as inventory that is also being produced. For example, if overhead is charged to the manufacture of inventory at $1.50 per hour of direct labour, the same allocation procedure is used to charge overhead to the capital asset; thus, the cost of the asset includes $1.50 of overhead per hour of direct labour. While this method is widely used in practice, it is difficult to

---

[5]"Capital Assets, Acquisition, Construction or Development Over Time," CICA *Handbook*, Paragraph 3060.22, October 1990.

justify if production below capacity is a reason for constructing the asset internally. Absorbing the cost of idle capacity in the cost of the internally constructed asset relieves current income and inventory of charges that would otherwise have been made to them, and results in a higher cost of the constructed asset. This process increases income of the current and near-future years (by reducing costs of sales and inventory) and reduces income of distant-future years (by increasing depreciation charges). Authoritative accounting pronouncements do not resolve the issue. Proper accounting is, thus, a matter of professional judgement in applying the concept of full cost. The authors believe that the full-cost concept should be generally followed and that the total cost of internally developed assets should include materials, labour, and overhead prorated in the same manner as for inventory being manufactured. A logical exception to this general policy would arise if a company were operating below capacity and constructing a capital asset internally in order to utilize more efficiently its employees and facilities. In such a case, if it is *practical* to determine the incremental overhead, only the incremental overhead associated with the manufacture of the asset should be included in the cost of the asset.

What amount should be capitalized as the cost of an internally constructed asset when the internal costs total more than the price at which the asset could have been purchased externally? Accountants generally agree that the *maximum* amount at which the asset should be established is its *market value*. Any costs beyond that amount represent inefficiencies of internal construction and should not be included in the cost of the asset. Future periods should not be burdened with the greater depreciation charges that would result from the capitalization of those costs. Any costs beyond the external market price of the internally constructed asset should be treated as expenses in the period in which they are incurred.

Capitalization of Interest

Our earlier discussion of deferred payment for capital assets emphasized the importance of distinguishing between expenditures that represent payments for interest on money borrowed and expenditures that are made to acquire the productive services of various types of assets. Controversy has surrounded the determination of the historical cost of assets, however, when interest costs are incurred specifically for the acquisition and preparation of assets for their intended use.

Historically, most enterprises have treated all interest as expense when incurred. The **capitalization of interest** as part of the historical cost of assets has been a common practice among public utilities, however, because customers are charged regulated rates based on costs incurred and designed to provide shareholders of the utilities with a fair rate of return on their investment. When interest costs are incurred to construct utility facilities, interest is capitalized as part of the cost of those facilities. Therefore, utility rates on the new facilities are based on higher asset-acquisition costs, and future utility users in those areas will pay rates that cover the interest costs required to finance the facilities that produce the services they consume.

The practice of capitalizing interest has not been limited to public utilities. An increasing number of other enterprises began adopting the policy of capitalizing interest in certain circumstances. The CICA *Handbook* allows for the inclusion of carrying costs, but does not outline any specific procedures.[6] Standards of accounting and reporting in this area were established in the United States by the Financial Accounting Standards Board

---

[6]"Capital Assets," CICA *Handbook*, Paragraph 3060.26, October 1990.

in its *Statement of Financial Accounting Standards No. 34.*[7] These standards are used by many Canadian corporations. This pronouncement requires the capitalization of interest by all enterprises in certain circumstances on the premise that the historical cost of acquiring an asset includes all costs necessary to bring the asset to the condition and location required for its intended use. In addition, the capitalization of interest cost in certain

Matching

circumstances is necessary to achieve a proper matching of revenues and expenses as the asset costs are depreciated in future periods.

Interest is capitalized as part of the cost of acquiring an asset if an **extended period** is required to prepare the asset for its intended use and **significant expenditures** related to the asset take place during that period. The objectives of capitalizing interest in such cases are (1) to obtain a cost that reflects the enterprise's total investment in the asset and (2) to recognize depreciation expense in future periods that adequately measures the cost

Measurement

of services provided by the asset. Interest should be capitalized only if the amounts are material and the benefits of capitalization exceed the costs of accumulating the required information. Within those constraints, capitalization of interest is appropriate in situations such as the following:

1. Assets constructed by the enterprise for its own use.
2. Assets constructed for an enterprise by another enterprise if the acquiring enterprise makes deposits or progress payments.
3. Land under development for a particular use.
4. Assets intended for sale or lease that are constructed as discrete projects.

Common characteristics of these assets are (1) they are not yet being used in earning activities and (2) they are undergoing preparation for use in earning activities in the future. If the production of an asset is complete, if the asset is not being changed in some way, or if obsolescence, excess capacity, or need of repair prevents an asset from being used in earning activities, the asset does not qualify for the capitalization of interest. Also, interest is not capitalized on inventories that are routinely manufactured or otherwise produced in large quantities on a repetitive basis.

Theoretically, capitalized interest is the interest that was actually incurred during a period but that *could have been avoided* if expenditures related to the qualifying asset had not been made. Interest is based on the average accumulated expenditures for the asset during the development period, including interest capitalized in prior periods.

If specific borrowings are associated with an asset for which interest is being capitalized, the interest rates on these borrowings are used. If this direct association cannot be made, a **weighted average interest rate** on all borrowings of the company will determine the amount of interest to be capitalized. Because the interest to be capitalized is based on actual outstanding debt, the amount capitalized cannot exceed the interest incurred during the period. Interest capitalization begins when the initial expenditure related to the development of the asset is made, and continues as long as the asset is undergoing active development. Interest capitalization ends when the asset is ready for its intended use, whether or not it is placed in service at that time.

To illustrate interest capitalization, assume that Elmwood Production Limited is constructing a warehouse for use in its own operations. Costs of materials, labour, and overhead of $160 000 have been identified and charged to the asset account. Initial expenditures in early January 1995 were $70 000. In early May of that year, $50 000 more

---

[7]"Capitalization of Interest Cost," *FASB Statement of Financial Accounting Standards No. 34,* 1979.

was invested; in early October, an additional $40 000. On January 2, 1995, the company arranged for a 12 percent, $100 000 loan to partially finance the construction. In January, the company borrowed the full amount of the loan and used it to finance the first $100 000 of expenditures in the warehouse. The remaining investment in the project came from available cash within the company. The company has a substantial amount of additional debt outstanding at an average interest rate of 10 percent. The amount of interest to be capitalized is as follows:

Period of Time	Investment	No. of months	Investment × No. of Months
January–April	$ 70 000	4	$ 280 000
	50 000		
May-September	$120 000	5	600 000
	40 000		
October–December	$160 000	3	480 000
			$1 360 000

Average expenditure for 1995:
  $1 360 000/12 months = $113 333
Interest capitalization for 1995:
  $100 000 × 12% = $12 000
  13 333 × 10% =   1 333
  $113 333   = $13 333

The average accumulated expenditure for the construction of the asset during 1995 is $113 333. This amount is determined by computing the amount of the investment for three periods of time during the year, the end of the first two periods being determined when an additional investment was made in the asset, and the end of the last period being determined by the end of the financial reporting period. A weighted average investment is then computed and interest is determined in two steps: (1) on the first $100 000 investment in the asset at the 12 percent rate on the $100 000 loan taken out specifically for this project, and (2) on the remaining $13 333 ($113 333 − $100 000) at the 10 percent rate on the remaining debt of the company.

If we assume that interest on the $100 000 debt incurred specifically for this asset is charged directly to the asset account as incurred and that other interest is allocated from interest expense previously recognized, the entry to record the capitalization of interest is as follows:

Warehouse	13 333	
Cash (or Interest Payable)		12 000
Interest Expense		1 333

In reality, several entries totalling the amounts in the above entry may be made at different points in time. The $12 000 interest on debt incurred specifically for this asset would be charged to the asset as it was paid or accrued. The transfer of $1333 interest previously recognized as an expense would most likely be made when the asset is complete or at the end of the accounting period if the asset is still in process. This is necessary in order to state properly the asset cost and the interest expense for the period.

When the $13 333 interest is combined with the $160 000 of materials, labour, and overhead costs that are capitalized as part of the cost of the asset, the total asset cost is

$173 333 ($160 000 + $13 333). This amount is the basis for financial statement presentation and depreciation calculation.

In this case, the investment in the asset for which interest is being capitalized is greater than the debt directly related to that project. In addition, Elmwood has other debt outstanding that provides the basis for the capitalization of interest on the additional investment of $60 000 ($160 000 investment less $100 000 of directly related debt). If the company had no debt beyond the $100 000 directly related to the asset under construction, no additional interest could be capitalized, because the amount of capitalized interest is limited to the amount of interest actually incurred during the construction period.

Disclosure

When a company has capitalized a part of interest incurred during an accounting period in accordance with CICA *Handbook* Section 3850, special disclosure must be made in the notes to the financial statements.[8] Exhibit 12.2 presents an example of this disclosure from the 1991 financial statements of Torstar Corporation. Torstar is a broadly based information and entertainment communications company.

Acquisition by Issuing Securities

Capital assets may be acquired by issuing securities (e.g., share certificates) rather than by paying cash or transferring other assets to the seller. In such transactions, accountants record the equivalent amount of cash that would have been transferred in a comparable cash transaction. Several problems may obscure the determination of the cash-equivalent amount. Market values of either the securities or the asset(s) exchanged may not be readily available. On the other hand, although the market value of the securities may be readily determinable from a market quotation, such a value may be based on a level of market activity substantially different from the number of shares involved in the acquisition. In such situations, the market price may not indicate the value of the shares if the number issued in the acquisition had been included in the transactions determining the market price.

When securities are issued in exchange for assets, the market value of the shares issued should normally be used as the basis for recording both the assets acquired and the shares issued. When the market value of the property exchanged is more objectively determinable than the market value of the shares, the value of the property should be used.[9] If the market value of the shares is based on a level of market activity so far below the number of shares included in the transaction that the current market value is not appropriate, the estimated valuation of the property exchanged or an estimate of the value of the shares apart from the original market value should be made by the officers of the issuing corporation. This value is used in recording the transaction. Generally, neither the **par** or **stated value** nor the current book value of the shares is an appropriate base for recording transactions in which securities are exchanged for capital assets.

To illustrate, assume that Elmwood Production Limited purchases land from another enterprise by issuing 22 000 shares of its no-par-value shares. The market price of the shares is $32 at the time of the transaction. The 22 000 shares do not represent a substantial number of shares in relation to the volume of shares activity in the market. The capital structure of most Canadian corporations has no-par value, so in Canada the entire market value would be credited to the Common Shares account. The purchase of the land is recorded by the following entry:

---

[8]"Interest Capitalized— Disclosure Considerations," CICA *Handbook,* Section 3850, August 1987.
  [9]"Non-monetary Transactions," CICA *Handbook,* Paragraph 3830.05, December 1989.

Exhibit 12.2 Torstar Corporation: Capitalization of Interest Disclosure

5. Property, Plant and Equipment

	Cost	Accumulated Depreciation	Net
	(thousands of dollars)		
1991			
Land	$7 758		$7 758
Buildings and leasehold improvements	43 057	$15 242	27 815
Machinery and equipment	149 385	96 888	52 497
Construction in progress	311 179		311 179
Total	$511 379	$112 130	$399 249
1990			
Land	$7 604		$7 604
Buildings and leasehold improvements	42 024	$13 416	28 608
Machinery and equipment	142 759	85 474	57 285
Construction in progress	105 932		105 932
Total	$298 319	$98 890	$199 429

A new press facility is being constructed for The Toronto Star. Production from this facility is expected to begin in the latter part of 1992 with the plant fully completed in 1993. The total cost of this facility will be approximately $415 million (including capitalized interest).

Interest capitalized on construction in progress in 1991 was $22.1 million (1990– $5.8 million).

Source: Torstar Corporation, *1991 Annual Report.*

Land	704 000	
Common Shares (22 000 × $32)		704 000

Basket Purchases

Asset/Liability Measurement

The term **basket purchase** refers to the acquisition of several assets for a single price. The primary accounting problem arising from the basket (lump sum) purchase is the apportionment of the total price paid to the individual assets acquired. Sometimes several assets can be purchased in a single transaction for less than the individual assets could be acquired separately. In such cases, the allocation of the total price paid for the group of assets to the individual assets is based on the relative values of the individual assets acquired. In accordance with the historical cost method of measuring assets, the total cost recorded must not exceed the total price paid, even if the total appraised value exceeds that amount. The individual asset values that are assigned for purposes of allocation may be based on current market prices, appraisal values, the present values of expected future benefits, or other appropriate estimations.[10]

To illustrate, we will assume that Elmwood Production Limited acquires several assets in a single transaction from a competitor who is going out of business. The total purchase price is $855 000. The acquired assets and their individually estimated values, based on current market prices and independent appraisals, are as follows:

---

[10]"Capital Assets, Measurement," CICA *Handbook,* Paragraph 3060.20, October 1990.

Inventory	$100 000
Building	500 000
Land	150 000
Fixtures	200 000

The allocation of the $855 000 cost to the individual assets is based on the relative esti-mated value of the individual assets, as follows:

Asset	Appraisal Value	Cost Allocation	
Inventory	$100 000	(100/950) $855 000 =	$ 90 000
Building	500 000	(500/950) $855 000 =	450 000
Land	150 000	(150/950) $855 000 =	135 000
Fixtures	200 000	(200/950) $855 000 =	180 000
	$950 000		$855 000

Alternatively, a percentage of cost to total appraisal value may be computed as fol-lows: $855 000/$950 000 = 90%. This percentage is then applied to the estimated value of each asset to determine the portion of the total cost allocated to that asset. For example, land would be allocated $135 000 as follows: $150 000 × 90% = $135 000. The entry to record the basket purchase in this example is as follows:

Inventory	90 000	
Building	450 000	
Land	135 000	
Fixtures	180 000	
Cash		855 000

Although this illustration deals with a purchase of several different classes of assets, the same procedure may be used to allocate the cost of several items of the same type to individual items, such as several inventory items or pieces of machinery.

When a company makes a basket purchase of assets, it may also make expenditures that relate to only one of the assets. Accountants must carefully distinguish between the common price paid for several assets and any related expenditures that apply only to a single asset. The former should be allocated among the assets acquired, as illustrated in the example. Any related expenditures that apply to specific assets should be associated entirely with those assets. For example, a company may acquire inventory, furniture, and land in a single purchase transaction. The price paid should be allocated among these assets based on their individual relative fair values. Legal fees paid to transfer title of the land, however, should be assigned only to the land and should not affect the recorded cost of the inventory and furniture.

Installation, Preparation, and Start-up Costs

Under the full-cost concept, capital assets are established at the cost of acquisition. This includes expenditures necessary to bring them to the appropriate location and to prepare them for their intended use. Substantial outlays for transportation, installation, remod-elling, and reconditioning may be required to advance the asset to the point of becoming a positive factor in the generation of revenue.

Significant time may elapse between the purchase of an asset and the placement of the asset into service. This is particularly true in the case of buildings undergoing extensive renovation. Costs related to the asset incurred during this period (e.g., insurance, taxes, and supervisory salaries) are capitalized as part of the cost of the asset. For some assets, such as machinery, trial runs and other tests may be necessary before the asset can be put into full service. These tests may require supplies, materials, and other assets. Such costs are also part of the cost of acquiring the asset and preparing it for its intended use. Since the asset is not in use, the start-up costs can be capitalized and amortized over future periods. However, in practice many companies expense the start-up costs as part of their overhead.

Depreciation is not recognized on assets until they are placed into service, even if they were acquired at some previous date. No depreciation is recognized during a period of remodelling or renovation between the time the asset is acquired and is placed into service. In compliance with the matching principle, recognition of depreciation is deferred until the asset becomes a part of the revenue-producing process.

Post-Acquisition Expenditures

After capital assets are acquired and placed into service, additional costs may be related to the continued use of the assets. There is an important distinction between capital and revenue expenditures. **Capital expenditures** are those expected to benefit *future* periods and, thus, are recorded as assets and depreciated over those periods. **Revenue expenditures** are normal, recurring expenditures designed to sustain the usefulness of the asset through the *current* accounting period and, thus, are charged to expense as incurred.

In distinguishing between capital and revenue expenditures, accountants commonly identify capital expenditures as those expenditures expected to allow the related asset to render greater future benefits to the enterprise. Accordingly, capital expenditures are expected to have one or both of the following positive impacts on future operations:

1. The *quantity* of services received from the asset will be increased. This may take the form of a longer useful life or more units of output.
2. The *quality* of the services received from the asset will be increased.

If neither of these conditions is met, the expenditure is intended to maintain the present level and quality of services rendered by the asset. These expenditures are appropriately designated as revenue expenditures and charged to expense as incurred.

Materiality   A common practice for distinguishing between capital and revenue expenditures is to establish a dollar amount that represents a materiality threshold. Expenditures that are less than the designated amount are treated as expenses when incurred, even if they are beneficial to future periods. The designated level for this distinction varies with the size of the enterprise. For example, a small company might expense all amounts below $100, while a large company might follow the same practice for amounts below $10 000. While this practice is justifiable only on grounds of materiality, it also eliminates the practical problem of judging the nature of a large number of small dollar amounts.

Expenditures related to capital assets incurred after the original acquisition may be classified into four categories: (1) additions, (2) replacements and betterments, (3) rearrangements and relocations, and (4) repair and maintenance. The following discussion of post-acquisition expenditures in terms of these four categories will help you distinguish between capital and revenue expenditures and identify the period over which capital expenditures should be allocated.

Additions

Additions represent major expenditures that, by definition, are capital in nature because they increase the service potential of the related asset. Additions to buildings are common when the size of the asset can be increased by adding a new wing or level to the existing facility.

Two major problems exist in relation to additions. First, the period over which the expenditure is to be depreciated must be determined. If the estimated useful life of the addition is independent of the asset to which it relates, the addition is treated as a *separate* asset and depreciated over its estimated useful life, regardless of the life of the original asset. This is common practice when structures are built as components and the addition would continue to exist even if the original structure were removed. In many cases, however, the addition is not independent of the original structure, and the period of depreciation for the addition must be determined in relation to the original structure. In such cases, the cost of the addition is depreciated over the shorter of the estimated life of the addition or the remaining life of the original asset.

The second problem related to additions is the identification of the costs that are to be appropriately capitalized. Adding to a facility frequently requires alteration of the original structure. For example, the addition of a new wing may involve removing walls or rerouting plumbing. If the original unit was constructed with a plan to expand, costs related to the original asset incurred when the addition is constructed are appropriately capitalized as part of the cost of the addition. On the other hand, costs incurred that could have been avoided if appropriate planning had taken place at an earlier date should be expensed rather than carried forward as part of the addition. Distinguishing between such costs requires judgement, and care should be taken to ensure proper classification.

Replacements and Betterments

Replacements and betterments represent the substitution of a new part of an asset for an existing part. For example, the base of a machine may be replaced with a new base, or the roof of a building may be replaced with a new roof.

If the new part of the asset is similar in nature to the part being eliminated, the substitution is called a **replacement**. If the new part represents an improvement in quality over the part being eliminated, the substitution is called a **betterment**.[11] An important consideration in determining the appropriate accounting treatment of replacements and betterments is whether the original part of the existing asset is separately identifiable. If separate identification is possible, the new expenditure should be substituted for the portion of the book value being replaced or improved. This is possible when the components of the asset have been separately identified and depreciated.

To illustrate, assume that Fagan Limited acquires a building at a cost of $250 000. Separate identification of the cost components indicates that $30 000 of the cost relates to the roof of the building. The building is being depreciated over a 25-year life by the straight-line method, with an estimated salvage value of $20 000. The roof, however, is being depreciated over a ten-year life by the straight-line method, with no estimated salvage value. After nine years, the roof is replaced at a cost of $50 000. The replacement

[11]"Capital Assets, Betterment," CICA *Handbook,* Paragraph 3060.29, October 1990.

is expected to last twenty years, but it must be written off for the remaining years of the original estimate of the building's life.

The replacement is substituted in the accounts as follows:

Building (new roof)	50 000	
Accumulated Depreciation (0.9 × $30 000)	27 000	
Loss on Replacement of Roof	3 000	
Building (old roof)		30 000
Cash		50 000

The cost of the building, other than that allocated to the roof, should continue to be depreciated over the remaining unchanged useful life. The roof is depreciated at $3125 per year ($50 000/16) over the remaining sixteen years of the life of the building.

While this substitution approach is logical in accounting for replacements and betterments, the separate identification of elements of an asset is frequently not possible due to the lack of separate records of the components of the asset or the integrated nature of the asset. Also, the parts of an asset changed by replacements and betterments during remodelling or renovation are generally difficult to separate in the manner we have described.

If separate identification is not possible or practical, the costs of replacements and betterments are treated as increases in the book value of the asset, thereby increasing the basis for depreciation over the remaining life of the asset. If the replacement or betterment is designed primarily to enhance the *quality* of the service potential of the asset, the cost is charged to the asset account, and an appropriate increase in depreciation expense is recognized in future years. Although the book value of the replaced or improved portion remains in the asset and accumulated depreciation accounts, the replacement or betterment usually takes place when the original expenditure is nearing the point of full depreciation and book value is a relatively small amount.

If the replacement is designed primarily to *extend the length of the service life* of the asset rather than to enhance the quality of the service rendered, the book value should be increased by charging Accumulated Depreciation. The accountant then depreciates the revised book value, less any salvage value, over the revised useful life.

As an example, assume that Singh, Inc. replaces the electrical system in its building at a cost of $100 000. The building originally cost $800 000 and had $425 000 accumulated depreciation at the time of the replacement. The company has no record of the separate components of the building. Prior to the replacement, the asset had a remaining life of ten years, with an expected $50 000 residual value.

If the replacement is made in order to enhance the quality of service potential in the future, the replacement is accounted for as follows:

Building	100 000	
Cash		100 000

This entry increases the book value to $475 000, as follows:

Original cost of building	$ 800 000
Cost of replacement of electrical system	100 000
	900 000
Accumulated depreciation	(425 000)
	$ 475 000

Depreciation expense thereafter is recognized at $42 500 per year [($475 000 − $50 000) ÷ 10 years]. If the replacement is made in order to extend the useful life, the replacement is accounted for as follows:

Accumulated Depreciation—Building	100 000	
Cash		100 000

This entry also increases the book value to $475 000, as follows:

Original cost of building		$800 000
Accumulated depreciation prior to replacement	$425 000	
Cost of replacement of electrical system	(100 000)	325 000
		$475 000

If we further assume that the replacement adds seven years to the current estimated service period of ten years, and that the estimated residual value is unchanged, the depreciation thereafter is recognized at $25 000 per year [($475 000 − $50 000) ÷ 17].

The distinction between charging the asset account or accumulated depreciation with the cost of the replacement is one of classification, because the impact on book value is identical. Capitalization by debiting the asset (i.e., the Building account) provides recognition of the increased value of the asset to the enterprise in terms of future service potential. Alternatively, capitalization by charging Accumulated Depreciation recognizes that costs extending the asset's life are essentially a recovery of past depreciation charges.

Rearrangements and Relocations

Materiality

Matching

Rearrangements and **relocations** frequently occur to facilitate future operations. If the costs of such activities are material and can be separated from recurring operating expenses, they should be capitalized and recognized as expenses over the periods expected to benefit in accordance with the matching principle. Alternatively, if the costs are *not* material, if they are *inseparable* from recurring operating expenses, or if the future benefits in terms of increased efficiency are *questionable,* they should be expensed in the period in which they are incurred.

The unamortized portion of costs of previously capitalized rearrangement and relocation costs is sometimes presented as an intangible asset, but it is more appropriately described as a **deferred charge** (i.e., an unamortized balance awaiting amortization). Deferred charges are usually presented in the balance sheet as a part of an "other assets" category. Chapter 14 discusses this balance sheet category in more detail.

Repair and Maintenance

Repair and **maintenance** expenditures are necessary to maintain the current operating capabilities of capital assets. Such expenditures range from custodial care and recurring minor repairs on buildings to periodic inspection and servicing of machinery and equipment. Repair and maintenance expenditures are treated as expenses when incurred, since they are designed to ensure continued and dependable service of an asset.

Materiality

Distinguishing between repair and maintenance expenditures and those expenditures that should be capitalized is sometimes difficult. Major repairs that take on the characteristics of replacements and betterments in terms of the expected future use of the asset are capitalized if the impact on future income is judged to be material.

The treatment of repair and maintenance as expenses when incurred is based on the assumption that such expenses are evenly distributed over time and that individual expenditures are relatively small. Expenditures made in one period that provide for the use of the asset in a subsequent period are usually small or are offset by similar expenditures incurred during the subsequent period. If financial statements are prepared on a monthly or quarterly basis, the assumptions of immateriality and even distribution over time may be less appropriate. In these cases, repair and maintenance expense may be accrued on an estimated basis by establishing an Allowance account, with actual expenditures charged to that allowance when made.

To illustrate the accrual of repair and maintenance, assume that Elmwood Production Limited incurs substantial amounts of repair and maintenance related to its equipment. Because of the size of the expenditures, their relative infrequency, and the need to prepare monthly financial statements, the company recognizes the estimated annual cost of $120 000 for 1995 on a monthly basis. Actual costs incurred during January, February, and March 1995 are $500, $18 500, and $1200, respectively. Entries to recognize the expenses and related expenditures are as follows:

January

Various dates	Allowance for Repair and Maintenance	500	
	Cash (or other asset, liability, or		
	expense account, as appropriate)		500
	Repair and Maintenance Expense		
31	($120 000/12)	10 000	
	Allowance for Repair and Maintenance		10 000

February

Various dates	Allowance for Repair and Maintenance	18 500	
	Cash (or other appropriate account)		18 500
28	Repair and Maintenance Expense	10 000	
	Allowance for Repair and Maintenance		10 000

March

Various dates	Allowance for Repair and Maintenance	1 200	
	Cash (or other appropriate account)		1 200
31	Repair and Maintenance Expense	10 000	
	Allowance for Repair and Maintenance		10 000

This method results in equal recognition of repair and maintenance expense of $10 000 each month, even though expenditures vary considerably between periods. A question arises, however, as to the balance in the Allowance for Repair and Maintenance account at the end of a reporting period. For Elmwood Production Limited, this amount is as follows:

		Balance in Allowance Account
January	Expense recognized	$(10 000)
	Costs charged to allowance	500
	Balance in allowance at January 31	(9 500)
February	Expense recognized	(10 000)
	Costs charged to allowance	18 500
	Balance in allowance at February 28	(1 000)
March	Expense recognized	(10 000)
	Costs charged to allowance	1 200
	Balance in allowance at March 31	$ (9 800)

In practice, diversity exists in the treatment of the Allowance account in balance sheets prepared at the end of each month. The nature of the item, as well as the process giving rise to it, suggests treating the allowance in the same way that accumulated depreciation is treated (i.e., as a deduction in determining the book value of the related asset). An alternative interpretation of treating the allowance as a liability is difficult to justify, because expenditure in the future depends on future events. Also, the notion that the enterprise has a liability to itself for repair and maintenance on its assets is difficult to support. A related question concerns the treatment of any balance in the Allowance account at the end of the *annual* reporting period. If the estimated accrual method is used to spread the expense over the interim periods of the year, the estimated amount should be continually evaluated and adjusted in the final month or quarter so that the Allowance account is eliminated at year-end. This way, the problem of balance sheet classification in annual financial statements is avoided.

Matching

Consistency

Materiality

Careful judgement is required in accounting for capital-asset-related expenditures made subsequent to original acquisition. The overriding objective is to match properly the cost of the expiration of the service potential with the revenue generated by that effort. Consistency in application is also important, because inconsistent treatment may materially affect the financial position and the results of operation. Accounting policies should reflect the most logical and realistic assumptions available.

Accounting for the various types of capital and revenue expenditures discussed in this section is summarized in Exhibit 12.3. In some cases, companies present their accounting policies concerning repairs, maintenance, and other post-acquisition expenditures in notes to the financial statements. Exhibit 12.4 includes a section of the accounting policy statement from the 1991 annual report of The Oshawa Group Limited, "a Canadian company operating in eight provinces with more than 16 000 employees. Over the last 80 years, it has become a major distributor of food and pharmaceutical products to retailers and consumers."[12] The disclosure makes specific reference to the accounting treatment of repairs and maintenance, as well as other aspects of accounting for capital assets.

Disposals of Capital Assets

Capital assets are disposed of for a variety of reasons and in a variety of ways. They may be **sold,** or they may be **abandoned** or **converted involuntarily,** as in the case of loss by fire, flood, or other natural disaster. They can also be **exchanged.** Regardless of the cause, two basic steps are followed in accounting for disposals. First, depreciation is recognized to the date of a disposal. This is necessary in order to reflect properly the cost of operations for that portion of the year in which the asset is used and to correctly establish the book value of the asset at the time of disposal. Second, the cost and accumulated depreciation of the asset are eliminated from the accounts, any cash received is recorded, and a gain or loss on the disposal is recognized. In exchanges, other assets are received and cash may be paid, both requiring accounting recognition.

---

[12]The Oshawa Group Limited, *1991 Annual Report* (Etobicoke, ON: 1992).

Exhibit 12.3 Summary of Accounting for Postacquisition Expenditures

Type of Expenditure	Circumstances	Accounting Treatment
Additions	Useful life is *independent* of original asset.	Capitalize expenditure in separate account and depreciate over the estimated useful life.
	Useful life is *limited* to remaining life of original asset.	Capitalize expenditure as part of the original asset and increase the depreciation recognized over the remaining useful life.
Replacement and Betterment	*Separate* identification of portion of asset substituted is possible.	Capitalize expenditure to asset account and depreciate over shorter of the estimated useful life of (1) the replacement/betterment or (2) the original asset. Cost and accumulated depreciation on portion of asset being replaced are removed, and gain or loss is recognized.
	Separate identification of portion of asset substituted is *not* possible; service *potential* of asset is improved.	Charge expenditure to asset account and depreciate over the shorter of the estimated life of (1) the replacement/betterment or (2) the original asset.
	Separate identification of portion substituted is *not* possible; service *life* of asset is extended.	Charge expenditure to Accumulated Depreciation and depreciate book value over revised estimated life.
Rearrangement and Relocation	Costs are *identifiable* and *material* in amount; changes are expected to produce *discernible* future benefits.	Capitalize expenditure and amortize over the period expected to benefit.
	Costs are *not* separately identifiable nor material in amount; future benefits are *not* discernible.	Treat expenditure as expense when incurred.
Repair and maintenance	Incurrence of costs is *evenly* distributed over the annual period.	Treat expenditures as expenses when incurred.
	Incurrence of costs is *not* evenly distributed over the annual period	Accrue periodic expense on an estimated basis and charge actual expenditures to Allowance. (No allowance should be carried forward from one annual period to the next.)

> ## Exhibit 12.4 The Oshawa Group Limited: Capital Asset Policy Disclosure
>
> **Fixed Assets and Depreciation**
>
> Major enlargements, remodelings and improvements are charged to the appropriate fixed asset accounts. The cost of maintenance and repairs which does not extend the life of an asset is charged against earnings.
>
> Fixed assets are recorded at cost, which in the case of land and buildings includes carrying costs incurred during development, construction and the initial leasing period, and are depreciated on a straight-line basis at rates sufficient to amortize the cost of the assets over their estimated useful lives as follows:
>
> | **Classification** | **Estimated Useful Life** |
> | --- | --- |
> | Buildings | 20 to 40 years |
> | Equipment | 3 to 10 years |
> | Leasehold improvements | term of lease plus first option to a maximum of 20 years |
>
> *Source:* The Oshawa Group Limited, *1991 Annual Report.*

To illustrate, assume that Hosang Corporation acquired a building in January 1987 at a total cost of $510 000. The building has been depreciated by the straight-line method using a twenty-year life, with an estimated residual value of $60 000. On June 30, 1995, the building is sold for $425 000. The company reports on a calendar-year basis.

Depreciation must be brought up to date prior to recording the sale itself. To account for the half-year depreciation in 1995, the following entry is made:

Depreciation Expense		
[½ × ($510 000 − $60 000)/20]	11 250	
Accumulated Depreciation		11 250

This brings accumulated depreciation on the asset up to $146 250, determined as follows:

Depreciation, 1987–1994	
$[($510 000 − $60 000)/20 years (6 years)]	$135 000
Depreciation, partial year 1995	
[($510 000 − $60 000)/20 years (½ year)]	11 250
	146 250

Many companies would defer recording the depreciation of $11 250 until the end of the year, when depreciation on all capital assets is recognized. Regardless of when the entry is made, the accumulated depreciation used in recording the sale of the asset is $146 250. The entry for the sale of the asset is then recorded as follows:

Cash	425 000	
Accumulated Depreciation—Building	146 250	
Building		510 000
Gain on Sale of Building		61 250

The gain is measured by subtracting the book value from the proceeds of the sale:

$$\text{Gain} = \$425\ 000 - (\$510\ 000 - \$146\ 250) = \$61\ 250$$

Sometimes assets are abandoned without being sold or otherwise disposed of. The process of recording a disposal by abandonment is the same as that illustrated above, except that no proceeds are received. In this case, the loss equals the book value of the asset after depreciation is updated to the date of abandonment.

Sometimes an enterprise loses an asset due to factors out of its control; that is, by involuntary conversion. Examples are loss by fire, flood, or other disaster. The accounting procedures parallel those for abandonment if no insurance proceeds are received; if insurance proceeds are received, the accounting procedures are much like those for the sale of capital assets.[13]

To illustrate an exchange transaction, we assume that on June 30, 1995, Hosang Corporation exchanges the building described above for a building valued at $750 000. Hosang paid $350 000 in the exchange. Depreciation must first be updated to the date of the transaction, as in previous examples. The exchange is then recorded as follows:

June 30, 1995	Building (new)	750 000	
	Accumulated Depreciation	146 250	
	Building (old)		510 000
	Cash		350 000
	Gain on Exchange of Buildings		36 250

This transaction is a **monetary exchange,** because a significant portion of the value Hosang is giving up is in the form of cash. A **nonmonetary exchange** is one in which little or no cash is involved. Special valuation problems in nonmonetary exchanges arise when fair value of the assets in the exchange cannot be determined or the exchange involves similar assets, and thus, the earning process is considered incomplete. The subject of nonmonetary exchanges is covered in greater depth later in this chapter.

Materiality

Gains and losses on capital assets are ordinarily not considered to be extraordinary items in the income statement. Depending on the extent of detail in the income statement, such items may be separately disclosed, however. If a gain or loss of this type is material in amount and is judged to be either unusual in nature or infrequent in occurrence and not subject to a management decision or determination, separate disclosure should be made. An occasion in which such gains and losses are presented as extraordinary items is found in involuntary conversions.[14] One example is the destruction of a capital asset by an earthquake. Therefore, it is important to consider the underlying cause of a write-down or write-off of a capital asset in judging whether it is an extraordinary item or not. While such write-downs or write-offs are usually not presented as extraordinary items, they may be considered such if they result from a major casualty *and* are clearly unusual in nature, infrequent in occurrence, and not determined by management.

Departures from Historical Cost

Asset/Liability Measurement

Historical cost is well established as the basis for measuring and reporting property, plant, and equipment and is supported by authoritative pronouncements. As with most accounting principles, however, there are exceptions to the general practice of recording and depreciating assets at cost. Although departures from historical cost are not frequent, this

---

[13]Property, or casualty, insurance, including the computation of amounts to be received on insurance policies that include co-insurance requirements, is covered in Chapter 13. In Chapter 11, any situation involving insurance proceeds states the amount to be received from the insurance recovery.

[14]"Income Statement," CICA *Handbook,* Paragraph 1520.03(l), August 1991.

Fair Value Measures a Fair Exchange

The AcSC introduces a new *Handbook* section for recording nonmonetary transactions.

Published in December and effective this month, new *Handbook* Section 3830, "Nonmonetary Transactions," is designed to ensure these transactions are usually measured at fair value. The Recommendations, which appear in almost the same form as those proposed in the November 1988 exposure draft of the same name, may be applied retroactively or prospectively.

The Accounting Standards Committee (AcSC) embarked on the project in 1987 to close a perceived gap in the *Handbook*. The then recent revision to Section 1540, "Statement of Changes in Financial Position," shifted the reporting focus in that statement from working capital to cash flows, giving nonmonetary transactions greater prominence.

The new section recommends measuring nonmonetary transactions at the fair value of the assets or services involved and recognizing any consequent gain or loss in the income statement. Nonmonetary transactions are exchanges of assets, liabilities or services for other assets, liabilities or services with little or no monetary consideration—generally, less than 10% of the total consideration. They can also be nonmonetary nonreciprocal transfers, which are transfers of nonmonetary assets, liabilities or services without consideration.

The new requirement to record such transactions at fair value excludes:

- Nonmonetary transactions between an entity and its controlling shareholder or transactions between entities under common control. Such transactions, since they are outside the scope of the new section, may or may not be measured at fair value.
- Nonmonetary exchanges that don't represent the culmination of the earnings process, such as the exchange of a factory in Montreal for one of similar capacity and functions in Halifax. These would be measured at the carrying value of the asset or service relinquished. No gain or loss would be recognized, except to the extent that any monetary consideration received exceeds carrying value. In those cases, a gain would be recorded to the extent of the excess.
- Nonmonetary, nonreciprocal transfers to owners that represent a spinoff or other form of restructuring or liquidation, as in the distribution to owners of shares in a subsidiary corporation. These transfers would be recorded at the carrying value of the asset or liability given up and no gain or loss would be recognized.

The new section recommends disclosing the nature, measurement basis, amount and related gains and losses

of nonmonetary transactions, except for those that don't represent the culmination of the earnings process.

The AcSC received 53 responses to the exposure draft, most of which were favourable. Thirty-eight generally agreed with the ED proposals, 12 claimed there were fundamental problems with them, and three gave no opinion.

Concerns about the proposals concentrated on certain definitions, their application to related parties, circumstances under which fair value can't be determined, how to record exchanges of similar assets and business combinations, accounting for nonprofit organizations and, finally, disclosure requirements.

The definitions that drew the most comment were "nonmonetary exchanges," and "monetary" and "nonmonetary" assets and liabilities. Twelve respondents expressed concern about the "little or no" clause regarding the former. They suggested the definition should indicate how much of the exchange has to be monetary before the transaction itself becomes monetary. The committee agreed and added a general rule indicating that 10% marked the threshold of monetary consideration. While US accounting standards set 25% as the limit, the AcSC believes a lower proportion is more appropriate.

It was suggested that the definitions of monetary and nonmonetary assets would be improved with examples, which the AcSC also added.

Several respondents questioned why the ED proposed to exclude nonmonetary transactions between an entity and its controlling shareholder or between entities under common control. They focused on the need for guidance in accounting for nonmonetary transactions between related parties, arguing that those form the bulk of all such transactions. Some suggested the AcSC should initiate a *Handbook* project on the measurement of related party transactions; others preferred to expand the ED's scope to include all nonmonetary transactions.

Four respondents said they believed nonmonetary transactions between commonly controlled enterprises should be measured at fair value, and that transactions should be measured the same way regardless of whether an enterprise is 49% or 51% owned. The ED, they argued, should apply to exchanges between commonly controlled enterprises just as it does to nonmonetary transactions between other entities.

Others agreed that transactions between commonly controlled enterprises should be excluded, but argued that

Continued

the AcSC should undertake a separate project to deal with such transactions.

The committee concluded that common control transactions should continue to be excluded from the section's scope. Special considerations in measuring such transactions may make it impossible to arbitrarily recommend the use of fair value. The AcSC, as a result, has now added a project to its work program to study common control transactions.

Most respondents supported the ED proposal to measure nonmonetary transactions at fair value, looking first to the value of the asset given up and, if it isn't clearly determinable, using the fair value of the asset received. Several, however, included suggestions for improving the Recommendations.

Some argued the ED wasn't forceful enough in requiring enterprises to use the fair value of the asset given up. They also found the proposal to use the value of assets received when the value is clearly determinable to be too subjective. They argued that:

• Because of confusion over the meaning of "determinable," the Recommendation might effectively offer enterprises a choice between using the value of the asset given up or that received.

• Enterprises might write up their assets in questionable circumstances (as when an exchange of similar property—not a nonmonetary transaction—has actually occurred).

• The same transaction might be recorded at different values in the books of two different enterprises.

The AcSC made no changes to the ED proposals. It didn't think the words "clearly determinable" would cause the problems cited by the respondents; instead, it found that the Recommendation would still result in fair value being used to measure nonmonetary transactions.

Some respondents suggested the ED should have allowed for the use of carrying value when fair value can't be determined or when a major uncertainty exists about the fair value's realizability. The current US standard, APB 29, "Nonmonetary Transactions," includes such an exception.

The AcSC made no provision for using carrying values. It concluded that enterprises wouldn't normally enter into a transaction without knowing either the value of the asset or service received or the value of that being given up. If major uncertainty arose concerning the realizability of an asset's fair value, then the asset would be written down under generally accepted accounting principles (as required by *Handbook* Section 3050, "Long-term Investments," and the proposed revision to Section 3060, "Capital Assets," on property, plant and equipment).

Many respondents requested more guidance on how to determine fair value. The committee considered adding more background to the Recommendations, but concluded such guidance was already widely available.

Respondents generally agreed carrying value should be used for exchanges of assets that don't result in the culmination of the earnings process. Eight, however, disagreed with the proposal that, where a partial monetary consideration exits, it should be added to the asset's carrying value. These respondents supported the US treatment, which requires recognizing a portion of the gain and all of a loss (APB 29). Not to recognize the gain, they argued, might result in carrying the asset at nil or negative value. Besides, they added, Canadian accounting standards should be similar to US standards unless there are persuasive reasons for a difference.

The AcSC concluded that exchanges of similar property shouldn't result in the recognition of a gain or loss because they're made at carrying value. The amendment to the definition of nonmonetary exchanges, which limits the amount of monetary consideration to 10% of the fair value, would also mean there would be fewer gains on exchanges of similar property. Unrealized losses would already be written off under the auspices of other *Handbook* requirements. As for the rare situations when monetary considerations exceed carrying value, the *Handbook* now allows that excess to be treated as a gain. The AcSC doesn't believe a divergence from the US position will cause significant reporting problems in practice.

The ED proposed amending *Handbook* section 1580, "Business Combinations," so that it would advise against using fair value for combinations that are, in effect, an exchange of similar businesses; and to add background paragraphs explaining this recommendation. Half the respondents supported this proposal, half did not.

Those who disagreed argued that the amended Recommendation would be too loosely interpreted; exchanges that should be accounted for at fair value might be recorded at carrying value. Others suggested that different forms of exchange transactions might be accounted for differently even though their substance was the same; for example, a share-for-share exchange might be recorded at carrying value while a share-for-net-assets exchange would be recorded at fair value.

The AcSC disagreed that the proposed Recommendation would cause problems in practice. Section 1580 needed to be revised to provide for those unusual situations when a business is exchanged for a similar business.

Continued

For that reason, the substance of the ED proposals remains unchanged. The committee amended the wording of the material, however, because it agreed with respondents' assertions that any nonmonetary transaction should be subject to all the requirements of the relevant section, not just a single paragraph. The ED's proposed background paragraphs to Section 1580 were removed, and the Recommendation now refers to all of Section 3830, rather than just the one paragraph.

Five respondents believed the ED should have addressed nonprofit organization issues. In particular, they claimed, guidance was needed regarding donations of nonmonetary assets and services. Some noted that *Handbook* Section 4230, "Nonprofit Organizations—Specific Items," permits a donation to be recorded at no value when an estimate of cost cannot be made. Would the ED, they asked, override Section 4230?

The AcSC believes that Section 4230, by virtue of dealing explicitly with the issue of accounting for donations for nonprofit organizations, would override the general provisions of the new section on nonmonetary transactions. When accounting for nonmonetary exchanges, however, nonprofit organizations would be required to use fair value in accordance with Section 3830.

The ED proposed to require disclosure of the nature, basis of measurement, amount and related gains and losses of nonmonetary transactions. Nine respondents found such disclosures excessive and claimed they would provide no meaningful information. Also, they suggested, highlighting nonmonetary transactions in the financial statements would lead users to infer there was something dubious or questionable about such transactions. Disclosure, when the transaction doesn't result in the culmination of earnings, would be particularly onerous and meaningless (as, for example, in a car dealership, where significant portions of inventory may be "swapped" regularly). The AcSC agreed with the last point and dropped the requirement to make disclosures about exchanges that don't result in the culmination of the earnings process.

Source: Reprinted, with permission, from "Fair Value Measures a Fair Exchange," *CA Magazine*, January 1990, pp. 49–51. Published by the Canadian Institute of Chartered Accountants, Toronto, Canada.

section discusses several situations representing departures from the general concepts developed earlier in this chapter.

Donated Assets

Enterprises may receive assets by donation, such as when land is donated to an enterprise by a city as an inducement to locate a facility in the city. The advantages to the city in the future result from increased property-tax revenues, increased levels of employment, improved reputation, and other positive aspects of increased business activity.

Strict adherence to historical cost in such cases would result in recording the asset acquired at a zero cost or at an amount equal to the relatively minor costs incidental to the acceptance of the land, such as the cost of transferring title. Accounting for donated assets at a zero cost, however, is not generally thought to represent the substance of the transaction in terms of the fair value of the donated asset received by the enterprise.

Substance Over Form

Accounting for **nonreciprocal transfers,** which are transfers of assets or services in one direction, either to or from the enterprise, is also discussed in Section 3830 of the CICA *Handbook,* which concludes that the receipt of an asset in a nonreciprocal transfer should be based on the fair value of the asset received.[15] The CICA relied heavily on the modifying convention of substance over form in reaching this conclusion.

To illustrate the receipt of a donated asset, assume that Elmwood Production Limited receives land appraised at $130 000 as an inducement to locate a manufacturing facility in the city of Manchester. The receipt of the land and the related contribution by the city is recorded as follows:

---

[15]"Non-monetary Transactions," CICA *Handbook,* Paragraph 3830.05, December 1989.

Land	130 000	
Donated Capital—Plant Site		130 000

Costs incurred relative to the transfer that *would have been incurred* had the asset been purchased are also charged to the asset account. Any other costs are treated as expenses in the current period. The Donated Capital account becomes a part of the shareholders' equity of the enterprise that receives the donated asset.

Permanent Impairment in Value

The price that an enterprise pays for a capital asset is based on estimates of future use, of future demand for products and services, and of other considerations of future events. When circumstances dramatically change, capital assets may experience a **permanent impairment in value.**

A permanent impairment in value may occur when the demand for products or services significantly declines, when assets become obsolete or inadequate, or when other circumstances change. Depreciation (allocating cost to the periods benefiting from the use of the asset) is designed to facilitate the determination of net income via the matching principle. Although depreciation accounting is not designed primarily as a method of asset valuation, generally assets are not carried in the balance sheet at amounts exceeding their value. We have already seen this practice in the rule of applying the lower of cost or market value to inventory and marketable securities.

Matching

In the case of capital assets, this general rule discourages carrying assets in the accounts or in the balance sheet at amounts exceeding the value of the assets. This sometimes means that the future value of the assets has been reduced from that originally expected, even though the assets will continue to be used. In other cases, the assets have become valueless for their original purpose and are worth only their salvage value.

If a permanent impairment in value has occurred, the book value of the asset is reduced by crediting the accumulated depreciation and recognizing a loss. If the asset is to continue to be used, future depreciation charges may require adjustment to account for revised estimates of useful life, salvage value, and other factors.

To illustrate, we will assume that Elmwood Production Limited acquired machinery in 1992 for use in producing a line of toys. The asset cost $100 000 and had an expected $20 000 residual value at the end of an expected eight-year life. At the end of 1994, the machinery had a book value of $70 000, computed as follows:

Asset cost in 1992	$100 000
Accumulated depreciation at December 31, 1994	
[($100 000 − $20 000)/8 (3 years)]	(30 000)
Book value at December 31, 1994	$ 70 000

Because of changes in consumer demand, management determines in early 1995 that the asset is worth substantially less than originally expected. Specifically, it is determined that the book value should be reduced to $20 000; the remaining life, to two years; and the salvage value, to $2000. The entry to record this impairment in value is as follows:

Loss—Obsolescence of Machinery ($70 000 − $20 000)	50 000	
Accumulated Depreciation—Machinery		50 000

Materiality

Depreciation recognized in 1995 and 1996 will be $9000 [($20 000 − $2000)/2 years]. If material, the loss of $50 000 should be separately disclosed in the income statement on the basis that it is not a typical transaction that reflects normal business operations. However, this type of loss should *not* be treated as extraordinary.

If the book value of an asset is being reduced to the salvage value and no future use of the asset is expected, an entry similar to the previous one is made for the amount that leaves the estimated residual value as the book value. No further depreciation is recognized on the asset after it has been retired.

Acquisitions and Disposals by Exchange

A business enterprise can participate in an exchange transaction whereby it simultaneously acquires an asset and disposes of another asset. For example, an enterprise may exchange land that it owns for land held by another enterprise. Also, used machinery may be exchanged for other used machinery. These transactions may include either the receipt or payment of a small amount of cash (not exceeding 10 percent of the value given or received), sometimes referred to as **boot,**[16] to adjust for the perceived difference in the value of the assets exchanged. Transactions like this are called **nonmonetary transactions.** The CICA *Handbook* established the proper accounting for nonmonetary transactions in Section 3830, which was cited earlier in this chapter.

Concepts Underlying Exchange Transactions

The general principle governing the recording of a nonmonetary exchange is to record the acquired asset at the **fair value** of the assets involved in the exchange. Accordingly, the fair value of the surrendered asset is used as a measure of the historical cost of the acquired asset, and a gain or loss may be recognized on the exchange. This principle was illustrated earlier in this chapter when we recorded the exchange of buildings. However, if the fair value of the asset received is more clearly evident than the fair value of the asset surrendered, the former amount is used.[17] Fair value of a nonmonetary asset may be established by estimated realizable value in cash transactions of similar assets, quoted market prices, independent appraisals, and other available evidence.

Modification of this fair value concept is required in several circumstances, including instances in which fair value is not determinable or the transaction does not result in the culmination of an earning process. In some circumstances, the fair value of assets surrendered or received cannot be determined within reasonably objective limits. In these cases, the acquired asset is recorded at the book value of the surrendered asset. No gain or loss on the exchange is recorded, because the new asset is simply substituted for the old asset in the accounts.

Two types of nonmonetary exchanges are not considered to result in the completion of an earning process:

1. An exchange of a product or property held for sale in the ordinary course of business for a product or property to be sold in the same line of business to facilitate sales to customers other than parties to the exchange.

---

[16]"Boot" is an archaic term for benefit or profit.

[17]"Non-monetary Transactions," CICA *Handbook,* Paragraph 3830.05, December 1989.

2. An exchange of a productive asset not held for sale in the ordinary course of business for a similar productive asset or an equivalent interest in the same or similar productive asset.[18]

In the first case, inventory is exchanged for inventory. A subsequent transaction in which the inventory is sold to the ultimate customer must take place before the earning process is considered complete. In the second case, productive assets are exchanged for productive assets of the same general type performing essentially the same function. The earning process is not considered complete until these assets are used in the production of goods or services that are sold. These transactions are sometimes referred to as **swaps** of inventory or similar productive assets.

Assets acquired in swaps are generally recorded at the book value of the assets surrendered, and no gain is recognized as a result of the exchange. If boot is received in a transaction in which a gain is apparent (i.e., the fair value received exceeds the book value surrendered), the recipient of the boot deducts the boot from the book value of the surrendered asset.

Conservatism

In certain circumstances, the fair value inherent in a swap of inventory or capital assets may indicate that a loss would be recorded if fair value were the basis for recording the transaction. In such cases, fair value is used and the loss is recognized in accordance with the modifying convention of conservatism. Methods of accounting for assets acquired through nonmonetary exchanges are summarized in Exhibit 12.5.

Revenue Realization

In summary, recording nonmonetary transactions represents an interesting application of the accounting principles of revenue realization and asset measurement and of the modifying convention of conservatism. Transactions are generally recorded on the basis of fair value, which is consistent with revenue realization and historical cost if the transaction represents the culmination of an earning process. If the earning process is not

Asset/Liability Measurement Conservatism Revenue Realization

complete, however, the acquired asset is recorded at the book value of the surrendered asset unless a loss is apparent; in that case, the loss is recorded in accordance with the modifying convention of conservatism. In a nonmonetary transaction that does not complete the earning process and in which boot is received, the revenue realization principle has not been met. Each company receiving an asset would record its new asset at the carrying value of the asset given up plus any monetary consideration received or minus any monetary consideration paid. A gain would be recorded if the monetary consideration received exceeds the carrying value of the asset.

Illustrations of Exchange Transactions

This section analyzes a number of transactions, each of which illustrates a different concept in recording exchange transactions. In each independent case, Elmwood Production Limited is trading equipment. The following information is common to all cases:

Cost of equipment traded	$100 000
Accumulated depreciation to date of trade	40 000
Book value of equipment traded	$ 60 000

Example 1. Elmwood trades the equipment for several trucks. The value of the equipment is not determinable, but the trucks have a total estimated market value of $75 000. No cash is involved in the transaction.

---

[18]"Non-monetary Transactions," CICA *Handbook,* Paragraph 3830.09, December 1989.

Review

Exhibit 12.5 Non-Monetary Exchange of Assets

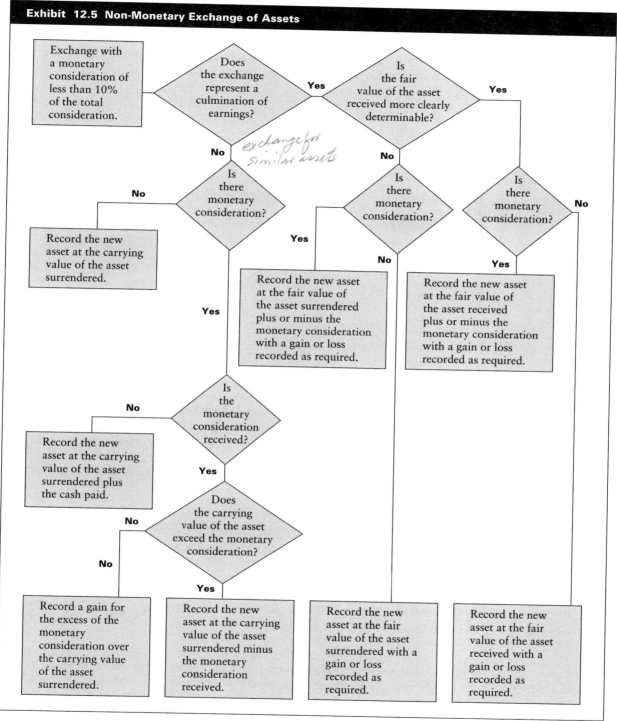

Exchange with a monetary consideration of less than 10% of the total consideration.

Does the exchange represent a culmination of earnings?

Yes

Is the fair value of the asset received more clearly determinable?

Yes

No

exchange for similar assets

No

Is there monetary consideration?

No

Is there monetary consideration?

Is there monetary consideration?

No

Record the new asset at the carrying value of the asset surrendered.

Yes

Yes

No

Yes

Record the new asset at the fair value of the asset surrendered plus or minus the monetary consideration with a gain or loss recorded as required.

Record the new asset at the fair value of the asset received plus or minus the monetary consideration with a gain or loss recorded as required.

Is the monetary consideration received?

No

Yes

Record the new asset at the carrying value of the asset surrendered plus the cash paid.

Does the carrying value of the asset exceed the monetary consideration?

No

No

Yes

Record a gain for the excess of the monetary consideration over the carrying value of the asset surrendered.

Record the new asset at the carrying value of the asset surrendered minus the monetary consideration received.

Record the new asset at the fair value of the asset surrendered with a gain or loss recorded as required.

Record the new asset at the fair value of the asset received with a gain or loss recorded as required.

This transaction is a nonmonetary exchange that represents the **culmination** of an earning process, because the assets exchanged are **not similar in nature.** Since the fair value of the equipment is not determinable, the fair value of the trucks received is used as the value inherent in the transaction. The assets acquired are recorded at fair value, and any resulting gain or loss is recorded as indicated in the following entry:

Trucks	75 000	
Accumulated Depreciation—Equipment	40 000	
Equipment		100 000
Gain on Exchange of Assets		15 000

If boot had been either received or paid, cash would have been either debited or credited as part of the entry.

Example 2. Elmwood trades the equipment for office furniture. The value of neither the equipment nor the office furniture can be determined objectively.

This transaction is recorded on the basis of the book value of the assets surrendered, because the fair value being exchanged cannot be determined. No gain or loss is recognized. The following entry is appropriate:

Office Furniture	60 000	
Accumulated Depreciation—Equipment	40 000	
Equipment		100 000

Example 3. Elmwood exchanges the equipment, which has an appraised value of $50 000, and pays an additional $4000 in exchange for similar equipment for which a value cannot be readily determined.

This transaction does not represent the completion of an earning process, because similar assets are exchanged. While such transactions would normally be recorded on the basis of the book value of the assets surrendered, any loss indicated must be recorded. In this case a loss is indicated, determined as follows:

Recorded amount of assets surrendered		
Equipment	$60 000	
Cash	4 000	$64 000
Fair value inherent in transaction		
Fair value of equipment surrendered	50 000	
Cash paid	4 000	(54 000)
Loss indicated		$10 000

However, the loss is not recorded, because the *earning process has not been completed.* Paragraph 3830.10 of the CICA *Handbook* requires the new asset to be recorded at the carrying value given up plus the cash paid:

Equipment (new)	64 000	
Accumulated Depreciation—Equipment	40 000	
Equipment (old)		100 000
Cash		4 000

Example 4. Elmwood trades the equipment, valued at $67 000, for similar equipment for which no fair value is determinable. A gain is apparent in the transaction, computed as follows:

Fair value inherent in transaction	
Fair value of asset surrendered	$67 000
Recorded amount of asset surrendered	
Equipment	(60 000)
Gain indicated	$ 7 000

However, the gain is not recorded, because the *earning process has not been completed*. The transaction is recorded as follows:

Equipment (new)	60 000	
Accumulated Depreciation—Equipment	40 000	
Equipment (old)		100 000

Example 5. Elmwood exchanges the equipment, valued at $65 000, and $4000 cash for similar equipment for which a market value is not determinable.

This transaction *does not represent the culmination of the earning process* because similar items of equipment are being exchanged. A gain is indicated because the fair value inherent in the transaction exceeds the recorded amounts of assets surrendered.

Fair value inherent in transaction		
Fair value of equipment surrendered	$65 000	
Cash	4 000	$69 000
Recorded amount of assets surrendered		
Equipment	60 000	
Cash	4 000	(64 000)
Gain indicated		$ 5 000

The *gain is not recorded,* and the equipment acquired is recorded at the book value of the equipment surrendered plus the $4000 cash paid:

Equipment (new)	64 000	
Accumulated Depreciation—Equipment	40 000	
Equipment (old)		100 000
Cash		4 000

Example 6. Elmwood trades the equipment for similar productive equipment valued at $69 000. In addition, Elmwood receives $6000 in cash.

Although this is a nonmonetary exchange that does not represent the completion of an earning process, the **receipt of boot in a gain situation** requires an adjustment to the value of the asset received. Normally, no gain or loss is recorded in recognition of the exchange of similar assets, because the earnings process is not complete. The value exchanged in the transaction is computed as follows:

Fair value inherent in transaction		
Cash received	$ 6 000	
Fair value of equipment received	69 000	$75 000
Recorded amount of asset surrendered		
Equipment		(60 000)
Gain indicated		$15 000

The gain is recorded with an adjustment to the value of the asset received. No gain or loss should be recorded unless the value received is lower than the value surrender. The asset received should not be recorded at a value that exceeds its fair value.

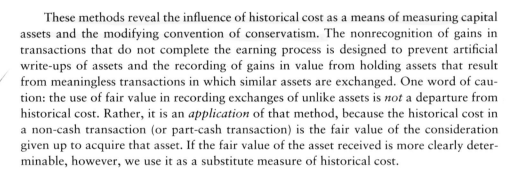

Equipment (new)	54 000	
Accumulated Depreciation—Equipment	40 000	
Cash	6 000	
Equipment (old)		100 000

Asset/Liability Measurement

Conservatism

These methods reveal the influence of historical cost as a means of measuring capital assets and the modifying convention of conservatism. The nonrecognition of gains in transactions that do not complete the earning process is designed to prevent artificial write-ups of assets and the recording of gains in value from holding assets that result from meaningless transactions in which similar assets are exchanged. One word of caution: the use of fair value in recording exchanges of unlike assets is *not* a departure from historical cost. Rather, it is an *application* of that method, because the historical cost in a non-cash transaction (or part-cash transaction) is the fair value of the consideration given up to acquire that asset. If the fair value of the asset received is more clearly determinable, however, we use it as a substitute measure of historical cost.

Quasi Reorganization

A **quasi reorganization** is a specialized situation in which assets are reduced from their book values to lower estimates of future value. To this extent, the quasi reorganization is similar to a permanent impairment in value.

The quasi reorganization, however, is different in that it involves a simultaneous adjustment in the book values of several assets. It represents a general decline in the value of the enterprise rather than a decline in usefulness of one asset or a few specific assets. The quasi reorganization involves adjustments to several shareholders' equity accounts, including Retained Earnings, as part of the process by which the book values of assets are reduced. The circumstances that call for the quasi reorganization process are considered in the Chapter 18 Appendix.

Discovery Value

The **discovery value** is the hidden amount by which a property may increase significantly subsequent to acquisition. An example is the discovery of a valuable natural resource on land subsequent to acquisition. Since the existence of the resource was unknown when the land was acquired, the original cost would not reflect the value exchanged.

The accounting treatment of assets discovered subsequent to acquisition varies considerably, ranging from nonrecognition to the complete recognition of the estimated value of the discovered assets. Accountants generally hesitate to record increases in asset values that have not been verified by transactions with other enterprises. Discovery value is not an acceptable method of revenue recognition under GAAP. Thus, the most common treatment of discovery is nonrecognition. This is consistent with the APB's conclusion:

> The Board is of the opinion that property, plant and equipment should not be written up by an entity to reflect appraisal, market or current values which are above cost to the entity. . . . Whenever appreciation has been recorded on the books, income should be charged with depreciation computed on the written up amounts.[19]

Some increases in value were recorded prior to this APB pronouncement. In addition, some accountants believe that the discovery of assets that were unknown at the time of acquisition is different from the appreciation in asset value that results from changing market conditions, changes in consumer tastes, or other factors occurring after acquisition. Therefore, an accountant may occasionally encounter an increase in the recorded basis of a capital asset that represents the recording of discovery value. As indicated in *Accounting Principles Board Opinion No. 6,* depreciation (or depletion) of the asset should reflect the increased cost basis of the asset. Accountants generally agree that when such asset write-ups are appropriate, the credit side of the entry should be to the shareholders' equity rather than to a revenue or gain account.

To illustrate, assume that Royal Mining Limited acquired land for $200 000 in 1993. In 1993, mineral deposits in the estimated amount of 75 000 tonnes and appraised at $4.25 per tonne (net of anticipated extraction costs) were discovered on the land. Management estimates that the land will be worth its original cost of $200 000 after the exploitation of the mineral deposits. The entries to record these events assume that 15 700 tonnes were extracted and sold in 1993:

1993	Land	200 000	
	Cash		200 000
	Land—Mineral Deposits Discovered	318 750	
	Unrealized Capital Increment—Discovery of		
	Mineral Deposits		318 750
	(75 000 × $4.25 = $318 750)		
	Depletion Expense	66 725	
	Land—Mineral Deposits Discovered		66 725
	[(15 700/75 000) × $318 750 = $66 725]		

The capital account, Unrealized Capital Increment—Discovery of Mineral Deposits, is presented as part of the shareholders' equity section in the balance sheet.

Government Assistance

Several levels of government offer assistance programs. These programs range from subsidies for pollution devices to grants for termite treatment. New programs are continually introduced to meet ecological and social needs.

In 1975, Section 3800 of the CICA *Handbook* was introduced to deal with the accounting for government assistance. This section replaced Section 3065, which only dealt with fixed assets. There are two approaches to the accounting treatment of govern-

---

[19]"Omnibus Opinion," *APB Opinion No. 6,* 1965, Paragraph 17.

Exhibit 12.6 TransCanada PipeLines Limited: Capital Assets Disclosure

Note 3 Plant, Property and Equipment	Cost	1991 Accumulated Depreciation	Net Book Value	1990 Net Book Value
		December 31 (millions of dollars)		
Gas Transmission				
Gas plant in service				
Mainline	4637.3	(1077.6)	3559.7	2645.8
Compression	994.2	(321.9)	672.3	535.3
Metering and other	188.4	(51.1)	137.3	115.9
	5819.9	(1450.6)	4369.3	3297.0
Gas plant under construction	357.7	—	357.7	172.5
	6177.6	(1450.6)	4727.0	3469.5
Gas Sales, Marketing and Other	173.1	(53.2)	119.9	100.6
	6350.7	(1503.8)	4846.9	3570.1

Source: TransCanada PipeLines Limited, *1991 Annual Report.*

ment assistance. The capital approach considers this assistance as a reduction of the amount of capital required to finance the expenditure, or as not earned. The income approach assumes the assistance is a revenue or expense item and confers a benefit to the recipient company. The CICA favours the income approach, with the assistance being applied in the period in which the related expenses are incurred.[20]

Financial Statement Disclosure

At the end of Chapter 13, after completing our study of tangible assets and depreciation, we look more carefully at the disclosure requirements for property, plant, and equipment. Many companies include only total amounts for property, plant, and equipment in their balance sheets and then provide more detailed information in notes to the financial statements. In Exhibit 12.6, we illustrate this type of presentation for TransCanada PipeLines Limited. TransCanada PipeLines has brought together Western Canadian natural gas producers and consumers in Saskatchewan, Manitoba, Ontario, and Quebec.

Concluding Remarks

Asset/Liability Measurement

Several accounting principles are significant in accounting for capital assets. This chapter has focussed primarily on the determination of *historical cost* as the principal means of measuring capital assets. While historical cost may seem to be a relatively simple and straightforward principle, complications may arise in a variety of circumstances, such as the purchase of more than one asset in a single transaction, the treatment of costs related to acquisition, the internal construction of capital assets, the incurrence of interest cost in the construction of capital assets, and post-acquisition expenditures that may have an impact on the historical cost of capital assets. Generally accepted accounting principles

[20]"Accounting for Government Assistance," CICA *Handbook*, Section 3800, May 1988.

in all of these situations reflect the considered judgement of accountants in determining historical cost.

Consistency

In determining historical cost, *objectivity* is important. Accountants base their measurements on objective, verifiable evidence to the extent possible. The *consistency principle* is also important in the treatment of capital assets expenditures since similar expenditures are made from period to period. The *materiality principle* comes into play in accounting for capital assets, as it does in virtually all areas of accounting. The strict application of the principles discussed in this chapter is not required if the results are insignificant and, therefore, not cost-effective.

Materiality

Matching

One of the primary purposes for carefully establishing the correct historical cost of capital assets is to determine the appropriate amount for depreciation in accordance with the matching principle. In the next chapter, we consider depreciation of capital assets in depth, building on the general principles of historical cost determination discussed in this chapter.

Key Points	1. Property, plant, and equipment and intangible assets are long-lived assets that are acquired for use in the production and distribution of goods and services. (Objective 1)

1. Property, plant, and equipment and intangible assets are long-lived assets that are acquired for use in the production and distribution of goods and services. (Objective 1)
2. Several basic accounting principles have an impact on the proper accounting for tangible and intangible assets. Most notable are the historical cost method of measuring and reporting and the matching principle. (Objective 2)
3. Several unique problems may be encountered in attempting to apply historical cost to specific types of capital assets, such as land, buildings, machinery, equipment, furniture, fixtures, and natural resources. (Objective 3)
4. General problems of establishing historical cost include the treatment of:
   a. Cash discounts.
   b. Deferred-payment plans.
   c. Internally constructed capital assets.
   d. Capitalization of interest.
   e. Acquisition by issuing securities.
   f. Basket purchases.
   g. Installation, preparation, and start-up costs. (Objective 3)
5. An important distinction in accounting for post-acquisition expenditures is to separate capital expenditures from revenue expenditures. Capital expenditures are amortized over their estimated useful lives, whereas revenue expenditures are charged to expense as incurred. (Objective 4)
6. Disposals of capital assets may result from sales, abandonments, involuntary conversions, or exchanges. Disposals may result in gains or losses, which are presented as part of net income. (Objective 5)
7. Certain specialized situations dictate a departure from historical cost in accounting for capital assets. These exceptions are found in the cases of donated assets, permanent impairments in value, quasi reorganizations, and discovery value. (Objective 6)

Questions	Q12.1 Identify the two primary characteristics of all tangible and intangible assets.

Q12.1 Identify the two primary characteristics of all tangible and intangible assets.
Q12.2 Distinguish between tangible and intangible assets and identify several types of each.

Q12.3 Identify four principles that underlie accounting for tangible and intangible assets within generally accepted accounting principles.

Q12.4 What is the "full-cost" interpretation of historical cost, as applied to capital assets?

Q12.5 In determining the full cost of land, what expenditures in addition to the bargained acquisition price might be included?

Q12.6 Why is it generally desirable for land improvements to be capitalized in a separate account from the Land account?

Q12.7 How should land that is held for investment or speculative purposes be classified in the balance sheet?

Q12.8 For items of machinery, equipment, furniture, and fixtures, what expenditures may be included in the cost figure in addition to the original acquisition price?

Q12.9 What is the preferred treatment of cash discounts in determining the cost of capital assets?

Q12.10 In what circumstances may it be necessary to impute interest included in the payments in a deferred-payment plan for capital assets? What is the purpose of imputing interest?

Q12.11 What distortions will exist in the financial statements of the buyer of a capital asset if interest is not imputed in an installment contract for which interest should have been imputed?

Q12.12 As a general rule, a careful distinction is made between interest and the cost of capital assets. In certain circumstances, however, it is appropriate to capitalize interest in establishing the correct historical cost of an asset. What are these circumstances?

Q12.13 When a capital asset is acquired by issuing capital shares, what is the appropriate basis for recording the asset acquired?

Q12.14 If several assets are acquired in a single transaction for one price, how is the historical cost of the individual assets determined?

Q12.15 Enterprises may produce their own capital assets for use in future operations. Determining the cost of such assets is complicated by the fact that production activities of capital assets may be mixed with production activities of inventory items. Describe how the cost of internally developed assets should be determined, including an identification of specific costs to be included.

Q12.16 Distinguish between capital expenditures and revenue expenditures, citing several examples of each.

Q12.17 Distinguish between the accounting treatment of the following three types of betterments:
(a) Substitution of part of an asset when separate cost identification is possible.
(b) Substitution of part of an asset when separate cost identification is not possible and the advantage of the expenditure is improved quality of future services.
(c) Substitution of part of an asset when separate cost identification is not possible and the advantage of the expenditure is an extension of the useful life of the asset.

Q12.18 Under what circumstances should the allowance method of recognizing repair and maintenance expense be used as an alternative to recognition as costs are incurred? What is the purpose of the allowance method?

Q12.19 Assets acquired in exchange transactions may be recorded in one of several ways, depending on the circumstances of the exchange. Identify the circumstances in which each of the following bases is appropriate for recording an asset acquired in a nonmonetary exchange:
(a) Fair value inherent in the exchange.

(b) Book value of asset(s) surrendered.

(c) Recording the asset received at below its fair value.

Q12.20 Cardwell Limited acquired a 3 hectare site for the construction of a new branch plant. Which of the following costs (or groups of costs) should *not* be charged to the Land account of the company?

(a) Title examination fees, recording fees, and surveying fees.

(b) Costs of grading, clearing, and draining the property.

(c) Costs of removing the old, unwanted building from the land.

(d) Property taxes accruing during the period of plant construction.

(Adapted from AICPA.)

Q12.21 Horwitz Limited received $20 000 in cash and a used computer with a fair value of $150 000 from Harvest Corporation in exchange for Horwitz's existing computer, which had a fair value of $180 000 and an undepreciated cost of $160 000 recorded on its books. Which of the following answers shows at what amount the acquired computer should be recorded?

(a) $140 000
(c) $160 000
(b) $144 000
(d) $180 000

(Adapted from AICPA.)

Q12.22 Sipp Limited exchanged inventory items that cost $8000 and normally sold for $12 000 for a new delivery truck with a list price of $13 000. At which of the following figures should the delivery truck be recorded on Sipp's books?

(a) $8000
(c) $12 000
(b) $8667
(d) $13 000

(Adapted from AICPA.)

Exercises

E12.1 Building and Land Cost. Weber Limited acquired land and a building for $275 000 on October 15, 1994. The land was appraised at $125 000 and the building at $175 000. Unpaid property taxes assumed by Weber were $12 000, 40 percent allocated to the land and 60 percent to the building. Additional costs incurred were:

(1) Building renovation, $57 500.
(2) Option on alternative land and building which were not acquired, $1750.
(3) Cost of survey, $210.

Instructions

Determine the cost of the building and the land, identifying the individual elements of cost included in each asset.

E12.2 Capital Asset Acquisition Cost. Anders Co. recently acquired several items of property, plant, and equipment. The transactions were as follows:

June 5   Purchased land appraised at $175 000 and machinery appraised at $50 000 for a total of $195 000.

July 16   Purchased a building for $185 000 in cash and 100 000 of the company's common shares trading at $10 on the Toronto Stock Exchange.

Aug. 21   Received a parcel of land from the city of Hillsboro as an inducement to locate a plant in the city. No payment was required. The land was appraised at $65 000.

Sept. 25   Acquired furniture and fixtures by issuing a $75 000, two-year, noninterest-bearing note. In similar transactions, the company has paid 8 percent interest.

Instructions
Prepare the journal entry appropriate in each case to record the acquisition of property, plant, and equipment.

E12.3 Land Cost. Paulson Limited acquired land on June 1, 1995, for $170 000, on which a new building will be immediately constructed. Costs related to the acquisition include:

(1) A commission of 4 percent of the price for the location of the land and the negotiation of the acquisition price.
(2) $1700 for legal fees related to the transfer of the title of the land and other matters.
(3) $350 for a survey pursuant to the closing of the transaction.
(4) $2500 for options acquired at an earlier date: $1500 for the land acquired and $1000 for an alternative parcel of land that was seriously considered but not acquired.
(5) $16 000 for removal of an existing building; $2750 was received from the salvage of materials.
(6) $2400 for 1994 property taxes that were delinquent on June 1, 1995. Taxes for 1995 are expected to be $3000 and will be paid by Paulson before December 31, 1995.

Instructions
Determine the historical cost of the land as it should be presented in the company's balance sheet on December 31, 1995.

E12.4 Fixtures Cost. Wexler Limited acquired several fixtures for its new building, including display cases, shelves, and hanging racks. The invoice price of the fixtures was $72 500. The company received a 2 percent cash discount by paying within the discount period. Freight and insurance during shipment totalled $352. Costs of assembling and installing the fixtures were $475. While installing a display case, a new employee carelessly broke a glass top. This top was replaced at a cost of $185.

Instructions
Determine the total cost of the fixtures, identifying the individual elements that make up the total.

E12.5 Equipment Transactions. On January 1, 1995, Presser Ltd. acquired used equipment by issuing the seller a two-year, noninterest-bearing note for $200 000. The value of the equipment is apparently less than $200 000, but a specific amount cannot be determined. In recent borrowings, Presser has paid 10 percent interest.

On January 7, the company installed the equipment. Estimated costs of installation were $1750 for labour and $670 for materials, both included in the manufacturing accounts. On January 12, the company paid $675 for freight and insurance charges during shipment.

Instructions
(a) Prepare general journal entries for the above transactions and for adjustments required on December 31, 1995, including supporting computations. The company plans to depreciate the asset over eight years, with the salvage value being approxi-

mately equal to the costs of removal. Straight-line depreciation should be used. Interest is recognized by the effective interest method.

(b) What amount of interest expense will be recognized at December 31, 1996, on the equipment note?

E12.6 Capital Asset Transactions. Clyde Products acquired the following capital assets during 1995:

Equipment. Acquired at an invoice price of $60 000, subject to a 1 percent cash discount that was not taken. Freight and insurance during shipment cost $350. The equipment has a five-year life expectancy and a salvage value of 10 percent of the invoice price.

Land. Acquired by issuing 10 000 common shares when the market price of the shares was $11.

Machinery. Acquired at a cost of $27 600. Installation costs were $770. Trial runs and other testing cost $510. These expenses have been included in the Manufacturing Overhead account. The machinery is expected to be useful for ten years, at the end of which it will have a $2500 salvage value.

Instructions

Prepare all general journal entries needed to record the acquisition and depreciation of the assets for 1995. Straight-line depreciation should be used, with a full year recognized.

E12.7 Internally Constructed Assets. Wicker Ltd. decided to construct its own equipment rather than acquire similar assets from other companies. Management believed that the assets could be built for less than they could be bought. Material and labour costs were determined to be $195 000 and $220 000, respectively. Overhead is normally charged to production at the rate of 85 percent of the direct labour cost. The actual increment in overhead resulting from the construction was determined to be $162 000.

Instructions

(a) Assuming the company is operating at full capacity and must curtail production operations to construct the equipment, determine the appropriate amounts to be capitalized as the cost of the equipment. Justify your treatment of overhead costs.

(b) How would the capitalized amount change if the company were not operating at capacity?

E12.8 Nonmonetary Exchange. Mannis Limited recently swapped used machinery for similar used machinery with a competing company. Mannis's previous machinery cost $7000 and had a book value of $5500 at the time of the trade. The machinery's estimated value was $6200, and Mannis paid $500 in cash as part of the transaction. Machinery received in the trade had not been appraised recently. Mannis's accountant recorded the trade as follows:

Machinery (new)	6 700	
Accumulated Depreciation	1 500	
Machinery (old)		7 000
Cash		500
Gain on Exchange of Machinery		700

594 Intermediate Accounting

Instructions

(a) Prepare the general journal entry you would suggest for recording the transaction.
(b) Explain the fallacy, if any, in the accountant's entry and how your entry would correct the problem.

E12.9 Replacement. Bills Enterprise replaced a portion of its building for $675 000. Before the replacement, the Building and Accumulated Depreciation accounts were as follows:

Building	$3 500 000
Accumulated depreciation	(2 250 000)
	$1 250 000

Instructions

Prepare the general journal entry to record the $675 000 expenditure in each of the following independent cases:

(a) Separate identification of the portion of the building being replaced is not possible. The replacement was designed to improve the service potential of the total facility for the remainder of its original expected useful life.
(b) The portion of the building being replaced accounts for $1 million and $785 000 of the Building and Accumulated Depreciation accounts, respectively.
(c) Separate identification of the portion of the building being replaced is not possible. The primary purpose of the expenditure is to lengthen the life of the building from that originally estimated.

E12.10 Miscellaneous Capital Asset Entries. Reese, Inc., engaged in the following transactions involving capital assets during the current year:

(1) A building expansion costing $260 000 is expected to provide service for twenty years, even though the original building will be useful for only ten more years.
(2) The base of a machine was replaced for $7000. The portion of the original cost allocated to the base was $5000, and the cost of the asset was 40 percent depreciated at the time of the replacement. The old base was sold for $800. The new base is expected to serve the machine to the end of its useful life.
(3) A number of improvements were made in a building for $87 400. The cost of items replaced could not be determined. The improvements were made to ensure the original estimated useful life of the building.
(4) The reorganization required to move into the new addition cost $12 500. Management believes that the rearrangement will benefit the company for at least three years.
(5) Servicing of machinery on a regular basis resulted in expenditures of $4200.

Instructions

(a) Prepare the general journal entry to record each transaction.
(b) Describe the appropriate period of depreciation or amortization of any items capitalized in each entry.

E12.11 Impairment in Value. CD, Inc. invested heavily in equipment that was needed to produce a new line of stereo equipment. On January 1, 1995, the cost and accumulated depreciation balances on the equipment were as follows:

Equipment	$5 250 000
Accumulated depreciation	(2 700 000)
	$2 550 000

Due to changes in consumer tastes and unexpected advances in electronics, CD's management now believes that the future service potential of the equipment is greatly reduced and the useful life is much shorter than originally estimated. Specifically, management believes the future service potential of the asset is limited to $1 million and the future life extends only through 1996.

Instructions

Determine the amounts that should be presented in the company's balance sheet and income statement relative to the equipment at December 31, 1995.

E12.12 Correction of Errors. Fulmer, Inc., carried out a number of transactions involving the acquisition of several assets. All expenditures were recorded in the following single asset account, identified as Fixed Assets:

Fixed Assets

Acquisition price of land and building	$120 000
Options taken out on several pieces of property	2 000
List price of machinery purchased	39 800
Freight on machinery purchased	625
Repair to machinery resulting from damage during shipment	185
Cost of removing old machinery	600
Driveways and sidewalks	12 750
Building remodelling	50 000
Utilities paid since acquisition of building	2 600
	$228 560

Based on property tax assessments, which are believed to fairly represent the relative values involved, the building is worth twice as much as the land. The machinery was subject to a 2 percent cash discount, which was taken and credited to Purchases Discounts. Of the two options, $750 related to the building and land purchased and $1250 related to those not purchased. The old machinery was sold at book value.

Instructions

Prepare the general journal entry or entries to correct the Fixed Asset account. Provide supporting calculations for the amounts capitalized in individual capital asset accounts. All expenditures were made in the current year and the books have not been closed.

E12.13 Building Disposals. Estes, Incorporated, owns a building with a book value of $85 000 on October 31, 1994, the end of the company's fiscal year, computed as follows:

Building	$180 000
Accumulated depreciation	(95 000)
	$ 85 000

Depreciation is computed by the straight-line method at $1500 per month.

Instructions
Prepare the general journal entry or entries to record the disposal of the building under each of the following independent cases:

(a) The building is sold on June 30, 1995, for $105 000.
(b) The company incurs costs of $15 800 to improve the building in preparation for its sale. The building is sold on August 31, 1995, for $97 000.
(c) The building is destroyed by fire on March 31, 1995. Proceeds from insurance total $67 800.

E12.14 Capitalization of Interest Cost. Cale Ltd. entered into a contract with Moncton Limited to construct a building for Cale. The contract called for work to begin on June 1, 1994, and for Cale to make an initial payment of $100 000 at that time. Another $50 000 was to be paid by Cale at the end of each three-month period until May 31, 1995, when the building was to be completed, transferred to Cale, and placed into service.

All aspects of the contract were completed on schedule. Cale Ltd. made the payments from existing working capital and did not incur any additional debt for the specific purpose of financing the construction of the building. Throughout the construction period, however, Cale had $750 000 of debt outstanding at an average interest rate of 10 percent.

Instructions
(a) Determine the appropriate cost of the building on the books of Cale Ltd..
(b) Explain the rationale for the various components of cost in (a).

E12.15 Machinery Disposals. Powell Manufacturing Limited has a machine that it plans to eliminate. The machine has the following cost and accumulated depreciation at the time of the anticipated transaction:

Machinery	$25 000
Accumulated depreciation	(12 500)
	$12 500

Instructions
Prepare the general journal entry to record the disposal in each of the following independent cases:

(a) The machine is appraised at $17 000 and is traded for a patent with an unknown value.
(b) The machine is appraised at $5000 and is traded for a similar machine with an indeterminate value. In addition, cash of $27 000 is paid.
(c) The machine is sold for $13 700 cash.
(d) The machine is traded, along with $700 cash, for a similar machine with an appraisal value of $15 000.

(e) The machine is traded for a similar machine with a value of $15 000. In addition, $1000 cash is received.

E12.16 Repair and Maintenance Expense. The controller of Tucker, Inc., asked you to review the Repair and Maintenance Expense account for the year to determine whether all of the charges are appropriate. You have identified the following ten transactions for further scrutiny. All of these transactions are considered material in amount.

Date	Amount	Description
Jan. 3	$10 000	Service contract on office equipment.
Mar. 7	10 000	Initial design fee for proposed extension of office building.
Apr. 12	18 500	New condenser for central air conditioning unit located on the roof of office building.
Apr. 20	7 000	Purchase of two executive chairs and desks.
May 12	40 850	Purchase of storm windows and screens and their installation on all office windows.
May 18	38 450	Sealing of roof leaks in production plant.
June 19	28 740	Replacement of large door to production area.
July 3	11 740	Installation of automatic door-opening system on the above door to speed opening.
Sept. 14	38 500	Overhead crane for the assembly department to speed up production.
Oct. 18	11 000	Replacement of broken gear on machine in the machining department.

Instructions

For each of the above transactions, indicate whether the Repair and Maintenance Expense account is properly charged, and if not, indicate the appropriate account to which the transaction should be charged. Explain your reasoning in each case.
(Adapted from CMA.)

Problems

P12.1 Historical Cost Determination. The determination of historical cost may be complicated by a number of factors related to the transaction in which the asset is acquired. Chumley Limited has been involved in a number of transactions in which capital assets have been acquired.

Instructions

In each of the following independent situations, determine the historical cost of the capital assets to Chumley Limited:

(a) Land and building are acquired by Chumley for $580 000. The building is destroyed at a cost of $37 000 to make way for a new facility that is to be constructed in the future. Proceeds of $10 000 are received from salvaged materials from the old building.

(b) Land and building are acquired by Chumley for $500 000 and are appraised at $200 000 and $350 000, respectively. Plans call for the renovation of the building, after which it will be used in future operations.

(c) Land is acquired by Chumley at a cost of $125 000. An option had been taken out earlier for $5000 that guaranteed the purchase price for 90 days. Another option for $5000 was negotiated on an alternative land site that was not acquired. Legal costs related to the transaction were $650.

(d) Land was purchased by Chumley by issuing 1300 common shares. The shares have a market value of $16 per share. No independent appraisal has been made on the land.

(e) Equipment was purchased by Chumley by issuing a $67 000, three-year, noninterest-bearing note. The purchaser's borrowing rate is estimated to be 12 percent, based on other recent borrowing. Transportation and installation costs incurred by the purchase totalled $2100.

(f) Equipment was acquired by Chumley at an invoice price of $85 000. A 1 percent cash discount was taken by payment within the ten-day period required under the terms of the agreement. Damage to the asset during shipment required a $125 payment by the purchaser. The costs of installation were $2450. Insurance on the equipment for one year ($350) was paid.

(g) Chumley exchanged items of specialized equipment with another company; in addition, Chumley paid $50 000 cash. The book value of the equipment surrendered was $88 000. Market value approximates book value.

(h) Upon the advice of a management consulting firm, Chumley reorganized its production facilities. Costs of $18 775 were incurred for rearrangement activities. At the same time, equipment costing $47 500 was acquired, on which an available 2 percent cash discount was not taken due to an oversight by the bookkeeper. The equipment that was being replaced was sold at a price that resulted in a $1000 loss.

P12.2 Miscellaneous Capital Asset Transactions. Dinville Ltd. recently acquired land and a building in a single transaction.

Instructions

Prepare the journal entry to record the acquired assets in each of the following independent situations:

(a) Cash of $285 000 is paid. The land is appraised at $250 000, and an existing building, which will be destroyed to make room for a new one, is appraised at $50 000.

(b) Cash of $275 000 is paid. The land is appraised at $175 000 and an existing building, which will be retained and used, is appraised at $125 000.

(c) Cash of $285 000 is paid. In addition, $15 000 is received from the salvage of an existing building that was destroyed to make room for a new one. The land is appraised at $250 000 and the old building at $35 000.

(d) A $370 000 noninterest-bearing note that requires a single payment at the end of three years is given for the land. No appraisal on the land is available. Dinville Ltd. has recently borrowed money at 10 percent.

(e) Cash of $500 000 is paid. The land is appraised at $250 000; other assets acquired in the same transaction are appraised as follows:

Equipment	$100 000
Fixtures	115 000
Patent	85 000

P12.3 Miscellaneous Capital Asset Transactions. Barth Limited acquired several items of property, plant, and equipment during 1995, its first year of operation:

Jan. 5 The city of Montreal donated land to the company as an inducement to locate facilities in the city. The land was appraised at $215 000 and resulted in no cash payment by the company.

Jan. 12 Issued 50 000 no-par value common shares and paid $500 000 cash for assets appraised as follows:

Building	$1 700 000
Land	850 000
Machinery	150 000
Inventory	450 000

At the time of the transaction, the common shares were selling for $51 per share.

Feb. 5 Acquired machinery on account for $145 000, terms 2/10, n/30. Payment was made on Mar. 2.

July 17 Machinery priced at $30 000 was acquired by issuing a 90-day, 10 percent note. The note was paid at maturity.

Aug. 1 Machinery was purchased by issuing a noninterest-bearing note for $85 000, payable at the end of two years. In similar transactions, the company paid an interest rate of 10 percent.

Instructions

Prepare the journal entries necessary to record the acquisitions of property, plant, and equipment indicated above. Also, prepare any additional entries that would be required during 1995 as a result of the information given. Do not prepare adjusting entries to recognize depreciation at the end of 1995.

P12.4 Correction of Errors. McClain Limited recently acquired a building and the surrounding land. The company's accountant established a single Land and Building account and has made the following entries:

1995		**Land and Building Account**	
Jan.	3	Acquisition price	$425 000
	3	Prepayment of insurance on building (2 years)	10 500
Feb.	1	Payment of property taxes ($2400 delinquent for 1994; $3600 for 1995)	6 000
Mar.	7	Renovation costs on building	42 500
Apr.	1	Cost of open house to familiarize the public with new facility opened that day	2 000
			486 000
Dec. 31		Depreciation for 1995, computed by straight-line method with twenty-year life	(24 300)
			$461 700

McClain's accountant has shown the $461 700 Land and Building account in the balance sheet and the $24 300 as Depreciation Expense in the income statement. As a staff member of the CA firm responsible for auditing the financial statements of the company, you must propose any adjustments you consider necessary. Your investigation reveals the following:

(1) Upon acquisition, the land was independently appraised at $115 000 and the building at $325 000.

(2) McClain's policy calls for depreciation by the straight-line method, computed monthly.
(3) The building is expected to have a residual value of 10 percent of its cost basis at the end of its twenty-year life. The building was placed in service on April 1, 1995.
(4) Property taxes are allocated 74 percent to the building and 26 percent to the land.

Instructions

Prepare any adjusting entry or entries that you think are necessary. Provide computations that you would present to your supervisor to support your position. (All amounts may be rounded to the nearest dollar.)

P12.5   Nonmonetary Exchanges.   You have been retained by Royal Metal Products Limited to evaluate its accounting procedures in several areas. One area is nonmonetary transactions. Andy Jack, President of Royal Metal, has met with you concerning these transactions and indicated that in his opinion no "sale" has taken place until at least 50 percent of the transactions are represented in cash. Therefore, in accounting for exchanges of assets that do not meet this 50 percent test, he has instructed his accountant to simply transfer the book value of the surrendered asset, plus cash (if any), into the new asset account. In Jack's opinion, ". . . this makes a lot of sense and is really easy. In addition, it does not clutter up the income statement with gains and losses that are meaningless in that they have no significant cash consequences."

In evaluating the company's financial records, you discover the following transactions:

(1) Royal Metal traded metal inventory to a competitor for a small strip of land adjacent to Royal's warehouse. The metal had a cost of $10 000; the strip of land had been appraised at $18 000. Royal's accountant had recorded the land at $10 000 as instructed by Jack.
(2) Royal Metal had several unneeded trucks that were traded to a competitor for some metal inventory that was difficult to obtain. The trucks had a book value of $45 000 (cost, $120 000; accumulated depreciation, $75 000). While no appraisal value was available for the trucks, the metal was valued at $42 000. Royal paid $3500 boot in addition to the trucks to complete the transaction. Jack instructed the accountant to record the metal inventory at $48 500 ($45 000 + $3500) since the cash did not constitute 50 percent of the transaction.

Instructions

(a) React to Andy Jack's rule concerning accounting for nonmonetary exchanges. Do you agree or disagree with it? Why?
(b) Evaluate Royal's accounting treatment of each of the exchanges described above. What changes, if any, would you suggest to bring Royal's accounting into conformity with generally accepted accounting principles?
(c) For each of the two exchanges described above, state briefly the theoretical justification for recording the required asset in the way you have suggested it should be recorded.

P12.6   Nonmonetary Exchanges.   Rothchild, Inc. plans to dispose of certain gymnastics equipment in one of several ways. The equipment originally cost $200 000, and depreciation recognized to date is $70 000. A recent appraisal values the equipment at approximately $150 000 on the used equipment market. Rothchild's owner wants to know the impact of various methods of disposal on the company's financial statements.

Instructions

Prepare the general journal entry or entries for the following independent alternative methods of disposal. Following each entry, comment on the impact the alternative would have on the income statement for the year in which the transaction took place.

(a) Rothchild trades the equipment for a vacant lot whose current value is not known.
(b) Rothchild trades the equipment for similar equipment valued at $160 000 and pays $8000 in the exchange.
(c) Rothchild trades the equipment for similar equipment valued at $140 000 and receives $10 000 cash.
(d) Rothchild sells the equipment for $170 000. The proceeds are combined with an additional $50 000 cash and a $125 000, five-year, 10 percent note to purchase new equipment. The 10 percent interest rate on the note appears fair.
(e) Rothchild trades the equipment for similar equipment also valued at $150 000. No cash is included in the transaction.

P12.7 Repair and Maintenance. Neptune Limited uses the allowance method of accounting for equipment repair and maintenance expenditures. A monthly amount of $1200 is recognized as an expense and credited to the allowance on a quarterly basis. Expenditures for repairs and maintenance are charged to this allowance. Any existing balance in the allowance is adjusted to zero through the expense at the end of the company's fiscal year, March 31. Depreciation on equipment is computed at 2 percent of the gross asset balance at the end of each quarter. Account balances on April 1, 1994, are as follows:

Equipment	$125 000
Accumulated depreciation	(57 200)
	$ 67 800

Neptune engaged in the following transactions involving equipment from April 1, 1994, through March 31, 1995:

Apr. 18	Repair costs	$ 550
May 17	Equipment acquisition	5 275
July 30	Repair costs	3 620
Oct. 19	Repair costs	5 200
Dec. 17	Equipment acquisition	10 900
Feb. 18	Repair costs	4 990

Instructions

(a) Determine the amounts to be included in the company's balance sheet based on the equipment accounts at the end of each quarter from April 1, 1994, through March 31, 1995. Round all amounts to the nearest dollar.
(b) What amount of repair and maintenance expense will appear in the annual income statement on March 31, 1995?
(c) Briefly explain the rationale for the allowance method of accounting for repairs and maintenance in this situation, as opposed to simply recognizing repair and maintenance expenditures as expenses when they are incurred.

P12.8 Capitalization of Interest Cost. Ritter, Inc., contracted a company to build a warehouse in 1995. Construction began on January 2 and Ritter paid $50 000 on that date. Ritter then made additional payments as follows, based on progress made toward completion of the structure:

Apr. 1	$50 000
June 1	75 000
Sept. 1	85 000
Nov. 1	45 000

Ritter arranged for an 8 percent loan of $120 000 on January 2 and borrowed the total amount at that time. The proceeds were used to partially finance the construction. Amounts invested in the project in excess of $120 000 were financed from available working capital. During 1995, the company had debt obligations, other than the one related directly to the construction project of $1 million, on which interest expense of $120 000 was recognized. Completion of the project is expected sometime during 1996. Ritter's reporting period ends on December 31.

Instructions

(a) Prepare a schedule to determine the cost of the construction in progress at December 31, 1995.
(b) Prepare general journal entries to record the above events, assuming all interest has been charged to interest expense as incurred. Capitalized interest is to be recognized at year-end.
(c) Prepare the note disclosure that should accompany the financial statements relative to this construction project.

P12.9 Miscellaneous Capital Asset Transactions. Sidler Ltd. presented the following items of property, plant, and equipment in its balance sheet on December 31, 1994:

Property, Plant, and Equipment

Equipment	$ 126 250	
Accumulated depreciation	(32 500)	$ 93 750
Buildings	751 000	
Accumulated depreciation	(251 500)	499 500
Land		162 720

During 1995, the company engaged in the following transactions involving property, plant, and equipment:

Jan. 1 Construction of a small office building was begun and a $10 000 initial payment was made. (The project was completed on August 1.)

2 Bonds in the face amount of $200 000 were sold at par value. Annual interest of 6 percent is to be paid semi-annually on June 30 and Dec. 31. Sidler plans to use the proceeds to purchase several property, plant, and equipment items in the near future and to finance construction of the office building.

Feb. 5 A piece of equipment with a list price of $35 250 was acquired. A 2 percent cash discount was received by paying on Feb. 10, within the ten-day discount period.

28 The second progress payment ($20 000) was made on the office building.

Apr. 30 The third progress payment ($20 000) was made on the office building.

May   1   A piece of used equipment was acquired in a trade for a similar asset that the company had owned for several years. The newly acquired asset had a market value of $18 000. The asset surrendered had a book value of $15 000 (cost, $25 000; accumulated depreciation, $10 000). Sidler paid $750 in cash. (*Hint:* The proper amount for recording the newly acquired asset is the book value of the asset surrendered plus cash paid. This transaction represents the exchange of similar productive assets in which the earning process is not complete.)

June 30   The fourth progress payment ($20 000) was made on the office building.

July   1   Land was acquired by issuing a $55 000, two-year, noninterest-bearing note. The note calls for two payments of $27 500, one and two years after the date of the note. A recent appraisal of the land indicates an estimated value of $49 040.

Aug.   1   The office building was completed and placed in service. The building had been constructed by another company between January 1 and August 1. Sidler made the final payment of $10 000 on August 1.

Instructions

(a) Prepare all journal entries for the preceding transactions and any additional necessary entries.

(b) Prepare any adjusting entries required on December 31, 1995. Depreciation is computed at 10 percent of the ending account balance for equipment and 4 percent of the ending account balance for buildings, approximating straight-line depreciation with 10- and 25-year lives for equipment and buildings, respectively.

(c) Prepare the presentation of property, plant, and equipment to be included in the December 31, 1995, balance sheet.

(d) Prepare the note, to be included with the 1995 financial statements, on the accounting policies with reference to property, plant, and equipment.

P12.10   Correction of Errors.   Simcoe Ltd. purchased land and a building, demolished the existing building, and immediately constructed a new building. All of this occurred in the first eight months of 1994. In evaluating the company's Building account at year-end, you find the following amounts make up the $954 800 balance:

Jan. 5	Purchase price of land and building	$175 000
15	Demolition cost of old building, net of $10 000 salvage	54 000
Sept. 1	Cost of new building	630 000
1	Insurance on new building	12 000
5	Display fixtures in new building	62 800
Dec. 31	Interest expense on new building	21 000
		$954 800

Upon further analysis, you discover the following explanations for these amounts:

$175 000—The land was appraised at $150 000 and the existing building, $50 000. A combined purchase price of $175 000 was negotiated because the seller was anxious to sell the property as soon as possible.

$ 54 000—The company negotiated a price of $64 000 for demolition of the old building, with the contractor retaining all salvageable materials. The latter were estimated to be worth $10 000.

$630 000—This represents the contract price for the new building, which was put into service on September 1. No interest was paid directly or was related indirectly to this building prior to September 1.

$ 12 000—Insurance was taken out on the building and its contents at $12 000 for a twelve-month period.

$ 62 800—Display fixtures, which are separate from the building itself, were installed.

$ 21 000—A loan was taken out when the building was put into service to cover the $630 000 contract price. Interest was calculated at $630 000 at the effective 10 percent interest rate for four months, or $21 000.

Simcoe Ltd. depreciates all capital assets by the straight-line method. Useful lives are twenty years for buildings and ten years for all others. Expected salvage values are 25 percent of cost for buildings and 10 percent of cost for all others.

Instructions

(a) Prepare individual correcting entries for each item in the Building account that was incorrectly charged to that account. Provide a one-sentence explanation of your reasoning in each case.

(b) Prepare depreciation adjusting entries for all capital assets, assuming depreciation is computed to the nearest whole month.

P12.11   Nonmonetary Exchanges.   Leroux, Inc. owns Asset A, a used asset for which no current market value is readily determinable. Asset A cost $125 000 several years ago, and has a book value of $65 000 on June 30, 1995. The company is considering alternative opportunities to dispose of Asset A in an exchange transaction that would result in the acquisition of a similar asset.

Instructions

For each of the following independent cases, prepare the general journal entry necessary to record the exchange of Asset A for the appropriate alternative asset. For each alternative, briefly explain the amount at which the new asset is capitalized.

	Asset B	Asset C	Asset D	Asset E	Asset F
Original cost	$145 000	$90 000	$100 000	$165 000	$110 000
Accumulated depreciation	(75 000)	—	(25 000)	(100 000)	(10 000)
Book value	$ 70 000	$90 000	$ 75 000	$ 65 000	$100 000
Current market value	*	$90 000	$ 50 000	$ 90 000	$100 000
Cash paid by (received by) Leroux, Inc.	—	$20 000	$ (3000)	$(10 000)	$ 45 000

*Unable to determine.

P12.12   Miscellaneous Capital Asset Transactions.   Cronan Manufacturing Limited had several transactions during 1994 and 1995 concerning capital assets. Several of these transactions are described below, followed by the entry or entries made by the company's accountant.

Equipment.   Several used items were acquired on February 1, 1994, by issuing a $100 000 noninterest-bearing note. The note is due one year from the date of issuance. No market value of the note or the equipment is available. Cronan's most recent borrowing rate was 8 percent.

Feb. 1, 1994	Equipment	100 000	
	Notes Payable		100 000
Dec. 31, 1994	Depreciation Expense	10 000	
	Accumulated Depreciation—		
	Equipment		10 000

Buildings. A building was acquired on June 1, 1994, by issuing 100 000 of the company's no-par value common shares. The common shares are not widely traded, therefore no market price is available. The average amount of the outstanding common shares is $5.00. The building was appraised on the transaction date at $650 000.

June 1, 1994	Building	500 000	
	Common Shares (100 000 × $5)		500 000
Dec. 31, 1994	Depreciation Expense	20 000	
	Accumulated Depreciation—		
	Building		20 000

Inventory/Fixtures. Inventory and display fixtures were acquired for $125 000 cash on April 1, 1995, from a competitor who was liquidating her business. The estimated value of the inventory was $85 000 and the value of the fixtures was $55 000.

Apr. 1, 1995	Inventory	85 000	
	Display Fixtures	55 000	
	Cash		125 000
	Gain on Acquisition of Inventory and		
	Fixtures		15 000

Land. Land was donated to Cronan by the city of North Bay in September 1995 as an inducement to build a facility there. Plans call for construction at an undetermined future date. The land was appraised at $48 500. No entry was made.

Machinery. Machinery was acquired in an exchange for similar equipment on October 12, 1995. The assets surrendered had originally cost $52 500, had $16 000 accumulated depreciation, and were appraised at $45 000 on the date of the exchange. Cronan received machinery valued at $40 000 and $5000 in cash in the transaction.

Oct. 12, 1994	Machinery	40 000	
	Cash	5 000	
	Accumulated Depreciation—Machinery	16 000	
	Machinery		52 500
	Gain on Exchange of Machinery		8 500
Dec. 31, 1994	Depreciation Expense	4 000	
	Accumulated Depreciation—		
	Machinery		4 000

Additional Information

Cronan uses straight-line depreciation applied to all assets as follows:

(1) A full year's depreciation taken in the year of acquisition and no depreciation taken in the year of disposal.
(2) Estimated life: 25 years for buildings; 10 years on all other assets. (No salvage values are assumed.)

Instructions

For each of the items of property, plant, and equipment above.

(a) Describe the error(s) made in recording the assets and related depreciation, if any.
(b) Prepare journal entries to correct the accounts and to properly record depreciation for 1995. The books for 1995 have not been adjusted or closed.

Cases

C12.1 Internally Constructed Assets. Five years ago, Martin Manufacturing, Inc. began producing "probos," a new type of instrument it hoped to sell to doctors, dentists, and hospitals. The demand for probos far exceeded initial expectations, and the company was unable to produce enough probos to meet the demand.

The company was manufacturing its product on equipment that it built at the start of its operations. To meet demand, more efficient equipment was needed. The company decided to design and build the equipment, since what was currently available on the market was unsuitable.

In 1995, a section of the plant was devoted to development of the new equipment and a special staff was hired. Within six months, a machine was developed at a cost of $170 000 that successfully increased production and reduced labour costs. Sparked by the success, the company built three more machines at a cost of $80 000 each.

Instructions

(a) In addition to satisfying a need that outsiders cannot meet within the desired time, why might a firm construct capital assets for its own use?
(b) In general, what costs should be capitalized for a self-constructed capital asset?
(c) Discuss the reasonableness of including in the capitalized cost of self-constructed assets
  (1) The increase in overhead caused by the self-construction of capital assets.
  (2) A proportionate share of overhead on the same basis as that applied to goods manufactured for sale.
(d) Discuss the proper accounting treatment of the $90 000 difference by which the cost of the first machine exceeded the cost of the subsequent machines.
(Adapted from AICPA.)

C12.2 Land and Building Cost. Travis Limited purchased land for use as its corporate headquarters. A small factory that was on the land when it was purchased was torn down before construction of the office building began. A substantial amount of rock blasting and removal had to be done before construction of the building foundation could begin. Because the office building was set back on the land far from the public road, Travis had the contractor construct a paved road that led from the public road to the parking lot of the office building.

Three years after the office building was occupied, Travis added four storeys to it. The four storeys had an estimated useful life of five years more than the remaining estimated useful life of the original office building.

Ten years later, the land and building were sold at an amount more than their net book value, and Travis had a new office building constructed in another province for use as its new corporate headquarters.

Instructions

(a) Which of the above expenditures should be capitalized? How should each be depreciated or amortized? Discuss the rationale for your answers.

(b) How would the sale of the land and building be accounted for? Include in your answer how to determine the net book value at the date of sale. Discuss the rationale for your answer.

(Adapted from AICPA.)

Judgement Cases **J12.1 Repair and Maintenance.** Seaborne Carriers, Inc., is involved in the transport of petroleum by oil tankers throughout the world. The company has typically accounted for its major repair and maintenance costs by charging them to expense when related liabilities are incurred. Seaborne has become aware of the generally accepted accounting practice in the airline industry, by which the anticipated costs of major repairs and maintenance are charged to operations as an expense over the period that the asset is used prior to the actual repair or maintenance activity being performed. For example, jet engines must be maintained carefully and at precise points of use measured in hours. The costs of the maintenance are charged as an expense while the aircraft is used, rather than only at the point at which the maintenance must be performed. The propriety of this accounting is well recognized in the airline industry.

Seaborne Carriers wishes to use the same type of accounting for the regularly scheduled maintenance and repairs that are performed on its vessels. The president says to you, "What's good for the goose is good for the gander, and this will more closely match the costs of our operations with the revenues that are generated at the same time. Further, with all the present environmental concerns, we can demonstrate our commitment to proper maintenance programs."

You have not thought about this idea before as you are not skilled in airline industry accounting. As a result of a discussion with a staff person at the CICA, you are now aware that such accounting is considered appropriate for airlines but that other industries typically have not adopted such procedures because no liability has been incurred prior to the performance of the maintenance and no obligation exists to maintain equipment. Generally, the charge for depreciation expense is thought to measure the cost of using the asset during a period of time. You are aware that airlines do depreciate their equipment in normal fashion.

Instructions

Would you be willing to accept the accounting proposed by Seaborne Carriers for their scheduled maintenance and repair activities? Explain the rationale for your position.

J12.2 Capitalization of Interest. Adaptable, Inc., is a real estate developer that constructs and, on occasion, operates large commercial buildings (e.g., warehouses, office buildings, and apartment complexes). One of the buildings that the company recently completed and is operating is a medical office building near a large hospital. Interest and other construction costs were appropriately charged to the building during its construction. The original plan was to lease office space to physicians and other professionals associated with the hospital. That plan, however, has not proven successful, and occupancy rates have remained relatively low.

Now, Adaptable has decided to convert the building into an apartment complex to rent primarily to hospital employees and students enrolled in the hospital's nursing school. The company estimates that the conversion will take about a year, and it is wondering whether it will be able to capitalize interest on the entire cost of the asset during its conversion period. That is, will the entire cost of the asset now recorded on the books of the company and the costs incurred on the conversion qualify as expenditures on which interest should be capitalized during the construction period? The president of Adaptable is particularly anxious to capitalize as much interest as possible. He tells you, "We are going to have a small bottom line next year anyway, and this would certainly help keep income as high as possible."

Instructions

Should interest be capitalized during the conversion period? If so, what amount of average accumulated expenditures should be used to calculate the amount of interest to be capitalized? That is, should the amount of average accumulated expenditures include the total cost of the asset to Adaptable or be limited to the new expenditures made to accomplish the conversion?

Chapter 13

Property, Plant, and Equipment: Depreciation, Depletion, and Special Problems

Objectives

1. To describe the depreciation process as an application of the matching principle in accounting for property, plant, and equipment.

2. To describe and illustrate depreciation methods that are commonly used in practice, including methods based on time and on activity level.

3. To discuss accounting for natural resources and the related amortization of historical cost through the depletion process.

4. To illustrate typical presentations of capital assets and related disclosures of depreciation in the primary financial statements and related notes.

5. To introduce the accounting treatment of changes in estimates and corrections of errors affecting capital assets.

Revenue–Expense Association

Matching principle is a term used to identify the process by which accountants determine net income. Matching involves recognizing revenues associated with business activities during a certain period and identifying expenses related to the generation of those revenues. The difference between these revenues and expenses is the **net income** of the enterprise for that period.

Three principles govern the inclusion of an expenditure (or part of an expenditure) as an expense in the matching process for a particular time period. The principles are (1) associating cause and effect, (2) systematic and rational allocation, and (3) immediate recognition.[1]

Associating cause and effect refers to the fact that some expenditures are directly associated with specific revenues and, thus, are included in determining net income for the period in which those revenues are received. For example, certain manufacturing costs, such as direct materials and direct labour, are directly related to items of inventory produced and help to determine income when those items are sold.

Systematic and rational allocation explains the accounting recognition of those costs that do not have a direct cause-and-effect relationship on the generation of revenue but that are recognized as expenses in an attempt to allocate costs in a systematic and rational manner among several accounting periods. An expenditure that is made in one period but provides benefits to several accounting periods, such as the cost of a capital asset, provides an example of the need for interperiod allocations in the determination of income.

Immediate recognition explains the inclusion of certain costs in determining income, because expenditures of the current period (or those carried forward from previous periods) have no discernible future benefits. The recognition of certain expenses, such as research and development, and the expensing of items that do not result in increased revenues, such as the write-off of obsolete equipment, exemplify the immediate recognition of costs in determining income.

The Depreciation Process

Accounting for property, plant, and equipment when they enter the productive processes of an enterprise is best described by systematic and rational allocation. We have seen in Chapter 12 that capital assets are acquired for the purpose of being used in the production or distribution of other goods or services and are expected to provide service over a relatively long period. With the exception of land, plant assets are believed to possess valuable but limited economic usefulness to the enterprise holding the rights to the service potential of the assets.

Depreciation Defined

Asset/Liability Measurement

Capital assets are measured and recorded at historical cost, and that cost is allocated to the periods that benefit from the use of the assets on the basis of several estimates concerning their use. In theory, the accountant prefers to allocate the cost of property, plant, and equipment in a manner that is proportionate to the contribution that the assets make to the generation of revenue each period. In other words, the greater the contribution to

---

[1]"Financial Statement Concepts," CICA *Handbook*, Paragraphs 1000.50–51, March 1991.

revenue for a particular accounting period, the more depreciation expense should be charged for a given asset. However, because of the uncertainties surrounding the precise pattern in which a given asset contributes to revenue, accountants estimate periodic depreciation by methods that include simplifying assumptions and that are both systematic and rational.

Cost allocation via depreciation does not measure the value of an asset; it is intended to recognize a portion of the cost of the asset as an expense each period in determining net income. Accordingly, **depreciation** is defined as the process of allocating the cost of property, plant, and equipment as an expense in a systematic and rational manner to those periods expected to benefit from the use of these assets.

A common misconception is that the depreciation process provides a cash fund that is available for the replacement of the asset at the end of its useful life. Depreciation is a process of cost allocation intended primarily to determine net income during those accounting periods in which the asset is used as part of the revenue-producing process. When **periodic depreciation** is recognized, cash is not affected. The company may set aside cash for the replacement of depreciable assets at the end of their useful lives, but this would be done in addition to the recognition of depreciation expense for purposes of determining income. Setting aside cash to replace capital assets is not a common practice among business enterprises.

The assumption that the economic usefulness or service potential of capital assets declines over time is supported by the realities of the process of producing and distributing goods and services. Declining service potential is caused by changes in both the asset and the environment in which the asset is used.

The changes in property, plant, and equipment that support the notion of declining service potential result from routine wear and tear, deterioration, and other effects of constant use in normal business operations. Over time, these **physical factors** result in a decline in the future service potential of the assets and provide support for allocating the acquisition cost of capital assets as an expense. Due to the finite service potential of most capital assets, use of the assets in one period results in a decline in the service potential available for use in future periods.

Changes in the environment in which property, plant, and equipment are used, sometimes called **functional factors**, also influence the amount of future service potential present in an asset at a given time. Business expansion and growth may render a capital asset obsolete. At that time the asset is **inadequate for the intended purpose**, although it may still be suitable for its original purpose and may prove quite useful to another enterprise. For example, adequate buildings acquired at the inception of a business may become limited in their future service potential when unexpected growth requires larger facilities for efficient operation.

Supercession, on the other hand, results when an enterprise acquires improved assets that are capable of providing the same service as present capital assets at an increased level of efficiency or at a significantly reduced cost. **Obsolescence** broadly refers to the decline in future service potential due to the functional factors relating to the environment in which the enterprise operates rather than to a decrease in the asset's physical utility. Functional factors include inadequacy, supercession, and other changes that affect the asset's potential to provide future service.

Estimates Required in the Depreciation Process

Asset/Liability Measurement

The depreciation process requires several estimates concerning property, plant, and equipment. Measuring capital assets at historical cost involves estimates, assumptions, and allocations, many of which are described in Chapter 12. These include the treatment of acquisition-related costs, the capitalization of interest costs, the treatment of overhead for internally constructed assets, and others. Nevertheless, the historical cost of capital assets is better described as an actual or computed figure than an estimate. However, other figures necessary to apply the depreciation process (i.e., the useful life and salvage value of the asset) are clearly estimates of future events.

Allocating the cost of an asset over future periods requires an estimate of its **useful life**, which may be expressed in **time** (e.g., months or years), **productive output** (e.g., units produced), or **service quantities** (e.g., machine hours operated or kilometres driven). The logical basis for estimating useful life varies from asset to asset. Accountants attempt to identify the measure of useful life that is most closely associated with the decline in the service potential of the asset. Time is usually the measure used for buildings, furniture, and fixtures. The useful life of machinery that turns out identifiable products may be appropriately stated in terms of a variable measuring productive output. In still other cases, service capacity (determined by some physical quantity used or consumed) may be appropriate; for example, kilometres driven may provide the best estimate of the useful life of a vehicle. Regardless of the nature of the depreciable asset, however, **an estimate of the useful life must be made** in order to identify the period over which the asset will be depreciated. This life may be identified by a number of titles, all of which have common meanings: service life, economic life, estimated useful life, and other similar terms.

In all widely used methods, the depreciation amount is the difference between the historical cost of the asset and the estimated salvage value expected to accrue to the asset holder at the end of the useful life. Thus, the residual value of the asset when it is no longer useful to the enterprise must be estimated. In some methods, this estimate must be made initially, when the depreciation schedule is established. In other cases, this estimate can be deferred until later in the life of the asset.

The amount expected to be available at the end of the service life is identified by a variety of terms with common meanings: residual value, salvage value, and other similar terms. Any anticipated costs of preparing the asset for disposal at the end of its expected useful life should be treated as reductions in the residual value for purposes of determining depreciation. The estimates of useful life and residual value are based on the expected usefulness of the asset to the present owner.

Regardless of the method selected, depreciation is recorded at the end of each accounting period by an adjusting entry in which Depreciation Expense is debited and Accumulated Depreciation is credited, as discussed in Chapter 6. The depreciation expense then becomes a component of income determination for that period and represents an application of the matching principle. The increase in accumulated depreciation further reduces the book value of the asset as presented in the balance sheet.

Matching

Depreciation Estimation Methods: Individual Assets

Several methods have been developed to apply the general concept of depreciation to property, plant, and equipment. These methods combine the historical cost, the estimated useful life, and the estimated residual value of the asset with certain assumptions about the pattern of decline in the asset's service potential.

This section discusses several methods for determining periodic depreciation for individual assets. These methods can be classified as those based on time and those based on activity level:

Depreciation Methods Based on Time

1. Straight line
2. Accelerated
   a. Double-declining balance (diminishing)
   b. Sum-of-the-years'-digits (Appendix A at the end of this chapter)
3. Annuity or sinking fund (Appendix A at the end of this chapter)

Depreciation Methods Based on Activity Level

1. Productive output
2. Service quantity

Several additional depreciation methods are discussed briefly in Appendix A at the end of this chapter. Many of these are infrequently used methods for depreciating individual assets. The other methods presented in Appendix A are applied to capital assets in groups rather than individually.

Exhibit 13.1 contains a summary of the results from a survey of 300 Canadian companies. It is clear from these findings that it is important for Canadian accounting students to have a good understanding of the three methods of depreciation that are most widely used in Canada. These three methods will be presented in this chapter.

Periodic depreciation expense determined by any of the methods based on time can be computed in advance and will be the same regardless of the level of activity during the period. Depreciation determined by any method based on activity level results in the determination of a constant depreciation charge per unit of activity. Depreciation expense for any single period is then computed at the end of that period and is based on the activity level achieved during the period.

To illustrate the depreciation methods in this section, the following asset is assumed:

Asset 147

Cost	$12 000
Estimated salvage value	$ 2 000
Estimated life	
In years	5
In units of output	25 000
In service hours	60 000

It would be unusual to have a depreciable asset for which the useful life could be stated equally well in terms of years, units of output, and service hours. The example here includes all three only to facilitate the illustration and comparison of the different methods, and we indicate the circumstances most appropriate for applying an individual method.

Straight-Line Method

The **straight-line method** of depreciation is simple and results in the same amount of depreciation expense for each full year in the life of an asset. The depreciation charge is based on the **passage of time** rather than the level of productive activity.

Periodic depreciation under the straight-line method is computed as follows (D = depreciation):

$$D = \frac{Cost - Salvage\ value}{Number\ of\ years\ in\ asset's\ life}$$

Exhibit 13.1 Disclosure of Depreciation, Depletion, and Amortization Methods Used in Canada

| | Percentage | | | |
	1990	1989	1988	1987
Straight-line	61.8	61.1	61.0	60.0
Diminishing balance	21.0	21.6	21.3	21.5
Unit of production	16.3	16.4	16.8	17.6
Sinking fund	0.9	0.9	0.9	0.9
	100.0	100.0	100.0	100.0

Source: Reprinted from *Financial Reporting in Canada,* Nineteenth Edition (Toronto: CICA, 1991), p. 151.

Depreciation for the first year (D_1) for Asset 147 is computed as follows:

$$D_1 = \frac{\$12\,000 - \$2000}{5}$$
$$= \$2000$$

Due to the straightforward nature of the calculation, the absence of complicating assumptions, and the ease of understanding, the straight-line method is widely practised. The method is conceptually appropriate if the decline in service potential relates primarily to the passage of time rather than to the level of activity, and if the decline is thought to be approximately the same amount each period. The straight-line method may also provide a reasonable basis for depreciation when the level of activity is important but the use of the asset is relatively constant from period to period.

Applying the straight-line method to the five-year life of Asset 147, we arrive at the schedule in Exhibit 13.2. The book value at the end of the fifth year is the $2000 salvage value originally used to determine the total depreciation to be charged ($10 000). The book value at the end of each year is the amount presented as an asset in the enterprise's balance sheet. The financial statement disclosure requirements for capital assets are covered in a later section of this chapter.

Accelerated Method

Accelerated depreciation methods, sometimes referred to as **diminishing-charge methods,** are designed to recognize greater amounts of depreciation in the early years of an asset's life and smaller amounts in the later years. Of the several variations of accelerated depreciation, the most widely used is the double-declining balance method, which is presented in this section. Even though the amount of depreciation varies from year to year with accelerated methods, depreciation is still based on the passage of time; it is computed in advance and is based on the estimated of useful life. The salvage value is not included in the calculation of the annual depreciation. The salvage value should equal the undepreciated balance that remains at the end of the asset's useful life.

Accelerated depreciation methods emerged out of income tax law, which allows companies to take more depreciation in the early years of an asset's life than in later years. As we discuss later in this section, the use of accelerated depreciation for income tax purposes does not necessitate its use for financial reporting purposes. However, acceler-

Exhibit 13.2 Depreciation Schedule for Asset 147: Straight-Line Method

End of Year	Depreciation Entry: Dr.: Depreciation Expense Cr.: Accumulated Depreciation	Balance: Accumulated Depreciation	Book Value
			$12 000
1	$2 000	$ 2 000	10 000
2	2 000	4 000	8 000
3	2 000	6 000	6 000
4	2 000	8 000	4 000
5	2 000	10 000	2 000

ated depreciation may be conceptually sound if the declining pattern of expense recognition is consistent with the actual contribution the asset makes to the revenue-generating process.

Accelerated depreciation methods are conceptually attractive when an asset is believed to provide superior performance (i.e., operate with greater efficiency) in the early years of its life. Further support for accelerated depreciation is found in the expected pattern of repair and maintenance. If repair and maintenance costs are expected to increase during the life of the asset, declining depreciation charges coupled with increasing repair and maintenance charges result in a pattern of expense recognition that may relate more closely to the decline in service potential than would result from other depreciation methods. The potential for obsolescence is also cited as a reason for using accelerated depreciation: the greater charges to income in the early years of the asset's life reduce the book value early, and reduce the probability that a significant write-off will have to be made later because of a permanent impairment in value due to obsolescence.

Double-Declining Balance Method

The **double-declining balance method** is a type of accelerated depreciation in which the charge in early years exceeds that of later years. In the double-declining balance method, a **constant percentage** is multiplied by a **declining base**. The most common application of this method uses the constant percentage based on twice some multiple of the straight-line rate.

The difference between the double-declining balance and the declining-balance methods is that the declining-balance method only uses some multiple of the straight-line rate; the rate is not doubled. This fixed percentage is then applied to the declining book value of the asset, giving a depreciation figure that declines throughout the life of the asset. **The book value, however, should never be reduced below the estimated salvage value.**

The double-declining balance rate is computed as twice the straight-line rate, as follows (DDB = double-declining balance):

$$\text{DDB\%} = \frac{100\%}{\text{Life in years}} \times 2$$

For Asset 147, this rate is 40 percent:

$$\text{DDB\%} = \frac{100\%}{5} \times 2$$

$$= 40\%$$

Applying 40 percent to the declining book value of Asset 147 and ignoring salvage value until the book value is reduced to salvage value, we compute the depreciation for each year in the asset's life as follows:

$$D_1 = 40\% \ (\$12 \ 000) = \$4800$$
$$D_2 = 40\% \ (\$12 \ 000 - \$4800) = \$2880$$
$$D_3 = 40\% \ [\$12 \ 000 - (\$4800 + \$2880)] = \$1728$$
$$D_4 = \$10 \ 000 - (\$4800 + \$2880 + \$1728) = \$592$$

Depreciation at 40% of the book value cannot be taken in Year 4 because this would reduce book value below the $2000 salvage value expected. Likewise, no depreciation can be taken in Year 5. Some companies avoid this problem by systematically switching to straight-line at the point where it exceeds declining balance.

Exhibit 13.3 shows a schedule for Asset 147 that results from applying the double-declining balance method.

Productive-Output Method

The **productive-output** (or **units of output**) **method** uses the output of capital assets as a basis for recognizing periodic depreciation. The rationale is that some assets are capable of producing a determinable number of units of productive output, and depreciation should be recognized in relation to the portion of that output that occurs in each accounting period.

A cost factor **per unit of output** is first calculated. This factor is then applied to the actual output for the period to determine the depreciation charge. Depreciation expense cannot be determined in advance, because it is dependent on the level of output during the period. The depreciation computation using the productive-output method is generalized as follows:

$$D = \frac{Cost - Salvage \ value}{Life \ in \ units \ of \ output} \times Units \ of \ output \ for \ period$$

The first element in the computation may be stated as depreciation rate per unit of output. Applying this concept to Asset 147 results in a cost per unit of $0.40:

$$Estimated \ cost \ per \ unit \ of \ output = \frac{\$12 \ 000 - \$2 \ 000}{25 \ 000 \ units}$$
$$= \$0.40$$

We will assume that units are produced in Years 1 to 5 in the following pattern: 4000, 9000, 8000, 2000, and 2000. Depreciation can then be computed for each year by applying the $0.40 cost per unit to the units of output:

$$D_1 = \$0.40 \times 4000 = \$1600$$
$$D_2 = \$0.40 \times 9000 = \$3600$$
$$D_3 = \$0.40 \times 8000 = \$3200$$
$$D_4 = \$0.40 \times 2000 = \$800$$
$$D_5 = \$0.40 \times 2000 = \$800$$

Exhibit 13.3 Depreciation Schedule for Asset 147: Double-Declining Balance Method

End of Year	Depreciation Entry: Dr.: Depreciation Expense Cr.: Accumulated Depreciation	Balance: Accumulated Depreciation	Book Value
—	—	—	$12 000
1	$4 800	$ 4 800	7 200
2	2 880	7 680	4 320
3	1 728	9 408	2 592
4	592	10 000	2 000
5	—	10 000	2 000

Exhibit 13.4 shows the schedule that results for Asset 147 when the productive-output method is applied to the five years in the asset's life. As in the other methods, the book value at the end of five years equals the expected salvage value of $2000, because the total amount of the recognized depreciation expense is $10 000.

The productive-output method is suitable only if the asset provides a separate, identifiable unit of product, as is the case with equipment used to manufacture items of inventory. The productivity of many capital assets, such as buildings and fixtures, however, cannot be measured in terms of a unit of output. In such cases, the productive-output method is *not* appropriate. For those assets whose contribution to operations can best be measured in terms of units of productive output, this method is particularly suitable if the decline in service potential is thought to be more closely tied to the production of units than to the passage of time. If an asset is used very little in a period, depreciation by the productive-output method will be low; if the level of activity is high, depreciation will be high. If obsolescence or additional factors other than physical output are considered important in determining the pattern of decline in the asset's service potential from period to period, the productive-output method is not suitable.

Service-Quantity Method

The productivity of some assets is best measured in terms of service quantity; for example, we state the productivity of certain machinery in terms of operating hours and the productivity of vehicles in terms of kilometres. While the mechanics of applying the service-quantity method are similar to those of the productive-output method, the concepts underlying the methods are somewhat different.

Under the **service-quantity method,** the contribution to operations is stated in terms of **productive-input factors** rather than output of the production process. Accordingly, depreciation recognized in any period is dependent on the quantity of the productive-input factor consumed in the use of the asset during that period. The amount of the productive input is limited, and the depreciable amount (cost less salvage value) is recognized as an expense on the basis of the expiration of this limited quantity of productive inputs.

Depreciation under the service-quantity method is generalized as follows:

$$D = \frac{\text{Cost } - \text{ Salvage value}}{\text{Total quantity of productive service}} \times \text{Productive service for period}$$

Exhibit 13.4 Depreciation Schedule for Asset 147: Productive-Output Method

End of Year	Depreciation Entry: Dr.: Depreciation Expense Cr.: Accumulated Depreciation	Balance: Accumulated Depreciation	Book Value
—	—	—	$12 000
1	$1 600	$ 1 600	10 400
2	3 600	5 200	6 800
3	3 200	8 400	3 600
4	800	9 200	2 800
5	800	10 000	2 000

As in the productive-output method, the first factor may be stated as a depreciation rate per unit of productive service. For Asset 147, the appropriate service quantity is 60 000 service hours, resulting in a cost per hour of $0.1667:

$$\text{Estimated cost per unit of productive service} = \frac{\$12\ 000 - \$2000}{60\ 000\ \text{hours}}$$
$$= \$0.1667$$

The asset is used during Years 1 to 5 for the following service hours: 14 000, 15 000, 20 000, 4000, and 7000. Depreciation is computed for each year as follows:

$$D_1 = \$0.1667 \times 14\ 000 = \$2334$$
$$D_2 = \$0.1667 \times 15\ 000 = \$2501$$
$$D_3 = \$0.1667 \times 20\ 000 = \$3334$$
$$D_4 = \$0.1667 \times \ 4\ 000 = \$\ 667$$
$$D_5 = \$0.1667 \times \ 7\ 000 = \$1164$$

A $3 rounding adjustment is made in the D_5 computation.

Exhibit 13.5 shows the schedule for Asset 147 that results when we apply the service-quantity method to the five years in the asset's life.

The depreciation varies annually depending on the level of use of the asset during the period. If the decline in service potential relates to the physical use of the asset, the service-quantity method is appropriate. In particular, if the use of the asset varies from period to period, this method more realistically reflects the decline in service potential through depreciation expense than does a method that recognizes depreciation based on the passage of time but disregards the level of activity. If the decline in the service potential relates more to the passage of time or obsolescence, however, the straight-line or an accelerated method is more suitable, even when the contribution of the asset is stated in terms of service quantities.

In our discussion of depreciation methods, we have used the same asset throughout, assuming that we could estimate useful life in terms of time, units of production, and service quantities. This was done for purposes of illustration only. As stated earlier, in practice only one of these would be used for any particular asset. In these illustrations, the fact that the exhaustion of service quantities or the completion of units of production took place precisely over a five-year period is of no particular relevance, because depre-

	Exhibit 13.5 Depreciation Schedule for Asset 147: Service-Quantity Method			
End of Year	Depreciation Entry: Dr.: Depreciation Expense Cr.: Accumulated Depreciation		Balance: Accumulated Depreciation	Book Value
—	—		—	$12 000
1	$2 334		$ 2 334	9 666
2	2 501		4 835	7 165
3	3 334		8 169	3 831
4	667		8 836	3 164
5	1 164		10 000	2 000

ciation would be based on only one of these variables (service quantities, units of production, or passage of time) for any particular asset.

What is the proper accounting treatment when fully depreciated assets continue to be used by an enterprise? Obviously, the estimate of useful life in terms of either time or activity level proved to be inaccurate, even if it was based on the best information available at the time. The cost and accumulated depreciation of fully depreciated assets should remain in the accounts as long as the assets are actively used, even though these figures effectively cancel each other out in the determination of book value. The use of fully depreciated capital assets in the revenue-producing process presents a theoretical problem, because no portion of the cost of these assets is included among expenses. This violates the matching principle. If fully depreciated assets make significant contributions to revenue, this fact should be disclosed in the financial statements. This is usually not a major problem, because fully depreciated assets still in use are usually not an important part of total assets.

Matching

Disclosure

Capital Cost Allowance

Capital cost allowance (CCA) is the term used to depreciate assets under Canadian income tax laws. The rates and rules of CCA have no direct relationship to the depreciation methods used under GAAP. CCA is organized into classes, with each class having a different rate. Some of the classes were introduced to stimulate certain sectors of the economy. The same type of equipment used for the same purpose, but purchased in different years, may qualify as a different class of asset under the income tax act. The following are two examples of CCA classes:

Class	Rate(%)	Description
22	50	Most power operated movable equipment you bought before 1988 that you use for excavating, moving, placing or compacting earth, rock, concrete or asphalt.
38	30	Most power operated movable equipment you bought after 1987 that you use for excavating, moving, placing or compacting earth, rock, concrete or asphalt.[2]

CCA should only be deducted on assets available for use with "available for use" being when an enterprise first earns income from the assets or the second year after the

[2]Canada, *Canadian Income Tax Act 1991*, Bill C-28 (Ottawa: May 30, 1991, amended Dec. 17, 1991).

year in which it acquires the assets in question. In the year of acquisition, CCA is the rate for the class multiplied by the acquisition cost less any proceeds of disposal for the class times one-half. In other words, in the first year of the use of an asset, only half of the CCA amount can be deducted for tax purposes.

Assume that Asset 147 qualifies under Class 28. Applying 30 percent to the cost of Asset 147 ($12 000), we compute the CCA for each year in the asset's life as follows:

$$D_1 = 30\% \ (\$12\ 000) = \$3600 \times \tfrac{1}{2} = \$1800$$
$$D_2 = 30\% \ (\$12\ 000 - \$1800) = \$3060$$
$$D_3 = 30\% \ [\$12\ 000 - (\$1800 + \$3060)] = \$2142$$
$$D_4 = 30\% \ [\$12\ 000 - (\$1800 + \$3060 + \$2142)] = \$1499.40$$

The differences between CCA and the depreciation methods used for the preparation of the financial statements results in the need for **deferred tax allocation credits and/or debits** in the accounting records. This topic will be covered in more depth in Chapter 19, which deals with accounting for income taxes in financial reporting. Companies may use different accounting methods for financial reporting and for income tax purposes. Regardless of this option, many small companies use their tax methods for their financial statements to avoid keeping two sets of records. The objective of selecting a depreciation method for financial reporting purposes is to properly match revenues and expenses. The inability to directly associate the decline in service potential of capital assets with revenues produced by those assets, however, precludes precise measurements of the amount of cost to treat as depreciation each period. Thus, methods designed primarily for income tax purposes frequently become a part of financial reporting on the basis that the tax methods are consistent with the matching principle. Also, the differences in amounts between accounting and income tax methods may be immaterial when placed in the context of a company's financial statements.

Matching

Materiality

Chapter 19 discusses capital cost allowance in greater detail and considers more carefully the differences between the way the cost of capital assets is recognized in financial statements and the way cost is recognized in preparing tax returns. At this point, simply keep in mind that it is acceptable and, in fact, sometimes even mandatory for companies to use different methods in preparing financial statements from those used in preparing income tax returns. Depreciation is one of those areas in which this frequently occurs.

Selecting an Appropriate Depreciation Method

We have discussed several factors that should be considered when a company selects a depreciation method: physical use, expected obsolescence, expected pattern of decline in usefulness, periodic contribution of the asset to the revenue-producing process, and others. These considerations are often difficult, if not impossible, to quantify, and they sometimes offset one another, resulting in some uncertainty about the most appropriate method in a given set of circumstances. The authoritative literature suggests only that the depreciation method be both systematic and rational.

Often, *practical* rather than conceptual considerations govern the selection of a depreciation method. For example, the simplicity of the straight-line method explains its frequent use in accounting practice. Companies may deduct the maximum amount permitted by CCA for income tax purposes and use straight-line depreciation for financial reporting, thereby reducing taxable income and deferring income tax payments without reducing the net income reported in the early years of the assets' lives. This combination is particularly popular among rapidly expanding companies that invest additional amounts in capital assets on a continuous basis. In other cases, however, when simplicity influences the choice, a company will use CCA for both income tax reporting and financial reporting to avoid the cost and inconvenience of retaining two sets of depreciation records. In many cases, depreciation methods used in the past are applied to new assets without any real consideration of the appropriateness of those methods. In some cases, depreciation methods used by other companies with which the enterprise may be compared may influence the choice of depreciation method.

Consistency

Consistency is an important accounting principle when considering the depreciation of capital assets or any accounting policy. Once a depreciation method is selected for a particular asset or class of assets, that method should be used consistently from period to period so that the net incomes of successive accounting periods are comparable.

In summary, it is difficult to generalize about how companies determine the depreciation methods they use. Conceptual as well as practical considerations are important, and consistency over time must also be considered.

Fractional-Year Problems

In the previous examples, we have assumed that the **depreciation year** and the **financial reporting period** are the same. That is, Asset 147 was acquired at the beginning of a reporting period and a full year's depreciation was taken in that year. However, capital assets are not always acquired at the beginning of a fiscal period. Likewise, assets are not always disposed of at the end of the period. The problem of accounting for depreciation for assets acquired and disposed of at various times during the year is frequently encountered in applying all of the methods that were discussed in the previous section. The computation of depreciation expense differs, however, only for those methods in which depreciation is based on the passage of time. Depreciation for partial years under the activity-based methods is computed in the same way as for full years of use, because the expense is based on productive output or service quantity rather than a time period.

Numerous policies may be adopted in applying depreciation methods in reporting periods when assets have been held for only part of the period. This may occur twice in the life of every asset: once in the period of acquiring the asset and once in the period of disposing of the asset. Only if acquisition and disposal transactions occur on or very close to the first and last days of the financial reporting period are the problems of depreciation for partial years avoided.

To illustrate several problems and alternative approaches to depreciation for partial years, we will use the example of Asset 286.

Asset 286

Cost	$100 000
Estimated salvage value	None
Estimated life in years	4
Date of acquisition	Aug. 10
Financial reporting period	Jan. 1–Dec. 31

A fractional-year problem exists because the four years in the asset's life do not correspond precisely to four financial reporting years.

Financial reporting years:

Depreciation years:

The first depreciation year begins during the first financial reporting year and ends during the second financial reporting year. This sequence continues throughout the life of Asset 286, with the financial reporting periods following a January-through-December pattern and the depreciation years following an August-to-August pattern.

A number of policies may be adopted for the fractional-year problem that exists in the first and last years of the asset's life. Several of these are applied to Asset 286 in Exhibit 13.6, which uses the straight-line method of depreciation.

Several observations are possible concerning these approaches to the fractional-year problem. Policy 1 is widely practised and results in the most precise recognition of depreciation in terms of time. Because depreciation computations incorporate numerous assumptions and estimates, computations based on a period of time shorter than one month are rarely made. In the case of Asset 286, five months (August–December) of depreciation are recognized in the first financial reporting period, because the asset was acquired in the first half of August. Seven months of depreciation remain to be recognized in the fifth financial reporting period. Under Policy 2, no depreciation is taken in the first year, because the enterprise acquired the asset in the last half of the year. If the asset had been acquired in the first half, a full year's depreciation would have been taken in the first year and none in the last year. Under Policy 3, depreciation is recognized to the nearest half year. Thus, if the asset is acquired in the period of January–March, a full year's depreciation is taken in the first year. If the asset is acquired in the period April–September, a half year's depreciation is taken; and if the asset is acquired in the period October–December, no depreciation is taken. Under Policies 1, 2, and 3, the date of the acquisition of the asset influences the amount of depreciation recognized in the first and last years.

Policies 4, 5, and 6 differ from Policies 1, 2, and 3 in that assets are treated in the same way, regardless of when they are acquired. Under Policy 4, a half-year's depreciation is taken in the first year and the same in the last year. Under Policy 5, a full year's depreciation is taken in the first year and none in the last year. Under Policy 6, no depreciation is taken in the first year, and a full year's depreciation is taken in the last year. Policies 5 and 6 resolve the fractional-year problem by forcing the depreciation year and the financial reporting year to coincide.

Applying fractional-year policies where accelerated depreciation methods are used varies only in that the amount of depreciation recognized declines each year. For example, with the double-declining balance method, Asset 286 would be depreciated as follows under Policies 1 and 3:

	Policy 1 **Nearest Full Month**	**Policy 3** **Nearest Half Year**
Year 1	$\$100\ 000 \times 50\% \times \dfrac{5\ \text{mo.}}{12\ \text{mo.}} = \underline{\underline{\$20\ 833}}$	$\$100\ 000 \times 50\% \times \frac{1}{2} = \underline{\underline{\$25\ 000}}$
Year 2	$\$100\ 000 \times 50\% \times \dfrac{7\ \text{mo.}}{12\ \text{mo.}} = \$29\ 167$	$\$100\ 000 \times 50\% \times \frac{1}{2} = \$25\ 000$
	$(\$100\ 000 - \$50\ 000) \times 50\% \times \dfrac{5\ \text{mo.}}{12\ \text{mo.}} = \underline{\quad 10\ 417}$	$(\$100\ 000 - \$50\ 000) \times 50\% \times \frac{1}{2} = \underline{\quad 12\ 500}$
	$\underline{\underline{\$39\ 584}}$	$\underline{\underline{\$37\ 500}}$

Exhibit 13.6 Alternative Approaches to Fractional-Year Problem for Asset 286: Straight-Line Method

Fractional-Year Policy (13)	Depreciation: Recognized in Financial Reporting Periods				
	1	2	3	4	5
1. Recognize depreciation to nearest full month.	10 417*	25 000**	25 000	25 000	14 583†
2. Recognize depreciation to nearest full year.	—	25 000	25 000	25 000	25 000
3. Recognize depreciation to nearest half year.	12 500‡	25 000	25 000	25 000	12 500
4. Recognize one-half year's depreciation in period of acquisition and one-half in period of disposal.	12 500	25 000	25 000	25 000	12 500
5. Recognize full-year's depreciation in period of acquisition and none in period of disposal.	25 000	25 000	25 000	25 000	—
6. Recognize no depreciation in period of acquisition and full year in period of disposal.	—	25 000	25 000	25 000	25 000

*$^{5}/_{12}$ (100 000/4)

** (100 000/4)

†$^{7}/_{12}$ (100 000/4)

‡(25 000 × ½)

Review

In the case of declining-balance, depreciation for the second and subsequent years can be computed directly by multiplying the percentage times the book value at the beginning of the year. For example, under Policy 1, the second year's depreciation is computed as follows: ($100 000 − $20 833) × 50% = $39 584. Under Policy 3, the second year's depreciation is computed as follows: ($100 000 − $25 000) × 50% = $37 500.

Consistency

The keys to applying fractional-year policies are practicality, logic, and consistency. If numerous assets are acquired and disposed of frequently and during various times of the year, all of the policies in Exhibit 13.6 are suitable for coping with the fractional-year problem. However, the policy selected must be applied consistently. Infrequent acquisitions and disposals of major assets that individually have a material impact on financial position and results of operations should be depreciated under an appropriate depreciation method to the nearest full month. *Policy #1*

Materiality

Natural Resources and Depletion

Business operations frequently use **natural resources,** sometimes referred to as **wasting assets.** Natural resources include coal, oil, ore, precious metals (e.g., silver, gold), and timber, and are characterized by their removal and consumption and, thus, the loss of physical characteristics. The replacement of natural resources comes about only by the process of nature and is not subject to human production. **Depletion** is the term used to describe the accounting procedure by which the costs of natural resources are allocated to expense as they contribute to the revenue-producing process.

(16)

Asset/Liability Measurement (16)

Accounting for natural resources parallels closely accounting for property, plant, and equipment. The measurement of a natural resource at historical cost is based on the sacrifice made to acquire the asset. The allocation of this cost over the quantities of the natural resource used to produce revenue (i.e., depletion) is typically computed on a unit basis, much like the units of output method of depreciation. This allocation matches revenues with expenses in the determination of periodic income. The book value of the natural resource at any time is that portion of the cost that has not been charged to income. Book value does not necessarily represent the current market value of the natural resource, because the book value is only a portion of the original cost of the asset. The

Matching

similarity between capital assets and natural resources is further emphasized by the fact that they are usually presented together in the balance sheet, with separate disclosure by major categories.

The **depletion rate,** an estimate of the cost per unit of the natural resource, is based on the historical cost reduced by any expected residual value after the natural resource has been fully exploited. The depletion rate is then applied to the number of units of the natural resource withdrawn during the period.

To illustrate the depletion process, we will assume that Universal Mining Company acquired the rights to mineral deposits for $2 250 000. Management expected 500 000 tonnes of the mineral to be economically removed and sold. If, during 1995, 65 000 tonnes are removed and sold, the depletion rate and depletion charge for the year are computed as follows:

$$\text{Depletion rate per tonne} = \frac{\$2\ 250\ 000}{500\ 000\ \text{t}} = \$4.50 \text{ per tonne}$$

$$\text{Cost of mineral removed in 1995} = (\$4.50 \times 65\ 000\ \text{t})$$
$$= \$292\ 500$$

Depletion is recognized by the following general journal entry:

Depletion Expense	292 500	
Accumulated Depletion		292 500

The natural resource and related depletion are shown in the balance sheet as follows:

Mineral deposits	$2 250 000	
Less: Accumulated depletion	(292 500)	$1 957 500

The depletion expense for the period ($292 500) is presented as a cost of production in the income statement.

If some portion of the natural resource is not sold and remains in inventory, that portion of the depletion will be included in the inventory cost and not charged to income as a cost in the period of production. For example, in the previous case, if 15 000 of the 65 000 tonnes extracted in 1995 remained in inventory at the end of the year, depletion expense and the cost of the depletable resource held in inventory would be as follows:

$$\begin{array}{lll}
\text{Depletion expense} = 50\ 000\ \text{t} \times \$4.50 & = & \$225\ 000 \\
\text{Inventory} = \underline{15\ 000}\ \text{t} \times \$4.50 & = & \underline{67\ 500} \\
\underline{\underline{65\ 000}} & & \underline{\underline{\$292\ 500}}
\end{array}$$

Although this process appears relatively straightforward and analogous to the depreciation process presented earlier in this chapter, several unique aspects of natural resources are frequently encountered. These aspects are discussed individually in the following sections:

1. The costs of exploration, development, and restoration.
2. The discovery of natural resources subsequent to acquisition.
3. The distribution of liquidating dividends.

Exploration, Development, and Restoration Costs

The cost of natural resources may include a variety of expenditures after the initial acquisition of a property or the purchase of rights to explore on another's property. **Exploration costs** are frequently incurred in attempts to locate the reserves of the natural resource that can be economically extracted. Sometimes these costs result in the location of reserves that can be economically exploited, and at other times, in the failure to locate reserves that can be economically exploited. This difference has led to two accounting methods for exploration costs. Under the **successful-efforts method,** only those exploration costs that can be associated with the discovery of producible reserves are considered to be a part of the depletion base of the natural resource; costs not associated with the discovery of producible reserves are expensed as incurred on the basis that they fail to represent future expected benefits. The alternative, the **full-cost method,** assumes that all exploration costs are necessary expenditures to discover the location of producible reserves and thus are a part of the cost of those producible reserves. Both methods are used in practice, and a great deal of controversy has surrounded the use of the two methods, particularly in the oil and gas industry. We discuss this controversy in greater depth in Chapter 14.

Development costs are expenditures that are necessary to exploit reserves of natural resources that have been located through successful exploration activities. Development costs in the form of tangible assets, such as machinery and equipment, tunnels, shafts, and wells, should be separately classified in appropriate asset accounts and depreciated over their estimated useful lives in accordance with normal depreciation policies. If these assets are limited in their usefulness to the development of a specific natural resource project, however, they should be depreciated over the life of that project by the same method used for the natural resource.

The property containing a natural resource may be sold after extraction activities are complete. The amount expected to be derived from such sale represents the salvage or residual value and reduces the depletion base. To prepare the property for sale, however, **restoration costs** may be necessary to return the property to its natural state. Restoration costs reduce the net amount expected to be received in the form of a salvage value, and therefore the calculation of depletion includes an amount of an accrued liability to cover restoration costs.

To illustrate, assume that for $1 750 000 Willow Mines acquires property believed to contain valuable minerals. The company incurs $500 000 in exploration costs and an additional $1 550 000 in tangible development costs before the mineral can be successfully extracted. Geological estimates indicate that 75 000 tonnes of the mineral is a reasonable estimate of the amount that can be economically extracted. Willow Mines expects to sell the property for $500 000 after exploitation. However, restoration costs of $150 000 will be required to prepare the property for sale. The depletion base and depletion rate per tonne are computed as follows:

Initial acquisition price		$1 750 000
Exploration costs		500 000
Development costs		1 550 000
Total acquisition cost		$3 800 000
Less: Estimated residual value	$ 500 000	
Restoration costs	(150 000)	(350 000)
Depletion base		$3 450 000
Depletion rate per tonne ($3 450 000/75 000 t)		$46

Assume 10 000 tonnes are mined and sold during the current year. The entry to record the depletion would be as follows:

Depletion Expense (10 000 t × $46)	460 000	
Accumulated Depletion		440 000
Accrued Liability for Restoration		20 000
(*Restoration*: $150 000/75 000 t = $2 per t)		

Discovery Subsequent to Acquisition

Natural resource reserves may be discovered on previously acquired property. In this case, the historical cost of the property does not include a price paid for the natural resource, because that resource was not known to exist at the time of purchase. In terms of including a reasonable depletion charge in the determination of income in future years, support exists for capitalizing discovery value and including it in the depletion base on which the periodic depletion charge is computed. Where the existence of the natural resource was known at the time of acquisition, the historical cost of the asset would reflect that fact and depletion should be based on cost.

Distribution of Liquidating Dividends

In some cases, the major business activity of a company centres around the exploitation of natural resources, and no plans exist for the replacement of the resource upon exhaustion. A common practice is to distribute dividends to shareholders in amounts up to the total of the retained earnings plus accumulated depletion. To the extent that dividends exceed the amount of retained earnings, however, distributions represent **liquidating dividends** or a **return of shareholders' investments** to them rather than a return on their investments.

To illustrate, we will assume that Huffman Limited has a retained earnings balance of $1 200 000 at December 31, 1995. Accumulated depletion on natural resources totals $1 million. Cash dividends of $2 million are declared. Common shares outstanding total 1 million. The entry to record the dividend is as follows, assuming that paid-in capital in excess of par of at least $800 000 exists:

Retained Earnings (or Dividends Declared)	1 200 000	
Common Shares	800 000	
Dividends Payable		2 000 000

Care must be taken to inform shareholders that the $2.00 dividend per share represents a $1.20 per share return on the investment and an $0.80 per share liquidating dividend.

The Allocation Problem

Matching

This chapter frequently points out that depreciation and depletion are cost allocation processes. They are an integral part of applying the matching principle to an enterprise's nonmonetary inputs, such as inventories and capital assets, to accounting periods for the purpose of determining net income. The costs that have not yet been assigned as expenses to an accounting period are maintained as assets in anticipation of future assignment as expenses. We are attempting to match the various **inputs** (costs) into an enterprise's revenue-producing process with the **outputs** (revenues) of that process.

As Arthur L. Thomas has indicated, however, the outputs of a process are the result of not only a number of inputs but also the *interaction* of those inputs:

> The allocation problem has several dimensions, some of which are subtle. But one is easily described: to match costs with revenues, we must know what the contributions of the firm's individual inputs are. Unfortunately. . . . there is no way to know this.
>
> Seeing why this is so requires introducing a final concept, interaction. Inputs to a process interact whenever they generate an output different from the total of what they would yield separately. For instance, labor and equipment interact whenever people and machines working together produce more goods than the total of what people could make with their bare hands and machines could make untended. As this example suggests, interaction is extremely common. Almost all of a firm's inputs interact with each other—their failure to do so would ordinarily signal their uselessness.
>
> Surprising as it may seem, it can be proved that whenever inputs interact, calculations of how much total revenue or cash flow has been contributed by any individual input are as meaningless as, say, calculations of the proportion of a worker's services due to any one internal organ: heart, liver or lungs. Thus, despite all textbooks and American Institute of CPAs or FASB releases to the contrary—despite what you have been trained to believe—our attempts to match costs with revenues must almost always fail.[3]

Matching

Does this interaction mean that the allocation of asset costs is futile and that we should not attempt to apply the matching principle? Not necessarily, but understanding the limitations of matching and cost allocation is important. Thomas further suggests that, wherever possible, the Financial Accounting Standards Board should develop accounting standards that do not rely on arbitrary allocation. Two primary allocation-free alternatives to conventional financial reporting exist: current value accounting and reporting of fund flows based on cash and near-cash assets. Where allocations cannot be eliminated in financial reporting, allocations should be kept simple. Complex cost allocation methods should be avoided, and care should be taken not to extend allocation methods to additional areas of financial reporting wherever possible.[4]

Financial Statement Presentation

Property, plant, and equipment have a significant impact on the financial position of business enterprises. For many enterprises, the investment in plant assets exceeds that of any other asset category. The method of depreciation used may also significantly influence the financial position and results of operations of the reporting enterprise.

Disclosure

The CICA *Handbook* identifies the following disclosure requirements in relation to capital assets to be included in the financial statements or in related notes:[5]

1. Depreciation expense for the period.
2. Balances of major classes of depreciable assets, by nature or function, at the balance sheet date.

---

[3]Arthur L. Thomas, "The FASB and the Allocation Fallacy," *Journal of Accountancy* (November 1975), p. 66.

[4]Arthur L. Thomas, "The FASB and the Allocation Fallacy," *Journal of Accountancy* (November 1975), p. 68.

[5]"Capital Assets," CICA *Handbook,* Paragraphs 3060.58–64, October 1990.

3. Accumulated depreciation, either by major classes of depreciable assets or in total, at the balance sheet date.

4. A general description in the method or methods used in computing depreciation with respect to major classes of depreciable assets.

Due to differences in assets of various enterprises and the flexibility permitted by the authoritative literature, information about capital assets is presented in numerous ways in financial statements. In Chapter 12, we reviewed the capital asset disclosure of TransCanada PipeLines Limited, in which only total amounts were presented in the balance sheet with detailed amounts for types of capital assets presented in a note to the financial statements (Exhibit 12.5). In Exhibit 13.7, we present the capital asset disclosure from the 1991 annual report of Petro-Canada. Petro-Canada is the largest Canadian-owned oil and gas company, with assets of $6 billion and revenue of nearly $5 billion in 1991. Exhibit 13.7 includes Note 14 from the 1991 annual report and an excerpt from the summary of accounting policies concerning property, plant and equipment, including depreciation. The consolidated balance sheet includes a single asset line, property, plant and equipment, at cost less accumulated depreciation and depletion, at $4.084 billion (1991) and $4.778 billion (1990). These amounts equal the totals in the third and sixth columns in Exhibit 13.7. In the consolidated income statement, depreciation and depletion are presented as one of several expense items at $396 million, $373 million and $407 million in 1989, 1990, and 1991, respectively.

Asset categories that are closely related are frequently combined to avoid unnecessary detail in the balance sheet. For example, land may be combined with land improvements or other closely related assets. Buildings may be combined with improvements, equipment, or other closely related assets.

Changes in Estimates and Corrections of Errors

Companies often have to change estimates incorporated in depreciation methods. They may also have to correct errors in past historical cost and depreciation amounts.

Changes in Estimates

Matching

Asset/Liability Measurement

As we have seen in studying depreciation and depletion, matching revenues and expenses requires several estimates. Measuring the asset at historical cost may involve estimates, assumptions, and allocations. Furthermore, estimates of useful life—in terms of either time or service quantities—must be made, as well as estimates of the residual value of the asset.

These estimates are made when the asset is placed into service, and they are based on information available at that time. As conditions change, however, estimates of useful lives may need to be either lengthened or shortened. Likewise, estimates of salvage value may also require revision. Management has a responsibility to continuously monitor its operations and to periodically reevaluate the estimates used in recognizing depreciation and depletion.

A change in estimated life or salvage value is not a correction of an error if the estimate was originally made in good faith and was based on all information available at the time. The change simply verifies the fact that as time passes and more information becomes available, more accurate estimates are possible. Changes in estimates of useful

Accounting for Oilpatch Site Restoration Costs

Accounting for the environment is here to stay, providing new challenges to the financially beleaguered oil and gas industry.

"Alberta's oilpatch has begun declaring a painful, $4.5 billion financial liability: the price tag for cleaning up the province's 90,000 well sites . . . This means $4.5 billion for an industry struggling to remain in the black." (*Calgary Herald,* January 18, 1992.)

Accounting for the environment has become increasingly important to organizations operating in the natural resources sector. Changes in society's perceptions and in the legal environment have forced management accountants to begin grappling with the costs associated with environmental cleanups. As the *Calgary Herald* quote suggests, site restoration costs are particularly important to the oil and gas industry, given the magnitude of the costs and the financial health of the industry itself.

A few years ago, the CICA introduced a standard on accounting for future removal and site restoration costs. CICA *Handbook* sections 3060.39 to .41 came into effect for fiscal years beginning on or after December 1, 1990, and require publicly traded oil and gas companies to begin making provisions for these costs. As with most CICA standards, managers are allowed some discretion on how this one is to be implemented.

This article summarizes the range of accounting alternatives permitted and describes the results of our study concerning the standard's impact on 95 publicly traded oil and gas companies. We will discuss how these organizations chose to apply the standard, as well as its impact on the financial health of Canada's oil and gas industry in 1991.

Accounting Methods Permitted

Handbook section 3060.39 states that, "when reasonably determinable, provisions should be made for future removal and site restoration costs, net of expected recoveries, in a rational and systematic manner by charges to income." This wording implicitly provides a range of possible methods to account for these costs.

In particular, management can choose between the deferred charge approach and note disclosure. Under the deferred charge approach, a yearly expense for site restoration costs is determined and charged against current income. The offsetting amount is credited to a deferred charge account on the balance sheet; this will increase over

time until the company actually incurs the costs associated with site restoration. While section 3060.39 recommends the deferred charge method, firms may opt for the off-balance-sheet approach of note disclosure if future site restoration costs cannot be reasonably determined.

Managers using the deferred charge approach must also choose between retrospective and prospective application. Under retrospective application, asset and liability accounts are adjusted to reflect site restoration costs as if the company had been applying section 3060.39 all along. This results in an immediate decrease in retained earnings to reflect the site restoration costs that should have been charged against previous earnings. Note, however, that retrospective application has less impact on future earnings.

Under prospective application, no adjustment is made to retained earnings. Instead, the entire amount of site restoration costs is amortized against future earnings. Management's choice of prospective or retrospective application will therefore influence the timing of expense recognition, as well as the financial impact on the balance sheet.

Method Selected

To find out how managers of oil and gas companies have chosen to account for site restoration costs, we identified the population of 125 oil and gas exploration companies that were publicly traded on either the Toronto Stock Exchange or Alberta Stock Exchange and had a December 31, 1991, fiscal year end. We then called these firms and asked them to send us a copy of their annual report. Those not responding received a second call within the following two weeks. This resulted in a final sample of 95 firms.

As **Table 1** shows, the majority of responding firms chose to use the deferred charge method, rather than note disclosure. The 10 firms that used note disclosure tended to be much smaller than the other firms, in terms of total assets and total revenues. They were also both relatively and absolutely less profitable than firms that chose the deferred charge method. Because they were smaller, it is possible that these firms used less sophisticated accounting

Continued

systems, making it more difficult for them to estimate site restoration costs. Alternatively, their weaker financial condition may have encouraged them to defer recognizing these costs.

TABLE 1
Company Facts and Accounting Method Chosen*

	Deferred Charge Method	Note Disclosure Method
Number of firms	85	10
1991 median assets	$80 million	$7 million
1991 median revenues	$22 million	$2 million
1991 median net loss prior to applying standard	$22 000	$600 000
1990 total debt/equity ratio	0.93	0.66

*Multivariate tests using logistic regression indicated that the differences between the two groups were mostly significant.

Although most of the firms opted to account for site restoration costs on the balance sheet, we saw more variation in the decision of whether to account for these costs retrospectively or prospectively. Of the 85 firms using the deferred charge method, 66 applied the recommendations prospectively and 19 retrospectively (**Table 2**). The firms choosing retrospective disclosure tended to be larger in terms of total assets and total revenues. They also tended to be less profitable than the firms that applied the standard prospectively. It is possible that firms with large losses prior to applying the standard chose retrospective application because it effectively shifts a portion of site restoration costs to previous periods, decreasing the costs to be recognized in the current period. However, in addition to being less profitable, retrospective disclosers tended to have a lower debt/equity ratio prior to applying the standard. One possible interpretation is that managers of firms that already had a high debt/equity ratio decided to apply the standard prospectively since prospective application has less impact on financial ratios, especially ratios that might be used in debt covenants.

The Cost of Site Restoration

For 79 of the 85 firms that used the deferred charge method, we were able to estimate the total magnitude of site restoration costs. Since most companies indicated that these costs would be amortized against income on a unit of production basis, we started from the estimated current costs and divided by current production to arrive at an estimated cost per equivalent barrel of oil. This number

was then multiplied by total proven reserves to get an estimate of total costs. For retrospective disclosers, we also added on the amount of the retrospective adjustment.

TABLE 2
Company Facts and Prospective v. Retrospective Application*

	Retrospective Application	Prospective Application
Number of firms	19	66
1991 median assets	$220 million	$55 million
1991 median revenues	$ 72 million	$15 million
1991 median net loss prior to applying standard	$ 6 million	$99 000
1990 debt/equity ratio	0.73	0.98

*Multivariate tests using logistic regression indicated that the differences between the two groups were mostly significant.

The total estimated site restoration cost for the 79 firms was $6.2 billion, $377 million of which was expensed in 1991 (**Table 3**). These results suggest that the preliminary estimate of $4.5 billion mentioned by the *Calgary Herald* may have understated the actual costs associated with site restoration.

Looking at individual firms, immediate recognition of site restoration costs would result, on average, in a 14% decrease in shareholders' equity. A portion of these costs pertain to future revenues, so this figure overstates the impact of site restoration costs. However, it does provide some indication of their magnitude.

In 1991, the amount of site restoration costs expensed was two per cent of revenues. On the surface, this doesn't seem like a large cost increase for oil and gas producers to absorb. However, the majority of the oil and gas firms that we examined were in a net loss position to start with. These firms may not have the financial slack needed to absorb site restoration costs at the present time.

TABLE 3
Facts on Site Restoration Costs

Total estimated costs (79 firms)	$6.2 billion
Costs as a percentage of shareholders' equity	14%
Estimated costs for 1991 year (79 firms)	$377 million
Percentage of 1991 revenues	2%
Estimated median cost per equivalent barrel	0.15

Continued

A Greener Oilpatch?

CICA's introduction of section 3060.39 indicates that accounting for the environment is here to stay. Within the oil and gas industry, the magnitude of site restoration costs appears to be even larger than previously estimated. For managers working in the oilpatch, accounting for these costs is just one more challenge that must be faced in returning the industry to profitability.

Source: Reprinted from Dean Neu and Bill Thon, "Accounting for Oilpatch Site Restoration Costs," *CGA Magazine,* December 1992, pp. 41–43 and 71–72.

Exhibit 13.7 Petro-Canada: Capital Assets Disclosure (stated in millions of dollars)

Note 14: Property, Plant and Equipment

	1991			1990			1991	1990
	Cost	Accumulated Depreciation, Depletion and Amortization	Net	Cost	Accumulated Depreciation, Depletion and Amortization	Net	Capital Expenditures	
Natural Resources								
Oil and gas								
Canada—nonfrontier	$3 417	$1 987	$1 430	$3 549	$1 972	$1 577	$127	$223
—frontier	182	—	182	120	—	120	62	14
Foreign	21	6	15	18	3	15	3	5
Oil sands								
Syncrude Project	812	330	482	787	197	590	25	23
Other	218	218	—	217	217	—	1	5
Natural gas liquids	237	125	112	228	114	114	9	11
Other	78	57	21	77	56	21	1	1
	4 965	2 723	2 242	4 996	2 559	2 437	228	282
Refined Products								
Refining	1 886	1 079	807	1 838	579	1 259	81	89
Marketing and other	1 093	299	794	1 060	246	814	206	132
	2 979	1 378	1 601	2 898	825	2 073	287	221
Other property, plant and equipment	525	284	241	509	241	268	24	29
	$8 469	$4 385	$4 084	$8 403	$3 625	$4 778	$539	$532

Interest capitalized for the year ended December 31, 1991 amounted to $10 million (year ended December 31, 1990—$2 million; year ended December 31, 1989—$nil).

Note 1: Summary of Significant Accounting Policies

(e) Depreciation, Depletion and Amortization

The carrying amounts of significant unproved properties are evaluated periodically for impairment with any such impairment being charged to earnings. The cost of other unproved properties is amortized over their average holding period.

Depreciation and depletion of capitalized costs of oil and gas producing properties is calculated using the unit of production method.

Depreciation of other plant and equipment is provided on either the unit of production method or the straight line method as appropriate. Straight line depreciation rates are based on the estimated service lives of the related assets.

Source: Petro-Canada, *1991 Annual Report.*

lives and salvage values should be treated on a **prospective basis,** according to CICA *Handbook* Section 1506.[6] This means that the effect of the change is recognized in the period in which the change is made and future periods. No recognition is made of the depreciation or depletion that would have been recognized in the past if new estimates had been in effect.

To illustrate the change in depreciation estimates, we will assume that Mosteller Company acquired machinery in early 1992 for $275 000. The machinery was expected to have a five-year life and a salvage value of $25 000. Depreciation recognized in 1992, 1993, and 1994 was based on these estimates. The depreciation entries at the end of 1992, 1993, and 1994 were as follows:

Depreciation Expense	50 000	
Accumulated Depreciation		50 000

In 1995, management determines that the machine can be used for four more years, after which it will have an approximate salvage value of $5000. Depreciation for 1995 and the remaining years in the asset's life is $30 000:

Cost	$275 000
Depreciation, 1992–94	
[($275 000 − $25 000)/5 years × 3 years]	(150 000)
Book value at beginning of 1995	125 000
Expected salvage value, end of 1998	(5 000)
Depreciation base, 1995–98	$120 000
Depreciation expense, 1995–98 ($120 000/4 years)	$ 30 000

The book value ($125 000) at the time of the change in estimate is used as the cost figure in the revised depreciation computation, and the depreciation method is applied as usual. At the end of 1998, the book value of the asset will be $5000, which is the expected salvage value:

$$\$275\ 000 - [(\$50\ 000 \times 3\ \text{years}) + (\$30\ 000 \times 4\ \text{years})] = \$5000$$

The same basic process is followed with other depreciation methods if either the useful life or the salvage value is changed.

Corrections of Errors

Corrections of past errors in recording assets, depreciation, and depletion are treated as a correction of an error in **prior period statements** in accordance with CICA *Handbook* Section 1506.[7] Errors involving property, plant, and equipment frequently result from the expensing of asset costs that should have been capitalized and from the incorrect application of depreciation methods.

We illustrate the correction of capital asset and depreciation errors by assuming that Watson Corporation acquired equipment in 1992 that was expected to be used for ten

---

[6]"Accounting Changes, Change in an Accounting Estimate" CICA *Handbook* Paragraphs 1506.22–25, March 1991.

[7]"Accounting Changes, Correction of an Error in Prior Period Financial Statements," CICA *Handbook* Paragraphs 1506.26–30, March 1991.

years. The asset cost $150 000 and was expected to have a $10 000 salvage value at the end of its ten-year life. During the 1995 audit, management discovered that the equipment had been incorrectly expensed in 1992. Correct depreciation policy called for the use of the straight-line method of depreciation with a half-year depreciation taken in the first and last years of the asset's life.

Disregarding any income tax effects of the error, we can determine the appropriate corrections to the accounts and the proper depreciation expense for 1995:

Cost of equipment					$150 000
Depreciation expense					
1992: [($150 000 − $10 000)/10] ½		=	$ 7 000		
1993: [($150 000 − $10 000)/10]		=	$14 000		
1994: [($150 000 − $10 000)/10]		=	$14 000	(35 000)	
Book value at beginning of 1995				115 000	
Depreciation expense					
1995: [($150 000 − $10 000)/10]				(14 000)	
Book value at end of 1995				$101 000	

The following entry records the asset and related depreciation of 1992–94:

Equipment	150 000	
Accumulated Depreciation *92-94 depreciation*		35 000
Retained Earnings (or Correction of Prior Period) *BV at beginning/95*		115 000

The credit to retained earnings represents the net effect of the $150 000 understatement of income resulting from the expensing of the asset in 1992, less the $35 000 overstatement to income in 1992, 1993, and 1994 resulting from the failure to record depreciation ($7000 + $14 000 + $14 000).[8] The entry to record depreciation for 1995 is made as if the asset and related depreciation had been properly recorded in the past:

Depreciation Expense	14 000	
Accumulated Depreciation		14 000

The prior period correction of an error is presented on the statement of retained earnings as a restatement of the beginning balance, as discussed in Chapter 4. In the Watson case, the adjustment of the beginning retained earnings of 1995 would be $115 000, the amount credited to retained earnings in the entry above.

A second illustration of a prior period correction assumes that Goren Limited capitalized the $42 000 cost of painting the interior of its administrative office building in 1992. The interior of the building is painted every five years, so management decided to write off the painting at $8400 a year for five years.

The $42 000 capitalization was discovered in 1994, and the entry to correct this error is recorded as follows:

---

[8]The income tax consequences of the correction are not considered in this illustration. As we have seen in Chapter 4, the correction should be presented in the financial statements on a net-of-tax basis. The subject of correction of errors, including income tax implications, is covered more extensively in Chapters 19 and 20.

Accumulated Depreciation — *(2 yrs)*   16 800
Retained Earnings (or Prior Period Correction) *expensed*   25 200
    Building   42 000

The location of errors and the analysis required to determine the impact of errors on the financial statements may be quite complicated, particularly if comparative financial statements are presented. Companies may also change accounting methods (e.g., depreciation method), a subject not covered at this point. Accounting changes and correction of errors are covered more extensively in Chapter 20.

Concluding Remarks

Matching

The *matching principle* is the primary accounting principle that explains the process of depreciation. In this chapter, we have illustrated several methods of depreciation. We have also discussed problems inherent in applying the matching principle, such as partial-year depreciation. The *consistency principle* is particularly important in depreciation because consistent application of accounting methods over time is necessary to generate information for successive accounting periods that can be compared in evaluating the financial progress of the reporting entity. The *disclosure principle* also presents capital assets in the financial statements. Companies typically include important information concerning capital assets in both the financial statements and in related notes.

Consistency

Disclosure

Asset/Liability Measurement

We can see the problems inherent in applying the *asset/liability measurement, matching, and consistency principles* in situations where errors of previous periods are discovered and where changes in estimates required to apply these accounting principles are made. These accounting problems are only introduced in this chapter, and are addressed and illustrated more completely in Chapter 20.

Matching

Consistency

Key Points

1. Depreciation is the process of allocating the cost of property, plant, and equipment as an expense in a systematic and rational manner to those periods expected to benefit from the use of the assets. (Objective 1)

2. Depreciation is a necessary part of applying the matching principle to long-lived assets that are used in the production of revenue. (Objective 1)

3. Several accounting methods are used to allocate the historical cost of individual capital assets to the periods that benefit from their use. These methods can be divided into methods based on time and those based on activity level. (Objective 2)

4. Special accounting policies must be adopted to handle situations in which capital assets are used for less than a complete accounting period. Consistency is an important accounting principle in handling this special accounting problem. (Objective 2)

5. Natural resources are a special type of property, plant, and equipment. The allocation of the historical cost of natural resources is called depletion and is similar to depreciation of other capital assets. (Objective 3)

6. Authoritative accounting pronouncements require several specific items of information concerning capital assets to be disclosed in the financial statements. These include the balances in major classes of depreciable assets, accumulated depreciation, depreciation expense, and a general description of the depreciation methods used. (Objective 4)

7. Changes in estimates required to recognize depreciation and depletion are handled on a prospective basis and, therefore, recognized in the period of the change and in future periods. (Objective 5)

8. Corrections of errors in accounting for capital assets, depreciation, and depletion are treated as corrections to a prior period. Previously issued financial statements are restated, and retained earnings are corrected for the past errors. (Objective 5)

Appendix A: Alternative Depreciation Methods

Additional Individual Asset Methods

Several alternatives to the depreciation methods presented in this chapter are available. While these methods are not as widely used in practice, they do meet the criteria of being both systematic and rational. Three of these alternatives are presented here: the sum-of-the-years'-digits, annuity, and sinking fund methods.

To illustrate these methods, Asset 147 is again used. The necessary information, again, is as follows:

Asset 147

Cost	$12 000
Estimated salvage value	2 000
Estimated life in years	5

An assumed interest rate of 10 percent is used for the annuity and sinking fund methods.

Sum-of-the-Years'-Digits Method

The **sum-of-the-years'-digits method** is a type of accelerated depreciation in which the charge in early years exceeds that of later years. In this method, a *declining fraction* is multiplied by a *constant base*. In the declining-balance method the opposite is true: a *constant percentage* is multiplied by a *declining base*.

The sum-of-the-years'-digits method is applied by computing a fraction, the denominator of which equals the **life of the asset in years plus all digits between that number and zero.** The numerator of the fraction represents the **specific number of the year** in the useful life of the asset, but the numbers are applied in **descending order** throughout the life of the asset. For example, if the useful life is ten years, the number 10 would be the numerator in D_1, the number 9 in D_2, etc. This fraction is then multiplied by **depreciable cost** (i.e., cost minus salvage value). Thus, depreciation is computed as follows:

$$D = \frac{\text{Current year digit}}{\text{Sum-of-the-years'-digits}} \times (\text{Cost} - \text{Salvage value})$$

Applying these concepts to Asset 147, we find that the denominator (the sum of the digits: 5 + 4 + 3 + 2 + 1) equals 15. Depreciation is determined for each year by multiplying the appropriate fraction by the depreciable amount. Remember that the numerator is selected in *reverse,* or *descending* order, resulting in the following computations:

$$D_1 = 5/15 \times (\$12\,000 - \$2000) = \$\ 3\,333$$
$$D_2 = 4/15 \times (\$12\,000 - \$2000) = \ \ 2\,667$$
$$D_3 = 3/15 \times (\$12\,000 - \$2000) = \ \ 2\,000$$
$$D_4 = 2/15 \times (\$12\,000 - \$2000) = \ \ 1\,333$$
$$D_5 = 1/15 \times (\$12\,000 - \$2000) = \ \ \underline{\ \ \ \ 667}$$
$$\underline{\$10\,000}$$

These computations result in the schedule for Asset 147 presented in Exhibit 13.8. As with straight-line depreciation, the book value of $2000 at the end of the five years equals the salvage value anticipated at the beginning of the asset's life.

For assets with relatively long lives, determining the sum of the digits as computed above may be burdensome. In these cases, the denominator in the fraction may be determined as follows (n = years in asset's life, N = years in asset's life, SYD = sum-of-the-years'-digits):

$$SYD = n\left(\frac{N+1}{2}\right)$$

For example, for an asset with a 35-year life, the sum of the digits is computed as follows:

$$SYD = 35\left(\frac{35+1}{2}\right)$$
$$= 630$$

The depreciation rate is 35/630 for the first year, 34/630 for the second year, and so on.

Fractional-Year Problems

In the previous example, we assumed that the depreciation year and the financial reporting period are the same. To illustrate the problem of approaches to sum-of-the-years'-digits depreciation for partial years, the example of Asset 286 will be used.

Asset 286

Cost	$100 000
Estimated salvage value	None
Estimated life in years	4
Date of acquisition	Aug. 10
Financial reporting period	Jan. 1–Dec. 31

A fractional-year problem exists because the four years in the asset's life do not correspond precisely to four financial reporting years. The first depreciation year begins during the first financial reporting year and ends during the second financial reporting year. This sequence continues throughout the life of Asset 286, with the financial reporting periods following a January-through-December pattern and the depreciation years following an August-to-August pattern.

Applying the fractional-year policies outlined in the chapter to the sum-of-the-years'-digits method, Asset 286 would be depreciated as follows under Policies 1 and 3:

Exhibit 13.8 Depreciation Schedule for Asset 147: Sum-of-the-Years'-Digits Method

End of Year	Depreciation Entry: Dr.: Depreciation Expense Cr.: Accumulated Depreciation	Balance: Accumulated Depreciation	Book Value
1	—	—	$12 000
1	$3 333	$ 3 333	8 667
2	2 667	6 000	6 000
3	2 000	8 000	4 000
4	1 333	9 333	2 667
5	667	10 000	2 000

Policy 1
Nearest Full Month

Year 1 $\$100\ 000 \times \dfrac{4}{10} \times \dfrac{5\ \text{mo.}}{12\ \text{mo.}} = \underline{\underline{\$16\ 667}}$

Year 2 $\$100\ 000 \times \dfrac{4}{10} \times \dfrac{7\ \text{mo.}}{12\ \text{mo.}} = \$23\ 333$

$\$100\ 000 \times \dfrac{3}{10} \times \dfrac{5\ \text{mo.}}{12\ \text{mo.}} = \underline{\quad 12\ 500\quad}$

$\underline{\underline{\$35\ 833}}$

Policy 3
Nearest Half Year

$\$100\ 000 \times \dfrac{4}{10} \times \dfrac{1}{2} = \underline{\underline{\$20\ 000}}$

$\$100\ 000 \times \dfrac{4}{10} \times \dfrac{1}{2} = \$20\ 000$

$\$100\ 000 \times \dfrac{3}{10} \times \dfrac{1}{2} = \underline{\quad 15\ 000\quad}$

$\underline{\underline{\$35\ 000}}$

Annuity Method

The **annuity method** of depreciation is based on the assumption that in acquiring property, plant, and equipment, an enterprise makes an investment much like an annuity (i.e., an investment yielding a fixed return for a stated period of time). Periodic returns on the investment are separated into two elements: a return of the principal amount and an interest revenue on the investment. Throughout the life of the asset, the interest revenue diminishes as the return of the principal reduces the investment.

Under the annuity method, periodic depreciation is computed by using the equation shown below, where PV is equal to the present value of 1 at the assumed rate for the estimated life of the asset, and $PVOA$ is equal to the present value of an ordinary annuity of 1 at the assumed rate for the estimated life of the asset:

$$D = \frac{\text{Cost} - (\text{Salvage value} \times PV)}{PVOA}$$

Applying this equation to Asset 147 at an assumed 10 percent interest rate and using Tables 7.2 and 7.4, we determine depreciation as $2838:

$$D_1 = \frac{\$12\ 000 - (\$2000 \times 0.62092)}{3.79079}$$
$$= \$2838$$

Depreciation is recognized at the constant amount of $2838 each year. Interest revenue is recognized each year in an amount equal to the book value of the asset times the appropriate interest rate, and Accumulated Depreciation is credited for the difference between the depreciation expense ($2838) and the interest revenue. Since interest revenue declines each year, the credit to Accumulated Depreciation increases each year. The application of these concepts to Asset 147 is illustrated in Exhibit 13.9.

The primary limitation of the annuity method, in addition to the judgement involved in selecting an appropriate interest rate, is that total depreciation expense recognized over the life of the asset exceeds the cost of the asset by the amount of the interest revenue recognized. In the case of Asset 147, this relationship is as follows:

Total depreciation expense recognized ($2838 × 5 years)	$14 190
Total interest revenue recognized	
($1200 + $1036 + $856 + $658 + $440)	(4 190)
Cost less estimated salvage value of Asset 147	$10 000

Also, the net effect on income is an *increasing* charge, since depreciation expense remains constant while interest revenue declines over time. These problems of the amount and pattern of depreciation recognition raise questions as to the appropriateness of the method under current generally accepted accounting principles, which stress matching and historical cost.

Sinking Fund Method

The **sinking fund method** is a variation of the annuity method wherein interest revenue and depreciation expense are not recognized as separate elements in the determination of income during the life of the asset. The computations under the sinking fund method are the same as those for the annuity method.

Applying the sinking fund method to Asset 147, we find that the depreciation expense is the difference between the $2838 depreciation cost and the interest revenue each year. This is the same as the credit to the accumulated depreciation column of Exhibit 13.9.

The concept of establishing a sinking fund to provide for the replacement of property, plant, and equipment is rarely applied in practice. However, the existence of the fund is not a prerequisite to the use of the depreciation method derived from this concept.

The sinking fund method poses the same questions as does the annuity method in regard to an increasing depreciation charge during the life of the asset and the appropriate interest rate for applying the method.

Group-Depreciation Systems

The depreciation methods discussed earlier apply the concept of depreciation to specific individual assets. In some cases, however, it is impractical or even impossible to apply one of the generally accepted depreciation methods to individual assets or to individual components of a complex asset. Several systems are available to compute depreciation for groups of assets that are treated as a single asset for purposes of determining periodic depreciation expense.

Of the many variations of group-depreciation systems, the following are included in this section: inventory system, retirement and replacement systems, and group and composite systems.

Inventory System

The **inventory system** of determining periodic depreciation of capital assets closely parallels the determination of expense and the related asset for supplies. As assets are acquired, an asset account is debited. At the end of the financial reporting period, an

Exhibit 13.9 Depreciation Schedule for Asset 147: Annuity Method

Equals to Depreciation Expense under Sinking Fund

End of Year	Dr.: Depreciation Expense	Cr.: Interest Revenue	Cr.: Accumulated Depreciation	Balance: Accumulated Depreciation	Book Value
	—	—	—	—	$12 000
1	$2 838	$1 200	$1 638	$1 638	10 362
2	2 838	1 036	1 802	3 440	8 560
3	2 838	856	1 982	5 422	6 578
4	2 838	658	2 180	7 602	4 398
5	2 838	440	2 398	10 000	2 000

Computations

Interest revenue is the book value of the asset multiplied by the interest rate.

Example—Year 1: $12 000 × 10% = $1200
Year 2: ($12 000 − $1638) × 10% = $1036

The credit to Accumulated Depreciation is the difference between the Depreciation Expense and the Interest Revenue.

Example—Year 1: $2838 − $1200 = $1638
Year 2: $2838 − $1036 = $1802

inventory count is taken of the items on hand. The difference between the asset balance and the cost of the items on hand, possibly adjusted to an amount below cost to reflect wear and tear, represents the depreciation charge for the period.

The inventory system is appropriate if a large number of items with a small unit cost are used in the productive process and if the application of a depreciation method to individual assets is impractical. Examples are machine tools, hand tools, and patterns used in the manufacturing process. The inventory method approximates the depreciation amount that would have resulted from depreciating the assets on an individual basis.

To illustrate, we assume that Tyson Manufacturing Company uses a large number of small hand tools in its manufacturing process. Rather than compute depreciation individually on these relatively inexpensive tools, the company uses the inventory method of depreciating them. The asset account reflects the following activity during 1995:

Small Tools Account

Balance, January 1, 1995	$12 750
Acquisitions	
March 5, 1995	1 300
August 29, 1995	5 420
October 7, 1995	3 500
	$22 970

An inventory on December 31, 1995, reveals that hand tools costing $17 250 are in use. Management determines that these assets should be reduced by 20 percent due to wear and tear on them to date. Depreciation expense to be recognized in 1995 is determined as follows:

Balance in Small Tools account	$22 970
Value of ending inventory	
[$17 250 − 0.20($17 250)]	13 800
Depreciation for 1995	$ 9 170

The entry to recognize depreciation is as follows:

Depreciation Expense	9170	
Small Tools		9170

No accumulated depreciation account is maintained, and Depreciation Expense is debited periodically for the reduction in the asset account necessary to bring it to the appropriate balance.

Cash may be received when assets are sold. In the entry debiting Cash, the asset account is credited. This effectively reduces the difference between the ending balance in the asset account and the value of the inventory of tools on hand, thus reducing the depreciation recognized.

For example, for the Tyson case, we will assume that the beginning balance and acquisitions are the same as previously stated but, in addition, that $1500 was received from the sale of used hand tools at December 31, 1995. The following general journal entries would be required:

Cash	1500	
Small Tools		1500
Depreciation Expense	7670	
Small Tools		7670

The $1500 from the cash sale is credited directly into the asset account (Small Tools), reducing the balance from $22 970 to $21 470. Depreciation is then computed as $7670 ($21 470 − $13 800).

Retirement and Replacement Systems

The retirement and replacement systems may be used in much the same situations as the inventory system. They are suitable depreciation systems if a large number of similar items are employed by the enterprise and the items are being replaced on a relatively constant schedule. Under both systems, no depreciation is recognized until items are replaced.

The retirement and replacement systems are frequently used by public utilities, which have large numbers of virtually identical items that are constantly being installed and retired: utility poles, utility lines, accessories used in utility lines, meters (gas, water, electric), and telephone receivers.

Under the **retirement system,** the cost of retired items is debited to Depreciation Expense at the time of retirement, and the asset account is reduced by the same amount. The cost of the new items that replace the existing ones is debited to the asset account, and the process continues. No identification of depreciation by individual unit is kept, no accumulated depreciation account is maintained, and no depreciation is taken until units are replaced.

Assume that Jasper Utility Company uses the retirement system to determine depreciation on a large number of utility poles located throughout the city of Jasper. The balance in the Utility Pole account is $250 000 at the beginning of 1995. During the year, poles originally costing $72 500 are replaced with new poles costing $97 000. In addition, new poles that are installed in a new service area cost $19 600.

The following entries are necessary to recognize these events:

Depreciation Expense	72 500	
Utility Poles		72 500
Utility Poles	97 000	
Cash		97 000
Utility Poles	19 600	
Cash		19 600

Any cash received from the salvage of the poles being replaced is treated as a reduction in the $72 500 depreciation expense.

The **replacement system** is similar to the retirement system in terms of the circumstances in which it is appropriate. Under the replacement system, however, the cost of replacing the assets—not the cost of the original assets—is treated as the periodic depreciation. In applying the replacement system to the Jasper situation, we need to record the following entries:

Depreciation Expense	97 000	
Cash		97 000
Utility Poles	19 600	
Cash		19 600

The original cost of the utility poles is left in the asset account and the cost of replacement ($97 000) is the depreciation amount recognized. Normally the asset account would be affected only if new poles were acquired for purposes other than replacement of existing poles (such as those for $19 600 in the Jasper case).

As is the case with the retirement system, in the replacement system no identification or depreciation by individual unit is kept, no accumulated depreciation account is maintained, and depreciation expense is not recognized until existing units are replaced. Also, any cash received from the salvage of individual units is treated as a reduction of depreciation expense.

A criticism of both the retirement and the replacement systems is that they do not present the allocation of historical cost as an expense during the period of time when the assets are being used to produce revenue. The reasonableness of either system as an approximation of the allocation of cost depends on the constancy of retirement and replacement over time on a continuous basis. If this continuous retirement and replacement of a large number of similar assets does not apply, these systems should not be used.

The retirement system is a type of first-in, first-out (FIFO) cost determination, since the oldest costs are charged to expense and the most recent costs are maintained in the asset account. In the case of Jasper Utility Company, the 1995 depreciation expense is $72 500 (made up of the oldest costs), and the balance sheet asset is $294 100 ($250 000 − $72 500 + $97 000 + $19 600), which includes the more recent costs of replacement. On the other hand, the replacement system is a form of last-in, first-out (LIFO), since the most recent costs are charged as an expense and the older costs are retained in the asset account. In the case of Jasper Utility Company, the 1995 depreciation expense is $97 000 (made up of the most recent costs), and the balance sheet asset is $269 600 ($250 000 + $19 600), including the original cost of those items that have now been replaced.

Group and Composite Systems

In some cases, individual assets are combined and depreciated at an average depreciation rate for the assets included. When assets are combined in this manner because of their similarity (e.g., a fleet of vehicles), the depreciation system is called a **group system**. Dissimilar assets may be combined for depreciation purposes if they are used in operations as an integrated unit (e.g., components of an integrated manufacturing assembly). In such cases, the depreciation system is called a **composite system.**

The group and composite systems differ from the other methods of multiple-asset depreciation that we discussed earlier in that an Accumulated Depreciation account is kept for the **group of assets** involved. However, the accumulated depreciation does not relate to any particular asset within the group. The mechanics of applying the group and composite systems are outlined in the following steps:

1. The cost of individual assets that comprise the group are debited to a single asset account.
2. An average depreciation rate is determined by stating the total of the annual depreciation of the individual assets as a percentage of a total cost of the assets included in the group.
3. Depreciation on the group of assets is charged to the Depreciation Expense account and credited to the Accumulated Depreciation account in an amount equal to the percentage computed in Step 2 multiplied by the cost of the assets.
4. The removal of an individual asset from the group is recorded as a debit to the Accumulated Depreciation account and a credit to the asset account in an amount equal to the cost of the individual asset removed. No gain or loss is recognized. Any proceeds received on the asset removal are debited to Cash and serve to reduce the amount that would otherwise be charged to Accumulated Depreciation.

To illustrate, we will assume that Tyson Manufacturing Company has a number of small production processes that operate simultaneously to produce several consumer products. The composite depreciation system is used for the assets employed in each process. Information concerning the components of the integrated production assembly for digital watches is presented in Exhibit 13.10.

The five components have been debited to a single asset account, Digital-Watch Production Assembly. We compute the depreciation per year on each component by using the straight-line method. The average depreciation rate is 9 percent, determined by dividing the total depreciation per year of $11 750 by the historical cost of the assets, $125 000. The composite life is 9.7 years ($114 000/$11 750). This indicates that the group of assets will be fully depreciated in approximately ten years if the 9 percent depreciation rate is applied to the historical cost annually.

A single depreciation entry is made each year for the group of assets, as follows:

Depreciation Expense	11 750	
Accumulated Depreciation—Digital-Watch Production		
Assembly		11 750

Exhibit 13.10 Digital-Watch Production Assembly

Component	Historical Cost	Estimated Salvage Value	Estimated Depreciable Amount	Useful Life in Years	Depreciation per Year
L	$ 27 000	$ 3 000	$ 24 000	8	$ 3 000
M	19 000	4 000	15 000	10	1 500
N	5 000	—	5 000	5	1 000
O	62 000	2 000	60 000	12	5 000
P	12 000	2 000	10 000	8	1 250
	$125 000	$11 000	$114 000		$11 750

The disposal of a component of the group of assets is recorded by charging the Accumulated Depreciation account. No gain or loss is recognized, because the accumulated depreciation cannot be associated with any particular asset or component of the group. For example, if Component P is sold for $1000 after five years of service, the following entry is made:

Cash	1000	
Accumulated Depreciation—Digital-Watch Production Assembly	11 000	
Digital-Watch Production Assembly		12 000

The cost of replacing removed components is debited into the composite asset account. When the components of a composite asset change significantly, as might be the case after several components have been replaced, the depreciation rate may require revision. A recalculation of the depreciation amount should be made periodically, based on the existing components at that time. The periodic depreciation amount is then updated to reflect the current makeup of the composite asset.

The major advantage of the group and composite method is the clerical cost savings that result from maintaining a single asset account and single accumulated depreciation account for several individual assets. In our example of the Digital-Watch Production Assembly, only five components exist, so the cost savings would not be very great. This example is intended to illustrate an approach, however, and if the composite asset had many parts, the clerical savings could be significant. A major problem in the case of the composite method is the application of a single depreciation rate, based on a weighted average life, to diverse components whose lives may vary considerably. This variance is illustrated in the Tyson Manufacturing example, in which the estimated lives of the components range from five to twelve years, but the same rate of depreciation is applied to all components. This problem does not arise in the group method, because the basis for combining the assets is their similarity; therefore, the life of each asset is similar to that of the other assets in the group.

Another problem with both the group method and the composite method is that no gain or loss is recorded on the disposal of individual assets within the group, because the cost of the individual asset, minus any proceeds from disposal, is charged to the Accumulated Depreciation account. Inaccurate estimates of useful lives and individual assets that are not productive may go unnoticed more easily under the group and composite methods than they would if the assets were depreciated on an individual basis.

Appendix B: Casualty Insurance

To reduce the risk of financial loss due to casualties (e.g., from fires, thefts, floods, or accidents), business enterprises commonly acquire **casualty insurance.** The purpose of this insurance is to shift to an insurance company the burden of a potential loss from such unexpected occurrences. The **face value** of the insurance policy is the maximum amount that the insurance company is required to pay if a loss occurs. Payments made to the insurance company are called **premiums** and are paid in advance of the period of insurance coverage. Thus, payments represent prepaid expenses when they are made. Since premiums are typically lower when insurance contracts provide for coverage over longer periods of time (i.e., more than one year) and payment for the entire period may be made in advance, the current portion of the prepayments appears in the balance sheet as a current asset and the remainder as a noncurrent asset (i.e., other asset or deferred charge).

We are accustomed to thinking in terms of historical cost or book value of property, plant, and equipment. For insurance purposes, however, the relevant dollar measurement of these assets is **fair market value.** The amount recoverable from an insurance company is the lesser of the loss based on fair market value or the face value of the insurance policy, unless the policy includes a co-insurance clause, which is discussed in the next section. The recorded basis of the asset—the historical cost or book value—is *not* the basis for determining the insurance reimbursement and is used only to determine the book gain or loss resulting from the asset loss and related insurance reimbursement.

Common complexities in accounting for casualty insurance are co-insurance and coverage by multiple insurance policies. These topics are discussed in the following sections, after which the accounting process for recording an insured casualty loss is illustrated.

Co-insurance

Casualty insurance policies frequently contain **co-insurance requirements** to encourage companies to insure assets at amounts based on their fair market value. Companies realize that many casualties result in only partial destruction of capital assets. In the absence of co-insurance requirements, companies are inclined to insure assets at less than their fair market value, because they would receive full reimbursement for any losses up to the face amounts of the insurance policies.

The co-insurance requirement is stated as a percentage of fair market value of the insured asset and requires the property to be insured to at least the percentage indicated, or the insured must share in any loss that occurs. For example, if an asset with a fair market value of $100 000 is insured under a policy including an 80 percent co-insurance requirement, the asset must be insured for at least $80 000 ($100 000 × 0.80) to collect the full amount of any loss from the insurance company. The amount paid, however, will not exceed the face value of the insurance policy in any case.

The amount recoverable under a co-insurance situation is computed by multiplying the loss incurred (based on fair market value at the time of the casualty) by the percentage of face value of the policy to the co-insurance requirement, in dollars. The amount actually reimbursed is the smallest of three amounts: the amount recoverable under the co-insurance requirements, the amount of the loss, or the face value of the policy. These relationships are presented in Exhibit 13.11.

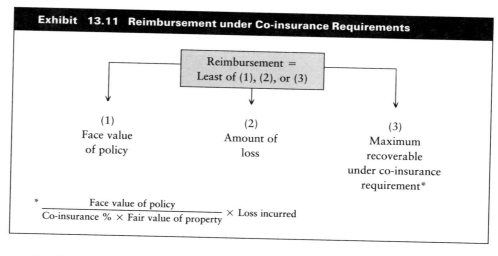

Exhibit 13.11 Reimbursement under Co-insurance Requirements

Reimbursement =
Least of (1), (2), or (3)

(1)
Face value
of policy

(2)
Amount of
loss

(3)
Maximum
recoverable
under co-insurance
requirement*

$$* \quad \frac{\text{Face value of policy}}{\text{Co-insurance \% } \times \text{ Fair value of property}} \times \text{Loss incurred}$$

To illustrate, we assume that Mosteller Company has insurance for several of its assets under separate insurance policies containing co-insurance requirements. These policies are described below, including losses incurred from casualties on each asset.

	Asset A	**Asset B**	**Asset C**
Fair market value of asset	$200 000	$250 000	$300 000
Face value of policy	$180 000	$150 000	$250 000
Co-insurance requirement	90%	70%	80%
Amount of loss from casualty (based on fair market value)	$150 000	$120 000	$290 000

For Asset A, the co-insurance requirement is met, since the $180 000 face value of the policy is exactly equal to the co-insurance requirement ($200 000 × 90%). Thus, the computation of the amount recoverable under the co-insurance requirement is not necessary, and the insurance company will pay $150 000, the smaller of the face value of the policy ($180 000) or the amount of the loss ($150 000).

For Asset B, the co-insurance requirement is not met, since the $150 000 face value of the policy is less than the co-insurance requirement of $175 000 ($250 000 × 0.70). The maximum amount recoverable is computed as follows:

$$\frac{\$150\ 000}{\$250\ 000 \times 70\%} \times \$120\ 000 = \$102\ 840$$

Since the policy will pay the least of the face value of the policy ($150 000), the amount of the loss ($120 000), or the amount recoverable under the co-insurance requirement ($102 857), only $102 857 will be recovered. The insured party will share in any loss, with the insurance company paying 85.7 percent of the loss ($102 857/$120 000) and the insured paying 14.3 percent of the loss [($120 000 − $102 857)/$120 000].

For Asset C, the coinsurance requirement is met, because the $250 000 face value of the policy is greater than the co-insurance requirement of $240 000 ($300 000 × 0.80). Thus, the computation of the amount recoverable is not necessary, and the insurance company will pay the $250 000 face value of the policy, since it is less than the $290 000 loss.

Coverage by Multiple Insurance Policies

If more than one insurance policy covers the same property, the amount reimbursable under each policy is determined in the same way as described in the previous section. Each policy will pay the least of the following: (1) the face value of the policy; (2) an allocated portion of the loss; or (3) the maximum recoverable under a co-insurance requirement.

The allocated portion of the loss is based on the face value of the policies. For example, if a company has a $100 000 policy on a piece of property and another policy of $50 000 on the same property, the first policy would be allocated two-thirds ($100 000/$150 000) of any loss and the second policy would be allocated one-third ($50 000/$150 000) of the loss. The maximum recoverable under a co-insurance requirement is computed as illustrated in the previous section, with the face value of the individual policy used in the numerator of the computation.

Accounting for Casualties

The following steps summarize the process of accounting for a casualty:

1. Depreciation expense is recognized to the date of the casualty; other adjustments, such as the expiration of prepaid insurance, are made.
2. A Casualty account is established to serve as a clearing account for amounts relative to the casualty.
3. The Casualty account is debited and credited for appropriate amounts, as follows:
    Debits
    a. Book value of the asset(s) destroyed or damaged.
    b. Adjustments to prepaid insurance resulting from the reduction in insurance coverage for the remainder of the period for which premiums have been paid. Other costs incidental to the settlement.
    Credits
    a. Amounts recoverable from insurance companies.
    b. Amounts recoverable from the salvage of damaged assets.
4. The Casualty account is closed into the Income Summary as a single amount representing the net loss or gain on the casualty and related insurance settlement.

Since the amounts relative to the casualty and related insurance settlement become available over an extended period of time, the Casualty account is used temporarily to house the various components as they become available. A debit balance in the account represents a loss, and a credit balance represents a gain. The latter results when insurance is based on the fair market value of assets and the final settlement from the insurance company exceeds the book value of the lost asset(s) and other costs related to the settlement.

Amounts recoverable from the insurance company are classified as current assets when collection is anticipated in the near future. The loss or gain resulting from the closing of the Casualty account is presented as an extraordinary item in the income statement only if it meets the criteria of Paragraph 3480.02.

To illustrate the process of recording a casualty, we will assume that Mosteller Manufacturing Company, a calendar-year corporation, has a building that was damaged by fire on May 1, 1995. Specific information on the building and the fire loss are as follows:

Cost of building	$450 000	
Accumulated depreciation through December 31, 1994	125 000	$325 000
Fair value of building at May 1, 1995		$700 000
Face value of insurance policy		$500 000
Amount of fire loss (based on fair value)		$350 000
Co-insurance requirement		80%
Prepaid insurance at January 1, 1995		$ 1 800

Depreciation expense is computed on a monthly basis at an annual rate of $45 000. The prepaid insurance at January 1 represents the premium for the calendar year 1995 that was paid in advance in late 1994. The insurance policy continues in effect after the loss for the remainder of 1995 in an amount adjusted forward for the payment for the fire loss.

The building is determined to have been a 50 percent loss, based on the relationship of the fire loss to the fair value of the building ($350 000/$700 000). The following general journal entries are required to record the casualty if we assume that depreciation expense is computed to the nearest full month:

To Adjust Accounts to the Date of the Fire Loss

Depreciation Expense	15 000	
Accumulated Depreciation		15 000
[4 months × ($45 000/12) = $15 000]		

Insurance Expense	600	
Prepaid Insurance		600
(4/12 × $1800 = $600)		

To Close Accounts to Casualty Account

Casualty ($225 000 − $70 000)	155 000	
Accumulated Depreciation [½ ($125 000 + $15 000)]	70 000	
Building (½ × $450 000)		225 000

Receivable from Insurance Company	312 500	
Casualty		312 500

$$\left(\frac{\$500\ 000 \times \$350\ 000}{\$700\ 000 \times 80\%} = \$312\ 500 \right)$$

Casualty	750	
Prepaid Insurance		750
[($312 500/$500 000) × $1200 = $750]		

To Close Casualty to Income Summary

Casualty	156 750	
Income Summary		156 750
($155 000 + $750 − $312 500)		

The entry for $750 to reduce prepaid insurance and adjust the Casualty account is necessary because the insurance in effect after the payment of $312 500 is reduced to

$187 500 ($500 000 − $312 500). The Casualty account is charged with a pro rata share of the premium related to the remainder of the year. The balance in the Prepaid Insurance account after this adjustment is $450 ($1200 − $750), representing the premium related to insurance coverage of $187 500 for the remainder of 1995.

In this situation, the Casualty account had a credit balance, indicating that the company had a gain rather than a loss. This gain is presented in the income statement as "proceeds from insurance in excess of book value of building destroyed by fire" or another appropriate title.

Questions

Q13.1 What is the primary theoretical justification for recognizing the cost of property, plant, and equipment as expense over their estimated useful lives?

Q13.2 Identify the specific elements in the definition of the term "depreciation."

Q13.3 Under the matching principle, what distortion in income would take place if capital assets were written off as expenses when they were acquired rather than during their estimated useful lives through depreciation?

Q13.4 Distinguish between "physical" and "functional" factors as they relate to the decline in usefulness of property, plant, and equipment.

Q13.5 What specific estimates are required to apply the widely used methods of depreciation?

Q13.6 What is the primary justification for using the straight-line depreciation method?

Q13.7 What are the primary justifications for using the accelerated depreciation methods?

Q13.8 (Appendix A) For an asset with a relatively long life, computing the denominator base for the sum-of-the-years'-digits depreciation method can be burdensome if done by adding the digits from zero to the number of years in the asset's life. Apply the shortcut method of determining the denominator for an asset with an estimated useful life of eighteen years.

Q13.9 The double-declining balance depreciation rate can be computed by dividing the dollar amount of straight-line depreciation by the cost less the estimated salvage value of the asset, and then doubling the resulting rate. How can the same rate be computed without using the dollar amount of depreciation?

Q13.10 What is the primary impetus behind the use of accelerated depreciation methods?

Q13.11 What justification exists for the use of depreciation methods based on productive output or service quantities?

Q13.12 Under all depreciation methods, the book value of a capital asset declines through the life of the asset. What does this declining book value represent?

Q13.13 When a capital asset is acquired or disposed of at a time other than the beginning or end of a year, how should depreciation be handled for the first and last financial reporting periods during which the asset is used?

Q13.14 (Appendix A) What is the justification for group depreciation systems in which numerous assets are depreciated as a single asset?

Q13.15 (Appendix A) Describe the amount that represents the debit to depreciation expense in each of the following group-depreciation methods:
(a) Inventory system.   (c) Replacement system.
(b) Retirement system.   (d) Group and composite systems.

Q13.16 What is depletion, and how is it different from or similar to depreciation?

Q13.17 What is a change in an accounting estimate, and how should such changes be treated in the financial statements of the period of change?

Q13.18 If an accountant determines in 1995 that a depreciable asset with a ten-year life was incorrectly treated as an expense in 1992, what accounting treatment is appropriate in 1995 and future years?

Q13.19 (Appendix B) What is co-insurance, and how does it affect the amount that a company will receive from the insurer in the event of a loss?

Q13.20 (Appendix A) Which of the following depreciation methods does not result in decreasing charges?
- (a) Double-declining balance.
- (b) Sum-of-the-years'-digits.
- (c) Sinking fund.
- (d) Annuity.

Q13.21 Property, plant, and equipment are conventionally presented in the balance sheet at which of the following amounts?
- (a) Replacement cost less accumulated depreciation.
- (b) Historical cost less salvage value.
- (c) Original cost adjusted for general price-level changes.
- (d) Acquisition cost less depreciation recognized to date.

(Adapted from AICPA.)

Q13.22 In general accounting usage, which statement(s) applies (apply) to depreciation?
- (a) It is a process of asset valuation for balance sheet purposes.
- (b) It applies only to long-lived intangible assets.
- (c) It is used to indicate a decline in market value of a long-lived asset.
- (d) It is an accounting process that allocates long-lived asset cost to accounting periods.

(Adapted from AICPA.)

Q13.23 Which of the following four statements is the assumption on which straight-line depreciation is based?
- (a) The operating efficiency of an asset decreases in later years.
- (b) Service value declines as a function of time rather than use.
- (c) Service value declines as a function of obsolescence rather than time.
- (d) Physical wear and tear are more important than economic obsolescence.

(Adapted from AICPA.)

Q13.24 A graph is set up with "depreciation expense" on the vertical axis and the years along the horizontal axis. Assuming linear relationships, how would the graphs for straight-line and double-declining balance depreciation, respectively, be drawn?
- (a) Vertically and sloping down to the right.
- (b) Vertically and sloping up to the right.
- (c) Horizontally and sloping down to the right.
- (d) Horizontally and sloping up to the right.

(Adapted from AICPA.)

Exercises

E13.1 Depreciation Computations. Walker Ltd. acquired a new machine costing $147 500. The machine is expected to have a $20 000 residual value at the end of its six-year life and is expected to provide 17 000 hours of useful service or 50 000 units.

Instructions

Determine the first full year's depreciation, to the nearest dollar, under each of the following methods. The machine was used for 2750 hours during the year and produced 8000 units.
- (a) Straight line.
- (b) Double-declining balance.
- (c) Productive-output method.
- (d) Service hours.

E13.2 Depreciation Computations. The *Red Deer Daily News* acquired a delivery truck to distribute newspapers throughout the city of Red Deer. The truck cost $12 500 and is expected to last approximately four years, during which it will be driven approximately 80 000 km. The estimated salvage value of the truck is $1500. The truck was driven 14 500 and 17 600 km in its first two years. Assume the company has a 10 percent interest rate.

Instructions
Determine annual depreciation for the first two years of the truck's life using each of the following methods:
(a) Straight line.
(b) Service kilometres.
(c) Double-declining balance.
(d) Annuity. (Appendix A)

E13.3 Cost Determination and Depreciation. Winfred Products Ltd. purchased machinery that had a cash selling price of $175 000 by paying $85 000 cash and issuing $108 000 of face-value, noninterest-bearing notes. The company paid an additional $5000 for delivery and installation. A service contract was taken out, calling for $2500 annual payments; the first year's payment was made at the time the machinery was acquired. The machinery is expected to have a useful life of ten years and an estimated salvage value at the end of that time of $20 000. This asset qualifies for Class 8 at 20 percent with the limitation of a 50 percent deduction in the year of acquisition.

Instructions
(a) Determine the cost of the machinery for the purpose of computing depreciation.
(b) Prepare general journal entries to record the above events.
(c) Determine the first-year deduction using each of the following methods:
   (1) Straight-line.
   (2) Capital cost allowance.
   (3) Declining balance at 150 percent the straight-line rate.

E13.4 Partial Year Depreciation. Roth Ltd. acquired equipment for $500 000 on April 8, 1994. The asset is expected to have a four-year life and a salvage value of $60 000. Straight-line depreciation is to be used. The company reports on a calendar-year basis.

Instructions
(a) Compute depreciation to be recognized in 1994, 1995, 1996, 1997, and 1998 under each of the following independent fractional-year policies:
   (1) Depreciation recognized to nearest full month.
   (2) Depreciation recognized to nearest full year.
   (3) Half-year depreciation taken in the year of acquisition and in the year of disposal.
   (4) Full-year depreciation taken in the year of acquisition and none in the year of disposal.
(b) If the asset had been acquired on November 20, 1994, instead of April 8, under which policies would depreciation in 1994 and 1998 differ from that computed in (a)? Why?

E13.5 Partial Year Depreciation. On January 1, 1994, Fenner, Inc. purchased a new machine for $600 000. The machine has an estimated useful life of eight years with an expected salvage value at the end of that time of $25 000. Management specifies depreciation of machinery by the double-declining balance method.

Instructions

(a) What amount should be shown on Fenner's balance sheet on December 31, 1995, net of accumulated depreciation, for this asset?

(b) Assume the asset was acquired on August 5, 1994, rather than January 1. Compute the projected book value of the machine on December 31, 1994, 1995, and 1996 under each of the following independent fractional-year policies:

(1) A half-year's depreciation is taken in the year of acquisition and disposal.

(2) Depreciation is computed to the nearest full month.

E13.6 Cost Determination and Depreciation. The Building account of Cochran Ltd. includes the following items on December 31, 1995:

Building

Contract price	225 000	Gain on sale of old building	17 500
Options	7 000		
Repair and maintenance	12 000		

The building was acquired in early 1995 and all entries have been made since the acquisition. The options include $5000 on the building acquired and $2000 on a building that was not acquired. Repair and maintenance costs relate to routine activities occurring after the building was occupied.

Instructions

(a) Prepare the entry (or entries) needed to correct the Building account on December 31, 1995, before the books are closed.

(b) Determine depreciation expense for 1995 using each of the following methods, assuming a twenty-year life and $80 000 salvage value. A half-year depreciation is taken in the year of acquisition and the year of disposal.

(1) Straight line.

(2) Double-declining balance.

(3) Sum-of-the-years'-digits (Appendix A).

E13.7 Cost Determination and Depreciation. Oakville, Inc., a calendar-year company, purchased a machine for $65 000 on January 1, 1993. On that day, Oakville incurred the following additional costs:

Loss on sale of old machinery	$1000
Freight-in on new machinery	500
Installation	2000
Testing before regular operation	300

The estimated salvage value of the new machine was $5000. Oakville estimates that the machine will have a useful life of twenty years, with depreciation being computed on the straight-line method. In January 1995, accessories costing $5400 were added to the machine to reduce its operating costs. The accessories neither prolonged the machine's life nor provided salvage value.

Instructions

(a) Compute depreciation expense for 1993.
(b) Compute depreciation expense for 1995.
(Adapted from AICPA.)

E13.8 Cost Determination and Depreciation. On January 1, 1994, Phillips, Inc. purchased a machine for $50 000. Phillips paid shipping expenses of $500 and installation costs of $1200. The machine was estimated to have a ten-year life and a salvage value of $3000. In January 1995, additions costing $3600 were made to comply with pollution control laws. These additions neither prolonged the life of the machine nor provided salvage value.

Instructions

Prepare a schedule showing the components of book value for the machine at the end of years 1994 through 1997 under the straight-line method of depreciation.
(Adapted from AICPA.)

E13.9 Asset Exchanges and Depreciation. Carter Ltd. acquired a used machine in exchange for a similar machine from Darter Ltd. Just before the exchange, the book values of the respective assets were as follows:

	Cost	Accumulated Depreciation	Book Value
Carter Ltd.	$55 000	$25 000	$30 000
Darter Ltd.	47 500	22 500	25 000

Instructions

Prepare the journal entries to record the exchange and the first year's depreciation expense on the books of both companies in each of the following independent situations:

(a) No market value of either asset is available. Carter Ltd. uses straight-line depreciation with a six-year life for the asset acquired. Darter Ltd. uses double-declining balance depreciation with a ten-year life for the asset acquired. No salvage value is expected from either asset. (*Hint:* Because no market value information is available, the acquired assets must be recorded at the book value of the assets surrendered.)

(b) The asset relinquished by Carter Ltd. is valued at $22 000 (both parties are aware of this value). No value can be determined for the asset relinquished by Darter Ltd. Carter Ltd. uses straight-line depreciation with an eight-year life and a $4000 salvage value on the asset acquired. Darter Ltd. uses double-declining balance depreciation with a six-year life and no salvage value on the asset acquired. Assume the assets are dissimilar.

E13.10 **(Appendix A) Inventory Depreciation Method.**   Stark Co. uses the inventory system to account for numerous small tools used by employees. Under this system, depreciation is based on an inventory of tools on hand at the end of the year. Expenditures are charged to a Tools account throughout the year. The balance in the Tools account at the beginning of 1995 was $35 000. The following activity concerning small tools occurred during 1995:

Acquisitions (at cost)	
Mar. 12	$18 750
Aug. 28	6 300
Sale of used tools (at salvage value)	
Dec. 19	4 600

An inventory at the end of the year revealed that tools costing $34 800 were on hand and in use.

Instructions

(a) Prepare all general journal entries for activities related to small tools during 1995.
(b) Prepare the balance sheet and income statement for small tools for 1995.

E13.11   **(Appendix A) Retirement and Replacement Methods.**   Mack Utility Ltd. has a balance in its Water Meter account of $1 790 000 on January 1, 1995. This balance represents a large number of items, each with a small dollar value. The company is continually replacing the meters as its service employees identify units that are not functioning properly. During 1995 the company installed new meters in three different geographical areas, as follows:

Date of Job Completion	Cost of New Meters Installed	Cost of Old Meters Replaced	Proceeds from Sale of Old Meters
Feb. 17	$265 000	$192 000	$17 000
May 28	350 000	—	—
Oct. 30	160 000	93 000	5 000

The May 28 installation of new meters was in a new service area.

Instructions

(a) Prepare all journal entries for these transactions using the following depreciation methods:
   (1) Retirement method.
   (2) Replacement method.
(b) Prepare the balance sheet and income statement amounts using both of the above methods for the year ended December 31, 1995.

E13.12   **(Appendix A) Composite Depreciation Method.**   A schedule of machinery owned by Remdal Manufacturing Ltd. for its Assembly P is presented below:

	Total Cost	Estimated Salvage Value	Estimated Life in Years
Component P1	$440 000	$40 000	10
Component P2	280 000	20 000	5
Component P3	175 000	—	4

Remdal computes depreciation by the straight-line method.

Instructions
(a) Compute the composite life of the machines (in years) and the average depreciation rate for the machines (as a percentage).
(b) Prepare the general journal entry to record depreciation on the machines as a group for one year.

E13.13 Correction of Errors. On January 2, 1994, Winnipeg Ltd. exchanged a used truck for a similar truck. The original cost of Winnipeg's truck was $7000. It had accumulated depreciation of $3800 and a market value of approximately $4200 at the time of the exchange. Winnipeg paid an additional $4400 cash for the "new" truck, which was valued at approximately $8600.

The accountant for Winnipeg Ltd. recorded the truck at $7600, the total of the cash paid and the book value of the old truck. He recorded depreciation on the basis of kilometres driven, assuming a total useful life of 50 000 km, with 12 200 km driven in 1994. However, he failed to consider the $2700 expected salvage value after the 50 000 km life.

Instructions
(a) At what amount should the acquired truck have been recorded by Winnipeg? Why?
(b) Assume that the accountant's errors are found in 1995 before depreciation expense has been recorded for that year. Prepare the journal entries necessary to correct the accounts and to properly recognize depreciation expense for 1995, assuming that 17 200 km were driven that year.

E13.14 Cost Determination and Depreciation. Mandell Ltd. acquired a used delivery truck for $14 350. The following expenditures were made upon acquisition:

New tires	$425
Body repair and paint	515
Installation of special shelves	375
One-year insurance premium	450

Management expects that the truck will be of service for four years and will be driven a total of 60 000 km. A $3000 salvage value is expected.

Instructions
(a) Determine the cost of the truck for financial accounting purposes.
(b) Determine the depreciation expense for the first and second years using each of the following methods:
    (1) Straight-line.

(2) Service quantity in kilometres. (The truck was driven 9760 and 13 950 km in the first and second years, respectively.)

E13.15 Change in Asset Life. Gatan, Inc. purchased machinery in January of 1993 and applied straight-line depreciation during 1993 and 1994. The machinery cost $128 400, had an estimated six-year life, and was expected to be worth $8400 at the end of six years. In 1995, management reevaluated its capital assets and determined that this machinery would be useful for seven more years, including 1995. At the end of that period a salvage value of only $2000 is expected.

Instructions

(a) What amount of depreciation was recorded in 1993 and in 1994?
(b) When the change in estimated useful life is made in 1995, what entry, if any, should be made to account for the difference between annual depreciation taken in previous years and what will be taken in future years?
(c) Prepare the general journal entry to record depreciation expense for 1995.

E13.16 Change in Asset Life. Wellman Corporation purchased a machine on January 1, 1990, for $160 000. Upon acquisition, the machine had an estimated useful life of ten years with no salvage value. The machine is being depreciated on a straight-line basis. On January 1, 1995, as a result of experience with the machine, management decided that the machine had an estimated useful life of fifteen years from the date of purchase.

Instructions

(a) Prepare the general journal entry to record depreciation for 1995.
(b) Independent of your answer to (a), assume that on January 1, 1995, Wellman determines that it can extend the asset's life ten years beyond that date only by investing an additional $15 000 in the asset. The company anticipates a residual value at the end of the revised life of $5000. Prepare the journal entries required in 1995, including the recognition of depreciation for the year.
(Adapted from AICPA.)

E13.17 Correction of Errors. In 1993, North Ltd. bought a piece of machinery that was erroneously charged to Depreciation Expense in 1993. The company depreciates this class of assets by the double-declining balance method, with a half year's depreciation taken in the year of acquisition and in the year of disposal. This particular machine cost $62 000 and is expected to have an $8000 residual value at the end of eight years, at which time the company plans to dispose of it.

The error was discovered in 1995 as a result of the periodic evaluation of the estimated useful life of all capital assets.

Instructions

Prepare the general journal entries to correct the accounts and to properly record depreciation expense for 1995.

E13.18 Depletion. Worsham Ltd. acquired a tract of land containing an extractable natural resource. The purchase contract requires Worsham to restore the land to a condition suitable for recreation after it has extracted the natural resource. Geological surveys estimate recoverable reserves of 4 million tonnes and a land value of $1 million after restoration. Relevant cost information follows:

Land purchase price	$10 000 000
Estimated restoration costs	1 200 000

Instructions
(a) What is the depletion charge per tonne of the recoverable reserves?
(b) If the company extracts 550 000 t in the first year and sells 525 000 t, determine the following amounts:
   (1) Depletion expense.
   (2) Inventory cost of the recovered natural resource.
(Adapted from AICPA.)

E13.19 Depletion. Farr Corporation quarries limestone at two locations, crushes it, and sells it to be used in road building. Quarry No. 1 is leased, and Farr is paying a royalty of $0.01 per tonne of limestone quarried. Quarry No. 2 is owned, Farr having paid $100 000 for the site; the company estimates that the property can be sold for $30 000 after production ceases. Other data follow:

	Quarry No. 1	**Quarry No. 2**
Estimated total reserves (tonnes)	30 000 000	100 000 000
Tonnes quarried through Dec. 31, 1994	2 000 000	40 000 000
Tonnes quarried, 1995	800 000	1 380 000
Sales, 1995	$600 000	$1 000 000

All of the quarried stone is sold by the end of the year.

Instructions
(a) Determine the 1995 depletion for Quarry No. 1 for financial reporting purposes.
(b) Determine the 1995 depletion for Quarry No. 2 for financial reporting purposes.
(c) Assume the same information except that a new engineering study performed early in 1995 indicated that as of January 1, 1995, 75 million t of limestone were available in Quarry No. 2. How much would depletion of Quarry No. 2 be in 1995 for financial reporting purposes?
(Adapted from AICPA.)

E13.20 (Appendix B) Property Insurance. Information about four independent cases concerning casualty insurance on equipment is presented below.

	Case A	Case B	Case C	Case D
Fair market value of equipment at date of fire	$75 000	$100 000	$120 000	$150 000
Amount of fire loss	65 000	80 000	70 000	120 000
Face value of insurance policy	50 000	90 000	75 000	110 000
Co-insurance requirement	None	80%	90%	70%

Instructions

(a) For each case, determine the amount that would be recoverable from the insurance company.

(b) Prepare the general journal entry to record the fire loss and insurance recovery for Case B. Assume that the equipment destroyed had originally cost $155 000 and had accumulated depreciation of $86 700. No adjustment to prepaid insurance is required.

Problems

P13.1   Depreciation Computations.   Fox Machine Ltd. acquired heavy machinery at a cost of $160 000. In addition to the purchase price, $5000 was paid for delivery of the machinery and $2000 was paid for training company personnel to operate the equipment. The machinery was expected to provide 10 000 machine hours of service for five years, after which the machine can be sold for approximately $17 000. Actual machine operating hours during the first five years were as follows: 2700, 2200, 2400, 1600, and 1500. The company's borrowing rate is 8 percent.

Instructions

(a) Compute depreciation for each of the five years using the following depreciation methods:
   (1) Straight-line.
   (2) Service quantity—machine hours.
   (3) Double-declining balance.
   (4) Annuity (Appendix A).

(b) Comment briefly on the impact on book value that you see when comparing the four methods.

P13.2   Capital Asset Cost and Depreciation.   Information pertaining to Rand Corporation's property, plant, and equipment for 1995 is presented below.

Account Balances at January 1, 1995

	Debit	Credit
Land	$ 150 000	
Building	1 200 000	
Accumulated depreciation		$263 100
Machinery and equipment	900 000	
Accumulated depreciation		250 000
Automotive equipment	115 000	
Accumulated depreciation		84 600

Depreciation Method and Useful Life

Building—150% declining balance, 25 years.
Machinery and equipment—Straight-line, 10 years.
Automotive equipment—Double-declining balance, 4 years.

The salvage value of the depreciable assets is immaterial. Depreciation is computed to the nearest month.

Additional Information

On January 2, 1995, Rand purchased a new car for $10 000 cash and the trade-in of a two-year-old car with a cost of $9000 and a book value of $2250. The new car has a cash price of $12 000; the market value of the trade-in is not known.

On April 1, 1995, a machine purchased for $23 000 on April 1, 1990, was destroyed by fire. Rand recovered $15 500 from its insurance company.

On July 1, 1995, machinery and equipment were purchased at a total invoice cost of $280 000; additional costs of $5000 for freight and $25 000 for installation were incurred.

Instructions

(a) For each asset classification, prepare schedules showing depreciation expense and accumulated depreciation that would appear on Rand's income statement for the year ended December 31, 1995, and balance sheet at December 31, 1995, respectively.

(b) Prepare a schedule showing the gain or loss from disposal of assets that would appear in Rand's income statement for the year ended December 31, 1995.

(c) Prepare the property, plant, and equipment section of Rand's December 31, 1995, balance sheet.

(Adapted from AICPA.)

P13.3 Miscellaneous Transactions. Rosman Supply Ltd. entered into a series of transactions involving capital assets during 1994, its first year of operations. These transactions are summarized as follows:

Jan. 10 Machinery was acquired for $10 250 on account, terms 2/10, n/30.
 12 Freight-in of $250 on machinery acquired on January 10 was paid. The machine was immediately put into service.
 18 The account related to the machinery acquired on January 10 was paid.
Mar. 19 Inventory, fixtures, a building, and land were acquired for a single price of $520 000. The assets were appraised as follows:

Inventory	$150 000
Fixtures	70 000
Building	250 000
Land	100 000

May 1 Renovation costs of $50 000 on the building acquired on March 19 were completed, and the fixtures, building, and land placed into service.
Nov. 1 A truck was acquired and immediately placed into service. The truck had a list price of $9000 and was purchased by issuing an $8200, 12 percent, two-year note. The 12 percent interest rate was typical for this type of transaction and is payable annually. The truck was driven 2750 km in 1994.
Dec. 5 A second machine was acquired similar to that acquired on January 10 (both machines will be used). The machine was acquired on account for $10 700, terms 2/10, n/30. Payment was not made until 1995. Rosman did not incur a freight charge on this machine.
 31 The executive group of Rosman Supply Ltd. decided that the following policies should be used to determine the periodic depreciation on capital assets:

Asset	Life	Salvage	Method	Fractional-Year Policy
Machinery	8 yrs.	None	Double-declining balance	Nearest full month
Fixtures	10 yrs.	$10 000	Double-declining balance	Half year in years of acquisition and disposal
Buildings	25 yrs.	$60 000	Straight-line	Half year in years of acquisition and disposal
Truck	50 000 km	$800	Service quantity—kilometres	None

Instructions

(a) Prepare general journal entries to record the transactions described above.
(b) Prepare all adjusting entries.
(c) Prepare the property, plant, and equipment section of the balance sheet for Rosman Supply Ltd. on December 31, 1994.
(d) Briefly describe the meaning of the book values you included in (c). Explain their relationship to the current market value of the assets.

P13.4 Cost and Depreciation Calculations.   On January 1, 1994, Mock Corporation purchased a tract of land (site number 101) with a building for $650 000. Additionally, Mock paid a real estate broker's commission of $36 000, legal fees of $6000, and title guarantee insurance of $18 000. The closing statement indicated that the land value was $500 000 and the building value was $100 000. Shortly after acquisition, the building was torn down at a cost of $75 000.

Mock entered into a $3 million fixed-price contract with Smart Builders, Inc. on March 1, 1994, for the construction of an office building on land site number 101. The building was completed and occupied on September 30, 1995. Additional construction costs were incurred as follows:

Plans, specifications, and blueprints	$ 17 000
Architect's fees for design and supervision	112 000

The building is estimated to have a 40-year life from date of completion and will be depreciated using the declining balance method at 150 percent of the straight-line rate.

To finance the construction cost, Mock borrowed $3 million on March 1, 1994. The loan is payable in ten annual installments of $300 000 plus interest at the rate of 7 percent. Mock's average amounts of accumulated building construction expenditures were as follows:

For the period March 1 to December 31, 1994	$ 900 000
For the period January 1 to September 30, 1995	2 300 000

Instructions

(a) Prepare a schedule to determine the individual costs making up the balance in the land account in respect of land site number 101 as of September 30, 1995.
(b) Prepare a schedule that discloses the individual costs that should be capitalized in the office building account as of September 30, 1995. Show supporting computations.
(c) Comment briefly on the rationale for capitalizing interest as part of the building as you have done in (b).

(d) Prepare a schedule showing the depreciation expense computation of the office building for the year ended December 31, 1995.
(Adapted from AICPA.)

P13.5 Miscellaneous Transactions. Swenson Manufacturing Ltd. produces tools that are sold to a variety of manufacturing companies for use in their production operations. Many items of machinery are used to manufacture these tools. Presented below is information from the Machinery account and the related Accumulated Depreciation account on January 1, 1995, the beginning of the company's fiscal year.

Machinery	$725 400
Accumulated depreciation	(276 100)
	$449 300

The company uses the straight-line method of depreciation. The machinery is expected to have a ten-year life and no salvage value. Each piece of machinery is accounted for individually with a half year's depreciation taken in the years of acquisition and disposal. Depreciation is recorded on December 31 of each year.

The following transactions involving machinery took place during 1995:

Feb. 1 A machine acquired in 1993 for $10 500 was sold for $4860.
    15 New machinery costing $15 750 was acquired to replace the machine sold February 1.
Mar. 25 Repair and maintenance costs of $7500 were incurred.
Nov. 7 A machine costing $25 500, acquired in 1992, was traded for a similar machine. The acquired machine had a fair market value of $20 000. Swenson paid $1000 as a part of the exchange.
    11 Repair and maintenance costs of $7260 were incurred.
Dec. 5 A machine acquired in 1992 for $7250 was sold for $2500.
    10 New machinery costing $12 500 was acquired.
    31 Depreciation for all machinery for 1995 was recorded.

Instructions
(a) Prepare general journal entries for all machine-related transactions for 1995, including the recognition of depreciation for the year. Provide supporting computations for your entries. (*Hint:* In the November 7 transaction, the machine acquired should be recorded at the book value surrendered, plus cash paid.)
(b) Determine the balances in the Machinery and Accumulated Depreciation accounts for the December 31, 1995, balance sheet.

P13.6 Miscellaneous Transactions and Corrections. Parnell Ltd. takes a full year's depreciation in the year of acquisition and no depreciation in the year of disposal for all long-lived assets. During 1995, Parnell had five assets, described below.

	Asset V	Asset W	Asset X	Asset Y	Asset Z
Historical cost	$92 000	$127 500	$27 800	$70 000	$110 000
Year of acquisition	1992	1995	1990	1991	1995
Depreciation method	Straight-line	Double-declining balance	Units of production	Straight-line	Double-declining balance
Estimated life	10 yrs.	5 yrs.	100 000 units	7 yrs.	5 yrs.
Estimated salvage value	None	$5000	$3800	None	$20 000

Additional information about four of the assets has been collected to facilitate making the appropriate journal entries at the end of 1995:

Asset V Management has determined that the asset will be useful for a total of seventeen years rather than the ten years originally estimated. No salvage value is expected at the end of the asset's life.

Asset X During 1995, $10 000 was spent to improve the asset, adding 40 000 units of output to its total expected capacity. Before 1995, 65 000 units had been produced; during 1995, 20 000 units were produced. The estimated salvage value remained unchanged as a result of the improvement in 1995, which was recorded as a debit to accumulated depreciation.

Asset Y During 1995, Asset Y was sold for $25 000. The bookkeeper recorded the sale as follows:

Depreciation Expense	10 000	
Cash	25 000	
Asset Y		35 000

Asset Z Asset Z was acquired in late 1995 to replace Asset Y, which was sold.

Instructions
Prepare general journal entries for each asset on December 31, 1995, the end of Parnell Ltd.'s reporting period, to correct any errors made during the year and to properly record depreciation for the year. Show supporting computations.

P13.7 Correction of Errors. You have been assigned to help audit Mallard for 1994. Part of your responsibility is to evaluate the accounting procedures used to record capital assets and depreciation during 1992 and 1993, the first two years of the company's existence. No audit was made during those years.

The company applies the straight-line method of depreciation to buildings and the double-declining balance method to equipment. A full year's depreciation is taken in the year of acquisition and none is taken in the year of disposal. Balances in these accounts at the end of 1994 (before 1994 depreciation has been recognized) are as follows:

	Building (10-year life)	Equipment (5-year life)
Cost	$400 000	$160 000
Accumulated depreciation	(75 000)	(102 400)
	$325 000	$ 57 600

Your analysis of the company's records reveals the following:

Building.   The building was acquired before the beginning of operations on January 1, 1992, for $400 000. Of this amount, $50 000 was allocable to the land on which the building is situated. Transaction costs were an additional $25 000. Another $152 000 in renovation costs were incurred before the building was placed into service. The transaction and renovation costs were charged to expense in 1992. The building was originally expected to have a residual value of $25 000, which appears to have been a reasonable estimate at that time. Recent changes in economic conditions during 1994 indicate that the building will likely be disposable at $100 000 at the end of its ten-year life.

Equipment.   No salvage value was expected from the equipment at the end of its five-year life. Now, in 1994, it appears that the equipment will be worth $40 000 at the end of that period. It is also determined that machinery acquired during 1994 for $40 000 was incorrectly recorded as repair and maintenance expense. This mistake has not been corrected.

Instructions

Prepare all general journal entries necessary to correct the accounts and to properly record depreciation for 1994 for the separate Building and Equipment accounts. Present supporting computations with your entries.

P13.8   Correction of Errors.   Dobson Co. acquired the assets of a competitor in order to establish a branch of Dobson's main store. Dobson paid $500 000 in cash and issued 10 000 no-par common shares, which had an average paid in amount of $25 and a $30 market value at the date of issuance. The market value is based on active trading of the shares in quantities far in excess of the 10 000 shares exchanged in the acquisition. An appraisal of the assets, used by Dobson to negotiate the purchase price, reveals the following values on the transaction date:

Inventory	$200 000
Accounts receivable	100 000
Display fixtures	100 000
Building	300 000
Land	100 000
	$800 000

An inexperienced bookkeeper for Dobson recorded the acquisition as follows:

Inventory	200 000	
Accounts Receivable	100 000	
Capital Assets	450 000	
Cash		500 000
Common Shares		250 000
(10 000 shares × $25)		

A further analysis of the Capital Asset account reveals that the same bookkeeper entered the following items in the account during 1994:

Debit Entries		
May 1 Acquisition price	$450 000	
May 1 Insurance on building and fixtures		
(May 1, 1994, to April 30, 1995)	10 000	$460 000

Credit Entries

May 1   Proceeds from the sale of unneeded display
            fixtures   17 500
Dec. 31 Depreciation for 1994   22 125

                                                                      (39 625)
Balance, December 31, 1994 $420 375

A computation accompanying the depreciation figure for 1994 is as follows: ($460 000 − $17 500)/20 years = $22 125. You have determined that the unneeded display fixtures that were sold represent 10 percent of the fixtures acquired from the competitor on May 1.

You have also learned that Dobson depreciates fixtures over a ten-year life by the double-declining balance method and assumes a salvage value of 10 percent of the cost of items on hand when the depreciation calculation is made. The building is subject to straight-line depreciation over a twenty-year life. The building has an estimated $50 000 residual value at the end of the twenty years. All depreciation is computed to the nearest full month. This information was apparently ignored by the bookkeeper.

Instructions

(a) Prepare general journal entries to correct the accounts on December 31, 1994, assuming the books have not been closed. For each entry, explain to the bookkeeper why the entry is necessary and what error(s) were made in the original recording of the item.
(b) Prepare the balance sheet for property, plant, and equipment on December 31, 1994.
(c) Determine the appropriate depreciation expense amounts for the display fixtures and building for 1995.

P13.9   Depletion and Depreciation. Rim Mine Corporation acquired property in 1995 that is believed to include valuable mineral deposits. The cost of the property was $900 000. Geological estimates indicate that approximately 10 million tonnes of the mineral may be economically extracted in eight years. It is further estimated that the property can be sold for $250 000 to be used for commercial development following mineral extraction. For $80 000, Rim expects to restore the land to a condition appropriate for resale.

After initial acquisition, the following costs were incurred:

Exploration costs $350 000 (related to expected producible mineral reserves).
Development costs $325 000 (related to development of tunnels and shafts in the ground); $460 000 (related to specialized production equipment).

Instructions

(a) Prepare general journal entries necessary to record the above transactions, beginning with the initial acquisition and including depletion and depreciation for 1995 using the following additional information:
(1) 3 720 000 tonnes of the mineral are extracted and sold during 1995.
(2) The specialized production equipment will be useful in ongoing production operations and has a ten-year life expectancy and a $35 000 salvage value. Double-declining balance depreciation is to be used, with a full year's depreciation taken in 1995.

(b) How would your entries in (a) differ if the specialized production equipment were acquired exclusively for use in the extraction of the mineral for this project? (The $35 000 salvage value is still a reasonable estimate.)

P13.10 Income Statment. Wilman Mining Ltd. went into business in January 1994 to mine and sell a mineral. Assets were acquired as follows:

Asset	Cost	Estimated Useful Life	Residual Value
Land and mineral deposit	$1 000 000(a)	10 000 000 t	$200 000(b)
Mine building	75 000	life of mine	5 000
Equipment	650 000	8 years	65 000

(a) Additional costs

Exploration costs (related to minerals discovered)	$ 88 000
Development costs	110 000

(b) Restoration costs (estimated cost of preparing land for sale at $200 000)

	75 000

Depreciation policies of the company are as follows:

Mineral deposits—tonnes-extracted basis.
Mine building—same basis as mineral deposits.
Equipment—double-declining balance.

Operating data for 1994 and 1995 are as follows:

	1994	1995
Tonnes of mineral extracted	1 500 000	2 500 000
Tonnes of mineral sold at $4 per tonne	1 200 000	2 000 000
Costs of mineral extraction, exclusive of depreciation and depletion (labour, maintenance, etc.)	$1 175 000	$2 260 000
Selling and administrative costs	$985 000	$1 660 000

Inventory of extracted minerals is carried on the first-in, first-out basis. The cost basis for inventory produced during a given period is computed at the average production cost for that period.

Wilman had 500 000 common shares outstanding in 1994 and 1995.

Instructions

Prepare comparative income statements for 1994 and 1995, providing computations to support your entries and disregarding income taxes. The company's year-end is December 31.

P13.11 (Appendix A) Composite Depreciation Method. Wong Manufacturing Ltd. uses the composite depreciation method for its Production Assembly L35. The individual components in the assembly and their estimated residual values and estimated lives are presented below.

Component	Cost	Estimated Salvage Value	Estimated Useful Life in Years
L35-1	$125 000	$25 000	5
L35-2	36 000	1 000	7
L35-3	117 000	17 000	10
L35-4	42 000	—	6
L35-5	19 500	1 500	6
L35-6	211 250	11 250	8
L35-7	82 600	1 600	9

Instructions

(a) Determine the composite life of Assembly L35 and the annual depreciation rate.

(b) Prepare the adjusting entry to record depreciation for the first year of the assembly's life. Depreciation is recorded to the nearest hundred dollars.

(c) During the second year of the asset's life, Component L35-2 is determined to be incompatible with the other components and is sold for $20 000. Record the disposal of Component L35-2.

(d) Component L35-2 is replaced with a new component costing $50 000 and having an estimated nine-year life and a $500 salvage value. Record this replacement and depreciation for the second year.

(e) Disregard the information in (d). Management determines that Component L35-2 must be replaced with a highly specialized piece of equipment that is now in the experimental stage. This component costs $100 000, is expected to be useful for only two years, and will have no salvage value. Record the replacement and depreciation for the second year.

P13.12 (Appendix A) Group Depreciation Methods. Maples Ltd. is considering the use of a group depreciation method for Asset X. The company has many units of Asset X in use at all times and is constantly replacing the units, each of which has a relatively low price. Statistics about Asset X for 1995 have been estimated as follows:

	Units
Beginning balance	100 000
Additions	78 000
Retirements	(62 000)
Ending balance	116 000

Asset X is replaced on a FIFO basis. The beginning balance in Asset X is $250 000, indicating a $2.50 unit cost. Additions were made at a $2.60 unit cost during 1995. Retirements were salvaged for $5000.

Instructions

(a) Prepare the general journal entries to record additions, retirements, and depreciation for the year using each of the following group depreciation methods:
   (1) Inventory system.
   (2) Replacement system.
   (3) Retirement system.

(b) Determine the depreciation expense and the asset balance to be presented in the 1995 financial statements under each depreciation method in (a).

(c) Why might a company choose to use a group depreciation method rather than treating each asset as an individual unit?

P13.13   (Appendix B) Property Insurance.   This problem contains two independent parts.

Part 1.   Blue Ltd. has several assets under separate insurance policies that contain co-insurance requirements. Descriptions of these policies and insurable losses sustained on each asset are as follows:

	Asset W	Asset X	Asset Y
Fair market value of asset	$45 000	$25 000	$40 000
Face value of policy	$40 000	$22 500	$25 000
Co-insurance requirement	80%	90%	85%
Amount of casualty loss	$25 000	$25 000	$30 000

Instructions

Determine the amount to be reimbursed by the insurance company for Assets W, X, and Y.

Part 2.   Red Ltd. has two insurance policies on its building. Policy 1 has a face value of $500 000; Policy 2 has a face value of $300 000. The estimated value of the building is $1 million. A loss of $750 000 was recently sustained when a fire destroyed a major portion of the building.

Instructions

Determine the amount to be received from each policy in the following independent cases:

(a)   The policies contain no co-insurance requirements.
(b)   Both policies have 90 percent co-insurance requirements.
(c)   Policy 1 has a 90 percent co-insurance requirement and Policy 2 has a 70 percent co-insurance requirement.

P13.14   (Appendix A) Alternative Depreciation Mehtods.   Wampler Corporation bought a new asset on January 1, 1995, which it plans to put into service immediately. The following information is available:

Cost	$100 000
Expected salvage value	$5 000
Estimated life in years	15
Current corporate interest rate	12%

Instructions

Calculate the depreciation for the first two years of the asset's life using each of the following methods:

(1)   Sum-of-the-years'-digits.
(2)   Annuity method. (Show both the depreciation expense and accumulated depreciation amounts.)
(3)   Sinking fund method.

P13.15   Asset Section of Balance Sheet.   Mallory, Inc. manufactures a variety of medical instruments and supplies. The company uses the calendar year for reporting purposes.

Information regarding Mallory's assets as of December 31, 1995, before any year-end adjustments, is given below.

Short- and Long-term Investments. Mallory invests excess funds in short-term marketable securities. The company also has long-term investments in the common shares of other companies. Mallory's holdings of common shares represent less than 5 percent ownership in those companies. Details are shown below.

Information on Mallory's Holdings of Common Shares

Investments	Acquisition Date	Purchase Price	Market Values Dec. 31, 1994	Market Values Dec. 31, 1995
Short-Term				
PWR, Inc.	Mar. 1, 1995	$ 130 000	—	$ 123 000
Tyra Ltd.	Aug. 15, 1995	80 000	—	75 500
Marank Ltd.	Nov. 20, 1995	50 000	—	51 500
Total short-term investments		260 000		250 000
Long-Term				
Grabill Ltd.	July 1, 1994	117 000	$112 000	113 000
Mikott, Inc.	Mar. 1, 1993	242 000	260 000	252 000
Stanor Ltd.	Dec. 15, 1992	165 000	168 000	170 000
Clarmit, Inc.	Aug. 22, 1991	286 000	272 000	260 000
Total long-term investments		810 000	812 000	795 000
Total investments		$1 070 000	$812 000	$1 045 000

None of the declines in market prices are considered permanent. Dividends that have been declared but have not been received as of December 31, 1995, total $10 300.

Accounts Receivable. The outstanding accounts receivable as of December 31, 1995, total $304 000. The allowance for uncollectable accounts had a credit balance of $16 800 on December 31, 1994. A total of $6400 in uncollectable accounts was written off during 1995. An aging of the accounts receivable on December 31, 1995, shows a total of $12 400 of the accounts receivable will be uncollectable.

Notes Receivable. Mallory holds two notes from trade customers that are due in 1996. In addition, Mallory holds a note that resulted from the sale of some of its manufacturing equipment. This note is not due until 1998. Interest is due on the anniversary date of the note and has not been accrued as of December 31, 1995. Details are given below, with the two trade notes listed first.

Date of Note	Maturity Date	Face Amount	Annual Interest Rate
Apr. 1, 1995	Mar. 31, 1996	$150 000	8%
July 1, 1995	June 30, 1996	275 000	8%
Jan. 1, 1994	Dec. 31, 1998	450 000	9%
		$875 000	

Inventories. Inventories are valued at the lower of cost or market value. Cost is determined by the FIFO method. Mallory's physical count of inventory reflects that merchandise with a cost of $2 500 000 and market value of $3 200 000 was on hand on December 31, 1995. In addition to this inventory, Mallory had merchandise still out on consignment. The cost of this merchandise was $240 000, the handling and shipping charges to get the merchandise to the consignee totalled $8000, and the market value was $300 000.

Property, Plant, and Equipment.   Mallory states all property at cost. The property and related account balances before the current year's depreciation expense are shown below. The depreciation expense for 1995 is $125 000 for the building and $150 000 for the equipment and furniture.

	Cost	Accumulated Depreciation (before adjustment)
Land	$1 450 000	—
Buildings	3 600 000	$1 425 000
Equipment and furniture	1 750 000	785 000
	$6 800 000	$2 210 000

Included in the amount for land is $250 000 for a parcel of land acquired on December 28, 1995, as a potential building site. As part of the contract to acquire the land, Mallory also had to pay $20 000 in delinquent property taxes; this amount was recorded as an expense.

Additional Information

Cash.   The total in the various bank accounts and imprest petty cash funds amounts to $165 000.

Insurance.   Mallory has purchased insurance to protect its assets and operations. The policies that will be in effect during 1996 are shown below:

Policy No.	Date of Policy	Premium Amount	Coverage in Years
JNA-XY5782	July 1, 1993	$18 000	3
DOME-NX85472	Apr. 1, 1994	30 000	3
FMC-BD287X	Oct. 1, 1995	8 000	1

Patent.   Mallory acquired patent rights on January 2, 1995, for $75 000. At that time, management estimated that the patent would provide economic benefits to the company for the next five years.

Instructions

(a) Prepare a classified asset section of the statement of financial position for Mallory, Inc. on December 31, 1995, as it should appear in the annual report to shareholders.

(b) Describe the information pertaining to Mallory's assets that must be disclosed in the notes to the 1995 financial statements in the annual report to shareholders.

(Adapted from CMA.)

Cases

C13.1   Expensing Versus Amortizing Asset Costs.   Constructo Corporation sells and erects "shell houses." These are frame structures that are completely finished on the outside and are finished on the inside except for flooring, partition studding, and ceiling joists. Shell houses are sold chiefly to customers who are handy with tools and who have time to do the interior wiring, plumbing, wall finishing, and other work necessary to complete the houses.

Constructo buys shell houses from a manufacturer in unassembled packages consisting of all lumber, roofing, doors, windows, and similar materials. Upon commencing operations in a new area, Constructo buys or leases land for its local warehouse, field office, and display houses. Sample houses are erected for $6000 to $10 000. The unassembled packages constitute the majority of the expense; erection is a short, low-cost operation. Old models are torn down or altered every three to seven years. They have little salvage value, because dismantling and moving costs nearly equal the cost of an unassembled package.

Instructions

(a) A choice must be made between (1) expensing the costs of sample houses in the period in which the expenditure is made and (2) spreading the costs over more than one period. Discuss the advantages of each method.

(b) Should Constructo amortize the cost of sample houses on the basis of (1) the passage of time or (2) the number of shell houses sold? Explain.

(Adapted from AICPA.)

C13.2 Depreciation Policy. Ron's Manufacturing Ltd. was organized January 1, 1994. During 1994, it has used in its reports to management the straight-line method of depreciating its capital assets.

On November 8, you meet with Ron's officers to discuss the depreciation method to be used for income tax and shareholder reporting. Ron's president has suggested a new method that he feels is more suitable than the straight-line method for the period of rapid expansion of production and capacity that he foresees. Below, the proposed method is applied to a capital asset with an original cost of $32 000, an estimated useful life of five years, and an estimated salvage value of $3000.

Year	Depreciation Expense	Accumulated Depreciation at Year-End	Book Value at Year-End
1	$12 800.00	$12 800.00	$19 200.00
2	7 680.00	20 480.00	11 520.00
3	4 608.00	25 088.00	6 912.00
4	2 764.80	27 852.80	4 147.20
5	1 147.20	29 000.00	3 000.00

The president favours the new method because he has heard that

(1) It will increase the funds recovered during the years near the end of the assets' useful lives, when maintenance and replacement disbursements will be high.

(2) It will result in increased write-offs in later years and tax benefits.

Instructions

(a) What is the purpose of accounting for depreciation?

(b) Is the president's proposal within the scope of generally accepted accounting principles? Discuss the circumstances under which the method would be reasonable and those under which it would not be reasonable.

(c) The president asks your advice concerning the following:

  (1) Do depreciation charges recover or create funds? Explain.

  (2) How does a change in the method of depreciation affect the company's tax liability? If the method were used for shareholders, how would it affect the availability of funds generated by operations?

(Adapted from AICPA.)

C13.3 Significance of Book Value. When John Severance, President of Severance, Inc. opened his office on Monday, March 8, he discovered that a robbery had occurred over the weekend. Someone had entered the office through a back window and stolen a computer. After notifying authorities, Severance identified the serial number on those computers that were not taken and compared them with the capital asset records that were kept in the company vault. After doing this, Severance said to his employees: "Thank goodness the thief took one of the computers that was almost fully depreciated. That serves him right and certainly eases our situation, since the computers are not insured."

Instructions

(a) What is your reaction to Severance's evaluation of this situation?

(b) Is Severance, Inc. "better off" because a thief stole a computer on which more depreciation has already been taken (as opposed to one with less depreciation taken)? Why or why not?

Judgement Cases

J13.1 Gain Recognition and Depletion. White Paper Ltd. owns large holdings of forest lands in the Pacific Northwest that are used to supply the company's mills with various types of pulp. The company has recently received an offer on some of its least productive land and has decided to sell.

Specifically, the company has received an offer to sell a portion of one large forest that it has owned for many decades. The president wants to determine how the sale will be reported in the company's financial statements and the amount of gain to be recognized. The current carrying amount of the forest on the company's books of $8 million represents the cost of the forest, less charges for depletion, plus improvements (such as roads and reforestation) and cultivation costs. The portion to be sold represents about one-eighth of the total forest land and the proposed sales price is $5 million. The land subject to the sale is mountainous, near a river, and is in a particularly remote area that does not currently have roads developed on it. Recent geological tests, however, reveal that substantial and valuable mineral deposits exist on the land, which the buyer plans to exploit.

Your assistant has prepared the following proposed accounting for the sale. He has assigned a pro rata share of the carrying amount of the tract of ($8 million × ⅛) $1 million to the sale and proposes importing a gain of $4 million on the transaction. You believe the problem is rather simple and are satisfied with this suggestion. You have arranged a meeting with the president to discuss the proposed accounting.

You are surprised when the president points out a number of considerations that he believes are important to the determination of the proper accounting treatment for the transaction. He states that the land has been virtually worthless to the company up to this point. He believes that the other factors and considerations as to the newly found minerals should be recognized in accounting for the sale, and argues that only a nominal amount, if any, of the carrying amount of the forest should be attributed to the portion sold, resulting in a gain of virtually all of the $5 million sales price. He reasons:

The land we are selling has never been of value to us in our productive processes. Indeed, we never would have bought it if we could have avoided doing so when we acquired the large tract from the federal government many years ago. The fact that mineral deposits have now been found on it is simply fortuitous for us. The productivity of this forest to our company will remain unchanged by the sale, and therefore, the entire sales price of $5 million is simply a windfall gain that we are receiving. Finally, if we allocate the cost as you suggest, this will leave a relatively small amount of original cost for us to allocate to the revenues generated by the timber production that we will sell in the future on other parts of the land. We will report much higher profitability on the sale of timber than we actually achieve, and you don't want that, do you?

Instructions

React to the president's proposal. Do you think that his proposed accounting for the sale is acceptable?

J13.2 Depreciating and Valuing Inactive Assets.   High Flyer Aviation has a group of airplanes of various designs and ages. Some of the older planes are not fuel-efficient and have lately been used only when all other aircraft are already in use and for charter flights when other more efficient planes are not readily available in the location desired.

Recently, an oil crisis has arisen due to the invasion of one Middle-Eastern country by another. One result of this crisis has been a dramatic increase in the cost of petroleum products, including aircraft fuel. In fact, the cost of fuel has become so high that the older, less efficient aircraft are not being used at all because they simply cannot be operated at a positive contribution margin due to the high fuel prices and the effects of intense charter competition. At the time that the company's financial statements are being prepared, the crisis shows no signs of relenting. In fact, the situation appears to be worsening and most oil analysts predict that the price of petroleum products will remain very high for the foreseeable future.

As a result of these factors, High Flyer Aviation has "mothballed" all of its older, inefficient airplanes and is attempting to sell them. No buyers have been found, however, and prospects look dim for finding a buyer in the near future. You are concerned with whether the carrying amounts in the financial statements of these older aircraft should continue to be depreciated or whether they have been impaired and should be written down to lower figures than their current carrying values. The aircraft have been depreciated by a combination of methods. The engines, controls, and avionics are depreciated over flying hours, while the airframes are depreciated over a period of ten years by the straight-line method. The president of the company has indicated to you that if she cannot sell the planes at a gain, she will hold them until fuel prices come back down and things stabilize:

> At that time, we will begin to use these planes again profitably. Until then, I don't believe that any aspect of the aircraft should be depreciated or written down to some arbitrary amount that has nothing to do with their value in use. I certainly don't think that the components of the aircraft that are ordinarily depreciated over flying hours should be depreciated when no flying is conducted—that just doesn't make sense.

Despite the president's assurances, you still have concerns about both appropriate depreciation policy and the realizability of the carrying amount of the aircraft. You are aware, for example, that replacing the old engines with new, fuel-efficient ones is one way of making the aircraft more serviceable. You also know that this is a very expensive alternative.

Instructions

Should any (or all) of the components of the inactive aircraft continue to be depreciated while they are not being used? Should the value of the aircraft be written down to an amount lower than their undepreciated cost? If so, describe the conceptual amount at which they should be carried on the financial statements of High Flyer Aviation. If you believe that continued depreciation and/or a write-down is appropriate, how will you convince the president to accept this accounting treatment?

J13.3   Depreciating a Leased Asset.   Dryden Petroleum Ltd. has constructed equipment for a large offshore drilling platform that it planned to use in its exploration and production efforts. The company has now decided, however, to lease this equipment to another company because of unanticipated cash-flow needs. This lease has a term of five years, and the company expects to be able to lease the equipment to other companies for its entire economic life of approximately fifteen years. If fact, management believes that it will be possible to negotiate leases with higher payments through other companies after the initial five-year lease is complete. The total amount of the lease payments that the company expects to receive over the economic life of the equipment exceeds the current carrying amount of the equipment on the financial statements of Dryden by only a small amount. If those anticipated cash receipts were discounted at any reasonable rate of interest, however, the present value of the future cash receipts would be substantially less than the carrying value of the equipment.

The company is in the process of preparing its annual financial statements, and you wonder how the equipment that was constructed to be used but that is now being leased should be depreciated and whether it should be considered impaired in value at this time. That is, the net present value of the expected future cash flows from the leases, some of which are yet to be negotiated, are less than the carrying value of the asset.

Instructions
Should the equipment be depreciated in a normal fashion? Should any recognition be given in the selection of a depreciation method to the belief that the leases following the first lease will result in substantially greater lease payments? Should a loss be recognized now in these circumstances? If so, how will this loss affect the amount of depreciation to be recognized on the equipment in the future? If you believe that a loss should be recognized, be sure to describe how the amount of the loss should be measured.

Chapter 14

Intangible Assets

Objectives

1. To distinguish between intangible assets and property, plant, and equipment and to explain how intangible assets contribute to the revenue-producing process.

2. To distinguish between separately identifiable intangible assets and goodwill, an intangible asset that relates to the enterprise as a whole.

3. To apply basic accounting principles, such as matching and asset/liability measurement, in accounting for intangible assets.

4. To illustrate the preparation of the financial statement items and accompanying disclosures for intangible assets.

5. To explain goodwill, including how it arises, how to estimate its value, and how to determine its cost.

6. To discuss the accounting problems associated with several special areas of accounting that involve intangible assets, including research and development, development-stage enterprises, and oil and gas industry accounting.

Defining Intangible Assets

Intangible assets are factors in the production or distribution of goods or services that generate revenue. Most intangible assets have relatively long lives and are subject to amortization over several periods subsequent to their acquisition, as are property, plant, and equipment. However, the distinguishing feature of intangibles is their **lack of physical characteristics.** Additionally, the uncertainty of the amount and timing of future benefits is generally thought to be greater with intangible assets than with other long-lived assets. The value of an intangible asset accrues primarily from the rights or privileges that it provides the owner.

The absence of physical existence alone does not qualify an asset to be presented as an intangible. Assets that lack physical existence are also found in several balance sheet categories other than intangibles. For example, receivables, short-term investments, and prepaid expenses are presented as current assets; noncurrent receivables and investments in shares and bonds are classified as investments and funds; and long-term prepayments are presented as other assets or deferred charges. Thus, in addition to the lack of physical existence, assets classified as intangible must be used in the production or distribution of other goods or services and have relatively long lives, making them subject to amortization.

Intangible assets are frequently divided into those that are separately identifiable and those that lack specific identification. Examples of **separately identifiable intangible assets** are patents, copyrights, franchises, licensing agreements, trade names, trademarks, and organization costs. Intangible assets that lack specific identification are inherent in a continuing business and relate to an enterprise as a whole. While the name given to such assets varies from entity to entity, a common name for this type of intangible asset is **goodwill,** the term used in this chapter.

Despite the fact that intangible assets lacking specific identification vary considerably in nature from separately identifiable intangibles, standards that guide the accounting for *all* intangibles have been developed by the accounting profession. The most significant of these standards are in CICA *Handbook,* Section 3060, which provides the basis for much of the material in this chapter.[1]

Accounting Standards for Intangible Assets

Asset/Liability Measurement

Matching

Generally accepted standards of accounting for intangible assets incorporate historical cost in applying the asset/liability measurement and matching principles. In much the same way as with property, plant, and equipment, intangible assets are recorded initially at historical cost, the fair value at the time of acquisition. This cost is subsequently amortized over those periods in which the assets are used as factors in the production or distribution of goods and services. Accounting for intangible assets is described in the following sections in terms of acquisition, amortization, disposal, and financial statement presentation.

Acquisition of Intangible Assets

An intangible asset is recorded at cost, which may be described as the sacrifice in assets or the incurrence of liabilities that are necessary to acquire the asset. Intangible assets

<hr>

[1]"Capital Assets," CICA *Handbook,* Paragraph 3060.06, December 1992.

may be acquired from other enterprises, in which case cost is normally the fair value of consideration given in the exchange transaction. In unusual circumstances, the value of the intangible asset received may be more readily determinable than the value of the consideration given, and in these cases the former should be used to record the cost of the intangible asset received.

Intangible assets may also be acquired as part of a group of assets or as part of the acquisition of an entire enterprise. Separately identifiable assets and liabilities, including intangible assets, acquired in such transactions are assigned part of the total cost of the group of assets or enterprise acquired. This assignment is normally based on the fair value of individual assets. The cost of an intangible asset not specifically identifiable that is acquired in this manner is measured by the difference between the total cost of the group of assets and the cost assigned to the other assets, including the separately identifiable intangible assets. This process is developed in greater depth in a subsequent section of this chapter.

Some intangible assets are developed internally. Costs of developing, maintaining, or restoring intangible assets that can be separately identified and have determinate lives are capitalized in appropriate intangible asset accounts. Similar costs that do not relate to separately identifiable, intangible assets, that have indeterminate lives, or that are inherent in a continuing business should not be capitalized as intangible assets.

 We must take care in distinguishing between costs of intangible assets and other expenditures that should be charged to expense when incurred under generally accepted accounting principles (GAAP). Examples of the latter are advertising and research costs. Frequently, these expenses are closely related to the development of intangible assets and are sometimes confused with them.

The initial accounting for potential intangible asset acquisition costs is summarized in Exhibit 14.1. Separately identifiable intangible assets with determinable lives are capitalized in specific intangible asset accounts, whether they were acquired from another entity or developed internally. Patents, for example, may be acquired from other enterprises or developed internally. Intangible assets, such as goodwill, that cannot be separately identified but result from transactions with other entities should be established in appropriate intangible asset accounts. Costs relating to internally developed intangibles that cannot be separately identified are treated as expenses when incurred, even though they may have many of the characteristics of goodwill. For example, a company may develop an outstanding reputation, much like one that it could acquire through a business merger. The costs incurred to develop this reputation internally are normally expensed as incurred. Expenditures that are charged to expense when incurred under generally accepted accounting principles, such as research or advertising, are not established as intangible assets, even though they may relate closely to the development, maintenance, or enhancement of certain intangible assets.

Amortization of Intangible Assets

CICA *Handbook,* Section 3060, includes the recommendations for all capital assets, both tangibles and intangibles. Amortization of all these assets is required for *all* assets used to generate income. Before the CICA issued Section 3060, companies divided intangible assets into those with determinable lives and those without determinable lives. Those with determinable lives were amortized, whereas those without determinable lives were not amortized. Under Section 3060, however, intangible assets must be amortized over

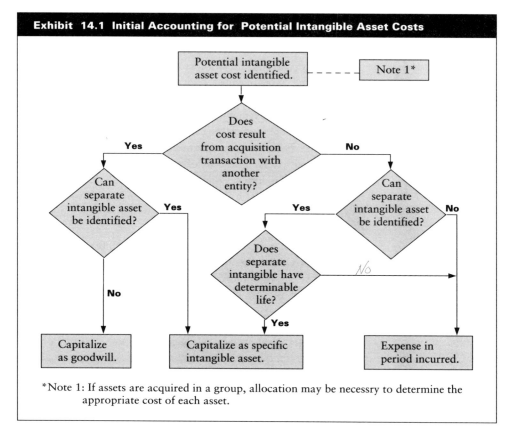

Exhibit 14.1 Initial Accounting for Potential Intangible Asset Costs

*Note 1: If assets are acquired in a group, allocation may be necessry to determine the appropriate cost of each asset.

the periods that benefit from their use.[2] In establishing this requirement, the CICA made the following observation:

> Different methods of amortizing a capital asset result in different patterns of charges to income. The objective is to provide a rational and systematic basis for allocating the amortizable amount of a capital asset over its estimated life and useful life.[3]

A number of pertinent factors must be considered in establishing the periods expected to benefit from intangible assets. These are outlined by the Accounting Principles Board in the United States and include the following:[4]

1. Legal, regulatory, or contractual provisions may limit the maximum useful life.
2. Provisions for renewal or extension may alter a specified limit on useful life.
3. Obsolescence, demand, competition, and other economic factors may affect useful life.

---

[2]In requiring the amortization of intangible assets, the CICA indicated that companies were not required to amortize intangibles acquired before December 1, 1990, the effective date of Section 3060. Because some companies began amortizing intangibles that previously had not been amortized whereas others continued to carry these intangibles at their historical cost, some intangible assets may still be found on some companies' balance sheets at unamortized historical cost.

[3]"Capital Assets," CICA *Handbook,* Paragraph 3060.35, October 1990.

[4]"Accounting for Intangible Assets," *APB Opinion No. 17,* 1970.

4. Useful life may parallel the service life expectancies of individuals or groups of employees.

5. Present competitive advantage may be restricted by expected actions of competitors or others.

6. An apparent unlimited life may in fact be indefinite and benefits cannot be reasonably projected.

7. An intangible may be a composite of any individual factors with varying effective lives.

The CICA supports these factors and also has established a maximum period of 40 years for the amortization of intangible assets. Thus, an intangible asset should be amortized over the shorter of its economic life (which may be influenced by legal or contractual limitations) or 40 years. The CICA offered little justification for the 40-year maximum amortization period; however, several explanations appear reasonable.

Intangible assets with indeterminate lives, such as goodwill, are frequently amortized over the maximum period. These assets may relate to individual employees or groups of employees and other conditions that are of limited duration. These same conditions are not likely to continue beyond a period of 40 years. Amortization over a 40-year period, even though this is an arbitrary assignment of cost, prevents any one accounting period from being burdened with such a significant amortization charge that income is materially affected. Also, few intangible assets are useful to an enterprise for more than 40 years. In fact, the makeup of a corporation in terms of asset structure, personnel, production processes, marketing strategy, and many other aspects will generally be significantly different when viewed in 40-year intervals.

Materiality

Matching

Although the 40-year maximum amortization period appears somewhat arbitrary, justification exists for amortization over a relatively long period. Also, if the value of intangible assets does in fact diminish over time, the matching principle requires some portion of the cost of such assets to enter into the determination of income in the periods that are benefited. This is true even if the life of the asset is not precisely determinable when it is acquired.

An enterprise should continuously evaluate the period over which intangible assets are being amortized. If estimates of useful lives change due to subsequent events and circumstances, the unamortized cost remaining at that point should be allocated to the increased or reduced number of periods in the remaining expected life.[5] The period of amortization should never exceed 40 years from the date of acquisition.

Paragraph 3060.35 of the CICA *Handbook* also recommends the straight-line method of amortization unless a company can specifically demonstrate that another method is more appropriate. Accountants typically ignore residual values in applying the straight-line method in the amortization of intangible assets. Policies followed in recognizing amortization for partial years vary, but the alternatives available parallel closely those for property, plant, and equipment as discussed in Chapter 13. Amortization may be computed to the nearest full month, half year, or full year in applying the straight-line method in periods during which the intangible asset is disposed of or acquired. Expenditures during the life of the intangible asset that are considered to increase the cost of the asset should be amortized over the remaining life of the related asset.

To illustrate the process of acquiring and amortizing an intangible asset, we will assume that Howard Limited acquired a patent in 1994 from another enterprise for

---

[5]"Capital Assets," CICA *Handbook,* Paragraphs 3060.37-38, October 1990.

$10 000. Production personnel estimate that the patent will be used for ten years and will be worthless at the end of that time. Howard Limited uses the straight-line method of amortizing intangibles, with a full year's amortization in the first year.

Entries to record the acquisition of the patent and the amortization for 1994 are:

Patent	10 000	
Cash		10 000
Amortization Expense	1 000	
Patent		1 000
($10 000/10 years = $1000)		

Chapters 12 and 13 explain that accumulated depreciation of property, plant, and equipment must be disclosed in the financial statements. No similar requirement exists, however, for intangible assets, so we usually credit amortization directly to the asset account, as illustrated in the Howard example. Although this approach is commonly practised, an Accumulated Amortization account for intangible assets is acceptable and is sometimes encountered in business. In fact, if a clear record of the relationship of the historical cost of an intangible asset and its related accumulated amortization is particularly important, such an account is preferable. Unless indicated otherwise, this text follows the procedure of crediting amortization directly to the intangible asset account.

Continuing the example of Howard Limited, assume that in 1996 the company incurs $2000 in legal costs for successfully defending the patent when a competitor charges that it violates a patent held by the competitor. Entries to record the $2000 additional cost of the patent and amortization expense for 1996 are as follows:

Patent	2000	
Cash		2000
Amortization Expense	1250	
Patent		1250
[($8000 + $2000)/8 years = $1250]		

The $8000 book value of the patent and the $2000 additional cost are totalled and amortized over the remaining life of eight years. Amortization of 1996 is thus $1250.

Amortization Expense	4375	
Patent		4375
($8750/2 years = $4375)		

Patent

1994	10 000	1994 Amortization	1 000
		1995 Amortization	1 000
1996	2 000	1996 Amortization	1 250
	8 750		

In the previous example, assume further that a competitor introduces a similar product at the beginning of 1997. The competitor's product should replace Howard Limited's product within two years. This new situation requires a change in the remaining life of the patent to two years.

Disposal of Intangible Assets

Companies may sell separately identified intangible assets in the same way as other assets. When such a transaction occurs, the **unamortized cost** of an asset must be removed from the books; the proceeds from the sale or exchange must be recorded; and a gain or loss, if any, must be must be recognized. The company's amortization policy may require the recording of amortization before the sales transaction is recorded.

The cost of intangible assets should not be written off as a loss in the period of acquisition, as was sometimes done before the revision of CICA *Handbook,* Section 3060. Estimates of value and future benefits of intangible assets may indicate that the unamortized cost should be reduced significantly by a charge against income at some point in the expected useful life. Unwarranted losses based on temporary conditions or other circumstances that do not support a diminished value of intangible assets are not recorded.

Financial Statement Presentation of Intangible Assets

Financial statement disclosures include the method, period, and rate of amortization of intangible assets. While balance sheet presentations of intangible assets vary, typical presentations include a general category designated "intangible assets" or "other assets," in which the various specific intangible assets held by the enterprise are listed.

Exhibit 14.2 presents the disclosure of intangible assets and change in accounting policy from the notes to the financial statements in Maclean Hunter Limited's 1991 annual report. "Maclean Hunter Limited is a diversified communications company operating in Canada, the United States and Europe with 12 000 employees and revenue of $1.5 billion. The company publishes leading consumer magazines in Canada and numerous business publications, and is involved in broadcasting, cable television, business forms, commercial printing, radio paging, and trade and consumer shows."[6] A single line labelled "Intangible Assets" appears in the company's 1990–91 comparative statement of financial position. Note 8 in Exhibit 14.2 details the specific intangible assets held by the company and the cost, accumulated depreciation, and net dollar amounts of each one. (The word "depreciation" is occasionally used in practice in place of "amortization." Conceptually, the word amortization is preferable for the writing-off of intangible assets.) Note 2 presents the change in accounting policy and the method of amortizing the intangible assets. Alternatively, it is acceptable to include the detailed information on individual intangible assets in the body of the balance sheet and to present the accounting policy employed in the intangibles note.

Separately Identifiable Intangible Assets

Companies may acquire separately identifiable intangible assets from other enterprises or governmental entities, or they may develop them internally. Separately identifiable intangibles that are developed internally and have determinable lives or that are acquired from others should be established in separate intangible asset accounts that describe the nature of the right or privilege involved.

---

[6]Maclean Hunter Limited, *Annual Report 1991*, inside front cover.

Exhibit 14.2 Maclean Hunter Limited: Intangible Asset Disclosure

8. Intangible Assets
(millions)

		1991		1990
	Cost	**Accumulated Depreciation**	**Net**	**Net**
Cable television franchises	$312.6	$13.5	$299.1	$303.2
Broadcast licences	43.7	7.0	36.7	36.0
Circulation and subscriber bases	43.9	15.5	28.4	29.2
Paging frequencies	7.3	0.6	6.7	6.8
Others	12.8	6.5	6.3	5.6
Total 1991	$420.3	$43.1	$377.2	$380.8
Total 1990	$424.5	$43.7	$380.8	

The Company has changed its accounting policy pertaining to the amortization of intangible assets, as described in note 2.

2. Change in Accounting Policy

Effective January 1, 1991, the Company changed its accounting policy pertaining to the amortization of intangible assets, which include broadcast licences, cable television franchises, circulation bases, subscriber lists and radio paging frequencies, to comply with the recommendations of the Canadian Institute of Chartered Accountants *Handbook* Section 3060. Previously, if the life of the intangible asset was considered to be indefinite, the asset was not amortized. Under the new accounting policy, intangible assets are amortized on a straight-line basis over their estimated economic life up to a maximum of 40 years, except for cable television franchises which are amortized using the sinking fund method with an interest rate of 4% over periods not exceeding 40 years.

   The effect of this change in accounting policy has been to reduce net income in 1991 by $6.0 million (4¢ per share) and to reduce net income in 1990 by $5.4 million (3¢ per share). The new requirements have been applied retroactively, so the results for 1990 have been restated and retained earnings at January 1, 1990 have been reduced by $7.7 million.

Source: Maclean Hunter Limited, *1991 Annual Report.*

Several different types of separately identifiable intangible assets are encountered in practice. The following sections explore some of the most common types of intangibles: patents, copyrights, trade names and trademarks, franchises, licensing agreements, and leaseholds. We also discuss organization costs and deferred charges, assets that are frequently presented with or close to intangible assets in the balance sheet.[7]

Patents

A **patent** is a document issued by the Patent Office of Consumer and Corporate Affairs that grants the holder the right to exclude others from making, using, or selling the item that is the subject of the patent. Patents are frequently received on new and innovative products for which a market may exist. Prior to October 1989, the legal life of a patent was seventeen years from the day of issue. In October 1989, the legislation was changed to twenty years from the day of application. The accounting for a patent begins only after it is issued, and the time between application and issue is approximately three years. A patent is not renewable, but during the legal life of the original patent the holder can

---

[7]"Capital Assets," CICA *Handbook*, Paragraph 3060.62, October 1990.

sometimes extend its life effectively by obtaining a new patent that includes slight variations.

Many of the consumer products we use every day are manufactured under patents granted to the producing companies. For example, cameras, household appliances, and hair dryers are frequently produced under patents.

Obtaining a patent does not guarantee that the holder has something of value. The value of a patent stems from its potential for creating competitive advantage, which may include the ability to produce and sell a different or superior product, obtain a higher selling price for the product, produce it at a lower cost, and exclude competition from producing a specific product or utilizing a specific process.

A patent acquired from another enterprise is recorded at the fair value of consideration given in the purchasing transaction unless the fair value of the assets received is more readily determinable. A patent exchanged for $50 000 cash and that was developed internally by the vendor for $30 000, would be recorded at $50 000. However, the same patent exchanged for common shares with no recent market value, would be recorded at $30 000 or the market value of the patent if it was available. The cost of internally developed patents includes legal and registration fees, including the cost of models and drawings that accompany registration applications. Research and development costs incurred in the generation of patents, however, are charged to expense as incurred. (We will cover this topic later in the chapter.)

The costs of successful legal defences of a patent are capitalized as part of the patent cost, because such action supports the inherent value of the patent. The costs of unsuccessful legal defences of a patent, however, are expensed as incurred. In addition, the unsuccessful defence of a patent raises a question concerning the existence of an asset and usually implies that the unamortized patent cost should be written off as a loss. If a new patent is obtained as a result of refinement, improvement, or another modification of an existing patent, the unamortized cost of the existing patent is considered part of the cost of the new patent if the benefits provided by the two patents are essentially the same. Sample patent entries were presented earlier in this chapter.

The cost of a patent is amortized over the shorter of its economic or its legal life. Numerous factors tend to reduce the useful life of a patent, including

1. Technical progress that results in new and more efficient inventions.
2. Substitute products that become available for current products.
3. Changes in customer demand.
4. Developments by competitors that are sufficiently different to qualify for different patents.

Thus, the economic life of a patent is frequently less than its maximum legal life.

Copyrights

A **copyright** provides the holder with exclusive rights to the publication, production, and sale of the rights for a literary, dramatic, musical, or artistic work. **Exclusive right** means that the holder can use the work and **preclude others from using it.** Individuals holding copyrights typically use them to reproduce, sell or otherwise distribute, and perform or record the work.

The Copyright Office of Consumer and Corporate Affairs issues copyrights for the length of the copyright creator's life plus 50 years. The cost of acquired copyrights includes the acquisition price and any related expenditure. The cost of internally developed copyrights includes legal and other registration costs. Generally, the cost is amortized over the economic life of the copyright, which is the period over which the copyright is expected to produce revenue. If the economic life exceeds 40 years, a 40-year period is used for amortization. Due to the limited period of time over which most copyrights are expected to generate revenue, however, the economic life is usually much shorter than the legal life. From a practical point of view, the cost of a copyright is often amortized over a relatively short period.

Trade Names and Trademarks

A **trade name** or **trademark** is a symbol, design, word, or phrase that is used by an enterprise to distinguish itself or its product from other enterprises. Trademarks frequently consist of designs or other unique symbols to encourage public identification of products or enterprises. Legal protection for trade names and trademarks is granted by registration with the Consumer and Corporate Affairs Office.

We are all familiar with many trade names, such as Coca-Cola, Loblaw's President's Choice, Shoppers Drug Mart's Life products, and Zenith. These, along with other recognizable trade names, create immediate product identification.

Registration of trade names and trademarks provides continuous protection, subject to periodic renewal every fifteen years. Capitalizable costs of trade names and trademarks include legal fees, registration costs, design costs, acquisition costs, successful legal defence, and other expenditures directly related to the acquisition of the right to use the trade name or trademark. Although advertising expenditures may enhance the value or extend the life of a trade name or trademark, this association is generally believed to be too indirect to warrant the capitalization of such costs.

The cost of a trade name or trademark is amortized over the shorter of 40 years or the economic life of the asset. Due to the uncertainties inherent in estimating useful life when factors such as consumer demand are important, the cost of a trade name or trademark is typically amortized over a relatively short period of time.

Franchises

A **franchise** is a contractual agreement that allows the holder to perform certain functions, to sell certain products or services, to use certain trade names or trademarks, or to do other specific things identified in the franchise agreement. Many of the businesses we encounter daily operate under franchises. Examples are Second Cup, McDonald's, and Kentucky Fried Chicken restaurants.

Some enterprises enter into franchise agreements with other enterprises to sell products, use trade names, or engage in other activities in exchange for specific payments and the fulfillment of other obligations. In other cases, enterprises enter into franchise agreements with governmental units to use public property or to furnish certain types of services, such as water, gas, electricity, public transportation, and waste disposal.

The initial cost of a franchise is recorded as an intangible asset to be amortized over future periods. The franchise cost is then amortized over the shorter of 40 years or the economic life of the franchise. In computing the economic life of the franchise, the holder must consider the time (if any) specified in the franchise contract. If the franchise can be terminated at the option of the entity granting the franchise, the holder should amortize the cost of the franchise over a relatively short period of time. Periodic payments made under a franchise agreement should generally be charged to expense as incurred.

To illustrate the process of accounting for a franchise, we will assume that Warren Limited purchased a franchise from Muffin Magic. The conditions of the four-year agreement include an initial payment of $40 000 and a royalty charge of 5 percent of sales. The following entries are recorded during the first year of the agreement with sales of $85 000:

Jan. 2	Franchise Fees	40 000	
	Cash		40 000
Dec. 31	Amortization of Franchise Fees	10 000	
	Franchise Fees		10 000
	($40 000/4 years)		
	Royalty Expense	4 250	
	Cash		4 250
	($85 000 × 0.05)		

Licensing Agreements

Some enterprises obtain licensing agreements to engage in certain lines of business or to use properties or rights owned by other entities. For example, radio and television stations obtain licences from the Canadian Radio-Television and Telecommunications Commission (CRTC). The cost of such licences represents an intangible asset, the accounting for which parallels closely the accounting for franchises. The cost is amortized over the shorter of the economic life or 40 years.

Leaseholds

Leasehold costs are frequently found in balance sheets as either property, plant, and equipment or intangible assets. A **lease** is a contract in which the owner of the property (**lessor**) grants another party (**lessee**) the right to use the property for a specified period of time for fixed or determinable payments. The lease typically states other rights and obligations of both the lessor and lessee.

In accounting for leases, some are treated as purchases of the property by the lessee. We follow this accounting treatment if the lease contract is similar to an acquisition of the property by the lessee and includes certain specified characteristics. This is called the **capitalization of the lease** and is a clear example of substance over form, the modifying convention discussed in Chapter 2. In these cases, the capitalized cost of the lease, which is usually the present value of the required lease payments, is presented as an asset in the lessee's balance sheet. This is a complex subject, which we treat extensively in Chapter 23. Leases that are not capitalized are called **operating leases.**

Substance Over Form

With both capital and operating leases, lessees may have costs that are presented as intangible assets. Lease contracts frequently call for lessees to prepay lease payments. Such payments must be associated with the appropriate periods and represent intangible assets prior to amortization. Some portion of these prepayments may be appropriately classified as current assets.

Leaseholds may arise from the purchase of the right to lease a property from the lessee. Assume that Gants Inc. holds the ten-year lease on a property in a popular shopping mall. Gants has outgrown these premises and has subleased this location to Boisvert

Ltd. for a fee of $10 000. The $10 000 fee is an intangible asset on the balance sheet of Boisvert Ltd. and would be amortized over the ten-year term of the lease.

Lessees frequently make expenditures that improve the quality of service rendered by leased property. Examples of such leasehold improvements include improvements to building space and improvements to land, such as driveways, landscaping, and parking lots. Although these expenditures are made in anticipation of benefits to be derived by the lessee, the improvements typically become the property of the lessor at the end of the lease term. Leasehold improvements are capitalized by the lessee in a separate Leasehold Improvement account and amortized over the shorter of the lease term, the life of the property resulting from the improvement, or 40 years.

Organization Costs

Numerous costs are incurred in organizing a business enterprise, particularly a corporation. Such **organization costs** include the following:

1. Legal fees of drafting the corporate charter and by-laws.
2. Legal fees of corporate registration.
3. Compensation to promoters of the enterprise and other promotional costs.
4. Initial share-issuance costs.
5. Miscellaneous costs of organization.

One can argue that, theoretically, all periods in which an enterprise operates benefit from the incurrence of these costs. In practice, however, the life of the enterprise is usually not known or determinable at the inception of the enterprise, when these costs are incurred. On the other hand, support exists for the position that the early years in the enterprise's life benefit most from organization costs and that such costs lose significance once the enterprise becomes an established operating unit.

Organization costs are frequently treated as deferred charges and are amortized over a relatively short period in the early years of an enterprise's life. Organization costs are frequently amortized over a period of five or ten years for financial reporting purposes.

Distinguishing between organization costs and costs that relate to normal operations is a difficult determination that requires the accountant to use judgement. Costs of normal operations should not be capitalized as organization costs or any other type of intangible asset.

Deferred Charges

Deferred charges, sometimes called **deferred costs, deferred debits,** or **other assets,** may be found in balance sheets with or near the intangible assets. As we saw in Chapter 4, "deferred charge" is a broad term used to identify a number of different items with debit balances that do not fit well into any of the other asset categories of the balance sheet. Organization costs are sometimes referred to as deferred charges. Other costs, such as financing charges, discounts and expenses on long-term prepayments, plant rearrangement costs, and accumulated tax allocation debits, are sometimes referred to as deferred charges.

The presence of deferred charges indicates the problem of attempting to define all costs that have not been amortized in one of the common asset categories. The deferred-charge category is necessary because some debit-balance accounts simply do not fit elsewhere.

Exhibit 14.3 contains the "other assets" section from the 1990–91 balance sheet of Petro-Canada. Petro-Canada is the largest Canadian-owned oil and gas company, with assets of $6 billion and revenue of nearly $5 billion in 1991. Exhibit 14.3 includes Note 15 from the 1991 annual report. The remaining assets described as "other" are not separately disclosed because of the materiality of the individual amounts.

Materiality

Intangible Assets not Separately Identifiable: Goodwill

Certain transactions give rise to intangible assets that are not separately identifiable as are patents, copyrights, and other intangibles discussed previously. Intangible assets that cannot be separately identified relate to the enterprise as a whole. They frequently exist because of the unique combination of separate assets and personnel of the enterprise, and their synergy explains why the value of an enterprise as a whole—measured in terms of its anticipated earning capacity—may be greater than the sum of the values of the individual parts of the enterprise. While such intangible assets are identified with a variety of titles, a commonly used term, goodwill, is used throughout this text.

Goodwill Concept

Goodwill is the capability of an enterprise to produce earnings in excess of normal for the industry in which the enterprise operates. This unique earning capability results from intangible advantages working for the enterprise in conjunction with the separately identifiable tangible and intangible assets. We apply the excess-earning-capacity concept in the various techniques of estimating the dollar amount of goodwill. A closely related notion is that the value of an enterprise as a whole may exceed the value of the sum of the market value of the individual assets less the liabilities of the enterprise. Such situations result from the existence of intangible qualities, such as an outstanding reputation, superior managerial capability, and ability to operate at an above-normal level of efficiency. Any characteristic or combination of characteristics that gives an enterprise a competitive advantage over other enterprises, thereby allowing a higher level of earnings than would normally be expected, supports the existence of goodwill.

Goodwill has been described as a master valuation account, which indicates that it provides a reconciliation of the difference between the value of an enterprise as a whole and the aggregate value of the individual parts of the enterprise. When viewed in this context, goodwill explains the difference between enterprises with above-normal earnings and those with normal earnings. The goodwill at work for an enterprise with above-normal earnings represents an additional **working asset** that contributes to the enterprise's ability to earn a return on specific individual assets at a level in excess of that normally expected.

Because the value of goodwill is identified with an enterprise as a whole, the asset goodwill is inseparable from that enterprise. Thus, goodwill is not exchangeable in the same sense as separately identifiable assets. In certain circumstances, however, goodwill is exchanged when an entire enterprise is acquired. Therefore, when the cost results from the acquisition transaction with another entity and a separate intangible asset cannot be identified, an appropriate goodwill account is established. As depicted in Exhibit 14.1, internally developed qualities similar to acquired goodwill are expensed in the current period.

Exhibit 14.3 Petro-Canada: Disclosure of Other Assets for the Years Ended December 31 (stated in millions of dollars)

Note 15: Other Assets

	1991	1990
At cost		
Oil sands overburden removal costs	$ 15	$ 47
Less portion related to oil sands to be mined within one year	7	21
	8	26
Deferred pension funding	40	32
At amortized cost		
Goodwill	64	72
Deferred financing costs	19	18
Other	36	27
	$167	$175

Source: Petro-Canada, *1991 Annual Report.*

When an enterprise contemplates the acquisition of another business, it must determine the value of that business. A starting point is to estimate the current value of all specific assets to be received and liabilities to be assumed. This amount is identified as the fair value of **net assets** received. The seller will want to include any existing goodwill in determining the exchange price, whether or not the goodwill has previously been recorded as an asset. Once an exchange price is agreed upon and the sale has taken place, the purchaser acquires the goodwill to the extent that the overall purchase price exceeds the current value of the other net assets received. Goodwill is then recorded by the purchaser. The recorded cost of the goodwill may vary from the valuation of the goodwill estimated to be inherent in the business being acquired, because the goodwill recorded is the amount necessary to reconcile the total purchase price to the current value of the other net assets received.

Conceptually, goodwill should be measured by identifying those factors that offer a competitive advantage to an enterprise, such as superior managerial efficiency, an excellent reputation among customers, and the ability to operate at a high level of efficiency.[8] By placing a monetary valuation on these features and aggregating these amounts, the value of goodwill can be established.

Realistically, valuing the individual intangible qualities that support the existence of goodwill involves measurement problems too complex for present accounting practice. Accountants have therefore turned to an indirect method of valuing goodwill, whereby they estimate the total anticipated excess earning capability rather than the individual elements that support the existence of goodwill. This process involves estimating future periodic earnings from an investment in another enterprise, comparing this estimation with what would normally be expected, and aggregating the excess of anticipated earnings over normal earnings. The estimation of excess earning capacity is made for purposes of determining a price to pay for the enterprise rather than for purposes of financial statement presentation.

---

[8]"Business Combinations," CICA *Handbook*, Paragraph 1580.54, April 1986.

For example, assume that Red Limited is considering the acquisition of Blue Inc. Red Limited will take over all the assets and will assume all the liabilities of Blue Inc. Red Limited estimates the current value of the net assets (assets less liabilities) of Blue Inc. at $750 000. In addition, Red Limited believes it will be able to achieve a level of earnings substantially in excess of normal on its investment due to Blue Inc.'s outstanding reputation. Specifically, the excess earnings are estimated to total $100 000. Red Limited is therefore willing to pay up to $850 000 for the net assets of Blue Inc. If an amount greater than $750 000 is paid, the excess is identified as the cost of goodwill resulting from the transaction. In this case, goodwill should not exceed $100 000, since that is the value that has been estimated for goodwill. The cost of goodwill is less than $100 000, however, if the final bargained exchange price is less than $850 000. For example, if the agreed-upon purchase price is $780 000, the amount of goodwill is $30 000 ($780 000 − $750 000). On the other hand, if the agreed-upon price is $840 000, the amount of goodwill is $90 000 ($840 000 − $750 000).

Accounting for Goodwill

Once acquired, goodwill is accounted for as outlined in Paragraphs 1580.54–62 of the CICA *Handbook*. Exhibit 14.1 indicates that goodwill acquired from another enterprise is recorded at cost in an appropriate intangible asset account. The life of goodwill is not constrained by legal or contractual limitations and therefore may be judged by management to be indeterminate. In such cases, we would amortize the goodwill over a period not to exceed 40 years. In other cases, management may decide that the period over which excess earnings can be anticipated is limited to a period shorter than 40 years, and we would amortize the goodwill over the expected period of advantageous operations.

In taking the position that goodwill should be treated as an asset and amortized over its estimated useful life, the CICA considered several alternative treatments. These included (1) retaining the cost of goodwill as an asset indefinitely unless a reduction in value becomes evident and (2) deducting the cost of goodwill from shareholders' equity when it is acquired. Supporting the nonamortization approach is the notion that until the future value becomes less than the historical cost, no loss should be recognized. The basis for deducting the cost of goodwill from shareholders' equity at the time of purchase is that the nature of goodwill differs from other assets and warrants special accounting treatment; since goodwill relates to the business as a whole and its value fluctuates widely, estimates of either its value or term of existence are too unreliable for purposes of income determination.[9] These positions were rejected by the Accounting Principles Board in favour of the amortization approach we describe in this text and as outlined in Paragraph 1580.58 of the CICA *Handbook*.

Many of the advantages of goodwill that can be acquired externally may be developed internally. For example, a company may develop an excellent reputation, superior managerial capability, and other attributes that allow it to earn at an above-normal level without acquiring another enterprise. Despite the similarity between these internally developed characteristics and goodwill acquired from another enterprise, only the latter is capitalized in an intangible asset account. The costs of internally developed attributes that are similar to acquired goodwill are recognized as expenses when incurred.

The reason for not recognizing internally developed goodwill as an asset is primarily the **lack of objective evidence**. In an external acquisition, the two enterprises agree on the

---

[9]"Business Combinations," CICA *Handbook*, Paragraph 1580.55, April 1986.

existence and amount of goodwill. Thus, the difference in accounting for goodwill acquired externally and that developed internally is based primarily on differences in the verifiability of the existence of an asset.

Goodwill Example: Diversified Enterprises/Single Product, Inc.

In the following paragraphs, we use an example involving Diversified Enterprises and Single Product, Inc. to illustrate various computational considerations in accounting for goodwill. Diversified Enterprises is considering the acquisition of Single Product, Inc., a relatively small company that has an excellent reputation. Single Product deals in a product line Diversified wants to move into. Diversified would acquire all the assets and assume all the liabilities of Single Product. The balance sheet of Single Product is presented in Exhibit 14.4. Single Product has no cash to be transferred to Diversified Enterprises.

Two questions must be answered by Diversified Enterprises in determining a reasonable price to pay for the net assets of Single Product, Inc. First, to what extent do the balance sheet figures represent the current value of the individual assets and liabilities? Second, is goodwill evident in the past performance of Single Product, Inc.? The price that Diversified is willing to pay should be based on the current value of Single Product's net identifiable assets (assets less liabilities) plus the value of any excess earning capability included in the acquisition. The total of the two elements establishes an amount around which to negotiate an acquisition price.

Because the purchase of Single Product, Inc. by Diversified Enterprises represents an acquisition transaction, the recorded amounts of assets on the books of Single Product are of no particular importance to Diversified except as a possible starting point for establishing the current value of the acquired assets. Based on appraisals, current market prices, and the application of specific price indices to historical cost figures, Diversified has established the values presented in Exhibit 14.5 for the assets of Single Product. We will assume that the amounts of liabilities on Single's books fairly reflect the obligations Diversified is assuming.

Asset/Liability Measurement

Why are the recorded amounts of assets in the balance sheet of Single Product, Inc. different from the current value estimates in Exhibit 14.5? The balance sheet amounts are based on GAAP, which usually do not reflect the current value of the assets. The basis for measuring and recording most assets is historical cost. Adjustments to costs are made to reflect market declines in applying the lower of cost or market method to marketable securities, inventories, and other assets whose realizabilities have been impaired. The balance sheet amounts for many items, however, may be significantly different from their current market values. Also, the accounting method used to account for inventories may cause a difference between recorded amounts and current market values. If the last-in, first-out (LIFO) method is used, for example, the balance sheet amount may be well below the current value, whereas the first-in, first-out (FIFO) method would normally cause the recorded amount to be closer to the current value. If the inventory to be acquired will be used in a different way by the acquiring enterprise, it may have a greater or lesser value than the amount recorded on the books of the acquired company. Differences in the valuation of receivables most likely reflect differences in the assessment of uncollectable accounts, because the receivables amount reflects the net realizable value of the asset.

Asset/Liability Measurement

Differences between the recorded amounts and the current values of capital assets or of separately identifiable intangible assets are due primarily to the initial measuring and recording of these assets at historical cost and the subsequent depreciation and amortization of the cost figures. The market prices of the assets may remain constant, decline

Exhibit 14.4

Single Product, Inc.
BALANCE SHEET
June 30, 1992

Assets			Liabilities	
Marketable securities		$ 5 000	Accounts payable	$ 99 000
Accounts receivable		28 000	Bonds payable	112 000
Inventories		140 000		$211 000
Property, plant, and equipment	$275 000			
			Shareholders' Equity	
Accumulated depreciation	(125 000)	150 000	Capital shares	$150 000
Patents		85 000	Retained earnings	47 000
				$197 000
			Total liabilities and shareholders' equity	
Total assets		$408 000		$408 000

Exhibit 14.5   Current Value of Net Assets of Single Product, Inc.

Assets		
Marketable securities	$ 6 000	
Accounts receivable	25 000	
Inventories	125 000	
Property, plant, and equipment	182 000	
Patents	100 000	$438 000

Liabilities		
Accounts payable	99 000	
Bonds payable	112 000	(211 000)
Estimated current value of net assets		$227 000

at a different rate from the book value, or actually increase. The book values as presented in the balance sheet are not designed to reflect current value.

If Diversified pays a price believed fair in light of the earning potential of Single Product, goodwill will emerge only if that price exceeds $227 000. For example, if the two enterprises agree on a $250 000 cash purchase price, goodwill is $23 000, computed as follows:

Purchase price	$ 250 000
Less: Estimated current value of net assets received	(227 000)
Cost of goodwill	$ 23 000

In this case, the journal entry to record the acquisition of the net assets and the assumption of liabilities of Single Product, Inc. by Diversified Enterprises is as follows:

Marketable Securities	6 000	
Accounts Receivable	25 000	
Inventories	125 000	
Property, Plant, and Equipment	182 000	
Patents	100 000	
Goodwill	23 000	
Accounts Payable		99 000
Bonds Payable		112 000
Cash		250 000

If Diversified pays a higher price, the implied goodwill will be more. For example, if $275 000 is paid, the cost of goodwill will be $48 000, determined by the excess of the $275 000 purchase price over the $227 000 estimated value of the net assets received.

Implicit in this transaction is Diversified's belief that the value of goodwill is at least equal to the cost implied in the transaction. Diversified should not pay a price in excess of the estimated current value of the identifiable net assets unless its management believes that the earning potential accruing to it in the transaction equals or exceeds the acquisition price.

Exhibit 14.6 presents an actual purchase transaction involving goodwill. In 1991, CAE Industries Ltd. purchased Vanguard Pacific Group of Companies for $16 695 000. The purchase price was paid in $2 283 000 cash with the balance of $14 412 000 payable in 1993. The excess of cost over the estimated fair value of the net assets, goodwill of $14 233 000, is being amortized on a straight-line basis over 40 years.

Estimating the Value of Goodwill

For goodwill to exist, evidence of the capability to earn amounts in excess of what would normally be expected must exist. An evaluation of the existence of goodwill therefore requires a comparison of expected earnings with normal earnings. If the anticipated earnings exceed the norm, evidence of goodwill is present.

How is the **normal rate of earnings** for an enterprise determined? The normal rate used for goodwill estimation is typically an approximation of the rate required to attract capital into the company that is acquiring another company. The risk associated with the enterprise is a major variable in determining the cost of capital: the higher the risk associated with the company, the higher the cost of capital. Risk, in turn, is assessed by considering the company's line of business, existing debt–equity relationships, past profitability, and other variables. In determining the normal rate, a common approach is to consult financial services and other sources for an average cost of capital for other companies in the same industry. Of course, care must be taken that industry figures represent companies that are truly comparable.

Projecting expected future earnings for purposes of comparison with normal earnings involves a careful analysis of past earnings and projected changes in future conditions. Although information about the past may be useful in estimating future earnings, unadjusted past earnings would rarely be an appropriate measure of expected future earnings. Trends in the past, however, may be projected into the future and may serve as a reasonable basis for estimating future profitability. Extraordinary items and other infrequently recurring items included in past earnings are usually excluded when using the past to project the future.

Exhibit 14.6 CAE Industries Ltd.: Purchase of Business Resulting in Goodwill, Years Ended March 31 (amounts in thousands of dollars)

2. Acquisition

On September 7, 1991, the corporation purchased the principal business assets of the Vanguard Pacific Group of companies, a major supplier of axle services for railways in the United States.

The transaction has been accounted for by the purchase method and accordingly the operating results have been included in the consolidated financial statements from the date of purchase. The financial summary of the acquisition is as follows:

Assets acquired, at fair values:	
Net working capital	$ 1 481
Net fixed assets	981
Goodwill	14 233
	$16 695

Consideration for the net assets acquired was a cash payment of $2283 with the majority of the balance of $14 412 payable in 1993.

Source: CAE Industries Ltd., *1992 Annual Report.*

Several methods of estimating the goodwill in an acquisition are discussed in this section. The following four steps are common to all methods:

Step 1. Estimate the periodic earnings that are expected to be achieved on the investment in the current value of the net assets to be received.

Step 2. Estimate the periodic earnings that would normally be expected on the investment in the current value of the net assets to be received.

Step 3. Comparing amounts in Steps 1 and 2, compute the amount of anticipated periodic excess earnings over normal earnings.

Step 4. Convert the amount computed in Step 3 from a periodic figure to an aggregate figure that represents an estimate of the total anticipated excess earnings (i.e., goodwill).

Several methods are available for making the conversion required in Step 4 of the **periodic** anticipated excess value of future anticipated excess earnings.

Estimating Expected Periodic Earnings

A starting point for **estimating expected future earnings** is past performance. However, our intent is to estimate *future* earnings to an **aggregate** figure that represents the total earnings, and in the future the factors that influence earnings may be different from those in the past. When we base assessments of future earnings on past earnings, we should use several periods in an attempt to eliminate the impact of nonrecurring events and to identify significant trends in earnings or components of earnings.

Continuing the Diversified Enterprises example, we will assume the earnings information for Single Product for the past four years as given in Exhibit 14.7 on page 694.

The average net income for the four years is $50 000, or a 22 percent return on the current value of the net assets of Single Product. These amounts are computed as follows:

Accounting for Brands: A Call for Clarity

Requiring greater disclosure of companies' accounting treatment of brand names would help to lessen discrepancies and help investors and creditors to make more informed judgments

How to account for brand names in financial statements? As with accounting for goodwill, various countries' opinions on the subject differ. The differences show up in their rules governing brand treatment—including Canada's—and in how closely they adhere to the rules. The discrepancies might best be addressed by increasing disclosure of brand accounting requirements, and by examining brands' indefinite lives.

A discussion of accounting for brands begins with a look at accounting for goodwill. When the value of a business on a going-concern basis exceeds the value of all its identifiable assets and liabilities, then the business has goodwill. Although its value constantly changes, goodwill exists in most businesses (negative goodwill, while rare, can also exist).

Accounting authorities agree that internally generated goodwill, or inherent goodwill, should be ignored for reporting purposes. For example, the United Kingdom's Exposure Draft #47 notes the following:

"Internally generated goodwill should not be recognized and included in the balance sheet. In a cost-based accounting model, it does not pass the criteria for recognition in the balance sheet because neither its cost nor the transaction which gave rise to it can be identified." (ED #47, part 1, para. 9)[1]

When one company acquires another, goodwill exists if the fair value of the identifiable assets less liabilities exceeds the purchase price. As both the cost and the transaction can be identified, this purchased goodwill meets the above criteria for recognition. However, opinion differs among countries on how to account for this goodwill in financial statements.

Goodwill Accounting Anomalies

In the United States, Opinion #17 issued in 1970 by the Accounting Principles Board requires companies to amortize purchased goodwill over a maximum of 40 years.[2] (Although an "opinion" is superseded by any Financial Accounting Standards Board (FASB) pronouncement, no such pronouncement has yet been made.)

In the U.K., accounting for goodwill is specified in the Standard Statement of Accounting Practice #22 and Exposure Draft #47.[3] Published in 1984 and revised in 1989, SSAP #22 permits two options. Purchased goodwill is usually written off against reserves at the time of the acquisition. But the company can also capitalize goodwill and write it off over its useful economic life. ED #47 published

in 1990 permits only the latter treatment. "Useful economic life" is a maximum of 20 years, or up to 40 years under unusual circumstances.

In Canada, accounting for goodwill is addressed in the Canadian Institute of Chartered Accountants (CICA) Handbook.[4] Paragraphs 1580.54 to 1580.62 instruct a company to capitalize and write off purchased goodwill rationally and systematically over its effective life for up to 40 years.

In all three countries, the customary emphasis on the bottom line motivates companies to choose whichever method minimizes current charges against income. Thus, a company usually amortizes purchased goodwill over the longest possible period. Ideally, the company with the highest net income would take the lowest charge, and the company with the lowest net income would take the highest charge. In practice, the company most motivated to extend its amortization period in order to reduce amortization expense is that with the lowest net income, or the least goodwill. Conversely, a company reporting reasonable or good net income—the one with the greater goodwill—can better withstand a high amortization charge and is therefore more likely to report a high charge.

Before publication of Opinion #17 in the U.S., a struggling company would retain goodwill at cost on its balance sheet until it became obvious that its value had been impaired. At that point, obliged to recognize that its goodwill had evaporated, the company had to write it down to its current value. The fact that a struggling company already reporting net losses had to make such large downward adjustments led to publication of Opinion #17.

Treatment of goodwill under the U.K.'s SSAP #22 also posed a significant problem (Pizzey, 1990).[5] Writing off goodwill to reserves could severely reduce a company's equity, perhaps causing it to contravene debt ratio requirements in debenture agreements, bank loan agreements, and the like. In any event, this treatment would cause misleading leverage ratios. In extreme cases, when a company purchased substantial goodwill, it could eliminate the value of its equity—an anomalous effect. Pizzey points out that using an arbitrary life for the amortization charge contravenes the matching principle. And as the company makes ongoing expenditures to maintain the value of goodwill, charging amortization of its original cost constitutes double-counting.

Continued

The Value of Brands

Goodwill exists because an organization has specific attributes, identifiable or not. Examples of identifiable factors mentioned in the U.K.'s ED #47 include a well-trained workforce, location near a port and high cost of market entry. Another identifiable factor is a brand.

The brand may be a registered trademark in which the company has proprietary rights. Nevertheless, brand names sometimes become so closely associated with a product that consumers use them generally. Many instant coffees are called "Nescafe" although this name is the trademark of the Nestle company. Consumers refer to "snowmobiles," a name specifically chosen by Bombadier for its product.

When a brand becomes widely known, it acquires value, allowing the owner to profit more by his assets than if he had marketed them as no-name products. A brand is at the local level what goodwill is at the corporate level. And, like accounting for goodwill, accounting for brands poses its share of problems.

As with goodwill, a company's brand value might be either internally generated or purchased. When a company purchases both goodwill and brands, how they are recorded can affect its reported results. If the brands are considered part of the goodwill, then both would be amortized over the same time period. But if they are recorded separately, the amortization charges would probably differ.

Treatment of brands in the U.K. is covered in Exposure Draft #52 issued in 1991.[6] If approved as an SSAP, this document will require companies to treat purchased brands not separately but as part of goodwill. Thus they would be amortized as outlined in ED #47. Internally created brands would not be capitalized at all. Despite these promulgations, several U.K. companies have not only recognized purchased brands, but even capitalized internally created brands. In an extreme example, Cadbury-Schweppes PLC capitalized internally created brands in 1989 and 1990 to a total of more than 1 billion British pounds.

In the U.S., Opinion #17 distinguishes between goodwill and other identifiable intangible assets, but applies the same rules to each. Purchased brands are capitalized and amortized either explicitly or implicitly as part of goodwill. And, because of bottom-line pressure, they are usually written off over the maximum allowable period of 40 years.

In Canada, Section 3060 of the CICA Handbook treats brands as intangible assets. Companies must carry brands on their balance sheet at cost, less accumulated amortization and write-downs. They are to be amortized rationally and systematically over their useful lives for up to 40 years. In practice, most brands are represented by registered trademarks. A trademark is initially registered for 15 years and may be renewed under federal law for subsequent 15-year periods, effectively giving the trademark an indefinite life.[7] In this respect, a brand resembles land (which is not amortized) more than other long-term assets.

A Call for Greater Disclosure

Just as in maintaining its goodwill, a company invests heavily to create and maintain its brands. But a brand is more immediately identifiable, even if the steps in its development are not always identifiable. If the expenditures incurred in developing a brand can be identified, both Canadian and American companies can capitalize the cost and amortize it over its economic life for up to 40 years. Because they are not required to provide detailed disclosure of the development, it is impossible to determine what has occurred just by examining the financial reports.

These points are illustrated by two major brewing companies, Molson Companies Ltd. and John Labatt Ltd. Both companies are widely diversified. Both own a wide range of recognizable brands and intangible assets. Labatt's notes on its 1990 financial report state the following:

"Goodwill and other proprietary rights are amortized using the straight line method over the lesser of their useful lives and forty years." (Labatt's, 1990)[8]

Molson's notes to its 1991 financial report state the following:

"Intangible assets, which principally include goodwill, brand names and hockey franchises, are carried at cost. Goodwill is amortized on a straight line basis over periods not exceeding forty years. Brand names and hockey franchises are not being amortized as there has been no decrease in their value." (Molson's, 1991)[9]

The discrepancy is clear: two companies with similar situations report on entirely different bases. By failing to amortize its brands or hockey franchises, Molson's appears to contravene Generally Accepted Accounting Principles. Conversely, one could argue (following Pizzey, 1990) that if Molson's did amortize its brands and hockey franchises while incurring expenditures to maintain their value, the company would be double-counting.

Requiring greater disclosure of brand accounting would clarify this situation. Because brand capitalization is a matter of judgment and not easy to verify, its objec-

Continued

tivity will always be in doubt. And as with Cadbury-Schweppes PLC, brand capitalization can represent a significant amount of money. In an efficient market with full disclosure, investors and creditors can make their own judgments and adjustments to value. Without full disclosure, they are working in the dark. Companies should also fully disclose their amortization periods, even when they are probably using the maximum term permitted under GAAP. Another question to be addressed: should brands have indefinite lives?

[1] The Accounting Standards Committee, *Exposure Draft #47: Accounting for Goodwill*, 1990.

[2] The Accounting Principles Board, *Opinion #17*, 1970.

[3] The Accounting Standards Committee, *Standard Statement of Accounting Practice #22: Accounting for Goodwill, (revised)*, 1989.

[4] Canadian Institute of Chartered Accountants, *Handbook*.

[5] Pizzey, A. *Accounting for Goodwill and Brands, Management Accounting* (U.K.), September 1919, pp. 22–26.

[6] The Accounting Standards Committee, *Exposure Draft #52: Accounting for Intangible Fixed Assets*, 1991.

[7] Trade Marks Act, R.S.C., 1985, T-13.

[8] John Labatt Ltd., Consolidated Financial Statements, 1990.

[9] Molson Companies Ltd., Consolidated Financial Statements, 1991.

Source: Reprinted from an article in *CMA Magazine*, by Dr. John M. Macintosh and Dr. John M. Parkinson. "Accounting for Brands: A Call for Clarity," July/August 1992, pp. 13–15.

Exhibit 14.7   Single Product, Inc.: Income Data for Years Ending June 30, 1991–94

	1991	1992	1993	1994
Revenues	$ 255 000	$ 262 000	$ 212 000	$ 238 000
Expenses	(204 000)	(224 000)	(160 000)	(182 000)
Income before extraordinary items		38 000	52 000	
Extraordinary gain (loss)		12 000	(9 000)	
Net income	$ 51 000	$ 50 000	$ 43 000	$ 56 000

$$\text{Average net income} = \frac{\$51\ 000 + \$50\ 000 + \$43\ 000 + \$56\ 000}{4 \text{ years}} = \$50\ 000$$

$$\text{Return on current value of net assets} = \frac{\$50\ 000}{\$227\ 000} = 22\%$$

Several factors should be considered in deciding on the appropriateness of using $50 000 as an expected level of earnings in the future. The inclusion of the extraordinary items is questionable, because they are by definition not expected to recur. Also, the accounting policies followed by Diversified to determine net income may be different from those used by Single Product. Such a difference could influence the assessment of future earnings. Other factors could also affect the expected future earnings. For example, in the future, depreciation and amortization on property, plant, and equipment and patents will be based on the **new cost basis** (i.e., the estimated fair value), and the estimated lives of these assets may be extended or reduced.

Furthermore, trends in the components of earnings may reveal that conditions in 1994 are more indicative of the future than the average of several periods. Considerations that are not apparent in the financial statements and that are discernible only through careful consideration of the operating characteristics of the enterprise being acquired may affect the evaluation of expected earnings. For example, the management of Diversified may believe Single Product could be even more profitable with the incorporation of more efficient production processes.

To continue our example, we will assume that the average earnings of Single Product during 1991–94, after the elimination of extraordinary items and the inclusion of an additional charge of $3850 per year for expected increases in depreciation and amortization, represent a reasonable estimate of future earnings. This amount is computed as follows:

Average annual income		
before extraordinary items	1991	$ 51 000
	1992	38 000
	1993	52 000
	1994	56 000
		$197 000 ÷ 4 years = $49 250
Less: Additional depreciation and amortization		(3 850)
Estimated future annual income		$45 400

This estimate reflects a rate of return on the estimated current value of the net assets being acquired of 20 percent ($45 400/$227 000 = 0.2). These amounts are used in the continuation of the Diversified Enterprise example.

Estimating Normal Periodic Earnings

The selection of a normal rate of earnings should reflect an estimate of the rate necessary to attract capital into the business under existing circumstances. As with determining all interest rates, the risk taken in the investment is an important consideration. A related consideration is the industry in which the enterprise operates.

Published rates that represent averages of a number of similar enterprises can usually be obtained from various financial services (e.g., Statistics Canada, Dun & Bradstreet, or Standard & Poor's). However, rates obtained in this manner are based on historical figures and may be different from rates based on current values. Also, the unique features of the enterprise under consideration may make the identification of comparable enterprises difficult. Any valid rate must be based on companies that are similar to the one for which goodwill is being computed.

In continuing the example of Diversified Enterprises, we will assume 12 percent as the rate that represents a normal cost of attracting capital into enterprises similar to Single Product. Thus, normal annual earnings on the $227 000 investment are $27 240 ($227 000 × 0.12).

Computing the Anticipated Annual Excess Earnings

The amounts computed in Steps 1 and 2 are combined to determine the **anticipated annual earnings in excess of normal.** In the case of Single Product, Inc., this computation is as follows:

Estimated future annual earnings ($227 000 ×0.2)	$45 400
Estimated normal annual earnings ($227 000 × 0.12)	(27 240)
Estimated excess of expected annual earnings over normal	$18 160

Estimating Total Excess Earnings

Several methods are available to convert the annual amount of anticipated excess earnings to an estimate of total goodwill. Three methods are explained in the following sections.

Method 1. Years Multiple of Excess Earnings. This method is based on the assumption that the excess earnings will continue for a determinable number of periods. Goodwill is computed by multiplying the excess annual earnings by the number of years management believes it can sustain the advantages acquired.

For Diversified Enterprises we assume for this calculation that management believes it can sustain the anticipated level of excess earnings for six years, after which it will disappear. In this case, goodwill is valued as follows:

$$Goodwill = 6 \text{ years} \times \$18\ 160 = \$108\ 960$$

A deficiency in this method is its failure to recognize the difference between the value of the excess earnings of the first year after the acquisition and that of subsequent years (i.e., the time value of money). Also, the difficulty in accurately estimating the number of years over which the excess earnings can be sustained indicates that this method contains an implementation problem.

Method 2. Present Value of Excess Earnings. Recognition of the time value of the excess earnings is a major advantage of basing the value of goodwill on the present value of excess earnings rather than on the total amount as in Method 1. The period over which the excess earnings can be sustained must be estimated. The amount of annual excess earnings is then discounted to its present value by an appropriate interest rate.

Assuming that Diversified estimates that the excess earnings will continue for six years, we discount at the normal rate (i.e., the estimated cost of capital, which in this case is 12 percent), and compute goodwill as follows:

$$Goodwill = 4.11141 \times \$18\ 160 = \$74\ 663$$

Table 7.4 shows that the present value of an annuity factor for six periods at 12 percent is 4.11141. This figure is used because the estimated excess earnings of $18 160 per year will accrue to Diversified Enterprises over a six-year period.

The greater risk inherent in the continuation of the excess earnings in the future may encourage the use of a higher interest rate in estimating the total value of goodwill. For example, if a 20 percent rate is used in estimating the goodwill in the Diversified acquisition of Single Product, goodwill is estimated as follows using an annuity factor of 3.32551 from Table 7.4:

$$Goodwill = 3.32551 \times \$18\ 160 = \$60\ 391$$

Conceptually, the present value method has merit because explicit recognition is given to the limited life of the excess earnings and the time value of money is considered. Practical problems of implementation are the estimations of the number of years and the interest rate. As seen in the Method 2 examples, judgements about these factors can significantly affect the resulting goodwill estimate.

Method 3. Capitalization of Excess Earnings. The assumption that the excess earnings will continue indefinitely leads to estimating goodwill by capitalizing the excess earnings at an appropriate rate. If the normal rate is used in the Diversified example, then

$$Goodwill = \frac{\$18\ 160}{12\%} = \$151\ 333$$

Goodwill computed in this manner represents the amount that would have to be invested to yield a return equal to the **excess earnings in perpetuity.** In other words, an investment of $151 333 that yields a 12 percent return will yield $18 160 annually ($151 333 × 0.12 per year in perpetuity). The primary flaws in this computation are (1) that the computed goodwill figure is based on the assumption that estimated excess earnings will continue indefinitely and (2) that this perpetual advantage relates entirely to conditions that exist when goodwill is acquired.

The uncertainty concerning the continuity of excess future earnings may encourage the use of a higher interest rate, indicating the higher level of risk. In the Diversified Enterprises example, a 20 percent rate for capitalizing excess earnings results in the following computation:

$$\text{Goodwill} = \frac{\$18\ 160}{20\%} = \$90\ 800$$

We have used two different interest rates in the previous examples to point out the difficulty of selecting the appropriate rate for purposes of applying this method. One study on valuing a closely held business suggests that the rate used should represent the expected yield on an investment in the company and can be selected by either the summation or the direct market comparison methods. Under the summation method, the accountant determines the required rate of return and then adjusts that rate for any portion of the expected return that may not be reflected in the earnings stream being capitalized. To illustrate this method, the authors of the study suggest the following approach:

Long-term government bond rate	6%
Plus: Average premium return on small corporation shares over government bonds	5
Expected total rate of return on small publicly held shares	11
Plus: Premium for greater risk and liquidity	6
Total required expected rate of return for subject company	17
Less: Consensus long-term inflation expectation	2
Capitalization rate to apply to current earnings	15%

The direct market comparison method requires the accountant to develop a rate, or range of rates, based on information from comparable companies. One of the implementation problems associated with this method is the difficulty of getting information about other similar companies, particularly if the company for which goodwill is being estimated is not publicly held.[10]

In summary, the assumptions underlying the various methods of estimating goodwill and the judgements required in the implementation of the methods demonstrate the difficulty of measuring goodwill. The estimates of goodwill in the Diversified and Single Product examples range from $60 391 to $151 333. At best, these figures represent a rough approximation of the range into which goodwill falls. An important point to remember is that the amount recorded as goodwill is the actual cost that is implied in the purchase transaction. The estimation procedures we have just illustrated are used to

Asset/Liability Measurement

[10]Warren Kissin and Ronald Zulli, "Valuation of a Closely Held Business," *Journal of Accountancy* (June 1988), p. 42. (The example presented here differs only in the numbers used.)

quantify the value of goodwill to assist management in determining an appropriate amount for negotiating a purchase price of another enterprise. Estimates of the value of goodwill may also be useful to auditors in assessing the appropriateness of the recorded amount of goodwill in the balance sheet.

"Negative Goodwill"

Asset/Liability Measurement

In the previous examples, we have assumed that the price paid for an enterprise *exceeds* the sum of the current value of the individual identifiable assets, less liabilities. If the sum of the values of the individual assets, less liabilities, is *greater* than the price paid, does "negative goodwill" exist? Presumably the answer is no, because this would result in assets being recorded at amounts in excess of the prices paid for them, a violation of applying the asset/liability measurement principle using historical cost.

If the price paid for an enterprise is *less* than the sum of the values of the individual identifiable assets, less liabilities, the difference should be allocated as a reduction of the recorded cost of those separately identifiable noncurrent assets other than investments. If, in an unusual case, this allocation reduces noncurrent assets (other than investments) to zero, the difference should be recorded as a deferred credit and amortized as an *addition* to future income over a period not to exceed 40 years. Such a deferred credit would be identified as an "excess of book value over cost of purchased subsidiary" or another appropriate title. (The terms "negative goodwill" or "badwill" are not usually found in published financial statements.) This item is placed in the balance sheet among noncurrent liabilities or in a separate deferred credit section between liabilities and shareholders' equity.

Special Problem Areas

Several special problem areas exist in accounting for intangible assets and related costs. Accounting for research and development costs is closely related to accounting for intangible assets, particularly because some intangible assets are developed internally through research and development. Also, intangible assets are often used in research and development activities. Accounting for development-stage enterprises is another area closely related to accounting for intangible assets. Accounting for costs in the oil and gas industry relates to intangible asset accounting and represents an area of continuing controversy for the accounting profession. Since some understanding of all of these areas is necessary to gain an appreciation of proper accounting for intangible assets, these subjects are discussed in the remaining sections of this chapter.

Research and Development Costs

Research and development (R & D) is an important aspect of business operations for many enterprises. The CICA defines research and development as follows:

> Research is planned investigation undertaken with the hope of gaining new scientific or technical knowledge and understanding. Such investigation may or may not be directed towards a specific practical aim or application.

Development is the translation of research findings or other knowledge into a plan or design for new or substantially improved materials, devices, products, processes, systems or services prior to the commencement of commercial production or use.[11]

Distinguishing between R & D costs and expenditures that are capitalized in various asset categories requires that the accountant use careful judgement. Identifying R & D costs is facilitated by understanding the activities that lead to R & D costs. Such activities typically occur **prior to the beginning of commercial production and distribution of a product or process.** Various activities can result in R & D costs.[12]

Research activities typically include the following:

1. Laboratory research aimed at the discovery of new knowledge.
2. Searching for applications of new research findings or other knowledge.
3. Conceptual formulation and design of possible product or process alternatives.

Development activities typically include the following:

1. Testing in search for, or evaluation of, product or process alternatives.
2. Design, construction, and testing of preproduction prototypes and models.
3. Design of tools, jigs, moulds, and dies involving new technology.

Activities that relate to commercial production do not result in the incurrence of R & D costs, even though many are similar in nature to activities giving rise to R & D costs.

The following are examples of activities that do *not* result in R & D costs:[13]

1. Engineering follow-through in an early stage of commercial production.
2. Quality control during commercial production, including routine testing of products.
3. Trouble-shooting in connection with breakdowns during commercial production.
4. Routine or periodic alterations to existing products, production lines, manufacturing processes and other ongoing operations, even though such alterations may represent improvements.
5. Adaptation of an existing capacity to a particular requirement or customer's need as part of a continuing commercial activity.
6. Routine design of tools, jigs, moulds, and dies.
7. Activity, including design and construction engineering, related to the construction, relocation, rearrangement, or start-up of facilities or equipment other than facilities or equipment whose sole use is for a particular research and development project.

Several elements of costs identified with R & D activities can be identified: (1) materials, equipment, and facilities; (2) personnel; (3) intangibles purchased from others; (4) contract services; and (5) indirect costs. R & D expense of an enterprise includes some or all of the above costs in a given reporting period. If a cost is considered to be R & D, that cost is charged to expense when incurred. The development costs included in these

---

[11]"Research and Development Costs," CICA *Handbook,* Paragraph 3450.02, September 1985.

[12]"Research and Development Costs," CICA *Handbook,* Paragraphs 3450.04-05, September 1985.

[13]"Research and Development Costs," CICA *Handbook,* Paragraph 3450.06, September 1985.

R & D costs should be deferred to future periods if all of the criteria in Section 3450.21 are satisfied.[14]

Materials, Equipment, and Facilities

Materials, equipment, and facilities acquired for use in R & D activities that have future benefits—either in other R & D activities or in non-R & D activities—are capitalized in appropriate asset categories when acquired. The cost of materials subsequently used in R & D activities and depreciation on equipment and facilities used in R & D activities are classified as R & D expense when recognized. Costs of materials, equipment, and facilities acquired for particular R & D projects that have no alternative use are expensed as R & D when incurred.

Personnel

Salaries, wages, and other personnel costs of employees involved in R & D activities are charged to R & D expense as incurred.

Intangibles Purchased from Others

The costs of **purchased intangible assets** used in R & D activities that have future benefits in other R & D activities or non-R & D activities are capitalized in appropriate asset categories. As these intangible assets are amortized, R & D expense is charged. The amortization of the intangibles used in R & D thus becomes part of R & D expense as the assets are used. The costs of intangible assets that are purchased for use only in present R & D projects and that have no future benefits are charged to R & D expense as incurred.

Contract Services

Enterprises may engage others to perform R & D activities for them. The costs of such **contract services** are treated as R & D expenses when incurred.

Indirect Costs

A reasonable allocation of **indirect costs** that relate to R & D activities is included in the R & D expense in determining net income. Indirect costs include general and administrative expenses not directly related to R & D activity. To be included in R & D expense, however, general and administrative expenses must have some relationship to R & D activity.

In summary, whether costs represent R & D in the period acquired or in a subsequent period through amortization depends on whether the items have future benefits to ongoing R & D activities or in other activities of the enterprise.

To illustrate the identification of R & D costs, we will assume that Energy-Efficient Limited is involved in the production of high-efficiency home-heating and air-conditioning equipment. Energy-Efficient incurs a number of expenditures related to its activities, which are listed on the left in Exhibit 14.8. The proper accounting for these activities is described in the analysis on the right.

Numerous examples can be cited to illustrate the distinction between R & D costs and other expenditures. Most of the items in the Energy-Efficient example are obvious from the previous discussion. The capitalization of legal costs (item 5) and the cost of acquiring a competing patent (item 7) are appropriately capitalized in the Patent account.

---

[14]"Research and Development Costs," CICA *Handbook*, Paragraph 3450.21, September 1985.

Exhibit 14.8 Cost Analysis for Energy-Efficient Company

Expenditure	Capitalize as	Expense as
1. Acquisition of equipment and building to be used in ongoing research activity.	Building, equipment	
2. Salaries of research staff responsible for the design of new heating unit.		R&D
3. Material, labour, and overhead of model of new heating unit.		R&D
4. Costs of testing of model of new heating unit.		R&D
5. Legal fees related to patent on new heating unit.	Patent	
6. Costs of research on marketability of new heating unit.		Operating expense
7. Cost of acquiring patent believed to compete with one on new heating unit.	Patent	
8. Costs of engineering activity necessary to advance heating unit to point of commercial production.		R&D
9. Costs of quality control in early stages of commercial production.		Manufacturing cost
10. Depreciation of equipment and building acquired in 1.		R&D
11. Amortization of patent acquired in 5.		Manufacturing cost
12. Salaries of salespeople selling new heating unit.		Operating expense
13. Warranty costs on heating units sold.		Operating expense

Because this patent is related to a product that is being produced for sale, the amortization of the cost (item 11) is treated as a manufacturing cost. If the patent had been used in R & D activities, the amortization would have been classified as R & D expense. The cost of market research (item 6) on the new product is not included as R & D, because the research relates to the *marketability* of the product, not to its technical development. The costs of engineering activity (item 8) are development costs and can be capitalized provided the conditions of Section 3450.21 are satisfied. In summary, those costs incurred prior to the beginning of commercial production are either capitalized in appropriate asset accounts or charged to R & D expense. Amortization of the cost of assets used in R & D activities is included in R & D expense when recognized.

Why did the CICA take the position that R & D costs are to be expensed as incurred unless they are for specific assets that have identifiable future benefits? The institute carefully considered several capitalization alternatives for R & D expenditures: (1) capitalization of all costs when incurred, (2) capitalization of costs when specified conditions are present, and (3) accumulation of all R & D costs in a special category until the existence of future benefits can be determined. Applying the asset/liability measurement principle is particularly difficult, because the future benefits of individual R & D projects involve

Asset/Liability Measurement

a high degree of uncertainty and estimates of the rates of success of R & D projects vary considerably. Also, a direct relationship between R & D costs and specific future revenue generally cannot be determined. Even if a relationship between present R & D costs and future revenue can be demonstrated, the problem of measuring the asset still exists. Generally, an expenditure is not treated as an asset unless the future economic benefits can be identified and objectively measured at the time of the expenditure. Although the CICA *Handbook* provides clear conditions for capitalization of development costs, Section 3450.25 prohibits the capitalization of development costs expensed in prior years.[15]

Conservatism

This position is consistent with the modifying convention of conservatism, which states that the least favourable alternative presentation should be followed when significant doubt exists about the appropriate accounting principle to be applied.

In recent years, one area of particular difficulty in accounting for R & D has been the treatment of the costs of developing computer software. If software is developed in conjunction with activities typically associated with R & D, the development costs can be capitalized if the conditions of Paragraph 3450.21 are satisfied. For example, if software is developed to create a new or significantly improved product or process without any contractual arrangement for sale or cost reimbursement, the development costs are considered to be R & D costs. Likewise, the costs of developing software that is intended for use in the company's ongoing R & D activities are expensed as R & D as they are incurred.

The accounting for the costs of computer software to be sold, leased, or otherwise marketed as a separate product or as part of a product or process can be capitalized when technological feasibility has been established. Technological feasibility is established upon completion of a detailed program design or working model. Thereafter, all software production costs are capitalized and subsequently reported at the lower of unamortized cost or net realizable value. Capitalized software development costs are amortized based on current and expected future revenue for each product, subject to a minimum amortization equal to straight-line amortization over the remaining estimated economic life of the product.[16]

Development-Stage Enterprises

A **development-stage enterprise** is either (1) an organization that is devoting almost all of its effort to establishing a new business and that has not begun planned principal operations; or (2) an organization that has begun planned principal operations but that has not yet generated significant revenue from those operations. The CICA has no specific requirements affecting companies in the development stage. Specialized reporting practices have become accepted in Canada, however, and the Emerging Issues Committee has reviewed certain issues and reached a consensus on deferral of expenses during the development stage.[17]

The FASB issued *Statement of Financial Accounting Standards No. 7* in 1975 to standardize accounting and reporting practices by newly developed companies. Devel-

---

[15]"Research and Development Costs," CICA *Handbook,* Paragraph 3450.25, December 1985.

[16]"Accounting for the Costs of Computer Software To Be Sold, Leased, or Otherwise Marketed," *FASB Statement of Financial Accounting Standards No. 86,* Paragraphs 3, 5, and 8, 1985.

[17]"Revenue and Expenditures During the Pre-operating Period," *CICA Handbook, Emerging Issues Committee 27.1* (Toronto: CICA, April 1991), pp. EIC 27.1–4.

opment-stage enterprises typically devote a substantial amount of effort to activities such as the following:

1. Financial planning.
2. Raising capital.
3. Exploring for natural resources.
4. Developing natural resources.
5. Research and development.
6. Establishing sources of supply.
7. Acquiring property, plant, equipment, and other operating assets.
8. Recruiting and training personnel.
9. Starting up production.

Matching

Development-stage enterprises engaged in these activities incur significant costs but generate little or no revenue. Thus, these enterprises typically incur operating losses during the development stage.

EIC No. 27 requires development-stage enterprises to account and report on much the same basis as do established operating enterprises. The same generally accepted accounting principles that apply to established enterprises govern the recognition of revenue and expense and the capitalization of costs for development-stage enterprises. The financial statements issued by a development-stage enterprise should present **financial position, results of operations, and cash flows** as do those issued by established enterprises. Additional disclosures that are necessary because of the unique nature of the development-stage enterprise are summarized in Exhibit 14.9.

The financial statements must clearly indicate that the enterprise is in the development stage and must also include a description of the specific developmental activities in which the enterprise is involved. In the first year that the enterprise is no longer considered to be in the development stage, disclosure should indicate that in previous years it had been a development-stage enterprise.

The reporting recommendations of *EIC No. 27* simply apply generally accepted accounting principles of established operating enterprises to development-stage enterprises. Past practices of capitalizing operating losses and nonrecoverable costs as intangible assets are not acceptable. The treatment of a cost should be governed by the nature of the cost rather than the degree of maturity of the company incurring the cost. Under certain circumstances, however, a development-stage enterprise may prepare financial statements on a basis other than generally accepted accounting principles.

In Chapter 1, we discussed the economic impact of accounting principles and raised the question of whether the CICA and FASB should be concerned with the economic impact of the standards they set. This issue is important with respect to financial reporting by development-stage enterprises. Some accountants have pointed out that applying generally accepted accounting principles to developing enterprises frequently results in reporting net losses, which may not be fully understood by investors and creditors who could supply capital for these companies. If these reported losses influenced investors and creditors to withhold or delay investments in developing companies, new companies would have an even more difficult time getting started.

In an attempt to consider this issue, the FASB questioned officers of fifteen venture-capital enterprises. The conclusion of this limited research was that the accounting treatment of preoperating losses has little effect, if any, on the amount of capital that would be provided or the terms under which it would be provided to newly developed

Exhibit 14.9 Financial Reporting Requirements of Development-Stage Enterprises

Financial Statements	Special Disclosure Requirements*
Balance sheet	Cumulative net losses reported with a descriptive title, such as "deficit accumulated during the development stage" in shareholders' equity.
Income statement	Cumulative amounts of revenues and expenses from enterprise's inception.
Statement of changes in financial position	Cumulative amounts of sources and uses of cash since the enterprise's inception.
Statement of shareholders' equity	For each issuance of shares, the date, number of shares, warrants, rights, or other equity securities issued.
	For each issuance, the dollar amounts assigned to the consideration received (per share and in total).
	For each issuance involving noncash consideration, the nature of the transaction and the basis for assigning a dollar amount.

*These special disclosures are required *in addition* to those normally required under generally accepted accounting principles.

companies. According to these officers, the venture-capital investor typically relies on an assessment of cash flows based on an investigation of the technological, marketing, management, and financial aspects of the enterprise.[18] Other research in this general area tends to support these conclusions.

The FASB concluded that requiring cumulative figures in the financial statements, as described in Figure 14.9, would be useful in understanding the position of the developing company until it reached the position of being fully operative. The FASB determined, in addition, that the special report forms used in the past were less useful than were the financial statement forms of established operating enterprises with which investors were already familiar.

Accounting by Oil- and Gas-Producing Companies

Oil- and gas-producing companies incur substantial costs in locating and developing oil and gas reserves. Given the current state of technology, exploration requires many drilling efforts, only some of which locate producible oil and gas reserves. Other such efforts result in "dry holes" that provide no producible oil and gas.

Two methods of accounting for costs incurred in exploration activities are used in the oil and gas industry. The **successful-efforts method** is based on the theory that only the costs of locating producing wells (i.e., those wells from which gas and oil can economically be extracted) should be capitalized and amortized over future periods. Under this method, costs associated with activities that do not result in the location of producible oil and gas reserves are treated as expenses when they are incurred.

Under the alternative **full-cost method,** the costs of *all* efforts are treated as the costs of locating producing wells. Because many unsuccessful efforts are usually necessary to locate reserves that can be successfully exploited, exploration costs that would be treated

---

[18]"Accounting and Reporting by Development Stage Enterprises," *FASB Statement of Financial Accounting Standards No. 7, Paragraph 49, 1975.*

as expenses when incurred under the successful-efforts method are treated as assets and amortized over future periods under the full-cost method.

Both the successful-efforts and the full-cost methods have been widely used in accounting for the numerous costs incurred in oil and gas exploration. In practice, the successful-efforts method has been widely adopted by larger companies, while smaller companies have favoured the full-cost method. CICA *Handbook,* Section 3060.25 states that either method may be used, but the selected method must be applied to all properties.[19]

Costs in oil- and gas-producing activities fall into several classifications: acquisitions, explorations, development, production, support equipment, and facilities. Under the successful-efforts method, the costs of acquiring oil and gas rights are capitalized when incurred. These costs are amortized as a part of the cost of oil and gas produced. Exploration costs, except for the costs of drilling an exploratory well, are expensed as incurred. The costs of drilling an exploratory well are **temporarily deferred** until a determination is made on whether or not the well is producible. If producible reserves exist, the costs of the exploratory well are capitalized and amortized as part of the cost of oil and gas produced. If producible reserves do not exist, the costs of the exploratory well are expensed when this determination is made.

Costs of developing proven reserves are capitalized and depreciated as part of the cost of oil and gas produced. Production costs are treated as part of the cost of oil and gas produced and are expensed as incurred. Costs of support equipment and facilities are capitalized and depreciated as costs of oil and gas produced to the extent that they are used in oil- and gas-producing activities.

The application of the basic concept underlying the successful-efforts method is apparent in the accounting for exploration costs as previously described. All exploration costs, *except* those for drilling exploratory wells that result in producible oil and gas reserves, are treated as expenses as incurred. Thus, costs that are capitalized and amortized over a long period relate only to recoverable oil and gas reserves, the basic concept underlying the successful-efforts method.

Proponents of the full-cost method argue that the required expensing of the costs of unsuccessful efforts discourages exploration in the oil and gas industry at times when exploration is greatly needed. A related argument is that the reduced profitability of companies under the successful-efforts method discourages investment in oil- and gas-producing companies. These arguments are particularly significant for newer, developing companies that have aggressive exploration policies and, therefore, have a greater need for outside capital than do established enterprises.

Does the accounting method used by a company for exploration activities in the oil and gas industry identify those companies that are aggressive in exploration? One researcher concluded that full-cost companies are not more aggressive in exploration than successful-effort companies, although full-cost companies do make greater use of outside capital.[20] One interpretation of this research is that the method used to account for oil and gas production costs is not necessarily a factor that encourages or discourages exploration in the oil and gas industry.

A more recent study examined the circumstances surrounding voluntary changes from the successful-efforts to the full-cost method of accounting by oil- and gas-producing

---

[19]"Capital Assets," CICA *Handbook,* Paragraph 3060.25, October 1990.

[20]Edward B. Deakin III, "An Analysis of Differences Between Non-Major Oil Firms Using Successful-Efforts and Full Cost Methods," *Accounting Review* (October 1979), pp. 722–34.

companies. One explanation offered for such changes is that highly leveraged companies (i.e., those with high levels of debt financing) or those with high drilling risk prefer full-cost accounting in an attempt to reduce the probability of violating accounting-based debt covenant restrictions. The research suggests that full-cost adoption is associated not only with high leverage but also with current increases in debt financing and, to a lesser extent, with exploration activities. The researchers concluded that we can expect full-cost method adoptions to occur concurrently with abnormal increases in debt financing and exploration activities.[21] Thus, oil- and gas-producing companies continue to choose either the full-cost method or the successful-efforts method.

Conceptual Considerations

**Asset/Liability
Measurement**

Accounting for intangible assets is governed primarily by the accounting principles of asset/liability measurement, matching, and consistency, much like tangible assets. In measuring intangible assets, the accountant must exercise significant judgement, particularly in accounting for goodwill.

As with tangible assets, reliable evidence is important in accounting for intangible assets. Recorded assets should be based on verifiable evidence. Also, careful distinctions must be made between the cost of intangible assets and other expenditures, such as research and development, that are modifying expenses as incurred. The convention of

Conservatism

conservatism is also apparent in accounting for research and development and other costs often associated with intangible assets.

Matching

The matching principle is apparent in the required amortization of intangible assets over the shortest of the asset's useful life, its legal or contractual period, or 40 years. The

Consistency

consistency principle requires that intangible assets be treated alike from period to period so that the resulting financial information will be comparable.

Concluding Remarks

In studying a company's balance sheet, remember that the principles underlying accounting for different types of assets vary. These differing principles are used in recognition of the fact that the values of various assets are realized in several ways. For example, receivables are shown in the balance sheet at their net realizable value (gross amount less an estimate of the portion that will not be collected). Inventories are shown at the lower of cost or market. We have seen, however, that cost can be determined by several different flow assumptions and that variations also exist in the methods of determining the lower of cost or market once the cost has been determined. Concerning investments, we learned that a number of different methods are applied. These methods vary, depending on whether the investment is in debt or equity securities and whether it is current or noncurrent.

Now that we have studied the major asset categories, it is useful to review the significance of the dollar amounts to the various types of assets included in a company's balance sheet. The primary valuation techniques included within generally accepted accounting principles are presented in Exhibit 14.10.

---

[21]W. Bruce Johnson and Ramachandran Ramanan, "Discretionary Accounting Changes From 'Successful-Efforts' to 'Full-Cost' Methods: 1970–1976," *Accounting Review* (January 1988), p. 108.

Exhibit 14.10   Review of Asset Valuation Techniques

Type of Asset	Basis of Valuation Generally Found in Balance Sheet
Current Assets	
Cash	Face amount
Marketable securities	
Debt securities	Cost
Equity securities	Lower of cost or market
Receivables	Net realizable value
Inventories	Lower of cost or market
Prepaid expenses	Unexpired cost
Investments	
Debt securities	Cost, adjusted for unamortized premium or discount
Equity securities	
Investments lacking significant influence	Lower of cost or market*
Investments providing significant influence	Equity method
Tangible and Intangible Assets	
Property, plant, and equipment	Portion of cost not yet recognized as depreciation
Natural resources	Portion of cost not yet recognized as depletion
Intangibles	Portion of cost not yet recognized as amortization
Other Assets	Miscellaneous, depending on nature of specific asset

*When the decline is not temporary.

Key Points

1. Intangible assets differ from property, plant, and equipment primarily because the intangibles lack physical substance. Both types of assets have relatively long lives and are used in the production and distribution of goods and services. (Objective 1)
2. Some intangible assets (e.g., patents, copyrights, and franchises) are separately identifiable. Some intangibles, usually identified as goodwill, are associated with an enterprise as a whole and cannot be separated from that enterprise. (Objective 2)
3. Intangible assets acquired from other enterprises or developed internally that can be separately identified and have determinable lives are recorded as assets. Other costs related to internally developed intangibles, including those with characteristics similar to those of goodwill, are treated as expenses when they are incurred. (Objective 2)
4. Intangible assets are initially recorded at historical cost and then amortized over their estimated useful lives. The period of amortization cannot exceed 40 years, and the straight-line method is typically used. (Objective 3)
5. Financial statement disclosure of intangible assets includes the method and period of amortization. Intangibles are typically presented in a separate asset section designated as "intangible assets" or "other assets." (Objective 4)
6. Goodwill is an intangible asset representing anticipated excess earning capacity. It arises when the price paid for another business exceeds the current value of the

identifiable net assets acquired. Goodwill is recorded at cost and amortized over its estimated useful life in the same manner as other intangible assets. (Objective 5)

7. The value of goodwill can be estimated by several methods that are based on a comparison between anticipated earnings and normal earnings. (Objective 5)

8. All research costs are treated as expenses when they are incurred. Some development costs related to R & D activities, however, are capitalized in appropriate asset categories and amortized as expense over their estimated useful lives. (Objective 6)

9. Development-stage enterprises must apply generally accepted accounting principles in preparing financial statements purporting to present financial position and results of operations in much the same way as do established enterprises. In addition, development-stage enterprises must disclose certain cumulative figures that relate to the enterprise since its inception. (Objective 6)

10. Oil- and gas-producing companies may account for exploration costs under either the successful-efforts or the full-cost method within current GAAP. (Objective 6)

Questions

In questions Q14.1 through Q14.4, circle the letter of the correct answer.

Q14.1 The following procedure best describes the proper accounting for the cost of intangible assets subsequent to acquisition:
(a) Amortize over the longer of 40 years or the estimated useful life.
(b) Amortize over 40 years.
(c) Amortize over the shorter of the estimated useful life or 40 years.
(d) Amortize over ten years.

Q14.2 Assets that should be presented in the intangible-asset category of the balance sheet include all of the following *except*
(a) Goodwill   (b) Copyrights
(c) Patents   (d) Accounts receivable

Q14.3 The following characteristic is *not* necessary for an asset to qualify as intangible:
(a) Has a determinable life.
(b) Conveys a right or privilege.
(c) Has a relatively long life.
(d) Is used in the production of other goods or services.

Q14.4 The following statement best describes proper accounting by development-stage enterprises:
(a) The same as established operating enterprises except for the capitalization of R & D.
(b) The same as established operating enterprises except for the capitalization of operating losses in early years of operation.
(c) The same as established operating enterprises except for the requirement of additional disclosures in the financial statements and related notes.
(d) The same as established operating enterprises except that the statement of changes in financial position is not required.

Q14.5 Briefly identify the key elements in the definition of "intangible asset."

Q14.6 What basic feature distinguishes intangible assets from tangible capital assets?

Q14.7 Distinguish between intangible assets that can be separately identified and those that cannot be separately identified, indicating the type(s) of transactions in which each typically arises.

Q14.8 Identify several types of expenditures that are closely related to intangible assets but that should *not* be capitalized and amortized over periods after their incurrence. Advertising & Research

Q14.9 With regard to Section 3060 of the CICA *Handbook,* what is the basic rationale for requiring the amortization of intangible assets, even in cases in which the life of the intangible is apparently unlimited?

Q14.10 Identify several factors that should be considered in estimating the useful life of a separately identifiable intangible asset.

Q14.11 Indicate the current legal life of the following intangible assets: patents, copyrights, and trademarks. *Renewable every 15 yrs.*

Q14.12 Cite several examples of intangible assets whose lives may be limited through contractual arrangements between two enterprises or between an enterprise and a governmental unit. *A 5-yr. franchise; licensing agreement.*

Q14.13 What types of individual costs are properly included in organization costs?

Q14.14 How should organization costs be treated subsequent to the beginning of operations?

Q14.15 Define goodwill, and then identify any specific circumstances that must be met for goodwill to be established as an asset in the balance sheet.

Q14.16 Briefly outline specific procedures that are followed in accounting for goodwill, including the determination of cost and the recognition of periodic amortization.

Q14.17 Briefly outline the steps that should be followed in placing an estimate on the value of goodwill existing in a potential acquisition.

Q14.18 Of the various methods of estimating the value of goodwill presented in this chapter, which appears to have the greatest merit on a conceptual basis? Why?

Q14.19 Research and development costs are classified in five categories: (1) materials, equipment, and facilities; (2) personnel costs; (3) intangibles purchased from others; (4) contract services; and (5) indirect costs. Describe the items included in each category and provide one or more examples of each.

Q14.20 Distinguish between the full-cost method and the successful-efforts method of accounting by oil- and gas-producing companies.

Q14.21 Define the term "development-stage enterprise" and suggest several activities in which such an enterprise would typically be engaged.

Q14.22 To what extent do the accounting and reporting standards that are applicable to established operating enterprises apply to development-stage enterprises?

Exercises

E14.1 Franchise. On January 2, 1994, East Limited entered into a franchise agreement to operate a fast-food restaurant called Hot Dog Haven. The franchisee paid an initial fee of $12 000 in anticipation of earning revenue from the use of the name Hot Dog Haven for the term of the franchise contract.

The franchise contract is for a five-year period, at the end of which a new agreement will be negotiated, if desired, by the original parties. The franchise also calls for payment of 5 percent of gross revenues by East Limited each year. Revenues for 1994 and 1995 were $89 500 and $128 600, respectively. Straight-line amortization is used on all intangible assets. East Limited reports on a calendar-year basis.

Instructions

(a) Prepare all journal entries for East Limited relative to the franchise agreement for 1994 and 1995.

(b) Determine the amounts to be included in the 1995 financial statements relative to the franchise.

E14.2 Research and Development. Distinguishing between R & D expense and other related costs is sometimes difficult. Identify the accounts that should be debited in each of the following transactions or adjustments:

(1) Cost of models of products under development. A market for this product exists and the company hopes to sell the product as soon as the development stage is complete.
(2) Cost of patent usable only in a current R & D project.
(3) Legal fees paid to successfully defend a patent used in ongoing R & D activities.
(4) Amortization of a patent on a product currently being manufactured and sold.
(5) Costs of quality control over the production process.
(6) Amortization of a patent used in ongoing R & D activities.
(7) Warranty costs on products sold.
(8) Costs of R & D contract services expected to be of continuing benefit.
(9) Materials expected to be used only in a current development project. The marketing department is hoping to find a market for this product.

E14.3 Patents. Wells Manufacturing Inc. acquired three patents in January 1994. The patents have different lives, as indicated in the following schedule:

	Cost	Estimated Useful Life in Years	Remaining Legal Life in Years
Patent X	$12 500	10	17
Patent Y	27 250	5	7
Patent Z	65 620	Indefinite	17

Patent Z is believed to be uniquely useful as long as the company retains the right to use it. In June 1995, the company unsuccessfully attempted to defend its right to Patent Y. Legal fees of $12 700 were incurred in this action.

The company's policy is to amortize intangible assets by the straight-line method to the nearest half year. The company reports on a calendar-year basis.

Instructions
Determine the amount of amortization that should be recognized for 1994, 1995, and 1996.

E14.4 Patent. Lance Corporation acquired a patent on June 25, 1992, for $13 000. Management expects the patent to be useful to the company for its remaining legal life of thirteen years.

On January 12, 1994, the company spent $5000 to successfully defend the patent against a competing company.

During 1995, management determines that the estimated remaining life of the patent should be reduced to only five remaining years, including the current year. This decision was made after careful consideration of the actions of various competing companies.

Instructions
Prepare all journal entries relating to the patent for 1992 through 1995, assuming the company's year-end is December 31. Company policy is to amortize intangible assets by the straight-line method, computed to the nearest full month.

E14.5   Organization Costs.   Williard Manufacturing Limited was organized during 1994. In assisting in the preparation of the financial statements for the year ending December 31, you discover that the following items were debited to the Organization Cost account during early January 1994:

Legal fees of corporate registration	$27 500
Compensation of promoters of corporation	13 800
Salaries of employees before the beginning of operations	5 600
Discount on 10-year bonds issued before the beginning of operations	2 770
	$49 670

Plans call for the amortization of organization costs over a five-year period by the straight-line method. The company's accountant does not plan to begin this amortization until 1995, however, due to the large operating loss that the company sustained in 1994. No amortization of the discount on the bonds has been made. The straight-line method is considered appropriate.

Instructions

Prepare all correcting and adjusting entries that you would propose on December 31, 1994. Closing entries for the year have not been made.

E14.6   Leasehold.   Presser Enterprises Inc. has leased several items of equipment under a lease that does not qualify for capitalization. The lease was entered into on May 1, 1992. Presser paid the $150 000 rental for the first year in advance; a similar payment is made each year on May 1. The lease term is 10 years, and the equipment is expected to have a useful life of 25 years.

On May 1, 1994, the company spent $36 000 to make certain improvements on the equipment. These improvements are expected to guarantee the maximum usefulness of the equipment for the duration of the lease term.

Leasehold improvements are amortized by the straight-line method, computed to the nearest half year.

Instructions

Determine the balance sheet and income statement amounts related to the equipment lease for the years ending December 31, 1992–95.

E14.7   Goodwill.   Ramsey Corporation is considering acquisition of the net assets of Fuller Limited to expand its operations. The book value and current value of the net assets of Fuller Limited are $165 000 and $200 000, respectively. The normal rate of return is believed to be 9 percent, but Ramsey believes it can earn 12 percent annually on its investment due to Fuller's excellent reputation.

Instructions

Compute the goodwill that results from applying the following methods to the situation described:

(a) Years multiple of excess earnings, assuming a ten-year period of excess earnings.
(b) Present value of excess earnings at the expected rate, assuming an eight-year period of excess earnings.
(c) Capitalization of excess earnings at the normal rate.
(d) Capitalization of excess earnings at 12 percent.

E14.8 Goodwill. Filson Inc. is considering acquiring the net assets of Roth Limited as part of a diversification program. The management of Filson believes Roth's excellent reputation provides an opportunity to achieve a level of earnings in excess of the normal rate of 10 percent. In fact, Filson expects to earn a rate of return of 16 percent on its investment.

The following information is available on Roth Limited:

	Estimated Current Value
Current assets	$175 000
Noncurrent assets	280 000
Total reported assets	455 000
Liabilities	(272 000)
Net assets	$183 000

In determining the amount it should bid for Roth Limited, the management of Filson is attempting to estimate a value for goodwill.

Instructions

Compute the goodwill resulting from each of the following methods:

(a) Years multiple of excess earnings, assuming a five-year period.
(b) Present value of excess earnings at the expected rate, assuming a five-year period.
(c) Capitalization of excess earnings at the normal rate.
(d) Capitalization of excess earnings at the expected rate.

E14.9 Goodwill. St. Johns Diversified acquired Simplified Products Inc. on January 1, 1995. Conditions of the acquisition include the following:

(1) St. Johns issued $1 200 000 of twenty-year bonds to finance the transaction. The $1 200 000 was transferred to Simplified Products Inc. to complete the acquisition. Interest is payable annually on December 31 at 13 percent.
(2) St. Johns is to take over all assets (except cash) and all liabilities of Simplified Products Inc. Simplified Products is then to liquidate its assets by distributing cash to shareholders in retirement of their shares.
(3) St. Johns has established the following current valuations on assets and liabilities to be assumed:

	Book Value on Simplified's Books	Estimated Current Value
Receivables	$ 100 000	$ 90 000
Inventory	550 000	720 000
Property, plant, and equipment	900 000	1 300 000
Current liabilities	(300 000)	(250 000)
Noncurrent liabilities	(1 000 000)	(1 000 000)
Net assets	$ 250 000	$ 860 000

(4) St. Johns has determined through various estimation techniques that goodwill inherent in the transaction has a value of at least $400 000. Goodwill is to be amortized over a twenty-year period by the straight-line method.

Instructions

Prepare all journal entries on the books of St. Johns Diversified for the year ended December 31, 1995. Include amortization of goodwill for the full year.

E14.10 Research and Development. An account for a research project identified as AM423 is included on the trial balance of your client, Buckley Limited. The account balance consists of the following charges:

Salaries of research staff	$28 500
Patent acquired solely for use in project AM423	12 000
Patent acquired for use in several research projects, including AM423	16 200
Cost of models	8 950
	$65 650

Intangible assets are amortized by the straight-line method over the shorter of the legal life or estimated useful life. The company's patents have generally been found to be useful for approximately ten years. You determined that both of the patents were acquired in early 1995 and all other costs were incurred throughout 1995.

Instructions

Determine the items that should be presented in the Buckley's balance sheet and income statement on December 31, 1995.

E14.11 Copyright. Storeytime Limited incorrectly charged the $60 000 cost of a copyright acquired in early 1994 to the retained earnings account. The error was discovered during the 1995 audit. The company holds several copyrights and follows the policy of amortizing their cost by the straight-line method over the period expected to benefit, computed to the nearest whole year. The $60 000 copyright was expected to be useful in producing revenue for 12 years from the time of acquisition, even though the legal life is longer.

Instructions

(a) Prepare the 1995 entry that is necessary to correct the 1994 error.
(b) Prepare the entry to record amortization of the copyright for 1995.

E14.12 Amortization of Intangibles. Borton Limited acquired three intangible assets from other enterprises during 1995: patent, $15 270; leasehold improvement, $18 975; and goodwill, $248 000. The patent has a remaining legal life of six years. The leasehold improvement has an expected life of 25 years. The goodwill is expected to provide benefits in the form of high earnings indefinitely. The leasehold improvement is on property that Borton has leased for fifteen years; renewal depends on the intent of both parties at that time. No further information on the lives of the various intangible assets is available or determinable.

Instructions
(a) State your recommendations for the useful life to use for amortization of the three intangible assets. Justify your recommendations.
(b) Assuming that straight-line amortization is used, with a full year taken in the year of acquisition, prepare the entry or entries necessary to record the amortization of the intangible assets at the end of 1995, based on your recommendations in (a).

E14.13 Research and Development. For several years, Martin Manufacturing Inc. has been expensing R & D costs. In 1995, research efforts materialize and three patents are acquired. Patent 87-1 will be used in the ongoing R & D activities of the enterprise. Patent 87-2 will be used in one specific research project that is currently underway. Patent 87-3 will be used in the company's manufacturing process.

Company officials suggest that the patent costs be established as follows:

Patent	Legal Costs of Obtaining Patents	Costs Previously Charged to R & D	Total Cost
87-1	$ 6 500	$17 625	$24 125
87-2	2 000	—	2 000
87-3	4 250	19 000	23 250
	$12 750	$36 625	$49 375

Because legal costs were charged to the Legal Fees account when they were incurred, the company's accountant recommends the following entry:

Patents	49 375	
Legal Fees		12 750
Retained Earnings		36 625

Instructions
(a) Evaluate the suggested entry to record the patents, and justify your position.
(b) Suggest alternative entries for the capitalization of the patents.
(c) How should the amortization of the patent costs be treated in subsequent years?

E14.14 Trademark. Fisher, Inc. has developed a trademark to distinguish its products from those of its competitors. Through advertising and other means, the company is seeking to establish significant product identification to increase future sales.

The similarity between the trademark costs and other intangible and operating costs has caused some confusion about proper accounting. The following items are being treated as part of the cost of the trademark:

Marketing research to study consumer tastes	$32 500
Design costs of trademark	17 800
Legal fees of registering trademark	850
Advertising to establish recognition of trademark	17 800
Registration fee with the Office of Consumer and Corporate Affairs	1 200

Through renewals, the trademark is expected to have an unlimited life.

Instructions

(a) Evaluate each of the costs as appropriate for capitalization in the Trademark account.
(b) Recommend the period of amortization for the cost of the trademark. Justify your recommendation.

E14.15 Oil and Gas Costs.   Alberta Oil Corporation is involved in oil and gas production activities. The following costs were incurred during 1995:

Acquiring mineral rights	$13 500 000
Exploration	
Drilling exploratory wells resulting in recoverable reserves	8 400 000
Drilling exploratory wells not resulting in recoverable reserves	5 550 000
Other costs	7 890 000
Developing recoverable oil reserves	9 375 000
Producing oil and gas (after extraction)	10 550 000
Acquiring equipment for use in oil- and gas-producing activities	17 650 000

Instructions

For each of the above cost categories, indicate the proper accounting treatment within the (1) successful-efforts method and (2) full-cost method by choosing among the following:

(a) Expense as incurred.
(b) Capitalize and amortize as a cost of oil and gas produced.
(c) Treat as a cost of oil and gas produced as incurred.

Problems

P14.1 Intangible Asset Cost.   Superco, Inc. has accumulated a number of costs in a single Intangibles account. As a new employee in the company's accounting department, you have been asked to analyze the account and recommend any corrections you think should be made. The Intangibles account for 1995 is presented to you as follows:

Intangibles

Date	Transaction Description	Dr.	Cr.	Balance
Jan. 2	Legal fees related to organization of business	10 500		10 500
Jan. 2	Prepayment of lease on building for one year	18 000		28 500
Feb. 1	Prepayment of insurance for two years	1 800		30 300
Feb. 28	Advertising expenses (radio, television, and newspaper)	8 000		38 300
Apr. 7	Premium on bonds issued		10 500	27 800
Apr. 25	Interest paid on short-term notes	2 500		30 300
May 5	Legal fees in filing for trade name (Superco)	7 200		37 500
June 30	Cash discount on merchandise purchased		175	37 325

The company plans to present financial statements as of June 30, 1995, to a local bank to support a request for additional financing. Company policy is to amortize intangible asset costs over a ten-year period, computed to the nearest full month. The president suggests an amortization on June 30, 1995, of $1866 (rounded), computed as follows: ($37 325/10 years) × ½ year = $1866

Instructions

(a) Prepare an analysis of the entries in the Intangibles account and indicate corrections you would propose, including reclassifications of items.

(b) Based on your response to (a), prepare the entries to properly record amortization of intangible assets on June 30, 1995. Assume all amounts are material and that straight-line amortization is to be used.

P14.2 Miscellaneous Intangible Assets. Sanders Limited acquired three intangible assets before 1995. The company is involved in the preparation of financial statements on June 30, 1995. Before that date, no formal statements were prepared and the cost of intangible assets had been charged (debited) to retained earnings when acquired.

The following intangible assets were accounted for in this manner:

Asset	Acquisition Date	Estimated Useful Life in Years	Cost
Copyright No. 1	Jan. 2, 1991	25	$30 000
Copyright No. 2	July 15, 1992	15	33 000
Goodwill	Feb. 28, 1993	Indeterminate	32 000

Management has now decided to correct the past accounting treatment and to account for the intangibles as if they had been properly capitalized at the time of acquisition and subsequently amortized. The straight-line method of amortization is to be used, computed to the nearest half year. The company has selected July 1–June 30 for its financial reporting period.

Instructions

(a) Prepare the entries necessary to reclassify the intangible assets and to record amortization for 1995. Provide adequate support for your entries.

(b) Briefly explain in a written paragraph the process you followed in preparing the entry or entries in (a).

P14.3 Research and Development. Calgary Sound, Inc., has initiated an extensive research program to develop a more efficient method of recording compact disks. Management expects to be able to lease its production facilities, when completely refined, to the many record-producing companies in the area.

You have been asked to assist in the preparation of financial statements for the year ended December 31, 1995. Costs related to the project have been accumulated in a master account identified simply as "Recording" since the beginning of the project in early 1995, as follows:

Debits

$185 000—Equipment purchased for use in many research projects over a five-year period.

78 000—Salaries of staff working on research project.

17 500—Computer program services purchased through a contract with another enterprise.

24 800—Legal fees related to the patent acquired on the new production process, which is expected to be useful in producing revenue for ten years.

Credits

$ 88 000—Down payments received from other companies that have contracted to use the new production process in the future.

Management has determined that general and administrative expenses of $175 500 were incurred during 1995. Based on the time spent on the various enterprise functions, you estimate that 25 percent of this amount relates to the research project identified as "recording."

Discussions with corporate officials reveal that all long-lived assets are depreciated with a full year's amortization taken in the year of acquisition and none in the year of disposal. You determine that the process began to generate revenue in 1995, and therefore, the amortization of the patent should begin this year.

Instructions

(a) Prepare all journal entries you would suggest to correct the Recording account and other accounts related to the company's research and development effort.
(b) Prepare all adjusting entries that should be made on December 31, 1995, to reflect amortization and depreciation for the year.
(c) Identify all items that will appear in the financial statements on December 31, 1995, related to plant, intangible assets, and research and development.
(d) Describe in a short paragraph your treatment of items that are included in the research and development expense in (c).

P14.4   Patents.   On April 27, 1993, Ontario Supply Inc. acquired two patents, several items of equipment, and a parcel of land for a total of $137 500. Appraisal values of the assets on the date of acquisition are as follows:

Patent A	$30 000
Patent B	40 000
Equipment	19 700
Land	62 000

By acquiring the assets in a group, the company was able to get a favourable price. Patent A has a five-year remaining life and Patent B a twelve-year remaining life. Amortization on intangible assets is determined on a straight-line basis, computed in whole dollars to the nearest full month.

During 1994, the company became involved in two lawsuits resulting in the successful defence of Patent B but the unsuccessful defence of Patent A. Total legal fees of $17 600 were incurred. Management estimates that approximately equal effort went into defending each patent. The established date of these settlements was March 7, 1994.

No further transactions affecting the patents occurred through October 31, 1995.

Instructions

(a) Prepare journal entries for the years 1993, 1994, and 1995, relating to the intangible asset accounts. The company's reporting year ends on October 31.

(b) Briefly explain any difference in your treatment of the legal costs of the defences of Patents A and B.

P14.5 Goodwill. Manitoba Corporation is negotiating to acquire Clarke Inc. Manitoba Corporation manufactures and sells wood-burning stoves, and Clarke Inc. produces parts that are required to manufacture the stoves. Clarke Inc. enjoys an exceptional reputation, and the management of Manitoba Corporation believes it can continue the level of income currently experienced by Clarke Inc. and satisfy its own need for parts.

Under the contemplated arrangement, Manitoba Corporation will negotiate for the acquisition of the net assets of Clarke Inc. The following information has been developed to determine the appropriate price:

(1) Recorded amounts and estimated current values of assets and liabilities of Clarke Inc. are as follows:

	Recorded Amounts	Estimated Current Values
Assets to be received	$1 485 000	$1 925 000
Liabilities to be assumed	510 000	510 000
	$ 975 000	$1 415 000

(2) Earnings of Clarke Inc. for the past five years averaged $192 000. This is believed to be a reasonable estimate of future income.
(3) The level of income normally experienced by companies similar to Clarke Inc. is 9 percent.

Instructions
(a) Compute the estimated value of goodwill under each of the following methods and assumptions:
   (1) Years multiple of excess earnings, assuming a five-year period of excess earnings.
   (2) Present value of excess earnings, assuming a seven-year period of excess earnings and a 10 percent interest rate.
   (3) Capitalization of excess earnings at the normal rate.
   (4) Capitalization of excess earnings at twice the normal rate.
(b) If the present value of excess earnings method is accepted by management as the appropriate value of goodwill for negotiation purposes, what is the maximum price Manitoba Corporation should pay for the net assets of Clarke Inc.?

P14.6 Goodwill. Trudeau Limited is considering the acquisition of Martin Inc. A considerable amount of information about Martin Inc. has been accumulated, including the following:

Net Income. Net income figures are:

Year	Net Income
1990	$78 500
1991	59 000
1992	67 200
1993	51 500
1994	72 000

Net income for 1990 included a $12 500 extraordinary gain; 1992 net income included a $14 000 extraordinary gain.

Selected Balance Sheet Data. As of the transaction date, recorded amounts and estimated current values of assets are:

	Recorded Amount	Estimated Current Value
Receivables	$125 000	$120 000
Inventories	216 000	415 000
Property, plant, and equipment	300 000	425 000
Patents	10 000	75 000

Liabilities to be assumed are $665 000.

Management of Trudeau Limited believes the investment in Martin Inc. will provide a return in excess of the 10 percent that is normal for the industry. Analysis of the components of earnings indicates that average net income for the past five years is a reasonable basis for estimating future income. It is believed, however, that the effect of extraordinary items should be eliminated and that depreciation and amortization can be expected to increase by $12 500 annually.

Instructions

(a) Estimate the amount of goodwill in the Martin Inc. acquisition by each of the following methods:
  (1) Years multiple of estimated excess earnings, assuming a five-year period of excess earnings.
  (2) Present value of estimated excess earnings, discounted at the normal rate over a five-year period.
  (3) Capitalization of the estimated excess earnings at a 15 percent rate.
(b) For each category of assets, indicate the probable reason for the difference between the recorded amount and the estimated current value.
(c) After extended negotiations, a price of $400 000 is finally agreed upon by the two companies. Prepare the journal entry to record the acquisition by Trudeau Limited. You may include all liabilities in a single Liability account. The agreement calls for a cash payment of $175 000 and the issuance of 10 000 no-par value shares of Trudeau Limited. The current market price of the shares is $22.50.

P14.7 Goodwill. Pearson Inc. has negotiated to acquire the net assets of Robbins Corp. The companies have agreed that the purchase price should be established at the fair market value of the assets, less liabilities, plus the value of the goodwill of Robbins Corp. The value of the goodwill has been agreed upon as the average of the last three years' excess of income from normal operations over 10 percent of shareholders' equity at the beginning of the year, discounted to the present at 10 percent for a five-year period. The last three years are 1992, 1993, and 1994.

The following figures have been taken from the last four years' financial statements of Robbins Corp. (December 31 year-end):

	1991	1992	1993	1994
Net income	$ 225 000	$ 250 000	$ 350 000	$ 550 000
Shareholders' equity				
Common shares	1 500 000	1 500 000	1 800 000	1 800 000
Retained earnings	125 000	250 000	400 000	500 000
	$1 625 000	$1 750 000	$2 200 000	$2 300 000

Additional Information

You have been engaged as an independent CA to determine the total purchase price that has apparently been agreed upon by both parties. As part of your investigation, you discover the following:

(1) The two companies have agreed on the following estimates of the current value of the assets to be transferred (other than goodwill):

Receivables	$150 000	Buildings	$1 400 000
Inventory	400 000	Land	1 600 000
Equipment	500 000	Franchise	150 000

(2) Liabilities to be assumed by Pearson Inc. total $1 200 000.
(3) Additional shares were sold in May 1993.
(4) The following questionable items have been recorded by year:

1992.   An extraordinary gain of $25 500 was included in net income. This represents the excess of the proceeds over cost of land purchased by the city under expropriation proceedings.

1993.   A franchise agreement was entered into in January and $100 000 paid in advance. The period of the franchise is five years. No amortization has been taken. The $100 000 was debited to an Intangible Asset Account.

1994.   A sum of $15 000 was received from a customer whose account had been erroneously written off as uncollectable in 1993 by a direct charge to Bad Debts Expense. The arrangement with the customer had explicitly called for repayment in 1994. The $15 000 was credited to Miscellaneous Income when received.

An insurance recovery of $125 000 was received on inventory that was totally destroyed by a flood. The $125 000 was presented as an extraordinary gain due to the unusual circumstances surrounding the flood. The cost of the inventory, $75 000, was debited to Retained Earnings. The flood was extremely unusual; a similar event has never occurred in the location of the company during this century and is not expected to recur.

An additional tax assessment of $97 000 was paid. Of this amount, $25 000 related to 1991, $35 000 to 1992, and $37 000 to 1993. Retained Earnings was debited for the total of $97 000, since this adjustment resulted from an accounting error.

Instructions

(a) Prepare a schedule that includes:
   (1) The corrected net income for 1991, 1992, 1993, and 1994.
   (2) The amount to be used for computing goodwill for 1992, 1993, and 1994. A conference with officials of the two companies reveals that the phrase "income from normal operations" appears to have meant income before extraordinary items.
(b) Prepare a schedule restating retained earnings for 1991, 1992, 1993, and 1994 at year-end.
(c) Based on information from your schedules in (a), compute goodwill as agreed upon by the two companies.

(d) Prepare the journal entry to record the net assets of Robbins Corp. acquired by Pearson Inc., assuming payment is made by issuing 100 000 of Pearson Inc. common shares and the remainder in cash. The no-par value common shares have a market price of $25. The transaction was finalized on January 5, 1995.

(e) Prepare the adjusting entry one year after the acquisition to record amortization on the intangible assets acquired. The franchise is expected to have a six-year life, and the goodwill is to be amortized over a period consistent with the method by which it was computed.

P14.8 Miscellaneous Intangible Assets. Information concerning Roach Inc.'s intangible assets follows:

(1) On January 1, 1994, Roach signed an agreement to operate as a franchisee of Rapid Copy Service, Inc. for an initial franchise fee of $80 200. Of this amount, $25 000 was paid when the agreement was signed, and the balance is payable in four annual payments of $13 800 each beginning January 1, 1995. The agreement provides that the down payment is not refundable and no future services are required of the franchisor. The present value at January 1, 1994, of the four annual payments discounted at 10 percent (the implicit rate for a loan of this type) is $43 700. The agreement also provides that 5 percent of the revenue from the franchise must be paid to the franchisor annually. Roach's revenue from the franchise for 1994 was $900 000. Roach estimates the useful life of the franchise to be ten years.

(2) Roach incurred $78 000 of experimental and development costs in its laboratory to develop a patent that was granted on January 2, 1994. Legal fees and other costs associated with registration of the patent totalled $16 400. Management estimates that the useful life of the patent will be eight years.

(3) A trademark was purchased from Sampson Corp. for $40 000 on July 1, 1991. Expenditures for successful litigation in defence of the trademark totalling $10 000 were paid on July 1, 1994. Management estimates that the useful life of the trademark will be twenty years from the date of acquisition.

Instructions

(a) Prepare a schedule showing the intangible assets section of Roach's balance sheet at December 31, 1994. Show supporting computations in good form.

(b) Prepare a schedule showing all expenses resulting from the transactions that would appear on Roach's income statement for the year ended December 31, 1994. Show supporting computations in good form.

(Adapted from AICPA.)

P14.9 Miscellaneous Intangible Assets. Barber Inc. was organized and began operations in 1995. Selected transactions for the first year of operation are listed below.

Jan. 5 Paid $5000 to the lawyers who assisted in preparing the corporate by-laws, obtaining the corporate charter, and generally advising the company on several legal matters.

Jan. 10 Issued 1000 shares of the company's no-par value common shares to promoters of the corporation. In another recent transaction, shares sold at $12 per share.

Feb. 5 Paid $10 000 to develop and acquire the exclusive right to use the company's trademark.

Mar. 21 Paid $8500 to an advertising agency to promote the company and its products, emphasizing the new trademark recently developed. A second installment is to be paid in six months.

Apr.   1 A licence to operate a shop in the local airport was obtained for $12 000 from the city on April 1. The licence covers a five-year period, at the end of which the company must pay $12 000 for renewal for five years. In addition, the company must pay 5 percent of gross revenues to the city to cover utilities, maintenance, and other operating expenses. An estimated amount of $15 000 for April 1 to December 31 was paid on April 15. In subsequent years, this payment will be made at the end of the calendar year.

July   25 A marketing research firm was hired to help survey potential customers and assess ways to capitalize more on consumer demand. An initial payment of $3250 was made to the firm.

Sept. 30 A second payment of $8500 was made to the advertising agency for promotional services rendered. The advertising is expected to enhance the value of the trademark and to generally benefit the company for several years.

Oct.   5 Another company, Malott Enterprises, was acquired. In the transaction, $265 000 cash was paid to acquire assets valued as follows: inventory, $97 500; property, plant, and equipment, $180 000; franchise rights, $42 500. Noncurrent liabilities assumed totalled $96 000. Management has placed an estimated value of $80 000 on goodwill, based on the present value of excess future earnings over a ten-year period. The franchise has a five-year remaining life.

Nov.   7 Paid $2500 in legal fees to successfully defend the trademark against a competitor who had begun using an identical diagram in a different colour to market similar products.

Instructions

(a) Prepare general journal entries to record these transactions.

(b) Prepare any adjusting entries necessary for intangible assets on December 31, 1995, in anticipation of the preparation of financial statements. Consider the following information:

(1) Revenues for 1995 were $336 000.

(2) Intangible assets are to be amortized by the straight-line method, computed to the nearest full month. Intangibles are to be amortized over the contractual period, if any. Other intangibles, including goodwill, are to be amortized over a ten-year period.

(3) Amortization should be rounded to the nearest dollar.

(c) Indicate items and amounts relative to intangible assets that should be presented in the company's balance sheet and income statement on December 31, 1995.

P14.10 Research and Development. Loszynski Corporation was founded in 1982 and experienced only moderate growth during its first ten years. However, Loszynski was able to attract several scientists and researchers with technical experience and ability and became a pioneer in the field of robotics.

Loszynski experienced a 30 percent annual growth in revenue for the years 1992–94 due to the increased demand for its products and consulting services. The company, assured of sufficient financing, planned several expenditures in 1994 that would enable it to meet increased demand and continue its excellent growth rate through the rest of the decade.

Ron Griffin of Loszynski's general accounting department is experiencing difficulty in understanding several transactions made during the first quarter of 1995, some of which include expenditures that were planned in 1994. Griffin has asked the controller for assistance in determining how to record the six transactions listed below, and how they will affect the financial statements of Loszynski Corporation in both current and future periods. All amounts are considered material.

(1) Loszynski paid $260 000 for land on which to build a new research facility. The cost to raze and remove an old building on the site of the newly proposed research facility was $50 000. Lumber, copper tubing, and a few remaining usable fixtures from the old building were salvaged and sold for $10 000. Loszynski paid $4000 to the architect who designed the new building, $30 000 for excavation of the basement, and $420 000 to a contractor for construction of the building. Due to the foundation, construction, and materials used, the new building is expected to last for at least 60 years. Loszynski's research director, however, believes the building will not be appropriate for the needs of the company after twenty years.

(2) Loszynski gave a one-year noninterest-bearing note for $165 000 to Roberts Industries in exchange for a conveyor to be installed in the new research facility and a temperature monitoring system (TMS). The imputed interest rate on the note is 10 percent per year. At the date of the exchange, the remaining life of both items on the books of Roberts Industries was seven years. The conveyor had an estimated value of $60 000 at the date of the exchange, is expected to last 30 years, and will be needed as long as the new research facility is used by the company. The TMS had an estimated value of $100 000 at the date of the exchange and is expected to last five years.

(3) Loszynski incurred the following costs in securing a trademark.

Design costs	$2000
Registration fees	300
Lawyer's fees	700

Loszynski's lawyer informed the company that the trademark registration system provides for an initial registration term of fifteen years and an indefinite number of renewals for periods of fifteen years each. Loszynski's marketing manager believes the trademark will be of value to the company for 50 years.

(4) Loszynski incurred $9000 of legal fees in defending the rights to a patent. The patent was purchased in the first quarter of 1993 at a cost of $15 000 and is being amortized over a period of twelve years.

(5) Loszynski made improvements to a building it has occupied since the first quarter of 1991 under the terms of a twenty-year lease. Carpeting installed at a cost of $2800 is expected to last 10 years and shelving installed at a cost of $4200 is expected to last 30 years.

(6) Loszynski spent $37 000 searching for practical applications of new research findings that are believed to be of use to the company for the next twenty years.

Instructions

As controller for Loszynski Corporation, review the six transactions brought to your attention by Ron Griffin. For each of the six transactions:

(a) Identify whether the item is to be expensed or capitalized in 1995.
(b) Identify the amount to be expensed or capitalized (other than depreciation or amortization).
(c) Identify the number of years to be used to write off the items that are capitalized.
(d) Justify your answers by reference to underlying accounting theory or to relevant sections of the CICA *Handbook*. You need not cite the section(s) by number.

Income tax implications and calculation of annual depreciation or amortization charges for capitalized items are to be ignored. Use the following format to present your answer.

Item Number	Amount to Be Expensed (if any)	Capitalized Items (if any)		Justification of Treatment and/or Life
		Amount	Life	

(Adapted from CMA.)

P14.11 Patents. Malik Inc. is involved in the development, manufacture, and sale of burglar alarm systems, ranging from relatively simple units for private residences to sophisticated units for large office buildings. The company's operations depend largely on an ongoing research and development program, resulting in the internal development of patents. Also, the company occasionally acquires patents from other companies.

As the accountant for Malik Inc., you are responsible for the proper accounting of many transactions relative to research and operating activities. The following activities have taken place over several years:

1991

Continuous research to develop improved alarm systems	$179 000
May 31 Acquisition of Patent A, with a 12-year remaining legal life, from a competitor	72 000

1992

Feb. 28 Costs of models of new alarm system	32 250
Oct. 31 Legal fees for acquisition of Patent B on new alarm system	38 000

1993

Continuous development to advance new alarm system to commercial production	38 000
June 30 Initiation of advertising campaign to promote new alarm system, enhancing the value of Patents A and B	42 000
Oct. 25 Legal expenses for the successful defence of Patent B	18 000

1994

Mar. 19 Legal expenses for the unsuccessful defence of Patent A	8 500
May 24 Acquisition of Patent C, with a six-year remaining legal life, from a competitor in anticipation that it will replace Patent A	43 500

1995

Continuous research on improved alarm system to replace Patent B	82 650

In 1995, management determined that the remaining life of Patent B was only three years, including the current year. Research was begun in that year to prepare for the replacement of Patent B with a new patent—presumably Patent D—at some future date.

Instructions

Prepare the Patent account for 1991 through December 1995—the end of Malik's current reporting year—following these guidelines:

(a) Amortization is to be made by the straight-line method, with no assumed residual value.

(b) Amortization is to be based on the shorter of the legal life or ten years, unless indicated otherwise, computed to the nearest half year from acquisition or to disposal.

(c) The book value to be presented in the balance sheet on December 31 of each year should be indicated.

P14.12 Miscellaneous Intangible Assets. Victory Diversified Inc. has been in business for several years. A trial balance prepared by the company's staff accountant for December 31, 1995, is presented below.

Victory Diversified Inc.
UNADJUSTED TRIAL BALANCE
December 31, 1995
(in thousands of dollars)

Account	Dr.	Cr.
Cash	$20	
Accounts receivable	50	
Inventory	120	
Equipment	800	
Accumulated depreciation—Equipment		$ 250
Buildings	1200	
Accumulated depreciation—Buildings		400
Patents	550	
Franchise agreement	95	
Organization costs	102	
Goodwill	345	
Accounts payable		12
Accrued wages payable		5
Accrued taxes payable		60
Bonds payable		500
Premium on bonds payable		35
Preferred shares (no-par value)		100
Common shares (no-par value)		1320
Retained earnings (as of January 1)		400
Sales revenue		900
Cost of goods sold	400	
Selling and administrative expenses	300	
	$3982	$3982

Additional Information

Before 1995, Victory Diversified Inc. prepared financial statements internally. The company has not been audited because the ownership is held completely by one family and is not actively sold. As of 1995, however, in anticipation of bank loans and a possible public offering of common shares, the company needs audited financial statements prepared in conformity with generally accepted accounting principles.

As a member of the team of independent auditors responsible for Victory Diversified, you have been assigned to audit the intangible assets. You have observed that four intangible asset accounts appear on the unadjusted trial balance. Additional investigation reveals the following:

Patents. All patents were purchased from another company when Victory Diversified began operations on January 2, 1988. These patents are being amortized over an expected useful life of fourteen years. Improvements made to equipment covered by the patents costing $75 000 were debited to the account in January 1992. Amortization in 1992–94 included amortization on the $75 000 for the remaining life of the relevant patent. It is determined that the $75 000 should have been expensed in 1992. It is further determined on December 31, 1995, that one of the patents has a remaining life of only two years. This patent was originally assigned a cost of $210 000.

Franchise Agreement. A franchise agreement was signed on January 1, 1995. A $50 000 fee was paid, covering a five-year period, at the end of which the company may renew the agreement by paying $50 000. A decision on renewal has not been made as of December 31, 1995. The agreement calls for an annual payment of 5 percent of revenue. An entry debiting the account for $45 000 was made at the time of the cash payment for 1995.

Organization Costs. Organization costs include the unamortized portion of amounts paid to promoters for services rendered at the inception of the corporation. These fees have been amortized since inception over an estimated 40-year life. The decision is made, as of December 31, 1995, to reduce the total period of amortization of organization costs to twelve years.

Goodwill. The Goodwill account includes three items:

$ 45 000—Legal expenses relative to incorporation. These were assigned to the account in January 1988.

200 000—Excess of cost over assigned net asset values of an enterprise acquired in early 1993, expected to be of value for an indefinite period.

100 000—Paid to an advertising consulting firm in early 1994 for a major advertising effort expected to be beneficial for an indefinite period.

No amortization has been taken on any amount in the Goodwill account.

Instructions

(a) Prepare an analysis of each intangible asset, indicating (1) the changes needed to restate each intangible account on a corrected basis for determining the amount of amortization for 1995, and (2) the proper amount of amortization for 1995.

(b) Prepare two compound journal entries (1) to correct the intangible asset account balances before the recording of 1995 amortization, and (2) to record 1995 amortization.

Cases

C14.1 Intangible Costs. Honeyall Inc. is a large publicly held corporation. Listed below are six selected expenditures made by the company during the current fiscal year ended April 30, 1994. The proper accounting treatment of these transactions must be determined in order for Honeyall's annual financial statements to be prepared in accordance with generally accepted accounting principles.

(1) Honeyall Inc. spent $2 million on a program designed to improve relations with its dealers. This project was favourably received by the dealers, and Honeyall's management believes that significant future benefits will be obtained from this program. The program was conducted during the fourth quarter of the current fiscal year.

(2) A pilot plant to test a new production process was constructed during 1993–94 at a cost of $4 million. The plant will operate for approximately five years. At the end of that time, the company will make a decision regarding the economic value of the process. The pilot plant is too small for commercial production, so it will be dismantled when the test is over.

(3) A new product will be introduced next year. The company spent $3 million during the current year for design of tools, jigs, moulds, and dies for this product.

(4) Honeyall, Inc. purchased Merit Corp. for $5 million in cash in early August 1993. The fair market value of the identifiable assets of Merit was $4 million.
(5) A large advertising campaign was conducted during April 1994 to introduce a new product to be released during the first quarter of the 1994–95 fiscal year. The advertising campaign cost $2.5 million.
(6) During the first six months of the 1993–94 fiscal year, $500 000 was spent on legal work in connection with a successful patent application. The patent became effective November 1, 1993. The legal life of the patent is seventeen years, while the economic life of the patent is expected to be approximately ten years.

Instructions

For each of the six transactions, determine the amount that should be included on Honeyall's April 30, 1994, balance sheet and income statement.
(Adapted from CMA.)

C14.2 Research and Development. Burke Limited is in the process of developing a revolutionary new product. A division of the company was formed to develop, manufacture, and market this product. As of year-end (December 31, 1995), the new product has not been manufactured for resale; however, a prototype unit is in operation.

Throughout 1995, the new division incurred certain costs, including the costs of design and engineering studies, prototype manufacturing costs, administrative expenses (including salaries of administrative personnel), and market research costs. In addition, approximately $800 000 in equipment (with an estimated useful life of ten years) was purchased for use in developing and manufacturing the new product. Approximately $300 000 of this equipment was built specifically for the design development of the new product. The remaining $500 000 was used to manufacture the preproduction prototype and will be used to manufacture the new product once it is in commercial production.

Instructions

(a) What are the definitions of "research" and "development" as defined in Section 3450 of the CICA *Handbook?*
(b) In accordance with Section 3450 of the CICA *Handbook,* how should the various costs described above be recorded on the financial statements for the year ended December 31, 1995?
(Adapted from AICPA.)

C14.3 Development-Stage Enterprise. The president of New Limited, Thomas P. New, has engaged you to assist in the preparation of financial statements to be used in conjunction with a proposed bank loan. Officials of the bank have requested financial statements that are "based on good accounting."

New Limited was organized during 1995. The company has been raising capital, acquiring assets, developing personnel, and developing products that it plans to market in the future. Only insignificant amounts of revenue have been generated to date.

Mr. New has prepared the following balance sheet which he considers adequate for purposes of the proposed bank loan. He also offers the information that accompanies the balance sheet as an explanation of some of the activities of the enterprise to date.

New Limited
BALANCE SHEET
October 31, 1995

Assets

Cash	$ 17 650
Machinery (at cost)	59 350
Land (at cost)	15 000
Intangibles	41 400
	$133 400

Liabilities

Accrued expenses	$ 11 975
Notes payable (90-day)	21 425
	33 400

Shareholders' Equity

Common shares	100 000
	$133 400

Notes

(1) Intangible assets consist of the following:

Research and development	$15 400
Marketing research	3 400
Personnel recruitment and training	12 600
Legal fees relative to organization of corporation	4 750
Operating expenses incurred through October 31, 1995	5 250
	$41 400

(2) Common shares have been issued as follows:
   (a) Thomas P. New, President, acquired 8000 no-par value shares for $10 per share.
   (b) George M. New, brother of Thomas, received 2000 shares in exchange for land that he had purchased five years earlier for $15 000.
   (c) John X. New, a cousin of Thomas and George, received 1000 shares for managerial services rendered in operating the enterprise to date. John will become the general manager at some future date when he quits his current position with another company.

Thomas New asks you to verify the authenticity of his balance sheet and send it to the bank as soon as possible so that he can proceed with his application for the much-needed bank loan.

Instructions
(a) Identify the deficiencies in Mr. New's balance sheet, considering both his draft of the statement and the additional information that he has provided. Indicate the proper treatment of each item you have listed as a deficiency.
(b) In addition to the changes you propose in (a), what items must be included to provide the bank with financial statements that are prepared in conformity with generally accepted accounting principles?

Judgement Cases

J14.1 Organization Costs. Big Time Co. Inc. was formed during the previous year and you, the newly appointed controller of the company, have encountered a thorny issue involving a large series of payments to the founder and chief executive officer (CEO) for his work in establishing the company and attracting investors. The CEO has directed you to treat all the amounts paid to him as "organization costs" and to amortize them over a five-year period. He stated,

Without my strenuous efforts this company wouldn't even exist. I worked night and day to find investors and put these deals together. I developed corporate by-laws, obtained the corporate charter, and simply got the wheels rolling. When we start generating revenue next year, I want to match it with these costs in an appropriate manner. If any costs were necessary to form and organize this business, the amounts paid to me are it.

You are more than a little concerned, because the amounts paid to the CEO constitute 10 percent of the total shareholders' equity of $6 million contributed by the other investors. Indeed, this is the manner by which the amounts paid to the CEO were determined. He has consistently had cheques written to himself in the amount of 10 percent of all payments received for the issuance of capital shares. The corporate charter and by-laws do not specifically prohibit such withdrawals and, in fact, provide that the CEO and other officers will be compensated adequately for the services they render to the company.

Instructions

How should you account for these amounts? If you believe that they cannot be considered organization costs and reported as assets, what treatment do you recommend? Be sure to address the theoretical as well as the practical issues inherent in the case.

J14.2 Capitalization Versus Expense. Fast Change Inc. has just undergone substantial personnel changes in its executive leadership. The board of directors has replaced the chief executive officer (CEO); the vice-presidents for production, marketing, and finance; and a number of other high-level positions. The executive search costs involved in the personnel changes, as well as severance pay to those whose contracts were prematurely terminated, are both individually material to the company. The changes were made because the company's poor performance in recent years has come close to violating several of its lending covenants relating to debt–equity ratios and the rate of return on assets employed (net income divided by total assets).

The new CEO would like the company to stop perceiving itself as a "loser" and wants to avoid issuing financial statements that reveal the violations of lending covenants and avoid the attendant negotiations with the banks that will follow. He observes that if the personnel costs involved in changing the management team were capitalized rather than charged to expense, the company's financial statements would not depict a violation of the lending covenants. He calls you, the new chief accounting officer, to his office and instructs you to research the possibility of appropriately capitalizing these costs. He tells you,

All of these costs were incurred by the company to remedy a bad management situation. The result of incurring these costs is the excellent management team that is now in place and those costs will continue to benefit the company throughout our tenure. I personally believe that these costs should be reported as an intangible asset and amortized over the next five years (the length of my contract). As you know, however, I'm not an accountant by any means, and I don't want to do anything wrong by issuing financial statements that contain departures from GAAP. However, I also want to put our best foot forward as we move to improve the operating performance of this business. We're all new here, and I know you want to get off on the right foot. Because of the importance of this matter to me, I know I can count on you, as a valuable member of our team, to leave no stone unturned in justifying our position in treating these costs as intangible assets.

Instructions

Perform the research requested by the CEO. Be sure to consider the appropriate technical and conceptual issues that underly the preparation of financial statements in accordance with GAAP. Also consider any ethical issues that come to mind as you consider the wishes of your new boss.

Appendix A

Canadian Pacific Limited

1992 Financial Report

Consolidated Balance Sheet
December 31

Assets

(in millions)	1992	1991
Current Assets		
Cash and temporary investments	$ **1,387.3**	$ 1,603.0
Accounts receivable	**1,090.7**	1,559.2
Inventories (Note 8)	**611.5**	925.9
	3,089.5	4,088.1
Investments (Note 9)	**1,189.6**	924.1
Properties, at cost (Note 10)		
Transportation	**7,970.1**	7,770.2
Energy	**5,601.1**	5,727.9
Forest Products	**4,188.3**	4,088.4
Real Estate and Hotels	**4,088.4**	3,899.8
Telecommunications and Manufacturing	**1,357.4**	1,591.7
Other	**57.9**	53.0
	23,263.2	23,131.0
Less: Accumulated depreciation, depletion and amortization	**8,221.1**	8,323.9
	15,042.1	14,807.1
Other Assets and Deferred Charges (Note 11)	**902.6**	767.8
	$ 20,223.8	$ 20,587.1

Auditors' Report

To the Shareholders of Canadian Pacific Limited
We have audited the consolidated balance sheets of Canadian Pacific Limited as at December 31, 1992 and 1991 and the statements of consolidated income, consolidated retained income and changes in consolidated financial position for each of the three years in the period ended December 31, 1992. These consolidated financial statements are the responsibility of the Corporation's management. Our responsibility is to express an opinion on these financial statements based on our audits.

We conducted our audits in accordance with generally accepted auditing standards. Those standards require that we plan and perform an audit to obtain reasonable assurance whether the financial statements are free of material misstatement. An audit includes examining, on a test basis, evidence supporting the amounts and disclosures in the financial statements. An audit also includes assessing the accounting principles used and significant estimates made by management as well as evaluating the overall financial statement presentation.

In our opinion, these consolidated financial statements present fairly, in all material respects, the financial position of Canadian Pacific Limited as at December 31, 1992 and 1991 and the results of its operations and the changes in its financial position for each of the three years in the period ended December 31, 1992 in accordance with generally accepted accounting principles in Canada.

Price Waterhouse

Chartered Accountants
Montreal, Quebec
March 5, 1993

Liabilities and Shareholders' Equity

(in millions)

	1992	1991
Current Liabilities		
Bank loans		
Accounts payable and accrued liabilities	$ 149.6	$ 360.3
Income and other taxes payable	1,790.4	2,009.8
Dividends payable	159.7	69.1
Long term debt maturing within one year (Note 12)	29.7	29.5
	694.1	405.5
	2,823.5	2,874.2
Deferred Liabilities (Note 13)	753.2	502.0
Long Term Debt (Note 12)	7,021.8	6,809.8
Perpetual 4% Consolidated Debenture Stock (Note 14)	172.4	176.4
Deferred Income Taxes	1,930.6	2,203.3
Deferred Income Credits (Note 15)	420.8	440.5
Minority Shareholders' Interest in Subsidiary Companies (Note 16)	815.2	867.0
Shareholders' Equity (Note 17)		
Preference Shares	14.9	14.9
Ordinary Shares		
Issued – 319,053,305 (1991 – 318,677,431) shares		
Premium on securities	1,241.1	1,234.9
Other paid-in surplus	1,174.5	1,174.5
Foreign currency translation adjustments	154.1	154.1
Retained income	219.4	72.4
	3,482.3	4,063.1
	6,286.3	6,713.9
Commitments (Note 21)		
	$ 20,223.8	$ 20,587.1

See Notes to Consolidated Financial Statements.

Approved on behalf of the Board:

J.F. Hankinson, Director

W.W. Stinson, Director

(in millions)	1992	1991	1990
Operating Activities			
Net income (loss)	$ (478.3)	$ (913.8)	$ 355.3
Depreciation, depletion and amortization	915.1	906.6	795.2
Deferred income taxes	(362.0)	(276.6)	169.7
Minority interest share of income (losses) of subsidiaries	(57.3)	(135.1)	21.3
Equity in losses of associates	48.3	152.3	38.5
Write-down of assets and restructuring costs	615.0	1,270.0	61.9
Reduction in restructuring accruals	(127.5)	—	—
Amortization of exchange losses (gains)	0.9	(55.3)	(70.9)
Gains from sales of businesses,			
investments and properties	(17.2)	(160.3)	(93.9)
Other operating cash items, net	(84.6)	(35.7)	(17.7)
Cash from operations, before changes			
in working capital	452.4	752.1	1,259.4
Decrease (increase) in non-cash working capital			
balances relating to operations (Note 6)	316.1	(3.0)	24.6
Cash from operations	768.5	749.1	1,284.0
Dividends			
Paid to shareholders of the Corporation	(102.1)	(249.1)	(292.9)
Paid to minority shareholders of subsidiaries	(21.3)	(26.0)	(41.9)
	(123.4)	(275.1)	(334.8)
Financing Activities			
Issuance of long term debt	1,688.0	3,718.7	1,372.7
Repayment of long term debt	(1,182.8)	(1,064.6)	(1,074.1)
Issuance of shares by subsidiaries	285.5	6.8	2.0
Redemption of Preferred Shares by subsidiaries	(1.1)	(23.7)	(62.5)
Issuance of Ordinary Shares by the Corporation	6.2	8.9	13.3
Repurchase of Ordinary Shares by the Corporation	—	—	(10.3)
	795.8	2,646.1	241.1
Investing Activities			
Business acquisitions and investments (Note 7)	(376.9)	(139.9)	(284.8)
Additions to properties (Note 2)	(1,397.2)	(1,690.8)	(1,953.9)
Sales of businesses, investments and properties	328.2	463.8	373.7
	(1,445.9)	(1,366.9)	(1,865.0)
Cash Position*			
Increase (decrease) in cash	(5.0)	1,753.2	(674.7)
Cash (deficit) at beginning of year	1,242.7	(510.5)	164.2
Cash (deficit) at end of year	$ 1,237.7	$ 1,242.7	$ (510.5)

*Cash comprises cash and temporary investments net of
bank loans and notes payable.

See Notes to Consolidated Financial Statements.

Statement of Consolidated Income
For the Year ended December 31

(in millions, except amounts per share)	1992	1991	1990
Revenues			
Goods sold	$ **3,790.7**	$ 4,903.1	$ 5,292.3
Services	**5,172.9**	5,168.4	5,164.0
	8,963.6	10,071.5	10,456.3
Costs and Expenses			
Cost of goods sold	**2,836.1**	3,787.9	3,686.3
Cost of services	**3,571.5**	3,597.9	3,473.0
Selling, general and administrative	**1,747.2**	1,755.4	1,466.9
Depreciation, depletion and amortization	**915.1**	1,435.8	795.2
	9,069.9	10,577.0	9,421.4
Operating income (loss) (Note 2)	**(106.3)**	(505.5)	1,034.9
Interest expense, net (Note 3)	**592.8**	540.0	487.6
Other expenses (income) (Note 4)	**146.7**	(122.8)	(17.3)
Income (loss) before income taxes, minority interest and equity in income	**(845.8)**	(922.7)	564.6
Income tax expense (recovery) (Note 5)	**(278.7)**	(263.5)	220.4
Minority interest share of income (losses) of subsidiaries	**(57.3)**	(135.1)	21.3
Income (loss) before equity in income of associates	**(509.8)**	(524.1)	322.9
Equity in income (loss) of Laidlaw Inc.	**22.4**	(98.9)	32.4
Equity in income of United Dominion Industries Limited	**9.1**	—	—
Write-down of investment in Laidlaw Inc. (Note 9)	**—**	(290.8)	—
Net income (loss)	$ **(478.3)**	$ (913.8)	$ 355.3
Earnings (loss) per Ordinary Share	$ **(1.50)**	$ (2.87)	$ 1.11

Statement of Consolidated Retained Income
For the Year ended December 31

(in millions, except amounts per share)	1992	1991	1990
Balance, January 1	$ **4,063.1**	$ 5,178.0	$ 5,116.2
Net income (loss)	**(478.3)**	(913.8)	355.3
	3,584.8	4,264.2	5,471.5
Dividends			
4% Preference Shares	**0.5**	0.5	0.5
Ordinary Shares (per share: 1992 – $0.32; 1991 – $0.63; 1990 – $0.92)	**102.0**	200.6	293.0
Total dividends	**102.5**	201.1	293.5
Balance, December 31	$ **3,482.3**	$ 4,063.1	$ 5,178.0

See Notes to Consolidated Financial Statements.

NOTES TO CONSOLIDATED FINANCIAL STATEMENTS

1. Significant Accounting Policies

Principles of Consolidation

The consolidated financial statements have been prepared in accordance with accounting principles generally accepted in Canada and include the accounts of Canadian Pacific Limited (the "Corporation") and all of its subsidiaries ("CP Limited").

All significant inter-company transactions and balances have been eliminated.

The principal companies and divisions included in each business segment are as follows:

December 31	1992	1991	1990
	Percentage Ownership		
Transportation			
CP Rail System			
CP Rail – a division of the Corporation			
Soo Line Corporation (Note 7)	**100.0%**	100.0%	100.0%
Delaware and Hudson Railway Company, Inc.	**100.0**	100.0	—
CP Ships			
Canada Maritime Limited	**57.0**[1]	57.0	57.0
Racine Terminal (Montreal) Limited	**100.0**	100.0	100.0
CP Trucks			
Canadian Pacific Express & Transport Ltd.	**100.0**	100.0	100.0
Energy			
PanCanadian Petroleum Limited	**87.1**	87.1	87.1
Fording Coal			
Fording Coal Holdings Inc.	**100.0**	100.0	100.0
NYCO Minerals, Inc.	**100.0**	100.0	100.0
Forest Products			
Canadian Pacific Forest Products Limited	**70.0**[2]	79.7	79.7
Real Estate and Hotels			
Marathon Realty Holdings Inc.	**100.0**	100.0	100.0
CP Rail System (see above)			
Canadian Pacific Hotels & Resorts Inc.	**100.0**	100.0	100.0
Telecommunications and Manufacturing			
Unitel Communications Holdings Inc.	**60.0**[3]	60.0	60.0
United Dominion Industries Limited	**45.4**[4]	55.4	55.4

[1] In February 1993, the Corporation increased its ownership to 100% by acquiring the remaining 43% of the shares.

[2] In February 1992, Canadian Pacific Forest Products Limited (CP Forest) issued 8.5 million Common Shares. The Corporation through a wholly-owned subsidiary bought 1.7 million Common Shares, or 20%, thereby decreasing its ownership in CP Forest to 70.0% from 79.7%.

[3] In January 1993, Unitel Communications Holdings Inc. issued common shares thereby decreasing the Corporation's ownership to 48%. CP Limited will account for this investment on the equity method in 1993 (Note 22).

[4] In May 1992, United Dominion Industries Limited (United Dominion) issued 6.5 million Common Shares. The Corporation did not purchase any of the shares, thereby decreasing its ownership to 45.4% from 55.4%. CP Limited changed its method of accounting, effective June 1, 1992, for its investment in United Dominion to the equity method.

CP Limited changed its method of accounting, effective December 10, 1992, for its investment in United Dominion to the cost method and wrote down its carrying value to net realizable value as determined by the conversion price set in the equity exchangeable debentures issued in December 1992 (Notes 4, 9 and 12).

CP Limited accounts for its investment in its associated company, Laidlaw Inc., on the equity method. CP Forest follows the equity method of accounting for its investments in joint ventures. A significant part of CP Limited's exploration, development and production of oil and gas and investment in real estate is carried out as joint ventures and partnerships. These investments are accounted for through proportional consolidation.

The major differences between Canadian and United States generally accepted accounting principles, insofar as they apply to CP Limited, are described under Supplementary Data (see page 76).

Unless otherwise specified, all dollar amounts are expressed in Canadian dollars.

1. Significant Accounting Policies (cont'd)

Revenue Recognition

Transportation: Railway freight revenues are recognized upon the completion of movements.

Revenues from shipping operations, costs directly attributable to loaded moves and vessel costs are accounted for on the basis of voyages completed in the period.

Revenues from trucking operations are recognized, and related costs are provided for, when the goods to be delivered are picked up.

Energy: Revenues from oil and gas operations are recognized at the time the oil is sold or natural gas is delivered.

Coal sales revenues are recognized when the coal has been loaded and has departed the shipping location.

Forest Products: Revenues are recognized at the later of the bill of lading date and the release date to the customer, which usually coincides with the date the goods are accepted by the purchaser or common carrier.

Real Estate and Hotels: Revenues from income-producing properties are generally recognized upon the earlier of attaining an occupancy level of 80% or the expiration of a one-year period following substantial completion. Prior to such time, rental revenues and operating costs are capitalized as part of the cost of the project. Income from sales of properties is fully recognized at the time of sale, provided that estimated future cash flows from the properties are adequate to service any vendor financing.

Revenues from hotel operations are recognized when services are provided and ultimate collection is reasonably assured.

Telecommunications and Manufacturing: Revenues from telecommunications activities are recognized when the services are provided.

Income on construction contracts is recognized on the percentage-of-completion basis.

Earnings per Ordinary Share

Earnings per Ordinary Share are calculated after providing for dividends on the Corporation's Preference Shares using the weighted average number of Ordinary Shares outstanding during the year.

Foreign Currency Translation

Foreign currency assets and liabilities of CP Limited's operations, other than through self-sustained foreign subsidiaries, are translated into Canadian dollars at the year-end exchange rate for monetary items and at the historical exchange rates for non-monetary ones. Foreign currency revenues and expenses are translated at the exchange rate in effect on the dates of the related transactions except for provisions for depreciation and depletion which are translated on the same basis as the related assets. With the exception of unrealized gains and losses on long term monetary assets and liabilities, which are being amortized to income over the remaining lives of the related items, foreign currency gains and losses are included in income immediately.

The accounts of CP Limited's self-sustained foreign subsidiaries are translated into Canadian dollars using the year-end exchange rate for assets and liabilities and the average exchange rates in effect for the year for revenues and expenses. Exchange gains or losses arising from translation are deferred and included under Shareholders' Equity as Foreign Currency Translation Adjustments. Also included as a foreign currency translation adjustment is the exchange credit arising from translation of the Corporation's Perpetual 4% Consolidated Debenture Stock.

Post Retirement Benefits

For defined benefit plans, pension costs are actuarially determined on the basis of management's best estimates using the projected benefit method prorated over the service lives of employees. Pension expense includes the cost of pension benefits earned during the current year and the amortization of adjustments arising from pension plan amendments, experience gains and losses and changes in assumptions. The amortization period covers the expected average remaining service lives of employees covered by the various plans. The difference between the market related value of pension fund assets and the present value of accrued pension benefits, at the date the present accounting policy was adopted, is also being amortized over the expected average remaining service lives of plan employees.

For defined contribution plans, pension costs generally equal plan contributions made during the current year.

For post retirement health care and life insurance benefits, costs are based on the annual insurance premium paid to provide these benefits.

Inventories

Raw materials, rail materials and supplies are valued at the lower of average cost and replacement cost.

Finished goods are valued at the lower of average cost and net realizable value.

Properties

Transportation: Accounting for railway properties is carried out in accordance with the Uniform Classification of Accounts issued by the National Transportation Agency in Canada and in accordance with Interstate Commerce Commission rules in the United States. Fixed asset additions and major renewals are recorded at cost. Maintenance and repairs are charged to expense as incurred with the exception of material costs of programmed track replacement in Canada which are capitalized. When depreciable property is retired or otherwise disposed of in the normal course of business, the book value, less salvage, is charged to accumulated depreciation.

Depreciation is calculated on the straight-line basis at rates based upon the estimated service lives of depreciable property, except for rail and other track material in the United States which is based on usage. For railway properties, the rates used by CP Rail System are as authorized by the National Transportation Agency of Canada for CP Rail, and by

1. Significant Accounting Policies (cont'd)

the Interstate Commerce Commission for the Soo Line Railroad Company (a wholly-owned subsidiary of Soo Line Corporation) and the Delaware and Hudson Railway Company, Inc.

Estimated service lives used for principal categories of transportation properties are as follows:

	Years
Railway	
Road diesel locomotives	27 to 40
Freight cars	17 to 51
Ties	28 to 60
Rails – in first position	21 to 29
– in other than first position	45 to 60
Ships	20
Trucks and trailers	7 to 12

Energy: CP Limited follows the full cost method of accounting for oil and gas properties, whereby all costs relating to the exploration for, and the development of, conventional crude oil and natural gas reserves are capitalized on a country-by-country cost centre basis. Costs accumulated within each cost centre are depleted and depreciated using the unit of production method, based on estimated proved reserves, with net production and reserves volumes of natural gas converted to equivalent energy units of crude oil. Proceeds from disposal of properties are normally deducted from the full cost pool without recognition of gain or loss.

Acquisitions and exploration costs in new cost centres are excluded from costs subject to depletion until it is determined whether or not proved reserves are attributable to the properties, or if impairment has occurred.

In determining depletion and depreciation provisions for conventional oil and natural gas assets, CP Limited includes any excess of the net book value of those oil and natural gas assets over the unescalated, undiscounted future net operating revenues from its proved oil and natural gas reserves for each cost centre (ceiling test). A second ceiling test calculation is conducted on an enterprise basis, by including in the depletion and depreciation provisions any excess of the net book value of conventional oil and natural gas assets for all cost centres over the total unescalated, undiscounted future net operating revenues from proved oil and natural gas reserves, less future general and administrative expenses, financing costs and income taxes. The ceiling test calculations utilize CP Limited's weighted average product prices prevailing at year end.

Depreciation of conventional crude oil and natural gas plant, production and other equipment is provided for using the unit of production method. Natural gas liquids extraction and Syncrude oil sands facilities are depreciated on a straight-line basis over the estimated service lives of the assets.

Commencing in 1991, estimated future dismantlement and site restoration costs of conventional crude oil, natural gas and Syncrude oil sands assets are provided for using the unit of production method. Such costs for extraction facilities of natural gas liquids are provided for over the estimated service lives of the assets. Expenditures incurred to dismantle facilities and restore well sites are charged against the related restoration liability.

Expenditures by CP Limited to acquire, explore for and develop identified mineral properties are capitalized, net of costs relating to production during the development phase, pending evaluation and completion. Expenditures on general exploration for producing properties and abandoned properties are charged against income.

Depletion on producing properties is provided using a unit of production method based upon the proven mineral reserve position.

CP Limited provides for the eventual reclamation of mineral properties based on current production.

Interest on funds borrowed to finance major energy projects is capitalized during the development and construction periods.

Forest Products: Plants and properties are stated at cost which is after the deduction of investment tax credits. Plants and properties are depreciated over their estimated useful lives using the unit of production method for pulp and paper mills and the straight-line method for other plant and properties. During the construction period, interest is capitalized on major improvements and expansions.

Real Estate and Hotels: Real estate held for investment is stated at the lower of cost less accumulated depreciation, and net recoverable amount which is the estimated future cash flow from the ongoing use and residual value of a capital asset. Real estate held for sale is stated at the lower of cost and estimated net realizable value. Cost includes carrying costs, principally real estate taxes, interest, the imputed value of free rent, directly attributable salaries and expenses of development personnel and, for income properties, initial leasing costs.

Hotel properties are recorded at cost including interest capitalized during major renewals.

The sinking fund method of providing depreciation is used for buildings. This method will amortize the cost of the buildings over a maximum period of 40 years in a series of annual instalments increasing at the rate of 5% compounded annually.

Telecommunications and Manufacturing: Property, plant and equipment are recorded at cost which, in the case of new manufacturing facilities, includes interest during construction. Maintenance and repairs are expensed as incurred.

Depreciation of plant and equipment is provided principally on a straight-line basis at rates intended to amortize the cost of these assets over their estimated economic lives. Rates for telecommunications equipment are approved by the Canadian Radio-television and Telecommunications Commission.

2. Segmented Information

Business Segments

CP Limited carries on its operating activities through the following classes of business: Transportation, Energy, Forest Products, Real Estate and Hotels, and Telecommunications and Manufacturing. The business segments are based upon the major activities of significant subsidiaries and divisions of CP Limited.

The results of CP Rail System reflect interest, corporate overhead and income tax allocations made by the Corporation. The results of all other entities are based upon their reported net incomes adjusted, where applicable, for acquisition-related costs. Interest charges allocated to CP Rail System are based principally on cash flow, corporate overhead on the basis of cost of operations, and income taxes on the basis of CP Rail's accounting income as adjusted for non-taxable items.

Charges between entities within the same business segment, which are made at normal tariff or other arm's length rates, are eliminated in reporting revenues and expenses by business segment. Services provided by entities in the Transportation segment to other entities in this segment yielded revenues in 1992 of $61.5 million (1991 – $65.1 million; 1990 – $60.3 million).

Charges between entities in different business segments, which are made at normal tariff or other arm's length rates, are not eliminated in reporting revenues and expenses by business segment but are eliminated in reporting total consolidated revenues and expenses. Consolidated net income is not affected by this practice. Services provided by the Corporation's Transportation segment to other business segments yielded revenues in 1992 of $90.2 million (1991 – $179.3 million; 1990 – $167.4 million). Other charges between business segments amounted to $47.7 million in 1992 (1991 – $48.4 million; 1990 – $49.1 million).

(in millions)		Revenues	Cost of Goods and Services	Selling, General and Administrative	Depreciation, Depletion and Amortization	Operating Income (Loss)
Transportation						
CP Rail System	**1992**	**$ 3,181.3**	**$ 2,219.7**	**$ 1,104.8**	**$ 200.1**	**$ (343.3)**
	1991	3,339.8	2,227.4	894.7	193.2	24.5
	1990	3,247.6	2,130.3	611.0	190.2	316.1
CP Ships	**1992**	**359.0**	**268.3**	**61.5**	**10.9**	**18.3**
	1991	319.8	248.5	68.1	10.1	(6.9)
	1990	322.5	237.3	74.6	8.9	1.7
CP Trucks	**1992**	**419.5**	**436.1**	**65.9**	**17.4**	**(99.9)**
	1991	480.4	440.6	52.6	19.6	(32.4)
	1990	518.9	459.4	63.9	19.1	(23.5)
Total (after elimination of intra-segment charges)	**1992**	**$ 3,898.3**	**$ 2,862.6**	**$ 1,232.2**	**$ 228.4**	**$ (424.9)**
	1991	4,074.9	2,851.4	1,015.4	222.9	(14.8)
	1990	4,028.7	2,766.7	749.5	218.2	294.3
Energy						
PanCanadian Petroleum Limited	**1992**	**$ 953.0**	**$ 311.6**	**$ 51.2**	**$ 310.3**	**$ 279.9**
	1991	846.4	292.6	75.9	363.0	114.9
	1990	948.4	303.6	43.8	246.8	354.2
Fording Coal	**1992**	**262.5**	**118.2**	**83.4**	**19.1**	**41.8**
	1991	434.3	172.1	168.0	24.6	69.6
	1990	404.1	154.4	158.1	21.8	69.8
Total	**1992**	**$ 1,215.5**	**$ 429.8**	**$ 134.6**	**$ 329.4**	**$ 321.7**
	1991	1,280.7	464.7	243.9	387.6	184.5
	1990	1,352.5	458.0	201.9	268.6	424.0
Forest Products						
Canadian Pacific Forest Products Limited	**1992**	**$ 1,825.5**	**$ 1,871.6**	**$ 70.1**	**$ 153.3**	**$ (269.5)**
	1991	2,083.3	2,210.7	86.4	631.6	(845.4)
	1990	2,269.2	2,016.3	97.0	141.0	14.9

2. Segmented Information (cont'd)

(in millions)		Revenues		Cost of Goods and Services		Selling, General and Administrative		Depreciation, Depletion and Amortization		Operating Income (Loss)
Real Estate and Hotels										
Marathon Realty Holdings Inc.	**1992**	$	**492.6**	$	**243.8**	$	**13.7**	$	**53.1**	$ **182.0**
	1991		414.4		259.1		16.4		50.1	88.8
	1990		423.8		240.6		16.1		47.8	119.3
CP Rail System	**1992**		**21.2**		**—**		**—**		**—**	**21.2**
	1991		21.1		—		—		—	21.1
	1990		86.9		—		—		—	86.9
Canadian Pacific Hotels & Resorts Inc.	**1992**		**455.2**		**293.8**		**73.7**		**37.7**	**50.0**
	1991		443.2		292.3		89.4		37.0	24.5
	1990		416.8		263.1		68.4		27.1	58.2
Total	**1992**	$	**969.0**	$	**537.6**	$	**87.4**	$	**90.8**	$ **253.2**
	1991		878.7		551.4		105.8		87.1	134.4
	1990		927.5		503.7		84.5		74.9	264.4
Telecommunications and Manufacturing										
Unitel Communications Holdings Inc.	**1992**	$	**440.5**	$	**209.5**	$	**129.4**	$	**99.1**	$ **2.5**
	1991		435.2		236.5		103.8		81.7	13.2
	1990		418.3		241.5		122.5		66.0	(11.7)
United Dominion Industries Limited	**1992**		**752.7**		**634.4**		**93.5**		**14.1**	**10.7**
	1991		1,546.4		1,298.8		200.1		24.9	22.6
	1990		1,676.6		1,389.6		211.5		26.5	49.0
Total	**1992**	$	**1,193.2**	$	**843.9**	$	**222.9**	$	**113.2**	$ **13.2**
	1991		1,981.6		1,535.3		303.9		106.6	35.8
	1990		2,094.9		1,631.1		334.0		92.5	37.3
Consolidated Total (after elimination of inter-segment charges)	**1992**	$	**8,963.6**	$	**6,407.6**	$	**1,747.2**	$	**915.1**	$ **(106.3)**
	1991		10,071.5		7,385.8		1,755.4		1,435.8	(505.5)
	1990		10,456.3		7,159.3		1,466.9		795.2	1,034.9

Notes:

Transportation: Included in selling, general and administrative expenses of CP Rail System is a $453.6 million provision in 1992 for a reduction in train crew sizes, expected rail line rationalization in eastern Canada and other cost reduction initiatives and a $250.9 million provision in 1991 for Angus Shops closure and other restructuring charges.

- Included in cost of goods and services is a $36.2 million provision, and included in selling, general and administrative expenses is a $24.7 million provision, for asset disposals and other restructuring charges of CP Trucks in 1992.

Energy: Included in depreciation, depletion and amortization expenses of PanCanadian Petroleum Limited, in 1991, is a $100.0 million write-down of United States assets and investment in OSLO project.

- Included in selling, general and administrative expenses of PanCanadian Petroleum Limited, in 1991, is a $22.0 million provision for organizational effectiveness program.

Forest Products: Included in cost of goods and services are equity in losses of joint ventures amounting to $79.8 million in 1992, $53.4 million in 1991 and $70.9 million in 1990.

- Included in depreciation, depletion and amortization expenses is a $429.2 million provision and included in cost of goods and services is a $99.1 million provision for shutdown of the Trois-Rivières mill, downsizing of the Dalhousie mill and write-down of the paperboard and packaging business in 1991.

Real Estate and Hotels: Included in Marathon's cost of goods and services are provisions for write-down of income properties and sites and land amounting to $28.3 million in 1992, $58.5 million in 1991 and $39.6 million in 1990.

Telecommunications and Manufacturing: The 1992 results for United Dominion Industries Limited are for the period January 1 to May 31, 1992. Effective June 1, 1992, this investment was accounted for on the equity method (Note 1).

2. Segmented Information (cont'd)

(in millions)

Identifiable Assets	1992	1991	1990
Transportation			
CP Rail System	$ 5,542.3	$ 5,802.2	$ 5,573.0
CP Ships	136.2	128.3	129.5
CP Trucks	150.9	181.5	213.5
	5,829.4	6,112.0	5,916.0
Energy			
PanCanadian Petroleum Limited	3,250.3	3,099.2	3,072.8
Fording Coal	524.6	450.0	393.3
	3,774.9	3,549.2	3,466.1
Forest Products			
Canadian Pacific Forest Products Limited	3,110.4	3,089.9	3,388.2
Real Estate and Hotels			
Marathon Realty Holdings Inc.	3,016.0	2,901.5	2,720.6
Canadian Pacific Hotels & Resorts Inc.	1,013.9	1,010.6	923.5
	4,029.9	3,912.1	3,644.1
Telecommunications and Manufacturing			
Unitel Communications Holdings Inc.	1,120.0	974.3	866.6
United Dominion Industries Limited	—	941.7	1,100.0
	1,120.0	1,916.0	1,966.6
Other	5,167.2	4,377.3	3,555.8
Inter-company eliminations	(2,808.0)	(2,369.4)	(1,713.3)
	$ 20,223.8	$ 20,587.1	$ 20,223.5

(in millions)

Additions to Properties	1992	1991	1990
Transportation			
CP Rail System	$ 209.5	$ 252.6	$ 265.4
CP Ships	6.0	21.8	13.5
CP Trucks	8.0	4.9	12.9
	223.5	279.3	291.8
Energy			
PanCanadian Petroleum Limited	344.3	390.0	339.6
Fording Coal	91.4	67.3	39.8
	435.7	457.3	379.4
Forest Products			
Canadian Pacific Forest Products Limited	240.5	349.8	428.6
Real Estate and Hotels			
Marathon Realty Holdings Inc.	243.8	318.7	396.2
Canadian Pacific Hotels & Resorts Inc.	35.8	108.1	166.4
	279.6	426.8	562.6
Telecommunications and Manufacturing			
Unitel Communications Holdings Inc.	207.2	150.8	256.4
United Dominion Industries Limited	6.5	17.9	31.6
	213.7	168.7	288.0
Other	4.2	8.9	3.5
	$ 1,397.2	$ 1,690.8	$ 1,953.9

2. Segmented Information (cont'd)

(in millions)	1992	1991	1990
Geographic Segments			
Canada			
Revenues			
Domestic	$ **4,835.9**	$ 5,311.1	$ 5,622.1
Export	**2,203.8**	2,433.2	2,491.5
Inter-company revenues	**(199.4)**	(292.8)	(276.8)
	$ **6,840.3**	$ 7,451.5	$ 7,836.8
Operating income (loss)	$ **(84.4)**	$ (409.3)	$ 949.6
Identifiable assets	$ **17,981.1**	$ 17,704.6	$ 16,968.7
United States			
Revenues	$ **1,640.4**	$ 1,993.4	$ 1,945.6
Operating income (loss)	$ **(44.4)**	$ (99.5)	$ 64.2
Identifiable assets	$ **3,647.1**	$ 3,679.6	$ 3,025.2
Other Countries			
Revenues	$ **482.9**	$ 626.6	$ 673.9
Operating income	$ **22.5**	$ 3.3	$ 21.1
Identifiable assets	$ **493.1**	$ 928.9	$ 888.6
Summary			
Revenues	$ **8,963.6**	$ 10,071.5	$ 10,456.3
Operating income (loss)	$ **(106.3)**	$ (505.5)	$ 1,034.9
Identifiable assets	$ **22,121.3**	$ 22,313.1	$ 20,882.5
Investment in Laidlaw Inc.	**739.8**	643.4	1,054.3
Investment in United Dominion Industries Limited	**170.7**	—	—
Inter-company eliminations	**(2,808.0)**	(2,369.4)	(1,713.3)
	$ **20,223.8**	$ 20,587.1	$ 20,223.5

3. Interest Expense, Net

(in millions)	1992	1991	1990
Long term debt and debenture stock	$ **742.7**	$ 658.5	$ 547.0
Short term debt	**19.6**	81.7	143.6
	762.3	740.2	690.6
Less: Interest income	**102.4**	116.1	104.5
Interest capitalized	**67.1**	84.1	98.5
	$ **592.8**	$ 540.0	$ 487.6

4. Other Expenses (Income)

(in millions)	1992	1991	1990
Corporate expenses	$ **45.6**	$ 56.8	$ 50.4
Amortization of exchange losses (gains)	**0.9**	(55.3)	(70.9)
Amortization of the discount of the present value of the restructuring accruals	**15.7**	—	—
Loss on dilution of ownership in subsidiaries	**12.5**	—	—
Write-down of investment in United Dominion Industries Limited	**72.2**	—	—
Gain on sale of businesses			
Canadian Pacific Forest Products Limited			
Tissue business	**—**	(86.4)	—
United Dominion Industries Limited			
Packaging Equipment division	**—**	(40.5)	—
Other	**(0.2)**	2.6	3.2
	$ **146.7**	$ (122.8)	$ (17.3)

5. Income Tax Expense (Recovery)

(in millions)	1992	1991	1990
Canadian			
Current	$ **75.1**	$ 0.9	$ 42.9
Deferred	**(354.9)**	(260.3)	167.9
	$ **(279.8)**	$ (259.4)	$ 210.8
Foreign			
Current	$ **8.2**	$ 12.2	$ 7.8
Deferred	**(7.1)**	(16.3)	1.8
	$ **1.1**	$ (4.1)	$ 9.6
Total			
Current	$ **83.3**	$ 13.1	$ 50.7
Deferred	**(362.0)**	(276.6)	169.7
	$ **(278.7)**	$ (263.5)	$ 220.4

The deferred income tax expense (recovery) arose from the following:

	1992	1991	1990
Excess of tax over book depreciation	$ **76.8**	$ (3.8)	$ 66.3
Exploration and development allowances	**6.8**	26.0	38.9
Losses tax affected	**(288.2)**	(95.0)	34.0
Write-down of assets and restructuring costs	**(210.8)**	(230.7)	(12.3)
Reduction in restructuring accruals	**44.7**	—	—
Other	**8.7**	26.9	42.8
	$ **(362.0)**	$ (276.6)	$ 169.7

The difference between the income tax expense (recovery)
    and the provision obtained by applying
    the statutory tax rate is as follows:

	1992	1991	1990
Provision at the statutory rate	$ **(383.8)**	$ (390.4)	$ 243.2
Depletion and resource allowances	**(53.7)**	(39.4)	(63.0)
Foreign tax differentials	**2.2**	(7.2)	(11.7)
Royalties and mineral reserve tax	**25.7**	22.1	27.9
Manufacturing and processing credits	**16.8**	32.9	—
Loss carryforwards recognized	**(1.5)**	(17.6)	(20.6)
Losses not tax affected	**94.3**	43.1	29.6
Capital gains rate differential	**(21.5)**	(7.5)	(23.2)
Large corporations tax	**26.7**	24.2	21.3
Effect of non-deductible portion of asset write-downs and restructuring costs	**3.3**	73.3	—
Other	**12.8**	3.0	16.9
Income tax expense (recovery)	$ **(278.7)**	$ (263.5)	$ 220.4

6. Changes in Non-Cash Working Capital Balances

(in millions)	1992	1991	1990
Decrease (increase) in current assets			
Accounts receivable	$ 468.5	$ 27.5	$ 60.4
Inventories	314.4	120.3	(27.2)
Increase (decrease) in current liabilities			
Accounts payable and accrued liabilities	(219.4)	153.0	(13.0)
Income and other taxes payable	90.6	(46.9)	44.8
Decrease in non-cash working capital balances during the year	654.1	253.9	65.0
Decrease in non-cash working capital balances due to change in accounting method for the Corporation's investment in United Dominion Industries Limited (Note 1)	(270.9)	—	—
Decrease in non-cash working capital balances relating to write-downs of assets and restructuring costs	(191.4)	(191.7)	(22.3)
Increase in non-cash working capital balances relating to reduction in restructuring accruals	127.5	—	—
Non-cash working capital balances of businesses disposed	(12.6)	(62.9)	(18.3)
Other changes in non-cash working capital balances not relating to operations	9.4	(2.3)	0.2
Decrease (increase) in non-cash working capital balances relating to operations	$ 316.1	$ (3.0)	$ 24.6

7. Business Acquisitions and Investments

(in millions)	1992	1991	1990
Expenditures on business acquisitions and investments comprise the following:			
Acquisitions by United Dominion Industries Limited	$ 180.7	$ —	$ —
Investment by a subsidiary in subordinated notes of a joint venture	61.8	85.4	43.1
Investment by the Corporation in Laidlaw Inc.	50.1	—	—
Acquisition of:			
Soo Line Corporation	—	—	108.2
Doubletree Hotels Corporation	—	—	62.6
Other acquisitions and investments by subsidiaries	84.3	54.5	70.9
	$ 376.9	$ 139.9	$ 284.8

In January 1992, United Dominion Industries Limited (United Dominion) acquired the net assets of the door and architectural and industrial wall systems and floor decking businesses of the Robertson-CECO Corporation, and the stock of Bredel Exploitatie B.V. These acquisitions have been accounted for by the purchase method and are included in United Dominion's results from the dates of acquisition.

On various dates in 1992 and 1991 and on December 27, 1990, Canadian Pacific Forest Products Limited invested $61.8 million, $85.4 million and $43.1 million, respectively, in interest-bearing subordinated notes of Gold River Newsprint Limited Partnership.

On February 20, 1992, the Corporation acquired 4,550,000 Class B Non-Voting Shares of Laidlaw Inc. for cash consideration of $50.1 million or $11.00 per share.

On January 24, 1990, the Corporation increased its ownership interest in its subsidiary, Soo Line Corporation, from 55.8% to 96%. On April 9, 1990, the remaining 4% was acquired. Total cost of the acquisition amounted to $108.2 million. The excess of book value over total cost, which amounts to approximately $16 million, has been allocated to depreciable assets. The results of the Soo Line Corporation are reported with those of CP Rail System.

On December 6, 1990, the Corporation, through its wholly-owned subsidiary, Canadian Pacific Hotels & Resorts Inc., acquired an 80% equity interest in Doubletree Hotels Corporation (Doubletree). The total acquisition cost of $62.6 million was allocated to management contracts – $47.8 million, goodwill – $24.2 million, other – $3.8 million and assumption of long term debt of $13.2 million. The results of Doubletree have been included in the Real Estate and Hotels segment from the date of acquisition, and goodwill is being amortized over forty years.

8. Inventories

(in millions)

	1992	1991
Rail materials and supplies	$ 183.9	$ 220.1
Raw materials	150.5	247.0
Work in progress	9.4	82.1
Finished goods	131.2	235.8
Stores and materials	136.5	140.9
	$ 611.5	$ 925.9

9. Investments

(in millions)

	1992	1991
Accounted for on the equity basis:		
Laidlaw Inc.*	$ 739.8	$ 643.4
Gold River Newsprint Limited Partnership**	(81.8)	(13.1)
Ponderay Newsprint Company**	8.3	18.0
Other	66.0	67.2
Accounted for on the cost basis:		
United Dominion Industries Limited	170.7	—
Subordinated Notes of Gold River Newsprint Limited Partnership	210.9	136.9
Other	75.7	71.7
	$ 1,189.6	$ 924.1

*The Corporation owns 22,500,000 Class A voting shares, which represent 47.2% of Laidlaw's Class A voting shares outstanding, and 29,711,034 Class B non-voting shares, which represent 12.9% of Laidlaw's Class B non-voting shares outstanding. The Corporation's ownership interest in Laidlaw, based on the combined number of Class A and Class B shares outstanding, was 18.8% at December 31, 1992 and 1991, and 19.9% at December 31, 1990.

The quoted market value of the Corporation's investment in Laidlaw at December 31, 1992, was $612.6 million.

At December 31, 1992, the difference of approximately $292 million between the carrying amount of the Corporation's investment in Laidlaw and its share of the underlying equity in net assets of Laidlaw has been assigned to goodwill and is being written off over forty years.

The following is a summary of the reported results and financial position of Laidlaw:

For the Year ended August 31

(U.S. $ in millions)

	1992	1991	1990
Revenues	$ 1,925.6	$ 1,882.4	$ 1,737.5
Income from operations	237.7	246.8	291.2
Net income (loss)	132.4	(344.4)	214.5
Net income (loss) applicable to Class A and Class B shares	131.8	(348.9)	206.0

August 31

(U.S. $ in millions)

	1992	1991
Total assets	$ 3,658.9	$ 3,595.3
Total liabilities	1,699.0	1,913.2
Shareholders' equity	1,959.9	1,682.1

Dividends received by the Corporation from Laidlaw amounted to $8.2 million in 1992, $13.3 million in 1991 and $13.3 million in 1990.

In 1991, the Corporation wrote down the carrying value of its investment in Laidlaw to reflect a decline that management considers to be other than temporary.

**Canadian Pacific Forest Products Limited's share of losses from these joint ventures of $79.8 million in 1992 (1991 – $53.4 million; 1990 – $70.9 million) is included in cost of goods sold of the Forest Products segment.

10. Properties and Accumulated Depreciation, Depletion and Amortization

(in millions)		1992		1991
	Cost	Accumulated Depreciation, Depletion and Amortization	Net	Net
Transportation				
CP Rail System	$ 7,583.1	$ 2,766.9	$ 4,816.2	$ 4,754.8
CP Ships	170.8	113.4	57.4	63.2
CP Trucks	216.2	127.3	88.9	99.2
	7,970.1	3,007.6	4,962.5	4,917.2
Energy				
PanCanadian Petroleum Limited	4,913.2	2,029.4	2,883.8	2,879.5
Fording Coal	687.9	259.6	428.3	356.6
	5,601.1	2,289.0	3,312.1	3,236.1
Forest Products				
Canadian Pacific Forest Products Limited	4,188.3	1,960.3	2,228.0	2,197.6
Real Estate and Hotels				
Marathon Realty Holdings Inc.	3,064.7	298.4	2,766.3	2,650.6
Canadian Pacific Hotels & Resorts Inc.	1,023.7	197.6	826.1	825.5
	4,088.4	496.0	3,592.4	3,476.1
Telecommunications and Manufacturing				
Unitel Communications Holdings Inc.	1,357.4	445.2	912.2	802.4
United Dominion Industries Limited	—	—	—	144.4
	1,357.4	445.2	912.2	946.8
Other	57.9	23.0	34.9	33.3
	$ 23,263.2	$ 8,221.1	$ 15,042.1	$ 14,807.1

11. Other Assets and Deferred Charges

(in millions)	1992	1991
Unrealized exchange gains	$ 193.4	$ 154.6
Unamortized exchange loss	187.2	1.9
Prepaid pension cost	145.4	137.7
Long term receivables	81.3	75.3
Management contracts	54.4	53.2
Goodwill	31.7	122.5
Other	209.2	222.6
	$ 902.6	$ 767.8

12. Long Term Debt

(in millions)	1992	1991
Canadian Pacific Limited		
7½% – 10½% Debentures due 1994-2022	$ 1,426.3	$ 1,061.2
8½% Debentures due 1995	105.0	—
8½% – 9.45% Equipment Trust Certificates due 1993-1998	127.5	119.6
8⅞% – 11¼% Collateral Trust Bonds	—	56.8
Obligations under capital leases due 1993-2000	39.1	43.0
Soo Line Corporation		
12.95% Notes due 1993-2005	35.5	138.2
8¼% – 13⅝% Equipment Trust Certificates due 1993-1996	14.2	18.9
Obligations under capital leases due 1993-1999	15.8	17.8
PanCanadian Petroleum Limited		
10.55% Debentures due 2000	150.0	181.4
7.9% – 8.1% Medium term notes due 2002	127.0	—
Notes due after 1993	75.8	124.1
Canadian Pacific Forest Products Limited		
9.22% – 10⅝% Notes payable due 1996-2011	676.1	614.8
9.25% – 10.85% Debentures due 2002-2014	411.0	125.0
Syndicated loan due 1999	127.1	115.6
Bank loans due 1993-1998	123.7	288.8
Bank term loan due 1993-1996	63.5	57.7
Sundry due 1993-1998	15.9	17.4
Marathon Realty Holdings Inc.		
7⅝% – 13⅜% Mortgages due 1993-2020	547.9	441.6
Bank term loans due 1994-1999	390.8	511.5
9.85% – 11¼% Secured bonds and debentures due 1995-2006	362.0	386.6
9% – 14¾% First mortgage bonds due 1997-2007	218.6	251.7
Canadian Pacific Hotels & Resorts Inc.		
Promissory note due after 1993	12.7	11.6
Unitel Communications Holdings Inc.		
Bank loans due 1993	353.0	423.8
Obligations under capital leases due 1993-2007	24.0	13.6
United Dominion Industries Limited		
Notes due 1998	—	58.0
7⅜% Deutsche Mark Bonds	—	114.6
Bank loans due 1994	—	25.0
Canadian Pacific Securities Limited		
9.85% – 11.6% Guaranteed debentures due 1994-2026	765.4	559.9
Canadian Pacific Enterprises Limited		
Notes due 1996	1,270.0	1,160.0
Notes due 1993	220.1	245.1
Other	17.9	32.0
	7,715.9	7,215.3
Less: Long term debt maturing within one year	694.1	405.5
	$ 7,021.8	$ 6,809.8

12. Long Term Debt (cont'd)

The Corporation's debentures are unsecured, but carry a negative pledge.

Equipment Trust Certificates are secured by specific units of railway rolling stock.

On December 10, 1992, the Corporation issued $105 million of 8.5% unsecured equity exchangeable debentures maturing December 15, 1995. The debentures are exchangeable at maturity into a maximum of 10 million common shares of United Dominion Industries Limited (United Dominion) (approximately 28% of the common shares outstanding). If all exchangeable debentures were ultimately exchanged for United Dominion shares, the Corporation's interest in United Dominion would decrease to approximately 17.5%.

Canadian Pacific Forest Products Limited (CP Forest) has entered into an interest rate swap agreement with one of its bankers which converts the $127.1 million syndicated loan to a fixed rate debt of 9.71% up to 1999. CP Forest has also entered into several interest rate swap agreements with its bankers which convert $286.0 million of 9.25% debentures into floating rate until June 1995.

Substantially all of Marathon Realty Holdings Inc.'s long term debt is secured by income properties and income properties under construction. Unitel Communications Holdings Inc.'s credit facility has a floating charge over all of its assets.

At December 31, 1992, foreign currency long term debt, denominated principally in United States dollars, amounted to $4,509.6 million (1991 – $4,128.0 million).

Unless otherwise specified, notes payable bear interest at rates which fluctuate with money market rates. Under currency swap agreements, Japanese yen denominated fixed interest payments with respect to Canadian Pacific Enterprises Limited's (CP Enterprises) notes due in 1993 have been converted to Canadian dollar fixed payments and, in 1992, the effective interest cost was 11.77%. Under interest rate swap agreements, $254 million of CP Enterprises' notes due 1996 have been converted from floating rates to fixed rates averaging 8.49%.

Of the aggregate bank loans of $938.6 million included above, approximately $931.8 million bear interest at rates which fluctuate with bank prime or money market rates. CP Limited has entered into a series of interest rate swaps for periods of one to five years, in order to fix the interest rate, at a weighted average rate of approximately 11.7%, on $405 million of its bank loans.

Annual maturities and sinking fund requirements for each of the five years following 1992 are: 1993 – $694.1 million; 1994 – $732.3 million; 1995 – $466.5 million; 1996 – $2,023.5 million; 1997 – $224.9 million.

The Corporation and a number of its subsidiaries are parties with major financial institutions to financial instruments with off-balance-sheet risk. These financial instruments include forward exchange contracts and interest rate and currency swap agreements principally associated with certain of CP Limited's long term debt and future commodity revenue, with a principal amount at December 31, 1992 of approximately $1,700 million in addition to the interest rate swaps on notes payable and bank loans referred to above. These instruments, which have maturities between 1993 and 2002, involve to varying degrees elements of credit or market risk in excess of the amount recognized in the consolidated balance sheet. CP Limited is exposed to credit loss in the event of nonperformance by the counterparties; however, CP Limited does not anticipate such nonperformance. CP Limited is also exposed to market loss due to movements in currency values.

13. Deferred Liabilities

(in millions)	1992	1991
Provision for restructuring costs	$ **451.6**	$ 160.7
Deferred workmen's compensation	**61.0**	59.4
Future removal and site restoration costs	**56.6**	45.4
Deferred exchange gain	**44.5**	44.4
Accrued pension cost	**37.7**	48.6
Other	**101.8**	143.5
	$ **753.2**	$ 502.0

14. Perpetual 4% Consolidated Debenture Stock

(in millions)	1992			1991
		United States		
Currency of Issue	Sterling	Dollar	Total	Total
Issued	£ 46.8	$ 65.0	$ **172.4**	$ 304.5
Less: Pledged as collateral	—	—	**—**	128.1
	£ 46.8	$ 65.0	$ **172.4**	$ 176.4

The consolidated debenture stock, created by an Act of Parliament of 1889, constitutes a first charge upon and over the whole of the undertaking, railways, works, rolling stock, plant, property and effects of the Corporation, with certain exceptions.

15. Deferred Income Credits

Deferred Income Credits include $181.1 million (1991 – $186.3 million) from the Federal Government primarily for the rehabilitation of certain western branch lines, $94.7 million (1991 – $96.3 million) from other bodies, mainly for reloca- tion of railway lines, and $72.5 million (1991 – $74.7 million) in investment tax credits. These amounts are being amor- tized to income on the same basis as the related fixed assets are being depreciated.

16. Minority Shareholders' Interest in Subsidiary Companies

(in millions)	1992	1991
Canada Maritime Limited	$ **14.8**	$ 10.7
PanCanadian Petroleum Limited	**216.5**	204.1
Canadian Pacific Forest Products Limited	**312.9**	226.6
Marathon Realty Holdings Inc.		
7.5% Cumulative redeemable preferred shares	**25.0**	—
Canadian Pacific Hotels & Resorts Inc.	**4.2**	3.5
Unitel Communications Holdings Inc.		
Preferred shares	**30.0**	—
Common share equity	**211.8**	179.0
United Dominion Industries Limited		
9.5% Cumulative redeemable convertible preferred shares	**—**	71.7
Common share equity	**—**	171.4
	$ **815.2**	$ 867.0

17. Shareholders' Equity

Preferred Shares: At December 31, 1992, the Corporation was authorized to issue 20,381,788 Cumulative Redeemable Preference Shares without nominal or par value. No shares of this class are outstanding.

Preference Shares: 4% Non-Cumulative
Authorized: an amount not exceeding one-half the aggre- gate amount of Ordinary Shares outstanding.

(in millions)	1992	1991	1990
Issued:			
2,561,769 Sterling Preference Shares	$ **4.2**	$ 4.2	$ 4.2
10,696,941 Canadian Dollar Preference Shares	**10.7**	10.7	10.7
	$ **14.9**	$ 14.9	$ 14.9

Every Sterling Preference Share and every Canadian Dollar Preference Share gives the same rights as to voting as is given by an Ordinary Share.

At December 31, 1992, Chemainus Towing Co. Ltd. (an indirect subsidiary of the Corporation) held 33,000 Sterling and 842,250 Canadian Dollar Preference Shares in the Corporation at a total cost of $487,000.

17. Shareholders' Equity (cont'd)

Ordinary Shares: At December 31, 1992, the Corporation was authorized to issue an unlimited number of shares without nominal or par value.

An analysis of Ordinary Share balances is as follows:

(in millions)	1992 Number	1992 Amount	1991 Number	1991 Amount	1990 Number	1990 An
Balance, January 1	**318.7**	**$ 1,234.9**	318.2	$ 1,226.0	318.2	$ 1,2
Issued under dividend reinvestment and share purchase, and stock option plans*	**0.4**	**6.2**	0.5	8.9	0.6	
Stock repurchase program**	**—**	**—**	—	—	(0.6)	
Balance, December 31	**319.1**	**$ 1,241.1**	318.7	$ 1,234.9	318.2	$ 1,2

*Effective July 1, 1992, the Corporation amended its Dividend Reinvestment and Share Purchase Plan to reinstitute the provision which permitted participants to acquire new Ordinary Shares of the Corporation by investing optional cash payments, to a maximum of $30,000 in any calendar year.

**In 1990, the Corporation repurchased 567,200 shares u■ a Normal Course Issuer Bid at a cost of $10.3 million. ■ million was allocated to Ordinary Shares and $8.1 millic■ Premium on Securities.

Foreign Currency Translation Adjustments: An analysis of the Foreign Currency Translation Adjustments balance is as follows:

(in millions)	1992	1991	1
Balance, January 1	$ 72.4	$ 79.9	$ 1■
Effect of exchange rate changes	**171.0**	(7.5)	(■
Other	**(24.0)**	—	(■
Balance, December 31	**$ 219.4**	$ 72.4	$ ■

18. Stock Options

Under the Corporation's stock option plan, options may be granted to certain key employees to purchase Ordinary Shares of the Corporation at a price not less than 90% of the market value of the share at the grant date. Each option may be exercised after two years in respect of one-half of the number of shares to which it relates and after three years in respect of the balance. Options expire ten years after the grant date.

Simultaneously with the grant of an option, employees are also granted Share Appreciation Rights (SARs) equivalent to one-half the number of shares to which each option relates. An SAR entitles the holder to receive payment of an amount equal to the excess of the market value of an Ordinary Share at the time of exercise of the SAR over the related option price. SARs may be exercised no earlier than three years and no later than ten years after the grant date.

Where an option has been exercised as to one-half the number of shares to which it relates, any further exercise reduces the number of SARs granted on a one-for-one basis. At all times the exercise of an SAR reduces the number of shares covered by an option on a one-for-one basis.

In the event of a change in control of the Corporation, all outstanding options and SARs become immediately exercisable.

Under a senior executive long term incentive plan, certain senior executives of the Corporation are entitled, under certain conditions, to purchase Ordinary Shares. During 1992, no Ordinary Shares (1991 – nil; 1990 – 155,500) were purchased under this plan.

The number of Ordinary Shares authorized for issuance under the stock option and senior executive long term incentive plans at December 31, 1992 was 5,000,000 (1991 – 5,000,000), of which 1,046,400 shares (1991 – 1,655,680) were available for the granting of future options and future share purchases under the senior executive long term incentive plan.

At December 31, 1992, options covering 3,369,307 Ordinary Shares (1991 – 2,493,057) were outstanding. These options expire in the years 1996 to 2002 and are exercisable at prices ranging from $16.813 to $27.875 per share.

Options covering 1,290,251 Ordinary Shares were exercisable at December 31, 1992 as follows: 210,720 shares at $16.813 per share; 1,060 shares at $17.813 per share; 7,193 shares at $18.563 per share; 2,409 shares at $19.250 per share; 215,911 shares at $19.875 per share; 260,806 shares at $20.375 per share; 27,316 shares at $20.563 per share; 212,622 shares at $23.188 per share; 301,284 shares at $24.188 per share; 1,688 shares at $25.688 per share; 15,278 shares at $27.250 per share; 33,964 shares at $27.875 per share.

A summary of option activity during 1992 is as follows:

	Number of Shares covered by Options
Outstanding at beginning of year	2,493,057
Granted	958,902
Exercised	—
Cancelled	(82,652)
Outstanding at end of year	3,369,307

19. Shareholder Protection Rights Plan

On May 2, 1990, the shareholders of the Corporation approved a Shareholder Protection Rights Plan (the Rights Plan). Under the Rights Plan, one right was issued for each Ordinary Share and holders of Preference Shares received convertible rights which will be automatically converted into ordinary rights based on the value of the Preference Shares relative to the Ordinary Shares.

The rights issued to shareholders under the Rights Plan entitle the holder, upon the occurrence of certain triggering events, to acquire equity interests in the Corporation at a 50% discount to the market. Triggering events include the acquisition of 15% or more of the Ordinary Shares alone, or of the Ordinary and Preference Shares together, in a transac-

tion not approved by the Board of Directors of the Corporation. However, the rights are not triggered by certain permitted bids that are made to all holders of Ordinary Shares and which must be approved by a majority vote of independent shareholders.

Alexander Centre Industries Limited has applied to the Supreme Court of Ontario for certain orders, including an order declaring the Rights Plan to be oppressive and in disregard of the interest of the Preference shareholders, an order restraining the Corporation from taking any action in connection with the Rights Plan and an order amending the Rights Plan so as to treat the Preference shareholders on an equal basis in relation to the Ordinary shareholders.

20. Pensions

The Corporation and the majority of its subsidiaries have defined benefit plans which provide for pensions based principally on years of service and compensation rates near retirement. Annual contributions to these plans, which are based on various actuarial cost methods, are made on the basis of not less than the minimum amounts required by Federal or Provincial pe supervisory authorities.

Net pension expense for the year for such defined b plans includes the following components:

(in millions)	1992	1991	
Service cost-benefits earned during the year	$ 38.9	$ 50.8	$
Interest cost on projected benefit obligation	455.1	474.8	
Actual return on pension fund assets	(377.5)	(542.1)	(
Net amortization and deferrals	(40.9)	86.0	
Net pension expense	$ 75.6	$ 69.5	$

The following table sets forth the plans' funded status and the amounts recognized in CP Limited's consolidated balance sheet as at December 31:

(in millions)	1992		1991	
	Plans having assets in excess of accumulated benefits	Plans having accumulated benefits in excess of assets	Plans having assets in excess of accumulated benefits	Plans accum b in of
Actuarial present value of benefit obligation:				
Vested	$ 4,398.4	$ 361.0	$ 4,470.6	$
Non-vested	23.2	1.7	31.3	
Accumulated benefit obligation	4,421.6	362.7	4,501.9	
Effect of projected future salary increases	626.8	14.1	685.2	
Projected benefit obligation (based on a weighted average discount rate of approximately 9% and salary increases ranging from 5% to 6%)	5,048.4	376.8	5,187.1	
Pension fund assets at market related values	4,976.8	286.7	5,177.8	
Pension fund assets less than projected benefit obligation	(71.6)	(90.1)	(9.3)	
Unamortized portion of net (asset) obligation at January 1, 1987*	162.2	(17.2)	125.5	
Unamortized prior service cost*	244.7	18.8	307.6	
Unamortized net (gain) loss*	(189.9)	50.8	(286.1)	
Prepaid (accrued) pension cost in Consolidated Balance Sheet	$ 145.4	$ (37.7)	$ 137.7	$

*Being amortized over expected average remaining service lives of employees, generally 15 years.

Pension fund assets consist primarily of listed stocks and bonds. The assumed weighted average long term rate of return on pension fund assets is approximately 9%.

CP Limited also has subsidiary-sponsored defined contribution plans. Pension expense for such plans, which generally equals the employer's required contribution, was $12.1 million, $7.7 million and $6.1 million in 1992, 1991 and 1990, respectively.

In addition to pension benefits, the Corporation and se of its subsidiaries provide health care and life insurance ben for certain retired employees. The cost of providing benefits is recognized by expensing the annual insu premiums which were approximately $11 million, $7 million $8 million in 1992, 1991 and 1990, respectively.

21. Commitments

At December 31, 1992, commitments for capital expenditures amounted to $233.7 million and minimum payments under operating leases were estimated at $618.0 million in the aggregate, with annual payments in each of the five years following 1992 of: 1993 – $124.0 million; 1994 – $94.3 million; 1995 – $74.6 million; 1996 – $60.1 million; 1997 – $44.0 million.

At December 31, 1992, unused commitments for long term financing amounted to $1,146.1 million at interest rates varying with bank prime or money market rates, with commitment fees on $542.1 million ranging from .125% to .25%.

Unused lines of credit for short term financing, subject to periodic review, repayable on demand and at various maturities up to 365 days, amounted to $738.9 million on which interest rates vary with bank prime or money market rates.

22. Subsequent Events

On January 29, 1993, Unitel Communications Holdings Inc. (Unitel) issued common shares to AT&T Canada Inc. in exchange for the contribution of intelligent network equipment, software and related services valued at $150 million. This common share issue reduced the Corporation's ownership in Unitel to 48% from 60%. Also on January 29, 1993, the Corporation purchased $36 million of common shares and $36 million of preferred shares of Unitel. CP Limited will account for this investment on the equity method in 1993.

On March 5, 1993, Canadian Pacific Forest Products Limited (CP Forest) entered into an agreement to issue 8 million Common Shares to the public for $20 a share. The Corporation will not purchase any shares under this offering, thereby decreasing its ownership in CP Forest to 60.7% from 70.0%.

23. Reclassification

Certain prior years' figures have been reclassified to conform with the presentation adopted for 1992.

24. Supplementary Data

The discussion of Canadian and United States accounting principles and the reconciliation of net income between United States and Canadian generally accepted accounting principles for the years included in Supplementary Data are an integral part of these financial statements.

The following data are provided to comply with certain disclosure requirements of the Securities and Exchange Commission (SEC) of the United States.

Canadian and United States Accounting Principles
The consolidated financial statements of CP Limited have been prepared in accordance with generally accepted accounting principles (GAAP) in Canada, as promulgated by the Canadian Institute of Chartered Accountants. Over the years, a number of differences have developed between Canadian and United States GAAP. For the information of the Corporation's United States shareholders, the major differences are described below and their effect on CP Limited's operating income and net income is summarized, the effect on the statement of changes in consolidated financial position and consolidated balance sheet not being significant, except that dividends are treated as a financing activity in the statement of changes in consolidated financial position under United States GAAP.

The full cost methods of accounting for conventional oil and gas operations promulgated under Canadian and United States GAAP differ in the following respect. Ceiling test calculations are performed by comparing the net book value of conventional petroleum and natural gas properties with the future net revenues expected to be generated from proven developed reserves, discounted at ten percent for United States reporting purposes, and undiscounted for Canadian reporting. Any excess of net book value over future net revenues is recognized as additional depletion expense in both reporting jurisdictions.

The sinking fund method of providing depreciation followed by the Real Estate and Hotels business segment in accordance with Canadian GAAP is not an acceptable method under United States GAAP, which requires that the straight-line method be used.

CP Limited follows the Canadian practice of deferring amortizing unrealized exchange gains and losses relate long term foreign currency assets and liabilities, whe under United States GAAP such gains and losses are incl in income immediately.

The principal difference between Canadian and Un States GAAP in accounting for pension costs is in the ch of discount rate used for computing the benefit obliga and the service and interest cost components of net peri pension expense. Under Canadian GAAP, the discount used represents management's best estimate of the l term rate of return on pension fund assets, whereas un United States GAAP the discount rate reflects the rat which pension benefits can be effectively settled at the of the financial statements. The impact of this differenc CP Limited's pension expense is included in the follov table. The impact of the difference on the funded statu CP Limited's plans is not material.

CP Limited follows the Canadian practice of expen costs related to post retirement health care and life insura benefits when they are paid, whereas under the new Un States accounting standard these costs, based on the te of the plan, are recognized on an accrual basis during years the plan participants provide the services. The cum tive effect of prior years' differences is charged aga earnings in 1992 which is the first year of adoption of the United States standard.

Canadian and United States Accounting Principles (cont'd)

For the Year ended December 31 (in millions, except amounts per share)	1992	1991	1990
Operating income (loss)			
Canadian GAAP	$ (106.3)	$ (505.5)	$ 1,034.9
United States GAAP	(254.2)	(717.2)	984.3
Net income (loss)			
Canadian GAAP	(478.3)	(913.8)	355.3
United States GAAP	(693.9)	(1,037.4)	320.3
Earnings (loss) per Ordinary Share			
Canadian GAAP	(1.50)	(2.87)	1.11
United States GAAP	(2.18)	(3.26)	1.00

The following is a reconciliation of net income (loss) under
  Canadian GAAP to net income (loss) under United States GAAP:

	1992	1991	1990
Net income (loss) – Canadian GAAP	$ (478.3)	$ (913.8)	$ 355.3
Increased or (decreased) by:			
Oil and gas	10.2	(63.6)	(2.1)
Real estate and hotels	(16.3)	(24.6)	(18.3)
Foreign exchange	(131.1)	(10.4)	(11.2)
Pension costs	(21.3)	(28.6)	(9.9)
Post retirement benefits	(58.3)	—	—
Other	1.2	3.6	6.5
Net income (loss) – United States GAAP	$ (693.9)	$ (1,037.4)	$ 320.3

A new United States standard on accounting for income taxes (SFAS 109) was issued February 1992 to become effective for fiscal years beginning after December 15, 1992. CP Limited has completed a preliminary study of the effect SFAS 109 will have on its financial position. CP Limited expects that adoption of this new standard in 1993 will not have a significant impact on its financial position as determined following United States GAAP.

Quarterly Financial Information (unaudited)

For the Year ended December 31 (in millions)	1992		1991	
	Canadian GAAP	United States GAAP	Canadian GAAP	United States GAAP
Operating income (loss)				
First quarter	$ 61.4	$ 47.6	$ 83.0	$ 61.8
Second quarter	151.6	143.9	167.6	154.6
Third quarter	(165.9)	(167.6)	144.2	125.6
Fourth quarter	(153.4)	(278.1)	(900.3)	(1,059.2)
	$ (106.3)	$ (254.2)	$ (505.5)	$ (717.2)
Net income (loss)				
First quarter	$ (39.7)	$ (89.0)	$ (5.3)	$ (17.5)
Second quarter	21.0	5.3	30.9	32.9
Third quarter	(205.6)	(317.0)	(51.8)	(45.8)
Fourth quarter	(254.0)	(293.2)	(887.6)	(1,007.0)
	$ (478.3)	$ (693.9)	$ (913.8)	$ (1,037.4)

Quarterly Financial Information (unaudited)
Statement of Consolidated Income

For the three months ended (in millions, except amounts per share)	March 31	June 30	Sept. 30	Dec. 31
		1992		
Revenues				
Goods sold	$ 1,164.3	$ 1,113.3	$ 730.4	$ 782.7
Services	1,253.0	1,357.9	1,293.5	1,268.5
	2,417.3	2,471.2	2,023.9	2,051.2
Costs and Expenses				
Cost of goods sold	893.9	835.9	543.9	562.4
Cost of services	857.2	895.6	883.2	935.5
Selling, general and administrative	372.6	362.3	543.1	469.2
Depreciation, depletion and amortization	232.2	225.8	219.6	237.5
	2,355.9	2,319.6	2,189.8	2,204.6
Operating income (loss)	61.4	151.6	(165.9)	(153.4)
Interest expense, net	142.1	144.3	148.6	157.8
Other expenses (income)	6.7	10.0	27.5	102.5
Income (loss) before income taxes, minority interest and equity in income	(87.4)	(2.7)	(342.0)	(413.7)
Income tax expense (recovery)	(21.6)	(2.6)	(118.4)	(136.1)
Minority interest share of income (losses) of subsidiaries	(22.3)	(12.4)	(11.5)	(11.1)
Income (loss) before equity in income of associates	(43.5)	12.3	(212.1)	(266.5)
Equity in income of Laidlaw Inc.	3.8	6.3	3.3	9.0
Equity in income of United Dominion Industries Limited	—	2.4	3.2	3.5
Net income (loss)	$ (39.7)	$ 21.0	$ (205.6)	$ (254.0)
Earnings (loss) per Ordinary Share	$ (0.12)	$ 0.06	$ (0.64)	$ (0.80)

Operating income includes write-downs and restructuring costs of $270.2 million for the three months ended September 30, 1992, and $272.6 million for the three months ended December 31, 1992, as described in Note 2.

Other expenses for the three months ended December 31, 1992, include a $72.2 million write-down of investment in United Dominion Industries Limited.

Quarterly Financial Information (unaudited)
Statement of Consolidated Income

For the three months ended (in millions, except amounts per share)	1991 March 31	June 30	Sept. 30	Dec. 31
Revenues				
Goods sold	$ 1,246.4	$ 1,267.1	$ 1,202.3	$ 1,187.3
Services	1,214.3	1,330.1	1,298.4	1,325.6
	2,460.7	2,597.2	2,500.7	2,512.9
Costs and Expenses				
Cost of goods sold	905.6	936.0	915.6	1,030.7
Cost of services	869.9	895.3	878.3	954.4
Selling, general and administrative	375.4	368.1	347.1	664.8
Depreciation, depletion and amortization	226.8	230.2	215.5	763.3
	2,377.7	2,429.6	2,356.5	3,413.2
Operating income (loss)	83.0	167.6	144.2	(900.3)
Interest expense, net	130.6	135.1	135.8	138.5
Other expenses (income)	(46.8)	(2.3)	(88.5)	14.8
Income (loss) before income taxes, minority interest and equity in income	(0.8)	34.8	96.9	(1,053.6)
Income tax expense (recovery)	(2.5)	16.2	41.5	(318.7)
Minority interest share of income (losses) of subsidiaries	3.1	(7.5)	2.8	(133.5)
Income (loss) before equity in income of associates	(1.4)	26.1	52.6	(601.4)
Equity in income (loss) of Laidlaw Inc.	(3.9)	4.8	(104.4)	4.6
Write-down of investment in Laidlaw Inc.	—	—	—	(290.8)
Net income (loss)	$ (5.3)	$ 30.9	$ (51.8)	$ (887.6)
Earnings (loss) per Ordinary Share	$ (0.02)	$ 0.10	$ (0.16)	$ (2.79)

Operating income for the three months ended December 31, 1991, includes write-downs and restructuring costs of $959.7 million described in Note 2.

Other income for the three months ended March 31, 1991, includes a gain of $40.5 million on sale of business by United Dominion Industries Limited.

Other income for the three months ended September 30, 1991, includes a gain of $86.2 million on sale of the tissue business by Canadian Pacific Forest Products Limited.

TEN-YEAR SUMMARY

(dollars in millions, except amounts per share)	1992	1991	1990	1989
Revenues				
Continuing operations	$ **8,963.6**	$ 10,071.5	$ 10,456.3	$ 10,831.6
Operating income (loss) from:				
Transportation	$ **(424.9)**	$ (14.8)	$ 294.3	$ 263.4
Energy	**321.7**	184.5	424.0	297.6
Forest Products	**(269.5)**	(845.4)	14.9	377.1
Real Estate and Hotels	**253.2**	134.4	264.4	354.6
Telecommunications and				
Manufacturing	**13.2**	35.8	37.3	84.2
	$ **(106.3)**	$ (505.5)	$ 1,034.9	$ 1,376.9
Income (loss) from				
continuing operations	$ **(478.3)**	$ (913.8)	$ 355.3	$ 664.6
Net income (loss)	$ **(478.3)**	$ (913.8)	$ 355.3	$ 745.2
United States GAAP				
Income (loss) from				
continuing operations	$ **(693.9)**	$ (1,037.4)	$ 320.3	$ 687.7
Net income (loss)	$ **(693.9)**	$ (1,037.4)	$ 320.3	$ 768.3
Total assets	$ **20,223.8**	$ 20,587.1	$ 20,223.5	$ 19,048.3
Total capitalization				
Total long term debt	$ **7,715.9**	$ 7,215.3	$ 4,564.4	$ 4,256.4
Perpetual 4% Consolidated				
Debenture Stock	**172.4**	176.4	180.1	162.9
Minority shareholders' interest				
in subsidiary companies	**815.2**	867.0	1,043.3	1,238.8
Shareholders' equity	**6,286.3**	6,713.9	7,827.4	7,796.5
	$ **14,989.8**	$ 14,972.6	$ 13,615.2	$ 13,454.6
Per Ordinary Share:				
Income (loss) from				
continuing operations				
Canadian GAAP	$ **(1.50)**	$ (2.87)	$ 1.11	$ 2.09
United States GAAP	$ **(2.18)**	$ (3.26)	$ 1.00	$ 2.17
Net income (loss)				
Canadian GAAP	$ **(1.50)**	$ (2.87)	$ 1.11	$ 2.35
United States GAAP	$ **(2.18)**	$ (3.26)	$ 1.00	$ 2.42
Dividends	$ **0.32**	$ 0.63	$ 0.92	$ 0.84
Number of Ordinary Shares (in millions)				
Actual	**319.1**	318.7	318.2	318.2
Average	**318.8**	318.5	318.5	317.3
Rate of return on				
average shareholders' equity	**(7.4%)**	(12.6%)	4.5%	9.9%
Debt: equity ratio	**53:47**	49:51	35:65	33:67

	1988		1987		1986		1985		1984		1983
$	10,730.0	$	10,089.7	$	10,484.2	$	10,359.5	$	9,736.6	$	8,472.3
$	488.4	$	602.9	$	466.4	$	420.0	$	469.0	$	424.0
	234.4		323.5		310.1		626.8		586.5		479.1
	587.4		476.6		215.6		117.6		149.6		(13.2)
	298.5		205.2		199.2		179.9		158.9		140.7
	78.8		53.3		70.5		91.2		56.7		(21.3)
$	1,687.5	$	1,661.5	$	1,261.8	$	1,435.5	$	1,420.7	$	1,009.3
$	683.9	$	441.7	$	186.4	$	357.3	$	380.9	$	242.6
$	820.1	$	826.3	$	(80.3)	$	252.7	$	366.2	$	129.0
$	747.1	$	526.7	$	244.6	$	336.0	$	372.9	$	204.9
$	887.6	$	923.5	$	(5.5)	$	230.9	$	340.4	$	90.3
$	17,650.8	$	18,000.7	$	17,698.7	$	21,331.5	$	18,670.7	$	17,486.4
$	3,836.0	$	4,469.8	$	5,114.7	$	6,683.5	$	5,609.0	$	5,536.4
	178.1		197.7		184.6		185.0		157.8		292.5
	1,073.4		1,139.0		1,344.7		2,031.7		2,981.3		2,660.2
	7,303.1		6,433.0		5,753.4		6,032.5		4,387.8		3,928.2
$	12,390.6	$	12,239.5	$	12,397.4	$	14,932.7	$	13,135.9	$	12,417.3
$	2.21	$	1.47	$	0.62	$	1.62	$	1.77	$	1.12
$	2.42	$	1.75	$	0.82	$	1.52	$	1.73	$	0.95
$	2.65	$	2.75	$	(0.27)	$	1.14	$	1.70	$	0.59
$	2.87	$	3.07	$	(0.02)	$	1.04	$	1.58	$	0.41
$	0.68	$	0.54	$	0.48	$	0.48	$	0.47	$	0.47
	316.9		302.8		299.5		297.7		215.0		215.0
	309.1		300.5		298.3		220.8		215.0		215.0
	11.9%		13.6%		(1.4%)		4.9%		8.8%		3.3%
	32:68		38:62		43:57		46:54		44:56		47:53

GEOGRAPHIC DISTRIBUTION OF
NET PROPERTY INVESTMENT

At December 31, 1992	Properties, at Cost less Depreciation	Percent of Total
	(in millions)	
Canada		
Atlantic Provinces	$ 192.4	2
Quebec	1,597.3	11
Ontario	3,478.0	23
Manitoba	270.8	2
Saskatchewan	631.6	4
Alberta	3,529.3	23
British Columbia	2,264.9	15
N.W.T., Yukon & Offshore	44.5	–
Transportation Equipment	896.8	6
	12,905.6	86
Outside Canada		
United States	2,060.3	14
Other	36.8	–
Ocean Ships	39.4	–
	2,136.5	14
Total	$ 15,042.1	100

Consolidated Balance Sheet
December 31

Assets

(in millions)	1992	1991
Current Assets		
Cash and temporary investments	$ **1,387.3**	$ 1,603.0
Accounts receivable	**1,090.7**	1,559.2
Inventories (Note 8)	**611.5**	925.9
	3,089.5	4,088.1
Investments (Note 9)	**1,189.6**	924.1
Properties, at cost (Note 10)		
Transportation	**7,970.1**	7,770.2
Energy	**5,601.1**	5,727.9
Forest Products	**4,188.3**	4,088.4
Real Estate and Hotels	**4,088.4**	3,899.8
Telecommunications and Manufacturing	**1,357.4**	1,591.7
Other	**57.9**	53.0
	23,263.2	23,131.0
Less: Accumulated depreciation, depletion and amortization	**8,221.1**	8,323.9
	15,042.1	14,807.1
Other Assets and Deferred Charges (Note 11)	**902.6**	767.8
	$ 20,223.8	$ 20,587.1

Auditors' Report

To the Shareholders of Canadian Pacific Limited
We have audited the consolidated balance sheets of Canadian Pacific Limited as at December 31, 1992 and 1991 and the statements of consolidated income, consolidated retained income and changes in consolidated financial position for each of the three years in the period ended December 31, 1992. These consolidated financial statements are the responsibility of the Corporation's management. Our responsibility is to express an opinion on these financial statements based on our audits.

We conducted our audits in accordance with generally accepted auditing standards. Those standards require that we plan and perform an audit to obtain reasonable assurance whether the financial statements are free of material misstatement. An audit includes examining, on a test basis, evidence supporting the amounts and disclosures in the financial statements. An audit also includes assessing the accounting principles used and significant estimates made by management as well as evaluating the overall financial statement presentation.

In our opinion, these consolidated financial statements present fairly, in all material respects, the financial position of Canadian Pacific Limited as at December 31, 1992 and 1991 and the results of its operations and the changes in its financial position for each of the three years in the period ended December 31, 1992 in accordance with generally accepted accounting principles in Canada.

Price Waterhouse

Chartered Accountants
Montreal, Quebec
March 5, 1993

Liabilities and Shareholders' Equity

(in millions)	1992	1991
Current Liabilities		
Bank loans	$ 149.6	$ 360.3
Accounts payable and accrued liabilities	1,790.4	2,009.8
Income and other taxes payable	159.7	69.1
Dividends payable	29.7	29.5
Long term debt maturing within one year (Note 12)	694.1	405.5
	2,823.5	2,874.2
Deferred Liabilities (Note 13)	753.2	502.0
Long Term Debt (Note 12)	7,021.8	6,809.8
Perpetual 4% Consolidated Debenture Stock (Note 14)	172.4	176.4
Deferred Income Taxes	1,930.6	2,203.3
Deferred Income Credits (Note 15)	420.8	440.5
Minority Shareholders' Interest in Subsidiary Companies (Note 16)	815.2	867.0
Shareholders' Equity (Note 17)		
Preference Shares	14.9	14.9
Ordinary Shares		
Issued – 319,053,305 (1991 – 318,677,431) shares	1,241.1	1,234.9
Premium on securities	1,174.5	1,174.5
Other paid-in surplus	154.1	154.1
Foreign currency translation adjustments	219.4	72.4
Retained income	3,482.3	4,063.1
	6,286.3	6,713.9

Commitments (Note 21)

	$ 20,223.8	$ 20,587.1

See Notes to Consolidated Financial Statements.

Approved on behalf of the Board:

[signature]

J.F. Hankinson, Director

[signature]

W.W. Stinson, Director

(in millions, except amounts per share)	1992	1991	1990
Revenues			
Goods sold	$ 3,790.7	$ 4,903.1	$ 5,292.3
Services	5,172.9	5,168.4	5,164.0
	8,963.6	10,071.5	10,456.3
Costs and Expenses			
Cost of goods sold	2,836.1	3,787.9	3,686.3
Cost of services	3,571.5	3,597.9	3,473.0
Selling, general and administrative	1,747.2	1,755.4	1,466.9
Depreciation, depletion and amortization	915.1	1,435.8	795.2
	9,069.9	10,577.0	9,421.4
Operating income (loss) (Note 2)	(106.3)	(505.5)	1,034.9
Interest expense, net (Note 3)	592.8	540.0	487.6
Other expenses (income) (Note 4)	146.7	(122.8)	(17.3)
Income (loss) before income taxes, minority interest and equity in income	(845.8)	(922.7)	564.6
Income tax expense (recovery) (Note 5)	(278.7)	(263.5)	220.4
Minority interest share of income (losses) of subsidiaries	(57.3)	(135.1)	21.3
Income (loss) before equity in income of associates	(509.8)	(524.1)	322.9
Equity in income (loss) of Laidlaw Inc.	22.4	(98.9)	32.4
Equity in income of United Dominion Industries Limited	9.1	—	—
Write-down of investment in Laidlaw Inc. (Note 9)	—	(290.8)	—
Net income (loss)	$ (478.3)	$ (913.8)	$ 355.3
Earnings (loss) per Ordinary Share	$ (1.50)	$ (2.87)	$ 1.11

Statement of Consolidated Retained Income
For the Year ended December 31

(in millions, except amounts per share)	1992	1991	1990
Balance, January 1	$ 4,063.1	$ 5,178.0	$ 5,116.2
Net income (loss)	(478.3)	(913.8)	355.3
	3,584.8	4,264.2	5,471.5
Dividends			
4% Preference Shares	0.5	0.5	0.5
Ordinary Shares (per share: 1992 – $0.32; 1991 – $0.63; 1990 – $0.92)	102.0	200.6	293.0
Total dividends	102.5	201.1	293.5
Balance, December 31	$ 3,482.3	$ 4,063.1	$ 5,178.0

See Notes to Consolidated Financial Statements.

(in millions)	1992	1991	1990
Operating Activities			
Net income (loss)	$ **(478.3)**	$ (913.8)	$ 355.3
Depreciation, depletion and amortization	**915.1**	906.6	795.2
Deferred income taxes	**(362.0)**	(276.6)	169.7
Minority interest share of income (losses) of subsidiaries	**(57.3)**	(135.1)	21.3
Equity in losses of associates	**48.3**	152.3	38.5
Write-down of assets and restructuring costs	**615.0**	1,270.0	61.9
Reduction in restructuring accruals	**(127.5)**	—	—
Amortization of exchange losses (gains)	**0.9**	(55.3)	(70.9)
Gains from sales of businesses,			
investments and properties	**(17.2)**	(160.3)	(93.9)
Other operating cash items, net	**(84.6)**	(35.7)	(17.7)
Cash from operations, before changes			
in working capital	**452.4**	752.1	1,259.4
Decrease (increase) in non-cash working capital			
balances relating to operations (Note 6)	**316.1**	(3.0)	24.6
Cash from operations	**768.5**	749.1	1,284.0
Dividends			
Paid to shareholders of the Corporation	**(102.1)**	(249.1)	(292.9)
Paid to minority shareholders of subsidiaries	**(21.3)**	(26.0)	(41.9)
	(123.4)	(275.1)	(334.8)
Financing Activities			
Issuance of long term debt	**1,688.0**	3,718.7	1,372.7
Repayment of long term debt	**(1,182.8)**	(1,064.6)	(1,074.1)
Issuance of shares by subsidiaries	**285.5**	6.8	2.0
Redemption of Preferred Shares by subsidiaries	**(1.1)**	(23.7)	(62.5)
Issuance of Ordinary Shares by the Corporation	**6.2**	8.9	13.3
Repurchase of Ordinary Shares by the Corporation	**—**	—	(10.3)
	795.8	2,646.1	241.1
Investing Activities			
Business acquisitions and investments (Note 7)	**(376.9)**	(139.9)	(284.8)
Additions to properties (Note 2)	**(1,397.2)**	(1,690.8)	(1,953.9)
Sales of businesses, investments and properties	**328.2**	463.8	373.7
	(1,445.9)	(1,366.9)	(1,865.0)
Cash Position*			
Increase (decrease) in cash	**(5.0)**	1,753.2	(674.7)
Cash (deficit) at beginning of year	**1,242.7**	(510.5)	164.2
Cash (deficit) at end of year	$ **1,237.7**	$ 1,242.7	$ (510.5)

*Cash comprises cash and temporary investments net of
bank loans and notes payable.

See Notes to Consolidated Financial Statements.

Appendix B

Present Value Tables

Table B.1 Amount of 1

$$fvf_{\overline{n}|i} = (1 + i)^n$$

Periods (n)	1%	2%	2.5%	3%	4%	5%
1	1.01000	1.02000	1.02500	1.03000	1.04000	1.05000
2	1.02010	1.04040	1.05063	1.06090	1.08160	1.10250
3	1.03030	1.06121	1.07689	1.09273	1.12486	1.15763
4	1.04060	1.08243	1.10381	1.12551	1.16986	1.21551
5	1.05101	1.10408	1.13141	1.15927	1.21665	1.27628
6	1.06152	1.12616	1.15969	1.19405	1.26532	1.34010
7	1.07214	1.14869	1.18869	1.22987	1.31593	1.40710
8	1.08286	1.17166	1.21840	1.26677	1.36857	1.47746
9	1.09369	1.19509	1.24886	1.30477	1.42331	1.55133
10	1.10462	1.21899	1.28008	1.34392	1.48024	1.62889
11	1.11567	1.24337	1.31209	1.38423	1.53945	1.71034
12	1.12683	1.26824	1.34489	1.42576	1.60103	1.79586
13	1.13809	1.29361	1.37851	1.46853	1.66507	1.88565
14	1.14947	1.31948	1.41297	1.51259	1.73168	1.97993
15	1.16097	1.34587	1.44830	1.55797	1.80094	2.07893
16	1.17258	1.37279	1.48451	1.60471	1.87298	2.18287
17	1.18430	1.40024	1.52162	1.65285	1.94790	2.29202
18	1.19615	1.42825	1.55966	1.70243	2.02582	2.40662
19	1.20811	1.45681	1.59865	1.75351	2.10685	2.52695
20	1.22019	1.48595	1.63862	1.80611	2.19112	2.65330
21	1.23239	1.51567	1.67958	1.86029	2.27877	2.78596
22	1.24472	1.54598	1.72157	1.91610	2.36992	2.92526
23	1.25716	1.57690	1.76461	1.97359	2.46472	3.07152
24	1.26973	1.60844	1.80873	2.03279	2.56330	3.22510
25	1.28243	1.64061	1.85394	2.09378	2.66584	3.38635
26	1.29526	1.67342	1.90029	2.15659	2.77247	3.55567
27	1.30821	1.70689	1.94780	2.22129	2.88337	3.73346
28	1.32129	1.74102	1.99650	2.28793	2.99870	3.92013
29	1.33450	1.77584	2.04641	2.35657	3.11865	4.11614
30	1.34785	1.81136	2.09757	2.42726	3.24340	4.32194
31	1.36133	1.84759	2.15001	2.50008	3.37313	4.53804
32	1.37494	1.88454	2.20376	2.57508	3.50806	4.76494
33	1.38869	1.92223	2.25885	2.65234	3.64838	5.00319
34	1.40258	1.96068	2.31532	2.73191	3.79432	5.25335
35	1.41660	1.99989	2.37321	2.81386	3.94609	5.51602
36	1.43077	2.03989	2.43254	2.89828	4.10393	5.79182
37	1.44508	2.08069	2.49335	2.98523	4.26809	6.08141
38	1.45953	2.12230	2.55568	3.07478	4.43881	6.38548
39	1.47412	2.16474	2.61957	3.16703	4.61637	6.70475
40	1.48886	2.20804	2.68506	3.26204	4.80102	7.03999

Table B.1   Amount of 1

6%	8%	10%	12%	16%	20%	24%	Periods (n)
1.06000	1.08000	1.10000	1.12000	1.16000	1.20000	1.24000	1
1.12360	1.16640	1.21000	1.25440	1.34560	1.44000	1.53760	2
1.19102	1.25971	1.33100	1.40493	1.56090	1.72800	1.90662	3
1.26248	1.36049	1.46410	1.57352	1.81064	2.07360	2.36421	4
1.33823	1.46933	1.61051	1.76234	2.10034	2.48832	2.93163	5
1.41852	1.58687	1.77156	1.97382	2.43640	2.98598	3.63522	6
1.50363	1.71382	1.94872	2.21068	2.82622	3.58318	4.50767	7
1.59385	1.85093	2.14359	2.47596	3.27841	4.29982	5.58951	8
1.68948	1.99900	2.35795	2.77308	3.80296	5.15978	6.93099	9
1.79085	2.15892	2.59374	3.10585	4.41144	6.19174	8.59443	10
1.89830	2.33164	2.85312	3.47855	5.11726	7.43008	10.65709	11
2.01220	2.51817	3.13843	3.89598	5.93603	8.91610	13.21479	12
2.13293	2.71962	3.45227	4.36349	6.88579	10.69932	16.38634	13
2.26090	2.93719	3.79750	4.88711	7.98752	12.83918	20.31906	14
2.39656	3.17217	4.17725	5.47357	9.26552	15.40702	25.19563	15
2.54035	3.42594	4.59497	6.13039	10.74800	18.48843	31.24259	16
2.69277	3.70002	5.05447	6.86604	12.46768	22.18611	38.74081	17
2.85434	3.99602	5.55992	7.68997	14.46251	26.62333	48.03860	18
3.02560	4.31570	6.11591	8.61276	16.77652	31.94800	59.56786	19
3.20714	4.66096	6.72750	9.64629	19.46076	38.33760	73.86415	20
3.39956	5.03383	7.40025	10.80385	22.57448	46.00512	91.59155	21
3.60354	5.43654	8.14027	12.10031	26.18640	55.20614	113.57352	22
3.81975	5.87146	8.95430	13.55235	30.37622	66.24737	140.83116	23
4.04893	6.34118	9.84973	15.17863	35.23642	79.49685	174.63064	24
4.29187	6.84848	10.83471	17.00006	40.87424	95.39622	216.54199	25
4.54938	7.39635	11.91818	19.04007	47.41412	114.47546	268.51207	26
4.82235	7.98806	13.10999	21.32488	55.00038	137.37055	332.95497	27
5.11169	8.62711	14.42099	23.88387	63.80044	164.84466	412.86416	28
5.41839	9.31727	15.86309	26.74993	74.00851	197.81359	511.95156	29
5.74349	10.06266	17.44940	29.95992	85.84988	237.37631	634.81993	30
6.08810	10.86767	19.19434	33.55511	99.58586	284.85158	787.17672	31
6.45339	11.73708	21.11378	37.58173	115.51959	341.82189	976.09913	32
6.84059	12.67605	23.22515	42.09153	134.00273	410.18627	1210.36292	33
7.25103	13.69013	25.54767	47.14252	155.44317	492.22352	1500.85002	34
7.68609	14.78534	28.10244	52.79962	180.31407	590.66823	1861.05403	35
8.14725	15.96817	30.91268	59.13557	209.16432	708.80187	2307.70699	36
8.63609	17.24563	34.00395	66.23184	242.63062	850.56225	2861.55667	37
9.15425	18.62528	37.40434	74.17966	281.45151	1020.67470	3548.33027	38
9.70351	20.11530	41.14478	83.08122	326.48376	1224.80964	4399.92954	39
10.28572	21.72452	45.25926	93.05097	378.72116	1469.77157	5455.91262	40

Table B.2 Present Value of 1

$$pvf_{\overline{n}|\,i} = \frac{1}{(1 + i)^n}$$

Periods (n)	1%	2%	2.5%	3%	4%	5%
1	0.99010	0.98039	0.97561	0.97087	0.96154	0.95238
2	0.98030	0.96117	0.95181	0.94260	0.92456	0.90703
3	0.97059	0.94232	0.92860	0.91514	0.88900	0.86384
4	0.96098	0.92385	0.90595	0.88849	0.85480	0.82270
5	0.95147	0.90573	0.88385	0.86261	0.82193	0.78353
6	0.94205	0.88797	0.86230	0.83748	0.79031	0.74622
7	0.93272	0.87056	0.84127	0.81309	0.75992	0.71068
8	0.92348	0.85349	0.82075	0.78941	0.73069	0.67684
9	0.91434	0.83676	0.80073	0.76642	0.70259	0.64461
10	0.90529	0.82035	0.78120	0.74409	0.67556	0.61391
11	0.89632	0.80426	0.76214	0.72242	0.64958	0.58468
12	0.88745	0.78849	0.74356	0.70138	0.62460	0.55684
13	0.87866	0.77303	0.72542	0.68095	0.60057	0.53032
14	0.86996	0.75788	0.70773	0.66112	0.57748	0.50507
15	0.86135	0.74301	0.69047	0.64186	0.55526	0.48102
16	0.85282	0.72845	0.67362	0.62317	0.53391	0.45811
17	0.84438	0.71416	0.65720	0.60502	0.51337	0.43630
18	0.83602	0.70016	0.64117	0.58739	0.49363	0.41552
19	0.82774	0.68643	0.62553	0.57029	0.47464	0.39573
20	0.81954	0.67297	0.61027	0.55368	0.45639	0.37689
21	0.81143	0.65978	0.59539	0.53755	0.43883	0.35894
22	0.80340	0.64684	0.58086	0.52189	0.42196	0.34185
23	0.79544	0.63416	0.56670	0.50669	0.40573	0.32557
24	0.78757	0.62172	0.55288	0.49193	0.39012	0.31007
25	0.77977	0.60953	0.53939	0.47761	0.37512	0.29530
26	0.77205	0.59758	0.52623	0.46369	0.36069	0.28124
27	0.76440	0.58586	0.51340	0.45019	0.34682	0.26785
28	0.75684	0.57437	0.50088	0.43708	0.33348	0.25509
29	0.74934	0.56311	0.48866	0.42435	0.32065	0.24295
30	0.74192	0.55207	0.47674	0.41199	0.30832	0.23138
31	0.73458	0.54125	0.46511	0.39999	0.29646	0.22036
32	0.72730	0.53063	0.45377	0.38834	0.28506	0.20987
33	0.72010	0.52023	0.44270	0.37703	0.27409	0.19987
34	0.71297	0.51003	0.43191	0.36604	0.26355	0.19035
35	0.70591	0.50003	0.42137	0.35538	0.25342	0.18129
36	0.69892	0.49022	0.41109	0.34503	0.24367	0.17266
37	0.69200	0.48061	0.40107	0.33498	0.23430	0.16444
38	0.68515	0.47119	0.39128	0.32523	0.22529	0.15661
39	0.67837	0.46195	0.38174	0.31575	0.21662	0.14915
40	0.67165	0.45289	0.37243	0.30656	0.20829	0.14205

Table B.2 Present Value of 1

6%	8%	10%	12%	16%	20%	24%	Periods (n)
0.94340	0.92593	0.90909	0.89286	0.86207	0.83333	0.80645	1
0.89000	0.85734	0.82645	0.79719	0.74316	0.69444	0.65036	2
0.83962	0.79383	0.75131	0.71178	0.64066	0.57870	0.52449	3
0.79209	0.73503	0.68301	0.63552	0.55229	0.48225	0.42297	4
0.74726	0.68058	0.62092	0.56743	0.47611	0.40188	0.34111	5
0.70496	0.63017	0.56447	0.50663	0.41044	0.33490	0.27509	6
0.66506	0.58349	0.51316	0.45235	0.35383	0.27908	0.22184	7
0.62741	0.54027	0.46651	0.40388	0.30503	0.23257	0.17891	8
0.59190	0.50025	0.42410	0.36061	0.26295	0.19381	0.14428	9
0.55839	0.46319	0.38554	0.32197	0.22668	0.16151	0.11635	10
0.52679	0.42888	0.35049	0.28748	0.19542	0.13459	0.09383	11
0.49697	0.39711	0.31863	0.25668	0.16846	0.11216	0.07567	12
0.46884	0.36770	0.28966	0.22917	0.14523	0.09346	0.06103	13
0.44230	0.34046	0.26333	0.20462	0.12520	0.07789	0.04921	14
0.41727	0.31524	0.23939	0.18270	0.10793	0.06491	0.03969	15
0.39365	0.29189	0.21763	0.16312	0.09304	0.05409	0.03201	16
0.37136	0.27027	0.19784	0.14564	0.08021	0.04507	0.02581	17
0.35034	0.25025	0.17986	0.13004	0.06914	0.03756	0.02082	18
0.33051	0.23171	0.16351	0.11611	0.05961	0.03130	0.01679	19
0.31180	0.21455	0.14864	0.10367	0.05139	0.02608	0.01354	20
0.29416	0.19866	0.13513	0.09256	0.04430	0.02174	0.01092	21
0.27751	0.18394	0.12285	0.08264	0.03819	0.01811	0.00880	22
0.26180	0.17032	0.11168	0.07379	0.03292	0.01509	0.00710	23
0.24698	0.15770	0.10153	0.06588	0.02838	0.01258	0.00573	24
0.23300	0.14602	0.09230	0.05882	0.02447	0.01048	0.00462	25
0.21981	0.13520	0.08391	0.05252	0.02109	0.00874	0.00372	26
0.20737	0.12519	0.07628	0.04689	0.01818	0.00728	0.00300	27
0.19563	0.11591	0.06934	0.04187	0.01567	0.00607	0.00242	28
0.18456	0.10733	0.06304	0.03738	0.01351	0.00506	0.00195	29
0.17411	0.09938	0.05731	0.03338	0.01165	0.00421	0.00158	30
0.16425	0.09202	0.05210	0.02980	0.01004	0.00351	0.00127	31
0.15496	0.08520	0.04736	0.02661	0.00866	0.00293	0.00102	32
0.14619	0.07889	0.04306	0.02376	0.00746	0.00244	0.00083	33
0.13791	0.07305	0.03914	0.02121	0.00643	0.00203	0.00067	34
0.13011	0.06763	0.03558	0.01894	0.00555	0.00169	0.00054	35
0.12274	0.06262	0.03235	0.01691	0.00478	0.00141	0.00043	36
0.11579	0.05799	0.02941	0.01510	0.00412	0.00118	0.00035	37
0.10924	0.05369	0.02673	0.01348	0.00355	0.00098	0.00028	38
0.10306	0.04971	0.02430	0.01204	0.00306	0.00082	0.00023	39
0.09722	0.04603	0.02209	0.01075	0.00264	0.00068	0.00018	40

Table B.3   Amount of an Ordinary Annuity of 1

$$aoaf_{\overline{n}|i} = \frac{(1 + i)^n - 1}{i}$$

Periods (n)	1%	2%	2.5%	3%	4%	5%
1	1.00000	1.00000	1.00000	1.00000	1.00000	1.00000
2	2.01000	2.02000	2.02500	2.03000	2.04000	2.05000
3	3.03010	3.06040	3.07562	3.09090	3.12160	3.15250
4	4.06040	4.12161	4.15252	4.18363	4.24646	4.31012
5	5.10101	5.20404	5.25633	5.30914	5.41632	5.52563
6	6.15202	6.30812	6.38774	6.46841	6.63298	6.80191
7	7.21354	7.43428	7.54743	7.66246	7.89829	8.14201
8	8.28567	8.58297	8.73612	8.89234	9.21423	9.54911
9	9.36853	9.75463	9.95452	10.15911	10.58280	11.02656
10	10.46221	10.94972	11.20338	11.46388	12.00611	12.57789
11	11.56683	12.16872	12.48347	12.80780	13.48635	14.20679
12	12.68250	13.41209	13.79555	14.19203	15.02581	15.91713
13	13.80933	14.68033	15.14044	15.61779	16.62684	17.71298
14	14.94742	15.97394	16.51895	17.08632	18.29191	19.59863
15	16.09690	17.29342	17.93193	18.59891	20.02359	21.57856
16	17.25786	18.63929	19.38022	20.15688	21.82453	23.65749
17	18.43044	20.01207	20.86473	21.76159	23.69751	25.84037
18	19.61475	21.41231	22.38635	23.41444	25.64541	28.13238
19	20.81090	22.84056	23.94601	25.11687	27.67123	30.53900
20	22.01900	24.29737	25.54466	26.87037	29.77808	33.06595
21	23.23919	25.78332	27.18327	28.67649	31.96920	35.71925
22	24.47159	27.29898	28.86286	30.53678	34.24797	38.50521
23	25.71630	28.84496	30.58443	32.45288	36.61789	41.43048
24	26.97346	30.42186	32.34904	34.42647	39.08260	44.50200
25	28.24320	32.03030	34.15776	36.45926	41.64591	47.72710
26	29.52563	33.67091	36.01171	38.55304	44.31174	51.11345
27	30.82089	35.34432	37.91200	40.70963	47.08421	54.66913
28	32.12910	37.05121	39.85980	42.93092	49.96758	58.40258
29	33.45039	38.79223	41.85630	45.21885	52.96629	62.32271
30	34.78489	40.56808	43.90270	47.57542	56.08494	66.43885
31	36.13274	42.37944	46.00027	50.00268	59.32834	70.76079
32	37.49407	44.22703	48.15028	52.50276	62.70147	75.29883
33	38.86901	46.11157	50.35403	55.07784	66.20953	80.06377
34	40.25770	48.03380	52.61289	57.73018	69.85791	85.06696
35	41.66028	49.99448	54.92821	60.46208	73.65222	90.32031
36	43.07688	51.99437	57.30141	63.27594	77.59831	95.83632
37	44.50765	54.03425	59.73395	66.17422	81.70225	101.62814
38	45.95272	56.11494	62.22730	69.15945	85.97034	107.70955
39	47.41225	58.23724	64.78298	72.23423	90.40915	114.09502
40	48.88637	60.40198	67.40255	75.40126	95.02552	120.79977

Table B.3 Amount of an Ordinary Annuity of 1

6%	8%	10%	12%	16%	20%	24%	Periods (n)
1.00000	1.00000	1.00000	1.00000	1.00000	1.00000	1.00000	1
2.06000	2.08000	2.10000	2.12000	2.16000	2.20000	2.24000	2
3.18360	3.24640	3.31000	3.37440	3.50560	3.64000	3.77760	3
4.37462	4.50611	4.64100	4.77933	5.06650	5.36800	5.68422	4
5.63709	5.86660	6.10510	6.35285	6.87714	7.44160	8.04844	5
6.97532	7.33593	7.71561	8.11519	8.97748	9.92992	10.98006	6
8.39384	8.92280	9.48717	10.08901	11.41387	12.91590	14.61528	7
9.89747	10.63663	11.43589	12.29969	14.24009	16.49908	19.12294	8
11.49132	12.48756	13.57948	14.77566	17.51851	20.79890	24.71245	9
13.18079	14.48656	15.93742	17.54874	21.32147	25.95868	31.64344	10
14.97164	16.64549	18.53117	20.65458	25.73290	32.15042	40.23787	11
16.86994	18.97713	21.38428	24.13313	30.85017	39.58050	50.89495	12
18.88214	21.49530	24.52271	28.02911	36.78620	48.49660	64.10974	13
21.01507	24.21492	27.97498	32.39260	43.67199	59.19592	80.49608	14
23.27597	27.15211	31.77248	37.27971	51.65951	72.03511	100.81514	15
25.67253	30.32428	35.94973	42.75328	60.92503	87.44213	126.01077	16
28.21288	33.75023	40.54470	48.88367	71.67303	105.93056	157.25336	17
30.90565	37.45024	45.59917	55.74971	84.14072	128.11667	195.99416	18
33.75999	41.44626	51.15909	63.43968	98.60323	154.74000	244.03276	19
36.78559	45.76196	57.27500	72.05244	115.37975	186.68800	303.60062	20
39.99273	50.42292	64.00250	81.69874	134.84051	225.02560	377.46477	21
43.39229	55.45676	71.40275	92.50258	157.41499	271.03072	469.05632	22
46.99583	60.89330	79.54302	104.60289	183.60138	326.23686	582.62984	23
50.81558	66.76476	88.49733	118.15524	213.97761	392.48424	723.46100	24
54.86451	73.10594	98.34706	133.33387	249.21402	471.98108	898.09164	25
59.15638	79.95442	109.18177	150.33393	290.08827	567.37730	1114.63363	26
63.70577	87.35077	121.09994	169.37401	337.50239	681.85276	1383.14570	27
68.52811	95.33883	134.20994	190.69889	392.50277	819.22331	1716.10067	28
73.63980	103.96594	148.63093	214.58275	456.30322	984.06797	2128.96483	29
79.05819	113.28321	164.49402	241.33268	530.31173	1181.88157	2640.91639	30
84.80168	123.34587	181.94342	271.29261	616.16161	1419.25788	3275.73632	31
90.88978	134.21354	201.13777	304.84772	715.74746	1704.10946	4062.91304	32
97.34316	145.95062	222.25154	342.42945	831.26706	2045.93135	5039.01217	33
104.18375	158.62667	245.47670	384.52098	965.26979	2456.11762	6249.37509	34
111.43478	172.31680	271.02437	431.66350	1120.71295	2948.34115	7750.22511	35
119.12087	187.10215	299.12681	484.46312	1301.02703	3539.00937	9611.27913	36
127.26812	203.07032	330.03949	543.59869	1510.19135	4247.81125	11918.98612	37
135.90421	220.31595	364.04343	609.83053	1752.82197	5098.37350	14780.54279	38
145.05846	238.94122	401.44778	684.01020	2034.27348	6119.04820	18328.87306	39
154.76197	259.05652	442.59256	767.09142	2360.75724	7343.85784	22728.80260	40

Table B.4   Present Value of an Ordinary Annuity of 1

$$pvoaf_{\overline{n}|\,i} = \frac{1 - \dfrac{1}{(1 + i)^n}}{i}$$

Periods (n)	1%	2%	2.5%	3%	4%	5%
1	0.99010	0.98039	0.97561	0.97087	0.96154	0.95238
2	1.97040	1.94156	1.92742	1.91347	1.88609	1.85941
3	2.94099	2.88388	2.85602	2.82861	2.77509	2.72325
4	3.90197	3.80773	3.76197	3.71710	3.62990	3.54595
5	4.85343	4.71346	4.64583	4.57971	4.45182	4.32948
6	5.79548	5.60143	5.50813	5.41719	5.24214	5.07569
7	6.72819	6.47199	6.34939	6.23028	6.00205	5.78637
8	7.65168	7.32548	7.17014	7.01969	6.73274	6.46321
9	8.56602	8.16224	7.97087	7.78611	7.43533	7.10782
10	9.47130	8.98259	8.75206	8.53020	8.11090	7.72173
11	10.36763	9.78685	9.51421	9.25262	8.76048	8.30641
12	11.25508	10.57534	10.25776	9.95400	9.38507	8.86325
13	12.13374	11.34837	10.98318	10.63496	9.98565	9.39357
14	13.00370	12.10625	11.69091	11.29607	10.56312	9.89864
15	13.86505	12.84926	12.38138	11.93794	11.11839	10.37966
16	14.71787	13.57771	13.05500	12.56110	11.65230	10.83777
17	15.56225	14.29187	13.71220	13.16612	12.16567	11.27407
18	16.39827	14.99203	14.35336	13.75351	12.65930	11.68959
19	17.22601	15.67846	14.97889	14.32380	13.13394	12.08532
20	18.04555	16.35143	15.58916	14.87747	13.59033	12.46221
21	18.85698	17.01121	16.18455	15.41502	14.02916	12.82115
22	19.66038	17.65805	16.76541	15.93692	14.45112	13.16300
23	20.45582	18.29220	17.33211	16.44361	14.85684	13.48857
24	21.24339	18.91393	17.88499	16.93554	15.24696	13.79864
25	22.02316	19.52346	18.42438	17.41315	15.62208	14.09394
26	22.79520	20.12104	18.95061	17.87684	15.98277	14.37519
27	23.55961	20.70690	19.46401	18.32703	16.32959	14.64303
28	24.31644	21.28127	19.96489	18.76411	16.66306	14.89813
29	25.06579	21.84438	20.45355	19.18845	16.98371	15.14107
30	25.80771	22.39646	20.93029	19.60044	17.29203	15.37245
31	26.54229	22.93770	21.39541	20.00043	17.58849	15.59281
32	27.26959	23.46833	21.84918	20.38877	17.87355	15.80268
33	27.98969	23.98856	22.29188	20.76579	18.14765	16.00255
34	28.70267	24.49859	22.72379	21.13184	18.41120	16.19290
35	29.40858	24.99862	23.14516	21.48722	18.66461	16.37419
36	30.10751	25.48884	23.55625	21.83225	18.90828	16.54685
37	30.79951	25.96945	23.95732	22.16724	19.14258	16.71129
38	31.48466	26.44064	24.34860	22.49246	19.36786	16.86789
39	32.16303	26.90259	24.73034	22.80822	19.58448	17.01704
40	32.83469	27.35548	25.10278	23.11477	19.79277	17.15909

Table B.4   Present Value of an Ordinary Annuity of 1

6%	8%	10%	12%	16%	20%	24%	Periods (n)
0.94340	0.92593	0.90909	0.89286	0.86207	0.83333	0.80645	1
1.83339	1.78326	1.73554	1.69005	1.60523	1.52778	1.45682	2
2.67301	2.57710	2.48685	2.40183	2.24589	2.10648	1.98130	3
3.46511	3.31213	3.16987	3.03735	2.79818	2.58873	2.40428	4
4.21236	3.99271	3.79079	3.60478	3.27429	2.99061	2.74538	5
4.91732	4.62288	4.35526	4.11141	3.68474	3.32551	3.02047	6
5.58238	5.20637	4.86842	4.56376	4.03857	3.60459	3.24232	7
6.20979	5.74664	5.33493	4.96764	4.34359	3.83716	3.42122	8
6.80169	6.24689	5.75902	5.32825	4.60654	4.03097	3.56550	9
7.36009	6.71008	6.14457	5.65022	4.83323	4.19247	3.68186	10
7.88687	7.13896	6.49506	5.93770	5.02864	4.32706	3.77569	11
8.38384	7.53608	6.81369	6.19437	5.19711	4.43922	3.85136	12
8.85268	7.90378	7.10336	6.42355	5.34233	4.53268	3.91239	13
9.29498	8.24424	7.36669	6.62817	5.46753	4.61057	3.96160	14
9.71225	8.55948	7.60608	6.81086	5.57546	4.67547	4.00129	15
10.10590	8.85137	7.82371	6.97399	5.66850	4.72956	4.03330	16
10.47726	9.12164	8.02155	7.11963	5.74870	4.77463	4.05911	17
10.82760	9.37189	8.20141	7.24967	5.81785	4.81219	4.07993	18
11.15812	9.60360	8.36492	7.36578	5.87746	4.84350	4.09672	19
11.46992	9.81815	8.51356	7.46944	5.92884	4.86958	4.11026	20
11.76408	10.01680	8.64869	7.56200	5.97314	4.89132	4.12117	21
12.04158	10.20074	8.77154	7.64465	6.01133	4.90943	4.12998	22
12.30338	10.37106	8.88322	7.71843	6.04425	4.92453	4.13708	23
12.55036	10.52876	8.98474	7.78432	6.07263	4.93710	4.14281	24
12.78336	10.67478	9.07704	7.84314	6.09709	4.94759	4.14742	25
13.00317	10.80998	9.16095	7.89566	6.11818	4.95632	4.15115	26
13.21053	10.93516	9.23722	7.94255	6.13636	4.96360	4.15415	27
13.40616	11.05108	9.30657	7.98442	6.15204	4.96967	4.15657	28
13.59072	11.15841	9.36961	8.02181	6.16555	4.97472	4.15853	29
13.76483	11.25778	9.42691	8.05518	6.17720	4.97894	4.16010	30
13.92909	11.34980	9.47901	8.08499	6.18724	4.98245	4.16137	31
14.08404	11.43500	9.52638	8.11159	6.19590	4.98537	4.16240	32
14.23023	11.51389	9.56943	8.13535	6.20336	4.98781	4.16322	33
14.36814	11.58693	9.60857	8.15656	6.20979	4.98984	4.16389	34
14.49825	11.65457	9.64416	8.17550	6.21534	4.99154	4.16443	35
14.62099	11.71719	9.67651	8.19241	6.22012	4.99295	4.16486	36
14.73678	11.77518	9.70592	8.20751	6.22424	4.99412	4.16521	37
14.84602	11.82887	9.73265	8.22099	6.22779	4.99510	4.16549	38
14.94907	11.87858	9.75696	8.23303	6.23086	4.99592	4.16572	39
15.04630	11.92461	9.77905	8.24378	6.23350	4.99660	4.16590	40

Index of Financial Statement Excerpts

Subject Index

READER REPLY CARD

We are interested in your reaction to *Intermediate Accounting, First Canadian Edition* by Williams, Deutsch, Stanga, and Holder. You can help us to improve this book in future editions by completing this questionnaire.

1. What was your reason for using this book?

   ☐ university course   ☐ college course   ☐ continuing education course
   ☐ professional   ☐ personal   ☐ other (please specify) _____
      development   interest   _____

2. If you are a student, please identify your school and the course. If you used this book for a program, what was the name of the program?

3. Which chapters or parts of this book did you use?

4. If you omitted any chapters or parts, which ones?

5. What did you like best about this book? What did you like the least? Please identify any topics you think should be added to future editions.

6. Were the boxed articles in each chapter of interest to you?

   Was the information in this textbook presented in an interesting manner? Was the textbook easier to use as two volumes rather than one?

8. Add any comments or suggestions.

(fold here and tape shut)

- -

MAIL ⮞ POSTE

Canada Post Corporation / Société canadienne des postes

Postage paid	**Port payé**
If mailed in Canada	si posté au Canada
Business	**Réponse**
Reply	**d'affaires**

0116870399

0116870399-M8Z4X6-BR01

Scott Duncan
Publisher, College Division
HOLT RINEHART AND WINSTON OF CANADA, LIMITED
55 HORNER AVENUE
TORONTO, ONTARIO
M8Z 9Z9